Matters Computational

Jörg Arndt

Matters Computational

Ideas, Algorithms, Source Code

 Springer

Jörg Arndt
Rothenburger Strasse 174
90439 Nürnberg
Germany
arndt@jjj.de

ISBN 978-3-662-50662-2   ISBN 978-3-642-14764-7 (eBook)
DOI 10.1007/978-3-642-14764-7
Springer Heidelberg Dordrecht London New York

Cover design: KuenkelLopka GmbH

Printed on acid-free paper

Springer is part of Springer Science+Business Media (www.springer.com)

Preface

This is a book for the *computationalist*, whether a working programmer or anyone interested in methods of computation. The focus is on material that does not usually appear in textbooks on algorithms.

Where necessary the underlying *ideas* are explained and the *algorithms* are given formally. It is assumed that the reader is able to understand the given *source code*, it is considered part of the text. We use the C++ programming language for low-level algorithms. However, only a minimal set of features beyond plain C is used, most importantly classes and templates. For material where technicalities in the C++ code would obscure the underlying ideas we use either pseudocode or, with arithmetical algorithms, the GP language. Appendix C gives an introduction to GP.

Example computations are often given with an algorithm, these are usually made with the demo programs referred to. Most of the listings and figures in this book were created with these programs. A recurring topic is practical efficiency of the implementations. Various optimization techniques are described and the actual performance of many given implementations is indicated.

The accompanying software, the FXT [21] and the hfloat [22] libraries, are written for POSIX compliant platforms such as the Linux and BSD operating systems. The license is the GNU General Public License (GPL), version 3 or later, see http://www.gnu.org/licenses/gpl.html.

Individual chapters are self-contained where possible and references to related material are given where needed. The symbol '‡' marks sections that can be skipped at first reading. These typically contain excursions or more advanced material.

Each item in the bibliography is followed by a list of page numbers where citations occur. With papers that are available for free download the respective URL is given. Note that the URL may point to a preprint which can differ from the final version of the paper.

An electronic version of this book is available online, see appendix A. Given the amount of material treated there must be errors in this book. Corrections and suggestions for improvement are appreciated, the preferred way of communication is electronic mail. A list of errata is online at http://www.jjj.de/fxt/#fxtbook.

Many people helped to improve this book. It is my pleasure to thank them all, particularly helpful were

Igal Aharonovich, Max Alekseyev, Marcus Blackburn, Nathan Bullock, Dominique Delande, Mike Engber, Torsten Finke, Sean Furlong, Almaz Gaifullin, Pedro Gimeno, Alexander Glyzov, R. W. Gosper, Andreas Grünbacher, Lance Gurney, Markus Gyger, Christoph Haenel, Tony Hardie-Bick, Laszlo Hars, Thomas Harte, Stephen Hartke, Christian Hey, Jeff Hurchalla, Derek M. Jones, Gideon Klimer, Richard B. Kreckel, Mike Kundmann, Gál László, Dirk Lattermann, Avery Lee, Brent Lehman, Marc Lehmann, Paul C. Leopardi, John Lien, Mirko Liss, Robert C. Long, Fred Lunnon, Johannes Middeke, Doug Moore, Fábio Moreira, Andrew Morris, David Nalepa, Samuel Neves, Matthew Oliver, Mirosław Osys, Christoph Pacher, Krisztián Paczári, Scott Paine, Yves Paradis, Gunther Piez, André Piotrowski, David García Quintas, Andreas Raseghi, Tony Reix, Johan Rönnblom, Uwe Schmelich, Thomas Schraitle, Clive Scott, Mukund Sivaraman, Michal Staruch, Ralf Stephan, Mikko Tommila, Sebastiano

Vigna, Michael Roby Wetherfield, Jim White, Vinnie Winkler, John Youngquist, Rui Zhang, and Paul Zimmermann.

Special thanks go to Edith Parzefall and Michael Somos for independently proofreading the whole text (the remaining errors are mine), and to Neil Sloane for creating the On-Line Encyclopedia of Integer Sequences [312].

jj   Nürnberg, Germany, June 2010

"Why make things difficult, when it is possible to make them cryptic and totally illogical, with just a little bit more effort?"

— Aksel Peter Jørgensen

Contents

Part I

Low level algorithms

Chapter 1

Bit wizardry

We give low-level functions for binary words, such as isolation of the lowest set bit or counting all set bits. Sometimes the term 'one' is used for a set bit and 'zero' for an unset bit. Where it cannot cause confusion, the term 'bit' is used for a set bit (as in "counting the bits of a word").

The C-type `unsigned long` is abbreviated as `ulong` as defined in [FXT: fxttypes.h]. It is assumed that `BITS_PER_LONG` reflects the size of an `unsigned long`. It is defined in [FXT: bits/bitsperlong.h] and usually equals the machine word size: 32 on 32-bit architectures, and 64 on 64-bit machines. Further, the quantity `BYTES_PER_LONG` reflects the number of bytes in a machine word: it equals `BITS_PER_LONG` divided by eight. For some functions it is assumed that `long` and `ulong` have the same number of bits.

Many functions will only work on machines that use two's complement, which is used by all of the current general purpose computers (the only machines using one's complement appear to be some successors of the UNIVAC system, see [358, entry "UNIVAC 1100/2200 series"]).

The examples of assembler code are for the x86 and the AMD64 architecture. They should be simple enough to be understood by readers who know assembler for any CPU.

1.1 Trivia

1.1.1 Little endian versus big endian

The order in which the bytes of an integer are stored in memory can start with the least significant byte (*little endian* machine) or with the most significant byte (*big endian* machine). The hexadecimal number `0x0D0C0B0A` will be stored in the following manner if memory addresses grow from left to right:

```
adr:    z    z+1   z+2   z+3
mem:    0D    0C    0B    0A    // big endian
mem:    0A    0B    0C    0D    // little endian
```

The difference becomes visible when you cast pointers. Let `V` be the 32-bit integer with the value above. Then the result of `char c = *(char *)(&V);` will be `0x0A` (value modulo 256) on a little endian machine but `0x0D` (value divided by 2^{24}) on a big endian machine. Though friends of big endian sometimes refer to little endian as 'wrong endian', the desired result of the shown pointer cast is much more often the modulo operation.

Whenever words are serialized into bytes, as with transfer over a network or to a disk, one will need two code versions, one for big endian and one for little endian machines. The C-type `union` (with words and bytes) may also require separate treatment for big and little endian architectures.

1.1.2 Size of pointer is not size of int

If programming for a 32-bit architecture (where the size of `int` and `long` coincide), casting pointers to integers (and back) will usually work. The same code *will* fail on 64-bit machines. If you have to cast pointers to an integer type, cast them to a sufficiently big type. For portable code it is better to avoid casting pointers to integer types.

J. Arndt, *Matters Computational: Ideas, Algorithms, Source Code*,
DOI 10.1007/978-3-642-14764-7_1, © Springer-Verlag Berlin Heidelberg 2011

1.1.3 Shifts and division

With two's complement arithmetic division and multiplication by a power of 2 is a right and left shift, respectively. This is true for unsigned types and for multiplication (left shift) with signed types. Division with signed types rounds toward zero, as one would expect, but right shift is a division (by a power of 2) that rounds to $-\infty$:

```
int a = -1;
int c = a >> 1;    // c == -1
int d = a / 2;     // d ==  0
```

The compiler still uses a shift instruction for the division, but with a 'fix' for negative values:

```
 9:test.cc   @ int foo(int a)
10:test.cc   @ {
285 0003 8B442410            movl 16(%esp),%eax  // move argument to %eax
11:test.cc   @     int s = a >> 1;
289 0007 89C1               movl %eax,%ecx
290 0009 D1F9               sarl $1,%ecx
12:test.cc   @     int d = a / 2;
293 000b 89C2               movl %eax,%edx
294 000d C1EA1F             shrl $31,%edx  // fix: %edx=(%edx<0?1:0)
295 0010 01D0               addl %edx,%eax // fix: add one if a<0
296 0012 D1F8               sarl $1,%eax
```

For unsigned types the shift would suffice. One more reason to use unsigned types whenever possible.

The assembler listing was generated from C code via the following commands:

```
# create assembler code:
c++ -S -fverbose-asm -g -O2  test.cc -o test.s
# create asm interlaced with source lines:
as -alhnd test.s  > test.lst
```

There are two types of *right* shifts: a *logical* and an *arithmetical* shift. The logical version (`shrl` in the above fragment) always fills the higher bits with zeros, corresponding to division of unsigned types. The arithmetical shift (`sarl` in the above fragment) fills in ones or zeros, according to the most significant bit of the original word.

Computing remainders modulo a power of 2 with unsigned types is equivalent to a bit-and:

```
ulong a = b % 32;   // == b & (32-1)
```

All of the above is done by the compiler's optimization wherever possible.

Division by (compile time) constants can be replaced by multiplications and shifts. The compiler does it for you. A division by the constant 10 is compiled to:

```
 5:test.cc   @ ulong foo(ulong a)
 6:test.cc   @ {
 7:test.cc   @     ulong b = a / 10;
290 0000 8B442404            movl 4(%esp),%eax
291 0004 F7250000            mull .LC33   // value == 0xcccccccd
292 000a 89D0               movl %edx,%eax
293 000c C1E803             shrl $3,%eax
```

Therefore it is sometimes reasonable to have separate code branches with explicit special values. Similar optimizations can be used for the modulo operation if the modulus is a compile time constant. For example, using modulus 10,000:

```
 8:test.cc   @ ulong foo(ulong a)
 9:test.cc   @ {
53 0000 8B4C2404            movl 4(%esp),%ecx
10:test.cc   @     ulong b = a % 10000;
57 0004 89C8               movl %ecx,%eax
58 0006 F7250000            mull .LC0   // value == 0xd1b71759
59 000c 89D0               movl %edx,%eax
60 000e C1E80D             shrl $13,%eax
61 0011 69C01027            imull $10000,%eax,%eax
62 0017 29C1               subl %eax,%ecx
63 0019 89C8               movl %ecx,%eax
```

Algorithms to replace divisions by a constant with multiplications and shifts are given in [168], see also [346].

Note that the C standard leaves the behavior of a right shift of a signed integer as 'implementation-defined'. The described behavior (that a negative value remains negative after right shift) is the default behavior of many commonly used C compilers.

1.1.4 A pitfall (two's complement)

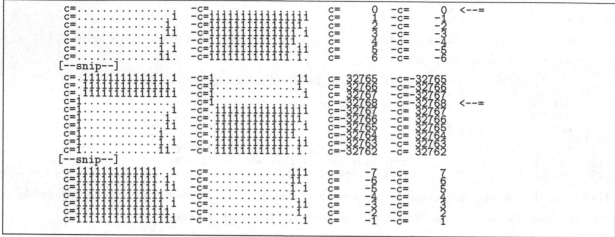

Figure 1.1-A: With two's complement there is one nonzero value that is its own negative.

In two's complement zero is not the only number that is equal to its negative. The value with just the highest bit set (the most negative value) also has this property. Figure 1.1-A (the output of [FXT: bits/gotcha-demo.cc]) shows the situation for words of 16 bits. This is why innocent looking code like the following can simply fail:

```
if ( x<0 )  x = -x;
// assume x positive here (WRONG!)
```

1.1.5 Another pitfall (shifts in the C-language)

A shift by more than BITS_PER_LONG−1 is undefined by the C-standard. Therefore the following function can fail if k is zero:

```
1    static inline ulong first_comb(ulong k)
2    // Return the first combination of (i.e. smallest word with) k bits,
3    // i.e.  00..001111..1 (k low bits set)
4    {
5        ulong t = ~0UL >> ( BITS_PER_LONG - k );
6        return t;
7    }
```

Compilers usually emit just a shift instruction which on certain CPUs does *not* give zero if the shift is equal to or greater than BITS_PER_LONG. This is why the line

```
if ( k==0 )  t = 0;  // shift with BITS_PER_LONG is undefined
```

has to be inserted just before the return statement.

1.1.6 Shortcuts

Test whether at least one of a and b equals zero with

```
if ( !(a && b) )
```

This works for both signed and unsigned integers. Check whether both are zero with

```
if ( (a|b)==0 )
```

This obviously generalizes for several variables as

```
if ( (a|b|c|..|z)==0 )
```

Test whether exactly one of two variables is zero using

```
        if ( (!a) ^ (!b) )
```

1.1.7   Average without overflow

A routine for the computation of the average $(x+y)/2$ of two arguments x and y is [FXT: bits/average.h]

```
1    static inline ulong average(ulong x, ulong y)
2    // Return floor( (x+y)/2 )
3    // Use:       x+y == ((x&y)<<1) + (x^y)
4    // that is:  sum ==  carries   + sum_without_carries
5    {
6        return (x & y) + ((x ^ y) >> 1);
7    }
```

The function gives the correct value even if $(x + y)$ does not fit into a machine word. If it is known that $x \geq y$, then we can use the simpler statement `return y+(x-y)/2`. The following version rounds to infinity:

```
1    static inline ulong ceil_average(ulong x, ulong y)
2    // Use:       x+y == ((x|y)<<1) - (x^y)
3    // ceil_average(x,y) == average(x,y) + ((x^y)&1))
4    {
5        return (x | y) - ((x ^ y) >> 1);
6    }
```

1.1.8   Toggling between values

To toggle an integer x between two values a and b, use:

```
pre-calculate:  t  = a ^ b;
toggle:         x ^= t;   // a <--> b
```

The equivalent trick for floating-point types is

```
pre-calculate:  t = a + b;
toggle:         x = t - x;
```

Here an overflow could occur with a and b in the allowed range if both are close to overflow.

1.1.9   Next or previous even or odd value

Compute the next or previous even or odd value via [FXT: bits/evenodd.h]:

```
1    static inline ulong next_even(ulong x)  { return x+2-(x&1); }
2    static inline ulong prev_even(ulong x)  { return x-2+(x&1); }
3
4    static inline ulong next_odd(ulong x)  { return x+1+(x&1); }
5    static inline ulong prev_odd(ulong x)  { return x-1-(x&1); }
```

The following functions return the unmodified argument if it has the required property, else the nearest such value:

```
1    static inline ulong next0_even(ulong x)  { return x+(x&1); }
2    static inline ulong prev0_even(ulong x)  { return x-(x&1); }
3
4    static inline ulong next0_odd(ulong x)  { return x+1-(x&1); }
5    static inline ulong prev0_odd(ulong x)  { return x-1+(x&1); }
```

Pedro Gimeno gives [priv. comm.] the following optimized versions:

```
1    static inline ulong next_even(ulong x)  { return (x|1)+1; }
2    static inline ulong prev_even(ulong x)  { return (x-1)&~1; }
3
4    static inline ulong next_odd(ulong x)  { return (x+1)|1; }
5    static inline ulong prev_odd(ulong x)  { return (x&~1)-1; }
```

```
1    static inline ulong next0_even(ulong x)  { return (x+1)&~1; }
2    static inline ulong prev0_even(ulong x)  { return x&~1; }
3
4    static inline ulong next0_odd(ulong x)  { return x|1; }
5    static inline ulong prev0_odd(ulong x)  { return (x-1)|1; }
```

1.1.10   Integer versus float multiplication

The floating-point multiplier gives the highest bits of the product. Integer multiplication gives the result modulo 2^b where b is the number of bits of the integer type used. As an example we square the number 111111111 using a 32-bit integer type and floating-point types with 24-bit and 53-bit mantissa (significand):

```
  a =  111111111          // assignment
a*a == 12345678987654321  // true result

a*a == 1653732529                 // result with 32-bit integer multiplication
(a*a)%(2**32) == 1653732529       // ... which is modulo (2**bits_per_int)

a*a == 1.23456794814405440e+16 // result with float multiplication (24 bit mantissa)
a*a == 1.2345678987654320e+16  // result with float multiplication (53 bit mantissa)
```

1.1.11   Double precision float to signed integer conversion

Conversion of double precision floats that have a 53-bit mantissa to signed integers via [11, p.52-53]

```
1    #define DOUBLE2INT(i, d)  { double t = ((d) + 6755399441055744.0); i = *((int *)(&t)); }
2    double x = 123.0;
3    int i;
4    DOUBLE2INT(i, x);
```

can be a faster alternative to

```
1    double x = 123.0;
2    int i = x;
```

The constant used is $6755399441055744 = 2^{52} + 2^{51}$. The method is machine dependent as it relies on the binary representation of the floating-point mantissa. Here it is assumed that, the floating-point number has a 53-bit mantissa with the most significant bit (that is always one with normalized numbers) omitted, and that the address of the number points to the mantissa.

1.1.12   Optimization considerations

Never assume that some code is the 'fastest possible'. There is always another trick that can still improve performance. Many factors can have an influence on performance, like the number of CPU registers or cost of branches. Code that performs well on one machine might perform badly on another. The old trick to swap variables without using a temporary is pretty much out of fashion today:

```
        //     a=0, b=0    a=0, b=1    a=1, b=0    a=1, b=1
a ^= b; //      0    0      1    1      1    0      0    1
b ^= a; //      0    0      1    0      1    1      0    1
a ^= b; //      0    0      1    0      0    1      1    1

// equivalent to:  tmp = a;  a = b;  b = tmp;
```

However, under some conditions (like extreme register pressure) it may be the way to go. Note that if both operands are identical (memory locations) then the result is zero.

The only way to find out which version of a function is faster is to actually do benchmarking (timing). The performance does depend on the sequence of instructions surrounding the machine code, assuming that all of these low-level functions get inlined. Studying the generated CPU instructions helps to understand what happens, but can never replace benchmarking. This means that benchmarks for just the isolated routine can at best give a rough indication. Test your application using different versions of the routine in question.

Never ever delete the unoptimized version of some code fragment when introducing a streamlined one. Keep the original in the source. If something nasty happens (think of low level software failures when porting to a different platform), you will be *very* grateful for the chance to temporarily resort to the slow but correct version.

Study the optimization recommendations for your CPU (like [11] and [12] for the AMD64, see also [144]). You can also learn a lot from the documentation for other architectures.

Proper documentation is an absolute must for optimized code. Always assume that nobody will understand the code without comments. You may not be able to understand uncommented code written by yourself after enough time has passed.

1.2 Operations on individual bits

1.2.1 Testing, setting, and deleting bits

The following functions should be self-explanatory. Following the spirit of the C language there is no check whether the indices used are out of bounds. That is, if any index is greater than or equal to BITS_PER_LONG, the result is undefined [FXT: bits/bittest.h]:

```
1    static inline ulong test_bit(ulong a, ulong i)
2    // Return zero if bit[i] is zero,
3    //   else return one-bit word with bit[i] set.
4    {
5        return  (a & (1UL << i));
6    }
```

The following version returns either zero or one:

```
1    static inline bool test_bit01(ulong a, ulong i)
2    // Return whether bit[i] is set.
3    {
4        return ( 0 != test_bit(a, i) );
5    }
```

Functions for setting, clearing, and changing a bit are:

```
1    static inline ulong set_bit(ulong a, ulong i)
2    // Return a with bit[i] set.
3    {
4        return  (a | (1UL << i));
5    }
```

```
1    static inline ulong clear_bit(ulong a, ulong i)
2    // Return a with bit[i] cleared.
3    {
4        return  (a & ~(1UL << i));
5    }
```

```
1    static inline ulong change_bit(ulong a, ulong i)
2    // Return a with bit[i] changed.
3    {
4        return  (a ^ (1UL << i));
5    }
```

1.2.2 Copying a bit

To copy a bit from one position to another, we generate a one if the bits at the two positions differ. Then an XOR changes the target bit if needed [FXT: bits/bitcopy.h]:

```
1    static inline ulong copy_bit(ulong a, ulong isrc, ulong idst)
2    // Copy bit at [isrc] to position [idst].
3    // Return the modified word.
4    {
5        ulong x = ((a>>isrc) ^ (a>>idst)) & 1;  // one if bits differ
6        a ^= (x<<idst); // change if bits differ
7        return  a;
8    }
```

The situation is more tricky if the bit positions are given as (one bit) masks:

```
1    static inline ulong mask_copy_bit(ulong a, ulong msrc, ulong mdst)
2    // Copy bit according at src-mask (msrc)
3    //   to the bit according to the dest-mask (mdst).
4    // Both msrc and mdst must have exactly one bit set.
5    {
6        ulong x = mdst;
7        if ( msrc & a )  x = 0;  // zero if source bit set
8        x ^= mdst;  // ==mdst if source bit set, else zero
9        a &= ~mdst;  // clear dest bit
```

```
10       a |= x;
11       return a;
12  }
```

The compiler generates branch-free code as the conditional assignment is compiled to a `cmov` (conditional move) assembler instruction. If one or both masks have several bits set, the routine will set all bits of `mdst` if any of the bits in `msrc` is one, or else clear all bits of `mdst`.

1.2.3 Swapping two bits

A function to swap two bits of a word is [FXT: bits/bitswap.h]:

```
1   static inline ulong bit_swap(ulong a, ulong k1, ulong k2)
2   // Return a with bits at positions [k1] and [k2] swapped.
3   // k1==k2 is allowed (a is unchanged then)
4   {
5       ulong x = ((a>>k1) ^ (a>>k2)) & 1;  // one if bits differ
6       a ^= (x<<k2); // change if bits differ
7       a ^= (x<<k1); // change if bits differ
8       return  a;
9   }
```

If it is known that the bits do have different values, the following routine should be used:

```
1   static inline ulong bit_swap_01(ulong a, ulong k1, ulong k2)
2   // Return a with bits at positions [k1] and [k2] swapped.
3   // Bits must have different values (!)
4   // (i.e. one is zero, the other one)
5   // k1==k2 is allowed (a is unchanged then)
6   {
7       return  a ^ ( (1UL<<k1) ^ (1UL<<k2) );
8   }
```

1.3 Operations on low bits or blocks of a word

The underlying idea of functions operating on the lowest set bit is that addition and subtraction of 1 always changes a burst of bits at the lower end of the word. The functions are given in [FXT: bits/bitlow.h].

1.3.1 Isolating, setting, and deleting the lowest one

The lowest one (set bit) is isolated via

```
1   static inline ulong lowest_one(ulong x)
2   // Return word where only the lowest set bit in x is set.
3   // Return 0 if no bit is set.
4   {
5       return  x & -x;  // use: -x == ~x + 1
6   }
```

The lowest zero (unset bit) is isolated using the equivalent of `lowest_one( ~x )`:

```
1   static inline ulong lowest_zero(ulong x)
2   // Return word where only the lowest unset bit in x is set.
3   // Return 0 if all bits are set.
4   {
5       x = ~x;
6       return  x & -x;
7   }
```

Alternatively, we can use either of

```
return  (x ^ (x+1)) & ~x;
return  ((x ^ (x+1)) >> 1 ) + 1;
```

The sequence of returned values for $x = 0, 1, \ldots$ is the highest power of 2 that divides $x + 1$, entry A006519 in [312] (see also entry A001511):

```
x:  ==   x            lowest_zero(x)
0:  == ........        .......1
1:  == .......1        ......1.
2:  == ......1.        .......1
3:  == ......11        .....1..
4:  == .....1..        .......1
5:  == .....1.1        ......1.
6:  == .....11.        .......1
7:  == .....111        ....1...
8:  == ....1...        .......1
9:  == ....1..1        ......1.
10: == ....1.1.        .......1
```

The lowest set bit in a word can be cleared by

```
1    static inline ulong clear_lowest_one(ulong x)
2    // Return word where the lowest bit set in x is cleared.
3    // Return 0 for input == 0.
4    {
5        return  x & (x-1);
6    }
```

The lowest unset bit can be set by

```
1    static inline ulong set_lowest_zero(ulong x)
2    // Return word where the lowest unset bit in x is set.
3    // Return ~0 for input == ~0.
4    {
5        return  x | (x+1);
6    }
```

1.3.2 Computing the index of the lowest one

We compute the index (position) of the lowest bit with an assembler instruction if available [FXT: bits/bitasm-amd64.h]:

```
1    static inline ulong asm_bsf(ulong x)
2    // Bit Scan Forward
3    {
4        asm ("bsfq %0, %0" : "=r" (x) : "0" (x));
5        return x;
6    }
```

Without the assembler instruction an algorithm that involves $O(\log_2 \text{BITS\_PER\_LONG})$ operations can be used. The function can be implemented as follows (suggested by Nathan Bullock [priv. comm.], 64-bit version) [FXT: bits/bitlow.h]:

```
1    static inline ulong lowest_one_idx(ulong x)
2    // Return index of lowest bit set.
3    // Examples:
4    //    ***1 --> 0
5    //    **10 --> 1
6    //    *100 --> 2
7    // Return 0 (also) if no bit is set.
8    {
9        ulong r = 0;
10       x &= -x;  // isolate lowest bit
11       if ( x & 0xffffffff00000000UL )  r += 32;
12       if ( x & 0xffff0000ffff0000UL )  r += 16;
13       if ( x & 0xff00ff00ff00ff00UL )  r += 8;
14       if ( x & 0xf0f0f0f0f0f0f0f0UL )  r += 4;
15       if ( x & 0xccccccccccccccccUL )  r += 2;
16       if ( x & 0xaaaaaaaaaaaaaaaaUL )  r += 1;
17       return r;
18   }
```

The function returns zero for two inputs, one and zero. If a special value for the input zero is needed, a statement as the following should be added as the first line of the function:

```
    if ( 1>=x )  return  x-1; // 0 if 1, ~0 if 0
```

The following function returns the parity of the index of the lowest set bit in a binary word

```
1    static inline ulong lowest_one_idx_parity(ulong x)
2    {
3        x &= -x;  // isolate lowest bit
```

```
4        return  0 != (x & 0xaaaaaaaaaaaaaaaaUL);
5    }
```

The sequence of values for $x = 0, 1, 2, \ldots$ is

00100010101000100010001010100010101000101010001000100010101000010...

This is the complement of the *period-doubling sequence*, entry A035263 in [312]. See section 38.5.1 on page 735 for the connection to the towers of Hanoi puzzle.

1.3.3   Isolating blocks of zeros or ones at the low end

Isolate the burst of low ones as follows [FXT: bits/bitlow.h]:

```
1    static inline ulong low_ones(ulong x)
2    // Return word where all the (low end) ones are set.
3    // Example:  01011011 --> 00000011
4    // Return 0 if lowest bit is zero:
5    //         10110110 --> 0
6    {
7        x = ~x;
8        x &= -x;
9        --x;
10       return x;
11   }
```

The isolation of the low zeros is slightly cheaper:

```
1    static inline ulong low_zeros(ulong x)
2    // Return word where all the (low end) zeros are set.
3    // Example:  01011000 --> 00000111
4    // Return 0 if all bits are set.
5    {
6        x &= -x;
7        --x;
8        return x;
9    }
```

The lowest block of ones (which may have zeros to the right of it) can be isolated by

```
1    static inline ulong lowest_block(ulong x)
2    // Isolate lowest block of ones.
3    // e.g.:
4    // x   = *****011100
5    // l   = 00000000100
6    // y   = *****100000
7    // x^y = 00000111100
8    // ret = 00000011100
9    {
10       ulong l = x & -x;  // lowest bit
11       ulong y = x + l;
12       x ^= y;
13       return  x & (x>>1);
14   }
```

1.3.4   Creating a transition at the lowest one

Use the following routines to set a rising or falling edge at the position of the lowest set bit [FXT: bits/bitlow-edge.h]:

```
1    static inline ulong lowest_one_10edge(ulong x)
2    // Return word where all bits from (including) the
3    //    lowest set bit to most significant bit are set.
4    // Return 0 if no bit is set.
5    // Example:  00110100 --> 11111100
6    {
7        return ( x | -x );
8    }
```

```
1    static inline ulong lowest_one_01edge(ulong x)
2    // Return word where all bits from  (including) the
3    //    lowest set bit to the least significant are set.
4    // Return 0 if no bit is set.
5    // Example:  00110100 --> 00000111
```

```
6    {
7        if ( 0==x )  return 0;
8        return  x^(x-1);
9    }
```

1.3.5   Isolating the lowest run of matching bits

Let $x = *0W$ and $y = *1W$, the following function computes W:

```
1    static inline ulong low_match(ulong x, ulong y)
2    {
3        x ^= y;   // bit-wise difference
4        x &= -x;  // lowest bit that differs in both words
5        x -= 1;   // mask that covers equal bits at low end
6        x &= y;   // isolate matching bits
7        return x;
8    }
```

1.4   Extraction of ones, zeros, or blocks near transitions

We give functions for the creation or extraction of bit-blocks and the isolation of values near transitions. A transition is a place where adjacent bits have different values. A block is a group of adjacent bits of the same value.

1.4.1   Creating blocks of ones

The following functions are given in [FXT: bits/bitblock.h].

```
1    static inline ulong bit_block(ulong p, ulong n)
2    // Return word with length-n bit block starting at bit p set.
3    // Both p and n are effectively taken modulo BITS_PER_LONG.
4    {
5        ulong x = (1UL<<n) - 1;
6        return  x << p;
7    }
```

A version with indices wrapping around is

```
1    static inline ulong cyclic_bit_block(ulong p, ulong n)
2    // Return word with length-n bit block starting at bit p set.
3    // The result is possibly wrapped around the word boundary.
4    // Both p and n are effectively taken modulo BITS_PER_LONG.
5    {
6        ulong x = (1UL<<n) - 1;
7        return  (x<<p) | (x>>(BITS_PER_LONG-p));
8    }
```

1.4.2   Finding isolated ones or zeros

The following functions are given in [FXT: bits/bit-isolate.h]:

```
1    static inline ulong single_ones(ulong x)
2    // Return word with only the isolated ones of x set.
3    {
4        return x & ~( (x<<1) | (x>>1) );
5    }
```

We can assume a word is embedded in zeros or ignore the bits outside the word:

```
1    static inline ulong single_zeros_xi(ulong x)
2    // Return word with only the isolated zeros of x set.
3    {
4        return  single_ones( ~x );  // ignore outside values
5    }
```

```
1    static inline ulong single_zeros(ulong x)
2    // Return word with only the isolated zeros of x set.
3    {
4        return  ~x & ( (x<<1) & (x>>1) );  // assume outside values == 0
5    }
```

```
1    static inline ulong single_values(ulong x)
2    // Return word where only the isolated ones and zeros of x are set.
3    {
4        return  (x ^ (x<<1)) & (x ^ (x>>1));  // assume outside values == 0
5    }
```

```
1    static inline ulong single_values_xi(ulong x)
2    // Return word where only the isolated ones and zeros of x are set.
3    {
4        return  single_ones(x) | single_zeros_xi(x);  // ignore outside values
5    }
```

1.4.3 Isolating single ones or zeros at the word boundary

```
1    static inline ulong border_ones(ulong x)
2    // Return word where only those ones of x are set that lie next to a zero.
3    {
4        return  x & ~( (x<<1) & (x>>1) );
5    }
```

```
1    static inline ulong border_values(ulong x)
2    // Return word where those bits of x are set that lie on a transition.
3    {
4        return  (x ^ (x<<1)) | (x ^ (x>>1));
5    }
```

1.4.4 Isolating transitions

```
1    static inline ulong high_border_ones(ulong x)
2    // Return word where only those ones of x are set
3    //    that lie right to (i.e. in the next lower bin of) a zero.
4    {
5        return  x & ( x ^ (x>>1) );
6    }
```

```
1    static inline ulong low_border_ones(ulong x)
2    // Return word where only those ones of x are set
3    //    that lie left to (i.e. in the next higher bin of) a zero.
4    {
5        return  x & ( x ^ (x<<1) );
6    }
```

1.4.5 Isolating ones or zeros at block boundaries

```
1    static inline ulong block_border_ones(ulong x)
2    // Return word where only those ones of x are set
3    //    that are at the border of a block of at least 2 bits.
4    {
5        return  x & ( (x<<1) ^ (x>>1) );
6    }
```

```
1    static inline ulong low_block_border_ones(ulong x)
2    // Return word where only those bits of x are set
3    //    that are at left of a border of a block of at least 2 bits.
4    {
5        ulong t = x & ( (x<<1) ^ (x>>1) );  // block_border_ones()
6        return  t & (x>>1);
7    }
```

```
1    static inline ulong high_block_border_ones(ulong x)
2    // Return word where only those bits of x are set
3    //    that are at right of a border of a block of at least 2 bits.
4    {
5        ulong t = x & ( (x<<1) ^ (x>>1) );  // block_border_ones()
6        return  t & (x<<1);
7    }
```

```
1    static inline ulong block_ones(ulong x)
2    // Return word where only those bits of x are set
3    //    that are part of a block of at least 2 bits.
4    {
5        return  x & ( (x<<1) | (x>>1) );
6    }
```

1.5 Computing the index of a single set bit

In the function `lowest_one_idx()` given in section 1.3.2 on page 9 we first isolated the lowest one of a word x by first setting `x&=-x`. At this point, x contains just one set bit (or `x==0`). The following lines in the routine compute the index of the only bit set. This section gives some alternative techniques to compute the index of the one in a single-bit word.

1.5.1 Cohen's trick

```
modulus m=11
     k =  0  1  2  3  4  5  6  7
mt[k]=  0  0  1  8  2  4  9  7

Lowest bit == 0:        x= .......1 =    1    x % m=  1 ==> lookup = 0
Lowest bit == 1:        x= ......1. =    2    x % m=  2 ==> lookup = 1
Lowest bit == 2:        x= .....1.. =    4    x % m=  4 ==> lookup = 2
Lowest bit == 3:        x= ....1... =    8    x % m=  8 ==> lookup = 3
Lowest bit == 4:        x= ...1.... =   16    x % m=  5 ==> lookup = 4
Lowest bit == 5:        x= ..1..... =   32    x % m= 10 ==> lookup = 5
Lowest bit == 6:        x= .1...... =   64    x % m=  9 ==> lookup = 6
Lowest bit == 7:        x= 1....... =  128    x % m=  7 ==> lookup = 7
```

Figure 1.5-A: Determination of the position of a single bit with 8-bit words.

A nice trick is presented in [110]: for N-bit words find a number m such that all powers of 2 are different modulo m. That is, the (multiplicative) order of 2 modulo m must be greater than or equal to N. We use a table `mt[]` of size m that contains the power of 2: `mt[(2**j) mod m] = j` for $j > 0$. To look up the index of a one-bit-word x it is reduced modulo m and `mt[x]` is returned.

We demonstrate the method for $N = 8$ where $m = 11$ is the smallest number with the required property. The setup routine for the table is

```
1    const ulong m = 11; // the modulus
2    ulong mt[m+1];
3    static void mt_setup()
4    {
5        mt[0] = 0;  // special value for the zero word
6        ulong t = 1;
7        for (ulong i=1; i<m; ++i)
8        {
9            mt[t] = i-1;
10           t *= 2;
11           if ( t>=m )  t -= m;  // modular reduction
12       }
13   }
```

The entry in `mt[0]` will be accessed when the input is the zero word. We can use any value to be returned for input zero. Here we simply use zero to always have the same return value as with `lowest_one_idx()`. The index can be computed by

```
1    static inline ulong m_lowest_one_idx(ulong x)
2    {
3        x &= -x;  // isolate lowest bit
4        x %= m;   // power of 2 modulo m
5        return  mt[x]; // lookup
6    }
```

The code is given in the program [FXT: bits/modular-lookup-demo.cc], the output with $N = 8$ (edited for size) is shown in figure 1.5-A. The following moduli $m(N)$ can be used for N-bit words:

```
N:   4    8   16   32   64  128  256  512  1024
m:   5   11   19   37   67  131  269  523  1061
```

The modulus $m(N)$ is the smallest prime greater than N such that 2 is a primitive root modulo $m(N)$.

```
db=...1.111   (De Bruijn sequence)
   k  = 0  1  2  3  4  5  6  7
dbt[k] = 0  1  2  4  7  3  6  5

Lowest bit == 0:   x = .......1   db * x = ...1.111   shifted = ........ == 0 ==> lookup = 0
Lowest bit == 1:   x = ......1.   db * x = ..1.111.   shifted = .......1 == 1 ==> lookup = 1
Lowest bit == 2:   x = .....1..   db * x = .1.111..   shifted = ......1. == 2 ==> lookup = 2
Lowest bit == 3:   x = ....1...   db * x = 1.111...   shifted = .....1.1 == 5 ==> lookup = 3
Lowest bit == 4:   x = ...1....   db * x = .111....   shifted = .....11 == 3 ==> lookup = 4
Lowest bit == 5:   x = ..1.....   db * x = 111.....   shifted = ....111 == 7 ==> lookup = 5
Lowest bit == 6:   x = .1......   db * x = 11......   shifted = .....11. == 6 ==> lookup = 6
Lowest bit == 7:   x = 1.......   db * x = 1.......   shifted = .....1.. == 4 ==> lookup = 7
```

Figure 1.5-B: Computing the position of the single set bit in 8-bit words with a De Bruijn sequence.

1.5.2   Using De Bruijn sequences

The following method (given in [228]) is even more elegant. It uses binary De Bruijn sequences of size N. A binary De Bruijn sequence of length 2^N contains all binary words of length N, see section 41.1 on page 864. These are the sequences for 32 and 64 bit, as binary words:

```
#if BITS_PER_LONG == 32
const ulong db = 0x4653ADFUL;
// == 00000100011001010011101011011111
const ulong s = 32-5;
#else
const ulong db = 0x218A392CD3D5DBFUL;
// == 0000001000011000101000111001001011001101001111010101110110111111
const ulong s = 64-6;
#endif
```

Let w_i be the i-th sub-word from the left (high end). We create a table such that the entry with index w_i points to i:

```
1    ulong dbt[BITS_PER_LONG];
2    static void dbt_setup()
3    {
4        for (ulong i=0; i<BITS_PER_LONG; ++i)  dbt[ (db<<i)>>s ] = i;
5    }
```

The computation of the index involves a multiplication and a table lookup:

```
1    static inline ulong db_lowest_one_idx(ulong x)
2    {
3        x &= -x;   // isolate lowest bit
4        x *= db;   // multiplication by a power of 2 is a shift
5        x >>= s;   // use log_2(BITS_PER_LONG) highest bits
6        return dbt[x];   // lookup
7    }
```

The used sequences must start with at least $\log_2(N) - 1$ zeros because in the line x *= db the word x is shifted (not rotated). The code is given in the demo [FXT: bits/debruijn-lookup-demo.cc], the output with $N = 8$ (edited for size, dots denote zeros) is shown in figure 1.5-B.

1.5.3   Using floating-point numbers

Floating-point numbers are normalized so that the highest bit in the mantissa is set. Therefore if we convert an integer into a float, the position of the *highest* set bit can be read off the exponent. By isolating the lowest bit before that operation, the index can be found with the same trick. However, the conversion between integers and floats is usually slow. Further, the technique is highly machine dependent.

1.6   Operations on high bits or blocks of a word

For functions operating on the highest bit there is no method as trivial as shown for the lower end of the word. With a bit-reverse CPU-instruction available life would be significantly easier. However, almost no CPU seems to have it.

1.6.1 Isolating the highest one and finding its index

```
..............1111....1111.111 = 0xf0f7   == word
................1............. = highest_one
..............1111111111111111 = highest_one_01edge
1111111111111111.............. = highest_one_10edge
                           15 = highest_one_idx
.............................. 111 = low_zeros
.......................111 = low_ones
.........................1 = lowest_one
.........................1 = lowest_one_01edge
1111111111111111111111111111111 = lowest_one_10edge
                            0 = lowest_one_idx
.......................111 = lowest_block
............1111....1111.11. = clear_lowest_one
...................1.... = lowest_zero
............1111....11111111 = set_lowest_zero
.............................. = high_ones
1111111111111111.............. = high_zeros
1............................. = highest_zero
1.............1111....1111.111 = set_highest_zero
```

```
1111111111111111....1111....1... = 0xffff0f08   == word
1............................. = highest_one
11111111111111111111111111111111 = highest_one_01edge
1............................. = highest_one_10edge
                           31 = highest_one_idx
..........................111 = low_zeros
.............................. = low_ones
.................1... = lowest_one
................1111 = lowest_one_01edge
11111111111111111111111111111... = lowest_one_10edge
                            3 = lowest_one_idx
.................1... = lowest_block
1111111111111111....1111...... = clear_lowest_one
.........................1 = lowest_zero
1111111111111111....1111....1..1 = set_lowest_zero
1111111111111111.............. = high_ones
.............................. = high_zeros
.................1............. = highest_zero
1111111111111111...1111....1... = set_highest_zero
```

Figure 1.6-A: Operations on the highest and lowest bits (and blocks) of a binary word for two different 32-bit input words. Dots denote zeros.

Isolation of the highest set bit is easy if a bit-scan instruction is available [FXT: bits/bitasm-i386.h]:

```
1    static inline ulong asm_bsr(ulong x)
2    // Bit Scan Reverse
3    {
4        asm ("bsrl %0, %0" : "=r" (x) : "0" (x));
5        return x;
6    }
```

Without a bit-scan instruction, we use the auxiliary function [FXT: bits/bithigh-edge.h]

```
1    static inline ulong highest_one_01edge(ulong x)
2    // Return word where all bits from (including) the
3    //   highest set bit to bit 0 are set.
4    // Return 0 if no bit is set.
5    {
6        x |= x>>1;
7        x |= x>>2;
8        x |= x>>4;
9        x |= x>>8;
10       x |= x>>16;
11   #if  BITS_PER_LONG >= 64
12       x |= x>>32;
13   #endif
14       return  x;
15   }
```

The resulting code is [FXT: bits/bithigh.h]

```
1    static inline ulong highest_one(ulong x)
2    // Return word where only the highest bit in x is set.
3    // Return 0 if no bit is set.
4    {
5    #if defined  BITS_USE_ASM
6        if ( 0==x )  return 0;
7        x = asm_bsr(x);
8        return  1UL<<x;
9    #else
10        x = highest_one_01edge(x);
11        return  x ^ (x>>1);
12   #endif // BITS_USE_ASM
13   }
```

To determine the index of the highest set bit, use

```
1    static inline ulong highest_one_idx(ulong x)
2    // Return index of highest bit set.
3    // Return 0 if no bit is set.
4    {
5    #if defined  BITS_USE_ASM
6        return  asm_bsr(x);
7    #else // BITS_USE_ASM
8
9        if ( 0==x )  return  0;
10
11       ulong r = 0;
12   #if  BITS_PER_LONG >= 64
13       if ( x & 0xffffffff00000000UL )  { x >>= 32;  r += 32; }
14   #endif
15       if ( x & 0xffff0000UL )  { x >>= 16;  r += 16; }
16       if ( x & 0x0000ff00UL )  { x >>=  8;  r +=  8; }
17       if ( x & 0x000000f0UL )  { x >>=  4;  r +=  4; }
18       if ( x & 0x0000000cUL )  { x >>=  2;  r +=  2; }
19       if ( x & 0x00000002UL )  {           r +=  1; }
20       return r;
21   #endif // BITS_USE_ASM
22   }
```

The branches in the non-assembler part of the routine can be avoided by a technique given in [215, rel.96, sect.7.1.3] (version for 64-bit words):

```
1    static inline ulong highest_one_idx(ulong x)
2    {
3    #define MU0 0x5555555555555555UL  // MU0 == ((-1UL)/3UL)  == ...01010101_2
4    #define MU1 0x3333333333333333UL  // MU1 == ((-1UL)/5UL)      == ...00110011_2
5    #define MU2 0x0f0f0f0f0f0f0f0fUL  // MU2 == ((-1UL)/17UL)   == ...00001111_2
6    #define MU3 0x00ff00ff00ff00ffUL  // MU3 == ((-1UL)/257UL)   == (8 ones)
7    #define MU4 0x0000ffff0000ffffUL  // MU4 == ((-1UL)/65537UL) == (16 ones)
8    #define MU5 0x00000000ffffffffUL  // MU5 == ((-1UL)/4294967297UL) == (32 ones)
9        ulong r = ld_neq(x, x & MU0)
10           + (ld_neq(x, x & MU1) << 1)
11           + (ld_neq(x, x & MU2) << 2)
12           + (ld_neq(x, x & MU3) << 3)
13           + (ld_neq(x, x & MU4) << 4)
14           + (ld_neq(x, x & MU5) << 5);
15       return r;
16   }
```

The auxiliary function `ld_neq()` is given in [FXT: bits/bitldeq.h]:

```
1    static inline bool ld_neq(ulong x, ulong y)
2    // Return whether floor(log2(x))!=floor(log2(y))
3    { return  ( (x^y) > (x&y) ); }
```

The following version for 64-bit words provided by Sebastiano Vigna [priv. comm.] is an implementation of Brodal's algorithm [215, alg.B, sect.7.1.3]:

```
1    static inline ulong highest_one_idx(ulong x)
2    {
3        if ( x == 0 )  return 0;
4        ulong r = 0;
5        if ( x & 0xffffffff00000000UL )  { x >>= 32;  r += 32; }
6        if ( x & 0xffff0000UL )          { x >>= 16;  r += 16; }
7        x |= (x << 16);
8        x |= (x << 32);
9        const ulong y = x & 0xff00f0f0ccccaaaaUL;
```

```
10      const ulong z = 0x8000800080008000UL;
11      ulong t = z & ( y | (( y | z ) - ( x ^ y )));
12      t |= (t << 15);
13      t |= (t << 30);
14      t |= (t << 60);
15      return  r + ( t >> 60 );
16  }
```

1.6.2 Isolating the highest block of ones or zeros

Isolate the left block of zeros with the function

```
1   static inline ulong high_zeros(ulong x)
2   // Return word where all the (high end) zeros are set.
3   // e.g.:  00011001 --> 11100000
4   // Returns 0 if highest bit is set:
5   //        11011001 --> 00000000
6   {
7       x |= x>>1;
8       x |= x>>2;
9       x |= x>>4;
10      x |= x>>8;
11      x |= x>>16;
12  #if  BITS_PER_LONG >= 64
13      x |= x>>32;
14  #endif
15      return  ~x;
16  }
```

The left block of ones can be isolated using arithmetical right shifts:

```
1   static inline ulong high_ones(ulong x)
2   // Return word where all the (high end) ones are set.
3   // e.g.  11001011 --> 11000000
4   // Returns 0 if highest bit is zero:
5   //        01110110 --> 00000000
6   {
7       long y = (long)x;
8       y &= y>>1;
9       y &= y>>2;
10      y &= y>>4;
11      y &= y>>8;
12      y &= y>>16;
13  #if  BITS_PER_LONG >= 64
14      y &= y>>32;
15  #endif
16      return  (ulong)y;
17  }
```

If arithmetical shifts are more expensive than unsigned shifts, use

```
1   static inline ulong high_ones(ulong x)  { return  high_zeros( ~x ); }
```

A demonstration of selected functions operating on the highest or lowest bit (or block) of binary words is given in [FXT: bits/bithilo-demo.cc]. Part of its output is shown in figure 1.6-A.

1.7 Functions related to the base-2 logarithm

The following functions are given in [FXT: bits/bit2pow.h]. A function that returns $\lfloor \log_2(x) \rfloor$ can be implemented using the obvious algorithm:

```
1   static inline ulong ld(ulong x)
2   // Return floor(log2(x)),
3   // i.e. return k so that 2^k <= x < 2^(k+1)
4   // If x==0, then 0 is returned (!)
5   {
6       ulong k = 0;
7       while ( x>>=1 )  { ++k; }
8       return k;
9   }
```

The result is the same as returned by `highest_one_idx()`:

```
1    static inline ulong ld(ulong x) { return  highest_one_idx(x); }
```

The bit-wise algorithm can be faster if the average result is known to be small.

Use the function `one_bit_q()` to determine whether its argument is a power of 2:

```
1    static inline bool one_bit_q(ulong x)
2    // Return whether x \in {1,2,4,8,16,...}
3    {
4        ulong m = x-1;
5        return   (((x^m)>>1) == m);
6    }
```

The following function does the same except that it returns `true` also for the zero argument:

```
1    static inline bool is_pow_of_2(ulong x)
2    // Return whether x == 0(!) or x == 2**k
3    { return   !(x & (x-1)); }
```

With FFTs where the length of the transform is often restricted to power of 2 the following functions are useful:

```
1    static inline ulong next_pow_of_2(ulong x)
2    // Return x if x=2**k
3    // else return 2**ceil(log_2(x))
4    // Exception: returns 0 for x==0
5    {
6        if ( is_pow_of_2(x) )  return x;
7        x |= x >> 1;
8        x |= x >> 2;
9        x |= x >> 4;
10       x |= x >> 8;
11       x |= x >> 16;
12   #if BITS_PER_LONG == 64
13       x |= x >> 32;
14   #endif
15       return   x + 1;
16   }
```

```
1    static inline ulong next_exp_of_2(ulong x)
2    // Return k if x=2**k else return k+1.
3    // Exception: returns 0 for x==0.
4    {
5        if ( x <= 1 )   return 0;
6        return ld(x-1) + 1;
7    }
```

The following version should be faster if inline assembler is used for `ld()`:

```
1    static inline ulong next_pow_of_2(ulong x)
2    {
3        if ( is_pow_of_2(x) )   return x;
4        ulong n = 1UL<<ld(x);   // n<x
5        return   n<<1;
6    }
```

The following routine for comparison of base-2 logarithms without actually computing them is suggested by [215, rel.58, sect.7.1.3] [FXT: bits/bitldeq.h]:

```
1    static inline bool ld_eq(ulong x, ulong y)
2    // Return whether floor(log2(x))==floor(log2(y))
3    { return   ( (x^y) <= (x&y) ); }
```

1.8   Counting the bits and blocks of a word

The following functions count the ones in a binary word. They need $O\left(\log_2(\text{BITS\_PER\_LONG})\right)$ operations. We give mostly the 64-bit versions [FXT: bits/bitcount.h]:

```
1    static inline ulong bit_count(ulong x)
2    // Return number of bits set
3    {
4        x = (0x5555555555555555UL & x) + (0x5555555555555555UL & (x>> 1));  // 0-2 in 2 bits
5        x = (0x3333333333333333UL & x) + (0x3333333333333333UL & (x>> 2));  // 0-4 in 4 bits
6        x = (0x0f0f0f0f0f0f0f0fUL & x) + (0x0f0f0f0f0f0f0f0fUL & (x>> 4));  // 0-8 in 8 bits
7        x = (0x00ff00ff00ff00ffUL & x) + (0x00ff00ff00ff00ffUL & (x>> 8));  // 0-16 in 16 bits
```

```
8        x = (0x0000ffff0000ffffUL & x) + (0x0000ffff0000ffffUL & (x>>16));   // 0-32 in 32 bits
9        x = (0x00000000ffffffffUL & x) + (0x00000000ffffffffUL & (x>>32));   // 0-64 in 64 bits
10       return x;
11   }
```

The underlying idea is to do a search via bit masks. The code can be improved to either

```
1        x = ((x>>1) & 0x5555555555555555UL) + (x & 0x5555555555555555UL);   // 0-2 in 2 bits
2        x = ((x>>2) & 0x3333333333333333UL) + (x & 0x3333333333333333UL);   // 0-4 in 4 bits
3        x = ((x>>4) + x) & 0x0f0f0f0f0f0f0f0fUL;                            // 0-8 in 8 bits
4        x +=  x>> 8;                                                        // 0-16 in 8 bits
5        x +=  x>>16;                                                        // 0-32 in 8 bits
6        x +=  x>>32;                                                        // 0-64 in 8 bits
7        return  x & 0xff;
```

or (taken from [10])

```
1        x -=  (x>>1) & 0x5555555555555555UL;                               // 0-2 in 2 bits
2        x  = ((x>>2) & 0x3333333333333333UL) + (x & 0x3333333333333333UL);  // 0-4 in 4 bits
3        x  = ((x>>4) + x) & 0x0f0f0f0f0f0f0f0fUL;                          // 0-8 in 8 bits
4        x *= 0x0101010101010101UL;
5        return  x>>56;
```

Which of the latter two versions is faster mainly depends on the speed of integer multiplication.

The following code for 32-bit words (given by Johan Rönnblom [priv. comm.]) may be advantageous if loading constants is expensive. Note some constants are in octal notation:

```
1    static inline uint CountBits32(uint a)
2    {
3        uint mask = 011111111111UL;
4        a = (a - ((a&~mask)>>1)) - ((a>>2)&mask);
5        a += a>>3;
6        a = (a & 070707) + ((a>>18) & 070707);
7        a *= 010101;
8        return  ((a>>12) & 0x3f);
9    }
```

If the table holds the bit-counts of the numbers 0...255, then the bits can be counted as follows:

```
1    ulong bit_count(ulong x)
2    {
3        unsigned char ct = 0;
4        ct += tab[ x & 0xff ];   x >>= 8;
5        ct += tab[ x & 0xff ];   x >>= 8;
6    [--snip--]  /* BYTES_PER_LONG times */
7        ct += tab[ x & 0xff ];
8        return ct;
9    }
```

However, while table driven methods tend to excel in synthetic benchmarks, they can be very slow if they cause cache misses.

We give a method to count the bits of a word of a special form:

```
1    static inline ulong bit_count_01(ulong x)
2    // Return number of bits in a word
3    // for words of the special form 00...0001...11
4    {
5        ulong ct = 0;
6        ulong a;
7    #if  BITS_PER_LONG == 64
8        a = (x & (1UL<<32)) >> (32-5);   // test bit 32
9        x >>= a;   ct += a;
10   #endif
11       a = (x & (1UL<<16)) >> (16-4);   // test bit 16
12       x >>= a;   ct += a;
13
14       a = (x & (1UL<<8)) >> (8-3);   // test bit 8
15       x >>= a;   ct += a;
16
17       a = (x & (1UL<<4)) >> (4-2);   // test bit 4
18       x >>= a;   ct += a;
19
20       a = (x & (1UL<<2)) >> (2-1);   // test bit 2
21       x >>= a;   ct += a;
22
23       a = (x & (1UL<<1)) >> (1-0);   // test bit 1
```

```
24        x >>= a;  ct += a;
25
26        ct += x & 1; // test bit 0
27
28        return ct;
29    }
```

All branches are avoided, thereby the code may be useful on a planet with pink air, for further details
see [301].

1.8.1   Sparse counting

If the (average input) word is known to have only a few bits set, the following sparse count variant can
be advantageous:

```
1    static inline ulong bit_count_sparse(ulong x)
2    // Return number of bits set.
3    {
4        ulong n = 0;
5        while ( x )  { ++n;  x &= (x-1); }
6        return  n;
7    }
```

The loop will execute once for each set bit. Partial unrolling of the loop should be an improvement for
most cases:

```
1        ulong n = 0;
2        do
3        {
4            n += (x!=0);  x &= (x-1);
5            n += (x!=0);  x &= (x-1);
6            n += (x!=0);  x &= (x-1);
7            n += (x!=0);  x &= (x-1);
8        }
9        while ( x );
10       return  n;
```

If the number of bits is close to the maximum, use the given routine with the complement:

```
1    static inline ulong bit_count_dense(ulong x)
2    // Return number of bits set.
3    // The loop (of bit_count_sparse()) will execute once for
4    //   each unset bit (i.e. zero) of x.
5    {
6        return  BITS_PER_LONG - bit_count_sparse( ~x );
7    }
```

If the number of ones is guaranteed to be less than 16, then the following routine (suggested by Gunther
Piez [priv. comm.]) can be used:

```
1    static inline ulong bit_count_15(ulong x)
2    // Return number of set bits, must have at most 15 set bits.
3    {
4        x -=  (x>>1) & 0x5555555555555555UL;                                   // 0-2 in 2 bits
5        x = ((x>>2) & 0x3333333333333333UL) + (x & 0x3333333333333333UL);  // 0-4 in 4 bits
6        x *= 0x1111111111111111UL;
7        return  x>>60;
8    }
```

A routine for words with no more than 3 set bits is

```
1    static inline ulong bit_count_3(ulong x)
2    {
3        x -=  (x>>1) & 0x5555555555555555UL;  // 0-2 in 2 bits
4        x *= 0x5555555555555555UL;
5        return  x>>62;
6    }
```

1.8.2   Counting blocks

Compute the number of bit-blocks in a binary word with the following function:

```
1    static inline ulong bit_block_count(ulong x)
2    // Return number of bit blocks.
3    // E.g.:
4    // ..1..11111...111.  -> 3
```

```
5  // ...1..11111...111  -> 3
6  // ......1.....1.1..  -> 3
7  // .........111.1111  -> 2
8  {
9      return  (x & 1) + bit_count( (x^(x>>1)) ) / 2;
10 }
```

Similarly, the number of blocks with two or more bits can be counted via:

```
1   static inline ulong bit_block_ge2_count(ulong x)
2   // Return number of bit blocks with at least 2 bits.
3   // E.g.:
4   // ..1..11111...111.  -> 2
5   // ...1..11111...111  -> 2
6   // ......1.....1.1..  -> 0
7   // .........111.1111  -> 2
8   {
9       return  bit_block_count( x & ( (x<<1) & (x>>1) ) );
10  }
```

1.8.3   GCC built-in functions ‡

Newer versions of the C compiler of the GNU Compiler Collection (GCC [146], starting with version 3.4) include a function `__builtin_popcountl(ulong)` that counts the bits of an unsigned long integer. The following list is taken from [147]:

```
int __builtin_ffs (unsigned int x)
    Returns one plus the index of the least significant 1-bit of x,
    or if x is zero, returns zero.

int __builtin_clz (unsigned int x)
    Returns the number of leading 0-bits in x, starting at the
    most significant bit position.  If x is 0, the result is undefined.

int __builtin_ctz (unsigned int x)
    Returns the number of trailing 0-bits in x, starting at the
    least significant bit position.  If x is 0, the result is undefined.

int __builtin_popcount (unsigned int x)
    Returns the number of 1-bits in x.

int __builtin_parity (unsigned int x)
    Returns the parity of x, i.e. the number of 1-bits in x modulo 2.
```

The names of the corresponding versions for arguments of type unsigned long are obtained by adding '`l`' (ell) to the names, for the type unsigned long long append '`ll`'. Two more useful built-ins are:

```
void __builtin_prefetch (const void *addr, ...)
    Prefetch memory location addr

long __builtin_expect (long exp, long c)
    Function to provide the compiler with branch prediction information.
```

1.8.4   Counting the bits of many words ‡

```
x[ 0]=11111111  a0=11111111  a1=........  a2=........  a3=........  a4=........
x[ 1]=11111111  a0=........  a1=11111111  a2=........  a3=........  a4=........
x[ 2]=11111111  a0=11111111  a1=11111111  a2=........  a3=........  a4=........
x[ 3]=11111111  a0=........  a1=........  a2=11111111  a3=........  a4=........
x[ 4]=11111111  a0=11111111  a1=........  a2=11111111  a3=........  a4=........
x[ 5]=11111111  a0=........  a1=11111111  a2=11111111  a3=........  a4=........
x[ 6]=11111111  a0=11111111  a1=11111111  a2=11111111  a3=........  a4=........
x[ 7]=11111111  a0=........  a1=........  a2=........  a3=11111111  a4=........
x[ 8]=11111111  a0=11111111  a1=........  a2=........  a3=11111111  a4=........
x[ 9]=11111111  a0=........  a1=11111111  a2=........  a3=11111111  a4=........
x[10]=11111111  a0=11111111  a1=11111111  a2=........  a3=11111111  a4=........
x[11]=11111111  a0=........  a1=........  a2=11111111  a3=11111111  a4=........
x[12]=11111111  a0=11111111  a1=........  a2=11111111  a3=11111111  a4=........
x[13]=11111111  a0=........  a1=11111111  a2=11111111  a3=11111111  a4=........
x[14]=11111111  a0=11111111  a1=11111111  a2=11111111  a3=11111111  a4=........
x[15]=11111111  a0=........  a1=........  a2=........  a3=........  a4=11111111
x[16]=11111111  a0=11111111  a1=........  a2=........  a3=........  a4=11111111
```

Figure 1.8-A: Counting the bits of an array (where all bits are set) via vertical addition.

For counting the bits in a long array the technique of *vertical addition* can be useful. For ordinary addition the following relation holds:

```
a + b  ==  (a^b) + ((a&b)<<1)
```

The carry term (a&b) is propagated to the left. We now replace this 'horizontal' propagation by a 'vertical' one, that is, propagation into another word. An implementation of this idea is [FXT: bits/bitcount-v-demo.cc]:

```
1    ulong
2    bit_count_leq31(const ulong *x, ulong n)
3    // Return sum(j=0, n-1, bit_count(x[j]) )
4    // Must have  n<=31
5    {
6        ulong a0=0, a1=0, a2=0, a3=0, a4=0;
7        //      1,    3,    7,   15,   31,  <--= max n
8        for (ulong k=0; k<n; ++k)
9        {
10           ulong cy = x[k];
11           { ulong t = a0 & cy;  a0 ^= cy;  cy = t; }
12           { ulong t = a1 & cy;  a1 ^= cy;  cy = t; }
13           { ulong t = a2 & cy;  a2 ^= cy;  cy = t; }
14           { ulong t = a3 & cy;  a3 ^= cy;  cy = t; }
15           { a4 ^= cy; }
16           // [ PRINT x[k], a0, a1, a2, a3, a4 ]
17       }
18
19       ulong b = bit_count(a0);
20       b += (bit_count(a1)<<1);
21       b += (bit_count(a2)<<2);
22       b += (bit_count(a3)<<3);
23       b += (bit_count(a4)<<4);
24       return  b;
25   }
```

Figure 1.8-A shows the intermediate values with the computation of a length-17 array of all-ones words. After the loop the values of the variables a0, ..., a4 are

```
a4=11111111
a3=........
a2=........
a1=........
a0=11111111
```

The columns, read as binary numbers, tell us that in all positions of all words there were a total of $17 = 10001_2$ bits. The remaining instructions compute the total bit-count.

After some simplifications and loop-unrolling a routine for counting the bits of 15 words can be given as [FXT: bits/bitcount-v.cc]:

```
1    static inline ulong bit_count_v15(const ulong *x)
2    // Return sum(j=0, 14, bit_count(x[j]) )
3    // Technique is "vertical" addition.
4    {
5    #define VV(A) { ulong t = A & cy;  A ^= cy;  cy = t; }
6        ulong a1, a2, a3;
7        ulong a0=x[0];
8        { ulong cy = x[ 1];   VV(a0);  a1 = cy; }
9        { ulong cy = x[ 2];   VV(a0);  a1 ^= cy; }
10       { ulong cy = x[ 3];   VV(a0);  VV(a1);  a2 = cy; }
11       { ulong cy = x[ 4];   VV(a0);  VV(a1);  a2 ^= cy; }
12       { ulong cy = x[ 5];   VV(a0);  VV(a1);  a2 ^= cy; }
13       { ulong cy = x[ 6];   VV(a0);  VV(a1);  a2 ^= cy; }
14       { ulong cy = x[ 7];   VV(a0);  VV(a1);  VV(a2);  a3 = cy; }
15       { ulong cy = x[ 8];   VV(a0);  VV(a1);  VV(a2);  a3 ^= cy; }
16       { ulong cy = x[ 9];   VV(a0);  VV(a1);  VV(a2);  a3 ^= cy; }
17       { ulong cy = x[10];   VV(a0);  VV(a1);  VV(a2);  a3 ^= cy; }
18       { ulong cy = x[11];   VV(a0);  VV(a1);  VV(a2);  a3 ^= cy; }
19       { ulong cy = x[12];   VV(a0);  VV(a1);  VV(a2);  a3 ^= cy; }
20       { ulong cy = x[13];   VV(a0);  VV(a1);  VV(a2);  a3 ^= cy; }
21       { ulong cy = x[14];   VV(a0);  VV(a1);  VV(a2);  a3 ^= cy; }
22   #undef VV
23
24       ulong b = bit_count(a0);
25       b += (bit_count(a1)<<1);
```

```
26         b += (bit_count(a2)<<2);
27         b += (bit_count(a3)<<3);
28         return  b;
29  }
```

Each of the macros VV gives three machine instructions, one AND, XOR, and MOVE. The routine for the user is

```
1   ulong
2   bit_count_v(const ulong *x, ulong n)
3   // Return sum(j=0, n-1, bit_count(x[j]) )
4   {
5       ulong b = 0;
6       const ulong *xe = x + n + 1;
7       while ( x+15 < xe )  // process blocks of 15 elements
8       {
9           b += bit_count_v15(x);
10          x += 15;
11      }
12
13      // process remaining elements:
14      const ulong r = (ulong)(xe-x-1);
15      for (ulong k=0; k<r; ++k)  b+=bit_count(x[k]);
16
17      return  b;
18  }
```

Compared to the obvious method of bit-counting

```
1   ulong bit_count_v2(const ulong *x, ulong n)
2   {
3       ulong b = 0;
4       for (ulong k=0; k<n; ++k)  b += bit_count(x[k]);
5       return  b;
6   }
```

our routine uses roughly 30 percent less time when an array of 100,000,000 words is processed. There are many possible modifications of the method. If the bit-count routine is rather slow, one may want to avoid the four calls to it after the processing of every 15 words. Instead, the variables $a0, \ldots, a3$ could be added (vertically!) to an array of more elements. If that array has n elements, then only with each block of $2^n - 1$ words n calls to the bit-count routine are necessary.

1.9   Words as bitsets

1.9.1   Testing whether subset of given bitset

The following function tests whether a word u, as a bitset, is a subset of the bitset given as the word e [FXT: bits/bitsubsetq.h]:

```
1   static inline bool is_subset(ulong u, ulong e)
2   // Return whether the set bits of u are a subset of the set bits of e.
3   // That is, as bitsets, test whether u is a subset of e.
4   {
5       return  ( (u & e)==u );
6   //    return  ( (u & ~e)==0 );
7   //    return  ( (~u | e)!=0 );
8   }
```

If u contains any bits not set in e, then these bits are cleared in the AND-operation and the test for equality will fail. The second version tests whether no element of u lies outside of e, the third is obtained by complementing the equality. A proper subset of e is a subset $\neq e$:

```
1   static inline bool is_proper_subset(ulong u, ulong e)
2   // Return whether u (as bitset) is a proper subset of e.
3   {
4       return  ( (u<e) && ((u & e)==u) );
5   }
```

The generated machine code contains a branch:

```
101    xorl    %eax, %eax      # prephitmp.71
102    cmpq    %rsi, %rdi      # e, u
```

```
103    jae      .L6                 #,  /* branch to end of function */
104    andq     %rdi, %rsi          # u, e
106    xorl     %eax, %eax          # prephitmp.71
107    cmpq     %rdi, %rsi          # u, e
108    sete     %al                 #, prephitmp.71
```

Replace the Boolean operator '&&' by the bit-wise operator '&' to obtain branch-free machine code:

```
101    cmpq     %rsi, %rdi          # e, u
102    setb     %al                 #, tmp63
103    andq     %rdi, %rsi          # u, e
105    cmpq     %rdi, %rsi          # u, e
106    sete     %dl                 #, tmp66
107    andl     %edx, %eax          # tmp66, tmp63
108    movzbl   %al, %eax           # tmp63, tmp61
```

1.9.2   Testing whether an element is in a given set

We determine whether a given number is an element of a given set (which must be a subset of the set $\{0, 1, 2, \ldots, \text{BITS\_PER\_LONG}-1\}$). For example, to determine whether x is a prime less than 32, use the function

```
1    ulong m = (1UL<<2) | (1UL<<3) | (1UL<<5) | ... | (1UL<<31);  // precomputed
2    static inline ulong is_tiny_prime(ulong x)
3    {
4        return  m & (1UL << x);
5    }
```

The same idea can be applied to look up tiny factors [FXT: bits/tinyfactors.h]:

```
1    static inline bool is_tiny_factor(ulong x, ulong d)
2    // For x,d < BITS_PER_LONG (!)
3    // return whether d divides x  (1 and x included as divisors)
4    // no need to check whether d==0
5    //
6    {
7        return  ( 0 != ( (tiny_factors_tab[x]>>d) & 1 ) );
8    }
```

The function uses the precomputed array [FXT: bits/tinyfactors.cc]:

```
1    extern const ulong tiny_factors_tab[] =
2    {
3                         0x0UL,    // x = 0:              ( bits: ........)
4                         0x2UL,    // x = 1:  1           ( bits: ......1.)
5                         0x6UL,    // x = 2:  1 2         ( bits: .....11.)
6                         0xaUL,    // x = 3:  1 3         ( bits: ....1.1.)
7                         0x16UL,   // x = 4:  1 2 4       ( bits: ...1.11.)
8                         0x22UL,   // x = 5:  1 5         ( bits: ..1...1.)
9                         0x4eUL,   // x = 6:  1 2 3 6     ( bits: .1..111.)
10                        0x82UL,   // x = 7:  1 7         ( bits: 1.....1.)
11                        0x116UL,  // x = 8:  1 2 4 8
12                        0x20aUL,  // x = 9:  1 3 9
13   [--snip--]
14            0x20000002UL,    // x = 29:  1 29
15            0x4000846eUL,    // x = 30:  1 2 3 5 6 10 15 30
16            0x80000002UL,    // x = 31:  1 31
17   #if  ( BITS_PER_LONG > 32 )
18            0x100010116UL,   // x = 32:  1 2 4 8 16 32
19            0x20000080aUL,   // x = 33:  1 3 11 33
20   [--snip--]
21    0x2000000000000002UL,    // x = 61:  1 61
22    0x4000000080000006UL,    // x = 62:  1 2 31 62
23    0x800000000020028aUL     // x = 63:  1 3 7 9 21 63
24   #endif // ( BITS_PER_LONG > 32 )
25    };
```

Bit-arrays of arbitrary size are discussed in section 4.6 on page 164.

1.10 Index of the *i*-th set bit

To determine the index of the *i*-th set bit, we use a technique similar to the method for counting the bits of a word. Only the 64-bit version is shown [FXT: bits/ith-one-idx.h]:

```
1   static inline ulong ith_one_idx(ulong x, ulong i)
2   // Return index of the i-th set bit of x where 0 <= i < bit_count(x).
3   {
4       ulong x2 = x - ((x>>1) & 0x5555555555555555UL);     // 0-2 in 2 bits
5       ulong x4 = ((x2>>2) & 0x3333333333333333UL) +
6                   (x2 & 0x3333333333333333UL);            // 0-4 in 4 bits
7       ulong x8 = ((x4>>4) + x4) & 0x0f0f0f0f0f0f0f0fUL;   // 0-8 in 8 bits
8       ulong ct = (x8 * 0x0101010101010101UL) >> 56;       // bit count
9
10      ++i;
11      if ( ct < i )  return ~0UL;  // less than i bits set
12
13      ulong x16 = (0x00ff00ff00ff00ffUL & x8) + (0x00ff00ff00ff00ffUL & (x8>>8));     // 0-16
14      ulong x32 = (0x0000ffff0000ffffUL & x16) + (0x0000ffff0000ffffUL & (x16>>16));  // 0-32
15
16      ulong w, s = 0;
17
18      w = x32 & 0xffffffffUL;
19      if ( w < i )  { s += 32;  i -= w; }
20
21      x16 >>= s;
22      w = x16 & 0xffff;
23      if ( w < i )  { s += 16;  i -= w; }
24
25      x8 >>= s;
26      w = x8 & 0xff;
27      if ( w < i )  { s += 8;  i -= w; }
28
29      x4 >>= s;
30      w = x4 & 0xf;
31      if ( w < i )  { s += 4;  i -= w; }
32
33      x2 >>= s;
34      w = x2 & 3;
35      if ( w < i )  { s += 2;  i -= w; }
36
37      x >>= s;
38      s += ( (x&1) != i );
39
40      return s;
41  }
```

1.11 Avoiding branches

Branches are expensive operations with many CPUs, especially if the CPU pipeline is very long. A useful trick is to replace

```
if ( (x<0) || (x>m) )  { ... }
```

where x might be a signed integer, by

```
if ( (unsigned)x > m )  { ... }
```

The obvious code to test whether a point (x, y) lies outside a square box of size m is

```
if ( (x<0) || (x>m) || (y<0) || (y>m) )  { ... }
```

If m is a power of 2, it is better to use

```
if ( ( (ulong)x | (ulong)y ) > (unsigned)m )  { ... }
```

The following functions are given in [FXT: bits/branchless.h]. This function returns $\max(0, x)$. That is, zero is returned for negative input, else the unmodified input:

```
1   static inline long max0(long x)
2   {
3       return  x & ~(x >> (BITS_PER_LONG-1));
4   }
```

There is no restriction on the input range. The trick used is that with negative x the arithmetic shift will give a word of all ones which is then negated and the AND-operation clears all bits. Note this function will only work if the compiler emits an arithmetic right shift, see section 1.1.3 on page 3. The following routine computes $\min(0, x)$:

```
1    static inline long min0(long x)
2    // Return min(0, x), i.e. return zero for positive input
3    {
4        return  x & (x >> (BITS_PER_LONG-1));
5    }
```

The following `upos_*()` functions only work for a limited range. The highest bit must not be set as it is used to emulate the carry flag. Branchless computation of the absolute difference $|a - b|$:

```
1    static inline ulong upos_abs_diff(ulong a, ulong b)
2    {
3        long d1 = b - a;
4        long d2 = (d1 & (d1>>(BITS_PER_LONG-1)))<<1;
5        return  d1 - d2; // == (b - d) - (a + d);
6    }
```

The following routine sorts two values:

```
1    static inline void upos_sort2(ulong &a, ulong &b)
2    // Set {a, b} := {min(a, b), max(a,b)}
3    // Both a and b must not have the most significant bit set
4    {
5        long d = b - a;
6        d &= (d>>(BITS_PER_LONG-1));
7        a += d;
8        b -= d;
9    }
```

Johan Rönnblom gives [priv. comm.] the following versions for signed integer minimum, maximum, and absolute value, that can be advantageous for CPUs where immediates are expensive:

```
1    #define B1   (BITS_PER_LONG-1) // bits of signed int minus one
2    #define MINI(x,y) (((x) &  (((int)((x)-(y)))>>B1)) + ((y) & ~(((int)((x)-(y)))>>B1)))
3    #define MAXI(x,y) (((x) & ~(((int)((x)-(y)))>>B1)) + ((y) &  (((int)((x)-(y)))>>B1)))
4    #define ABSI(x)   (((x) & ~(((int)(x))>>B1))        - ((x) &  (((int)(x))>>B1)))
```

Your compiler may be smarter than you thought

The machine code generated for

```
    x =  x & ~(x >> (BITS_PER_LONG-1));  // max0()
```

is

```
35:    48 99                cqto
37:    48 83 c4 08          add      $0x8,%rsp // stack adjustment
3b:    48 f7 d2             not      %rdx
3e:    48 21 d0             and      %rdx,%rax
```

The variable `x` resides in the register `rAX` both at start and end of the function. The compiler uses a special (AMD64) instruction `cqto`. Quoting [13]:

> Copies the sign bit in the rAX register to all bits of the rDX register. The effect of this instruction is to convert a signed word, doubleword, or quadword in the rAX register into a signed doubleword, quadword, or double-quadword in the rDX:rAX registers. This action helps avoid overflow problems in signed number arithmetic.

Now the equivalent

```
    x = ( x<0 ? 0 : x );  // max0()  "simple minded"
```

is compiled to:

```
35:    ba 00 00 00 00       mov      $0x0,%edx
3a:    48 85 c0             test     %rax,%rax
3d:    48 0f 48 c2          cmovs    %rdx,%rax // note %edx is %rdx
```

A conditional move (`cmovs`) instruction is used here. That is, the optimized version is (on my machine) actually worse than the straightforward equivalent.

A second example is a function to adjust a given value when it lies outside a given range [FXT: bits/branchless.h]:

```
1   static inline long clip_range(long x, long mi, long ma)
2   // Code equivalent to (for mi<=ma):
3   //    if ( x<mi )  x = mi;
4   //    else if ( x>ma )  x = ma;
5   {
6       x -= mi;
7       x = clip_range0(x, ma-mi);
8       x += mi;
9       return  x;
10  }
```

The auxiliary function used involves one branch:

```
1   static inline long clip_range0(long x, long m)
2   // Code equivalent (for m>0) to:
3   //    if ( x<0 )  x = 0;
4   //    else if ( x>m )  x = m;
5   //    return  x;
6   {
7       if ( (ulong)x > (ulong)m )  x = m & ~(x >> (BITS_PER_LONG-1));
8       return  x;
9   }
```

The generated machine code is

```
0:    48 89 f8          mov     %rdi,%rax
3:    48 29 f2          sub     %rsi,%rdx
6:    31 c9             xor     %ecx,%ecx
8:    48 29 f0          sub     %rsi,%rax
b:    78 0a             js      17 <_Z2CLlll+0x17>  // the branch
d:    48 39 d0          cmp     %rdx,%rax
10:   48 89 d1          mov     %rdx,%rcx
13:   48 0f 4e c8       cmovle  %rax,%rcx
17:   48 8d 04 0e       lea     (%rsi,%rcx,1),%rax
```

Now we replace the code by

```
1    static inline long clip_range(long x, long mi, long ma)
2    {
3        x -= mi;
4        if ( x<0 )  x = 0;
5    //    else  // commented out to make (compiled) function really branchless
6        {
7            ma -= mi;
8            if ( x>ma )  x = ma;
9        }
10       x += mi;
11   }
```

Then the compiler generates branchless code:

```
0:    48 89 f8             mov     %rdi,%rax
3:    b9 00 00 00 00       mov     $0x0,%ecx
8:    48 29 f0             sub     %rsi,%rax
b:    48 0f 48 c1          cmovs   %rcx,%rax
f:    48 29 f2             sub     %rsi,%rdx
12:   48 39 d0             cmp     %rdx,%rax
15:   48 0f 4f c2          cmovg   %rdx,%rax
19:   48 01 f0             add     %rsi,%rax
```

Still, with CPUs that do not have a conditional move instruction (or some branchless equivalent of it) the techniques shown in this section can be useful.

1.12   Bit-wise rotation of a word

Neither C nor C++ have a statement for bit-wise rotation of a binary word (which may be considered a missing feature). The operation can be emulated via [FXT: bits/bitrotate.h]:

```
1   static inline ulong bit_rotate_left(ulong x, ulong r)
2   // Return word rotated r bits to the left
3   // (i.e. toward the most significant bit)
```

```
4   {
5       return  (x<<r) | (x>>(BITS_PER_LONG-r));
6   }
```

As already mentioned, GCC emits exactly the CPU instruction that is *meant* here, even with non-constant argument r. Explicit use of the corresponding assembler instruction should not do any harm:

```
1   static inline ulong bit_rotate_right(ulong x, ulong r)
2   // Return word rotated r bits to the right
3   // (i.e. toward the least significant bit)
4   {
5   #if defined  BITS_USE_ASM     // use x86 asm code
6       return asm_ror(x, r);
7   #else
8       return  (x>>r) | (x<<(BITS_PER_LONG-r));
9   #endif
10  }
```

Here we use an assembler instruction when available [FXT: bits/bitasm-amd64.h]:

```
1   static inline ulong asm_ror(ulong x, ulong r)
2   {
3       asm ("rorq   %%cl, %0" : "=r" (x) : "0" (x), "c" (r));
4       return x;
5   }
```

Rotation using only a part of the word length can be implemented as

```
1   static inline ulong bit_rotate_left(ulong x, ulong r, ulong ldn)
2   // Return ldn-bit word rotated r bits to the left
3   // (i.e. toward the most significant bit)
4   // Must have  0 <= r <= ldn
5   {
6       ulong m = ~0UL >> ( BITS_PER_LONG - ldn );
7       x &= m;
8       x = (x<<r) | (x>>(ldn-r));
9       x &= m;
10      return  x;
11  }
```

and

```
1   static inline ulong bit_rotate_right(ulong x, ulong r, ulong ldn)
2   // Return ldn-bit word rotated r bits to the right
3   // (i.e. toward the least significant bit)
4   // Must have  0 <= r <= ldn
5   {
6       ulong m = ~0UL >> ( BITS_PER_LONG - ldn );
7       x &= m;
8       x = (x>>r) | (x<<(ldn-r));
9       x &= m;
10      return  x;
11  }
```

Finally, the functions

```
1   static inline ulong bit_rotate_sgn(ulong x, long r, ulong ldn)
2   // Positive r --> shift away from element zero
3   {
4       if ( r > 0 )  return  bit_rotate_left(x, (ulong)r, ldn);
5       else          return  bit_rotate_right(x, (ulong)-r, ldn);
6   }
```

and (full-word version)

```
1   static inline ulong bit_rotate_sgn(ulong x, long r)
2   // Positive r --> shift away from element zero
3   {
4       if ( r > 0 )  return  bit_rotate_left(x, (ulong)r);
5       else          return  bit_rotate_right(x, (ulong)-r);
6   }
```

are sometimes convenient.

1.13   Binary necklaces ‡

We give several functions related to cyclic rotations of binary words and a class to generate binary necklaces.

1.13.1   Cyclic matching, minimum, and maximum

The following function determines whether there is a cyclic right shift of its second argument so that it matches the first argument. It is given in [FXT: bits/bitcyclic-match.h]:

```
1   static inline ulong bit_cyclic_match(ulong x, ulong y)
2   // Return  r if x==rotate_right(y, r) else return ~0UL.
3   // In other words: return
4   //   how often the right arg must be rotated right (to match the left)
5   // or, equivalently:
6   //   how often the left arg must be rotated left (to match the right)
7   {
8       ulong r = 0;
9       do
10      {
11          if ( x==y )  return r;
12          y = bit_rotate_right(y, 1);
13      }
14      while ( ++r < BITS_PER_LONG );
15
16      return ~0UL;
17  }
```

The functions shown work on the full length of the words, equivalents for the sub-word of the lowest `ldn` bits are given in the respective files. Just one example:

```
1   static inline ulong bit_cyclic_match(ulong x, ulong y, ulong ldn)
2   // Return  r if x==rotate_right(y, r, ldn) else return ~0UL
3   // (using ldn-bit words)
4   {
5       ulong r = 0;
6       do
7       {
8           if ( x==y )  return r;
9           y = bit_rotate_right(y, 1, ldn);
10      }
11      while ( ++r < ldn );
12
13      return ~0UL;
14  }
```

The minimum among all cyclic shifts of a word can be computed via the following function given in [FXT: bits/bitcyclic-minmax.h]:

```
1   static inline ulong bit_cyclic_min(ulong x)
2   // Return minimum of all rotations of x
3   {
4       ulong r = 1;
5       ulong m = x;
6       do
7       {
8           x = bit_rotate_right(x, 1);
9           if ( x<m )  m = x;
10      }
11      while ( ++r < BITS_PER_LONG );
12
13      return  m;
14  }
```

1.13.2 Cyclic period and binary necklaces

Selecting from all n-bit words those that are equal to their cyclic minimum gives the sequence of the binary length-n necklaces, see chapter 18 on page 370. For example, with 6-bit words we find:

word	period	word	period
`......`	1	`..111.`	6
`.....1`	6	`.1111.`	6
`....11`	6	`.1.1.1`	6
`...111`	6	`.11.11`	3
`..1.1.`	3	`.11111`	6
`..1.11`	6	`111111`	1

The values in each right column can be computed using [FXT: bits/bitcyclic-period.h]:

```
1   static inline ulong bit_cyclic_period(ulong x, ulong ldn)
2   // Return minimal positive bit-rotation that transforms x into itself.
3   //   (using ldn-bit words)
4   // The returned value is a divisor of ldn.
5   {
6       ulong y = bit_rotate_right(x, 1, ldn);
7       return  bit_cyclic_match(x, y, ldn) + 1;
8   }
```

It is possible to completely avoid the rotation of partial words: let d be a divisor of the word length n. Then the rightmost $(n-1)\,d$ bits of the word computed as `x^(x>>d)` are zero if and only if the word has period d. So we can use the following function body:

```
1       ulong sl = BITS_PER_LONG-ldn;
2       for (ulong s=1; s<ldn; ++s)
3       {
4           ++sl;
5           if ( 0==( (x^(x>>s)) << sl ) )  return s;
6       }
7       return ldn;
```

Testing for periods that are not divisors of the word length can be avoided as follows:

```
1       ulong f = tiny_factors_tab[ldn];
2       ulong sl = BITS_PER_LONG-ldn;
3       for (ulong s=1; s<ldn; ++s)
4       {
5           ++sl;
6           f >>= 1;
7           if ( 0==(f&1) )  continue;
8           if ( 0==( (x^(x>>s)) << sl ) )  return s;
9       }
10      return ldn;
```

The table of tiny factors used is shown in section 1.9.2 on page 24.

The version for `ldn==BITS_PER_LONG` can be optimized similarly:

```
1   static inline ulong bit_cyclic_period(ulong x)
2   // Return minimal positive bit-rotation that transforms x into itself.
3   // (same as bit_cyclic_period(x, BITS_PER_LONG) )
4   //
5   // The returned value is a divisor of the word length,
6   //   i.e. 1,2,4,8,...,BITS_PER_LONG.
7   {
8       ulong r = 1;
9       do
10      {
11          ulong y = bit_rotate_right(x, r);
12          if ( x==y )  return r;
13          r <<= 1;
14      }
15      while ( r < BITS_PER_LONG );
16
17      return r;  // == BITS_PER_LONG
18  }
```

1.13.3 Generating all binary necklaces

We can generate all necklaces by the FKM algorithm given in section 18.1.1 on page 371. Here we specialize the method for binary words. The words generated are the cyclic maxima [FXT: class bit_necklace in bits/bit-necklace.h]:

```
1   class bit_necklace
2   {
3   public:
4       ulong a_;    // necklace
5       ulong j_;    // period of the necklace
6       ulong n2_;   // bit representing n: n2==2**(n-1)
7       ulong j2_;   // bit representing j: j2==2**(j-1)
8       ulong n_;    // number of bits in words
9       ulong mm_;   // mask of n ones
10      ulong tfb_;  // for fast factor lookup
11
12  public:
13      bit_necklace(ulong n)  { init(n); }
14      ~bit_necklace()  { ; }
15
16      void init(ulong n)
17      {
18          if ( 0==n )  n = 1;  // avoid hang
19          if ( n>=BITS_PER_LONG )  n = BITS_PER_LONG;
20          n_ = n;
21
22          n2_ = 1UL<<(n-1);
23          mm_ = (~0UL) >> (BITS_PER_LONG-n);
24          tfb_ = tiny_factors_tab[n] >> 1;
25          tfb_ |= n2_;  // needed for n==BITS_PER_LONG
26          first();
27      }
28
29      void first()
30      {
31          a_  = 0;
32          j_  = 1;
33          j2_ = 1;
34      }
35
36      ulong data() const { return  a_; }
37      ulong period() const { return j_; }
```

The method for computing the successor is

```
1       ulong next()
2       // Create next necklace.
3       // Return the period, zero when current necklace is last.
4       {
5           if ( a_==mm_ )  { first();  return 0; }
6
7           do
8           {
9               // next lines compute index of highest zero, same result as
10              // j_ = highest_zero_idx( a_ ^ (~mm_)  );
11              // but the direct computation is faster:
12              j_ = n_ - 1;
13              ulong jb = 1UL << j_;
14              while ( 0!=(a_ & jb) )  { --j_;  jb>>=1; }
15
16              j2_ = 1UL << j_;
17              ++j_;
18              a_ |= j2_;
19              a_ = bit_copy_periodic(a_, j_, n_);
20          }
21          while ( 0==(tfb_ & j2_) );  // necklaces only
22
23          return  j_;
24      }
```

It uses the following function for periodic copying [FXT: bits/bitperiodic.h]:

```
1   static inline ulong bit_copy_periodic(ulong a, ulong p, ulong ldn)
2   // Return word that consists of the lowest p bits of a repeated
3   // in the lowest ldn bits (higher bits are zero).
4   // E.g.: if p==3, ldn=7 and a=*****xyz (8-bit), the return 0zxyzxyz.
5   // Must have p>0 and ldn>0.
6   {
7       a &= ( ~0UL >> (BITS_PER_LONG-p) );
```

```
8        for (ulong s=p; s<ldn; s<<=1)  { a |= (a<<s); }
9        a &= ( ~0UL >> (BITS_PER_LONG-ldn) );
10       return a;
11   }
```

Finally, we can easily detect whether a necklace is a Lyndon word:

```
1        ulong is_lyndon_word()  const  { return (j2_ & n2_); }
2
3        ulong next_lyn()
4        // Create next Lyndon word.
5        // Return the period (==n), zero when current necklace is last.
6        {
7            if ( a_==mm_ )  { first();  return 0; }
8            do  { next(); }  while ( !is_lyndon_word() );
9            return  n_;
10       }
11   };
```

About 54 million necklaces per second are generated (with $n = 32$), corresponding to a rate of 112 M/s for pre-necklaces [FXT: bits/bit-necklace-demo.cc].

1.13.4   Computing the cyclic distance

A function to compute the cyclic distance between two words [FXT: bits/bitcyclic-dist.h] is:

```
1    static inline ulong bit_cyclic_dist(ulong a, ulong b)
2    // Return minimal bitcount of (t ^ b)
3    // where t runs through the cyclic rotations of a.
4    {
5        ulong d = ~0UL;
6        ulong t = a;
7        do
8        {
9            ulong z = t ^ b;
10           ulong e = bit_count( z );
11           if ( e < d )  d = e;
12           t = bit_rotate_right(t, 1);
13       }
14       while ( t!=a );
15       return  d;
16   }
```

If the arguments are cyclic shifts of each other, then zero is returned. A version for partial words is

```
1    static inline ulong bit_cyclic_dist(ulong a, ulong b, ulong ldn)
2    {
3        ulong d = ~0UL;
4        const ulong m = (~0UL>>(BITS_PER_LONG-ldn));
5        b &= m;
6        a &= m;
7        ulong t = a;
8        do
9        {
10           ulong z = t ^ b;
11           ulong e = bit_count( z );
12           if ( e < d )  d = e;
13           t = bit_rotate_right(t, 1, ldn);
14       }
15       while ( t!=a );
16       return  d;
17   }
```

1.13.5   Cyclic XOR and its inverse

The functions [FXT: bits/bitcyclic-xor.h]

```
1    static inline ulong bit_cyclic_rxor(ulong x)
2    {
3        return x ^ bit_rotate_right(x, 1);
4    }
```

and

```
1    static inline ulong bit_cyclic_lxor(ulong x)
2    {
3        return x ^ bit_rotate_left(x, 1);
4    }
```

return a word whose number of set bits is even. A word and its complement produce the same result.

The inverse functions need no rotation at all, the inverse of `bit_cyclic_rxor()` is the inverse Gray code (see section 1.16 on page 41):

```
1    static inline ulong bit_cyclic_inv_rxor(ulong x)
2    // Return v so that bit_cyclic_rxor(v) == x.
3    {
4        return inverse_gray_code(x);
5    }
```

The argument x must have an even number of bits. If this is the case, the lowest bit of the result is zero. The complement of the returned value is also an inverse of `bit_cyclic_rxor()`.

The inverse of `bit_cyclic_lxor()` is the inverse reversed code (see section 1.16.6 on page 45):

```
1    static inline ulong bit_cyclic_inv_lxor(ulong x)
2    // Return v so that bit_cyclic_lxor(v) == x.
3    {
4        return inverse_rev_gray_code(x);
5    }
```

We do not need to mask out the lowest bit because for valid arguments (that have an even number of bits) the high bits of the result are zero. This function can be used to solve the quadratic equation $v^2 + v = x$ in the finite field $GF(2^n)$ when normal bases are used, see section 42.6.2 on page 903.

1.14   Reversing the bits of a word

The bits of a binary word can efficiently be reversed by a sequence of steps that reverse the order of certain blocks. For 16-bit words, we need $4 = \log_2(16)$ such steps [FXT: bits/revbin-steps-demo.cc]:

```
[ 0 1 2 3 4 5 6 7 8 9 a b c d e f ]
[ 1 0 3 2 5 4 7 6 9 8 b a d c f e ]   <--= pairs swapped
[ 3 2 1 0 7 6 5 4 b a 9 8 f e d c ]   <--= groups of 2 swapped
[ 7 6 5 4 3 2 1 0 f e d c b a 9 8 ]   <--= groups of 4 swapped
[ f e d c b a 9 8 7 6 5 4 3 2 1 0 ]   <--= groups of 8 swapped
```

1.14.1   Swapping adjacent bit blocks

We need a couple of auxiliary functions given in [FXT: bits/bitswap.h]. Pairs of adjacent bits can be swapped via

```
1    static inline ulong bit_swap_1(ulong x)
2    // Return x with neighbor bits swapped.
3    {
4    #if  BITS_PER_LONG == 32
5        ulong m = 0x55555555UL;
6    #else
7    #if  BITS_PER_LONG == 64
8        ulong m = 0x5555555555555555UL;
9    #endif
10   #endif
11       return  ((x & m) << 1) | ((x & (~m)) >> 1);
12   }
```

The 64-bit branch is omitted in the following examples. Adjacent groups of 2 bits are swapped by

```
1    static inline ulong bit_swap_2(ulong x)
2    // Return x with groups of 2 bits swapped.
3    {
4        ulong m = 0x33333333UL;
5        return  ((x & m) << 2) | ((x & (~m)) >> 2);
6    }
```

Equivalently,

```
1    static inline ulong bit_swap_4(ulong x)
2    // Return x with groups of 4 bits swapped.
3    {
4        ulong m = 0x0f0f0f0fUL;
5        return  ((x & m) << 4) | ((x & (~m)) >> 4);
6    }
```

and

```
1    static inline ulong bit_swap_8(ulong x)
2    // Return x with groups of 8 bits swapped.
3    {
4        ulong m = 0x00ff00ffUL;
5        return  ((x & m) << 8) | ((x & (~m)) >> 8);
6    }
```

When swapping half-words (here for 32-bit architectures)

```
1    static inline ulong bit_swap_16(ulong x)
2    // Return x with groups of 16 bits swapped.
3    {
4        ulong m = 0x0000ffffUL;
5        return  ((x & m) << 16) | ((x & (m<<16)) >> 16);
6    }
```

we could also use the bit-rotate function from section 1.12 on page 27, or

```
    return (x << 16) | (x >> 16);
```

The GCC compiler recognizes that the whole operation is equivalent to a (left or right) word rotation and indeed emits just a single rotate instruction.

1.14.2   Bit-reversing binary words

The following is a function to reverse the bits of a binary word [FXT: bits/revbin.h]:

```
1    static inline ulong revbin(ulong x)
2    // Return x with reversed bit order.
3    {
4        x = bit_swap_1(x);
5        x = bit_swap_2(x);
6        x = bit_swap_4(x);
7        x = bit_swap_8(x);
8        x = bit_swap_16(x);
9    #if  BITS_PER_LONG >= 64
10        x = bit_swap_32(x);
11   #endif
12       return x;
13   }
```

The steps after `bit_swap_4()` correspond to a byte-reverse operation. This operation is just one assembler instruction for many CPUs. The inline assembler with GCC for AMD64 CPUs is given in [FXT: bits/bitasm-amd64.h]:

```
1    static inline ulong asm_bswap(ulong x)
2    {
3        asm ("bswap %0" : "=r" (x) : "0" (x));
4        return x;
5    }
```

We use it for byte reversal if available:

```
1    static inline ulong bswap(ulong x)
2    // Return word with reversed byte order.
3    {
4    #ifdef BITS_USE_ASM
5        x = asm_bswap(x);
6    #else
7        x = bit_swap_8(x);
8        x = bit_swap_16(x);
9    #if  BITS_PER_LONG >= 64
10        x = bit_swap_32(x);
11   #endif
12   #endif // def BITS_USE_ASM
13       return x;
```

```
14   }
```

The function actually used for bit reversal is good for both 32 and 64 bit words:

```
1   static inline ulong revbin(ulong x)
2   {
3        x = bit_swap_1(x);
4        x = bit_swap_2(x);
5        x = bit_swap_4(x);
6        x = bswap(x);
7        return x;
8   }
```

The masks can be generated in the process:

```
1   static inline ulong revbin(ulong x)
2   {
3        ulong s = BITS_PER_LONG >> 1;
4        ulong m = ~0UL >> s;
5        while ( s )
6        {
7            x = ( (x & m) << s ) ^ ( (x & (~m)) >> s );
8            s >>= 1;
9            m ^= (m<<s);
10       }
11       return  x;
12   }
```

The above function will not always beat the obvious, bit-wise algorithm:

```
1   static inline ulong revbin(ulong x)
2   {
3        ulong r = 0,  ldn = BITS_PER_LONG;
4        while ( ldn-- != 0 )
5        {
6            r <<= 1;
7            r += (x&1);
8            x >>= 1;
9        }
10       return  r;
11   }
```

Therefore the function

```
1   static inline ulong revbin(ulong x, ulong ldn)
2   // Return word with the ldn least significant bits
3   //   (i.e. bit_0 ... bit_{ldn-1})  of x reversed,
4   //   the other bits are set to zero.
5   {
6        return  revbin(x) >> (BITS_PER_LONG-ldn);
7   }
```

should only be used if `ldn` is not too small, else be replaced by the trivial algorithm.

We can use table lookups so that, for example, eight bits are reversed at a time using a 256-byte table. The routine for full words is

```
1   unsigned char revbin_tab[256]; // reversed 8-bit words
2   ulong revbin_t(ulong x)
3   {
4        ulong r = 0;
5        for (ulong k=0; k<BYTES_PER_LONG; ++k)
6        {
7            r <<= 8;
8            r |= revbin_tab[ x & 255 ];
9            x >>= 8;
10       }
11       return r;
12   }
```

The routine can be optimized by unrolling to avoid all branches:

```
1   static inline ulong revbin_t(ulong x)
2   {
3        ulong r      = revbin_tab[ x & 255 ];   x >>= 8;
4        r <<= 8;   r |= revbin_tab[ x & 255 ];   x >>= 8;
5        r <<= 8;   r |= revbin_tab[ x & 255 ];   x >>= 8;
6   #if BYTES_PER_LONG > 4
```

```
 7          r <<= 8;  r |= revbin_tab[ x & 255 ];  x >>= 8;
 8          r <<= 8;  r |= revbin_tab[ x & 255 ];  x >>= 8;
 9          r <<= 8;  r |= revbin_tab[ x & 255 ];  x >>= 8;
10          r <<= 8;  r |= revbin_tab[ x & 255 ];  x >>= 8;
11      #endif
12          r <<= 8;  r |= revbin_tab[ x ];
13          return r;
14      }
```

However, reversing the first 2^{30} binary words with this routine takes (on a 64-bit machine) longer than with the routine using the `bit_swap_NN()` calls, see [FXT: bits/revbin-tab-demo.cc].

1.14.3   Generating the bit-reversed words in order

If the bit-reversed words have to be generated in the (reversed) counting order, there is a significantly cheaper way to do the update [FXT: bits/revbin-upd.h]:

```
1    static inline ulong revbin_upd(ulong r, ulong h)
2    // Let n=2**ldn and h=n/2.
3    // Then, with r == revbin(x, ldn) at entry, return revbin(x+1, ldn)
4    // Note: routine will hang if called with r the all-ones word
5    {
6        while ( !((r^=h)&h) )  h >>= 1;
7        return  r;
8    }
```

Now assume we want to generate the bit-reversed words of all $N = 2^n - 1$ words less than 2^n. The total number of branches with the `while`-loop can be estimated by observing that for half of the updates just one bit changes, two bits change for a quarter, three bits change for one eighth of all updates, and so on. So the loop executes less than $2N$ times:

$$N \left(\frac{1}{2} + \frac{2}{4} + \frac{3}{8} + \frac{4}{16} + \cdots + \frac{\log_2(N)}{N} \right) \;=\; N \sum_{j=1}^{\log_2(N)} \frac{j}{2^j} < 2N \qquad (1.14\text{-}1)$$

For large values of N the following method can be significantly faster if a fast routine is available for the computation of the least significant bit in a word. The underlying observation is that for a fixed word of size n there are just n different patterns of bit-changes with incrementing. We generate a lookup table of the bit-reversed patterns, `utab[]`, an array of `BITS_PER_LONG` elements:

```
1    static inline void make_revbin_upd_tab(ulong ldn)
2    // Initialize lookup table used by revbin_tupd()
3    {
4        utab[0] = 1UL<<(ldn-1);
5        for (ulong k=1; k<ldn; ++k)  utab[k] = utab[k-1] | (utab[k-1]>>1);
6    }
```

The change patterns for $n = 5$ start as

```
pattern   reversed pattern
 ...i1     1i:::
 ::ii1     1ii::
 ...i1     1i:::
 :iiii     1iii:
 ...i1     1i:::
```

The pattern with x set bits is used for the update of k to $k + 1$ when the lowest zero of k is at position $x - 1$:

	reversed	used when the lowest zero of k is at index:
utab[0]=	1....	0
utab[1]=	11...	1
utab[2]=	111..	2
utab[3]=	1111.	3
utab[4]=	11111	4

The update routine can now be implemented as

```
1   static inline ulong revbin_tupd(ulong r, ulong k)
2   // Let r==revbin(k, ldn) then
3   // return revbin(k+1, ldn).
4   // NOTE 1: need to call make_revbin_upd_tab(ldn) before usage
5   //         where ldn=log_2(n)
6   // NOTE 2: different argument structure than revbin_upd()
7   {
8       k = lowest_one_idx(~k);  // lowest zero idx
9       r ^= utab[k];
10      return r;
11  }
```

The revbin-update routines are used for the revbin permutation described in section 2.6.

	30 bits	16 bits	8 bits	
Update, bit-wise	1.00	1.00	1.00	`revbin_upd()`
Update, table	0.99	1.08	1.15	`revbin_tupd()`
Full, masks	0.74	0.81	0.86	`revbin()`
Full, 8-bit table	1.77	1.94	2.06	`revbin_t()`
Full32, 8-bit table	0.83	0.90	0.96	`revbin_t_le32()`
Full16, 8-bit table	—	0.54	0.58	`revbin_t_le16()`
Full, generated masks	2.97	3.25	3.45	[page 35]
Full, bit-wise	8.76	5.77	2.50	[page 35]

Figure 1.14-A: Relative performance of the revbin-update and (full) revbin routines. The timing of the bit-wise update routine is normalized to 1. Values in each column should be compared, smaller values correspond to faster routines. A column labeled "*N* bits" gives the timing for reversing the *N* least significant bits of a word.

The relative performance of the different revbin routines is shown in figure 1.14-A. As a surprise, the full-word revbin function is consistently faster than both of the update routines, mainly because the machine used (see appendix B on page 922) has a byte swap instruction. As the performance of table lookups is highly machine dependent your results can be very different.

1.14.4 Alternative techniques for in-order generation

The following loop, due to Brent Lehmann [priv. comm.], also generates the bit-reversed words in succession:

```
1   ulong n = 32;  // a power of 2
2   ulong p = 0, s = 0, n2 = 2*n;
3   do
4   {
5       // here: s is the bit-reversed word
6       p += 2;
7       s ^= n - (n / (p&-p));
8   }
9   while ( p<n2 );
```

The revbin-increment is branchless but involves a division which usually is an expensive operation. With a fast bit-scan function the loop should be replaced by

```
1   do
2   {
3       p += 1;
4       s ^= n - (n >> (lowest_one_idx(p)+1));
5   }
6   while ( p<n );
```

A recursive algorithm for the generation of the bit-reversed words in order is given in [FXT: bits/revbin-rec-demo.cc]:

```
1   ulong N;
2   void revbin_rec(ulong f, ulong n)
3   {
4       // visit( f )
5       for (ulong m=N>>1; m>n; m>>=1)  revbin_rec(f+m, m);
```

```
6   }
```

Call `revbin_rec(0, 0)` to generate all N-bit bit-reversed words.

A technique to generate all revbin pairs in a pseudo random order is given in section 41.4 on page 873.

1.15   Bit-wise zip

The bit-wise zip (bit-zip) operation moves the bits in the lower half to even indices and the bits in the upper half to odd indices. For example, with 8-bit words the permutation of bits is

```
    [ a b c d A B C D ]   |--> [ a A b B c C d D ]
```

A straightforward implementation is

```
1   ulong bit_zip(ulong a, ulong b)
2   {
3       ulong x = 0;
4       ulong m = 1, s = 0;
5       for (ulong k=0; k<(BITS_PER_LONG/2); ++k)
6       {
7           x |= (a & m) << s;
8           ++s;
9           x |= (b & m) << s;
10          m <<= 1;
11      }
12      return  x;
13  }
```

Its inverse (bit-unzip) moves even indexed bits to the lower half-word and odd indexed bits to the upper half-word:

```
1   void bit_unzip(ulong x, ulong &a, ulong &b)
2   {
3       a = 0;  b = 0;
4       ulong m = 1, s = 0;
5       for (ulong k=0; k<(BITS_PER_LONG/2); ++k)
6       {
7           a |= (x & m) >> s;
8           ++s;
9           m <<= 1;
10          b |= (x & m) >> s;
11          m <<= 1;
12      }
13  }
```

For a faster implementation we will use the `butterfly_*()`-functions which are defined in [FXT: bits/bitbutterfly.h] (64-bit version):

```
1   static inline ulong butterfly_4(ulong x)
2   // Swap in each block of 16 bits the two central blocks of 4 bits.
3   {
4       const ulong ml = 0x0f000f000f000f00UL;
5       const ulong s = 4;
6       const ulong mr = ml >> s;
7       const ulong t = ((x & ml) >> s ) | ((x & mr) << s );
8       x = (x & ~(ml | mr)) | t;
9       return  x;
10  }
```

The following version of the function may look more elegant but is actually slower:

```
1   static inline ulong butterfly_4(ulong x)
2   {
3       const ulong m = 0x0ff00ff00ff00ffUL;
4       ulong c = x & m;
5       c ^= (c<<4) ^ (c>>4);
6       c &= m;
7       return  x ^ c;
8   }
```

The optimized versions of the bit-zip and bit-unzip routines are [FXT: bits/bitzip.h]:

```
1   static inline ulong bit_zip(ulong x)
2   {
```

```
3    #if  BITS_PER_LONG == 64
4        x = butterfly_16(x);
5    #endif
6        x = butterfly_8(x);
7        x = butterfly_4(x);
8        x = butterfly_2(x);
9        x = butterfly_1(x);
10       return  x;
11   }
```

and

```
1    static inline ulong bit_unzip(ulong x)
2    {
3        x = butterfly_1(x);
4        x = butterfly_2(x);
5        x = butterfly_4(x);
6        x = butterfly_8(x);
7    #if  BITS_PER_LONG == 64
8        x = butterfly_16(x);
9    #endif
10       return  x;
11   }
```

Laszlo Hars suggests [priv. comm.] the following routine (version for 32-bit words), which can be obtained by making the compile-time constants explicit:

```
1    static inline uint32 bit_zip(uint32 x)
2    {
3        x = ((x & 0x0000ff00) << 8) | ((x >> 8) & 0x0000ff00) | (x & 0xff0000ff);
4        x = ((x & 0x00f000f0) << 4) | ((x >> 4) & 0x00f000f0) | (x & 0xf00ff00f);
5        x = ((x & 0x0c0c0c0c) << 2) | ((x >> 2) & 0x0c0c0c0c) | (x & 0xc3c3c3c3);
6        x = ((x & 0x22222222) << 1) | ((x >> 1) & 0x22222222) | (x & 0x99999999);
7        return x;
8    }
```

A bit-zip version for words whose upper half is zero is (64-bit version)

```
1    static inline ulong bit_zip0(ulong x)
2    // Return word with lower half bits in even indices.
3    {
4        x = (x | (x<<16)) & 0x0000ffff0000ffffUL;
5        x = (x | (x<<8))  & 0x00ff00ff00ff00ffUL;
6        x = (x | (x<<4))  & 0x0f0f0f0f0f0f0f0fUL;
7        x = (x | (x<<2))  & 0x3333333333333333UL;
8        x = (x | (x<<1))  & 0x5555555555555555UL;
9        return  x;
10   }
```

Its inverse is

```
1    static inline ulong bit_unzip0(ulong x)
2    // Bits at odd positions must be zero.
3    {
4        x = (x | (x>>1))  & 0x3333333333333333UL;
5        x = (x | (x>>2))  & 0x0f0f0f0f0f0f0f0fUL;
6        x = (x | (x>>4))  & 0x00ff00ff00ff00ffUL;
7        x = (x | (x>>8))  & 0x0000ffff0000ffffUL;
8        x = (x | (x>>16)) & 0x00000000ffffffffUL;
9        return  x;
10   }
```

The simple structure of the routines suggests trying the following versions of bit-zip and its inverse:

```
1    static inline ulong bit_zip(ulong x)
2    {
3        ulong y =  (x >> 32);
4        x &= 0xffffffffUL;
5        x = (x | (x<<16)) & 0x0000ffff0000ffffUL;
6        y = (y | (y<<16)) & 0x0000ffff0000ffffUL;
7        x = (x | (x<<8))  & 0x00ff00ff00ff00ffUL;
8        y = (y | (y<<8))  & 0x00ff00ff00ff00ffUL;
9        x = (x | (x<<4))  & 0x0f0f0f0f0f0f0f0fUL;
10       y = (y | (y<<4))  & 0x0f0f0f0f0f0f0f0fUL;
11       x = (x | (x<<2))  & 0x3333333333333333UL;
12       y = (y | (y<<2))  & 0x3333333333333333UL;
13       x = (x | (x<<1))  & 0x5555555555555555UL;
```

```
14        y = (y | (y<<1))  & 0x5555555555555555UL;
15        x |= (y<<1);
16        return  x;
17    }
```

```
1     static inline ulong bit_unzip(ulong x)
2     {
3         ulong y = (x >> 1) & 0x5555555555555555UL;
4         x &= 0x5555555555555555UL;
5         x = (x | (x>>1))  & 0x3333333333333333UL;
6         y = (y | (y>>1))  & 0x3333333333333333UL;
7         x = (x | (x>>2))  & 0x0f0f0f0f0f0f0f0fUL;
8         y = (y | (y>>2))  & 0x0f0f0f0f0f0f0f0fUL;
9         x = (x | (x>>4))  & 0x00ff00ff00ff00ffUL;
10        y = (y | (y>>4))  & 0x00ff00ff00ff00ffUL;
11        x = (x | (x>>8))  & 0x0000ffff0000ffffUL;
12        y = (y | (y>>8))  & 0x0000ffff0000ffffUL;
13        x = (x | (x>>16)) & 0x00000000ffffffffUL;
14        y = (y | (y>>16)) & 0x00000000ffffffffUL;
15        x |= (y<<32);
16        return  x;
17    }
```

As the statements involving the variables x and y are independent the CPU-internal parallelism can be used. However, these versions turn out to be slightly slower than those given before.

The following function moves the bits of the lower half-word of x into the even positions of lo and the bits of the upper half-word into hi (two versions given):

```
1     #define  BPLH  (BITS_PER_LONG/2)
2
3     static inline void bit_zip2(ulong x, ulong &lo, ulong &hi)
4     {
5     #if 1
6         x = bit_zip(x);
7         lo = x & 0x5555555555555555UL;
8         hi = (x>>1) & 0x5555555555555555UL;
9     #else
10        hi = bit_zip0( x >> BPLH );
11        lo = bit_zip0( (x << BPLH) >> (BPLH) );
12    #endif
13    }
```

The inverse function is

```
1     static inline ulong bit_unzip2(ulong lo, ulong hi)
2     // Inverse of bit_zip2(x, lo, hi).
3     {
4     #if 1
5         return  bit_unzip( (hi<<1) | lo  );
6     #else
7         return  bit_unzip0(lo) | (bit_unzip0(hi) << BPLH);
8     #endif
9     }
```

Functions that zip/unzip the bits of the lower half of two words are

```
1     static inline ulong bit_zip2(ulong x, ulong y)
2     // 2-word version:
3     // only the lower half of x and y are merged
4     {
5         return  bit_zip( (y<<BPLH) + x );
6     }
```

and (64-bit version)

```
1     static inline void bit_unzip2(ulong t, ulong &x, ulong &y)
2     // 2-word version:
3     // only the lower half of x and y are filled
4     {
5         t = bit_unzip(t);
6         y = t >> BPLH;
7         x = t & 0x00000000ffffffffUL;
8     }
```

1.16 Gray code and parity

```
        k:     bin(k)      g(k)     g^-1(k)    g(2*k)   g(2*k+1)
        0:    .......    .......    .......    .......    ......1
        1:    ......1    ......1    ......1    .....11    .....1.
        2:    .....1.    .....11    .....11    ....11.    ....111
        3:    .....11    .....1.    .....1.    ....1.1    ....1..
        4:    ....1..    ....11.    ....111    ...11..    ...11.1
        5:    ....1.1    ....111    ....11.    ...1111    ...111.
        6:    ....11.    ....1.1    ....1..    ...1.1.    ...1.11
        7:    ....111    ....1..    ....1.1    ...1..1    ...1...
        8:    ...1...    ...11..    ...1111    ..11...    ..11..1
        9:    ...1..1    ...11.1    ...111.    ..11.11    ..11.1.
       10:    ...1.1.    ...1111    ...11..    ..1111.    ..11111
       11:    ...1.11    ...111.    ...11.1    ..111.1    ..111..
       12:    ...11..    ...1.1.    ...1...    ..1.1..    ..1.1.1
       13:    ...11.1    ...1.11    ...1..1    ..1.111    ..1.11.
       14:    ...111.    ...1..1    ...1.11    ..1..1.    ..1..11
       15:    ...1111    ...1...    ...1.1.    ..1...1    ..1....
       16:    ..1....    ..11...    ..11111    .11....    .11...1
       17:    ..1...1    ..11..1    ..1111.    .11..11    .11..1.
       18:    ..1..1.    ..11.11    ..111..    .11.11.    .11.111
       19:    ..1..11    ..11.1.    ..111.1    .11.1.1    .11.1..
       20:    ..1.1..    ..1111.    ..11...    .1111..    .1111.1
       21:    ..1.1.1    ..11111    ..11..1    .111111    .11111.
       22:    ..1.11.    ..111.1    ..11.11    .111.1.    .111.11
       23:    ..1.111    ..111..    ..11.1.    .111..1    .111...
       24:    ..11...    ..1.1..    ..1....    .1.1...    .1.1..1
       25:    ..11..1    ..1.1.1    ..1...1    .1.1.11    .1.1.1.
       26:    ..11.1.    ..1.111    ..1..11    .1.111.    .1.1111
       27:    ..11.11    ..1.11.    ..1..1.    .1.11.1    .1.11..
       28:    ..111..    ..1..1.    ..1.111    .1..1..    .1..1.1
       29:    ..111.1    ..1..11    ..1.11.    .1..111    .1..11.
       30:    ..1111.    ..1...1    ..1.1..    .1...1.    .1...11
       31:    ..11111    ..1....    ..1.1.1    .1....1    .1.....
```

Figure 1.16-A: Binary words, their Gray code, inverse Gray code, and Gray codes of even and odd values (from left to right).

The *Gray code* of a binary word can easily be computed by [FXT: bits/graycode.h]

```
1    static inline ulong gray_code(ulong x)  { return  x ^ (x>>1); }
```

Gray codes of consecutive values differ in one bit. Gray codes of values that differ by a power of 2 differ in two bits. Gray codes of even/odd values have an even/odd number of bits set, respectively. This is demonstrated in [FXT: bits/gray-demo.cc], whose output is given in figure 1.16-A.

To produce a random value with an even/odd number of bits set, set the lowest bit of a random number to 0/1, respectively, and return its Gray code.

Computing the inverse Gray code is slightly more expensive. As the Gray code is the bit-wise difference modulo 2, we can compute the inverse as bit-wise sums modulo 2:

```
1    static inline ulong inverse_gray_code(ulong x)
2    {
3        // VERSION 1 (integration modulo 2):
4        ulong h=1, r=0;
5        do
6        {
7            if ( x & 1 )  r^=h;
8            x >>= 1;
9            h = (h<<1)+1;
10       }
11       while ( x!=0 );
12       return r;
13   }
```

For n-bit words, n-fold application of the Gray code gives back the original word. Using the symbol G for the Gray code (operator), we have $G^n = \mathrm{id}$, so $G^{n-1} \circ G = \mathrm{id} = G^{-1} \circ G$. That is, applying the Gray code computation $n - 1$ times gives the inverse Gray code. Thus we can simplify to

```
1        // VERSION 2 (apply graycode BITS_PER_LONG-1 times):
2        ulong r = BITS_PER_LONG;
3        while ( --r )  x ^= x>>1;
4        return x;
```

Applying the Gray code twice is identical to `x^=x>>2;`, applying it four times is `x^=x>>4;`, and the idea holds for all power of 2. This leads to the most efficient way to compute the inverse Gray code:

```
1        // VERSION 3 (use: gray ** BITSPERLONG == id):
2        x ^= x>>1;   // gray ** 1
3        x ^= x>>2;   // gray ** 2
4        x ^= x>>4;   // gray ** 4
5        x ^= x>>8;   // gray ** 8
6        x ^= x>>16;  // gray ** 16
7        // here: x = gray**31(input)
8        // note: the statements can be reordered at will
9   #if  BITS_PER_LONG >= 64
10       x ^= x>>32;   // for 64bit words
11  #endif
12       return  x;
```

1.16.1   The parity of a binary word

The *parity* of a word is its bit-count modulo 2. The lowest bit of the inverse Gray code of a word contains the parity of the word. So we can compute the parity as [FXT: bits/parity.h]:

```
1   static inline ulong parity(ulong x)
2   // Return 0 if the number of set bits is even, else 1
3   {
4        return  inverse_gray_code(x) & 1;
5   }
```

Each bit of the inverse Gray code contains the parity of the partial input left from it (including itself).

Be warned that the parity flag of many CPUs is the complement of the above. With the x86-architecture the parity bit also only takes into account the lowest byte. The following routine computes the parity of a full word [FXT: bits/bitasm-i386.h]:

```
1   static inline ulong asm_parity(ulong x)
2   {
3        x ^= (x>>16);
4        x ^= (x>>8);
5        asm ("addl  $0, %0  \n"
6             "setnp %%al    \n"
7             "movzx %%al, %0"
8             : "=r" (x) : "0" (x) : "eax");
9        return x;
10  }
```

The equivalent code for the AMD64 CPU is [FXT: bits/bitasm-amd64.h]:

```
1   static inline ulong asm_parity(ulong x)
2   {
3        x ^= (x>>32);
4        x ^= (x>>16);
5        x ^= (x>>8);
6        asm ("addq  $0, %0  \n"
7             "setnp %%al    \n"
8             "movzx %%al, %0"
9             : "=r" (x) : "0" (x) : "rax");
10       return x;
11  }
```

1.16.2   Byte-wise Gray code and parity

A byte-wise Gray code can be computed using (32-bit version)

```
1   static inline ulong byte_gray_code(ulong x)
2   // Return the Gray code of bytes in parallel
3   {
4        return  x ^ ((x & 0xfefefefe)>>1);
5   }
```

Its inverse is

```
1   static inline ulong byte_inverse_gray_code(ulong x)
2   // Return the inverse Gray code of bytes in parallel
3   {
```

```
4        x ^= ((x & 0xfefefefeUL)>>1);
5        x ^= ((x & 0xfcfcfcfcUL)>>2);
6        x ^= ((x & 0xf0f0f0f0UL)>>4);
7        return  x;
8    }
```

And the parities of all bytes can be computed as

```
1    static inline ulong byte_parity(ulong x)
2    // Return the parities of bytes in parallel
3    {
4        return  byte_inverse_gray_code(x) & 0x01010101UL;
5    }
```

1.16.3 Incrementing (counting) in Gray code

```
      k:      g(k)        g(2*k)         g(k) p       diff p     set
      0:    .......      .......       ....... .     ....... .   {}
      1:    ......1      .....11       .....1 1      .....+ 1    {0}
      2:    .....11      ....11.       ....11 .      ....+1 .    {0, 1}
      3:    .....1.      ....1.1       ....1. 1      ....1- 1    {1}
      4:    ....11.      ...11..       ...11. .      ...+1. .    {1, 2}
      5:    ....111      ...1111       ...111 1      ...11+ 1    {0, 1, 2}
      6:    ....1.1      ...1.1.       ...1.1 .      ...1-1 .    {0, 2}
      7:    ....1..      ...1..1       ...1.. 1      ...1.- 1    {2}
      8:    ...11..      ...11..       ..11... .     ..+1... .   {2, 3}
      9:    ...11.1      ..11.11       ..11.1 1      ..11.+ 1    {0, 2, 3}
     10:    ...1111      ..1111.       ..1111 .      ..11+1 .    {0, 1, 2, 3}
     11:    ...111.      ..111.1       ..111. 1      ..111- 1    {1, 2, 3}
     12:    ...1.1.      ..1.1..       ..1.1. .      ..1-1. .    {1, 3}
     13:    ...1.11      ..1.111       ..1.11 1      ..1.1+ 1    {0, 1, 3}
     14:    ...1..1      ..1..1.       ..1..1 .      ..1.-1 .    {0, 3}
     15:    ...1...      ..1...1       ..1... 1      ..1..- 1    {3}
     16:    ..11...      .11....       ..11... .     .+1... .    {3, 4}
     17:    ..11..1      .11..11       .11..1 1      .11..+ 1    {0, 3, 4}
```

Figure 1.16-B: The Gray code equals the Gray code of doubled value shifted to the right once. Equivalently, we can separate the lowest bit which equals the parity of the other bits. The last column shows that the changes with each increment always happen one position left of the rightmost bit.

Let $g(k)$ be the Gray code of a number k. We are interested in efficiently generating $g(k+1)$. We can implement a fast Gray counter if we use a spare bit to keep track of the parity of the Gray code word, see figure 1.16-B The following routine does this [FXT: bits/nextgray.h]:

```
1    static inline ulong next_gray2(ulong x)
2    // With input x==gray_code(2*k) the return is gray_code(2*k+2).
3    // Let x1 be the word x shifted right once
4    // and i1 its inverse Gray code.
5    // Let r1 be the return r shifted right once.
6    // Then r1 = gray_code(i1+1).
7    // That is, we have a Gray code counter.
8    // The argument must have an even number of bits.
9    {
10       x ^= 1;
11       x ^= (lowest_one(x) << 1);
12       return x;
13   }
```

Start with x=0, increment with x=next_gray2(pg) and use the words g=x>>1:

```
1        ulong x = 0;
2        for (ulong k=0; k<n2; ++k)
3        {
4            ulong g = x>>1;
5            x = next_gray2(x);
6            // here:  g == gray_code(k);
7        }
8
```

This is shown in [FXT: bits/bit-nextgray-demo.cc]. To start at an arbitrary (Gray code) value g, compute

```
    x = (g<<1) ^ parity(g)
```

Then use the statement x=next_gray2(x) for later increments.

If working with a set whose elements are the set bits in the Gray code, the parity is the set size k modulo 2. Compute the increment as follows:

1. If k is even, then goto step 2, else goto step 3.

2. If the first element is zero, then remove it, else prepend the element zero.

3. If the first element equals the second minus one, then remove the second element, else insert at the second position the element equal to the first element plus one.

A method to decrement is obtained by simply swapping the actions for even and odd parity.

When working with an array that contains the elements of the set, it is more convenient to do the described operations at the end of the array. This leads to the (loopless) algorithm for subsets in minimal-change order given in section 8.2.2 on page 206. Properties of the Gray code are discussed in [127].

1.16.4   The Thue-Morse sequence

The sequence of parities of the binary words

        0110100110010110100101100110100110010110011010101...

is called the *Thue-Morse sequence* (entry A010060 in [312]). It appears in various seemingly unrelated contexts, see [8] and section 38.1 on page 726. The sequence can be generated with [FXT: class thue_morse in bits/thue-morse.h]:

```
1    class thue_morse
2    // Thue-Morse sequence
3    {
4    public:
5        ulong k_;
6        ulong tm_;
7
8    public:
9        thue_morse(ulong k=0)  { init(k); }
10       ~thue_morse()  { ; }
11
12       ulong init(ulong k=0)
13       {
14           k_ = k;
15           tm_ = parity(k_);
16           return tm_;
17       }
18
19       ulong data()  { return tm_; }
20
21       ulong next()
22       {
23           ulong x = k_ ^ (k_ + 1);
24           ++k_;
25           x ^= x>>1;           // highest bit that changed with increment
26           x &= 0x5555555555555555UL;  // 64-bit version
27           tm_ ^= ( x!=0 );   // change if highest changed bit was at even index
28           return tm_;
29       }
30   };
```

The rate of generation is about 366 M/s (6 cycles per update) [FXT: bits/thue-morse-demo.cc].

1.16.5   The Golay-Rudin-Shapiro sequence ‡

The function [FXT: bits/grsnegative.h]

```
1    static inline ulong grs_negative_q(ulong x)  { return  parity( x & (x>>1) ); }
```

returns +1 for indices where the *Golay-Rudin-Shapiro sequence* (or *GRS sequence*, entry A020985 in [312]) has the value −1. The algorithm is to count the bit-pairs modulo 2. The pairs may overlap: the

```
                  ++
                  +++-
                  +++- ++-+
                  +++- ++-+  +++- --+-
                  +++- ++-+  +++- --+-  +++- ++-+  ---+ ++-+
                  +++- ++-+  +++- --+-  +++- ++-+  ---+ ++-+  +++- ++-+  +++- --+- ...
                    ^         ^     ^^ ^       ^         ^
                     3,   6,  11,12,13,15,  19,  22,  ...
```

Figure 1.16-C: A construction for the Golay-Rudin-Shapiro (GRS) sequence.

---

sequence [1111] contains the three bit-pairs [11..], [.11.], and [..11]. The function returns +1 for x in the sequence

3, 6, 11, 12, 13, 15, 19, 22, 24, 25, 26, 30, 35, 38, 43, 44, 45, 47, 48, 49, 50, 52, 53, ...

This is entry A022155 in [312], see also section 38.3 on page 731. The sequence can be computed by starting with two ones, and appending the left half and the negated right half of the values so far in each step, see figure 1.16-C. To compute the successor in the GRS sequence, use

```
1    static inline ulong grs_next(ulong k, ulong g)
2    // With g == grs_negative_q(k), compute grs_negative_q(k+1).
3    {
4        const ulong cm = 0x5555555555555554UL;  // 64-bit version
5        ulong h = ~k;  h &= -h;  // == lowest_zero(k);
6        g ^= ( ((h&cm) ^ ((k>>1)&h)) !=0 );
7        return  g;
8    }
```

With incrementing k, the lowest run of ones of k is replaced by a one at the lowest zero of k. If the length of the lowest run is odd and ≥ 2 then a change of parity happens. This is the case if the lowest zero of k is at one of the positions

bin 0101 0101 0101 0100 == hex 5 5 5 4 == cm

If the position of the lowest zero is adjacent to the next block of ones, another change of parity will occur. The element of the GRS sequence changes if exactly one of the parity changes takes place.

The update function can be used as shown in [FXT: bits/grs-next-demo.cc]:

```
1        ulong n = 65;  // Generate this many values of the sequence.
2        ulong k0 = 0;  // Start point of the sequence.
3        ulong g = grs_negative_q(k0);
4        for (ulong k=k0;  k<k0+n;  ++k)
5        {
6            // Do something with g here.
7            g = grs_next(k, g);
8        }
```

The rate of generation is about 347 M/s, direct computation gives a rate of 313 M/s.

1.16.6   The reversed Gray code

We define the *reversed Gray code* to be the bit-reversed word of the Gray code of the bit-reversed word. That is,

rev_gray_code(x) := revbin(gray_code(revbin(x)))

It turns out that the corresponding functions are identical to the Gray code versions up to the reversed shift operations (C-language operators '>>' replaced by '<<'). So computing the reversed Gray code is as easy as [FXT: bits/revgraycode.h]:

```
1    static inline ulong rev_gray_code(ulong x)  { return  x ^ (x<<1); }
```

Its inverse is

```
1    static inline ulong inverse_rev_gray_code(ulong x)
2    {
3        // use: rev_gray ** BITSPERLONG == id:
4        x ^= x<<1;  // rev_gray ** 1
5        x ^= x<<2;  // rev_gray ** 2
6        x ^= x<<4;  // rev_gray ** 4
```

```
111.1111....1111............... = 0xef0f0000  == word
1..11...1...1...1............... = gray_code
..11...1...1...1................ = rev_gray_code
1.11.1.11111.1.11111111111111111 = inverse_gray_code
1.1..1.1.....1.1................ = inverse_rev_gray_code
-------------------------------------------------------
...1....1111....11111111111111111 = 0x10f0ffff  == word
...11...1...1...1................ = gray_code
..11...1...1...1...............1 = rev_gray_code
...11111.1.11111.1.1.1.1.1.1.1.1 = inverse_gray_code
1111.....1.1.....1.1.1.1.1.1.1.1 = inverse_rev_gray_code
-------------------------------------------------------
......1......................... = 0x2000000  == word
......11........................ = gray_code
......11........................ = rev_gray_code
......11111111111111111111111111 = inverse_gray_code
1111111......................... = inverse_rev_gray_code
-------------------------------------------------------
111111.1111111111111111111111111 = 0xfdffffff  == word
1.....11........................ = gray_code
......11.......................1 = rev_gray_code
1.1.1..1.1.1.1.1.1.1.1.1.1.1.1.1 = inverse_gray_code
1.1.1.11.1.1.1.1.1.1.1.1.1.1.1.1 = inverse_rev_gray_code
-------------------------------------------------------
```

Figure 1.16-D: Examples of the Gray code, reversed Gray code, and their inverses with 32-bit words.

```
7        x ^= x<<8;   // rev_gray ** 8
8        x ^= x<<16;  // rev_gray ** 16
9        // here: x = rev_gray**31(input)
10       // note: the statements can be reordered at will
11   #if  BITS_PER_LONG >= 64
12       x ^= x<<32;  // for 64bit words
13   #endif
14       return  x;
15   }
```

Some examples with 32-bit words are shown in figure 1.16-D.

Let G and E denote be the Gray code and reversed Gray code of a word X, respectively. Write G^{-1} and E^{-1} for their inverses. Then E preserves the lowest bit of X, while E preserves the highest. Also E preserves the lowest *set* bit of X, while E preserves the highest. Further, E^{-1} contains at each bit the parity of all bits of X right from it, including the bit itself. Especially, the word parity can be found in the highest bit of E^{-1}.

Let $\overline{X}$ denote the complement of X, p its parity, and let S the right shift by one of G^{-1}. Then we have

$$G^{-1} \text{ XOR } E^{-1} = \begin{cases} X & \text{if } p = 0 \\ \overline{X} & \text{otherwise} \end{cases} \tag{1.16-1a}$$

$$S \text{ XOR } E^{-1} = \begin{cases} 0 & \text{if } p = 0 \\ \overline{0} & \text{otherwise} \end{cases} \tag{1.16-1b}$$

We note that taking the reversed Gray code of a binary word corresponds to multiplication with the binary polynomial $x + 1$ and the inverse reversed Gray code is a method for fast exact division by $x + 1$, see section 40.1.6 on page 826. The inverse reversed Gray code can be used to solve the reduced quadratic equation for binary normal bases, see section 42.6.2 on page 903.

1.17 Bit sequency ‡

The *sequency* of a binary word is the number of zero-one transitions in the word. A function to determine the sequency is [FXT: bits/bitsequency.h]:

```
1    static inline ulong bit_sequency(ulong x)  { return bit_count( gray_code(x) ); }
```

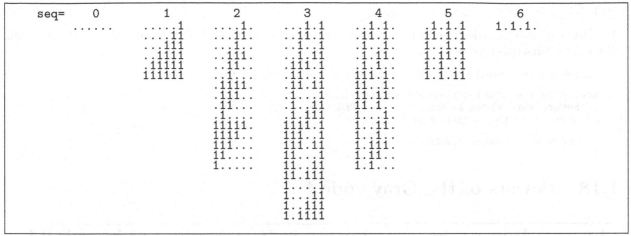

Figure 1.17-A: 6-bit words of prescribed sequence as generated by `next_sequence()`.

The function assumes that all bits to the left of the word are zero and all bits to the right are equal to the lowest bit, see figure 1.17-A. For example, the sequence of the 8-bit word [00011111] is one. To take the lowest bit into account, add it to the sequence (then all sequences are even).

The minimal binary word with given sequence can be computed as follows:

```
1    static inline ulong first_sequence(ulong k)
2    // Return the first (i.e. smallest) word with sequence k,
3    // e.g.  00..00010101010 (seq 8)
4    // e.g.  00..00101010101 (seq 9)
5    // Must have:  0 <= k <= BITS_PER_LONG
6    {
7         return inverse_gray_code( first_comb(k) );
8    }
```

A faster version is (32-bit branch only):

```
1         if ( k==0 )  return 0;
2         const ulong m = 0xaaaaaaaaUL;
3         return  m >> (BITS_PER_LONG-k);
```

The maximal binary word with given sequence can be computed via

```
1    static inline ulong last_sequence(ulong k)
2    // Return the last (i.e. biggest) word with sequence k.
3    {
4         return inverse_gray_code( last_comb(k) );
5    }
```

The functions `first_comb(k)` and `last_comb(k)` return a word with k bits set at the low and high end, respectively (see section 1.24 on page 62).

For the generation of all words with a given sequence, starting with the smallest, we use a function that computes the next word with the same sequence:

```
1    static inline ulong next_sequence(ulong x)
2    {
3         x = gray_code(x);
4         x = next_colex_comb(x);
5         x = inverse_gray_code(x);
6         return x;
7    }
```

The inverse function, returning the previous word with the same sequence, is

```
1    static inline ulong prev_sequence(ulong x)
2    {
3         x = gray_code(x);
4         x = prev_colex_comb(x);
5         x = inverse_gray_code(x);
6         return x;
```

```
7   }
```

The list of all 6-bit words ordered by sequence is shown in figure 1.17-A. It was created with the program [FXT: bits/bitsequence-demo.cc].

The sequence of a word can be complemented as follows (32-bit version):

```
1   static inline ulong complement_sequence(ulong x)
2   // Return word whose sequence is BITS_PER_LONG - s
3   // where s is the sequence of x
4   {
5       return x ^ 0xaaaaaaaaUL;
6   }
```

1.18   Powers of the Gray code ‡

Figure 1.18-A: Powers of the matrices for the Gray code (top) and the reversed Gray code (bottom).

The Gray code is a bit-wise linear transform of a binary word. The 2^k-th power of the Gray code of x can be computed as x ^ (x>>k). The e-th power can be computed as the bit-wise sum of the powers corresponding to the bits in the exponent. This motivates [FXT: bits/graypower.h]:

```
1   static inline ulong gray_pow(ulong x, ulong e)
2   // Return (gray_code**e)(x)
3   // gray_pow(x, 1) == gray_code(x)
4   // gray_pow(x, BITS_PER_LONG-1) == inverse_gray_code(x)
5   {
6       e &= (BITS_PER_LONG-1);  // modulo BITS_PER_LONG
7       ulong s = 1;
8       while ( e )
9       {
10          if ( e & 1 )  x ^= x >> s;  // gray ** s
11          s <<= 1;
12          e >>= 1;
13      }
14      return x;
15  }
```

The Gray code $g = [g_0, g_1, \ldots, g_7]$ of a 8-bit binary word $x = [x_0, x_1, \ldots, x_7]$ can be expressed as a matrix multiplication over GF(2) (dots for zeros):

```
    g    =        G          x
   [g0]       [ 11...... ]  [x0]
   [g1]       [ .11..... ]  [x1]
   [g2]       [ ..11.... ]  [x2]
   [g3]  =    [ ...11... ]  [x3]
   [g4]       [ ....11.. ]  [x4]
   [g5]       [ .....11. ]  [x5]
   [g6]       [ ......11 ]  [x6]
   [g7]       [ .......1 ]  [x7]
```

The powers of the Gray code correspond to multiplication with powers of the matrix G, shown in figure 1.18-A (bottom). The powers of the inverse Gray code for N-bit words (where N is a power of 2) can be computed by the relation $G^e\, G^{N-e} = G^N = \mathrm{id}$.

```
1    static inline ulong inverse_gray_pow(ulong x, ulong e)
2    // Return (inverse_gray_code**(e))(x)
3    //    == (gray_code**(-e))(x)
4    // inverse_gray_pow(x, 1) == inverse_gray_code(x)
5    // inverse_gray_pow(x, BITS_PER_LONG-1) == gray_code(x)
6    {
7        return  gray_pow(x, -e);
8    }
```

The matrices corresponding to the powers of the reversed Gray code are shown in figure 1.18-A (bottom). We just have to reverse the shift operator in the functions:

```
1    static inline ulong rev_gray_pow(ulong x, ulong e)
2    // Return (rev_gray_code**e)(x)
3    {
4        e &= (BITS_PER_LONG-1);  // modulo BITS_PER_LONG
5        ulong s = 1;
6        while ( e )
7        {
8            if ( e & 1 )  x ^= x << s;  // rev_gray ** s
9            s <<= 1;
10           e >>= 1;
11       }
12       return  x;
13   }
```

The inverse function is

```
1    static inline ulong inverse_rev_gray_pow(ulong x, ulong e)
2    // Return (inverse_rev_gray_code**(e))(x)
3    {
4        return  rev_gray_pow(x, -e);
5    }
```

1.19 Invertible transforms on words ‡

The functions presented in this section are invertible transforms on binary words. The names are chosen as 'some code', emphasizing the result of the transforms, similar to the convention used with the name 'Gray code'. The functions are given in [FXT: bits/bittransforms.h].

In the transform (*blue code*)

```
1    static inline ulong blue_code(ulong a)
2    {
3        ulong s = BITS_PER_LONG >> 1;
4        ulong m = ~0UL << s;
5        do
6        {
7            a ^= ( (a&m) >> s );
8            s >>= 1;
9            m ^= (m>>s);
10       }
11       while ( s );
12       return  a;
13   }
```

the masks 'm' are (32-bit binary)

```
11111111111111111...............
11111111........1111111...........
1111....1111....1111....1111.....
1.1.1.1.1.1.1.1.1.1.1.1.1.1.1.1.
```

The same masks are used in the *yellow code*

```
1    static inline ulong yellow_code(ulong a)
2    {
3        ulong s = BITS_PER_LONG >> 1;
4        ulong m = ~0UL >> s;
5        do
6        {
7            a ^= ( (a&m) << s );
8            s >>= 1;
```

```
9              m ^= (m<<s);
10         }
11     while ( s );
12     return  a;
13  }
```

Both need $O(\log_2 \mathtt{BITS\_PER\_LONG})$ operations. The `blue_code` can be used as a fast implementation for the composition of a binary polynomial with $x + 1$, see section 40.7.2 on page 845. The yellow code can also be computed by the statement

```
revbin( blue_code( revbin(x) ) );
```

So we could have called it *reversed blue code*. Note the names 'blue code' etc. are ad hoc terminology and not standard. See section 23.11 on page 486 for the closely related Reed-Muller transform.

```
                  blue                  yellow
      0:    ....... 0*   1111111111111111111111111111111  0
      1:    ......1 1*   1111111111111111111111111111111 32
      2:    .....11 2    1.1.1.1.1.1.1.1.1.1.1.1.1.1.1.1. 16
      3:    .....1. 1    .1.1.1.1.1.1.1.1.1.1.1.1.1.1.1.1 16
      4:    ...1.1  2    11..11..11..11..11..11..11..11.. 16
      5:    ...1..  1    ..11..11..11..11..11..11..11..11 16
      6:    ...11.  2*   .11..11..11..11..11..11..11..11. 16
      7:    ...111  3*   1..11..11..11..11..11..11..11..1 16
      8:    ..1111  4    1.1.1.1.1.1.1.1.1.1.1.1.1.1.1. 8
      9:    ..111.  3    .111.111.111.111.111.111.111.111 24
     10:    ..11..  2    ..1.1.1.1.1.1.1.1.1.1.1.1.1.1.1. 8
     11:    ..11.1  3    11.111.111.111.111.111.111.111.1 24
     12:    ..1.1.  2    .1.1.1.1.1.1.1.1.1.1.1.1.1.1.1. 8
     13:    ..1.11  3    1.111.111.111.111.111.111.111.11 24
     14:    ..1..1  2    111.111.111.111.111.111.111.111. 24
     15:    ..1...  1    .1...1.1...1.1...1.1...1.1...1.1 8
     16:    .1...1  2    1111....1111....1111....1111.... 16
     17:    .1....  1    ....1111....1111....1111....1111 16
     18:    .1..1.  2*   .1.11.1.1.11.1.1.11.1.1.11.1.1. 16
     19:    .1..11  3*   1.1.11.1.1.11.1.1.11.1.1.11.1.1 16
     20:    .1.1..  2*   .1111....1111....1111....1111.. 16
     21:    .1.1.1  3*   11....1111....1111....1111....11 16
     22:    .1.111  4    1..1.11.1..1.11.1..1.11.1..1.11. 16
     23:    .1.11.  3    .11..1..11..1..11..1..11..1..11. 16
     24:    .1111.  4    .1111....1111....1111....1111. 16
     25:    .11111  5    1....1111....1111....1111....111 16
     26:    .111.1  4    11.1..11.1..11.1..11.1..11.1..1 16
     27:    .111..  3    .1.11.1..11.1..11.1..11.1..11.1 16
     28:    .11.11  4    1.11.1..11.1..11.1..11.1..11.1.. 16
     29:    .11.1.  3    .1..11.1..11.1..11.1..11.1..11 16
     30:    .11...  2    ..1111....1111....1111....1111. 16
     31:    .11..1  3    111....1111....1111....1111....1 16
```

Figure 1.19-A: Blue and yellow transforms of the binary words 0, 1, ..., 31. Bit-counts are shown at the right of each column. Fixed points are marked with asterisks.

The transforms of the binary words up to 31 are shown in figure 1.19-A, the lists were created with the program [FXT: bits/bittransforms-blue-demo.cc]. The parity of $B(a)$ is equal to the lowest bit of a. Up to the $a = 47$ the bit-count varies by ± 1 between successive values of $B(a)$, the transition $B(47) \to B(48)$ changes the bit-count by 3. The sequence of the indices a where the bit-count changes by more than one is

47, 51, 59, 67, 75, 79, 175, 179, 187, 195, 203, 207, 291, 299, 339, 347, 419, 427, ...

The yellow code might be a good candidate for 'randomization' of binary words. The blue code maps any range $[0 \ldots 2^k - 1]$ onto itself. Both the blue code and the yellow code are involutions (self-inverse).

The transforms (*red code*)

```
1   static inline ulong red_code(ulong a)
2   {
3       ulong s = BITS_PER_LONG >> 1;
4       ulong m = ~0UL >> s;
5       do
6       {
7           ulong u = a & m;
8           ulong v = a ^ u;
9           a = v ^ (u<<s);
10          a ^= (v>>s);
11          s >>= 1;
```

```
                 red                                  green
  0:  ................................  0   ..............................  0
  1:  1...............................  1   11111111111111111111111111111111 32
  2:  11..............................  2   .1.1.1.1.1.1.1.1.1.1.1.1.1.1.1.1 16
  3:  .1..............................  1   1.1.1.1.1.1.1.1.1.1.1.1.1.1.1.1. 16
  4:  1.1.............................  2   ..11..11..11..11..11..11..11..11 16
  5:  ..1.............................  1   11..11..11..11..11..11..11..11.. 16
  6:  .11.............................  2   .11..11..11..11..11..11..11..11. 16
  7:  111.............................  3   1..11..11..11..11..11..11..11..1 16
  8:  1111............................  4   ...1...1...1...1...1...1...1...1  8
  9:  .111............................  3   111.111.111.111.111.111.111.111. 24
 10:  ..11............................  2   .1...1...1...1...1...1...1...1..  8
 11:  1.11............................  3   1.111.111.111.111.111.111.111.11 24
 12:  ..1.............................  2   ...1...1...1...1...1...1...1...1  8
 13:  11.1............................  3   11.111.111.111.111.111.111.111.1 24
 14:  1..1............................  2   .111.111.111.111.111.111.111.111 24
 15:  ...1............................  2   1...1...1...1...1...1...1...1...  8
 16:  1...1...........................  2   ....1111....1111....1111....1111 16
 17:  ....1...........................  1   1111....1111....1111....1111.... 16
 18:  .1..1...........................  2   .1.11.1..1.11.1..1.11.1..1.11.1. 16
 19:  11..1...........................  3   1.1..1.11.1..1.11.1..1.11.1..1.1 16
 20:  ...1.1..........................  2   ...1111....1111....1111....1111. 16
 21:  1..1.1..........................  3   11..1111....1111....1111....11.. 16
 22:  111.1...........................  4   .11.1..1.11.1..1.11.1..1.11.1..1 16
 23:  ..11.1..........................  3   1..11.1..1.11.1..1.11.1..1.11... 16
 24:  .1111...........................  4   ....1111....1111....1111....1111 16
 25:  11111...........................  5   111....1111....1111....1111....1 16
 26:  1.111...........................  4   .1...1..1.11.1..1.11.1..1.11..11 16
 27:  ..111...........................  3   1.11..1.11.1..1.11.1..1.11..11.1 16
 28:  11.11...........................  4   .1.11..1.11.1..1.11.1..1.11..1.1 16
 29:  .1.11...........................  3   11.1..1.11.1..1.11.1..1.11.1..1. 16
 30:  ...11...........................  2   .1111....1111....1111....1111... 16
 31:  1..11...........................  3   1....1111....1111....1111....111 16
```

Figure 1.19-B: Red and green transforms of the binary words 0, 1, ..., 31.

```
12        m ^= (m<<s);
13     }
14     while ( s );
15     return  a;
16  }
```

and (*green code*)

```
 1   static inline ulong green_code(ulong a)
 2   {
 3       ulong s = BITS_PER_LONG >> 1;
 4       ulong m = ~0UL << s;
 5       do
 6       {
 7           ulong u = a & m;
 8           ulong v = a ^ u;
 9           a = v ^ (u>>s);
10           a ^= (v<<s);
11           s >>= 1;
12           m ^= (m>>s);
13       }
14       while ( s );
15       return  a;
16   }
```

use the masks

```
........:11111111111111111
....::11111111....11111111
::11:11::11:11::11:11::11:11
:1.1.1.1.1.1.1.1.1.1.1.1.1.1
```

The transforms of the binary words up to 31 are shown in figure 1.19-B, which was created with the program [FXT: bits/bittransforms-red-demo.cc]. The red code can also be computed by the statement

```
revbin( blue_code( x ) );
```

and the green code by

```
blue_code( revbin( x ) );
```

	i	r	B	Y	R	E
i	i	r	B	Y	R	E
r	r	i	R*	E*	B*	Y*
B	B	E*	i	R*	Y*	r*
Y	Y	R*	E*	i	r*	B*
R	R	Y*	r*	B*	E	i
E	E	B*	Y*	r*	i	R

Figure 1.19-C: Multiplication table for the transforms.

1.19.1   Relations between the transforms

We write B for the blue code (transform), Y for the yellow code and r for bit-reversal (the `revbin`-function). We have the following relations between B and Y:

$$B \;=\; YrY \quad = rYr \tag{1.19-1a}$$
$$Y \;=\; BrB \quad = rBr \tag{1.19-1b}$$
$$r \;=\; YBY \quad = BYB \tag{1.19-1c}$$

As said, B and Y are self-inverse:

$$B^{-1} \;=\; B, \qquad BB = \text{id} \tag{1.19-2a}$$
$$Y^{-1} \;=\; Y, \qquad YY = \text{id} \tag{1.19-2b}$$

We write R for the red code, and E for the green code. The red code and the green code are not involutions (square roots of identity) but third roots of identity:

$$RRR \;=\; \text{id}, \qquad R^{-1} = RR = E \tag{1.19-3a}$$
$$EEE \;=\; \text{id}, \qquad E^{-1} = EE = R \tag{1.19-3b}$$
$$RE \;=\; ER = \text{id} \tag{1.19-3c}$$

Figure 1.19-C shows the multiplication table. The R in the third column of the second row says that $rB = R$. The letter i is used for identity (id). An asterisk says that $x\,y \neq y\,x$.

By construction we have

$$R \;=\; rB \tag{1.19-4a}$$
$$E \;=\; rY \tag{1.19-4b}$$

Relations between R and E are:

$$R \;=\; ErE \quad = rEr \tag{1.19-5a}$$
$$E \;=\; RrR \quad = rRr \tag{1.19-5b}$$
$$R \;=\; RER \tag{1.19-5c}$$
$$E \;=\; ERE \tag{1.19-5d}$$

For the bit-reversal we have

$$r \;=\; YR = RB = BE = EY \tag{1.19-6}$$

Some products for the transforms are

$$B \;=\; RY = YE = RBR = EBE \tag{1.19-7a}$$
$$Y \;=\; EB = BR = RYR = EYE \tag{1.19-7b}$$
$$R \;=\; BY = BEB = YEY \tag{1.19-7c}$$
$$E \;=\; YB = BRB = YRY \tag{1.19-7d}$$

Some triple products that give the identical transform are

$$\text{id} \;=\; BYE \;=\; RYB \tag{1.19-8a}$$

$$\text{id} \;=\; EBY \;=\; BRY \tag{1.19-8b}$$

$$\text{id} \;=\; YEB \;=\; YBR \tag{1.19-8c}$$

1.19.2 Relations to Gray code and reversed Gray code

Write g for the Gray code, then:

$$g\,B\,g\,B \;=\; \text{id} \tag{1.19-9a}$$

$$g\,B\,g \;=\; B \tag{1.19-9b}$$

$$g^{-1}\,B\,g^{-1} \;=\; B \tag{1.19-9c}$$

$$g\,B \;=\; B\,g^{-1} \tag{1.19-9d}$$

Let S_k be the operator that rotates a word by k bits (bit 0 is moved to position k), then

$$Y\,S_{+1}\,Y \;=\; g \tag{1.19-10a}$$

$$Y\,S_{-1}\,Y \;=\; g^{-1} \tag{1.19-10b}$$

$$Y\,S_k\,Y \;=\; g^k \tag{1.19-10c}$$

Shift in the sequency domain is bit-wise derivative in time domain. Relation 1.19-10c, together with an algorithm to generate the cycle leaders of the Gray permutation (section 2.12.1 on page 128) gives a curious method to generate the binary necklaces whose length is a power of 2, described in section 18.1.6 on page 376. Let e be the operator for the reversed Gray code, then

$$B\,S_{+1}\,B \;=\; e^{-1} \tag{1.19-11a}$$

$$B\,S_{-1}\,B \;=\; e \tag{1.19-11b}$$

$$B\,S_k\,B \;=\; e^{-k} \tag{1.19-11c}$$

1.19.3 Fixed points of the blue code ‡

```
 0 = ......  : ..........  =   0     16 = .1....  : .1...1...  = 272
 1 = .....1  : .........1  =   1     17 = .1...1  : .1.11.1..  = 360
 2 = ....1.  : ........11.  =   6    18 = .1..1.  : .1.....1..  = 260
 3 = ....11  : ........111  =   7    19 = .1..11  : .1.11111..  = 380
 4 = ...1..  : ......1.1..  =  20    20 = .1.1..  : .1...1.11.  = 278
 5 = ...1.1  : ......1..1.  =  18    21 = .1.1.1  : .1.11.111.  = 366
 6 = ...11.  : ......1.1.1  =  21    22 = .1.11.  : .1......1.  = 258
 7 = ...111  : .......1.11  =  19    23 = .1.111  : .1.1111.1.  = 378
 8 = ..1...  : ....1111...  = 120    24 = ..11..  : .1...1...1  = 273
 9 = ..1..1  : ...11.11..  = 108     25 = ..11.1  : .1.11.1..1  = 361
10 = ..1.1.  : ...111111.  = 126     26 = ..11.1  : .1.....1.1  = 261
11 = ..1.11  : ...11.1.1.  = 106     27 = ..11.11  : .1.11111.1  = 381
12 = ..11..  : ...1111..1  = 121     28 = ..111.  : .1...1.111  = 279
13 = ..11.1  : ...11.11.1  = 109     29 = ..111.1  : .1.11.1111  = 367
14 = ..111.  : ...1111111  = 127     30 = ..1111.  : .1......11  = 259
15 = ..1111  : ...11.1.11  = 107     31 = ..11111  : .1.1111.11  = 379
```

Figure 1.19-D: The first fixed points of the blue code. The highest bit of all fixed points lies at an even index. There are $2^{n/2}$ fixed points with highest bit at index n.

The sequence of fixed points of the blue code is (entry A118666 in [312])

$$0,\ 1,\ 6,\ 7,\ 18,\ 19,\ 20,\ 21,\ 106,\ 107,\ 108,\ 109,\ 120,\ 121,\ 126,\ 127,\ 258,\ 259,\ \ldots$$

If f is a fixed point, then f XOR 1 is also a fixed point. Further, $2\,(f$ XOR $(2\,f))$ is a fixed point. These facts can be cast into a function that returns a unique fixed point for each argument [FXT: bits/blue-fixed-points.h]:

```
1    static inline ulong blue_fixed_point(ulong s)
2    {
3        if ( 0==s )  return 0;
4        ulong f = 1;
5        while ( s>1 )
6        {
7            f ^= (f<<1);
8            f <<= 1;
9            f |= (s&1);
10           s >>= 1;
11       }
12       return f;
13   }
```

The output for the first few arguments is shown in figure 1.19-D. Note that the fixed points are not in ascending order. The list was created by the program [FXT: bits/bittransforms-blue-fp-demo.cc].

Now write $f(x)$ for the binary polynomial corresponding to f (see chapter 40 on page 822), if $f(x)$ is a fixed point (that is, $B\,f(x) = f(x+1) = f(x)$), then both $(x^2+x)\,f(x)$ and $1 + (x^2+x)\,f(x)$ are fixed points. The function `blue_fixed_point()` repeatedly multiplies by x^2+x and adds one if the corresponding bit of the argument is set.

For the inverse function, we exploit that polynomial division by $x+1$ can be done with the inverse reversed Gray code (see section 1.16.6 on page 45) if the polynomial is divisible by $x+1$:

```
1    static inline ulong blue_fixed_point_idx(ulong f)
2    // Inverse of blue_fixed_point()
3    {
4        ulong s = 1;
5        while ( f )
6        {
7            s <<= 1;
8            s ^= (f & 1);
9            f >>= 1;
10           f = inverse_rev_gray_code(f);   // == bitpol_div(f, 3);
11       }
12       return s >> 1;
13   }
```

1.19.4 More transforms by symbolic powering

The idea of powering a transform (as with the Gray code, see section 1.18 on page 48) can be applied to the 'color'-transforms as exemplified for the blue code:

```
1    static inline ulong blue_xcode(ulong a, ulong x)
2    {
3        x &= (BITS_PER_LONG-1);  // modulo BITS_PER_LONG
4        ulong s = BITS_PER_LONG >> 1;
5        ulong m = ~0UL << s;
6        while ( s )
7        {
8            if ( x & 1 )  a ^= ( (a&m) >> s );
9            x >>= 1;
10           s >>= 1;
11           m ^= (m>>s);
12       }
13       return a;
14   }
```

The result is *not* the power of the blue code which would be pretty boring as $B\,B = \text{id}$. The transforms (and the equivalents for Y, R and E, see [FXT: bits/bitxtransforms.h]) are more interesting: all relations between the transforms are still valid, if the symbolic exponent is identical with all terms in the relation. For example, we had $B\,B = \text{id}$, now $B^x\,B^x = \text{id}$ is true for all x. Similarly, $E\,E = R$ now has to be $E^x\,E^x = R^x$. That is, we have BITS_PER_LONG different versions of our four transforms that share their properties with the 'simple' versions. Among them are BITS_PER_LONG transforms B^x and Y^x that are involutions and E^x and R^x that are third roots of the identity: $E^x\,E^x\,E^x = R^x\,R^x\,R^x = \text{id}$.

While not powers of the simple versions, we still have $B^0 = Y^0 = R^0 = E^0 = \text{id}$. Further, let e be the 'exponent' of all ones and Z be any of the transforms, then $Z^e = Z$. Writing '+' for the XOR operation, we have $Z^x Z^y = Z^{x+y}$ and so $Z^x Z^y = Z$ whenever $x + y = e$.

1.19.5   The building blocks of the transforms

Consider the following transforms on 2-bit words where addition is bit-wise (that is, XOR):

$$\text{id}_2\, v \;=\; \begin{bmatrix} 1 & 0 \\ 0 & 1 \end{bmatrix} \begin{bmatrix} a \\ b \end{bmatrix} = \begin{bmatrix} a \\ b \end{bmatrix} \tag{1.19-12a}$$

$$r_2\, v \;=\; \begin{bmatrix} 0 & 1 \\ 1 & 0 \end{bmatrix} \begin{bmatrix} a \\ b \end{bmatrix} = \begin{bmatrix} b \\ a \end{bmatrix} \tag{1.19-12b}$$

$$B_2\, v \;=\; \begin{bmatrix} 1 & 1 \\ 0 & 1 \end{bmatrix} \begin{bmatrix} a \\ b \end{bmatrix} = \begin{bmatrix} a+b \\ b \end{bmatrix} \tag{1.19-12c}$$

$$Y_2\, v \;=\; \begin{bmatrix} 1 & 0 \\ 1 & 1 \end{bmatrix} \begin{bmatrix} a \\ b \end{bmatrix} = \begin{bmatrix} a \\ a+b \end{bmatrix} \tag{1.19-12d}$$

$$R_2\, v \;=\; \begin{bmatrix} 0 & 1 \\ 1 & 1 \end{bmatrix} \begin{bmatrix} a \\ b \end{bmatrix} = \begin{bmatrix} b \\ a+b \end{bmatrix} \tag{1.19-12e}$$

$$E_2\, v \;=\; \begin{bmatrix} 1 & 1 \\ 1 & 0 \end{bmatrix} \begin{bmatrix} a \\ b \end{bmatrix} = \begin{bmatrix} a+b \\ a \end{bmatrix} \tag{1.19-12f}$$

It can easily be verified that for these the same relations hold as for id, r, B, Y, R, E. In fact the 'color-transforms', bit-reversal, and identity are the transforms obtained as repeated Kronecker-products of the matrices (see section 23.3 on page 462). The transforms are linear over GF(2):

$$Z(\alpha\, a + \beta\, b) \;=\; \alpha\, Z(a) + \beta\, Z(b) \tag{1.19-13}$$

The corresponding version of the bit-reversal is [FXT: bits/revbin.h]:

```
1    static inline ulong xrevbin(ulong a, ulong x)
2    {
3        x &= (BITS_PER_LONG-1);   // modulo BITS_PER_LONG
4        ulong s = BITS_PER_LONG >> 1;
5        ulong m = ~0UL >> s;
6        while ( s )
7        {
8            if ( x & 1 )  a = ( (a & m) << s ) ^ ( (a & (~m)) >> s );
9            x >>= 1;
10           s >>= 1;
11           m ^= (m<<s);
12       }
13       return  a;
14   }
```

Then, for example, $R^x = r^x B^x$ (see relation 1.19-4a on page 52). The yellow code is the bit-wise Reed-Muller transform (described in section 23.11 on page 486) of a binary word. The symbolic powering is equivalent to selecting individual levels of the transform.

1.20   Scanning for zero bytes

The following function (32-bit version) determines if any sub-byte of the argument is zero from [FXT: bits/zerobyte.h]:

```
1    static inline ulong contains_zero_byte(ulong x)
2    {
3        return  ((x-0x01010101UL)^x) & (~x) & 0x80808080UL;
4    }
```

It returns zero when x contains no zero-byte and nonzero when it does. The idea is to subtract one from each of the bytes and then look for bytes where the borrow propagated all the way to the most significant bit. A simplified version is given in [215, sect.7.1.3, rel.90]:

```
1        return  0x80808080UL & ( x - 0x01010101UL ) & ~x;
```

To scan for other values than zero (e.g. 0xa5), we can use

```
contains_zero_byte( x ^ 0xa5a5a5a5UL )
```

For very long strings and word sizes of 64 or more bits the following function may be a win [FXT: aux1/bytescan.cc]:

```
1    ulong long_strlen(const char *str)
2    // Return length of string starting at str.
3    {
4        ulong x;
5        const char *p = str;
6
7        // Alignment: scan bytes up to word boundary:
8        while ( (ulong)p % BYTES_PER_LONG )
9        {
10           if ( 0 == *p )  return  (ulong)(p-str);
11           ++p;
12       }
13
14       x = *(ulong *)p;
15       while ( ! contains_zero_byte(x) )
16       {
17           p += BYTES_PER_LONG;
18           x = *(ulong *)p;
19       }
20
21       // now a zero byte is somewhere in x:
22       while ( 0 != *p )  { ++p; }
23
24       return  (ulong)(p-str);
25   }
```

1.21   Inverse and square root modulo 2^n

1.21.1   Computation of the inverse

The inverse modulo 2^n where n is the number of bits in a word can be computed using an iteration (see section 29.1.5 on page 569) with quadratic convergence. The number to be inverted has to be odd [FXT: bits/bit2adic.h]:

```
1    static inline ulong inv2adic(ulong x)
2    // Return inverse modulo 2**BITS_PER_LONG
3    // x must be odd
4    // The number of correct bits is doubled with each step
5    // ==> loop is executed prop. log_2(BITS_PER_LONG) times
6    // precision is 3, 6, 12, 24, 48, 96, ... bits (or better)
7    {
8        if ( 0==(x&1) )  return 0;  // not invertible
9        ulong i = x;  // correct to three bits at least
10       ulong p;
11       do
12       {
13           p = i * x;
14           i *= (2UL - p);
15       }
16       while ( p!=1 );
17       return  i;
18   }
```

Let m be the modulus (a power of 2), then the computed value i is the inverse of x modulo m: $i \equiv x^{-1} \bmod m$. It can be used for the *exact division*: to compute the quotient a/x for a number a that is known to be divisible by x, simply multiply by i. This works because $a = b\,x$ (a is divisible by x), so $a\,i \equiv b\,x\,i \equiv b \bmod m$.

1.21.2 Exact division by $C = 2^k \pm 1$

We use the following relation where $Y = 1 - C$:

$$\frac{A}{C} = \frac{A}{1-Y} = A(1+Y)(1+Y^2)(1+Y^4)(1+Y^8)\dots(1+Y^{2^n}) \mod Y^{2^{n+1}} \quad (1.21\text{-}1)$$

The relation can be used for efficient exact division over $\mathbb{Z}$ by $C = 2^k \pm 1$. For $C = 2^k + 1$ use

$$\frac{A}{C} = A(1-2^k)(1+2^{k\,2})(1+2^{k\,4})(1+2^{k\,8})\cdots(1+2^{k\,2^u}) \mod 2^N \quad (1.21\text{-}2)$$

where $k\,2^u \geq N$. For $C = 2^k - 1$ use $(A/C = -A/-C)$

$$\frac{A}{C} = -A(1+2^k)(1+2^{k\,2})(1+2^{k\,4})(1+2^{k\,8})\cdots(1+2^{k\,2^u}) \mod 2^N \quad (1.21\text{-}3)$$

The equivalent method for exact division by polynomials (over GF(2)) is given in section 40.1.6 on page 826.

1.21.3 Computation of the square root

Figure 1.21-A: Examples of the inverse and square root modulo 2^n of x where $-9 \leq x \leq +9$. Where no inverse or square root is given, it does not exist.

With the inverse square root we choose the start value to match $\lfloor d/2 \rfloor + 1$ as that guarantees four bits of initial precision. Moreover, we control which of the two possible values of the inverse square root is computed. The argument modulo 8 has to be equal to 1.

```
1    static inline ulong invsqrt2adic(ulong d)
2    // Return inverse square root modulo 2**BITS_PER_LONG
3    // Must have:  d==1 mod 8
4    // The number of correct bits is doubled with each step
5    // ==> loop is executed prop. log_2(BITS_PER_LONG) times
6    // precision is 4, 8, 16, 32, 64, ... bits (or better)
7    {
8        if ( 1 != (d&7) )  return 0;  // no inverse sqrt
9        // start value: if d == ****10001 ==> x := ****1001
10       ulong x = (d >> 1) | 1;
11       ulong p, y;
12       do
13       {
14           y = x;
15           p = (3 - d * y * y);
16           x = (y * p) >> 1;
17       }
18       while ( x!=y );
19       return x;
20   }
```

The square root is computed as $d \cdot 1/\sqrt{d}$:

```
1    static inline ulong sqrt2adic(ulong d)
2    // Return square root modulo 2**BITS_PER_LONG
3    // Must have: d==1 mod 8  or  d==4 mod 32,  d==16 mod 128
4    //   ... d==4**k mod 4**(k+3)
5    // Result undefined if condition does not hold
6    {
7        if ( 0==d ) return  0;
8        ulong s = 0;
9        while ( 0==(d&1) )  { d >>= 1; ++s; }
10       d *= invsqrt2adic(d);
11       d <<= (s>>1);
12       return   d;
13   }
```

Note that the square root modulo 2^n is something completely different from the integer square root in general. If the argument d is a perfect square, then the result is $\pm\sqrt{d}$. The output of the program [FXT: bits/bit2adic-demo.cc] is shown in figure 1.21-A. For further information see [213, ex.31, p.213], [135, chap.6, p.126], and also [208].

1.22   Radix -2 (minus two) representation

The radix -2 representation of a number n is

$$n = \sum_{k=0}^{\infty} t_k (-2)^k \tag{1.22-1}$$

where the t_k are zero or one. For integers n the sum is terminating: the highest nonzero t_k is at most two positions beyond the highest bit of the binary representation of the absolute value of n (with two's complement).

1.22.1   Conversion from binary

```
      k:      bin(k)     m=bin2neg(k)    g=gray(m)     dec(g)
      0:      .......     .......        .......        0 <= 0
      1:      ......1     ......1        ......1        1 <= 1
      2:      .....1.     ....11.        ....1.1        5
      3:      .....11     ....111        ....1..        4
      4:      ....1..     ....1..        ....11.        2
      5:      ....1.1     ....1.1        ...1111        3 <= 5
      6:      ....11.     ..11.1.        ..1.111        19
      7:      ....111     ..11.11        ..1.11.        18
      8:      ...1...     ..11...        ..1.1..        20
      9:      ...1..1     ..11..1        ..1.1.1        21
     10:      ...1.1.     ..1111.        ..1...1        17
     11:      ...1.11     ..11111        ..1....        16
     12:      ...11..     ..111..        ..1..1.        14
     13:      ...11.1     ..111.1        ..1..11        15
     14:      ...111.     ..1..1.        ..11.11        7
     15:      ...1111     ..1..11        ..11.1.        6
     16:      ..1....     ..1....        ..11...        8
     17:      ..1...1     ..1...1        ..11..1        9
     18:      ..1..1.     ...1.11.       ..111.1        13
     19:      ..1..11     ...1.111       ..111..        12
     20:      ..1.1..     ...1.1..       ..1111.        10
     21:      ..1.1.1     ...1.1.1       ..11111        11 <= 21
     22:      ..1.11.     11.1.1.        1.11111        75
     23:      ..1.111     11.1.11        1.11111.       74
     24:      ..11...     11.1...        1.111..        76
     25:      ..11..1     11.1..1        1.111.1        77
     26:      ..11.1.     11.111.        1.11..1        73
     27:      ..11.11     11.1111        1.11...        72
     28:      ..111..     11.11..        1.11.1.        70
     29:      ..111.1     11.11.1        1.11.11        71
     30:      ..1111.     11...1.        1.1..11        79
     31:      ..11111     11...11        1.1..1.        78
```

Figure 1.22-A: Radix -2 representations and their Gray codes. Lines ending in '<=N' indicate that all values $\leq N$ occur in the last column up to that point.

A surprisingly simple algorithm to compute the coefficients t_k of the radix -2 representation of a binary number is [39, item 128] [FXT: bits/negbin.h]:

```
1   static inline ulong bin2neg(ulong x)
2   // binary --> radix(-2)
3   {
4       const ulong m = 0xaaaaaaaaUL; // 32 bit version
5       x += m;
6       x ^= m;
7       return  x;
8   }
```

An example:

```
    14 -->   ..1..1. == 16 - 2 = =(-2)^4 + (-2)^1
```

The inverse routine executes the inverse of the two steps in reversed order:

```
1   static inline ulong neg2bin(ulong x)
2   // radix(-2) --> binary
3   // inverse of bin2neg()
4   {
5       const ulong m = 0xaaaaaaaaUL;  // 32-bit version
6       x ^= m;
7       x -= m;
8       return  x;
9   }
```

Figure 1.22-A shows the output of the program [FXT: bits/negbin-demo.cc]. The sequence of Gray codes of the radix -2 representation is a Gray code for the numbers in the range $0, \ldots, k$ for the following values of k (entry A002450 in [312]):

$$k \;=\; 1, 5, 21, 85, 341, 1365, 5461, 21845, 87381, 349525, 1398101, \ldots, (4^n - 1)/3$$

1.22.2 Fixed points of the conversion ‡

```
  0: ..........    64: ....1.....    256: ..1.......    320: ..1.1.....
  1: .........1    65: ....1....1    257: ..1......1    321: ..1.1....1
  4: ........1..    68: ....1...1..    260: ..1.....1..    324: ..1.1...1..
  5: ........1.1    69: ....1...1.1    261: ..1.....1.1    325: ..1.1...1.1
 16: ......1....    80: ....1.1....    272: ..1...1....    336: ..1.1.1....
 17: ......1...1    81: ....1.1...1    273: ..1...1...1    337: ..1.1.1...1
 20: ......1.1..    84: ....1.1.1..    276: ..1...1.1..    340: ..1.1.1.1..
 21: ......1.1.1    85: ....1.1.1.1    277: ..1...1.1.1    341: ..1.1.1.1.1
```

Figure 1.22-B: The fixed points of the conversion and their binary representations (dots denote zeros).

The sequence of fixed points of the conversion starts as

```
 0, 1, 4, 5, 16, 17, 20, 21, 64, 65, 68, 69, 80, 81, 84, 85, 256, ...
```

The binary representations have ones only at even positions (see figure 1.22-B). This is the *Moser – De Bruijn sequence*, entry A000695 in [312]. The generating function of the sequence is

$$\frac{1}{1-x} \sum_{j=0}^{\infty} \frac{4^j \, x^{2^j}}{1 + x^{2^j}} \;=\; x + 4x^2 + 5x^3 + 16x^4 + 17x^5 + 20x^6 + 21x^7 + 64x^8 + 65x^9 + \ldots \quad (1.22\text{-}2)$$

The sequence also appears as exponents in the power series (see also section 38.10.1 on page 750)

$$\prod_{k=0}^{\infty} \left(1 + x^{4^k}\right) \;=\; 1 + x + x^4 + x^5 + x^{16} + x^{17} + x^{20} + x^{21} + x^{64} + x^{65} + x^{68} + \ldots \quad (1.22\text{-}3)$$

The k-th fixed point is computed by moving all bits of the binary representation of k to position $2x$ where $x \geq 0$ is the index of the bit under consideration:

```
1    static inline ulong negbin_fixed_point(ulong k)
2    {
3        return bit_zip0(k);
4    }
```

The bit-zip function is given in section 1.15 on page 39. The sequence of radix -2 representations of $0, 1, 2, \ldots$, interpreted as binary numbers, is entry A005351 in [312]:

  0,1,6,7,4,5,26,27,24,25,30,31,28,29,18,19,16,17,22,23,20,21,106,107,104,105,110,111, ...

The corresponding sequence for the negative numbers $-1, -2, -3, \ldots$ is entry A005352:

  3,2,13,12,15,14,9,8,11,10,53,52,55,54,49,48,51,50,61,60,63,62,57,56,59,58,37,36,39,38, ...

More information about 'non-standard' representations of numbers can be found in [213].

1.22.3   Generating negbin words in order

Figure 1.22-C: Radix -2 representations of the numbers $0 \ldots + 63$ (top) and $0 \ldots - 63$ (bottom).

A radix -2 representation can be incremented by the function [FXT: bits/negbin.h] (32-bit versions in what follows):

```
1    static inline ulong next_negbin(ulong x)
2    // With x the radix(-2) representation of n
3    // return radix(-2) representation of n+1.
4    {
5        const ulong m = 0xaaaaaaaaUL;
6        x ^= m;
7        ++x;
8        x ^= m;
9        return x;
10   }
```

A version without constants is

```
1        ulong s = x << 1;
2        ulong y = x ^ s;
3        y += 1;
4        s ^= y;
5        return s;
```

Decrementing can be done via

```
1    static inline ulong prev_negbin(ulong x)
2    // With x the radix(-2) representation of n
3    // return radix(-2) representation of n-1.
4    {
5        const ulong m = 0xaaaaaaaaUL;
6        x ^= m;
7        --x;
8        x ^= m;
9        return x;
10   }
```

or via

```
1        const ulong m = 0x55555555UL;
2        x ^= m;
3        ++x;
4        x ^= m;
5        return x;
```

The functions are quite fast, about 730 million words per second are generated (3 cycles per increment or decrement). Figure 1.22-C shows the generated words in forward (top) and backward (bottom) order. It was created with the program [FXT: bits/negbin2-demo.cc].

1.23 A sparse signed binary representation

```
 0:  .......   .......    0 =
 1:  ......1   ......P    1 =  +1
 2:  .....1.   .....P.    2 =  +2
 3:  .....11   ....P.M    3 =  +4 -1
 4:  ....1..   ....P..    4 =  +4
 5:  ....1.1   ....P.P    5 =  +4 +1
 6:  ....11.   ...P.M.    6 =  +8 -2
 7:  ....111   ...P..M    7 =  +8 -1
 8:  ...1...   ...P...    8 =  +8
 9:  ...1..1   ...P..P    9 =  +8 +1
10:  ...1.1.   ...P.P.   10 =  +8 +2
11:  ...1.11   ..P.M.M   11 = +16 -4 -1
12:  ...11..   ..P.M..   12 = +16 -4
13:  ...11.1   ..P.M.P   13 = +16 -4 +1
14:  ...111.   ..P..M.   14 = +16 -2
15:  ...1111   ..P...M   15 = +16 -1
16:  ..1....   ..P....   16 = +16
17:  ..1...1   ..P...P   17 = +16 +1
18:  ..1..1.   ..P..P.   18 = +16 +2
19:  ..1..11   ..P.P.M   19 = +16 +4 -1
20:  ..1.1..   ..P.P..   20 = +16 +4
21:  ..1.1.1   ..P.P.P   21 = +16 +4 +1
22:  ..1.11.   .P.M.M.   22 = +32 -8 -2
23:  ..1.111   .P.M..M   23 = +32 -8 -1
24:  ..11...   .P.M...   24 = +32 -8
25:  ..11..1   .P.M..P   25 = +32 -8 +1
26:  ..11.1.   .P.M.P.   26 = +32 -8 +2
27:  ..11.11   .P..M.M   27 = +32 -4 -1
28:  ..111..   .P..M..   28 = +32 -4
29:  ..111.1   .P..M.P   29 = +32 -4 +1
30:  ..1111.   .P...M.   30 = +32 -2
31:  ..11111   .P....M   31 = +32 -1
32:  .1.....   .P.....   32 = +32
```

Figure 1.23-A: Sparse signed binary representations (nonadjacent form, NAF). The symbols 'P' and 'M' are respectively used for +1 and −1, dots denote zeros.

```
 0:  ........   ........    0 =
 1:  .......1   .......P    1 =  +1
 2:  ......1.   ......P.    2 =  +2
 4:  .....1..   .....P..    4 =  +4
 5:  .....1.1   .....P.P    5 =  +4 +1
 8:  ....1...   ....P...    8 =  +8
 9:  ....1..1   ....P..P    9 =  +8 +1
10:  ....1.1.   ....P.P.   10 =  +8 +2
16:  ...1....   ...P....   16 = +16
17:  ...1...1   ...P...P   17 = +16 +1
18:  ...1..1.   ...P..P.   18 = +16 +2
20:  ...1.1..   ...P.P..   20 = +16 +4
21:  ...1.1.1   ...P.P.P   21 = +16 +4 +1
32:  ..1.....   ..P.....   32 = +32
33:  ..1....1   ..P....P   33 = +32 +1
34:  ..1...1.   ..P...P.   34 = +32 +2
36:  ..1..1..   ..P..P..   36 = +32 +4
37:  ..1..1.1   ..P..P.P   37 = +32 +4 +1
40:  ..1.1...   ..P.P...   40 = +32 +8
41:  ..1.1..1   ..P.P..P   41 = +32 +8 +1
42:  ..1.1.1.   ..P.P.P.   42 = +32 +8 +2
64:  .1......   .P......   64 = +64
```

Figure 1.23-B: The numbers whose negative part in the NAF representation is zero.

An algorithm to compute a representation of a number x as

$$x = \sum_{k=0}^{\infty} s_k \cdot 2^k \quad \text{where} \quad s_k \in \{-1, 0, +1\} \tag{1.23-1}$$

such that two consecutive digits s_k, s_{k+1} are never simultaneously nonzero is given in [275]. Figure 1.23-A gives the representation of several small numbers. It is the output of [FXT: bits/bin2naf-demo.cc].

We can convert the binary representation of x into a pair of binary numbers that correspond to the positive and negative digits [FXT: bits/bin2naf.h]:

```
1   static inline void bin2naf(ulong x, ulong &np, ulong &nm)
2   // Compute (nonadjacent form, NAF) signed binary representation of x:
3   // the unique representation of x as
4   //    x=\sum_{k}{d_k*2^k} where d_j \in {-1,0,+1}
5   //    and no two adjacent digits d_j, d_{j+1} are both nonzero.
6   // np has bits j set where d_j==+1
7   // nm has bits j set where d_j==-1
8   // We have:  x = np - nm
9   {
10      ulong xh = x >> 1;   // x/2
11      ulong x3 = x + xh;   // 3*x/2
12      ulong c = xh ^ x3;
13      np = x3 & c;
14      nm = xh & c;
15  }
```

Converting back to binary is trivial:

```
1   static inline ulong naf2bin(ulong np, ulong nm)  { return ( np - nm ); }
```

The representation is one example of a *nonadjacent form* (NAF). A method for the computation of certain nonadjacent forms (w-NAF) is given in [255]. A Gray code for the signed binary words is described in section 14.7 on page 315.

If a binary word contains no consecutive ones, then the negative part of the NAF representation is zero. The sequence of values is $[0, 1, 2, 4, 5, 8, 9, 10, 16, \ldots]$, entry A003714 in [312], see figure 1.23-B. The numbers are called the *Fibbinary numbers*.

1.24 Generating bit combinations

1.24.1 Co-lexicographic (colex) order

Given a binary word with k bits set the following routine computes the binary word that is the next combination of k bits in co-lexicographic order. In the co-lexicographic order the reversed sets are sorted, see figure 1.24-A. The method to determine the successor is to determine the lowest block of ones and move its highest bit one position up. Then the rest of the block is moved to the low end of the word [FXT: bits/bitcombcolex.h]:

```
1   static inline ulong next_colex_comb(ulong x)
2   {
3       ulong r = x & -x;        // lowest set bit
4       x += r;                  // replace lowest block by a one left to it
5
6       if ( 0==x )  return 0;   // input was last combination
7
8       ulong z = x & -x;        // first zero beyond lowest block
9       z -= r;                  // lowest block  (cf. lowest_block())
10
11      while ( 0==(z&1) )  { z >>= 1; }  // move block to low end of word
12      return  x | (z>>1);      // need one bit less of low block
13  }
```

One could replace the while-loop by a bit scan and shift combination. The combinations $\binom{32}{20}$ are generated at a rate of about 142 million per second. The rate is about 120 M/s for the combinations $\binom{32}{12}$, the rate with $\binom{60}{7}$ is 70 M/s, and with $\binom{60}{53}$ it is 160 M/s.

```
            word   =      set      =  set (reversed)
    1:      ...111 =  { 0, 1, 2 }  =  { 2, 1, 0 }
    2:      ..1.11 =  { 0, 1, 3 }  =  { 3, 1, 0 }
    3:      ..11.1 =  { 0, 2, 3 }  =  { 3, 2, 0 }
    4:      ..111. =  { 1, 2, 3 }  =  { 3, 2, 1 }
    5:      .1..11 =  { 0, 1, 4 }  =  { 4, 1, 0 }
    6:      .1.1.1 =  { 0, 2, 4 }  =  { 4, 2, 0 }
    7:      .1.11. =  { 1, 2, 4 }  =  { 4, 2, 1 }
    8:      .11..1 =  { 0, 3, 4 }  =  { 4, 3, 0 }
    9:      .11.1. =  { 1, 3, 4 }  =  { 4, 3, 1 }
   10:      .111.. =  { 2, 3, 4 }  =  { 4, 3, 2 }
   11:      1...11 =  { 0, 1, 5 }  =  { 5, 1, 0 }
   12:      1..1.1 =  { 0, 2, 5 }  =  { 5, 2, 0 }
   13:      1..11. =  { 1, 2, 5 }  =  { 5, 2, 1 }
   14:      1.1..1 =  { 0, 3, 5 }  =  { 5, 3, 0 }
   15:      1.1.1. =  { 1, 3, 5 }  =  { 5, 3, 1 }
   16:      1.11.. =  { 2, 3, 5 }  =  { 5, 3, 2 }
   17:      11...1 =  { 0, 4, 5 }  =  { 5, 4, 0 }
   18:      11..1. =  { 1, 4, 5 }  =  { 5, 4, 1 }
   19:      11.1.. =  { 2, 4, 5 }  =  { 5, 4, 2 }
   20:      111... =  { 3, 4, 5 }  =  { 5, 4, 3 }
```

Figure 1.24-A: Combinations $\binom{6}{3}$ in co-lexicographic order. The reversed sets are sorted.

A variant of the method which involves a division appears in [39, item 175]. The routine given here is due to Doug Moore and Glenn Rhoads.

The following routine computes the predecessor of a combination:

```
1    static inline ulong prev_colex_comb(ulong x)
2    // Inverse of next_colex_comb()
3    {
4        x = next_colex_comb( ~x );
5        if ( 0!=x )  x = ~x;
6        return  x;
7    }
```

The first and last combination can be computed via

```
1    static inline ulong first_comb(ulong k)
2    // Return the first combination of (i.e. smallest word with) k bits,
3    // i.e.   00..001111..1 (k low bits set)
4    // Must have:   0 <= k <= BITS_PER_LONG
5    {
6        ulong t = ~0UL >> ( BITS_PER_LONG - k );
7        if ( k==0 )  t = 0;  // shift with BITS_PER_LONG is undefined
8        return t;
9    }
```

and

```
1    static inline ulong last_comb(ulong k, ulong n=BITS_PER_LONG)
2    // return the last combination of (biggest n-bit word with) k bits
3    // i.e.   1111..100..00 (k high bits set)
4    // Must have:   0 <= k <= n <= BITS_PER_LONG
5    {
6        return  first_comb(k) << (n - k);
7    }
```

The if-statement in `first_comb()` is needed because a shift by more than BITS_PER_LONG-1 is undefined by the C-standard, see section 1.1.5 on page 4.

The listing in figure 1.24-A can be created with the program [FXT: bits/bitcombcolex-demo.cc]:

```
1        ulong n = 6,  k = 3;
2        ulong last = last_comb(k, n);
3        ulong g = first_comb(k);
4        ulong gg = 0;
5        do
6        {
7            // visit combination given as word g
8            gg = g;
```

```
9           g = next_colex_comb(g);
10      }
11      while ( gg!=last );
```

1.24.2 Lexicographic (lex) order

```
            lex (5, 3)                    colex (5, 2)
          word  =    set                word  =    set
     1:  ..111  = { 0, 1, 2 }          ...11  = { 0, 1 }
     2:  .1.11  = { 0, 1, 3 }          ..1.1  = { 0, 2 }
     3:  1..11  = { 0, 1, 4 }          ..11.  = { 1, 2 }
     4:  .11.1  = { 0, 2, 3 }          .1..1  = { 0, 3 }
     5:  1.1.1  = { 0, 2, 4 }          .1.1.  = { 1, 3 }
     6:  11..1  = { 0, 3, 4 }          .11..  = { 2, 3 }
     7:  .111.  = { 1, 2, 3 }          1...1  = { 0, 4 }
     8:  1.11.  = { 1, 2, 4 }          1..1.  = { 1, 4 }
     9:  11.1.  = { 1, 3, 4 }          1.1..  = { 2, 4 }
    10:  111..  = { 2, 3, 4 }          11...  = { 3, 4 }
```

Figure 1.24-B: Combinations $\binom{5}{3}$ in lexicographic order (left). The sets are sorted. The binary words with lex order are the bit-reversed complements of the words with colex order (right).

The binary words corresponding to combinations $\binom{n}{k}$ in lexicographic order are the bit-reversed complements of the words for the combinations $\binom{n}{n-k}$ in co-lexicographic order, see figure 1.24-B. A more precise term for the order is subset-lex (for sets written with elements in increasing order). The sequence is identical to the delta-set-colex order backwards.

The program [FXT: bits/bitcomblex-demo.cc] shows how to compute the subset-lex sequence efficiently:

```
1     ulong n = 5,  k = 3;
2     ulong x = first_comb(n-k);      // first colex (n-k choose n)
3     const ulong m = first_comb(n);  // aux mask
4     const ulong l = last_comb(k, n); // last colex
5     ulong ct = 0;
6     ulong y;
7     do
8     {
9         y = revbin(~x, n) & m;  // lex order
10        // visit combination given as word y
11        x = next_colex_comb(x);
12    }
13    while ( y != l );
```

The bit-reversal routine `revbin()` is shown in section 1.14 on page 33. Sections 6.2.1 on page 177 and section 6.2.2 give iterative algorithms for combinations (represented by arrays) in lex and colex order, respectively.

1.24.3 Shifts-order

```
 1:  1....      1:  11...      1:  111..      1:  1111.
 2:  .1...      2:  .11..      2:  .111.      2:  .1111
 3:  ..1..      3:  ..11.      3:  ..111      3:  111.1
 4:  ...1.      4:  ...11      4:  11..1      4:  11.11
 5:  ....1      5:  1.1..      5:  .11.1      5:  1.111
                6:  .1.1.      6:  11..1
                7:  ..1.1      7:  1.11.
                8:  1..1.      8:  .1.11
                9:  .1..1      9:  1.1.1
               10:  1...1     10:  1..11
```

Figure 1.24-C: Combinations $\binom{5}{k}$, for $k = 1, 2, 3, 4$ in shifts-order.

Figure 1.24-C shows combinations in *shifts-order*. The order for combinations $\binom{n}{k}$ is obtained from the shifts-order for subsets (section 8.4 on page 208) by discarding all subsets whose number of elements are $\neq k$ and reversing the list order. The first combination is $[1^k 0^{n-k}]$ and the successor is computed as follows (see figure 1.24-D):

```
 1:  1111...              18:  .11..11
 2:  .1111..              19:  11..1.1   < S
 3:  ..1111.              20:  11...11   < S-2
 4:  ...1111              21:  1.111..   < S-2
 5:  111.1..   < S        22:  .1.111.
 6:  .111.1.              23:  ..1.111
 7:  ..111.1              24:  1.11.1.   < S
 8:  111..1.   < S        25:  .1.11.1
 9:  .111..1              26:  1.11..1   < S
10:  111...1   < S        27:  1.1.11.   < S-2
11:  11.11..   < S-2      28:  .1.1.11
12:  .11.11.              29:  1.1.1.1   < S
13:  ..11.11              30:  1.1..11   < S-2
14:  11.1.1.   < S        31:  1..111.   < S-2
15:  .11.1.1              32:  .1..111
16:  11.1..1   < S        33:  1..11.1   < S
17:  11..11.   < S-2      34:  1..1.11   < S-2
18:  .11..11              35:  1...111   < S-2
```

Figure 1.24-D: Updates with combinations $\binom{7}{4}$: simple split 'S', split second 'S-2', easy case unmarked.

1. Easy case: if the rightmost one is not in position zero (least significant bit), then shift the word to the right and return the combination.

2. Finished?: if the combination is the last one ($[0^n]$, $[0^{n-1}1]$, $[10^{n-k}1^{k-1}]$), then return zero.

3. Shift back: shift the word to the left such that the leftmost one is in the leftmost position (this can be a no-op).

4. Simple split: if the rightmost one is not the least significant bit, then move it one position to the right and return the combination.

5. Split second block: move the rightmost bit of the second block (from the right) of ones one position to the right and attach the lowest block of ones and return the combination.

An implementation is given in [FXT: bits/bitcombshifts.h]:

```
 1   class bit_comb_shifts
 2   {
 3   public:
 4       ulong x_;   // the combination
 5       ulong s_;   // how far shifted to the right
 6       ulong n_, k_;  // combinations (n choose k)
 7       ulong last_;   // last combination
 8
 9   public:
10       bit_comb_shifts(ulong n, ulong k)
11       {
12           n_ = n;  k_ = k;
13           first();
14       }
15
16       ulong first(ulong n, ulong k)
17       {
18           s_ = 0;
19           x_ =  last_comb(k, n);
20
21           if ( k>1 )  last_ = first_comb(k-1) | (1UL<<(n_-1));  // [10000111]
22           else        last_ = k;  // [000001] or [000000]
23
24           return x_;
25       }
26
27       ulong first()  { return first(n_, k_); }
28
29       ulong next()
30       {
31           if ( 0==(x_&1) )  // easy case:
32           {
33               ++s_;
34               x_ >>= 1;
35               return  x_;
36           }
37           else  // splitting cases:
```

```
38          {
39                  if ( x_ == last_ )  return 0;  // combination was last
40
41                  x_ <<= s_;  s_ = 0;  // shift back to the left
42                  ulong b = x_ & -x_;  // lowest bit
43
44
45                  if ( b!=1UL )  // simple split
46                  {
47                      x_ -= (b>>1);  // move rightmost bit to the right
48                      return x_;
49                  }
50                  else  // split second block and attach first
51                  {
52                      ulong t = low_ones(x_);  //  block of ones at lower end
53                      x_ ^= t;  // remove block
54                      ulong b2 = x_ & -x_;  // (second) lowest bit
55
56                      b2 >>= 1;
57                      x_ -= b2;  // move bit to the right
58
59                      // attach block:
60                      do  { t<<=1; }  while ( 0==(t&x_) );
61                      x_ |= (t>>1);
62                      return x_;
63                  }
64          }
65      }
66  };
```

The combinations $\binom{32}{20}$ are generated at a rate of about 150 M/s, for the combinations $\binom{32}{12}$ the rate is about 220 M/s [FXT: bits/bitcombshifts-demo.cc]. The rate with the combinations $\binom{60}{7}$ is 415 M/s and with $\binom{60}{53}$ it is 110 M/s. The generation is very fast for the sparse case.

1.24.4   Minimal-change order ‡

The following routine is due to Doug Moore [FXT: bits/bitcombminchange.h]:

```
1   static inline ulong igc_next_minchange_comb(ulong x)
2   // Return the inverse Gray code of the next combination in minimal-change order.
3   // Input must be the inverse Gray code of the current combination.
4   {
5       ulong g = rev_gray_code(x);
6       ulong i = 2;
7       ulong cb; // ==candidate bits;
8       do
9       {
10          ulong y = (x & ~(i-1)) + i;
11          ulong j = lowest_one(y) << 1;
12          ulong h = !!(y & j);
13          cb = ((j-h) ^ g) & (j-i);
14          i = j;
15      }
16      while ( 0==cb );
17
18      return  x + lowest_one(cb);
19  }
```

It can be used as suggested by the routine

```
1   static inline ulong next_minchange_comb(ulong x, ulong last)
2   // Not efficient, just to explain the usage of igc_next_minchange_comb()
3   // Must have: last==igc_last_comb(k, n)
4   {
5       x = inverse_gray_code(x);
6       if ( x==last )  return 0;
7       x = igc_next_minchange_comb(x);
8       return  gray_code(x);
9   }
```

The auxiliary function igc_last_comb() is (32-bit version only)

```
1   static inline ulong igc_last_comb(ulong k, ulong n)
2   // Return the (inverse Gray code of the) last combination
```

```
3    // as in igc_next_minchange_comb()
4    {
5        if ( 0==k )  return 0;
6
7        const ulong f = 0xaaaaaaaaUL >> (BITS_PER_LONG-k);  // == first_sequence(k);
8        const ulong c = ~0UL >> (BITS_PER_LONG-n);  // == first_comb(n);
9        return c ^ (f>>1);
10       // =^=  (by Doug Moore)
11   //      return  ((1UL<<n) - 1) ^ ((((1UL<<k) - 1) / 3);
12   }
```

Successive combinations differ in exactly two positions. For example, with $n = 5$ and $k = 3$:

```
   x          inverse_gray_code(x)
..111          ..1.1 == first_sequence(k)
.11.1          .1..1
.1111          .11.1
11..1          1...1
11.1.          1..11
111.1          1.111
1.1.1          11..1
1.111          11.11
1..11          111.1 == igc_last_comb(k, n)
```

The same run of bit combinations would be generated by going through the Gray codes and omitting all words where the bit-count is not equal to k. The algorithm shown here is much more efficient.

For greater efficiency one may prefer code which avoids the repeated computation of the inverse Gray code, for example:

```
1    ulong last = igc_last_comb(k, n);
2    ulong c, nc = first_sequence(k);
3    do
4    {
5        c = nc;
6        nc = igc_next_minchange_comb(c);
7        ulong g = gray_code(c);
8        // Here g contains the bit-combination
9    }
10   while ( c!=last );
```

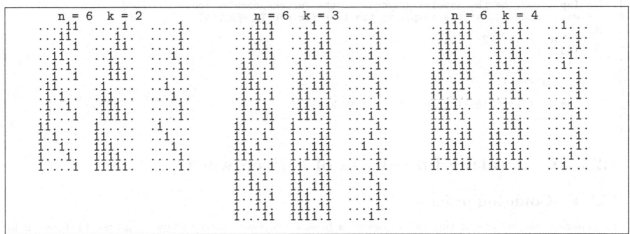

Figure 1.24-E: Minimal-change combinations, their inverse Gray codes, and the differences of the inverse Gray codes. The differences are powers of 2.

The difference of the inverse Gray codes of two successive combinations is always a power of 2, see figure 1.24-E (the listings were created with the program [FXT: bits/bitcombminchange-demo.cc]). With this observation we can derive a different version that checks the pattern of the change:

```
1    static inline ulong igc_next_minchange_comb(ulong x)
2    // Alternative version.
3    {
4        ulong gx = gray_code( x );
5        ulong i = 2;
6        do
7        {
```

```
8            ulong y = x + i;
9            i <<= 1;
10           ulong gy = gray_code( y );
11           ulong r = gx ^ gy;
12
13           // Check that change consists of exactly one bit
14           // of the new and one bit of the old pattern:
15           if ( is_pow_of_2( r & gy ) && is_pow_of_2( r & gx ) )  break;
16           // is_pow_of_2(x):=((x & -x) == x)  returns 1 also for x==0.
17           // But this cannot happen for both tests at the same time
18       }
19       while ( 1 );
20       return  y;
21   }
```

This version is the fastest: the combinations $\binom{32}{12}$ are generated at a rate of about 96 million per second, the combinations $\binom{32}{20}$ at a rate of about 83 million per second.

Here is another version which needs the number of set bits as a second parameter:

```
1    static inline ulong igc_next_minchange_comb(ulong x, ulong k)
2    // Alternative version, uses the fact that the difference
3    // of two successive x is the smallest possible power of 2.
4    {
5        ulong y, i = 2;
6        do
7        {
8            y = x + i;
9            i <<= 1;
10       }
11       while ( bit_count( gray_code(y) ) != k );
12       return  y;
13   }
```

The routine will be fast if the CPU has a bit-count instruction. The necessary modification for the generation of the previous combination is trivial:

```
1    static inline ulong igc_prev_minchange_comb(ulong x, ulong k)
2    // Returns the inverse graycode of the previous combination in minimal-change order.
3    // Input must be the inverse graycode of the current combination.
4    // With input==first the output is the last for n=BITS_PER_LONG
5    {
6        ulong y, i = 2;
7        do
8        {
9            y = x - i;
10           i <<= 1;
11       }
12       while ( bit_count( gray_code(y) ) != k );
13       return  y;
14   }
```

1.25 Generating bit subsets of a given word

1.25.1 Counting order

To generate all subsets of the set of ones of a binary word we use the sparse counting idea shown in section 1.8.1 on page 20. The implementation is [FXT: class bit_subset in bits/bitsubset.h]:

```
1    class bit_subset
2    {
3    public:
4        ulong u_;  // current subset
5        ulong v_;  // the full set
6
7    public:
8        bit_subset(ulong v) : u_(0), v_(v)  { ; }
9        ~bit_subset() { ; }
10       ulong current()  const  { return u_; }
11       ulong next()  { u_ = (u_ - v_) & v_;  return u_; }
12       ulong prev()  { u_ = (u_ - 1 ) & v_;  return u_; }
13
```

```
14      ulong first(ulong v)  { v_=v;  u_=0;  return u_; }
15      ulong first()  { first(v_);  return u_; }
16
17      ulong last(ulong v)  { v_=v;  u_=v;  return u_; }
18      ulong last()  { last(v_);  return u_; }
19  };
```

With the word [...11.1.] the following sequence of words is produced by subsequent `next()`-calls:

```
. . . . . . . .1.
. . . . . .1.:1.
. . . 1.:1.
. . .1.:1.
. . .11.:1.
. . . . . . .
```

A block of ones at the right will result in the binary counting sequence. About 1.1 billion subsets per second are generated with both `next()` and `prev()` [FXT: bits/bitsubset-demo.cc].

1.25.2 Minimal-change order

We use a method to isolate the changing bit from counting order that does not depend on shifting:

```
*******0111  =  u
*******1000  =  u+1
00000001111  =  (u+1) ^ u
00000001000  =  ((u+1) ^ u) & (u+1)   <--= bit to change
```

The method still works if the set bits are separated by any amount of zeros. In fact, we want to find the single bit that changed from 0 to 1. The bits that switched from 0 to 1 in the transition from the word A to B can also be isolated via X=B&~A. The implementation is [FXT: class `bit_subset_gray` in bits/bitsubset-gray.h]:

```
1   class bit_subset_gray
2   {
3   public:
4       bit_subset S_;
5       ulong g_;  // subsets in Gray code order
6       ulong h_;  // highest bit in S_.v_;  needed for the prev() method
7
8   public:
9       bit_subset_gray(ulong v) : S_(v), g_(0), h_(highest_one(v))  { ; }
10      ~bit_subset_gray()  { ; }
11
12      ulong current()  const { return g_; }
13      ulong next()
14      {
15          ulong u0 = S_.current();
16          if ( u0 == S_.v_ )  return first();
17          ulong u1 = S_.next();
18          ulong x = ~u0 & u1;
19          g_ ^= x;
20          return g_;
21      }
22
23      ulong first(ulong v)  { S_.first(v);  h_=highest_one(v);  g_=0;  return g_; }
24      ulong first()  { S_.first();  g_=0;  return g_; }
25      [--snip--]
```

With the word [...11.1.] the following sequence of words is produced by subsequent `next()`-calls:

```
. . . . . .1.
. . . . .1.:1.
. . . .11.:.
. . .11.:1.
. . .1.:1.
. . . . .
```

A block of ones at the right will result in the binary Gray code sequence, see [FXT: bits/bitsubset-gray-demo.cc]. The method `prev()` computes the previous word in the sequence, note the swapped roles of the variables u0 and u1:

```
1       [--snip--]
2       ulong prev()
3       {
```

```
4              ulong u1 = S_.current();
5              if ( u1 == 0 )  return last();
6              ulong u0 = S_.prev();
7              ulong x = ~u0 & u1;
8              g_ ^= x;
9              return g_;
10         }
11
12         ulong last(ulong v)  { S_.last(v);  h_=highest_one(v);  g_=h_;  return g_; }
13         ulong last()  { S_.last();  g_=h_;  return g_; }
14     };
```

About 365 million subsets per second are generated with both `next()` and `prev()`.

1.26 Binary words in lexicographic order for subsets

1.26.1 Next and previous word in lexicographic order

```
 1:   1...  =  8    {0}
 2:   11..  = 12    {0, 1}
 3:   111.  = 14    {0, 1, 2}
 4:   1111  = 15    {0, 1, 2, 3}
 5:   11.1  = 13    {0, 1, 3}
 6:   1.1.  = 10    {0, 2}
 7:   1.11  = 11    {0, 2, 3}
 8:   1..1  =  9    {0, 3}
 9:   .1..  =  4    {1}
10:   .11.  =  6    {1, 2}
11:   .111  =  7    {1, 2, 3}
12:   .1.1  =  5    {1, 3}
13:   ..1.  =  2    {2}
14:   ..11  =  3    {2, 3}
15:   ...1  =  1    {3}
```

Figure 1.26-A: Binary words corresponding to nonempty subsets of the 4-element set in lexicographic order with respect to subsets. Note the first element of the subsets corresponds to the highest set bit.

```
[0:  .....   =  0 *]    16: .1...1 = 17      32: 1....1 = 33      48: 11..11 = 51
 1:  .....1  =  1 *     17: .1..11 = 19      33: 1...11 = 35      49: 11..1. = 50
 2:  ....11  =  3       18: .1..1. = 18 *    34: 1...1. = 34 *    50: 11.1.1 = 53
 3:  ....1.  =  2       19: .1.1.1 = 21      35: 1..1.1 = 37      51: 11.111 = 55
 4:  ...1.1  =  5       20: .1.111 = 23      36: 1..111 = 39      52: 11.11. = 54
 5:  ...111  =  7       21: .1.11. = 22      37: 1..11. = 38      53: 11.1.. = 52
 6:  ...11.  =  6 *     22: .1.1.. = 20      38: 1..1.. = 36      54: 111..1 = 57
 7:  ...1..  =  4       23: .11..1 = 25      39: 1.1..1 = 41      55: 111.11 = 59
 8:  ..1..1  =  9       24: .11.11 = 27      40: 1.1.11 = 43      56: 111.1. = 58
 9:  ..1.11  = 11       25: .11.1. = 26      41: 1.1.1. = 42      57: 1111.1 = 61
10:  ..1.1.  = 10 *     26: .111.1 = 29      42: 1.11.1 = 45      58: 111111 = 63
11:  ..11.1  = 13       27: .11111 = 31      43: 1.1111 = 47      59: 11111. = 62
12:  ..1111  = 15       28: .1111. = 30      44: 1.111. = 46      60: 1111.. = 60 *
13:  ..111.  = 14       29: .111.. = 28      45: 1.11.. = 44      61: 111... = 56
14:  ..11..  = 12       30: .11... = 24      46: 1.1... = 40      62: 11.... = 48
15:  ..1...  =  8       31: .1.... = 16      47: 11...1 = 49      63: 1..... = 32
```

Figure 1.26-B: Binary words corresponding to the subsets of the 6-element set, as generated by `prev_lexrev()`. Fixed points are marked with asterisk.

The (bit-reversed) binary words in lexicographic order with respect to the subsets shown in figure 1.26-A can be generated by successive calls to the following function [FXT: bits/bitlex.h]:

```
1    static inline ulong next_lexrev(ulong x)
2    // Return next word in subset-lex order.
3    {
4        ulong x0 = x & -x;  // lowest bit
5        if ( 1!=x0 )  // easy case: set bit right of lowest bit
6        {
7            x0 >>= 1;
8            x ^= x0;
9            return  x;
```

```
10        }
11        else  // lowest bit at word end
12        {
13            x ^= x0;  // clear lowest bit
14            x0 = x & -x;  // new lowest bit ...
15            x0 >>= 1;  x -= x0;  // ... is moved one to the right
16            return  x;
17        }
18    }
```

The bit-reversed representation was chosen because the isolation of the lowest bit is often cheaper than the same operation on the highest bit. Starting with a one-bit word at position $n - 1$, we generate the 2^n subsets of the word of n ones. The function is used as follows [FXT: bits/bitlex-demo.cc]:

```
ulong n = 4;  // n-bit binary words
ulong x = 1UL<<(n-1);  // first subset
do
{
    // visit word x
}
while ( (x=next_lexrev(x)) );
```

The following function goes backward:

```
1     static inline ulong prev_lexrev(ulong x)
2     // Return previous word in subset-lex order.
3     {
4         ulong x0 = x & -x;  // lowest bit
5         if ( x & (x0<<1) )  // easy case: next higher bit is set
6         {
7             x ^= x0;  // clear lowest bit
8             return x;
9         }
10        else
11        {
12            x += x0;  // move lowest bit to the left
13            x |= 1;  // set rightmost bit
14            return x;
15        }
16    }
```

The sequence of all n-bit words is generated by 2^n calls to `prev_lexrev()`, starting with zero. The words corresponding to subsets of the 6-element set are shown in figure 1.26-B. The sequence $[1, 3, 2, 5, 7, 6, 4, 9, \dots]$ in the right column is entry A108918 in [312].

The rate of generation using `next()` is about 274 million per second and about 253 million per second with `prev()`. An equivalent routine for arrays is given in section 8.1.2 on page 203. The routines are useful for a special version of fast Walsh transforms described in section 23.5.3 on page 472.

1.26.2 Conversion between binary and lex-ordered words

A little contemplation on the structure of the binary words in lexicographic order leads to the routine that allows random access to the k-th lex-rev word (unrank algorithm) [FXT: bits/bitlex.h]:

```
1     static inline ulong negidx2lexrev(ulong k)
2     {
3         ulong z = 0;
4         ulong h = highest_one(k);
5         while ( k )
6         {
7             while ( 0==(h&k) )  h >>= 1;
8             z ^= h;
9             ++k;
10            k &= h - 1;
11        }
12        return  z;
13    }
```

Let the inverse function be $T(x)$, then we have $T(0) = 0$ and, with $h(x)$ being the highest power of 2 not greater than x,

$$T(x) \;=\; h(x) - 1 + \begin{cases} T\left(x - h(x)\right) & \text{if } x - h(x) \neq 0 \\ h(x) & \text{otherwise} \end{cases} \tag{1.26-1}$$

The ranking algorithm starts with the lowest bit:

```
1   static inline ulong lexrev2negidx(ulong x)
2   {
3       if ( 0==x )  return 0;
4       ulong h = x & -x;  // lowest bit
5       ulong r = (h-1);
6       while ( x^=h )
7       {
8           r += (h-1);
9           h = x & -x;  // next higher bit
10      }
11      r += h;  // highest bit
12      return  r;
13  }
```

1.26.3   Minimal decompositions into terms $2^k - 1$ ‡

```
      ....1 1       ....1 =  1    =  1
      ...11 2       ....1. =  2    =  1 + 1
      ...1. 1       ...11 =  3    =  3
      ..1.1 2       ...1. =  4    =  3 + 1
      ..111 3       ..1.1 =  5    =  3 + 1 + 1
      ..11. 2       ..11. =  6    =  3 + 3
      ..1.. 1       ..111 =  7    =  7
      .1..1 2       .1... =  8    =  7 + 1
      .1.11 3       .1..1 =  9    =  7 + 1 + 1
      .1.1. 2       .1.1. = 10    =  7 + 3
      .11.1 3       .1.11 = 11    =  7 + 3 + 1
      .1111 4       .11.. = 12    =  7 + 3 + 1 + 1
      .111. 3       .11.1 = 13    =  7 + 3 + 3
      .11.. 2       .111. = 14    =  7 + 7
      .1... 1       .1111 = 15    = 15
      1...1 2       1.... = 16    = 15 + 1
      1..11 3       1...1 = 17    = 15 + 1 + 1
      1..1. 2       1..1. = 18    = 15 + 3
      1.1.1 3       1..11 = 19    = 15 + 3 + 1
      1.111 4       1.1.. = 20    = 15 + 3 + 1 + 1
      1.11. 3       1.1.1 = 21    = 15 + 3 + 3
      1.1.. 2       1.11. = 22    = 15 + 7
      11..1 3       1.111 = 23    = 15 + 7 + 1
      11.11 4       11... = 24    = 15 + 7 + 1 + 1
      11.1. 3       11..1 = 25    = 15 + 7 + 3
      111.1 4       11.1. = 26    = 15 + 7 + 3 + 1
      11111 5       11.11 = 27    = 15 + 7 + 3 + 1 + 1
      1111. 4       111.. = 28    = 15 + 7 + 3 + 3
      111.. 3       111.1 = 29    = 15 + 7 + 7
      11... 2       1111. = 30    = 15 + 15
      1.... 1       11111 = 31    = 31
```

Figure 1.26-C: Binary words in subset-lex order and their bit counts (left columns). The least number of terms of the form $2^k - 1$ needed in the sum $x = \sum_k \left(2^k - 1\right)$ (right columns) equals the bit count.

The least number of terms needed in the sum $x = \sum_k \left(2^k - 1\right)$ equals the number of bits of the lex-word as shown in figure 1.26-C. The number can be computed as

```
c = bit_count( negidx2lexrev( x ) );
```

Alternatively, we can subtract the greatest integer of the form $2^k - 1$ until x is zero and count the number of subtractions. The sequence of these numbers is entry A100661 in [312]:

1,2,1,2,3,2,1,2,3,2,3,4,3,2,1,2,3,2,3,4,3,2,3,4,3,4,5,4,3,2,1,2,3,2,3,...

The following function can be used to compute the sequence:

```
1   void S(ulong f, ulong n)  // A100661
2   {
3       static int s = 0;
4       ++s;
5       cout << s << ",";
6       for (ulong m=1; m<n; m<<=1)  S(f+m, m);
7       --s;
8       cout << s << ",";
9   }
```

If called with arguments $f = 0$ and $n = 2^k$, it prints the first $2^{k+1} - 1$ numbers of the sequence followed by a zero. A generating function of the sequence is given by

$$Z(x) \;:=\; \frac{-1 + 2\,(1 - x)\,\prod_{n=1}^{\infty}\left(1 + x^{2^n - 1}\right)}{(1 - x)^2} \;= \tag{1.26-2}$$

$$1 + 2x + x^2 + 2x^3 + 3x^4 + 2x^5 + x^6 + 2x^7 + 3x^8 + 2x^9 + 3x^{10} + 4x^{11} + 3x^{12} + 2x^{13} \quad + \ldots$$

1.26.4 The sequence of fixed points ‡

```
    0:   ..........;            514:   .1.......1.
    1:   .........1             540:   .1....111..
    6:   ........11.            556:   .1...1.11..
   10:   .......1.1.           [--snip--]
   18:   ......1..1.           1556:   .11....1.1..
   34:   .....1...1.           1572:   .11...1.1..
   60:   .....1111..           1604:   .11..1...1..
   66:   ....1....1.           1668:   .11.1....1..
   92:   ....1.111..           1796:   .111.....1..
  108:   ....11.11..           2040:   .11111111..
  116:   ....111.1..           2050:   1.........1.
  130:   ...1....1.            2076:   1.......111.
  156:   ...1..111.            2092:   1.....1.11.
  172:   ...1.1.11..           2100:   1.....11.1..
  180:   ...1.11.1..           2124:   1....1..11..
  204:   ...11..11..           2132:   1....1.1.1..
  212:   ...11.1.1..           2148:   1....11..1..
  228:   ...111..1..          [--snip--]
  258:   ..1.......1.          4644:   1..1...1..1..
  284:   ..1....111.           4676:   1..1..1....1..
  300:   ..1...1.11.           4740:   1..1.1.1...1..
  308:   ..1...11.1.           4868:   1..11.....1..
  332:   ..1..1..1.1.          5112:   1.1111111...
  340:   ..1..1.1.1.           5132:   1.1.......11.
  356:   ..1..11...1.          5140:   1.1......1.1.
  396:   ..11...11..           5156:   1.1.....1..1.
  404:   ..11..1.1..           5188:   1.1....1....1.
  420:   ..11.1...1..          5252:   1.1..1..1.....1.
  452:   ..111...1..           5380:   1.1.1.....1..
```

Figure 1.26-D: Fixed points of the binary to lex-rev conversion.

The sequence of fixed points of the conversion to and from indices starts as

0, 1, 6, 10, 18, 34, 60, 66, 92, 108, 116, 130, 156, 172, 180, 204, 212,
228, 258, 284, 300, 308, 332, 340, 356, 396, 404, 420, 452, 514, 540, 556, ...

This sequence is entry A079471 in [312]. The values as bit patterns are shown in figure 1.26-D. The crucial observation is that a word is a fixed point if it equals zero or its bit-count equals 2^j where j is the index of the lowest set bit.

Now we can find out whether x is a fixed point of the sequence by the following function:

```
1    static inline bool is_lexrev_fixed_point(ulong x)
2    // Return whether x is a fixed point in the prev_lexrev() - sequence
3    {
4        if ( x & 1 )
5        {
6            if ( 1==x )  return  true;
7            else         return  false;
8        }
9        else
10       {
11           ulong w = bit_count(x);
12           if ( w != (w & -w) ) return  false;
13           if ( 0==x )  return  true;
14           return  0 != ( (x & -x) & w );
15       }
16   }
```

Alternatively, use either of the following tests:

```
    x == negidx2lexrev(x)
    x == lexrev2negidx(x)
```

1.26.5   Recursive generation and relation to a power series ‡

```
Start: 1
Rules:
   0 --> 0
   1 --> 110
-------------
0:    (#=2)
   1
1:    (#=4)
   110
2:    (#=8)
   1101100
3:    (#=16)
   110110011011000
4:    (#=32)
   11011001101100011011001101100000
5:    (#=64)
   1101100110110001101100110110000110110011011000110110011011100000
```

Figure 1.26-E: String substitution with rules $\{0 \to 0, 1 \mapsto 110\}$.

The following function generates the bit-reversed binary words in reversed lexicographic order:

```
1    void C(ulong f, ulong n, ulong w)
2    {
3        for (ulong m=1; m<n; m<<=1)  C(f+m, m, w^m);
4        print_bin(" ", w, 10);  // visit
5    }
```

By calling `C(0, 64, 0)` we generate the list of words shown in figure 1.26-B with the all-zeros word moved to the last position. A slight modification of the function

```
1    void A(ulong f, ulong n)
2    {
3        cout << "1,";
4        for (ulong m=1; m<n; m<<=1)  A(f+m, m);
5        cout << "0,";
6    }
```

generates the power series (sequence A079559 in [312])

$$\prod_{n=1}^{\infty} \left(1 + x^{2^n-1}\right) \;=\; 1 + x + x^3 + x^4 + x^7 + x^8 + x^{10} + x^{11} + x^{15} + x^{16} + \dots \qquad (1.26\text{-}3)$$

By calling `A(0, 32)` we generate the sequence

   1,1,0,1,1,0,0,1,1,0,1,1,0,0,0,1,1,0,1,1,0,0,1,1,0,1,1,0,0,0,0, ...

Indeed, the lowest bit of the k-th word of the bit-reversed sequence in reversed lexicographic order equals the $(k-1)$-st coefficient in the power series. The sequence can also be generated by the string substitution shown in figure 1.26-E.

The sequence of sums, prepended by 1,

$$1 + x \, \frac{\prod_{n=1}^{\infty} \left(1 + x^{2^n-1}\right)}{1-x} \;=\; 1 + 1\,x + 2\,x^2 + 2\,x^3 + 3\,x^4 + 4\,x^5 + 4\,x^6 + \dots \qquad (1.26\text{-}4)$$

has series coefficients

   1, 1, 2, 2, 3, 4, 4, 4, 5, 6, 6, 7, 8, 8, 8, 8, 9, 10, 10, 11, 12, 12, 12, 13, ...

This sequence is entry A046699 in [312]. We have $a(1) = a(2) = 1$ and the sequence satisfies the peculiar recurrence

$$a(n) \;=\; a(n - a(n-1)) + a(n - 1 - a(n-2)) \qquad \text{for} \quad n > 2 \qquad (1.26\text{-}5)$$

1.27   Fibonacci words ‡

A Fibonacci word is a word that does not contain two successive ones. Whether a given binary word is a Fibonacci word can be tested with the function [FXT: bits/fibrep.h]

```
1    static inline bool is_fibrep(ulong f)
2    {
3        return  ( 0==(f&(f>>1)) );
4    }
```

The following functions convert between the binary and the Fibonacci representation:

```
1    static inline ulong bin2fibrep(ulong b)
2    // Return Fibonacci representation of b
3    // Limitation: the first Fibonacci number greater
4    //   than b must be representable as ulong.
5    // 32 bit:  b < 2971215073=F(47)  [F(48)=4807526976 > 2^32]
6    // 64 bit:  b < 12200160415121876738=F(93)  [F(94) > 2^64]
7    {
8        ulong f0=1, f1=1, s=1;
9        while ( f1<=b )  { ulong t = f0+f1;  f0=f1;  f1=t;  s<<=1; }
10       ulong f = 0;
11       while ( b )
12       {
13           s >>= 1;
14           if ( b>=f0 )  { b -= f0;  f^=s; }
15           { ulong t = f1-f0;  f1=f0;  f0=t; }
16       }
17       return f;
18   }
```

```
1    static inline ulong fibrep2bin(ulong f)
2    // Return binary representation of f
3    // Inverse of bin2fibrep().
4    {
5        ulong f0=1, f1=1;
6        ulong b = 0;
7        while ( f )
8        {
9            if ( f&1 )   b += f1;
10           { ulong t=f0+f1;  f0=f1;  f1=t; }
11           f >>= 1;
12       }
13       return b;
14   }
```

1.27.1 Lexicographic order

```
 0: ........    11: ...1.1..    22: .1.....1    33: .1.1.1.1    44: 1..1..1.
 1: .......1    12: ...1.1.1    23: .1....1.    34: 1.......    45: 1..1.1..
 2: ......1.    13: ..1....1    24: .1....1.    35: 1......1    46: 1..1.1.1
 3: .....1..    14: ..1....1    25: .1....1.1   36: 1.....1.    47: 1.1.....
 4: .....1.1    15: ..1...1.    26: .1...1..    37: 1.....1..   48: 1.1....1
 5: ....1...    16: ..1..1.1    27: .1...1.1    38: 1....1.1    49: 1.1...1.
 6: ....1..1    17: ..1..1.1    28: .1..1.1.    39: 1....1..1   50: 1.1..1..
 7: ....1.1.    18: ..1.1...    29: .1..1...    40: 1...1..1    51: 1.1..1.1
 8: ...1....    19: ..1.1..1    30: .1.1...1    41: 1...1.1.    52: 1.1.1...
 9: ...1...1    20: ..1.1.1.    31: .1.1..1.    42: 1..1....    53: 1.1.1..1
10: ...1..1.    21: .1......    32: .1.1.1..    43: 1..1...1    54: 1.1.1.1.
```

Figure 1.27-A: All 55 Fibonacci words with 8 bits in lexicographic order.

The 8-bit Fibonacci words are shown in figure 1.27-A. To generate all Fibonacci words in lexicographic order, use the function [FXT: bits/fibrep.h]

```
1    static inline ulong next_fibrep(ulong x)
2    // With x the Fibonacci representation of n
3    // return Fibonacci representation of n+1.
4    {
5        // 2 examples:          // ex. 1          // ex.2
6        //                      // x == [*]0 010101  // x == [*]0 01010
7        ulong y = x | (x>>1);   // y == [*]? 011111  // y == [*]? 01111
8        ulong z = y + 1;        // z == [*]? 100000  // z == [*]? 10000
9        z = z & -z;             // z == [0]0 100000  // z == [0]0 10000
10       x ^= z;                 // x == [*]0 110101  // x == [*]0 11010
11       x &= ~(z-1);            // x == [*]0 100000  // x == [*]0 10000
12
13       return x;
14   }
```

The routine can be used to generate all *n*-bit words as shown in [FXT: bits/fibrep2-demo.cc]:

```
const ulong f = 1UL << n;
ulong t = 0;
do
{
    // visit(t)
    t = next_fibrep(t);
}
while ( t!=f );
```

The reversed order can be generated via

```
ulong f = 1UL << n;
do
{
    f = prev_fibrep(f);
    // visit(f)
}
while ( f );
```

which uses the function (64-bit version)

```
1    static inline ulong prev_fibrep(ulong x)
2    // With x the Fibonacci representation of n
3    // return Fibonacci representation of n-1.
4    {
5        // 2 examples:        //  ex. 1              //  ex.2
6        //                    // x == [*]0 100000    // x == [*]0 10000
7        ulong y = x & -x;     // y == [0]0 100000    // y == [0]0 10000
8        x ^= y;               // x == [*]0 000000    // x == [*]0 00000
9        ulong m = 0x5555555555555555UL;   // m == ...01010101
10       if ( m & y )  m >>= 1; // m == ...01010101   // m == ...0101010
11       m &= (y-1);           // m == [0]0 010101    // m == [0]0 01010
12       x ^= m;               // x == [*]0 010101    // x == [*]0 01010
13       return x;
14   }
```

The forward version generates about 180 million words per second, the backward version about 170 million words per second.

1.27.2   Gray code order ‡

A Gray code for the binary Fibonacci words (shown in figure 1.27-B) can be derived from the Gray code of the radix −2 representations (see section 1.22 on page 58) of binary words whose difference is of the form

```
  1     ...................1
  3     ..................;i1
  5     .................;1.1
  8     ...............;1.;1
 19     .............;1.;i1
 37     ...........;1.;1.1
 73     .........;1.;1.;1
147     .......;1.;1.;i1
293     .....;1.;1.;1.1
```

The algorithm is to try these values as increments starting from the least, same as for the minimal-change combination described in section 1.24.4 on page 66. The next valid word is encountered if it is a valid Fibonacci word, that is, if it does not contain two consecutive set bits. The implementation is [FXT: class bit_fibgray in bits/bitfibgray.h]:

```
1    class bit_fibgray
2    // Fibonacci Gray code with binary words.
3    {
4    public:
5        ulong x_;  // current Fibonacci word
6        ulong k_;  // aux
7        ulong fw_, lw_;  // first and last Fibonacci word in Gray code
8        ulong mw_;  // max(fw_, lw_)
9        ulong n_;   // Number of bits
10
11   public:
12       bit_fibgray(ulong n)
13       {
14           n_ = n;
15           fw_ = 0;
```

```
  j:        k(j)        k(j)-k(j-1)   x=bin2neg(k)      gray(x)
  1:    ....11...1    .........1    ...111...1    ...1..1..1  =  27
  2:    ....11....    .........1    ...111...     ...1..1...  =  26
  3:    ....1.1111    ........1     ...111..11    ...1..1.1.  =  28
  4:    ....1.11..    .......11     ..11111.      ...1...1.   =  23
  5:    ....1.1.11    .........1    ..1111111     ...1....1   =  21
  6:    ....1.1.1.    .........1    ..111111.     ...1....1   =  22
  7:    ....1.1..1    .........1    ..1111..1     ...1...1.1  =  25
  8:    ....1.1...    .........1    ..1111        ...1...1.   =  24
  9:    ....1...11    ......1.1     ..11..111     ...1.1.1..  =  32
 10:    ....1...1.    .........1    ..11..11.     ...1.1.1.1  =  33
 11:    ....1....1    .........1    ..11...1      ...1.1..1   =  30
 12:    ....1         .........1    ..11          ...1.1..    =  29
 13:    .....11111    .........1    ..11..11      ...1.1.1.   =  31
 14:    ......11..    ....1..11     .....111      ......1..1. =  10
 15:    .....1.11     .........1    .....11111    .......1..1 =   8
 16:    .....1.1.     .........1    .....1111.    .......1..1 =   9
 17:    .....1..1     .........1    .....11..1    ......1..1.1=  12
 18:    .....1        .........1    .....11       ......1..1. =  11
 19:    ......11      ....1..1      .....111      .......1.1. =   3
 20:    ......1.      .........1    .....11.      .......1.1.1=   4
 21:    ......1       .........1    .....1        .......1.1  =   1
 22:                  .........1    .....         .......1    =   0
 23:    1111111111    .........1    .......11     .......1..  =   2
 24:    111111111.    ....1..11     .......11.    ......1.1.  =   7
 25:    11111111.11   .........1    .......1111   ......1...  =   5
 26:    1111111.1.    .........1    .......111.   ......1...1 =   6
 27:    111111...1    ....1..1.1    ..11...1      ...1.1..1   =  19
 28:    111111.       .........1    ..11...        ...1.1..    =  18
 29:    11111.1111    .........1    ..11..11      ...1.1.1.   =  20
 30:    11111.11..    ........11    ..1111.       ...1...1.   =  15
 31:    11111.1.11    .........1    ..111111      ...1...1    =  13
 32:    11111.1.1.    .........1    ..11111.      ...1...1    =  14
 33:    11111.1..1    .........1    ..111..1      ...1..1.1   =  17
 34:    11111.1...    ........1     ..111...      ...1..1..   =  16
```

Figure 1.27-B: Gray code for the binary Fibonacci words (rightmost column).

```
16         for (ulong m=(1UL<<(n-1)); m!=0; m>>=3)  fw_ |= m;
17         lw_ = fw_ >> 1;
18         if ( 0==(n&1) )  { ulong t=fw_; fw_=lw_; lw_=t; }  // swap first/last
19         mw_ = ( lw_>fw_ ? lw_ : fw_ );
20         x_ = fw_;
21         k_ = inverse_gray_code(fw_);
22         k_ = neg2bin(k_);
23     }
24
25     ~bit_fibgray()  {;}
26
27     ulong next()
28     // Return next word in Gray code.
29     // Return ~0 if current word is the last one.
30     {
31         if ( x_ == lw_ )  return ~0UL;
32         ulong s = n_;  // shift
33         while ( 1 )
34         {
35             --s;
36             ulong c = 1 | (mw_ >> s);  // possible difference for negbin word
37             ulong i = k_ - c;
38             ulong x = bin2neg(i);
39             x ^= (x>>1);
40
41             if ( 0==(x&(x>>1)) )  // is_fibrep(x)
42             {
43                 k_ = i;
44                 x_ = x;
45                 return x;
46             }
47         }
48     }
49 };
```

About 130 million words per second are generated. The program [FXT: bits/bitfibgray-demo.cc] shows how to use the class, figure 1.27-B was created with it. Section 14.2 on page 305 gives a recursive algorithm for Fibonacci words in Gray code order.

1.28 Binary words and parentheses strings ‡

```
  0    .... P  [empty string]       .....   [empty string]
  1    ...1 P  ()                    ....1   ()
  2    ..1.                          ...11   (())
  3    ..11 P  (())                  ..1.1   ()()
  4    .1..                          ..111   ((()))
  5    .1.1 P  ()()                  .1.11   (()())
  6    .11.                          .11.1   ()(())
  7    .111 P  ((()))                .1111   ((()))
  8    1...                          1..11   (())()
  9    1..1                          1.1.1   ()()()
 10    1.1.                          1.111   ((()()))
 11    1.11 P  (()())                11.11   (()(()))
 12    11..                          111.1   ()((()))
 13    11.1 P  ()(())                11111   (((())))
 14    111.
 15    1111 P  (((())))
```

Figure 1.28-A: Left: some of the 4-bit binary words can be interpreted as a string parentheses (marked with 'P'). Right: all 5-bit words that correspond to well-formed parentheses strings.

A subset of the binary words can be interpreted as a (well formed) string of parentheses. The 4-bit binary words that have this property are marked with a 'P' in figure 1.28-A (left) [FXT: bits/parenword-demo.cc]. The strings are constructed by scanning the word from the low end and printing a '(' with each one and a ')' with each zero. To find out when to terminate, one adds up +1 for each opening parenthesis and −1 for a closing parenthesis. After the ones in the binary word have been scanned, the s closing parentheses have to be added where s is the value of the sum [FXT: bits/parenwords.h]:

```
1    static inline void parenword2str(ulong x, char *str)
2    {
3        int s = 0;
4        ulong j = 0;
5        for (j=0; x!=0; ++j)
6        {
7            s += ( x&1 ? +1 : -1 );
8            str[j] = ")("[x&1];
9            x >>= 1;
10       }
11       while ( s-- > 0 )  str[j++] = ')';  // finish string
12       str[j] = 0;  // terminate string
13   }
```

The 5-bit binary words that are valid 'paren words' together with the corresponding strings are shown in figure 1.28-A (right). Note that the lower bits in the word (right end) correspond to the beginning of the string (left end). If a negative value for the sums occurs at any time of the computation, the word is not a paren word. A function to determine whether a word is a paren word is

```
1    static inline bool is_parenword(ulong x)
2    {
3        int s = 0;
4        for (ulong j=0; x!=0; ++j)
5        {
6            s += ( x&1 ? +1 : -1 );
7            if ( s<0 )  break;  // invalid word
8            x >>= 1;
9        }
10       return  (s>=0);
11   }
```

The sequence

   1, 3, 5, 7, 11, 13, 15, 19, 21, 23, 27, 29, 31, 39, 43, 45, 47, 51, 53, 55, 59, 61, 63, ...

of nonzero integers x so that is_parenword(x) returns true is entry A036991 in [312]. If we fix the number of paren pairs, then the following functions generate the least and biggest valid paren words. The first paren word is a block of n ones at the low end:

```
1    static inline ulong first_parenword(ulong n)
2    // Return least binary word corresponding to n pairs of parens
3    // Example, n=5:  .....11111   ((((()))))
```

```
4    {
5        return first_comb(n);
6    }
```

The last paren word is the word with a sequence of n blocks '01' at the low end:

```
1    static inline ulong last_parenword(ulong n)
2    // Return biggest binary word corresponding to n pairs of parens.
3    // Must have: 1 <= n <= BITS_PER_LONG/2.
4    // Example, n=5:  .1.1.1.1.1    ()()()()()
5    {
6        return  0x5555555555555555UL >> (BITS_PER_LONG-2*n);
7    }
```

```
......11111 = (((((())))))   ...1...1111 = (((())))()   ..1....1111 = (((()))))()
.....1.1111 = ((((()))))    ...1..1.111 = ((()())())   ..1...1.111 = (((()))()()
.....11.111 = (((()())))    ...1..11.11 = ((()())())   ..1...11.11 = (()(())())
.....111.11 = (()((())))    ...1..111.1 = ()((()))()   ..1...111.1 = ()(()))()
.....1111.1 = ()((((()))    ...1.1..111 = ((())()())   ..1..1..111 = (())())()()
....1..1111 = (((())))()    ...1.1.1.11 = ()()()()()   ..1..1.1.11 = (())()()()
....1.1.111 = ((()()))()    ...1.1.11.1 = ()()(())()   ..1..1.11.1 = (()(())()()
....1.11.11 = (()()())()    ...1.11..11 = ()(()()())   ..1..11..11 = (()()()())
....1.111.1 = ()(()()()    ...1.11.1.1 = ()(())()()   ..1..11.1.1 = (()()()()()
....11..111 = (((()()())   ...11...111 = ((())())()   ..1.1...111 = ((())()())
....11.1.11 = ()()((()))   ...11..1.11 = ()()()()()   ..1.1..1.11 = (())()()()
....11.11.1 = ()(()(())   ...11.11.1 = ()(())()()   ..1.1.1.11.1 = ()(())()()
....111..11 = (()((())))   ...11.1..11 = ()()()()()   ..1.1.1..11 = (()()()()()
....111.1.1 = ()()((()))   ...11.1.1.1 = ()()()(())   ..1.1.1.1.1 = ()()()()()
```

Figure 1.28-B: The 42 binary words corresponding to all valid pairings of 5 parentheses, in colex order.

The sequence of all binary words corresponding to n pairs of parens in colex order can be generated with the following (slightly cryptic) function:

```
1    static inline ulong next_parenword(ulong x)
2    // Next (colex order) binary word that is a paren word.
3    {
4        if ( x & 2 )  // Easy case, move highest bit of lowest block to the left:
5        {
6            ulong b = lowest_zero(x);
7            x ^= b;
8            x ^= (b>>1);
9            return x;
10       }
11       else // Gather all low "01"s and split lowest nontrivial block:
12       {
13           if ( 0==(x & (x>>1)) )  return 0;
14           ulong w = 0;  // word where the bits are assembled
15           ulong s = 0;  // shift for lowest block
16           ulong i = 1;  // == lowest_one(x)
17           do  // collect low "01"s:
18           {
19               x ^= i;
20               w <<= 1;
21               w |= 1;
22               ++s;
23               i <<= 2;  // == lowest_one(x);
24           }
25           while ( 0==(x&(i<<1)) );
26
27           ulong z = x ^ (x+i);  // lowest block
28           x ^= z;
29           z &= (z>>1);
30           z &= (z>>1);
31           w ^= (z>>s);
32           x |= w;
33           return x;
34       }
35   }
```

The program [FXT: bits/parenword-colex-demo.cc] shows how to create a list of binary words corresponding to n pairs of parens (code slightly shortened):

```
1        ulong n = 4;  // Number of paren pairs
```

```
 2        ulong pn = 2*n+1;
 3        char *str = new char[n+1];  str[n] = 0;
 4        ulong x = first_parenword(n);
 5        while ( x )
 6        {
 7            print_bin("  ", x, pn);
 8            parenword2str(x, str);
 9            cout << " = " << str << endl;
10
11            x = next_parenword(x);
12        }
```

Its output with $n = 5$ is shown in figure 1.28-B. The 1,767,263,190 paren words for $n = 19$ are generated at a rate of about 169 million words per second. Chapter 15 on page 323 gives a different formulation of the algorithm.

Knuth [215, ex.23, sect.7.1.3] gives a very elegant routine for generating the next paren word, the comments are MMIX instructions:

```
 1    static inline ulong next_parenword(ulong x)
 2    {
 3        const ulong m0 = -1UL/3;
 4        ulong t = x ^ m0;               // XOR t, x, m0;
 5        if ( (t&x)==0 ) return 0;       // current is last
 6        ulong u = (t-1) ^ t;            // SUBU u, t, 1;  XOR u, t, u;
 7        ulong v = x | u;                // OR v, x, u;
 8        ulong y = bit_count( u & m0 );  // SADD y, u, m0;
 9        ulong w = v + 1;                // ADDU w, v, 1;
10        t = v & ~w;                     // ANDN t, v, w;
11        y = t >> y;                     // SRU y, t, y;
12        y += w;                         // ADDU y, w, y;
13        return y;
14    }
```

The routine is slower, however, about 81 million words per second are generated. A bit-count instruction in hardware would speed it up significantly. Treating the case of easy update separately as in the other version, we get a rate of about 137 million words per second.

1.29 Permutations via primitives ‡

We give two methods to specify permutations of the bits of a binary word via one or more control words. The methods are suggestions for machine instructions that can serve as primitives for permutations of the bits of a word.

1.29.1 A restricted method

```
........,.......,iiiiii,11111111111111111
......,,.iiiiiiii........,.11111111
..,,,1111....1111....,1111...,1111
.,11..11..11..11..11..11..11..11
.1.1.1.1.1.1.1.1.1.1.1.1.1.1.1.1

........,.......,1...............,....    bits   15 ...
......,,....1.........,.......1........    bits    7 ...
..,,.1.......1.......1.......1.......1.    bits    3  11 ...
.,1..1..1..1..1..1..1..1..1..1..1..1.    bits    1   5   9  13 ...
.1.1.1.1.1.1.1.1.1.1.1.1.1.1.1.1    bits    0   2   4   6   8  10  12  14 ...
```

Figure 1.29-A: Mask with primitives for permuting bits with 32-bit words (top), and words with ones at the highest bit of each block (bottom).

We can specify a subset of all permutations by selecting bit-blocks of the masks as shown for 32-bit words in figure 1.29-A (top). Subsets of the blocks of the masks can be determined with the bits of a word by considering the highest bit of each block (bottom of the figure). We use all bits of a word (except for the highest bit) to select the blocks where the bits defined by the block and those left to it should be swapped. An implementation of the implied algorithm is given in [FXT: bits/bitperm1-demo.cc]. Arrays are used to give more readable code:

```
1    void perm1(uchar *a, ulong ldn, const uchar *x)
2    // Permute a[] according to the 'control word' x[].
3    // The length of a[] must be 2**ldn.
4    {
5        long n = 1L<<ldn;
6        for (long s=n/2; s>0; s/=2)
7        {
8            for (long k=0; k<n; k+=s+s)
9            {
10               if ( x[k+s-1]!='0' )
11               {
12                   // swap regions [a+k,...,a+k+s-1], [a+k+s,...,a+k+2*s-1]:
13                   swap(a+k, a+k+s, s);
14               }
15           }
16       }
17   }
```

The routine for the inverse permutation differs in a single line:

```
    for (long s=1; s<n; s+=s)
```

No attempt has been made to optimize or parallelize the algorithm. We just explore how useful a machine instruction for the permutation of bits would be.

The program uses a fixed size of 16 bits, an 'x' is printed whenever the corresponding bit is set:

```
a=0123456789ABCDEF    bits of the input word
x=0010011000110110    control word
      8:      7    11x
      4:    3   5x  9      13x
      2:  1     5x  9      13x
      1: 0    2x  4    6x  8   10x 12   14x
a=01326754CDFEAB98    result
```

This control word leads to the Gray permutation (see 2.12 on page 128). Assume we use words with N bits. We cannot (for $N > 2$) specify all $N!$ permutations as we can choose between only 2^{N-1} control words. Now set the word length to $N := 2^n$. The reachable permutations are those where the intervals $[k \cdot 2^j, \ldots, (k+1) \cdot 2^j - 1]$ contain all numbers $[p \cdot 2^j, \ldots, (p+1) \cdot 2^j - 1]$ for all $j \leq n$ and $0 \leq k < 2^{n-j}$, choosing p for each interval arbitrarily ($0 \leq p < 2^{n-j}$). For example, the lower half of the permuted array must contain a permutation of either the lower or the upper half ($j = n - 1$) and each pair a_{2y}, a_{2y+1} must contain two elements $2z, 2z + 1$ ($j = 1$). The bit-reversal is computed with a control word where all bits are set. Alas, the (important!) zip permutation (bit-zip, see section 1.15 on page 38) is unreachable.

A machine instruction could choose between the two routines via the highest bit in the control word.

1.29.2 A general method

All permutations of $N = 2^n$ elements can be specified with n control words of N bits. Assume we have a machine instruction that collects bits according to a control word. An eight bit example:

```
a = abcdefgh    input data
x = ..1.11.1    control word (dots for zeros)
      cefh      bits of a where x has a one
    abdg        bits of a where x has a zero
    abdgcefh    result, bits separated according to x
```

We need n such instructions that work on all length-2^k sub-words for $1 \leq k \leq n$. For example, the instruction working on half words of a 16-bit word would work as

```
a = abcdefgh ABCDEFGH    input data
x = ..1.11.1 1111....    control word (dots for zeros)
      cefh   ABCD        bits of a where x has a one
    abdg     EFGH        bits of a where x has a zero
    abdgcefh EFGHABCD    result, bits separated according to x
```

Note the bits of the different sub-words are not mixed. Now all permutations can be reached if the control word for the 2^k-bit sub-words have exactly 2^{k-1} bits set in all ranges $[j \cdot 2^k, \ldots, (j+1) \cdot 2^k]$.

A control word together with the specification of the instruction used defines the action taken. The following leads to a swap of adjacent bit pairs

```
    1.1.1.1.1.1.1.1.1.1.1.1.1.1.1.1.    k= 1  (2-bit sub-words)
```

while this

```
    1.1.1.1.1.1.1.1.1.1.1.1.1.1.1.1.    k= 5 (32 bit sub-words)
```

results in gathering the even and odd indexed bits in the halfwords.

A complete set of permutation primitives for 16-bit words and their effect on a symbolic array of bits (split into groups of four elements for readability) is

```
                                0123 4567 89ab cdef
    11111111........    k= 4  ==> 89ab cdef 0123 4567
    1111....1111....    k= 3  ==> cdef 89ab 4567 0123
    11..11..11..11..    k= 2  ==> efcd ab89 6745 2301
    1.1.1.1.1.1.1.1.    k= 1  ==> fedc ba98 7654 3210
```

The top primitive leads to a swap of the left and right half of the bits, the next to a swap of the halves of the half words and so on. The computed permutation is array reversal. Note that we use array notation (least index left) here.

The resulting permutation depends on the order in which the primitives are used. When starting with full words we get:

```
                                      0123 4567 89ab cdef
    1.1. 1.1. 1.1. 1.1.  k= 4  ==>    1357 9bdf 0246 8ace
    1.1. 1.1. 1.1. 1.1.  k= 3  ==>    37bf 159d 26ae 048c
    1.1. 1.1. 1.1. 1.1.  k= 2  ==>    7f3b 5d19 6e2a 4c08
    1.1. 1.1. 1.1. 1.1.  k= 1  ==>    f7b3 d591 e6a2 c480
```

The result is different when starting with 2-bit sub-words:

```
                                      0123 4567 89ab cdef
    1.1. 1.1. 1.1. 1.1.  k= 1  ==>    1032 5476 98ba dcfe
    1.1. 1.1. 1.1. 1.1.  k= 2  ==>    0213 4657 8a9b cedf
    1.1. 1.1. 1.1. 1.1.  k= 3  ==>    2367 0145 abef 89cd
    1.1. 1.1. 1.1. 1.1.  k= 4  ==>    3715 bf9d 2604 ae8c
```

There are $\binom{2z}{z}$ possibilities to have z bits set in a $2z$-bit word. There are 2^{n-k} length-2^k sub-words in a 2^n-bit word so the number of valid control words for that step is

$$\left[\binom{2^k}{2^{k-1}} \right]^{2^{n-k}}$$

The product of the number of valid words in all steps gives the number of permutations:

$$(2^n)! \;=\; \prod_{k=1}^{n} \left[\binom{2^k}{2^{k-1}} \right]^{2^{n-k}} \tag{1.29-1}$$

1.30 CPU instructions often missed

1.30.1 Essential

- Bit-shift and bit-rotate instructions that work properly for shifts greater than or equal to the word length: the shift instruction should zero the word, the rotate instruction should take the shift modulo word length. The C-language standards leave the results for these operations undefined and compilers simply emit the corresponding assembler instructions. The resulting CPU dependent behavior is both a source of errors and makes certain optimizations impossible.

- A bit-reverse instruction. A fast byte-swap mitigates the problem, see section 1.14 on page 33.

- Instructions that return the index of highest or lowest set bit in a word. They must execute fast.

- Fast conversion from integer to float and double (both directions).

- A fused multiply-add instruction for floats.

- Instructions for the multiplication of complex floating-point numbers, computing $A \cdot C - B \cdot D$ and $A \cdot D + B \cdot C$ from A, B, C, and D.

- A sum-diff instruction, computing $A + B$ and $A - B$ from A and B. This can serve as a primitive for fast orthogonal transforms.

- An instruction to swap registers. Even better, a conditional version of that.

1.30.2 Nice to have

- A parity bit for the complete machine word. The parity of a word is the number of bits modulo 2, not the complement of it. Even better, an instruction for the inverse Gray code, see section 1.16 on page 41.

- A bit-count instruction, see section 1.8 on page 18. This would also give the parity at bit zero.

- An instruction for computing the index of the i-th set bit of a word, see section 1.10 on page 25. This would be useful even if execution takes a dozen cycles.

- A random number generator, LHCAs (see section 41.8 on page 878) may be candidates. At the very least: a decent entropy source.

- A conditional version of more than just the move instruction, possibly as an instruction prefix.

- A bit-zip and a bit-unzip instruction, see section 1.15 on page 38. Note this is polynomial squaring over $GF(2)$.

- Primitives for permutations of bits, see section 1.29.2 on page 81. A bit-gather and a bit-scatter instruction for sub-words of all sizes a power of 2 would allow for arbitrary permutations (see [FXT: bits/bitgather.h] and [FXT: bits/bitseparate.h] for versions working on complete words).

- Multiplication corresponding to XOR as addition. This is the multiplication without carries used for polynomials over $GF(2)$, see section 40.1 on page 822.

1.31 Some space filling curves ‡

1.31.1 The Hilbert curve

A rendering of the Hilbert curve (named after David Hilbert [182]) is shown in figure 1.31-A. An efficient algorithm to compute the direction of the n-th move of the Hilbert curve is based on the parity of the number of threes in the radix-4 representation of n (see section 38.9.1 on page 748).

Let d_x and d_y correspond to the moves at step n in the Hilbert curve. Then $d_x, d_y \in \{-1, 0, +1\}$ and exactly one of them is zero. So for both $p := d_x + d_y$ and $m := d_x - d_y$ we have $p, m \in \{-1, +1\}$.

The following function computes p and returns $0, 1$ if $p = -1, +1$, respectively [FXT: bits/hilbert.h]:

```
1    static inline ulong hilbert_p(ulong t)
2    // Let dx,dy be the horizontal,vertical move
3    // with step t of the Hilbert curve.
4    // Return  zero if (dx+dy)==-1, else one (then: (dx+dy)==+1).
5    // Algorithm: count number of threes in radix 4
6    {
7        ulong d = (t & 0x5555555555555555UL) & ((t & 0xaaaaaaaaaaaaaaaaUL) >> 1);
8        return  parity( d );
9    }
```

If 1 is returned the step is to the right or upwards. The function can be slightly optimized as follows (64-bit version only):

```
1    static inline ulong hilbert_p(ulong t)
2    {
3        t &= ((t & 0xaaaaaaaaaaaaaaaaUL) >> 1);
```

Figure 1.31-A: The first 255 segments of the Hilbert curve.

```
dx+dy:  ++-+++-+++----++++-+++-+++---+++++-+++-+++----+---+---+---++++-
dx-dy:  +----+++-+++-+++-++++----+---+----++++---+---+----++++---+---+--
   dir: >^<^^>v>^>vv<v>>^<^>^<<v<^^^>v>>^<^>^<<v<^<<v>vv<^<v<^^>^<
  turn: 0--+0++--++0+--0-++-0--++--0-++00++-0--++--0-++-0--+0++--++0+--
```

Figure 1.31-B: Moves and turns of the Hilbert curve.

```
4       t ^= t>>2;
5       t ^= t>>4;
6       t ^= t>>8;
7       t ^= t>>16;
8       t ^= t>>32;
9       return  t & 1;
10   }
```

The corresponding value for m can be computed as:

```
1    static inline ulong hilbert_m(ulong t)
2    // Let dx,dy be the horizontal,vertical move
3    // with step t of the Hilbert curve.
4    // Return  zero if (dx-dy)==-1, else one (then: (dx-dy)==+1).
5    {
6        return  hilbert_p( -t );
7    }
```

If the values for p and m are equal the step is in horizontal direction. It remains to merge the values of p and m into a 2-bit value d that encodes the direction of the move:

```
1    static inline ulong hilbert_dir(ulong t)
2    // Return d encoding the following move with the Hilbert curve.
3    //
4    // d \in {0,1,2,3} as follows:
5    //    d : direction
6    //    0 : right (+x:  dx=+1, dy= 0)
7    //    1 : down  (-y:  dx= 0, dy=-1)
8    //    2 : up    (+y:  dx= 0, dy=+1)
9    //    3 : left  (-x:  dx=-1, dy= 0)
10   {
```

```
11        ulong p = hilbert_p(t);
12        ulong m = hilbert_m(t);
13        ulong d = p ^ (m<<1);
14        return  d;
15    }
```

To print the value of d symbolically, we can print the value of `(">v^<")[d]`. The sequence of moves can also be generated by the string substitution process shown in figure 1.31-C.

```
    Start:  A
    Rules:
      A --> D>A^A<C
      B --> C<BvB>D
      C --> BvC<C^A
      D --> A^D>DvB
      > --> >
      < --> <
      ^ --> ^
      v --> v
    --------------
 0:    (#=1)
     A
 1:    (#=7)
    D>A^A<C
 2:    (#=31)
    A^D>DvB>D>A^A<C^D>A^A<C<BvC<C^A
 3:    (#=127)
    D>A^A<C^A^D>DvB>A^D>DvBvC<BvB>D>A^D>DvB>D>A^A<C^D>A^A<C<BvC<C^A^A^D>DvB>D>A^A<C^D> ...
```

Figure 1.31-C: Moves of the Hilbert curve by a string substitution process, the symbols 'A', 'B', 'C', and 'D', are ignored when drawing the curve.

The turn u between steps can be computed as

```
1    static inline int hilbert_turn(ulong t)
2    // Return the turn (left or right) with the steps
3    //    t and t-1 of the Hilbert curve.
4    // Returned value is
5    //    0 for no turn
6    //   +1 for right turn
7    //   -1 for left turn
8    {
9        ulong d1 = hilbert_dir(t);
10       ulong d2 = hilbert_dir(t-1);
11       d1 ^= (d1>>1);
12       d2 ^= (d2>>1);
13       ulong u = d1 - d2;
14       // at this point, symbolically:  cout << ("+.-0+.-")[ u + 3 ];
15       if ( 0==u )  return 0;
16       if ( (long)u<0 )  u += 4;
17       return  (1==u ? +1 : -1);
18   }
```

To print the value of u symbolically, we can print `("-0+")[u+1];`.

The values of p and m, followed by the direction and turn of the Hilbert curve are shown in figure 1.31-B. The list was created with the program [FXT: bits/hilbert-moves-demo.cc]. Figure 1.31-A was created with the program [FXT: bits/hilbert-texpic-demo.cc]. The computation of a function whose series coefficients are ± 1 and $\pm i$ according to the Hilbert curve is described in section 38.9 on page 747.

A finite state machine (FSM) for the conversion from a 1-dimensional coordinate (linear coordinate of the curve) to the pair of coordinates x and y of the Hilbert curve is described in [39, item 115]. At each step two bits of input are processed. The array `htab[]` serves as lookup table for the next state and two bits of the result. The FSM has an internal state of two bits [FXT: bits/lin2hilbert.cc]:

```
1    void
2    lin2hilbert(ulong t, ulong &x, ulong &y)
3    // Transform linear coordinate t to Hilbert x and y
4    {
5        ulong xv = 0, yv = 0;
6        ulong c01 = (0<<2);  // (2<<2) for transposed output (swapped x, y)
7        for (ulong i=0; i<BITS_PER_LONG/2; ++i)
8        {
9            ulong abi = t >> (BITS_PER_LONG-2);
10           t <<= 2;
```

```
11
12              ulong st = htab[ (c01<<2) | abi ];
13              c01 = st & 3;
14
15              yv <<= 1;
16              yv |= ((st>>2) & 1);
17              xv <<= 1;
18              xv |= (st>>3);
19          }
20      x = xv;  y = yv;
21  }
```

OLD				NEW				NEW				OLD			
C_0	C_1	A_I	B_I	X_I	Y_I	C_0	C_1	C_0	C_1	X_I	Y_I	A_I	B_I	C_0	C_1
0	0	0	0	0	0	1	0	0	0	0	0	0	0	1	0
0	0	0	1	0	1	0	0	0	0	0	1	0	1	0	0
0	0	1	0	1	1	0	0	0	0	1	0	1	1	0	0
0	0	1	1	1	0	0	1	0	0	1	1	1	0	0	0
0	1	0	0	1	1	1	1	0	1	0	0	1	0	0	1
0	1	0	1	0	1	0	1	0	1	0	1	0	1	0	1
0	1	1	0	0	0	0	1	0	1	1	0	1	1	0	0
0	1	1	1	1	0	0	0	0	1	1	1	0	0	1	1
1	0	0	0	0	0	0	0	1	0	0	0	0	0	0	0
1	0	0	1	1	0	1	0	1	0	0	1	1	1	1	1
1	0	1	0	1	1	1	0	1	0	1	0	0	1	1	0
1	0	1	1	0	1	1	1	1	0	1	1	1	0	1	0
1	1	0	0	1	1	0	1	1	1	0	0	1	0	1	1
1	1	0	1	1	0	1	1	1	1	0	1	1	0	0	1
1	1	1	0	0	0	1	1	1	1	1	0	0	1	1	1
1	1	1	1	0	1	1	0	1	1	1	1	0	0	0	1

Figure 1.31-D: The original table from [39] for the finite state machine for the 2-dimensional Hilbert curve (left). All sixteen 4-bit words appear in both the 'OLD' and the 'NEW' column. So the algorithm is invertible. Swap the columns and sort numerically to obtain the two columns at the right, the table for the inverse function.

The table used is defined (see figure 1.31-D) as

```
1   static const ulong htab[] = {
2   #define HT(xi,yi,c0,c1) ((xi<<3)+(yi<<2)+(c0<<1)+(c1))
3       // index == HT(c0,c1,ai,bi)
4       HT( 0, 0,  1, 0 ),
5       HT( 0, 1,  0, 0 ),
6       HT( 1, 1,  0, 0 ),
7       HT( 1, 0,  0, 1 ),
8   [--snip--]
9       HT( 0, 0,  1, 1 ),
10      HT( 0, 1,  1, 0 )
11  };
```

As indicated in the code, the table maps every four bits c0,c1,ai,bi to four bits xi,yi,c0,c1. The table for the inverse function (again, see figure 1.31-D) is

```
1   static const ulong ihtab[] = {
2   #define IHT(ai,bi,c0,c1) ((ai<<3)+(bi<<2)+(c0<<1)+(c1))
3       // index == HT(c0,c1,xi,yi)
4       IHT( 0, 0,  1, 0 ),
5       IHT( 0, 1,  0, 0 ),
6       IHT( 1, 1,  0, 1 ),
7       IHT( 1, 0,  0, 0 ),
8       [--snip--]
9       IHT( 0, 1,  1, 1 ),
10      IHT( 0, 0,  0, 1 )
11  };
```

The words have to be processed backwards:

```
1   ulong
2   hilbert2lin(ulong x, ulong y)
3   // Transform Hilbert x and y to linear coordinate t
4   {
5       ulong t = 0;
6       ulong c01 = 0;
```

```
7        for (ulong i=0; i<(BITS_PER_LONG/2); ++i)
8        {
9            t <<= 2;
10           ulong xi = x >> (BITS_PER_LONG/2-1);
11           xi &= 1;
12           ulong yi = y >> (BITS_PER_LONG/2-1);
13           yi &= 1;
14           ulong xyi = (xi<<1) | yi;
15           x <<= 1;
16           y <<= 1;
17
18           ulong st = ihtab[ (c01<<2) | xyi ];
19           c01 = st & 3;
20
21           t |= (st>>2);
22       }
23
24       return t;
25   }
```

1.31.2   The Z-order

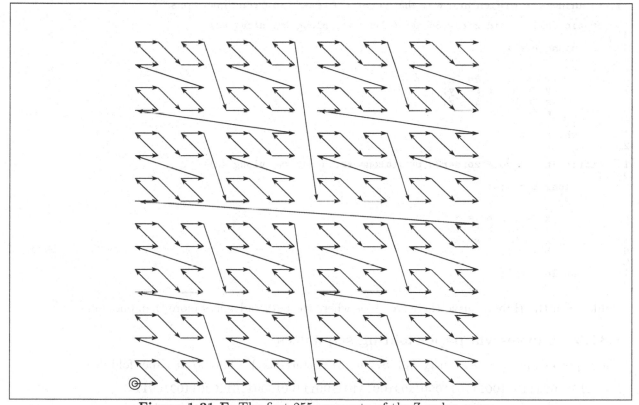

Figure 1.31-E: The first 255 segments of the Z-order curve.

A 2-dimensional space-filling curve in *Z-order* traverses all points in each quadrant before it enters the next. Figure 1.31-E shows a rendering of the Z-order curve, created with the program [FXT: bits/zorder-texpic-demo.cc]. The conversion between a linear parameter to a pair of coordinates is done by separating the bits at the even and odd indices [FXT: bits/zorder.h]:

```
static inline void lin2zorder(ulong t, ulong &x, ulong &y)  { bit_unzip2(t, x, y); }
```

The routine `bit_unzip2()` is described in section 1.15 on page 38. The inverse is

```
static inline ulong zorder2lin(ulong x, ulong y)  { return bit_zip2(x, y); }
```

The next pair can be computed with the following (constant amortized time) routine:

```
1    static inline void zorder_next(ulong &x, ulong &y)
2    {
```

```
 3        ulong b = 1;
 4        do
 5        {
 6            x ^= b;   b &= ~x;
 7            y ^= b;   b &= ~y;
 8            b <<= 1;
 9        }
10        while ( b );
11   }
```

The previous pair is computed similarly:

```
 1   static inline void zorder_prev(ulong &x, ulong &y)
 2   {
 3        ulong b = 1;
 4        do
 5        {
 6            x ^= b;   b &= x;
 7            y ^= b;   b &= y;
 8            b <<= 1;
 9        }
10        while ( b );
11   }
```

The routines are written in a way that generalizes easily to more dimensions:

```
 1   static inline void zorder3d_next(ulong &x, ulong &y, ulong &z)
 2   {
 3        ulong b = 1;
 4        do
 5        {
 6            x ^= b;   b &= ~x;
 7            y ^= b;   b &= ~y;
 8            z ^= b;   b &= ~z;
 9            b <<= 1;
10        }
11        while ( b );
12   }
```

```
 1   static inline void zorder3d_prev(ulong &x, ulong &y, ulong &z)
 2   {
 3        ulong b = 1;
 4        do
 5        {
 6            x ^= b;   b &= x;
 7            y ^= b;   b &= y;
 8            z ^= b;   b &= z;
 9            b <<= 1;
10        }
11        while ( b );
12   }
```

Unlike with the Hilbert curve there are steps where the curve advances more than one unit.

1.31.3   Curves via paper-folding sequences

The *paper-folding sequence*, entry A014577 in [312], starts as [FXT: bits/bit-paper-fold-demo.cc]:

    1101100111001001110110001100100111011001110010001101100011001001 ...

The k-th element $(k > 0)$ is one if $k = 2^t \cdot (4u + 1)$, entry A091072 in [312]:

    1, 2, 4, 5, 8, 9, 10, 13, 16, 17, 18, 20, 21, 25, 26, 29, 32, 33, ...

The k-th element of the paper-folding sequence can be computed by testing the value of the bit left to the lowest (that is, rightmost) one in the binary expansion of k [FXT: bits/bit-paper-fold.h]:

```
 1   static inline bool bit_paper_fold(ulong k)
 2   {
 3        ulong h = k & -k;   // == lowest_one(k)
 4        k &= (h<<1);
 5        return   ( k==0 );
 6   }
```

About 550 million values per second are generated. We use `bool` as return type to indicate that only zero or one is returned. The value can be used as an integer of arbitrary type, there is no need for a cast.

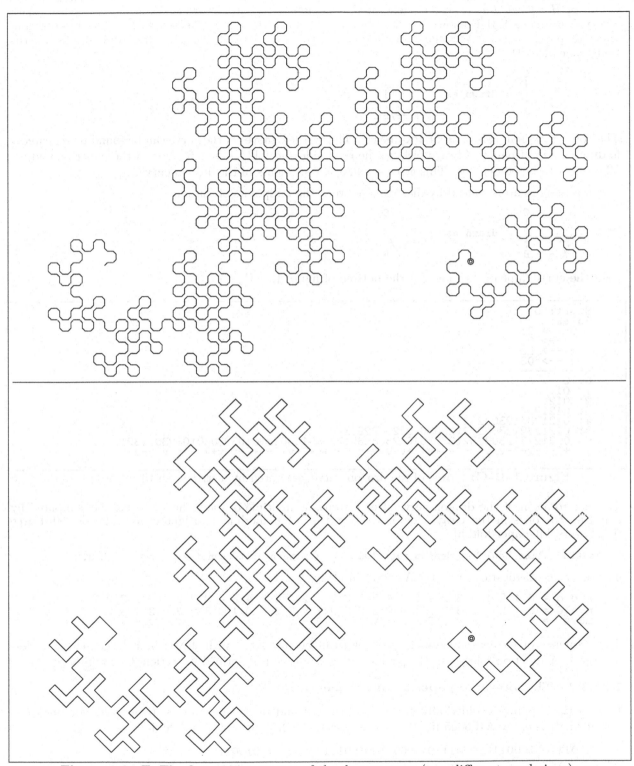

Figure 1.31-F: The first 1024 segments of the dragon curve (two different renderings).

1.31.3.1   The dragon curve

Another name for the sequence is *dragon curve sequence*, because a space filling curve known as dragon curve (or *Heighway dragon*) can be generated if we interpret a one as 'turn left' and a zero as 'turn right'. The top of figure 1.31-F shows the first 1024 segments of the curve (created with [FXT: bits/dragon-curve-texpic-demo.cc]). As some points are visited twice we draw the turns with cut off corners, for the (left) turn $A \to B \to C$:

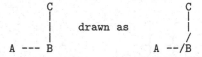

The code is given in [FXT: aux0/tex-line.cc]. The first few moves of the curve can be found by repeatedly folding a strip of paper. Always pick up the right side and fold to the left. Unfold the paper and adjust all corners to be 90 degrees. This gives the first few segments of the dragon curve.

When all angles are replaced by diagonals between the midpoints of the lines

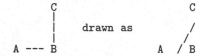

then the curve appears as shown at the bottom of figure 1.31-F.

```
Start: 0
Rules:
   0 --> 01
   1 --> 21
   2 --> 23
   3 --> 03
   --------------
0: 0
1: 01
2: 0121
3: 01212321
4: 0121232123032321
5: 0121232123032321230301032303232 321
6: 0121232123032321230301032303232123030103012101032303010323032321
   +^-^-v-^-v+v-v-^-v+v+^+v-v+v-v-^-v+v+^+v+^-^+^+v-v+v+^+v-v+v-v-^
```

Figure 1.31-G: Moves of the dragon curve generated by a string substitution process.

The net rotation of the dragon-curve after k steps, as multiple of the right angle, can be computed by counting the ones in the Gray code of k. Take the result modulo 4 to ignore multiples of 360 degree [FXT: bits/bit-paper-fold.h]:

```
1    static inline bool bit_dragon_rot(ulong k)  { return  bit_count( k ^ (k>>1) ) & 3; }
```

The sequence of rotations is entry A005811 in [312]:

```
s e q = 0 1 2 1 2 3 2 1 2 3 4 3 2 3 2 1 2 3 4 3 4 5 4 3 2 3 4 3 2 3 2 1 2 3 ...
m o d = 0 1 2 1 2 3 2 1 2 3 0 3 2 3 2 1 2 3 0 3 0 1 0 3 2 3 0 3 2 3 2 1 2 3 ...
move  = + ^ - ^ - v - ^ - v + v - v - ^ - v + v + ^ + v - v + v - v - ^ - v ...
```

The sequence of moves (as symbols, last row) can be computed with [FXT: bits/dragon-curve-moves-demo.cc]. A function related to the paper-folding sequence is described in section 38.8.3 on page 744.

1.31.3.2   The alternate paper-folding sequence

If the strip of paper is folded alternately from the left and right, then another paper-folding sequence is obtained. It is entry A106665 in [312] and it starts as [FXT: bits/bit-paper-fold-alt-demo.cc]:

```
1001110010001101100111011000110010011100100011001001110110001011 ...
```

Compute the sequence via [FXT: bits/bit-paper-fold.h]

```
1    static inline bool bit_paper_fold_alt(ulong k)
2    {
3        ulong h = k & -k;   // == lowest_one(k)
```

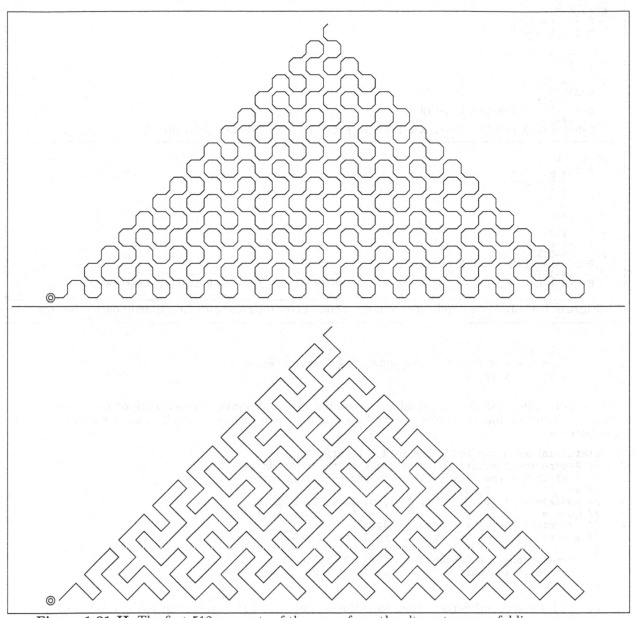

Figure 1.31-H: The first 512 segments of the curve from the alternate paper-folding sequence.

```
    Start: 0
    Rules:
        0 --> 01
        1 --> 03
        2 --> 23
        3 --> 21
        -------------
    0: 0
    1: 01
    2: 0103
    3: 01030121
    4: 0103012101032303
    5: 010301210103230301030121232101 21
    6: 0103012101032303010301212321012101030121010323032321230301032303
       +^+v+^-^+^+v-v+v+^+v+^-^-v-^+^-^+^+v+^-^+^+v-v+v-v-^-v+v+^+v-v+v
```

Figure 1.31-I: Moves of the alternate curve generated by a string substitution process.

```
Start: L
Rules:
   L --> L+R+L-R
   R --> L+R-L-R
   + --> +
   - --> -
-------------
0:     (#=1)
   L
1:     (#=7)
   L+R+L-R
2:     (#=31)
   L+R+L-R+L+R-L-R+L+R+L-R-L+R-L-R
3:     (#=127)
   L+R+L-R+L+R-L-R+L+R+L-R-L+R-L-R+L+R+L-R+L+R-L-R-L+R+L-R-L+R-L-R+L+ ...
```

```
Start: L
Rules:
   L --> R+L+R-L
   R --> R+L-R-L
   + --> +
   - --> -
-------------
0:     (#=1)
   L
1:     (#=7)
   R+L+R-L
2:     (#=31)
   R+L-R-L+R+L+R-L+R+L-R-L-R+L+R-L
3:     (#=127)
   R+L-R-L+R+L+R-L-R+L-R-L-R+L+R-L+R+L+R-L+R+L-R-L-R+L+R-L+R+L-R-L-R+ ...
```

Figure 1.31-J: Moves and turns of the dragon curve (top) and alternate dragon curve (bottom).

```
4        h <<= 1;
5        ulong t = h & (k ^ 0xaaaaaaaaUL);   // 32-bit version
6        return ( t!=0 );
7    }
```

About 413 million values per second are generated. By interpreting the sequence of zeros and ones as turns we again obtain triangular space-filling curves shown in figure 1.31-H. The orientations can be computed as

```
1    static inline ulong bit_paper_fold_alt_rot(ulong k)
2    // Return total rotation (as multiple of the right angle)
3    //    after k steps in the alternate paper-folding curve.
4    // k=        0, 1, 2, 3, 4, 5, ...
5    // seq(k)= 0, 1, 0, 3, 0, 1, 2, 1, 0, 1, 0, 3, 2, 3, 0, ...
6    // move =  +  ^  +  v  +  ^  -  ^  +  ^  +  v  -  v  +
7    // (+==right, -==left, ^==up, v==down).
8    // Algorithm: count the ones in  (w ^ gray_code(k)).
9    {
10       const ulong w = 0xaaaaaaaaUL;  // 32-bit version
11       return  bit_count( w ^ (k ^ (k>>1)) ) & 3;  // modulo 4
12   }
```

Figure 1.31-J shows a different string substitution process for the generation of the rotations (symbols '+' and '-') for the paper-folding sequences, both symbols 'L' and 'R' are interpreted as a unit move in the current direction.

If the constant in the routine is replaced by a parameter w, then its bits determine whether a left or a right fold was made at each step:

```
1    static inline bool bit_paper_fold_general(ulong k, ulong w)
2    {
3        ulong h = k & -k;   // == lowest_one(k)
4        h <<= 1;
5        ulong t = h & (k^w);
6        return ( t!=0 );
7    }
```

1.31.4   Terdragon and hexdragon

The *terdragon* curve turns to the left or right by 120 degrees depending to the sequence

$$0, 1, 0, 0, 1, 1, 0, 1, 0, 0, 1, 0, 0, 1, 1, 0, 1, 1, 0, 1, 0, 0, 1, 1, 0, 1, \dots$$

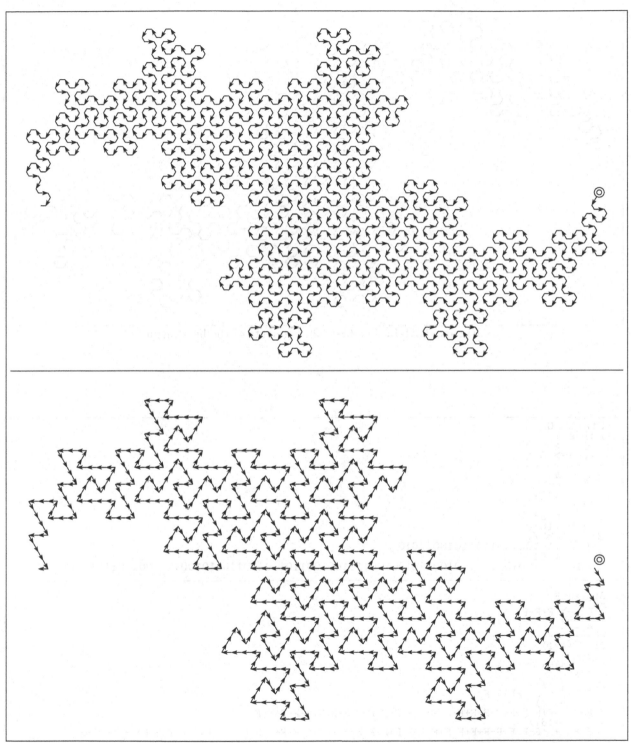

Figure 1.31-K: The first 729 segments of the terdragon (two different renderings).

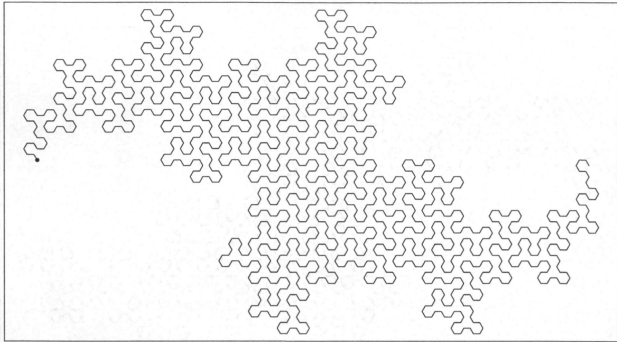

Figure 1.31-L: The first 729 segments of the hexdragon.

```
Start: 0
Rules:
   0 --> 010
   1 --> 011
-------------
0:   (#=1)
   0
1:   (#=3)
   010
2:   (#=9)
   010011010
3:   (#=27)
   010011010010011011010011010
4:   (#=81)
   010011010010011011010011010010011011010011011010011010010011011010011010010011011010011010
```
```
Start: F
Rules:
   F --> F+F-F
   + --> +
   - --> -
-------------
0:   (#=1)
   F
1:   (#=5)
   F+F-F
2:   (#=17)
   F+F-F+F+F-F-F+F-F
3:   (#=53)
   F+F-F+F+F-F-F+F-F+F+F-F+F+F-F-F+F-F-F+F-F+F+F-F-F+F-F
4:   (#=161)
   F+F-F+F+F-F-F+F-F+F+F-F+F+F-F-F+F-F-F+F-F+F+F-F-F+F-F+F+F-F+F+F-F-F+F-F+F+F-F+F+F-F-F+F-F-F+F-F+F+F-F-F+F-F-F+F-F+F+F-F-F+F-  ...
```

Figure 1.31-M: Turns of the terdragon curve, generated by string substitution (top), alternative process for the moves and turns (bottom, identify '+' with '0' and '-' with '1').

```
Start: F
Rules:
    F --> F+L+F-L-F
    + --> +
    - --> -
    L --> L
    ----------------
0:    (#=1)
    F
1:    (#=9)
    F+L+F-L-F
2:    (#=33)
    F+L+F-L-F+L+F+L+F-L-F-L-F+L+F-L-F
3:    (#=105)
    F+L+F-L-F+L+F+L+F-L-F-L-F+L+F-L-F+L+F+L+F-L-F-L-F+L+F-L-F-L-F+L+F-L-F+ ...
```

Figure 1.31-N: String substitution process for the hexdragon.

The sequence is entry A080846 in [312], it can be generated via the string substitution with rules $0 \mapsto 101$ and $1 \mapsto 011$, see figure 1.31-M. A fast method to compute the sequence is based on radix-3 counting: let $C_1(k)$ be the number of ones in the radix-3 expansion of k, the sequence is one if $C_1(k+1) < C_1(k)$ [FXT: bits/bit-dragon3.h]:

```
1    static inline bool bit_dragon3_turn(ulong &x)
2    // Increment the radix-3 word x and
3    // return whether the number of ones in x is decreased.
4    {
5        ulong s = 0;
6        while ( (x & 3) == 2 )  { x >>= 2;  ++s; }  // scan over nines
7    //     if ( (x & 3) == 0 )  ==> incremented word will have one more 1
8    //     if ( (x & 3) == 1 )  ==> incremented word will have one less 1
9        bool tr = ( (x & 3) != 0 );  // incremented word will have one less 1
10       ++x;  // increment next digit
11       x <<= (s<<1);  // shift back
12       return  tr;
13   }
```

About 220 million values per second are generated. Two renderings of the first 729 segments of the curve are shown in figure 1.31-K (created with [FXT: bits/dragon3-texpic-demo.cc]).

If we replace each turn by 120 degrees (followed by a line) by two turns by 60 degrees (each followed by a line) we obtain what may be called a *hexdragon*, shown in figure 1.31-L (created with [FXT: bits/dragon-hex-texpic-demo.cc]). A string substitution process for the hexdragon is shown in figure 1.31-N.

1.31.5   Dragon curves based on radix-R counting

Another dragon curve can be generated on radix-5 counting (we will call the curve *R5-dragon*) [FXT: bits/bit-dragon-r5.h]:

```
1    static inline bool bit_dragon_r5_turn(ulong &x)
2    // Increment the radix-5 word x and
3    // return (tr) whether the lowest nonzero digit
4    // of the incremented word is > 2.
5    {
6        ulong s = 0;
7        while ( (x & 7) == 4 )  { x >>= 3;  ++s; }  // scan over nines
8        bool tr = ( (x & 7) >= 2 );  // whether digit will be > 2
9        ++x;  // increment next digit
10       x <<= (3*s);  // shift back
11       return  tr;
12   }
```

About 310 million values per second are generated. The turns are by 90 degrees. Two renderings of the R5-dragon are shown in figure 1.31-O (created with [FXT: bits/dragon-r5-texpic-demo.cc]). The sequence of returned values (entry A175337 in [312]) can be computed via the string substitution shown in figure 1.31-R (top).

Based on radix-7 counting we can generate a curve that will be called the *R7-dragon*, the turns are be 120 degrees [FXT: bits/bit-dragon-r7.h]:

```
1    static inline bool bit_dragon_r7_turn(ulong &x)
2    // Increment the radix-7 word x and
```

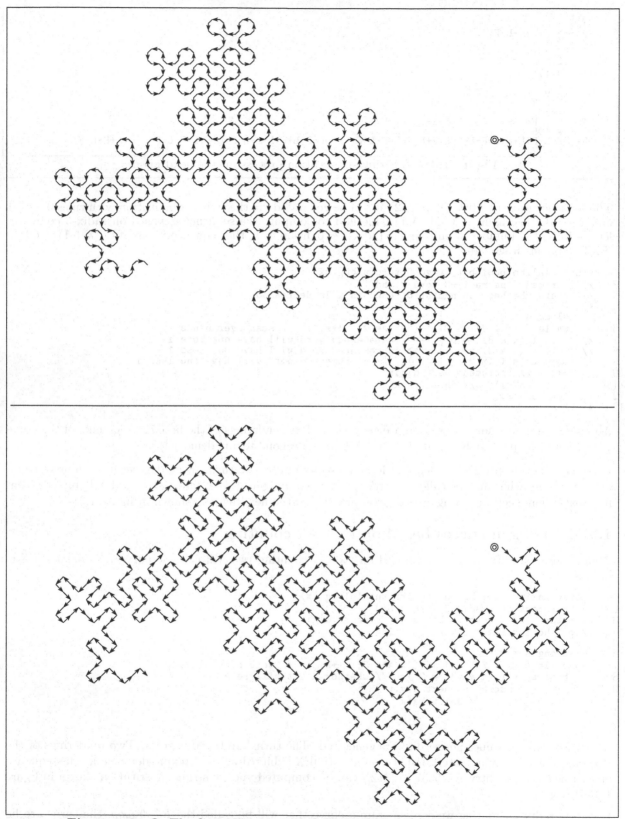

Figure 1.31-O: The first 625 segments of the R5-dragon (two different renderings).

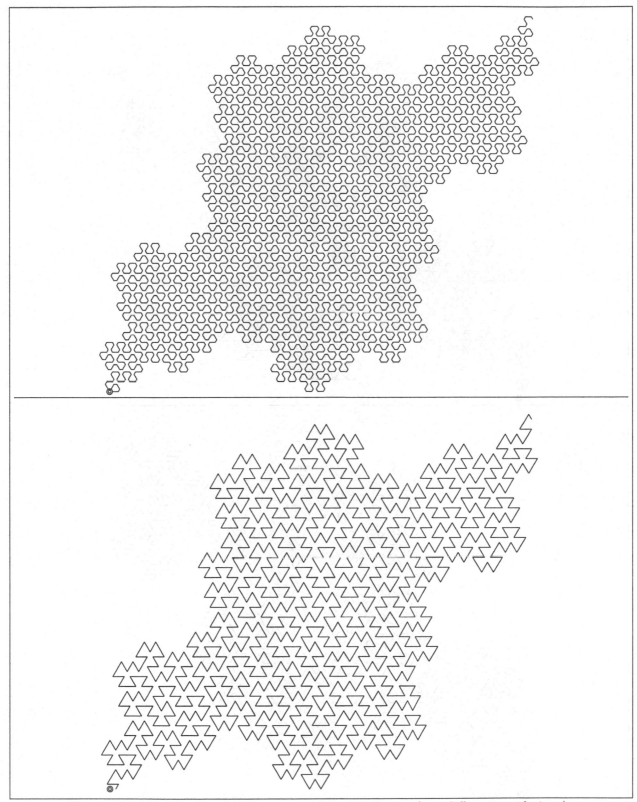

Figure 1.31-P: The first 2401 segments of the R7-dragon (two different renderings).

```
3    // return (tr) whether the lowest nonzero digit
4    // of the incremented word is either 2, 3, or 6.
```

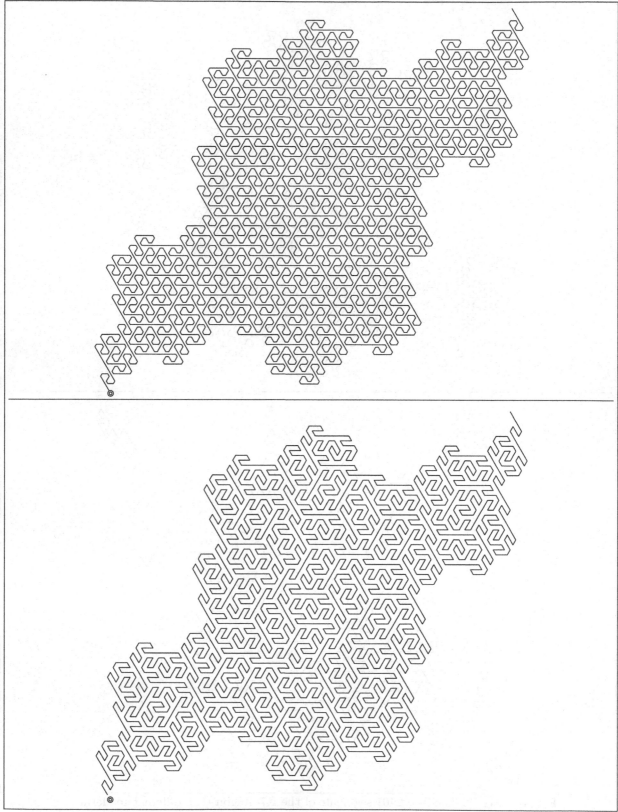

Figure 1.31-Q: The first 2401 segments of the second R7-dragon (two different renderings).

```
Start: 0
Rules:
  0 --> 00110
  1 --> 00111
-------------
0:   (#=1)
  0
1:   (#=5)
  00110
2:   (#=25)
  0011000110001110011100110
3:   (#=125)
  0011000110001110011100110001100011000111001110011000110001100011000111001110011100  \
  11000110001110011100111001100011000111001110011100110
```

```
Start: 0
Rules:
  0 --> 0100110
  1 --> 0110110
-------------
0:   (#=1)
  0
1:   (#=7)
  0100110
2:   (#=49)
  0100110011011001001100100110011011001101100100110
3:   (#=343)
  0100110011011001001100100110011011001101100100110010011001101100110110011011001001 ...
```

```
Start: 0
Rules:
  0 --> 0++--00
  + --> 0++--0+
  - --> 0++--0-
-------------
0:   (#=1)
  0
1:   (#=7)
  0++--00
2:   (#=49)
  0++--000++--0+0++--0+0++--0-0++--0-0++--000++--00
3:   (#=343)
  0++--000++--0+0++--0+0++--0-0++--0-0++--000++--000++--000++--0+0++--0+0++-- ...
```

Figure 1.31-R: Turns of the R5-dragon (top), the R7-dragon (middle), and the second R7-dragon (bottom), generated by string substitution.

```
5    {
6        ulong s = 0;
7        while ( (x & 7) == 6 )  { x >>= 3;  ++s; } // scan over nines
8        ++x;  // increment next digit
9        bool tr = ( x & 2 );  // whether digit is either 2, 3, or 6
10       x <<= (3*s);  // shift back
11       return  tr;
12   }
13
```

Two renderings of the R7-dragon are shown in figure 1.31-P (created with [FXT: bits/dragon-r7-texpic-demo.cc]). The sequence of returned values (entry A176405 in [312]) can be computed via the string substitution shown in figure 1.31-R (middle). Turns for another curve based on radix-7 counting (shown in figure 1.31-Q, created with [FXT: bits/dragon-r7-2-texpic-demo.cc]) can be computed as follows:

```
1    static inline int bit_dragon_r7_2_turn(ulong &x)
2    // Increment the radix-7 word x and
3    // return (tr) according to the lowest nonzero digit d
4    // of the incremented word:
5    //   d==[1,2,3,4,5,6]  ==>  rt:=[0,+1,+1,-1,-1,0]
6    // (tr * 120deg) is the turn with the second R7-dragon.
7    {
8        ulong s = 0;
9        while ( (x & 7) == 6 )  { x >>= 3;  ++s; } // scan over nines
10       ++x;  // increment next digit
11       int tr = 2 - ( (0x2f58 >> (2*(x&7)) ) & 3 );
12       x <<= (3*s);  // shift back
13       return  tr;
14   }
```

The sequence of turns can be generated by the string substitution shown in figure 1.31-R (bottom), it is

```
Start: F
Rules: F --> F+F+F-F-F     + --> +     - --> -
-------------
0:    (#=1)
   F
1:    (#=9)
  F+F+F-F-F
2:    (#=49)
  F+F+F-F-F+F+F+F-F-F+F+F+F-F-F+F+F+F-F-F+F+F-F-F
3:    (#=249)
  F+F+F-F-F+F+F+F-F-F+F+F+F-F-F+F+F+F-F-F+F+F-F-F+F+F+F-F-F+F+F+F-F-F+F+F+F-F-F-F+  ...
```
```
Start: F
Rules: F --> F+F-F-F+F+F-F     + --> +     - --> -
-------------
0:    (#=1)
   F
1:    (#=13)
  F+F-F-F+F+F-F
2:    (#=97)
  F+F-F-F+F+F-F+F+F-F-F+F+F-F-F+F+F-F-F+F+F-F+F+F-F-F+F+F-F+F+F-F-F+F+F-  ...
```
```
Start: F
Rules: F --> FOF+F+F-F-FOF     + --> +     - --> -     O --> O
-------------
0:    (#=1)
   F
1:    (#=13)
  FOF+F+F-F-FOF
2:    (#=97)
  FOF+F+F-F-FOFOFOF+F+F-F-FOF+FOF+F+F-F-FOF+FOF+F+F-F-FOF-FOF+F+F-F-FOF-FOF+F+F-F-FO  ...
```

Figure 1.31-S: String substitution processes for the turns (symbols '+' and '-') and moves (symbol 'F' is a unit move in the current direction) of the R5-dragon (top), the R7-dragon (middle), and the second R7-dragon (bottom).

entry A176416 in [312].

Two curves respectively based on radix-9 and radix-13 counting are shown in figure 1.31-T. The corresponding routines are given in [FXT: bits/bit-dragon-r9.h]

```
1   static inline bool bit_dragon_r9_turn(ulong &x)
2   // Increment the radix-9 word x and
3   // return (tr) whether the lowest nonzero digit
4   // of the incremented word is either 2, 3, 5, or 8.
5   // tr determines whether to turn left or right (by 120 degrees)
6   // with the R9-dragon fractal.
7   // The sequence tr is the fixed point
8   // of the morphism  0 |--> 011010010,  1 |--> 011010011.
9   // Also fixed point of morphism (identify + with 0 and - with 1)
10  // F |--> F+F-F-F+F-F+F+F-F,  + |--> +,  - |--> -
11  // Also fixed point of morphism
12  // F |--> G+G-G,  G |--> F-F+F,  + |--> +,  - |--> -
13  {
14      ulong s = 0;
15      while ( (x & 15) == 8 )  { x >>= 4;  ++s; }  // scan over nines
16      ++x;   // increment next digit
17      bool tr = ( (0x12c >> (x&15)) & 1 );  // whether digit is either 2, 3, 5, or 8
18      x <<= (4*s);  // shift back
19      return  tr;
20  }
```

and [FXT: bits/bit-dragon-r13.h]

```
1   static inline bool bit_dragon_r13_turn(ulong &x)
2   // Increment the radix-13 word x and
3   // return (tr) whether the lowest nonzero digit
4   // of the incremented word is either 3, 6, 8, 9, 11, or 12.
5   // tr determines whether to turn left or right (by 90 degrees)
6   // with the R13-dragon fractal.
7   // The sequence tr is the fixed point
8   // of the morphism  0 |--> 0010010110110,  1 |--> 0010010110111.
9   // Also fixed point of morphism (identify + with 0 and - with 1)
10  // F |--> F+F+F-F+F+F-F+F-F+F-F-F,  + |--> +,  - |--> -
11  {
12      ulong s = 0;
```

```
13          while ( (x & 15) == 12 ) { x >>= 4;  ++s; }  // scan over nines
14          ++x;  // increment next digit
15          bool tr = ( (0x1b48 >> (x&15)) & 1 );  // whether digit is either 3, 6, 8, 9, 11, or 12
16          x <<= (4*s);  // shift back
17          return  tr;
18    }
```

Figure 1.31-T: The R9-dragon (top) and the R13-dragon (bottom).

Chapter 2

Permutations and their operations

We study permutations together with the operations on them, like composition and inversion. We further discuss the decomposition of permutations into cycles and give methods for generating random permutations, cyclic permutations, involutions, and derangements. In-place algorithms for applying several special permutations like the revbin permutation, the Gray permutation, and matrix transposition are given.

Algorithms for the generation of all permutations of a given number of objects and bijections between permutations and mixed radix numbers in factorial base are given in chapter 10.

2.1 Basic definitions and operations

A permutation of n elements can be represented by an array $X = [x_0, x_1, \ldots, x_{n-1}]$. When the permutation X is *applied* to $F = [f_0, f_1, \ldots, f_{n-1}]$, then the element at position k is moved to position x_k. A routine for the operation is [FXT: perm/permapply.h]:

```
1    template <typename Type>
2    void apply_permutation(const ulong *x, const Type *f, Type * restrict g, ulong n)
3    // Apply the permutation x[] to the array f[],
4    // i.e. set g[x[k]] <-- f[k]   for all k
5    {
6        for (ulong k=0; k<n; ++k)  g[x[k]] = f[k];
7    }
```

Routines to test various properties of permutations are given in [FXT: perm/permq.cc]. The length-n sequence $[0, 1, 2, \ldots, n - 1]$ represents the *identical permutation* which leaves all elements in their position. To check whether a given permutation is the identity is trivial:

```
1    bool is_identity(const ulong *f, ulong n)
2    // Return whether f[] is the identical permutation,
3    // i.e. whether f[k]==k for all k= 0...n-1
4    {
5        for (ulong k=0; k<n; ++k)  if ( f[k] != k )  return false;
6        return true;
7    }
```

A fixed point of a permutation is an index where the element is not moved:

```
1    ulong count_fixed_points(const ulong *f, ulong n)
2    // Return number of fixed points in f[]
3    {
4        ulong ct = 0;
5        for (ulong k=0; k<n; ++k)  ct += ( f[k] == k );
6        return ct;
7    }
```

A *derangement* is a permutation that has no fixed points. A routine to check whether a permutation is a derangement is

```
1    bool is_derangement(const ulong *f, ulong n)
2    // Return whether f[] is a derangement of identity,
3    // i.e. whether f[k]!=k for all k
4    {
5        for (ulong k=0; k<n; ++k)  if ( f[k] == k )  return false;
```

J. Arndt, *Matters Computational: Ideas, Algorithms, Source Code*,
DOI 10.1007/978-3-642-14764-7_2, © Springer-Verlag Berlin Heidelberg 2011

```
6        return true;
7    }
```

Whether two arrays are mutual derangements (that is, $f_k \neq g_k$ for all k) can be determined by:

```
1    bool is_derangement(const ulong *f, const ulong *g, ulong n)
2    // Return whether f[] is a derangement of g[],
3    // i.e. whether f[k]!=g[k] for all k
4    {
5        for (ulong k=0; k<n; ++k)  if ( f[k] == g[k] )  return false;
6        return true;
7    }
```

A *connected* (or *indecomposable*) permutation contains no proper prefix mapped to itself. We test whether $\max(f_0, f_1, \ldots, f_k) > k$ for all $k < n - 1$:

```
1    bool
2    is_connected(const ulong *f, ulong n)
3    {
4        if ( n<=1 )  return true;
5        ulong m = 0;  // maximum
6        for (ulong k=0; k<n-1; ++k)  // for all proper prefixes
7        {
8            const ulong fk = f[k];
9            if ( fk>m )   m = fk;
10           if ( m<=k )  return false;
11       }
12       return true;
13   }
```

To check whether an array is a valid permutation, we need to verify that each index in the valid range appears exactly once. The bit-array described in section 4.6 on page 164 allows doing the job without modifying the input:

```
1    bool
2    is_valid_permutation(const ulong *f, ulong n, bitarray *bp/*=0*/)
3    // Return whether all values 0...n-1 appear exactly once,
4    // i.e. whether f represents a permutation of [0,1,...,n-1].
5    {
6        // check whether any element is out of range:
7        for (ulong k=0; k<n; ++k)  if ( f[k]>=n )  return false;
8
9        // check whether values are unique:
10       bitarray *tp = bp;
11       if ( 0==bp )  tp = new bitarray(n);  // tags
12       tp->clear_all();
13
14       ulong k;
15       for (k=0; k<n; ++k)  if ( tp->test_set(f[k]) )  break;
16
17       if ( 0==bp )  delete tp;
18
19       return  (k==n);
20   }
```

The *complement* of a permutation is computed by replacing every element v by $n - 1 - v$ [FXT: perm/permcomplement.h]:

```
1    inline void make_complement(const ulong *f, ulong *g, ulong n)
2    // Set (as permutation) g to the complement of f.
3    // Can have f==g.
4    {
5        for (ulong k=0; k<n; ++k)  g[k] = n - 1 - f[k];
6    }
```

The *reversal* of a permutation is simply the reversed array [FXT: perm/reverse.h]:

```
1    template <typename Type>
2    inline void reverse(Type *f, ulong n)
3    // Reverse order of array f.
4    {
5        for (ulong k=0, i=n-1;  k<i;  ++k, --i)  swap2(f[k], f[i]);
6    }
```

2.2   Representation as disjoint cycles

Every permutation consists entirely of disjoint cycles. A *cycle* of a permutation is a subset of the indices
that is rotated (by one position) by the permutation. The term *disjoint* means that the cycles do not
'cross' each other. While this observation may appear trivial it gives a recipe for many operations: follow
the cycles of the permutation, one by one, and do the necessary operation on each of them.

Consider the following permutation of length 8:

```
[ 0 ,2 ,4 ,6 ,1 ,3 ,5, 7 ]
```

There are two fixed points (0 and 7, which we omit) and these cycles:

```
( 1 --> 2 --> 4 )
( 3 --> 6 --> 5 )
```

The cycles do 'wrap around', for example, the final 4 of the fist cycle goes to position 1, the first element
of the cycle. The inverse permutation is found by reversing every arrow in each cycle:

```
( 1 <-- 2 <-- 4 )
( 3 <-- 6 <-- 5 )
```

Equivalently, we can reverse the order of the elements in each cycle:

```
( 4 --> 2 --> 1 )
( 5 --> 6 --> 3 )
```

If we begin each cycle with its smallest element, the inverse permutation is written as

```
( 1 --> 4 --> 2 )
( 3 --> 5 --> 6 )
```

This form is obtained by reversing all elements except the first in each cycle of the (forward) permutation.
The last three sets of cycles all describe the same permutation, it is

```
[ 0 ,4 ,1 ,5 ,2 ,6, 3 ,7 ]
```

```
Permutation:
[ 0 2 4 6 1 3 5 7 ]
Inverse:
[ 0 4 1 5 2 6 3 7 ]

Cycles:
  (0) #=1
  (1, 2, 4) #=3
  (3, 6, 5) #=3
  (7) #=1

Code:
template <typename Type>
inline void foo_perm_8(Type *f)
{
  { Type t=f[1];   f[1]=f[4];   f[4]=f[2];   f[2]=t; }
  { Type t=f[3];   f[3]=f[5];   f[5]=f[6];   f[6]=t; }
}
```

Figure 2.2-A: A permutation of 8 elements, its inverse, its cycles, and code for the permutation.

The cycles form of a permutation can be printed with [FXT: perm/printcycles.cc]:

```
1    void
2    print_cycles(const ulong *f, ulong n, bitarray *tb/*=0*/)
3    // Print cycle form of the permutation in f[].
4    // Examples (first permutations of 4 elements in lex order):
5    //        array form        cycle form
6    //   0:  [ 0 1 2 3 ]      (0) (1) (2) (3)
7    //   1:  [ 0 1 3 2 ]      (0) (1) (2, 3)
8    //   2:  [ 0 2 1 3 ]      (0) (1, 2) (3)
9    //   3:  [ 0 2 3 1 ]      (0) (1, 2, 3)
10   //   4:  [ 0 3 1 2 ]      (0) (1, 3, 2)
11   //   5:  [ 0 3 2 1 ]      (0) (1, 3) (2)
12   //   6:  [ 1 0 2 3 ]      (0, 1) (2) (3)
13   //   7:  [ 1 0 3 2 ]      (0, 1) (2, 3)
14   //   8:  [ 1 2 0 3 ]      (0, 1, 2) (3)
15   {
16       bitarray *b = tb;
```

```
17          if ( tb==0 )  b = new bitarray(n);
18          b->clear_all();
19
20          for (ulong k=0; k<n; ++k)
21          {
22              if ( b->test(k) )  continue; // already processed
23
24              cout << "(";
25              ulong i = k;  // next in cycle
26              const char *cm = "";
27              do
28              {
29                  cout << cm << i;
30                  cm = ", ";
31                  b->set(i);
32              }
33              while ( (i=f[i]) != k );  // until we meet cycle leader again
34              cout << ") ";
35          }
36
37          if ( tb==0 )  delete b;
38      }
```

The bit-array (see section 4.6 on page 164 for the implementation) is used to keep track of the elements already processed. The routine can be modified to generate code for applying a given permutation to an array. The program [FXT: perm/cycles-demo.cc] prints cycles and code for a permutation, see figure 2.2-A.

2.2.1   Cyclic permutations

A permutation consisting of exactly one cycle is called *cyclic*. Whether a given permutation has this property can be tested with [FXT: perm/permq.cc]:

```
1   bool
2   is_cyclic(const ulong *f, ulong n)
3   // Return whether permutation is exactly one cycle.
4   {
5       if ( n<=1 )  return true;
6       ulong k = 0,  e = 0;
7       do  { e=f[e]; ++k; }  while ( e!=0 );
8       return  (k==n);
9   }
```

The method used is to follow the cycle starting at position zero and counting how long it is. If the length found equals the array length, then the permutation is cyclic. There are $(n-1)!$ cyclic permutations of n elements.

2.2.2   Sign and parity of a permutation

Every permutation can be written as a composition of *transpositions* (cycles of length 2). This number of transpositions is not unique, but modulo 2 it is unique. The *sign* of a permutation is defined to be $+1$ if the number is even and -1 if the number is odd. The minimal number of transpositions whose composition give a cycle of length l is $l-1$. So the minimal number of transpositions for a permutation consisting of k cycles where the length of the j-th cycle is l_j equals $\sum_{j=1}^{k}(l_j - 1) = (\sum_{j=1}^{k} l_j) - k$. The transposition count modulo 2 is called the *parity* of a permutation.

2.3   Compositions of permutations

We can apply several permutations to an array, one by one. The resulting permutation is called the *composition* of the applied permutations. The operation of composition is not commutative: in general $f \cdot g \neq g \cdot f$ for $f \neq g$. We note that the permutations of n elements form a group (of $n!$ elements), the group operation is composition.

2.3.1   The inverse of a permutation

A permutation f is the *inverse* of the permutation g if it undoes its effect: $f \cdot g = \text{id}$. A test whether two permutations f and g are mutual inverses is

```
1    bool is_inverse(const ulong *f, const ulong *g, ulong n)
2    // Return whether f[] is the inverse of g[]
3    {
4        for (ulong k=0; k<n; ++k)  if ( f[g[k]] != k )  return false;
5        return true;
6    }
```

We have $g \cdot f = f \cdot g = \text{id}$, in a group the left-inverse is equal to the right-inverse, so we can simply call g 'the inverse' of f.

A permutation which is its own inverse is called an *involution*. Checking for this is easy:

```
1    bool is_involution(const ulong *f, ulong n)
2    // Return whether max cycle length is <= 2,
3    // i.e. whether f * f = id.
4    {
5        for (ulong k=0; k<n; ++k)  if ( f[f[k]] != k )  return false;
6        return true;
7    }
```

The following routine computes the inverse of a given permutation [FXT: perm/perminvert.cc]:

```
1    void make_inverse(const ulong *f, ulong * restrict g, ulong n)
2    // Set (as permutation) g to the inverse of f
3    {
4        for (ulong k=0; k<n; ++k)  g[f[k]] = k;
5    }
```

For the in-place computation of the inverse we have to reverse each cycle [FXT: perm/perminvert.cc]:

```
1    void make_inverse(ulong *f, ulong n, bitarray *bp/*=0*/)
2    // Set (as permutation) f to its own inverse.
3    {
4        bitarray *tp = bp;
5        if ( 0==bp )  tp = new bitarray(n);  // tags
6        tp->clear_all();
7
8        for (ulong k=0; k<n; ++k)
9        {
10           if ( tp->test_clear(k) )  continue;  // already processed
11           tp->set(k);
12
13           // invert a cycle:
14           ulong i = k;
15           ulong g = f[i];  // next index
16           while ( 0==(tp->test_set(g)) )
17           {
18               ulong t = f[g];
19               f[g] = i;
20               i = g;
21               g = t;
22           }
23           f[g] = i;
24       }
25
26       if ( 0==bp )  delete tp;
27   }
```

The extra array of tag-bits can be avoided by using the highest bit of each word as a tag-bit. The scheme would fail if any word of the permutation array had the highest bit set. However, on byte-addressable machines such an array will not fit into memory (for word sizes of 16 or more bits). To keep the code similar to the version using the bit-array, we define

```
1    static const ulong s1 = 1UL << (BITS_PER_LONG - 1);  // highest bit is tag-bit
2    static const ulong s0 = ~s1;  // all bits but tag-bit
3
4    static inline void SET(ulong *f, ulong k)  { f[k&s0] |= s1; }
5    static inline void CLEAR(ulong *f, ulong k)  { f[k&s0] &= s0; }
6    static inline bool TEST(ulong *f, ulong k)  { return (0!=(f[k&s0]&s1)); }
```

We have to mask out the tag-bit when using the index variable k. The routine can be implemented as

```
1    void
2    make_inverse(ulong *f, ulong n)
3    // Set (as permutation) f to its own inverse.
4    // In-place version using highest bits of array as tag-bits.
5    {
6        for (ulong k=0; k<n; ++k)
7        {
8            if ( TEST(f, k) ) { CLEAR(f, k);  continue; } // already processed
9            SET(f, k);
10
11           // invert a cycle:
12           ulong i = k;
13           ulong g = f[i];  // next index
14           while ( 0==TEST(f, g) )
15           {
16               ulong t = f[g];
17               f[g] = i;
18               SET(f, g);
19               i = g;
20               g = t;
21           }
22           f[g] = i;
23
24           CLEAR(f, k);  // leave no tag-bits set
25       }
26   }
```

The extra `CLEAR()` statement at the end removes the tag-bit of the cycle minima. Its effect is that no tag-bits are set after the routine has finished. This routine has about the same performance as the bit-array version.

2.3.2   The square of a permutation

The *square* of a permutation is the composition with itself. The routine for squaring is [FXT: perm/permcompose.cc]

```
1    void make_square(const ulong *f, ulong * restrict g, ulong n)
2    // Set (as permutation) g = f * f
3    {
4        for (ulong k=0; k<n; ++k)  g[k] = f[f[k]];
5    }
```

The in-place version is

```
1    void make_square(ulong *f, ulong n, bitarray *bp/*=0*/)
2    // Set (as permutation) f = f * f
3    // In-place version.
4    {
5        bitarray *tp = bp;
6        if ( 0==bp )  tp = new bitarray(n);  // tags
7        tp->clear_all();
8
9        for (ulong k=0; k<n; ++k)
10       {
11           if ( tp->test_clear(k) )  continue;  // already processed
12           tp->set(k);
13
14           // square a cycle:
15           ulong i = k;
16           ulong t = f[i];  // save
17           ulong g = f[i];  // next index
18           while ( 0==(tp->test_set(g)) )
19           {
20               f[i] = f[g];
21               i = g;
22               g = f[g];
23           }
24           f[i] = t;
25       }
26
27       if ( 0==bp )  delete tp;
```

```
28   }
```

2.3.3   Composing and powering permutations

The composition of two permutations can be computed as

```
1   void
2   compose(const ulong *f, const ulong *g, ulong * restrict h, ulong n)
3   // Set (as permutation) h = f * g
4   {
5       for (ulong k=0; k<n; ++k)  h[k] = f[g[k]];
6   }
```

The following version will be used in the powering routine for permutations:

```
1   void
2   compose(const ulong *f, ulong * restrict g, ulong n)
3   // Set (as permutation) g = f * g
4   {
5       for (ulong k=0; k<n; ++k)  g[k] = f[g[k]]; // yes, this works
6   }
```

The e-th power of a permutation f is computed (and returned in g) by a version of the binary exponentiation algorithm described in section 28.5 on page 563 [FXT: perm/permcompose.cc]:

```
1   void
2   power(const ulong *f, ulong * restrict g, ulong n, long e,
3         ulong * restrict t/*=0*/)
4   // Set (as permutation) g = f ** e
5   {
6       if ( e==0 )
7       {
8           for (ulong k=0; k<n; ++k)  g[k] = k;
9           return;
10      }
11
12      if ( e==1 )
13      {
14          acopy(f, g, n);
15          return;
16      }
17
18      if ( e==-1 )
19      {
20          make_inverse(f, g, n);
21          return;
22      }
23
24      // here:  abs(e) > 1
25      ulong x = e>0 ? e : -e;
26
27      if ( is_pow_of_2(x) )  // special case x==2^n
28      {
29          make_square(f, g, n);
30          while ( x>2 )  { make_square(g, n);   x /= 2; }
31      }
32      else
33      {
34          ulong *tt = t;
35          if ( 0==t )  { tt = new ulong[n]; }
36          acopy(f, tt, n);
37
38          int firstq = 1;
39          while ( 1 )
40          {
41              if ( x&1 )  // odd
42              {
43                  if ( firstq )  // avoid multiplication by 1
44                  {
45                      acopy(tt, g, n);
46                      firstq = 0;
47                  }
48                  else  compose(tt, g, n);
49
50                  if ( x==1 )   goto dort;
51              }
52
```

```
53              make_square(tt, n);
54              x /= 2;
55          }
56
57      dort:
58          if ( 0==t )  delete [] tt;
59      }
60
61      if ( e<0 )  make_inverse(g, n);
62  }
```

The routine involves $O(n \log(n))$ operations. By extracting the cycles of the permutation, computing their e-th powers, and copying them back, we could reduce the complexity to only $O(n)$. The e-th power of a cycle is a cyclic shift by e positions, as described in section 2.9 on page 123.

2.4 In-place methods to apply permutations to data

We repeat the routine for applying a permutation [FXT: perm/permapply.h]:

```
1   template <typename Type>
2   void apply_permutation(const ulong *x, const Type *f, Type * restrict g, ulong n)
3   // Apply the permutation x[] to the array f[],
4   // i.e. set g[x[k]] <-- f[k]  for all k
5   {
6       for (ulong k=0; k<n; ++k)  g[x[k]] = f[k];
7   }
```

The in-place version follows the cycles of the permutation:

```
1   template <typename Type>
2   void apply_permutation(const ulong *x, Type * restrict f, ulong n, bitarray *bp=0)
3   {
4       bitarray *tp = bp;
5       if ( 0==bp )  tp = new bitarray(n);  // tags
6       tp->clear_all();
7
8       for (ulong k=0; k<n; ++k)
9       {
10          if ( tp->test_clear(k) )  continue;  // already processed
11          tp->set(k);
12
13          // --- do cycle: ---
14          ulong i = k;  // start of cycle
15          Type t = f[i];
16          ulong g = x[i];
17          while ( 0==(tp->test_set(g)) )  // cf. gray_permute()
18          {
19              Type tt = f[g];
20              f[g] = t;
21              t = tt;
22              g = x[g];
23          }
24          f[g] = t;
25          // --- end (do cycle) ---
26      }
27
28      if ( 0==bp )  delete tp;
29  }
```

To apply the inverse of a permutation without inverting the permutation itself, use

```
1   template <typename Type>
2   void apply_inverse_permutation(const ulong *x, const Type *f, Type * restrict g, ulong n)
3   {
4       for (ulong k=0; k<n; ++k)  g[k] = f[x[k]];
5   }
```

The in-place version is

```
1   template <typename Type>
2   void apply_inverse_permutation(const ulong *x, Type * restrict f, ulong n, bitarray *bp=0)
3   {
4       bitarray *tp = bp;
```

```
5        if ( 0==bp )  tp = new bitarray(n);   // tags
6        tp->clear_all();
7
8        for (ulong k=0; k<n; ++k)
9        {
10           if ( tp->test_clear(k) )  continue;   // already processed
11           tp->set(k);
12
13           // --- do cycle: ---
14           ulong i = k;  // start of cycle
15           Type t = f[i];
16           ulong g = x[i];
17           while ( 0==(tp->test_set(g)) )  // cf. inverse_gray_permute()
18           {
19               f[i] = f[g];
20               i = g;
21               g = x[i];
22           }
23           f[i] = t;
24           // --- end (do cycle) ---
25       }
26
27       if ( 0==bp )  delete tp;
28   }
```

A permutation of n elements can be given as a function $X(k)$ (where $0 \leq X(k) <= n$ for $0 \leq k < n$, and $X(i) \neq X(j)$ for $i \neq j$). The permutation given as function X can be applied to an array f via [FXT: perm/permapplyfunc.h]:

```
1    template <typename Type>
2    void apply_permutation(ulong (*x)(ulong), const Type *f, Type * restrict g, ulong n)
3    // Set g[x(k)] <-- f[k]  for all k
4    {
5        for (ulong k=0; k<n; ++k)  g[x(k)] = f[k];
6    }
```

For example, the following statements are equivalent:

```
apply_permutation(gray_code, f, g, n);
gray_permute(f, g, n);
```

The inverse routine is

```
1    template <typename Type>
2    void apply_inverse_permutation(ulong (*x)(ulong), const Type *f, Type * restrict g, ulong n)
3    {
4        for (ulong k=0; k<n; ++k)  g[k] = f[x(k)];
5    }
```

The in-place versions of these routines are almost identical to the routines that apply permutations given as arrays. Only a tiny change must be made in the processing of the cycles. For example, the fragment

```
1    void apply_permutation(const ulong *x, Type * restrict f, ulong n, bitarray *bp=0)
2      [--snip--]
3           ulong i = k;  // start of cycle
4           Type t = f[i];
5           ulong g = x[i];
6           while ( 0==(tp->test_set(g)) )  // cf. gray_permute()
7           {
8               Type tt = f[g];
9               f[g] = t;
10              t = tt;
11              g = x[g];
12          }
13          f[g] = t;
14      [--snip--]
```

must be modified by replacing all occurrences of 'x[i]' with 'x(i)':

```
1    void apply_permutation(ulong (*x)(ulong), Type *f, ulong n, bitarray *bp=0)
2      [--snip--]
3           ulong i = k;  // start of cycle
4           Type t = f[i];
5           ulong g = x(i);   // <--=
6           while ( 0==(tp->test_set(g)) )  // cf. gray_permute()
```

```
7        {
8            Type tt = f[g];
9            f[g] = t;
10           t = tt;
11           g = x(g);   // <--=
12       }
13       f[g] = t;
14   [--snip--]
```

2.5 Random permutations

The following routine randomly permutes an array with arbitrary elements [FXT: perm/permrand.h]:

```
1   template <typename Type>
2   void random_permute(Type *f, ulong n)
3   {
4       for (ulong k=n; k>1; --k)
5       {
6           const ulong i = rand_idx(k);
7           swap2(f[k-1], f[i]);
8       }
9   }
```

An alternative version for the loop is:

```
1       for (ulong k=1; k<n; ++k)
2       {
3           const ulong i = rand_idx(k+1);
4           swap2(f[k], f[i]);
5       }
```

The method is given in [132], it is sometimes called *Knuth shuffle* or *Fisher-Yates shuffle*, see [213, alg.P, sect.3.4.2]. We use the auxiliary routine [FXT: aux0/rand-idx.h]

```
1   inline ulong rand_idx(ulong m)
2   // Return random number in the range [0, 1, ..., m-1].
3   // Must have m>0.
4   {
5       if ( m==1 )  return 0;   // could also use % 1
6       ulong x = (ulong)rand();
7       x ^= x>>16;      // avoid using low bits of rand() alone
8       return  x % m;
9   }
```

A random permutation is computed by applying the function to the identical permutation:

```
1   void random_permutation(ulong *f, ulong n)
2   // Create a random permutation
3   {
4       for (ulong k=0; k<n; ++k)  f[k] = k;
5       random_permute(f, n);
6   }
```

A slight modification of the underlying idea can be used for a routine for *random selection* from a list with only one linear read. Let L be a list of n items $L_1, \ldots, L_n$.

1. Set $t = L_1$, set $k = 1$.

2. Set $k = k + 1$. If $k > n$ return t.

3. With probability $1/k$ set $t = L_k$.

4. Go to step 2.

Note that one does not need to know n, the number of elements in the list, in advance: replace the second statement in step 2 by "If there are no more elements, return t".

2.5.1 Random cyclic permutation

A routine to apply a random cyclic permutation (as defined in section 2.2.1 on page 105) to an array is
[FXT: perm/permrand-cyclic.h]

```
1    template <typename Type>
2    void random_permute_cyclic(Type *f, ulong n)
3    // Permute the elements of f by a random cyclic permutation.
4    {
5        for (ulong k=n-1; k>0; --k)
6        {
7            const ulong i = rand_idx(k);
8            swap2(f[k], f[i]);
9        }
10   }
```

The method is called *Sattolo's algorithm*, see [296], and also [171] and [362]. It can be described as a
method to arrange people in a cycle: Assume there are n people in a room. Let the first person choose
a successor out of the remaining persons not yet chosen. Then let the person just chosen make the next
choice of a successor. Repeat until everyone has been chosen. Finally, let the first person be the successor
of the last person chosen.

The cycle representation of a random cyclic permutation can be computed by applying a random permutation to all elements (of the identical permutation) except for the first element.

2.5.2 Random prefix of a permutation

A length-m prefix of a random permutation of n elements is computed by the following routine that uses
just $O(m)$ operations [FXT: perm/permrand-pref.h]:

```
1    template <typename Type>
2    void random_permute_pref(Type *f, ulong n, ulong m)
3    // Set the first m elements to a prefix of a random permutation.
4    // Same as: set the first m elements of f to a random permutation
5    // of a random selection of all n elements.
6    // Must have m<=n-1.
7    // Same as random_permute() if m>=n-1.
8    {
9        if ( m>n-1 )  m = n-1;  // m>n is not admissable
10       for (ulong k=0,j=n; k<m; ++k,--j)
11       {
12           const ulong i = k + rand_idx(j);  // k<=i<n
13           swap2(f[k], f[i]);
14       }
15   }
```

The first element is randomly selected from all n elements, the second from the remaining $n-1$ elements,
and so on. Thus there are $n\,(n-1)\,\ldots\,(n-m+1) = n!/(n-m)!$ length-m prefixes of permutations of
n elements.

2.5.3 Random permutation with prescribed parity

To compute a random permutation with prescribed parity (as defined in section 2.2.2 on page 105) we
keep track of the parity of the generated permutation and change it via a single transposition if necessary
[FXT: perm/permrand-parity.h]:

```
1    template <typename Type>
2    void random_permute_parity(Type *f, ulong n, bool par)
3    // Randomly permute the elements of f, such that the
4    // parity of the permutation equals par.
5    // I.e. the minimal number of transpositions of the
6    //  permutation is even if par==0, else odd.
7    // Note: with n<=1 there is no odd permutation.
8    {
9        if ( (par==1) && (n<2) )  return;  // not admissable
10
11       bool pr = 0;  // identity has even parity
12       for (ulong k=1; k<n; ++k)
```

```
13    {
14        const ulong i = rand_idx(k+1);
15        swap2(f[k], f[i]);
16        pr ^= ( k != i );   // parity changes with swap
17    }
18
19    if ( par!=pr )  swap2(f[0], f[1]);  // need to change parity
20  }
```

2.5.4 Random permutation with m smallest elements in prescribed order

In the last algorithm we conditionally changed the positions 0 and 1. Now we conditionally change the elements 0 and 1 to preserve their relative order [FXT: perm/permrand-ord.h]:

```
1   template <typename Type>
2   void random_ord01_permutation(Type *f, ulong n)
3   // Random permutation such that elements 0 and 1 are in order.
4   {
5       random_permutation(f, n);
6       ulong t = 0;
7       while ( f[t]>1 )  ++t;
8       if ( f[t]==0 )  return;  // already in correct order
9       f[t] = 0;
10      do { ++t; }  while ( f[t]!=0 );
11      f[t] = 1;
12  }
```

The routine generates half of all the permutations but not their reversals. The following routine fixes the relative order of the m smallest elements:

```
1   template <typename Type>
2   void random_ordm_permutation(Type *f, ulong n, ulong m)
3   // Random permutation such that the m smallest elements are in order.
4   // Must have m<=n.
5   {
6       random_permutation(f, n);
7       for (ulong t=0,j=0; j<m; ++t)  if ( f[t]<m )  { f[t]=j; ++j; }
8   }
```

A random permutation where 0 appears as the last of the m smallest elements is computed by:

```
1   template <typename Type>
2   void random_lastm_permutation(Type *f, ulong n, ulong m)
3   // Random permutation such that 0 appears as last of the m smallest elements.
4   // Must have m<=n.
5   {
6       random_permutation(f, n);
7       if ( m<=1 )  return;
8
9       ulong p0=0, pl=0;  // position of 0, and last (in m smallest elements)
10      for (ulong t=0, j=0;  j<m;  ++t)
11      {
12          if ( f[t]<m )
13          {
14              pl = t;  // update position of last
15              if ( f[t]==0 )  { p0 = t; }  // record position of 0
16              ++j;   // j out of m smallest found
17          }
18      }
19      // here t is the position of the last of the m smallest elements
20      swap2( f[p0], f[pl] );
21  }
```

2.5.5 Random permutation with prescribed cycle type

To create a random permutation with given cycle type (see section 11.1.2 on page 278) we first give a routine for permuting by one cycle of prescribed length. We need to keep track of the set of unprocessed elements. The positions of those (available) elements are stored in an array r[]. After an element is processed its index is swapped with the last available index [FXT: perm/permrand-cycle-type.h]:

```
1   template <typename Type>
2   inline ulong random_cycle(Type *f, ulong cl, ulong *r, ulong nr)
3   // Permute a random set of elements (whose positions are given in
```

```
4     // r[0], ..., r[nr-1]) by a random cycle of length cl.
5     // Must have  nr >= cl  and  cl != 0.
6     {
7         if ( cl==1 )  // just remove a random position from r[]
8         {
9             const ulong i = rand_idx(nr);
10            --nr;  swap2( r[nr], r[i] );  // remove position from set
11        }
12        else  // cl >= 2
13        {
14            const ulong i0 = rand_idx(nr);
15            const ulong k0 = r[i0];  // position of cycle leader
16            const Type f0 = f[k0];  // cycle leader
17            --cl;
18            --nr;  swap2( r[nr], r[i0] );  // remove position from set
19
20            ulong kp = k0;  // position of predecessor in cycle
21            do  // create cycle
22            {
23                const ulong i = rand_idx(nr);
24                const ulong k = r[i]; // random available position
25                f[kp] = f[k];         // move element
26                --nr;  swap2( r[nr], r[i] );  // remove position from set
27                kp = k;  // update predecessor
28            }
29            while ( --cl );
30
31            f[kp] = f0;    // close cycle
32        }
33
34        return nr;
35    }
```

To permute according to a cycle type, we call the routine according to the elements of an array c[] that specifies how many cycles of each length are required:

```
1     template <typename Type>
2     inline void random_permute_cycle_type(Type *f, ulong n, const ulong *c, ulong *tr=0)
3     // Permute the elements of f by a random permutation of prescribed cycle type.
4     // The permutation will have c[k] cycles of length k+1.
5     // Must have s <= n where s := sum(k=0, n-1, c[k]).
6     // If s < n then the permutation will have n-s fixed points.
7     {
8         ulong *r = tr;
9         if ( tr==0 )  r = new ulong[n];
10        for (ulong k=0; k<n; ++k)  r[k] = k;  // initialize set
11        ulong nr = n;  // number of elements available
12        // available positions are  r[0], ..., r[nr-1]
13
14        for (ulong k=0; k<n; ++k)
15        {
16            ulong nc = c[k];  // number of cycles of length k+1;
17            if ( nc==0 )  continue;  // no cycles of this length
18            const ulong cl = k+1;  // cycle length
19            do
20            {
21                nr = random_cycle(f, cl, r, nr);
22            }
23            while ( --nc );
24        }
25
26        if ( tr==0 )  delete [] r;
27    }
```

2.5.6   Random self-inverse permutation

For the self-inverse permutations (involutions) we need to compute certain branch probabilities. At each step either a 2-cycle or a fixed point is generated. The probability that the next step generates a fixed point is $R(n) = I(n-1)/I(n)$ where $I(n)$ is the number of involutions of n elements. This can be seen by dividing relation 11.1-6 on page 279 by $I(n)$:

$$1 = \frac{I(n-1)}{I(n)} + \frac{(n-1)\,I(n-2)}{I(n)} \tag{2.5-1}$$

At each step we generate a random number t where $0 \leq t < 1$, if $t > R(n)$ then a 2-cycle is created, else a fixed point. The quantities $I(n)$ cannot be used with fixed precision arithmetic because an overflow would occur for large n. Instead, we update $R(n)$ via

$$R(n+1) \;=\; \frac{1}{1 + n\,R(n)} \tag{2.5-2}$$

The recurrence is numerically stable [FXT: perm/permrand-self-inverse.h]:

```
1    inline void next_involution_branch_ratio(double &rat, double &n1)
2    {
3        n1 += 1.0;
4        rat = 1.0/( 1.0 + n1*rat );
5    }
```

The following routine initializes the array of values $R(n)$:

```
1    inline void init_involution_branch_ratios(double *b, ulong n)
2    {
3        b[0] = 1.0;
4        double rat = 0.5,  n1 = 1.0;
5        for (ulong k=1; k<n; ++k)
6        {
7            b[k] = rat;
8            next_involution_branch_ratio(rat, n1);
9        }
10   }
```

```
1    template <typename Type>
2    inline void random_permute_self_inverse(Type *f, ulong n,
3                                            ulong *tr=0, double *tb=0, bool bi=false)
4    // Permute the elements of f by a random self-inverse permutation (an involution).
5    // Set bi:=true to signal that the branch probabilities in tb[]
6    //   have been precomputed (via init_involution_branch_ratios()).
7    {
8        ulong *r = tr;
9        if ( tr==0 )  r = new ulong[n];
10       for (ulong k=0; k<n; ++k)  r[k] = k;
11       ulong nr = n;  // number of elements available
12       // available positions are  r[0], ..., r[nr-1]
13
14       double *b = tb;
15       if ( tb==0 )  { b = new double[n];  bi=false; }
16       if ( !bi )  init_involution_branch_ratios(b, n);
17
18       while ( nr>=2 )
19       {
20           const ulong x1 = nr-1;
21           const ulong r1 = r[x1];  // available position
22           --nr;  // no swap needed if x1==last
23
24           const double rat = b[nr];  // probability to choose fixed point
25
26           const double t = rnd01();  // 0 <= t < 1
27           if ( t > rat )  // 2-cycle
28           {
29               const ulong x2 = rand_idx(nr);
30               const ulong r2 = r[x2];  // random available position != r1
31               --nr;  swap2(r[x2], r[nr]);
32               swap2( f[r1], f[r2] );
33           }
34           // else // fixed point, nothing to do
35       }
36
37       if ( tr==0 )  delete [] r;
38       if ( tb==0 )  delete [] b;
39   }
```

The auxiliary function rand01() returns a random number t where $0 \leq t < 1$ [FXT: aux0/randf.cc].

2.5.7 Random derangement

In each step of the routine for a random permutation without fixed points (a derangement) we join two cycles and decide whether to close the resulting cycle. The probability of closing is $B(n) = (n-1)\,D(n-$

$2)/D(n)$ where $D(n)$ is the number of derangements of n elements. This can be seen by dividing relation 11.1-12a on page 280 by $D(n)$:

$$1 \;=\; \frac{(n-1)\,D(n-1)}{D(n)} + \frac{(n-1)\,D(n-2)}{D(n)} \tag{2.5-3}$$

The probability $B(n)$ is close to $1/n$ for large n. Already for $n > 30$ the relative error (for $B(n)$ versus $1/n$) is less than 10^{-32}, so $B(n)$ is indistinguishable from $1/n$ with floating-point types where the mantissa has at most 106 bits. We compute a table of just 32 values $B(n)$ [FXT: perm/permrand-derange.h]:

```
1    // number of precomputed branch ratios:
2    #define NUM_PBR 32  // OK for up to 106-bit mantissa
3
4    inline void init_derange_branch_ratios(double *b)
5    {
6        b[0] = 0.0;  b[1] = 1.0;
7        double dn0 = 1.0,  dn1 = 0.0,  n1 = 1.0;
8        for (ulong k=2; k<NUM_PBR; ++k)
9        {
10           const double dn2 = dn1;
11           next_num_derangements(dn0, dn1, n1);
12           const double rat = (n1) * dn2/dn0;   // == (n-1) * D(n-2) / D(n)
13           b[k] = rat;
14       }
15   }
```

The $D(n)$ are updated using $D(n) = (n-1)\,[D(n-1) + D(n-2)]$:

```
1    inline void next_num_derangements(double &dn0, double &dn1, double &n1)
2    {
3        const double dn2 = dn1;  dn1 = dn0;  n1 += 1.0;
4        dn0 = n1*(dn1 + dn2);
5    }
```

Now the $B(n)$ are computed as

```
1    inline double derange_branch_ratio(const double *b, ulong n)
2    {
3        if ( n<NUM_PBR )  return b[n];
4        else              return 1.0/(double)n;  // relative error < 1.0e-32
5    }
```

The routine for a random derangement is

```
1    template <typename Type>
2    inline void random_derange(Type *f, ulong n,
3                               ulong *tr=0,
4                               double *tb=0, bool bi=false)
5    // Permute the elements of f by a random derangement.
6    // Set bi:=true to signal that the branch probabilities in tb[]
7    //    have been precomputed (via init_derange_branch_ratios()).
8    // Must have n > 1.
9    {
10       ulong *r = tr;
11       if ( tr==0 )  r = new ulong[n];
12       for (ulong k=0; k<n; ++k)  r[k] = k;
13       ulong nr = n;  // number of elements available
14       // available positions are  r[0], ..., r[nr-1]
15
16       double *b = tb;
17       if ( tb==0 )  { b = new double[NUM_PBR];  bi=false; }
18       if ( !bi )  init_derange_branch_ratios(b);
19
20       while ( nr>=2 )
21       {
22           const ulong x1 = nr-1;  // last element
23           const ulong r1 = r[x1];
24
25           const ulong x2 = rand_idx(nr-1);  // random element !=last
26           const ulong r2 = r[x2];
27
28           swap2( f[r1], f[r2] );  // join cycles containing f[r1] and f[r2]
29
30           // remove r[x1]=r1 from set:
31           --nr;  // swap2(r[x1], r[nr]);  // swap not needed if x1==last
```

```
32
33               const double rat = derange_branch_ratio(b, nr);
34               const double t = rnd01();  // 0 <= t < 1
35               if ( t < rat )  // close cycle
36               {
37                   // remove r[x2]=r2 from set:
38                   --nr;  swap2(r[x2], r[nr]);
39               }
40               // else  cycle stays open
41           }
42
43       if ( tr==0 )  delete [] r;
44       if ( tb==0 )  delete [] b;
45   }
```

The method is (essentially) given in [245]. A generalization for permutations with all cycles of length $\geq m$ is given in [24].

2.5.8   Random connected permutation

A random connected (indecomposable) permutation can be computed via the *rejection method*: create a random permutation, if it is not connected, repeat. An implementation is [FXT: perm/permrand-connected.h]

```
1   inline void random_connected_permutation(ulong *f, ulong n)
2   {
3       for (ulong k=0; k<n; ++k)  f[k] = k;
4       do  { random_permute(f, n); }  while ( ! is_connected(f, n) );
5   }
```

The method is efficient because the number of connected permutations is (asymptotically) given by

$$C(n) \;=\; n! \left(1 - \frac{2}{n} - O\left(\frac{1}{n^2}\right) \right) \tag{2.5-4}$$

That is, the test for connectedness is expected to fail with a probability of about $2/n$ for large n. The probability of failure can be reduced to about $2/n^2$ by avoiding the permutations that fix either the first or the last element. The small cases ($n \leq 3$) are treated separately:

```
1   if ( n<=3 )
2   {
3       for (ulong k=0; k<n; ++k)  f[k] = k;
4       if ( n<2 )  return;   // [] or [0]
5       swap2(f[0], f[n-1]);
6       if ( n==2 )  return;  // [1,0]
7       // here: [2,1,0]
8       const ulong i = rand_idx(3);
9       swap2(f[1], f[i]);
10      // i = 0  ==>  [1,2,0]
11      // i = 1  ==>  [2,1,0]
12      // i = 2  ==>  [2,0,1]
13      return;
14  }
15
16  do
17  {
18      for (ulong k=0; k<n; ++k)  f[k] = k;
19
20      while ( 1 )
21      {
22          const ulong i0 = 1 + rand_idx(n-1);  // first element must move
23          const ulong i1 = 1 + rand_idx(n-1);  // f[1] will be last element
24          swap2( f[0], f[i0] );
25          swap2( f[1], f[i1] );
26          if ( f[1]==n-1 )  // undo swap and repeat (here: f[0]!=0)
27          {
28              swap2( f[1], f[i1] );
29              swap2( f[0], f[i0] );
30              continue;    // probability 1/n but work only O(1)
31          }
32          else  break;
33      }
```

```
34
35          swap2(f[1], f[n-1]);  // move f[1] to last
36          // here:  f[0] != 0  and  f[n-1] != n-1
37          random_permute(f+1, n-2);  // permute 2nd ... 2nd last element
38      }
39      while ( ! is_connected(f, n) );
```

2.6 The revbin permutation

```
    0: [ *                         ]
    1: [              *            ]
    2: [      *                    ]
    3: [                *          ]
    4: [    *                      ]
    5: [            *              ]
    6: [        *                  ]
    7: [                  *        ]
    8: [  *                        ]   0: [ *              ]
    9: [                *          ]   1: [        *       ]
   10: [         *                 ]   2: [   *            ]
   11: [                   *       ]   3: [            *   ]
   12: [       *                   ]   4: [ *              ]   0: [ *        ]
   13: [                  *        ]   5: [          *     ]   1: [     *    ]
   14: [          *                ]   6: [     *          ]   2: [  *       ]
   15: [                       * ]     7: [              * ]   3: [      *   ]
```

Figure 2.6-A: Permutation matrices of the revbin permutation for sizes 16, 8 and 4. The permutation is self-inverse.

The permutation that swaps elements whose binary indices are mutual reversals is called *revbin permutation* (sometimes also *bit-reversal* or *bitrev* permutation). For example, for length $n = 256$ the element with index $x = 43_{10} = 00101011_2$ is swapped with the element whose index is $\tilde{x} = 11010100_2 = 212_{10}$. Note that $\tilde{x}$ depends on both x and on n. Pseudocode for a naive implementation is

```
1    procedure revbin_permute(a[], n)
2    // a[0..n-1] input,result
3    {
4        for x:=0 to n-1
5        {
6            r := revbin(x, n)
7            if r>x then  swap(a[x], a[r])
8        }
9    }
```

The condition `r>x` before the `swap()` statement makes sure that the swapping is not undone later when the loop variable `x` has the value of the present `r`.

2.6.1 Computation using revbin-update

The key ingredient for a fast permutation routine is the observation that we only need to update the bit-reversed values: given $\tilde{x}$ we can compute $\widetilde{x+1}$ efficiently as described in section 1.14.3 on page 36. A faster routine will be of the form

```
1    procedure revbin_permute(a[], n)
2    // a[0..n-1] input,result
3    {
4        if n<=2  return
5        r := 0  // the reversed 0
6        for x:=1 to n-1
7        {
8            r := revbin_upd(r, n/2)
9            if r>x then  swap(a[x], a[r])
10       }
11   }
```

About $(n - \sqrt{n})/2$ `swap()` statements are executed with the revbin permutation of n elements. That is, almost every element is moved for large n, as there are only a few numbers with symmetric bit patterns:

n:	2 # swaps	# symm. pairs
2:	0	2
4:	2	2
8:	4	4
16:	12	4
32:	24	8
64:	56	8
2^{10}:	992	32
2^{20}:	$0.999 \cdot 2^{20}$	2^{10}
∞:	$n - \sqrt{n}$	$\sqrt{n}$

The sequence is entry A045687 in [312]:

0, 2, 4, 12, 24, 56, 112, 238, 480, 992, 1980, 4032, 8064, 16242, 32512, 65280, ...

2.6.2 Exploiting the symmetries of the permutation

Symmetry can be used for further optimization: if for even $x < \frac{n}{2}$ there is a swap for the pair $(x, \tilde{x})$, then there is also a swap for the pair $(n-1-x, n-1-\tilde{x})$. As $x < \frac{n}{2}$ and $\tilde{x} < \frac{n}{2}$, one has $n-1-x > \frac{n}{2}$ and $n-1-\tilde{x} > \frac{n}{2}$. That is, the swaps are independent. A routine that uses these observations is

```
1   procedure revbin_permute(a[], n)
2   {
3       if n<=2  return
4       nh := n/2
5       r := 0  // the reversed 0
6       x := 1
7       while x<nh
8       {
9           // x odd:
10          r := r + nh
11          swap(a[x], a[r])
12          x := x + 1
13
14          // x even:
15          r := revbin_upd(r, n/2)
16          if r>x then
17          {
18              swap(a[x], a[r])
19              swap(a[n-1-x], a[n-1-r])
20          }
21          x := x + 1
22      }
23  }
```

The code above can be used to derive an optimized version for zero padded data (used with linear convolution, see section 22.1.4 on page 443):

```
1   procedure revbin_permute0(a[], n)
2   {
3       if n<=2  return
4       nh := n/2
5       r := 0  // the reversed 0
6       x := 1
7       while x<nh
8       {
9           // x odd:
10          r := r + nh
11          a[r] := a[x]
12          a[x] := 0
13          x := x + 1
14
15          // x even:
16          r := revbin_upd(r, n)
17          if r>x then  swap(a[x], a[r])
18          // Omit swap of a[n-1-x] and a[n-1-r] as both are zero
19          x := x + 1
20      }
21  }
```

We can carry the scheme further, distinguishing whether $x \bmod 4 = 0, 1, 2$, or 3, as done in the implementation [FXT: perm/revbinpermute.h]. The following parameters determine how much of the symmetry is used and which version of the revbin-update routine is chosen:

```
1   #define  RBP_SYMM  4  // amount of symmetry used: 1, 2, 4 (default is 4)
2   #define  FAST_REVBIN  // define if using revbin(x, ldn) is faster than updating
```

We further define a macro to swap elements:

```
1   #define  idx_swap(k, r)  { ulong kx=(k), rx=(r);  swap2(f[kx], f[rx]); }
```

The main routine uses unrolled versions of the revbin permutation for small values of n. These are given in [FXT: perm/shortrevbinpermute.h]. For example, the unrolled routine for $n = 16$ is

```
1    template <typename Type>
2    inline void revbin_permute_16(Type *f)
3    {
4         swap2(f[1], f[8]);
5         swap2(f[2], f[4]);
6         swap2(f[3], f[12]);
7         swap2(f[5], f[10]);
8         swap2(f[7], f[14]);
9         swap2(f[11], f[13]);
10   }
```

The code was generated with the program [FXT: perm/cycles-demo.cc], see section 2.2 on page 104. The routine `revbin_permute_leq_64(f,n)`, which is called for $n \leq 64$, selects the correct routine for the parameter n:

```
1    template <typename Type>
2    void revbin_permute(Type *f, ulong n)
3    {
4         if ( n<=64 )
5         {
6              revbin_permute_leq_64(f, n);
7              return;
8         }
9        [--snip--]
```

In what follows we set `RBP_SYMM` to 4, define `FAST_REVBIN`, and omit the corresponding preprocessor statements. Some auxiliary constants have to be computed:

```
1         const ulong ldn = ld(n);
2         const ulong nh = (n>>1);
3         const ulong n1  = n - 1;    // = 11111111
4         const ulong nx1 = nh - 2;   // = 01111110
5         const ulong nx2 = n1 - nx1; // = 10111101
```

The main loop is

```
1         ulong k = 0,  r = 0;
2         while ( k < (n/RBP_SYMM)  )  // n>=16, n/2>=8, n/4>=4
3         {
4              // ----- k%4 == 0:
5              if ( r>k )
6              {
7                   idx_swap(k, r);  // <nh, <nh 11
8                   idx_swap(n1^k, n1^r);  // >nh, >nh 00
9                   idx_swap(nx1^k, nx1^r);  // <nh, <nh 11
10                  idx_swap(nx2^k, nx2^r);  // >nh, >nh 00
11             }
12
13             ++k;
14             r ^= nh;
15
16             // ----- k%4 == 1:
17             if ( r>k )
18             {
19                  idx_swap(k, r);  // <nh, >nh 10
20                  idx_swap(n1^k, n1^r);  // >nh, <nh 01
21             }
22
23             ++k;
24             r = revbin(k, ldn);
25
26             // ----- k%4 == 2:
27             if ( r>k )
28             {
29                  idx_swap(k, r);  // <nh, <nh 11
30                  idx_swap(n1^k, n1^r); // >nh, >nh 00
```

```
31            }
32
33            ++k;
34            r ^= nh;
35
36            // ----- k%4 == 3:
37            if ( r>k )
38            {
39                idx_swap(k, r);        // <nh, >nh 10
40                idx_swap(nx1^k, nx1^r);   // <nh, >nh 10
41            }
42
43            ++k;
44            r = revbin(k, ldn);
45        }
46    }  // end of the routine
```

For large n the routine takes about six times longer than a simple array reversal. Much of the time is spent waiting for memory which suggests that further optimizations would best be attempted with special machine instructions to bypass the cache or with non-temporal writes.

A specialized implementation optimized for zero padded data is given in [FXT: perm/revbinpermute0.h]. Some memory accesses can be avoided for that case. For example, revbin-pairs with both indices greater than $n/2$ need no processing at all.

2.6.3   A pitfall

When working with separate arrays for the real and imaginary parts of complex data, one could remove half of the bookkeeping as follows:

```
1    procedure revbin_permute(a[], b[], n)
2    {
3        if n<=2  return
4        r := 0  // the reversed 0
5        for x:=1 to n-1
6        {
7            r := revbin_upd(r, n/2)  // inline me
8            if r>x then
9            {
10               swap(a[x], a[r])
11               swap(b[x], b[r])
12           }
13       }
14   }
```

If both the real and the imaginary part fit into level-1 cache the method can lead to a speedup. However, for large arrays the routine can be much *slower* than two separate calls of the simple method: with FFTs the real and imaginary element for the same index typically lie apart in memory by a power of 2, leading to a high percentage of cache misses with large arrays.

2.7   The radix permutation

The *radix permutation* is the generalization of the revbin permutation to arbitrary radices. Pairs of elements are swapped when their indices, written in radix r, are reversed. For example, in radix 10 and $n = 1000$ the elements with indices 123 and 321 will be swapped. The radix permutation is self-inverse.

Code for the radix r permutation of the array f[] is given in [FXT: perm/radixpermute.h]. The routine must be called with n a perfect power of the radix r. Radix $r = 2$ gives the revbin permutation.

```
1    extern ulong radix_permute_nt[];  // == 9, 90, 900, ...  for r=10
2    extern ulong radix_permute_kt[];  // == 1, 10, 100, ...  for r=10
3    #define  NT  radix_permute_nt
4    #define  KT  radix_permute_kt
5
6    template <typename Type>
7    void radix_permute(Type *f, ulong n, ulong r)
8    {
9        ulong x = 0;
10       NT[0]  = r-1;
11       KT[0]  = 1;
```

```
12      while ( 1 )
13      {
14          ulong z = KT[x] * r;
15          if ( z>n )  break;
16          ++x;
17          KT[x] = z;
18
19          NT[x] = NT[x-1] * r;
20      }
21      // here: n == p**x
22
23      for (ulong i=0, j=0;  i < n-1;  i++)
24      {
25          if ( i<j )  swap2(f[i], f[j]);
26
27          ulong t = x - 1;
28          ulong k = NT[t];   // =^=  k = (r-1) * n / r;
29
30          while ( k<=j )
31          {
32              j -= k;
33              k = NT[--t];   // =^=  k /= r;
34          }
35
36          j += KT[t]; // =^=  j += (k/(r-1));
37      }
38  }
```

2.8 In-place matrix transposition

Transposing a matrix is easy when it is not done in-place. The following routine does the job [FXT: aux2/transpose.h]:

```
1   template <typename Type>
2   void transpose(const Type * restrict f, Type * restrict g, ulong nr, ulong nc)
3   // Transpose nr x nc matrix f[]  into an nc x nr matrix g[].
4   {
5       for (ulong r=0; r<nr; r++)
6       {
7           ulong isrc = r * nc;
8           ulong idst = r;
9           for (ulong c=0; c<nc; c++)
10          {
11              g[idst] = f[isrc];
12              isrc += 1;
13              idst += nr;
14          }
15      }
16  }
```

Matters get more complicated for the in-place equivalent. We have to find the cycles (see section 2.2 on page 104) of the underlying permutation. To transpose a $n_r \times n_c$ matrix first identify the position i of the entry in row r and column c:

$$i \;=\; r \cdot n_c + c \tag{2.8-1}$$

After the transposition the element will be at position i' in the transposed $n_r' \times n_c'$ matrix

$$i' \;=\; r' \cdot n_c' + c' \tag{2.8-2}$$

We have $r' = c$, $c' = r$, $n_r' = n_c$ and $n_c' = n_r$, so

$$i' \;=\; c \cdot n_r + r \tag{2.8-3}$$

Multiplying the last equation by n_c gives

$$i' \cdot n_c \;=\; c \cdot n_r \cdot n_c + r \cdot n_c \tag{2.8-4}$$

With $n := n_r \cdot n_c$ and $r \cdot n_c = i - c$ we find

$$i' \cdot n_c \;=\; c \cdot n + i - c \tag{2.8-5}$$
$$i \;=\; i' \cdot n_c - c \cdot (n - 1) \tag{2.8-6}$$

Take the equation modulo $n - 1$ to obtain

$$i \;\equiv\; i' \cdot n_c \bmod n - 1 \tag{2.8-7}$$

That is, the transposition moves the element $i = i' \cdot n_c$ to position i'. Multiply by n_r to find the inverse:

$$i \cdot n_r \;\equiv\; i' \cdot n_c \cdot n_r \;\equiv\; i' \cdot (n - 1 + 1) \;\equiv\; i' \tag{2.8-8}$$

That is, element i will be moved to $i' = i \cdot n_r \bmod n - 1$. The following routine uses a bit-array to keep track of the elements processed so far [FXT: aux2/transpose.h]:

```
1    #define  SRC(k)  (((unsigned long long)(k)*nc)%n1)
2
3    template <typename Type>
4    void transpose(Type *f, ulong nr, ulong nc, bitarray *ba=0)
5    // In-place transposition of an  nr X nc  array
6    //    that lies in contiguous memory.
7    {
8        if ( 1>=nr )  return;
9        if ( 1>=nc )  return;
10
11       if ( nr==nc )  transpose_square(f, nr);
12       else
13       {
14           const ulong n1 = nr * nc - 1;
15
16           bitarray *tba = 0;
17           if ( 0==ba )  tba = new bitarray(n1);
18           else          tba = ba;
19           tba->clear_all();
20
21           for (ulong k=1;  k<n1;  k=tba->next_clear(++k) )  // 0 and n1 are fixed points
22           {
23               // do a cycle:
24               ulong ks = SRC(k);
25               ulong kd = k;
26               tba->set(kd);
27               Type t = f[kd];
28               while ( ks != k )
29               {
30                   f[kd] = f[ks];
31                   kd = ks;
32                   tba->set(kd);
33                   ks = SRC(ks);
34               }
35               f[kd] = t;
36           }
37
38           if ( 0==ba )  delete tba;
39       }
40   }
```

One should take care of possible overflows in the calculation of $i \cdot n_c$. In case that n is a power of 2 (and so are both n_r and n_c) the multiplications modulo $n - 1$ are cyclic shifts. Thus any overflow can be avoided and the computation is also significantly cheaper. An implementation is given in [FXT: aux2/transpose2.h].

2.9   Rotation by triple reversal

To rotate a length-n array by s positions without using any temporary memory, reverse three times as in the following routine [FXT: perm/rotate.h]:

```
1    template <typename Type>
2    void rotate_left(Type *f, ulong n, ulong s)
```

```
Rotate left by 3 positions:
   [ 1 2 3 4 5 6 7 8 ]   original array
   [ 3 2 1 4 5 6 7 8 ]   reverse first 3 elements
   [ 3 2 1 8 7 6 5 4 ]   reverse last 8-3=5 elements
   [ 4 5 6 7 8 1 2 3 ]   reverse whole array

Rotate right by 3 positions:
   [ 1 2 3 4 5 6 7 8 ]   original array
   [ 5 4 3 2 1 6 7 8 ]   reverse first 8-3=5 elements
   [ 5 4 3 2 1 8 7 6 ]   reverse last 3 elements
   [ 6 7 8 1 2 3 4 5 ]   reverse whole array
```

Figure 2.9-A: Rotation of a length-8 array by 3 positions to the left (top) and right (bottom).

```
3    // Rotate towards element #0
4    // Shift is taken modulo n
5    {
6        if ( s>=n )
7        {
8            if (n<2) return;
9            s %= n;
10       }
11       if ( s==0 )  return;
12
13       reverse(f,    s);
14       reverse(f+s, n-s);
15       reverse(f,    n);
16   }
```

We will call this trick the *triple reversal technique*. For example, left-rotating an 8-element array by 3 positions is achieved by the steps shown in figure 2.9-A (top). A right rotation of an n-element array by s positions is identical to a left rotation by $n - s$ positions (bottom of figure 2.9-A):

```
1    template <typename Type>
2    void rotate_right(Type *f, ulong n, ulong s)
3    // Rotate away from element #0
4    // Shift is taken modulo n
5    {
6        if ( s>=n )
7        {
8            if (n<2) return;
9            s %= n;
10       }
11       if ( s==0 )  return;
12
13       reverse(f,      n-s);
14       reverse(f+n-s, s);
15       reverse(f,      n);
16   }
```

We could also execute the (self-inverse) steps of the left-shift routine in reversed order:

```
reverse(f,    n);
reverse(f+s, n-s);
reverse(f,    s);
```

```
               v v v v v     v v v v        <--= want to swap these blocks
   [ 0 1 2 3 4  a b c d e 7 8 w x y z  N N ]  original array
   [ 0 1 2 3 4  e d c b a 7 8 w x y z  N N ]  reverse first block
   [ 0 1 2 3 4  e d c b a 8 7 w x y z  N N ]  reverse range between blocks
   [ 0 1 2 3 4  e d c b a 8 7 z y x w  N N ]  reverse second block
   [ 0 1 2 3 4  w x y z 7 8 a b c d e  N N ]  reverse whole range
               ^ ^ ^ ^     ^ ^ ^ ^ ^        <--= the swapped blocks
```

Figure 2.9-B: Swapping the blocks [a b c d e] and [w x y z] via 4 reversals.

The triple reversal trick can also be used to swap two blocks in an array: first reverse the three ranges (first blocks, range between blocks, last block), then reverse the range that consists of all three. We will call this trick the *quadruple reversal technique*. The corresponding code is given in [FXT: perm/swapblocks.h]:

```
1    template <typename Type>
2    void swap_blocks(Type *f, ulong x1, ulong n1, ulong x2, ulong n2)
3    // Swap the blocks starting at indices x1 and x2
4    // n1 and n2 are the block lengths
5    {
6        if ( x1>x2 ) { swap2(x1,x2); swap2(n1,n2); }
7        f += x1;
8        x2 -= x1;
9        ulong n = x2 + n2;
10       reverse(f, n1);
11       reverse(f+n1, n-n1-n2);
12       reverse(f+x2, n2);
13       reverse(f, n);
14   }
```

The elements before x1 and after x2+n2 are not accessed. An example is shown in figure 2.9-B. The listing was created with the program [FXT: perm/swap-blocks-demo.cc].

A routine to undo the effect of swap_blocks(f, x1, n1, x2, n2) can be obtained by reversing the order of the steps:

```
1    template <typename Type>
2    void inverse_swap_blocks(Type *f, ulong x1, ulong n1, ulong x2, ulong n2)
3    {
4        if ( x1>x2 ) { swap2(x1,x2); swap2(n1,n2); }
5        f += x1;
6        x2 -= x1;
7        ulong n = x2 + n2;
8        reverse(f, n);
9        reverse(f+x2, n2);
10       reverse(f+n1, n-n1-n2);
11       reverse(f, n1);
12   }
```

An alternative method is to call swap_blocks(f, x1, n2, x2+n2-n1, n1).

2.10 The zip permutation

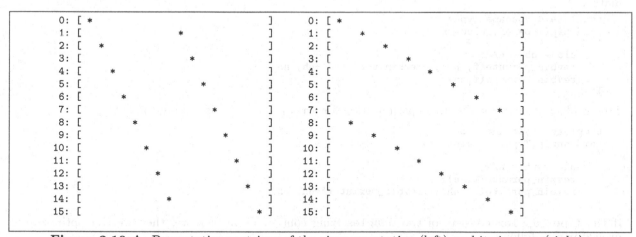

Figure 2.10-A: Permutation matrices of the zip permutation (left) and its inverse (right).

The *zip permutation* moves the elements from the lower half to the even indices and the elements from the upper half to the odd indices. Symbolically,

```
[ a b c d A B C D ]  |--[>a A b B c C d D ]
```

The size of the array must be even. A routine for the permutation is [FXT: perm/zip.h]

```
1    template <typename Type>
2    void zip(const Type * restrict f, Type * restrict g, ulong n)
3    {
4        ulong nh = n/2;
5        for (ulong k=0,  k2=0;  k<nh;  ++k, k2+=2)  g[k2] = f[k];
```

```
6        for (ulong k=nh, k2=1;  k<n;    ++k, k2+=2)  g[k2] = f[k];
7    }
```

The inverse of the zip permutation is the *unzip permutation*, it moves the even indices to the lower half and the odd indices to the upper half:

```
1    template <typename Type>
2    void unzip(const Type * restrict f, Type * restrict g, ulong n)
3    {
4        ulong nh = n/2;
5        for (ulong k=0,  k2=0;   k<nh;  ++k, k2+=2)  g[k] = f[k2];
6        for (ulong k=nh, k2=1;   k<n;   ++k, k2+=2)  g[k] = f[k2];
7    }
```

```
 0: [ *                      ]    0: [ *                      ]
 1: [          *             ]    1: [                 *      ]
 2: [     *                  ]    2: [         *              ]
 3: [               *        ]    3: [                  *     ]
 4: [   *                    ]    4: [      *                 ]
 5: [            *           ]    5: [                *       ]
 6: [       *                ]    6: [           *            ]
 7: [              *         ]    7: [                    *   ]
 8: [               *        ]    8: [  *                     ]
 9: [                *       ]    9: [              *         ]
10: [          *             ]   10: [          *             ]
11: [               *        ]   11: [                 *      ]
12: [          *             ]   12: [       *                ]
13: [             *          ]   13: [              *         ]
14: [           *            ]   14: [          *             ]
15: [                *  ]        15: [                  *  ]
```

Figure 2.10-B: Revbin permutation matrices that, when multiplied together, give the zip permutation and its inverse. Let L and R be the permutations given on the left and right side, respectively. Then $Z = R\,L$ and $Z^{-1} = L\,R$.

If the array size n is a power of 2, we can compute the zip permutation as a transposition of a $2 \times n/2$-matrix:

```
1    template <typename Type>
2    void zip(Type *f, ulong n)
3    {
4        ulong nh = n/2;
5        revbin_permute(f, nh);  revbin_permute(f+nh, nh);
6        revbin_permute(f, n);
7    }
```

The in-place version for the unzip permutation for arrays whose size is a power of 2 is

```
1    template <typename Type>
2    void unzip(Type *f, ulong n)
3    {
4        ulong nh = n/2;
5        revbin_permute(f, n);
6        revbin_permute(f, nh);  revbin_permute(f+nh, nh);
7    }
```

If the type Complex consists of two doubles lying contiguous in memory, then we can optimize the procedures as follows:

```
1    void zip(double *f, long n)
2    {
3        revbin_permute(f, n);
4        revbin_permute((Complex *)f, n/2);
5    }
```

```
1    void unzip(double *f, long n)
2    {
3        revbin_permute((Complex *)f, n/2);
4        revbin_permute(f, n);
5    }
```

For arrays whose size n is not a power of 2 the in-place zip permutation can be computed by transposing the data as a $2 \times n/2$ matrix:

```
transpose(f, 2, n/2);   // =^= zip(f, n)
```

The routines for in-place transposition are given in section 2.8 on page 122. The inverse is computed by transposing the data as an $n/2 \times 2$ matrix:

```
transpose(f, n/2, 2);   // =^= unzip(f, n)
```

While the above mentioned technique is usually *not* a gain for doing a transposition it may be used to speed up the revbin permutation itself.

2.11 The XOR permutation

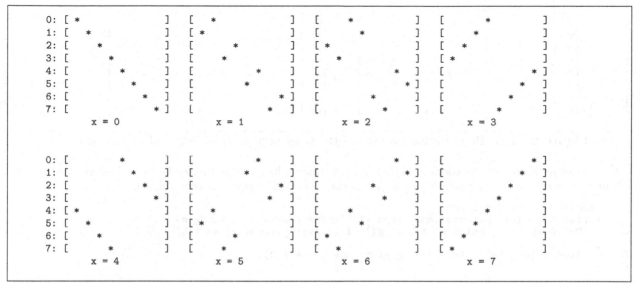

Figure 2.11-A: Permutation matrices of the XOR permutation for length 8 with parameter $x = 0 \ldots 7$. Compare to the table for the dyadic convolution shown in figure 23.8-A on page 481.

The *XOR permutation* (with parameter x) swaps the element at index k with the element at index x XOR k (see figure 2.11 A). The implementation is easy [FXT: perm/xorpermute.h]:

```
1   template <typename Type>
2   void xor_permute(Type *f, ulong n, ulong x)
3   {
4       if ( 0==x )  return;
5       for (ulong k=0; k<n; ++k)
6       {
7           ulong r = k^x;
8           if ( r>k )  swap2(f[r], f[k]);
9       }
10  }
```

The XOR permutation is clearly self-inverse. The array length n must be divisible by the smallest power of 2 that is greater than x. For example, n must be even if $x = 1$ and n must be divisible by 4 if $x = 2$ or $x = 3$. With n a power of 2 and $x < n$ one is on the safe side.

The XOR permutation contains a few other permutations as important special cases (for simplicity assume that the array length n is a power of 2): If the third argument x equals $n - 1$, the permutation is the reversal. With $x = 1$ neighboring even and odd indexed elements are swapped. With $x = n/2$ the upper and the lower half of the array are swapped.

We have

$$X_a X_b = X_b X_a = X_c \quad \text{where} \quad c = a \text{ XOR } b \qquad (2.11\text{-}1)$$

For the special case $a = b$ the relation does express the self-inverse property as X_0 is the identity. The XOR permutation occurs in relations between other permutations where we will use the symbol X_a, the subscript a denoting the third argument in the given routine.

2.12   The Gray permutation

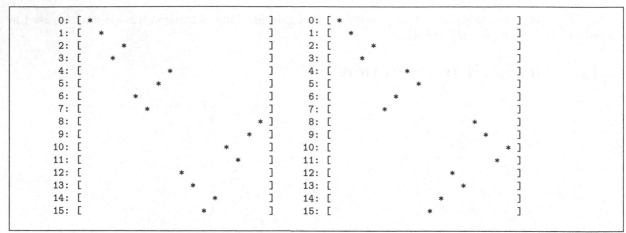

Figure 2.12-A: Permutation matrices of the Gray permutation (left) and its inverse (right).

The *Gray permutation* reorders (length-2^n) arrays according to the binary Gray code described in section 1.16 on page 41. A routine for the permutation is [FXT: perm/graypermute.h]:

```
1    template <typename Type>
2    inline void gray_permute(const Type *f, Type * restrict g, ulong n)
3    // Put Gray permutation of f[] to g[], i.e. g[gray_code(k)] == f[k]
4    {
5        for (ulong k=0; k<n; ++k)  g[gray_code(k)] = f[k];
6    }
```

Its inverse is

```
1    template <typename Type>
2    inline void inverse_gray_permute(const Type *f, Type * restrict g, ulong n)
3    // Put inverse Gray permutation of f[] to g[], i.e. g[k] == f[gray_code(k)]
4    // (same as: g[inverse_gray_code(k)] == f[k])
5    {
6        for (ulong k=0; k<n; ++k)  g[k] = f[gray_code(k)];
7    }
```

We again use calls to the routine to compute the Gray code because they are cheaper than the computations of the inverse Gray code.

2.12.1   Cycles of the permutation

We want to create in-place versions of the Gray permutation routines. It is necessary to identify the cycle leaders of the permutation (see section 2.2 on page 104) and find an efficient way to generate them.

It is instructive to study the complementary masks that occur for cycles of different lengths. The cycles of the Gray permutation for length 128 are shown in figure 2.12-B. No structure is immediately visible. However, we can generate the cycle maxima as follows: for each range $2^k \ldots 2^{k+1} - 1$ generate a bit-mask z that consists of the $k + 1$ leftmost bits of the infinite word that has ones at positions $0, 1, 2, 4, 8, \ldots, 2^i, \ldots$:

$$[1110100010000000100000000000000001000\ldots]$$

An example: for $k = 6$ we have $z = [1110100]$. Then take v to be $k + 1$ leftmost bits of the complement, $v = [0001011]$ in our example. Now the set of words $c = z + s$ where s is a subset of v contains exactly one element of each cycle in the range $2^k \ldots 2^{k+1} - 1 = 64 \ldots 127$, indeed the maximum of the cycle:

```
         cycle      #=length                          cycle-min  cycle-max

  0:  (  2,   3 ) #=2                                      2          3

  1:  (  4,   7,   5,   6 ) #=4                            4          7

  2:  (  8,  15,  10,  12 ) #=4                            8         15
  3:  (  9,  14,  11,  13 ) #=4                            9         14

  4:  ( 16,  31,  21,  25,  17,  30,  20,  24 ) #=8      16         31
  5:  ( 18,  28,  23,  26,  19,  29,  22,  27 ) #=8      18         29

  6:  ( 32,  63,  42,  51,  34,  60,  40,  48 ) #=8      32         63
  7:  ( 33,  62,  43,  50,  35,  61,  41,  49 ) #=8      33         62
  8:  ( 36,  56,  47,  53,  38,  59,  45,  54 ) #=8      36         59
  9:  ( 37,  57,  46,  52,  39,  58,  44,  55 ) #=8      37         58

 10:  ( 64,127,  85,102,  68,120,  80,  96 ) #=8         64        127
 11:  ( 65,126,  84,103,  69,121,  81,  97 ) #=8         65        126
 12:  ( 66,124,  87,101,  70,123,  82,  99 ) #=8         66        124
 13:  ( 67,125,  86,100,  71,122,  83,  98 ) #=8         67        125
 14:  ( 72,112,  95,106,  76,119,  90,108 ) #=8          72        119
 15:  ( 73,113,  94,107,  77,118,  91,109 ) #=8          73        118
 16:  ( 74,115,  93,105,  78,116,  88,111 ) #=8          74        116
 17:  ( 75,114,  92,104,  79,117,  89,110 ) #=8          75        117
126 elements in  18 nontrivial cycles.
cycle lengths:   2 ... 8;    2 fixed points: [0. 1]
```

Figure 2.12-B: Cycles of the Gray permutation of length 128.

```
.111.1.. = 116
.111.1.1 = 117
.111.11. = 118
.111.111 = 119
.11111.. = 124
.11111.1 = 125
.1111111 = 126
.1111111 = 127
maxima := z XOR subsets(v)  where  z = .111.1..  and  v = ....1.11
```

The sequence of cycle maxima is entry A175339 in [312]. The minima (entry A175338) of the cycles can be computed similarly:

```
.1......  = 64
.1.....1  = 65
.1....1.  = 66
.1....11  = 67
.1...1..  = 72
.1...1.1  = 73
.1...11.  = 74
.1...1.11 = 75
minima := z XOR subsets(v)  where  z = .1......  and  v = ....1.11
```

The list can be generated with the program [FXT: perm/permgray-leaders-demo.cc] which uses the routine [FXT: class gray_cycle_leaders in comb/gray-cycle-leaders.h]:

```
1   class gray_cycle_leaders
2   // Generate cycle leaders for Gray permutation
3   // where highest bit is at position ldn.
4   {
5   public:
6       bit_subset b_;
7       ulong za_;  // mask for cycle maxima
8       ulong zi_;  // mask for cycle minima
9       ulong len_; // cycle length
10      ulong num_; // number of cycles
11
12  public:
13      gray_cycle_leaders(ulong ldn)   // 0<=ldn<BITS_PER_LONG
14          : b_(0)
15      { init(ldn); }
16
17      ~gray_cycle_leaders() {;}
18
19      void init(ulong ldn)
20      {
21          za_ = 1;
22          ulong cz = 0;    // ~z
23          len_ = 1;
24          num_ = 1;
25          for (ulong ldm=1; ldm<=ldn; ++ldm)
```

```
26        {
27            za_ <<= 1;
28            cz <<= 1;
29            if ( is_pow_of_2(ldm) )
30            {
31                ++za_;
32                len_ <<= 1;
33            }
34            else
35            {
36                ++cz;
37                num_ <<= 1;
38            }
39        }
40
41        zi_ = 1UL << ldn;
42
43        b_.first(cz);
44    }
45
46    ulong current_max()  const  { return b_.current() | za_; }
47    ulong current_min()  const  { return b_.current() | zi_; }
48
49    bool next()  { return ( 0!=b_.next() ); }
50
51    ulong num_cycles()  const  { return num_; }
52    ulong cycle_length()  const  { return len_; }
53  };
```

The implementation uses the class for subsets of a bitset described in section 1.25 on page 68.

2.12.2 In-place routines

The in-place versions of the permutation routines are obtained by inlining the generation of the cycle
leaders. The forward version is [FXT: perm/graypermute.h]:

```
1   template <typename Type>
2   void gray_permute(Type *f, ulong n)
3   {
4       ulong z = 1; // mask for cycle maxima
5       ulong v = 0; // ~z
6       ulong cl = 1;  // cycle length
7       for (ulong ldm=1, m=2;  m<n;  ++ldm, m<<=1)
8       {
9           z <<= 1;
10          v <<= 1;
11          if ( is_pow_of_2(ldm) )
12          {
13              ++z;
14              cl <<= 1;
15          }
16          else  ++v;
17
18          bit_subset b(v);
19          do
20          {
21              // --- do cycle: ---
22              ulong i = z | b.next();  // start of cycle
23              Type t = f[i];            // save start value
24              ulong g = gray_code(i);   // next in cycle
25              for (ulong k=cl-1; k!=0; --k)
26              {
27                  Type tt = f[g];
28                  f[g] = t;
29                  t = tt;
30                  g = gray_code(g);
31              }
32              f[g] = t;
33              // --- end (do cycle) ---
34          }
35          while ( b.current() );
36      }
37  }
```

The function `is_pow_of_2()` is described in section 1.7 on page 17. The inverse routine differs only in
the block that processes the cycles:

```
1    template <typename Type>
2    void inverse_gray_permute(Type *f, ulong n)
3    {
4        [--snip--]
5                // --- do cycle: ---
6                ulong i = z | b.next();   // start of cycle
7                Type t = f[i];            // save start value
8                ulong g = gray_code(i);   // next in cycle
9                for (ulong k=cl-1; k!=0; --k)
10               {
11                   f[i] = f[g];
12                   i = g;
13                   g = gray_code(i);
14               }
15               f[i] = t;
16               // --- end (do cycle) ---
17       [--snip--]
18   }
```

The Gray permutation is used with certain Walsh transforms, see section 23.7 on page 474.

2.12.3 Performance of the routines

We use the convention that the time for an array reversal is 1.0. The operation is completely cache-friendly and therefore fast. A simple benchmark gives for 16 MB arrays:

```
arg 1: 21 == ldn  [Using 2**ldn elements]  default=21
arg 2: 10 == rep  [Number of repetitions]  default=10
Memsize = 16384 kiloByte  ==  2097152 doubles
                     reverse(f,n);     dt=  0.0103524   MB/s= 1546   rel=         1
                revbin_permute(f,n);   dt=  0.0674235   MB/s=  237   rel=   6.51282
               revbin_permute0(f,n);   dt=   0.061507   MB/s=  260   rel=   5.94131
                  gray_permute(f,n);   dt=  0.0155019   MB/s= 1032   rel=   1.49742
          inverse_gray_permute(f,n);   dt=  0.0150641   MB/s= 1062   rel=   1.45512
```

The revbin permutation takes about 6.5 units, due to its memory access pattern that is very problematic with respect to cache usage. The Gray permutation needs only 1.50 units. The difference gets bigger for machines with relatively slow memory with respect to the CPU.

The relative speeds are quite different for small arrays. With 16 kB (2048 doubles) we obtain

```
arg 1: 11 == ldn  [Using 2**ldn elements]  default=21
arg 2: 100000 == rep  [Number of repetitions]  default=512
Memsize = 16 kiloByte  ==  2048 doubles
                     reverse(f,n);     dt=1.88726e-06   MB/s= 8279   rel=         1
                revbin_permute(f,n);   dt=3.22166e-06   MB/s= 4850   rel=   1.70706
               revbin_permute0(f,n);   dt=2.69212e-06   MB/s= 5804   rel=   1.42647
                  gray_permute(f,n);   dt=4.75155e-06   MB/s= 3288   rel=   2.51769
          inverse_gray_permute(f,n);   dt=3.69237e-06   MB/s= 4232   rel=   1.95647
```

Due to the small size, the cache problems are gone.

2.13 The reversed Gray permutation

The *reversed Gray permutation* of a length-n array is computed by permuting the elements in the way that the Gray permutation would permute the upper half of an array of length $2n$. The array size n must be a power of 2. An implementation is [FXT: perm/grayrevpermute.h]:

```
1    template <typename Type>
2    inline void gray_rev_permute(const Type *f, Type * restrict g, ulong n)
3    // gray_rev_permute() =^=
4    //   { reverse(); gray_permute(); }
5    {
6        for (ulong k=0, m=n-1;  k<n;  ++k, --m)  g[gray_code(m)] = f[k];
7    }
```

All cycles have the same length, the cycles with $n = 64$ elements are

```
 0: [                              * ]      0: [                    *                ]
 1: [                            *   ]      1: [                  *                  ]
 2: [                        *       ]      2: [                *                    ]
 3: [                      *         ]      3: [              *                      ]
 4: [              *                 ]      4: [                          *   ]      
 5: [              *                 ]      5: [                          *     ]      
 6: [                *               ]      6: [                        *       ]      
 7: [                *               ]      7: [                      *         ]      
 8: [ *                              ]      8: [            *                    ]      
 9: [   *                            ]      9: [          *                      ]      
10: [     *                          ]     10: [          *                      ]      
11: [     *                          ]     11: [          *                      ]      
12: [         *                      ]     12: [    *                            ]      
13: [         *                      ]     13: [      *                          ]      
14: [       *                        ]     14: [  *                              ]      
15: [           *                    ]     15: [ *                               ]      
```

Figure 2.13-A: Permutation matrices of the reversed Gray permutation (left) and its inverse (right).

```
0:  (  0, 63, 21, 38,   4, 56, 16, 32) #=8
1:  (  1, 62, 20, 39,   5, 57, 17, 33) #=8
2:  (  2, 60, 23, 37,   6, 59, 18, 35) #=8
3:  (  3, 61, 22, 36,   7, 58, 19, 34) #=8
4:  (  8, 48, 31, 42,  12, 55, 26, 44) #=8
5:  (  9, 49, 30, 43,  13, 54, 27, 45) #=8
6:  ( 10, 51, 29, 41,  14, 52, 24, 47) #=8
7:  ( 11, 50, 28, 40,  15, 53, 25, 46) #=8
64 elements in   8 nontrivial cycles.
cycle length is == 8
No fixed points.
```

If 64 is added to the indices, the cycles in the upper half of the array as in `gray_permute(f, 128)` are reproduced. The in-place version of the permutation routine is

```cpp
1    template <typename Type>
2    void gray_rev_permute(Type *f, ulong n)
3    // n must be a power of 2, n<=2**(BITS_PER_LONG-2)
4    {
5        f -= n;  // note!
6
7        ulong z = 1; // mask for cycle maxima
8        ulong v = 0; // ~z
9        ulong cl = 1;  // cycle length
10       ulong ldm, m;
11       for (ldm=1, m=2;  m<=n;  ++ldm, m<<=1)
12       {
13           z <<= 1;  v <<= 1;
14           if ( is_pow_of_2(ldm) )  { ++z;  cl<<=1; }
15           else   ++v;
16       }
17
18       ulong tv = v, tu = 0;  // cf. bitsubset.h
19       do
20       {
21           tu = (tu-tv) & tv;
22           ulong i = z | tu;  // start of cycle
23
24           // --- do cycle: ---
25           ulong g = gray_code(i);
26           Type t = f[i];
27           for (ulong k=cl-1; k!=0; --k)
28           {
29               Type tt = f[g];
30               f[g] = t;
31               t = tt;
32               g = gray_code(g);
33           }
34           f[g] = t;
35           // --- end (do cycle) ---
36       }
37       while ( tu );
```

38   }

The routine for the inverse permutation again differs only in the way the cycles are processed:

```
1    template <typename Type>
2    void inverse_gray_rev_permute(Type *f, ulong n)
3    {
4       [--snip--]
5            // --- do cycle: ---
6            Type t = f[i];            // save start value
7            ulong g = gray_code(i);   // next in cycle
8            for (ulong k=cl-1; k!=0; --k)
9            {
10               f[i] = f[g];
11               i = g;
12               g = gray_code(i);
13           }
14           f[i] = t;
15           // --- end (do cycle) ---
16      [--snip--]
17   }
```

Let G denote the Gray permutation, $\overline{G}$ the reversed Gray permutation, r be the reversal, h the swap of the upper and lower halves, and X_a the XOR permutation (with parameter a) from section 2.11 on page 127. We have

$$\overline{G} \;=\; G\,r \;=\; h\,G \tag{2.13-1a}$$

$$\overline{G}^{-1} \;=\; r\,G^{-1} \tag{2.13-1b}$$

$$\overline{G}^{-1}G \;=\; G^{-1}\overline{G} \;=\; r \;=\; X_{n-1} \tag{2.13-1c}$$

$$G\,\overline{G}^{-1} \;=\; \overline{G}\,G^{-1} \;=\; h \;=\; X_{n/2} \tag{2.13-1d}$$

Chapter 3

Sorting and searching

We give various sorting algorithms and some practical variants of them, like sorting index arrays and pointer sorting. Searching methods both for sorted and for unsorted arrays are described. Finally we give methods for the determination of equivalence classes.

3.1 Sorting algorithms

We give sorting algorithms like selection sort, quicksort, merge sort, counting sort and radix sort. A massive amount of literature exists about the topic so we will not explore the details. Very readable texts are [115] and [306], while in-depth information can be found in [214].

3.1.1 Selection sort

```
[ n o w s o r t m e ]
[ e o w s o r t m n ]
[   m w s o r t o n ]
[     n s o r t o w ]
[       o o r t s w ]
[         o r t s w ]
[           r t s w ]
[             s t w ]
[               t w ]
[                 w ]
[ e m n o o r s t w ]
```

Figure 3.1-A: Sorting the string 'nowsortme' with the selection sort algorithm.

There are a several algorithms for sorting that have complexity $O\left(n^2\right)$ where n is the size of the array to be sorted. Here we use *selection sort*, where the idea is to find the minimum of the array, swap it with the first element, and repeat for all elements but the first. A demonstration of the algorithm is shown in figure 3.1-A, this is the output of [FXT: sort/selection-sort-demo.cc]. The implementation is straightforward [FXT: sort/sort.h]:

```
1    template <typename Type>
2    void selection_sort(Type *f, ulong n)
3    // Sort f[] (ascending order).
4    // Algorithm is O(n*n), use for short arrays only.
5    {
6        for (ulong i=0; i<n; ++i)
7        {
8            Type v = f[i];
9            ulong m = i; // position of minimum
10           ulong j = n;
11           while ( --j > i )  // search (index of) minimum
12           {
13               if ( f[j]<v )
14               {
15                   m = j;
16                   v = f[m];
17               }
18           }
```

J. Arndt, *Matters Computational: Ideas, Algorithms, Source Code*,
DOI 10.1007/978-3-642-14764-7_3, © Springer-Verlag Berlin Heidelberg 2011

```
19
20          swap2(f[i], f[m]);
21      }
22  }
```

A verification routine is always handy:

```
1   template <typename Type>
2   bool is_sorted(const Type *f, ulong n)
3   // Return whether the sequence f[0], f[1], ..., f[n-1] is ascending.
4   {
5       for (ulong k=1; k<n; ++k)  if ( f[k-1] > f[k] )  return false;
6       return  true;
7   }
```

A test for descending order is

```
1   template <typename Type>
2   bool is_falling(const Type *f, ulong n)
3   // Return whether the sequence f[0], f[1], ..., f[n-1] is descending.
4   {
5       for (ulong k=1; k<n; ++k)  if ( f[k-1] < f[k] )  return false;
6       return  true;
7   }
```

3.1.2 Quicksort

The *quicksort* algorithm is given in [183], it has complexity $O(n \log(n))$ (in the average case). It does not obsolete the simpler schemes, because for small arrays the simpler algorithms are usually faster, due to their minimal bookkeeping overhead.

The main activity of quicksort is *partitioning* the array. The corresponding routine reorders the array and returns a *pivot* index p so that $\max(f_0, \ldots, f_{p-1}) \le \min(f_p, \ldots, f_{n-1})$ [FXT: sort/sort.h]:

```
1   template <typename Type>
2   ulong partition(Type *f, ulong n)
3   {
4       // Avoid worst case with already sorted input:
5       const Type v = median3(f[0], f[n/2], f[n-1]);
6
7       ulong i = 0UL - 1;
8       ulong j = n;
9       while ( 1 )
10      {
11          do  { ++i; }  while ( f[i]<v );
12          do  { --j; }  while ( f[j]>v );
13
14          if ( i<j )  swap2(f[i], f[j]);
15          else        return j;
16      }
17  }
```

The function `median3()` is defined in [FXT: sort/minmaxmed23.h]:

```
1   template <typename Type>
2   static inline Type median3(const Type &x, const Type &y, const Type &z)
3   // Return median of the input values
4   { return  x<y ? (y<z ? y : (x<z ? z : x)) : (z<y ? y : (z<x ? z : x)); }
```

The function does 2 or 3 comparisons, depending on the input. One could simply use the element `f[0]` as pivot. However, the algorithm will need $O(n^2)$ operations when the array is already sorted.

Quicksort calls `partition` on the whole array, then on the two parts left and right from the partition index, then for the four, eight, etc. parts, until the parts are of length one. Note that the sub-arrays are usually of different lengths.

```
1   template <typename Type>
2   void quick_sort(Type *f, ulong n)
3   {
4       if ( n<=1 )  return;
5
6       ulong p = partition(f, n);
7       ulong ln = p + 1;
8       ulong rn = n - ln;
```

```
9       quick_sort(f, ln);   // f[0]   ... f[ln-1]  left
10      quick_sort(f+ln, rn);  // f[ln] ... f[n-1]   right
11   }
```

The actual implementation uses two optimizations: Firstly, if the number of elements to be sorted is less than a certain threshold, selection sort is used. Secondly, the recursive calls are made for the smaller of the two sub-arrays, thereby the stack size is bounded by $\lceil \log_2(n) \rceil$.

```
1    template <typename Type>
2    void quick_sort(Type *f, ulong n)
3    {
4      start:
5          if ( n<8 ) // parameter: threshold for nonrecursive algorithm
6          {
7              selection_sort(f, n);
8              return;
9          }
10
11         ulong p = partition(f, n);
12         ulong ln = p + 1;
13         ulong rn = n - ln;
14
15         if ( ln>rn )  // recursion for shorter sub-array
16         {
17              quick_sort(f+ln, rn);  // f[ln] ... f[n-1]   right
18              n = ln;
19         }
20         else
21         {
22              quick_sort(f, ln);  // f[0]   ... f[ln-1]  left
23              n = rn;
24              f += ln;
25         }
26
27         goto start;
28   }
```

The quicksort algorithm *will* be quadratic with certain inputs. A clever method to construct such inputs is described in [247]. The *heapsort* algorithm is in-place and $O(n \log(n))$ (also in the worst case). It is described in section 3.1.5 on page 141. Inputs that lead to quadratic time for the quicksort algorithm with median-of-3 partitioning are described in [257]. The paper suggests to use quicksort, but to detect problematic behavior during runtime and switch to heapsort if needed. The corresponding algorithm is called *introsort* (for *introspective sorting*).

3.1.3   Counting sort and radix sort

We want to sort an n-element array F of (unsigned) 8-bit values. A sorting algorithm which involves only 2 passes through the data proceeds as follows:

1. Allocate an array C of 256 integers and set all its elements to zero.

2. Count: for $k = 0, 1, \ldots, n-1$ increment $C[F[k]]$.
    Now $C[x]$ contains the number of bytes in F with the value x.

3. Set $r = 0$. For $j = 0, 1, \ldots, 255$
    set $k = C[j]$, then set the elements $F[r], F[r+1], \ldots, F[r+k-1]$ to j, and add k to r.

For large values of n this method is significantly faster than any other sorting algorithm. Note that no comparisons are made between the elements of F. Instead they are counted, the algorithm is the *counting sort* algorithm.

It might seem that the idea applies only to very special cases but with a little care it can be used in more general situations. We modify the method so that we are able to sort also (unsigned) integer variables whose range of values would make the method impractical with respect to a subrange of the bits in each word. We need an array G that has as many elements as F:

1. Choose any consecutive run of b bits, these will be represented by a bit mask m. Allocate an array C of 2^b integers and set all its elements to zero.

2. Let M be a function that maps the (2^b) values of interest (the bits masked out by m) to the range $0, 1, \ldots, 2^b - 1$.

3. Count: for $k = 0, 1, \ldots, n-1$ increment $C[M(F[k])]$.
   Now $C[x]$ contains how many values of $M(F[.])$ equal x.

4. Cumulate: for $j = 1, 2, \ldots, 2^b - 1$ (second to last) add $C[j-1]$ to $C[j]$.
   Now $C[x]$ contains the number of values $M(F[.])$ less than or equal to x.

5. Copy: for $k = n-1, \ldots, 2, 1, 0$ (last to first), do as follows:
   set $x := M(F[k])$, decrement $C[x]$, set $i := C[x]$, and set $G[i] := F[x]$.

A crucial property of the algorithm is that it is *stable*: if two (or more) elements compare equal (with respect to a certain bit-mask m), then the relative order between these elements is preserved.

```
Input                 Counting sort wrt. two lowest bits
                      m = .....11
0:   11111.11<        0:   ....11..
1:   ...1.1.1          1:   ..1111..
2:   ...1.1.1          2:   .111....
3:   ..1.1111<         3:   ..1.1.1
4:   ..1.1111<         4:   .1.1.1.1
5:   .1111..1          5:   .1...1.1
6:   .1.1.11.1         6:   11.1.11.
7:   .11.1..11<        7:   1111.111<
8:   .111...11<        8:   .1.1111<
9:   .111....          9:   .11...11<
```

The relative order of the three words ending with two set bits (marked with '<') is preserved.

A routine that verifies whether an array is sorted with respect to a bit range specified by the variable b0 and m is [FXT: sort/radixsort.cc]:

```
1   bool
2   is_counting_sorted(const ulong *f, ulong n, ulong b0, ulong m)
3   // Whether f[] is sorted wrt. bits b0,...,b0+z-1
4   //   where z is the number of bits set in m.
5   // m must contain a single run of bits starting at bit zero.
6   {
7       m <<= b0;
8       for (ulong k=1; k<n; ++k)
9       {
10          ulong xm = (f[k-1] & m ) >> b0;
11          ulong xp = (f[k] & m ) >> b0;
12          if ( xm>xp )  return false;
13      }
14      return true;
15  }
```

The function M is the combination of a mask-out and a shift operation. A routine that sorts according to b0 and m is:

```
1   void
2   counting_sort_core(const ulong * restrict f, ulong n, ulong * restrict g, ulong b0, ulong m)
3   // Write to g[] the array f[] sorted wrt. bits b0,...,b0+z-1
4   //   where z is the number of bits set in m.
5   // m must contain a single run of bits starting at bit zero.
6   {
7       ulong nb = m + 1;
8       m <<= b0;
9       ALLOCA(ulong, cv, nb);
10      for (ulong k=0; k<nb; ++k)  cv[k] = 0;
11
12      // --- count:
13      for (ulong k=0; k<n; ++k)
14      {
15          ulong x = (f[k] & m ) >> b0;
16          ++cv[ x ];
17      }
18
19      // --- cumulative sums:
20      for (ulong k=1; k<nb; ++k)  cv[k] += cv[k-1];
21
22      // --- reorder:
23      ulong k = n;
24      while ( k-- )  // backwards ==> stable sort
25      {
```

```
26          ulong fk = f[k];
27          ulong x = (fk & m) >> b0;
28          --cv[x];
29          ulong i = cv[x];
30          g[i] = fk;
31      }
32  }
```

```
        Input        Stage 1      Stage 2      Stage 3
                     m = ....11   m = ..11..   m = 11....
                        vv           vv           vv
        111.11       ...1..       11....       ..1...
        ..1...       1111..       1...1.       ..1...1
        .1.1.1       11....       1...11       .1.1.1
        1...1.       .1.1.1       .1.1.1       .1.11.
        1.1111       ...1.1       .1.11.       1...1.
        1111..       1...1.       ...1..       1...11
        ..1...1      .1.11.       ...1...1     1.1111
        .1.11.       111.11       111.11       111.11
        1...11       1.1111       1111..       111..11
        11....       1...11       1.1111       1111..
```

Figure 3.1-B: Radix sort of 10 six-bit values when using two-bit masks.

Now we can apply counting sort to a set of bit masks that cover the whole range. Figure 3.1-B shows an example with 10 six-bit values and 3 two-bit masks, starting from the least significant bits. This is the output of the program [FXT: sort/radixsort-demo.cc].

The following routine uses 8-bit masks to sort unsigned integers [FXT: sort/radixsort.cc]:

```
1   void
2   radix_sort(ulong *f, ulong n)
3   {
4       ulong nb = 8;   // Number of bits sorted with each step
5       ulong tnb = BITS_PER_LONG; // Total number of bits
6
7       ulong *fi = f;
8       ulong *g = new ulong[n];
9
10      ulong m = (1UL<<nb) - 1;
11      for (ulong k=1, b0=0;  b0<tnb;  ++k, b0+=nb)
12      {
13          counting_sort_core(f, n, g, b0, m);
14          swap2(f, g);
15      }
16
17      if ( f!=fi )  // result is actually in g[]
18      {
19          swap2(f, g);
20          for (ulong k=0; k<n; ++k)  f[k] = g[k];
21      }
22
23      delete [] g;
24  }
```

There is room for optimization. Combining copying with counting for the next pass (where possible) would reduce the number of passes almost by a factor of 2.

A version of radix sort that starts from the most significant bits is given in [306].

3.1.4 Merge sort

The *merge sort* algorithm is a method for sorting with complexity $O(n \log(n))$. We need a routine that copies two sorted arrays A and B into an array T such that T is in sorted order. The following implementation requires that A and B are adjacent in memory [FXT: sort/merge-sort.h]:

```
1   template  <typename Type>
2   void merge(Type * const restrict f, ulong na, ulong nb, Type * const restrict t)
3   // Merge the (sorted) arrays
4   //   A[] := f[0], f[1], ..., f[na-1]  and  B[] := f[na], f[na+1], ..., f[na+nb-1]
5   // into  t[] := t[0], t[1], ..., t[na+nb-1]  such that t[] is sorted.
6   // Must have: na>0 and nb>0
```

```
[ n o w s o r t m e A D B A C D 5 4 3 2 1 ]
[ n o o s w                                 ]
[             A e m r t                      ]
[ A e m n o o r s t w                        ]

[                       A B C D D            ]
[                               1 2 3 4 5    ]
[                       1 2 3 4 5 A B C D D  ]

[ A e m n o o r s t w                        ]
[                       1 2 3 4 5 A B C D D  ]
[ 1 2 3 4 5 A A B C D D e m n o o r s t w    ]
```

Figure 3.1-C: Sorting with the merge sort algorithm.

```
 7    {
 8        const Type * const A = f;
 9        const Type * const B = f + na;
10        ulong nt = na + nb;
11        Type ta = A[--na],  tb = B[--nb];
12
13        while ( true )
14        {
15            if ( ta > tb )  // copy ta
16            {
17                t[--nt] = ta;
18                if ( na==0 )  // A[] empty?
19                {
20                    for (ulong j=0; j<=nb; ++j)  t[j] = B[j];  // copy rest of B[]
21                    return;
22                }
23
24                ta = A[--na];  // read next element of A[]
25            }
26            else  // copy tb
27            {
28                t[--nt] = tb;
29                if ( nb==0 )  // B[] empty?
30                {
31                    for (ulong j=0; j<=na; ++j)  t[j] = A[j];  // copy rest of A[]
32                    return;
33                }
34
35                tb = B[--nb];  // read next element of B[]
36            }
37        }
38    }
```

Two branches are involved, the unavoidable branch with the comparison of the elements, and the test for empty array where an element has been removed.

We could sort by merging adjacent blocks of growing size as follows:

```
[ h g f e d c b a ]  // input
[ g h e f c d a b ]  // merge pairs
[ e f g h a b c d ]  // merge adjacent runs of two
[ a b c d e f g h ]  // merge adjacent runs of four
```

For a more localized memory access, we use a depth first recursion (compare with the binsplit recursion in section 34.1.1.1 on page 651):

```
 1    template <typename Type>
 2    void merge_sort_rec(Type *f, ulong n, Type *t)
 3    {
 4        if ( n<8 )
 5        {
 6            selection_sort(f, n);
 7            return;
 8        }
 9
10        const ulong na = n>>1;
11        const ulong nb = n - na;
12
```

```
13        // PRINT  f[0], f[1], ..., f[na-1]
14        merge_sort_rec(f, na, t);
15        // PRINT  f[na], f[na+1], ..., f[na+nb-1]
16        merge_sort_rec(f+na, nb, t);
17
18        merge(f, na, nb, t);
19        for (ulong j=0; j<n; ++j)  f[j] = t[j];     // copy back
20        // PRINT  f[0], f[1], ..., f[na+nb-1]
21    }
```

The comments PRINT indicate the print statements in the program [FXT: sort/merge-sort-demo.cc] that was used to generate figure 3.1-C. The method is (obviously) not in-place. The routine called by the user is

```
1    template <typename Type>
2    void merge_sort(Type *f, ulong n, Type *tmp=0)
3    {
4        Type *t = tmp;
5        if ( tmp==0 )  t = new Type[n];
6        merge_sort_rec(f, n, t);
7        if ( tmp==0 )  delete [] t;
8    }
```

Optimized algorithm

```
F :[ n o w s o r t m e A D B A C D 5 4 3 2 1 ]

F :[ n o o s w                                 ]
F :[           A e m r t                        ]
T :[ A e m n o o r s t w                        ]
F :[                     A B C D D              ]
F :[                                 1 2 3 4 5 ]
T :[                     1 2 3 4 5 A B C D D ]
F :[ 1 2 3 4 5 A A B C D D e m n o o r s t w ]
```

Figure 3.1-D: Sorting with the 4-way merge sort algorithm.

The copying from T to F in the recursive routine can be avoided by a 4-way splitting scheme. We sort the left two quarters and merge them into T, then we sort the right two quarters and merge them into $T + n_a$. Then we merge T and $T + n_a$ into F. Figure 3.1-D shows an example where only one recursive step is involved. It was generated with the program [FXT: sort/merge-sort4-demo.cc]. The recursive routine is [FXT: sort/merge-sort.h]

```
1    template <typename Type>
2    void merge_sort_rec4(Type *f, ulong n, Type *t)
3    {
4        if ( n<8 )  // threshold must be at least 8
5        {
6            selection_sort(f, n);
7            return;
8        }
9
10       // left and right half:
11       const ulong na = n>>1;
12       const ulong nb = n - na;
13
14       // left quarters:
15       const ulong na1 = na>>1;
16       const ulong na2 = na - na1;
17       merge_sort_rec4(f, na1, t);
18       merge_sort_rec4(f+na1, na2, t);
19
20       // right quarters:
21       const ulong nb1 = nb>>1;
22       const ulong nb2 = nb - nb1;
23       merge_sort_rec4(f+na, nb1, t);
24       merge_sort_rec4(f+na+nb1, nb2, t);
25
26       // merge quarters (F-->T):
27       merge(f, na1, na2, t);
28       merge(f+na, nb1, nb2, t+na);
29
```

```
30          // merge halves (T-->F):
31          merge(t, na, nb, f);
32      }
```

The routine called by the user is `merge_sort4()`.

3.1.5 Heapsort

The *heapsort* algorithm has complexity $O(n \log(n))$. It uses the heap data structure introduced in section 4.5.2 on page 160. A heap can be sorted by swapping the first (and biggest) element with the last and restoring the heap property for the array of size $n - 1$. Repeat until there is nothing more to sort [FXT: sort/heapsort.h]:

```
1   template <typename Type>
2   void heap_sort(Type *x, ulong n)
3   {
4       build_heap(x, n);
5       Type *p = x - 1;
6       for (ulong k=n; k>1; --k)
7       {
8           swap2(p[1], p[k]);  // move largest to end of array
9           --n;                // remaining array has one element less
10          heapify(p, n, 1);   // restore heap-property
11      }
12  }
```

Sorting into descending order is not any harder:

```
1   template <typename Type>
2   void heap_sort_descending(Type *x, ulong n)
3   // Sort x[] into descending order.
4   {
5       build_heap(x, n);
6       Type *p = x - 1;
7       for (ulong k=n; k>1; --k)
8       {
9           ++p;  --n;          // remaining array has one element less
10          heapify(p, n, 1);   // restore heap-property
11      }
12  }
```

A program that demonstrates the algorithm is [FXT: sort/heapsort-demo.cc].

3.2 Binary search

Searching for an element in a sorted array can be done in $O(\log(n))$ operations. The *binary search* algorithm uses repeated subdivision of the data [FXT: sort/bsearch.h]:

```
1
2   template <typename Type>
3   ulong bsearch(const Type *f, ulong n, const Type v)
4   // Return index of first element in f[] that equals v
5   // Return n if there is no such element.
6   // f[] must be sorted in ascending order.
7   // Must have  n!=0
8   {
9       ulong nlo=0, nhi=n-1;
10      while ( nlo != nhi )
11      {
12          ulong t = (nhi+nlo)/2;
13
14          if ( f[t] < v )  nlo = t + 1;
15          else             nhi = t;
16      }
17
18      if ( f[nhi]==v )  return nhi;
19      else              return n;
20  }
```

Only simple modifications are needed to search, for example, for the first element greater than or equal to a given value:

```
1    template <typename Type>
2    ulong bsearch_geq(const Type *f, ulong n, const Type v)
3    {
4        ulong nlo=0, nhi=n-1;
5        while ( nlo != nhi )
6        {
7            ulong t = (nhi+nlo)/2;
8
9            if ( f[t] < v )  nlo = t + 1;
10           else             nhi = t;
11       }
12
13       if ( f[nhi]>=v )  return nhi;
14       else              return n;
15   }
```

For very large arrays the algorithm can be improved by selecting the new index t different from the midpoint (nhi+nlo)/2, depending on the value sought and the distribution of the values in the array. As a simple example consider an array of floating-point numbers that are equally distributed in the interval $[\min(v), \max(v)]$. If the sought value equals v, one starts with the relation

$$\frac{n - \min(n)}{\max(n) - \min(n)} \;=\; \frac{v - \min(v)}{\max(v) - \min(v)} \tag{3.2-1}$$

where n denotes an index and $\min(n), \max(n)$ denote the minimal and maximal index of the current interval. Solving for n gives the linear interpolation formula

$$n \;=\; \min(n) + \frac{\max(n) - \min(n)}{\max(v) - \min(v)} \, (v - \min(v)) \tag{3.2-2}$$

The corresponding *interpolation binary search* algorithm would select the new subdivision index t according to the given relation. One could even use quadratic interpolation schemes for the selection of t. For the majority of practical applications the midpoint version of the binary search will be good enough.

Approximate matches are found by the following routine [FXT: sort/bsearchapprox.h]:

```
1    template <typename Type>
2    ulong bsearch_approx(const Type *f, ulong n, const Type v, Type da)
3    // Return index of first element x in f[] for which  |(x-v)| <= da
4    // Return n if there is no such element.
5    // f[] must be sorted in ascending order.
6    // da must be positive.
7    //
8    // Makes sense only with inexact types (float or double).
9    // Must have  n!=0
10   {
11       ulong k = bsearch_geq(f, n, v-da);
12       if ( k<n )  k = bsearch_leq(f+k, n-k, v+da);
13       return k;
14   }
```

3.3   Variants of sorting methods

Some practical variants of sorting algorithms are described, like sorting index arrays, pointer sorting, and sorting with a supplied comparison function.

3.3.1   Index sorting

With normal sorting we order the elements of an array f so that $f[k] \le f[k + 1]$. The *index-sort* routines order the indices in an array x so that the sequence $f[x[k]]$ is in ascending order, we have $f[x[k]] \le f[x[k + 1]]$. The implementation for the selection sort algorithm is [FXT: sort/sortidx.h]:

```
1    template <typename Type>
2    void idx_selection_sort(const Type *f, ulong n, ulong *x)
3    // Sort x[] so that the sequence f[x[0]], f[x[1]], ... f[x[n-1]] is ascending.
4    // Algorithm is O(n*n), use for short arrays only.
```

```
5    {
6        for (ulong i=0; i<n; ++i)
7        {
8            Type v = f[x[i]];
9            ulong m = i; // position-ptr of minimum
10           ulong j = n;
11           while ( --j > i )  // search (index of) minimum
12           {
13               if ( f[x[j]]<v )
14               {
15                   m = j;
16                   v = f[x[m]];
17               }
18           }
19
20           swap2(x[i], x[m]);
21       }
22   }
```

The verification code is

```
1    template  <typename Type>
2    bool is_idx_sorted(const Type *f, ulong n, const ulong *x)
3    // Return whether the sequence f[x[0]], f[x[1]], ... f[x[n-1]] is ascending order.
4    {
5        for (ulong k=1; k<n; ++k) if ( f[x[k-1]] > f[x[k]] ) return false;
6        return  true;
7    }
```

The transformation of the partition() routine is straightforward:

```
1    template <typename Type>
2    ulong idx_partition(const Type *f, ulong n, ulong *x)
3    // rearrange index array, so that for some index p
4    // max(f[x[0]] ... f[x[p]]) <= min(f[x[p+1]] ... f[x[n-1]])
5    {
6        // Avoid worst case with already sorted input:
7        const Type v = median3(*x[0], *x[n/2], *x[n-1], cmp);
8
9        ulong i = OUL - 1;
10       ulong j = n;
11       while ( 1 )
12       {
13           do  ++i;
14           while ( f[x[i]]<v );
15
16           do  --j;
17           while ( f[x[j]]>v );
18
19           if ( i<j )  swap2(x[i], x[j]);
20           else         return j;
21       }
22   }
```

The index-quicksort itself deserves a minute of contemplation comparing it to the plain version:

```
1    template <typename Type>
2    void idx_quick_sort(const Type *f, ulong n, ulong *x)
3    // Sort x[] so that the sequence f[x[0]], f[x[1]], ... f[x[n-1]] is ascending.
4    {
5    start:
6        if ( n<8 ) // parameter: threshold for nonrecursive algorithm
7        {
8            idx_selection_sort(f, n, x);
9            return;
10       }
11
12       ulong p = idx_partition(f, n, x);
13       ulong ln = p + 1;
14       ulong rn = n - ln;
15
16       if ( ln>rn )  // recursion for shorter sub-array
17       {
18           idx_quick_sort(f, rn, x+ln);  // f[x[ln]] ... f[x[n-1]]  right
19           n = ln;
20       }
21       else
22       {
```

```
23              idx_quick_sort(f, ln, x);  // f[x[0]]  ... f[x[ln-1]] left
24
25              n = rn;
26              x += ln;
27          }
28
29      goto start;
30  }
```

Note that the index-sort routines work perfectly for non-contiguous data. The index-analogues of the
binary search algorithms are again straightforward, they are given in [FXT: sort/bsearchidx.h].

The sorting routines do not change the array f, the actual data is not modified. To bring f into sorted
order, apply the *inverse* permutation of x to f (see section 2.4 on page 109):

```
apply_inverse_permutation(x, f, n);
```

To copy f in sorted order into g, use:

```
apply_inverse_permutation(x, f, n, g);
```

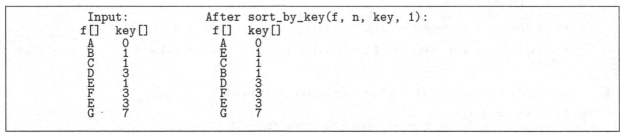

Figure 3.3-A: Sorting an array according to an array of keys.

The array x can be used for *sorting by keys*, see figure 3.3-A. The routine is [FXT: sort/sortbykey.h]:

```
1   template <typename Type1, typename Type2>
2   void sort_by_key(Type1 *f, ulong n, Type2 *key, bool skq=true)
3   // Sort f[] according to key[] in ascending order:
4   //   f[k] precedes f[j] if key[k]<key[j].
5   // If skq is true then key[] is also sorted.
6   {
7       ALLOCA(ulong, x, n);
8       for (ulong k=0; k<n; ++k)  x[k] = k;
9       idx_quick_sort(key, n, x);
10      apply_inverse_permutation(x, f, n);
11      if ( skq )  apply_inverse_permutation(x, key, n);
12  }
```

3.3.2 Pointer sorting

Pointer sorting is similar to index sorting. The array of indices is replaced by an array of pointers [FXT:
sort/sortptr.h]:

```
1   template <typename Type>
2   void ptr_selection_sort(/*const Type *f,*/ ulong n, const Type **x)
3   // Sort x[] so that the sequence *x[0], *x[1], ..., *x[n-1] is ascending.
4   {
5       for (ulong i=0; i<n; ++i)
6       {
7           Type v = *x[i];
8           ulong m = i; // position-ptr of minimum
9           ulong j = n;
10          while ( --j > i )  // search (index of) minimum
11          {
12              if ( *x[j]<v )
13              {
14                  m = j;
15                  v = *x[m];
16              }
17          }
18          swap2(x[i], x[m]);
```

```
19      }
20  }
```

The first argument (`const Type *f`) is not necessary with pointer sorting, it is indicated as a comment to make the argument structure uniform. The verification routine is

```
1  template <typename Type>
2  bool is_ptr_sorted(/*const Type *f,*/ ulong n, Type const*const*x)
3  // Return whether the sequence *x[0], *x[1], ..., *x[n-1] is ascending.
4  {
5      for (ulong k=1; k<n; ++k)  if ( *x[k-1] > *x[k] )  return false;
6      return true;
7  }
```

The pointer versions of the search routines are given in [FXT: sort/bsearchptr.h].

3.3.3 Sorting by a supplied comparison function

The routines in [FXT: sort/sortfunc.h] are similar to the C-quicksort `qsort` that is part of the standard library. A comparison function `cmp` has to be supplied by the caller. This allows, for example, sorting compound data types with respect to some key contained within them. Citing the manual page for `qsort`:

> The comparison function must return an integer less than, equal to, or greater than zero if the first argument is considered to be respectively less than, equal to, or greater than the second. If two members compare as equal, their order in the sorted array is undefined.

As a prototypical example we give the selection sort routine:

```
1  template <typename Type>
2  void selection_sort(Type *f, ulong n, int (*cmp)(const Type &, const Type &))
3  // Sort f[] (ascending order) with respect to comparison function cmp().
4  {
5      for (ulong i=0; i<n; ++i)
6      {
7          Type v = f[i];
8          ulong m = i; // position of minimum
9          ulong j = n;
10         while ( --j > i )   // search (index of) minimum
11         {
12             if ( cmp(f[j],v) < 0 )
13             {
14                 m = j;
15                 v = f[m];
16             }
17         }
18
19         swap2(f[i], f[m]);
20     }
21 }
```

The other routines are rather straightforward translations of the (plain) sort analogues. Replace the comparison operations involving elements of the array as follows:

```
(a < b)        cmp(a,b) < 0
(a > b)        cmp(a,b) > 0
(a == b)       cmp(a,b) == 0
(a <= b)       cmp(a,b) <= 0
(a >= b)       cmp(a,b) >= 0
```

The verification routine is

```
1  template <typename Type>
2  bool is_sorted(const Type *f, ulong n, int (*cmp)(const Type &, const Type &))
3  // Return whether the sequence f[0], f[1], ..., f[n-1]
4  // is sorted in ascending order with respect to comparison function cmp().
5  {
6      for (ulong k=1; k<n; ++k)  if ( cmp(f[k-1], f[k]) > 0 )  return false;
7      return true;
8  }
```

The numerous calls to `cmp()` do have a negative impact on the performance. With C++ you can provide a comparison 'function' for a class by overloading the comparison operators `<`, `<`, `<=`, `>=`, and `==` and use the plain sort version. That is, the comparisons are inlined and the performance should be fine.

3.3.3.1   Sorting complex numbers

You want to sort complex numbers? Fine with me, but *don't* tell your local mathematician. To see the mathematical problem, we ask whether i is less than or greater than zero. Assuming $i > 0$ it follows that $i \cdot i > 0$ (we multiplied with a positive value) which is $-1 > 0$ and that is false. So, is $i < 0$? Then $i \cdot i > 0$ (multiplication with a negative value, as assumed), thereby $-1 > 0$. Oops! The lesson is that there is no way to impose an order on the complex numbers that would justify the usage of the symbols '$<$' and '$>$' consistent with the rules to manipulate inequalities.

Nevertheless we can invent a relation for sorting: arranging (sorting) the complex numbers according to their absolute value (modulus) leaves infinitely many numbers in one 'bucket', namely all those that have the same distance from zero. However, one could use the modulus as the *major* ordering parameter, the argument (angle) as the *minor*. Or the real part as the major and the imaginary part as the minor. The latter is realized in

```
1    static inline int
2    cmp_complex(const Complex &f, const Complex &g)
3    {
4        const double fr = f.real(),  gr = g.real();
5        if ( fr!=gr )  return  (fr>gr ? +1 : -1);
6
7        const double fi = f.imag(),  gi = g.imag();
8        if ( fi!=gi )  return  (fi>gi ? +1 : -1);
9
10       return  0;
11   }
```

This function, when used as comparison with the following routine, can indeed be the practical tool you had in mind:

```
1    void complex_sort(Complex *f, ulong n)
2    // major order wrt. real part
3    // minor order wrt. imag part
4    {
5        quick_sort(f, n, cmp_complex);
6    }
```

3.3.3.2   Index and pointer sorting

The index sorting routines that use a supplied comparison function are given in [FXT: sort/sortidxfunc.h]:

```
1    template <typename Type>
2    void idx_selection_sort(const Type *f, ulong n, ulong *x,
3                            int (*cmp)(const Type &, const Type &))
4    // Sort x[] so that the sequence f[x[0]], f[x[1]], ... f[x[n-1]]
5    // is ascending with respect to comparison function cmp().
6    {
7        for (ulong i=0; i<n; ++i)
8        {
9            Type v = f[x[i]];
10           ulong m = i; // position-ptr of minimum
11           ulong j = n;
12           while ( --j > i )  // search (index of) minimum
13           {
14               if ( cmp(f[x[j]], v) < 0 )
15               {
16                   m = j;
17                   v = f[x[m]];
18               }
19           }
20
21           swap2(x[i], x[m]);
22       }
23   }
```

The verification routine is:

```
1    template  <typename Type>
2    bool is_idx_sorted(const Type *f, ulong n, const ulong *x,
3                       int (*cmp)(const Type &, const Type &))
4    // Return whether the sequence f[x[0]], f[x[1]], ... f[x[n-1]] is ascending
```

```
5   // with respect to comparison function cmp().
6   {
7       for (ulong k=1; k<n; ++k)  if ( cmp(f[x[k-1]], f[x[k]]) > 0 )  return false;
8       return  true;
9   }
```

The pointer sorting versions are given in [FXT: sort/sortptrfunc.h]

```
1   template <typename Type>
2   void ptr_selection_sort(/*const Type *f,*/ ulong n, const Type **x,
3                           int (*cmp)(const Type &, const Type &))
4   // Sort x[] so that the sequence *x[0], *x[1], ..., *x[n-1]
5   // is ascending with respect to comparison function cmp().
6   {
7       for (ulong i=0; i<n; ++i)
8       {
9           Type v = *x[i];
10          ulong m = i; // position-ptr of minimum
11          ulong j = n;
12          while ( --j > i )  // search (index of) minimum
13          {
14              if ( cmp(*x[j],v)<0 )
15              {
16                  m = j;
17                  v = *x[m];
18              }
19          }
20
21          swap2(x[i], x[m]);
22      }
23  }
```

The verification routine is:

```
1   template  <typename Type>
2   bool is_ptr_sorted(/*const Type *f,*/ ulong n, Type const*const*x,
3                       int (*cmp)(const Type &, const Type &))
4   // Return whether the sequence *x[0], *x[1], ..., *x[n-1]
5   // is ascending with respect to comparison function cmp().
6   {
7       for (ulong k=1; k<n; ++k)  if ( cmp(*x[k-1],*x[k]) > 0 )  return false;
8       return  true;
9   }
```

The corresponding versions of the binary search algorithm are given in [FXT: sort/bsearchidxfunc.h] and [FXT: sort/bsearchptrfunc.h].

3.4   Searching in unsorted arrays

To find the first occurrence of a certain value in an unsorted array use the routine [FXT: sort/usearch.h]

```
1   template <typename Type>
2   inline ulong first_geq_idx(const Type *f, ulong n, Type v)
3   // Return index of first element == v
4   // Return n if all !=v
5   {
6       ulong k = 0;
7       while ( (k<n) && (f[k]!=v) )  k++;
8       return k;
9   }
```

The functions `first_neq_idx()`, `first_geg_idx()` and `first_leq_idx()` find the first occurrence of an element unequal (to v), greater than or equal and less than or equal, respectively.

If the last bit of speed matters, one could use a sentinel, as suggested in [210, p.267]:

```
1   template <typename Type>
2   inline ulong first_eq_idx(/* NOT const */ Type *f, ulong n, Type v)
3   {
4       Type s = f[n-1];
5       f[n-1] = v;  // sentinel to guarantee that the search stops
6       ulong k = 0;
7       while ( f[k]!=v )  ++k;
```

```
 8        f[n-1] = s;  // restore value
 9        if ( (k==n-1) && (v!=s) )  ++k;
10        return k;
11   }
```

There is only one branch in the inner loop, this can give a significant speedup. However, the technique is only applicable if writing to the array 'f[]' is allowed.

Another way to optimize the search is *partial unrolling* of the loop:

```
 1   template <typename Type>
 2   inline ulong first_eq_idx_large(const Type *f, ulong n, Type v)
 3   {
 4        ulong k;
 5        for (k=0; k<(n&3); ++k)  if ( f[k]==v )  return k;
 6
 7        while ( k!=n )  // 4-fold unrolled
 8        {
 9            Type t0 = f[k],  t1 = f[k+1],  t2 = f[k+2],  t3 = f[k+3];
10            bool qa = ( (t0==v) | (t1==v) );  // note bit-wise OR to avoid branch
11            bool qb = ( (t2==v) | (t3==v) );
12            if ( qa | qb )  // element v found
13            {
14                while ( 1 )  { if ( f[k]==v )  return k;  else ++k; }
15            }
16            k += 4;
17        }
18
19        return n;
20   }
```

The search requires only two branches with every four elements. By using two variables qa and qb better usage of the CPU internal parallelism is attempted. Depending on the data type and CPU architecture 8-fold unrolling may give a speedup.

3.5   Determination of equivalence classes

Let S be a set and $C := S \times S$ the set of all ordered pairs (x, y) with $x, y \in S$. A *binary relation* R on S is a subset of C. An *equivalence relation* is a binary relation with the following properties:

- *reflexive*: $x \equiv x\ \forall x$.

- *symmetric*: $x \equiv y \iff y \equiv x\ \forall x, y$.

- *transitive*: $x \equiv y,\ y \equiv z \implies x \equiv z\ \forall x, y, z$.

Here we wrote $x \equiv y$ for $(x, y) \in R$ where $x, y \in S$.

We want to determine the *equivalence classes*: an equivalence relation partitions a set into $1 \leq q \leq n$ subsets $E_1, E_2, \ldots, E_q$ so that $x \equiv y$ whenever both x and y are in the same subset but $x \not\equiv y$ if x and y are in different subsets.

For example, the usual equality relation is an equivalence relation, with a set of (different) numbers each number is in its own class. With the equivalence relation that $x \equiv y$ whenever $x - y$ is a multiple of some fixed integer $m > 0$ and the set $\mathbb{Z}$ of all natural numbers we obtain m subsets and $x \equiv y$ if and only if $x \equiv y \bmod m$.

3.5.1   Algorithm for decomposition into equivalence classes

Let S be a set of n elements, represented as a vector. On termination of the following algorithm $Q_k = j$ if j is the least index such that $S_j \equiv S_k$ (note that we consider the elements of S to be in a fixed but arbitrary order here):

1. Put each element in its own equivalence class: $Q_k := k$ for all $0 \leq k < n$

2. Set $k := 1$ (index of the second element).

3. (Search for an equivalent element:)

   (a) Set $j := 0$.

   (b) If $S_k \equiv S_j$ set $Q_k = Q_j$ and goto step 4.

   (c) Set $j := j + 1$ and goto step 3b

4. Set $k := k + 1$ and if $k < n$ goto step 3, else terminate.

The algorithm needs $n - 1$ equivalence tests when all elements are in the same equivalence class and $n(n-1)/2$ equivalence tests when each element is alone in its own equivalence class.

In the following implementation the equivalence relation must be supplied as a function `equiv_q()` that returns true when its arguments are equivalent [FXT: sort/equivclasses.h]:

```
1    template <typename Type>
2    void equivalence_classes(const Type *s, ulong n, bool (*equiv_q)(Type,Type), ulong *q)
3    // Given an equivalence relation '==' (as function equiv_q())
4    //   and a set s[] with n elements,
5    // write to q[k] the index j of the first element s[j] such that s[k]==s[j].
6    {
7        for (ulong k=0; k<n; ++k)  q[k] = k;  // each in own class
8        for (ulong k=1; k<n; ++k)
9        {
10           ulong j = 0;
11           while ( ! equiv_q(s[j], s[k]) )  ++j;
12           q[k] = q[j];
13       }
14   }
```

3.5.2 Examples of equivalence classes

3.5.2.1 Integers modulo m

Choose an integer $m \geq 1$ and let any two integers a and b be equivalent if $a - b$ is an integer multiple of m (with $m = 1$ all integers are in the same class). We can choose the numbers $0, 1 \ldots, m - 1$ as *representatives* of the m classes obtained. Now we can do computations with those classes via the modular arithmetic as described in section 39.1 on page 764. This is easily the most important example of all equivalence relations.

The concept also make sense for a real (non-integral) modulus $m > 0$. We still put two numbers a and b into the same class if $a - b$ is an *integer* multiple of m. Finally, the modulus $m = 0$ leads to the equivalence relation 'equality'.

3.5.2.2 Binary necklaces

Consider the set S of n-bit binary words with the equivalence relation in which two words x and y are equivalent if and only if there is a cyclic shift $h_k(x)$ by $0 \leq k < n$ positions such that $h_k(x) = y$. The equivalence relation is supplied as the function [FXT: sort/equivclass-necklaces-demo.cc]:

```
1    static ulong nb;  // number of bits
2    bool n_equiv_q(ulong x, ulong y)  // necklaces
3    {
4        ulong d = bit_cyclic_dist(x, y, nb);
5        return  (0==d);
6    }
```

The function `bit_cyclic_dist()` is given in section 1.13.4 on page 32. For $n = 4$ we find the following list of equivalence classes:

```
    0:   ....  [#=1]
    1:   1...  .1..  ...1  ..1.  [#=4]
    3:   1..1  11..  ..11  .11.  [#=4]
    5:   .1.1  1.1.  [#=2]
    7:   11.1  111.  1.11  .111  [#=4]
   15:   1111  [#=1]
  # of equivalence classes = 6
```

These correspond to the *binary necklaces* of length 4. One usually chooses the cyclic minima (or maxima) among equivalent words as representatives of the classes.

3.5.2.3   Unlabeled binary necklaces

Same set but the equivalence relation is defined to identify two words x and y when there is a cyclic shift $h_k(x)$ by $0 \le k < n$ positions so that either $h_k(x) = y$ or $h_k(x) = \overline{y}$ where $\overline{y}$ is the complement of y:

```
1    static ulong mm;  // mask to complement
2    bool nu_equiv_q(ulong x, ulong y)  // unlabeled necklaces
3    {
4        ulong d = bit_cyclic_dist(x, y, nb);
5        if ( 0!=d )  d = bit_cyclic_dist(mm^x, y, nb);
6        return  (0==d);
7    }
```

With $n = 4$ we find

```
    0:    1111   ....   [#=2]
    1:    111.   11.1   1.11   1...   .111   ...1   ..1.   .1..   [#=8]
    3:    .11.   1..1   11..   ..11   [#=4]
    5:    .1.1   1.1.   [#=2]
  # of equivalence classes = 4
```

These correspond to the *unlabeled binary necklaces* of length 4.

3.5.2.4   Binary bracelets

The *binary bracelets* are obtained by identifying two words that are identical up to rotation and possible reversal. The corresponding comparison function is

```
1    bool b_equiv_q(ulong x, ulong y)  // bracelets
2    {
3        ulong d = bit_cyclic_dist(x, y, b);
4        if ( 0!=d )  d = bit_cyclic_dist(revbin(x,b), y, b);
5        return  (0==d);
6    }
```

There are six binary bracelets of length 4:

```
    0:    ....   [#=1]
    1:    1...   .1..   ...1   ..1.   [#=4]
    3:    1..1   11..   ..11   .11.   [#=4]
    5:    .1.1   1.1.   [#=2]
    7:    11.1   111.   1.11   .111   [#=4]
   15:    1111   [#=1]
```

The *unlabeled binary bracelets* are obtained by additionally allowing for bit-wise complementation:

```
1    bool bu_equiv_q(ulong x, ulong y)  // unlabeled bracelets
2    {
3        ulong d = bit_cyclic_dist(x, y, b);
4        x ^= mm;
5        if ( 0!=d )  d = bit_cyclic_dist(x, y, b);
6
7        x = revbin(x,b);
8        if ( 0!=d )  d = bit_cyclic_dist(x, y, b);
9        x ^= mm;
10        if ( 0!=d )  d = bit_cyclic_dist(x, y, b);
11
12        return  (0==d);
13    }
```

There are four unlabeled binary bracelets of length 4:

```
    0:    1111   ....   [#=2]
    1:    111.   11.1   1.11   1...   .111   ...1   ..1.   .1..   [#=8]
    3:    .11.   1..1   11..   ..11   [#=4]
    5:    .1.1   1.1.   [#=2]
```

The shown functions are given in [FXT: sort/equivclass-bracelets-demo.cc] which can be used to produce listings of the equivalence classes.

The sequences of numbers of labeled and unlabeled necklaces and bracelets are shown in figure 3.5-A.

n:	N	B	N/U	B/U
[312]#	A000031	A000029	A000013	A000011
1:	2	2	1	1
2:	3	3	2	2
3:	4	4	2	2
4:	6	6	4	4
5:	8	8	4	4
6:	14	13	8	8
7:	20	18	10	9
8:	36	30	20	18
9:	60	46	30	23
10:	108	78	56	44
11:	188	126	94	63
12:	352	224	180	122
13:	632	380	316	190
14:	1182	687	596	362
15:	2192	1224	1096	612

Figure 3.5-A: The number of binary necklaces 'N', bracelets 'B', unlabeled necklaces 'N/U', and unlabeled bracelets 'B/U'. The second row gives the sequence number in [312].

3.5.2.5   Binary words with reversal and complement

The set S of n-bit binary words and the equivalence relation identifying two words x and y whenever they are mutual complements or bit-wise reversals.

```
3 classes with 3-bit words:              10 classes with 5-bit words:
   0:   111   ...                           0:   11111   .....
   1:   ..1   .11   1..   11.                1:   1111.   1....   .1111   ....1
   2:   1.1   .1.                            2:   1.111   111.1   .1...   ...1.
                                             3:   111..   ...11   ..111   11...
                                             4:   ..1..   11.11
6 classes with 4-bit words:                  5:   11.1.   1.1..   ..1.1   .1.11
   0:   1111   ....                           6:   ..11.   .11..   11..1   1..11
   1:   111.   1...   .111   ...1             9:   .11.1   1.11.   .1..1   1..1.
   2:   ..1.   .1..   1.11   11.1            10:   .1.1.   1.1.1
   3:   11..   ..11                          14:   1...1   .111.
   5:   1.1.   .1.1
   6:   .11.   1..1
```

Figure 3.5-B: Equivalence classes of binary words where words are identified if either their reversals or complements are equal.

For example, the equivalence classes with 3-, 4- and 5-bit words are shown in figure 3.5-B. The sequence of numbers of equivalence classes for word-sizes n is (entry A005418 in [312])

```
n:  1, 2, 3, 4,  5,  6,  7,  8,   9,  10,  11,   12,   13,   14,    15,    16, ...
#:  1, 2, 3, 6, 10, 20, 36, 72, 136, 272, 528, 1056, 2080, 4160, 8256, 16512, ...
```

The equivalence classes can be computed with the program [FXT: sort/equivclass-bitstring-demo.cc].

We have chosen examples where the resulting equivalence classes can be verified by inspection. For example, we could create the subsets of equivalent necklaces by simply rotating a given word and marking the words visited so far. Such an approach, however, is not possible if the equivalence relation does not have an obvious structure.

3.5.3   The number of equivalence relations for a set of n elements

We write $B(n)$ for the number of possible partitionings (and thereby equivalence relations) of the set $\{1, 2, \ldots, n\}$. These are called *Bell numbers*. The sequence of Bell numbers is entry A000110 in [312], it starts as ($n \geq 1$):

1, 2, 5, 15, 52, 203, 877, 4140, 21147, 115975, 678570, 4213597, ...

The can be computed easily as indicated in the following table:

```
0:  [ 1]
1:  [ 1,  2]
2:  [ 2,  3,  5]
3:  [ 5,  7, 10,  15]
4:  [15, 20, 27,  37,  52]
5:  [52, 67, 87, 114, 151, 203]
n:  [B(n), ... ]
```

The first element in each row is the last element of the previous row, the remaining elements are the sum of their left and upper left neighbors. As GP code:

```
1    N=7;   v=w=b=vector(N);   v[1]=1;
2    { for(n=1,N-1,
3         b[n] = v[1];
4         print(n-1, ":  ", v); \\ print row
5         w[1] = v[n];
6         for(k=2,n+1, w[k]=w[k-1]+v[k-1]);
7         v=w;
8      ); }
```

An implementation in C++ is given in [FXT: comb/bell-number-demo.cc]. An alternative way to compute the Bell numbers is shown in section 17.2 on page 358.

Chapter 4

Data structures

We give implementations of selected data structures like stack, ring buffer, queue, double-ended queue (deque), bit-array, heap and priority queue.

4.1 Stack (LIFO)

```
push(  1)  1   -   -   -                    #=1
push(  2)  1   2   -   -                    #=2
push(  3)  1   2   3   -                    #=3
push(  4)  1   2   3   4                    #=4
push(  5)  1   2   3   4   5   -   -   -    #=5
push(  6)  1   2   3   4   5   6   -   -    #=6
push(  7)  1   2   3   4   5   6   7   -    #=7
pop==  7   1   2   3   4   5   6            #=6
pop==  6   1   2   3   4   5   -   -   -    #=5
push(  8)  1   2   3   4   5   8   -   -    #=6
pop==  8   1   2   3   4   5   -   -   -    #=5
pop==  5   1   2   3   4   -   -   -   -    #=4
push(  9)  1   2   3   4   9   -   -   -    #=5
pop==  9   1   2   3   4   -   -   -   -    #=4
pop==  4   1   2   3   -   -   -   -   -    #=3
push( 10)  1   2   3  10   -   -   -   -    #=4
pop== 10   1   2   3   -   -   -   -   -    #=3
pop==  3   1   2   -   -   -   -   -   -    #=2
push( 11)  1   2  11   -   -   -   -   -    #=3
pop== 11   1   2   -   -   -   -   -   -    #=2
pop==  2   1   -   -   -   -   -   -   -    #=1
push( 12)  1  12   -   -   -   -   -   -    #=2
pop== 12   1   -   -   -   -   -   -   -    #=1
pop==  1   -   -   -   -   -   -   -   -    #=0
push( 13) 13   -   -   -   -   -   -   -    #=1
pop== 13   -   -   -   -   -   -   -   -    #=0
pop==  0   -   -   -   -   -   -   -   -    #=0
  (stack was empty)
push( 14) 14   -   -   -   -   -   -   -    #=1
pop== 14   -   -   -   -   -   -   -   -    #=0
pop==  0   -   -   -   -   -   -   -   -    #=0
  (stack was empty)
push( 15) 15   -   -   -   -   -   -   -    #=1
```

Figure 4.1-A: Inserting and retrieving elements with a stack.

A *stack* (or LIFO, for *last-in, first-out*) is a data structure that supports the operations: `push()` to save an entry, `pop()` to retrieve and remove the entry that was entered last, and `peek()` to retrieve the element that was entered last without removing it. The method `poke()` modifies the last entry. An implementation with the option to let the stack grow when necessary is [FXT: **class stack** in ds/stack.h]:

```
1    template <typename Type>
2    class stack
3    {
4    public:
5        Type  *x_;  // data
6        ulong  s_;  // size
```

J. Arndt, *Matters Computational: Ideas, Algorithms, Source Code*,
DOI 10.1007/978-3-642-14764-7_4, © Springer-Verlag Berlin Heidelberg 2011

```
 7        ulong  p_;  // stack pointer (position of next write), top entry @ p-1
 8        ulong  gq_; // grow gq elements if necessary, 0 for "never grow"
 9
10    public:
11        stack(ulong n, ulong growq=0)
12        {
13            s_ = n;
14            x_ = new Type[s_];
15            p_ = 0;  // stack is empty
16            gq_ = growq;
17        }
18
19        ~stack()  { delete [] x_; }
20
21        ulong num()  const  { return p_; }  // Return number of entries.
```

Insertion and retrieval from the top of the stack are implemented as follows:

```
 1        ulong push(Type z)
 2        // Add element z on top of stack.
 3        // Return size of stack, zero on stack overflow.
 4        // If gq_ is nonzero the stack grows if needed.
 5        {
 6            if ( p_ >= s_ )
 7            {
 8                if ( 0==gq_ )  return 0;  // overflow
 9                grow();
10            }
11
12            x_[p_] = z;
13            ++p_;
14
15            return  s_;
16        }
17
18        ulong pop(Type &z)
19        // Retrieve top entry and remove it.
20        // Return number of entries before removing element.
21        // If empty return zero and leave z is undefined.
22        {
23            ulong ret = p_;
24            if ( 0!=p_ )  { --p_;  z = x_[p_]; }
25            return  ret;
26        }
27
28        ulong poke(Type z)
29        // Modify top entry.
30        // Return number of entries.
31        // If empty return zero and do nothing.
32        {
33            if ( 0!=p_ )  x_[p_-1] = z;
34            return p_;
35        }
36
37        ulong peek(Type &z)
38        // Read top entry, without removing it.
39        // Return number of entries.
40        // If empty return zero and leave z undefined.
41        {
42            if ( 0!=p_ )  z = x_[p_-1];
43            return p_;
44        }
```

The growth routine is implemented as

```
 1    private:
 2        void grow()
 3        {
 4            ulong ns = s_ + gq_;  // new size
 5            x_ = ReAlloc<Type>(x_, ns, s_);
 6            s_ = ns;
 7        }
 8    };
```

here we use the function `ReAlloc()` that imports the C function `realloc()`.

```
% man realloc
```

```
#include <stdlib.h>

void *realloc(void *ptr, size_t size);
```

realloc() changes the size of the memory block pointed to by ptr to size
bytes. The contents will be unchanged to the minimum of the old and new
sizes; newly allocated memory will be uninitialized. If ptr is NULL, the
call is equivalent to malloc(size); if size is equal to zero, the call is
equivalent to free(ptr). Unless ptr is NULL, it must have been returned by
an earlier call to malloc(), calloc() or realloc().

A program that shows the working of the stack is [FXT: ds/stack-demo.cc]. An example output where
the initial size is 4 and the growth-feature enabled (in increments of 4 elements) is shown in figure 4.1-A.

4.2 Ring buffer

A *ring buffer* is an array together with read and write operations that wrap around. That is, when the
last position of the array is reached, writing continues at the begin of the array, thereby erasing the oldest
entries. The read operation starts at the oldest entry in the array.

```
            array x[]         x[] ordered     n   wpos  fpos
insert(A)   A                 A               1    1     0
insert(B)   A  B              A  B            2    2     0
insert(C)   A  B  C           A  B  C         3    3     0
insert(D)   A  B  C  D        A  B  C  D      4    0     0
insert(E)   E  B  C  D        B  C  D  E      4    1     1
insert(F)   E  F  C  D        C  D  E  F      4    2     2
insert(G)   E  F  G  D        D  E  F  G      4    3     3
insert(H)   E  F  G  H        E  F  G  H      4    0     0
insert(I)   I  F  G  H        F  G  H  I      4    1     1
insert(J)   I  J  G  H        G  H  I  J      4    2     2
```

Figure 4.2-A: Writing to a ring buffer.

Figure 4.2-A shows the contents of a length-4 ring buffer after insertion of the symbols 'A', 'B', ..., 'J'.
The listing was created with the program [FXT: ds/ringbuffer-demo.cc]. The implementation used is
[FXT: **class ringbuffer** in ds/ringbuffer.h]:

```
1   template <typename Type>
2   class ringbuffer
3   {
4   public:
5       Type *x_;   // data (ring buffer)
6       ulong s_;   // allocated size (# of elements)
7       ulong n_;   // current number of entries in buffer
8       ulong wpos_;  // next position to write in buffer
9       ulong fpos_;  // first position to read in buffer
10
11  public:
12      ringbuffer(ulong n)
13      {
14          s_ = n;
15          x_ = new Type[s_];
16          n_ = 0;
17          wpos_ = 0;
18          fpos_ = 0;
19      }
20
21      ~ringbuffer()  { delete [] x_; }
22
23      ulong num()  const  { return n_; }
```

If an entry is inserted, it is written to index wpos:

```
1       void insert(const Type &z)
2       {
3           x_[wpos_] = z;
4           if ( ++wpos_>=s_ )  wpos_ = 0;
5           if ( n_ < s_ )  ++n_;
```

```
 6              else  fpos_ = wpos_;
 7          }
 8
 9      ulong read(ulong k, Type &z)  const
10      // Read entry k (that is, [(fpos_ + k)%s_]).
11      // Return 0 if k>=n, else return k+1.
12      {
13          if ( k>=n_ )  return 0;
14          ulong j = fpos_ + k;
15          if ( j>=s_ )  j -= s_;
16          z = x_[j];
17          return  k + 1;
18      }
19  };
```

Ring buffers are, for example, useful for logging purposes, if only a certain number of lines can be saved. To do so, enhance the `ringbuffer` class so that it uses an additional array of (fixed width) strings. The message to log is copied into the array and the pointer set accordingly. A read returns the pointer to the string.

4.3   Queue (FIFO)

A *queue* (or FIFO for first-in, first-out) is a data structure that supports the following operations: `push()` saves an entry, `pop()` retrieves (and removes) the entry that was entered least recently, and `peek()` retrieves the least recently entered element without removing it.

```
                  array x[]                    n    rpos   wpos
   push( 1)   1   -   -   -                     1     0      1
   push( 2)   1   2   -   -                     2     0      2
   push( 3)   1   2   3   -                     3     0      3
   push( 4)   1   2   3   4                     4     0      0
   push( 5)   1   2   3   4   5   -   -   -     5     0      5
   push( 6)   1   2   3   4   5   6   -   -     6     0      6
   push( 7)   1   2   3   4   5   6   7   -     7     0      7
   pop== 1    -   2   3   4   5   6   7   -     6     1      7
   pop== 2    -   -   3   4   5   6   7   -     5     2      7
   push( 8)   -   -   3   4   5   6   7   8     6     2      0
   pop== 3    -   -   -   4   5   6   7   8     5     3      0
   pop== 4    -   -   -   -   5   6   7   8     4     4      0
   push( 9)   9   -   -   -   5   6   7   8     5     4      1
   pop== 5    9   -   -   -   -   6   7   8     4     5      1
   pop== 6    9   -   -   -   -   -   7   8     3     6      1
   push(10)   9  10   -   -   -   -   7   8     4     6      2
   pop== 7    9  10   -   -   -   -   -   8     3     7      2
   pop== 8    9  10   -   -   -   -   -   -     2     0      2
   push(11)   9  10  11   -   -   -   -   -     3     0      3
   pop== 9    -  10  11   -   -   -   -   -     2     1      3
   pop==10    -   -  11   -   -   -   -   -     1     2      3
   push(12)   -   -  11  12   -   -   -   -     2     2      4
   pop==11    -   -   -  12   -   -   -   -     1     3      4
   pop==12    -   -   -   -   -   -   -   -     0     4      4
   push(13)   -   -   -   -  13   -   -   -     1     4      5
   pop==13    -   -   -   -   -   -   -   -     0     5      5
   pop== 0    -   -   -   -   -   -   -   -     0     5      5
      (queue was empty)
   push(14)   -   -   -   -   -  14   -   -     1     5      6
   pop==14    -   -   -   -   -   -   -   -     0     6      6
   pop== 0    -   -   -   -   -   -   -   -     0     6      6
      (queue was empty)
   push(15)   -   -   -   -   -   -  15   -     1     6      7
```

Figure 4.3-A: Inserting and retrieving elements with a queue.

We describe a queue with an optional feature of growing when necessary. Figure 4.3-A shows the data for a queue where the initial size is four and the growth-feature enabled (in steps of four elements). The listing was created with the program [FXT: ds/queue-demo.cc].

The implementation is [FXT: class queue in ds/queue.h]:

```
1   template <typename Type>
2   class queue
3   {
4   public:
5       Type *x_;    // pointer to data
6       ulong s_;    // allocated size (# of elements)
7       ulong n_;    // current number of entries in buffer
8       ulong wpos_;  // next position to write in buffer
9       ulong rpos_;  // next position to read in buffer
10      ulong gq_;  // grow gq elements if necessary, 0 for "never grow"
11
12  public:
13      explicit queue(ulong n, ulong growq=0)
14      {
15          s_ = n;
16          x_ = new Type[s_];
17          n_ = 0;
18          wpos_ = 0;
19          rpos_ = 0;
20          gq_ = growq;
21      }
22
23      ~queue()  { delete [] x_; }
24
25      ulong num()  const  { return n_; }
```

The method push() writes to x[wpos], peek() and pop() read from x[rpos]:

```
1       ulong push(const Type &z)
2       // Return number of entries.
3       // Zero is returned on failure
4       //   (i.e. space exhausted and 0==gq_)
5       {
6           if ( n_ >= s_ )
7           {
8               if ( 0==gq_ )  return 0;  // growing disabled
9               grow();
10          }
11
12          x_[wpos_] = z;
13          ++wpos_;
14          if ( wpos_>=s_ )  wpos_ = 0;
15
16          ++n_;
17          return n_;
18      }
19
20      ulong peek(Type &z)
21      // Return number of entries.
22      // if zero is returned the value of z is undefined.
23      {
24          z = x_[rpos_];
25          return n_;
26      }
27
28      ulong pop(Type &z)
29      // Return number of entries before pop
30      // i.e. zero is returned if queue was empty.
31      // If zero is returned the value of z is undefined.
32      {
33          ulong ret = n_;
34          if ( 0!=n_ )
35          {
36              z = x_[rpos_];
37              ++rpos_;
38              if ( rpos_ >= s_ )  rpos_ = 0;
39              --n_;
40          }
41
42          return ret;
43      }
```

The growing feature is implemented as follows:

```
1   private:
```

```
2        void grow()
3        {
4            ulong ns = s_ + gq_;  // new size
5            // move read-position to zero:
6            rotate_left(x_, s_, rpos_);
7            x_ = ReAlloc<Type>(x_, ns, s_);
8            wpos_ = s_;
9            rpos_ = 0;
10           s_ = ns;
11       }
12   };
```

4.4   Deque (double-ended queue)

A *deque* (for *double-ended queue*) combines the data structures stack and queue: insertion and deletion in time $O(1)$ is possible both at the first and the last position. An implementation with the option to let the deque grow when necessary is [FXT: `class deque` in ds/deque.h]

```
1    template <typename Type>
2    class deque
3    {
4    public:
5        Type *x_;    // data (ring buffer)
6        ulong s_;    // allocated size (# of elements)
7        ulong n_;    // current number of entries in buffer
8        ulong fpos_; // position of first element in buffer
9        // insert_first() will write to (fpos-1)%n
10       ulong lpos_; // position of last element in buffer plus one
11       // insert_last() will write to  lpos,  n==(lpos-fpos) (mod s)
12       // entries are at [fpos, ..., lpos-1]  (range may be empty)
13
14       ulong  gq_; // grow gq elements if necessary, 0 for "never grow"
15
16   public:
17       explicit deque(ulong n, ulong growq=0)
18       {
19           s_ = n;
20           x_ = new Type[s_];
21           n_ = 0;
22           fpos_ = 0;
23           lpos_ = 0;
24           gq_ = growq;
25       }
26
27       ~deque()  { delete [] x_; }
28
29       ulong num()  const { return n_; }
```

The insertion at the front and end are implemented as

```
1        ulong insert_first(const Type &z)
2        // Return number of entries after insertion.
3        // Zero is returned on failure
4        //    (i.e. space exhausted and 0==gq_)
5        {
6            if ( n_ >= s_ )
7            {
8                if ( 0==gq_ )  return 0;  // growing disabled
9                grow();
10           }
11
12           --fpos_;
13           if ( fpos_ == -1UL )  fpos_ = s_ - 1;
14           x_[fpos_] = z;
15           ++n_;
16           return  n_;
17       }
18
19
20       ulong insert_last(const Type &z)
21       // Return number of entries after insertion.
22       // Zero is returned on failure
23       //    (i.e. space exhausted and 0==gq_)
```

```
24        {
25            if ( n_ >= s_ )
26            {
27                if ( 0==gq_ )  return 0;   // growing disabled
28                grow();
29            }
30
31            x_[lpos_] = z;
32            ++lpos_;
33            if ( lpos_>=s_ )  lpos_ = 0;
34            ++n_;
35            return  n_;
36        }
```

The extraction methods are

```
1        ulong extract_first(Type & z)
2        // Return number of elements before extract.
3        // Return 0 if extract on empty deque was attempted.
4        {
5            if ( 0==n_ )  return 0;
6            z = x_[fpos_];
7            ++fpos_;
8            if ( fpos_ >= s_ )  fpos_ = 0;
9            --n_;
10           return  n_ + 1;
11       }
12
13       ulong extract_last(Type & z)
14       // Return number of elements before extract.
15       // Return 0 if extract on empty deque was attempted.
16       {
17           if ( 0==n_ )  return 0;
18           --lpos_;
19           if ( lpos_ == -1UL )  lpos_ = s_ - 1;
20           z = x_[lpos_];
21           --n_;
22           return  n_ + 1;
23       }
```

We can read at the front, end, or an arbitrary index, without changing any data:

```
1        ulong read_first(Type & z)  const
2        // Read (but don't remove) first entry.
3        // Return number of elements (i.e. on error return zero).
4        {
5            if ( 0==n_ )  return 0;
6            z = x_[fpos_];
7            return n_;
8        }
9
10       ulong read_last(Type & z)  const
11       // Read (but don't remove) last entry.
12       // Return number of elements (i.e. on error return zero).
13       {
14           return  read(n_-1, z);  // ok for n_==0
15       }
16
17       ulong read(ulong k, Type & z)  const
18       // Read entry k (that is, [(fpos_ + k)%s_]).
19       // Return 0 if k>=n_ else return k+1
20       {
21           if ( k>=n_ )  return 0;
22           ulong j = fpos_ + k;
23           if ( j>=s_ )  j -= s_;
24           z = x_[j];
25           return  k + 1;
26       }
```

```
1    private:
2        void grow()
3        {
4            ulong ns = s_ + gq_;  // new size
5            // Move read-position to zero:
6            rotate_left(x_, s_, fpos_);
7            x_ = ReAlloc<Type>(x_, ns, s_);
8            fpos_ = 0;
```

```
 9          lpos_ = n_;
10          s_ = ns;
11      }
12  };
```

```
    insert_first( 1)       1
    insert_last(51)        1 51
    insert_first( 2)       2  1 51
    insert_last(52)        2  1 51 52
    insert_first( 3)       3  2  1 51 52
    insert_last(53)        3  2  1 51 52 53
    extract_first()= 3     2  1 51 52 53
    extract_last()= 53     2  1 51 52
    insert_first( 4)       4  2  1 51 52
    insert_last(54)        4  2  1 51 52 54
    extract_first()= 4     2  1 51 52 54
    extract_last()= 54     2  1 51 52
    extract_first()= 2     1 51 52
    extract_last()= 52     1 51
    extract_first()= 1     51
    extract_last()= 51
    insert_first( 5)       5
    insert_last(55)        5 55
    extract_first()= 5     55
    extract_last()= 55
    extract_first()= (deque is empty)
    extract_last()=  (deque is empty)
    insert_first( 7)       7
    insert_last(57)        7 57
```

Figure 4.4-A: Inserting and retrieving elements with a queue.

Its working is shown in figure 4.4-A which was created with the program [FXT: ds/deque-demo.cc].

4.5   Heap and priority queue

4.5.1   Indexing scheme for binary trees

```
                              1:[...1]

            2:[..1.]                          3:[..11]

    4:[.1..]        5:[.1.1]        6:[.11.]        7:[.111]

8:[1...]  9:[1..1]
```

Figure 4.5-A: Indexing a binary tree: the left child of node k is node $2k$, the right child is node $2k + 1$.

A one-based index array with n elements can be identified with a binary tree as shown in figure 4.5-A. Node 1 is the root node. The left child of node k is node $2k$ and the right child is node $2k + 1$. The parent of node k is node $\lfloor k/2 \rfloor$.

We require that consecutive array indices 1, 2, ..., n are used. Therefore all nodes k where $k \leq \lfloor n/2 \rfloor$ have at least one child.

4.5.2   The binary heap

A *binary heap* is a binary tree of the form just described, where both children are less than or equal to their parent. Figure 4.5-B shows an example of a heap with nine elements.

The following function determines whether a given array is a heap [FXT: ds/heap.h]:

```
1  template <typename Type>
2  ulong test_heap(const Type *x, ulong n)
```

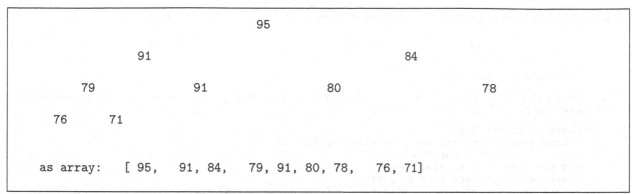

Figure 4.5-B: A heap with nine elements, the left or right child is never greater than the parent.

```
3      // Return 0 if x[] has heap property
4      // else index of node found to be greater than its parent.
5      {
6          const Type *p = x - 1;  // make one-based
7          for (ulong k=n; k>1; --k)
8          {
9              ulong t = (k>>1); // parent(k)
10             if ( p[t]<p[k] )  return k-1;  // in {1, 2, ..., n}
11         }
12         return 0;  // has heap property
13     }
```

Let $L = 2k$ and $R = 2k + 1$ be the left and right children of node k, respectively. Now assume that the subtrees whose roots are L and R already have the heap property, but node k is less than either L or R. We can restore the heap property between k, L, and R by swapping element k downwards (with L or R, as needed). The process is repeated if necessary until the bottom of the tree is reached:

```
1      template <typename Type>
2      void heapify(Type *z, ulong n, ulong k)
3      // Data expected in z[1,2,...,n].
4      {
5          ulong m = k;  // index of max of k, left(k), and right(k)
6
7          const ulong l = (k<<1); // left(k);
8          if ( (l <= n) && (z[l] > z[k]) )  m = l;  // left child (exists and) greater than k
9
10         const ulong r = (k<<1) + 1; // right(k);
11         if ( (r <= n) && (z[r] > z[m]) )  m = r;  // right child (ex. and) greater than max(k,l)
12
13         if ( m != k )  // need to swap
14         {
15             swap2(z[k], z[m]);
16             heapify(z, n, m);
17         }
18     }
```

To reorder an array into a heap, we restore the heap property from the bottom up:

```
1      template <typename Type>
2      void build_heap(Type *x, ulong n)
3      // Reorder data to a heap.
4      // Data expected in x[0,1,...,n-1].
5      {
6          Type *z = x - 1;   // make one-based
7          ulong j = (n>>1);  // max index such that node has at least one child
8          while ( j > 0 )
9          {
10             heapify(z, n, j);
11             --j;
12         }
13     }
```

The routine has complexity $O(n)$. Let the *height* of node k be the maximal number of swaps that can happen with `heapify(k)`. There are less than $n/2$ elements of height 1, $n/4$ of height 2, $n/8$ of height 3, and so on. Let $W(n)$ be the maximal number of swaps with n elements, we have

$$W(n) \quad < \quad 1\,n/2 + 2\,n/4 + 3\,n/8 + \ldots + \log_2(n)\,1 \quad < \quad 2\,n \tag{4.5-1}$$

So the complexity is indeed linear.

A new element can be inserted into a heap in $O(\log n)$ time by appending it and moving it towards the root as necessary:

```
1    template <typename Type>
2    bool heap_insert(Type *x, ulong n, ulong s, Type t)
3    // With x[] a heap of current size n
4    // and max size s (i.e. space for s elements allocated),
5    // insert t and restore heap-property.
6    // Return true if successful, else (i.e. if space exhausted) false.
7    {
8        if ( n > s )  return false;
9        ++n;
10       Type *x1 = x - 1;  // make one-based
11       ulong j = n;
12       while ( j > 1 )  // move towards root as needed
13       {
14           ulong k = (j>>1);  // k==parent(j)
15           if ( x1[k] >= t )  break;
16           x1[j] = x1[k];
17           j = k;
18       }
19       x1[j] = t;
20       return true;
21   }
```

Similarly, the maximal element can be removed in time $O(\log n)$:

```
1    template <typename Type>
2    Type heap_extract_max(Type *x, ulong n)
3    // Return maximal element of heap and restore heap structure.
4    // Return value is undefined for 0==n.
5    {
6        Type m = x[0];
7        if ( 0 != n )
8        {
9            Type *x1 = x - 1;
10           x1[1] = x1[n];
11           --n;
12           heapify(x1, n, 1);
13       }
14       return m;
15   }
```

4.5.3 Priority queue

A *priority queue* is a data structure that supports insertion of an element and extraction of its maximal element, both in time $O(\log(n))$. A priority queue can be used to schedule an event for a certain time and return the next pending event.

We use a binary heap to implement a priority queue. Two modifications seem appropriate: Firstly, replace `extract_max()` by `extract_next()`, leaving it as a compile time option whether to extract the minimal or the maximal element. We need to change the comparison operators at a few strategic places so that the heap is built either with its maximal or its minimal element first [FXT: class priority_queue in ds/priorityqueue.h]:

```
1    #if  1
2    // next() is the one with the smallest key
3    // i.e.  extract_next()  is  extract_min()
4    #define _CMP_ <
5    #define _CMPEQ_ <=
6    #else
7    // next() is the one with the biggest key
8    // i.e.  extract_next()  is  extract_max()
9    #define _CMP_ >
10   #define _CMPEQ_ >=
11   #endif
```

Secondly, augment the elements by an event description that can be freely defined:

```
1    template <typename Type1, typename Type2>
2    class priority_queue
3    {
4    public:
5        Type1 *t1_;  // time:   t1[1..s]  one-based array!
6        Type2 *e1_;  // events: e1[1..s]  one-based array!
7        ulong s_;    // allocated size (# of elements)
8        ulong n_;    // current number of events
9        ulong gq_;   // grow gq elements if necessary, 0 for "never grow"
10
11   public:
12       priority_queue(ulong n, ulong growq=0)
13       {
14           s_ = n;
15           t1_ = new Type1[s_] - 1;
16           e1_ = new Type2[s_] - 1;
17
18           n_ = 0;
19           gq_ = growq;
20       }
21
22       ~priority_queue()
23       {
24           delete [] (t1_+1);
25           delete [] (e1_+1);
26       }
27   [--snip--]
```

The extraction and insertion operations are

```
1        bool extract_next(Type1 &t, Type2 &e)
2        {
3            if ( n_ == 0 )  return false;
4
5            t = t1_[1];
6            e = e1_[1];
7            t1_[1] = t1_[n_];
8            e1_[1] = e1_[n_];
9            --n_;
10           heapify(1);
11
12           return true;
13       }
14
15       bool insert(const Type1 &t, const Type2 &e)
16       // Insert event e at time t.
17       // Return true if successful, else false (space exhausted and growth disabled).
18       {
19           if ( n_ >= s_ )
20           {
21               if ( 0==gq_ )  return false;  // growing disabled
22               grow();
23           }
24
25           ++n_;
26           ulong j = n_;
27           while ( j > 1 )
28           {
29               ulong k = (j>>1);  // k==parent(j)
30               if ( t1_[k] _CMPEQ_ t )  break;
31               t1_[j] = t1_[k];  e1_[j] = e1_[k];
32               j = k;
33           }
34           t1_[j] = t;
35           e1_[j] = e;
36
37           return true;
38       }
39
40       void reschedule_next(Type1 t)
41       {
42           t1_[1] = t;
43           heapify(1);
44       }
```

The member function `reschedule_next()` is more efficient than the sequence `extract_next();` `insert();`, as it calls `heapify()` only once. The `heapify()` function is tail-recursive, so we make it iterative:

```
1    private:
2        void heapify(ulong k)
3        {
4            ulong m = k;
5
6        hstart:
7            ulong l = (k<<1);  // left(k);
8            ulong r = l + 1;  // right(k);
9            if ( (l <= n_) && (t1_[l] _CMP_ t1_[k]) )  m = l;
10           if ( (r <= n_) && (t1_[r] _CMP_ t1_[m]) )  m = r;
11
12           if ( m != k )
13           {
14               swap2(t1_[k], t1_[m]);  swap2(e1_[k], e1_[m]);
15 //              heapify(m);
16               k = m;
17               goto hstart;  // tail recursion
18           }
19       }
```

The second argument of the constructor determines the number of elements added in case of growth, it is disabled (equals zero) by default.

```
1    private:
2        void grow()
3        {
4            ulong ns = s_ + gq_;  // new size
5            t1_ = ReAlloc<Type1>(t1_+1, ns, s_) - 1;
6            e1_ = ReAlloc<Type2>(e1_+1, ns, s_) - 1;
7            s_ = ns;
8        }
9    };
```

The `ReAlloc()` routine is described in section 4.1 on page 153.

```
        Inserting into piority_queue:            Extracting from piority_queue:
        # :    event  @        time             # :    event  @        time
        0:       A     @    0.840188             9:       F     @    0.197551
        1:       B     @    0.394383             8:       I     @    0.277775
        2:       C     @    0.783099             7:       G     @    0.335223
        3:       D     @    0.79844              6:       B     @    0.394383
        4:       E     @    0.911647             5:       J     @    0.55397
        5:       F     @    0.197551             4:       H     @    0.76823
        6:       G     @    0.335223             3:       C     @    0.783099
        7:       H     @    0.76823              2:       D     @    0.79844
        8:       I     @    0.277775             1:       A     @    0.840188
        9:       J     @    0.55397              0:       E     @    0.911647
```

Figure 4.5-C: Insertion of events labeled 'A', 'B', ..., 'J' scheduled for random times into a priority queue (left) and subsequent extraction (right).

The program [FXT: ds/priorityqueue-demo.cc] inserts events at random times $0 \le t < 1$, then extracts all of them. It gives the output shown in figure 4.5-C. A more typical usage would intermix the insertions and extractions.

4.6 Bit-array

The use of *bit-arrays* should be obvious: an array of tag values (like 'seen' versus 'unseen') where all standard data types would be a waste of space. Besides reading and writing individual bits one should implement a convenient search for the next set (or cleared) bit.

The class [FXT: `class bitarray` in ds/bitarray.h] is used, for example, for lists of small primes [FXT: mod/primes.cc], for in-place transposition routines [FXT: aux2/transpose.h] (see section 2.8 on page 122) and several operations on permutations (see section 2.4 on page 109).

```
1    class bitarray
```

```
2    // Bit-array class mostly for use as memory saving array of Boolean values.
3    // Valid index is 0...nb_-1 (as usual in C arrays).
4    {
5    public:
6        ulong *f_;    // bit bucket
7        ulong n_;     // number of bits
8        ulong nfw_;   // number of words where all bits are used, may be zero
9        ulong mp_;    // mask for partially used word if there is one, else zero
10       // (ones are at the positions of the _unused_ bits)
11       bool myfq_;   // whether f[] was allocated by class
12   [--snip--]
```

The constructor allocates memory by default. If the second argument is nonzero, it must point to an accessible memory range:

```
1        bitarray(ulong nbits, ulong *f=0)
2        // nbits must be nonzero
3        {
4            ulong nw = ctor_core(nbits);
5            if ( f!=0 )
6            {
7                f_ = (ulong *)f;
8                myfq_ = false;
9            }
10           else
11           {
12               f_ = new ulong[nw];
13               myfq_ = true;
14           }
15       }
```

The public methods are

```
1    // operations on bit n:
2        ulong test(ulong n)  const // Test whether n-th bit set
3        void set(ulong n)          // Set n-th bit
4        void clear(ulong n)        // Clear n-th bit
5        void change(ulong n)       // Toggle n-th bit
6        ulong test_set(ulong n)    // Test whether n-th bit is set and set it
7        ulong test_clear(ulong n)  // Test whether n-th bit is set and clear it
8        ulong test_change(ulong n) // Test whether n-th bit is set and toggle it
9
10   // Operations on all bits:
11       void clear_all()           // Clear all bits
12       void set_all()             // Set all bits
13       int all_set_q()  const;    // Return whether all bits are set
14       int all_clear_q()  const;  // Return whether all bits are clear
15
16   // Scanning the array:
17       // Note: the given index n is included in the search
18       ulong next_set_idx(ulong n)  const   // Return index of next set or value beyond end
19       ulong next_clear_idx(ulong n)  const // Return index of next clear or value beyond end
```

Combined operations like 'test-and-set-bit', 'test-and-clear-bit', 'test-and-change-bit' are often needed in applications that use bit-arrays. This is why modern CPUs often have instructions implementing these operations.

The class does not supply overloading of the array-index operator [] because the writing variant would cause a performance penalty. One might want to add 'sparse'-versions of the scan functions (next_set_idx() and next_clear_idx()) for large bit-arrays with only few bits set or unset.

On the AMD64 architecture the corresponding CPU instructions are used [FXT: bits/bitasm-amd64.h]:

```
1    static inline ulong asm_bts(ulong *f, ulong i)
2    // Bit Test and Set
3    {
4        ulong ret;
5        asm ( "btsq %2, %1 \n"
6              "sbbq %0, %0"
7              : "=r" (ret)
8              : "m" (*f), "r" (i) );
9        return ret;
10   }
```

If no specialized CPU instructions are available, the following two macros are used:

```
1    #define  DIVMOD(n, d, bm) \
2    ulong d = n / BITS_PER_LONG; \
3    ulong bm = 1UL << (n % BITS_PER_LONG);
```

```
1    #define  DIVMOD_TEST(n, d, bm) \
2    ulong d = n / BITS_PER_LONG; \
3    ulong bm = 1UL << (n % BITS_PER_LONG); \
4    ulong t = bm & f_[d];
```

The macro `BITS_USE_ASM` determines whether the CPU instruction is available:

```
1        ulong test_set(ulong n)  // Test whether n-th bit is set and set it.
2        {
3    #ifdef  BITS_USE_ASM
4            return asm_bts(f_, n);
5    #else
6            DIVMOD_TEST(n, d, bm);
7            f_[d] |= bm;
8            return  t;
9    #endif
10       }
```

Performance is still good in that case as the modulo operation and division by `BITS_PER_LONG` (a power of 2) are replaced with cheap (bit-and and shift) operations. On the machine described in appendix B on page 922 both versions give practically identical performance.

The way that out of bounds are handled can be defined at the beginning of the header file:

```
#define CHECK  0  // define to disable check of out of bounds access
//#define CHECK  1  // define to handle out of bounds access
//#define CHECK  2  // define to fail with out of bounds access
```

4.7 Left-right array

The *left-right array* (or *LR-array*) keeps track of a range of indices $0, \ldots, n-1$. Every index can have two states, *free* or *set*. The LR-array implements the following operations in time $O(\log n)$: marking the k-th free index as set; marking the k-th set index as free; for the i-th (absolute) index, finding how many indices of the same type (free or set) are left (or right) to it (including or excluding i).

The implementation is given as [FXT: class `left_right_array` in ds/left-right-array.h]:

```
1    class left_right_array
2    {
3    public:
4        ulong *fl_;  // Free indices Left (including current element) in bsearch interval
5        bool *tg_;   // tags: tg[i]==true if and only if index i is free
6        ulong n_;    // total number of indices
7        ulong f_;    // number of free indices
```

The arrays used have n elements:

```
1    public:
2        left_right_array(ulong n)
3        {
4            n_ = n;
5            fl_ = new ulong[n_];
6            tg_ = new bool[n_];
7            free_all();
8        }
9
10       ~left_right_array()
11       {
12           delete [] fl_;
13           delete [] tg_;
14       }
15
16       ulong num_free() const  { return f_; }
17       ulong num_set() const  { return  n_ - f_; }
```

The initialization routine `free_all()` of the array fl[] uses a variation of the binary search algorithm described in section 3.2 on page 141:

```
1    private:
2        void init_rec(ulong i0, ulong i1)
3        // Set elements of fl[0,...,n-2] according to empty array a[].
4        // The element fl[n-1] needs to be set to 1 afterwards.
5        // Work is O(n).
6        {
7            if ( (i1-i0)!=0 )
8            {
9                ulong t = (i1+i0)/2;
10               init_rec(i0, t);
11               init_rec(t+1, i1);
12           }
13           fl_[i1] = i1-i0+1;
14       }
15
16   public:
17       void free_all()
18       // Mark all indices as free.
19       {
20           f_ = n_;
21           for (ulong j=0; j<n_; ++j)  tg_[j] = true;
22           init_rec(0, n_-1);
23           fl_[n_-1] = 1;
24       }
```

The crucial observation is that the set of all intervals occurring with binary search is fixed if the size of the searched array is fixed. For any interval $[i_0, i_1]$ the element fl[t] where $t = \lfloor (i_0 + i_1)/2 \rfloor$ contains the number of free positions in $[i_0, t]$. The following method returns the k-th free index:

```
1        ulong get_free_idx(ulong k)  const
2        // Return the k-th ( 0 <= k < num_free() ) free index.
3        // Return ~0UL if k is out of bounds.
4        // Work is O(log(n)).
5        {
6            if ( k >= num_free() )  return ~0UL;
7
8            ulong i0 = 0,  i1 = n_-1;
9            while ( 1 )
10           {
11               ulong t = (i1+i0)/2;
12               if ( (fl_[t] == k+1) && (tg_[t]) )  return t;
13
14               if ( fl_[t] > k )  // left:
15               {
16                   i1 = t;
17               }
18               else   // right:
19               {
20                   i0 = t+1;  k-=fl_[t];
21               }
22           }
23       }
```

Usually one would have an extra array where one actually does write to the position returned above. Then the data of the LR-array has to be modified accordingly. The following method does this:

```
1        ulong get_free_idx_chg(ulong k)
2        // Return the k-th ( 0 <= k < num_free() ) free index.
3        // Return ~0UL if k is out of bounds.
4        // Change the arrays and fl[] and tg[] reflecting
5        //    that index i will be set afterwards.
6        // Work is O(log(n)).
7        {
8            if ( k >= num_free() )  return ~0UL;
9
10           --f_;
11
12           ulong i0 = 0,  i1 = n_-1;
13           while ( 1 )
14           {
15               ulong t = (i1+i0)/2;
16
17               if ( (fl_[t] == k+1) && (tg_[t]) )
18               {
19                   --fl_[t];
20                   tg_[t] = false;
21                   return t;
```

```
22          }
23
24          if ( fl_[t] > k )  // left:
25          {
26              --fl_[t];
27              i1 = t;
28          }
29          else     // right:
30          {
31              i0 = t+1;  k-=fl_[t];
32          }
33      }
34  }
```

```
fl[]= 1 2 3 1 5 1 2 1 1
a [ ]*=* * * * * * * *                        (continued)

------- first: -------                        ------- last: -------
fl[]= 0 1 2 1 4 1 2 1 1                        fl[]= 0 0 0 1 2 1 1 0 0
a [ ]1=* * * * * * * *                         a[]= 1 3 5 * * * 6 4 2

------- last: -------                          ------- first: -------
fl[]= 0 1 2 1 4 1 2 1 0                         fl[]= 0 0 0 0 1 1 1 0 0
a [ ]1=* * * * * * * 2                          a[]= 1 3 5 7 * * 6 4 2

------- first: -------                         ------- last: -------
fl[]= 0 0 1 1 3 1 2 1 0                         fl[]= 0 0 0 0 1 0 0 0 0
a [ ]1=3 * * * * * * 2                          a[]= 1 3 5 7 * 8 6 4 2

------- last: -------                          ------- first: -------
fl[]= 0 0 1 1 3 1 2 0 0                         fl[]= 0 0 0 0 0 0 0 0 0
a [ ]1=3 * * * * * 4 2                          a[]= 1 3 5 7 9 8 6 4 2

------- first: -------
fl[]= 0 0 0 1 2 1 2 0 0
a [ ]1=3 5 * * * * 4 2
```

Figure 4.7-A: Alternately setting the first and last free position in an LR-array. Asterisks denote free positions, indices i where tg[i] is true.

For example, the following program sets alternately the first and last free position until no free position is left [FXT: ds/left-right-array-demo.cc]:

```
1   ulong n = 9;
2   ulong *A = new ulong[n];
3   left_right_array LR(n);
4   LR.free_all();
5
6   // PRINT
7   for (ulong e=0; e<n; ++e)
8   {
9       ulong s = 0;  // first free
10      if ( 0!=(e&1) )  s = LR.num_free()-1;  // last free
11
12      ulong idx2 = LR.get_free_idx_chg(s);
13      A[idx2] = e+1;
14      // PRINT
15  }
```

Its output is shown in figure 4.7-A. For large n the method get_free_idx_chg() runs at a rate of (very roughly) 2 million per second. The method to free the k-th set position is

```
1   ulong get_set_idx_chg(ulong k)
2   // Return the k-th ( 0 <= k < num_set() ) set index.
3   // Return ~OUL if k is out of bounds.
4   // Change the arrays and fl[] and tg[] reflecting
5   //    that index i will be freed afterwards.
6   // Work is O(log(n)).
7   {
8       if ( k >= num_set() )  return ~OUL;
9
10      ++f_;
11
12      ulong i0 = 0,  i1 = n_-1;
13      while ( 1 )
14      {
```

```
15          ulong t = (i1+i0)/2;
16          // how many elements to the left are set:
17          ulong slt = t-i0+1 - fl_[t];
18
19          if ( (slt == k+1) && (tg_[t]==false) )
20          {
21              ++fl_[t];
22              tg_[t] = true;
23              return t;
24          }
25
26          if ( slt > k )  // left:
27          {
28              ++fl_[t];
29              i1 = t;
30          }
31          else   // right:
32          {
33              i0 = t+1;   k-=slt;
34          }
35      }
36  }
```

The following method returns the number of free indices left of i (and excluding i):

```
1   ulong num_FLE(ulong i)  const
2   // Return number of Free indices Left of (absolute) index i (Excluding i).
3   // Work is O(log(n)).
4   {
5       if ( i >= n_ )  { return ~0UL; }  // out of bounds
6
7       ulong i0 = 0,  i1 = n_-1;
8       ulong ns = i;  // number of set element left to i (including i)
9       while ( 1 )
10      {
11          if ( i0==i1 )  break;
12
13          ulong t = (i1+i0)/2;
14          if ( i<=t )  // left:
15          {
16              i1 = t;
17          }
18          else   // right:
19          {
20              ns -= fl_[t];
21              i0 = t+1;
22          }
23      }
24
25      return  i-ns;
26  }
```

Based on it are methods to determine the number of free/set indices to the left/right, including/excluding the given index. We omit the out-of-bounds clauses in the following:

```
1   ulong num_FLI(ulong i)  const
2   // Return number of Free indices Left of (absolute) index i (Including i).
3   { return num_FLE(i) + tg_[i]; }
4
5   ulong num_FRE(ulong i)  const
6   // Return number of Free indices Right of (absolute) index i (Excluding i).
7   { return  num_free() - num_FLI(i); }
8
9   ulong num_FRI(ulong i)  const
10  // Return number of Free indices Right of (absolute) index i (Including i).
11  { return  num_free() - num_FLE(i); }
12
13  ulong num_SLE(ulong i)  const
14  // Return number of Set indices Left of (absolute) index i (Excluding i).
15  { return i - num_FLE(i); }
16
17  ulong num_SLI(ulong i)  const
18  // Return number of Set indices Left of (absolute) index i (Including i).
19  { return i - num_FLE(i) + !tg_[i]; }
20
21  ulong num_SRE(ulong i)  const
22  // Return number of Set indices Right of (absolute) index i (Excluding i).
```

```
23            { return  num_set() - num_SLI(i); }
24
25       ulong num_SRI(ulong i)  const
26       // Return number of Set indices Right of (absolute) index i (Including i).
27            { return  num_set() - i + num_FLE(i); }
```

These can be used for the fast conversion between permutations and inversion tables, see section 10.1.1.1 on page 235.

Part II

Combinatorial generation

Chapter 5

Conventions and considerations

We give algorithms for the generation of all combinatorial objects of certain types such as combinations, compositions, subsets, permutations, integer partitions, set partitions, restricted growth strings and necklaces. Finally, we give some constructions for Hadamard and conference matrices. Several (more esoteric) combinatorial objects that are found via searching in directed graphs are presented in chapter 20.

These routines are useful in situations where an exhaustive search over all configurations of a certain kind is needed. Combinatorial algorithms are also fundamental to many programming problems and they can simply be fun!

5.1   Representations and orders

For a set of n elements we will take either $\{0, 1, \ldots, n-1\}$ or $\{1, 2, \ldots, n\}$. Our convention for the set notation is to start with the smallest element. Often there is more than one useful way to represent a combinatorial object. For example the subset $\{1, 4, 6\}$ of the set $\{0, 1, 2, 3, 4, 5, 6\}$ can also be written as a *delta set* [0100101]. Some sources use the term *bit string*. We often write dots instead of zeros for readability: [.1..1.1]. Note that in the delta set we put the first element to the left side (*array notation*), this is in contrast to the usual way of printing binary numbers, where the least significant bit (bit number zero) is shown on the right side.

For most objects we will give an algorithm for generation in *lexicographic* (or simply *lex*) order. In lexicographic order a string $X = [x_0, x_1, \ldots]$ precedes the string $Y = [y_0, y_1, \ldots]$ if for the smallest index k where the strings differ we have $x_k < y_k$. Further, the string X precedes $X.W$ (the concatenation of X with W) for any nonempty string W. The *co-lexicographic* (or simply *colex*) order is obtained by sorting with respect to the reversed strings. The order sometimes depends on the representation that is used, for an example see figure 8.1-A on page 202.

In a *minimal-change* order the amount of change between successive objects is the least possible. Such an order is also called a (combinatorial) *Gray code*. There is in general more than one such order. Often we can impose even stricter conditions, like that (with permutations) the changes are between adjacent positions. The corresponding order is a *strong minimal-change order*. A very readable survey of Gray codes is given in [343], see also [298].

5.2   Ranking, unranking, and counting

For a particular ordering of combinatorial objects (say, lexicographic order for permutations) we can ask which position in the list a given object has. An algorithm for finding the position is called a *ranking* algorithm. A method to determine the object, given its position, is called an *unranking* algorithm.

Given both ranking and unranking methods, one can compute the successor of a given object by computing its rank r and unranking $r + 1$. While this method is usually slow the idea can be used to find more efficient algorithms for computing the successor. In addition the idea often suggests interesting orderings for combinatorial objects.

J. Arndt, *Matters Computational: Ideas, Algorithms, Source Code*,
DOI 10.1007/978-3-642-14764-7_5, © Springer-Verlag Berlin Heidelberg 2011

We sometimes give ranking or unranking methods for numbers in special forms such as factorial representations for permutations. Ranking and unranking methods are implicit in generation algorithms based on mixed radix counting given in section 10.9 on page 258.

A simple but surprisingly powerful way to discover isomorphisms (one-to-one correspondences) between combinatorial objects is counting them. If the sequences of numbers of two kinds of objects are identical, chances are good of finding a conversion routine between the corresponding objects. For example, there are 2^n permutations of n elements such that no element lies more than one position to the right of its original position. With this observation an algorithm for generating these permutations via binary counting can be found, see section 11.2 on page 282.

The representation of combinatorial objects as restricted growth strings (as shown in section 15.2 on page 325) follows from the same idea. The resulting generation methods can be very fast and flexible.

The number of objects of a given size can often be given by an explicit expression (for example, the number of parentheses strings of n pairs is the Catalan number $C_n = \binom{2n}{n}/(n+1)$, see section 15.4 on page 331). The *ordinary generating function* (OGF) for a combinatorial object has a power series whose coefficients count the objects: for the Catalan numbers we have the OGF

$$C(x) \;=\; \sum_{n=0}^{\infty} C_n\, x^n \;=\; \frac{1 - \sqrt{1 - 4\,x}}{2\,x} \tag{5.2-1}$$

Generating functions can often be given even though no explicit expression for the number of the objects is known. The generating functions sometimes can be used to observe nontrivial identities, for example, that the number of partitions into distinct parts equals the number of partitions into odd parts, given as relation 16.4-23 on page 348. An *exponential generating function* (EGF) for a type of object where there are E_n objects of size n has the power series of the form (see, for example, relation 11.1-7 on page 279)

$$\sum_{n=0}^{\infty} E_n\, \frac{x^n}{n!} \tag{5.2-2}$$

An excellent introduction to generating functions is given in [166], for in-depth information see [167, vol.2, chap.21, p.1021], [143], and [319].

5.3 Characteristics of the algorithms

In almost all cases we produce the combinatorial objects one by one. Let n be the size of the object. The successor (with respect to the specified order) is computed from the object itself and additional data of a size less than a constant multiple of n.

Let B be the total number of combinatorial objects under consideration. Sometimes the cost of a successor computation is $O(n)$. Then the total cost for generating all objects is $O(n \cdot B)$.

If the successor computation takes a fixed number of operations (independent of the object size), then we say the algorithm is $O(1)$. If so, there can be no loop in the implementation, we say the algorithm is *loopless*. Then the total cost for all objects is $c \cdot B$ for some constant c, independent of the object size. A loopless algorithm can only exist if the amount of change between successive objects is bounded by a constant that does not depend on the object size. Natural candidates for loopless algorithms are Gray codes.

In many cases the cost of computing all objects is also $c \cdot B$ while the computation of the successor does involve a loop. As an example consider incrementing in binary using arrays: in half of the cases just the lowest bit changes, for half of the remaining cases just two bits change, and so on. The total cost is $B \cdot (1 + \frac{1}{2}(1 + \frac{1}{2}(\cdots))) = 2 \cdot B$, independent of the number of bits used. So the total cost is as in the loopless case while the successor computation can be expensive in some cases. Algorithms with this characteristic are said to be *constant amortized time* (or CAT). Often CAT algorithms are faster than loopless algorithms, typically if their structure is simpler.

5.4   Optimization techniques

Let x be an array of n elements. The loop

```
ulong k = 0;
while ( (k<n) && (x[k]!=0) )  ++k;  // find first zero
```

can be replaced by

```
ulong k = 0;
while ( x[k]!=0 )  ++k;  // find first zero
```

if a single *sentinel* element x[n]=0 is appended to the end of the array. The latter version will often be faster as less branches occur.

The test for equality as in

```
ulong k = 0;
while ( k!=n )  { /*...*/  ++k; }
```

is more expensive than the test for equality with zero as in

```
ulong k = n;
while ( --k!=0 )  { /*...*/ }
```

Therefore the latter version should be used when applicable.

To reduce the number of branches, replace the two tests

```
if ( (x<0) || (x>m) )  { /*...*/ }
```

by the following single test where unsigned integers are used:

```
if ( x>m )  { /*...*/ }
```

Use a do-while construct instead of a while-do loop whenever possible because the latter also tests the loop condition at entry. Even if the do-while version causes some additional work, the gain from avoiding a branch may outweigh it. Note that in the C language the for-loop also tests the condition at loop entry.

When computing the next object there may be special cases where the update is easy. If the percentage of these 'easy cases' is not too small, an extra branch in the update routine should be created. The performance gain is very visible in most cases (section 10.4 on page 245) and can be dramatic (section 10.5 on page 248).

Recursive routines can be quite elegant and versatile, see, for example, section 6.4 on page 182 and section 13.2.1 on page 297. However, expect only about half the speed of a good iterative implementation of the same algorithm. The notation for *list recursions* is given in section 14.1 on page 304.

Address generation can be simpler if arrays are used instead of pointers. This technique is useful for many permutation generators, see chapter 10 on page 232. Change the pointer declarations to array declarations in the corresponding class as follows:

```
//ulong *p_;    // permutation data (pointer version)
ulong p_[32];   // permutation data (array version)
```

Here we assume that nobody would attempt to compute all permutations of 31 or more elements ($31! \approx 8.22 \cdot 10^{33}$, taking about $1.3 \cdot 10^{18}$ years to finish). To use arrays uncomment (in the corresponding header files) a line like

```
#define PERM_REV2_FIXARRAYS // use arrays instead of pointers (speedup)
```

This will also disable the statements to allocate and free memory with the pointers. Whether the use of arrays tends to give a speedup is noted in the comment. The performance gain can be spectacular, see section 7.1 on page 194.

5.5   Implementations, demo-programs, and timings

Most combinatorial generators are implemented as C++ classes. The first object in the given order is created by the method first(). The method to compute the successor is usually next(). If a method for the computation of the predecessor is given, then it is called `prev()` and a method `last()` to compute the last element in the list is given.

The current combinatorial object can be accessed through the method `data()`. To make all data of a class accessible the data is declared `public`. This way the need for various `get_something()` methods is avoided. To minimize the danger of accidental modification of class data the variable names end with an underscore. For example, the class for the generation of combinations in lexicographic order starts as

```
class combination_lex
{
public:
    ulong *x_;     // combination: k elements 0<=x[j]<k in increasing order
    ulong n_, k_; // Combination (n choose k)
```

The methods for the user of the class are `public`, the internal methods (which can leave the data in an inconsistent state) are declared `private`.

Timings for the routines are given with most demo-programs. For example, the timings for the generation of subsets in minimal-change order (as delta sets, implemented in [FXT: **class subset_gray_delta** in comb/subset-gray-delta.h]) are given near the end of [FXT: comb/subset-gray-delta-demo.cc], together with the parameters used:

```
Timing:

  time ./bin 30
  arg 1: 30 == n  [Size of the set]  default=5
  arg 2: 0 == cq  [Whether to start with full set]  default=0
  ./bin 30  5.90s user 0.02s system 100% cpu 5.912 total
   ==> 2^30/5.90 == 181,990,139 per second

// with SUBSET_GRAY_DELTA_MAX_ARRAY_LEN defined:
  time ./bin 30
  arg 1: 30 == n  [Size of the set]  default=5
  arg 2: 0 == cq  [Whether to start with full set]  default=0
  ./bin 30  5.84s user 0.01s system 99% cpu 5.853 total
   ==>  2^30/5.84 == 183,859,901 per second
```

For your own measurements simply uncomment the line

```
//#define TIMING // uncomment to disable printing
```

near the top of the demo-program. The rate of generation for a certain object is occasionally given as 123 M/s, meaning that 123 million objects are generated per second.

If a generator routine is used in an application, one must do the benchmarking with the application. Choosing the optimal ordering and type of representation (for example, delta sets versus sets) for the given task is crucial for good performance. Further optimization will very likely involve the surrounding code rather than the generator alone.

Chapter 6

Combinations

We give algorithms to generate all subsets of the n-element set that contain k elements. For brevity we sometimes refer to the $\binom{n}{k}$ combinations of k out of n elements as "the combinations $\binom{n}{k}$".

6.1 Binomial coefficients

```
n \ k 0   1    2    3    4    5    6    7    8    9   10   11   12   13   14   15
 0:   1
 1:   1   1
 2:   1   2    1
 3:   1   3    3    1
 4:   1   4    6    4    1
 5:   1   5   10   10    5    1
 6:   1   6   15   20   15    6    1
 7:   1   7   21   35   35   21    7    1
 8:   1   8   28   56   70   56   28    8    1
 9:   1   9   36   84  126  126   84   36    9    1
10:   1  10   45  120  210  252  210  120   45   10    1
11:   1  11   55  165  330  462  462  330  165   55   11    1
12:   1  12   66  220  495  792  924  792  495  220   66   12    1
13:   1  13   78  286  715 1287 1716 1716 1287  715  286   78   13    1
14:   1  14   91  364 1001 2002 3003 3432 3003 2002 1001  364   91   14    1
15:   1  15  105  455 1365 3003 5005 6435 6435 5005 3003 1365  455  105   15    1
```

Figure 6.1-A: The binomial coefficients $\binom{n}{k}$ for $0 \leq n, k \leq 15$.

The number of ways to choose k elements from a set of n elements equals the binomial coefficient ('n choose k', or 'k out of n'):

$$\binom{n}{k} \;=\; \frac{n!}{k!\,(n-k)!} \;=\; \frac{n\,(n-1)\,(n-2)\,\ldots\,(n-k+1)}{k\,(k-1)\,(k-2)\,\ldots\,1} \;=\; \frac{\prod_{j=1}^{k}(n-j+1)}{k!} \;=\; \frac{n^{\underline{k}}}{k^{\underline{k}}} \qquad (6.1\text{-}1)$$

The last equality uses the *falling factorial* notation $a^{\underline{b}} := a\,(a-1)\,(a-2)\,\ldots\,(a-b+1)$. Equivalently, a set of n elements has $\binom{n}{k}$ subsets of exactly k elements. These subsets are called the *k-subsets* (where k is fixed) or *k-combinations* of an n-set (a set with n elements).

To avoid overflow during the computation of the binomial coefficient, use the form

$$\binom{n}{k} \;=\; \frac{(n-k+1)^{\overline{k}}}{1^{\overline{k}}} \;=\; \frac{n-k+1}{1} \cdot \frac{n-k+2}{2} \cdot \frac{n-k+3}{3} \,\ldots\, \frac{n}{k} \qquad (6.1\text{-}2)$$

An implementation is given in [FXT: aux0/binomial.h]:

```
1   inline ulong binomial(ulong n, ulong k)
2   {
3       if ( k>n ) return 0;
4       if ( (k==0) || (k==n) ) return 1;
5       if ( 2*k > n ) k = n-k;  // use symmetry
6
7       ulong b = n - k + 1;
8       ulong f = b;
9       for (ulong j=2; j<=k; ++j)
```

J. Arndt, *Matters Computational: Ideas, Algorithms, Source Code*,
DOI 10.1007/978-3-642-14764-7_6, © Springer-Verlag Berlin Heidelberg 2011

```
10      {
11          ++f;
12          b *= f;
13          b /= j;
14      }
15      return  b;
16  }
```

The table of the first binomial coefficients is shown in figure 6.1-A. This table is called *Pascal's triangle*, it was generated with the program [FXT: comb/binomial-demo.cc]. Observe that

$$\binom{n}{k} \;=\; \binom{n-1}{k-1} + \binom{n-1}{k} \tag{6.1-3}$$

That is, each entry is the sum of its upper and left upper neighbor. The generating function for the k-combinations of an n-set is

$$(1+x)^n \;=\; \sum_{k=0}^{n} \binom{n}{k} x^k \tag{6.1-4}$$

6.2 Lexicographic and co-lexicographic order

```
              lexicographic                          co-lexicographic
          set        delta set              set        delta set    set reversed
   1:  { 0, 1, 2 }   111...        1:  { 0, 1, 2 }   111...    { 2, 1, 0 }
   2:  { 0, 1, 3 }   11.1..        2:  { 0, 1, 3 }   11.1..    { 3, 1, 0 }
   3:  { 0, 1, 4 }   11..1.        3:  { 0, 2, 3 }   1.11..    { 3, 2, 0 }
   4:  { 0, 1, 5 }   11...1        4:  { 1, 2, 3 }   .111..    { 3, 2, 1 }
   5:  { 0, 2, 3 }   1.11..        5:  { 0, 1, 4 }   11..1.    { 4, 1, 0 }
   6:  { 0, 2, 4 }   1.1.1.        6:  { 0, 2, 4 }   1.1.1.    { 4, 2, 0 }
   7:  { 0, 2, 5 }   1.1..1        7:  { 1, 2, 4 }   .11.1.    { 4, 2, 1 }
   8:  { 0, 3, 4 }   1..11.        8:  { 0, 3, 4 }   1..11.    { 4, 3, 0 }
   9:  { 0, 3, 5 }   1..1.1        9:  { 1, 3, 4 }   .1.11.    { 4, 3, 1 }
  10:  { 0, 4, 5 }   1...11       10:  { 2, 3, 4 }   ..111.    { 4, 3, 2 }
  11:  { 1, 2, 3 }   .111..       11:  { 0, 1, 5 }   11...1    { 5, 1, 0 }
  12:  { 1, 2, 4 }   .11.1.       12:  { 0, 2, 5 }   1.1..1    { 5, 2, 0 }
  13:  { 1, 2, 5 }   .11..1       13:  { 1, 2, 5 }   .11..1    { 5, 2, 1 }
  14:  { 1, 3, 4 }   .1.11.       14:  { 0, 3, 5 }   1..1.1    { 5, 3, 0 }
  15:  { 1, 3, 5 }   .1.1.1       15:  { 1, 3, 5 }   .1.1.1    { 5, 3, 1 }
  16:  { 1, 4, 5 }   .1..11       16:  { 2, 3, 5 }   ..11.1    { 5, 3, 2 }
  17:  { 2, 3, 4 }   ..111.       17:  { 0, 4, 5 }   1...11    { 5, 4, 0 }
  18:  { 2, 3, 5 }   ..11.1       18:  { 1, 4, 5 }   .1..11    { 5, 4, 1 }
  19:  { 2, 4, 5 }   ..1.11       19:  { 2, 4, 5 }   ..1.11    { 5, 4, 2 }
  20:  { 3, 4, 5 }   ...111       20:  { 3, 4, 5 }   ...111    { 5, 4, 3 }
```

Figure 6.2-A: All combinations $\binom{6}{3}$ in lexicographic order (left) and co-lexicographic order (right).

The combinations of three elements out of six in *lexicographic* (or simply *lex*) order are shown in figure 6.2-A (left). The sequence is such that the sets are ordered lexicographically. Note that for the delta sets the element zero is printed first whereas with binary words (section 1.24 on page 62) the least significant bit (bit zero) is printed last. The sequence for *co-lexicographic* (or *colex*) order is such that the sets, when written reversed, are ordered lexicographically.

6.2.1 Lexicographic order

The following implementation generates the combinations in lexicographic order as sets [FXT: **class combination_lex** in comb/combination-lex.h]:

```
1   class combination_lex
2   {
3   public:
4       ulong *x_;      // combination: k elements 0<=x[j]<k in increasing order
```

```
 5        ulong n_, k_;  // Combination (n choose k)
 6
 7    public:
 8        combination_lex(ulong n, ulong k)
 9        {
10            n_ = n;   k_ = k;
11            x_ = new ulong[k_];
12            first();
13        }
14
15        ~combination_lex()  { delete [] x_; }
16
17        void first()
18        {
19            for (ulong k=0; k<k_; ++k)  x_[k] = k;
20        }
21
22        void last()
23        {
24            for (ulong i=0; i<k_; ++i)  x_[i] = n_ - k_ + i;
25        }
26
```

Computation of the successor and predecessor:

```
 1        ulong next()
 2        // Return smallest position that changed, return k with last combination
 3        {
 4            if ( x_[0] == n_ - k_ )  // current combination is the last
 5            { first();  return k_; }
 6
 7            ulong j = k_ - 1;
 8            // easy case:  highest element != highest possible value:
 9            if ( x_[j] < (n_-1) )  { ++x_[j];  return j; }
10
11            // find highest falling edge:
12            while ( 1 == (x_[j] - x_[j-1]) )  { --j; }
13
14            // move lowest element of highest block up:
15            ulong ret = j - 1;
16            ulong z = ++x_[j-1];
17
18            // ... and attach rest of block:
19            while ( j < k_ )  { x_[j] = ++z;   ++j; }
20
21            return  ret;
22        }
```

```
 1        ulong prev()
 2        // Return smallest position that changed, return k with last combination
 3        {
 4            if ( x_[k_-1] == k_-1 )  // current combination is the first
 5            { last();  return k_; }
 6
 7            // find highest falling edge:
 8            ulong j = k_ - 1;
 9            while ( 1 == (x_[j] - x_[j-1]) )  { --j; }
10
11            ulong ret = j;
12            --x_[j];  // move down edge element
13
14            // ... and move rest of block to high end:
15            while ( ++j < k_ )  x_[j] = n_ - k_ + j;
16
17            return  ret;
18        }
```

The listing in figure 6.2-A was created with the program [FXT: comb/combination-lex-demo.cc]. The routine generates the combinations $\binom{32}{20}$ at a rate of about 104 million per second. The combinations $\binom{32}{12}$ are generated at a rate of 166 million per second.

6.2.2 Co-lexicographic order

The combinations of three elements out of six in *co-lexicographic* (or *colex*) order are shown in figure 6.2-A (right). Algorithms to compute the successor and predecessor are implemented in [FXT: class combination_colex in comb/combination-colex.h]:

```
1    class combination_colex
2    {
3    public:
4        ulong *x_;     // combination: k elements 0<=x[j]<k in increasing order
5        ulong n_, k_; // Combination (n choose k)
6
7        combination_colex(ulong n, ulong k)
8        {
9            n_ = n;  k_ = k;
10           x_ = new ulong[k_+1];
11           x_[k_] = n_ + 2;  // sentinel
12           first();
13       }
14
15   [--snip--]
16     ulong next()
17     // Return greatest position that changed, return k with last combination
18     {
19
20         if ( x_[0] == n_ - k_ )  // current combination is the last
21         { first();  return k_; }
22
23         ulong j = 0;
24         // until lowest rising edge:  attach block at low end
25         while ( 1 == (x_[j+1] - x_[j]) ) { x_[j] = j;  ++j; }  // can touch sentinel
26
27         ++x_[j];  // move edge element up
28
29         return  j;
30     }
31
32     ulong prev()
33     // Return greatest position that changed, return k with last combination
34     {
35         if ( x_[k_-1] == k_-1 )  // current combination is the first
36         { last();  return k_; }
37
38         // find lowest falling edge:
39         ulong j = 0;
40         while ( j == x_[j] )  ++j;  // can touch sentinel
41
42         --x_[j];  // move edge element down
43         ulong ret = j;
44
45         // attach rest of low block:
46         while ( 0!=j-- )  x_[j] = x_[j+1] - 1;
47
48         return  ret;
49     }
50   [--snip--]
```

The listing in figure 6.2-A was created with the program [FXT: comb/combination-colex-demo.cc]. The combinations are generated $\binom{32}{20}$ at a rate of about 140 million objects per second, the combinations $\binom{32}{12}$ are generated at a rate of 190 million objects per second.

As a toy application of the combinations in co-lexicographic order we compute the products of k of the n smallest primes. We maintain an array of k products shown at the right of figure 6.2-B. If the return value of the method next() is j, then $j+1$ elements have to be updated from right to left [FXT: comb/kproducts-colex-demo.cc]:

```
1        combination_colex C(n, k);
2        const ulong *c = C.data();  // combinations as sets
3
4        ulong *tf = new ulong[n];  // table of Factors (primes)
5        // fill in small primes:
6        for (ulong j=0,f=2; j<n; ++j)  { tf[j] = f;  f=next_small_prime(f+1); }
7
8        ulong *tp = new ulong[k+1];  // table of Products
9        tp[k] = 1; // one appended (sentinel)
10
11       ulong j = k-1;
12       do
13       {
14           // update products from right:
15           ulong x = tp[j+1];
16           { ulong i = j;
```

```
            combination  j     delta-set      products
   1:     { 0,  1,  2 }  2     111....     [     30    15     5     1 ]
   2:     { 0,  1,  3 }  2     11.1...     [     42    21     7     1 ]
   3:     { 0,  2,  3 }  1     1.11...     [     70    35     7     1 ]
   4:     { 1,  2,  3 }  0     .111...     [    105    35     7     1 ]
   5:     { 0,  1,  4 }  2     11..1..     [     66    33    11     1 ]
   6:     { 0,  2,  4 }  1     1.1.1..     [    110    55    11     1 ]
   7:     { 1,  2,  4 }  0     .11.1..     [    165    55    11     1 ]
   8:     { 0,  3,  4 }  1     1..11..     [    154    77    11     1 ]
   9:     { 1,  3,  4 }  0     .1.11..     [    231    77    11     1 ]
  10:     { 2,  3,  4 }  0     ..111..     [    385    77    11     1 ]
  11:     { 0,  1,  5 }  2     11...1.     [     78    39    13     1 ]
  12:     { 0,  2,  5 }  1     1.1..1.     [    130    65    13     1 ]
  13:     { 1,  2,  5 }  0     .11..1.     [    195    65    13     1 ]
  14:     { 0,  3,  5 }  1     1..1.1.     [    182    91    13     1 ]
  15:     { 1,  3,  5 }  0     .1.1.1.     [    273    91    13     1 ]
  16:     { 2,  3,  5 }  0     ..11.1.     [    455    91    13     1 ]
  17:     { 0,  4,  5 }  1     1...11.     [    286   143    13     1 ]
  18:     { 1,  4,  5 }  0     .1..11.     [    429   143    13     1 ]
  19:     { 2,  4,  5 }  0     ..1.11.     [    715   143    13     1 ]
  20:     { 3,  4,  5 }  0     ...111.     [   1001   143    13     1 ]
  21:     { 0,  1,  6 }  2     11....1     [    102    51    17     1 ]
  22:     { 0,  2,  6 }  1     1.1...1     [    170    85    17     1 ]
  23:     { 1,  2,  6 }  0     .11...1     [    255    85    17     1 ]
  24:     { 0,  3,  6 }  1     1..1..1     [    238   119    17     1 ]
  25:     { 1,  3,  6 }  0     .1.1..1     [    357   119    17     1 ]
  26:     { 2,  3,  6 }  0     ..11..1     [    595   119    17     1 ]
  27:     { 0,  4,  6 }  1     1...1.1     [    374   187    17     1 ]
  28:     { 1,  4,  6 }  0     .1..1.1     [    561   187    17     1 ]
  29:     { 2,  4,  6 }  0     ..1.1.1     [    935   187    17     1 ]
  30:     { 3,  4,  6 }  0     ...11.1     [   1309   187    17     1 ]
  31:     { 0,  5,  6 }  1     1....11     [    442   221    17     1 ]
  32:     { 1,  5,  6 }  0     .1...11     [    663   221    17     1 ]
  33:     { 2,  5,  6 }  0     ..1..11     [   1105   221    17     1 ]
  34:     { 3,  5,  6 }  0     ...1.11     [   1547   221    17     1 ]
  35:     { 4,  5,  6 }  0     ....111     [   2431   221    17     1 ]
```

Figure 6.2-B: All products of $k = 3$ of the $n = 7$ smallest primes $(2, 3, 5, \ldots, 17)$. The products are the leftmost elements of the array on the right side.

```
17            do
18            {
19                ulong f = tf[ c[i] ];
20                x *= f;
21                tp[i] = x;
22            }
23            while ( i-- );
24        } // here: final product is x == tp[0]
25
26        // visit the product x here
27
28        j = C.next();
29    }
30    while ( j < k );
```

The leftmost element of this array is the desired product. A sentinel element at the end of the array is used to avoid an extra branch with the loop variable. With lexicographic order the update would go from left to right.

6.3   Order by prefix shifts (cool-lex)

An algorithm for generating combinations by prefix shifts is given in [291]. The ordering is called *cool-lex* in the paper. Figure 6.3-A shows some orders for $\binom{5}{2}$, figure 6.3-B shows the combinations $\binom{9}{3}$. The listings were created with the program [FXT: comb/combination-pref-demo.cc] which uses the implementation in [FXT: `class combination_pref` in comb/combination-pref.h]:

```
 1:  1....        1:  11...        1:  111..        1:  1111.
 2:  .1...        2:  .11..        2:  .111.        2:  .1111
 3:  ..1..        3:  1.1..        3:  1.11.        3:  1.111
 4:  ...1.        4:  .1.1.        4:  11.1.        4:  11.11
 5:  ....1        5:  ..11.        5:  .11.1        5:  111.1
                  6:  1..1.        6:  1.1.1
                  7:  .1..1        7:  .1.11
                  8:  ..1.1        8:  ..111
                  9:  ...11        9:  1..11
                 10:  1...1       10:  11..1
```

Figure 6.3-A: Combinations $\binom{5}{k}$, for $k = 1, 2, 3, 4$ in an ordering generated by prefix shifts.

```
.......................................................1111111111111111111111111111111
.........................................11111111111111111111111111............1111111.
..............1111111111111111........111111..............111111....1..
......1111111111....1111....111111....1111..11111...1...1....
...111111....1111....1111.1....111.1....1...1....1....1....
.111..111..111..1....111.1....1....1....111.1....1....1....1....1.....
111.11.1..11.1..1....11.1..1....1....11.1..1....1....1....1....1.....
11.11.1..11.1..1....11.1..1....1....11.1..1....1....1....1....1.....1
1.11.1..11.1..1....11.1..1....1....11.1..1....1....1....1.....11
```

Figure 6.3-B: Combinations $\binom{9}{3}$ via prefix shifts.

```
 1   class combination_pref
 2   {
 3   public:
 4       ulong *b_;  // data as delta set
 5       ulong s_, t_, n_;  // combination (n choose k) where n=s+t, k=t.
 6   private:
 7       ulong x, y;  // aux
 8
 9   public:
10       combination_pref(ulong n, ulong k)
11       // Must have: n>=2, k>=1  (i.e. s!=0 and t!=0)
12       {
13           s_ = n - k;
14           t_ = k;
15           n_ = s_ + t_;
16           b_ = new ulong[n_];
17           first();
18       }
19   [--snip--]
```

```
 1       void first()
 2       {
 3           for (ulong j=0; j<n_; ++j)  b_[j] = 0;
 4           for (ulong j=0; j<t_; ++j)  b_[j] = 1;
 5           x = 0;  y = 0;
 6       }
 7
 8       bool next()
 9       {
10           if ( x==0 )  { x=1;  b_[t_]=1;  b_[0]=0;  return true; }
11           else
12           {
13               if ( x>=n_-1 )  return false;
14               else
15               {
16                   b_[x] = 0;  ++x;  b_[y] = 1;  ++y; // X(s,t)
17                   if ( b_[x]==0 )
18                   {
19                       b_[x] = 1;  b_[0] = 0;        // Y(s,t)
20                       if ( y>1 )  x = 1;            // Z(s,t)
21                       y = 0;
22                   }
23                   return true;
24               }
25           }
26       }
27   [--snip--]
```

The combinations $\binom{32}{20}$ and $\binom{32}{12}$ are generated at a rate of about 200 M/s.

6.4 Minimal-change order

```
                Gray code                              complemented Gray code
        1:   { 0, 1, 2 }   111...             1:   { 3, 4, 5 }    ...111
        2:   { 0, 2, 3 }   1.11..             2:   { 1, 4, 5 }    .1..11
        3:   { 1, 2, 3 }   .111..             3:   { 0, 4, 5 }    1...11
        4:   { 0, 1, 3 }   11.1..             4:   { 2, 4, 5 }    ..1.11
        5:   { 0, 3, 4 }   1..11.             5:   { 1, 2, 5 }    .11..1
        6:   { 1, 3, 4 }   .1.11.             6:   { 0, 2, 5 }    1.1..1
        7:   { 2, 3, 4 }   ..111.             7:   { 0, 1, 5 }    11...1
        8:   { 0, 2, 4 }   1.1.1.             8:   { 1, 3, 5 }    .1.1.1
        9:   { 1, 2, 4 }   .11.1.             9:   { 0, 3, 5 }    1..1.1
       10:   { 0, 1, 4 }   11..1.            10:   { 2, 3, 5 }    ..11.1
       11:   { 0, 4, 5 }   1...11            11:   { 1, 2, 3 }    .111..
       12:   { 1, 4, 5 }   .1..11            12:   { 0, 2, 3 }    1.11..
       13:   { 2, 4, 5 }   ..1.11            13:   { 0, 1, 3 }    11.1..
       14:   { 3, 4, 5 }   ...111            14:   { 0, 1, 2 }    111...
       15:   { 0, 3, 5 }   1..1.1            15:   { 1, 2, 4 }    .11.1.
       16:   { 1, 3, 5 }   .1.1.1            16:   { 0, 2, 4 }    1.1.1.
       17:   { 2, 3, 5 }   ..11.1            17:   { 0, 1, 4 }    11..1.
       18:   { 0, 2, 5 }   1.1..1            18:   { 1, 3, 4 }    .1.11.
       19:   { 1, 2, 5 }   .11..1            19:   { 0, 3, 4 }    1..11.
       20:   { 0, 1, 5 }   11...1            20:   { 2, 3, 4 }    ..111.
```

Figure 6.4-A: Combinations $\binom{6}{3}$ in Gray order (left) and complemented Gray order (right).

The combinations of three elements out of six in a *minimal-change* order (a *Gray code*) are shown in figure 6.4-A (left). With each transition exactly one element changes its position. We use a recursion for the list $C(n, k)$ of combinations $\binom{n}{k}$ (notation as in relation 14.1-1 on page 304):

$$C(n, k) \;=\; \begin{matrix}[C(n-1, k) &] \\ [(n) . C^{\mathbf{R}}(n-1, k-1)]\end{matrix} \;=\; \begin{matrix}[0 . C(n-1, k) &] \\ [1 . C^{\mathbf{R}}(n-1, k-1)]\end{matrix} \tag{6.4-1}$$

The first equality is for the set representation, the second for the delta-set representation. An implementation is given in [FXT: comb/combination-gray-rec-demo.cc]:

```
1    ulong *x;   // elements in combination at x[1] ... x[k]
2
3    void comb_gray(ulong n, ulong k, bool z)
4    {
5        if ( k==n )
6        {
7            for (ulong j=1; j<=k; ++j)  x[j] = j;
8            visit();
9            return;
10       }
11
12       if ( z )  // forward:
13       {
14           comb_gray(n-1, k, z);
15           if ( k>0 )  { x[k] = n;  comb_gray(n-1, k-1, !z); }
16       }
17       else      // backward:
18       {
19           if ( k>0 )  { x[k] = n;  comb_gray(n-1, k-1, !z); }
20           comb_gray(n-1, k, z);
21       }
22   }
```

The recursion can be partly unfolded as follows

$$C(n, k) \;=\; \begin{matrix}[C(n-2, k) &] \\ [(n-1) . C^{\mathbf{R}}(n-2, k-1)] \\ [(n) . C^{\mathbf{R}}(n-1, k-1) &]\end{matrix} \;=\; \begin{matrix}[0\,0 . C(n-2, k) &] \\ [0\,1 . C^{\mathbf{R}}(n-2, k-1)] \\ [1 . C^{\mathbf{R}}(n-1, k-1) &]\end{matrix} \tag{6.4-2}$$

A recursion for the complemented order is

$$C'(n, k) \;=\; \begin{array}{l} [(n) \cdot C'(n-1,\, k-1)] \\ [C'^{\mathbf{R}}(n-1,\, k) \qquad\quad] \end{array} \;=\; \begin{array}{l} [1 \cdot C'(n-1,\, k-1)] \\ [0 \cdot C'^{\mathbf{R}}(n-1,\, k) \quad] \end{array} \tag{6.4-3}$$

```
1   void comb_gray_compl(ulong n, ulong k, bool z)
2   {
3      [--snip--]
4      if ( z )  // forward:
5      {
6          if ( k>0 )  { x[k] = n;  comb_gray_compl(n-1, k-1, z); }
7          comb_gray_compl(n-1, k, !z);
8      }
9      else     // backward:
10     {
11         comb_gray_compl(n-1, k, !z);
12         if ( k>0 )  { x[k] = n;  comb_gray_compl(n-1, k-1, z); }
13     }
14  }
```

A very efficient (*revolving door*) algorithm to generate the sets for the Gray code is given in [269]. An implementation following [215, alg.R, sect.7.2.1.3] is [FXT: `class combination_revdoor` in comb/combination-revdoor.h]. Usage of the class is shown in [FXT: comb/combination-revdoor-demo.cc]. The routine generates the combinations $\binom{32}{20}$ at a rate of about 115 M/s, the combinations $\binom{32}{12}$ are generated at a rate of 181 M/s. An implementation geared for good performance for small values of k is given in [223], a C++ adaptation is [FXT: comb/combination-lam-demo.cc]. The combinations $\binom{32}{12}$ are generated at a rate of 190 M/s and the combinations $\binom{64}{7}$ at a rate of 250 M/s. The routine is limited to values $k \geq 2$.

6.5   The Eades-McKay strong minimal-change order

In any Gray code order for combinations just one element is moved between successive combinations. When an element is moved across any other, there is more than one change on the set representation. If i elements are crossed, then $i+1$ entries in the set change:

```
         set            delta set
    { 0, 1, 2, 3 }      1111..
    { 1, 2, 3, 4 }      .1111.
```

A *strong minimal-change order* is a Gray code where only one entry in the set representation is changed per step. That is, only zeros in the delta set representation are crossed, the moves are called *homogeneous*. One such order is the *Eades-McKay* sequence described in [134]. The Eades-McKay sequence for the combinations $\binom{7}{3}$ is shown in figure 6.5-A (left).

6.5.1   Recursive generation

The Eades-McKay order can be generated with the program [FXT: comb/combination-emk-rec-demo.cc]:

```
1   ulong *rv;  // elements in combination at rv[1] ... rv[k]
2
3   void
4   comb_emk(ulong n, ulong k, bool z)
5   {
6       if ( k==n )
7       {
8           for (ulong j=1; j<=k; ++j)  rv[j] = j;
9           visit();
10          return;
11      }
12
13      if ( z )  // forward:
14      {
15          if ( (n>=2) && (k>=2) )  { rv[k] = n;  rv[k-1] = n-1;  comb_emk(n-2, k-2, z); }
16          if ( (n>=2) && (k>=1) )  { rv[k] = n;  comb_emk(n-2, k-1, !z); }
17          if ( (n>=1) )            { comb_emk(n-1, k, z); }
18      }
19      else     // backward:
```

```
          Eades-McKay                         complemented Eades-McKay

      1:  { 4, 5, 6 }  ....111           1:  { 4, 5, 6 }  ....111
      2:  { 3, 5, 6 }  ...1.11           2:  { 3, 5, 6 }  ...1.11
      3:  { 2, 5, 6 }  ..1..11           3:  { 2, 5, 6 }  ..1..11
      4:  { 1, 5, 6 }  .1...11           4:  { 1, 5, 6 }  .1...11
      5:  { 0, 5, 6 }  1....11           5:  { 0, 5, 6 }  1....11
      6:  { 0, 1, 6 }  11....1           6:  { 0, 4, 6 }  1...1.1
      7:  { 0, 2, 6 }  1.1...1           7:  { 1, 4, 6 }  .1..1.1
      8:  { 1, 2, 6 }  .11...1           8:  { 2, 4, 6 }  ..1.1.1
      9:  { 1, 3, 6 }  .1.1..1           9:  { 3, 4, 6 }  ...11.1
     10:  { 0, 3, 6 }  1..1..1          10:  { 2, 3, 6 }  ..11..1
     11:  { 2, 3, 6 }  ..11..1          11:  { 1, 3, 6 }  .1.1..1
     12:  { 2, 4, 6 }  ..1.1.1          12:  { 0, 3, 6 }  1..1..1
     13:  { 1, 4, 6 }  .1..1.1          13:  { 0, 2, 6 }  1.1...1
     14:  { 0, 4, 6 }  1...1.1          14:  { 1, 2, 6 }  .11...1
     15:  { 3, 4, 6 }  ...11.1          15:  { 0, 1, 6 }  11....1
     16:  { 3, 4, 5 }  ...111.          16:  { 0, 1, 5 }  11...1.
     17:  { 2, 4, 5 }  ..1.11.          17:  { 0, 2, 5 }  1.1..1.
     18:  { 1, 4, 5 }  .1..11.          18:  { 1, 2, 5 }  .11..1.
     19:  { 0, 4, 5 }  1...11.          19:  { 2, 3, 5 }  ..11.1.
     20:  { 0, 1, 5 }  11...1.          20:  { 1, 3, 5 }  .1.1.1.
     21:  { 0, 2, 5 }  1.1..1.          21:  { 0, 3, 5 }  1..1.1.
     22:  { 1, 2, 5 }  .11..1.          22:  { 0, 4, 5 }  1...11.
     23:  { 1, 3, 5 }  .1.1.1.          23:  { 1, 4, 5 }  .1..11.
     24:  { 0, 3, 5 }  1..1.1.          24:  { 2, 4, 5 }  ..1.11.
     25:  { 2, 3, 5 }  ..11.1.          25:  { 3, 4, 5 }  ...111.
     26:  { 2, 3, 4 }  ..111..          26:  { 2, 3, 4 }  ..111..
     27:  { 1, 3, 4 }  .1.11..          27:  { 1, 3, 4 }  .1.11..
     28:  { 0, 3, 4 }  1..11..          28:  { 0, 3, 4 }  1..11..
     29:  { 0, 1, 4 }  11..1..          29:  { 0, 2, 4 }  1.1.1..
     30:  { 0, 2, 4 }  1.1.1..          30:  { 1, 2, 4 }  .11.1..
     31:  { 1, 2, 4 }  .11.1..          31:  { 0, 1, 4 }  11..1..
     32:  { 1, 2, 3 }  .111...          32:  { 0, 1, 3 }  11.1...
     33:  { 0, 2, 3 }  1.11...          33:  { 0, 2, 3 }  1.11...
     34:  { 0, 1, 3 }  11.1...          34:  { 1, 2, 3 }  .111...
     35:  { 0, 1, 2 }  111....          35:  { 0, 1, 2 }  111....
```

Figure 6.5-A: Combinations in Eades-McKay order (left) and complemented Eades-Mckay order (right).

```
20      {
21          if ( (n>=1) )               { comb_emk(n-1, k, z); }
22          if ( (n>=2) && (k>=1) )     { rv[k] = n;  comb_emk(n-2, k-1, !z); }
23          if ( (n>=2) && (k>=2) )     { rv[k] = n;  rv[k-1] = n-1;  comb_emk(n-2, k-2, z); }
24      }
25  }
```

The combinations $\binom{32}{20}$ are generated at a rate of about 44 million per second, the combinations $\binom{32}{12}$ at a rate of 34 million per second.

The underlying recursion for the list $E(n, k)$ of combinations $\binom{n}{k}$ is (notation as in relation 14.1-1 on page 304)

$$E(n,k) \;=\; \begin{bmatrix} (n) \cdot (n-1) \cdot E(n-2, k-2)] \\ (n) \cdot E^{\mathbf{R}}(n-2, k-1) \qquad] \\ E(n-1, k) \qquad\qquad\quad] \end{bmatrix} = \begin{bmatrix} 1\,1 \cdot E(n-2, k-2) \quad] \\ 1\,0 \cdot E^{\mathbf{R}}(n-2, k-1)] \\ 0 \cdot E(n-1, k) \qquad\quad] \end{bmatrix} \tag{6.5-1}$$

Again, the first equality is for the set representation, the second for the delta-set representation. Counting the elements on both sides gives the relation

$$\binom{n}{k} \;=\; \binom{n-2}{k-2} + \binom{n-2}{k-1} + \binom{n-1}{k} \tag{6.5-2}$$

which is an easy consequence of relation 6.1-3 on page 177. A recursion for the complemented sequence (with respect to the delta sets) is

$$E'(n,k) \;=\; \begin{matrix}[(n)\,.\,E'(n-1,k-1) &]\\ [(n-1)\,.\,E'^{\mathbf{R}}(n-2,k-1)]\\ [E'(n-2,k) &]\end{matrix} \;=\; \begin{matrix}[1\,.\,E'(n-1,k-1) &]\\ [0\,1\,.\,E'^{\mathbf{R}}(n-2,k-1)]\\ [0\,0\,.\,E'(n-2,k) &]\end{matrix} \tag{6.5-3}$$

Counting on both sides gives

$$\binom{n}{k} \;=\; \binom{n-2}{k} + \binom{n-2}{k-1} + \binom{n-1}{k-1} \tag{6.5-4}$$

The condition for the recursion end has to be modified:

```
1   void
2   comb_emk_compl(ulong n, ulong k, bool z)
3   {
4       if ( (k==0) || (k==n) )
5       {
6           for (ulong j=1; j<=k; ++j)  rv[j] = j;
7           ++ct;
8           visit();
9           return;
10      }
11
12      if ( z )  // forward:
13      {
14          if ( (n>=1) && (k>=1) )  { rv[k] = n;    comb_emk_compl(n-1, k-1, z); }    // 1
15          if ( (n>=2) && (k>=1) )  { rv[k] = n-1;  comb_emk_compl(n-2, k-1, !z); }   // 01
16          if ( (n>=2)  )           { comb_emk_compl(n-2, k-0, z); }                  // 00
17      }
18      else       // backward:
19      {
20          if ( (n>=2)  )           { comb_emk_compl(n-2, k-0, z); }                  // 00
21          if ( (n>=2) && (k>=1) )  { rv[k] = n-1;  comb_emk_compl(n-2, k-1, !z); }   // 01
22          if ( (n>=1) && (k>=1) )  { rv[k] = n;    comb_emk_compl(n-1, k-1, z); }    // 1
23      }
24  }
```

The complemented sequence is not a strong Gray code.

6.5.2   Iterative generation via modulo moves

An iterative algorithm for the Eades-McKay sequence is given in [FXT: class `combination_emk` in comb/combination-emk.h]:

```
1   class combination_emk
2   {
3   public:
4       ulong *x_;   // combination: k elements 0<=x[j]<k in increasing order
5       ulong *s_;   // aux: start of range for moves
6       ulong *a_;   // aux: actual start position of moves
7       ulong n_, k_; // Combination (n choose k)
8
9   public:
10      combination_emk(ulong n, ulong k)
11      {
12          n_ = n;
13          k_ = k;
14          x_ = new ulong[k_+1];  // incl. high sentinel
15          s_ = new ulong[k_+1];  // incl. high sentinel
16          a_ = new ulong[k_];
17          x_[k_] = n_;
18          first();
19      }
20      [--snip--]
21
22      void first()
23      {
24          for (ulong j=0; j<k_; ++j)  x_[j] = j;
25          for (ulong j=0; j<k_; ++j)  s_[j] = j;
26          for (ulong j=0; j<k_; ++j)  a_[j] = x_[j];
27      }
```

The computation of the successor uses modulo steps:

```
1      ulong next()
2      // Return position where track changed, return k with last combination
3      {
4          ulong j = k_;
5          while ( j-- )   // loop over tracks
6          {
7              const ulong sj = s_[j];
8              const ulong m = x_[j+1] - sj - 1;
9
10             if ( 0!=m )   // unless range empty
11             {
12                 ulong u = x_[j] - sj;
13
14                 // modulo moves:
15                 if ( 0==(j&1) )
16                 {
17                     ++u;
18                     if ( u>m )   u = 0;
19                 }
20                 else
21                 {
22                     --u;
23                     if ( u>m )   u = m;
24                 }
25                 u += sj;
26
27                 if ( u != a_[j] )   // next position != start position
28                 {
29                     x_[j] = u;
30                     s_[j+1] = u+1;
31                     return j;
32                 }
33             }
34             a_[j] = x_[j];
35         }
36
37         return  k_;   // current combination is last
38     }
39  };
```

The combinations $\binom{32}{20}$ are generated at a rate of about 60 million per second, the combinations $\binom{32}{12}$ at a rate of 85 million per second [FXT: comb/combination-emk-demo.cc].

6.5.3 Alternative order via modulo moves

A slight modification of the successor computation gives an ordering where the first and last combination differ by a single transposition (though not a homogeneous one), see figure 6.5-B. The generator is given in [FXT: class combination_mod in comb/combination-mod.h]:

```
1   class combination_mod
2   {
3     [--snip--]
4       ulong next()
5       {
6     [--snip--]
7                 // modulo moves:
8                 // if ( 0==(j&1) )   // gives EMK
9                 if ( 0!=(j&1) )   // mod
10    [--snip--]
```

The rate of generation is identical with the EMK order [FXT: comb/combination-mod-demo.cc].

6.6 Two-close orderings via endo/enup moves

6.6.1 The endo and enup orderings for numbers

The *endo* order of the set $\{0, 1, 2, \ldots, m\}$ is obtained by writing all odd numbers of the set in increasing order followed by all even numbers in decreasing order: $\{1, 3, 5, \ldots, 6, 4, 2, 0\}$. The term endo stands

```
          mod        EMK                          mod         EMK
 1:    111....    111....            1:    1111..      1111...
 2:    11....1    11.1...            2:    111.1..      111...1
 3:    11..1..    11..1..            3:    111..1.      111..1.
 4:    11...1.    11...1.            4:    111...1      111.1..
 5:    11.1...    11....1            5:    11...11      11.11..
 6:    1.11...    1....11            6:    11..1.1      11.1.1.
 7:    1.1..1.    1...1.1            7:    11..11.      11.1..1
 8:    1.1.1..    1...11.            8:    11.1.1.      11..1.11
 9:    1.1..1.    1..1.1.            9:    11.1..1      11..11.
10:    1..11.     1..1..1           10:    11.11..      11...11
11:    1..1.1     1.1.1..           11:    1.111..      1...111
12:    1.1.1.     1.1.1..           12:    1.11.1.      1..1.11
13:    1...11.    1.1...1           13:    1.11..1      1..11.1
14:    1..1.1     1.1.1..           14:    1.1..11      1.1...111
15:    1...11     1.11...           15:    1.1.1.1      1.1.11.
16:    ....111    .111...           16:    1.1..11      1.1..11
17:    ...1.11    .11..1.           17:    1..111.      1.1...11
18:    ...11.1    .11.1..           18:    1..11.1      1.11..1
19:    ...111.    .11...1           19:    1...111      1.11.1.
20:    ..1.11     .1...11           20:    1....111     1.11...
21:    ..1.1.1    .1..1.1           21:    ...1111      .1111..
22:    ..1..11    .1..11.           22:    ..1.111      .111..1
23:    ..11.1     .1.1.1.           23:    ..11.11      .111.1.
24:    ..11.1     .1.11..           24:    ..111.1      .11.11.
25:    ..111.     .1.1..1           25:    ..1111.      .11.1.1
26:    .1.11.     ...111.           26:    .1.111       .11..11
27:    .1.1.1     ...11.1           27:    .1.1.11      .1.1.111
28:    .1.1.1     ...1.11           28:    .1.1.11      .1.1.11
29:    .1...11    ...1.11           29:    .1..111      .1.11.1
30:    .1..1.1    ...1.1.1          30:    .11.1.1      .1.1111.
31:    .1..11     ...11.1.          31:    .11.1.1      ..1111.
32:    .11...1    ....111           32:    .11.11.      ..111.1
33:    .11..1.    ....11.1          33:    .111.1.      ..11.11
34:    .11.1..    ....1.11          34:    .111..1      ..1.111
35:    .111...    ....111           35:    .1111..      ...1111
```

Figure 6.5-B: All combinations $\binom{7}{3}$ (left) and $\binom{7}{4}$ (right) in mod order and EMK order.

```
     m    endo sequence              m    enup sequence
 1:     1 0                      1:     0 1
 2:     1 2 0                    2:     0 2 1
 3:     1 3 2 0                  3:     0 2 3 1
 4:     1 3 4 2 0               4:     0 2 4 3 1
 5:     1 3 5 4 2 0            5:     0 2 4 5 3 1
 6:     1 3 5 6 4 2 0          6:     0 2 4 6 5 3 1
 7:     1 3 5 7 6 4 2 0        7:     0 2 4 6 7 5 3 1
 8:     1 3 5 7 8 6 4 2 0      8:     0 2 4 6 8 7 5 3 1
 9:     1 3 5 7 9 8 6 4 2 0    9:     0 2 4 6 8 9 7 5 3 1
```

Figure 6.6-A: The endo (left) and enup (right) orderings with maximal value m.

for 'Even Numbers DOwn, odd numbers up'. A routine for generating the successor in endo order with maximal value m is [FXT: comb/endo-enup.h]:

```
1    inline ulong next_endo(ulong x, ulong m)
2    // Return next number in endo order
3    {
4        if ( x & 1 )  // x odd
5        {
6            x += 2;
7            if ( x>m )  x = m - (m&1);  // == max even <= m
8        }
9        else  // x even
10       {
11           x = ( x==0 ? 1 : x-2 );
12       }
13       return x;
14   }
```

The sequences for the first few m are shown in figure 6.6-A. The routine computes one for the input zero.

An ordering starting with the even numbers in increasing order will be called *enup* (for 'Even Numbers UP, odd numbers down'). The computation of the successor can be implemented as

```
1    static inline ulong next_enup(ulong x, ulong m)
2    {
```

```
3       if ( x & 1 )  // x odd
4       {
5           x = ( x==1 ? 0 : x-2 );
6       }
7       else  // x even
8       {
9           x += 2;
10          if ( x>m )  x = m - !(m&1);  // max odd <=m
11      }
12      return x;
13  }
```

The orderings are reversals of each other, so we define:

```
1   static inline ulong prev_endo(ulong x, ulong m)  { return next_enup(x, m); }
2   static inline ulong prev_enup(ulong x, ulong m)  { return next_endo(x, m); }
```

A function that returns the x-th number in enup order with maximal digit m is

```
1   static inline ulong enup_num(ulong x, ulong m)
2   {
3       ulong r = 2*x;
4       if  ( r>m )  r = 2*m+1 - r;
5       return r;
6   }
```

The function will only work if $x \leq m$. For example, with $m = 5$:

```
    x :  0 1 2 3 4 5
    r :  0 2 4 5 3 1
```

The inverse function is

```
1   static inline ulong enup_idx(ulong x, ulong m)
2   {
3       const ulong b = x & 1;
4       x >>= 1;
5       return  ( b ? m-x : x );
6   }
```

The function to map into endo order is

```
1   static inline ulong endo_num(ulong x, ulong m)
2   {
3       // return enup_num(m-x, m);
4       x = m - x;
5       ulong r = 2*x;
6       if  ( r>m )  r = 2*m+1 - r;
7       return  r;
8   }
```

For example,

```
    x :  0 1 2 3 4 5
    r :  1 3 5 4 2 0
```

Its inverse is

```
1   static inline ulong endo_idx(ulong x, ulong m)
2   {
3       const ulong b = x & 1;
4       x >>= 1;
5       return  ( b ? x : m-x );
6   }
```

6.6.2 The endo and enup orderings for combinations

Two strong minimal-change orderings for combinations can be obtained via moves in enup and endo order. Figure 6.6-B shows an ordering where the moves to the right are on even positions (enup order, left). If the moves to the right are on odd positions (endo order), then Chase's sequence is obtained (right). Both have the property of being *two-close*: an element in the delta set moves by at most two positions (and the move is homogeneous, no other element is crossed). An implementation of an iterative algorithm for the computation of the combinations in enup order is [FXT: class combination_enup in comb/combination-enup.h].

```
1   class combination_enup
2   {
```

	enup moves			endo moves	
1:	{ 0, 1, 2 }	111.....	1:	{ 0, 1, 2 }	111.....
2:	{ 0, 1, 4 }	11..1...	2:	{ 0, 1, 3 }	11.1....
3:	{ 0, 1, 6 }	11....1.	3:	{ 0, 1, 5 }	11...1..
4:	{ 0, 1, 7 }	11.....1	4:	{ 0, 1, 7 }	11.....1
5:	{ 0, 1, 5 }	11...1..	5:	{ 0, 1, 6 }	11....1.
6:	{ 0, 1, 3 }	11.1....	6:	{ 0, 1, 4 }	11..1...
7:	{ 0, 2, 3 }	1.11....	7:	{ 0, 3, 4 }	1..11...
8:	{ 0, 2, 4 }	1.1.1...	8:	{ 0, 3, 5 }	1..1.1..
9:	{ 0, 2, 6 }	1.1...1.	9:	{ 0, 3, 7 }	1..1...1
10:	{ 0, 2, 7 }	1.1....1	10:	{ 0, 3, 6 }	1..1..1.
11:	{ 0, 2, 5 }	1.1..1..	11:	{ 0, 5, 6 }	1....11.
12:	{ 0, 4, 5 }	1...11..	12:	{ 0, 5, 7 }	1....1.1
13:	{ 0, 4, 6 }	1...1.1.	13:	{ 0, 6, 7 }	1.....11
14:	{ 0, 4, 7 }	1...1..1	14:	{ 0, 4, 7 }	1...1..1
15:	{ 0, 6, 7 }	1.....11	15:	{ 0, 4, 6 }	1...1.1.
16:	{ 0, 5, 7 }	1....1.1	16:	{ 0, 4, 5 }	1...11..
17:	{ 0, 5, 6 }	1....11.	17:	{ 0, 2, 5 }	1.1..1..
18:	{ 0, 3, 6 }	1..1..1.	18:	{ 0, 2, 7 }	1.1....1
19:	{ 0, 3, 7 }	1..1...1	19:	{ 0, 2, 6 }	1.1...1.
20:	{ 0, 3, 5 }	1..1.1..	20:	{ 0, 2, 4 }	1.1.1...
21:	{ 0, 3, 4 }	1..11...	21:	{ 0, 2, 3 }	1.11....
22:	{ 2, 3, 4 }	..111...	22:	{ 1, 2, 3 }	.111....
23:	{ 2, 3, 6 }	..11..1.	23:	{ 1, 2, 5 }	.11..1..
24:	{ 2, 3, 7 }	..11...1	24:	{ 1, 2, 7 }	.11....1
25:	{ 2, 3, 5 }	..11.1..	25:	{ 1, 2, 6 }	.11...1.
26:	{ 2, 4, 5 }	..1.11..	26:	{ 1, 2, 4 }	.11.1...
27:	{ 2, 4, 6 }	..1.1.1.	27:	{ 1, 3, 4 }	.1.11...
28:	{ 2, 4, 7 }	..1.1..1	28:	{ 1, 3, 5 }	.1.1.1..
29:	{ 2, 6, 7 }	..1...11	29:	{ 1, 3, 7 }	.1.1...1
30:	{ 2, 5, 7 }	..1..1.1	30:	{ 1, 3, 6 }	.1.1..1.
31:	{ 2, 5, 6 }	..1..11.	31:	{ 1, 5, 6 }	.1...11.
32:	{ 4, 5, 6 }	....111.	32:	{ 1, 5, 7 }	.1...1.1
33:	{ 4, 5, 7 }	....11.1	33:	{ 1, 6, 7 }	.1....11
34:	{ 4, 6, 7 }	....1.11	34:	{ 1, 4, 7 }	.1..1..1
35:	{ 5, 6, 7 }	111	35:	{ 1, 4, 6 }	.1..1.1.
36:	{ 3, 6, 7 }	...1..11	36:	{ 1, 4, 5 }	.1..11..
37:	{ 3, 5, 7 }	...1.1.1	37:	{ 3, 4, 5 }	...111..
38:	{ 3, 5, 6 }	...1.11.	38:	{ 3, 4, 7 }	...11..1
39:	{ 3, 4, 6 }	...11.1.	39:	{ 3, 4, 6 }	...11.1.
40:	{ 3, 4, 7 }	...11..1	40:	{ 3, 5, 6 }	...1.11.
41:	{ 3, 4, 5 }	...111..	41:	{ 3, 5, 7 }	...1.1.1
42:	{ 1, 4, 5 }	.1..11..	42:	{ 3, 6, 7 }	...1..11
43:	{ 1, 4, 6 }	.1..1.1.	43:	{ 5, 6, 7 }	111
44:	{ 1, 4, 7 }	.1..1..1	44:	{ 4, 6, 7 }	....1.11
45:	{ 1, 6, 7 }	.1....11	45:	{ 4, 5, 7 }	....11.1
46:	{ 1, 5, 7 }	.1...1.1	46:	{ 4, 5, 6 }	....111.
47:	{ 1, 5, 6 }	.1...11.	47:	{ 2, 5, 6 }	..1..11.
48:	{ 1, 3, 6 }	.1.1..1.	48:	{ 2, 5, 7 }	..1..1.1
49:	{ 1, 3, 7 }	.1.1...1	49:	{ 2, 6, 7 }	..1...11
50:	{ 1, 3, 5 }	.1.1.1..	50:	{ 2, 4, 7 }	..1.1..1
51:	{ 1, 3, 4 }	.1.11...	51:	{ 2, 4, 6 }	..1.1.1.
52:	{ 1, 2, 4 }	.11.1...	52:	{ 2, 4, 5 }	..1.11..
53:	{ 1, 2, 6 }	.11...1.	53:	{ 2, 3, 5 }	..11.1..
54:	{ 1, 2, 7 }	.11....1	54:	{ 2, 3, 7 }	..11...1
55:	{ 1, 2, 5 }	.11..1..	55:	{ 2, 3, 6 }	..11..1.
56:	{ 1, 2, 3 }	.111....	56:	{ 2, 3, 4 }	..111...

Figure 6.6-B: Combinations $\binom{8}{3}$ via enup moves (left) and via endo moves (Chase's sequence, right).

```
3   public:
4       ulong *x_;  // combination: k elements 0<=x[j]<k in increasing order
5       ulong *s_;  // aux: start of range for enup moves
6       ulong *a_;  // aux: actual start position of enup moves
7       ulong n_, k_; // Combination (n choose k)

1   public:
2       combination_enup(ulong n, ulong k)
3       {
4           n_ = n;
5           k_ = k;
6           x_ = new ulong[k_+1];  // incl. padding x_[k]
7           s_ = new ulong[k_+1];  // incl. padding x_[k]
8           a_ = new ulong[k_];
9           x_[k_] = n_;
10          first();
11      }
12
13      [--snip--]
14
15      void first()
16      {
17          for (ulong j=0; j<k_; ++j)  x_[j] = j;
18          for (ulong j=0; j<k_; ++j)  s_[j] = j;
19          for (ulong j=0; j<k_; ++j)  a_[j] = x_[j];
20      }
21
```

The 'padding' elements x[k] and s[k] allow omitting a branch, similar to sentinel elements. The successor of the current combination is computed by finding the range of possible movements (variable m) and, unless the range is empty, move until we are back at the start position:

```
1           ulong next()
2           // Return position where track changed, return k with last combination
3           {
4               ulong j = k_;
5               while ( j-- )  // loop over tracks
6               {
7                   const ulong sj = s_[j];
8                   const ulong m = x_[j+1] - sj - 1;
9
10                  if ( 0!=m )  // unless range empty
11                  {
12                      ulong u = x_[j] - sj;
13
14                      // move right on even positions:
15                      if ( 0==(sj&1) )  u = next_enup(u, m);
16                      else              u = next_endo(u, m);
17
18                      u += sj;
19
20                      if ( u != a_[j] )  // next pos != start position
21                      {
22                          x_[j] = u;
23                          s_[j+1] = u+1;
24                          return j;
25                      }
26                  }
27
28                  a_[j] = x_[j];
29              }
30
31              return  k_;  // current combination is last
32          }
33      };
```

The combinations $\binom{32}{20}$ are generated at a rate of 45 million objects per second, the combinations $\binom{32}{12}$ at a rate of 55 million per second. The only change in the implementation for computing the endo ordering is (at the obvious place in the code) [FXT: comb/combination-endo.h]:

```
1                   // move right on odd positions:
2                   if ( 0==(sj&1) )  u = next_endo(u, m);
3                   else              u = next_enup(u, m);
```

The ordering with endo moves is called *Chase's sequence*. Figure 6.6-B was created with the programs

[FXT: comb/combination-enup-demo.cc] and [FXT: comb/combination-endo-demo.cc].

The underlying recursion for the list $U(n,k)$ of combinations $\binom{n}{k}$ in enup order is

$$U(n,k) \;=\; \begin{array}{l}[(n)\,.\,(n-1)\,.\,U(n-2,\,k-2)] \\ [(n)\,.\,U(n-2,\,k-1) \qquad\quad\;] \\ [U^{\mathbf{R}}(n-1,\,k) \qquad\qquad\qquad]\end{array} \;=\; \begin{array}{l}[11\,.\,U(n-2,\,k-2)] \\ [10\,.\,U(n-2,\,k-1)] \\ [0\,.\,U^{\mathbf{R}}(n-1,\,k)\quad\;]\end{array} \tag{6.6-1}$$

The recursion is very similar to relation 6.5-1 on page 184. The crucial part of the recursive routine is [FXT: comb/combination-enup-rec-demo.cc]:

```
1   void
2   comb_enup(ulong n, ulong k, bool z)
3   {
4       if ( k==n )  { visit();   return; }
5
6       if ( z )   // forward:
7       {
8           if ( (n>=2) && (k>=2) )   { rv[k] = n;   rv[k-1] = n-1;   comb_enup(n-2, k-2, z); }
9           if ( (n>=2) && (k>=1) )   { rv[k] = n;   comb_enup(n-2, k-1, z); }
10          if ( (n>=1) )             { comb_enup(n-1, k, !z); }
11      }
12      else       // backward:
13      {
14          if ( (n>=1) )             { comb_enup(n-1, k, !z); }
15          if ( (n>=2) && (k>=1) )   { rv[k] = n;   comb_enup(n-2, k-1, z); }
16          if ( (n>=2) && (k>=2) )   { rv[k] = n;   rv[k-1] = n-1;   comb_enup(n-2, k-2, z); }
17      }
18  }
```

A recursion for the complemented sequence (with respect to the delta sets) is

$$U'(n,k) \;=\; \begin{array}{l}[(n)\,.\,U'^{\mathbf{R}}(n-1,\,k-1) \quad\;] \\ [(n-1)\,.\,U'(n-2,\,k-1)] \\ [U'(n-2,\,k) \qquad\qquad\qquad]\end{array} \;=\; \begin{array}{l}[1\,.\,U'^{\mathbf{R}}(n-1,\,k-1)] \\ [01\,.\,U'(n-2,\,k-1)] \\ [00\,.\,U'(n-2,\,k)\quad\;]\end{array} \tag{6.6-2}$$

The condition for the recursion end has to be modified:

```
1   void
2   comb_enup_compl(ulong n, ulong k, bool z)
3   {
4       if ( (k==0) || (k==n) )  { visit();   return; }
5
6       if ( z )   // forward:
7       {
8           if ( (n>=1) && (k>=1) )   { rv[k] = n;   comb_enup_compl(n-1, k-1, !z); }   // 1
9           if ( (n>=2) && (k>=1) )   { rv[k] = n-1;   comb_enup_compl(n-2, k-1, z); }   // 01
10          if ( (n>=2) )             { comb_enup_compl(n-2, k-0, z); }                  // 00
11      }
12      else       // backward:
13      {
14          if ( (n>=2) )             { comb_enup_compl(n-2, k-0, z); }                  // 00
15          if ( (n>=2) && (k>=1) )   { rv[k] = n-1;   comb_enup_compl(n-2, k-1, z); }   // 01
16          if ( (n>=1) && (k>=1) )   { rv[k] = n;   comb_enup_compl(n-1, k-1, !z); }   // 1
17      }
18  }
```

An algorithm for Chase's sequence that generates delta sets is described in [215, alg.C, sect.7.2.1.3], an implementation is given in [FXT: `class combination_chase` in comb/combination-chase.h]. The routine generates about 80 million combinations per second for both $\binom{32}{20}$ and $\binom{32}{12}$ [FXT: comb/combination-chase-demo.cc].

6.7 Recursive generation of certain orderings

We give a simple recursive routine to generate the orders shown in figure 6.7-A. The combinations are generated as sets [FXT: `class comb_rec` in comb/combination-rec.h]:

```
1   class comb_rec
2   {
```

	lexicographic	Gray code	compl. enup	compl. Eades-McKay
1:	111....	1....11	1....11	111....
2:	11.1...	1...11.	1...1.1	11.1...
3:	11..1..	1...1.1	1...11.	11..1..
4:	11...1.	1..11..	1..11..	11...1.
5:	11....1	1..1.1.	1..1.1.	11....1
6:	1.11...	1..1..1	1..1..1	1.1...1
7:	1.1.1..	1.11...	1.1...1	1.1..1.
8:	1.1..1.	1.1.1..	1.1..1.	1.1.1..
9:	1.1...1	1.1..1.	1.1.1..	1.11...
10:	1..11..	1.1...1	1.11...	1..11..
11:	1..1.1.	111....	111....	1..1.1.
12:	1..1..1	11.1...	11.1...	1..1..1
13:	1...11.	11..1..	11..1..	1...1.1
14:	1...1.1	11...1.	11...1.	1...11.
15:	1....11	11....1	11....1	1....11
16:	.111...	.1...11	.11...1	.1...11
17:	.11.1..	.1..11.	.11..1.	.1..1.1
18:	.11..1.	.1..1.1	.11.1..	.1..11.
19:	.11...1	.1.11..	.111...	.1.11..
20:	.1.11..	.1.1.1.	.1.11..	.1.1.1.
21:	.1.1.1.	.1.1..1	.1.1.1.	.1.1..1
22:	.1.1..1	.111...	.1.1..1	.11...1
23:	.1..11.	.11.1..	.1..1.1	.11..1.
24:	.1..1.1	.11..1.	.1..11.	.11.1..
25:	.1...11	.11...1	.1...11	.111...
26:	..111..	..1..11	..1..11	..111..
27:	..11.1.	..1.11.	..1.1.1	..11.1.
28:	..11..1	..1.1.1	..1.11.	..11..1
29:	..1.11.	..111..	..111..	..1.1.1
30:	..1.1.1	..11.1.	..11.1.	..1.11.
31:	..1..11	..11..1	..11..1	..1..11
32:	...111.	...1.11	...11.1	...1.11
33:	...11.1	...11.1	...111.	...11.1
34:	...1.11	...111.	...1.11	...111.
35:	111	111	111	111

Figure 6.7-A: All combinations $\binom{7}{3}$ in lexicographic, minimal-change, complemented enup, and complemented Eades-McKay order (from left to right).

```
3   public:
4       ulong n_, k_; // (n choose k)
5       ulong *rv_;   //  combination: k elements 0<=x[j]<k in increasing order
6       // == Record of Visits in graph
7       ulong rq_;   // condition that determines the order:
8       // 0 ==> lexicographic order
9       // 1 ==> Gray code
10      // 2 ==> complemented enup order
11      // 3 ==> complemented Eades-McKay sequence
12      ulong nq_;   // whether to reverse order
13  [--snip--]
14      void (*visit_)(const comb_rec &);  // function to call with each combination
15  [--snip--]
16
17      void generate(void (*visit)(const comb_rec &), ulong rq, ulong nq=0)
18      {
19          visit_ = visit;
20          rq_ = rq;
21          nq_ = nq;
22          ct_ = 0;
23          rct_ = 0;
24          next_rec(0);
25      }
```

The recursion function is given in [FXT: comb/combination-rec.cc]:

```
1   void comb_rec::next_rec(ulong d)
2   {
3       ulong r = k_ - d;  // number of elements remaining
4       if ( 0==r )  visit_(*this);
5       else
6       {
7           ulong rv1 = rv_[d-1];  // left neighbor
8           bool q;
9           switch ( rq_ )
```

```
10              {
11                  case 0:  q = 1;  break;           //  0 ==> lexicographic order
12                  case 1:  q = !(d&1);  break;      //  1 ==> Gray code
13                  case 2:  q = rv1&1;  break;       //  2 ==> complemented enup order
14                  case 3:  q = (d^rv1)&1;  break;   //  3 ==> complemented Eades-McKay sequence
15                  default: q = 1;
16                  }
17                  q ^= nq_;  // reversed order if  nq == true
18
19                  if ( q )  // forward:
20                      for (ulong x=rv1+1; x<=n_-r; ++x)  { rv_[d] = x;  next_rec(d+1); }
21                  else      // backward:
22                      for (ulong x=n_-r; (long)x>=(long)rv1+1; --x)  { rv_[d] = x;  next_rec(d+1); }
23          }
24      }
```

Figure 6.7-A was created with the program [FXT: comb/combination-rec-demo.cc]. The routine generates the combinations $\binom{32}{20}$ at a rate of about 35 million objects per second. The combinations $\binom{32}{12}$ are generated at a rate of 64 million objects per second.

Chapter 7

Compositions

The *compositions* of n into at most k parts are the ordered tuples $(x_0, x_1, \ldots, x_{k-1})$ where $x_0 + x_1 + \ldots + x_{k-1} = n$ and $0 \le x_i \le n$. Order matters: one 4-composition of 7 is $(0, 1, 5, 1)$, different ones are $(5, 0, 1, 1)$ and $(0, 5, 1, 1)$. The compositions of n into at most k parts are also called 'k-compositions of n'. To obtain the compositions of n into exactly k parts (where $k \le n$) generate the compositions of $n - k$ into k parts and add one to each position.

7.1 Co-lexicographic order

```
          composition   chg  combination        composition chg  combination
   1 :  [ 3 . . . . ]    4   111....        1:  [ 7 . . ]   2   1111111..
   2 :  [ 2 1 . . . ]    1   11.1...        2:  [ 6 1 . ]   1   111111.1.
   3 :  [ 1 2 . . . ]    1   1.11...        3:  [ 5 2 . ]   1   11111.11.
   4 :  [ . 3 . . . ]    1   .111...        4:  [ 4 3 . ]   1   1111.111.
   5 :  [ 2 . 1 . . ]    2   11..1..        5:  [ 3 4 . ]   1   111.1111.
   6 :  [ 1 1 1 . . ]    1   1.1.1..        6:  [ 2 5 . ]   1   11.11111.
   7 :  [ . 2 1 . . ]    1   .11.1..        7:  [ 1 6 . ]   1   1.111111.
   8 :  [ 1 . 2 . . ]    2   1..11..        8:  [ . 7 . ]   1   .1111111.
   9 :  [ . 1 2 . . ]    1   .1.11..        9:  [ 6 . 1 ]   2   111111..1
  1 0 :  [ . . 3 . . ]   2   ..111..       10:  [ 5 1 1 ]   1   11111.1.1
  1 1 :  [ 2 . . 1 . ]   3   11...1.       11:  [ 4 2 1 ]   1   1111.11.1
  1 2 :  [ 1 1 . 1 . ]   1   1.1..1.       12:  [ 3 3 1 ]   1   111.111.1
  1 3 :  [ . 2 . 1 . ]   1   .11..1.       13:  [ 2 4 1 ]   1   11.1111.1
  1 4 :  [ 1 . 1 1 . ]   2   1..1.1.       14:  [ 1 5 1 ]   1   1.11111.1
  1 5 :  [ . 1 1 1 . ]   1   .1.1.1.       15:  [ . 6 1 ]   1   .111111.1
  1 6 :  [ . . 2 1 . ]   2   ..11.1.       16:  [ 5 . 2 ]   2   11111..11
  1 7 :  [ 1 . . 2 . ]   3   1...11.       17:  [ 4 1 2 ]   1   1111.1.11
  1 8 :  [ . 1 . 2 . ]   1   .1..11.       18:  [ 3 2 2 ]   1   111.11.11
  1 9 :  [ . . 1 2 . ]   2   ..1.11.       19:  [ 2 3 2 ]   1   11.111.11
  2 0 :  [ . . . 3 . ]   3   ...111.       20:  [ 1 4 2 ]   1   1.1111.11
  2 1 :  [ 2 . . . 1 ]   4   11....1       21:  [ . 5 2 ]   1   .11111.11
  2 2 :  [ 1 1 . . 1 ]   1   1.1...1       22:  [ 4 . 3 ]   2   1111..111
  2 3 :  [ . 2 . . 1 ]   1   .11...1       23:  [ 3 1 3 ]   1   111.1.111
  2 4 :  [ 1 . 1 . 1 ]   2   1..1..1       24:  [ 2 2 3 ]   1   11.11.111
  2 5 :  [ . 1 1 . 1 ]   1   .1.1..1       25:  [ 1 3 3 ]   1   1.111.111
  2 6 :  [ . . 2 . 1 ]   2   ..11..1       26:  [ . 4 3 ]   1   .1111.111
  2 7 :  [ 1 . . 1 1 ]   3   1...1.1       27:  [ 3 . 4 ]   2   111..1111
  2 8 :  [ . 1 . 1 1 ]   1   .1..1.1       28:  [ 2 1 4 ]   1   11.1.1111
  2 9 :  [ . . 1 1 1 ]   2   ..1.1.1       29:  [ 1 2 4 ]   1   1.11.1111
  3 0 :  [ . . . 2 1 ]   3   ...11.1       30:  [ . 3 4 ]   1   .111.1111
  3 1 :  [ 1 . . . 2 ]   4   1....11       31:  [ 2 . 5 ]   2   11..11111
  3 2 :  [ . 1 . . 2 ]   1   .1...11       32:  [ 1 1 5 ]   1   1.1.11111
  3 3 :  [ . . 1 . 2 ]   2   ..1..11       33:  [ . 2 5 ]   1   .11.11111
  3 4 :  [ . . . 1 2 ]   3   ...1.11       34:  [ 1 . 6 ]   2   1..111111
  3 5 :  [ . . . . 3 ]   4   ....111       35:  [ . 1 6 ]   1   .1.111111
                                           36:  [ . . 7 ]   2   ..1111111
```

Figure 7.1-A: The compositions of 3 into 5 parts in co-lexicographic order, positions of the rightmost change, and delta sets of the corresponding combinations (left); and the corresponding data for compositions of 7 into 3 parts (right). Dots denote zeros.

J. Arndt, *Matters Computational: Ideas, Algorithms, Source Code*,
DOI 10.1007/978-3-642-14764-7_7, © Springer-Verlag Berlin Heidelberg 2011

The compositions in co-lexicographic (colex) order are shown in figure 7.1-A. The generator is implemented as [FXT: class `composition_colex` in comb/composition-colex.h]:

```
1    class composition_colex
2    {
3    public:
4        ulong n_, k_;   // composition of n into k parts
5        ulong *x_;      // data (k elements)
6    [--snip--]
7
8        void first()
9        {
10           x_[0] = n_;   // all in first position
11           for (ulong k=1; k<k_; ++k)  x_[k] = 0;
12       }
13
14       void last()
15       {
16           for (ulong k=0; k<k_; ++k)  x_[k] = 0;
17           x_[k_-1] = n_;  // all in last position
18       }
19   [--snip--]
```

The methods to compute the successor and predecessor are:

```
1        ulong next()
2        // Return position of rightmost change, return k with last composition.
3        {
4            ulong j = 0;
5            while ( 0==x_[j] )  ++j;  // find first nonzero
6
7            if ( j==k_-1 )  return k_;  // current composition is last
8
9            ulong v = x_[j];  // value of first nonzero
10           x_[j] = 0;        // set to zero
11           x_[0] = v - 1;    // value-1 to first position
12           ++j;
13           ++x_[j];                   // increment next position
14
15           return j;
16       }
17
18       ulong prev()
19       // Return position of rightmost change, return k with last composition.
20       {
21           const ulong v = x_[0];   // value at first position
22
23           if ( n_==v )  return k_; // current composition is first
24
25           x_[0] = 0;            // set first position to zero
26           ulong j = 1;
27           while ( 0==x_[j] )  ++j;  // find next nonzero
28           --x_[j];                  // decrement value
29           x_[j-1] = 1 + v;          // set previous position
30
31           return  j;
32       }
```

With each transition at most 3 entries are changed. The compositions of 10 into 30 parts (sparse case) are generated at a rate of about 110 million per second, the compositions of 30 into 10 parts (dense case) at about 200 million per second [FXT: comb/composition-colex-demo.cc]. With the dense case (corresponding to the right of figure 7.1-A) the computation is faster as the position to change is found earlier.

Optimized implementation

An implementation that is efficient also for the sparse case (that is, k much greater than n) is [FXT: class `composition_colex2` in comb/composition-colex2.h]. One additional variable p0 records the position of the first nonzero entry. The method to compute the successor is:

```
1    class composition_colex2
2    {
3        [--snip--]
```

```
 4    ulong next()
 5    // Return position of rightmost change, return k with last composition.
 6    {
 7        ulong j = p0_;   // position of first nonzero
 8
 9        if ( j==k_-1 )  return k_;  // current composition is last
10
11        ulong v = x_[j];   // value of first nonzero
12        x_[j] = 0;         // set to zero
13        --v;
14        x_[0] = v;         // value-1 to first position
15
16        ++p0_;                     // first nonzero one more right except ...
17        if ( 0!=v )  p0_ = 0;   // ... if value v was not one
18
19        ++j;
20        ++x_[j];           // increment next position
21
22        return  j;
23    }
24  };
```

About 270 million compositions are generated per second, independent of either n and k [FXT: comb/composition-colex2-demo.cc]. With the line

```
#define COMP_COLEX2_MAX_ARRAY_LEN   128
```

just before the class definition an array is used instead of a pointer. The fixed array length limits the value of k so by default the line is commented out. Using an array gives a significant speedup, the rate is about 365 million per second (about 6 CPU cycles per update).

7.2 Co-lexicographic order for compositions into exactly k parts

The compositions of n into exactly k parts (where $k \geq n$) can be obtained from the compositions of $n - k$ into at most k parts as shown in figure 7.2-A. The listing was created with the program [FXT: comb/composition-ex-colex-demo.cc]. The compositions can be generated in co-lexicographic order using [FXT: class composition_ex_colex in comb/composition-ex-colex.h]:

```
 1    class composition_ex_colex
 2    {
 3    public:
 4        ulong n_, k_;   // composition of n into exactly k parts
 5        ulong *x_;      // data (k elements)
 6        ulong nk1_;     // ==n-k+1
 7
 8    public:
 9        composition_ex_colex(ulong n, ulong k)
10        // Must have n>=k
11        {
12            n_ = n;
13            k_ = k;
14            nk1_ = n - k + 1;  // must be >= 1
15            if ( (long)nk1_ < 1 )  nk1_ = 1;  // avoid hang with invalid pair n,k
16            x_ = new ulong[k_ + 1];
17            x_[k] = 0;  // not one
18            first();
19        }
20        [--snip--]
```

The variable nk1_ is the maximal entry in the compositions:

```
 1        void first()
 2        {
 3            x_[0] = nk1_;  // all in first position
 4            for (ulong k=1; k<k_; ++k)  x_[k] = 1;
 5        }
 6
 7        void last()
 8        {
 9            for (ulong k=0; k<k_; ++k)  x_[k] = 1;
10            x_[k_-1] = nk1_;  // all in last position
11        }
```

```
            exact comp.   chg      composition
   1 :  [ 4 1 1 1 1 ]  4      [ 3 . . . . ]
   2 :  [ 3 2 1 1 1 ]  1      [ 2 1 . . . ]
   3 :  [ 2 3 1 1 1 ]  1      [ 1 2 . . . ]
   4 :  [ 1 4 1 1 1 ]  1      [ . 3 . . . ]
   5 :  [ 3 1 2 1 1 ]  2      [ 2 . 1 . . ]
   6 :  [ 2 2 2 1 1 ]  1      [ 1 1 1 . . ]
   7 :  [ 1 3 2 1 1 ]  1      [ . 2 1 . . ]
   8 :  [ 2 1 3 1 1 ]  2      [ 1 . 2 . . ]
   9 :  [ 1 2 3 1 1 ]  1      [ . 1 2 . . ]
 1 0 :  [ 1 1 4 1 1 ]  2      [ . . 3 . . ]
 1 1 :  [ 3 1 1 2 1 ]  3      [ 2 . . 1 . ]
 1 2 :  [ 2 2 1 2 1 ]  1      [ 1 1 . 1 . ]
 1 3 :  [ 1 3 1 2 1 ]  1      [ . 2 . 1 . ]
 1 4 :  [ 2 1 2 2 1 ]  2      [ 1 . 1 1 . ]
 1 5 :  [ 1 2 2 2 1 ]  1      [ . 1 1 1 . ]
 1 6 :  [ 1 1 3 2 1 ]  2      [ . . 2 1 . ]
 1 7 :  [ 2 1 1 3 1 ]  3      [ 1 . . 2 . ]
 1 8 :  [ 1 2 1 3 1 ]  1      [ . 1 . 2 . ]
 1 9 :  [ 1 1 2 3 1 ]  2      [ . . 1 2 . ]
 2 0 :  [ 1 1 1 4 1 ]  3      [ . . . 3 . ]
 2 1 :  [ 3 1 1 1 2 ]  4      [ 2 . . . 1 ]
 2 2 :  [ 2 2 1 1 2 ]  1      [ 1 1 . . 1 ]
 2 3 :  [ 1 3 1 1 2 ]  1      [ . 2 . . 1 ]
 2 4 :  [ 2 1 2 1 2 ]  2      [ 1 . 1 . 1 ]
 2 5 :  [ 1 2 2 1 2 ]  1      [ . 1 1 . 1 ]
 2 6 :  [ 1 1 3 1 2 ]  2      [ . . 2 . 1 ]
 2 7 :  [ 2 1 1 2 2 ]  3      [ 1 . . 1 1 ]
 2 8 :  [ 1 2 1 2 2 ]  1      [ . 1 . 1 1 ]
 2 9 :  [ 1 1 2 2 2 ]  2      [ . . 1 1 1 ]
 3 0 :  [ 1 1 1 3 2 ]  3      [ . . . 2 1 ]
 3 1 :  [ 2 1 1 1 3 ]  4      [ 1 . . . 2 ]
 3 2 :  [ 1 2 1 1 3 ]  1      [ . 1 . . 2 ]
 3 3 :  [ 1 1 2 1 3 ]  2      [ . . 1 . 2 ]
 3 4 :  [ 1 1 1 2 3 ]  3      [ . . . 1 2 ]
 3 5 :  [ 1 1 1 1 4 ]  4      [ . . . . 3 ]
```

Figure 7.2-A: The compositions of $n = 8$ into exactly $k = 5$ parts (left) are obtained from the compositions of $n - k = 3$ into at most $k = 5$ parts (right). Co-lexicographic order. Dots denote zeros.

The methods for computing the successor and predecessor are adaptations from the routines from the compositions into at most k parts:

```
ulong next()
// Return position of rightmost change, return k with last composition.
{
    ulong j = 0;
    while ( 1==x_[j] )  ++j;  // find first greater than one

    if ( j==k_ )  return k_;  // current composition is last

    ulong v = x_[j];  // value of first greater one
    x_[j] = 1;        // set to 1
    x_[0] = v - 1;    // value-1 to first position
    ++j;
    ++x_[j];          // increment next position

    return  j;
}

ulong prev()
// Return position of rightmost change, return k with last composition.
{
    const ulong v = x_[0];  // value at first position

    if ( nk1_==v )  return k_; // current composition is first

    x_[0] = 1;        // set first position to 1
    ulong j = 1;
    while ( 1==x_[j] )  ++j;  // find next greater than one
    --x_[j];                  // decrement value
```

```
29        x_[j-1] = 1 + v;              // set previous position
30
31        return j;
32    }
33 };
```

The routines are as fast as the generation into at most k parts with the corresponding parameters: the compositions of 40 into 10 parts are generated at a rate of about 200 million per second.

7.3 Compositions and combinations

```
           combination    delta set       composition
      1 :   [ 0 1 2 ]      111...          [ 3 . . . ]
      2 :   [ 0 2 3 ]      1.11..          [ 1 2 . . ]
      3 :   [ 1 2 3 ]      .111..          [ . 3 . . ]
      4 :   [ 0 1 3 ]      11.1..          [ 2 1 . . ]
      5 :   [ 0 3 4 ]      1..11.          [ 1 . 2 . ]
      6 :   [ 1 3 4 ]      .1.11.          [ . 1 2 . ]
      7 :   [ 2 3 4 ]      ..111.          [ . . 3 . ]
      8 :   [ 0 2 4 ]      1.1.1.          [ 1 1 1 . ]
      9 :   [ 1 2 4 ]      .11.1.          [ . 2 1 . ]
    1 0 :   [ 0 1 4 ]      11..1.          [ 2 . 1 . ]
    1 1 :   [ 0 4 5 ]      1...11          [ 1 . . 2 ]
    1 2 :   [ 1 4 5 ]      .1..11          [ . 1 . 2 ]
    1 3 :   [ 2 4 5 ]      ..1.11          [ . . 1 2 ]
    1 4 :   [ 3 4 5 ]      ...111          [ . . . 3 ]
    1 5 :   [ 0 3 5 ]      1..1.1          [ 1 . 1 1 ]
    1 6 :   [ 1 3 5 ]      .1.1.1          [ . 1 1 1 ]
    1 7 :   [ 2 3 5 ]      ..11.1          [ . . 2 1 ]
    1 8 :   [ 0 2 5 ]      1.1..1          [ 1 1 . 1 ]
    1 9 :   [ 1 2 5 ]      .11..1          [ . 2 . 1 ]
    2 0 :   [ 0 1 5 ]      11...1          [ 2 . . 1 ]
```

Figure 7.3-A: Combinations 6 choose 3 (left) and the corresponding compositions of 3 into 4 parts (right). The sequence of combinations is a Gray code but the sequence of compositions is not.

Figure 7.3-A shows the correspondence between compositions and combinations. The listing was generated using the program [FXT: comb/comb2comp-demo.cc]. Entries in the left column are combinations of 3 parts out of 6. The middle column is the representation of the combinations as delta sets. It also is a binary representation of a composition: A run of r consecutive ones corresponds to an entry r in the composition at the right.

Now write $P(n, k)$ for the compositions of n into (at most) k parts and $B(N, K)$ for the combination $\binom{N}{K}$: A composition of n into at most k parts corresponds to a combination of $K = n$ parts from $N = n + k - 1$ elements, symbolically:

$$P(n, k) \quad \leftrightarrow \quad B(N, K) = B(n + k - 1, n) \tag{7.3-1a}$$

A combination of K elements out of N corresponds to a composition of n into at most k parts where $n = K$ and $k = N - K + 1$:

$$B(N, K) \quad \leftrightarrow \quad P(n, k) = P(K, N - K + 1) \tag{7.3-1b}$$

We give routines for the conversion between combinations and compositions. The following routine converts a composition into the corresponding combination [FXT: comb/comp2comb.h]:

```
1   inline void comp2comb(const ulong *p, ulong k, ulong *b)
2   // Convert composition P(*, k) in p[] to combination in b[]
3   {
4       for (ulong j=0,i=0,z=0; j<k; ++j)
5       {
6           ulong pj = p[j];
7           for (ulong w=0; w<pj; ++w)   b[i++] = z++;
8           ++z;
9       }
10  }
```

The conversion of a combination into the corresponding composition can be implemented as

```
1    inline void comb2comp(const ulong *b, ulong N, ulong K, ulong *p)
2    // Convert combination B(N, K) in b[] to composition P(*,k) in p[]
3    // Must have: K>0
4    {
5        ulong k = N-K+1;
6        for (ulong z=0; z<k; ++z)  p[z] = 0;
7        --k;
8        ulong c1 = N;
9        while ( K-- )
10       {
11           ulong c0 = b[K];
12           ulong d = c1 - c0;
13           k -= (d-1);
14           ++p[k];
15           c1 = c0;
16       }
17   }
```

7.4 Minimal-change orders

```
          composition      combination               composition      combination
  1 : [ .  .  .  3  . ]  ...111.  [ 3 4 5 ]     1: [ 3  .  .  .  . ]  111....  [ 0 1 2 ]
  2 : [ .  1  .  2  . ]  .1..11.  [ 1 4 5 ]     2: [ 2  1  .  .  . ]  11.1...  [ 0 1 3 ]
  3 : [ 1  .  .  2  . ]  1...11.  [ 0 4 5 ]     3: [ 1  2  .  .  . ]  1.11...  [ 0 2 3 ]
  4 : [ .  .  1  2  . ]  ..1.11.  [ 2 4 5 ]     4: [ .  3  .  .  . ]  .111...  [ 1 2 3 ]
  5 : [ .  .  2  1  . ]  ..11.1.  [ 2 3 5 ]     5: [ .  2  1  .  . ]  .11.1..  [ 1 2 4 ]
  6 : [ .  1  1  1  . ]  .1.1.1.  [ 1 3 5 ]     6: [ 1  1  1  .  . ]  1.1.1..  [ 0 2 4 ]
  7 : [ 1  .  1  1  . ]  1..1.1.  [ 0 3 5 ]     7: [ 2  .  1  .  . ]  11..1..  [ 0 1 4 ]
  8 : [ 2  .  .  1  . ]  11...1.  [ 0 1 5 ]     8: [ 1  .  2  .  . ]  1..11..  [ 0 3 4 ]
  9 : [ 1  1  .  1  . ]  1.1..1.  [ 0 2 5 ]     9: [ .  1  2  .  . ]  .1.11..  [ 1 3 4 ]
 1 0 : [ .  2  .  1  . ]  .11..1.  [ 1 2 5 ]    10: [ .  .  3  .  . ]  ..111..  [ 2 3 4 ]
 1 1 : [ .  3  .  .  . ]  .111...  [ 1 2 3 ]    11: [ .  .  2  1  . ]  ..11.1.  [ 2 3 5 ]
 1 2 : [ 1  2  .  .  . ]  1.11...  [ 0 2 3 ]    12: [ 1  .  1  1  . ]  1..1.1.  [ 0 3 5 ]
 1 3 : [ 2  1  .  .  . ]  11.1...  [ 0 1 3 ]    13: [ .  1  1  1  . ]  .1.1.1.  [ 1 3 5 ]
 1 4 : [ 3  .  .  .  . ]  111....  [ 0 1 2 ]    14: [ .  2  .  1  . ]  .11..1.  [ 1 2 5 ]
 1 5 : [ 2  .  1  .  . ]  11..1..  [ 0 1 4 ]    15: [ 1  1  .  1  . ]  1.1..1.  [ 0 2 5 ]
 1 6 : [ 1  1  1  .  . ]  1.1.1..  [ 0 2 4 ]    16: [ 2  .  .  1  . ]  11...1.  [ 0 1 5 ]
 1 7 : [ .  2  1  .  . ]  .11.1..  [ 1 2 4 ]    17: [ 1  .  .  2  . ]  1...11.  [ 0 4 5 ]
 1 8 : [ .  1  2  .  . ]  .1.11..  [ 1 3 4 ]    18: [ .  1  .  2  . ]  .1..11.  [ 1 4 5 ]
 1 9 : [ 1  .  2  .  . ]  1..11..  [ 0 3 4 ]    19: [ .  .  1  2  . ]  ..1.11.  [ 2 4 5 ]
 2 0 : [ .  .  3  .  . ]  ..111..  [ 2 3 4 ]    20: [ .  .  .  3  . ]  ...111.  [ 3 4 5 ]
 2 1 : [ .  .  2  .  1 ]  ..11..1  [ 2 3 6 ]    21: [ .  .  .  2  1 ]  ...11.1  [ 3 4 6 ]
 2 2 : [ .  1  1  .  1 ]  .1.1..1  [ 1 3 6 ]    22: [ 1  .  .  1  1 ]  1...1.1  [ 0 4 6 ]
 2 3 : [ 1  .  1  .  1 ]  1..1..1  [ 0 3 6 ]    23: [ .  1  .  1  1 ]  .1..1.1  [ 1 4 6 ]
 2 4 : [ 2  .  .  .  1 ]  11....1  [ 0 1 6 ]    24: [ .  .  1  1  1 ]  ..1.1.1  [ 2 4 6 ]
 2 5 : [ 1  1  .  .  1 ]  1.1...1  [ 0 2 6 ]    25: [ .  .  2  .  1 ]  ..11..1  [ 2 3 6 ]
 2 6 : [ .  2  .  .  1 ]  .11...1  [ 1 2 6 ]    26: [ 1  .  1  .  1 ]  1..1..1  [ 0 3 6 ]
 2 7 : [ .  1  .  1  1 ]  .1..1.1  [ 1 4 6 ]    27: [ .  1  1  .  1 ]  .1.1..1  [ 1 3 6 ]
 2 8 : [ 1  .  .  1  1 ]  1...1.1  [ 0 4 6 ]    28: [ .  2  .  .  1 ]  .11...1  [ 1 2 6 ]
 2 9 : [ .  .  1  1  1 ]  ..1.1.1  [ 2 4 6 ]    29: [ 1  1  .  .  1 ]  1.1...1  [ 0 2 6 ]
 3 0 : [ .  .  .  2  1 ]  ...11.1  [ 3 4 6 ]    30: [ 2  .  .  .  1 ]  11....1  [ 0 1 6 ]
 3 1 : [ .  .  .  1  2 ]  ...1.11  [ 3 5 6 ]    31: [ 1  .  .  .  2 ]  1....11  [ 0 5 6 ]
 3 2 : [ .  1  .  .  2 ]  .1...11  [ 1 5 6 ]    32: [ .  1  .  .  2 ]  .1...11  [ 1 5 6 ]
 3 3 : [ 1  .  .  .  2 ]  1....11  [ 0 5 6 ]    33: [ .  .  1  .  2 ]  ..1..11  [ 2 5 6 ]
 3 4 : [ .  .  1  .  2 ]  ..1..11  [ 2 5 6 ]    34: [ .  .  .  1  2 ]  ...1.11  [ 3 5 6 ]
 3 5 : [ .  .  .  .  3 ]  ....111  [ 4 5 6 ]    35: [ .  .  .  .  3 ]  ....111  [ 4 5 6 ]
```

Figure 7.4-A: Compositions of 3 into 5 parts and the corresponding combinations as delta sets and sets in two minimal-change orders: order with enup moves (left) and order with modulo moves (right). The ordering by enup moves is a two-close Gray code. Dots denote zeros.

A minimal-change order (Gray code) for compositions is such that with each transition one entry is increased by 1 and another is decreased by 1. A recursion for the compositions $P(n,k)$ of n into k parts

#	combination	composition	composition	#	combination	composition	composition
1:	[0 5 6]	1....11	[1 . . . 2]	1:	[0 1 2]	111....	[3 . . . .]
2:	[0 4 6]	1...1.1	[1 . . 1 1]	2:	[0 1 3]	11.1...	[2 1 . . .]
3:	[0 4 5]	1...11.	[1 . . 2 .]	3:	[0 1 4]	11..1..	[2 . 1 . .]
4:	[0 3 4]	1..11..	[1 . 2 . .]	4:	[0 1 5]	11...1.	[2 . . 1 .]
5:	[0 3 5]	1..1.1.	[1 . 1 1 .]	5:	[0 1 6]	11....1	[2 . . . 1]
6:	[0 3 6]	1..1..1	[1 . 1 . 1]	6:	[0 2 6]	1.1...1	[1 1 . . 1]
7:	[0 2 6]	1.1...1	[1 1 . . 1]	7:	[0 2 5]	1.1..1.	[1 1 . 1 .]
8:	[0 2 5]	1.1..1.	[1 1 . 1 .]	8:	[0 2 4]	1.1.1..	[1 1 1 . .]
9:	[0 2 4]	1.1.1..	[1 1 1 . .]	9:	[0 2 3]	1.11...	[1 2 . . .]
10	[0 2 3]	1.11...	[1 2 . . .]	10:	[0 3 4]	1..11..	[1 . 2 . .]
11	[0 1 2]	111....	[3 . . . .]	11:	[0 3 5]	1..1.1.	[1 . 1 1 .]
12	[0 1 3]	11.1...	[2 1 . . .]	12:	[0 3 6]	1..1..1	[1 . 1 . 1]
13	[0 1 4]	11..1..	[2 . 1 . .]	13:	[0 4 6]	1...1.1	[1 . . 1 1]
14	[0 1 5]	11...1.	[2 . . 1 .]	14:	[0 4 5]	1...11.	[1 . . 2 .]
15	[0 1 6]	11....1	[2 . . . 1]	15:	[0 5 6]	1....11	[1 . . . 2]
16	[1 2 6]	.11...1	[. 2 . . 1]	16:	[1 5 6]	.1...11	[. 1 . . 2]
17	[1 2 5]	.11..1.	[. 2 . 1 .]	17:	[1 4 6]	.1..1.1	[. 1 . 1 1]
18	[1 2 4]	.11.1..	[. 2 1 . .]	18:	[1 4 5]	.1..11.	[. 1 . 2 .]
19	[1 2 3]	.111...	[. 3 . . .]	19:	[1 3 4]	.1.11..	[. 1 2 . .]
20	[1 3 4]	.1.11..	[. 1 2 . .]	20:	[1 3 5]	.1.1.1.	[. 1 1 1 .]
21 :	[1 3 5]	.1.1.1.	[. 1 1 1 .]	21:	[1 3 6]	.1.1..1	[. 1 1 . 1]
22	[1 3 6]	.1.1..1	[. 1 1 . 1]	22:	[1 2 6]	.11...1	[. 2 . . 1]
23	[1 4 6]	.1..1.1	[. 1 . 1 1]	23:	[1 2 5]	.11..1.	[. 2 . 1 .]
24	[1 4 5]	.1..11.	[. 1 . 2 .]	24:	[1 2 4]	.11.1..	[. 2 1 . .]
25	[1 5 6]	.1...11	[. 1 . . 2]	25:	[1 2 3]	.111...	[. 3 . . .]
26	[2 5 6]	..1..11	[. . 1 . 2]	26:	[2 3 4]	..111..	[. . 3 . .]
27	[2 4 6]	..1.1.1	[. . 1 1 1]	27:	[2 3 5]	..11.1.	[. . 2 1 .]
28	[2 4 5]	..1.11.	[. . 1 2 .]	28:	[2 3 6]	..11..1	[. . 2 . 1]
29	[2 3 4]	..111..	[. . 3 . .]	29:	[2 4 6]	..1.1.1	[. . 1 1 1]
30	[2 3 5]	..11.1.	[. . 2 1 .]	30:	[2 4 5]	..1.11.	[. . 1 2 .]
31	[2 3 6]	..11..1	[. . 2 . 1]	31:	[2 5 6]	..1..11	[. . 1 . 2]
32	[3 4 6]	...11.1	[. . . 2 1]	32:	[3 5 6]	...1.11	[. . . 1 2]
33	[3 4 5]	...111.	[. . . 3 .]	33:	[3 4 6]	...11.1	[. . . 2 1]
34	[3 5 6]	...1.11	[. . . 1 2]	34:	[3 4 5]	...111.	[. . . 3 .]
35	[4 5 6]	111	[. . . . 3]	35:	[4 5 6]	111	[. . . . 3]

Figure 7.4-B: The (reversed) complemented enup ordering (left) and Eades-McKay sequence (right) for combinations correspond to compositions where only two adjacent entries change with each transition, but by more than 1 in general.

---

in lexicographic order is (notation as in relation 14.1-1 on page 304)

$$
P(n,k) \;=\;
\begin{array}{l}
[0 \,.\, P(n-0, k-1)] \\
[1 \,.\, P(n-1, k-1)] \\
[2 \,.\, P(n-2, k-1)] \\
[3 \,.\, P(n-3, k-1)] \\
[4 \,.\, P(n-4, k-1)] \\
\quad\vdots \\
[n \,.\, P(0, k-1)\;\;]
\end{array}
\tag{7.4-1}
$$

A Gray code is obtained by changing the direction if the element is even:

$$
P(n,k) \;=\;
\begin{array}{l}
[0 \,.\, P^{\mathbf{R}}(n-0, k-1)] \\
[1 \,.\, P(n-1, k-1)\;\;] \\
[2 \,.\, P^{\mathbf{R}}(n-2, k-1)] \\
[3 \,.\, P(n-3, k-1)\;\;] \\
[4 \,.\, P^{\mathbf{R}}(n-4, k-1)] \\
\quad\vdots
\end{array}
\tag{7.4-2}
$$

The ordering is shown in figure 7.4-A (left), the corresponding combinations are in the (reversed) enup order from section 6.6.2 on page 188. Now we change directions at the odd elements:

$$P(n,k) \quad = \quad \begin{array}{l} [0 \,.\, P(n-0,k-1) \ ] \\ [1 \,.\, P^{\mathbf{R}}(n-1,k-1)] \\ [2 \,.\, P(n-2,k-1) \ ] \\ [3 \,.\, P^{\mathbf{R}}(n-3,k-1)] \\ [4 \,.\, P(n-4,k-1) \ ] \\ \\ [\qquad \vdots \qquad \quad] \end{array} \qquad (7.4\text{-}3)$$

We get an ordering (right of figure 7.4-A) corresponding to the combinations are in the (reversed) Eades-McKay order from section 6.5 on page 183. The listings were created with the program [FXT: comb/composition-gray-rec-demo.cc].

Gray codes for combinations correspond to Gray codes for combinations where no element in the delta set crosses another. The standard Gray code for combinations does not lead to a Gray code for compositions as shown in figure 7.3-A on page 198. If the directions in the recursions are always changed, the compositions correspond to combinations that have the complemented delta sets of the standard Gray code in reversed order.

Orderings where the changes involve just one pair of adjacent entries (shown in figure 7.4-B) correspond to the complemented strong Gray codes for combinations. The amount of change is greater than 1 in general. The listings were created with the program [FXT: comb/combination-rec-demo.cc], see section 6.7 on page 191.

Chapter 8

Subsets

We give algorithms to generate all subsets of a set of n elements. There are 2^n subsets, including the empty set. We further give methods to generate all subsets with k elements where k lies in a given range: $k_{min} \leq k \leq k_{max}$. The subsets with exactly k elements are treated in chapter 6 on page 176.

8.1 Lexicographic order

```
 1:   1....    {0}                    1....    {0}
 2:   11...    {0, 1}                 .1...    {1}
 3:   111..    {0, 1, 2}             11...    {0, 1}
 4:   1111.    {0, 1, 2, 3}          ..1..    {2}
 5:   11111    {0, 1, 2, 3, 4}       1.1..    {0, 2}
 6:   111.1    {0, 1, 2, 4}          .11..    {1, 2}
 7:   11.1.    {0, 1, 3}             111..    {0, 1, 2}
 8:   11.11    {0, 1, 3, 4}          ...1.    {3}
 9:   11..1    {0, 1, 4}             1..1.    {0, 3}
10:   1.1..    {0, 2}                .1.1.    {1, 3}
11:   1.11.    {0, 2, 3}            11.1.    {0, 1, 3}
12:   1.111    {0, 2, 3, 4}          ..11.    {2, 3}
13:   1.1.1    {0, 2, 4}            1.11.    {0, 2, 3}
14:   1..1.    {0, 3}                .111.    {1, 2, 3}
15:   1..11    {0, 3, 4}            1111.    {0, 1, 2, 3}
16:   1...1    {0, 4}                ....1    {4}
17:   .1...    {1}                   1...1    {0, 4}
18:   .11..    {1, 2}                .1..1    {1, 4}
19:   .111.    {1, 2, 3}            11..1    {0, 1, 4}
20:   .1111    {1, 2, 3, 4}          ..1.1    {2, 4}
21:   .11.1    {1, 2, 4}            1.1.1    {0, 2, 4}
22:   .1.1.    {1, 3}                .11.1    {1, 2, 4}
23:   .1.11    {1, 3, 4}            111.1    {0, 1, 2, 4}
24:   .1..1    {1, 4}                ...11    {3, 4}
25:   ..1..    {2}                   1..11    {0, 3, 4}
26:   ..11.    {2, 3}                .1.11    {1, 3, 4}
27:   ..111    {2, 3, 4}            11.11    {0, 1, 3, 4}
28:   ..1.1    {2, 4}                ..111    {2, 3, 4}
29:   ...1.    {3}                   1.111    {0, 2, 3, 4}
30:   ...11    {3, 4}                .1111    {1, 2, 3, 4}
31:   ....1    {4}                  11111    {0, 1, 2, 3, 4}
```

Figure 8.1-A: Nonempty subsets of a 5-element set in lexicographic order for the sets (left) and in lexicographic order for the delta sets (right).

The (nonempty) subsets of a set of five elements in lexicographic order are shown in figure 8.1-A. Note that the lexicographic order with sets is different from the lexicographic order with delta sets.

8.1.1 Generation as delta sets

The listing on the right side of figure 8.1-A is with respect to the delta sets. It was created with the program [FXT: comb/subset-deltalex-demo.cc] which uses the generator [FXT: class subset_deltalex

J. Arndt, *Matters Computational: Ideas, Algorithms, Source Code*,
DOI 10.1007/978-3-642-14764-7_8, © Springer-Verlag Berlin Heidelberg 2011

in comb/subset-deltalex.h]:

```
1    class subset_deltalex
2    {
3    public:
4        ulong *d_;   // subset as delta set
5        ulong n_;    // subsets of the  n-set {0,1,2,...,n-1}
6
7    public:
8        subset_deltalex(ulong n)
9        {
10           n_ = n;
11           d_ = new ulong[n+1];
12           d_[n] = 0;  // sentinel
13           first();
14       }
15
16       ~subset_deltalex()  { delete [] d_; }
17
18       void first()  { for (ulong k=0; k<n_; ++k)  d_[k] = 0; }
```

The algorithm for the computation of the successor is binary counting:

```
1
2        bool next()
3        {
4            ulong k = 0;
5            while ( d_[k]==1 )  { d_[k]=0;  ++k; }
6
7            if ( k==n_ )  return false;  // current subset is last
8
9            d_[k] = 1;
10           return true;
11       }
12
13       const ulong * data()  const { return d_; }
14   };
```

About 176 million subsets per second are generated and 192 M/s if an array is used. A bit-level algorithm to compute the subsets in lexicographic order is given in section 1.26 on page 70.

8.1.2   Generation as sets

The lexicographic order with respect to the set representation is shown at the left side of figure 8.1-A. The routines in [FXT: class subset_lex in comb/subset-lex.h] compute the nonempty sets:

```
1    class subset_lex
2    {
3    public:
4        ulong *x_;   // subset of {0,1,2,...,n-1}
5        ulong n_;    // number of elements in set
6        ulong k_;    // index of last element in subset
7        // Number of elements in subset == k+1
8
9    public:
10       subset_lex(ulong n)
11       {
12           n_ = n;
13           x_ = new ulong[n_];
14           first();
15       }
16
17       ~subset_lex()  { delete [] x_; }
18
19       ulong first()
20       {
21           k_ = 0;
22           x_[0] = 0;
23           return  k_ + 1;
24       }
25
26       ulong last()
27       {
28           k_ = 0;
29           x_[0] = n_ - 1;
30           return  k_ + 1;
31       }
```

```
32      [--snip--]
```

The method `next()` computes the successor:

```
1       ulong next()
2       // Generate next subset
3       // Return number of elements in subset
4       // Return zero if current == last
5       {
6           if ( x_[k_] == n_-1 )  // last element is max ?
7           {
8               if ( k_==0 ) { first();  return 0; }
9
10              --k_;       // remove last element
11              x_[k_]++;   // increase last element
12          }
13          else  // add next element from set:
14          {
15              ++k_;
16              x_[k_] = x_[k_-1] + 1;
17          }
18
19          return  k_ + 1;
20      }
```

Computation of the predecessor:

```
1       ulong prev()
2       // Generate previous subset
3       // Return number of elements in subset
4       // Return zero if current == first
5       {
6           if ( k_ == 0 )  // only one element ?
7           {
8               if ( x_[0]==0 ) { last();  return 0; }
9
10              x_[0]--;  // decr first element
11              x_[++k_] = n_ - 1;      // add element
12          }
13          else
14          {
15              if ( x_[k_] == x_[k_-1]+1 )  --k_;  // remove last element
16              else
17              {
18                  x_[k_]--;  // decr last element
19                  x_[++k_] = n_ - 1;      // add element
20              }
21          }
22
23          return  k_ + 1;
24      }
25
26      const ulong * data()  const { return x_; }
27  };
```

About 270 million subsets per second are generated with `next()` and about 155 million with `prev()` [FXT: comb/subset-lex-demo.cc]. A generalization of this order with mixed radix numbers is described in section 9.3 on page 224. A bit-level algorithm is given in section 1.26 on page 70.

8.2 Minimal-change order

8.2.1 Generation as delta sets

The subsets of a set with 5 elements in minimal-change order are shown in figure 8.2-A. The implementation [FXT: class `subset_gray_delta` in comb/subset-gray-delta.h] uses the Gray code of binary words and updates the position corresponding to the bit that changes in the Gray code:

```
1   class subset_gray_delta
2   // Subsets of the set {0,1,2,...,n-1} in minimal-change (Gray code) order.
3   {
4   public:
5       ulong *x_;  // current subset as delta-set
6       ulong n_;   // number of elements in set <= BITS_PER_LONG
7       ulong j_;   // position of last change
```

```
 0:    .....  {}                      0:   11111  { 0, 1, 2, 3, 4 }
 1:    1....  {0}                     1:   .1111  { 1, 2, 3, 4 }
 2:    11...  {0, 1}                  2:   ..111  { 2, 3, 4 }
 3:    .1...  {1}                     3:   1.111  { 0, 2, 3, 4 }
 4:    .11..  {1, 2}                  4:   1..11  { 0, 3, 4 }
 5:    111..  {0, 1, 2}              5:   ...11  { 3, 4 }
 6:    1.1..  {0, 2}                  6:   .1.11  { 1, 3, 4 }
 7:    ..1..  {2}                     7:   11.11  { 0, 1, 3, 4 }
 8:    ..11.  {2, 3}                  8:   11..1  { 0, 1, 4 }
 9:    1.11.  {0, 2, 3}              9:   .1..1  { 1, 4 }
10:    1111.  {0, 1, 2, 3}          10:   ....1  { 4 }
11:    .111.  {1, 2, 3}             11:   1...1  { 0, 4 }
12:    .1.1.  {1, 3}                12:   1.1.1  { 0, 2, 4 }
13:    11.1.  {0, 1, 3}             13:   ..1.1  { 2, 4 }
14:    1..1.  {0, 3}                14:   .11.1  { 1, 2, 4 }
15:    ...1.  {3}                    15:   111.1  { 0, 1, 2, 4 }
16:    ...11  {3, 4}                 16:   111..  { 0, 1, 2 }
17:    1..11  {0, 3, 4}             17:   .11..  { 1, 2 }
18:    11.11  {0, 1, 3, 4}          18:   ..1..  { 2 }
19:    .1.11  {1, 3, 4}             19:   1.1..  { 0, 2 }
20:    .1111  {1, 2, 3, 4}          20:   1....  { 0 }
21:    11111  {0, 1, 2, 3, 4}       21:   .....  {   }
22:    1.111  {0, 2, 3, 4}          22:   .1...  { 1 }
23:    ..111  {2, 3, 4}             23:   11...  { 0, 1 }
24:    ...1.1 {2, 4}                 24:   11.1.  { 0, 1, 3 }
25:    1.1.1  {0, 2, 4}             25:   .1.1.  { 1, 3 }
26:    111.1  {0, 1, 2, 4}          26:   ...1.  { 3 }
27:    .11.1  {1, 2, 4}             27:   1..1.  { 0, 3 }
28:    .1..1  {1, 4}                28:   1.11.  { 0, 2, 3 }
29:    11..1  {0, 1, 4}             29:   ..11.  { 2, 3 }
30:    1...1  {0, 4}                30:   .111.  { 1, 2, 3 }
31:    ....1  {4}                    31:   1111.  { 0, 1, 2, 3 }
```

Figure 8.2-A: The subsets of the set {0, 1, 2, 3, 4} in minimal-change order (left) and complemented minimal-change order (right). The changes are on the same places for both orders.

```
 8        ulong ct_;  // gray_code(ct_) corresponds to the current subset
 9        ulong mct_; // max value of ct.
10
11    public:
12        subset_gray_delta(ulong n)
13        {
14            n_ = (n ? n : 1);  // not zero
15            x_ = new ulong[n_];
16            mct_ = (1UL<<n) - 1;
17            first(0);
18        }
19
20        ~subset_gray_delta()  { delete [] x_; }
21
```

In the initializer one can choose whether the first set is the empty or the full set (left and right of figure 8.2-A):

```
 1        void first(ulong v=0)
 2        {
 3            ct_ = 0;
 4            j_ = n_ - 1;
 5            for (ulong j=0; j<n_; ++j)  x_[j] = v;
 6        }
 7
 8        const ulong * data()  const  { return x_; }
 9        ulong pos()  const { return j_; }
10        ulong current()  const  { return ct_; }
11
12        ulong next()
13        // Return position of change, return n with last subset
14        {
15            if ( ct_ == mct_ )  { return n_; }
16
```

```
17              ++ct_;
18              j_ = lowest_one_idx( ct_ );
19              x_[j_] ^= 1;
20
21              return  j_;
22          }
23
24      ulong prev()
25      // Return position of change, return n with first subset
26          {
27              if ( ct_ == 0 )  { return n_; }
28
29              j_ = lowest_one_idx( ct_ );
30              x_[j_] ^= 1;
31              --ct_;
32
33              return  j_;
34          }
35  };
```

About 180 million subsets are generated per second [FXT: comb/subset-gray-delta-demo.cc].

8.2.2   Generation as sets

A generator for the subsets of $\{1, 2, \ldots, n\}$ in set representation is [FXT: class subset_gray in comb/subset-gray.h]:

```
1   class subset_gray
2   // Subsets of the set {1,2,...,n} in minimal-change (Gray code) order.
3   {
4   public:
5       ulong *x_;   // data k-subset of {1,2,...,n} in x[1,...,k]
6       ulong n_;    // subsets of n-set
7       ulong k_;    // number of elements in subset
8
9   public:
10      subset_gray(ulong n)
11          {
12              n_ = n;
13              x_ = new ulong[n_+1];
14              x_[0] = 0;
15              first();
16          }
17
18      ~subset_gray()  { delete [] x_; }
19
20      ulong first()  { k_ = 0;  return k_; }
21      ulong last()   { x_[1] = 1;  k_ = 1;  return k_; }
22
23      const ulong * data() const { return x_+1; }
24      const ulong num() const { return k_; }
25
```

The algorithm to compute the successor is described in section 1.16.3 on page 43, see also [192]:

```
1   private:
2       ulong next_even()
3           {
4               if ( x_[k_]==n_ ) // remove n (from end):
5               {
6                   --k_;
7               }
8               else  // append n:
9               {
10                  ++k_;
11                  x_[k_] = n_;
12              }
13              return  k_;
14          }
15
16      ulong next_odd()
17          {
18              if ( x_[k_]-1==x_[k_-1] ) // remove x[k]-1 (from position k-1):
19              {
20                  x_[k_-1] = x_[k_];
21                  --k_;
```

```
22          }
23          else // insert x[k]-1 as second last element:
24          {
25              x_[k_+1] = x_[k_];
26              --x_[k_];
27              ++k_;
28          }
29          return  k_;
30      }
31
 1  public:
 2      ulong next()
 3      {
 4          if ( 0==(k_&1 ) ) return next_even();
 5          else               return next_odd();
 6      }
 7
 8      ulong prev()
 9      {
10          if ( 0==(k_&1 ) )  // k even
11          {
12              if ( 0==k_ )  return last();
13              return next_odd();
14          }
15          else  return next_even();
16      }
17  };
```

About 241 million subsets per second are generated with **next()** and about 167 M/s with **prev()** [FXT: comb/subset-gray-demo.cc]. With arrays instead of pointers the rates are about 266 M/s and 179 M/s.

8.2.3 Computing just the positions of change

The following routine computes only the locations of the changes, it is given in [52]. It can also be obtained as a specialization (for radix 2) of the loopless algorithm for computing a Gray code ordering of mixed radix numbers given section 9.2 on page 220 [FXT: **class ruler_func** in comb/ruler-func.h]:

```
 1  class ruler_func
 2  // Ruler function sequence: 0 1 0 2 0 1 0 3 0 1 0 2 0 1 0 4 0 1 0 2 0 1 ...
 3  {
 4  public:
 5      ulong *f_;   // focus pointer
 6      ulong n_;
 7
 8  public:
 9      ruler_func(ulong n)
10      {
11          n_ = n;
12          f_ = new ulong[n+2];
13          first();
14      }
15
16      ~ruler_func()  { delete [] f_; }
17
18      void first()  { for (ulong k=0; k<n_+2; ++k)  f_[k] = k; }
19
20      ulong next()
21      {
22          const ulong j = f_[0];
23          //  if ( j==n_ )  { first(); return n_; }  // leave to user
24          f_[0] = 0;
25          const ulong nj = j+1;
26          f_[j] = f_[nj];
27          f_[nj] = nj;
28          return j;
29      }
30  };
```

The rate of generation is about 244 M/s and 293 M/s if an array is used [FXT: comb/ruler-func-demo.cc].

```
 0:  {0,  ,  ,  ,  }  #=1  {0}              0:  { ,  , 2,  , 4}  #=2  {2, 4}
 1:  { , 1,  ,  ,  }  #=1  {1}              1:  {0, 1, 2,  , 4}  #=4  {0, 1, 2, 4}
 2:  { ,  , 2,  ,  }  #=1  {2}              2:  {0,  ,  ,  , 4}  #=2  {0, 4}
 3:  { ,  ,  , 3,  }  #=1  {3}              3:  {0,  , 2, 3, 4}  #=4  {0, 2, 3, 4}
 4:  {0,  ,  ,  , 4}  #=2  {0, 4}           4:  { ,  , 2,  ,  }  #=1  {2}
 5:  {0, 1,  ,  ,  }  #=2  {0, 1}           5:  { , 1, 2,  , 4}  #=3  {1, 2, 4}
 6:  { , 1, 2,  ,  }  #=2  {1, 2}           6:  {0, 1,  ,  , 4}  #=3  {0, 1, 4}
 7:  { ,  , 2, 3,  }  #=2  {2, 3}           7:  {0,  ,  , 3, 4}  #=3  {0, 3, 4}
 8:  {0,  ,  , 3, 4}  #=3  {0, 3, 4}        8:  { ,  , 2, 3,  }  #=2  {2, 3}
 9:  { , 1,  ,  , 4}  #=2  {1, 4}           9:  {0, 1, 2,  ,  }  #=3  {0, 1, 2}
10:  {0,  , 2,  ,  }  #=2  {0, 2}          10:  { ,  ,  ,  , 4}  #=1  {4}
11:  { , 1,  , 3,  }  #=2  {1, 3}          11:  {0, 1, 2, 3, 4}  #=5  {0, 1, 2, 3, 4}
12:  { ,  , 2,  , 4}  #=2  {2, 4}          12:  {0,  ,  ,  ,  }  #=1  {0}
13:  {0,  ,  , 3,  }  #=2  {0, 3}          13:  { ,  , 2, 3, 4}  #=3  {2, 3, 4}
14:  {0, 1,  ,  , 4}  #=3  {0, 1, 4}       14:  { , 1, 2,  ,  }  #=2  {1, 2}
15:  {0, 1, 2,  ,  }  #=3  {0, 1, 2}       15:  { , 1,  ,  , 4}  #=2  {1, 4}
16:  { , 1, 2, 3,  }  #=3  {1, 2, 3}       16:  {0, 1,  , 3, 4}  #=4  {0, 1, 3, 4}
17:  {0,  , 2, 3, 4}  #=4  {0, 2, 3, 4}    17:  { ,  ,  , 3,  }  #=1  {3}
18:  { , 1,  , 3, 4}  #=3  {1, 3, 4}       18:  {0, 1, 2, 3,  }  #=4  {0, 1, 2, 3}
19:  {0,  , 2,  , 4}  #=3  {0, 2, 4}       19:  { ,  ,  ,  ,  }  #=0  {}
20:  {0, 1,  , 3,  }  #=3  {0, 1, 3}       20:  { , 1, 2, 3, 4}  #=4  {1, 2, 3, 4}
21:  { , 1, 2,  , 4}  #=3  {1, 2, 4}       21:  {0, 1,  ,  ,  }  #=2  {0, 1}
22:  {0,  , 2, 3,  }  #=3  {0, 2, 3}       22:  { ,  ,  , 3, 4}  #=2  {3, 4}
23:  {0, 1,  , 3, 4}  #=4  {0, 1, 3, 4}    23:  { , 1, 2, 3,  }  #=3  {1, 2, 3}
24:  {0, 1, 2,  , 4}  #=4  {0, 1, 2, 4}    24:  { , 1,  ,  ,  }  #=1  {1}
25:  {0, 1, 2, 3,  }  #=4  {0, 1, 2, 3}    25:  { , 1,  , 3, 4}  #=3  {1, 3, 4}
26:  {0, 1, 2, 3, 4}  #=5  {0, 1, 2, 3, 4} 26:  { , 1,  , 3,  }  #=2  {1, 3}
27:  { , 1, 2, 3, 4}  #=4  {1, 2, 3, 4}    27:  {0, 1,  , 3,  }  #=3  {0, 1, 3}
28:  { ,  , 2, 3, 4}  #=3  {2, 3, 4}       28:  {0,  ,  , 3,  }  #=2  {0, 3}
29:  { ,  ,  , 3, 4}  #=2  {3, 4}          29:  {0,  , 2, 3,  }  #=3  {0, 2, 3}
30:  { ,  ,  ,  , 4}  #=1  {4}             30:  {0,  , 2,  ,  }  #=2  {0, 2}
31:  { ,  ,  ,  ,  }  #=0  {}              31:  {0,  , 2,  , 4}  #=3  {0, 2, 4}
```

Figure 8.3-A: Subsets of a 5-element set in an order corresponding to a De Bruijn sequence (left), and alternative ordering obtained by complementing the elements at even indices (right).

8.3 Ordering with De Bruijn sequences

A curious ordering for all subsets of a given set can be generated using a binary *De Bruijn sequence* that is a cyclic sequence of zeros and ones that contains each n-bit word once. In figure 8.3-A the empty places of the subsets are included to make the nice feature apparent [FXT: comb/subset-debruijn-demo.cc]. The ordering has the *single track* property: each column in this (delta set) representation is a circular shift of the first column. Each subset is made from its predecessor by shifting it to the right and inserting the current element from the sequence. The underlying De Bruijn sequence is

```
. 1 0 0 0 1 1 0 0 1 0 1 0 0 1 1 1 0 1 0 1 1 0 1 1 1 1 1 0 0 0 0 0
```

The implementation [FXT: `class subset_debruijn` in comb/subset-debruijn.h] uses [FXT: `class binary_debruijn` in comb/binary-debruijn.h], described in section 18.2 on page 377.

Successive subsets differ in many elements if the sequency (see section 1.17 on page 46) is large. Using the 'sequency-complemented' subsets (see end of section 1.17), we obtain an ordering where more elements change with small sequencies, as shown at the right of figure 8.3-A. This ordering corresponds to the complement-shift sequence of section 20.2.3 on page 397.

8.4 Shifts-order for subsets

Figure 8.4-A shows an ordering (*shifts-order*) of the nonempty subsets of a 6-bit binary word where all linear shifts of a word appear in succession. The generation is done by a simple recursion [FXT: comb/shift-subsets-demo.cc]:

```
1    ulong n;  // number of bits
2    ulong N;  // 2**n
3
4    void A(ulong x)
5    {
6        if ( x>=N )  return;
```

```
 1:  .....1  1    17:  1..111  4    33:  ....11  2    49:  ...111  3
 2:  ....1.  1    18:  ...1.1  2    34:  ...11.  2    50:  ..111.  3
 3:  ...1..  1    19:  ..1.1.  2    35:  ..11..  2    51:  .111..  3
 4:  ..1...  1    20:  .1.1..  2    36:  .11...  2    52:  111...  3
 5:  .1....  1    21:  1.1...  2    37:  11....  2    53:  111..1  4
 6:  1.....  1    22:  1.1..1  3    38:  11...1  3    54:  .111.1  4
 7:  1....1  2    23:  .1.1.1  3    39:  .11..1  3    55:  111.1.  4
 8:  .1...1  2    24:  1.1.1.  3    40:  11..1.  3    56:  111.11  5
 9:  1...1.  2    25:  1.1.11  4    41:  11..11  4    57:  ..1111  4
10:  1...11  3    26:  ..1.11  3    42:  ..11.1  3    58:  .1111.  4
11:  .1..1.  2    27:  .1.11.  3    43:  .11.1.  3    59:  1111..  4
12:  .1.1..  2    28:  1.11..  3    44:  11.1..  3    60:  1111.1  5
13:  1..1..  2    29:  1.11.1  4    45:  11.1.1  4    61:  .11111  5
14:  1..1.1  3    30:  .1111.  4    46:  .11.11  4    62:  11111.  5
15:  .1.11.  3    31:  1.111.  4    47:  11.11.  4    63:  111111  6
16:  1..11.  3    32:  1.1111  5    48:  11.111  5
```

Figure 8.4-A: Nonempty subsets of a 6-bit binary word where all linear shifts of a word appear in succession (shifts-order). All shifts are left shifts.

```
 1:  .....1  1    17:  ..1..1  2    33:  ...111  3    49:  .11.1.  3
 2:  ....1.  1    18:  ..1.11  3    34:  ..1111  3    50:  11.1..  3
 3:  ...1..  1    19:  .1.11.  3    35:  .111..  3    51:  11.1.1  4
 4:  ..1...  1    20:  1.11..  3    36:  111...  3    52:  11.111  5
 5:  .1....  1    21:  1.11.1  4    37:  111..1  4    53:  11.11.  4
 6:  1.....  1    22:  1.1111  5    38:  111.11  5    54:  .11.11  4
 7:  1....1  2    23:  1.111.  4    39:  111.1.  4    55:  .11..1  3
 8:  1...11  3    24:  .1.111  4    40:  .111.1  4    56:  11..1.  3
 9:  1...1.  2    25:  .1.1.1  3    41:  .11111  5    57:  11..11  4
10:  .1...1  2    26:  1.1.1.  3    42:  11111.  5    58:  11...1  3
11:  .1..11  3    27:  1.1.11  4    43:  111111  6    59:  11....  2
12:  1..11.  3    28:  1.1.1.  3    44:  1111.1  5    60:  .11...  2
13:  1..111  4    29:  1.1..1  2    45:  1111..  4    61:  ..11..  2
14:  1..1.1  3    30:  .1.1..  2    46:  .1111.  4    62:  ...11.  2
15:  1..1..  2    31:  ..1.1.  2    47:  ..1111  4    63:  ....11  2
16:  .1..1.  2    32:  ...1.1  2    48:  ..11.1  3
```

Figure 8.4-B: Nonempty subsets of a 6-bit binary word where all linear shifts of a word appear in succession and transitions that are not shifts switch just one bit (minimal-change shifts-order).

```
 1:  .......1  1    17:  ..1...1.  2    33:  1..1.1..  3    49:  ..1.1.1.  3
 2:  ......1.  1    18:  .1...1..  2    34:  1..1.1.1  4    50:  .1.1.1..  3
 3:  .....1..  1    19:  1...1...  2    35:  ....1.1.  2    51:  1.1.1...  3
 4:  ....1...  1    20:  1...1..1  3    36:  ....1.1.  2    52:  1.1.1..1  4
 5:  ...1....  1    21:  .1...1.1  3    37:  ...1.1..  2    53:  .1.1.1.1  4
 6:  ..1.....  1    22:  1...1.1.  3    38:  ..1.1...  2    54:  1.1.1.1.  4
 7:  .1......  1    23:  ....1..1  2    39:  .1.1....  2
 8:  1.......  1    24:  ...1..1.  2    40:  1.1.....  2
 9:  1......1  2    25:  ..1..1..  2    41:  1.1....1  3
10:  .1.....1  2    26:  .1..1...  2    42:  .1.1...1  3
11:  1.....1.  2    27:  1..1....  2    43:  1.1...1.  3
12:  .1....1.  2    28:  1..1...1  3    44:  ..1.1..1  3
13:  .1...1..  2    29:  .1..1..1  3    45:  .1.1.1..  3
14:  1....1..  2    30:  1..1..1.  3    46:  1.1..1..  3
15:  1...1.1.  3    31:  .1..1.1.  3    47:  1.1..1.1  4
16:  ...1...1  2    32:  .1..1.1.  3    48:  ...1.1.1  3
```

Figure 8.4-C: Nonzero Fibonacci words in an order where all shifts appear in succession.

```
7        visit(x);
8        A(2*x);
9        A(2*x+1);
10   }
```

The function visit() prints the binary expansion of its argument. The initial call is A(1).

The transitions that are not shifts change just one bit if the following pair of functions is used for the recursion (*minimal-change shifts-order* shown in figure 8.4-B):

```
1    void F(ulong x)
2    {
3        if ( x>=N )  return;
4        visit(x);
5        F(2*x);
6        G(2*x+1);
```

```
7   }
8
9   void G(ulong x)
10  {
11      if ( x>=N )  return;
12      F(2*x+1);
13      G(2*x);
14      visit(x);
15  }
```

The initial call is `F(1)`, the reversed order can be generated via `G(1)`.

A simple variation can be used to generate the Fibonacci words in a shifts-order shown in figure 8.4-C. With transitions that are not shifts more than one bit is changed in general. The function used is [FXT: comb/shift-subsets-demo.cc]:

```
1   void B(ulong x)
2   {
3       if ( x>=N )  return;
4       visit(x);
5       B(2*x);
6       B(4*x+1);
7   }
```

A bit-level algorithm for combinations in shifts-order is given in section 1.24.3 on page 64.

8.5 k-subsets where k lies in a given range

We give algorithms for generating all k-*subsets* of the n-set where k lies in the range $k_{min} \leq k \leq k_{max}$. If $k_{min} = 0$ and $k_{max} = n$, we generate all subsets. If $k_{min} = k_{max} = k$, we get the k-combinations of n.

8.5.1 Recursive algorithm

A generator for all k-subsets where k lies in a prescribed range is [FXT: class `ksubset_rec` in comb/ksubset-rec.h]. The used algorithm can generate the subsets in 16 different orders. Figure 8.5-A shows the lexicographic orders, figure 8.5-B shows three Gray codes. The constructor has just one argument, the number of elements of the set whose subsets are generated:

```
1   class ksubset_rec
2   // k-subsets where kmin<=k<=kmax in various orders.
3   // Recursive CAT algorithm.
4   {
5   public:
6       long n_; // subsets of a n-element set
7       long kmin_, kmax_; //  k-subsets where kmin<=k<=kma
8       long *rv_;  // record of visits in graph (list of elements in subset)
9       ulong ct_;   // count subsets
10      ulong rct_;  // count recursions (==work)
11      ulong rq_;   // condition that determines the order
12      ulong pq_;   // condition that determines the (printing) order
13      ulong nq_;   // whether to reverse order
14      // function to call with each combination:
15      void (*visit_)(const ksubset_rec &, long);
16
17  public:
18      ksubset_rec(ulong n)
19      {
20          n_ = n;
21          rv_ = new long[n_+1];
22          ++rv_;
23          rv_[-1] = -1UL;
24      }
25
26      ~ksubset_rec()
27      {
28          --rv_;
29          delete [] rv_;
30      }
```

One has to supply the interval for k (variables `kmin` and `kmax`) and a function that will be called with each subset. The argument `rq` determines which of the sixteen different orderings is chosen, the order

```
                order #0:                                        order #8:
     0:   11....   ......   { 0, 1 }           111...   ......   { 0, 1, 2 }
     1:   111...   ..P...   { 0, 1, 2 }        11.1..   ..MP..   { 0, 1, 3 }
     2:   11.1..   ..MP..   { 0, 1, 3 }        11..1.   ...MP.   { 0, 1, 4 }
     3:   11..1.   ...MP.   { 0, 1, 4 }        11...1   ....MP   { 0, 1, 5 }
     4:   11...1   ....MP   { 0, 1, 5 }        11....   .....M   { 0, 1 }
     5:   1.1...   .MP..M   { 0, 2 }           1.11..   .MPP..   { 0, 2, 3 }
     6:   1.11..   ...P..   { 0, 2, 3 }        1.1.1.   ...MP.   { 0, 2, 4 }
     7:   1.1.1.   ...MP.   { 0, 2, 4 }        1.1..1   ....MP   { 0, 2, 5 }
     8:   1.1..1   ....MP   { 0, 2, 5 }        1.1...   .....M   { 0, 2 }
     9:   1..1..   ..MP.M   { 0, 3 }           1..11.   ..MPP.   { 0, 3, 4 }
    10:   1..11.   ....P.   { 0, 3, 4 }        1..1.1   ....MP   { 0, 3, 5 }
    11:   1..1.1   ....MP   { 0, 3, 5 }        1..1..   .....M   { 0, 3 }
    12:   1...1.   ...MPM   { 0, 4 }           1...11   ...MPP   { 0, 4, 5 }
    13:   1...11   .....P   { 0, 4, 5 }        1...1.   .....M   { 0, 4 }
    14:   1....1   .....M   { 0, 5 }           1....1   ....MP   { 0, 5 }
    15:   .11...   MPP..M   { 1, 2 }           .111..   MPPP.M   { 1, 2, 3 }
    16:   .111..   ...P..   { 1, 2, 3 }        .11.1.   ...MP.   { 1, 2, 4 }
    17:   .11.1.   ...MP.   { 1, 2, 4 }        .11..1   ....MP   { 1, 2, 5 }
    18:   .11..1   ....MP   { 1, 2, 5 }        .11...   .....M   { 1, 2 }
    19:   .1.1..   ..MP.M   { 1, 3 }           .1.11.   ..MPP.   { 1, 3, 4 }
    20:   .1.11.   ....P.   { 1, 3, 4 }        .1.1.1   ....MP   { 1, 3, 5 }
    21:   .1.1.1   ....MP   { 1, 3, 5 }        .1.1..   .....M   { 1, 3 }
    22:   .1..1.   ...MPM   { 1, 4 }           .1..11   ...MPP   { 1, 4, 5 }
    23:   .1..11   .....P   { 1, 4, 5 }        .1..1.   .....M   { 1, 4 }
    24:   .1...1   .....M   { 1, 5 }           .1...1   ....MP   { 1, 5 }
    25:   ..11..   .MPP.M   { 2, 3 }           ..111.   .MPPPM   { 2, 3, 4 }
    26:   ..111.   ....P.   { 2, 3, 4 }        ..11.1   ....MP   { 2, 3, 5 }
    27:   ..11.1   ....MP   { 2, 3, 5 }        ..11..   .....M   { 2, 3 }
    28:   ..1.1.   ...MPM   { 2, 4 }           ..1.11   ...MPP   { 2, 4, 5 }
    29:   ..1.11   .....P   { 2, 4, 5 }        ..1.1.   .....M   { 2, 4 }
    30:   ..1..1   .....M   { 2, 5 }           ..1..1   ....MP   { 2, 5 }
    31:   ...11.   ..MPPM   { 3, 4 }           ...111   ..MPP.   { 3, 4, 5 }
    32:   ...111   .....P   { 3, 4, 5 }        ...11.   .....M   { 3, 4 }
    33:   ...1.1   .....M   { 3, 5 }           ...1.1   ...MP   { 3, 5 }
    34:   ....11   ...MP.   { 4, 5 }           ....11   ...MP.   { 4, 5 }
```

Figure 8.5-A: The k-subsets (where $2 \leq k \leq 3$) of a 6-element set. Lexicographic order for sets (left) and reversed lexicographic order for delta sets (right).

can be reversed with nonzero **nq**.

```
 1        void generate(void (*visit)(const ksubset_rec &, long),
 2                    long kmin, long kmax, ulong rq, ulong nq=0)
 3        {
 4            ct_ = 0;
 5            rct_ = 0;
 6
 7            kmin_ = kmin;
 8            kmax_ = kmax;
 9            if ( kmin_ > kmax_ )  swap2(kmin_, kmax_);
10            if ( kmax_ > n_ )  kmax_ = n_;
11            if ( kmin_ > n_ )  kmin_ = n_;
12
13            visit_ = visit;
14            rq_ = rq % 4;
15            pq_ = (rq>>2) % 4;
16            nq_ = nq;
17            next_rec(0);
18        }
19
20    private:
21        void next_rec(long d);
22    };
```

The recursive routine itself is given in [FXT: comb/ksubset-rec.cc]:

```
 1    void
 2    ksubset_rec::next_rec(long d)
 3    {
 4        if ( d>kmax_ )  return;
```

```
        order #6:              order #7:              order #10:
 0:    1....1    ....1       11....    .....       1....1    ....1
 1:    1...11    ....P.      111...    ..P...      1...1.    ....PM
 2:    1...1.    ....M       11.1..    .MP...      1..11.    ....P
 3:    1..1..    ...PM.      11..1.    ...MP.      1..11.    ...P.M
 4:    1..11.    ....P.      11...1    ....MP      1..1.1    ....MP
 5:    1..1.1    ....MP      1.1..1    .MP...      1..1..    .....M
 6:    1.1..1    ...PM.      1.1.1.    ....PM      1.1...    ..PM..
 7:    1.1.1.    ....PM      1.11..    ...PM.      1.1..1    .....P
 8:    1.11..    ...PM.      1.1...    ...M..      1.1.1.    ....PM
 9:    1.1...    ....M..     1.1...    ..MP..      1.11..    ...PM.
10:    11....    .PM...      1..11.    ....P.      111...    .P.M..
11:    111...    .P...       1..1.1    ....MP      11.1..    ..MP..
12:    11.1..    ..MP..      1..11.    ..MP..      11..1.    ...MP.
13:    11..1.    ...MP..     1..1..    .....M      11...1    ...MP.
14:    11...1    ....MP      1..1.1    ....MP      11....    ......M
15:    .11..1    M.P...      .1...1    MP...       .11...    M.P...
16:    .11.1.    ....PM      .1..11    ....P.      .11..1    ....P
17:    .111..    ...PM.      .1..1.    .....M      .11.1.    ....PM
18:    .11...    ....M..     .1.1..    ...PM.      .111..    ....PM.
19:    .1.1..    ..MP..      .1.11.    ....P.      .1.11.    ..M.P.
20:    ..1.11    ...P..      .1.1.1    ....MP      .1.1.1    ....MP
21:    .1.1.1    ....MP      .11..1    ..PM..      .1.1..    ......M
22:    .1..11    ....MP      .11.1.    ....PM      .1.1..    ....MP.
23:    .1..1.    ....M.      .111..    ...PM.      .1..11    .....P
24:    .1...1    ....MP      .11...    ....M..     .1..1.    .....M.
25:    ..1..1    MP...       ..11..    M.P...      ..1..1    MP...
26:    ..1.11    ....P.      ..111.    .....P.     ..1.1.    ....PM
27:    ..1.1.    ....M       ..11.1    ....MP.     ..1.11    ....P.
28:    ...11.    ...PM.      ...1.11   ...MP.      ...111.   ...P.M
29:    ...111    ....P.      ..1.1.    .....M      ..11.1    ....MP
30:    ..11.1    ....MP      ..1.11    .....MP     ...11.    ......M
31:    ....111   M.P..       ..1.1.    ....MP.     ...11.    ...M.P.
32:    ....11.   .....M      ...111    ....P.      ....111   ......P
33:    ....1.1   .....MP     ....11.   .....M      ....1.1   .....M.
34:    ....11    ...MP.      ....11    ...M.P      ....11    ...MP.
```

Figure 8.5-B: Three minimal-change orders of the k-subsets (where $2 \le k \le 3$) of a 6-element set.

```
        order #7:
 0:   ......    .P....                32:  1....1    ...MP    0 5
 1:   1.....    .P....    0           33:  .1...11   MP...    1 5
 2:   11....    .P...     0 1         34:  .1..11    ....P.   1 4 5
 3:   111...    ..P...    0 1 2       35:  .1..1.    .....M   1 4
 4:   1111..    ...P..    0 1 2 3     36:  .1.1..    ...PM.   1 3
 5:   11111.    ....P.    0 1 2 3 4   37:  .1.11.    ....P.   1 3 4
 6:   111111    .....P    0 1 2 3 4 5 38:  .1.111    ....P    1 3 4 5
 7:   1111.1    .....M.   0 1 2 3 5   39:  .1.1.1    .....M   1 3 5
 8:   111.11    ...MP.    0 1 2 4 5   40:  .11..1    .PM..    1 2 5
 9:   111.1.    ......M   0 1 2 4     41:  .11...    .....PM  1 2 4
10:   111..1    ....MP    0 1 2 5     42:  .11.11    .....P   1 2 4 5
11:   11.1.1    ..MP..    0 1 3 5     43:  .111.1    ...PM.   1 2 3 5
12:   11.111    ....P.    0 1 3 4 5   44:  .11111    ...P.    1 2 3 4 5
13:   11.11.    ......M   0 1 3 4     45:  .1111.    .....M   1 2 3 4
14:   11.1..    .....M.   0 1 3       46:  .111..    .....M.  1 2 3
15:   11..1.    ..MP..    0 1 4       47:  .11...    ...M..   1 2
16:   11..11    .....P    0 1 4 5     48:  .1....    ..M...   1
17:   11...1    .....M.   0 1 5       49:  ...1.     .MP..    2
18:   1.1..1    .MP...    0 2 5       50:  ..11..    ..P..    2 3
19:   1.1.1.    ...PM     0 2 4       51:  ..111.    ...P.    2 3 4
20:   1.1.11    .....P    0 2 4 5     52:  ..1111    .....P   2 3 4 5
21:   1.11.1    ...PM.    0 2 3 5     53:  ..11.1    .....M   2 3 5
22:   1.1111    .....P.   0 2 3 4 5   54:  ..1.11    ...MP.   2 4 5
23:   1.111.    ......M   0 2 3 4     55:  ..1.1.    ......M  2 4
24:   1.11..    ......M.  0 2 3       56:  ..1..1    ....MP   2 5
25:   1.1...    ...M..    0 2         57:  ...1.1    .MP..    3 5
26:   1...1.    ..MP..    0 3         58:  ...111    ..P..    3 4 5
27:   1..11.    ....P.    0 3 4       59:  ...11.    .....M   3 4
28:   1..111    .....P    0 3 4 5     60:  ...1..    ....M.   3
29:   1..1.1    ...M..    0 3 5       61:  ....1.    ..MP..   4
30:   1...11    ...MP.    0 4 5       62:  ....11    .....P   4 5
31:   1...1.    ......M   0 4         63:  .....1    .....M.  5
```

Figure 8.5-C: With $k_{min} = 0$ and order number seven at each transition either one element is added or removed, or one element moves to an adjacent position.

```
5
6         ++rct_;   // measure computational work
7         long rv1 = rv_[d-1];  // left neighbor
8         bool q;
9         switch ( rq_ % 4 )
10        {
11        case 0:  q = 1;  break;
12        case 1:  q = !(d&1);  break;
13        case 2:  q = rv1&1;  break;
14        case 3:  q = (d^rv1)&1;  break;
15        }
16
17        if ( nq_ )  q = !q;
18
19        long x0 = rv1 + 1;
20        long rx = n_ - (kmin_ - d);
21        long x1 = min2( n_-1, rx );
22
23  #define PCOND(x) if ( (pq_==x) && (d>=kmin_) )  { visit_(*this, d);  ++ct_; }
24        PCOND(0);
25        if ( q )  // forward:
26        {
27            PCOND(1);
28            for (long x=x0; x<=x1; ++x)  { rv_[d] = x;  next_rec(d+1); }
29            PCOND(2);
30        }
31        else  // backward:
32        {
33            PCOND(2);
34            for (long x=x1; x>=x0; --x)  { rv_[d] = x;  next_rec(d+1); }
35            PCOND(1);
36        }
37        PCOND(3);
38  #undef PCOND
39  }
```

About 50 million subsets per second are generated [FXT: comb/ksubset-rec-demo.cc].

8.5.2   Iterative algorithm for a minimal-change order

```
        delta set   diff      set
    1:   ...11     .....     { 4, 5 }
    2:   ..11.     ..P.M     { 3, 4 }
    3:   ..111     ....P     { 3, 4, 5 }
    4:   ..1.1     ...M.     { 3, 5 }
    5:   .11..     .P..M     { 2, 3 }
    6:   .11.1     ....P     { 2, 3, 5 }
    7:   .1111     ...P.     { 2, 3, 4, 5 }
    8:   .111.     ....M     { 2, 3, 4 }
    9:   .1.1.     ..M..     { 2, 4 }
   10:   .1.11     ....P     { 2, 4, 5 }
   11:   .1..1     ...M.     { 2, 5 }
   12:   11...     P...M     { 1, 2 }
   13:   11..1     ....P     { 1, 2, 5 }
   14:   11.11     ...P.     { 1, 2, 4, 5 }
   15:   11.1.     ....M     { 1, 2, 4 }
   16:   1111.     ..P..     { 1, 2, 3, 4 }
   17:   111.1     ...MP     { 1, 2, 3, 5 }
   18:   111..     ....M     { 1, 2, 3 }
   19:   1.1..     .M...     { 1, 3 }
   20:   1.1.1     ....P     { 1, 3, 5 }
   21:   1.111     ...P.     { 1, 3, 4, 5 }
   22:   1.11.     ....M     { 1, 3, 4 }
   23:   1..1.     ..M..     { 1, 4 }
   24:   1..11     ....P     { 1, 4, 5 }
   25:   1...1     ...M.     { 1, 5 }
```

Figure 8.5-D: The (25) k-subsets where $2 \leq k \leq 4$ of a 5-element set in a minimal-change order.

A generator for subsets in Gray code order is [FXT: `class ksubset_gray` in comb/ksubset-gray.h]:

```
1     class ksubset_gray
2     {
3     public:
4         ulong n_;    // k-subsets of {1, 2, ..., n}
5         ulong kmin_, kmax_;  // kmin <= k <= kmax
6         ulong k_;    // k elements in current set
7         ulong *S_;   // set in S[1,2,...,k] with elements \in {1,2,...,n}
8         ulong j_;    // aux
9
10    public:
11        ksubset_gray(ulong n, ulong kmin, ulong kmax)
12        {
13            n_ = (n>0 ? n : 1);
14            // Must have 1<=kmin<=kmax<=n
15            kmin_ = kmin;
16            kmax_ = kmax;
17            if ( kmax_ < kmin_ )  swap2(kmin_, kmax_);
18            if ( kmin_==0 )  kmin_ = 1;
19
20            S_ = new ulong[kmax_+1];
21            S_[0] = 0;  // sentinel: != 1
22            first();
23        }
24
25        ~ksubset_gray()  { delete [] S_; }
26        const ulong *data()  const  { return S_+1; }
27        ulong num()  const  { return k_; }
28
29        ulong last()
30        {
31            S_[1] = 1;  k_ = kmin_;
32            if ( kmin_==1 )  { j_ = 1; }
33            else
34            {
35                for (ulong i=2; i<=kmin_; ++i)  { S_[i] = n_ - kmin_ + i; }
36                j_ = 2;
37            }
38            return k_;
39        }
40
41
42        ulong first()
43        {
44            k_ = kmin_;
45            for (ulong i=1; i<=kmin_; ++i)  { S_[i] = n_ - kmin_ + i; }
46            j_ = 1;
47            return k_;
48        }
49
50        bool is_first()  const  { return ( S_[1] == n_ - kmin_ + 1 ); }
51
52        bool is_last()  const
53        {
54            if ( S_[1] != 1  )   return 0;
55            if ( kmin_<=1 )  return (k_==1);
56            return  (S_[2]==n_-kmin_+2);
57        }
58    [--snip--]
```

The routines for computing the next or previous subset are adapted from a routine to compute the successor given in [192]. It is split into two auxiliary functions:

```
1     private:
2         void prev_even()
3         {
4             ulong &n=n_, &kmin=kmin_, &kmax=kmax_, &j=j_;
5             if ( S_[j-1] == S_[j]-1 )  // can touch sentinel S[0]
6             {
7                 S_[j-1] = S_[j];
8                 if ( j > kmin )
9                 {
10                    if ( S_[kmin] == n )  { j = j-2; } else  { j = j-1; }
11                }
12                else
13                {
14                    S_[j] = n - kmin + j;
15                    if ( S_[j-1]==S_[j]-1 )  { j = j-2; }
```

```
16                   }
17               }
18               else
19               {
20                   S_[j] = S_[j] - 1;
21                   if ( j < kmax )
22                   {
23                       S_[j+1] = S_[j] + 1;
24                       if ( j >= kmin-1 )  { j = j+1; }  else  { j = j+2; }
25                   }
26               }
27           }

1        void prev_odd()
2        {
3            ulong &n=n_, &kmin=kmin_, &kmax=kmax_, &j=j_;
4            if ( S_[j] == n )  { j = j-1; }
5            else
6            {
7                if ( j < kmax )
8                {
9                    S_[j+1] = n;
10                   j = j+1;
11               }
12               else
13               {
14                   S_[j] = S_[j]+1;
15                   if ( S_[kmin]==n )  { j = j-1; }
16               }
17           }
18       }
19       [--snip--]
```

The `next()` and `prev()` functions use these routines. Note that calls cannot not be mixed.

```
1        ulong prev()
2        {
3            if ( is_first() )  { last(); return 0; }
4            if ( j_&1 )  prev_odd();
5            else         prev_even();
6            if ( j_<kmin_ )  { k_ = kmin_; } else { k_ = j_; };
7            return k_;
8        }

1        ulong next()
2        {
3            if ( is_last() )  { first();  return 0; }
4            if ( j_&1 )  prev_even();
5            else         prev_odd();
6            if ( j_<kmin_ )  { k_ = kmin_; } else { k_ = j_; };
7            return k_;
8        }
9        [--snip--]
```

Usage of the class is shown in the program [FXT: comb/ksubset-gray-demo.cc], the k-subsets where $2 \le k \le 4$ in the order generated by the algorithm are shown in figure 8.5-D. About 150 million subsets per second can be generated with the routine `next()` and 130 million with `prev()`.

8.5.3   A two-close order with homogenous moves

Orderings of the k-subsets with k in a given range that are *two-close* are shown in figure 8.5-E: one element is inserted or removed or moves by at most two positions. The moves by two positions only cross a zero, the changes are *homogenous*. The list was produced with the program [FXT: comb/ksubset-twoclose-demo.cc] which uses [FXT: `class ksubset_twoclose` in comb/ksubset-twoclose.h]:

```
1    class ksubset_twoclose
2    // k-subsets (kmin<=k<=kmax) in a two-close order.
3    // Recursive algorithm.
4    {
5    public:
6        ulong *rv_;  // record of visits in graph (delta set)
7        ulong n_;    // subsets of the n-element set
8
9        // function to call with each combination:
```

```
          delta set  diff       set                        delta set  diff       set
  1:      .1111      .....    { 1, 2, 3, 4 }      1:       ....11     ......   { 4, 5 }
  2:      ..111      .M...    { 2, 3, 4 }         2:       ...1.1     ...PM.   { 3, 5 }
  3:      1.111      P....    { 0, 2, 3, 4 }      3:       .1...1     .P.M.    { 1, 5 }
  4:      11.11      .PM..    { 0, 1, 3, 4 }      4:       .....1     .M....   { 5 }
  5:      .1.11      M....    { 1, 3, 4 }         5:       1....1     P....    { 0, 5 }
  6:      ...11      .M...    { 3, 4 }            6:       ..1..1     M.P...   { 2, 5 }
  7:      1..11      P....    { 0, 3, 4 }         7:       ..11..     ...P.M   { 2, 3 }
  8:      11..1      .P.M.    { 0, 1, 4 }         8:       .1.1..     .PM...   { 1, 3 }
  9:      .1..1      M....    { 1, 4 }            9:       ...1..     .M....   { 3 }
 10:      1...1      PM...    { 0, 4 }           10:       1..1..     P.....   { 0, 3 }
 11:      ..1.1      M.P..    { 2, 4 }           11:       11....     .P.M.    { 0, 1 }
 12:      1.1.1      P....    { 0, 2, 4 }        12:       .1....     M.....   { 1 }
 13:      .11.1      MP...    { 1, 2, 4 }        13:       1.....     PM...    { 0 }
 14:      111.1      P....    { 0, 1, 2, 4 }     14:       ..1...     M.P...   { 2 }
 15:      1111.      ...PM    { 0, 1, 2, 3 }     15:       1.1...     P.....   { 0, 2 }
 16:      .111.      M....    { 1, 2, 3 }        16:       .11...     MP....   { 1, 2 }
 17:      ..11.      .M...    { 2, 3 }           17:       .1..1.     ..M.P.   { 1, 4 }
 18:      1.11.      P....    { 0, 2, 3 }        18:       ....1.     .M....   { 4 }
 19:      11.1.      .PM..    { 0, 1, 3 }        19:       1...1.     P.....   { 0, 4 }
 20:      .1.1.      M....    { 1, 3 }           20:       ..1.1.     M.P...   { 2, 4 }
 21:      1..1.      PM...    { 0, 3 }           21:       ...11.     ..MP..   { 3, 4 }
 22:      11...      .P.M.    { 0, 1 }
 23:      1.1..      .MP..    { 0, 2 }
 24:      .11..      MP...    { 1, 2 }
 25:      111..      P....    { 0, 1, 2 }
```

Figure 8.5-E: The k-subsets where $2 \leq k \leq 4$ of 5 elements (left) and the sets where $1 \leq k \leq 2$ of 6 elements (right) in two-close orders.

```
10          void (*visit_)(const ksubset_twoclose &);
11      [--snip--]
12
13          void generate(void (*visit)(const ksubset_twoclose &),
14                      ulong kmin, ulong kmax)
15      {
16          visit_ = visit;
17          ulong kmax0 = n_ - kmin;
18          next_rec(n_, kmax, kmax0, 0);
19      }
```

The recursion is:

```
 1   private:
 2       void next_rec(ulong d, ulong n1, ulong n0, bool q)
 3       // d:  remaining depth in recursion
 4       // n1: remaining ones to fill in
 5       // n0: remaining zeros to fill in
 6       // q:  direction in recursion
 7       {
 8           if ( 0==d )  { visit_(*this);  return; }
 9
10           --d;
11
12           if ( q )
13           {
14               if ( n0 )  { rv_[d]=0;  next_rec(d, n1-0, n0-1, d&1); }
15               if ( n1 )  { rv_[d]=1;  next_rec(d, n1-1, n0-0, q); }
16           }
17           else
18           {
19               if ( n1 )  { rv_[d]=1;  next_rec(d, n1-1, n0-0, q); }
20               if ( n0 )  { rv_[d]=0;  next_rec(d, n1-0, n0-1, d&1); }
21           }
22       }
23   };
```

About 75 million subsets per second can be generated. For $k_{min} = k_{max} =: k$ we obtain the enup order for combinations described in section 6.6.2 on page 188.

Chapter 9

Mixed radix numbers

The *mixed radix* representation $A = [a_0, a_1, a_2, \ldots, a_{n-1}]$ of a number x with respect to a radix vector $M = [m_0, m_1, m_2, \ldots, m_{n-1}]$ is given by

$$x = \sum_{k=0}^{n-1} a_k \prod_{j=0}^{k-1} m_j \tag{9.0-1}$$

where $0 \leq a_j < m_j$ (and $0 \leq x < \prod_{j=0}^{n-1} m_j$, so that n digits suffice). For $M = [r, r, r, \ldots, r]$ the relation reduces to the radix-r representation:

$$x = \sum_{k=0}^{n-1} a_k \, r^k \tag{9.0-2}$$

All 3-digit radix-4 numbers are shown in various orders in figure 9.0-A. Note that the least significant digit (a_0) is at the left side of each number (array representation).

9.1 Counting (lexicographic) order

An implementation for mixed radix counting is [FXT: class `mixedradix_lex` in comb/mixedradix-lex.h]:

```
1    class mixedradix_lex
2    {
3    public:
4        ulong *a_;  // digits
5        ulong *m1_; // radix (minus one) for each digit
6        ulong n_;   // Number of digits
7        ulong j_;   // position of last change
8
9    public:
10       mixedradix_lex(const ulong *m, ulong n, ulong mm=0)
11       {
12           n_ = n;
13           a_ = new ulong[n_+1];
14           m1_ = new ulong[n_+1];
15           a_[n_] = 1;    // sentinel: !=0, and !=m1[n]
16           m1_[n_] = 0;   // sentinel
17           mixedradix_init(n_, mm, m, m1_);
18           first();
19       }
20       [--snip--]
```

The initialization routine `mixedradix_init()` is given in [FXT: comb/mixedradix-init.cc]:

```
1    void
2    mixedradix_init(ulong n, ulong mm, const ulong *m, ulong *m1)
3    // Auxiliary function used to initialize vector of nines in mixed radix classes.
4    {
5        if ( m )  // all radices given
6        {
7            for (ulong k=0; k<n; ++k)  m1[k] = m[k] - 1;
8        }
9        else
```

J. Arndt, *Matters Computational: Ideas, Algorithms, Source Code*,
DOI 10.1007/978-3-642-14764-7_9, © Springer-Verlag Berlin Heidelberg 2011

	counting	Gray	modular Gray	gslex	endo	endo Gray
0:	[. . .]	[. . .]	[. . .]	[1 . .]	[. . .]	[. . .]
1:	[1 . .]	[1 . .]	[1 . .]	[2 . .]	[1 . .]	[1 . .]
2:	[2 . .]	[2 . .]	[2 . .]	[3 . .]	[3 . .]	[3 . .]
3:	[3 . .]	[3 . .]	[3 . .]	[1 1 .]	[2 . .]	[2 . .]
4:	[. 1 .]	[3 1 .]	[3 1 .]	[2 1 .]	[. 1 .]	[2 1 .]
5:	[1 1 .]	[2 1 .]	[. 1 .]	[3 1 .]	[1 1 .]	[3 1 .]
6:	[2 1 .]	[1 1 .]	[1 1 .]	[. 1 .]	[3 1 .]	[1 1 .]
7:	[3 1 .]	[. 1 .]	[2 1 .]	[1 2 .]	[2 1 .]	[. 1 .]
8:	[. 2 .]	[. 2 .]	[2 2 .]	[2 2 .]	[. 3 .]	[. 3 .]
9:	[1 2 .]	[1 2 .]	[3 2 .]	[3 2 .]	[1 3 .]	[1 3 .]
10	[2 2 .]	[2 2 .]	[. 2 .]	[. 2 .]	[3 3 .]	[3 3 .]
11	[3 2 .]	[3 2 .]	[1 2 .]	[1 3 .]	[2 3 .]	[2 3 .]
12	[. 3 .]	[3 3 .]	[1 3 .]	[2 3 .]	[. 2 .]	[2 2 .]
13	[1 3 .]	[2 3 .]	[2 3 .]	[3 3 .]	[1 2 .]	[3 2 .]
14	[2 3 .]	[1 3 .]	[3 3 .]	[. 3 .]	[3 2 .]	[1 2 .]
15	[3 3 .]	[. 3 .]	[. 3 .]	[1 . 1]	[2 2 .]	[. 2 .]
16	[. . 1]	[. 3 1]	[. 3 1]	[2 . 1]	[. . 1]	[. 2 1]
17	[1 . 1]	[1 3 1]	[1 3 1]	[3 . 1]	[1 . 1]	[1 2 1]
18	[2 . 1]	[2 3 1]	[2 3 1]	[1 1 1]	[3 . 1]	[3 2 1]
19	[3 . 1]	[3 3 1]	[3 3 1]	[2 1 1]	[2 . 1]	[2 2 1]
20	[. 1 1]	[3 2 1]	[3 . 1]	[3 1 1]	[. 1 1]	[2 3 1]
21	[1 1 1]	[2 2 1]	[. . 1]	[. 1 1]	[1 1 1]	[3 3 1]
22	[2 1 1]	[1 2 1]	[1 . 1]	[1 2 1]	[3 1 1]	[1 3 1]
23	[3 1 1]	[. 2 1]	[2 . 1]	[2 2 1]	[2 1 1]	[. 3 1]
24	[. 2 1]	[. 1 1]	[2 1 1]	[3 2 1]	[. 3 1]	[. 1 1]
25	[1 2 1]	[1 1 1]	[3 1 1]	[. 2 1]	[1 3 1]	[1 1 1]
26	[2 2 1]	[2 1 1]	[. 1 1]	[1 3 1]	[3 3 1]	[3 1 1]
27	[3 2 1]	[3 1 1]	[1 1 1]	[2 3 1]	[2 3 1]	[2 1 1]
28	[. 3 1]	[3 . 1]	[1 2 1]	[3 3 1]	[. 2 1]	[2 . 1]
29	[1 3 1]	[2 . 1]	[2 2 1]	[. 3 1]	[1 2 1]	[3 . 1]
30	[2 3 1]	[1 . 1]	[3 2 1]	[. . 1]	[3 2 1]	[1 . 1]
31	[3 3 1]	[. . 1]	[. 2 1]	[1 . 2]	[2 2 1]	[. . 1]
32	[. . 2]	[. . 2]	[. 2 2]	[2 . 2]	[. . 3]	[. . 3]
33	[1 . 2]	[1 . 2]	[1 2 2]	[3 . 2]	[1 . 3]	[1 . 3]
34	[2 . 2]	[2 . 2]	[2 2 2]	[1 1 2]	[3 . 3]	[3 . 3]
35	[3 . 2]	[3 . 2]	[3 2 2]	[2 1 2]	[2 . 3]	[2 . 3]
36	[. 1 2]	[3 1 2]	[3 3 2]	[3 1 2]	[. 1 3]	[2 1 3]
37	[1 1 2]	[2 1 2]	[. 3 2]	[. 1 2]	[1 1 3]	[3 1 3]
38	[2 1 2]	[1 1 2]	[1 3 2]	[1 2 2]	[3 1 3]	[1 1 3]
39	[3 1 2]	[. 1 2]	[2 3 2]	[2 2 2]	[2 1 3]	[. 1 3]
40	[. 2 2]	[. 2 2]	[2 . 2]	[3 2 2]	[. 3 3]	[. 3 3]
41	[1 2 2]	[1 2 2]	[3 . 2]	[. 2 2]	[1 3 3]	[1 3 3]
42	[2 2 2]	[2 2 2]	[. . 2]	[1 3 2]	[3 3 3]	[3 3 3]
43	[3 2 2]	[3 2 2]	[1 . 2]	[2 3 2]	[2 3 3]	[2 3 3]
44	[. 3 2]	[3 3 2]	[1 1 2]	[3 3 2]	[. 2 3]	[2 2 3]
45	[1 3 2]	[2 3 2]	[2 1 2]	[. 3 2]	[1 2 3]	[3 2 3]
46	[2 3 2]	[1 3 2]	[3 1 2]	[. . 2]	[3 2 3]	[1 2 3]
47	[3 3 2]	[. 3 2]	[. 1 2]	[1 . 3]	[2 2 3]	[. 2 3]
48	[. . 3]	[. 3 3]	[. 1 3]	[2 . 3]	[. . 2]	[. 2 2]
49	[1 . 3]	[1 3 3]	[1 1 3]	[3 . 3]	[1 . 2]	[1 2 2]
50	[2 . 3]	[2 3 3]	[2 1 3]	[1 1 3]	[3 . 2]	[3 2 2]
51	[3 . 3]	[3 3 3]	[3 1 3]	[2 1 3]	[2 . 2]	[2 2 2]
52	[. 1 3]	[3 2 3]	[3 2 3]	[3 1 3]	[. 1 2]	[2 3 2]
53	[1 1 3]	[2 2 3]	[. 2 3]	[. 1 3]	[1 1 2]	[3 3 2]
54	[2 1 3]	[1 2 3]	[1 2 3]	[1 2 3]	[3 1 2]	[1 3 2]
55	[3 1 3]	[. 2 3]	[2 2 3]	[2 2 3]	[2 1 2]	[. 3 2]
56	[. 2 3]	[. 1 3]	[2 3 3]	[3 2 3]	[. 3 2]	[. 1 2]
57	[1 2 3]	[1 1 3]	[3 3 3]	[. 2 3]	[1 3 2]	[1 1 2]
58	[2 2 3]	[2 1 3]	[. 3 3]	[1 3 3]	[3 3 2]	[3 1 2]
59	[3 2 3]	[3 1 3]	[1 3 3]	[2 3 3]	[2 3 2]	[2 1 2]
60	[. 3 3]	[3 . 3]	[1 . 3]	[3 3 3]	[. 2 2]	[2 . 2]
61	[1 3 3]	[2 . 3]	[2 . 3]	[. 3 3]	[1 2 2]	[3 . 2]
62	[2 3 3]	[1 . 3]	[3 . 3]	[. . 3]	[3 2 2]	[1 . 2]
63	[3 3 3]	[. . 3]	[. . 3]	[. . .]	[2 2 2]	[. . 2]

Figure 9.0-A: All 3-digit, radix-4 numbers in various orders (dots denote zeros): counting-, Gray-, modular Gray-, gslex-, endo-, and endo Gray order. The least significant digit is on the left of each word (array notation).

```
                      M = [2 3 4 ]        M = [4 3 2 ]
         0 :          [ . . . ]           [ . . . ]
         1 :          [ 1 . . ]           [ 1 . . ]
         2 :          [ . 1 . ]           [ 2 . . ]
         3 :          [ 1 1 . ]           [ 3 . . ]
         4 :          [ . 2 . ]           [ . 1 . ]
         5 :          [ 1 2 . ]           [ 1 1 . ]
         6 :          [ . . 1 ]           [ 2 1 . ]
         7 :          [ 1 . 1 ]           [ 3 1 . ]
         8 :          [ . 1 1 ]           [ . 2 . ]
         9 :          [ 1 1 1 ]           [ 1 2 . ]
       1 0 :          [ . 2 1 ]           [ 2 2 . ]
       1 1 :          [ 1 2 1 ]           [ 3 2 . ]
       1 2 :          [ . . 2 ]           [ . . 1 ]
       1 3 :          [ 1 . 2 ]           [ 1 . 1 ]
       1 4 :          [ . 1 2 ]           [ 2 . 1 ]
       1 5 :          [ 1 1 2 ]           [ 3 . 1 ]
       1 6 :          [ . 2 2 ]           [ . 1 1 ]
       1 7 :          [ 1 2 2 ]           [ 1 1 1 ]
       1 8 :          [ . . 3 ]           [ 2 1 1 ]
       1 9 :          [ 1 . 3 ]           [ 3 1 1 ]
       2 0 :          [ . 1 3 ]           [ . 2 1 ]
       2 1 :          [ 1 1 3 ]           [ 1 2 1 ]
       2 2 :          [ . 2 3 ]           [ 2 2 1 ]
       2 3 :          [ 1 2 3 ]           [ 3 2 1 ]
```

Figure 9.1-A: Mixed radix numbers in counting (lexicographic) order, dots denote zeros. The radix vectors are $M = [2, 3, 4]$ (rising factorial base, left) and $M = [4, 3, 2]$ (falling factorial base, right). The least significant digit is on the left of each word (array notation).

```
10      {
11          if ( mm>1 )  // use mm as radix for all digits:
12              for (ulong k=0; k<n; ++k)  m1[k] = mm - 1;
13          else
14          {
15              if ( mm==0 )  // falling factorial base
16                  for (ulong k=0; k<n; ++k)  m1[k] = n - k;
17              else // rising factorial base
18                  for (ulong k=0; k<n; ++k)  m1[k] = k + 1;
19          }
20      }
21  }
```

Instead of the vector of radices $M = [m_0, m_1, m_2, \ldots, m_{n-1}]$ the vector of 'nines' ($M' = [m_0 - 1, m_1 - 1, m_2 - 1, \ldots, m_{n-1} - 1]$, variable m1_) is used. This modification leads to slightly faster generation. The first n-digit in lexicographic order number is all-zero, the last is all-nines:

```
1   [--snip--]
2     void first()
3     {
4         for (ulong k=0; k<n_; ++k)  a_[k] = 0;
5         j_ = n_;
6     }
7
8     void last()
9     {
10        for (ulong k=0; k<n_; ++k)  a_[k] = m1_[k];
11        j_ = n_;
12    }
13  [--snip--]
```

A number is incremented by setting all nines (digits a_j that are equal to $m_j - 1$) at the lower end to zero and incrementing the next digit:

```
1   bool next()  // increment
2   {
3       ulong j = 0;
4       while ( a_[j]==m1_[j] ) { a_[j]=0; ++j; } // can touch sentinels
5       j_ = j;
6
7       if ( j==n_ ) return false;  // current is last
8
```

```
9              ++a_[j];
10             return true;
11         }
12     [--snip--]
```

A number is decremented by setting all zero digits at the lower end to nine and decrementing the next digit:

```
1      bool prev()  // decrement
2      {
3          ulong j = 0;
4          while ( a_[j]==0 )  { a_[j]=m1_[j];  ++j; }  // can touch sentinels
5          j_ = j;
6
7          if ( j==n_ )  return false;  // current is first
8
9          --a_[j];
10         return true;
11     }
12     [--snip--]
```

Figure 9.1-A shows the 3-digit mixed radix numbers for bases $M = [2, 3, 4]$ (left) and $M = [4, 3, 2]$ (right). The listings were created with the program [FXT: comb/mixedradix-lex-demo.cc].

The rate of generation for the routine `next()` is about 166 M/s (with radix-2 numbers, $M = [2, 2, 2, \ldots, 2]$), 257 M/s (radix-3), and about 370 M/s (radix-8). The slowest generation occurs for radix-2, as the number of carries is maximal. The number C of carries with incrementing is on average

$$C = \frac{1}{m_0}\left(1 + \frac{1}{m_1}\left(1 + \frac{1}{m_2}\left(1 + \frac{1}{m_3}(\ldots)\right)\right)\right) = \sum_{k=0}^{n}\frac{1}{\prod_{j=0}^{k} m_j} \qquad (9.1\text{-}1)$$

The number of digits changed on average equals $C + 1$. For $M = [r, r, r, \ldots, r]$ (and $n = \infty$) we have $C = \frac{1}{r-1}$. For the worst case ($r = 2$) we have $C = 1$, so two digits are changed on average.

9.2 Minimal-change (Gray code) order

9.2.1 Constant amortized time (CAT) algorithm

Figure 9.2-A shows the 3-digit mixed radix numbers for radix vectors $M = [2, 3, 4]$ (left) and $M = [4, 3, 2]$ (right) in Gray code order. A generator for the Gray code order is [FXT: class `mixedradix_gray` in comb/mixedradix-gray.h]:

```
1    class mixedradix_gray
2    {
3    public:
4        ulong *a_;   // mixed radix digits
5        ulong *m1_;  // radices (minus one)
6        ulong *i_;   // direction
7        ulong n_;    // n_ digits
8        ulong j_;    // position of last change
9        int dm_;     // direction of last move
10
11   public:
12       mixedradix_gray(const ulong *m, ulong n, ulong mm=0)
13       {
14           n_ = n;
15           a_ = new ulong[n_+1];
16           a_[n] = -1UL;   // sentinel
17           i_ = new ulong[n_+1];
18           i_[n_] = 0;     // sentinel
19           m1_ = new ulong[n_+1];
20
21           mixedradix_init(n_, mm, m, m1_);
22
23           first();
24       }
25   [--snip--]
```

```
        M = [ 2 3 4 ]     x      j   d     M=[ 4 3 2 ]     x      j   d
 0 :    [ .  .  . ]       0                 [ .  .  . ]     0
 1 :    [ 1  .  . ]       1      0   1      [ 1  .  . ]     1      0   1
 2 :    [ 1  1  . ]       3      1   1      [ 2  .  . ]     2      0   1
 3 :    [ .  1  . ]       2      0 - 1      [ 3  .  . ]     3      0   1
 4 :    [ .  2  . ]       4      1   1      [ 3  1  . ]     7      1   1
 5 :    [ 1  2  . ]       5      0   1      [ 2  1  . ]     6      0 - 1
 6 :    [ 1  2  1 ]      1 1     2   1      [ 1  1  . ]     5      0 - 1
 7 :    [ .  2  1 ]      1 0     0 - 1      [ .  1  . ]     4      0 - 1
 8 :    [ .  1  1 ]       8      1 - 1      [ .  2  . ]     8      1   1
 9 :    [ 1  1  1 ]       9      0   1      [ 1  2  . ]     9      0   1
1 0 :   [ 1  .  1 ]       7      1 - 1      [ 2  2  . ]    10      0   1
1 1 :   [ .  .  1 ]       6      0 - 1      [ 3  2  . ]    11      0   1
1 2 :   [ .  .  2 ]      1 2     2   1      [ 3  2  1 ]    23      2   1
1 3 :   [ 1  .  2 ]      1 3     0   1      [ 2  2  1 ]    22      0 - 1
1 4 :   [ 1  1  2 ]      1 5     1   1      [ 1  2  1 ]    21      0 - 1
1 5 :   [ .  1  2 ]      1 4     0 - 1      [ .  2  1 ]    20      0 - 1
1 6 :   [ .  2  2 ]      1 6     1   1      [ .  1  1 ]    16      1 - 1
1 7 :   [ 1  2  2 ]      1 7     0   1      [ 1  1  1 ]    17      0   1
1 8 :   [ 1  2  3 ]      2 3     2   1      [ 2  1  1 ]    18      0   1
1 9 :   [ .  2  3 ]      2 2     0 - 1      [ 3  1  1 ]    19      0   1
2 0 :   [ .  1  3 ]      2 0     1 - 1      [ 3  .  1 ]    15      1 - 1
2 1 :   [ 1  1  3 ]      2 1     0   1      [ 2  .  1 ]    14      0 - 1
2 2 :   [ 1  .  3 ]      1 9     1 - 1      [ 1  .  1 ]    13      0 - 1
2 3 :   [ .  .  3 ]      1 8     0 - 1      [ .  .  1 ]    12      0 - 1
```

Figure 9.2-A: Mixed radix numbers in Gray code order, dots denote zeros. The radix vectors are $M = [2, 3, 4]$ (left) and $M = [4, 3, 2]$ (right). Columns 'x' give the values, columns 'j' and 'd' give the position of last change and its direction, respectively.

The array `i_[]` contains the 'directions' for each digit: it contains +1 or -1 if the computation of the successor will increase or decrease the corresponding digit. It has to be filled when the first or last number is computed:

```
1    void first()
2    {
3        for (ulong k=0; k<n_; ++k)  a_[k] = 0;
4        for (ulong k=0; k<n_; ++k)  i_[k] = +1;
5        j_ = n_;
6        dm_ = 0;
7    }
8
9    void last()
10   {
11       // find position of last even radix:
12       ulong z = 0;
13       for (ulong i=0; i<n_; ++i)  if ( m1_[i]&1 )  z = i;
14       while ( z<n_ )  // last even .. end:
15       {
16           a_[z] = m1_[z];
17           i_[z] = +1;
18           ++z;
19       }
20
21       j_ = 0;
22       dm_ = -1;
23   }
24   [--snip--]
```

A sentinel element (`i_[n]`=0) is used to optimize the computations of the successor and predecessor. The method works in constant amortized time:

```
1    bool next()
2    {
3        ulong j = 0;
4        ulong ij;
5        while ( (ij=i_[j]) )  // can touch sentinel i[n]==0
6        {
7            ulong dj = a_[j] + ij;
8            if ( dj>m1_[j] )  // =^= if ( (dj>m1_[j]) || ((long)dj<0) )
9            {
10               i_[j] = -ij;  // flip direction
```

```
11              }
12              else  // can update
13              {
14                  a_[j] = dj;  // update digit
15                  dm_ = ij;    // save for dir()
16                  j_ = j;      // save for pos()
17                  return true;
18              }
19
20              ++j;
21          }
22          return false;
23      }
24      [--snip--]
```

Note the if-clause: it is an optimized expression equivalent to the one given as comment. The following methods are often useful:

```
1      ulong pos()  const  { return j_; }  // position of last change
2      int dir()  const  { return dm_; }   // direction of last change
```

The routine for the computation of the predecessor is obtained by changing the plus sign in the statement `ulong dj = a_[j] + ij;` to a minus sign. The rate of generation is about 128 M/s for radix 2, 243 M/s for radix 4, and 304 M/s for radix 8 [FXT: comb/mixedradix-gray-demo.cc].

9.2.2 Loopless algorithm

A loopless algorithm for the computation of the successor, taken from [215, alg.H, sect.7.2.1.1], is given in [FXT: comb/mixedradix-gray2.h]:

```
1    class mixedradix_gray2
2    {
3    public:
4        ulong *a_;  // digits
5        ulong *m1_; // radix minus one ('nines')
6        ulong *f_;  // focus pointer
7        ulong *d_;  // direction
8        ulong n_;   // number of digits
9        ulong j_;   // position of last change
10       int dm_;    // direction of last move
11       [--snip--]
12       void first()
13       {
14           for (ulong k=0; k<n_; ++k)  a_[k] = 0;
15           for (ulong k=0; k<n_; ++k)  d_[k] = 1;
16           for (ulong k=0; k<=n_; ++k)  f_[k] = k;
17           dm_ = 0;
18           j_ = n_;
19       }
20
21       bool next()
22       {
23           const ulong j = f_[0];
24           f_[0] = 0;
25
26           if ( j>=n_ )  { first();  return false; }
27
28           const ulong dj = d_[j];
29           const ulong aj = a_[j] + dj;
30           a_[j] = aj;
31
32           dm_ = (int)dj;  // save for dir()
33           j_ = j;         // save for pos()
34
35           if ( aj+dj > m1_[j] )  // was last move?
36           {
37               d_[j] = -dj;       // change direction
38               f_[j] = f_[j+1];   // lookup next position
39               f_[j+1] = j + 1;
40           }
41
42           return true;
43       }
```

The rate of generation is about 120 M/s for radix 2, 194 M/s for radix 4, and 264 M/s for radix 8 [FXT: comb/mixedradix-gray2-demo.cc].

9.2.3 Modular Gray code order

```
          M=[ 2 3 4 ]    j              M=[ 4 3 2 ]    j
      0 : [ .  .  . ]               0:  [ .  .  . ]
      1 : [ 1  .  . ]   0           1:  [ 1  .  . ]   0
      2 : [ 1  1  . ]   1           2:  [ 2  .  . ]   0
      3 : [ .  1  . ]   0           3:  [ 3  .  . ]   0
      4 : [ .  2  . ]   1           4:  [ 3  1  . ]   1
      5 : [ 1  2  . ]   0           5:  [ .  1  . ]   0
      6 : [ 1  2  1 ]   2           6:  [ 1  1  . ]   0
      7 : [ .  2  1 ]   0           7:  [ 2  1  . ]   0
      8 : [ .  .  1 ]   1           8:  [ 2  2  . ]   1
      9 : [ 1  .  1 ]   0           9:  [ 3  2  . ]   0
    1 0 : [ 1  1  1 ]   1          10:  [ .  2  . ]   0
    1 1 : [ .  1  1 ]   0          11:  [ 1  2  . ]   0
    1 2 : [ .  1  2 ]   2          12:  [ 1  2  1 ]   2
    1 3 : [ 1  1  2 ]   0          13:  [ 2  2  1 ]   0
    1 4 : [ 1  2  2 ]   1          14:  [ 3  2  1 ]   0
    1 5 : [ .  2  2 ]   0          15:  [ .  2  1 ]   0
    1 6 : [ .  .  2 ]   1          16:  [ .  .  1 ]   1
    1 7 : [ 1  .  2 ]   0          17:  [ 1  .  1 ]   0
    1 8 : [ 1  .  3 ]   2          18:  [ 2  .  1 ]   0
    1 9 : [ .  .  3 ]   0          19:  [ 3  .  1 ]   0
    2 0 : [ .  1  3 ]   1          20:  [ 3  1  1 ]   1
    2 1 : [ 1  1  3 ]   0          21:  [ .  1  1 ]   0
    2 2 : [ 1  2  3 ]   1          22:  [ 1  1  1 ]   0
    2 3 : [ .  2  3 ]   0          23:  [ 2  1  1 ]   0
```

Figure 9.2-B: Mixed radix numbers in modular Gray code order, dots denote zeros. The radix vectors are $M = [2, 3, 4]$ (left) and $M = [4, 3, 2]$ (right). The columns 'j' give the position of last change.

Figure 9.2-B shows the *modular Gray code* order for 3-digit mixed radix numbers with radix vectors $M = [2, 3, 4]$ (left) and $M = [4, 3, 2]$ (right). The transitions are either $k \to k+1$ or, if k is maximal, $k \to 0$. The mixed radix modular Gray code can be generated as follows [FXT: class mixedradix_modular_gray2 in comb/mixedradix-modular-gray2.h]:

```
1   class mixedradix_modular_gray2
2   {
3   public:
4       ulong *a_;   // digits
5       ulong *m1_;  // radix minus one ('nines')
6       ulong *x_;   // count changes of digit
7       ulong n_;    // number of digits
8       ulong j_;    // position of last change
9
10  public:
11      mixedradix_modular_gray2(ulong n, ulong mm, const ulong *m=0)
12      {
13          n_ = n;
14          a_ = new ulong[n_];
15          m1_ = new ulong[n_+1];  // incl. sentinel at m1[n]
16          x_ = new ulong[n_+1];   // incl. sentinel at x[n] (!= m1[n])
17
18          mixedradix_init(n_, mm, m, m1_);
19
20          first();
21      }
22      [--snip--]
```

The computation of the successor works in constant amortized time

```
1       bool next()
2       {
3           ulong j = 0;
4           while ( x_[j] == m1_[j] )  // can touch sentinels
5           {
6               x_[j] = 0;
```

```
7              ++j;
8            }
9          ++x_[j];
10
11         if ( j==n_ )  { first();  return false; }  // current is last
12
13         j_ = j;  // save position of change
14
15         // increment:
16         ulong aj = a_[j] + 1;
17         if ( aj>m1_[j] )  aj = 0;
18         a_[j] = aj;
19
20         return true;
21     }
22     [--snip--]
```

The rate of generation is about 151 M/s for radix 2, 254 M/s for radix 4, and 267 M/s for radix 8 [FXT: comb/mixedradix-modular-gray2-demo.cc].

The loopless implementation [FXT: `class mixedradix_modular_gray` in comb/mixedradix-modular-gray.h] was taken from [215, ex.77, sect.7.2.1.1]. The rate of generation is about 169 M/s with radix 2, 197 M/s with radix 4, and 256 M/s with radix 8 [FXT: comb/mixedradix-modular-gray-demo.cc].

9.3   gslex order

```
           M = [ 2 3 4 ]     x           M=[ 4 3 2 ]     x
     0 :     [ 1 . . ]       1      0:    [ 1 . . ]       1
     1 :     [ 1 1 . ]       3      1:    [ 2 . . ]       2
     2 :     [ . 1 . ]       2      2:    [ 3 . . ]       3
     3 :     [ 1 2 . ]       5      3:    [ 1 1 . ]       5
     4 :     [ . 2 . ]       4      4:    [ 2 1 . ]       6
     5 :     [ 1 . 1 ]       7      5:    [ 3 1 . ]       7
     6 :     [ 1 1 1 ]       9      6:    [ . 1 . ]       4
     7 :     [ . 1 1 ]       8      7:    [ 1 2 . ]       9
     8 :     [ 1 2 1 ]      11      8:    [ 2 2 . ]      10
     9 :     [ . 2 1 ]      10      9:    [ 3 2 . ]      11
   1 0 :     [ . . 1 ]       6     10:    [ . 2 . ]       8
   1 1 :     [ 1 . 2 ]      13     11:    [ 1 . 1 ]      13
   1 2 :     [ 1 1 2 ]      15     12:    [ 2 . 1 ]      14
   1 3 :     [ . 1 2 ]      14     13:    [ 3 . 1 ]      15
   1 4 :     [ 1 2 2 ]      17     14:    [ 1 1 1 ]      17
   1 5 :     [ . 2 2 ]      16     15:    [ 2 1 1 ]      18
   1 6 :     [ . . 2 ]      12     16:    [ 3 1 1 ]      19
   1 7 :     [ 1 . 3 ]      19     17:    [ . 1 1 ]      16
   1 8 :     [ 1 1 3 ]      21     18:    [ 1 2 1 ]      21
   1 9 :     [ . 1 3 ]      20     19:    [ 2 2 1 ]      22
   2 0 :     [ 1 2 3 ]      23     20:    [ 3 2 1 ]      23
   2 1 :     [ . 2 3 ]      22     21:    [ . 2 1 ]      20
   2 2 :     [ . . 3 ]      18     22:    [ . . 1 ]      12
   2 3 :     [ . . . ]       0     23:    [ . . . ]       0
```

Figure 9.3-A: Mixed radix numbers in gslex (generalized subset lex) order, dots denote zeros. The radix vectors are $M = [2,3,4]$ (left) and $M = [4,3,2]$ (right). Successive words differ in at most three positions. Columns 'x' give the values.

The algorithm for the generation of subsets in lexicographic order in set representation given in section 8.1.2 on page 203 can be generalized for mixed radix numbers. Figure 9.3-A shows the 3-digit mixed radix numbers for base $M = [2,3,4]$ (left) and $M = [4,3,2]$ (right). Note that zero is the last word in this order. For lack of a better name we call the order *gslex* (for *generalized subset-lex*) order. A generator for the gslex order is [FXT: `class mixedradix_gslex` in comb/mixedradix-gslex.h]:

```
1    class mixedradix_gslex
2    {
3    public:
4        ulong n_;   // n-digit numbers
5        ulong *a_;  // digits
6        ulong *m1_; // m1[k] == radix-1 at position k
```

```
7
8    public:
9        mixedradix_gslex(ulong n, ulong mm, const ulong *m=0)
10       {
11           n_ = n;
12           a_ = new ulong[n_ + 1];
13           a_[n_] = 1;  // sentinel
14           m1_ = new ulong[n_];
15           mixedradix_init(n_, mm, m, m1_);
16           first();
17       }
18   [--snip--]
19       void first()
20       {
21           for (ulong k=0; k<n_; ++k)   a_[k] = 0;
22           a_[0] = 1;
23       }
24
25       void last()
26       {
27           for (ulong k=0; k<n_; ++k)   a_[k] = 0;
28       }
```

The method **next()** computes the successor:

```
1        bool next()
2        {
3            ulong e = 0;
4            while ( 0==a_[e] )   ++e;  // can touch sentinel
5
6            if ( e==n_ )  { first();   return false; }  // current is last
7
8            ulong ae = a_[e];
9            if ( ae != m1_[e] )  // easy case: simple increment
10           {
11               a_[0] = 1;
12               a_[e] = ae + 1;
13           }
14           else
15           {
16               a_[e] = 0;
17               if ( a_[e+1]==0 )  // can touch sentinel
18               {
19                   a_[0] = 1;
20                   ++a_[e+1];
21               }
22           }
23           return true;
24       }
```

The predecessor is computed by the method prev():

```
1        bool prev()
2        {
3            ulong e = 0;
4            while ( 0==a_[e] )   ++e;  // can touch sentinel
5
6            if ( 0!=e )  // easy case: prepend nine
7            {
8                --e;
9                a_[e] = m1_[e];
10           }
11           else
12           {
13               ulong a0 = a_[0];
14               --a0;
15               a_[0] = a0;
16
17               if ( 0==a0 )
18               {
19                   do { ++e; } while ( 0==a_[e] );  // can touch sentinel
20                   if ( e==n_ )  { last();   return false; }  // current is first
21                   ulong ae = a_[e];
22                   --ae;
23                   a_[e] = ae;
24                   if ( 0==ae )
25                   {
26                       --e;
```

```
27                      a_[e] = m1_[e];
28                  }
29              }
30          }
31          return true;
32      }
```

The routine works in constant amortized time and is fast in practice. The worst performance occurs when all digits are radix 2, then about 123 million objects are created per second. With radix 4 the rate is about 198 M/s, with radix 16 about 273 M/s [FXT: comb/mixedradix-gslex-demo.cc].

Alternative gslex order

```
            M = [ 2  3  4 ]      x              M=[ 4  3  2 ]      x
      0 :   [  .  .  . ]         0         0:   [  .  .  . ]       0
      1 :   [  1  .  . ]         1         1:   [  1  .  . ]       1
      2 :   [  1  1  . ]         3         2:   [  1  1  . ]       5
      3 :   [  1  1  1 ]         9         3:   [  1  1  1 ]      17
      4 :   [  1  1  2 ]       1 5         4:   [  1  2  . ]       9
      5 :   [  1  1  3 ]       2 1         5:   [  1  2  1 ]      21
      6 :   [  1  2  . ]         5         6:   [  1  .  1 ]      13
      7 :   [  1  2  1 ]       1 1         7:   [  2  .  . ]       2
      8 :   [  1  2  2 ]       1 7         8:   [  2  1  . ]       6
      9 :   [  1  2  3 ]       2 3         9:   [  2  1  1 ]      18
    1 0 :   [  1  .  1 ]         7        10:   [  2  2  . ]      10
    1 1 :   [  1  .  2 ]        13        11:   [  2  2  1 ]      22
    1 2 :   [  1  .  3 ]        19        12:   [  2  .  1 ]      14
    1 3 :   [  .  1  . ]         2        13:   [  3  .  . ]       3
    1 4 :   [  .  1  1 ]         8        14:   [  3  1  . ]       7
    1 5 :   [  .  1  2 ]        14        15:   [  3  1  1 ]      19
    1 6 :   [  .  1  3 ]        20        16:   [  3  2  . ]      11
    1 7 :   [  .  2  . ]         4        17:   [  3  2  1 ]      23
    1 8 :   [  .  2  1 ]        10        18:   [  3  .  1 ]      15
    1 9 :   [  .  2  2 ]        16        19:   [  .  1  . ]       4
    2 0 :   [  .  2  3 ]        22        20:   [  .  1  1 ]      16
    2 1 :   [  .  .  1 ]         6        21:   [  .  2  . ]       8
    2 2 :   [  .  .  2 ]        12        22:   [  .  2  1 ]      20
    2 3 :   [  .  .  3 ]        18        23:   [  .  .  1 ]      12
```

Figure 9.3-B: Mixed radix numbers in alternative gslex order, dots denote zeros. The radix vectors are $M = [2, 3, 4]$ (left) and $M = [4, 3, 2]$ (right). Successive words differ in at most three positions. Columns 'x' give the values.

A variant of the gslex order is shown in figure 9.3-B. The ordering can be obtained from the gslex order by reversing the list, reversing the words, and replacing all nonzero digits d_i by $r_i - d_i$ where r_i is the radix at position i. The implementation is given in [FXT: class mixedradix_gslex_alt in comb/mixedradix-gslex-alt.h], the rate of generation is about the same as with gslex order [FXT: comb/mixedradix-gslex-alt-demo.cc].

9.4   endo order

The computation of the successor in mixed radix endo order (see section 6.6.1 on page 186) is very similar to the counting order described in section 9.1 on page 217. The implementation [FXT: class mixedradix_endo in comb/mixedradix-endo.h] uses an additional array le_[] of the last nonzero elements in endo order. Its entries are 2 for $m > 1$, else 1:

```
1    class mixedradix_endo
2    {
3    public:
4        ulong *a_;   // digits, sentinel a[n]
5        ulong *m1_;  // radix (minus one) for each digit
6        ulong *le_;  // last positive digit in endo order, sentinel le[n]
7        ulong n_;    // Number of digits
8        ulong j_;    // position of last change
9
10       mixedradix_endo(const ulong *m, ulong n, ulong mm=0)
```

```
            M = [ 5 6 ]       x                              x
    0 :     [ . . ]       0         15:     [ . 5 ]     25
    1 :     [ 1 . ]       1         16:     [ 1 5 ]     26
    2 :     [ 3 . ]       3         17:     [ 3 5 ]     28
    3 :     [ 4 . ]       4         18:     [ 4 5 ]     29
    4 :     [ 2 . ]       2         19:     [ 2 5 ]     27
    5 :     [ . 1 ]       5         20:     [ . 4 ]     20
    6 :     [ 1 1 ]       6         21:     [ 1 4 ]     21
    7 :     [ 3 1 ]       8         22:     [ 3 4 ]     23
    8 :     [ 4 1 ]       9         23:     [ 4 4 ]     24
    9 :     [ 2 1 ]       7         24:     [ 2 4 ]     22
   10:      [ . 3 ]      15         25:     [ . 2 ]     10
   11:      [ 1 3 ]      16         26:     [ 1 2 ]     11
   12:      [ 3 3 ]      18         27:     [ 3 2 ]     13
   13:      [ 4 3 ]      19         28:     [ 4 2 ]     14
   14:      [ 2 3 ]      17         29:     [ 2 2 ]     12
```

Figure 9.4-A: Mixed radix numbers in endo order, dots denote zeros. The radix vector is $M = [5,6]$. Columns 'x' give the values.

```
11          {
12              n_ = n;
13              a_ = new ulong[n_+1];
14              a_[n_] = 1;  // sentinel:  != 0
15              m1_ = new ulong[n_];
16
17              mixedradix_init(n_, mm, m, m1_);
18
19              le_ = new ulong[n_+1];
20              le_[n_] = 0;  // sentinel:  != a[n]
21              for (ulong k=0; k<n_; ++k)  le_[k] = 2 - (m1_[k]==1);
22
23              first();
24          }
25          [--snip--]
```

The first word is all zero, the last can be read from the array le_[]:

```
1           void first()
2           {
3               for (ulong k=0; k<n_; ++k)  a_[k] = 0;
4               j_ = n_;
5           }
6
7           void last()
8           {
9               for (ulong k=0; k<n_; ++k)  a_[k] = le_[k];
10              j_ = n_;
11          }
12          [--snip--]
```

In the computation of the successor the function next_endo() is used instead of a simple increment:

```
1           bool next()
2           {
3               bool ret = false;
4               ulong j = 0;
5
6               while ( a_[j]==le_[j] )  { a_[j]=0; ++j; }  // can touch sentinel
7               if ( j<n_ ) // only if no overflow
8               {
9                   a_[j] = next_endo(a_[j], m1_[j]);  // increment
10                  ret = true;
11              }
12
13              j_ = j;
14              return ret;
15          }
16
17          bool prev()
18          {
19              bool ret = false;
20              ulong j = 0;
21
22              while ( a_[j]==0 )  { a_[j]=le_[j]; ++j; }  // can touch sentinel
```

```
23          if ( j<n_ ) // only if no overflow
24          {
25              a_[j] = prev_endo(a_[j], m1_[j]);  // decrement
26              ret = true;
27          }
28
29          j_ = j;
30          return ret;
31      }
32  [--snip--]
```

The function **next()** generates between about 115 million (radix 2) and 180 million (radix 16) numbers per second. The listing in figure 9.4-A was created with the program [FXT: comb/mixedradix-endo-demo.cc].

9.5 Gray code for endo order

```
        M = [ 5 6 ]      x     j     d                       x     j     d
  0 :   [ . . ]          0                     15:   [ 2 5 ]  27    1     1
  1 :   [ 1 . ]          1     0     1         16:   [ 4 5 ]  29    0    -1
  2 :   [ 3 . ]          3     0     1         17:   [ 3 5 ]  28    0    -1
  3 :   [ 4 . ]          4     0     1         18:   [ 1 5 ]  26    0    -1
  4 :   [ 2 . ]          2     0     1         19:   [ . 5 ]  25    0    -1
  5 :   [ 2 1 ]          7     1     1         20:   [ . 4 ]  20    1     1
  6 :   [ 4 1 ]          9     0   - 1         21:   [ 1 4 ]  21    0     1
  7 :   [ 3 1 ]          8     0   - 1         22:   [ 3 4 ]  23    0     1
  8 :   [ 1 1 ]          6     0   - 1         23:   [ 4 4 ]  24    0     1
  9 :   [ . 1 ]          5     0   - 1         24:   [ 2 4 ]  22    0     1
 10:    [ . 3 ]         15     1     1         25:   [ 2 2 ]  12    1     1
 11:    [ 1 3 ]         16     0     1         26:   [ 4 2 ]  14    0    -1
 12:    [ 3 3 ]         18     0     1         27:   [ 3 2 ]  13    0    -1
 13:    [ 4 3 ]         19     0     1         28:   [ 1 2 ]  11    0    -1
 14:    [ 2 3 ]         17     0     1         29:   [ . 2 ]  10    0    -1
```

Figure 9.5-A: Mixed radix numbers in endo Gray code, dots denote zeros. The radix vector is $M = [4, 5]$. Columns 'x' give the values, columns 'j' and 'd' give the position of last change and its direction, respectively.

A Gray code for mixed radix numbers in endo order is a modification of the CAT algorithm for the Gray code described in section 9.2 on page 220 [FXT: **class mixedradix_endo_gray** in comb/mixedradix-endo-gray.h]:

```
1   class mixedradix_endo_gray
2   {
3   public:
4       ulong *a_;  // mixed radix digits
5       ulong *m1_; // radices (minus one)
6       ulong *i_;  // direction
7       ulong *le_; // last positive digit in endo order
8       ulong n_;   // n_ digits
9       ulong j_;   // position of last change
10      int dm_;    // direction of last move
11
12  [--snip--]
13      void first()
14      {
15          for (ulong k=0; k<n_; ++k)  a_[k] = 0;
16          for (ulong k=0; k<n_; ++k)  i_[k] = +1;
17          j_ = n_;
18          dm_ = 0;
19      }
```

In the computation of the last number the digits from the last even radix to the end have to be set to the last digit in endo order:

```
1       void last()
2       {
3           for (ulong k=0; k<n_; ++k)  a_[k] = 0;
4           for (ulong k=0; k<n_; ++k)  i_[k] = -1UL;
```

```
5
6            // find position of last even radix:
7            ulong z = 0;
8            for (ulong i=0; i<n_; ++i)  if ( m1_[i]&1 )  z = i;
9            while ( z<n_ )  // last even .. end:
10           {
11               a_[z] = le_[z];
12               i_[z] = +1;
13               ++z;
14           }
15
16           j_ = 0;
17           dm_ = -1;
18       }
19   [--snip--]
```

The successor is computed as follows:

```
1        bool next()
2        {
3            ulong j = 0;
4            ulong ij;
5            while ( (ij=i_[j]) )  // can touch sentinel i[n]==0
6            {
7                ulong dj;
8                bool ovq;  // overflow?
9                if ( ij == 1 )
10               {
11                   dj = next_endo(a_[j], m1_[j]);
12                   ovq = (dj==0);
13               }
14               else
15               {
16                   ovq = (a_[j]==0);
17                   dj = prev_endo(a_[j], m1_[j]);
18               }
19
20               if ( ovq )  i_[j] = -ij;
21               else
22               {
23                   a_[j] = dj;
24                   dm_ = ij;
25                   j_ = j;
26                   return true;
27               }
28
29               ++j;
30           }
31           return false;
32       }
33   [--snip--]
```

For the routine for computation of the predecessor change the test if (ij == 1) to if (ij != 1). About 65 million (radix 2) and 110 million (radix 16) numbers per second are generated. The listing in figure 9.5-A was created with the program [FXT: comb/mixedradix-endo-gray-demo.cc].

9.6   Fixed sum of digits

Mixed radix numbers with sum of digits 4 in lexicographic order are shown in figure 9.6-A. The numbers in falling factorial base correspond to length-6 permutations with 5 inversions (left, see section 10.1.1), the radix-4 numbers correspond to compositions of 4 into 4 parts of size at most 3 (middle, see section 7.1 on page 194), and the binary numbers correspond to combinations $\binom{7}{4}$ (right, see section 6.2 on page 177). The numbers also correspond to the k-subsets (combinations) of multisets, see section 13.1 on page 295. The listings were created with the program [FXT: comb/mixedradix-sod-lex-demo.cc].

The successor is computed by determining the position j of the leftmost nonzero digit whose right neighbor can be incremented. After the increment the digits at positions up to j are set to the (lexicographically) first string such that the sum of digits is preserved. Sentinels are used with the scans [FXT: class mixedradix_sod_lex in comb/mixedradix-sod-lex.h]:

```
1    class mixedradix_sod_lex
```

```
              ffact                    radix-4                   radix-2
 1:  [ 4 . . . . ]        1:  [ 3 1 . . ]          1:  [ 1 1 1 1 . . . ]
 2:  [ 3 1 . . . ]        2:  [ 2 2 . . ]          2:  [ 1 1 1 . 1 . . ]
 3:  [ 2 2 . . . ]        3:  [ 1 3 . . ]          3:  [ 1 1 . 1 1 . . ]
 4:  [ 1 3 . . . ]        4:  [ 3 . 1 . ]          4:  [ 1 . 1 1 1 . . ]
 5:  [ . 4 . . . ]        5:  [ 2 1 1 . ]          5:  [ . 1 1 1 1 . . ]
 6:  [ 3 . 1 . . ]        6:  [ 1 2 1 . ]          6:  [ 1 1 1 . . 1 . ]
 7:  [ 2 1 1 . . ]        7:  [ . 3 1 . ]          7:  [ 1 1 . 1 . 1 . ]
 8:  [ 1 2 1 . . ]        8:  [ 2 . 2 . ]          8:  [ 1 . 1 1 . 1 . ]
 9:  [ . 3 1 . . ]        9:  [ 1 1 2 . ]          9:  [ . 1 1 1 . 1 . ]
10:  [ 2 . 2 . . ]       10:  [ . 2 2 . ]         10:  [ 1 1 . . 1 1 . ]
11:  [ 1 1 2 . . ]       11:  [ 1 . 3 . ]         11:  [ 1 . 1 . 1 1 . ]
12:  [ . 2 2 . . ]       12:  [ . 1 3 . ]         12:  [ . 1 1 . 1 1 . ]
13:  [ 1 . 3 . . ]       13:  [ 3 . . 1 ]         13:  [ 1 . . 1 1 1 . ]
14:  [ . 1 3 . . ]       14:  [ 2 1 . 1 ]         14:  [ . 1 . 1 1 1 . ]
15:  [ 3 . . 1 . ]       15:  [ 1 2 . 1 ]         15:  [ . . 1 1 1 1 . ]
16:  [ 2 1 . 1 . ]       16:  [ . 3 . 1 ]         16:  [ 1 1 1 . . . 1 ]
17:  [ 1 2 . 1 . ]       17:  [ 2 . 1 1 ]         17:  [ 1 1 . 1 . . 1 ]
18:  [ . 3 . 1 . ]       18:  [ 1 1 1 1 ]         18:  [ 1 . 1 1 . . 1 ]
19:  [ 2 . 1 1 . ]       19:  [ . 2 1 1 ]         19:  [ . 1 1 1 . . 1 ]
20:  [ 1 1 1 1 . ]       20:  [ 1 . 2 1 ]         20:  [ 1 1 . . 1 . 1 ]
21:  [ . 2 1 1 . ]       21:  [ . 1 2 1 ]         21:  [ 1 . 1 . 1 . 1 ]
22:  [ 1 . 2 1 . ]       22:  [ . . 3 1 ]         22:  [ . 1 1 . 1 . 1 ]
23:  [ . 1 2 1 . ]       23:  [ 2 . . 2 ]         23:  [ 1 . . 1 1 . 1 ]
24:  [ . . 3 1 . ]       24:  [ 1 1 . 2 ]         24:  [ . 1 . 1 1 . 1 ]
25:  [ 2 . . 2 . ]       25:  [ . 2 . 2 ]         25:  [ . . 1 1 1 . 1 ]
26:  [ 1 1 . 2 . ]       26:  [ 1 . 1 2 ]         26:  [ 1 1 . . . 1 1 ]
27:  [ . 2 . 2 . ]       27:  [ . 1 1 2 ]         27:  [ 1 . 1 . . 1 1 ]
28:  [ 1 . 1 2 . ]       28:  [ . . 2 2 ]         28:  [ . 1 1 . . 1 1 ]
29:  [ . 1 1 2 . ]       29:  [ 1 . . 3 ]         29:  [ 1 . . 1 . 1 1 ]
30:  [ . . 2 2 . ]       30:  [ . 1 . 3 ]         30:  [ . 1 . 1 . 1 1 ]
31:  [ 3 . . . 1 ]       31:  [ . . 1 3 ]         31:  [ . . 1 1 . 1 1 ]
32:  [ 2 1 . . 1 ]                                 32:  [ 1 . . . 1 1 1 ]
33:  [ 1 2 . . 1 ]                                 33:  [ . 1 . . 1 1 1 ]
34:  [ . 3 . . 1 ]                                 34:  [ . . 1 . 1 1 1 ]
35:  [ 2 . 1 . 1 ]                                 35:  [ . . . 1 1 1 1 ]
36:  [ 1 1 1 . 1 ]
37:  [ . 2 1 . 1 ]
38:  [ 1 . 2 . 1 ]
39:  [ . 1 2 . 1 ]
40:  [ . . 3 . 1 ]
41:  [ 2 . . 1 1 ]
42:  [ 1 1 . 1 1 ]
43:  [ . 2 . 1 1 ]
44:  [ 1 . 1 1 1 ]
45:  [ . 1 1 1 1 ]
46:  [ . . 2 1 1 ]
47:  [ 1 . . 2 1 ]
48:  [ . 1 . 2 1 ]
49:  [ . . 1 2 1 ]
```

Figure 9.6-A: Mixed radix numbers with sum of digits 4 in lexicographic order: 5-digit falling factorial base (left), 4-digit radix 4 (middle), and 7-digit binary (right).

```
2    {
3    public:
4        ulong *a_;   // digits
5        ulong *m1_;  // nines (radix minus one) for each digit
6        ulong n_;    // Number of digits
7        ulong s_;    // Sum of digits
8        ulong j_;    // rightmost position of last change
9        ulong sm_;   // max possible sum of digits (arg s with first())
10
11   public:
12       mixedradix_sod_lex(ulong n, ulong mm, const ulong *m=0)
13       {
14           n_ = n;
15           a_[n_] = 1;    // sentinel !=0
16           m1_[n_] = 2;   // sentinel >a[n]
17           a_[n_+1] = 0;    // sentinel ==0
18           m1_[n_+1] = 1;   // sentinel >0
19
20           mixedradix_init(n_, mm, m, m1_);
21
22           ulong s = 0;
23           for (ulong i=0; i<n_; ++i)  s += m1_[i];
```

```
24            sm_ = s;
25
26            j_ = n_ - 1;
27        }
28    [--snip--]
```

The sum of digits is supplied with the method `first()`:

```
1     bool first(ulong k)
2     {
3         s_ = k;
4         if ( s_ > sm_ )  return false;  // too big
5
6         ulong i = 0;
7         ulong s = s_;
8         while ( s )
9         {
10            const ulong m1 = m1_[i];
11            if ( s >= m1 )  { a_[i] = m1;  s -= m1; }
12            else            { a_[i] = s;  break; }
13            ++i;
14        }
15
16        while ( ++i<n_ )  { a_[i] = 0; }
17
18        j_ = n_ - 1;
19        return true;
20    }
21
22    bool next()
23    {
24        ulong j = 0;
25        ulong s = 0;
26        while ( (a_[j]==0) || (a_[j+1]==m1_[j+1]) )  // can read sentinels
27        {
28            s += a_[j];
29            a_[j]=0;
30            ++j;
31        }
32        j_ = j+1;  // record rightmost position of change
33
34        if ( j_ >= n_ )  return false;  // current is last
35
36        s += (a_[j] - 1);
37        a_[j] = 0;
38        ++a_[j+1];  // increment next digit
39
40        ulong i = 0;
41        do  // set prefix to lex-first string
42        {
43            const ulong m1 = m1_[i];
44            if ( s >= m1 )  { a_[i] = m1;  s -= m1; }
45            else            { a_[i] = s;  s = 0; }
46            ++i;
47        }
48        while ( s );
49
50        return true;
51    }
52
53    [--snip--]
54 };
```

Chapter 10

Permutations

We present algorithms for the generation of all permutations in various orders such as lexicographic and minimal-change order. Several methods to convert permutations to and from mixed radix numbers with factorial base are described. Algorithms for application, inversion, and composition of permutations and for the generation of random permutations are given in chapter 2.

10.1 Factorial representations of permutations

The factorial number system corresponds to the mixed radix bases $M = [2, 3, 4, \ldots]$ (*rising factorial base*) or $M = [\ldots, 4, 3, 2]$ (*falling factorial base*). A factorial number with $(n-1)$-digits can have $n!$ different values. We develop different methods to convert factorial numbers to permutations and vice versa.

10.1.1 The Lehmer code (inversion table)

Each permutation of n elements can be converted to a unique $(n-1)$-digit factorial number $A = [a_0, a_1, \ldots, a_{n-2}]$ in the falling factorial base: for each index k (except the last) count the number of elements with indices to the right of k that are less than the current element [FXT: comb/fact2perm.cc]:

```
1    void perm2ffact(const ulong *x, ulong n, ulong *fc)
2    // Convert permutation in x[0,...,n-1] into
3    //    the (n-1) digit falling factorial representation in fc[0,...,n-2].
4    // We have: fc[0]<n, fc[1]<n-1, ..., fc[n-2]<2 (falling radices)
5    {
6        for (ulong k=0; k<n-1; ++k)
7        {
8            ulong xk = x[k];
9            ulong i = 0;
10           for (ulong j=k+1; j<n; ++j)  if ( x[j]<xk )  ++i;
11           fc[k] = i;
12       }
13   }
```

The routine works because all elements of the permutation are distinct. The factorial representation computed is called the *Lehmer code* of the permutation. For example, the permutation $P = [3, 0, 1, 4, 2]$ has the inversion table $I = [3, 0, 0, 1]$: three elements less than the first element (3) lie to the right of it, no elements less than the second (0) or third (1) elements lies right to them, and one element less than 4 lies right of it.

An alternative term for the Lehmer code is *inversion table*: an *inversion* of a permutation

$$[x_0, x_1, \ldots, x_{n-1}] \tag{10.1-1}$$

is a pair of indices k and j where $k < j$ and $x_j < x_k$. Now fix k and call such an inversion (where an element x_j right of k is less than x_k) a *right inversion* at k. The inversion table $[i_0, i_1, \ldots, i_{n-2}]$ of a permutation is computed by setting i_k to the number of right inversions at k. This is exactly what the given routine does.

A routine that computes the permutation for a given Lehmer code is

J. Arndt, *Matters Computational: Ideas, Algorithms, Source Code,*
DOI 10.1007/978-3-642-14764-7_10, © Springer-Verlag Berlin Heidelberg 2011

```
1    void ffact2perm(const ulong *fc, ulong n, ulong *x)
2    // Inverse of perm2ffact():
3    // Convert the (n-1) digit falling factorial representation in fc[0,...,n-2].
4    // into permutation in x[0,...,n-1]
5    // Must have: fc[0]<n, fc[1]<n-1, ..., fc[n-2]<2 (falling radices)
6    {
7        for (ulong k=0; k<n; ++k)  x[k] = k;
8        for (ulong k=0; k<n-1; ++k)
9        {
10           ulong i = fc[k];
11           if ( i )  rotate_right1(x+k, i+1);
12       }
13   }
```

A routine to compute the inverse permutation from the Lehmer code is

```
1    void ffact2invperm(const ulong *fc, ulong n, ulong *x)
2    // Convert the (n-1) digit falling factorial representation in fc[0,...,n-2]
3    // into permutation in x[0,...,n-1] such that
4    // the permutation is the inverse of the one computed via ffact2perm().
5    {
6        for (ulong k=0; k<n; ++k)  x[k] = k;
7        for (ulong k=n-2; (long)k>=0; --k)
8        {
9            ulong i = fc[k];
10           if ( i )  rotate_left1(x+k, i+1);
11       }
12   }
```

	ffact	permutation	rev.compl.perm.	rfact
0 :	[. . .]	[. 1 2 3]	[. 1 2 3]	[. . .]
1 :	[1 . .]	[1 . 2 3]	[. 1 3 2]	[. . 1]
2 :	[2 . .]	[2 . 1 3]	[. 2 3 1]	[. . 2]
3 :	[3 . .]	[3 . 1 2]	[1 2 3 .]	[. . 3]
4 :	[. 1 .]	[. 2 1 3]	[. 2 1 3]	[. 1 .]
5 :	[1 1 .]	[1 2 . 3]	[. 3 1 2]	[. 1 1]
6 :	[2 1 .]	[2 1 . 3]	[. 3 2 1]	[. 1 2]
7 :	[3 1 .]	[3 1 . 2]	[1 3 2 .]	[. 1 3]
8 :	[. 2 .]	[. 3 1 2]	[1 2 . 3]	[. 2 .]
9 :	[1 2 .]	[1 3 . 2]	[1 3 . 2]	[. 2 1]
1 0 :	[2 2 .]	[2 3 . 1]	[2 3 . 1]	[. 2 2]
1 1 :	[3 2 .]	[3 2 . 1]	[2 3 1 .]	[. 2 3]
1 2 :	[. . 1]	[. 1 3 2]	[1 . 2 3]	[1 . .]
1 3 :	[1 . 1]	[1 . 3 2]	[1 . 3 2]	[1 . 1]
1 4 :	[2 . 1]	[2 . 3 1]	[2 . 3 1]	[1 . 2]
1 5 :	[3 . 1]	[3 . 2 1]	[2 1 3 .]	[1 . 3]
1 6 :	[. 1 1]	[. 2 3 1]	[2 . 1 3]	[1 1 .]
1 7 :	[1 1 1]	[1 2 3 .]	[3 . 1 2]	[1 1 1]
1 8 :	[2 1 1]	[2 1 3 .]	[3 . 2 1]	[1 1 2]
1 9 :	[3 1 1]	[3 1 2 .]	[3 1 2 .]	[1 1 3]
2 0 :	[. 2 1]	[. 3 2 1]	[2 1 . 3]	[1 2 .]
2 1 :	[1 2 1]	[1 3 2 .]	[3 1 . 2]	[1 2 1]
2 2 :	[2 2 1]	[2 3 1 .]	[3 2 . 1]	[1 2 2]
2 3 :	[3 2 1]	[3 2 1 .]	[3 2 1 .]	[1 2 3]

Figure 10.1-A: Numbers in falling factorial base and permutations so that the number is the Lehmer code of it (left columns). Dots denote zeros. The rising factorial representation of the reversed and complemented permutation equals the reversed Lehmer code (right columns).

A similar method can compute a representation in the rising factorial base. We count the number of elements to the left of k that are greater than the element at k (the number of *left inversions* at k):

```
1    void perm2rfact(const ulong *x, ulong n, ulong *fc)
2    // Convert permutation in x[0,...,n-1] into
3    //    the (n-1) digit rising factorial representation in fc[0,...,n-2].
4    // We have: fc[0]<2, fc[1]<3, ..., fc[n-2]<n (rising radices)
5    {
6        for (ulong k=1; k<n; ++k)
7        {
8            ulong xk = x[k];
9            ulong i = 0;
```

```
               rfact        permutation    rev.compl.perm.    ffact
    0 :      [ . . . ]      [ . 1 2 3 ]     [ . 1 2 3 ]      [ . . . ]
    1 :      [ 1 . . ]      [ 1 . 2 3 ]     [ . 1 3 2 ]      [ . . 1 ]
    2 :      [ . 1 . ]      [ . 2 1 3 ]     [ . 2 1 3 ]      [ . 1 . ]
    3 :      [ 1 1 . ]      [ 2 . 1 3 ]     [ . 2 3 1 ]      [ . 1 1 ]
    4 :      [ . 2 . ]      [ 1 2 . 3 ]     [ . 3 1 2 ]      [ . 2 . ]
    5 :      [ 1 2 . ]      [ 2 1 . 3 ]     [ . 3 2 1 ]      [ . 2 1 ]
    6 :      [ . . 1 ]      [ . 1 3 2 ]     [ 1 . 2 3 ]      [ 1 . . ]
    7 :      [ 1 . 1 ]      [ 1 . 3 2 ]     [ 1 . 3 2 ]      [ 1 . 1 ]
    8 :      [ . 1 1 ]      [ . 3 1 2 ]     [ 1 2 . 3 ]      [ 1 1 . ]
    9 :      [ 1 1 1 ]      [ 3 . 1 2 ]     [ 1 2 3 . ]      [ 1 1 1 ]
  1 0 :      [ . 2 1 ]      [ 1 3 . 2 ]     [ 1 3 . 2 ]      [ 1 2 . ]
  1 1 :      [ 1 2 1 ]      [ 3 1 . 2 ]     [ 1 3 2 . ]      [ 1 2 1 ]
  1 2 :      [ . . 2 ]      [ . 2 3 1 ]     [ 2 . 1 3 ]      [ 2 . . ]
  1 3 :      [ 1 . 2 ]      [ 2 . 3 1 ]     [ 2 . 3 1 ]      [ 2 . 1 ]
  1 4 :      [ . 1 2 ]      [ . 3 2 1 ]     [ 2 1 . 3 ]      [ 2 1 . ]
  1 5 :      [ 1 1 2 ]      [ 3 . 2 1 ]     [ 2 1 3 . ]      [ 2 1 1 ]
  1 6 :      [ . 2 2 ]      [ 2 3 . 1 ]     [ 2 3 . 1 ]      [ 2 2 . ]
  1 7 :      [ 1 2 2 ]      [ 3 2 . 1 ]     [ 2 3 1 . ]      [ 2 2 1 ]
  1 8 :      [ . . 3 ]      [ 1 2 3 . ]     [ 3 . 1 2 ]      [ 3 . . ]
  1 9 :      [ 1 . 3 ]      [ 2 1 3 . ]     [ 3 . 2 1 ]      [ 3 . 1 ]
  2 0 :      [ . 1 3 ]      [ 1 3 2 . ]     [ 3 1 . 2 ]      [ 3 1 . ]
  2 1 :      [ 1 1 3 ]      [ 3 1 2 . ]     [ 3 1 2 . ]      [ 3 1 1 ]
  2 2 :      [ . 2 3 ]      [ 2 3 1 . ]     [ 3 2 . 1 ]      [ 3 2 . ]
  2 3 :      [ 1 2 3 ]      [ 3 2 1 . ]     [ 3 2 1 . ]      [ 3 2 1 ]
```

Figure 10.1-B: Numbers in rising factorial base and permutations so that the number is the Lehmer code of it (left columns). The reversed and complemented permutations and their falling factorial representations are shown in the right columns. They appear in lexicographic order.

```
10             for (ulong j=0; j<k; ++j)  if ( x[j]>xk )  ++i;
11             fc[k-1] = i;
12        }
13   }
```

The inverse routine is

```
1    void rfact2perm(const ulong *fc, ulong n, ulong *x)
2    {
3        for (ulong k=0; k<n; ++k)  x[k] = k;
4        ulong *y = x+n;
5        for (ulong k=n-1;  k!=0;  --k, --y)
6        {
7            ulong i = fc[k-1];
8            if ( i )  { ++i;  rotate_left1(y-i, i); }
9        }
10   }
```

A routine for the inverse permutation is

```
1    void rfact2invperm(const ulong *fc, ulong n, ulong *x)
2    // Convert the (n-1) digit rising factorial representation in fc[0,...,n-2].
3    //  into permutation in x[0,...,n-1] such that
4    // the permutation is the inverse of the one computed via rfact2perm().
5    {
6        for (ulong k=0; k<n; ++k)  x[k] = k;
7        ulong *y = x + 2;
8        for (ulong k=0;  k<n-1;  ++k, ++y)
9        {
10           ulong i = fc[k];
11           if ( i )  { ++i;  rotate_right1(y-i, i); }
12       }
13   }
```

The permutations corresponding to the Lehmer codes (in counting order) are shown in figure 10.1-A (left columns) which was created with the program [FXT: comb/fact2perm-demo.cc]. The permutation whose rising factorial representation is the digit-reversed Lehmer code is computed by reversing and complementing (replacing each element x by $n - 1 - x$) the original permutation:

Lehmer code	permutation	rev.perm	compl.rev.perm	rising fact
[3,0,0,1]	[3,0,1,4,2]	[2,4,1,0,3]	[2,0,3,4,1]	[1,0,0,3]

The permutations obtained from counting in the rising factorial base are shown in figure 10.1-B.

10.1.1.1 Computation with large arrays

With the left-right array described in section 4.7 on page 166 the conversion to and from the Lehmer code can be done in $O(n \log n)$ operations [FXT: comb/big-fact2perm.cc]:

```
1   void perm2ffact(const ulong *x, ulong n, ulong *fc, left_right_array &LR)
2   {
3       LR.set_all();
4       for (ulong k=0; k<n-1; ++k)
5       {
6           // i := number of Set positions Left of x[k], Excluding x[k].
7           ulong i = LR.num_SLE( x[k] );
8           LR.get_set_idx_chg( i );
9           fc[k] = i;
10      }
11  }
```

The LR-array passed as an extra argument has to be of size n. Conversion of an array of, say, 10 million entries is a matter of seconds if this routine is used [FXT: comb/big-fact2perm-demo.cc].

```
1   void ffact2perm(const ulong *fc, ulong n, ulong *x, left_right_array &LR)
2   {
3       LR.free_all();
4       for (ulong k=0; k<n-1; ++k)
5       {
6           ulong i = LR.get_free_idx_chg( fc[k] );
7           x[k] = i;
8       }
9       ulong i = LR.get_free_idx_chg( 0 );
10      x[n-1] = i;
11  }
```

The routines for rising factorials are

```
1   void perm2rfact(const ulong *x, ulong n, ulong *fc, left_right_array &LR)
2   {
3       LR.set_all();
4       for (ulong k=0, r=n-1;  k<n-1;  ++k, --r)  //  r == n-1-k;
5       {
6           // i := number of Set positions Left of x[r], Excluding x[r].
7           ulong i = LR.num_SLE( x[r] );
8           LR.get_set_idx_chg( i );
9           fc[r-1] = r - i;
10      }
11  }
```

and

```
1   void rfact2perm(const ulong *fc, ulong n, ulong *x, left_right_array &LR)
2   {
3       LR.free_all();
4       for (ulong k=0; k<n-1; ++k)
5       {
6           ulong i = LR.get_free_idx_chg( fc[n-2-k] );
7           x[n-1-k] = n-1-i;
8       }
9       ulong i = LR.get_free_idx_chg( 0 );
10      x[0] = n-1-i;
11  }
```

The conversion of the routines that compute permutations from factorial numbers into routines that compute the inverse permutations is especially easy, just change the code as follows:

```
        x[a] = b;      =-->     x[b] = a;
```

We obtain the routines

```
1   void ffact2invperm(const ulong *fc, ulong n, ulong *x, left_right_array &LR)
2   {
3       LR.free_all();
4       for (ulong k=0; k<n-1; ++k)
5       {
6           ulong i = LR.get_free_idx_chg( fc[k] );
7           x[i] = k;
```

```
 8          }
 9          ulong i = LR.get_free_idx_chg( 0 );
10          x[i] = n-1;
11      }
```

and

```
 1      void rfact2invperm(const ulong *fc, ulong n, ulong *x, left_right_array &LR)
 2      {
 3          LR.free_all();
 4          for (ulong k=0; k<n-1; ++k)
 5          {
 6              ulong i = LR.get_free_idx_chg( fc[n-2-k] );
 7              x[n-1-i] = n-1-k;
 8          }
 9          ulong i = LR.get_free_idx_chg( 0 );
10          x[n-1-i] = 0;
11      }
```

10.1.1.2   The number of inversions

The number of inversions of a permutation can be computed as follows [FXT: perm/permq.cc]:

```
 1      ulong
 2      count_inversions(const ulong *f, ulong n)
 3      // Return number of inversions in f[],
 4      // i.e. number of pairs k,j where k<j and f[k]>f[j]
 5      {
 6          ulong ct = 0;
 7          for (ulong k=1; k<n; ++k)
 8          {
 9              ulong fk = f[k];
10              for (ulong j=0; j<k; ++j)  ct += ( fk<f[j] );
11          }
12          return ct;
13      }
```

The algorithm is $O(n^2)$. For large arrays we can use the fact that the number of inversions equals the sum of digits of the Lehmer code, the algorithm is $O(n \log n)$:

```
 1      ulong
 2      count_inversions(const ulong *f, ulong n, left_right_array *tLR)
 3      {
 4          left_right_array *LR = tLR;
 5          if ( tLR==0 )  LR = new left_right_array(n);
 6
 7          ulong ct = 0;
 8          LR->set_all();
 9          for (ulong k=0; k<n-1; ++k)
10          {
11              ulong i = LR->num_SLE( f[k] );
12              LR->get_set_idx_chg( i );
13              ct += i;
14          }
15
16          if ( tLR==0 )  delete LR;
17          return ct;
18      }
```

10.1.2   A representation via reversals ‡

Replacing the rotations in the computation of a permutation from its Lehmer code by reversals gives a different one-to-one relation between factorial numbers and permutations. The routine for the falling factorial base is [FXT: comb/fact2perm-rev.cc]:

```
 1      void perm2ffact_rev(const ulong *x, ulong n, ulong *fc)
 2      {
 3          ALLOCA(ulong, ti, n);  // inverse permutation
 4          for (ulong k=0; k<n; ++k)  ti[x[k]] = k;
 5          for (ulong k=0; k<n-1; ++k)
 6          {
 7              ulong j; // find element k
 8              for (j=k; j<n; ++j)  if ( ti[j]==k )  break;
 9              j -= k;
```

```
              ffact        permutation      inv.perm.        ffact
 0 :   [ . . . ]   [ . 1 2 3 ]   [ . 1 2 3 ]   [ . . . ]
 1 :   [ 1 . . ]   [ 1 . 2 3 ]   [ 1 . 2 3 ]   [ 1 . . ]
 2 :   [ 2 . . ]   [ 2 1 . 3 ]   [ 2 1 . 3 ]   [ 2 . . ]
 3 :   [ 3 . . ]   [ 3 2 1 . ]   [ 3 2 1 . ]   [ 3 . . ]
 4 :   [ . 1 . ]   [ . 2 1 3 ]   [ . 2 1 3 ]   [ . 1 . ]
 5 :   [ 1 1 . ]   [ 1 2 . 3 ]   [ 2 . 1 3 ]   [ 2 1 . ]
 6 :   [ 2 1 . ]   [ 2 . 1 3 ]   [ 1 2 . 3 ]   [ 1 1 . ]
 7 :   [ 3 1 . ]   [ 3 1 2 . ]   [ 3 1 2 . ]   [ 3 1 . ]
 8 :   [ . 2 . ]   [ . 3 2 1 ]   [ . 3 2 1 ]   [ . 2 . ]
 9 :   [ 1 2 . ]   [ 1 3 2 . ]   [ 3 . 2 1 ]   [ 3 2 1 ]
10 :   [ 2 2 . ]   [ 2 3 . 1 ]   [ 2 3 . 1 ]   [ 2 2 . ]
11 :   [ 3 2 . ]   [ 3 . 1 2 ]   [ 1 2 3 . ]   [ 1 1 1 ]
12 :   [ . . 1 ]   [ . 1 3 2 ]   [ . 1 3 2 ]   [ . . 1 ]
13 :   [ 1 . 1 ]   [ 1 . 3 2 ]   [ 1 . 3 2 ]   [ 1 . 1 ]
14 :   [ 2 . 1 ]   [ 2 1 3 . ]   [ 3 1 . 2 ]   [ 3 1 1 ]
15 :   [ 3 . 1 ]   [ 3 2 . 1 ]   [ 2 3 1 . ]   [ 2 2 1 ]
16 :   [ . 1 1 ]   [ . 2 3 1 ]   [ . 3 1 2 ]   [ . 2 1 ]
17 :   [ 1 1 1 ]   [ 1 2 3 . ]   [ 3 . 1 2 ]   [ 3 2 . ]
18 :   [ 2 1 1 ]   [ 2 . 3 1 ]   [ 1 3 . 2 ]   [ 1 2 1 ]
19 :   [ 3 1 1 ]   [ 3 1 . 2 ]   [ 2 1 3 . ]   [ 2 . 1 ]
20 :   [ . 2 1 ]   [ . 3 1 2 ]   [ . 2 3 1 ]   [ . 1 1 ]
21 :   [ 1 2 1 ]   [ 1 3 . 2 ]   [ 2 . 3 1 ]   [ 2 1 1 ]
22 :   [ 2 2 1 ]   [ 2 3 1 . ]   [ 3 2 . 1 ]   [ 3 . 1 ]
23 :   [ 3 2 1 ]   [ 3 . 2 1 ]   [ 1 3 2 . ]   [ 1 2 . ]

              rfact        permutation      inv.perm.        rfact
 0 :   [ . . . ]   [ . 1 2 3 ]   [ . 1 2 3 ]   [ . . . ]
 1 :   [ 1 . . ]   [ 1 . 2 3 ]   [ 1 . 2 3 ]   [ 1 . . ]
 2 :   [ . 1 . ]   [ . 2 1 3 ]   [ . 2 1 3 ]   [ . 1 . ]
 3 :   [ 1 1 . ]   [ 2 . 1 3 ]   [ 1 2 . 3 ]   [ 1 2 . ]
 4 :   [ . 2 . ]   [ 2 1 . 3 ]   [ 2 1 . 3 ]   [ . 2 . ]
 5 :   [ 1 2 . ]   [ 1 2 . 3 ]   [ 2 . 1 3 ]   [ 1 1 . ]
 6 :   [ . . 1 ]   [ . 1 3 2 ]   [ . 1 3 2 ]   [ . . 1 ]
 7 :   [ 1 . 1 ]   [ 1 . 3 2 ]   [ 1 . 3 2 ]   [ 1 . 1 ]
 8 :   [ . 1 1 ]   [ . 3 1 2 ]   [ . 2 3 1 ]   [ . 1 2 ]
 9 :   [ 1 1 1 ]   [ 3 . 1 2 ]   [ 1 2 3 . ]   [ . 2 3 ]
10 :   [ . 2 1 ]   [ 3 1 . 2 ]   [ 2 1 3 . ]   [ 1 2 3 ]
11 :   [ 1 2 1 ]   [ 1 3 . 2 ]   [ 2 . 3 1 ]   [ 1 1 2 ]
12 :   [ . . 2 ]   [ . 3 2 1 ]   [ . 3 2 1 ]   [ . . 2 ]
13 :   [ 1 . 2 ]   [ 3 . 2 1 ]   [ 1 3 2 . ]   [ 1 1 3 ]
14 :   [ . 1 2 ]   [ . 2 3 1 ]   [ . 3 1 2 ]   [ . 1 1 ]
15 :   [ 1 1 2 ]   [ 2 . 3 1 ]   [ 1 3 . 2 ]   [ 1 2 1 ]
16 :   [ . 2 2 ]   [ 2 3 . 1 ]   [ 2 3 . 1 ]   [ . 2 2 ]
17 :   [ 1 2 2 ]   [ 3 2 . 1 ]   [ 2 3 1 . ]   [ 1 . 3 ]
18 :   [ . . 3 ]   [ 3 2 1 . ]   [ 3 2 1 . ]   [ . . 3 ]
19 :   [ 1 . 3 ]   [ 2 3 1 . ]   [ 3 2 . 1 ]   [ 1 2 2 ]
20 :   [ . 1 3 ]   [ 3 1 2 . ]   [ 3 1 2 . ]   [ . 1 3 ]
21 :   [ 1 1 3 ]   [ 1 3 2 . ]   [ 3 . 2 1 ]   [ 1 . 2 ]
22 :   [ . 2 3 ]   [ 1 2 3 . ]   [ 3 . 1 2 ]   [ 1 1 1 ]
23 :   [ 1 2 3 ]   [ 2 1 3 . ]   [ 3 1 . 2 ]   [ . 2 1 ]
```

Figure 10.1-C: Numbers in falling (top) and rising (bottom) factorial base and permutations so that the number is the alternative (reversal) code of it (left columns). The inverse permutations and their factorial representations are shown in the right columns. Dots denote zeros.

```
10              fc[k] = j;
11              reverse(ti+k, j+1);
12      }
13  }
```

The routine is the inverse of

```
1   void ffact2perm_rev(const ulong *fc, ulong n, ulong *x)
2   {
3       for (ulong k=0; k<n; ++k)  x[k] = k;
4       for (ulong k=0; k<n-1; ++k)
5       {
6           ulong i = fc[k];
7           // Lehmer: rotate_right1(x+k, i+1);
8           if ( i ) reverse(x+k, i+1);
9       }
10  }
```

Figure 10.1-C shows the permutations of 4 elements and their factorial representations. It was created with the program [FXT: comb/fact2perm-rev-demo.cc]. The routines for the rising factorial base are

```
1   void perm2rfact_rev(const ulong *x, ulong n, ulong *fc)
2   {
3       ALLOCA(ulong, ti, n);  // inverse permutation
4       for (ulong k=0; k<n; ++k)  ti[x[k]] = k;
5       for (ulong k=n-1; k!=0; --k)
6       {
7           ulong j; // find element k
8           for (j=0; j<=k; ++j)  if ( ti[j]==k )  break;
9           j = k - j;
10          fc[k-1] = j;
11          reverse(ti+k-j, j+1);
12      }
13  }
```

and

```
1   void rfact2perm_rev(const ulong *fc, ulong n, ulong *x)
2   {
3       for (ulong k=0; k<n; ++k)  x[k] = k;
4       ulong *y = x+n;
5       for (ulong k=n-1;  k!=0;  --k, --y)
6       {
7           ulong i = fc[k-1];
8           if ( i )
9           {
10              ++i;
11              // Lehmer: rotate_left1(y-i, i);
12              reverse(y-i, i);
13          }
14      }
15  }
```

10.1.3   A representation via rotations ‡

To compute permutations from the Lehmer code we used rotations by one position of length determined by the digits. If we fix the length and let the amount of rotation be the value of the digits, we obtain two more methods to compute permutations from factorial numbers [FXT: comb/fact2perm-rot.cc]:

```
1   void ffact2perm_rot(const ulong *fc, ulong n, ulong *x)
2   {
3       for (ulong k=0; k<n; ++k)  x[k] = k;
4       for (ulong k=0, len=n;  k<n-1;  ++k, --len)
5       {
6           ulong i = fc[k];
7           rotate_left(x+k, len, i);
8       }
9   }
```

```
1   void rfact2perm_rot(const ulong *fc, ulong n, ulong *x)
2   {
3       for (ulong k=0; k<n; ++k)  x[k] = k;
4       for (ulong k=n-2, len=n;  len>1;  --k, --len)
5       {
6           ulong i = fc[k];
```

```
        ffact       permutation    inv. perm.              rfact       permutation    inv. perm.
 0: [ .  .  . ]   [ .  1  2  3 ]  [ .  1  2  3 ]    0: [ .  .  . ]   [ .  1  2  3 ]  [ .  1  2  3 ]
 1: [ 1  .  . ]   [ 1  2  3  . ]  [ 3  .  1  2 ]    1: [ 1  .  . ]   [ .  1  3  2 ]  [ .  1  3  2 ]
 2: [ 2  .  . ]   [ 2  3  .  1 ]  [ 2  3  .  1 ]    2: [ .  1  . ]   [ .  2  3  1 ]  [ .  3  1  2 ]
 3: [ 3  .  . ]   [ 3  .  1  2 ]  [ 1  2  3  . ]    3: [ 1  1  . ]   [ .  2  1  3 ]  [ .  2  1  3 ]
 4: [ .  1  . ]   [ .  2  3  1 ]  [ .  3  1  2 ]    4: [ .  2  . ]   [ .  3  1  2 ]  [ .  2  3  1 ]
 5: [ 1  1  . ]   [ 1  3  .  2 ]  [ 2  .  3  1 ]    5: [ 1  2  . ]   [ .  3  2  1 ]  [ .  3  2  1 ]
 6: [ 2  1  . ]   [ 2  .  1  3 ]  [ 1  2  .  3 ]    6: [ .  .  1 ]   [ 1  2  3  . ]  [ 3  .  1  2 ]
 7: [ 3  1  . ]   [ 3  1  2  . ]  [ 3  1  2  . ]    7: [ 1  .  1 ]   [ 1  2  .  3 ]  [ 2  .  1  3 ]
 8: [ .  2  . ]   [ .  3  1  2 ]  [ .  2  3  1 ]    8: [ .  1  1 ]   [ 1  3  .  2 ]  [ 2  .  3  1 ]
 9: [ 1  2  . ]   [ 1  .  2  3 ]  [ 1  .  2  3 ]    9: [ 1  1  1 ]   [ 1  3  2  . ]  [ 3  .  2  1 ]
10  [ 2  2  . ]   [ 2  1  3  . ]  [ 3  1  .  2 ]   10: [ .  2  1 ]   [ 1  .  2  3 ]  [ 1  .  2  3 ]
11  [ 3  2  . ]   [ 3  2  .  1 ]  [ 2  3  1  . ]   11: [ 1  2  1 ]   [ 1  .  3  2 ]  [ 1  .  3  2 ]
12  [ .  .  1 ]   [ .  1  3  2 ]  [ .  1  3  2 ]   12: [ .  .  2 ]   [ 2  3  .  1 ]  [ 2  3  .  1 ]
13  [ 1  .  1 ]   [ 1  2  .  3 ]  [ 2  .  1  3 ]   13: [ 1  .  2 ]   [ 2  3  1  . ]  [ 3  2  .  1 ]
14  [ 2  .  1 ]   [ 2  3  1  . ]  [ 3  2  .  1 ]   14: [ .  1  2 ]   [ 2  .  1  3 ]  [ 1  2  .  3 ]
15  [ 3  .  1 ]   [ 3  .  2  1 ]  [ 1  3  2  . ]   15: [ 1  1  2 ]   [ 2  .  3  1 ]  [ 1  3  .  2 ]
16  [ .  1  1 ]   [ .  2  1  3 ]  [ .  2  1  3 ]   16: [ .  2  2 ]   [ 2  1  3  . ]  [ 3  1  .  2 ]
17  [ 1  1  1 ]   [ 1  3  2  . ]  [ 3  .  2  1 ]   17: [ 1  2  2 ]   [ 2  1  .  3 ]  [ 2  1  .  3 ]
18  [ 2  1  1 ]   [ 2  .  3  1 ]  [ 1  3  .  2 ]   18: [ .  .  3 ]   [ 3  .  1  2 ]  [ 1  2  3  . ]
19  [ 3  1  1 ]   [ 3  1  .  2 ]  [ 2  1  3  . ]   19: [ 1  .  3 ]   [ 3  .  2  1 ]  [ 1  3  2  . ]
20  [ .  2  1 ]   [ .  3  2  1 ]  [ .  3  2  1 ]   20: [ .  1  3 ]   [ 3  1  2  . ]  [ 3  1  2  . ]
21  [ 1  2  1 ]   [ 1  .  3  2 ]  [ 1  .  3  2 ]   21: [ 1  1  3 ]   [ 3  1  .  2 ]  [ 2  1  3  . ]
22  [ 2  2  1 ]   [ 2  1  .  3 ]  [ 2  1  .  3 ]   22: [ .  2  3 ]   [ 3  2  .  1 ]  [ 2  3  1  . ]
23  [ 3  2  1 ]   [ 3  2  1  . ]  [ 3  2  1  . ]   23: [ 1  2  3 ]   [ 3  2  1  . ]  [ 3  2  1  . ]
```

Figure 10.1-D: Falling (left) and rising (right) factorial numbers and permutations via rotation code.

```
7            rotate_left(x+n-len, len, i);
8      }
9   }
```

Figure 10.1-D shows the permutations of 4 elements corresponding to the falling and rising factorial numbers in lexicographic order [FXT: comb/fact2perm-rot-demo.cc]. The second half of the inverse permutations is the reversed permutations in the first half in reversed order. The columns of the inverse permutations with the falling factorials are cyclic shifts of each other, see section 10.12 on page 271 for more orderings with this property.

The routines to compute the factorial representation of a given permutation are

```
1   void perm2ffact_rot(const ulong *x, ulong n, ulong *fc)
2   {
3       ALLOCA(ulong, t, n);
4       for (ulong k=0; k<n; ++k)  t[x[k]] = k;  // inverse permutation
5       for (ulong k=0; k<n-1; ++k)
6       {
7           ulong s = 0;  while ( t[k+s] != k )  ++s;
8           if ( s!=0 )  rotate_left(t+k, n-k, s);
9           fc[k] = s;
10      }
11  }
```

and

```
void perm2rfact_rot(const ulong *x, ulong n, ulong *fc)
{
    ALLOCA(ulong, t, n);
    for (ulong k=0; k<n; ++k)  t[x[k]] = k;  // inverse permutation
    for (ulong k=0; k<n-1; ++k)
    {
        ulong s = 0;  while ( t[k+s] != k )  ++s;
        if ( s!=0 )  rotate_left(t+k, n-k, s);
        fc[n-2-k] = s;
    }
}
```

10.1.4 A representation via swaps

The following routines compute factorial representations via swaps, the method is adapted from [258]. The complexity of the direct implementation is $O(n)$ [FXT: comb/fact2perm-swp.cc]:

```
   ffact.          permutation        inv.perm.          rfact.
[ .  .  . ]       [ . 1 2 3 ]       [ . 1 2 3 ]       [ .  .  . ]
[ 1  .  . ]       [ 1 . 2 3 ]       [ 1 . 2 3 ]       [ .  .  1 ]
[ 2  .  . ]       [ 2 1 . 3 ]       [ 2 1 . 3 ]       [ .  .  2 ]
[ 3  .  . ]       [ 3 1 2 . ]       [ 3 1 2 . ]       [ .  .  3 ]
[ .  1  . ]       [ . 2 1 3 ]       [ . 2 1 3 ]       [ .  1  . ]
[ 1  1  . ]       [ 1 2 . 3 ]       [ 2 . 1 3 ]       [ .  1  1 ]
[ 2  1  . ]       [ 2 . 1 3 ]       [ 1 2 . 3 ]       [ .  1  2 ]
[ 3  1  . ]       [ 3 2 1 . ]       [ 3 2 1 . ]       [ .  1  3 ]
[ .  2  . ]       [ . 3 2 1 ]       [ . 3 2 1 ]       [ .  2  . ]
[ 1  2  . ]       [ 1 3 2 . ]       [ 3 . 2 1 ]       [ .  2  1 ]
[ 2  2  . ]       [ 2 3 . 1 ]       [ 2 3 . 1 ]       [ .  2  2 ]
[ 3  2  . ]       [ 3 . 2 1 ]       [ 1 3 2 . ]       [ .  2  3 ]
[ .  .  1 ]       [ . 1 3 2 ]       [ . 1 3 2 ]       [ 1  .  . ]
[ 1  .  1 ]       [ 1 . 3 2 ]       [ 1 . 3 2 ]       [ 1  .  1 ]
[ 2  .  1 ]       [ 2 1 3 . ]       [ 3 1 . 2 ]       [ 1  .  2 ]
[ 3  .  1 ]       [ 3 1 . 2 ]       [ 2 1 3 . ]       [ 1  .  3 ]
[ .  1  1 ]       [ . 2 3 1 ]       [ . 3 1 2 ]       [ 1  1  . ]
[ 1  1  1 ]       [ 1 2 3 . ]       [ 3 . 1 2 ]       [ 1  1  1 ]
[ 2  1  1 ]       [ 2 . 3 1 ]       [ 1 3 . 2 ]       [ 1  1  2 ]
[ 3  1  1 ]       [ 3 2 . 1 ]       [ 2 3 1 . ]       [ 1  1  3 ]
[ .  2  1 ]       [ . 3 1 2 ]       [ . 2 3 1 ]       [ 1  2  . ]
[ 1  2  1 ]       [ 1 3 . 2 ]       [ 2 . 3 1 ]       [ 1  2  1 ]
[ 2  2  1 ]       [ 2 3 1 . ]       [ 3 2 . 1 ]       [ 1  2  2 ]
[ 3  2  1 ]       [ 3 . 1 2 ]       [ 1 2 3 . ]       [ 1  2  3 ]

   rfact           permutation        inv.perm.          ffact
[ .  .  . ]       [ . 1 2 3 ]       [ . 1 2 3 ]       [ .  .  . ]
[ 1  .  . ]       [ . 1 3 2 ]       [ . 1 3 2 ]       [ .  .  1 ]
[ .  1  . ]       [ . 2 1 3 ]       [ . 2 1 3 ]       [ .  1  . ]
[ 1  1  . ]       [ . 3 1 2 ]       [ . 2 3 1 ]       [ .  1  1 ]
[ .  2  . ]       [ . 3 2 1 ]       [ . 3 2 1 ]       [ .  2  . ]
[ 1  2  . ]       [ . 2 3 1 ]       [ . 3 1 2 ]       [ .  2  1 ]
[ .  .  1 ]       [ 1 . 2 3 ]       [ 1 . 2 3 ]       [ 1  .  . ]
[ 1  .  1 ]       [ 1 . 3 2 ]       [ 1 . 3 2 ]       [ 1  .  1 ]
[ .  1  1 ]       [ 2 . 1 3 ]       [ 1 2 . 3 ]       [ 1  1  . ]
[ 1  1  1 ]       [ 3 . 1 2 ]       [ 1 2 3 . ]       [ 1  1  1 ]
[ .  2  1 ]       [ 3 . 2 1 ]       [ 1 3 2 . ]       [ 1  2  . ]
[ 1  2  1 ]       [ 2 . 3 1 ]       [ 1 3 . 2 ]       [ 1  2  1 ]
[ .  .  2 ]       [ 2 1 . 3 ]       [ 2 1 . 3 ]       [ 2  .  . ]
[ 1  .  2 ]       [ 3 1 . 2 ]       [ 2 1 3 . ]       [ 2  .  1 ]
[ .  1  2 ]       [ 1 2 . 3 ]       [ 2 . 1 3 ]       [ 2  1  . ]
[ 1  1  2 ]       [ 1 3 . 2 ]       [ 2 . 3 1 ]       [ 2  1  1 ]
[ .  2  2 ]       [ 2 3 . 1 ]       [ 2 3 . 1 ]       [ 2  2  . ]
[ 1  2  2 ]       [ 3 2 . 1 ]       [ 2 3 1 . ]       [ 2  2  1 ]
[ .  .  3 ]       [ 3 1 2 . ]       [ 3 1 2 . ]       [ 3  .  . ]
[ 1  .  3 ]       [ 2 1 3 . ]       [ 3 1 . 2 ]       [ 3  .  1 ]
[ .  1  3 ]       [ 3 2 1 . ]       [ 3 2 1 . ]       [ 3  1  . ]
[ 1  1  3 ]       [ 2 3 1 . ]       [ 3 2 . 1 ]       [ 3  1  1 ]
[ .  2  3 ]       [ 1 3 2 . ]       [ 3 . 2 1 ]       [ 3  2  . ]
[ 1  2  3 ]       [ 1 2 3 . ]       [ 3 . 1 2 ]       [ 3  2  1 ]
```

Figure 10.1-E: Numbers in falling (top) and rising (bottom) factorial base and permutations so that the number is the alternative (swaps) code of it (left columns). The inverse permutations and their factorial representations are shown in the right columns. Dots denote zeros.

```
1    void perm2ffact_swp(const ulong *x, ulong n, ulong *fc)
2    {
3        ALLOCA(ulong, t, n);
4        for (ulong k=0; k<n; ++k)  t[k] = x[k];
5        ALLOCA(ulong, ti, n);  // inverse permutation
6        for (ulong k=0; k<n; ++k)  ti[t[k]] = k;
7
8        for (ulong k=0; k<n-1; ++k)
9        {
10           ulong tk = t[k];  // >= k
11           fc[k] = tk - k;
12           ulong j = ti[k];  // location of element k, j>=k
13           ti[tk] = j;
14           t[j] = tk;
15       }
16   }
```

```
1    void perm2rfact_swp(const ulong *x, ulong n, ulong *fc)
2    {
3        ALLOCA(ulong, t, n);
4        for (ulong k=0; k<n; ++k)  t[k] = x[k];
5        ALLOCA(ulong, ti, n);  // inverse permutation
6        for (ulong k=0; k<n; ++k)  ti[t[k]] = k;
7
8        for (ulong k=0; k<n-1; ++k)
9        {
10           ulong j = ti[k];  // location of element k, j>=k
11           fc[n-2-k] = j - k;
12           ulong tk = t[k];  // >=k
13           ti[tk] = j;
14           t[j] = tk;
15       }
16   }
```

Their inverses also have linear complexity, and no additional memory is needed. The routine for falling base is

```
1    void ffact2perm_swp(const ulong *fc, ulong n, ulong *x)
2    {
3        for (ulong k=0; k<n; ++k)  x[k] = k;
4        for (ulong k=0; k<n-1; ++k)
5        {
6            ulong i = fc[k];
7            swap2( x[k], x[k+i] );
8        }
9    }
```

The routine for the rising base is

```
1    void rfact2perm_swp(const ulong *fc, ulong n, ulong *x)
2    {
3        for (ulong k=0; k<n; ++k)  x[k] = k;
4        for (ulong k=0,j=n-2; k<n-1; ++k,--j)
5        {
6            ulong i = fc[k];
7            swap2( x[j], x[j+i] );
8        }
9    }
```

The permutations corresponding to the alternative codes for the falling base are shown in figure 10.1-E (left columns, top). The inverse permutation has the rising factorial representation that is digit-reversed (right columns). The permutations corresponding to the alternative codes for rising base are shown at the bottom of figure 10.1-E The listings were created with the program [FXT: comb/fact2perm-swp-demo.cc]. The inverse permutations can be computed by applying the swaps (which are self-inverse) in reversed order, the routines are

```
1    void ffact2invperm_swp(const ulong *fc, ulong n, ulong *x)
2    // Generate inverse permutation wrt. ffact2perm_swp().
3    {
4        for (ulong k=0; k<n; ++k)  x[k] = k;
5        if ( n<=1 )  return;
6        ulong k = n-2;
7        do
8        {
```

```
 9              ulong i = fc[k];
10              swap2( x[k], x[k+1] );
11          }
12          while ( k-- );
13      }
```

and

```
 1      void rfact2invperm_swp(const ulong *fc, ulong n, ulong *x)
 2      // Generate inverse permutation wrt. rfact2perm_swp().
 3      {
 4          for (ulong k=0; k<n; ++k)  x[k] = k;
 5          if ( n<=1 )  return;
 6          ulong k = n-2, j=0;
 7          do
 8          {
 9              ulong i = fc[k];
10              swap2( x[j], x[j+i] );
11              ++j;
12          }
13          while ( k-- );
14      }
```

The routines can serve as a means to find interesting orders for permutations. Indeed, the permutation generator shown in section 10.4 on page 245 was found this way. A recursive algorithm for the (inverse) permutations shown at the lower right of figure 10.1-E is given in section 11.4.1 on page 285.

10.2 Lexicographic order

```
               permutation       inv. perm.     compl. inv. perm.    reversed perm.
      0 :    [ . 1 2 3 ]       [ . 1 2 3 ]       [ 3 2 1 . ]       [ 3 2 1 . ]
      1 :    [ . 1 3 2 ]       [ . 1 3 2 ]       [ 3 2 . 1 ]       [ 2 3 1 . ]
      2 :    [ . 2 1 3 ]       [ . 2 1 3 ]       [ 3 1 2 . ]       [ 3 1 2 . ]
      3 :    [ . 2 3 1 ]       [ . 3 1 2 ]       [ 3 . 2 1 ]       [ 1 3 2 . ]
      4 :    [ . 3 1 2 ]       [ . 2 3 1 ]       [ 3 1 . 2 ]       [ 2 1 3 . ]
      5 :    [ . 3 2 1 ]       [ . 3 2 1 ]       [ 3 . 1 2 ]       [ 1 2 3 . ]
      6 :    [ 1 . 2 3 ]       [ 1 . 2 3 ]       [ 2 3 1 . ]       [ 3 2 . 1 ]
      7 :    [ 1 . 3 2 ]       [ 1 . 3 2 ]       [ 2 3 . 1 ]       [ 2 3 . 1 ]
      8 :    [ 1 2 . 3 ]       [ 2 . 1 3 ]       [ 1 3 2 . ]       [ 3 . 2 1 ]
      9 :    [ 1 2 3 . ]       [ 3 . 1 2 ]       [ . 3 2 1 ]       [ . 3 2 1 ]
     1 0 :   [ 1 3 . 2 ]       [ 2 . 3 1 ]       [ 1 3 . 2 ]       [ 2 . 3 1 ]
     1 1 :   [ 1 3 2 . ]       [ 3 . 2 1 ]       [ . 3 1 2 ]       [ . 2 3 1 ]
     1 2 :   [ 2 . 1 3 ]       [ 1 2 . 3 ]       [ 2 1 3 . ]       [ 3 1 . 2 ]
     1 3 :   [ 2 . 3 1 ]       [ 1 3 . 2 ]       [ 2 . 3 1 ]       [ 1 3 . 2 ]
     1 4 :   [ 2 1 . 3 ]       [ 2 1 . 3 ]       [ 1 2 3 . ]       [ 3 . 1 2 ]
     1 5 :   [ 2 1 3 . ]       [ 3 1 . 2 ]       [ . 2 3 1 ]       [ . 3 1 2 ]
     1 6 :   [ 2 3 . 1 ]       [ 2 3 . 1 ]       [ 1 . 3 2 ]       [ 1 . 3 2 ]
     1 7 :   [ 2 3 1 . ]       [ 3 2 . 1 ]       [ . 1 3 2 ]       [ . 1 3 2 ]
     1 8 :   [ 3 . 1 2 ]       [ 1 2 3 . ]       [ 2 1 . 3 ]       [ 2 1 . 3 ]
     1 9 :   [ 3 . 2 1 ]       [ 1 3 2 . ]       [ 2 . 1 3 ]       [ 1 2 . 3 ]
     2 0 :   [ 3 1 . 2 ]       [ 2 1 3 . ]       [ 1 2 . 3 ]       [ 2 . 1 3 ]
     2 1 :   [ 3 1 2 . ]       [ 3 1 2 . ]       [ . 2 1 3 ]       [ . 2 1 3 ]
     2 2 :   [ 3 2 . 1 ]       [ 2 3 1 . ]       [ 1 . 2 3 ]       [ 1 . 2 3 ]
     2 3 :   [ 3 2 1 . ]       [ 3 2 1 . ]       [ . 1 2 3 ]       [ . 1 2 3 ]
```

Figure 10.2-A: All permutations of 4 elements in lexicographic order, their inverses, the complements of the inverses, and the reversed permutations. Dots denote zeros.

The permutations in lexicographic order appear as if (read as numbers and) sorted numerically in ascending order, see figure 10.2-A. The first half of the inverse permutations are the reversed inverse permutations in the second half: the position of zero in the first half of the inverse permutations lies in the first half of each permutation, so their reversal gives the second half. Write I for the operator that inverts a permutation, C for the complement, and R for reversal. Then we have

$$C \;=\; I R I \tag{10.2-1}$$

and thereby the first half of the permutations are the complements of the permutations in the second half. An implementation of an iterative algorithm is [FXT: class perm_lex in comb/perm-lex.h].

```
1    class perm_lex
2    {
3    public:
4        ulong *p_;   // permutation in 0, 1, ..., n-1, sentinel at [-1]
5        ulong n_;    // number of elements to permute
6
7    public:
8        perm_lex(ulong n)
9        {
10           n_ = n;
11           p_ = new ulong[n_+1];
12           p_[0] = 0;  // sentinel
13           ++p_;
14           first();
15       }
16
17       ~perm_lex() { --p_;  delete [] p_; }
18
19       void first()  { for (ulong i=0; i<n_; i++)  p_[i] = i; }
20
21       const ulong *data()  const { return p; }
22   [--snip--]
```

The method **next()** computes the next permutation with each call. The routine **perm_lex::next()** is based on code by Glenn Rhoads

```
1        bool next()
2        {
3            // find rightmost pair with p_[i] < p_[i+1]:
4            const ulong n1 = n_ - 1;
5            ulong i = n1;
6            do { --i; } while ( p_[i] > p_[i+1] );
7            if ( (long)i<0 ) return false;  // last sequence is falling seq.
8
9            // find rightmost element p[j] less than p[i]:
10           ulong j = n1;
11           while ( p_[i] > p_[j] ) { --j; }
12
13           swap2(p_[i], p_[j]);
14
15           // Here the elements p[i+1], ..., p[n-1] are a falling sequence.
16           // Reverse order to the right:
17           ulong r = n1;
18           ulong s = i + 1;
19           while ( r > s ) { swap2(p_[r], p_[s]);  --r;  ++s; }
20
21           return true;
22       }
```

Using the class is no black magic [FXT: comb/perm-lex-demo.cc]:

```
ulong n = 4;
perm_lex P(n);
do
{
    // visit permutation
}
while ( P.next() );
```

The routine generates about 130 million permutations per second. A faster algorithm is obtained by modifying the update operation for the co-lexicographic order (section 10.3) on the right end of the permutations [FXT: comb/perm-lex2.h]. The rate of generation is about 180 M/s when arrays are used and about 305 M/s with pointers [FXT: comb/perm-lex2-demo.cc].

The routine for computing the successor can easily be adapted for permutations of a multiset, see section 13.2.2 on page 298.

10.3 Co-lexicographic order

Figure 10.3-A shows the permutations of 4 elements in co-lexicographic (colex) order. An algorithm for the generation is implemented in [FXT: **class perm_colex** in comb/perm-colex.h]:

```
                permutation      rfact            inv. perm.
        0 :    [ 3 2 1 . ]     [ . . . ]         [ 3 2 1 . ]
        1 :    [ 2 3 1 . ]     [ 1 . . ]         [ 3 2 . 1 ]
        2 :    [ 3 1 2 . ]     [ . 1 . ]         [ 3 1 2 . ]
        3 :    [ 1 3 2 . ]     [ 1 1 . ]         [ 3 . 2 1 ]
        4 :    [ 2 1 3 . ]     [ . . 2 ]         [ 3 1 . 2 ]
        5 :    [ 1 2 3 . ]     [ 1 . 2 ]         [ 3 . 1 2 ]
        6 :    [ 3 2 . 1 ]     [ . . . 1 ]       [ 2 3 1 . ]
        7 :    [ 2 3 . 1 ]     [ 1 . . 1 ]       [ 2 3 . 1 ]
        8 :    [ 3 . 2 1 ]     [ . 1 . 1 ]       [ 1 3 2 . ]
        9 :    [ . 3 2 1 ]     [ 1 1 . 1 ]       [ . 3 2 1 ]
      1 0 :    [ 2 . 3 1 ]     [ . . 2 1 ]       [ 1 3 . 2 ]
      1 1 :    [ . 2 3 1 ]     [ 1 . 2 1 ]       [ . 3 1 2 ]
      1 2 :    [ 3 1 . 2 ]     [ . . . 2 ]       [ 2 1 3 . ]
      1 3 :    [ 1 3 . 2 ]     [ 1 . . 2 ]       [ 2 . 3 1 ]
      1 4 :    [ 3 . 1 2 ]     [ . 1 . 2 ]       [ 1 2 3 . ]
      1 5 :    [ . 3 1 2 ]     [ 1 1 . 2 ]       [ . 2 3 1 ]
      1 6 :    [ 1 . 3 2 ]     [ . . 2 2 ]       [ 1 . 3 2 ]
      1 7 :    [ . 1 3 2 ]     [ 1 . 2 2 ]       [ . 1 3 2 ]
      1 8 :    [ 2 1 . 3 ]     [ . . . 3 ]       [ 2 1 . 3 ]
      1 9 :    [ 1 2 . 3 ]     [ 1 . . 3 ]       [ 2 . 1 3 ]
      2 0 :    [ 2 . 1 3 ]     [ . . 1 3 ]       [ 1 2 . 3 ]
      2 1 :    [ . 2 1 3 ]     [ 1 . 1 3 ]       [ . 2 1 3 ]
      2 2 :    [ 1 . 2 3 ]     [ . . 2 3 ]       [ 1 . 2 3 ]
      2 3 :    [ . 1 2 3 ]     [ 1 . 2 3 ]       [ . 1 2 3 ]
```

Figure 10.3-A: The permutations of 4 elements in co-lexicographic order. Dots denote zeros.

```
1    class perm_colex
2    {
3    public:
4        ulong *d_;   // mixed radix digits with radix = [2, 3, 4, ...]
5        ulong *x_;   // permutation
6        ulong n_;    // permutations of n elements
7
8    public:
9        perm_colex(ulong n)
10       // Must have n>=2
11       {
12           n_ = n;
13           d_ = new ulong[n_];
14           d_[n-1] = 0;   // sentinel
15           x_ = new ulong[n_];
16           first();
17       }
18       [--snip--]
19
20       void first()
21       {
22           for (ulong k=0; k<n_; ++k)  x_[k] = n_-1-k;
23           for (ulong k=0; k<n_-1; ++k)  d_[k] = 0;
24       }
25
```

The update process uses rising factorial numbers. Let j be the position where the digit is incremented and d the value before the increment. The update

```
    permutation        rfact
                             v-- increment at j=3
    [ 0 3 4 5 2 1 ]    [ 1 2 3 1 1 ]   <--= digit before increment is d=1
    [ 5 4 2 0 3 1 ]    [ . . . 2 1 ]
```

is done in three steps:

```
    [ 0 3 4 5 2 1 ]    [ 1 2 3 1 1 ]
    [ 0 2 4 5 3 1 ]    [ 1 2 3 2 1 ]   <--= swap positions d=1 and j+1=4
    [ 5 4 2 0 3 1 ]    [ . . . 2 1 ]   <--= reverse range 0...j
```

The corresponding method is

```
1        bool next()
2        {
3            if ( d_[0]==0 ) // easy case
```

```
4      {
5          d_[0] = 1;
6          swap2(x_[0], x_[1]);
7          return true;
8      }
9      else
10     {
11         d_[0] = 0;
12         ulong j = 1;
13         ulong m1 = 2;   // nine in rising factorial base
14         while ( d_[j]==m1 )
15         {
16             d_[j] = 0;
17             ++m1;
18             ++j;
19         }
20
21         if ( j==n_-1 )  return false;  // current permutation is last
22
23         const ulong dj = d_[j];
24         d_[j] = dj + 1;
25
26         swap2( x_[dj], x_[j+1] );  // swap positions dj and j+1
27
28         { // reverse range [0...j]:
29             ulong a = 0,  b = j;
30             do
31             {
32                 swap2(x_[a], x_[b]);
33                 ++a;
34                 --b;
35             }
36             while ( a < b );
37         }
38
39         return true;
40     }
41 }
42 }
```

About 220 million permutations per second can be generated [FXT: comb/perm-colex-demo.cc]. With arrays instead of pointers the rate is 330 million per second.

10.4 An order from reversing prefixes

A surprisingly simple algorithm for the generation of all permutations uses mixed radix counting with the radices $[2, 3, 4, \ldots]$ (column digits in figure 10.4-A). Whenever the first j digits change with an increment, the permutation is updated by reversing the first $j+1$ elements (the method is given in [364]).

As with lex order the first half of the permutations are the complements of the permutations in the second half, now rewrite relation 10.2-1 on page 242 as

$$R = ICI \tag{10.4-1}$$

to see that the first half of the inverse permutations are the reversed inverse permutations in the second half. This can (for n even) also be observed from the positions of the largest element in the inverse permutations. A generator is [FXT: class perm_rev in comb/perm-rev.h]:

```
1   class perm_rev
2   {
3   public:
4       ulong *d_;   // mixed radix digits with radix = [2, 3, 4, ..., n-1, (sentinel=-1)]
5       ulong *p_;   // permutation
6       ulong n_;    // permutations of n elements
7
8   public:
9       perm_rev(ulong n)
10      {
11          n_ = n;
12          p_ = new ulong[n_];
13          d_ = new ulong[n_];
14          d_[n-1] = -1UL;  // sentinel
```

```
                permutation      rfact          inv. perm.
      0 :      [ . 1 2 3 ]    [ . . . ]       [ . 1 2 3 ]
      1 :      [ 1 . 2 3 ]    [ 1 . . ]       [ 1 . 2 3 ]
      2 :      [ 2 . 1 3 ]    [ . 1 . ]       [ 1 2 . 3 ]
      3 :      [ . 2 1 3 ]    [ 1 1 . ]       [ . 2 1 3 ]
      4 :      [ 1 2 . 3 ]    [ . 2 . ]       [ 2 . 1 3 ]
      5 :      [ 2 1 . 3 ]    [ 1 2 . ]       [ 2 1 . 3 ]
      6 :      [ 3 . 1 2 ]    [ . . 1 ]       [ 1 2 3 . ]
      7 :      [ . 3 1 2 ]    [ 1 . 1 ]       [ . 2 3 1 ]
      8 :      [ 1 3 . 2 ]    [ . 1 1 ]       [ 2 . 3 1 ]
      9 :      [ 3 1 . 2 ]    [ 1 1 1 ]       [ 2 1 3 . ]
    1 0 :      [ . 1 3 2 ]    [ . 2 1 ]       [ . 1 3 2 ]
    1 1 :      [ 1 . 3 2 ]    [ 1 2 1 ]       [ 1 . 3 2 ]
    1 2 :      [ 2 3 . 1 ]    [ . . 2 ]       [ 2 3 . 1 ]
    1 3 :      [ 3 2 . 1 ]    [ 1 . 2 ]       [ 2 3 1 . ]
    1 4 :      [ . 2 3 1 ]    [ . 1 2 ]       [ . 3 1 2 ]
    1 5 :      [ 2 . 3 1 ]    [ 1 1 2 ]       [ 1 3 . 2 ]
    1 6 :      [ 3 . 2 1 ]    [ . 2 2 ]       [ 1 3 2 . ]
    1 7 :      [ . 3 2 1 ]    [ 1 2 2 ]       [ . 3 2 1 ]
    1 8 :      [ 1 2 3 . ]    [ . . 3 ]       [ 3 . 1 2 ]
    1 9 :      [ 2 1 3 . ]    [ 1 . 3 ]       [ 3 1 . 2 ]
    2 0 :      [ 3 1 2 . ]    [ . 1 3 ]       [ 3 1 2 . ]
    2 1 :      [ 1 3 2 . ]    [ 1 1 3 ]       [ 3 . 2 1 ]
    2 2 :      [ 2 3 1 . ]    [ . 2 3 ]       [ 3 2 . 1 ]
    2 3 :      [ 3 2 1 . ]    [ 1 2 3 ]       [ 3 2 1 . ]
```

Figure 10.4-A: All permutations of 4 elements in an order where the first $j + 1$ elements are reversed when the first j digits change in the mixed radix counting sequence with radices $[2, 3, 4, \ldots]$.

```
15              first();
16          }
17
18          ~perm_rev()
19          {
20              delete [] p_;
21              delete [] d_;
22          }
23
24          void first()
25          {
26              for (ulong k=0; k<n_-1; ++k)  d_[k] = 0;
27              for (ulong k=0; k<n_; ++k)  p_[k] = k;
28          }
29
30          void last()
31          {
32              for (ulong k=0; k<n_-1; ++k)  d_[k] = k+1;
33              for (ulong k=0; k<n_; ++k)  p_[k] = n_-1-k;
34          }
```

The update routines are quite concise:

```
1          bool next()
2          {
3              // increment mixed radix number:
4              ulong j = 0;
5              while ( d_[j]==j+1 )  { d_[j]=0; ++j; }
6
7              // j==n-1 for last permutation
8              if ( j!=n_-1 ) // only if no overflow
9              {
10                 ++d_[j];
11                 reverse(p_, j+2); // update permutation
12                 return true;
13             }
14             else  return false;
15         }
16
17         bool prev()
18         {
19             // decrement mixed radix number:
20             ulong j = 0;
21             while ( d_[j]==0 )  { d_[j]=j+1; ++j; }
```

```
22
23              // j==n-1 for last permutation
24              if ( j!=n_-1 ) // only if no overflow
25              {
26                  --d_[j];
27                  reverse(p_, j+2); // update permutation
28                  return true;
29              }
30              else  return false;
31      }
32  };
```

Note that the routines work for arbitrary (distinct) entries of the array p_[].

An upper bound for the average number of elements that are moved in the transitions when generating all $N = n!$ permutations is $e \approx 2.7182818$ so the algorithm is CAT. The implementation generates more than 140 million permutations per second [FXT: comb/perm-rev-demo.cc]. Usage of the class is simple:

```
ulong n = 4;  // Number of elements to permute
perm_rev P(n);
P.first();
do
{
    // Use permutation here
}
while ( P.next() );
```

We note that the inverse permutations have the single-track property, see section 10.12 on page 271.

10.4.1   Method for unranking

Conversion of a rising factorial number into the corresponding permutation proceeds as exemplified for the 16-th permutation ($15 = 1 \cdot 1 + 1 \cdot 2 + 2 \cdot 6$, so d=[1,1,2]):

```
 1:   p=[ 0, 1, 2, 3 ]   d=[ 0, 0, 0 ] // start
13:   p=[ 2, 3, 0, 1 ]   d=[ 0, 0, 2 ] // right rotate all elements twice
15:   p=[ 0, 2, 3, 1 ]   d=[ 0, 1, 2 ] // right rotate first three elements
16:   p=[ 2, 0, 3, 1 ]   d=[ 1, 1, 2 ] // right rotate first two elements
```

The idea can be implemented as

```
1    void goto_rfact(const ulong *d)
2    // Goto permutation corresponding to d[] (i.e. unrank d[]).
3    // d[] must be a valid (rising) factorial mixed radix string:
4    // d[]==[d(0), d(1), d(2), ..., d(n-2)]  (n-1 elements) where 0<=d(j)<=j+1
5    {
6        for (ulong k=0; k<n_; ++k)  p_[k] = k;
7        for (ulong k=0; k<n_-1; ++k)  d_[k] = d[k];
8        for (long j=n_-2; j>=0; --j)  rotate_right(p_, j+2, d_[j]);
9    }
```

Compare to the method of section 10.1.3 on page 238.

10.4.2   Optimizing the update routine

We optimize the update routine by observing that 5 out of 6 updates are the swaps

```
(0,1)  (0,2)  (0,1)  (0,2)  (0,1)
```

We use a counter ct_ and modify the methods first() and next() accordingly [FXT: class perm_rev2 in comb/perm-rev2.h]:

```
1    class perm_rev2
2    {
3        perm_rev2(ulong n)
4        {
5            n_ = n;
6            const ulong s = ( n_<3 ? 3 : n_ );
7            p_ = new ulong[s+1];
8            d_ = new ulong[s];
9            first();
10       }
11
```

```
12    [--snip--]
13      ulong next()
14      // Return index of last element with reversal.
15      // Return n with last permutation.
16      {
17          if ( ct_!=0 )  // easy case(s)
18          {
19              --ct_;
20              const ulong e = 1 + (ct_ & 1);
21              swap2(p_[0], p_[e]);
22              return  e;
23          }
24          else
25          {
26              ct_ = 5;  // reset counter
27              ulong j = 2;  // note: start with 2
28              while ( d_[j]==j+1 )  { d_[j]=0; ++j; }  // can touch sentinel
29              ++d_[j];
30              reverse(p_, j+2); // update permutation
31              return  j + 1;
32          }
33      }
34
35    [--snip--]
```

The speedup is remarkable, about 275 million permutations per second are generated (about 8.5 cycles per update) [FXT: comb/perm-rev2-demo.cc]. If arrays are used instead of pointers, the rate drops to about 200 M/s.

10.5   Minimal-change order (Heap's algorithm)

```
              permutation     swap      digits     rfact(perm)    inv. perm.
   0 :      [ . 1 2 3 ]     ( 0 0 )    [ . . . ]    [ . . . ]    [ . 1 2 3 ]
   1 :      [ 1 . 2 3 ]     ( 1 0 )    [ 1 . . ]    [ 1 . . ]    [ 1 . 2 3 ]
   2 :      [ 2 . 1 3 ]     ( 2 0 )    [ . 1 . ]    [ 1 1 . ]    [ 1 2 . 3 ]
   3 :      [ . 2 1 3 ]     ( 1 0 )    [ 1 1 . ]    [ . 1 . ]    [ . 2 1 3 ]
   4 :      [ 1 2 . 3 ]     ( 2 0 )    [ . 2 . ]    [ . 2 . ]    [ 2 . 1 3 ]
   5 :      [ 2 1 . 3 ]     ( 1 0 )    [ 1 2 . ]    [ 1 2 . ]    [ 2 1 . 3 ]
   6 :      [ 3 1 . 2 ]     ( 3 0 )    [ . . 1 ]    [ 1 2 1 ]    [ 2 1 3 . ]
   7 :      [ 1 3 . 2 ]     ( 1 0 )    [ 1 . 1 ]    [ . 2 1 ]    [ 2 . 3 1 ]
   8 :      [ . 3 1 2 ]     ( 2 0 )    [ . 1 1 ]    [ . 1 1 ]    [ . 2 3 1 ]
   9 :      [ 3 . 1 2 ]     ( 1 0 )    [ 1 1 1 ]    [ 1 1 1 ]    [ 1 2 3 . ]
  1 0 :     [ 1 . 3 2 ]     ( 2 0 )    [ . 2 1 ]    [ 1 . 1 ]    [ 1 . 3 2 ]
  1 1 :     [ . 1 3 2 ]     ( 1 0 )    [ 1 2 1 ]    [ . . 1 ]    [ . 1 3 2 ]
  1 2 :     [ . 2 3 1 ]     ( 3 1 )    [ . . 2 ]    [ . . 2 ]    [ . 3 1 2 ]
  1 3 :     [ 2 . 3 1 ]     ( 1 0 )    [ 1 . 2 ]    [ 1 . 2 ]    [ 1 3 . 2 ]
  1 4 :     [ 3 . 2 1 ]     ( 2 0 )    [ . 1 2 ]    [ 1 1 2 ]    [ 1 3 2 . ]
  1 5 :     [ . 3 2 1 ]     ( 1 0 )    [ 1 1 2 ]    [ . 1 2 ]    [ . 3 2 1 ]
  1 6 :     [ 2 3 . 1 ]     ( 2 0 )    [ . 2 2 ]    [ . 2 2 ]    [ 2 3 . 1 ]
  1 7 :     [ 3 2 . 1 ]     ( 1 0 )    [ 1 2 2 ]    [ 1 2 2 ]    [ 2 3 1 . ]
  1 8 :     [ 3 2 1 . ]     ( 3 2 )    [ . . 3 ]    [ 1 2 3 ]    [ 3 2 1 . ]
  1 9 :     [ 2 3 1 . ]     ( 1 0 )    [ 1 . 3 ]    [ . 2 3 ]    [ 3 2 . 1 ]
  2 0 :     [ 1 3 2 . ]     ( 2 0 )    [ . 1 3 ]    [ . 1 3 ]    [ 3 . 2 1 ]
  2 1 :     [ 3 1 2 . ]     ( 1 0 )    [ 1 1 3 ]    [ 1 1 3 ]    [ 3 1 2 . ]
  2 2 :     [ 2 1 3 . ]     ( 2 0 )    [ . 2 3 ]    [ 1 . 3 ]    [ 3 1 . 2 ]
  2 3 :     [ 1 2 3 . ]     ( 1 0 )    [ 1 2 3 ]    [ . . 3 ]    [ 3 . 1 2 ]
```

Figure 10.5-A: The permutations of 4 elements in a minimal-change order. Dots denote zeros.

Figure 10.5-A shows the permutations of 4 elements in a *minimal-change order*: just 2 elements are swapped with each update. The column labeled `digits` shows the mixed radix numbers with rising factorial base in counting order. Let j be the position of the rightmost change of the mixed radix string R. Then the swap is $(j+1, x)$ where $x = 0$ if j is odd, and $x = R_j - 1$ if j is even. The sequence of values $j + 1$ starts

1, 2, 1, 2, 1, 3, 1, 2, 1, 2, 1, 3, 1, 2, 1, 2, 1, 3, 1, 2, 1, 2, 1, 4, 1, 2, 1, ...

The n-th value (starting with $n = 1$) is the largest z such that $z!$ divides n (entry A055881 in [312]).

The list rising factorial representations of the permutations is a Gray code only for permutations of up to four elements. (column labeled `rfact(perm)` in figure 10.5-A).

An implementation of the algorithm (given in [178]) is [FXT: class `perm_heap` in comb/perm-heap.h]:

```
1    class perm_heap
2    {
3    public:
4        ulong *d_;  // mixed radix digits with radix = [2, 3, 4, ..., n-1, (sentinel=-1)]
5        ulong *p_;  // permutation
6        ulong n_;   // permutations of n elements
7        ulong sw1_, sw2_;   // indices of swapped elements
8    [--snip--]
```

The computation of the successor is simple:

```
1        bool next()
2        {
3            // increment mixed radix number:
4            ulong j = 0;
5            while ( d_[j]==j+1 )  { d_[j]=0; ++j; }  // can touch sentinel
6
7            // j==n-1 for last permutation:
8            if ( j==n_-1 )  return false;
9
10           ulong k = j+1;
11           ulong x = ( k&1 ? d_[j] : 0 );
12           swap2(p_[k], p_[x]);  // omit statement to just compute swaps
13           sw1_ = k;   sw2_ = x;
14
15           ++d_[j];
16           return true;
17       }
18   [--snip--]
```

About 133 million permutations are generated per second. Often one will only use the indices of the swapped elements to update the visited configurations:

```
1        void get_swap(ulong &s1, ulong &s2)  const  { s1=sw1_; s2=sw2_; }
```

Then the statement `swap2(p_[k], p_[x]);` in the update routine can be omitted which leads to a rate of 215 M/s. Figure 10.5-A shows the permutations of 4 elements. It was created with the program [FXT: comb/perm-heap-demo.cc].

10.5.1 Optimized implementation

The algorithm can be optimized by treating 5 out of 6 cases separately, those where the first or second digit in the mixed radix number changes [FXT: class `perm_heap2` in comb/perm-heap2.h]:

```
1    class perm_heap2
2    {
3    public:
4        ulong *d_;  // mixed radix digits with radix = [2, 3, 4, 5, ..., n-1, (sentinel=-1)]
5        ulong *p_;  // permutation
6        ulong n_;   // permutations of n elements
7        ulong sw1_, sw2_;   // indices of swapped elements
8        ulong ct_;  // count 5,4,3,2,1,(0); nonzero ==> easy cases
9    [--snip--]
```

The counter is set to 5 in the method `first()`. The update routine is

```
1        ulong next()
2        // Return index of last element with reversal.
3        // Return n with last permutation.
4        {
5            if ( ct_!=0 )  // easy cases
6            {
7                --ct_;
8                sw1_ = 1 + (ct_ & 1);  // == 1,2,1,2,1
9                sw2_ = 0;
10               swap2(p_[sw1_], p_[sw2_]);
11               return  sw1_;
12           }
13           else
```

```
14      {
15          ct_ = 5;  // reset counter
16
17          // increment mixed radix number:
18          ulong j = 2;
19          while ( d_[j]==j+1 )  { d_[j]=0; ++j; }  // can touch sentinel
20
21          // j==n-1 for last permutation:
22          if ( j==n_-1 )  return  n_;
23
24          ulong k = j+1;
25          ulong x = ( k&1 ? d_[j] : 0 );
26          swap2(p_[k], p_[x]);
27          sw1_ = k;  sw2_ = x;
28
29          ++d_[j];
30
31          return k;
32      }
33  }
```

Usage of the class is shown in [FXT: comb/perm-heap2-demo.cc]:

```
1       do { /* visit permutation */ }  while ( P.next()!=n );
```

The rate of generation is about 280 M/s (7.85 cycles per update), and 460 M/s (4.78 cycles per update) with fixed arrays.

If only the swaps are of interest, we can simply omit all statements involving the permutation array p_[]. The implementation is [FXT: class **perm_heap2_swaps** in comb/perm-heap2-swaps.h], usage of the class is shown in [FXT: comb/perm-heap2-swaps-demo.cc].

Heap's algorithm and the optimization idea was taken from the excellent survey [305] which gives several permutation algorithms and implementations in pseudocode.

10.6   Lipski's Minimal-change orders

Several algorithms similar to Heap's method are given in Lipski's paper [235].

10.6.1   Variants of Heap's algorithm

Four orderings for the permutations of five elements are shown in figure 10.6-A. The leftmost order is Heap's order. The implementation is given in [FXT: class **perm_gray_lipski** in comb/perm-gray-lipski.h], the variable r determines the order that is generated:

```
1   class perm_gray_lipski
2   {
3     [--snip--]
4       ulong r_;    // order (0<=r<4):
5     [--snip--]
6
7     bool next()
8     {
9         // increment mixed radix number:
10        ulong j = 0;
11        while ( d_[j]==j+1 )  { d_[j]=0; ++j; }
12        if ( j<n_-1 ) // only if no overflow
13        {
14            const ulong d = d_[j];
15
16            ulong x;
17            switch ( r_ )
18            {
19            case 0:  x = (j&1 ? 0 : d);  break;     // Lipski(9) == Heap
20            case 1:  x = (j&1 ? 0 : j-d);  break;   // Lipski(16)
21            case 2:  x = (j&1 ? j-1 : d);  break;   // Lipski(10)
22            default: x = (j&1 ? j-1 : j-d);  break; // not in Lipski's paper
23            }
24            const ulong k = j+1;
25            swap2(p_[k], p_[x]);
26            sw1_ = k;  sw2_ = x;
```

	x=(j&1 ? 0 : d);		x=(j&1 ? 0 : j-d);		x=(j&1 ? j-1 : d);		x=(j&1 ? j-1 : j-d);	
1:	[. 1 2 3 4]		[. 1 2 3 4]		[. 1 2 3 4]		[. 1 2 3 4]	
2:	[1 . 2 3 4]	(1)	[1 . 2 3 4]	(1)	[1 . 2 3 4]	(1)	[1 . 2 3 4]	(1)
3:	[2 . 1 3 4]	(2)	[2 . 1 3 4]	(2)	[2 . 1 3 4]	(2)	[2 . 1 3 4]	(2)
4:	[. 2 1 3 4]	(1)	[. 2 1 3 4]	(1)	[. 2 1 3 4]	(1)	[. 2 1 3 4]	(1)
5:	[1 2 . 3 4]	(2)	[1 2 . 3 4]	(2)	[1 2 . 3 4]	(2)	[1 2 . 3 4]	(2)
6:	[2 1 . 3 4]	(1)	[2 1 . 3 4]	(1)	[2 1 . 3 4]	(1)	[2 1 . 3 4]	(1)
7:	[3 1 . 2 4]	(3)	[2 1 3 . 4]	(3,2)	[3 1 . 2 4]	(3)	[2 1 3 . 4]	(3,2)
8:	[1 3 . 2 4]	(1)	[1 2 3 . 4]	(1)	[1 3 . 2 4]	(1)	[1 2 3 . 4]	(1)
9:	[. 3 1 2 4]	(2)	[3 2 1 . 4]	(2)	[. 3 1 2 4]	(2)	[3 2 1 . 4]	(2)
10:	[3 . 1 2 4]	(1)	[2 3 1 . 4]	(1)	[3 . 1 2 4]	(1)	[2 3 1 . 4]	(1)
11:	[1 . 3 2 4]	(2)	[1 3 2 . 4]	(2)	[1 . 3 2 4]	(2)	[1 3 2 . 4]	(2)
12:	[. 1 3 2 4]	(1)	[3 1 2 . 4]	(1)	[. 1 3 2 4]	(1)	[3 1 2 . 4]	(1)
13:	[. 2 3 1 4]	(3,1)	[3 . 2 1 4]	(3,1)	[. 2 3 1 4]	(3,1)	[3 . 2 1 4]	(3,1)
14:	[2 . 3 1 4]	(1)	[. 3 2 1 4]	(1)	[2 . 3 1 4]	(1)	[. 3 2 1 4]	(1)
15:	[3 . 2 1 4]	(2)	[2 3 . 1 4]	(2)	[3 . 2 1 4]	(2)	[2 3 . 1 4]	(2)
16:	[. 3 2 1 4]	(1)	[3 2 . 1 4]	(1)	[. 3 2 1 4]	(1)	[3 2 . 1 4]	(1)
17:	[2 3 . 1 4]	(2)	[. 2 3 1 4]	(2)	[2 3 . 1 4]	(2)	[. 2 3 1 4]	(2)
18:	[3 2 . 1 4]	(1)	[2 . 3 1 4]	(1)	[3 2 . 1 4]	(1)	[2 . 3 1 4]	(1)
19:	[3 2 1 . 4]	(3,2)	[1 . 3 2 4]	(3)	[3 2 1 . 4]	(3,2)	[1 . 3 2 4]	(3)
20:	[2 3 1 . 4]	(1)	[. 1 3 2 4]	(1)	[2 3 1 . 4]	(1)	[. 1 3 2 4]	(1)
21:	[1 3 2 . 4]	(2)	[3 1 . 2 4]	(2)	[1 3 2 . 4]	(2)	[3 1 . 2 4]	(2)
22:	[3 1 2 . 4]	(1)	[1 3 . 2 4]	(1)	[3 1 2 . 4]	(1)	[1 3 . 2 4]	(1)
23:	[2 1 3 . 4]	(2)	[. 3 1 2 4]	(2)	[2 1 3 . 4]	(2)	[. 3 1 2 4]	(2)
24:	[1 2 3 . 4]	(1)	[3 . 1 2 4]	(1)	[1 2 3 . 4]	(1)	[3 . 1 2 4]	(1)
25:	[4 2 3 . 1]	(4)	[4 . 1 2 3]	(4)	[1 2 4 . 3]	(4,2)	[3 . 4 2 1]	(4,2)
26:	[2 4 3 . 1]	(1)	[. 4 1 2 3]	(1)	[2 1 4 . 3]	(1)	[. 3 4 2 1]	(1)
27:	[3 4 2 . 1]	(2)	[1 4 . 2 3]	(2)	[4 1 2 . 3]	(2)	[4 3 . 2 1]	(2)
28:	[4 3 2 . 1]	(1)	[4 1 . 2 3]	(1)	[1 4 2 . 3]	(1)	[3 4 . 2 1]	(1)
29:	[2 3 4 . 1]	(2)	[. 1 4 2 3]	(2)	[2 4 1 . 3]	(2)	[. 4 3 2 1]	(2)
30:	[3 2 4 . 1]	(1)	[1 . 4 2 3]	(1)	[4 2 1 . 3]	(1)	[4 . 3 2 1]	(1)
31:	[. 2 4 3 1]	(3)	[1 . 2 4 3]	(3,2)	[. 2 1 4 3]	(3)	[4 . 2 3 1]	(3,2)
32:	[2 . 4 3 1]	(1)	[. 1 2 4 3]	(1)	[2 . 1 4 3]	(1)	[. 4 2 3 1]	(1)
33:	[4 . 2 3 1]	(2)	[2 1 . 4 3]	(2)	[1 . 2 4 3]	(2)	[2 4 . 3 1]	(2)
34:	[. 4 2 3 1]	(1)	[1 2 . 4 3]	(1)	[. 1 2 4 3]	(1)	[4 2 . 3 1]	(1)
35:	[2 4 . 3 1]	(2)	[. 2 1 4 3]	(2)	[2 1 . 4 3]	(2)	[. 2 4 3 1]	(2)
36:	[4 2 . 3 1]	(1)	[2 . 1 4 3]	(1)	[1 2 . 4 3]	(1)	[2 . 4 3 1]	(1)
37:	[4 3 . 2 1]	(3,1)	[2 4 1 . 3]	(3,1)	[1 4 . 2 3]	(3,1)	[2 3 4 . 1]	(3,1)
38:	[3 4 . 2 1]	(1)	[4 2 1 . 3]	(1)	[4 1 . 2 3]	(1)	[3 2 4 . 1]	(1)
39:	[. 4 3 2 1]	(2)	[1 2 4 . 3]	(2)	[. 1 4 2 3]	(2)	[4 2 3 . 1]	(2)
40:	[4 . 3 2 1]	(1)	[2 1 4 . 3]	(1)	[1 . 4 2 3]	(1)	[2 4 3 . 1]	(1)
41:	[3 . 4 2 1]	(2)	[4 1 2 . 3]	(2)	[4 . 1 2 3]	(2)	[3 4 2 . 1]	(2)
42:	[. 3 4 2 1]	(1)	[1 4 2 . 3]	(1)	[. 4 1 2 3]	(1)	[4 3 2 . 1]	(1)
43:	[. 3 2 4 1]	(3,2)	[. 4 2 1 3]	(3)	[. 4 2 1 3]	(3,2)	[. 3 2 4 1]	(3)
44:	[3 . 2 4 1]	(1)	[4 . 2 1 3]	(1)	[4 . 2 1 3]	(1)	[3 . 2 4 1]	(1)
45:	[2 . 3 4 1]	(2)	[2 . 4 1 3]	(2)	[2 . 4 1 3]	(2)	[2 . 3 4 1]	(2)
46:	[. 2 3 4 1]	(1)	[. 2 4 1 3]	(1)	[. 2 4 1 3]	(1)	[. 2 3 4 1]	(1)
47:	[3 2 . 4 1]	(2)	[4 2 . 1 3]	(2)	[4 2 . 1 3]	(2)	[3 2 . 4 1]	(2)
48:	[2 3 . 4 1]	(1)	[2 4 . 1 3]	(1)	[2 4 . 1 3]	(1)	[2 3 . 4 1]	(1)
49:	[1 3 . 4 2]	(4)	[3 4 . 1 2]	(4)	[2 4 3 1 .]	(4,2)	[2 3 1 4 .]	(4,2)
50:	[3 1 . 4 2]	(1)	[4 3 . 1 2]	(1)	[4 2 3 1 .]	(1)	[3 2 1 4 .]	(1)
51:	[. 1 3 4 2]	(2)	[. 3 4 1 2]	(2)	[3 2 4 1 .]	(2)	[1 2 3 4 .]	(2)
52:	[1 . 3 4 2]	(1)	[3 . 4 1 2]	(1)	[2 3 4 1 .]	(1)	[2 1 3 4 .]	(1)
53:	[3 . 1 4 2]	(2)	[4 . 3 1 2]	(2)	[4 3 2 1 .]	(2)	[3 1 2 4 .]	(2)
54:	[. 3 1 4 2]	(1)	[. 4 3 1 2]	(1)	[3 4 2 1 .]	(1)	[1 3 2 4 .]	(1)
55:	[4 3 1 . 2]	(3)	[. 4 1 3 2]	(3,2)	[1 4 2 3 .]	(3)	[1 3 4 2 .]	(3,2)
56:	[3 4 1 . 2]	(1)	[4 . 1 3 2]	(1)	[4 1 2 3 .]	(1)	[3 1 4 2 .]	(1)
57:	[1 4 3 . 2]	(2)	[1 . 4 3 2]	(2)	[2 1 4 3 .]	(2)	[4 1 3 2 .]	(2)
58:	[4 1 3 . 2]	(1)	[. 1 4 3 2]	(1)	[1 2 4 3 .]	(1)	[1 4 3 2 .]	(1)
59:	[3 1 4 . 2]	(2)	[4 1 . 3 2]	(2)	[4 2 1 3 .]	(2)	[3 4 1 2 .]	(2)
60:	[1 3 4 . 2]	(1)	[1 4 . 3 2]	(1)	[2 4 1 3 .]	(1)	[4 3 1 2 .]	(1)
[--snip--]								
108:	[3 4 2 1 .]	(1)	[4 2 3 1 .]	(1)	[3 . 4 1 2]	(1)	[. 4 3 1 2]	(1)
109:	[3 1 2 4 .]	(3,1)	[4 1 3 2 .]	(3,1)	[3 1 4 . 2]	(3,1)	[. 1 3 4 2]	(3,1)
110:	[1 3 2 4 .]	(1)	[1 4 3 2 .]	(1)	[1 3 4 . 2]	(1)	[1 . 3 4 2]	(1)
111:	[2 3 1 4 .]	(2)	[3 4 1 2 .]	(2)	[4 3 1 . 2]	(2)	[3 . 1 4 2]	(2)
112:	[3 2 1 4 .]	(1)	[4 3 1 2 .]	(1)	[3 4 1 . 2]	(1)	[. 3 1 4 2]	(1)
113:	[1 2 3 4 .]	(2)	[1 3 4 2 .]	(2)	[1 4 3 . 2]	(2)	[1 3 . 4 2]	(2)
114:	[2 1 3 4 .]	(1)	[3 1 4 2 .]	(1)	[4 1 3 . 2]	(1)	[3 1 . 4 2]	(1)
115:	[2 1 4 3 .]	(3,2)	[2 1 4 3 .]	(3)	[4 1 . 3 2]	(3,2)	[4 1 . 3 2]	(3)
116:	[1 2 4 3 .]	(1)	[1 2 4 3 .]	(1)	[1 4 . 3 2]	(1)	[1 4 . 3 2]	(1)
117:	[4 2 1 3 .]	(2)	[4 2 1 3 .]	(2)	[. 4 1 3 2]	(2)	[. 4 1 3 2]	(2)
118:	[2 4 1 3 .]	(1)	[2 4 1 3 .]	(1)	[4 . 1 3 2]	(1)	[4 . 1 3 2]	(1)
119:	[1 4 2 3 .]	(2)	[1 4 2 3 .]	(2)	[1 . 4 3 2]	(2)	[1 . 4 3 2]	(2)
120:	[4 1 2 3 .]	(1)	[4 1 2 3 .]	(1)	[. 1 4 3 2]	(1)	[. 1 4 3 2]	(1)

Figure 10.6-A: First half and last few permutations of five elements generated by variants of Heap's method. Next to the permutations the swaps are shown as (x, y), a swap $(x, 0)$ is given as (x).

```
27
28                        d_[j] = d + 1;
29                        return true;
30                    }
31                else  return  false;  // j==n-1 for last permutation
32            }
33        [--snip--]
34    };
```

The top lines in figure 10.6-A repeat the statements in the switch-block. For three or less elements all orderings coincide, with $n = 4$ elements the orderings for $r = 0$ and $r = 2$, and the orderings for $r = 1$ and $r = 3$ coincide. About 110 million permutations per second are generated [FXT: comb/perm-gray-lipski-demo.cc]. Optimizations similar to those for Heaps method should be obvious.

10.6.2   Variants of Wells' algorithm

```
      x=( (j&1) || (d<=1) ? j : j-d );          x=( (j&1) || (d==0) ? 0 : d-1 );
       1 :   [ . 1 2 3 ]                         1:   [ . 1 2 3 ]
       2 :   [ 1 . 2 3 ]     ( 1 0)              2:   [ 1 . 2 3 ]     (1, 0)
       3 :   [ 1 2 . 3 ]     ( 2 1)              3:   [ 2 . 1 3 ]     (2, 0)
       4 :   [ 2 1 . 3 ]     ( 1 0)              4:   [ . 2 1 3 ]     (1, 0)
       5 :   [ 2 . 1 3 ]     ( 2 1)              5:   [ 1 2 . 3 ]     (2, 0)
       6 :   [ . 2 1 3 ]     ( 1 0)              6:   [ 2 1 . 3 ]     (1, 0)
       7 :   [ . 2 3 1 ]     ( 3 2)              7:   [ 3 1 . 2 ]     (3, 0)
       8 :   [ 2 . 3 1 ]     ( 1 0)              8:   [ 1 3 . 2 ]     (1, 0)
       9 :   [ 2 3 . 1 ]     ( 2 1)              9:   [ . 3 1 2 ]     (2, 0)
      1 0 :  [ 3 2 . 1 ]     ( 1 0)             10:   [ 3 . 1 2 ]     (1, 0)
      1 1 :  [ 3 . 2 1 ]     ( 2 1)             11:   [ 1 . 3 2 ]     (2, 0)
      1 2 :  [ . 3 2 1 ]     ( 1 0)             12:   [ . 1 3 2 ]     (1, 0)
      1 3 :  [ . 3 1 2 ]     ( 3 2)             13:   [ 2 1 3 . ]     (3, 0)
      1 4 :  [ 3 . 1 2 ]     ( 1 0)             14:   [ 1 2 3 . ]     (1, 0)
      1 5 :  [ 3 1 . 2 ]     ( 2 1)             15:   [ 3 2 1 . ]     (2, 0)
      1 6 :  [ 1 3 . 2 ]     ( 1 0)             16:   [ 2 3 1 . ]     (1, 0)
      1 7 :  [ 1 . 3 2 ]     ( 2 1)             17:   [ 1 3 2 . ]     (2, 0)
      1 8 :  [ . 1 3 2 ]     ( 1 0)             18:   [ 3 1 2 . ]     (1, 0)
      1 9 :  [ 2 1 3 . ]     ( 3 0)             19:   [ 3 . 2 1 ]     (3, 1)
      2 0 :  [ 1 2 3 . ]     ( 1 0)             20:   [ . 3 2 1 ]     (1, 0)
      2 1 :  [ 1 3 2 . ]     ( 2 1)             21:   [ 2 3 . 1 ]     (2, 0)
      2 2 :  [ 3 1 2 . ]     ( 1 0)             22:   [ 3 2 . 1 ]     (1, 0)
      2 3 :  [ 3 2 1 . ]     ( 2 1)             23:   [ . 2 3 1 ]     (2, 0)
      2 4 :  [ 2 3 1 . ]     ( 1 0)             24:   [ 2 . 3 1 ]     (1, 0)
```

Figure 10.6-B: Wells' order for the permutations of four elements (left) and an order where most swaps are with the first position (right). Dots denote the element zero.

A Gray code for permutations given by Wells [350] is shown in the left of figure 10.6-B. The following implementation includes two variants of the algorithm. We just give the crucial assignments in the computation of the successor [FXT: class `perm_gray_wells` in comb/perm-gray-wells.h]:

```
1        bool next()
2        {
3        [--snip--]
4            switch ( r_ )
5            {
6            case 1:  x = ( (j&1) || (d==0) ? 0 : d-1 );  break;  // Lipski(14)
7            case 2:  x = ( (j&1) || (d==0) ? j : d-1 );  break;  // Lipski(15)
8            default: x = ( (j&1) || (d<=1) ? j : j-d );  break;  // Wells' order == Lipski(8)
9            }
10       [--snip--]
11       }
```

Both expressions (`d==0`) can be changed to (`d<=1`) without changing the algorithm. About 105 million permutations per second are generated [FXT: comb/perm-gray-wells-demo.cc].

```
          permutation    swap     inverse p.    direction
  0 :    [ . 1 2 3 ]    (3, 2)    [ . 1 2 3 ]    + + + +
  1 :    [ 1 . 2 3 ]    (0, 1)    [ 1 . 2 3 ]    + + + +
  2 :    [ 1 2 . 3 ]    (1, 2)    [ 2 . 1 3 ]    + + + +
  3 :    [ 1 2 3 . ]    (2, 3)    [ 3 . 1 2 ]    + + + +
  4 :    [ 2 1 3 . ]    (0, 1)    [ 3 1 . 2 ]    − + + +
  5 :    [ 2 1 . 3 ]    (3, 2)    [ 2 1 . 3 ]    − + + +
  6 :    [ 2 . 1 3 ]    (2, 1)    [ 1 2 . 3 ]    − + + +
  7 :    [ . 2 1 3 ]    (1, 0)    [ . 2 1 3 ]    − + + +
  8 :    [ . 2 3 1 ]    (2, 3)    [ . 3 1 2 ]    + + + +
  9 :    [ . 2 3 1 ]    (0, 1)    [ 1 3 . 2 ]    + + + +
 1 0 :   [ 2 3 . 1 ]    (1, 2)    [ 2 3 . 1 ]    + + + +
 1 1 :   [ 2 3 1 . ]    (2, 3)    [ 3 2 . 1 ]    + + + +
 1 2 :   [ 3 2 1 . ]    (0, 1)    [ 3 2 1 . ]    − − + +
 1 3 :   [ 3 2 . 1 ]    (3, 2)    [ 2 3 1 . ]    − − + +
 1 4 :   [ 3 . 2 1 ]    (2, 1)    [ 1 3 2 . ]    − − + +
 1 5 :   [ . 3 2 1 ]    (1, 0)    [ . 3 2 1 ]    − − + +
 1 6 :   [ . 3 1 2 ]    (3, 2)    [ . 2 3 1 ]    + − + +
 1 7 :   [ 3 . 1 2 ]    (0, 1)    [ 1 2 3 . ]    + − + +
 1 8 :   [ 3 1 . 2 ]    (1, 2)    [ 2 1 3 . ]    + − + +
 1 9 :   [ 3 1 2 . ]    (2, 3)    [ 3 1 2 . ]    + − + +
 2 0 :   [ 1 3 2 . ]    (1, 0)    [ 3 . 2 1 ]    − − + +
 2 1 :   [ 1 3 . 2 ]    (3, 2)    [ 2 . 3 1 ]    − − + +
 2 2 :   [ 1 . 3 2 ]    (2, 1)    [ 1 . 3 2 ]    − − + +
 2 3 :   [ . 1 3 2 ]    (1, 0)    [ . 1 3 2 ]    − − + +
```

Figure 10.7-A: The permutations of 4 elements in a strong minimal-change order (smallest element moves most often). Dots denote zeros.

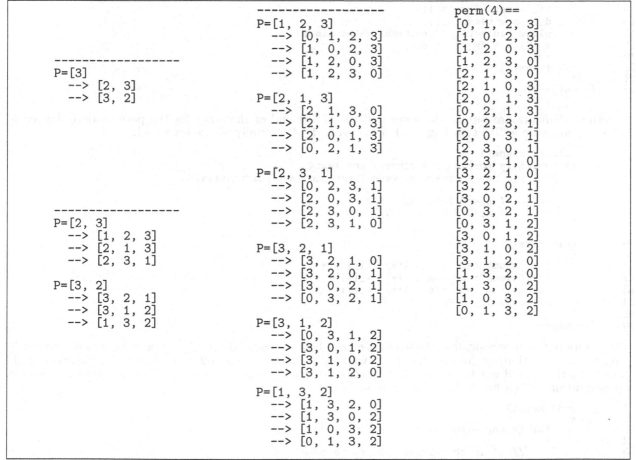

Figure 10.7-B: Trotter's construction as an interleaving process.

10.7   Strong minimal-change order (Trotter's algorithm)

Figure 10.7-A shows the permutations of 4 elements in a *strong minimal-change order*: just two elements
are swapped with each update and these are adjacent. In the sequence of the inverse permutations the
swapped pair always consists of elements x and $x + 1$. Also the first and last permutation differ by
an adjacent transposition (of the last two elements). The ordering can be obtained by an interleaving
process shown in figure 10.7-B. The first half of the permutations in this order are the reversals of the
second half: the relative order of the two smallest elements is changed only with the transition just after
the first half and reversal changes the order of these two elements. Mutually reversed permutations lie
$n!/2$ positions apart.

A computer program to generate all permutations in the shown order was given 1962 by H. F. Trotter [334],
see also [193] and [137]. We compute both the permutation and its inverse [FXT: class perm_trotter
in comb/perm-trotter.h]:

```
 1   class perm_trotter
 2   {
 3   public:
 4       ulong n_;      // number of elements to permute
 5       ulong *x_;     // permutation of {0, 1, ..., n-1}
 6       ulong *xi_;    // inverse permutation
 7       ulong *d_;     // auxiliary: directions
 8       ulong sw1_, sw2_; // indices of elements swapped most recently
 9
10   public:
11       perm_trotter(ulong n)
12       {
13           n_ = n;
14           x_ = new ulong[n_+2];
15           xi_ = new ulong[n_];
16           d_ = new ulong[n_];
17           ulong sen = 0;  // sentinel value minimal
18           x_[0] = x_[n_+1] = sen;
19           ++x_;
20           first();
21       }
22   [--snip--]
23
```

Sentinel elements are put at the lower and the higher end of the array for the permutation. For each
element we store a direction-flag $= \pm 1$ in an array d_[]. Initially all are set to $+1$:

```
 1       void fl_swaps()
 2       // Auxiliary routine for first() and last().
 3       // Set sw1, sw2 to swaps between first and last permutation.
 4       {
 5           sw1_ = ( n_==0 ? 0 : n_ - 1 );
 6           sw2_ = ( n_<2 ? 0 : n_ - 2 );
 7       }
 8
 9       void first()
10       {
11           for (ulong i=0; i<n_; i++)  xi_[i] = i;
12           for (ulong i=0; i<n_; i++)  x_[i] = i;
13           for (ulong i=0; i<n_; i++)  d_[i] = 1;
14           fl_swaps();
15       }
16   [--snip--]
```

To compute the successor, find the smallest element e1 whose neighbor e2 (left or right neighbor, according to the direction) is greater than e1. Swap the elements e1 and e2, and change the direction of all
elements that could not be moved. The locations of the elements, i1 and i2, are found with the inverse
permutation, which has to be updated accordingly:

```
 1       bool next()
 2       {
 3           for (ulong e1=0; e1<n_; ++e1)
 4           {
 5               // e1 is the element we try to move
 6               ulong i1 = xi_[e1];   // position of element e1
```

```
7          ulong d = d_[e1];      // direction to move e1
8          ulong i2 = i1 + d;     // position to swap with
9          ulong e2 = x_[i2];     // element to swap with
10
11         if ( e1 < e2 )  // can we swap?
12         {
13             xi_[e1] = i2;
14             xi_[e2] = i1;
15             x_[i1] = e2;
16             x_[i2] = e1;
17             sw1_ = i1;  sw2_ = i2;
18             while ( e1-- )  d_[e1] = -d_[e1];
19             return true;
20         }
21     }
22
23     first();
24     return false;
25 }
```

The locations of the swap are retrieved by the method

```
1     void get_swap(ulong &s1, ulong &s2)  const
2     { s1=sw1_; s2=sw2_; }
```

The last permutation is computed as follows:

```
1     void last()
2     {
3         for (ulong i=0; i<n_; i++)  xi_[i] = i;
4         for (ulong i=0; i<n_; i++)  x_[i] = i;
5         for (ulong i=0; i<n_; i++)  d_[i] = -1UL;
6         fl_swaps();
7         d_[sw1_] = +1;   d_[sw2_] = +1;
8         swap2(x_[sw1_], x_[sw2_]);
9         swap2(xi_[sw1_], xi_[sw2_]);
10    }
```

The routine for the predecessor is almost identical to the method next():

```
1     bool prev()
2     {
3 [--snip--]
4             ulong d = -d_[e1];      // direction to move e1 (NOTE: negated)
5 [--snip--]
6         last();
7         return false;
8     }
```

The routines next() and prev() generate about 145 million permutations per second. Figure 10.7-A was created with the program [FXT: comb/perm-trotter-demo.cc]:

```
ulong n = 4;
perm_trotter P(n);
do
{
    // visit permutation
}
while ( P.next() );
```

10.7.1 Optimized update routines

The element zero is moved most often, so we can treat that case separately [FXT: comb/perm-trotter.h]:

```
1     #define TROTTER_OPT  // much faster computations
2         [--snip--]
3     #ifdef TROTTER_OPT
4         ulong ctm_;  // counter to detect easy case
5         ulong xi0_;  // position of element zero
6         ulong d0_;   // direction of element zero
7     #endif // TROTTER_OPT
```

The counter ctm_ is initially set to n_. The update method becomes

```
1     bool next()
2     {
```

```
 3    #ifdef TROTTER_OPT
 4            if ( --ctm_ )  // easy case: move element 0
 5            {
 6                ulong i1 = xi0_;    // position of element 0
 7                ulong d = d0_;       // direction to move 0
 8                ulong i2 = i1 + d;   // position to swap with
 9                ulong e2 = x_[i2];   // element to swap with
10                xi_[0] = i2;
11                xi0_ = i2;
12                xi_[e2] = i1;
13                x_[i1] = e2;
14                x_[i2] = 0;
15                sw1_ = i1;  sw2_ = i2;
16                return true;
17            }
18            d0_ = -d0_;
19            ctm_ = n_;
20    #endif // TROTTER_OPT
21
22    #ifdef TROTTER_OPT
23            for (ulong e1=1; e1<n_; ++e1)  // note: start at e1=1
24    #else    // TROTTER_OPT
25            for (ulong e1=0; e1<n_; ++e1)
26    #endif // TROTTER_OPT
27            [--snip--]  // loop body as before
```

The very same modification can be applied to the method `prev()`, only the minus sign has to be added:

```
            ulong d = -d_[0];      // direction to move e1 (NOTE: negated)
```

Now both methods generate about 190 million permutations per second.

10.7.2 Variant where largest element moves most often

```
            permutation    swap       inverse p.    direction
   0 :    [ . 1 2 3 ]    ( 0 1 )    [ . 1 2 3 ]    - - - -
   1 :    [ . 1 3 2 ]    ( 3 2 )    [ . 1 3 2 ]    - - - -
   2 :    [ . 3 1 2 ]    ( 2 1 )    [ . 2 3 1 ]    - - - -
   3 :    [ 3 . 1 2 ]    ( 1 0 )    [ 1 2 3 . ]    - - - -
   4 :    [ 3 . 2 1 ]    ( 3 2 )    [ 1 3 2 . ]    - - - +
   5 :    [ . 3 2 1 ]    ( 0 1 )    [ . 3 2 1 ]    - - - +
   6 :    [ . 2 3 1 ]    ( 1 2 )    [ . 3 1 2 ]    - - - +
   7 :    [ . 2 1 3 ]    ( 2 3 )    [ . 2 1 3 ]    - - - +
   8 :    [ 2 . 1 3 ]    ( 1 0 )    [ 1 2 . 3 ]    - - - -
   9 :    [ 2 . 3 1 ]    ( 3 2 )    [ 1 3 . 2 ]    - - - -
  1 0 :  [ 2 3 . 1 ]    ( 2 1 )    [ 2 3 . 1 ]    - - - -
  1 1 :  [ 3 2 . 1 ]    ( 1 0 )    [ 2 3 1 . ]    - - - -
  1 2 :  [ 3 2 1 . ]    ( 3 2 )    [ 3 2 1 . ]    - - + +
  1 3 :  [ 2 3 1 . ]    ( 0 1 )    [ 3 2 . 1 ]    - - + +
  1 4 :  [ 2 1 3 . ]    ( 1 2 )    [ 3 1 . 2 ]    - - + +
  1 5 :  [ 2 1 . 3 ]    ( 2 3 )    [ 2 1 . 3 ]    - - + +
  1 6 :  [ 1 2 . 3 ]    ( 0 1 )    [ 2 . 1 3 ]    - - + -
  1 7 :  [ 1 2 3 . ]    ( 3 2 )    [ 3 . 1 2 ]    - - + -
  1 8 :  [ 1 3 2 . ]    ( 2 1 )    [ 3 . 2 1 ]    - - + -
  1 9 :  [ 3 1 2 . ]    ( 1 0 )    [ 3 1 2 . ]    - - + -
  2 0 :  [ 3 1 . 2 ]    ( 2 3 )    [ 2 1 3 . ]    - - + +
  2 1 :  [ 1 3 . 2 ]    ( 0 1 )    [ 2 . 3 1 ]    - - + +
  2 2 :  [ 1 . 3 2 ]    ( 1 2 )    [ 1 . 3 2 ]    - - + +
  2 3 :  [ 1 . 2 3 ]    ( 2 3 )    [ 1 . 2 3 ]    - - + +
```

Figure 10.7-C: The permutations of 4 elements in a strong minimal-change order (largest element moves most often). Dots denote zeros.

A variant of the ordering where the largest element moves most often is shown in figure 10.7-C. Only a few modifications have to be made [FXT: class `perm_trotter_lg` in comb/perm-trotter-lg.h]. The sentinel needs to be greater than all elements of the permutations, the directions start with −1, and in the update routine we look for the largest element whose neighbor is less than itself. Both `next()` and `prev()` generate about 146 million permutations per second [FXT: comb/perm-trotter-lg-demo.cc].

10.8   Star-transposition order

```
              permutation     swap      inverse p.
       0 :    [ . 1 2 3 ]              [ . 1 2 3 ]
       1 :    [ 1 . 2 3 ]    (0, 1)    [ 1 . 2 3 ]
       2 :    [ 2 . 1 3 ]    (0, 2)    [ 1 2 . 3 ]
       3 :    [ . 2 1 3 ]    (0, 1)    [ . 2 1 3 ]
       4 :    [ 1 2 . 3 ]    (0, 2)    [ 2 . 1 3 ]
       5 :    [ 2 1 . 3 ]    (0, 1)    [ 2 1 . 3 ]
       6 :    [ 3 1 . 2 ]    (0, 3)    [ 2 1 3 . ]
       7 :    [ . 1 3 2 ]    (0, 2)    [ . 1 3 2 ]
       8 :    [ 1 . 3 2 ]    (0, 1)    [ 1 . 3 2 ]
       9 :    [ 3 . 1 2 ]    (0, 2)    [ 1 2 3 . ]
     1 0 :    [ . 3 1 2 ]    (0, 1)    [ . 2 3 1 ]
     1 1 :    [ 1 3 . 2 ]    (0, 2)    [ 2 . 3 1 ]
     1 2 :    [ 2 3 . 1 ]    (0, 3)    [ 2 3 . 1 ]
     1 3 :    [ 3 2 . 1 ]    (0, 1)    [ 2 3 1 . ]
     1 4 :    [ . 2 3 1 ]    (0, 2)    [ . 3 1 2 ]
     1 5 :    [ 2 . 3 1 ]    (0, 1)    [ 1 3 . 2 ]
     1 6 :    [ 3 . 2 1 ]    (0, 2)    [ 1 3 2 . ]
     1 7 :    [ . 3 2 1 ]    (0, 1)    [ . 3 2 1 ]
     1 8 :    [ 1 3 2 . ]    (0, 3)    [ 3 . 2 1 ]
     1 9 :    [ 2 3 1 . ]    (0, 2)    [ 3 2 . 1 ]
     2 0 :    [ 3 2 1 . ]    (0, 1)    [ 3 2 1 . ]
     2 1 :    [ 1 2 3 . ]    (0, 2)    [ 3 . 1 2 ]
     2 2 :    [ 2 1 3 . ]    (0, 1)    [ 3 1 . 2 ]
     2 3 :    [ 3 1 2 . ]    (0, 2)    [ 3 1 2 . ]
```

Figure 10.8-A: The permutations of 4 elements in star-transposition order. Dots denote zeros.

Figure 10.8-A shows an ordering where successive permutations differ by a swap of the element at the first position with some other element (*star transposition*). In the list of the inverse permutations the zero is always moved, also the reversed permutations of the first half lie in the second half. An algorithm for the generation of such an ordering, attributed to Gideon Ehrlich, is given in [215, alg.E, sect.7.2.1.2]. An implementation is given in [FXT: class `perm_star` in comb/perm-star.h].

The listing shown in figure 10.8-A was created with [FXT: comb/perm-star-demo.cc]. About 190 million permutations per second are generated. If only the swaps are of interest, use [FXT: class `perm_star_swaps` in comb/perm-star-swaps.h], see [FXT: comb/perm-star-swaps-demo.cc] for its usage.

```
   S1 = 0 --> 0,1  == S2
   S2 = 01 --> 01,20,12  == S3
   S3 = 012012 --> 012012,301301,230230,123123  == S4
   S4 = (S3-0),(S3-1),(S3-2),(S3-3)  modulo 4
   S5 = (S4-0),(S4-1),(S4-2),(S4-3),(S4-4)  modulo 5
   == 012012301301230230123123,401401240240124124012012,340340134134013013401401, \
      234234023023402402340340,123123412412341341234234
```

Figure 10.8-B: Construction of the first column of the list of permutations, also sequence of positions of element zero in the inverse permutations.

The sequence of positions swapped with the first position, entry A123400 in [312], starts as

   1,2,1,2,1,3,2,1,2,1,2,3,1,2,1,2,1,3,2,1,2,1,2,4,3,1,3,1,3,2,1,3,1,3,1,2,3,1,3,1,3,2,1, ...

The sequence of positions of the element zero is entry A159880, it starts as

   0,1,2,0,1,2,3,0,1,3,0,1,2,3,0,2,3,0,1,2,3,1,2,3,4,0,1,4,0,1,2,4,0,2,4,0,1,2,4,1,2,4,0, ...

It can be constructed as shown in figure 10.8-B. The sequence can be generated via the permutations described in section 10.4 on page 245. Thus we can compute the inverse permutations as shown in figure 10.8-C. The listing was created with the program [FXT: comb/perm-star-inv-demo.cc]:

```
1      ulong n = 4;
2      perm_rev2 P(n);  P.first();
3      const ulong *r = P.data();
```

```
              inv. star-p.      swap       perm-rev
       1 :   [ . 1 2 3 ]                  [ . 1 2 3 ]
       2 :   [ 1 . 2 3 ]   ( 0 1 )        [ 1 . 2 3 ]
       3 :   [ 1 2 . 3 ]   ( 1 2 )        [ 2 . 1 3 ]
       4 :   [ . 2 1 3 ]   ( 2 0 )        [ . 2 1 3 ]
       5 :   [ 2 . 1 3 ]   ( 0 1 )        [ 1 2 . 3 ]
       6 :   [ 2 1 . 3 ]   ( 1 2 )        [ 2 1 . 3 ]
       7 :   [ 2 1 3 . ]   ( 2 3 )        [ 3 . 1 2 ]
       8 :   [ . 1 3 2 ]   ( 3 0 )        [ . 3 1 2 ]
       9 :   [ 1 . 3 2 ]   ( 0 1 )        [ 1 3 . 2 ]
      1 0 :  [ 1 2 3 . ]   ( 1 3 )        [ 3 1 . 2 ]
      1 1 :  [ . 2 3 1 ]   ( 3 0 )        [ . 1 3 2 ]
      1 2 :  [ 2 . 3 1 ]   ( 0 1 )        [ 1 . 3 2 ]
      1 3 :  [ 2 3 . 1 ]   ( 1 2 )        [ 2 3 . 1 ]
      1 4 :  [ 2 3 1 . ]   ( 2 3 )        [ 3 2 . 1 ]
      1 5 :  [ . 3 1 2 ]   ( 3 0 )        [ . 2 3 1 ]
      1 6 :  [ 1 3 . 2 ]   ( 0 2 )        [ 2 . 3 1 ]
      1 7 :  [ 1 3 2 . ]   ( 2 3 )        [ 3 . 2 1 ]
      1 8 :  [ . 3 2 1 ]   ( 3 0 )        [ . 3 2 1 ]
      1 9 :  [ 3 . 2 1 ]   ( 0 1 )        [ 1 2 3 . ]
      2 0 :  [ 3 2 . 1 ]   ( 1 2 )        [ 2 1 3 . ]
      2 1 :  [ 3 2 1 . ]   ( 2 3 )        [ 3 1 2 . ]
      2 2 :  [ 3 . 1 2 ]   ( 3 1 )        [ 1 3 2 . ]
      2 3 :  [ 3 1 . 2 ]   ( 1 2 )        [ 2 3 1 . ]
      2 4 :  [ 3 1 2 . ]   ( 2 3 )        [ 3 2 1 . ]
```

Figure 10.8-C: The inverse permutations of 4 elements with star-transposition order (left). The swaps are determined by the first element of the permutations generated via reversals (right).

```
4     ulong *x = new ulong[n];
5     for (ulong k=0; k<n; ++k)   x[k] = k;
6     ulong i0 = 0;  // position of element zero
7     do
8     {
9         ++ct;
10        ulong i1 = r[0];
11        swap2(x[i0], x[i1]);
12        // visit permutation in x[]
13        i0 = i1;
14    }
15    while ( P.next()!=n );
```

The rate of generation is about 155 million per second.

10.9   Minimal-change orders from factorial numbers

10.9.1   Permutations with falling factorial numbers

The Gray code for the mixed radix numbers with falling factorial base allows the computation of the permutations in Trotter's minimal-change order (see section 10.7 on page 254) in an elegant way. See figure 10.9-A which was created with the program [FXT: comb/perm-gray-ffact2-demo.cc]. The algorithm is implemented in [FXT: class perm_gray_ffact2 in comb/perm-gray-ffact2.h]:

```
1     class perm_gray_ffact2
2     {
3     public:
4         mixedradix_gray2 *mrg_;  // loopless routine
5         ulong n_;   // number of elements to permute
6         ulong *x_;  // current permutation (of {0, 1, ..., n-1})
7         ulong *ix_;  // inverse permutation
8         ulong sw1_, sw2_; // indices of elements swapped most recently
9
10    public:
11        perm_gray_ffact2(ulong n)
12        {
13            n_ = n;
```

	permutation	ffact	pos	dir	inverse perm.
0 :	[. 1 2 3]	[. . .]			[. 1 2 3]
1 :	[1 . 2 3]	[1 . .]	0	+1	[1 . 2 3]
2 :	[1 2 . 3]	[2 . .]	0	+1	[2 . 1 3]
3 :	[1 2 3 .]	[3 . .]	0	+1	[3 . 1 2]
4 :	[2 1 3 .]	[3 1 .]	1	+1	[3 1 . 2]
5 :	[2 1 . 3]	[2 1 .]	0	−1	[2 1 . 3]
6 :	[2 . 1 3]	[1 1 .]	0	−1	[1 2 . 3]
7 :	[. 2 1 3]	[. 1 .]	0	−1	[. 2 1 3]
8 :	[. 2 3 1]	[. 2 .]	1	+1	[. 3 1 2]
9 :	[2 . 3 1]	[1 2 .]	0	+1	[1 3 . 2]
1 0 :	[2 3 . 1]	[2 2 .]	0	+1	[2 3 . 1]
1 1 :	[2 3 1 .]	[3 2 .]	0	+1	[3 2 . 1]
1 2 :	[3 2 1 .]	[3 2 1]	2	+1	[3 2 1 .]
1 3 :	[3 2 . 1]	[2 2 1]	0	−1	[2 3 1 .]
1 4 :	[3 . 2 1]	[1 2 1]	0	−1	[1 3 2 .]
1 5 :	[. 3 2 1]	[. 2 1]	0	−1	[. 3 2 1]
1 6 :	[. 3 1 2]	[. 1 1]	1	−1	[. 2 3 1]
1 7 :	[3 . 1 2]	[1 1 1]	0	+1	[1 2 3 .]
1 8 :	[3 1 . 2]	[2 1 1]	0	+1	[2 1 3 .]
1 9 :	[3 1 2 .]	[3 1 1]	0	+1	[3 1 2 .]
2 0 :	[1 3 2 .]	[3 . 1]	1	−1	[3 . 2 1]
2 1 :	[1 3 . 2]	[2 . 1]	0	−1	[2 . 3 1]
2 2 :	[1 . 3 2]	[1 . 1]	0	−1	[1 . 3 2]
2 3 :	[. 1 3 2]	[. . 1]	0	−1	[. 1 3 2]

Figure 10.9-A: Permutations in minimal-change order (left) and Gray code for mixed radix numbers with falling factorial base. The two columns labeled 'pos' and 'dir' give the place of change with the mixed radix numbers and its direction. Whenever digit p (='pos') changes by $d = \pm 1$ (='dir') in the mixed radix sequence, then element p of the permutation is swapped with its right ($d = +1$) or left ($d = -1$) neighbor.

```
14              x_ = new ulong[n_];
15              ix_ = new ulong[n_];
16              mrg_ = new mixedradix_gray2(n_-1, 0);  // falling factorial base
17              first();
18          }
19
20          [--snip--]
21
22          void first()
23          {
24              mrg_->first();
25              for (ulong k=0; k<n_; ++k)  x_[k] = ix_[k] = k;
26              sw1_=n_-1;  sw2_=n_-2;
27          }
```

The crucial part is the computation of the successor:

```
1          bool next()
2          {
3              // Compute next mixed radix number in Gray code order:
4              if ( false == mrg_->next() )  { first(); return false; }
5              const ulong j = mrg_->pos();  // position of changed digit
6              const int d = mrg_->dir();    // direction of change
7
8              // swap:
9              const ulong x1 = j;          // element j
10             const ulong i1 = ix_[x1];    // position of j
11             const ulong i2 = i1 + d;     // neighbor
12             const ulong x2 = x_[i2];     // position of neighbor
13             x_[i1] = x2;   x_[i2] = x1;   // swap2(x_[i1], x_[i2]);
14             ix_[x1] = i2;  ix_[x2] = i1;  // swap2(ix_[x1], ix_[x2]);
15             sw1_=i1;  sw2_=i2;
16             return true;
17          }
```

The class uses the loopless algorithm for the computation of the mixed radix Gray code, so it is loopless itself. An alternative (CAT) algorithm is implemented in [FXT: class perm_gray_ffact in comb/perm-gray-ffact.h], we give just the routine for the successor:

```
1    private:
2        void swap(ulong j, ulong im)  // used with next() and prev()
3        {
4            const ulong x1 = j;         // element j
5            const ulong i1 = ix_[x1];   // position of j
6            const ulong i2 = i1 + im;   // neighbor
7            const ulong x2 = x_[i2];    // position of neighbor
8            x_[i1] = x2;   x_[i2] = x1;  // swap2(x_[i1], x_[i2]);
9            ix_[x1] = i2;  ix_[x2] = i1;  // swap2(ix_[x1], ix_[x2]);
10           sw1_=i1;  sw2_=i2;
11       }
12
13   public:
14       bool next()
15       {
16           ulong j = 0;
17           ulong m1 = n_ - 1;  // nine in falling factorial base
18           ulong ij;
19           while ( (ij=i_[j]) )
20           {
21               ulong im = i_[j];
22               ulong dj = d_[j] + im;
23               if ( dj>m1 )  // =^= if ( (dj>m1) || ((long)dj<0) )
24               {
25                   i_[j] = -ij;
26               }
27               else
28               {
29                   d_[j] = dj;
30                   swap(j, im);
31                   return true;
32               }
33
34               --m1;
35               ++j;
36           }
37           return false;
38       }
```

To compute the predecessor (method **prev()**), we only need to modify one statement as follows:

```
ulong im =  i_[j];  // next()
ulong im = -i_[j];  // prev()
```

The loopless routine computes about 80 million permutations per second, the CAT version about 160 million per second [FXT: comb/perm-gray-ffact-demo.cc]. Both are slower than the implementation given in section 10.7.1 on page 255.

10.9.2 Permutations with rising factorial numbers

Figure 10.9-B shows a Gray code for permutations based on the Gray code for numbers in rising factorial base. The ordering coincides with Heap's algorithm (see section 10.5 on page 248) for up to four elements. A recursive construction for the order is shown in figure 10.9-C. The figure was created with the program [FXT: comb/perm-gray-rfact-demo.cc]. A constant amortized time (CAT) algorithm for generating the permutations is [FXT: class **perm_gray_rfact** in comb/perm-gray-rfact.h]

```
1    class perm_gray_rfact
2    {
3    public:
4        mixedradix_gray *M_;  // loopless routine
5        ulong n_;    // number of elements to permute
6        ulong *x_;   // current permutation (of {0, 1, ..., n-1})
7        ulong *ix_;  // inverse permutation
8        ulong sw1_, sw2_; // indices of elements swapped most recently
9
10   public:
11       perm_gray_rfact(ulong n)
12       {
13           n_ = n;
14           x_ = new ulong[n_];
15           ix_ = new ulong[n_];
16           M_ = new mixedradix_gray(n_-1, 1);  // rising factorial base
```

	permutation	rfact	pos	dir	inverse perm.
0 :	[. 1 2 3]	[. . .]			[. 1 2 3]
1 :	[1 . 2 3]	[1 . .]	0	+1	[1 . 2 3]
2 :	[2 . 1 3]	[1 1 .]	1	+1	[1 2 . 3]
3 :	[. 2 1 3]	[. 1 .]	0	-1	[. 2 1 3]
4 :	[1 2 . 3]	[. 2 .]	1	+1	[2 . 1 3]
5 :	[2 1 . 3]	[1 2 .]	0	+1	[2 1 . 3]
6 :	[3 1 . 2]	[1 2 1]	2	+1	[2 1 3 .]
7 :	[1 3 . 2]	[. 2 1]	0	-1	[2 . 3 1]
8 :	[. 3 1 2]	[. 1 1]	1	-1	[. 2 3 1]
9 :	[3 . 1 2]	[1 1 1]	0	+1	[1 2 3 .]
1 0 :	[1 . 3 2]	[1 . 1]	1	-1	[1 . 3 2]
1 1 :	[. 1 3 2]	[. . 1]	0	-1	[. 1 3 2]
1 2 :	[. 2 3 1]	[. . 2]	2	+1	[. 3 1 2]
1 3 :	[2 . 3 1]	[1 . 2]	0	+1	[1 3 . 2]
1 4 :	[3 . 2 1]	[1 1 2]	1	+1	[1 3 2 .]
1 5 :	[. 3 2 1]	[. 1 2]	0	-1	[. 3 2 1]
1 6 :	[2 3 . 1]	[. 2 2]	1	+1	[2 3 . 1]
1 7 :	[3 2 . 1]	[1 2 2]	0	+1	[2 3 1 .]
1 8 :	[3 2 1 .]	[1 2 3]	2	+1	[3 2 1 .]
1 9 :	[2 3 1 .]	[. 2 3]	0	-1	[3 2 . 1]
2 0 :	[1 3 2 .]	[. 1 3]	1	-1	[3 . 2 1]
2 1 :	[3 1 2 .]	[1 1 3]	0	+1	[3 1 2 .]
2 2 :	[2 1 3 .]	[1 . 3]	1	-1	[3 1 . 2]
2 3 :	[1 2 3 .]	[. . 3]	0	-1	[3 . 1 2]

Figure 10.9-B: Permutations in minimal-change order (left) and Gray code for mixed radix numbers with rising factorial base. For even n the first and last permutations are cyclic shifts of each other.

```
                             append 3:
                              012 3
perm(2)=                      102 3
 01                           201 3                  ==> perm(4):
 10                           021 3                   0123
                              120 3                   1023
append 2:                     210 3                   2013
 01 2                                                 0213
 10 2                        reverse and swap (3,2):  1203
                              310 2                   2103
reverse and swap (2,1)        130 2                   3102
 20 1                         031 2                   1302
 02 1                         301 2                   0312
                              103 2                   3012
reverse and swap (1,0)        013 2                   1032
 12 0                                                 0132
 21 0                        reverse and swap (2,1):  0231
                              023 1                   2031
==> perm(3)                   203 1                   3021
 012                          302 1                   0321
 102                          032 1                   2301
 201                          230 1                   3201
 021                          320 1                   3210
 120                                                  2310
 210                         reverse and swap (1,0):  1320
                              321 0                   3120
                              231 0                   2130
                              132 0                   1230
                              312 0
                              213 0
                              123 0
```

Figure 10.9-C: Recursive construction of the permutations.

```
17              first();
18          }
19      [--snip--]
20          void first()
21          {
22              M_->first();
23              for (ulong k=0; k<n_; ++k)   x_[k] = ix_[k] = k;
24              sw1_=n_-1;  sw2_=n_-2;
25          }
```

Let $j \geq 0$ be the position of the digit changed with incrementing the mixed radix number, and $d = \pm 1$ the increment or decrement of that digit. The compute the next permutation, swap the element x_1 at position $j + 1$ with the element x_2 where x_2 is lying to the left of x_1 and it is the greatest element less than x_1 for $d > 0$, and the smallest element greater than x_1 for $d < 0$:

```
1       bool next()
2       {
3           // Compute next mixed radix number in Gray code order:
4           if ( false == M_->next() )  { first(); return false; }
5           ulong j = M_->pos();  // position of changed digit
6
7           if ( j<=1 )  // easy cases: swap == (0,j+1)
8           {
9               const ulong i2 = j+1;  // i1 == 0
10              const ulong x1 = x_[0],   x2 = x_[i2];
11              x_[0] = x2;    x_[i2] = x1;  // swap2(x_[i1], x_[i2]);
12              ix_[x1] = i2;  ix_[x2] = 0;  // swap2(ix_[x1], ix_[x2]);
13              sw1_=0;  sw2_=i2;
14              return true;
15          }
16          else
17          {
18              ulong i1 = j+1,  i2 = i1;
19              ulong x1 = x_[i1],  x2;
20              int d = M_->dir();    // direction of change
21              if ( d>0 )
22              {
23                  x2 = 0;
24                  for (ulong t=0; t<i1; ++t)  // search maximal smaller element left
25                  {
26                      ulong xt = x_[t];
27                      if ( (xt < x1) && (xt >= x2) )  { i2=t; x2=xt; }
28                  }
29              }
30              else
31              {
32                  x2 = n_;
33                  for (ulong t=0; t<i1; ++t)  // search minimal greater element
34                  {
35                      ulong xt = x_[t];
36                      if ( (xt > x1) && (xt <= x2) )  { i2=t; x2=xt; }
37                  }
38              }
39
40              x_[i1] = x2;    x_[i2] = x1;  // swap2(x_[i1], x_[i2]);
41              ix_[x1] = i2;  ix_[x2] = i1;  // swap2(ix_[x1], ix_[x2]);
42
43              sw1_=i2;  sw2_=i1;
44              return true;
45          }
46      }
```

There is a slightly more efficient algorithm to compute the successor using the inverse permutations:

```
1       bool next()
2       {
3       [--snip--]  /* easy cases as before */
4           else
5           {
6               ulong i1 = j+1,  i2 = i1;
7               ulong x1 = x_[i1],  x2;
8               int d = M_->dir();    // direction of change
9               if ( d>0 )  // in the inverse permutation search first smaller element left:
10              {
11                  for (x2=x1-1;  ; --x2)  if ( (i2=ix_[x2]) < i1 )  break;
12              }
13              else  // in the inverse permutation search first smaller element right:
```

```
14                        {
15                            for (x2=x1+1;  ; ++x2) if ( (i2=ix_[x2]) < i1 ) break;
16                        }
17      [--snip--]  /* swaps as before */
18                    }
19        }
```

The method is chosen by defining `SUCC_BY_INV` in the file [FXT: comb/perm-gray-rfact.h]. About 80 million permutations per second are generated, about 71 million with the first method.

10.9.3   Permutations with permuted factorial numbers

	permutation	swap	xfact	pos dir	inv.perm.
0 :	[. 1 2 3 4]		[. . . .]		[. 1 2 3 4]
1 :	[1 . 2 3 4]	(0 1)	[1 . . .]	0 +1	[1 . 2 3 4]
2 :	[2 . 1 3 4]	(0 2)	[1 1 . .]	1 +1	[1 2 . 3 4]
3 :	[. 2 1 3 4]	(0 1)	[. 1 . .]	0 -1	[. 2 1 3 4]
4 :	[1 2 . 3 4]	(0 2)	[. 2 . .]	1 +1	[2 . 1 3 4]
5 :	[2 1 . 3 4]	(0 1)	[1 2 . .]	0 +1	[2 1 . 3 4]
6 :	[2 1 . 4 3]	(3 4)	[1 2 1 .]	2 +1	[2 1 . 4 3]
7 :	[1 2 . 4 3]	(0 1)	[. 2 1 .]	0 -1	[2 . 1 4 3]
[--snip--]					
9 1 :	[3 4 2 1 .]	(0 1)	[. 2 4 3]	0 -1	[4 3 2 . 1]
9 2 :	[2 4 3 1 .]	(0 2)	[. 1 4 3]	1 -1	[4 3 . 2 1]
9 3 :	[4 2 3 1 .]	(0 1)	[1 1 4 3]	0 +1	[4 3 1 2 .]
9 4 :	[3 2 4 1 .]	(0 2)	[1 . 4 3]	1 -1	[4 3 1 . 2]
9 5 :	[2 3 4 1 .]	(0 1)	[. . 4 3]	0 -1	[4 3 . 1 2]
9 6 :	[2 3 4 . 1]	(3 4)	[. . 3 3]	2 -1	[3 4 . 1 2]
9 7 :	[3 2 4 . 1]	(0 1)	[1 . 3 3]	0 +1	[3 4 1 . 2]
[--snip--]					
106:	[3 1 4 . 2]	(0, 2)	[1 . 2 3]	1 -1	[3 1 4 . 2]
107:	[1 3 4 . 2]	(0, 1)	[. . 2 3]	0 -1	[3 . 4 1 2]
108:	[1 2 4 . 3]	(1, 4)	[. . 1 3]	2 -1	[3 . 1 4 2]
109:	[2 1 4 . 3]	(0, 1)	[1 . 1 3]	0 +1	[3 1 . 4 2]
110:	[4 1 2 . 3]	(0, 2)	[1 1 1 3]	1 +1	[3 1 2 4 .]
111:	[1 4 2 . 3]	(0, 1)	[. 1 1 3]	0 -1	[3 . 2 4 1]
112:	[2 4 1 . 3]	(0, 2)	[. 2 1 3]	1 +1	[3 2 . 4 1]
113:	[4 2 1 . 3]	(0, 1)	[1 2 1 3]	0 +1	[3 2 1 4 .]
114:	[3 2 1 . 4]	(0, 4)	[1 2 . 3]	2 -1	[3 2 1 . 4]
115:	[2 3 1 . 4]	(0, 1)	[. 2 . 3]	0 -1	[3 2 . 1 4]
116:	[1 3 2 . 4]	(0, 2)	[. 1 . 3]	1 -1	[3 . 2 1 4]
117:	[3 1 2 . 4]	(0, 1)	[1 1 . 3]	0 +1	[3 1 2 . 4]
118:	[2 1 3 . 4]	(0, 2)	[1 . . 3]	1 -1	[3 1 . 2 4]
119:	[1 2 3 . 4]	(0, 1)	[. . . 3]	0 -1	[3 . 1 2 4]

Figure 10.9-D: Permutations with mixed radix numbers with radix vector $[2, 3, 5, 4]$.

The rising and falling factorial numbers are special cases of factorial numbers with permuted digits. We give a method to compute the Gray code for permutations from the Gray code for permuted (falling) factorial numbers. A permutation of the radices determines how often a digit at any position is changed: the leftmost changes most often, the rightmost least often. The permutations corresponding to the mixed radix numbers with radix vector $[2, 3, 5, 4]$, the falling factorial last two radices swapped, is shown in figure 10.9-D [FXT: comb/perm-gray-rot1-demo.cc]. The desired property of this ordering is that the last permutation is as close to a cyclic shift by one position of the first as possible. With even n the Gray code with the falling factorial base the last permutation is a shift by one. With odd n no such Gray code exists: the total number of transpositions with any Gray code is odd for all $n > 1$, but the cyclic rotation by one corresponds to an even number of transpositions. The best we can get is that the first e elements where $e \leq n$ is the greatest possible even number. For example,

```
          first              last
n=6:   [ 0 1 2 3 4 5 ]    [ 1 2 3 4 5 0 ]
n=7:   [ 0 1 2 3 4 5 6 ]  [ 1 2 3 4 5 0 6 ]
```

We use this ordering to show the general method [FXT: class `perm_gray_rot1` in comb/perm-gray-rot1.h]:

```
1    class perm_gray_rot1
```

```
 2    {
 3    public:
 4        mixedradix_gray *M_;   // Gray code for factorial numbers
 5        ulong n_;    // number of elements to permute
 6        ulong *x_;   // current permutation (of {0, 1, ..., n-1})
 7        ulong *ix_;   // inverse permutation
 8        ulong sw1_, sw2_; // indices of elements swapped most recently
 9
10    public:
11        perm_gray_rot1(ulong n)
12        // Must have: n>=1
13        {
14            n_ = (n ? n : 1);  // at least one
15            x_ = new ulong[n_];
16            ix_ = new ulong[n_];
17
18            M_ = new mixedradix_gray(n_-1, 1);  // rising factorial base
19
20            // apply permutation of radix vector with mixed radix number:
21            if ( (n_ >= 3) && (n & 1) )  // odd n>=3
22            {
23                ulong *m1 = M_->m1_;
24                swap2(m1[n_-2], m1[n_-3]);  // swap last two factorial nines
25            }
26
27            first();
28        }
29    [--snip--]
```

The permutation applied here can be replaced by any permutation, the following update routines will still work:

```
 1        bool next()
 2        {
 3            // Compute next mixed radix number in Gray code order:
 4            if ( false == M_->next() )  { first();  return false; }
 5
 6            const ulong j = M_->pos();   // position of changed digit
 7            const ulong i1 = M_->m1_[j];  // valid for any permutation of factorial radices
 8
 9            const ulong x1 = x_[i1];
10            ulong  i2 = i1,  x2;
11            const int d = M_->dir();      // direction of change
12
13            if ( d>0 )  // in the inverse permutation search first smaller element left:
14            {
15                for (x2=x1-1;  ;  --x2)  if ( (i2=ix_[x2]) < i1 )  break;
16            }
17            else  // in the inverse permutation search first smaller element right:
18            {
19                for (x2=x1+1;  ;  ++x2)  if ( (i2=ix_[x2]) < i1 )  break;
20            }
21
22            x_[i1] = x2;     x_[i2] = x1;  // swap2(x_[i1], x_[i2]);
23            ix_[x1] = i2;   ix_[x2] = i1;  // swap2(ix_[x1], ix_[x2]);
24
25            sw1_=i2;   sw2_=i1;
26
27            return true;
28        }
29    [--snip--]
```

Note that instead of taking $j + 1$ as the position of the element to move, we take the value of the nine at the position j. The special ordering shown here can be used to construct a Gray code with the single track property, see section 10.12.2 on page 274.

10.10   Derangement order

In a *derangement order* for permutations two successive permutations have no element at the same position, as shown in figure 10.10-A. The listing was created with the program [FXT: comb/perm-derange-demo.cc]. There is no derangement order for $n = 3$. An implementation of the underlying algorithm (given in [298, p.611]) is [FXT: class perm_derange in comb/perm-derange.h]:

```
                permutation         inverse perm.
    0 :      [ . 1 2 3 ]         [ . 1 2 3 ]
    1 :      [ 3 . 1 2 ]         [ 1 2 3 . ]
    2 :      [ 1 2 3 . ]         [ 3 . 1 2 ]
    3 :      [ 2 3 . 1 ]         [ 2 3 . 1 ]
    4 :      [ 1 . 2 3 ]         [ 1 . 2 3 ]
    5 :      [ 3 1 . 2 ]         [ 2 1 3 . ]
    6 :      [ . 2 3 1 ]         [ . 3 1 2 ]
    7 :      [ 2 3 1 . ]         [ 3 2 . 1 ]
    8 :      [ 1 2 . 3 ]         [ 2 . 1 3 ]
    9 :      [ 3 1 2 . ]         [ 3 1 2 . ]
   1 0 :     [ 2 . 3 1 ]         [ 1 3 . 2 ]
   1 1 :     [ . 3 1 2 ]         [ . 2 3 1 ]
   1 2 :     [ 2 1 . 3 ]         [ 2 1 . 3 ]
   1 3 :     [ 3 2 1 . ]         [ 3 2 1 . ]
   1 4 :     [ 1 . 3 2 ]         [ 1 . 3 2 ]
   1 5 :     [ . 3 2 1 ]         [ . 3 2 1 ]
   1 6 :     [ 2 . 1 3 ]         [ 1 2 . 3 ]
   1 7 :     [ 3 2 . 1 ]         [ 2 3 1 . ]
   1 8 :     [ . 1 3 2 ]         [ . 1 3 2 ]
   1 9 :     [ 1 3 2 . ]         [ 3 . 2 1 ]
   2 0 :     [ . 2 1 3 ]         [ . 2 1 3 ]
   2 1 :     [ 3 . 2 1 ]         [ 1 3 2 . ]
   2 2 :     [ 2 1 3 . ]         [ 3 1 . 2 ]
   2 3 :     [ 1 3 . 2 ]         [ 2 . 3 1 ]
```

Figure 10.10-A: The permutations of 4 elements in derangement order.

```
1     class perm_derange
2     {
3     public:
4         ulong n_;   // number of elements
5         ulong *x_;  // current permutation
6         ulong ctm_; // counter modulo n
7         perm_trotter* T_;
8
9     public:
10        perm_derange(ulong n)
11        // Must have:  n>=4
12        // n=2: trivial, n=3: no solution exists,  n>=4: ok
13        {
14            n_ = n;
15            x_ = new ulong[n_];
16            T_ = new perm_trotter(n_-1);
17            first();
18        }
19    [--snip--]
```

The routine to update the permutation is

```
1     bool next()
2     {
3         ++ctm_;
4         if ( ctm_>=n_ ) // every n steps: need next perm_trotter
5         {
6             ctm_ = 0;
7             if ( ! T_->next() )  return false;  // current permutation is last
8             const ulong *t = T_->data();
9             for (ulong k=0; k<n_-1; ++k)  x_[k] = t[k];
10            x_[n_-1] = n_-1;  // last element
11        }
12        else  // rotate
13        {
14            if ( ctm_==n_-1 )  rotate_left1(x_, n_);
15            else // last two elements swapped
16            {
17                rotate_right1(x_, n_);
18                if ( ctm_==n_-2 )  rotate_right1(x_, n_);
19            }
20        }
21        return true;
22    }
```

The routines `rotate_right1()` and `rotate_last()` rotate the array `x_[]` by one position [FXT: perm/rotate.h]. These cyclic shifts are the performance bottleneck, one update of a length-n permutation is $O(n)$. Still, about 35 million permutations per second are generated for $n = 12$.

Gray codes have the minimal number of changes between successive permutations while derangement orders have the maximum. An algorithm for generating all permutations of n objects with k transitions (where $2 \le k \le n$ and $k \ne 3$) is given in [297].

Derangement order for even n ‡

```
        permutation   inv. perm.           permutation   inv. perm.
   0 : [ .  1  2  3 ] [ .  1  2  3 ]   0: [ .  1  2 ] [ .  1  2 ]
   1 : [ 1  2  3  . ] [ 3  .  1  2 ]   1: [ 1  2  . ] [ 2  .  1 ]
   2 : [ 2  3  .  1 ] [ 2  3  .  1 ]   2: [ 2  .  1 ] [ 1  2  . ] <<
   3 : [ 3  .  1  2 ] [ 1  2  3  . ]   3: [ 1  .  2 ] [ 1  .  2 ] <<
   4 : [ 1  2  .  3 ] [ 2  .  1  3 ]   4: [ .  2  1 ] [ .  2  1 ]
   5 : [ 2  .  3  1 ] [ 1  3  .  2 ]   5: [ 2  1  . ] [ 2  1  . ]
   6 : [ .  3  1  2 ] [ .  2  3  1 ]
   7 : [ 3  1  2  . ] [ 3  1  2  . ]
   8 : [ 2  .  1  3 ] [ 1  2  .  3 ]
   9 : [ .  1  3  2 ] [ .  1  3  2 ]
 1 0 :[ 1  3  2  . ] [ 3  .  2  1 ]
 1 1 :[ 3  2  .  1 ] [ 2  3  1  . ]
 1 2 :[ 1  .  2  3 ] [ 1  .  2  3 ]
 1 3 :[ .  2  3  1 ] [ .  3  1  2 ]
 1 4 :[ 2  3  1  . ] [ 3  2  .  1 ]
 1 5 :[ 3  1  .  2 ] [ 2  1  3  . ]
 1 6 :[ .  2  1  3 ] [ .  2  1  3 ]
 1 7 :[ 2  1  3  . ] [ 3  1  .  2 ]
 1 8 :[ 1  3  .  2 ] [ 2  .  3  1 ]
 1 9 :[ 3  .  2  1 ] [ 1  3  2  . ]
 2 0 :[ 2  1  .  3 ] [ 2  1  .  3 ]
 2 1 :[ 1  .  3  2 ] [ 1  .  3  2 ]
 2 2 :[ .  3  2  1 ] [ .  3  2  1 ]
 2 3 :[ 3  2  1  . ] [ 3  2  1  . ]
```

Figure 10.10-B: Permutations generated via cyclic shifts. The order is a derangement order for even n (left), but not for odd n (right). Dots denote zeros.

An algorithm for the generation of permutations via cyclic shifts suggested in [225] generates a derangement order if the number n of elements is even, see figure 10.10-B. An implementation of the algorithm, following [215, alg.C, sect.7.2.1.2], is [FXT: class `perm_rot` in comb/perm-rot.h]. For odd n the number of times that the successor is not a derangement of the predecessor equals $((n+1)/2)! - 1$. The program [FXT: comb/perm-rot-demo.cc] generates the permutations and counts those transitions.

An alternative ordering with the same number of transitions that are not derangements is obtained via mixed radix counting in falling factorial base and the routine [FXT: comb/perm-rot-unrank-demo.cc]

```
1    void ffact2perm_rot(const ulong *fc, ulong n, ulong *x)
2    // Convert falling factorial number fc[0, ..., n-2] into
3    // permutation of x[0, ..., n-1].
4    {
5        for (ulong k=0; k<n; ++k)   x[k] = k;
6        for (ulong k=n-1, j=2;  k!=0;  --k, ++j)  rotate_right(x+k-1, j, fc[k-1]);
7    }
```

Figure 10.10-C shows the generated ordering for $n = 4$ and $n = 3$. The observation that the permutations in second ordering are the complemented reversals of the first leads to the unranking routine

```
1    class perm_rot
2    {
3        ulong *a_;   // permutation of n elements
4        ulong n_;
5    [--snip--]
6
7        void goto_ffact(const ulong *d)
8        // Goto permutation corresponding to d[] (i.e. unrank d[]).
9        // d[] must be a valid (falling) factorial mixed radix string.
```

```
          ffact        permutation   inv. perm.          ffact      perm.      inv. perm.
 0 : [ .  .  . ]   [ . 1 2 3 ]   [ . 1 2 3 ]      0: [ .  . ]   [ . 1 2 ]   [ . 1 2 ]
 1 : [ 1  .  . ]   [ 3 . 1 2 ]   [ 1 2 3 . ]      1: [ 1  . ]   [ 2 . 1 ]   [ 1 2 . ]
 2 : [ 2  .  . ]   [ 2 3 . 1 ]   [ 2 3 . 1 ]      2: [ 2  . ]   [ 1 2 . ]   [ 2 . 1 ]  <<
 3 : [ 3  .  . ]   [ 1 2 3 . ]   [ 3 . 1 2 ]      3: [ .  1 ]   [ . 2 1 ]   [ . 2 1 ]  <<
 4 : [ .  1  . ]   [ . 3 1 2 ]   [ . 2 3 1 ]      4: [ 1  1 ]   [ 1 . 2 ]   [ 1 . 2 ]
 5 : [ 1  1  . ]   [ 2 . 3 1 ]   [ 1 3 . 2 ]      5: [ 2  1 ]   [ 2 1 . ]   [ 2 1 . ]
 6 : [ 2  1  . ]   [ 1 2 . 3 ]   [ 2 . 1 3 ]
 7 : [ 3  1  . ]   [ 3 1 2 . ]   [ 3 1 2 . ]
 8 : [ .  2  . ]   [ . 2 3 1 ]   [ . 3 1 2 ]
 9 : [ 1  2  . ]   [ 1 . 2 3 ]   [ 1 . 2 3 ]
10 : [ 2  2  . ]   [ 3 1 . 2 ]   [ 2 1 3 . ]
11 : [ 3  2  . ]   [ 2 3 1 . ]   [ 3 2 . 1 ]
12 : [ .  .  1 ]   [ . 1 3 2 ]   [ . 1 3 2 ]
13 : [ 1  .  1 ]   [ 2 . 1 3 ]   [ 1 2 . 3 ]
14 : [ 2  .  1 ]   [ 3 2 . 1 ]   [ 2 3 1 . ]
15 : [ 3  .  1 ]   [ 1 3 2 . ]   [ 3 . 2 1 ]
16 : [ .  1  1 ]   [ . 2 1 3 ]   [ . 2 1 3 ]
17 : [ 1  1  1 ]   [ 3 . 2 1 ]   [ 1 3 2 . ]
18 : [ 2  1  1 ]   [ 1 3 . 2 ]   [ 2 . 3 1 ]
19 : [ 3  1  1 ]   [ 2 1 3 . ]   [ 3 1 . 2 ]
20 : [ .  2  1 ]   [ . 3 2 1 ]   [ . 3 2 1 ]
21 : [ 1  2  1 ]   [ 1 . 3 2 ]   [ 1 . 3 2 ]
22 : [ 2  2  1 ]   [ 2 1 . 3 ]   [ 2 1 . 3 ]
23 : [ 3  2  1 ]   [ 3 2 1 . ]   [ 3 2 1 . ]
```

Figure 10.10-C: Alternative ordering for permutations generated via cyclic shifts. The order is a derangement order for even n (left), but not for odd n (right).

```
10      {
11              for (ulong k=0; k<n_; ++k)  a_[k] = k;
12              for (ulong k=n_-1, j=2;  k!=0;  --k, ++j)  rotate_right(a_+k-1, j, d[k-1]);
13              reverse(a_, n_);
14              make_complement(a_, a_, n_);
15      }
16  [--snip--]
17  }
```

Compare to the unranking for permutations by prefix reversals shown in section 10.4.1 on page 247.

10.11 Orders where the smallest element always moves right

10.11.1 A variant of Trotter's construction

An ordering for the permutations where the first element always moves right is produced by the interleaving process shown in figure 10.11-A. The process is similar to the one for Trotter's order shown in figure 10.7-B on page 253, but the directions are not changed. This ordering essentially appears in [259, p.7]. The second half of the permutations is the reversed list of the reversed permutations in the first half. The permutations are shown in figure 10.11-B, they are the inverses of the permutations corresponding to the falling factorial numbers, see figure 10.1-A on page 233. An implementation is [FXT: class perm_mv0 in comb/perm-mv0.h]:

```
1   class perm_mv0
2   {
3   public:
4       ulong *d_;   // mixed radix digits with radix = [n-1, n-2, n-3, ..., 2]
5       ulong *x_;   // permutation
6       ulong ect_;  // counter for easy case
7       ulong n_;    // permutations of n elements
8
9   public:
10      perm_mv0(ulong n)
11      // Must have n>=2
12      {
13          n_ = n;
14          d_ = new ulong[n_];
15          d_[n-1] = 1;  // sentinel (must be nonzero)
16          x_ = new ulong[n_];
```

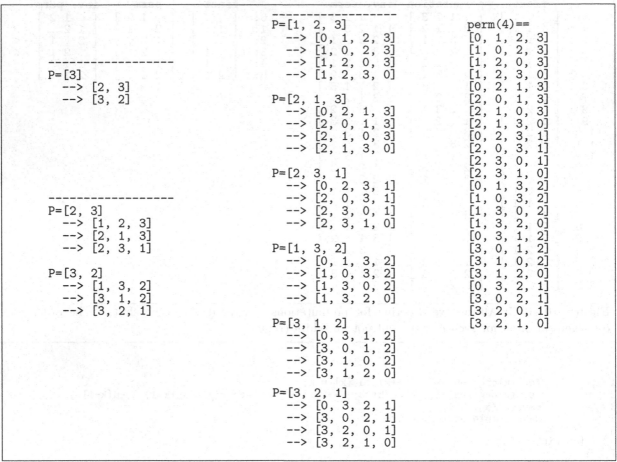

```
                                   -------------------
                                   P=[1, 2, 3]                    perm(4)==
                                     --> [0, 1, 2, 3]             [0, 1, 2, 3]
                                     --> [1, 0, 2, 3]             [1, 0, 2, 3]
         -------------------         --> [1, 2, 0, 3]             [1, 2, 0, 3]
         P=[3]                       --> [1, 2, 3, 0]             [1, 2, 3, 0]
           --> [2, 3]                                             [0, 2, 1, 3]
           --> [3, 2]               P=[2, 1, 3]                   [2, 0, 1, 3]
                                     --> [0, 2, 1, 3]             [2, 1, 0, 3]
                                     --> [2, 0, 1, 3]             [2, 1, 3, 0]
                                     --> [2, 1, 0, 3]             [0, 2, 3, 1]
                                     --> [2, 1, 3, 0]             [2, 0, 3, 1]
                                                                 [2, 3, 0, 1]
                                   P=[2, 3, 1]                    [2, 3, 1, 0]
         -------------------         --> [0, 2, 3, 1]             [0, 1, 3, 2]
         P=[2, 3]                     --> [2, 0, 3, 1]             [1, 0, 3, 2]
           --> [1, 2, 3]             --> [2, 3, 0, 1]             [1, 3, 0, 2]
           --> [2, 1, 3]             --> [2, 3, 1, 0]             [1, 3, 2, 0]
           --> [2, 3, 1]                                          [0, 3, 1, 2]
                                   P=[1, 3, 2]                    [3, 0, 1, 2]
         P=[3, 2]                     --> [0, 1, 3, 2]             [3, 1, 0, 2]
           --> [1, 3, 2]             --> [1, 0, 3, 2]             [3, 1, 2, 0]
           --> [3, 1, 2]             --> [1, 3, 0, 2]             [0, 3, 2, 1]
           --> [3, 2, 1]             --> [1, 3, 2, 0]             [3, 0, 2, 1]
                                                                 [3, 2, 0, 1]
                                   P=[3, 1, 2]                    [3, 2, 1, 0]
                                     --> [0, 3, 1, 2]
                                     --> [3, 0, 1, 2]
                                     --> [3, 1, 0, 2]
                                     --> [3, 1, 2, 0]

                                   P=[3, 2, 1]
                                     --> [0, 3, 2, 1]
                                     --> [3, 0, 2, 1]
                                     --> [3, 2, 0, 1]
                                     --> [3, 2, 1, 0]
```

Figure 10.11-A: Interleaving process to generate all permutations by right moves.

```
               permutation     ffact       inv. perm.
      0 :     [ . 1 2 3 ]     [ . . . ]    [ . 1 2 3 ]
      1 :     [ 1 . 2 3 ]     [ 1 . . ]    [ 1 . 2 3 ]
      2 :     [ 1 2 . 3 ]     [ 2 . . ]    [ 2 . 1 3 ]
      3 :     [ 1 2 3 . ]     [ 3 . . ]    [ 3 . 1 2 ]
      4 :     [ . 2 1 3 ]     [ . 1 . ]    [ . 2 1 3 ]
      5 :     [ 2 . 1 3 ]     [ 1 1 . ]    [ 1 2 . 3 ]
      6 :     [ 2 1 . 3 ]     [ 2 1 . ]    [ 2 1 . 3 ]
      7 :     [ 2 1 3 . ]     [ 3 1 . ]    [ 3 1 . 2 ]
      8 :     [ . 2 3 1 ]     [ . 2 . ]    [ . 3 1 2 ]
      9 :     [ 2 . 3 1 ]     [ 1 2 . ]    [ 1 3 . 2 ]
    1 0 :     [ 2 3 . 1 ]     [ 2 2 . ]    [ 2 3 . 1 ]
    1 1 :     [ 2 3 1 . ]     [ 3 2 . ]    [ 3 2 . 1 ]
    1 2 :     [ . 1 3 2 ]     [ . . 1 ]    [ . 1 3 2 ]
    1 3 :     [ 1 . 3 2 ]     [ 1 . 1 ]    [ 1 . 3 2 ]
    1 4 :     [ 1 3 . 2 ]     [ 2 . 1 ]    [ 2 . 3 1 ]
    1 5 :     [ 1 3 2 . ]     [ 3 . 1 ]    [ 3 . 2 1 ]
    1 6 :     [ . 3 1 2 ]     [ . 1 1 ]    [ . 2 3 1 ]
    1 7 :     [ 3 . 1 2 ]     [ 1 1 1 ]    [ 1 2 3 . ]
    1 8 :     [ 3 1 . 2 ]     [ 2 1 1 ]    [ 2 1 3 . ]
    1 9 :     [ 3 1 2 . ]     [ 3 1 1 ]    [ 3 1 2 . ]
    2 0 :     [ . 3 2 1 ]     [ . 2 1 ]    [ . 3 2 1 ]
    2 1 :     [ 3 . 2 1 ]     [ 1 2 1 ]    [ 1 3 2 . ]
    2 2 :     [ 3 2 . 1 ]     [ 2 2 1 ]    [ 2 3 1 . ]
    2 3 :     [ 3 2 1 . ]     [ 3 2 1 ]    [ 3 2 1 . ]
```

Figure 10.11-B: All permutations of 4 elements and falling factorial numbers used to update the permutations. Dots denote zeros.

```
17              first();
18        }
19     [--snip--]
20
21     void first()
22     {
23          for (ulong k=0; k<n_; ++k)   x_[k] = k;
24          for (ulong k=0; k<n_-1; ++k)  d_[k] = 0;
25          ect_ = 0;
26     }
27     [--snip--]
```

The update process uses the falling factorial numbers. Let j be the position where the digit is incremented and d the value before the increment. The update

```
permutation        ffact
                          v-- increment at j=2
[ 4 2 3 5 1 0 ]    [ 5 4 1 1 . ]  <--= digit before increment is d=1
[ 0 1 4 3 2 5 ]    [ . . 2 1 . ]
```

is done in three steps:

```
[ 4 2 3 5 1 0 ]    [ 5 4 1 1 . ]
[ 4 3 2 5 1 0 ]    [ 5 4 2 1 . ]   move element at position d=1 to the right
[ * * 4 3 2 5 ]    [ * * 2 1 . ]   move all but j=2 elements to end
[ 0 1 4 3 2 5 ]    [ . . 2 1 . ]   insert identical permutation at start
```

We treat the first digit separately as it changes most often (easy case):

```
1     bool next()
2     {
3          if ( ++ect_ < n_ ) // easy case
4          {
5               swap2(x_[ect_], x_[ect_-1]);
6               return true;
7          }
8          else
9          {
10              ect_ = 0;
11              ulong j = 1;
12              ulong m1 = n_ - 2;   // nine in falling factorial base
13              while ( d_[j]==m1 )  // find digit to increment
14              {
15                   d_[j] = 0;
16                   --m1;
17                   ++j;
18              }
19
20              if ( j==n_-1 )  return false;  // current permutation is last
21
22              const ulong dj = d_[j];
23              d_[j] = dj + 1;
24
25              // element at d[j] moves one position to the right:
26              swap2( x_[dj], x_[dj+1] );
27
28              { // move n-j elements to end:
29                   ulong s = n_-j,  d = n_;
30                   do
31                   {
32                        --s;
33                        --d;
34                        x_[d] = x_[s];
35                   }
36                   while ( s );
37              }
38
39              // fill in 0,1,2,..,j-1 at start:
40              for (ulong k=0; k<j; ++k)  x_[k] = k;
41
42              return true;
43          }
44     }
45   }
```

The routine generates about 210 million permutations per second [FXT: comb/perm-mv0-demo.cc].

10.11.2 Ives' algorithm

```
              permutation    inv. perm.
        1 : [ . 1 2 3 ]    [ . 1 2 3 ]
        2 : [ 1 . 2 3 ]    [ 1 . 2 3 ]
        3 : [ 1 2 . 3 ]    [ 2 . 1 3 ]
        4 : [ 1 2 3 . ]    [ 3 . 1 2 ]
        5 : [ . 2 3 1 ]    [ . 3 1 2 ]
        6 : [ 2 . 3 1 ]    [ 1 3 . 2 ]
        7 : [ 2 3 . 1 ]    [ 2 3 . 1 ]
        8 : [ 2 3 1 . ]    [ 3 2 . 1 ]
        9 : [ . 3 1 2 ]    [ . 2 3 1 ]
      1 0 : [ 3 . 1 2 ]    [ 1 2 3 . ]
      1 1 : [ 3 1 . 2 ]    [ 2 1 3 . ]
      1 2 : [ 3 1 2 . ]    [ 3 1 2 . ]   << only update with more
      1 3 : [ . 2 1 3 ]    [ . 2 1 3 ]   << than one transposition
      1 4 : [ 2 . 1 3 ]    [ 1 2 . 3 ]
      1 5 : [ 2 1 . 3 ]    [ 2 1 . 3 ]
      1 6 : [ 2 1 3 . ]    [ 3 1 . 2 ]
      1 7 : [ . 1 3 2 ]    [ . 1 3 2 ]
      1 8 : [ 1 . 3 2 ]    [ 1 . 3 2 ]
      1 9 : [ 1 3 . 2 ]    [ 2 . 3 1 ]
      2 0 : [ 1 3 2 . ]    [ 3 . 2 1 ]
      2 1 : [ . 3 2 1 ]    [ . 3 2 1 ]
      2 2 : [ 3 . 2 1 ]    [ 1 3 2 . ]
      2 3 : [ 3 2 . 1 ]    [ 2 3 1 . ]
      2 4 : [ 3 2 1 . ]    [ 3 2 1 . ]
```

Figure 10.11-C: All permutations of 4 elements in an order by Ives.

An ordering where most of the moves are a move by one position to the right of the smallest element is shown in figure 10.11-C. With n elements only one in $n(n-1)$ moves is more than a transposition (only the update from 12 to 13 in figure 10.11-C). The second half of the list of permutations is the reversed list of the reversed permutations in the first half. The algorithm, given by Ives [189], is implemented in [FXT: class perm_ives in comb/perm-ives.h]:

```
1    class perm_ives
2    {
3    public:
4        ulong *p_;    // permutation
5        ulong *ip_;   // inverse permutation
6        ulong n_;     // permutations of n elements
7
8    public:
9        perm_ives(ulong n)
10       // Must have: n >= 2
11       {
12           n_ = n;
13           p_ = new ulong[n_];
14           ip_ = new ulong[n_];
15           first();
16       }
17   [--snip--]
```

The computation of the successor is

```
1        bool next()
2        {
3            ulong e1 = 0,  u = n_ - 1;
4            do
5            {
6                const ulong i1 = ip_[e1];
7                const ulong i2 = (i1==u ? e1 : i1+1 );
8                const ulong e2 = p_[i2];
9                p_[i1] = e2;  p_[i2] = e1;
10               ip_[e1] = i2;  ip_[e2] = i1;
11
12               if ( (p_[e1]!=e1) || (p_[u]!=u) )  return true;
13
14               ++e1;
15               --u;
16           }
```

```
17          while ( u > e1 );
18
19          return false;
20      }
21  [--snip--]
```

The rate of generation is about 180 M/s [FXT: comb/perm-ives-demo.cc]. Using arrays instead of pointers increases the rate to about 190 M/s.

As the easy case with the update (when just the first element is moved) occurs so often it is natural to create an extra branch for it. If the define for `PERM_IVES_OPT` is made before the class definition, a counter is created:

```
1  class perm_ives
2  {
3     [--snip--]
4  #ifdef PERM_IVES_OPT
5     ulong ctm_;   // aux: counter for easy case
6     ulong ctm0_;  // aux: start value of ctm == n*(n-1)-1
7  #endif
8     [--snip--]
```

If the counter is nonzero, the following update can be used:

```
1      bool next()
2      {
3          if ( ctm_-- )  // easy case
4          {
5              const ulong i1 = ip_[0];   // e1 == 0
6              const ulong i2 = (i1==n_-1 ? 0 : i1+1);
7              const ulong e2 = p_[i2];
8              p_[i1] = e2;  p_[i2] = 0;
9              ip_[0] = i2;  ip_[e2] = i1;
10             return true;
11         }
12         ctm_ = ctm0_;
13
14     [--snip--]   // rest as before
15     }
```

If arrays are used, a minimal speedup is achieved (rate 192 M/s), if pointers are used, the effect is a notable slowdown (rate 163 M/s).

The greatest speedup comes from a modification of a condition in the loop:

```
if ( (p_[e1]^e1) | (p_[u]^u) )  return true;
// same as:   if ( (p_[e1]!=e1) || (p_[u]!=u) )  return true;
```

The rate is increased to almost 194 M/s. This optimization is activated by defining `PERM_IVES_OPT2`.

10.12 Single track orders

Figure 10.12-A shows a *single track order* for the permutations of four elements. Each column in the list of permutations is a cyclic shift of the first column. A recursive construction for the ordering is shown in figure 10.12-B. Figure 10.12-A was created with the program [FXT: comb/perm-st-demo.cc] which uses [FXT: class `perm_st` in comb/perm-st.h]:

```
1   class perm_st
2   {
3   public:
4       ulong *d_;   // mixed radix digits with radix = [2, 3, 4, ..., n-1, (sentinel=-1)]
5       ulong *p_;   // permutation
6       ulong *pi_;  // inverse permutation
7       ulong n_;    // permutations of n elements
8
9   public:
10      perm_st(ulong n)
11      {
12          n_ = n;
13          d_ = new ulong[n_];
14          p_ = new ulong[n_];
15          pi_ = new ulong[n_];
```

```
                   permutation                              inv. perm.
        0 :     [ . 2 3 1 ]        [ . . . ]          [ . 3 1 2 ]
        1 :     [ . 3 2 1 ]        [ 1 . . ]          [ . 3 2 1 ]
        2 :     [ . 3 1 2 ]        [ . 1 . ]          [ . 2 3 1 ]
        3 :     [ . 2 1 3 ]        [ 1 1 . ]          [ . 2 1 3 ]
        4 :     [ . 1 2 3 ]        [ . 2 . ]          [ . 1 2 3 ]
        5 :     [ . 1 3 2 ]        [ 1 2 . ]          [ . 1 3 2 ]
        6 :     [ 1 . 2 3 ]        [ . . 1 ]          [ 1 . 2 3 ]
        7 :     [ 1 . 3 2 ]        [ 1 . 1 ]          [ 1 . 3 2 ]
        8 :     [ 2 . 3 1 ]        [ . 1 1 ]          [ 1 3 . 2 ]
        9 :     [ 3 . 2 1 ]        [ 1 1 1 ]          [ 1 3 2 . ]
      1 0 :     [ 3 . 1 2 ]        [ . 2 1 ]          [ 1 2 3 . ]
      1 1 :     [ 2 . 1 3 ]        [ 1 2 1 ]          [ 1 2 . 3 ]
      1 2 :     [ 3 1 . 2 ]        [ . . 2 ]          [ 2 1 3 . ]
      1 3 :     [ 2 1 . 3 ]        [ 1 . 2 ]          [ 2 1 . 3 ]
      1 4 :     [ 1 2 . 3 ]        [ . 1 2 ]          [ 2 . 1 3 ]
      1 5 :     [ 1 3 . 2 ]        [ 1 1 2 ]          [ 2 . 3 1 ]
      1 6 :     [ 2 3 . 1 ]        [ . 2 2 ]          [ 2 3 . 1 ]
      1 7 :     [ 3 2 . 1 ]        [ 1 2 2 ]          [ 2 3 1 . ]
      1 8 :     [ 2 3 1 . ]        [ . . 3 ]          [ 3 2 . 1 ]
      1 9 :     [ 3 2 1 . ]        [ 1 . 3 ]          [ 3 2 1 . ]
      2 0 :     [ 3 1 2 . ]        [ . 1 3 ]          [ 3 1 2 . ]
      2 1 :     [ 2 1 3 . ]        [ 1 1 3 ]          [ 3 1 . 2 ]
      2 2 :     [ 1 2 3 . ]        [ . 2 3 ]          [ 3 . 1 2 ]
      2 3 :     [ 1 3 2 . ]        [ 1 2 3 ]          [ 3 . 2 1 ]
```

Figure 10.12-A: Permutations of 4 elements in single track order. Dots denote zeros.

```
      23   <--=  permutations of 2 elements
      32

      11 23 32   <--= concatenate rows and prepend new element

      112332    <--= shift  0
      321123    <--= shift  2
      233211    <--= shift  4


      000000 112332 321123 233211   <--= concatenate rows and prepend new element

      000000 112332 321123 233211   <--= shift  0
      233211 000000 112332 321123   <--= shift  6
      321123 233211 000000 112332   <--= shift 12
      112332 321123 233211 000000   <--= shift 18
```

Figure 10.12-B: Construction of the single track order for permutations of 4 elements.

```
16          d_[n-1] = -1UL;  // sentinel
17          first();
18      }
19    [--snip--]
```

The first permutation is in enup order (see section 6.6.1 on page 186):

```
1     const ulong *data()  const { return p_; }
2     const ulong *invdata()  const  { return pi_; }
3
4     void first()
5     {
6         for (ulong k=0; k<n_-1; ++k)  d_[k] = 0;
7         for (ulong k=0, e=0;  k<n_;  ++k)
8         {
9             p_[k] = e;
10            pi_[e] = k;
11            e = next_enup(e, n_-1);
12        }
13    }
14    [--snip--]
```

The swap with the inverse permutations are determined by the rightmost position j changing with mixed radix counting with rising factorial base. We write -1 for the last element, -2 for the second last, and so on:

```
j    swaps
0:   (-2,-1)
1:   (-3,-2)
2:   (-4,-3)  (-2,-1)
3:   (-5,-4)  (-3,-2)
4:   (-6,-5)  (-4,-3)  (-2,-1)
5:   (-7,-6)  (-5,-4)  (-3,-2)
j:   (-j-2, -j-1) ... (-2-(j%1), -1-(j%1))
```

The computation of the successor is CAT:

```
1      bool next()
2      {
3          // increment mixed radix number:
4          ulong j = 0;
5          while ( d_[j]==j+1 )  { d_[j]=0;  ++j; }
6
7          if ( j==n_-1 )  return false; // current permutation is last
8          ++d_[j];
9
10         for (ulong e1=n_-2-j, e2=e1+1;  e2<n_;  e1+=2, e2+=2)
11         {
12             const ulong i1 = pi_[e1];   // position of element e1
13             const ulong i2 = pi_[e2];   // position of element e2
14             pi_[e1] = i2;
15             pi_[e2] = i1;
16             p_[i1] = e2;
17             p_[i2] = e1;
18         }
19
20         return true;
21     }
```

All swaps with the inverse permutations are of adjacent pairs. The reversals of the first half of all permutations lie in the second half, the reversal of the k-th permutation lies at position $n! - 1 - k$

```
                 permutation                        inv. perm.
     0 :    [ . 1 2 3 ]     [ . . . ]        [ . 1 2 3 ]
     1 :    [ . 1 3 2 ]     [ 1 . . ]        [ . 1 3 2 ]
     2 :    [ . 2 3 1 ]     [ . 1 . ]        [ . 3 1 2 ]
     3 :    [ . 3 2 1 ]     [ 1 1 . ]        [ . 3 2 1 ]
     4 :    [ . 3 1 2 ]     [ . 2 . ]        [ . 2 3 1 ]
     5 :    [ . 2 1 3 ]     [ 1 2 . ]        [ . 2 1 3 ]
     6 :    [ 1 3 . 2 ]     [ . . 1 ]        [ 2 . 3 1 ]
     7 :    [ 1 2 . 3 ]     [ 1 . 1 ]        [ 2 . 1 3 ]
     8 :    [ 2 1 . 3 ]     [ . 1 1 ]        [ 2 1 . 3 ]
     9 :    [ 3 1 . 2 ]     [ 1 1 1 ]        [ 2 1 3 . ]
    1 0 :   [ 3 2 . 1 ]     [ . 2 1 ]        [ 2 3 1 . ]
    1 1 :   [ 2 3 . 1 ]     [ 1 2 1 ]        [ 2 3 . 1 ]
    1 2 :   [ 3 2 1 . ]     [ . . 2 ]        [ 3 2 1 . ]
    1 3 :   [ 2 3 1 . ]     [ 1 . 2 ]        [ 3 2 . 1 ]
    1 4 :   [ 1 3 2 . ]     [ . 1 2 ]        [ 3 . 2 1 ]
    1 5 :   [ 1 2 3 . ]     [ 1 1 2 ]        [ 3 . 1 2 ]
    1 6 :   [ 2 1 3 . ]     [ . 2 2 ]        [ 3 1 . 2 ]
    1 7 :   [ 3 1 2 . ]     [ 1 2 2 ]        [ 3 1 2 . ]
    1 8 :   [ 2 . 3 1 ]     [ . . 3 ]        [ 1 3 . 2 ]
    1 9 :   [ 3 . 2 1 ]     [ 1 . 3 ]        [ 1 3 2 . ]
    2 0 :   [ 3 . 1 2 ]     [ . 1 3 ]        [ 1 2 3 . ]
    2 1 :   [ 2 . 1 3 ]     [ 1 1 3 ]        [ 1 2 . 3 ]
    2 2 :   [ 1 . 2 3 ]     [ . 2 3 ]        [ 1 . 2 3 ]
    2 3 :   [ 1 . 3 2 ]     [ 1 2 3 ]        [ 1 . 3 2 ]
```

Figure 10.12-C: Permutations of 4 elements in single track order starting with the identical permutation.

The single track property is independent of the first permutation, we start with the identical permutation:

```
1      void first_id()  // start with identical permutation
2      {
3          for (ulong k=0; k<n_-1; ++k)  d_[k] = 0;
```

```
4        for (ulong k=0; k<n_; ++k)  p_[k] = pi_[k] = k;
5    }
```

The generated ordering is shown in figure 10.12-C. The reversal of the k-th permutation lies at position $(n!)/2 + k$. About 123 million permutations per second are generated.

10.12.1 Construction of all single track orders

```
112233
231312  <--= permutations of 3 elements in lex order (columns)
323121

000000 112233 231312 323121  <--= concatenate rows and prepend new element

000000 112233 231312 323121  <--= shift  0
323121 000000 112233 231312  <--= shift  6
231312 323121 000000 112233  <--= shift 12
112233 231312 323121 000000  <--= shift 18
```

Figure 10.12-D: Construction of a single track order for permutations of 4 elements from an arbitrary ordering of the permutations of 3 elements.

```
        single track ordering              modified single track ordering
......  112233 231312 323121         21.113 332.22 .212.1 1.333.
323121 ...... 112233 231312         1.333. 21.113 332.22 .212.1
231312 323121 ...... 112233         .212.1 1.333. 21.113 332.22
112233 231312 323121 ......         332.22 .212.1 1.333. 21.113

^^^^^^                               ^^^^^^
000000                               210321 <--= cyclic shifts
```

Figure 10.12-E: In each of the first $(n-1)!$ permutations in a single track ordering (first block left) an arbitrary rotation can be applied (first block right), leading to a different single track ordering.

A construction for a single track order of $n+1$ elements from an arbitrary ordering of n elements is shown in figure 10.12-D (for $n = 3$ and lexicographic order). Thereby we obtain as many single track orders for the permutations of n elements as there are orders of the permutations of $n-1$ elements, namely $((n-1)!)!$. One can apply cyclic shifts in each block as shown in figure 10.12-E. The shifts in the first $(n-1)!$ positions (first blocks in the figure) determine the shifts for the remaining permutations, and there are n different cyclic shifts in each position. Indeed all single track orderings are of this form, so their number is

$$N_s(n) \quad = \quad ((n-1)!)! \, n^{(n-1)!} \tag{10.12-1}$$

The number of single track orders that start with the identical permutation, and where the k-th run of $(n-1)!$ elements starts with k (and so all shifts between consecutive tracks are left shifts by $(n-1)!$ positions) is

$$N_s(n)/n! \quad = \quad ((n-1)! - 1)! \, n^{(n-1)!-1} \tag{10.12-2}$$

10.12.2 A single track Gray code

A Gray code with the single track property can be constructed by using a Gray code for the permutations of $n-1$ elements if the first and last permutation are cyclic shifts by one position of each other. Such Gray codes exist for even lengths only. Figure 10.12-F shows a single track Gray code for $n = 5$. For even n we use a Gray code where all but the last element are cyclically shifted between the first and last permutation. Such a Gray code is given in section 10.9.3 on page 263. The resulting single track order has just $n-1$ extra transpositions for all permutations of n elements, see figure 10.12-G. The listings were created with the program [FXT: comb/perm-st-gray-demo.cc] which uses [FXT: class **perm_st_gray** in comb/perm-st-gray.h]:

```
1    class perm_st_gray
2    {
```

```
[ . 1 2 3 4 ]   [ 1 2 3 4 . ]   [ 2 3 4 . 1 ]   [ 3 4 . 1 2 ]   [ 4 . 1 2 3 ]
[ 1 . 2 3 4 ]   [ . 2 3 4 1 ]   [ 2 3 4 1 . ]   [ 3 4 1 . 2 ]   [ 4 1 . 2 3 ]
[ 2 . 1 3 4 ]   [ . 1 3 4 2 ]   [ 1 3 4 2 . ]   [ 3 4 2 . 1 ]   [ 4 2 . 1 3 ]
[ . 2 1 3 4 ]   [ 2 1 3 4 . ]   [ 1 3 4 . 2 ]   [ 3 4 . 2 1 ]   [ 4 . 2 1 3 ]
[ 1 2 . 3 4 ]   [ 2 . 3 4 1 ]   [ . 3 4 1 2 ]   [ 3 4 1 2 . ]   [ 4 1 2 . 3 ]
[ 2 1 . 3 4 ]   [ 1 . 3 4 2 ]   [ . 3 4 2 1 ]   [ 3 4 2 1 . ]   [ 4 2 1 . 3 ]
[ 3 1 . 2 4 ]   [ 1 . 2 4 3 ]   [ . 2 4 3 1 ]   [ 2 4 3 1 . ]   [ 4 3 1 . 2 ]
[ 1 3 . 2 4 ]   [ 3 . 2 4 1 ]   [ . 2 4 1 3 ]   [ 2 4 1 3 . ]   [ 4 1 3 . 2 ]
[ . 3 1 2 4 ]   [ 3 1 2 4 . ]   [ 1 2 4 . 3 ]   [ 2 4 . 3 1 ]   [ 4 . 3 1 2 ]
[ 3 . 1 2 4 ]   [ . 1 2 4 3 ]   [ 1 2 4 3 . ]   [ 2 4 3 . 1 ]   [ 4 3 . 1 2 ]
[ 1 . 3 2 4 ]   [ . 3 2 4 1 ]   [ 3 2 4 1 . ]   [ 2 4 1 . 3 ]   [ 4 1 . 3 2 ]
[ . 1 3 2 4 ]   [ 1 3 2 4 . ]   [ 3 2 4 . 1 ]   [ 2 4 . 1 3 ]   [ 4 . 1 3 2 ]
[ . 2 3 1 4 ]   [ 2 3 1 4 . ]   [ 3 1 4 . 2 ]   [ 1 4 . 2 3 ]   [ 4 . 2 3 1 ]
[ 2 . 3 1 4 ]   [ . 3 1 4 2 ]   [ 3 1 4 2 . ]   [ 1 4 2 . 3 ]   [ 4 2 . 3 1 ]
[ 3 . 2 1 4 ]   [ . 2 1 4 3 ]   [ 2 1 4 3 . ]   [ 1 4 3 . 2 ]   [ 4 3 . 2 1 ]
[ . 3 2 1 4 ]   [ 3 2 1 4 . ]   [ 2 1 4 . 3 ]   [ 1 4 . 3 2 ]   [ 4 . 3 2 1 ]
[ 2 3 . 1 4 ]   [ 3 . 1 4 2 ]   [ . 1 4 2 3 ]   [ 1 4 2 3 . ]   [ 4 2 3 . 1 ]
[ 3 2 . 1 4 ]   [ 2 . 1 4 3 ]   [ . 1 4 3 2 ]   [ 1 4 3 2 . ]   [ 4 3 2 . 1 ]
[ 3 2 1 . 4 ]   [ 2 1 . 4 3 ]   [ 1 . 4 3 2 ]   [ . 4 3 2 1 ]   [ 4 3 2 1 . ]
[ 2 3 1 . 4 ]   [ 3 1 . 4 2 ]   [ 1 . 4 2 3 ]   [ . 4 2 3 1 ]   [ 4 2 3 1 . ]
[ 1 3 2 . 4 ]   [ 3 2 . 4 1 ]   [ 2 . 4 1 3 ]   [ . 4 1 3 2 ]   [ 4 1 3 2 . ]
[ 3 1 2 . 4 ]   [ 1 2 . 4 3 ]   [ 2 . 4 3 1 ]   [ . 4 3 1 2 ]   [ 4 3 1 2 . ]
[ 2 1 3 . 4 ]   [ 1 3 . 4 2 ]   [ 3 . 4 2 1 ]   [ . 4 2 1 3 ]   [ 4 2 1 3 . ]
[ 1 2 3 . 4 ]   [ 2 3 . 4 1 ]   [ 3 . 4 1 2 ]   [ . 4 1 2 3 ]   [ 4 1 2 3 . ]
```

Figure 10.12-F: A cyclic Gray code for the permutations of 5 elements with the single track property.

```
  1 :    [ 0 1 2 3 4 5 ]
  2 :    [ 1 0 2 3 4 5 ]
  3 :    [ 2 0 1 3 4 5 ]
  4 :    [ 0 2 1 3 4 5 ]
  5 :    [ 1 2 0 3 4 5 ]
        [--one transposition only--]
116:    [ 2 3 1 0 4 5 ]
117:    [ 1 3 2 0 4 5 ]
118:    [ 3 1 2 0 4 5 ]
119:    [ 2 1 3 0 4 5 ]
120:    [ 1 2 3 0 4 5 ]
121:    [ 1 2 3 4 5 0 ]   < <(0, 4, 5)
        [--one transposition only--]
240:    [ 2 3 0 4 5 1 ]
241:    [ 2 3 4 5 0 1 ]   < <(0, 4 ,5)
        [--one transposition only--]
360:    [ 3 0 4 5 1 2 ]
361:    [ 3 4 5 0 1 2 ]   < <(0, 4, 5)
        [--one transposition only--]
480:    [ 0 4 5 1 2 3 ]
481:    [ 4 5 0 1 2 3 ]   < <(0, 4 ,5)
        [--one transposition only--]
600:    [ 4 5 1 2 3 0 ]
601:    [ 5 0 1 2 3 4 ]   < <(0, 4, 5)
        [--one transposition only--]
720:    [ 5 1 2 3 0 4 ]
  1 :   [ 0 1 2 3 4 5 ]   << ( 0 4 ,5)
```

Figure 10.12-G: The single track ordering for even n with the least number of transpositions contains $n - 1$ extra transpositions. The transitions involving more than 2 elements are 3-cycles.

```
3    public:
4        perm_gray_rot1 *G;   // underlying permutations
5
6        ulong *x_;    // permutation
7        ulong *ix_;   // inverse permutation
8        ulong n_;     // number of elements
9        ulong sct_;   // count cyclic shifts
10
11   public:
12       perm_st_gray(ulong n)
13       // Must have n>=2
14       {
15           n_ = (n>=2 ? n : 2);
16           G = new perm_gray_rot1(n-1);
17           x_ = new ulong[n_];
18           ix_ = new ulong[n_];
19           first();
20       }
21       [--snip--]
22       void first()
23       {
24           G->first();
25           for (ulong j=0; j<n_; ++j)  ix_[j] = x_[j] = j;
26           sct_ = n_;
27       }
```

We define two auxiliary routines for swapping elements by their value and by their positions:

```
1    private:
2        void swap_elements(ulong x1, ulong x2)
3        {
4            const ulong i1 = ix_[x1],  i2 = ix_[x2];
5            x_[i1] = x2;   x_[i2] = x1;   // swap2(x_[i1], x_[i2]);
6            ix_[x1] = i2;  ix_[x2] = i1;  // swap2(ix_[x1], ix_[x2]);
7        }
8
9        void swap_positions(ulong i1, ulong i2)
10       {
11           const ulong x1 = x_[i1],  x2 = x_[i2];
12           x_[i1] = x2;   x_[i2] = x1;   // swap2(x_[i1], x_[i2]);
13           ix_[x1] = i2;  ix_[x2] = i1;  // swap2(ix_[x1], ix_[x2]);
14       }
```

The update routine consists of two cases. The frequent case is the update via the underlying permutation:

```
1    public:
2        bool next()
3        {
4            bool q = G->next();
5            if ( q )  // normal update (in underlying permutation of n-1 elements)
6            {
7                ulong i1, i2;  // positions of swaps
8                G->get_swap(i1, i2);
9
10               // rotate positions according to sct:
11               i1 += sct_;  if ( i1>=n_ )  i1-=n_;
12               i2 += sct_;  if ( i2>=n_ )  i2-=n_;
13
14               swap_positions(i1, i2);
15
16               return true;
17           }
```

The infrequent case happens when the last underlying permutation is encountered:

```
1            else  // goto next cyclic shift (once in (n-1)! updates, n-1 times in total)
2            {
3                G->first();  // restart underlying permutations
4                --sct_;      // adjust cyclic shift
5                swap_elements(0, n_-1);
6
7                if ( 0==(n_&1) )  // n even
8                    if ( n_>=4 )  swap_elements(n_-2, n_-1);  // one extra transposition
9
10               return ( 0!=sct_ );
11           }
12       }
```

Chapter 11

Permutations with special properties

11.1 The number of certain permutations

We give expressions for the number of permutations with special properties, such as involutions, derangements, permutations with prescribed cycle types, and permutations with distance restrictions.

11.1.1 Permutations with m cycles: Stirling cycle numbers

n:	total	m= 1	2	3	4	5	6	7	8	9
1:	1	1								
2:	2	1	1							
3:	: 6	2	3	1						
4:	24	6	11	6	1					
5:	120	24	50	35	10	1				
6:	720	120	274	225	85	15	1			
7:	5040	720	1764	1624	735	175	21	1		
8:	40320	5040	13068	13132	6769	1960	322	28	1	
9:	362880	40320	109584	118124	67284	22449	4536	546	36	1

Figure 11.1-A: Stirling numbers of the first kind $s(n, m)$ (Stirling cycle numbers).

The number of permutations of n elements into m cycles is given by the (unsigned) *Stirling numbers of the first kind* (or *Stirling cycle numbers*) $s(n, m)$. The first few are shown in figure 11.1-A which was created with the program [FXT: comb/stirling1-demo.cc]. We have $s(1, 1) = 1$ and

$$s(n, m) \quad - \quad s(n-1, m-1) + (n-1)\, s(n-1, m) \tag{11.1-1}$$

See entry A008275 in [312] and [1, p.824]. Many identities involving the Stirling numbers are given in [166, pp.243-253]. We note just a few, writing $S(n, k)$ for the Stirling set numbers (see section 17.2 on page 358):

$$x^n \;=\; \sum_{k=0}^{n} S(n, k)\, x^{\underline{k}} \;=\; \sum_{k=0}^{n} S(n, k)\, (-1)^{n-k}\, x^{\overline{k}} \tag{11.1-2a}$$

where $x^{\underline{k}} = x\,(x-1)\,(x-2)\cdots(x-k+1)$ and $x^{\overline{k}} = x\,(x+1)\,(x+2)\cdots(x+k-1)$. Also

$$x^{\underline{k}} \;=\; \sum_{k=0}^{n} s(n, k)\, (-1)^{n-k}\, x^k \tag{11.1-2b}$$

$$x^{\overline{k}} \;=\; \sum_{k=0}^{n} s(n, k)\, x^k \tag{11.1-2c}$$

J. Arndt, *Matters Computational: Ideas, Algorithms, Source Code*,
DOI 10.1007/978-3-642-14764-7_11, © Springer-Verlag Berlin Heidelberg 2011

With $D := \frac{d}{dz}$ and $\vartheta = z\frac{d}{dz}$, we have the operator identities [166, p.296]

$$\vartheta^n \;=\; \sum_{k=0}^{n} S(n,k)\, z^k\, D^k \tag{11.1-3a}$$

$$z^n\, D^n \;=\; \sum_{k=0}^{n} s(n,k)\,(-1)^{n-k}\, \vartheta^k \tag{11.1-3b}$$

11.1.2 Permutations with prescribed cycle type

A permutation of n elements is of *type* $C = [c_1, c_2, c_3, \ldots, c_n]$ if it has c_1 fixed points, c_2 cycles of length 2, c_3 cycles of length 3, and so on. The number $Z_{n,C}$ of permutations of n elements with type C equals [62, p.80]

$$Z_{n,C} \;=\; n!\,/\,(c_1!\,c_2!\,c_3!\,\ldots\,c_n!\; 1^{c_1}\,2^{c_2}\,3^{c_3}\,\ldots\,n^{c_n}) \;=\; n!\,/\prod_{k=1}^{n} (c_k!\,k^{c_k}) \tag{11.1-4}$$

We necessarily have $n = 1\,c_1 + 2\,c_2 + \ldots + n\,c_n$, that is, the c_j correspond to an integer partition of n.

The exponential generating function $\exp(L(z))$ where

$$L(z) \;=\; \sum_{k=1}^{\infty} \frac{t_k\, z^k}{k} \tag{11.1-5a}$$

gives detailed information about all cycle types:

$$\exp(L(z)) \;=\; \sum_{n=0}^{\infty} \left[\sum_{C} \left(Z_{n,C} \prod t_k^{c_k} \right) \right] \frac{z^n}{n!} \tag{11.1-5b}$$

That is, the exponent of t_k indicates how many cycles of length k are present in the given cycle type:

```
? n=8;R=O(z^(n+1));
? L=sum(k=1,n,eval(Str("t"k))*z^k/k)+R
  t1*z + 1/2*t2*z^2 + 1/3*t3*z^3 + 1/4*t4*z^4 +   [...]   + 1/8*t8*z^8 + O(z^9)

? serlaplace(exp(L))
  1
+ t1 *z
+ (t1^2 + t2) *z^2
+ (t1^3 + 3*t2*t1 + 2*t3) *z^3
+ (t1^4 + 6*t2*t1^2 + 8*t3*t1 + 3*t2^2 + 6*t4) *z^4
+ (t1^5 + 10*t2*t1^3 + 20*t3*t1^2 + 15*t1*t2^2 + 30*t1*t4 + 20*t3*t2 + 24*t5) *z^5
+ (t1^6 + 15*t2*t1^4 + 40*t3*t1^3 +   [...]   + 15*t2^3 + 90*t4*t2 + 40*t3^2 + 120*t6) *z^6
+ (t1^7 + 21*t2*t1^5 + 70*t3*t1^4 +   [...]   + 504*t5*t2 + 420*t4*t3 + 720*t7) *z^7
+ (t1^8 + 28*t2*t1^6 + 112*t3*t1^5 +   [...]   + 2688*t5*t3 + 1260*t4^2 + 5040*c8) *z^8
+ O(z^9)
```

Relation 11.1-5a is obtained by replacing t_k by $(k-1)!\,t_k$ in relation 17.2-7a on page 359 (for the EGF for set partitions of given type), which takes the order of the elements in each cycle into account.

11.1.3 Prefix conditions

Some types of permutations can be generated efficiently by a routine that produces the lexicographically ordered list of permutations subject to conditions for all prefixes. The implementation (following [215, alg.X, sect.7.2.1.2]) is [FXT: class **perm_restrpref** in comb/perm-restrpref.h]. The condition has to be supplied (as a function pointer) at creation of a class instance. The program [FXT: comb/perm-restrpref-demo.cc] demonstrates the usage, it can be used to generate all involutions, up-down permutations, connected permutations, or derangements, see figure 11.1-B..

```
      involutions                    up-down                      connected                   derangements
   1  :  1   2   3   4          1  :  1   3   2   4          1:   2   3   4   1          1:   2   1   4   3
   2  :  1   2   4   3          2  :  1   4   2   3          2:   2   4   1   3          2:   2   3   4   1
   3  :  1   3   2   4          3  :  2   3   1   4          3:   2   4   3   1          3:   2   4   1   3
   4  :  1   4   3   2          4  :  2   4   1   3          4:   3   1   4   2          4:   3   1   4   2
   5  :  2   1   3   4          5  :  3   4   1   2          5:   3   2   4   1          5:   3   4   1   2
   6  :  2   1   4   3        #perm = 5                      6:   3   4   1   2          6:   3   4   2   1
   7  :  3   2   1   4                                       7:   3   4   2   1          7:   4   1   2   3
   8  :  3   4   1   2                                       8:   4   1   2   3          8:   4   3   1   2
   9  :  4   2   3   1                                       9:   4   1   3   2          9:   4   3   2   1
   1  0  4   3   2   1                                      10:   4   2   1   3        #perm = 9
 #perm = 10                                                11:   4   2   3   1
                                                           12:   4   3   1   2
                                                           13:   4   3   2   1
                                                          #perm = 13
```

Figure 11.1-B: Examples of permutations subject to conditions on prefixes. From left to right: involutions, up-down permutations, connected permutations, and derangements.

11.1.3.1 Involutions

The sequence of numbers of involutions (self-inverse permutations), $I(n)$, starts as ($n \geq 1$)

$$1, \; 2, \; 4, \; 10, \; 26, \; 76, \; 232, \; 764, \; 2620, \; 9496, \; 35696, \; 140152, \; 568504, \; 2390480, \; \ldots$$

This is sequence A000085 in [312]. The first element in an involution can be a fixed point or a 2-cycle with any of the $n-1$ other elements, so

$$I(n) \;=\; I(n-1) + (n-1)\,I(n-2) \tag{11.1-6}$$

```
N=20; v=vector(N); v[1]=1; v[2]=2;
for(n=3,N,v[n]=v[n-1]+(n-1)*v[n-2]);  v  \\ ==  [1, 2, 4, 10, 26, 76, ... ]
```

Let $h_n(x)$ be the polynomial such that the coefficient of x^k gives the number of involutions of n elements with k fixed points. The polynomials can be computed recursively via $h_{n+1} = h_n' + x\,h_n$ (starting with $h_0 = 1$). We have $h_n(1) = I(n)$:

```
? h=1;for(k=1,8,h=(deriv(h)+x*h);print(subst(h,x,1),": ",h))
   1:  x
   2:  x^2 + 1
   4:  x^3 + 3*x
  10:  x^4 + 6*x^2 + 3
  26:  x^5 + 10*x^3 + 15*x
  76:  x^6 + 15*x^4 + 45*x^2 + 15
 232:  x^7 + 21*x^5 + 105*x^3 + 105*x
 764:  x^8 + 28*x^6 + 210*x^4 + 420*x^2 + 105
```

The exponential generating function (EGF) is

$$\sum_{k=0}^{\infty} \frac{I(k)\,x^k}{k!} \;=\; \exp\left(x + x^2/2\right) \tag{11.1-7}$$

We further have (set $c_1 = t$, $c_2 = 1$, and $c_k = 0$ for $k \geq 2$ in 11.1-5a)

$$\sum_{k=0}^{\infty} \frac{h_k(t)\,x^k}{k!} \;=\; \exp\left(t\,x + x^2/2\right) \tag{11.1-8}$$

The EGF for the number permutations whose m-th power is identity is [359, p.85]:

$$\exp\left(\sum_{d\backslash m} x^d/d\right) \tag{11.1-9}$$

The special case $m = 2$ gives relation 11.1-7. The condition function for involutions is

```
1    bool cond_inv(const ulong *a, ulong k)
2    {
```

```
3        ulong ak = a[k];
4        if ( (ak<=k) && (a[ak]!=k) )  return false;
5        return true;
6    }
```

The recurrence 11.1-6 can be generalized for permutations where only cycles of certain lengths are allowed. Set $t_k = 1$ if cycles of length k are allowed, else set $t_k = 0$. The recurrence relation for $P_T(n)$, the number of permutations corresponding to the vector $T = [t_1, t_2, \ldots, t_u]$ is (by relation 11.1-1)

$$P_T(n) \;=\; \sum_{k=1}^{u} t_k \, F\,(n-1, k-1) \, P_T(n-k) \quad \text{where} \tag{11.1-10a}$$

$$F(n-1, e) \;:=\; (n-1)\,(n-2)\,(n-3)\,\ldots\,(n-e+1) \quad \text{and} \quad F(n-1, 0) := 1 \tag{11.1-10b}$$

Initialize by setting $P_T(0) = 1$ and $P_T(n) = 0$ for $n < 0$. For example, if only cycles of length 1 or 3 are allowed ($t_1 = t_3 = 1$, else $t_k = 0$), the recurrence is

$$P(n) \;=\; P(n-1) + (n-1)\,(n-2)\,P(n-3) \tag{11.1-11}$$

The sequence of numbers of these permutations (whose order divides 3) is entry A001470 in [312]:

> 1, 1, 1, 3, 9, 21, 81, 351, 1233, 5769, 31041, 142011, 776601, 4874013, ...

11.1.3.2 Derangements

A permutation is a *derangement* if $a_k \neq k$ for all k:

```
1    bool cond_derange(const ulong *a, ulong k)  { return ( a[k] != k ); }
```

The sequence $D(n)$ of the number of derangements starts as ($n \geq 1$)

> 0, 1, 2, 9, 44, 265, 1854, 14833, 133496, 1334961, 14684570, 176214841, ...

This is sequence A000166 in [312], the *subfactorial numbers*. Compute $D(n)$ using either of

$$D(n) \;=\; (n-1)\,[D(n-1) + D(n-2)] \tag{11.1-12a}$$

$$\;=\; n\,D(n-1) + (-1)^n \tag{11.1-12b}$$

$$\;=\; \sum_{k=0}^{n} (-1)^{n-k} \frac{n!}{(n-k)!} \;=\; n! \sum_{k=0}^{n} \frac{(-1)^k}{k!} \tag{11.1-12c}$$

$$D(n) \;=\; \lfloor (n!+1)/e \rfloor \qquad \text{for} \quad n \geq 1 \tag{11.1-12d}$$

where $e = \exp(1)$. We use the recurrence 11.1-12a:

```
N=20;  v=vector(N);  v[1]=0;  v[2]=1;
for(n=3,N,v[n]=(n-1)*(v[n-1]+v[n-2]));  v  \\ == [0, 1, 2, 9, 44, 265, 1854, 14833, ... ]
```

The exponential generating function can be found by setting $t_1 = 0$ and $t_k = 1$ for $k \neq 1$ in relation 11.1-5a: we have $L(z) = \log\left(1/(1-z)\right) - z$ and

$$\sum_{k=0}^{\infty} \frac{D(n)\, z^n}{n!} \;=\; \exp L(z) \;=\; \frac{\exp(-z)}{1-z} \tag{11.1-13}$$

The number of derangements with prescribed first element is $K(n) := D(n)/(n-1)$, The sequence of values $K(n)$, entry A000255 in [312], starts as

> 1, 1, 3, 11, 53, 309, 2119, 16687, 148329, 1468457, 16019531, 190899411, ...

We have $K(n) = n\,K(n-1) + (n-1)\,K(n-2)$, and $K(n)$ counts the permutations with no occurrence of $[x, x+1]$, see figure 11.1-C. The condition used is

```
1    bool cond_xx1(const ulong *a, ulong k)
2    {
3        if ( k==1 )  return true;
4        return ( a[k-1] != a[k]-1 );  // must look backward
5    }
```

Note that the routine is for the permutations of the elements $1, 2, \ldots, n$ in a one-based array.

```
         no [x, x+1]              derangements with p(1)=2
     1  :1   3   2   4          1:   2   1   4   5   3
     2  :1   4   3   2          2:   2   1   5   3   4
     3  :2   1   4   3          3:   2   3   1   5   4
     4  :2   4   1   3          4:   2   3   4   5   1
     5  :2   4   3   1          5:   2   3   5   1   4
     6  :3   1   4   2          6:   2   4   1   5   3
     7  :3   2   1   4          7:   2   4   5   1   3
     8  :3   2   4   1          8:   2   4   5   3   1
     9  :4   1   3   2          9:   2   5   1   3   4
    1 0 4:  2   1   3         10:   2   5   4   1   3
    1 1 4:  3   2   1         11:   2   5   4   3   1
```

Figure 11.1-C: Permutations of 4 elements with no occurrence of $[x, x + 1]$ (left) and derangements of 5 elements starting with 2.

11.1.3.3 Connected permutations

The *connected* (or *indecomposable*) permutations satisfy, for $k = 0, 1, \ldots, n - 2$, the inequality of sets

$$\{a_0, a_1, \ldots, a_k\} \;\neq\; \{0, 1, \ldots, k\} \tag{11.1-14}$$

That is, there is no prefix of length $< n$ which is a permutation of itself. The condition function is

```
1   ulong N;  // set to n in main()
2   bool cond_indecomp(const ulong *a, ulong k)
3   // indecomposable condition: {a1,...,ak} != {1,...,k} for all k<n
4   {
5       if ( k==N )  return true;
6       for (ulong i=1; i<=k; ++i)  if ( a[i]>k )  return true;
7       return false;
8   }
```

The sequence of numbers $C(n)$ of indecomposable permutations starts as ($n \geq 1$)

  1, 1, 3, 13, 71, 461, 3447, 29093, 273343, 2829325, 31998903, 392743957, ...

This is entry A003319 in [312]. Compute $C(n)$ using

$$C(n) \;=\; n! - \sum_{k=1}^{n-1} k! \, C(n - k) \tag{11.1-15}$$

```
N=20; v=vector(N);
for(n=1,N,v[n]=n!-sum(k=1,n-1,k!*v[n-k]));   v  \\ == [1, 1, 3, 13, 71, 461, 3447, ... ]
```

The ordinary generating function can be given as

$$\sum_{n=1}^{\infty} C(n)\, z^n \;=\; 1 - \frac{1}{\sum_{k=0}^{\infty} k!\, z^k} \;=\; z + z^2 + 3\,z^3 + 13\,z^4 + 71\,z^5 + \ldots \tag{11.1-16}$$

The following recursion (and a Gray code for the connected permutations) is given in [205]:

$$C(n) \;=\; \sum_{k=1}^{n-1} (n - k)\,(k - 1)!\, C(n - k) \tag{11.1-17}$$

11.1.3.4 Alternating permutations

The *alternating permutations* (or *up-down permutations*) satisfy $a_0 < a_1 > a_2 < a_3 > \ldots$. The condition function is

```
1   bool cond_updown(const ulong *a, ulong k)
2   // up-down condition: a1 < a2 > a3 < a4 > ...
3   {
4       if ( k<2 )  return true;
5       if ( (k%2) )  return ( a[k]<a[k-1] );
6       else          return ( a[k]>a[k-1] );
7   }
```

The sequence $A(n)$ of the number of alternating permutations starts as $(n \geq 1)$

    1, 1, 2, 5, 16, 61, 272, 1385, 7936, 50521, 353792, 2702765, 22368256, ...

It is sequence A000111 in [312], the sequence of the *Euler numbers*. The list can be computed using the relation

$$A(n) = \frac{1}{2} \sum_{k=0}^{n-1} \binom{n-1}{k} A(k) A(n-1-k) \qquad (11.1\text{-}18)$$

```
N=20; v=vector(N+1); v[0+1]=1; v[1+1]=1; v[2+1]=1; \\ start with zero: v[x] == A(x-1)
for(n=3,N,v[n+1]=1/2*sum(k=0,n-1,binomial(n-1,k)*v[k+1]*v[n-1-k+1]));  v
  \\ ==  [1, 1, 1, 2, 5, 16, 61, 272, ... ]
```

An exponential generating function is

$$\frac{1 + \sin(z)}{\cos(z)} = \sum_{k=0}^{\infty} \frac{A(k) z^k}{k!} \qquad (11.1\text{-}19)$$

```
? serlaplace((1+sin(z))/cos(z))
  1 + z + z^2 + 2*z^3 + 5*z^4 + 16*z^5 + 61*z^6 + 272*z^7 + 1385*z^8 + 7936*z^9 + ...
```

11.2   Permutations with distance restrictions

We present constructions for Gray codes for permutations with certain restrictions. These are computed from Gray codes of mixed radix numbers with factorial base. We write $p(k)$ for the position of the element k in a given permutation.

11.2.1   Permutations where $p(k) \leq k + 1$

```
            ffact           perm            inv. perm       ffact(inv)
      1 :    . 3 . .    [ 0 4 1 2 3 ]    [ 0 2 3 4 1 ]     . 1 1 1
      2 :    . 2 . .    [ 0 3 1 2 4 ]    [ 0 2 3 1 4 ]     . 1 1 .
      3 :    . 1 . .    [ 0 2 1 3 4 ]    [ 0 2 1 3 4 ]     . 1 . .
      4 :    . 1 . 1    [ 0 2 1 4 3 ]    [ 0 2 1 4 3 ]     . 1 . 1
      5 :    . . . 1    [ 0 1 2 4 3 ]    [ 0 1 2 4 3 ]     . . . 1
      6 :    . . . .    [ 0 1 2 3 4 ]    [ 0 1 2 3 4 ]     . . . .
      7 :    . . 1 .    [ 0 1 3 2 4 ]    [ 0 1 3 2 4 ]     . . 1 .
      8 :    . . 2 .    [ 0 1 4 2 3 ]    [ 0 1 3 4 2 ]     . . 1 1
      9 :    1 . 2 .    [ 1 0 4 2 3 ]    [ 1 0 3 4 2 ]     1 . 1 1
     1 0 :   1 . 1 .    [ 1 0 3 2 4 ]    [ 1 0 3 2 4 ]     1 . 1 .
     1 1 :   1 . . .    [ 1 0 2 3 4 ]    [ 1 0 2 3 4 ]     1 . . .
     1 2 :   1 . . 1    [ 1 0 2 4 3 ]    [ 1 0 2 4 3 ]     1 . . 1
     1 3 :   2 . . 1    [ 2 0 1 4 3 ]    [ 1 2 0 4 3 ]     1 1 . 1
     1 4 :   2 . . .    [ 2 0 1 3 4 ]    [ 1 2 0 3 4 ]     1 1 . .
     1 5 :   3 . . .    [ 3 0 1 2 4 ]    [ 1 2 3 0 4 ]     1 1 1 .
     1 6 :   4 . . .    [ 4 0 1 2 3 ]    [ 1 2 3 4 0 ]     1 1 1 1
```

Figure 11.2-A: Gray code for the permutations of 5 elements where no element lies more than one place to the right of its position in the identical permutation.

Let $M(n)$ be the number of permutations of n elements where no element can move more than one place to the right. We have $M(n) = 2^{n-1}$, see entry A000079 in [312]. A Gray code for these permutations is shown in figure 11.2-A which was created with the program [FXT: comb/perm-right1-gray-demo.cc]. $M(n)$ also counts the permutations that start as a rising sequence (ending in the maximal element) and end as a falling sequence. The list in the leftmost column of figure 11.2-A can be generated by the recursion

```
1    void Y_rec(ulong d, bool z)
2    {
3        if ( d>=n )  visit();
4        else
5        {
6            if ( z )  // forward:
```

```
 7      {
 8              // words 0, 10, 200, 3000, 40000, ...
 9              ulong k = 0;
10              do
11              {
12                  ff[d] = k;
13                  Y_rec(d+k+1, !z);
14              }
15              while ( ++k <= (n-d) );
16          }
17          else       // backward:
18          {
19              // words ..., 40000, 3000, 200, 10, 0
20              ulong k = n-d+1;
21              do
22              {
23                  --k;
24                  ff[d] = k;
25                  Y_rec(d+k+1, !z);
26              }
27              while ( k != 0 );
28          }
29      }
30  }
```

The array `ff` (of length n) must be initialized with zeros and the initial call is `Y_rec(0, true);`. About 85 million words per second are generated. In the inverse permutations (where no element is more than one place left of its original position) the swaps are adjacent and their position is determined by the ruler function. Therefore the inverse permutations can be generated using [FXT: class `ruler_func` in comb/ruler-func.h] which is described in section 8.2.3 on page 207.

11.2.2 Permutations where $k - 1 \leq p(k) \leq k + 1$

```
        ffact            perm                      ffact            perm
  1 : 1 . . 1 . .    [ 1 0 2 4 3 5 6 ]      14:  . . . . . 1    [ 0 1 2 3 4 6 5 ]
  2 : 1 . . 1 . 1    [ 1 0 2 4 3 6 5 ]      15:  . . . 1 . 1    [ 0 1 2 4 3 6 5 ]
  3 : 1 . . . . 1    [ 1 0 2 3 4 6 5 ]      16:  . . . 1 . .    [ 0 1 2 4 3 5 6 ]
  4 : 1 . . . . .    [ 1 0 2 3 4 5 6 ]      17:  . 1 . 1 . .    [ 0 2 1 4 3 5 6 ]
  5 : 1 . . . 1 .    [ 1 0 2 3 5 4 6 ]      18:  . 1 . 1 . 1    [ 0 2 1 4 3 6 5 ]
  6 : 1 . 1 . 1 .    [ 1 0 3 2 5 4 6 ]      19:  . 1 . . . 1    [ 0 2 1 3 4 6 5 ]
  7 : 1 . 1 . . .    [ 1 0 3 2 4 5 6 ]      20:  . 1 . . . .    [ 0 2 1 3 4 5 6 ]
  8 : 1 . 1 . . 1    [ 1 0 3 2 4 6 5 ]      21:  . 1 . . 1 .    [ 0 2 1 3 5 4 6 ]
  9 : . . 1 . . 1    [ 0 1 3 2 4 6 5 ]
1 0 : . . 1 . . .    [ 0 1 3 2 4 5 6 ]
1 1 : . . 1 . 1 .    [ 0 1 3 2 5 4 6 ]
1 2 : . . . . 1 .    [ 0 1 2 3 5 4 6 ]
1 3 : . . . . . .    [ 0 1 2 3 4 5 6 ]
```

Figure 11.2-B: Gray code for the permutations of 7 elements where no element lies more than one place away from its position in the identical permutation. The permutations are self-inverse.

Let $F(n)$ the number of permutations of n elements where no element can move more than one place to the left. Then $F(n)$ is the $(n + 1)$-st Fibonacci number. A Gray code for these permutations is shown in figure 11.2-B which was created with the program [FXT: comb/perm-dist1-gray-demo.cc].

11.2.3 Permutations where $k - 1 \leq p(k) \leq k + d$

A Gray code for the permutations where no element lies more than one place to the left or d places to the right of its original position can be generated using the Gray codes for binary words with at most d consecutive ones given in section 14.3 on page 307. Figure 11.2-C shows the permutations of 6 elements with $d = 2$. It was created with the program [FXT: comb/perm-l1r2-gray-demo.cc]. The array shown leftmost in figure 11.2-C can be generated via the recursion

```
1   void Y_rec(ulong d, bool z)
2   {
3       if ( d>=n )  visit();
4       else
5       {
6           const ulong w = n-d;
```

```
              ffact              perm              inv. perm          ffact(inv)
      1 :   1 1 . . 1      [ 1 2 0 3 5 4 ]    [ 2 0 1 3 5 4 ]    2 . . . . 1
      2 :   1 1 . . .      [ 1 2 0 3 4 5 ]    [ 2 0 1 3 4 5 ]    2 . . . . .
      3 :   1 1 . 1 .      [ 1 2 0 4 3 5 ]    [ 2 0 1 4 3 5 ]    2 . . 1 . .
      4 :   1 1 . 1 1      [ 1 2 0 4 5 3 ]    [ 2 0 1 5 3 4 ]    2 . . 2 . .
      5 :   1 . . 1 1      [ 1 0 2 4 5 3 ]    [ 1 0 2 5 3 4 ]    1 . . 2 . .
      6 :   1 . . 1 .      [ 1 0 2 4 3 5 ]    [ 1 0 2 4 3 5 ]    1 . . 1 . .
      7 :   1 . . . .      [ 1 0 2 3 4 5 ]    [ 1 0 2 3 4 5 ]    1 . . . . .
      8 :   1 . . . 1      [ 1 0 2 3 5 4 ]    [ 1 0 2 3 5 4 ]    1 . . . . 1
      9 :   1 . 1 . 1      [ 1 0 3 2 5 4 ]    [ 1 0 3 2 5 4 ]    1 . 1 . . 1
   1 0 :   1 . 1 . .      [ 1 0 3 2 4 5 ]    [ 1 0 3 2 4 5 ]    1 . 1 . . .
   1 1 :   1 . 1 1 .      [ 1 0 3 4 2 5 ]    [ 1 0 4 2 3 5 ]    1 . 2 . . .
   1 2 :   . . 1 1 .      [ 0 1 3 4 2 5 ]    [ 0 1 4 2 3 5 ]    . . 2 . . .
   1 3 :   . . 1 . .      [ 0 1 3 2 4 5 ]    [ 0 1 3 2 4 5 ]    . . 1 . . .
   1 4 :   . . 1 . 1      [ 0 1 3 2 5 4 ]    [ 0 1 3 2 5 4 ]    . . 1 . . 1
   1 5 :   . . . . 1      [ 0 1 2 3 5 4 ]    [ 0 1 2 3 5 4 ]    . . . . . 1
   1 6 :   . . . . .      [ 0 1 2 3 4 5 ]    [ 0 1 2 3 4 5 ]    . . . . . .
   1 7 :   . . . 1 .      [ 0 1 2 4 3 5 ]    [ 0 1 2 4 3 5 ]    . . . 1 . .
   1 8 :   . . . 1 1      [ 0 1 2 4 5 3 ]    [ 0 1 2 5 3 4 ]    . . . 2 . .
   1 9 :   . 1 . 1 1      [ 0 2 1 4 5 3 ]    [ 0 2 1 5 3 4 ]    . 1 . 2 . .
   2 0 :   . 1 . 1 .      [ 0 2 1 4 3 5 ]    [ 0 2 1 4 3 5 ]    . 1 . 1 . .
   2 1 :   . 1 . . .      [ 0 2 1 3 4 5 ]    [ 0 2 1 3 4 5 ]    . 1 . . . .
   2 2 :   . 1 . . 1      [ 0 2 1 3 5 4 ]    [ 0 2 1 3 5 4 ]    . 1 . . . 1
   2 3 :   . 1 1 . 1      [ 0 2 3 1 5 4 ]    [ 0 3 1 2 5 4 ]    . 2 . . . 1
   2 4 :   . 1 1 . .      [ 0 2 3 1 4 5 ]    [ 0 3 1 2 4 5 ]    . 2 . . . .
```

Figure 11.2-C: Gray code for the permutations of 6 elements where no element lies more than one place to the left or two places to the right of its position in the identical permutation.

```
 7       if ( z )
 8       {
 9           if ( w>1 )  { ff[d]=1; ff[d+1]=1; ff[d+2]=0;  Y_rec(d+3, !z); }
10           ff[d]=1; ff[d+1]=0;  Y_rec(d+2, !z);
11           ff[d]=0;  Y_rec(d+1, !z);
12       }
13       else
14       {
15           ff[d]=0;  Y_rec(d+1, !z);
16           ff[d]=1; ff[d+1]=0;  Y_rec(d+2, !z);
17           if ( w>1 )  { ff[d]=1; ff[d+1]=1; ff[d+2]=0; Y_rec(d+3, !z); }
18       }
19   }
20   }
```

If the two lines starting with `if ( w>1 )` are omitted, the Fibonacci words are computed. About 100 million words per second are generated.

11.3 Self-inverse permutations (involutions)

```
        0 :  [ . 1 2 3 4 ]        1 3 : [ 3 4 2 . 1 ]
        1 :  [ . 1 2 4 3 ]        1 4 : [ . 2 1 3 4 ]
        2 :  [ . 1 4 3 2 ]        1 5 : [ . 2 1 4 3 ]
        3 :  [ . 4 2 3 1 ]        1 6 : [ 4 2 1 3 . ]
        4 :  [ 4 1 2 3 . ]        1 7 : [ 3 2 1 . 4 ]
        5 :  [ . 1 3 2 4 ]        1 8 : [ 2 1 . 3 4 ]
        6 :  [ . 4 3 2 1 ]        1 9 : [ 2 1 . 4 3 ]
        7 :  [ 4 1 3 2 . ]        2 0 : [ 2 4 . 3 1 ]
        8 :  [ . 3 2 1 4 ]        2 1 : [ 2 3 . 1 4 ]
        9 :  [ . 3 4 1 2 ]        2 2 : [ 1 . 2 3 4 ]
     1 0 : [ 4 3 2 1 . ]          2 3 : [ 1 . 2 4 3 ]
     1 1 : [ 3 1 2 . 4 ]          2 4 : [ 1 . 4 3 2 ]
     1 2 : [ 3 1 4 . 2 ]          2 5 : [ 1 . 3 2 4 ]
```

Figure 11.3-A: All self-inverse permutations of 5 elements.

An involution is a self-inverse permutation (see section 2.3.1 on page 106). The involutions of 5 elements are shown in figure 11.3-A. To generate all involutions, use [FXT: class **perm_involution** in comb/perm-involution.h]:

```
1    class perm_involution
2    {
3    public:
4        ulong *p_;   // self-inverse permutation in 0, 1, ..., n-1
5        ulong n_;    // number of elements to permute
6
7    public:
8        perm_involution(ulong n)
9        {
10           n_ = n;
11           p_ = new ulong[n_];
12           first();
13       }
14
15       ~perm_involution()  { delete [] p_; }
16       void first()  { for (ulong i=0; i<n_; i++)  p_[i] = i; }
17       const ulong * data()  const  { return p_; }
```

The successor of a permutation is computed as follows:

```
1        bool next()
2        {
3            for (ulong j=n_-1; j!=0; --j)
4            {
5                ulong ip = p_[j];   // inverse perm == perm
6                p_[j] = j;  p_[ip] = ip;  // undo prior swap
7                while ( (long)(--ip)>=0 )
8                {
9                    if ( p_[ip]==ip )
10                   {
11                       p_[j] = ip;  p_[ip] = j;  // swap2(p_[j], p_[ip]);
12                       return true;
13                   }
14               }
15           }
16           return false;  // current permutation is last
17       }
18   [--snip--]
19   };
```

The rate of generation is about 50 million per second [FXT: comb/perm-involution-demo.cc].

11.4   Cyclic permutations

Cyclic permutations consist of exactly one cycle of full length, see section 2.2.1 on page 105.

11.4.1   Recursive algorithm for cyclic permutations

A simple recursive algorithm for the generation of all (not only cyclic!) permutations of n elements can be described as follows: Put each of the n elements of the array to the first position and generate all permutations of the remaining $n - 1$ elements. If $n = 1$, print the permutation.

The generated order is shown in figure 11.4-A, it corresponds to the alternative (swaps) factorial representation with falling base, given in section 10.1.4 on page 239.

The algorithm is implemented in [FXT: class perm_rec in comb/perm-rec.h]:

```
1    class perm_rec
2    {
3    public:
4        ulong *x_;   // permutation
5        ulong n_;    // number of elements
6        void (*visit_)(const perm_lex_rec &);  // function to call with each permutation
7
8    public:
9        perm_rec(ulong n)
10       {
11           n_ = n;
12           x_ = new ulong[n_];
```

```
                permutation        inverse         ffact-swp
     0 :     [ . 1 2 3 ]      [ . 1 2 3 ]      [ . . . ]
     1 :     [ . 1 3 2 ]      [ . 1 3 2 ]      [ . . 1 ]
     2 :     [ . 2 1 3 ]      [ . 2 1 3 ]      [ . 1 . ]
     3 :     [ . 2 3 1 ]      [ . 3 1 2 ]      [ . 1 1 ]
     4 :     [ . 3 2 1 ]      [ . 3 2 1 ]      [ . 2 . ]
     5 :     [ . 3 1 2 ]      [ . 2 3 1 ]      [ . 2 1 ]
     6 :     [ 1 . 2 3 ]      [ 1 . 2 3 ]      [ 1 . . ]
     7 :     [ 1 . 3 2 ]      [ 1 . 3 2 ]      [ 1 . 1 ]
     8 :     [ 1 2 . 3 ]      [ 2 . 1 3 ]      [ 1 1 . ]
     9 :     [ 1 2 3 . ]      [ 3 . 1 2 ]      [ 1 1 1 ]
   1 0 :     [ 1 3 2 . ]      [ 3 . 2 1 ]      [ 1 2 . ]
   1 1 :     [ 1 3 . 2 ]      [ 2 . 3 1 ]      [ 1 2 1 ]
   1 2 :     [ 2 1 . 3 ]      [ 2 1 . 3 ]      [ 2 . . ]
   1 3 :     [ 2 1 3 . ]      [ 3 1 . 2 ]      [ 2 . 1 ]
   1 4 :     [ 2 . 1 3 ]      [ 1 2 . 3 ]      [ 2 1 . ]
   1 5 :     [ 2 . 3 1 ]      [ 1 3 . 2 ]      [ 2 1 1 ]
   1 6 :     [ 2 3 . 1 ]      [ 2 3 . 1 ]      [ 2 2 . ]
   1 7 :     [ 2 3 1 . ]      [ 3 2 . 1 ]      [ 2 2 1 ]
   1 8 :     [ 3 1 2 . ]      [ 3 1 2 . ]      [ 3 . . ]
   1 9 :     [ 3 1 . 2 ]      [ 2 1 3 . ]      [ 3 . 1 ]
   2 0 :     [ 3 2 1 . ]      [ 3 2 1 . ]      [ 3 1 . ]
   2 1 :     [ 3 2 . 1 ]      [ 2 3 1 . ]      [ 3 1 1 ]
   2 2 :     [ 3 . 2 1 ]      [ 1 3 2 . ]      [ 3 2 . ]
   2 3 :     [ 3 . 1 2 ]      [ 1 2 3 . ]      [ 3 2 1 ]
```

Figure 11.4-A: All permutations of 4 elements (left) and their inverses (middle), and their (swaps) representations as mixed radix numbers with falling factorial base. Permutations with common prefixes appear in succession. Dots denote zeros.

```
13        }
14
15        ~perm_rec()
16        { delete [] x_; }
17
18        void init()
19        {
20            for (ulong k=0; k<n_; ++k)  x_[k] = k;
21        }
22
23        void generate(void (*visit)(const perm_lex_rec &))
24        {
25            visit_ = visit;
26            init();
27            next_rec(0);
28        }
```

The recursive function `next_rec()` is

```
1        void next_rec(ulong d)
2        {
3            if ( d==n_-1 )  visit_(*this);
4            else
5            {
6                const ulong pd = x_[d];
7                for (ulong k=d; k<n_; ++k)
8                {
9
10                   ulong px = x_[k];
11                   x_[k] = pd;  x_[d] = px;   // =^= swap2(x_[d], x_[k]);
12                   next_rec(d+1);
13                   x_[k] = px;  x_[d] = pd;   // =^= swap2(x_[d], x_[k]);
14               }
15           }
16       }
```

The algorithm works because at each recursive call the elements x[d],...,x[n-1] are in a different order and when the function returns the elements are in the same order as they were initially. With the for-statement changed to

```
        for (ulong x=n_-1; (long)x>=(long)d; --x)
```

the permutations would appear in reversed order. Changing the loop in the function `next_rec()` to

```
            for (ulong k=d; k<n_; ++k)
            {
                swap2(x_[d], x_[k]);
                next_rec(d+1, qq);
            }
            rotate_left1(x_+d, n_-d);
```

produces lexicographic order.

```
          permutation            cycle              inverse          ffact-swp
  0 :   [ 1 2 3 4 . ]      (0 ,1 ,2 ,3 ,4)      [ 4 . 1 2 3 ]      [ 1 1 1 1 ]
  1 :   [ 1 2 4 . 3 ]      (0 ,1 ,2 ,4 ,3)      [ 3 . 1 4 2 ]      [ 1 1 2 1 ]
  2 :   [ 1 3 . 4 2 ]      (0 ,1 ,3 ,4 ,2)      [ 2 . 4 1 3 ]      [ 1 2 1 1 ]
  3 :   [ 1 3 4 2 . ]      (0 ,1 ,3 ,2 ,4)      [ 4 . 3 1 2 ]      [ 1 2 2 1 ]
  4 :   [ 1 4 3 . 2 ]      (0 ,1 ,4 ,2 ,3)      [ 3 . 4 2 1 ]      [ 1 3 1 1 ]
  5 :   [ 1 4 . 2 3 ]      (0 ,1 ,4 ,3 ,2)      [ 2 . 3 4 1 ]      [ 1 3 2 1 ]
  6 :   [ 2 . 3 4 1 ]      (0 ,2 ,3 ,4 ,1)      [ 1 4 . 2 3 ]      [ 2 1 1 1 ]
  7 :   [ 2 . 4 1 3 ]      (0 ,2 ,4 ,3 ,1)      [ 1 3 . 4 2 ]      [ 2 1 2 1 ]
  8 :   [ 2 3 1 4 . ]      (0 ,2 ,1 ,3 ,4)      [ 4 2 . 1 3 ]      [ 2 2 1 1 ]
  9 :   [ 2 3 4 . 1 ]      (0 ,2 ,4 ,1 ,3)      [ 3 4 . 1 2 ]      [ 2 2 2 1 ]
 1 0 :  [ 2 4 3 1 . ]      ( 0 2 ,3 ,1 ,4)      [ 4 3 . 2 1 ]      [ 2 3 1 1 ]
 1 1 :  [ 2 4 1 . 3 ]      ( 0 2 ,1 ,4 ,3)      [ 3 2 . 4 1 ]      [ 2 3 2 1 ]
 1 2 :  [ 3 2 . 4 1 ]      ( 0 3 ,4 ,1 ,2)      [ 2 4 1 . 3 ]      [ 3 1 1 1 ]
 1 3 :  [ 3 2 4 1 . ]      ( 0 3 ,1 ,2 ,4)      [ 4 3 1 . 2 ]      [ 3 1 2 1 ]
 1 4 :  [ 3 . 1 4 2 ]      ( 0 3 ,4 ,2 ,1)      [ 1 2 4 . 3 ]      [ 3 2 1 1 ]
 1 5 :  [ 3 . 4 2 1 ]      ( 0 3 ,2 ,4 ,1)      [ 1 4 3 . 2 ]      [ 3 2 2 1 ]
 1 6 :  [ 3 4 . 1 2 ]      ( 0 3 ,1 ,4 ,2)      [ 2 3 4 . 1 ]      [ 3 3 1 1 ]
 1 7 :  [ 3 4 1 2 . ]      ( 0 3 ,2 ,1 ,4)      [ 4 2 3 . 1 ]      [ 3 3 2 1 ]
 1 8 :  [ 4 2 3 . 1 ]      ( 0 4 ,1 ,2 ,3)      [ 3 4 1 2 . ]      [ 4 1 1 1 ]
 1 9 :  [ 4 2 . 1 3 ]      ( 0 4 ,3 ,1 ,2)      [ 2 3 1 4 . ]      [ 4 1 2 1 ]
 2 0 :  [ 4 3 1 . 2 ]      ( 0 4 ,2 ,1 ,3)      [ 3 2 4 1 . ]      [ 4 2 1 1 ]
 2 1 :  [ 4 3 . 2 1 ]      ( 0 4 ,1 ,3 ,2)      [ 2 4 3 1 . ]      [ 4 2 2 1 ]
 2 2 :  [ 4 . 3 1 2 ]      ( 0 4 ,2 ,3 ,1)      [ 1 3 4 2 . ]      [ 4 3 1 1 ]
 2 3 :  [ 4 . 1 2 3 ]      ( 0 4 ,3 ,2 ,1)      [ 1 2 3 4 . ]      [ 4 3 2 1 ]
```

Figure 11.4-B: All cyclic permutations of 5 elements and the permutations as cycles, their inverses, and their (swaps) representations as mixed radix numbers with falling factorial base (from left to right).

A modified function generates the cyclic permutations. We skip the case $x = d$ in the loop:

```
        for (ulong k=d+1; k<n_; ++k)  // omit k==d
```

The cyclic permutations of five elements are shown in figure 11.4-B. The program [FXT: comb/perm-rec-demo.cc] was used to create the figures in this section.

```
void visit(const perm_rec &P)  // function to call with each permutation
{
    // Print the permutation
}
int
main(int argc, char **argv)
{
    ulong n = 5;  // Number of elements to permute
    bool cq = 1;  // Whether to generate only cyclic permutations
    perm_rec P(n);
    if ( cq )  P.generate_cyclic(visit);
    else       P.generate(visit);
    return 0;
}
```

The routines generate about 57 million permutations and about 37 million cyclic permutations per second.

11.4.2 Minimal-change order for cyclic permutations

All cyclic permutations can be generated from a mixed radix Gray code with falling factorial base (see section 9.2 on page 220). Two successive permutations differ at three positions as shown in figure 11.4-C. A constant amortized time (CAT) implementation is [FXT: class cyclic_perm in comb/cyclic-perm.h]:

```
                    permutation        fact.num.              cycle
          0 :      [ 4 0 1 2 3 ]      [ . . . ]         (4, 3, 2, 1, 0)
          1 :      [ 3 4 1 2 0 ]      [ 1 . . ]         (4, 0, 3, 2, 1)
          2 :      [ 3 0 4 2 1 ]      [ 2 . . ]         (4, 1, 0, 3, 2)
          3 :      [ 3 0 1 4 2 ]      [ 3 . . ]         (4, 2, 1, 0, 3)
          4 :      [ 2 3 1 4 0 ]      [ 3 1 . ]         (4, 0, 2, 1, 3)
          5 :      [ 2 3 4 0 1 ]      [ 2 1 . ]         (4, 1, 3, 0, 2)
          6 :      [ 2 4 1 0 3 ]      [ 1 1 . ]         (4, 3, 0, 2, 1)
          7 :      [ 4 3 1 0 2 ]      [ . 1 . ]         (4, 2, 1, 3, 0)
          8 :      [ 4 0 3 1 2 ]      [ . 2 . ]         (4, 2, 3, 1, 0)
          9 :      [ 2 4 3 1 0 ]      [ 1 2 . ]         (4, 0, 2, 3, 1)
        1 0 :      [ 2 0 4 1 3 ]      [ 2 2 . ]         (4, 3, 1, 0, 2)
        1 1 :      [ 2 0 3 4 1 ]      [ 3 2 . ]         (4, 1, 0, 2, 3)
        1 2 :      [ 1 2 3 4 0 ]      [ 3 2 1 ]         (4, 0, 1, 2, 3)
        1 3 :      [ 1 2 4 0 3 ]      [ 2 2 1 ]         (4, 3, 0, 1, 2)
        1 4 :      [ 1 4 3 0 2 ]      [ 1 2 1 ]         (4, 2, 3, 0, 1)
        1 5 :      [ 4 2 3 0 1 ]      [ . 2 1 ]         (4, 1, 2, 3, 0)
        1 6 :      [ 4 3 0 2 1 ]      [ . 1 1 ]         (4, 1, 3, 2, 0)
        1 7 :      [ 1 4 0 2 3 ]      [ 1 1 1 ]         (4, 3, 2, 0, 1)
        1 8 :      [ 1 3 4 2 0 ]      [ 2 1 1 ]         (4, 0, 1, 3, 2)
        1 9 :      [ 1 3 0 4 2 ]      [ 3 1 1 ]         (4, 2, 0, 1, 3)
        2 0 :      [ 3 2 0 4 1 ]      [ 3 . 1 ]         (4, 1, 2, 0, 3)
        2 1 :      [ 3 2 4 1 0 ]      [ 2 . 1 ]         (4, 0, 3, 1, 2)
        2 2 :      [ 3 4 0 1 2 ]      [ 1 . 1 ]         (4, 2, 0, 3, 1)
        2 3 :      [ 4 2 0 1 3 ]      [ . . 1 ]         (4, 3, 1, 2, 0)
```

Figure 11.4-C: All cyclic permutations of 5 elements in a minimal-change order.

```
1    class cyclic_perm
2    {
3    public:
4        mixedradix_gray *M_;
5        ulong n_;    // number of elements to permute
6        ulong *ix_;  // current permutation (of {0, 1, ..., n-1})
7        ulong *x_;   // inverse permutation
8
9    public:
10       cyclic_perm(ulong n)
11           : n_(n)
12       {
13           ix_ = new ulong[n_];
14           x_ = new ulong[n_];
15           M_ = new mixedradix_gray(n_-2, 0);  // falling factorial base
16           first();
17       }
18    [--snip--]
```

The computation of the successor uses the position and direction of the mixed radix digit changed with the last increment:

```
1    private:
2        void setup()
3        {
4            const ulong *fc = M_->data();
5            for (ulong k=0; k<n_; ++k)  ix_[k] = k;
6
7            for (ulong k=n_-1; k>1; --k)
8            {
9                ulong z = n_-3-(k-2); // 0, ..., n-3
10               ulong i = fc[z];
11               swap2(ix_[k], ix_[i]);
12           }
13           if ( n_>1 )  swap2(ix_[0], ix_[1]);
14
15           make_inverse(ix_, x_, n_);
16       }
17
18    public:
19       void first()
20       {
21           M_->first();
```

```
22          setup();
23      }
24
25      bool next()
26      {
27          if ( false == M_->next() )  { first();  return false; }
28          ulong j = M_->pos();
29
30          if ( j && (x_[0]==n_-1) )  // once in 2*n cases
31          {
32              setup();  // work proportional to n
33              // only 3 elements are interchanged
34          }
35          else  // easy case
36          {
37              int d = M_->dir();
38              ulong x2 = (M_->data())[j];
39              ulong x1 = x2 - d,  x3 = n_-1;
40              ulong i1 = x_[x1], i2 = x_[x2], i3 = x_[x3];
41
42              swap2(x_[x1], x_[x2]);
43              swap2(x_[x1], x_[x3]);
44              swap2(ix_[i1], ix_[i2]);
45              swap2(ix_[i2], ix_[i3]);
46          }
47
48          return true;
49      }
50  [--snip--]
```

The listing in figure 11.4-C was created with the program [FXT: comb/cyclic-perm-demo.cc]. About 58 million permutations per second are generated.

11.4.3   Cyclic permutations from factorial numbers

falling fact.	permutation	cycle	inv.perm.
[. . .]	[1 2 3 4 0]	(0, 1, 2, 3, 4)	[4 0 1 2 3]
[1 . .]	[4 2 3 0 1]	(0, 4, 1, 2, 3)	[3 4 1 2 0]
[2 . .]	[1 4 3 0 2]	(0, 1, 4, 2, 3)	[3 0 4 2 1]
[3 . .]	[1 2 4 0 3]	(0, 1, 2, 4, 3)	[3 0 1 4 2]
[. 1 .]	[3 2 4 1 0]	(0, 3, 1, 2, 4)	[4 3 1 0 2]
[1 1 .]	[3 2 0 4 1]	(0, 3, 4, 1, 2)	[2 4 1 0 3]
[2 1 .]	[3 4 0 1 2]	(0, 3, 1, 4, 2)	[2 3 4 0 1]
[3 1 .]	[4 2 0 1 3]	(0, 4, 3, 1, 2)	[2 3 1 4 0]
[. 2 .]	[1 3 4 2 0]	(0, 1, 3, 2, 4)	[4 0 3 1 2]
[1 2 .]	[4 3 0 2 1]	(0, 4, 1, 3, 2)	[2 4 3 1 0]
[2 2 .]	[1 3 0 4 2]	(0, 1, 3, 4, 2)	[2 0 4 1 3]
[3 2 .]	[1 4 0 2 3]	(0, 1, 4, 3, 2)	[2 0 3 4 1]
[. . 1]	[2 3 1 4 0]	(0, 2, 1, 3, 4)	[4 2 0 1 3]
[1 . 1]	[2 3 4 0 1]	(0, 2, 4, 1, 3)	[3 4 0 1 2]
[2 . 1]	[4 3 1 0 2]	(0, 4, 2, 1, 3)	[3 2 4 1 0]
[3 . 1]	[2 4 1 0 3]	(0, 2, 1, 4, 3)	[3 2 0 4 1]
[. 1 1]	[2 4 3 1 0]	(0, 2, 3, 1, 4)	[4 3 0 2 1]
[1 1 1]	[2 0 3 4 1]	(0, 2, 3, 4, 1)	[1 4 0 2 3]
[2 1 1]	[4 0 3 1 2]	(0, 4, 2, 3, 1)	[1 3 4 2 0]
[3 1 1]	[2 0 4 1 3]	(0, 2, 4, 3, 1)	[1 3 0 4 2]
[. 2 1]	[3 4 1 2 0]	(0, 3, 2, 1, 4)	[4 2 3 0 1]
[1 2 1]	[3 0 4 2 1]	(0, 3, 2, 4, 1)	[1 4 3 0 2]
[2 2 1]	[3 0 1 4 2]	(0, 3, 4, 2, 1)	[1 2 4 0 3]
[3 2 1]	[4 0 1 2 3]	(0, 4, 3, 2, 1)	[1 2 3 4 0]

Figure 11.4-D: Numbers in falling factorial base and the corresponding cyclic permutations.

The cyclic permutations of n elements can be computed from length-$(n-2)$ factorial numbers. We give routines for both falling and rising base [FXT: comb/fact2cyclic.cc]:

```
1   void ffact2cyclic(const ulong *fc, ulong n, ulong *x)
2   // Generate cyclic permutation in x[]
3   //   from the (n-2) digit factorial number in fc[0,...,n-3].
4   // Falling radices:  [n-1, ..., 3, 2]
```

rising fact.	permutation	cycle	inv.perm.
[. . .]	[1 2 3 4 0]	(0 1, 2, 3, 4)	[4 0 1 2 3]
[1 . .]	[2 3 1 4 0]	(0 2, 1, 3, 4)	[4 2 0 1 3]
[. 1 .]	[3 2 4 1 0]	(0 3, 1, 2, 4)	[4 3 1 0 2]
[1 1 .]	[2 4 3 1 0]	(0 2, 3, 1, 4)	[4 3 0 2 1]
[. 2 .]	[1 3 4 2 0]	(0 1, 3, 2, 4)	[4 0 3 1 2]
[1 2 .]	[3 4 1 2 0]	(0 3, 2, 1, 4)	[4 2 3 0 1]
[. . 1]	[4 2 3 0 1]	(0 4, 1, 2, 3)	[3 4 1 2 0]
[1 . 1]	[2 3 4 0 1]	(0 2, 4, 1, 3)	[3 4 0 1 2]
[. 1 1]	[3 2 0 4 1]	(0 3, 4, 1, 2)	[2 4 1 0 3]
[1 1 1]	[2 0 3 4 1]	(0 2, 3, 4, 1)	[1 4 0 2 3]
[. 2 1]	[4 3 0 2 1]	(0 4, 1, 3, 2)	[2 4 3 1 0]
[1 2 1]	[3 0 4 2 1]	(0 3, 2, 4, 1)	[1 4 3 0 2]
[. . 2]	[1 4 3 0 2]	(0 1, 4, 2, 3)	[3 0 4 2 1]
[1 . 2]	[4 3 1 0 2]	(0 4, 2, 1, 3)	[3 2 4 1 0]
[. 1 2]	[3 4 0 1 2]	(0 3, 1, 4, 2)	[2 3 4 0 1]
[1 1 2]	[4 0 3 1 2]	(0 4, 2, 3, 1)	[1 3 4 2 0]
[. 2 2]	[1 3 0 4 2]	(0 1, 3, 4, 2)	[2 0 4 1 3]
[1 2 2]	[3 0 1 4 2]	(0 3, 4, 2, 1)	[1 2 4 0 3]
[. . 3]	[1 2 4 0 3]	(0 1, 2, 4, 3)	[3 0 1 4 2]
[1 . 3]	[2 4 1 0 3]	(0 2, 1, 4, 3)	[3 2 0 4 1]
[. 1 3]	[4 2 0 1 3]	(0 4, 3, 1, 2)	[2 3 1 4 0]
[1 1 3]	[2 0 4 1 3]	(0 2, 4, 3, 1)	[1 3 0 4 2]
[. 2 3]	[1 4 0 2 3]	(0 1, 4, 3, 2)	[2 0 3 4 1]
[1 2 3]	[4 0 1 2 3]	(0 4, 3, 2, 1)	[1 2 3 4 0]

Figure 11.4-E: Numbers in rising factorial base and corresponding cyclic permutations.

```
5   {
6       for (ulong k=0; k<n; ++k)  x[k] = k;
7
8       for (ulong k=n-1; k>1; --k)
9       {
10          ulong z = n-1-k; // 0, ..., n-3
11          ulong i = fc[z];
12          swap2(x[k], x[i]);
13      }
14
15      if ( n>1 )  swap2(x[0], x[1]);
16  }
```

```
1   void rfact2cyclic(const ulong *fc, ulong n, ulong *x)
2   // Rising radices:   [2, 3, ..., n-1]
3   {
4       for (ulong k=0; k<n; ++k)  x[k] = k;
5
6       for (ulong k=n-1; k>1; --k)
7       {
8           ulong i = fc[k-2];   // k-2 == n-3, ..., 0
9           swap2(x[k], x[i]);
10      }
11
12      if ( n>1 )  swap2(x[0], x[1]);
13  }
```

The cyclic permutations of 5 elements are shown in figures 11.4-D (falling base) and 11.4-E (rising base). The listings were created with the program [FXT: comb/fact2cyclic-demo.cc].

The cycle representation could be computed by applying the transformations in (all) permutations to all but the first element. That is, we can generate all cyclic permutations in cycle form by permuting all elements but the first with any permutation algorithm.

Chapter 12

k-permutations

```
            ffact. num.          permutation
   0 :  [ . . . . . ]     [ .  1 ] [2 3 4 5 ]
   1 :  [ 1 . . . . ]     [ 1  . ] [2 3 4 5 ]
   2 :  [ 2 . . . . ]     [ 2  . ] [1 3 4 5 ]
   3 :  [ 3 . . . . ]     [ 3  . ] [1 2 4 5 ]
   4 :  [ 4 . . . . ]     [ 4  . ] [1 2 3 5 ]
   5 :  [ 5 . . . . ]     [ 5  . ] [1 2 3 4 ]
   6 :  [ . 1 . . . ]     [ .  2 ] [1 3 4 5 ]
   7 :  [ 1 1 . . . ]     [ 1  2 ] [. 3 4 5 ]
   8 :  [ 2 1 . . . ]     [ 2  1 ] [. 3 4 5 ]
   9 :  [ 3 1 . . . ]     [ 3  1 ] [. 2 4 5 ]
 1 0 :  [ 4 1 . . . ]     [ 4  1 ] [. 2 3 5 ]
 1 1 :  [ 5 1 . . . ]     [ 5  1 ] [. 2 3 4 ]
 1 2 :  [ . 2 . . . ]     [ .  3 ] [1 2 4 5 ]
 1 3 :  [ 1 2 . . . ]     [ 1  3 ] [. 2 4 5 ]
 1 4 :  [ 2 2 . . . ]     [ 2  3 ] [. 1 4 5 ]
 1 5 :  [ 3 2 . . . ]     [ 3  2 ] [. 1 4 5 ]
 1 6 :  [ 4 2 . . . ]     [ 4  2 ] [. 1 3 5 ]
 1 7 :  [ 5 2 . . . ]     [ 5  2 ] [. 1 3 4 ]
 1 8 :  [ . 3 . . . ]     [ .  4 ] [1 2 3 5 ]
 1 9 :  [ 1 3 . . . ]     [ 1  4 ] [. 2 3 5 ]
 2 0 :  [ 2 3 . . . ]     [ 2  4 ] [. 1 3 5 ]
 2 1 :  [ 3 3 . . . ]     [ 3  4 ] [. 1 2 5 ]
 2 2 :  [ 4 3 . . . ]     [ 4  3 ] [. 1 2 5 ]
 2 3 :  [ 5 3 . . . ]     [ 5  3 ] [. 1 2 4 ]
 2 4 :  [ . 4 . . . ]     [ .  5 ] [1 2 3 4 ]
 2 5 :  [ 1 4 . . . ]     [ 1  5 ] [. 2 3 4 ]
 2 6 :  [ 2 4 . . . ]     [ 2  5 ] [. 1 3 4 ]
 2 7 :  [ 3 4 . . . ]     [ 3  5 ] [. 1 2 4 ]
 2 8 :  [ 4 4 . . . ]     [ 4  5 ] [. 1 2 3 ]
 2 9 :  [ 5 4 . . . ]     [ 5  4 ] [. 1 2 3 ]
```

Figure 12.0-A: The falling factorial numbers with $n-1$ digits where only k leading digits can be nonzero correspond to the k-permutations of n elements (here $n = 6$ and $k = 2$).

The length-k prefixes of the permutations of n elements are called k-*permutations*. The 2-permutations of 6 elements are shown in figure 12.0-A. We have n choices for the first element, $n - 1$ for the second, and so on. Therefore the number of the k-permutations of n elements is

$$n\,(n - 1)\,(n - 1)\,\dots\,(n - k + 1) \;=\; n^{\underline{k}} \;=\; \binom{n}{k}\,k! \tag{12.0-1}$$

The second equality shows that the k-permutations could be generated by listing all k-subsets of the n-set (combinations $\binom{n}{k}$), each in $k!$ orderings. The expression as falling factorial power shows that the k-permutations correspond to the falling factorial numbers where only the first k digits can be nonzero: the permutations in figure 12.0-A are obtained by converting the left column (as inversion table) into a permutation (by the routine `ffact2perm()` described in section 10.1.1 on page 232). This is done in the program [FXT: comb/ffact2kperm-demo.cc] which was used to create the figure.

J. Arndt, *Matters Computational: Ideas, Algorithms, Source Code,*
DOI 10.1007/978-3-642-14764-7_12, © Springer-Verlag Berlin Heidelberg 2011

```
               permutation              ffact                inv. perm.
    1 :    [  . 1 ] [2 3 4 5 ]    [ . . . . . ]      [ . 1 2 3 4 5 ]
    2 :    [  . 2 ] [1 3 4 5 ]    [ . 1 . . . ]      [ . 2 1 3 4 5 ]
    3 :    [  . 3 ] [1 2 4 5 ]    [ . 2 . . . ]      [ . 2 3 1 4 5 ]
    4 :    [  . 4 ] [1 2 3 5 ]    [ . 3 . . . ]      [ . 2 3 4 1 5 ]
    5 :    [  . 5 ] [1 2 3 4 ]    [ . 4 . . . ]      [ . 2 3 4 5 1 ]
    6 :    [ 1 . ]  [5 2 3 4 ]    [ 1 . . . . ]      [ 1 . 3 4 5 2 ]
    7 :    [ 1 2 ]  [5 . 3 4 ]    [ 1 1 . . . ]      [ 3 . 1 4 5 2 ]
    8 :    [ 1 3 ]  [5 . 2 4 ]    [ 1 2 . . . ]      [ 3 . 4 1 5 2 ]
    9 :    [ 1 4 ]  [5 . 2 3 ]    [ 1 3 . . . ]      [ 3 . 4 5 1 2 ]
  1 0 :    [ 1 5 ]  [4 . 2 3 ]    [ 1 4 . . . ]      [ 3 . 4 5 2 1 ]
  1 1 :    [ 2 . ]  [4 5 1 3 ]    [ 2 . . . . ]      [ 1 4 . 5 2 3 ]
  1 2 :    [ 2 1 ]  [4 5 . 3 ]    [ 2 1 . . . ]      [ 4 1 . 5 2 3 ]
  1 3 :    [ 2 3 ]  [4 5 . 1 ]    [ 2 2 . . . ]      [ 4 5 . 1 2 3 ]
  1 4 :    [ 2 4 ]  [3 5 . 1 ]    [ 2 3 . . . ]      [ 4 5 . 2 1 3 ]
  1 5 :    [ 2 5 ]  [3 4 . 1 ]    [ 2 4 . . . ]      [ 4 5 . 2 3 1 ]
  1 6 :    [ 3 . ]  [2 4 5 1 ]    [ 3 . . . . ]      [ 1 5 2 . 3 4 ]
  1 7 :    [ 3 1 ]  [2 4 5 . ]    [ 3 1 . . . ]      [ 5 1 2 . 3 4 ]
  1 8 :    [ 3 2 ]  [1 4 5 . ]    [ 3 2 . . . ]      [ 5 2 1 . 3 4 ]
  1 9 :    [ 3 4 ]  [1 2 5 . ]    [ 3 3 . . . ]      [ 5 2 3 . 1 4 ]
  2 0 :    [ 3 5 ]  [1 2 4 . ]    [ 3 4 . . . ]      [ 5 2 3 . 4 1 ]
  2 1 :    [ 4 . ]  [1 2 3 5 ]    [ 4 . . . . ]      [ 1 2 3 4 . 5 ]
  2 2 :    [ 4 1 ]  [. 2 3 5 ]    [ 4 1 . . . ]      [ 2 1 3 4 . 5 ]
  2 3 :    [ 4 2 ]  [. 1 3 5 ]    [ 4 2 . . . ]      [ 2 3 1 4 . 5 ]
  2 4 :    [ 4 3 ]  [. 1 2 5 ]    [ 4 3 . . . ]      [ 2 3 4 1 . 5 ]
  2 5 :    [ 4 5 ]  [. 1 2 3 ]    [ 4 4 . . . ]      [ 2 3 4 5 . 1 ]
  2 6 :    [ 5 . ]  [4 1 2 3 ]    [ 5 . . . . ]      [ 1 3 4 5 2 . ]
  2 7 :    [ 5 1 ]  [4 . 2 3 ]    [ 5 1 . . . ]      [ 3 1 4 5 2 . ]
  2 8 :    [ 5 2 ]  [4 . 1 3 ]    [ 5 2 . . . ]      [ 3 4 1 5 2 . ]
  2 9 :    [ 5 3 ]  [4 . 1 2 ]    [ 5 3 . . . ]      [ 3 4 5 1 2 . ]
  3 0 :    [ 5 4 ]  [3 . 1 2 ]    [ 5 4 . . . ]      [ 3 4 5 2 1 . ]
```

Figure 12.1-A: The 2-permutations of 6 elements in lexicographic order (left), the corresponding numbers in falling factorial basis (middle), and the inverse permutations (right).

12.1 Lexicographic order

For the generation of k-permutations in lexicographic order we use mixed radix numbers to determine the position of the leftmost change which is restricted to the first k elements. We also store the inverse permutation to simplify the update routine [FXT: comb/kperm-lex.h]:

```
1    class kperm_lex
2    {
3    public:
4        ulong *p_;   // permutation
5        ulong *ip_;  // inverse permutation
6        ulong *d_;   // falling factorial number
7        ulong n_;    // total number of elements
8        ulong k_;    // permutations of k elements
9        ulong u_;    // sort up to position u+1
10
11   public:
12       kperm_lex(ulong n)
13       {
14           n_ = n;
15           k_ = n;
16           p_ = new ulong[n_];
17           ip_ = new ulong[n_];
18           d_ = new ulong[n_+1];
19           d_[0] = 0;  // sentinel
20           ++d_;  // nota bene
21           first(k_);
22       }
23
24       ~kperm_lex()
25       {
26           delete [] p_;
27           delete [] ip_;
28           --d_;
29           delete [] d_;
```

```
30        }
31
32        void first(ulong k)
33        {
34            k_ = k;
35            u_ =  n_ - 1;
36            if ( k_ < u_ )  u_ = k_;  // == min(k, n-1)
37
38            for (ulong i=0; i<n_; i++)  p_[i] = i;
39            for (ulong i=0; i<n_; i++)  ip_[i] = i;
40            for (ulong i=0; i<n_; i++)  d_[i] = 0;
41        }
42
43        const ulong * data()  const  { return p_; }
44    [--snip--]
```

Note that k is determined only with the call to `first()`. In the update routine we swap the leftmost changed element (at position $i < k$) as for the lexicographic order of all permutations. Then we replace the elements up to position k by the smallest elements lying right of i. The positions $k, \ldots, n-1$ are not put in ascending order for reasons of efficiency. Therefore the falling factorial numbers in figure 12.1-A are not (in general) the inversion tables of the permutations.

```
1     bool next()
2     {
3         ulong i = k_ - 1;
4         ulong m1 = n_ - i - 1;
5         while ( d_[i] == m1 )  // increment mixed radix number
6         {
7             d_[i] = 0;
8             ++m1;
9             --i;
10        }
11
12        if ( (long)i<0 )  return false;  // current is last
13
14        ++d_[i];
15
16        { // find smallest element p[j] < p[i] that lies right of position i:
17            ulong z = p_[i];
18            do  { ++z; }  while ( ip_[z]<=i );
19            const ulong j = ip_[z];
20
21            swap2( p_[i], p_[j] );
22            swap2( ip_[p_[i]], ip_[p_[j]] );
23            ++i;
24        }
25
26
27        ulong z = 0;
28        while ( i < u_ )
29        {
30            // find smallest element right of position i:
31            while ( ip_[z] < i )  { ++z; }
32            const ulong j = ip_[z];
33
34            swap2( p_[i], p_[j] );
35            swap2( ip_[p_[i]], ip_[p_[j]] );
36            ++i;
37        }
38
39        return true;
40    }
41  };
```

The update is most efficient for small k, the rate of generation is about 80 M/s for $k = 4$ and $n = 100$ (best case), and about 30 M/s for $k = n = 12$ (worst case) [FXT: comb/kperm-lex-demo.cc].

12.2 Minimal-change order

A Gray code for k-permutations is given by the first inverse permutations in Trotter's order (see section 10.9.1 on page 258). The update routine in the generator [FXT: class `kperm_gray` in comb/kperm-gray.h] differs from that in [FXT: class `perm_gray_ffact` in comb/perm-gray-ffact.h] just be the test whether the left of the swapped elements lies inside the k-prefix:

```
                 permutation        swap        ffact            inv. perm.
     0 :    [ . 1 ][ 2 3 4 5 ]    (-, -)    [ . . . . . ]    [ . 1 2 3 4 5 ]
     1 :    [ 1 . ][ 2 3 4 5 ]    (0, 1)    [ 1 . . . . ]    [ 1 . 2 3 4 5 ]
     2 :    [ 2 . ][ 1 3 4 5 ]    (1, 2)    [ 2 . . . . ]    [ 1 2 . 3 4 5 ]
     3 :    [ 3 . ][ 1 2 4 5 ]    (2, 3)    [ 3 . . . . ]    [ 1 2 3 . 4 5 ]
     4 :    [ 4 . ][ 1 2 3 5 ]    (3, 4)    [ 4 . . . . ]    [ 1 2 3 4 . 5 ]
     5 :    [ 5 . ][ 1 2 3 4 ]    (4, 5)    [ 5 . . . . ]    [ 1 2 3 4 5 . ]
     6 :    [ 5 1 ][ . 2 3 4 ]    (0, 1)    [ 5 1 . . . ]    [ 2 1 3 4 5 . ]
     7 :    [ 4 1 ][ . 2 3 5 ]    (5, 4)    [ 4 1 . . . ]    [ 2 1 3 4 . 5 ]
     8 :    [ 3 1 ][ . 2 4 5 ]    (4, 3)    [ 3 1 . . . ]    [ 2 1 3 . 4 5 ]
     9 :    [ 2 1 ][ . 3 4 5 ]    (3, 2)    [ 2 1 . . . ]    [ 2 1 . 3 4 5 ]
   1 0 :    [ 1 2 ] [. 3 4 5 ]    ( 2 1 )   [ 1 1 . . . ]    [ 2 . 1 3 4 5 ]
   1 1 :    [ . 2 ] [1 3 4 5 ]    ( 1 0 )   [ . 1 . . . ]    [ . 2 1 3 4 5 ]
   1 2 :    [ . 3 ] [1 2 4 5 ]    ( 2 3 )   [ . 2 . . . ]    [ . 2 3 1 4 5 ]
   1 3 :    [ 1 3 ] [. 2 4 5 ]    ( 0 1 )   [ 1 2 . . . ]    [ 2 . 3 1 4 5 ]
   1 4 :    [ 2 3 ] [. 1 4 5 ]    ( 1 2 )   [ 2 2 . . . ]    [ 2 3 . 1 4 5 ]
   1 5 :    [ 3 2 ] [. 1 4 5 ]    ( 2 3 )   [ 3 2 . . . ]    [ 2 3 1 . 4 5 ]
   1 6 :    [ 4 2 ] [. 1 3 5 ]    ( 3 4 )   [ 4 2 . . . ]    [ 2 3 1 4 . 5 ]
   1 7 :    [ 5 2 ] [. 1 3 4 ]    ( 4 5 )   [ 5 2 . . . ]    [ 2 3 1 4 5 . ]
   1 8 :    [ 5 3 ] [. 1 2 4 ]    ( 2 3 )   [ 5 3 . . . ]    [ 2 3 4 1 5 . ]
   1 9 :    [ 4 3 ] [. 1 2 5 ]    ( 5 4 )   [ 4 3 . . . ]    [ 2 3 4 1 . 5 ]
   2 0 :    [ 3 4 ] [. 1 2 5 ]    ( 4 3 )   [ 3 3 . . . ]    [ 2 3 4 . 1 5 ]
   2 1 :    [ 2 4 ] [. 1 3 5 ]    ( 3 2 )   [ 2 3 . . . ]    [ 2 3 . 4 1 5 ]
   2 2 :    [ 1 4 ] [. 2 3 5 ]    ( 2 1 )   [ 1 3 . . . ]    [ 2 . 3 4 1 5 ]
   2 3 :    [ . 4 ] [1 2 3 5 ]    ( 1 0 )   [ . 3 . . . ]    [ . 2 3 4 1 5 ]
   2 4 :    [ . 5 ] [1 2 3 4 ]    ( 4 5 )   [ . 4 . . . ]    [ . 2 3 4 5 1 ]
   2 5 :    [ 1 5 ] [. 2 3 4 ]    ( 0 1 )   [ 1 4 . . . ]    [ 2 . 3 4 5 1 ]
   2 6 :    [ 2 5 ] [. 1 3 4 ]    ( 1 2 )   [ 2 4 . . . ]    [ 2 3 . 4 5 1 ]
   2 7 :    [ 3 5 ] [. 1 2 4 ]    ( 2 3 )   [ 3 4 . . . ]    [ 2 3 4 . 5 1 ]
   2 8 :    [ 4 5 ] [. 1 2 3 ]    ( 3 4 )   [ 4 4 . . . ]    [ 2 3 4 5 . 1 ]
   2 9 :    [ 5 4 ] [. 1 2 3 ]    ( 4 5 )   [ 5 4 . . . ]    [ 2 3 4 5 1 . ]
```

Figure 12.2-A: The 2-permutations of 6 elements in minimal-change order (left), the corresponding numbers in falling factorial basis (middle), and the inverse permutations (right).

```
1        bool next()
2        {
3          [--snip--]
4              if ( j>=k_ )  return false;
5          }
6          return false;
7        }
```

The rate of generation grows slightly with n and does not depend on k. For example, the rate is about 160 M/s (for $k = n = 12$) and 190 M/s (for $k = 4$ and $n = 100$) [FXT: comb/kperm-gray-demo.cc].

Chapter 13

Multisets

A *multiset* (or *bag*) is a collection of elements where elements can be repeated and order does not matter.

13.1 Subsets of a multiset

```
n == 630
primes    = [  2   3   5   7 ]
exponents = [  1   2   1   1 ]

          d     auxiliary products          exponents     change @
 1 :      1   [   1    1    1   1   1 ]   [ .  .  .  . ]      4
 2 :      2   [   2    1    1   1   1 ]   [ 1  .  .  . ]      0
 3 :      3   [   3    3    1   1   1 ]   [ .  1  .  . ]      1
 4 :      6   [   6    3    1   1   1 ]   [ 1  1  .  . ]      0
 5 :      9   [   9    9    1   1   1 ]   [ .  2  .  . ]      1
 6 :    1 8   [  18    9    1   1   1 ]   [ 1  2  .  . ]      0
 7 :      5   [   5    5    5   1   1 ]   [ .  .  1  . ]      2
 8 :    1 0   [  10    5    5   1   1 ]   [ 1  .  1  . ]      0
 9 :     15   [  15   15    5   1   1 ]   [ .  1  1  . ]      1
10 :     30   [  30   15    5   1   1 ]   [ 1  1  1  . ]      0
11 :     45   [  45   45    5   1   1 ]   [ .  2  1  . ]      1
12 :     90   [  90   45    5   1   1 ]   [ 1  2  1  . ]      0
1  3 :    7   [   7    7    7   7   1 ]   [ .  .  .  1 ]      3
14 :     14   [  14    7    7   7   1 ]   [ 1  .  .  1 ]      0
15 :     21   [  21   21    7   7   1 ]   [ .  1  .  1 ]      1
16 :     42   [  42   21    7   7   1 ]   [ 1  1  .  1 ]      0
17 :     63   [  63   63    7   7   1 ]   [ .  2  .  1 ]      1
18 :    126   [ 126   63    7   7   1 ]   [ 1  2  .  1 ]      0
19 :     35   [  35   35   35   7   1 ]   [ .  .  1  1 ]      2
20 :     70   [  70   35   35   7   1 ]   [ 1  .  1  1 ]      0
21 :    105   [ 105  105   35   7   1 ]   [ .  1  1  1 ]      1
22 :    210   [ 210  105   35   7   1 ]   [ 1  1  1  1 ]      0
23 :    315   [ 315  315   35   7   1 ]   [ .  2  1  1 ]      1
24 :    630   [ 630  315   35   7   1 ]   [ 1  2  1  1 ]      0
```

Figure 13.1-A: Divisors of $630 = 2^1 \cdot 3^2 \cdot 5^1 \cdot 7^1$ generated as subsets of the multiset of exponents.

A subset of a set of n elements can be identified with the bits of all n-bit binary words. The subsets of a multiset can be computed as mixed radix numbers: if the j-th element is repeated r_j times, then the radix of digit j has to be $r_j + 1$. Therefore all methods of chapter 9 on page 217 can be applied.

As an example, all divisors of a number x whose factorization $x = p_0^{e_0} \cdot p_1^{e_1} \cdots p_{n-1}^{e_{n-1}}$ is known can be computed via the length-n mixed radix numbers with radices $[e_0 + 1, e_1 + 1, \ldots, e_{n-1} + 1]$. The implementation [FXT: **class divisors** in mod/divisors.h] generates the subsets of the multiset of exponents in counting order (figure 13.1-A shows the data for $x = 630$). An auxiliary array T of products is updated with each step: if the changed digit (at position j) became 1, then set $t := T_{j+1} \cdot p_j$, else set $t := T_j \cdot p_j$. Set $T_i = t$ for all $0 \leq i \leq j$. A sentinel element $T_n = 1$ avoids unnecessary code. Figure 13.1-A was created with the program [FXT: mod/divisors-demo.cc]. The computation of all products of k out of n given factors is described in section 6.2.2 on page 178.

J. Arndt, *Matters Computational: Ideas, Algorithms, Source Code*,
DOI 10.1007/978-3-642-14764-7_13, © Springer-Verlag Berlin Heidelberg 2011

Subsets with prescribed number of elements

The *k-subsets* (or *combinations*) of a multiset are the subsets with k elements. They are one-to-one with the mixed radix numbers where the sum of digits equals k, see section 9.6 on page 229.

13.2 Permutations of a multiset

```
         (2, 2, 1)                    (6, 2)                    (1, 1, 1, 1)
  1 : [ . . 1 1 2 ]        1 : [ . . . . . . 1 1 ]      1: [ . 1 2 3 ]
  2 : [ . . 1 2 1 ]        2 : [ . . . . . . 1 . 1 ]    2: [ . 1 3 2 ]
  3 : [ . . 2 1 1 ]        3 : [ . . . . . . 1 1 . ]    3: [ . 2 1 3 ]
  4 : [ . 1 . 1 2 ]        4 : [ . . . . . 1 . . 1 ]    4: [ . 2 3 1 ]
  5 : [ . 1 . 2 1 ]        5 : [ . . . . . 1 . 1 . ]    5: [ . 3 1 2 ]
  6 : [ . 1 1 . 2 ]        6 : [ . . . . . 1 1 . . ]    6: [ . 3 2 1 ]
  7 : [ . 1 1 2 . ]        7 : [ . . . . 1 . . . 1 ]    7: [ 1 . 2 3 ]
  8 : [ . 1 2 . 1 ]        8 : [ . . . . 1 . . 1 . ]    8: [ 1 . 3 2 ]
  9 : [ . 1 2 1 . ]        9 : [ . . . . 1 . 1 . . ]    9: [ 1 2 . 3 ]
 1 0 : [ . 2 . 1 1 ]      1 0 : [ . . . . 1 1 . . . ]  10: [ 1 2 3 . ]
 1 1 : [ . 2 1 . 1 ]      1 1 : [ . . . 1 . . . . 1 ]  11: [ 1 3 . 2 ]
 1 2 : [ . 2 1 1 . ]      1 2 : [ . . . 1 . . . 1 . ]  12: [ 1 3 2 . ]
 1 3 : [ 1 . . 1 2 ]      1 3 : [ . . . 1 . . 1 . . ]  13: [ 2 . 1 3 ]
 1 4 : [ 1 . . 2 1 ]      1 4 : [ . . . 1 . 1 . . . ]  14: [ 2 . 3 1 ]
 1 5 : [ 1 . 1 . 2 ]      1 5 : [ . . . 1 1 . . . . ]  15: [ 2 1 . 3 ]
 1 6 : [ 1 . 1 2 . ]      1 6 : [ . . 1 . . . . . 1 ]  16: [ 2 1 3 . ]
 1 7 : [ 1 . 2 . 1 ]      1 7 : [ . . 1 . . . . 1 . ]  17: [ 2 3 . 1 ]
 1 8 : [ 1 . 2 1 . ]      1 8 : [ . . 1 . . . 1 . . ]  18: [ 2 3 1 . ]
 1 9 : [ 1 1 . . 2 ]      1 9 : [ . . 1 . . 1 . . . ]  19: [ 3 . 1 2 ]
 2 0 : [ 1 1 . 2 . ]      2 0 : [ . . 1 . 1 . . . . ]  20: [ 3 . 2 1 ]
 2 1 : [ 1 1 2 . . ]      2 1 : [ . . 1 1 . . . . . ]  21: [ 3 1 . 2 ]
 2 2 : [ 1 2 . . 1 ]      2 2 : [ . 1 . . . . . . 1 ]  22: [ 3 1 2 . ]
 2 3 : [ 1 2 . 1 . ]      2 3 : [ . 1 . . . . . 1 . ]  23: [ 3 2 . 1 ]
 2 4 : [ 1 2 1 . . ]      2 4 : [ . 1 . . . . 1 . . ]  24: [ 3 2 1 . ]
 2 5 : [ 2 . . 1 1 ]      2 5 : [ . 1 . . . 1 . . . ]
 2 6 : [ 2 . 1 . 1 ]      2 6 : [ . 1 . . 1 . . . . ]
 2 7 : [ 2 . 1 1 . ]      2 7 : [ . 1 . 1 . . . . . ]
 2 8 : [ 2 1 . . 1 ]      2 8 : [ . 1 1 . . . . . . ]
 2 9 : [ 2 1 . 1 . ]
 3 0 : [ 2 1 1 . . ]
```

Figure 13.2-A: Permutations of multisets in lexicographic order: the multiset $(2, 2, 1)$ (left), $(6, 2)$ (combinations $\binom{6+2}{2}$, middle), and $(1, 1, 1, 1)$ (permutations of four elements, right). Dots denote zeros.

We write $(r_0, r_1, \ldots, r_{k-1})$ for a multiset with r_0 elements of the first sort, r_1 of the second sort, $\ldots$, r_{k-1} elements of the k-th sort. The total number of elements is $n = \sum_{j=0}^{k-1} r_k$. For the elements of the j-th sort we always use the number j. The number of permutations $P(r_0, r_1, \ldots, r_{k-1})$ of the multiset $(r_0, r_1, \ldots, r_{k-1})$ is a *multinomial coefficient*:

$$P(r_0, r_1, \ldots, r_{k-1}) = \binom{n}{r_0, \, r_1, \, r_2, \ldots, \, r_{k-1}} = \frac{n!}{r_0! \, r_1! \, r_2! \cdots r_{k-1}!} \tag{13.2-1a}$$

$$= \binom{n}{r_0}\binom{n-r_0}{r_1}\binom{n-r_0-r_1}{r_2}\ldots\binom{r_{k-3}+r_{k-2}+r_{k-1}}{r_{k-3}}\binom{r_{k-2}+r_{k-1}}{r_{k-2}}\binom{r_{k-1}}{r_{k-1}} \tag{13.2-1b}$$

$$= \binom{r_0}{r_0}\binom{r_0+r_1}{r_1}\binom{r_0+r_1+r_2}{r_2}\binom{r_0+r_1+r_2+r_3}{r_3}\ldots\binom{n}{r_{k-1}} \tag{13.2-1c}$$

Relation 13.2-1a is obtained by observing that among the $n!$ ways to arrange all n elements $r_0!$ permutations of the first sort of elements, $r_1!$ of the second, and so on, lead to identical permutations.

13.2.1   Recursive generation

Let $[r_0, r_1, r_2, \ldots, r_{k-1}]$ denote the list of all permutations of the multiset $(r_0, r_1, r_2, \ldots, r_{k-1})$. We use the recursion

$$[r_0, r_1, r_2, \ldots, r_{k-1}] \quad = \quad \begin{matrix} r_0 \cdot [r_0 - 1, r_1, r_2, \ldots, r_{k-1}] \\ r_1 \cdot [r_0, r_1 - 1, r_2, \ldots, r_{k-1}] \\ r_2 \cdot [r_0, r_1, r_2 - 1, \ldots, r_{k-1}] \\ \vdots \\ r_{k-1} \cdot [r_0, r_1, r_2, \ldots, r_{k-1} - 1] \end{matrix} \tag{13.2-2}$$

The following routine generates all multiset permutations in lexicographic order when called with argument zero [FXT: comb/mset-perm-lex-rec-demo.cc]:

```
1   ulong n;     // number of objects
2   ulong *ms;   // multiset data in ms[0], ..., ms[n-1]
3   ulong k;     // number of different sorts of objects
4   ulong *r;    // number of elements '0' in r[0], '1' in r[1], ..., 'k-1' in r[k-1]
5
6   void mset_perm_rec(ulong d)
7   {
8       if ( d>=n ) visit();
9       else
10      {
11          for (ulong j=0; j<k; ++j)  // for all buckets
12          {
13              ++wct;
14              if ( r[j] )    // bucket has elements left
15              {
16                  ++rct;
17                  --r[j];        // take element from bucket
18                  ms[d] = j;  // put element in place
19                  mset_perm_rec(d+1);  // recursion
20                  ++r[j];        // put element back
21              }
22          }
23      }
24  }
```

As given the routine is inefficient when used with (many) small numbers r_j. An extreme case is $r_j = 1$ for all j, corresponding to the (usual) permutations: we have $n = k$ and the work for all $n!$ permutations is $O(n^n)$. The method can be made efficient by maintaining a list of pointers to the next nonzero 'bucket' nk[] [FXT: class mset_perm_lex_rec in comb/mset-perm-lex-rec.h]:

```
1   class mset_perm_lex_rec
2   {
3   public:
4       ulong k_;    // number of different sorts of objects
5       ulong *r_;   // number of elements '0' in r[0], '1' in r[1], ..., 'k-1' in r[k-1]
6       ulong n_;    // number of objects
7       ulong *ms_;  // multiset data in ms[0], ..., ms[n-1]
8       ulong *nn_;  // position of next nonempty bucket
9       void (*visit_)(const mset_perm_lex_rec &);  // function to call with each permutation
10      ulong ct_;   // count objects
11      ulong rct_;  // count recursions (==work)
12      [--snip--]
```

The initializer takes as arguments an array of multiplicities and its length:

```
1   public:
2       mset_perm_lex_rec(ulong *r, ulong k)
3       {
4           k_ = k;
5           r_ = new ulong[k];
6           for (ulong j=0; j<k_; ++j)  r_[j] = r[j];  // get buckets
7
8           n_ = 0;
9           for (ulong j=0; j<k_; ++j)  n_ += r_[j];
10          ms_ = new ulong[n_];
11
12          nn_ = new ulong[k_+1];  // incl sentinel
```

```
13          for (ulong j=0; j<k_; ++j)  nn_[j] = j+1;
14          nn_[k] = 0;  // pointer to first nonempty bucket
15      }
16   [--snip--]
```

The method to generate all permutations takes a 'visit' function as argument:

```
1        void generate(void (*visit)(const mset_perm_lex_rec &))
2        {
3            visit_ = visit;
4            ct_ = 0;
5            rct_ = 0;
6            mset_perm_rec(0);
7        }
8
9    private:
10       void mset_perm_rec(ulong d);
11   };
```

The recursion itself is [FXT: comb/mset-perm-lex-rec.cc]:

```
1    void mset_perm_lex_rec::mset_perm_rec(ulong d)
2    {
3        if ( d>=n_ )
4        {
5            ++ct_;
6            visit_( *this );
7        }
8        else
9        {
10           for (ulong jf=k_, j=nn_[jf];  j<k_;  jf=j, j=nn_[j])  // for all nonempty buckets
11           {
12               ++rct_;  // work == number of recursions
13
14               --r_[j];     // take element from bucket
15               ms_[d] = j;  // put element in place
16
17               if ( r_[j]==0 )  // bucket now empty?
18               {
19                   ulong f = nn_[jf]; // where we come from
20                   nn_[jf] = nn_[j];  // let recursions skip over j
21                   mset_perm_rec(d+1);     // recursion
22                   nn_[jf] = f;       // remove skip
23               }
24               else  mset_perm_rec(d+1);  // recursion
25
26               ++r_[j];        // put element back
27           }
28       }
29   }
```

The test whether the current bucket is nonempty is omitted, as empty buckets are skipped. Now the work involved with (regular) permutations is less than $e = 2.71828\ldots$ times the number of the generated permutations. Usage of the class is shown in [FXT: comb/mset-perm-lex-rec2-demo.cc]. The permutations of 12 elements are generated at a rate of about 25 million per second, the combinations $\binom{30}{15}$ at about 40 million per second, and the permutations of $(2,2,2,3,3,3)$ at about 20 million per second.

13.2.2 Iterative generation

The algorithm to generate the next permutation in lexicographic order given in section 10.2 on page 242 can be adapted for an iterative method for multiset permutations [FXT: class mset_perm_lex in comb/mset-perm-lex.h]:

```
1    class mset_perm_lex
2    {
3    public:
4        ulong k_;    // number of different sorts of objects
5        ulong *r_;   // number of elements '0' in r[0], '1' in r[1], ..., 'k-1' in r[k-1]
6        ulong n_;    // number of objects
7        ulong *ms_;  // multiset data in ms[0], ..., ms[n-1], sentinel at [-1]
8
9    public:
10       mset_perm_lex(const ulong *r, ulong k)
```

```
11          {
12              k_ = k;
13              r_ = new ulong[k];
14              for (ulong j=0; j<k_; ++j)  r_[j] = r[j];   // get buckets
15
16              n_ = 0;
17              for (ulong j=0; j<k_; ++j)  n_ += r_[j];
18              ms_ = new ulong[n_+1];
19              ms_[0] = 0;   // sentinel
20              ++ms_;   // nota bene
21
22              first();
23          }
24
25          void first()
26          {
27              for (ulong j=0, i=0;  j<k_;  ++j)
28                  for (ulong h=r_[j];  h!=0;  --h, ++i)  ms_[i] = j;
29          }
30      [--snip--]
```

The only change in the update routine is to replace the operators > by >= in the scanning loops:

```
1       bool next()
2       {
3           // find rightmost pair with ms[i] < ms[i+1]:
4           const ulong n1 = n_ - 1;
5           ulong i = n1;
6           do  { --i; }  while ( ms_[i] >= ms_[i+1] );   // can touch sentinel
7           if ( (long)i<0 )  return false;   // last sequence is falling seq.
8
9           // find rightmost element p[j] less than p[i]:
10          ulong j = n1;
11          while ( ms_[i] >= ms_[j] )  { --j; }
12
13          swap2(ms_[i], ms_[j]);
14
15          // Here the elements ms[i+1], ..., ms[n-1] are a falling sequence.
16          // Reverse order to the right:
17          ulong r = n1;
18          ulong s = i + 1;
19          while ( r > s )  { swap2(ms_[r], ms_[s]);  --r;  ++s; }
20
21          return true;
22      }
23  }
```

Usage of the class is shown in [FXT: comb/mset-perm-lex-demo.cc]:

```
ulong ct = 0;
do
{
    // visit
}
while ( P.next() );
```

The permutations of 12 elements are generated at a rate of about 127 million per second, the combinations $\binom{30}{15}$ at about 60 million per second, and the permutations of $(2, 2, 2, 3, 3, 3)$ at about 93 million per second.

13.2.3   Order by prefix shifts (cool-lex)

An ordering in which each transition involves a cyclic shift of a prefix is described in [360]. Figure 13.2-B shows examples of the ordering that were generated with the program [FXT: comb/mset-perm-pref-demo.cc]. The implementation is [FXT: comb/mset-perm-pref.h]:

```
1   class mset_perm_pref
2   {
3   public:
4       ulong k_;     // number of different sorts of objects
5       ulong *r_;    // number of elements '0' in r[0], '1' in r[1], ..., 'k-1' in r[k-1]
6       ulong n_;     // number of objects
7       ulong *ms_;   // multiset data in ms[0], ..., ms[n-1], sentinel at [n]
8
9   public:
10      mset_perm_pref(const ulong *r, ulong k)
```

```
                (2, 2, 1)                      (6, 2)                     (1, 1, 1, 1)
      1 : [ . 2 1 1 . ]         1 : [ . 1 1 . . . . . ]        1:  [ . 3 2 1 ]
      2 : [ 2 . 1 1 . ]         2 : [ 1 . 1 . . . . . ]        2:  [ 3 . 2 1 ]
      3 : [ 1 2 . 1 . ]         3 : [ . 1 . 1 . . . . ]        3:  [ 2 3 . 1 ]
      4 : [ . 1 2 1 . ]         4 : [ . . 1 1 . . . . ]        4:  [ . 2 3 1 ]
      5 : [ 1 . 2 1 . ]         5 : [ 1 . . 1 . . . . ]        5:  [ 2 . 3 1 ]
      6 : [ 2 1 . 1 . ]         6 : [ . 1 . . 1 . . . ]        6:  [ 3 2 . 1 ]
      7 : [ . 2 1 . 1 ]         7 : [ . . 1 . 1 . . . ]        7:  [ 1 3 2 . ]
      8 : [ 2 . 1 . 1 ]         8 : [ . . . 1 1 . . . ]        8:  [ 3 1 2 . ]
      9 : [ . 2 . 1 1 ]         9 : [ 1 . . . 1 . . . ]        9:  [ . 3 1 2 ]
    1 0 :[ . . 2 1 1 ]        1 0 :[ . 1 . . . 1 . . ]        10: [ 3 . 1 2 ]
    1 1 :[ 2 . . 1 1 ]        1 1 :[ . . 1 . . 1 . . ]        11: [ 1 3 . 2 ]
    1 2 :[ 1 2 . . 1 ]        1 2 :[ . . . 1 . 1 . . ]        12: [ . 1 3 2 ]
    1 3 :[ . 1 2 . 1 ]        1 3 :[ . . . . 1 1 . . ]        13: [ 1 . 3 2 ]
    1 4 :[ 1 . 2 . 1 ]        1 4 :[ 1 . . . . 1 . . ]        14: [ 3 1 . 2 ]
    1 5 :[ . 1 . 2 1 ]        1 5 :[ . 1 . . . . 1 . ]        15: [ 2 3 1 . ]
    1 6 :[ . . 1 2 1 ]        1 6 :[ . . 1 . . . 1 . ]        16: [ 1 2 3 . ]
    1 7 :[ 1 . . 2 1 ]        1 7 :[ . . . 1 . . 1 . ]        17: [ 2 1 3 . ]
    1 8 :[ 2 1 . . 1 ]        1 8 :[ . . . . 1 . 1 . ]        18: [ . 2 1 3 ]
    1 9 :[ 1 2 1 . . ]        1 9 :[ . . . . . 1 1 . ]        19: [ 2 . 1 3 ]
    2 0 :[ 1 1 2 . . ]        2 0 :[ 1 . . . . . 1 . ]        20: [ 1 2 . 3 ]
    2 1 :[ . 1 1 2 . ]        2 1 :[ . 1 . . . . . 1 ]        21: [ . 1 2 3 ]
    2 2 :[ 1 . 1 2 . ]        2 2 :[ . . 1 . . . . 1 ]        22: [ 1 . 2 3 ]
    2 3 :[ 1 1 . 2 . ]        2 3 :[ . . . 1 . . . 1 ]        23: [ 2 1 . 3 ]
    2 4 :[ . 1 1 . 2 ]        2 4 :[ . . . . 1 . . 1 ]        24: [ 3 2 1 . ]
    2 5 :[ 1 . 1 . 2 ]        2 5 :[ . . . . . 1 . 1 ]
    2 6 :[ . 1 . 1 2 ]        2 6 :[ . . . . . . 1 1 ]
    2 7 :[ . . 1 1 2 ]        2 7 :[ 1 . . . . . . 1 ]
    2 8 :[ 1 . . 1 2 ]        2 8 :[ 1 1 . . . . . . ]
    2 9 :[ 1 1 . . 2 ]
    3 0 :[ 2 1 1 . . ]
```

Figure 13.2-B: Permutations of multisets in 'cool-lex' order: the multiset $(2, 2, 1)$ (left), $(6, 2)$ (combinations $\binom{6+2}{2}$, middle), and $(1, 1, 1, 1)$ (permutations of four elements, right). Dots denote zeros.

```
11      {
12          k_ = k;
13          r_ = new ulong[k];
14          for (ulong j=0; j<k_; ++j)  r_[j] = r[j];  // get buckets
15
16          n_ = 0;
17          for (ulong j=0; j<k_; ++j)  n_ += r_[j];
18          ms_ = new ulong[n_+1];
19          ms_[n_] = k_;  // sentinel (must be greater than all elements)
20
21          first();
22      }
23
24      void first()
25      {
26          for (ulong j=0, i=0;  j<k_;  ++j)
27              for (ulong h=r_[j];  h!=0;  --h, ++i)  ms_[i] = j;
28
29          reverse(ms_, n_);   // non-increasing permutation
30          rotate_right1(ms_, n_); // ... shall be the last
31      }
32      [--snip--]
```

The cited paper uses a linked list for the multiset permutation. We simply use an array and determine the length of the longest non-increasing prefix in an unsophisticated way:

```
1       ulong next()
2       // Return length of rotated prefix, zero with last permutation.
3       {
4           // scan for prefix:
5           ulong i = -1UL;
6           do  { ++i; } while ( ms_[i] >= ms_[i+1] );  // can touch sentinel
7           ++i;
8           // here: i == length of longest non-increasing prefix
9
10          if ( i >= n_-1 )
11          {
```

```
12              rotate_right1(ms_, n_);
13              if ( i==n_ )  return 0;   // was last
14              return n_;
15          }
16          else
17          {
18              // compare last of prefix with element 2 positions right:
19              i += ( ms_[i+1] <= ms_[i-1] );
20              ++i;
21              rotate_right1(ms_, i);
22              return i;
23          }
24      }
25  };
```

The rate of generation is about 68 M/s for the permutations of 12 elements, 46 M/s for the combinations $\binom{30}{15}$, and 62 M/s for the permutations of $(2, 2, 2, 3, 3, 3)$. The equivalent order for combinations is given in section 6.3 on page 180.

As suggested in the paper, the length of the next longest non-increasing prefix can be computed with just one comparison, we store it in a variable `ln_`. Usage of the fast update is enabled via the line

```
#define MSET_PERM_PREF_LEN
```

near the top of the file [FXT: comb/mset-perm-pref.h]. The initialization has to be modified as follows:

```
1      void first()
2      {
3          [--snip--]   // as before
4  #ifdef MSET_PERM_PREF_LEN
5          ln_ = 1;
6          if ( k_ == 1 )  ln_ = n_;  // only one type of object
7  #endif
8      }
```

The computation of the successor can be implemented as

```
1      ulong next()
2      // Return length of rotated prefix, zero with last permutation.
3      {
4          const ulong i = ln_;
5          ulong nr;   // number of elements rotated
6          if ( i >= n_-1 )
7          {
8              nr = n_;
9              rotate_right1(ms_, nr);
10             if ( i==n_ )  return 0; // was last
11         }
12         else
13         {
14             nr = ln_ + 1 + ( ms_[i+1] <= ms_[i-1] );
15             rotate_right1(ms_, nr);
16         }
17
18         const bool cmp = ( ms_[0] < ms_[1] );
19         ln_ =  ( cmp ? 1 : ln_ + 1 );
20         return nr;
21     }
```

The rate of generation is improved to about 71 M/s for the permutations of 12 elements, 62 M/s for the combinations $\binom{30}{15}$, and 69 M/s for the permutations of $(2, 2, 2, 3, 3, 3)$.

13.2.4 Minimal-change order

An algorithm for the generation of a Gray code for the permutations of a multiset is given by Fred Lunnon [priv. comm.], figure 13.2-C shows examples of the ordering. It is a generalization of Trotter's order for permutations described in section 10.7 on page 254. The implementation is [FXT: class `mset_perm_gray` in comb/mset-perm-gray.h]:

```
1  class mset_perm_gray
2  {
3  public:
4      ulong *ms_;   // permuted elements (Lunnon's R_[])
5      ulong *P_;    // permutation
```

```
        (2, 2, 1)                          (6, 2)                      (1, 1, 1, 1)
 1 : [ . . 2 2 3 ]              1: [ . . . . . . 2 2 ]        1: [ . 2 3 4 ]
 2 : [ 2 . . 2 3 ]  ( 2 0 )     2: [ 2 . . . . . . 2 ]        2: [ 2 . 3 4 ]
 3 : [ . 2 . 2 3 ]  ( 0 1 )     3: [ . 2 . . . . . 2 ]        3: [ 2 3 . 4 ]
 4 : [ . 2 2 . 3 ]  ( 3 2 )     4: [ . . 2 . . . . 2 ]        4: [ 2 3 4 . ]
 5 : [ 2 . 2 . 3 ]  ( 1 0 )     5: [ . . . 2 . . . 2 ]        5: [ 3 2 4 . ]
 6 : [ 2 2 . . 3 ]  ( 2 1 )     6: [ . . . . 2 . . 2 ]        6: [ 3 2 . 4 ]
 7 : [ 2 2 3 . . ]  ( 4 2 )     7: [ . . . . . 2 . 2 ]        7: [ 3 . 2 4 ]
 8 : [ 2 2 . 3 . ]  ( 2 3 )     8: [ . . . . . 2 2 . ]        8: [ . 3 2 4 ]
 9 : [ 2 . 2 3 . ]  ( 1 2 )     9: [ 2 . . . . . 2 . ]        9: [ . 3 4 2 ]
10 :[ . 2 2 3 . ]  ( 0 1 )     10: [ . 2 . . . . 2 . ]       10: [ 3 . 4 2 ]
11 :[ . 3 2 2 . ]  ( 3 1 )     11: [ . . 2 . . . 2 . ]       11: [ 3 4 . 2 ]
12 :[ 3 . 2 2 . ]  ( 1 0 )     12: [ . . . 2 . . 2 . ]       12: [ 3 4 2 . ]
13 :[ 3 2 . 2 . ]  ( 2 1 )     13: [ . . . . 2 . 2 . ]       13: [ 4 3 2 . ]
14 :[ 3 2 2 . . ]  ( 3 2 )     14: [ . . . . 2 2 . . ]       14: [ 4 3 . 2 ]
15 :[ 3 2 . . 2 ]  ( 2 4 )     15: [ 2 . . . . 2 . . ]       15: [ 4 . 3 2 ]
16 :[ 3 . 2 . 2 ]  ( 1 2 )     16: [ . 2 . . . 2 . . ]       16: [ . 4 3 2 ]
17 :[ . 3 2 . 2 ]  ( 0 1 )     17: [ . . 2 . . 2 . . ]       17: [ . 4 2 3 ]
18 :[ . 3 . 2 2 ]  ( 2 3 )     18: [ . . . 2 . 2 . . ]       18: [ 4 . 2 3 ]
19 :[ 3 . . 2 2 ]  ( 1 0 )     19: [ . . . 2 2 . . . ]       19: [ 4 2 . 3 ]
20 :[ . . 3 2 2 ]  ( 0 2 )     20: [ 2 . . . 2 . . . ]       20: [ 4 2 3 . ]
21 :[ . . 2 3 2 ]  ( 2 3 )     21: [ . 2 . . 2 . . . ]       21: [ 2 4 3 . ]
22 :[ 2 . . 3 2 ]  ( 2 0 )     22: [ . . 2 . 2 . . . ]       22: [ 2 4 . 3 ]
23 :[ . 2 . 3 2 ]  ( 0 1 )     23: [ . . 2 2 . . . . ]       23: [ 2 . 4 3 ]
24 :[ . 2 3 . 2 ]  ( 3 2 )     24: [ 2 . . 2 . . . . ]       24: [ . 2 4 3 ]
25 :[ 2 . 3 . 2 ]  ( 1 0 )     25: [ . 2 . 2 . . . . ]
26 :[ 2 3 . . 2 ]  ( 2 1 )     26: [ . . 2 2 . . . . ]
27 :[ 2 3 2 . . ]  ( 4 2 )     27: [ 2 . 2 . . . . . ]
28 :[ 2 3 . 2 . ]  ( 2 3 )     28: [ 2 2 . . . . . . ]
29 :[ 2 . 3 2 . ]  ( 1 2 )
30 :[ . 2 3 2 . ]  ( 0 1 )
```

Figure 13.2-C: Gray code for permutations of multisets: the multiset $(2, 2, 1)$ (left, with swaps), $(6, 2)$ (combinations $\binom{6+2}{2}$, middle), and $(1, 1, 1, 1)$ (permutations of four elements, right). Dots denote ones.

```
6        ulong *Q_;    // inverse permutation
7        ulong *D_;    // direction
8        ulong k_;     // number of different sorts of objects
9        ulong n_;     // number of objects
10       ulong sw1_, sw2_;  // positions swapped with last update
11       ulong *r_;    // number of elements '1' in r[0], '2' in r[1], ..., 'k' in r[k-1]
12
13   public:
14       mset_perm_gray(const ulong *r, ulong k)
15       {
16           k_ = k;
17           r_ = new ulong[k_];
18           for (ulong j=0; j<k_; ++j)  r_[j] = r[j];
19           n_ = 0;
20           for (ulong j=0; j<k_; ++j)  n_ += r_[j];
21
22           ms_ = new ulong[n_+4];
23           P_ = new ulong[n_+4];
24           Q_ = new ulong[n_+4];
25           D_ = new ulong[n_+4];
26
27           first();
28       }
29       [--snip--]  // destructor
30
31       const ulong * data()  const { return ms_+1; }
32       void get_swaps(ulong &sw1, ulong &sw2)  const { sw1=sw1_;  sw2=sw2_; }
33
```

The arrays have four extra elements that are used as sentinels:

```
1        void first()
2        {
3            sw1_ = sw2_ = 0;
4
```

```
5          for (ulong j=0, i=1;  j<k_;  ++j)
6              for (ulong h=r_[j];  h!=0;   --h, ++i)  ms_[i] = j + 1;
7
8          const ulong n = n_;
9          for (ulong j=1;  j<=n;  ++j)  { P_[j] = j;  Q_[j] = j;  D_[j] = +1UL; }
10
11         // sentinels:
12         ms_[0] = 0;  P_[0] = 0;  Q_[0] = 0;  D_[0] = 0;
13         ulong j;
14         j = n+1;  ms_[j] = 0;      P_[j] = 0;    Q_[j] = n+2;  D_[j] = 0;
15         j = n+2;  ms_[j] = k_+1;   P_[j] = n+1;  Q_[j] = n+3;  D_[j] = +1;
16         j = n+3;  ms_[j] = k_+2;   P_[j] = n+2;  Q_[j] = 0;    D_[j] = +1;
17     }
```

To compute the successor we find the first run of identical elements that can be moved:

```
1       bool next()
2       {
3           // locate earliest unblocked element at j, starting at blocked element 0
4           ulong j = 0, i = 0, d = 0, l = 0; // init of l not needed
5           while ( ms_[j] >= ms_[i] )
6           {
7               D_[j] = -d;  // blocked at j; reverse drift d pre-emptively
8
9               // next element at j, neighbor at i:
10              j = Q_[P_[j]+1];
11              d = D_[j];
12              i = j+d;
13
14              if ( ms_[j-1] != ms_[j] )  l = j;  // save left end of run in l
15              else
16              {
17                  if ( (long)d < 0 )  i = l-1;
18              }
19          }
20
21          if ( j > n_ )  return false;  // current permutation is last
22
23          // restore left end at head of run
24          // shift run of equal rank from i-d,i-2d,...,l to i,i-d,...,l+d
25          if ( (long)d < 0 )  l = j;
26          ulong e = D_[i],  p = P_[i];  // save neighbor drift e and identifier p
27
28          for (ulong k=i;  k!=l;  k-=d)
29          {
30              P_[k]  = P_[k-d];
31              Q_[P_[k]] = k;
32              D_[k] = -1UL;  // reset drifts of run tail elements
33          }
34
35          sw1_ = i - 1;  sw2_ = l - 1;  // save positions swapped
36          swap2(ms_[i], ms_[l]);
37
38          D_[l] = e;  D_[i] = d;  // restore drifts of head and neighbor
39          P_[l] = p;  Q_[p] = l;  // wrap neighbor around to other end
40
41          return  true;
42      }
43   };
```

The rate of generation is roughly 40 M/s [FXT: comb/mset-perm-gray-demo.cc].

Chapter 14

Gray codes for strings with restrictions

We give constructions for Gray codes for strings with certain restrictions, such as forbidding two success-sive zeros or nonzero digits. The constraints considered are such that the number of strings of a given type satisfies a linear recursion with constant coefficients.

14.1 List recursions

```
11111111111111111111111.............
22222222.........111111111111111111.....:
11111.........222222...11111111:.
22...111..111111........111111..
..1111.....22..11111.....22.
1...22...11....11...22...11....11.

[120 W(n-3)]  +  rev([10 W(n-2)])  +  [00 W(n-2)]
  11111111         111111111111       ............
  22222222         ............       ............
  .......                             
                  .....11111111       11111111.....
  11111...        .......222          222.........
  22..1111         ..111111....       .....111111:.
  ..1111.           ..22....11         11....22...
  1...22..          .11....11...2      2...11....11.
```

$$W(n) \ ==$$

Figure 14.1-A: Computing a Gray code by a sublist recursion.

The algorithms are given as *list recursions*. For example, write $W(n)$ for the list of n-digit words (of a certain type), write $W^{\mathbf{R}}(n)$ for the reversed list, and $[x \, . \, W(n)]$ for the list with the word x prepended at each word. The recursion for a Gray code is

$$W(n) \ = \ \begin{array}{l} [0\,0\,.\,W(n-2)\ \ ] \\ [1\,0\,.\,W^{\mathbf{R}}(n-2)] \\ [1\,2\,0\,.\,W(n-3)] \end{array} \tag{14.1-1}$$

A relation like this always implies another version which is obtained by reversing the order of the sublists on the right side and additionally reversing each sublist

$$W^{\mathbf{R}}(n) \ = \ \begin{array}{l} [1\,2\,0\,.\,W^{\mathbf{R}}(n-3)] \\ [1\,0\,.\,W(n-2)\ \ ] \\ [0\,0\,.\,W^{\mathbf{R}}(n-2)\ \ ] \end{array} \tag{14.1-2}$$

The construction is illustrated in figure 14.1-A. An implementation of the algorithm is [FXT: comb/fib-alt-gray-demo.cc]:

```
1    void X_rec(ulong d, bool z)
2    {
```

J. Arndt, *Matters Computational: Ideas, Algorithms, Source Code,*
DOI 10.1007/978-3-642-14764-7_14, © Springer-Verlag Berlin Heidelberg 2011

```
 3          if ( d>=n )
 4          {
 5              if ( d<=n+1 )  // avoid duplicates
 6              {
 7                  visit();
 8              }
 9          }
10          else
11          {
12              if ( z )
13              {
14                  rv[d]=0;   rv[d+1]=0;   X_rec(d+2, z);
15                  rv[d]=1;   rv[d+1]=0;   X_rec(d+2,  ! z);
16                  rv[d]=1;   rv[d+1]=2;   rv[d+2]=0;   X_rec(d+3, z);
17              }
18              else
19              {
20                  rv[d]=1;   rv[d+1]=2;   rv[d+2]=0;   X_rec(d+3, z);
21                  rv[d]=1;   rv[d+1]=0;   X_rec(d+2,  ! z);
22                  rv[d]=0;   rv[d+1]=0;   X_rec(d+2, z);
23              }
24          }
25      }
```

The initial call is `X_rec(0, 0);`. The parameter `z` determines whether the list is generated in forward or backward order. No optimizations are made as these tend to obscure the idea. Here we could omit one statement `rv[d]=1;` in both branches, replace the arguments `z` and `!z` in the recursive calls by constants, or create an iterative version.

The number $w(n)$ of words $W(n)$ is determined by (some initial values and) a recursion. Counting the size of the lists on both sides of the recursion relation gives a relation for $w(n)$. Relation 14.1-1 leads to the recursion

$$w(n) \;=\; 2\,w(n-2) + w(n-3) \tag{14.1-3}$$

We can typically set $w(0) = 1$, there is one empty list and it satisfies all conditions. The numbers $w(n)$ are in fact the Fibonacci numbers.

14.2 Fibonacci words

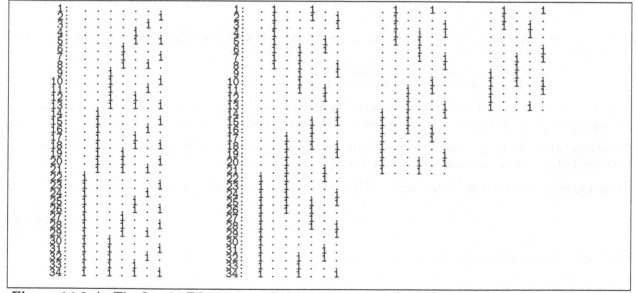

Figure 14.2-A: The first 34 Fibonacci words in counting order (left) and Gray codes through the first 34, 21, and 13 Fibonacci words (right). Dots are used for zeros.

A recursive routine to generate the Fibonacci words (binary words not containing two consecutive ones) can be given as follows:

```
1    ulong n;      // number of bits in words
2    ulong *rv;    // bits of the word
3
4    void fib_rec(ulong d)
5    {
6        if ( d>=n )  visit();
7        else
8        {
9            rv[d]=0;  fib_rec(d+1);
10           rv[d]=1;  rv[d+1]=0;  fib_rec(d+2);
11       }
12   }
```

We allocate one extra element (a sentinel) to reduce the number of if-statements in the code:

```
int main()
{
    n = 7;
    rv = new ulong[n+1];  // incl. sentinel rv[n]
    fib_rec(0);
    return 0;
}
```

The output (assuming `visit()` simply prints the array) is given in the left of figure 14.2-A.

A simple modification of the routine generates a Gray code through the Fibonacci words [FXT: comb/fibgray-rec-demo.cc]:

```
1    void fib_rec(ulong d, bool z)
2    {
3        if ( d>=n )  visit();
4        else
5        {
6            z = !z;  // change direction for Gray code
7            if ( z )
8            {
9                rv[d]=0;  fib_rec(d+1, z);
10               rv[d]=1;  rv[d+1]=0;  fib_rec(d+2, z);
11           }
12           else
13           {
14               rv[d]=1;  rv[d+1]=0;  fib_rec(d+2, z);
15               rv[d]=0;  fib_rec(d+1, z);
16           }
17       }
18   }
```

The variable `z` controls the direction in the recursion, it is changed unconditionally with each step. The `if-else` blocks can be merged into

```
1        rv[d]=!z;  rv[d+1]= z;  fib_rec(d+1+!z, z);
2        rv[d]= z;  rv[d+1]=!z;  fib_rec(d+1+ z, z);
```

In the n-bit Fibonacci Gray code the number of ones in the first and last, second and second-last, etc. tracks are equal. Therefore the sequence of reversed words is also a Fibonacci Gray code.

The algorithm needs constant amortized time and about 70 million objects are generated per second. A bit-level algorithm is given in section 1.27.2 on page 76.

The algorithm for the list of the length-n Fibonacci words $F(n)$ can be given as a recursion:

$$F(n) \;=\; \begin{matrix} [1\,0\,.\,F^{\mathbf{R}}(n-2)] \\ [0\,.\,F^{\mathbf{R}}(n-1)\ \ ] \end{matrix} \tag{14.2-1}$$

The generation can be sped up by merging two steps:

$$F(n) \;=\; \begin{matrix} [1\,0\,0\,.\,F(n-3)\ \ ] \\ [1\,0\,1\,0\,.\,F(n-4)] \\ [0\,0\,.\,F(n-2)\ \ \ ] \\ [0\,1\,0\,.\,F(n-3)\ \ ] \end{matrix} \tag{14.2-2}$$

14.3 Generalized Fibonacci words

```
............................iiiiiiiiiiiiiiiiiiiiii1111111111111111111111111111111111111111
.........................iiiiiiiiiiiiiiiiiiiiii..........................1111111111111111
......iiiiiiiiiii.......iiii....1111111............iiiiiiiiiii.....111111
....iiiiii......iiii.......iii...1111......iii....iii...iiiiii....iii....iiiiii
...ii..i..ii....ii...i...ii..ii...i...ii....ii...i...ii...i...ii....ii...ii...i...ii
.i.i.i....i.i.i.i.i.i..i.i.i.i.i.i..i.i.i.i.i.i..i.i.i.i.i..i.i.i.i.i.i..i.i.i.i.i..i.i.i

1111111111111111111111111111111111111111111111....................................
111111111111111....................................................
..........................................iiiiiiiiiiiiiiiiiiiiiii....iiiiiiiiiiiiiiiiiiiii
iii....iiiiiiiiiiii.......iiiiiii.........iiiiiiiiiiiii......iiiiiii....
1....iiii....1111......iiii.......111....iiii.......iiii...111111...ii
..ii..11..11..11...11..11...11..11...11..11..11...11...ii..ii...11..11....11..1
```

Figure 14.3-A: The 7-bit binary words with at most 2 consecutive ones in lexicographic (top) and minimal-change (bottom) order. Dots denote zeros.

```
111111111111111 1111111111111111111111111 ...............................................
111111111111111 .......................
.............. .......................
...............11111111111 iiiiiiiiiii.................1111111111111111111111
iii....111111 iiiiii..........iiiiii...........1111 1111.............iiiiiiiiiiii......1111111
1....iiii.......11 11...iiii....111111...iiii... ..iiii.....111111...iiii....1111....iiii...11
..11..11..11. .11..11...11...11..11...11..i 1...11..11...11..11...11..11..11....11..1
```

Figure 14.3-B: Recursive structure for the 7-bit binary words with at most 2 consecutive ones.

We generalize the Fibonacci words by allowing a fixed maximum value r of consecutive ones in a binary word. The Fibonacci words correspond to $r = 1$. Figure 14.3-A shows the 7-bit words with $r = 2$. The method to generate a Gray code for these words is a generalization of the recursion for the Fibonacci words. Write $L_r(n)$ for the list of n-bit words with at most r consecutive ones, then the recursive structure for the Gray code is

$$
L_r(n) \;=\;
\begin{array}{l}
[0 . L_r^{\mathbf{R}}(n-1) \qquad\qquad] \\
[1\,0 . L_r^{\mathbf{R}}(n-2) \qquad\quad\;] \\
[1\,1\,0 . L_r^{\mathbf{R}}(n-3) \qquad\;\;] \\
\;\; [\qquad \vdots \qquad\qquad\qquad] \\
[1^{r-2}0 . L_r^{\mathbf{R}}(n-1-r+2)] \\
[1^{r-1}0 . L_r^{\mathbf{R}}(n-1-r+1)] \\
[1^{r}0 . L_r^{\mathbf{R}}(n-1-r) \quad\;\;]
\end{array}
\tag{14.3-1}
$$

Figure 14.3-B shows the structure for $L_2(7)$, corresponding to the three lowest sublists on the right side of the equation. An implementation is [FXT: comb/maxrep-gray-demo.cc]:

```
1    ulong n;    // number of bits in words
2    ulong *rv;  // bits of the word
3    long mr;    // maximum number of consecutive ones

1    void maxrep_rec(ulong d, bool z)
2    {
3        if ( d>=n )  visit();
4        else
5        {
6            z = !z;
7
8            long km = mr;
9            if ( d+km > n )  km = n - d;
10
11           if ( z )
12           {
13               // words: 0, 10, 110, 1110, ...
14               for (long k=0; k<=km; ++k)
```

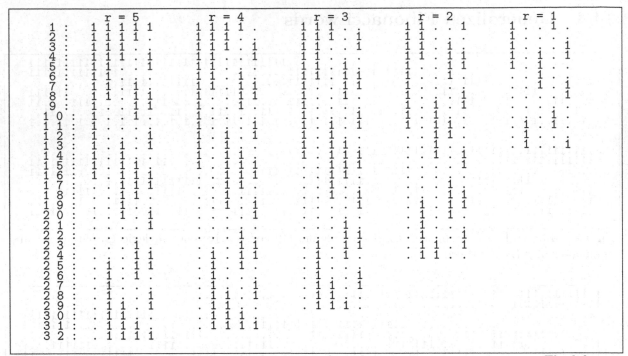

Figure 14.3-C: Gray codes of the 5-bit binary words with at most r consecutive ones. The leftmost column is the complement of the Gray code of all binary words, the rightmost column is the Gray code for the Fibonacci words.

```
15          {
16                  rv[d+k] = 0;
17                  maxrep_rec(d+1+k, z);
18                  rv[d+k] = 1;
19          }
20      }
21      else
22      {
23          // words: ... 1110, 110, 10, 0
24          for (long k=0; k<km; ++k)  rv[d+k] = 1;
25          for (long k=km; k>=0; --k)
26          {
27              rv[d+k] = 0;
28              maxrep_rec(d+1+k, z);
29          }
30      }
31  }
32 }
```

Figure 14.3-C shows the 5-bit Gray codes for $r \in \{1, 2, 3, 4, 5\}$. Observe that all sequences are subsequences of the leftmost column.

n:	0	1	2	3	4	5	6	7	8	9	10	11	12	13	14	15
r=1:	1	2	3	5	8	13	21	34	55	89	144	233	377	610	987	1597
r=2:	1	2	4	7	13	24	44	81	149	274	504	927	1705	3136	5768	10609
r=3:	1	2	4	8	15	29	56	108	208	401	773	1490	2872	5536	10671	20569
r=4:	1	2	4	8	16	31	61	120	236	464	912	1793	3525	6930	13624	26784
r=5:	1	2	4	8	16	32	63	125	248	492	976	1936	3840	7617	15109	29970

Figure 14.3-D: Number of length-n binary words with at most r consecutive ones.

Let $w_r(n)$ be the number of n-bit words $W_r(n)$ with $\leq r$ consecutive ones. Taking the length of the lists on both sides of relation 14.3-1 gives the recursion

$$w_r(n) = \sum_{j=0}^{r} w_r(n-1-j) \tag{14.3-2}$$

where we set $w_r(n) = 2^k$ for $0 \leq n \leq r$. The sequences for $r \leq 5$ start as shown in figure 14.3-D. The sequences are the following entries in [312]: $r = 1$ is entry A000045 (the Fibonacci numbers), $r = 2$ is A000073, $r = 3$ is A000078, $r = 4$ is A001591, and $r = 5$ is A001592. The variant of the Fibonacci sequence where each number is the sum of its k predecessors is also called *Fibonacci k-step sequence*. The generating function for $w_r(n)$ is

$$\sum_{n=0}^{\infty} w_r(n)\, x^n = \frac{\sum_{k=0}^{r} x^k}{1 - \sum_{k=1}^{r+1} x^k} \tag{14.3-3}$$

Alternative Gray code for words without substrings 111 ($r = 2$) ‡

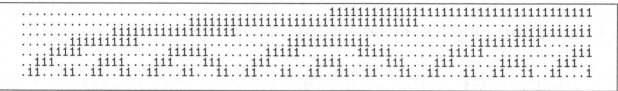

Figure 14.3-E: The 7-bit binary words with at most 2 consecutive ones in a minimal-change order.

The list recursion for the Gray code for binary words without substrings 111 is the special case $r = 2$ of relation 14.3-1 on page 307:

$$L_2(n) = \begin{matrix} [1\,1\,0\,.\,L_2^{\mathbf{R}}(n-3)] \\ [1\,0\,.\,L_2^{\mathbf{R}}(n-2)] \\ [0\,.\,L_2^{\mathbf{R}}(n-1)] \end{matrix} \tag{14.3-4}$$

A different Gray code is generated by the recursion

$$L_2'(n) = \begin{matrix} [1\,0\,.\,L_2'(n-2)] \\ [1\,1\,0\,.\,L_2'^{\mathbf{R}}(n-3)] \\ [0\,.\,L_2'(n-1)] \end{matrix} \tag{14.3-5}$$

The ordering is shown in figure 14.3-E. It was created with the program [FXT: comb/no111-gray-demo.cc].

Alternative Gray code for words without substrings 1111 ($r = 3$) ‡

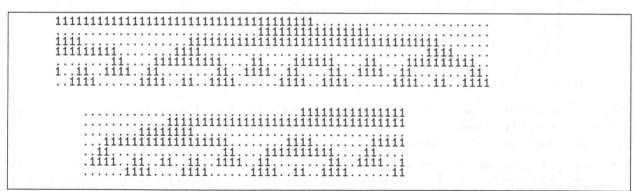

Figure 14.3-F: The 7-bit binary words with at most 3 consecutive ones in a minimal-change order.

A list recursion for an alternative Gray code for binary words without substrings 1111 ($r = 3$) is

$$L_3'(n) = \begin{matrix} [1\,1\,0\,.\,L_3'^{\mathbf{R}}(n-3)] \\ [0\,.\,L_3'^{\mathbf{R}}(n-1)] \\ [1\,1\,1\,0\,.\,L_3'^{\mathbf{R}}(n-4)] \\ [1\,0\,.\,L_3'^{\mathbf{R}}(n-2)] \end{matrix} \tag{14.3-6}$$

The ordering is shown in figure 14.3-F. It was created with the program [FXT: comb/no1111-gray-demo.cc]. For all odd $r \geq 3$ a Gray code is generated by a list recursion where the prefixes with an even number of ones are followed by those with an odd number of ones. For example, with $r = 5$ the recursion is

$$
L'_5(n) = \begin{array}{l}
[1\,1\,1\,1\,0\,.\,L'^{\mathbf{R}}_5(n-7)\ ] \\
[1\,1\,0\,.\,L'^{\mathbf{R}}_5(n-3)\quad\ ] \\
[0\,.\,L'^{\mathbf{R}}_5(n-1)\qquad\ ] \\
[1\,1\,1\,1\,1\,0\,.\,L'^{\mathbf{R}}_5(n-6)] \\
[1\,1\,1\,0\,.\,L'^{\mathbf{R}}_5(n-4)\quad\ ] \\
[1\,0\,.\,L'^{\mathbf{R}}_5(n-2)\qquad\ ]
\end{array}
\tag{14.3-7}
$$

14.4 Run-length limited (RLL) words

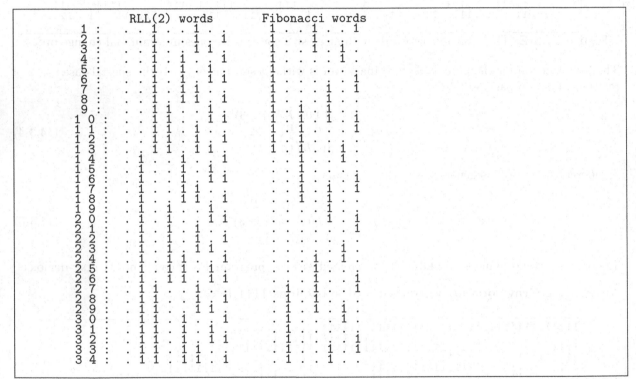

Figure 14.4-A: Lex order for RLL(2) words (left) corresponds to Gray code for Fibonacci words (right).

Words with conditions on the minimum and maximum number of repetitions of a value are called *run-length limited (RLL) words*. Here we consider only binary words where the number of both consecutive zeros and ones is at most r where $r \geq 2$. We call the RLL words starting with zero as RLL(r) words.

RLL(r) words of length n correspond to generalized Fibonacci words (with at most $r - 1$ ones) of length $n - 1$: the k-th digit ($k \geq 1$) of the Fibonacci word is one if the k-th digit of the RLL word is unchanged. The list of RLL(2) words in lexicographic order is shown in figure 14.4-A, note that the corresponding Fibonacci words are in minimal change order. The listing was generated by the following recursion [FXT: comb/rll-rec-demo.cc]:

```
1    ulong n;    // number of bits in words
2
3    void rll_rec(ulong d, bool z)
4    {
5        if ( d>=n )  visit();
6        else
7        {
```

```
                RLL(2) words   change   Fibonacci words
     1 :     . 1 1 . . 1 1        -      1 . 1 . 1 . 1
     2 :     . 1 1 . . 1 .        1      1 . 1 . 1 . .
     3 :     . 1 1 . 1 1 .        1      1 . 1 . . 1 .
     4 :     . 1 1 . 1 . .        1      1 . 1 . . . .
     5 :     . 1 1 . 1 . 1        1      1 . 1 . . . 1
     6 :     . 1 . . 1 1 .        3      1 . . 1 . 1 .
     7 :     . 1 . . 1 . .        1      1 . . 1 . . .
     8 :     . 1 . . 1 . 1        1      1 . . 1 . . 1
     9 :     . 1 . 1 1 . .        2      1 . . . 1 . 1
    1 0 :     . 1 . 1 1 . 1        1      1 . . . 1 . .
    1 1 :     . 1 . 1 . . 1        1      1 . . . . 1 .
    1 2 :     . 1 . 1 . 1 1        1      1 . . . . . 1
    1 3 :     . 1 . 1 . 1 .        1      1 . . . . . .
    1 4 :     1 1 . . 1 1 .        3      . 1 . 1 . 1 .
    1 5 :     1 1 . . 1 . .        1      . 1 . 1 . 1 .
    1 6 :     1 1 . . 1 . 1        1      . 1 . 1 . . 1
    1 7 :     1 1 . 1 1 . .        2      . 1 . . 1 . 1
    1 8 :     1 1 . 1 . . 1        1      . 1 . . 1 . .
    1 9 :     1 1 . 1 . 1 1        1      . 1 . . . 1 .
    2 0 :     1 1 . 1 . 1 1        1      . 1 . . . . 1
    2 1 :     1 1 . 1 . 1 .        1      . 1 . . . . .
    2 2 :     1 . . 1 1 .          3      . . 1 . 1 . 1
    2 3 :     1 . . 1 1 . 1        1      . . 1 . 1 . .
    2 4 :     1 . . 1 . .          1      . . 1 . . 1 .
    2 5 :     1 . . 1 . 1 1        1      . . 1 . . . 1
    2 6 :     1 . . 1 . 1 .        1      . . 1 . . . .
    2 7 :     1 . 1 1 . . 1        3      . . . 1 . 1 .
    2 8 :     1 . 1 1 . 1 1        1      . . . 1 . . 1
    2 9 :     1 . 1 1 . 1 .        1      . . . 1 . . .
    3 0 :     1 . 1 . . 1 1        2      . . . . 1 . 1
    3 1 :     1 . 1 . . 1 .        1      . . . . 1 . .
    3 2 :     1 . 1 . 1 1 .        1      . . . . . 1 .
    3 3 :     1 . 1 . 1 . .        1      . . . . . . 1
    3 4 :     1 . 1 . 1 . 1        1      . . . . . . .
```

Figure 14.4-B: Order for RLL(2) words (left) corresponding to lex order for Fibonacci words (right).

```
 8          if ( z==0 )
 9          {
10              rv[d]=0; rv[d+1]=1; rll_rec(d+2, 1);
11              rv[d]=1; rll_rec(d+1, 1);
12          }
13          else  // z==1
14          {
15              rv[d]=0; rll_rec(d+1, 0);
16              rv[d]=1; rv[d+1]=0; rll_rec(d+2, 0);
17          }
18      }
19  }
```

The variable z records whether the last bit was a one. By swapping the lines in the branch for $z = 1$ we obtain an ordering which corresponds to the (reversed) lexicographic order of the Fibonacci words shown in figure 14.4-B. The average number of changes per between successive elements tends to $1 + 1/\sqrt{5} \approx 1.44721$ for $n \to \infty$. The order is not a Gray code for the RLL words, the maximum number of changed bits among all transitions for $n \leq 30$ is

n: 1 2 3 4 5 6 7 8 9 10 11 12 13 14 15 16 17 18 19 20 21 22 23 24 25 26 27 28 29 30 ...
   1 1 1 2 3 3 3 4 5 5 5 5 6 7 7 7 8 9 9 9 10 11 11 11 12 13 13 13 14 15 15 ...

14.5   Digit x followed by at least x zeros

```
3333222222221111111111111..................................11111111111111111111111122222222222223333333
.....................123321......111123321111...............111111122223322221111111.......111123321111........
.123321.....123321....123321.....123321....123321.....123321.....123321....123321....123321....123321...123
```

Figure 14.5-A: Gray code for the length-6 words with maximal digit 3 where a digit x is followed by at least x zeros. Dots denote zeros.

Figure 14.5-A shows a Gray code for the length-5 words with maximal digit 3 where a digit x is followed by at least x zeros. For the Gray code list $Z_r(n)$ of the length-n words with maximal digit r we have

$$Z_r(n) = \begin{matrix} [0 \, . \, Z_r^{\mathbf{R}}(n-1) &] \\ [10 \, . \, Z_r^{\mathbf{R}}(n-2) &] \\ [200 \, . \, Z_r^{\mathbf{R}}(n-3) &] \\ [3000 \, . \, Z_r^{\mathbf{R}}(n-4) &] \\ [\quad \vdots &] \\ [r \, 0^r \, . \, Z_r^{\mathbf{R}}(n-r-1)] \end{matrix} \tag{14.5-1}$$

An implementation is [FXT: comb/gexz-gray-demo.cc]:

```
1    ulong n;    // number of digits in words
2    ulong *rv;  // digits of the word
3    ulong mr;   // radix== mr+1

1    void gexz_rec(ulong d, bool z)
2    {
3        if ( d>=n )  visit();
4        else
5        {
6            if ( z )
7            {
8                // words 0, 10, 200, 3000, 40000, ...
9                ulong k = 0;
10               do
11               {
12                   rv[d]=k;
13                   for (ulong j=1; j<=k; ++j)   rv[d+j] = 0;
14                   gexz_rec(d+k+1, !z);
15               }
16               while ( ++k <= mr );
17           }
18           else
19           {
20               // words ..., 40000, 3000, 200, 10, 0
21               ulong k = mr + 1;
22               do
23               {
24                   --k;
25                   rv[d]=k;
26                   for (ulong j=1; j<=k; ++j)   rv[d+j] = 0;
27                   gexz_rec(d+k+1, !z);
28               }
29               while ( k != 0 );
30           }
31       }
32   }
```

n:	0	1	2	3	4	5	6	7	8	9	10	11	12	13	14	15
r=1:	1	2	3	5	8	13	21	34	55	89	144	233	377	610	987	1597
r=2:	1	3	5	9	17	31	57	105	193	355	653	1201	2209	4063	7473	13745
r=3:	1	4	7	13	25	49	94	181	349	673	1297	2500	4819	9289	17905	34513
r=4:	1	5	9	17	33	65	129	253	497	977	1921	3777	7425	14597	28697	56417
r=5:	1	6	11	21	41	81	161	321	636	1261	2501	4961	9841	19521	38721	76806

Figure 14.5-B: Number of radix-$(r+1)$, length-n words where a digit x is followed by at least x zeros.

Let $z_r(n)$ be the number of n-bit words $Z_r(n)$, then

$$z_r(n) = \sum_{j=1}^{r+1} z_r(n-j) \tag{14.5-2}$$

where we set $z_r(n) = 1$ for $n \le 0$. The sequences for $r \le 5$ start as shown in figure 14.5-B. The sequences are the following entries in [312]: $r = 1$ is entry A000045 (the Fibonacci numbers), $r = 2$ is A000213, $r = 3$ is A000288, $r = 4$ is A000322, and $r = 5$ is A000383.

14.6 Generalized Pell words

14.6.1 Gray code for Pell words

```
.........................1111111111111111111222222..........1111111111111111111111111111111111  2222222
......1111111111111111112222222.............11111111111111111111  iiiiiii222......111111112222......1111111222......1111111222......111111122  iiii222
...1112..1112....1112...1112...1112....1112..1112...1112...1112..1112...1112...  1112..
.12.12..12.12..12.12.12..12.12..12.12.12..12.12..12.12.12..12.12..12.12.12..12.12..1  .12..12
```

```
.........................1111111111111111111111111111111111111111111111111111  2222222
.......11111111111111111111112222222222222211111111111111111111  iiiiiii2222221111111.............111111112222221111111  iiii222
..11122111...........11122111.......11122111.......11122111....  1.
.1221....1221..1221..1221....1221..1221...1221..1221....1221..1221..1221.  221..12
```

Figure 14.6-A: Start and end of the lists of 5-digit Pell words in counting order (top) and Gray code order (bottom). The lowest row is the least significant digit, dots denote zeros.

A Gray code of the Pell words (ternary words without the substrings "21" and "22") can be computed as follows:

```
1    ulong n;      // number of digits in words
2    ulong *rv;     // digits of the word
3    bool zq;       // order: 0==>Lex,  1==>Gray

1    void pell_rec(ulong d, bool z)
2    {
3        if ( d>=n )  visit();
4        else
5        {
6            if ( 0==z )
7            {
8                rv[d]=0;  pell_rec(d+1, z);
9                rv[d]=1;  pell_rec(d+1, zq^z);
10               rv[d]=2;  rv[d+1]=0;  pell_rec(d+2, z);
11           }
12           else
13           {
14               rv[d]=2;  rv[d+1]=0;  pell_rec(d+2, z);
15               rv[d]=1;  pell_rec(d+1, zq^z);
16               rv[d]=0;  pell_rec(d+1, z);
17           }
18       }
19   }
```

The global Boolean variable zq controls whether the counting order or the Gray code is generated. The code is given in [FXT: comb/pellgray-rec-demo.cc]. Both orderings are shown in figure 14.6-A. About 110 million words per second are generated. The computation of a function whose power series coefficients are related to the Pell Gray code is described in section 38.12.3 on page 760.

14.6.2 Gray code for generalized Pell words

```
3333222222222222221111111111111111.........................1111111111111111111111111111111111  
.....11112222332222111.......111122223322221111.......11112222332222  
.123321..123321....123321..123321..123321....123321..123321..123321....123  
```

```
1111111111112222222222222222222222222222222222222222222222222223333333333333  
222222223333333332222222222222211111111111111....................  
1111..........111122223322221111.......111122223322221111........  
321..123321..123321..123321....123321..123321..123321....123321..123  
```

Figure 14.6-B: Gray code for 4-digit radix-4 strings with no substring $3x$ with $x \neq 0$.

A generalization of the Pell words are the radix-$(r+1)$ strings where the substring rx with $x \neq 0$ is forbidden (that is, a nine can only be followed by a zero). Let $P_r(n)$ be the list of length-n words in Gray code order. The list can be generated by the recursion

$$P_r(n) = \begin{matrix} [0 \,.\, P_r(n-1) &] \\ [1 \,.\, P_r^{\mathbf{R}}(n-1) &] \\ [2 \,.\, P_r(n-1) &] \\ [3 \,.\, P_r^{\mathbf{R}}(n-1) &] \\ [\quad \vdots &] \\ [(r-1) \,.\, P_r^{\mathbf{R}}(n-1)] \\ [(r)\, 0 \,.\, P_r(n-2) &] \end{matrix} \tag{14.6-1a}$$

if r is even, and by the recursion

$$P_r(n) = \begin{matrix} [0 \,.\, P_r^{\mathbf{R}}(n-1) &] \\ [1 \,.\, P_r(n-1) &] \\ [2 \,.\, P_r^{\mathbf{R}}(n-1) &] \\ [3 \,.\, P_r(n-1) &] \\ [\quad \vdots &] \\ [(r-1) \,.\, P_r(n-1)] \\ [(r)\, 0 \,.\, P_r^{\mathbf{R}}(n-2) &] \end{matrix} \tag{14.6-1b}$$

if r is odd. Figure 14.6-B shows a Gray code for the 4-digit strings with $r = 3$. An implementation of the algorithm is [FXT: comb/pellgen-gray-demo.cc]:

```
1    ulong n;     // number of digits in words
2    ulong *rv;   // digits of the word (radix r+1)
3    long r;      // Forbidden substrings are [r, x] where x!=0

1    void pellgen_rec(ulong d, bool z)
2    {
3        if ( d>=n )  visit();
4        else
5        {
6            const bool p = r & 1;  // parity of r
7            rv[d] = 0;
8            if ( z )
9            {
10               for (long k=0; k<r; ++k)  { rv[d] = k;  pellgen_rec(d+1, z ^ p ^ (k&1)); }
11               { rv[d] = r;  rv[d+1] = 0;  pellgen_rec(d+2, p ^ z); }
12           }
13           else
14           {
15               { rv[d] = r;  rv[d+1] = 0;  pellgen_rec(d+2, p ^ z); }
16               for (long k=r-1; k>=0; --k)  { rv[d] = k;  pellgen_rec(d+1, z ^ p ^ (k&1)); }
17           }
18       }
19   }
```

With $r = 1$ we again get the Gray code for Fibonacci words.

n:	0	1	2	3	4	5	6	7	8	9	10	11
r=1:	1	2	3	5	8	13	21	34	55	89	144	233
r=2:	1	3	7	17	41	99	239	577	1393	3363	8119	19601
r=3:	1	4	13	43	142	469	1549	5116	16897	55807	184318	608761
r=4:	1	5	21	89	377	1597	6765	28657	121393	514229	2178309	9227465
r=5:	1	6	31	161	836	4341	22541	117046	607771	3155901	16387276	85092281

Figure 14.6-C: Number of length-n, radix-$(r+1)$ words with no substring $r\,x$ with $x \neq 0$.

Taking the number $p_r(n)$ of words $P_r(n)$ on both sides of relations 14.6-1a and 14.6-1b we find

$$p_r(n) = r\, p_r(n) + p_r(n-2) \tag{14.6-2}$$

where $p_r(0) = 1$ and $p_r(1) = r+1$. For $r \leq 5$ the sequences start as shown in figure 14.6-C. The sequences are the following entries in [312]: $r = 1$: A000045; $r = 2$: A001333; $r = 3$: A003688; $r = 4$: A015448;

$r = 5$: A015449. The generating function for $p_r(n)$ is

$$\sum_{n=0}^{\infty} p_r(n)\, x^n \;=\; \frac{1+x}{1 - r\,x - x^2} \qquad (14.6\text{-}3)$$

14.7 Sparse signed binary words

```
PPPPPPPPPPPPMMMMMMMMMMMM.................................MMMMMMMMMMMMMMMMMMMMMPPPPPPPPPPPPPPPPPPPPPP
PPPMMM..........MMMPPPPPPMMM......MMMMMPPPPPPPPPPPMMMMM...............MMMPPPPPPPMMM.......MMMMMPPPPP
PM..MPPM......MPPM..MPPM..MPPM......MPPM......MPPM......MPPM..MPPM..MPPM......MPPM...MP
PM..MPPM......MPPM..MPPM..MPPM......MPPM......MPPM......MPPM.MPPM.MPPM......MPPM...
```

Figure 14.7-A: A Gray code through the 85 sparse 6-bit signed binary words. Dots are used for zeros, the symbols 'P' and 'M' denote $+1$ and -1, respectively.

Figure 14.7-A shows a minimal-change order (Gray code) for the sparse signed binary words (nonadjacent form (NAF), see section 1.23 on page 61). Note that we allow a digit to switch between $+1$ and -1. If all words with any positive digit ('P') are omitted, we obtain the Gray code for Fibonacci words given in section 14.2 on page 305.

A recursive routine for the generation of the Gray code is given in [FXT: comb/naf-gray-rec-demo.cc]:

```
1    ulong n;    // number of digits of the string
2    int *rv;    // the string

1    void sb_rec(ulong d, bool z)
2    {
3        if ( d>=n )  visit();
4        else
5        {
6            if ( 0==z )
7            {
8                rv[d]=0;   sb_rec(d+1, 1);
9                rv[d]=-1;  rv[d+1]=0;  sb_rec(d+2, 1);
10               rv[d]=+1;  rv[d+1]=0;  sb_rec(d+2, 0);
11           }
12           else
13           {
14               rv[d]=+1;  rv[d+1]=0;  sb_rec(d+2, 1);
15               rv[d]=-1;  rv[d+1]=0;  sb_rec(d+2, 0);
16               rv[d]=0;   sb_rec(d+1, 0);
17           }
18       }
19   }
```

About 120 million words per second are generated.

Let $S(n)$ be the number of n-digit sparse signed binary numbers (of both signs) and $P(n)$ be the number of positive n-digit sparse signed binary numbers, then

n	0	1	2	3	4	5	6	7	8	9	10	11	12	13	14	15	16
S(n):	1	3	5	11	21	43	85	171	341	683	1365	2731	5461	10923	21845	43691	87381
P(n):	1	2	3	6	11	22	43	86	171	342	683	1366	2731	5462	10923	21846	43691

The sequence of values $S(n)$ and $P(n)$ are respectively entries A001045 and A005578 in [312]. We have

(with $e := n \bmod 2$)

$$S(n) = \frac{2^{n+2} - 1 + 2\,e}{3} = 2\,S(n-1) - 1 + 2\,e \tag{14.7-1a}$$

$$= S(n-1) + 2\,S(n-2) = 3\,S(n-2) + 2\,S(n-3) = 2\,P(n) - 1 \tag{14.7-1b}$$

$$P(n) = \frac{2^{n+1} + 1 + e}{3} = 2\,P(n-1) - 1 - e = S(n-1) + e \tag{14.7-1c}$$

$$= P(n-1) + S(n-2) = P(n-2) + S(n-2) + S(n-3) \tag{14.7-1d}$$

$$= S(n-2) + S(n-3) + S(n-4) + \ldots + S(2) + S(1) + 3 \tag{14.7-1e}$$

$$= 2\,P(n-1) + P(n-2) - 2\,P(n-3) \tag{14.7-1f}$$

Almost Gray code for positive words ‡

```
                  ><              ><
                                              ...........PPPPPPPPPPPPPPPPPPPPPPPPPPPPPPPPPPPPPPPPPPPP
PPPPPPPPPPPPPPPPPPPPPP.........................PPPPPPPPPPPPPPPPPPPPPPPMMMMMMMMMM.........................
PPPPPMMMM............PPPPP.........PPPPPPPPPPPPPPPPPPPPPPPPPPMMMMMMMMMM..........................MMMMMPPPPP
PM.......MPPM.........MMMPPP.......MPP...PPP....PM....MMMPPPPPPPMM.........MMMPPPPPPPMM........MPPM.......MP
...MPPM......MPPM....MPPM..MPPM.....PPM.....PM...MPPM...MPPM...MPPM......MPPM...MPPM...MPPM......MPPM...
                  ><              ><
```

Figure 14.7-B: An ordering of the 86 sparse 7-bit positive signed binary words that is almost a Gray code. The transitions that are not minimal are marked with '><'. Dots denote zeros.

If we start with the following routine that calls `sb_rec()` only after a one has been inserted, we get an ordering of the positive numbers:

```
1    void pos_rec(ulong d, bool z)
2    {
3        if ( d>=n )  visit();
4        else
5        {
6            if ( 0==z )
7            {
8                rv[d]=0;   pos_rec(d+1, 1);
9                rv[d]=+1;  rv[d+1]=0;  sb_rec(d+2, 1);
10           }
11           else
12           {
13               rv[d]=+1;  rv[d+1]=0;  sb_rec(d+2, 0);
14               rv[d]=0;   pos_rec(d+1, 0);
15           }
16       }
17   }
```

The ordering with n-digit words is a Gray code, except for $n - 4$ transitions. An ordering with only about $n/2$ non-Gray transitions is generated by the more complicated recursion [FXT: comb/naf-pos-rec-demo.cc]:

```
1    void pos_AAA(ulong d, bool z)
2    {
3        if ( d>=n )  visit();
4        else
5        {
6            if ( 0==z )
7            {
8                rv[d]=+1;  rv[d+1]=0;  sb_rec(d+2, 0);   // 0
9                rv[d]=0;   pos_AAA(d+1, 1);   // 1
10           }
11           else
12           {
13               rv[d]=0;   pos_BBB(d+1, 0);   // 0
14               rv[d]=+1;  rv[d+1]=0;  sb_rec(d+2, 1);   // 1
15           }
16       }
17   }
```

```
1    void pos_BBB(ulong d, bool z)
```

```
2     {
3         if ( d>=n ) visit();
4         else
5         {
6             if ( 0==z )
7             {
8                 rv[d]=+1;  rv[d+1]=0;  sb_rec(d+2, 1);  // 1
9                 rv[d]=0;  pos_BBB(d+1, 1);  // 1
10            }
11            else
12            {
13                rv[d]=0;  pos_AAA(d+1, 0);  // 0
14                rv[d]=+1;  rv[d+1]=0;  sb_rec(d+2, 0);  // 0
15            }
16        }
17    }
```

The initial call is `pos_AAA(0,0)`. The result for $n = 7$ is shown in figure 14.7-B. We list the number N of non-Gray transitions and the number of digit changes X in excess of a Gray code for $n \leq 30$:

```
n :1 2 3 4 5 6 7 8 9 1 01 11 213 1 41 516 17 18 19 20 21 22 23 24 25 26 27 28 29 30
N :0 0 0 0 1 2 2 2 3  4  4  4 5  6  6  6  7  8  8  8  9 10 10 10 11 12 12 12 13 14
X: 0 0 0 0 1 3 4 4 5  7  8  8 9 11 12 12 13 15 16 16 17 19 20 20 21 23 24 24 25 27
```

14.8 Strings with no two consecutive nonzero digits

```
 1:  .3..3      26:  ....1      51:  1.1.2      76:  2.3.2
 2:  .3..2      27:  ....2      52:  1.1.3      77:  2.3.1
 3:  .3..1      28:  ...3       53:  1...3      78:  2.3..
 4:  .3...      29:  ..1.3      54:  1...2      79:  3.3..
 5:  .3.1.      30:  ..1.2      55:  1...1      80:  3.3.1
 6:  .3.2.      31:  ..1.1      56:  1....      81:  3.3.2
 7:  .3.3.      32:  ..1..      57:  1..1.      82:  3.3.3
 8:  .2.3.      33:  ..2..      58:  1..2.      83:  3.2.3
 9:  .2.2.      34:  ..2.1      59:  1..3.      84:  3.2.2
10:  .2.1.      35:  ..2.2      60:  2..3.      85:  3.2.1
11:  .2...      36:  ..2.3      61:  2..2.      86:  3.2..
12:  .2..1      37:  ..3.3      62:  2..1.      87:  3.1..
13:  .2..2      38:  ..3.2      63:  2....      88:  3.1.1
14:  .2..3      39:  ..3.1      64:  2...1      89:  3.1.2
15:  .1..3      40:  ..3..      65:  2...2      90:  3.1.3
16:  .1..2      41:  1.3..      66:  2...3      91:  3...3
17:  .1..1      42:  1.3.1      67:  2.1.3      92:  3...2
18:  .1...      43:  1.3.2      68:  2.1.2      93:  3...1
19:  .1.1.      44:  1.3.3      69:  2.1.1      94:  3....
20:  .1.2.      45:  1.2.3      70:  2.1..      95:  3..1.
21:  .1.3.      46:  1.2.2      71:  2.2..      96:  3..2.
22:  ...3.      47:  1.2.1      72:  2.2.1      97:  3..3.
23:  ...2.      48:  1.2..      73:  2.2.2
24:  ...1.      49:  1.1..      74:  2.2.3
25:  .....      50:  1.1.1      75:  2.3.3
```

Figure 14.8-A: Gray code for the length-4 radix-4 strings with no two consecutive nonzero digits.

A Gray code for the length-n strings with radix $(r+1)$ and no two consecutive nonzero digits is generated by the following recursion for the list $D_r(n)$:

$$D_r(n) = \begin{array}{l}
[\, 0 \,.\, D_r^{\mathbf{R}}(n-1)] \\
[10 \,.\, D_r^{\mathbf{R}}(n-1)] \\
[20 \,.\, D_r(n-1)\ ] \\
[30 \,.\, D_r^{\mathbf{R}}(n-1)] \\
[40 \,.\, D_r(n-1)\ ] \\
[50 \,.\, D_r^{\mathbf{R}}(n-1)] \\
\quad[\quad \vdots \quad\quad]
\end{array} \tag{14.8-1}$$

An implementation is [FXT: comb/ntnz-gray-demo.cc]:

```
1    ulong n;      // length of strings
2    ulong *rv;    // digits of strings
3    ulong mr;     // max digit
```

```
1    void ntnz_rec(ulong d, bool z)
2    {
3        if ( d>=n )  visit();
4        else
5        {
6            if ( 0==z )
7            {
8                rv[d]=0;  ntnz_rec(d+1, 1);
9                for (ulong t=1; t<=mr; ++t)  { rv[d]=t;  rv[d+1]=0;  ntnz_rec(d+2, t&1); }
10           }
11           else
12           {
13               for (ulong t=mr; t>0; --t)  { rv[d]=t;  rv[d+1]=0;  ntnz_rec(d+2, !(t&1)); }
14               rv[d]=0;  ntnz_rec(d+1, 0);
15           }
16       }
17   }
```

Figure 14.8-A shows the Gray code for length-4, radix-4 ($r = 3$) strings. Setting $r = 2$, replacing 1 with -1, and 2 with $+1$, gives the Gray code for the sparse binary words (figure 14.7-A on page 315). With $r = 1$ we get the Gray code for the Fibonacci words.

n:	0	1	2	3	4	5	6	7	8	9	10	11	12	13	14
r=1:	1	2	3	5	8	13	21	34	55	89	144	233	377	610	987
r=2:	1	3	5	11	21	43	85	171	341	683	1365	2731	5461	10923	21845
r=3:	1	4	7	19	40	97	217	508	1159	2683	6160	14209	32689	75316	173383
r=4:	1	5	9	29	65	181	441	1165	2929	7589	19305	49661	126881	325525	833049
r=5:	1	6	11	41	96	301	781	2286	6191	17621	48576	136681	379561	1062966	2960771

Figure 14.8-B: Number of radix-$(r + 1)$, length-n words with no two consecutive nonzero digits.

Counting the elements on both sides of relation 14.8-1 we find that for the number $d_r(n)$ of strings in the list $D_r(n)$ we have

$$d_r(n) \;=\; d_r(n-1) + r\, d_r(n-2) \tag{14.8-2}$$

where $d_r(0) = 1$ and $d_r(1) = r+1$. The sequences of these numbers start as shown in figure 14.8-B. These are the following entries in [312]: $r = 1$: A000045; $r = 2$: A001045; $r = 3$: A006130; $r = 4$: A006131; $r = 5$: A015440; $r = 6$: A015441; $r = 7$: A015442; $r = 8$: A015443. The generating function for $d_r(n)$ is

$$\sum_{n=0}^{\infty} d_r(n)\, x^n \;=\; \frac{1 + r\,x}{1 - x - r\,x^2} \tag{14.8-3}$$

14.9 Strings with no two consecutive zeros

```
                 .....1111111111111112222222222222222333333333333333
1111222233333333322221111......1111222233333333322221111...
321..123321..123321..123321123321..123321..123321..123321


                    .....111111111111111111111111122222222222222222222222
iiiiiiii2222222222222222211111111......11111111222222222
222111...1112222222211....11122222211111112222221111....111222
21..12211221..1221..12211221..1221..1221..1221..12211221..12
```

Figure 14.9-A: Gray codes for strings with no two consecutive zeros: length-3 radix-4 (left) and length-4 radix-3 (right). Dots denote zeros.

Gray codes for strings with no two consecutive zeros are shown in figure 14.9-A. The recursion for the list $Z_r(n)$ with radix $(r+1)$ is

$$
Z_r(n) = \begin{matrix}
[0\,1\ .\ Z_r(n-2)\ ] \\
[0\,2\ .\ Z_r^{\mathbf{R}}(n-2)] \\
[0\,3\ .\ Z_r(n-2)\ ] \\
[0\,4\ .\ Z_r^{\mathbf{R}}(n-2)] \\
[0\,5\ .\ Z_r(n-2)\ ] \\
[\quad \vdots \quad] \\
[0\,r\ .\ Z_r^{\mathbf{R}}(n-2)] \\
[1\ .\ Z_r^{\mathbf{R}}(n-1)\ ] \\
[2\ .\ Z_r(n-1)\ ] \\
[3\ .\ Z_r^{\mathbf{R}}(n-1)\ ] \\
[4\ .\ Z_r(n-1)\ ] \\
[\quad \vdots \quad] \\
[r\ .\ Z_r^{\mathbf{R}}(n-1)\ ]
\end{matrix} \text{ for } r \text{ even,} \qquad
Z_r(n) = \begin{matrix}
[0\,1\ .\ Z_r^{\mathbf{R}}(n-2)] \\
[0\,2\ .\ Z_r(n-2)\ ] \\
[0\,3\ .\ Z_r^{\mathbf{R}}(n-2)] \\
[0\,4\ .\ Z_r(n-2)\ ] \\
[0\,5\ .\ Z_r^{\mathbf{R}}(n-2)] \\
[\quad \vdots \quad] \\
[0\,r\ .\ Z_r^{\mathbf{R}}(n-2)] \\
[1\ .\ Z_r(n-1)\ ] \\
[2\ .\ Z_r^{\mathbf{R}}(n-1)\ ] \\
[3\ .\ Z_r(n-1)\ ] \\
[4\ .\ Z_r^{\mathbf{R}}(n-1)\ ] \\
[\quad \vdots \quad] \\
[r\ .\ Z_r(n-1)\ ]
\end{matrix} \text{ for } r \text{ odd.} \qquad (14.9\text{-}1)
$$

An implementation is given in [FXT: comb/ntz-gray-demo.cc]:

```
ulong n;     // number of digits in words
ulong *rv;   // digits of the word (radix r+1)
long r;      // Forbidden substrings are [r, x] where x!=0

void ntz_rec(ulong d, bool z)
{
    if ( d>=n )  visit();
    else
    {
        bool w = 0;  // r-parity:  w depends on z ...
        if ( r&1 )  w = !z;   // ... if r odd

        if ( z )
        {
            // words 0X:
            rv[d] = 0;
            if ( d+2<=n )
            {
                for (long k=1; k<=r; ++k, w=!w)  { rv[d+1]=k;  ntz_rec(d+2, w); }
            }
            else
            {
                ntz_rec(d+1, w);
                w = !w;
            }

            w ^= (r&1);  //  r-parity:  change direction if r odd

            // words X:
            for (long k=1; k<=r; ++k, w=!w)  { rv[d]=k;  ntz_rec(d+1, w); }
        }
        else
        {
            // words X:
            for (long k=r; k>=1; --k, w=!w)  { rv[d]=k;  ntz_rec(d+1, w); }

            w ^= (r&1);  //  r-parity:  change direction if r odd

            // words 0X:
            rv[d] = 0;
            if ( d+2<=n )
            {
                for (long k=r; k>=1; --k, w=!w)  { rv[d+1]=k;  ntz_rec(d+2, w); }
            }
            else
            {
                ntz_rec(d+1, w);
                w = !w;
            }
        }
    }
}
```

With $r = 1$ we obtain the complement of the minimal-change list of Fibonacci words.

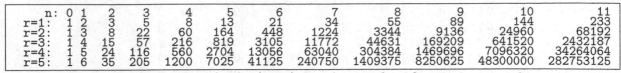

n:	0	1	2	3	4	5	6	7	8	9	10	11
r=1:	1	2	3	5	8	13	21	34	55	89	144	233
r=2:	1	3	8	22	60	164	448	1224	3344	9136	24960	68192
r=3:	1	4	15	57	216	819	3105	11772	44631	169209	641520	2432187
r=4:	1	5	24	116	560	2704	13056	63040	304384	1469696	7096320	34264064
r=5:	1	6	35	205	1200	7025	41125	240750	1409375	8250625	48300000	282753125

Figure 14.9-B: Number of radix-$(r+1)$, length-n words with no two consecutive zeros.

Let $z_r(n)$ be the number of words $W_r(n)$, we find

$$z_r(n) \;=\; r\,z_r(n-1) + r\,z_r(n-1) \tag{14.9-2}$$

where $z_r(0) = 1$ and $z_r(1) = r+1$. The sequences for $r \le 5$ start as shown in figure 14.9-B. These (for $r \le 4$) are the following entries in [312]: $r = 1$: A000045; $r = 2$: A028859; $r = 3$: A125145; $r = 4$: A086347. The generating function for $z_r(n)$ is

$$\sum_{n=0}^{\infty} z_r(n)\,x^n \;=\; \frac{1+x}{1-r\,x-r\,x^2} \tag{14.9-3}$$

14.10 Binary strings without substrings 1x1 or 1xy1 ‡

14.10.1 No substrings 1x1

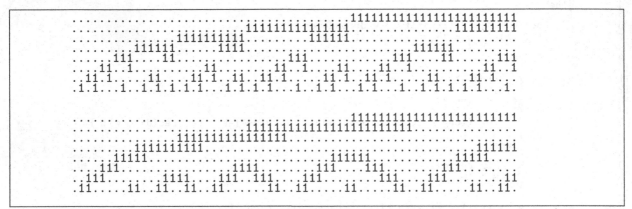

Figure 14.10-A: The length-8 binary strings with no substring 1x1 (where x is either 0 or 1): lex order (top) and minimal-change order (bottom). Dots denote zeros.

A Gray code for binary strings with no substring 1x1 is shown in figure 14.10-A. The recursive structure for the list $V(n)$ of the n-bit words is

$$V(n) \;=\; \begin{matrix} [1\,0\,0 \,.\, V(n-3) \quad] \\ [1\,1\,0\,0 \,.\, V^{\mathbf{R}}(n-4)] \\ [0 \,.\, V(n-1) \qquad\;] \end{matrix} \tag{14.10-1}$$

The implied algorithm can be implemented as [FXT: comb/no1x1-gray-demo.cc]:

```
1    ulong n;     // number of bits in words
2    ulong *rv;   // bits of the word

1    void no1x1_rec(ulong d, bool z)
2    {
3        if ( d>=n ) { if ( d<=n+2 ) visit(); }
4        else
5        {
6            if ( z )
7            {
```

```
8            rv[d]=1;  rv[d+1]=0;  rv[d+2]=0;  no1x1_rec(d+3, z);
9            rv[d]=1;  rv[d+1]=1;  rv[d+2]=0;  rv[d+3]=0;  no1x1_rec(d+4, !z);
10           rv[d]=0;  no1x1_rec(d+1, z);
11       }
12       else
13       {
14           rv[d]=0;  no1x1_rec(d+1, z);
15           rv[d]=1;  rv[d+1]=1;  rv[d+2]=0;  rv[d+3]=0;  no1x1_rec(d+4, !z);
16           rv[d]=1;  rv[d+1]=0;  rv[d+2]=0;  no1x1_rec(d+3, z);
17       }
18   }
19   }
```

The sequence of the numbers $v(n)$ of length-n strings starts as

n :	0	1	2	3	4	5	6	7	8	9	10	11	12	13	14	15	16	17
v(n):	1	2	4	6	9	15	25	40	64	104	169	273	441	714	1156	1870	3025	4895

This is entry A006498 in [312]. The recurrence relation is

$$v(n) \;=\; v(n-1) + v(n-3) + v(n-4) \qquad (14.10\text{-}2)$$

The generating function is

$$\sum_{n=0}^{\infty} v(n)\, x^n \;=\; \frac{1 + x + 2\,x^2 + x^3}{1 - x - x^3 - x^4} \qquad (14.10\text{-}3)$$

14.10.2   No substrings 1xy1

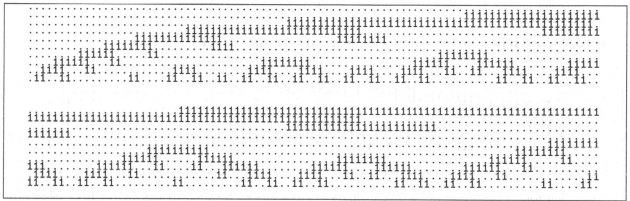

Figure 14.10-B: The length-10 binary strings with no substring 1xy1 (where x and y are either 0 or 1) in minimal-change order. Dots denote zeros.

Figure 14.10-B shows a Gray code for binary words with no substring 1xy1. The recursion for the list of n-bit words $Y(n)$ is

$$Y(n) \;=\; \begin{bmatrix} [1000\,.\,Y(n-4) &] \\ [101000\,.\,Y^{\mathbf{R}}(n-6)] \\ [111000\,.\,Y(n-6) &] \\ [11000\,.\,Y^{\mathbf{R}}(n-5) &] \\ [0\,.\,Y(n-1) &] \end{bmatrix} \qquad (14.10\text{-}4)$$

An implementation is given in [FXT: comb/no1xy1-gray-demo.cc]:

```
1   void Y_rec(long p1, long p2, bool z)
2   {
3       if ( p1>p2 )  { visit();  return; }
4
5   #define S1(a)     rv[p1+0]=a
6   #define S2(a,b)   S1(a);  rv[p1+1]=b;
7   #define S3(a,b,c) S2(a,b);  rv[p1+2]=c;
```

```
 8   #define S4(a,b,c,d)    S3(a,b,c); rv[p1+3]=d;
 9   #define S5(a,b,c,d,e)  S4(a,b,c,d); rv[p1+4]=e;
10   #define S6(a,b,c,d,e,f) S5(a,b,c,d,e); rv[p1+5]=f;
11
12       long d = p2 - p1;
13       if ( z )
14       {
15           if ( d >= 0 )  { S4(1,0,0,0);      Y_rec(p1+4, p2,  z); }   // 1 0 0 0
16           if ( d >= 2 )  { S6(1,0,1,0,0,0);  Y_rec(p1+6, p2, !z); }   // 1 0 1 0 0 0
17           if ( d >= 2 )  { S6(1,1,1,0,0,0);  Y_rec(p1+6, p2,  z); }   // 1 1 1 0 0 0
18           if ( d >= 1 )  { S5(1,1,0,0,0);    Y_rec(p1+5, p2, !z); }   // 1 1 0 0 0
19           if ( d >= 0 )  { S1(0);            Y_rec(p1+1, p2,  z); }   // 0
20       }
21       else
22       {
23           if ( d >= 0 )  { S1(0);            Y_rec(p1+1, p2,  z); }   // 0
24           if ( d >= 1 )  { S5(1,1,0,0,0);    Y_rec(p1+5, p2, !z); }   // 1 1 0 0 0
25           if ( d >= 2 )  { S6(1,1,1,0,0,0);  Y_rec(p1+6, p2,  z); }   // 1 1 1 0 0 0
26           if ( d >= 2 )  { S6(1,0,1,0,0,0);  Y_rec(p1+6, p2, !z); }   // 1 0 1 0 0 0
27           if ( d >= 0 )  { S4(1,0,0,0);      Y_rec(p1+4, p2,  z); }   // 1 0 0 0
28       }
29   }
```

Note the conditions i f(d > =?) that make sure that no string appears repeated. The initial call is
Y_rec(0, n-1, 0). The sequence of the numbers $y(n)$ of length-n strings starts as

n:	0	1	2	3	4	5	6	7	8	9	10	11	12	13	14	15	16	17
y(n):	1	2	4	8	12	17	25	41	69	114	180	280	440	705	1137	1825	2905	4610

The generating function is

$$\sum_{n=0}^{\infty} y(n)\,x^n \;=\; \frac{1 + x + 2\,x^2 + 4\,x^3 + 3\,x^4 + 2\,x^5}{1 - x - x^4 - x^5 - 2\,x^6} \tag{14.10-5}$$

14.10.3   Neither substrings 1x1 nor substrings 1xy1

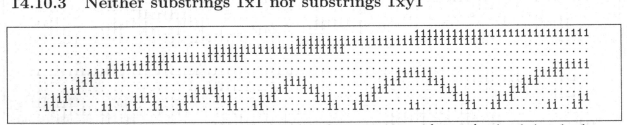

Figure 14.10-C: A Gray code for the length-10 binary strings with no substring 1x1 or 1xy1.

A recursion for a Gray code of the n-bit binary words $Z(n)$ with no substrings 1x1 or 1xy1 (shown in figure 14.10-C) is

$$Z(n) \;=\; \begin{matrix} [1000\,.\,Z(n-4) &] \\ [11000\,.\,Z^{\mathbf{R}}(n-5)] \\ [0\,.\,Z(n-1) &] \end{matrix} \tag{14.10-6}$$

The sequence of the numbers $z(n)$ of length-n strings starts as

n :	0	1	2	3	4	5	6	7	8	9	10	11	12	13	14	15	16	17
z(n):	1	2	4	6	8	11	17	27	41	60	88	132	200	301	449	669	1001	1502

The sequence is (apart from three leading ones) entry A079972 in [312] where two combinatorial interpretations are given:

```
Number of permutations satisfying -k<=p(i)-i<=r and p(i)-i not in I, i=1..n,
     with k=1, r=4, I={1,2}.
Number of compositions (ordered partitions) of n into elements of the set {1,4,5}.
```

The generating function is

$$\sum_{n=0}^{\infty} z(n)\,x^n \;=\; \frac{1 + x + 2\,x^2 + 2\,x^3 + x^4}{1 - x - x^4 - x^5} \tag{14.10-7}$$

Chapter 15

Parentheses strings

We give algorithms to list all well-formed strings of n pairs of parentheses. In the spirit of [211] we use the term *paren string* for a well-formed string of parentheses. A generalization, the k-ary Dyck words, is described at the end of the section.

If the problem at hand appears to be somewhat esoteric, then see [319, vol.2, exercise 6.19, p.219] for many kinds of objects isomorphic to our paren strings. Indeed, as of May 2010, 180 kinds of combinatorial objects counted by the Catalan numbers (which may be called *Catalan objects*) have been identified, see [321] and also [320].

15.1 Co-lexicographic order

```
 1:   (((((()))))    11111.....      22:   (()(()())    11..11.1..
 2:   ((((()()))))   1111.1....      23:   ()()(()())   1.1.11.1..
 3:   ((()(())))     111.11....      24:   ((())(())    111...11..
 4:   (()(((()))))   11.111....      25:   (()()(())    11.1..11..
 5:   ()(((()))))    1.1111....      26:   ()(()(())    1.11..11..
 6:   (((()()))))    1111..1...      27:   (())()(())   11..1.11..
 7:   ((()()()))     111.1.1...      28:   ()()()(())   1.1.1.11..
 8:   ()()(()))      11.11.1...      29:   (((())))()   1111....1.
 9:   ()(((())))     1.111.1...      30:   ((()()))()   111.1...1.
10:   (()()(()))     111..11...      31:   (()(()))()   11.11...1.
11:   ()()(())))     11.1.11...      32:   ()(((()))()  1.111...1.
12:   ()(()(()))     1.11.11...      33:   ((())())()   111..1..1.
13:   (())(((())))   11..111...      34:   (()()())()   11.1.1..1.
14:   ()(())(()))    1.1.111...      35:   ()(()()))()  1.11.1..1.
15:   ((()))(())     1111...1..      36:   (())(())()   11..11..1.
16:   (()()))(())    111.1..1..      37:   ()()(()))()  1.1.11..1.
17:   ()(()))(())    11.11..1..      38:   ((()))()()   111...1.1.
18:   ()(()())(())   1.111..1..      39:   (()())()()   11.1..1.1.
19:   (())()(())     111..1.1..      40:   ()(())()()   1.11..1.1.
20:   (()()()()      11.1.1.1..      41:   (())()()()   11..1.1.1.
21:   ()(()()()()    1.11.1.1..      42:   ()()()()()   1.1.1.1.1.
```

Figure 15.1-A: All (42) valid strings of 5 pairs of parentheses in co-lexicographic order.

An iterative scheme to generate all valid ways to group parentheses can be derived from a modified version of the combinations in co-lexicographic order (see section 6.2.2 on page 178). For $n = 5$ pairs the possible combinations are shown in figure 15.1-A. This is the output of [FXT: comb/paren-demo.cc].

Consider the sequences to the right of the paren strings as binary words (these are often called (binary) *Dyck words*). If the leftmost block has more than a single one, then its rightmost one is moved one position to the right. Otherwise (the leftmost block consists of a single one and) the ones of the longest run of the repeated pattern '1.' at the left are gathered at the left end and the rightmost one in the next block of ones (which contains at least two ones) is moved by one position to the right and the rest of the block is gathered at the left end (see the transitions from #14 to #15 or #37 to #38).

The generator is [FXT: **class paren** in comb/paren.h]:

J. Arndt, *Matters Computational: Ideas, Algorithms, Source Code*,
DOI 10.1007/978-3-642-14764-7_15, © Springer-Verlag Berlin Heidelberg 2011

```
1     class paren
2     {
3     public:
4         ulong k_;  // Number of paren pairs
5         ulong n_;  // ==2*k
6         ulong *x_; // Positions where an opening paren occurs
7         char *str_;  // String representation,  e.g. "((())()()()"
8
9     public:
10        paren(ulong k)
11        {
12            k_ = (k>1 ? k : 2);  // not zero (empty) or one (trivial: "()")
13            n_ = 2 * k_;
14            x_ = new ulong[k_ + 1];
15            x_[k_] = 999;  // sentinel
16            str_ = new char[n_ + 1];
17            str_[n_] = 0;
18            first();
19        }
20
21        ~paren()
22        {
23            delete [] x_;
24            delete [] str_;
25        }
26
27        void first()  { for (ulong i=0; i<k_; ++i)  x_[i] = i; }
28
29        void last()  { for (ulong i=0; i<k_; ++i)  x_[i] = 2*i; }
30
31        [--snip--]
```

The code for the computation of the successor and predecessor is quite concise. A sentinel x[k] is used
to save one branch in the generation of the next string

```
1     ulong next()  // return zero if current paren is the last
2     {
3         // if ( k_==1 )  return 0;  // uncomment to make algorithm work for k_==1
4
5         ulong j = 0;
6         if ( x_[1] == 2 )
7         {
8             // scan for low end == 010101:
9             j = 2;
10            while ( x_[j]==2*j )  ++j;  // can touch sentinel
11            if ( j==k_ )  { first();  return 0; }
12        }
13
14        // scan block:
15        while ( 1 == (x_[j+1] - x_[j]) )  { ++j; }
16
17        ++x_[j];  // move edge element up
18        for (ulong i=0; i<j; ++i)  x_[i] = i; // attach block at low end
19
20        return 1;
21    }
22
23    ulong prev()  // return zero if current paren is the first
24    {
25        // if ( k_==1 )  return 0;  // uncomment to make algorithm work for k_==1
26
27        ulong j = 0;
28        // scan for first gap:
29        while ( x_[j]==j )  ++j;
30        if ( j==k_ )  { last();  return 0; }
31
32        if ( x_[j]-x_[j-1] == 2 )  --x_[j];  // gap of length one
33        else
34        {
35            ulong i = --x_[j];
36            --j;
37            --i;
38            // j items to go, distribute as 1.1.1.11111
39            for ( ;  2*i>j;  --i,--j)  x_[j] = i;
40            for ( ;  i;  --i)  x_[i] = 2*i;
41            x_[0] = 0;
42        }
```

```
43
44          return 1;
45      }
46
47      const ulong * data()  const  { return x_; }
48      [--snip--]
49
```

The strings are set up on demand only:

```
1      const char * string()  // generate on demand
2      {
3          for (ulong j=0; j<n_; ++j)  str_[j] = ')';
4          for (ulong j=0; j<k_; ++j)  str_[x_[j]] = '(';
5          return str_;
6      }
7  };
```

The $477, 638, 700$ paren words for $n = 18$ are generated at a rate of about 67 million objects per second. Section 1.28 on page 78 gives a bit-level algorithm for the generation of the paren words in colex order.

15.2 Gray code via restricted growth strings

```
    1:    [ 0, 0, 0, 0, ]   ()()()()   1.1.1.1.
    2:    [ 0, 0, 0, 1, ]   ()()(())   1.1.11..
    3:    [ 0, 0, 1, 0, ]   ()(())()   1.11..1.
    4:    [ 0, 0, 1, 1, ]   ()(()())   1.11.1..
    5:    [ 0, 0, 1, 2, ]   ()((()))   1.111...
    6:    [ 0, 1, 0, 0, ]   (())()()   11..1.1.
    7:    [ 0, 1, 0, 1, ]   (())(())   11..11..
    8:    [ 0, 1, 1, 0, ]   (()())()   11.1..1.
    9:    [ 0, 1, 1, 1, ]   (()()())   11.1.1..
   10:    [ 0, 1, 1, 2, ]   (()(()))   11.11...
   11:    [ 0, 1, 2, 0, ]   ((()))()   111...1.
   12:    [ 0, 1, 2, 1, ]   ((())())   111..1..
   13:    [ 0, 1, 2, 2, ]   ((()()))   111.1...
   14:    [ 0, 1, 2, 3, ]   (((())))   1111....
```

Figure 15.2-A: Length-4 restricted growth strings in lexicographic order (left) and the corresponding paren strings (middle) and delta sets (right).

The valid paren strings can be represented by sequences $a_0, a_1, \ldots, a_n$ where $a_0 = 0$ and $a_k \leq a_{k-1} + 1$. These sequences are examples of *restricted growth strings* (RGS). Some sources use the term *restricted growth functions*.

The RGSs for $n = 4$ are shown in figure 15.2-A (left). The successor of an RGS is computed by incrementing the highest (rightmost in figure 15.2-A) digit a_j where $a_j \leq a_{j-1}$ and setting $a_i = 0$ for all $i > j$. The predecessor is computed by decrementing the highest digit $a_j \neq 0$ and setting $a_i = a_{i-1} + 1$ for all $i > j$.

The RGSs for a given n can be generated as follows [FXT: class `catalan` in comb/catalan.h]:

```
1   class catalan
2   // Catalan restricted growth strings (RGS)
3   // By default in near-perfect minimal-change order, i.e.
4   //   exactly two symbols in paren string change with each step
5   {
6   public:
7       int *as_;   // digits of the RGS: as_[k] <= as[k-1] + 1
8       int *d_;    // direction with recursion (+1 or -1)
9       ulong n_;   // Number of digits (paren pairs)
10      char *str_; // paren string
11      bool xdr_;  // whether to change direction in recursion (==> minimal-change order)
12      int dr0_;   // dr0: starting direction in each recursive step:
13      //    dr0=+1  ==> start with as[]=[0,0,0,...,0]  == "()()()...()"
14      //    dr0=-1  ==> start with as[]=[0,1,2,...,n-1] == "((( ... )))"
```

```
 1 : [ 0 1 2 3 4 ]   [ - - - - - ]   (((((()))))   11111.....
 2 : [ 0 1 2 3 3 ]   [ - - - - - ]   ((((()())))   1111.1....   ((((XA))))
 3 : [ 0 1 2 3 2 ]   [ - - - - - ]   (((()()()))   1111..1...   ((((()XA)))
 4 : [ 0 1 2 3 1 ]   [ - - - - - ]   ((((()))()))  1111...1..   ((((())XA))
 5 : [ 0 1 2 3 0 ]   [ - - - - - ]   ((((())))()   1111....1.   ((((()))XA)
 6 : [ 0 1 2 2 0 ]   [ - - - - + ]   ((((()()())))  111.1...1.   (((XA)))()
 7 : [ 0 1 2 2 1 ]   [ - - - - + ]   ((((()())))   111.1..1..   ((()())AX)
 8 : [ 0 1 2 2 2 ]   [ - - - - + ]   ((((()()()))   111.1.1...   ((()()AX))
 9 : [ 0 1 2 2 3 ]   [ - - - - + ]   ((((()()))))  111.11....   (((()(AX)))
10 : [ 0 1 2 1 2 ]   [ - - - - - ]   ((()(()()))   111..11...   (((()X(A)))    2
11 : [ 0 1 2 1 1 ]   [ - - - - - ]   ((()(())())   111..1.1..   ((()())XA))
12 : [ 0 1 2 1 0 ]   [ - - - - - ]   ((()(()))))   111...1.1.   ((()())()XA
13 : [ 0 1 2 0 0 ]   [ - - - - + ]   ((()())(())   111...1.1.   ((()))XA)()
14 : [ 0 1 2 0 1 ]   [ - - - - + ]   ((()()()())   111...11..   ((())) (AX)
15 : [ 0 1 1 0 1 ]   [ - - - + - ]   (()()()()())  11.1..11..   ((XA))(()()
16 : [ 0 1 1 0 0 ]   [ - - - + - ]   (()()()()())  11.1..1.1.   (()())(XA)
17 : [ 0 1 1 1 0 ]   [ - - - + + ]   (()()()()))   11.1.1..1.   (()()AX)()
18 : [ 0 1 1 1 1 ]   [ - - - + + ]   (()()()()))   11.1.1.1..   (()()(AX))
19 : [ 0 1 1 1 2 ]   [ - - - + + ]   (()()(()))   11.1.11...   (()()(AX))
20 : [ 0 1 1 2 3 ]   [ - - - + - ]   (()(()(())))  11.111....   (()(A(X)))    2
21 : [ 0 1 1 2 2 ]   [ - - - + - ]   (()(()()))   11.11.1...   (()((XA)))
22 : [ 0 1 1 2 1 ]   [ - - - + - ]   (()(()()())   11.11..1..   (()(()XA))
23 : [ 0 1 1 2 0 ]   [ - - - + - ]   (()(()))()   11.11...1.   (()(())XA
24 : [ 0 1 0 1 0 ]   [ - - - - + ]   (()()(())   11..11...1.   (()X(A))()    2
25 : [ 0 1 0 1 1 ]   [ - - - - + ]   (()()(())   11..11.1..   (()((()AX)
26 : [ 0 1 0 1 2 ]   [ - - - - + ]   (()()((()))  11..111...   (()((AX))
27 : [ 0 1 0 0 1 ]   [ - - - - - ]   (()()()())   11..1.11..   (()))(X(A))    2
28 : [ 0 1 0 0 0 ]   [ - - - - - ]   (()()()())   11..1.1.1.   (()))(XA)
29 : [ 0 0 0 0 0 ]   [ - - + + + ]   ()()()()()   1.1.1.1.1.   (XA)()()()
30 : [ 0 0 0 0 1 ]   [ - - + + - ]   ()()()()))   1.1.1.1.1.   ()()((AX)
31 : [ 0 0 0 1 2 ]   [ - - + + - ]   ()()((()))   1.1.111...   ()()(A(X))    2
32 : [ 0 0 0 1 1 ]   [ - - + + - ]   ()()(())())  1.1.11.1..   ()()((XA))
33 : [ 0 0 0 1 0 ]   [ - - + + - ]   ()()(()))   1.1.11..1.   ()()(()XA)
34 : [ 0 0 1 2 0 ]   [ - - + - + ]   ()(()((()))  1.111...1.   ()(A(X))()    2
35 : [ 0 0 1 2 1 ]   [ - - + - + ]   ()(()()()())  1.111..1..   ()((()()AX)
36 : [ 0 0 1 2 2 ]   [ - - + - + ]   ()(()()()))  1.111.1...   ()(()()AX))
37 : [ 0 0 1 2 3 ]   [ - - + - + ]   ()(()()()))  1.1111....   ()(((AX)))
38 : [ 0 0 1 1 2 ]   [ - - + - - ]   ()(()(()))   1.11.11...   ()((X(A)))    2
39 : [ 0 0 1 1 1 ]   [ - - + - - ]   ()(()()()())  1.11.1.1..   ()(()()XA))
40 : [ 0 0 1 1 0 ]   [ - - + - - ]   ()(()()()())  1.11.1..1.   ()(()()()XA
41 : [ 0 0 1 0 0 ]   [ - - + - + ]   ()(()()()())  1.11..1.1.   ()(()()XA)()
42 : [ 0 0 1 0 1 ]   [ - - + - + ]   ()(()()()())  1.11..11..   ()(()()(AX)
```

Figure 15.2-B: Minimal-change order for the paren strings of 5 pairs. From left to right: restricted growth strings, arrays of directions, paren strings, delta sets, and difference strings. If the changes are not adjacent, then the distance of changed positions is given at the right. The order corresponds to dr0=-1.

```
 1   public:
 2       catalan(ulong n, bool xdr=true, int dr0=+1)
 3       {
 4           n_ = n;
 5           as_ = new int[n_];
 6           d_ = new int[n_];
 7           str_ = new char[2*n_+1];   str_[2*n_] = 0;
 8           init(xdr, dr0);
 9       }
10
11       ~catalan()
12       {
13           delete [] as_;
14           delete [] d_;
15           delete [] str_;
16       }
17
18       void init(bool xdr, int dr0)
19       {
20           dr0_ = ( (dr0>=0) ? +1 : -1 );
21           xdr_ = xdr;
22
23           ulong n = n_;
24           if ( dr0_>0 )  for (ulong k=0; k<n; ++k)  as_[k] = 0;
25           else           for (ulong k=0; k<n; ++k)  as_[k] = k;
```

```
 1 : [ 0 0 0 0 0 ]   [ + + + + + ]   ()()()()()   1.1.1.1.1.
 2 : [ 0 0 0 0 1 ]   [ + + + + + ]   ()()()(())   1.1.1.11..   ()()()(AX)
 3 : [ 0 0 0 1 2 ]   [ + + + + - ]   ()()((()))   1.1.111...   ()()(A(X))    2
 4 : [ 0 0 0 1 1 ]   [ + + + + - ]   ()()(()())   1.1.11.1..   ()()((XA))
 5 : [ 0 0 0 1 0 ]   [ + + + + - ]   ()()(())()   1.1.11..1.   ()()(()XA)
 6 : [ 0 0 1 2 0 ]   [ + + + - + ]   ()((()))()   1.111...1.   ()(A(X))()    2
 7 : [ 0 0 1 2 1 ]   [ + + + - + ]   ()((())())   1.111..1..   ()((())AX)
 8 : [ 0 0 1 2 2 ]   [ + + + - + ]   ()((()()))   1.111.1...   ()((()AX))
 9 : [ 0 0 1 2 3 ]   [ + + + - + ]   ()(((())))   1.1111....   ()(((AX)))
10 : [ 0 0 1 1 2 ]   [ + + + - - ]   ()(()(()))   1.11.11...   ()((X(A)))    2
11 : [ 0 0 1 1 1 ]   [ + + + - - ]   ()(()()())   1.11.1.1..   ()(()(XA))
12 : [ 0 0 1 1 0 ]   [ + + + - - ]   ()(()())()   1.11.1..1.   ()(()()XA)
13 : [ 0 0 1 0 0 ]   [ + + + - + ]   ()(())()()   1.11..1.1.   ()(()XA)()
14 : [ 0 0 1 0 1 ]   [ + + + - + ]   ()(())(())   1.11..11..   ()(())(AX)
15 : [ 0 1 2 0 1 ]   [ + + - + - ]   ((()))(())   111...11..   (A(X))(())    2
16 : [ 0 1 2 0 0 ]   [ + + - + - ]   ((()))()()   111...1.1.   ((()))(XA)
17 : [ 0 1 2 1 0 ]   [ + + - + + ]   ((())())()   111..1..1.   ((())AX)()
18 : [ 0 1 2 1 1 ]   [ + + - + + ]   ((())()())   111..1.1..   ((())()AX)
19 : [ 0 1 2 1 2 ]   [ + + - + + ]   ((())(()))   111..11...   ((())(AX))
20 : [ 0 1 2 2 3 ]   [ + + - + - ]   ((()(())))   111.11....   ((()A(X)))    2
21 : [ 0 1 2 2 2 ]   [ + + - + - ]   ((()()()))   111.1.1...   ((()(XA)))
22 : [ 0 1 2 2 1 ]   [ + + - + - ]   ((()())())   111.1..1..   ((()()XA))
23 : [ 0 1 2 2 0 ]   [ + + - + - ]   ((()()))()   111.1...1.   ((()())XA)
24 : [ 0 1 2 3 0 ]   [ + + - + + ]   (((())))()   1111....1.   (((AX)))()
25 : [ 0 1 2 3 1 ]   [ + + - + + ]   (((()))())   1111...1..   (((()))AX)
26 : [ 0 1 2 3 2 ]   [ + + - + + ]   (((())()))   1111..1...   (((())AX))
27 : [ 0 1 2 3 3 ]   [ + + - + + ]   (((()())))   1111.1....   (((()AX)))
28 : [ 0 1 2 3 4 ]   [ + + - + + ]   ((((()))))   11111.....   ((((AX))))
29 : [ 0 1 1 2 3 ]   [ + + - - - ]   (()((())))   11.111....   ((X((A))))    3
30 : [ 0 1 1 2 2 ]   [ + + - - - ]   (()(()()))   11.11.1...   (()((XA)))
31 : [ 0 1 1 2 1 ]   [ + + - - - ]   (()(())())   11.11..1..   (()(()XA))
32 : [ 0 1 1 2 0 ]   [ + + - - - ]   (()(()))()   11.11...1.   (()(())XA)
33 : [ 0 1 1 1 0 ]   [ + + - - + ]   (()()())()   11.1.1..1.   (()(XA))()
34 : [ 0 1 1 1 1 ]   [ + + - - + ]   (()()()())   11.1.1.1..   (()()()AX)
35 : [ 0 1 1 1 2 ]   [ + + - - + ]   (()()(()))   11.1.11...   (()()(AX))
36 : [ 0 1 1 0 1 ]   [ + + - - - ]   (()())(())   11.1..11..   (()()X(A))    2
37 : [ 0 1 1 0 0 ]   [ + + - - - ]   (()())()()   11.1..1.1.   (()())(XA)
38 : [ 0 1 0 0 0 ]   [ + + - + + ]   (())()()()   11..1.1.1.   (()XA)()()
39 : [ 0 1 0 0 1 ]   [ + + - + + ]   (())()(())   11..1.11..   (())()(AX)
40 : [ 0 1 0 1 2 ]   [ + + - + - ]   (())((()))   11..111...   (())(A(X))    2
41 : [ 0 1 0 1 1 ]   [ + + - + - ]   (())(()())   11..11.1..   (())((XA))
42 : [ 0 1 0 1 0 ]   [ + + - + - ]   (())(())()   11..11..1.   (())(()XA)
```

Figure 15.2-C: Minimal-change order for the paren strings of 5 pairs. From left to right: restricted growth strings, arrays of directions, paren strings, delta sets, and difference strings. If the changes are not adjacent, then the distance of changed positions is given at the right. The order corresponds to dr0=1.

```
26
27           for (ulong k=0; k<n; ++k)  d_[k] = dr0_;
28      }
29
30      bool next()  { return next_rec(n_-1); }
31
32      const int *get()  const  { return as_; }
33
34      const char* str()  { make_str();  return (const char*)str_; }
35
36      [--snip--]
37      void make_str()
38      {
39          for (ulong k=0; k<2*n_; ++k)  str_[k] = ')';
40          for (ulong k=0,j=0; k<n_; ++k,j+=2)  str_[ j-as_[k] ] = '(';
41      }
42 };
```

The minimal-change order is obtained by changing the 'direction' in the recursion, an essentially identical mechanism (for the generation of set partitions) is shown in chapter 17 on page 354. The function is given in [FXT: comb/catalan.cc]:

```
1   bool
2   catalan::next_rec(ulong k)
3   {
```

```
4        if ( k<1 )  return false;  // current is last
5
6        int d = d_[k];
7        int as = as_[k] + d;
8        bool ovq = ( (d>0) ? (as>as_[k-1]+1) : (as<0) );
9        if ( ovq )  // have to recurse
10       {
11           ulong ns1 = next_rec(k-1);
12           if ( 0==ns1 )  return false;
13
14           d = ( xdr_ ? -d : dr0_ );
15           d_[k] = d;
16
17           as = ( (d>0) ? 0 : as_[k-1]+1 );
18       }
19       as_[k] = as;
20
21       return true;
22   }
```

The program [FXT: comb/catalan-demo.cc] demonstrates the usage:

```
ulong n = 4;
bool xdr = true;
int dr0 = -1;
catalan C(n, xdr, dr0);
do  { /* visit string */ }  while ( C.next() );
```

About 69 million strings per second are generated. Figure 15.2-B shows the minimal-change order for $n = 5$ and dr0=-1, and figure 15.2-C for dr0=+1.

More minimal-change orders

```
 1 :   0 0 0 0 0    1.1.1.1.1.      22:   0 1 2 2 1    111.1..1..
 2 :   0 0 0 0 1    1.1.1.11..      23:   0 1 2 2 0    111.1...1.
 3 :   0 0 0 1 2    1.1.111...      24:   0 1 2 1 0    111..1..1.
 4 :   0 0 0 1 1    1.1.11.1..      25:   0 1 2 1 1    111..1.1..
 5 :   0 0 0 1 0    1.1.11...1.     26:   0 1 2 1 2    111..11...
 6 :   0 0 1 2 3    1.1111....      27:   0 1 2 0 1    111...11..
 7 :   0 0 1 2 2    1.111.1...      28:   0 1 2 0 0    111...1.1.
 8 :   0 0 1 2 1    1.111..1..      29:   0 1 1 0 0    11.1..1.1.
 9 :   0 0 1 2 0    1.111...1.      30:   0 1 1 0 1    11.1..11..
10:    0 0 1 1 0    1.11.1..1.      31:   0 1 1 1 1    11.1.11...
11:    0 0 1 1 1    1.11.1.1..      32:   0 1 1 1 1    11.1.1.1..
12:    0 0 1 1 2    1.11.11...      33:   0 1 1 1 0    11.1.1..1.
13:    0 0 1 0 1    1.11..11..      34:   0 1 1 2 0    11.11...1.
14:    0 0 1 0 0    1.11..1.1.      35:   0 1 1 2 1    11.11..1..
15:    0 1 2 3 0    1111....1.      36:   0 1 1 2 2    11.11.1...
16:    0 1 2 3 1    1111...1..      37:   0 1 1 2 3    11.111....
17:    0 1 2 3 2    1111..1...      38:   0 1 0 1 0    11..11..1.
18:    0 1 2 3 3    1111.1....      39:   0 1 0 1 1    11..11.1..
19:    0 1 2 3 4    11111.....      40:   0 1 0 1 2    11..111...
20:    0 1 2 2 3    111.11....      41:   0 1 0 0 1    11..1.11..
21:    0 1 2 2 2    111.1.1...      42:   0 1 0 0 0    11..1.1.1.
```

Figure 15.2-D: Strings of 5 pairs of parentheses in a Gray code order.

The Gray code order shown in figure 15.2-D can be generated via a simple recursion:

```
1    ulong n;     // Number of paren pairs
2    ulong *rv;   // restricted growth strings
3
4    void next_rec(ulong d, bool z)
5    {
6        if ( d==n )  visit();
7        else
8        {
9            const long rv1 = rv[d-1];  // left neighbor
10           if ( 0==z )
11           {
12               for (long x=0; x<=rv1+1; ++x)  // forward
13               {
14                   rv[d] = x;
15                   next_rec(d+1, (x&1));
16               }
17           }
18           else
```

```
19              {
20                      for (long x=rv1+1; x>=0; --x)  // backward
21                      {
22                              rv[d] = x;
23                              next_rec(d+1, !(x&1));
24                      }
25              }
26      }
27  }
```

The initial call is `next_rec(0, 0);`. About 81 million strings per second are generated [FXT: comb/paren-gray-rec-demo.cc].

```
 1:  () () () () ()    1.1.1.1.1.      22:  () () () (())    11.1.11...
 2:  () () () (())     1.1.1.11..      23:  () () () () ()   11.1.1..1.
 3:  () () (()) ()     1.1.11.1..      24:  (()) () () ()    111..1..1.
 4:  () () (())        1.1.111...      25:  (()) () (())     111..11...
 5:  () () (()) ()     1.1.11..1.      26:  (()) () (())     111..1.1..
 6:  () (()) () ()     1.11.1..1.      27:  (()) () () ()    111.1..1..
 7:  () (()) (())      1.11.11...      28:  (()) () (())     111.1.1...
 8:  () (()) () ()     1.11.1.1..      29:  (()) () (())     111.11....
 9:  () (()) () ()     1.111..1..      30:  (()) () () ()    111.1...1.
10:  () (()) () ()     1.111.1...      31:  (()(())) ()      1111....1.
11:  () (()) ))        1.1111....      32:  (((()))))        11111.....
12:  () (()) () ()     1.111...1.      33:  (((()) ()))      1111.1....
13:  () (()) () ()     1.11..1.1.      34:  (((()) ()))      1111..1...
14:  () (()) (())      1.11..11..      35:  (((())) ()       1111...1..
15:  (()) () (())      11.1..11..      36:  (()) () ( () )   111...11..
16:  (()) () () ()     11.1..1.1.      37:  (()) () () ()    111...1.1.
17:  (()) (())         11.11...1.      38:  () () () () ()   11..1.1.1.
18:  (() ((())))       11.111....      39:  () () (())       11..1.11..
19:  (()) () () ()     11.11.1...      40:  () () (()) ()    11..11.1..
20:  (()) () () ()     11.11..1..      41:  () () (())       11..111...
21:  (() () () ())     11.1.1.1..      42:  () () (()) ()    11..11..1.
```

Figure 15.2-E: Strings of 5 pairs of parentheses in Gray code order as generated by a loopless algorithm.

A loopless algorithm (that does not use RGS) given in [329] is implemented in [FXT: class **paren_gray** in comb/paren-gray.h]. The generated order for five paren pairs is shown in figure 15.2-E. About 80 million strings per second are generated [FXT: comb/paren-gray-demo.cc]. Still more algorithms for the parentheses strings in minimal-change order are given in [90], [337], and [363].

```
 0:  ....1111 == (((())))
 1:  ...1.111 == (((()())))    ^= ...11...
 2:  ...11.11 == (()(()))      ^= ....11..
 3:  ...111.1 == ()(())        ^= .....11.
 4:  ..1.11.1 == ()(()) ()     ^= ..11....
 5:  ..1.1.11 == (() () ())    ^= .....11.
 6:  ..1..111 == (( () )( ))    ^= ....11..
 7:  .1...111 == (((()))()      ^= .11.....
 8:  .1..1.11 == (()()) ()      ^= .....11.
 9:  .1..11.1 == ()(()) ()      ^= .....11.
10:  .1.1.1.1 == () () () ()    ^= ...11...
11:  ..11.1.1 == () () (())     ^= .11.....
12:  ..11..11 == (()) ((())     ^= .....11.
13:  .1.1..11 == (()) () ()     ^= .11.....
```

Figure 15.2-F: A strong minimal-change order for the paren strings of 4 pairs.

For even values of n it is possible to generate paren strings in *strong minimal-change order* where changes occur only in adjacent positions. Figure 15.2-F shows an example for four pairs of parens. The listing was generated with [FXT: graph/graph-parengray-demo.cc] that uses directed graphs and the search algorithms described in chapter 20 on page 391.

```
 1:  ((((())))) 11111.....     22:  ((())()()) 111..1.1..
 2:  ()((((()))  1.1111....    23:  ()(()()()) 1.11..11..
 3:  (()((()))) 11.111....     24:  (()()(()) 11.1..11..
 4:  ((()((()))) 111.11....    25:  ()()()(()) 1.1.1.11..
 5:  (((()()))) 1111.1....     26:  (())()(()) 11..1.11..
 6:  ()(()()))) 1.111.1....    27:  ((())()()) 111...11..
 7:  ()(()()))) 11.11.1...     28:  ((())()()) 1111...1..
 8:  (()()()))) 111.1.1...     29:  ()(()()()) 1.111...1.
 9:  ()()(())()  1.11.11...    30:  (()()(()) 11.11...1.
10:  (()()(())) 11.1.11...     31:  (()()()()) 111.1...1.
11:  ()()((())) 1.1.111...     32:  ()()()(()) 1.11.1..1.
12:  (())((())) 11..111...     33:  (())()()() 11.1.1..1.
13:  ((())(())) 111..11...     34:  ()()(())() 1.1.11..1.
14:  ((()())()) 1111..1...     35:  (())()()() 11..11..1.
15:  ()(((())() 1.111..1..     36:  ((())()()) 111..1..1.
16:  ()(()()()  11.11..1..     37:  ()(())()() 1.11..1.1.
17:  (()()()()  111.1..1..     38:  (()()()()) 11.1..1.1.
18:  ()(()()()) 1.11.1.1..     39:  ()()()()() 1.1.1.1.1.
19:  (()()()()) 11.1.1.1..     40:  (())()()() 11..1.1.1.
20:  ()()(()()  1.1.11.1..     41:  ((())()()) 111...1.1.
21:  (())(()()  11..11.1..     42:  ((((())))() 1111....1.
```

Figure 15.3-A: All strings of 5 pairs of parentheses generated via prefix shifts.

15.3 Order by prefix shifts (cool-lex)

The binary words corresponding to paren strings can be generated in an order where each word differs from its successor by a cyclic shift of a prefix (ignoring the first bit which is always one). Moreover, each transition changes either two or four bits, see figure 15.3-A.

The (loopless) algorithm described in [292] can generate slightly more general objects: strings of t ones and s zeros where the number of zeros in any prefix does not exceed the number of ones. Paren strings correspond to $t = s$. The generator is implemented as follows [FXT: comb/paren-pref.h]:

```
1   class paren_pref
2   {
3   public:
4       const ulong t_, s_;  // t: number of ones, s: number of zeros
5       const ulong nq_;  // aux
6       ulong x_, y_;  // aux
7       ulong *b_;     // array of t ones and s zeros
8
9   public:
10
11      paren_pref(ulong t, ulong s)
12          // Must have: t >= s > 0
13          : t_(t), s_(s), nq_(s+t-(s==t))
14      {
15          b_ = new ulong[s_+t_+1];  // element [0] unused
16          first();
17      }
18
19      ~paren_pref()  { delete [] b_; }
20
21      const ulong * data()  const  { return b_+1; }
22
23      void first()
24      {
25          for (ulong j=0; j<=t_; ++j)  b_[j] = 1;
26          for (ulong j=t_+1; j<=s_+t_; ++j)  b_[j] = 0;
27          x_ = y_ = t_;
28      }
```

The method for updating is

```
1       bool next()
2       {
3           if ( x_ >= nq_ )  return false;
4           b_[x_] = 0;
5           b_[y_] = 1;
6           ++x_;
```

```
 7              ++y_;
 8              if ( b_[x_] == 0 )
 9              {
10                  if ( x_ == 2*y_ - 2 )  ++x_;
11                  else
12                  {
13                      b_[x_] = 1;
14                      b_[2] = 0;
15                      x_ = 3;
16                      y_ = 2;
17                  }
18              }
19              return true;
20          }
```

Note that the array b[] is one-based, as in the cited paper. A zero-based version is used if the line

`#define PAREN_PREF_BASE1  // default on (faster)`

near the top of the file is commented out. The rate of generation (with $t = s = 18$) is impressive: about 268 M/s when using a pointer and about 281 M/s when using an array [FXT: comb/paren-pref-demo.cc].

15.4 Catalan numbers

The number of valid combinations of n parentheses pairs is

$$C_n \;=\; \frac{\binom{2n}{n}}{n+1} \;=\; \frac{\binom{2n+1}{n}}{2n+1} \;=\; \frac{\binom{2n}{n-1}}{n} \;=\; \binom{2n}{n} - \binom{2n}{n-1} \qquad (15.4\text{-}1)$$

as nicely explained in [166, p.343-346]. These are the *Catalan numbers*, sequence A000108 in [312]:

$n:$	C_n	$n:$	C_n	$n:$	C_n
1:	1	11:	58786	21:	24466267020
2:	2	12:	208012	22:	91482563640
3:	5	13:	742900	23:	343059613650
4:	14	14:	2674440	24:	1289904147324
5:	42	15:	9694845	25:	4861946401452
6:	132	16:	35357670	26:	18367353072152
7:	429	17:	129644790	27:	69533550916004
8:	1430	18:	477638700	28:	263747951750360
9:	4862	19:	1767263190	29:	1002242216651368
10:	16796	20:	6564120420	30:	3814986502092304

The Catalan numbers are generated most easily with the relation

$$C_{n+1} \;=\; \frac{2\,(2\,n+1)}{n+2}\, C_n \qquad (15.4\text{-}2)$$

The generating function is

$$C(x) \;=\; \frac{1 - \sqrt{1-4\,x}}{2\,x} \;=\; \sum_{n=0}^{\infty} C_n\, x^n \;=\; 1 + x + 2\,x^2 + 5\,x^3 + 14\,x^4 + 42\,x^5 + \ldots \qquad (15.4\text{-}3)$$

The function $C(x)$ satisfies the equation $[x\,C(x)] = x + [x\,C(x)]^2$ which is equivalent to the following convolution property for the Catalan numbers:

$$C_n \;=\; \sum_{k=0}^{n-1} C_k\, C_{n-1-k} \qquad (15.4\text{-}4)$$

The quadratic equation has a second solution $(1 + \sqrt{1-4\,x})/(2\,x) = x^{-1} - 1 - x - 2\,x^2 - 5\,x^3 - 14\,x^4 - \ldots$ which we ignore here.

```
            RGS            Dyck word        positions
 1 :    [ 0 0 0 0 ]     1..1..1..1..     [ 0 3 6 9 ]
 2 :    [ 0 0 0 1 ]     1..1..1.1...     [ 0 3 6 8 ]
 3 :    [ 0 0 0 2 ]     1..1..11....     [ 0 3 6 7 ]
 4 :    [ 0 0 1 0 ]     1..1.1...1..     [ 0 3 5 9 ]
 5 :    [ 0 0 1 1 ]     1..1.1..1...     [ 0 3 5 8 ]
 6 :    [ 0 0 1 2 ]     1..1.1.1....     [ 0 3 5 7 ]
 7 :    [ 0 0 1 3 ]     1..1.11.....     [ 0 3 5 6 ]
 8 :    [ 0 0 2 0 ]     1..11....1..     [ 0 3 4 9 ]
 9 :    [ 0 0 2 1 ]     1..11...1...     [ 0 3 4 8 ]
1 0 :   [ 0 0 2 2 ]     1..11..1....     [ 0 3 4 7 ]
1 1 :   [ 0 0 2 3 ]     1..11.1.....     [ 0 3 4 6 ]
1 2 :   [ 0 0 2 4 ]     1..111......     [ 0 3 4 5 ]
1 3 :   [ 0 1 0 0 ]     1.1..1..1..     [ 0 2 6 9 ]
1 4 :   [ 0 1 0 1 ]     1.1..1.1...     [ 0 2 6 8 ]
1 5 :   [ 0 1 0 2 ]     1.1..11....     [ 0 2 6 7 ]
1 6 :   [ 0 1 1 0 ]     1.1.1...1..     [ 0 2 5 9 ]
1 7 :   [ 0 1 1 1 ]     1.1.1..1...     [ 0 2 5 8 ]
1 8 :   [ 0 1 1 2 ]     1.1.1.1....     [ 0 2 5 7 ]
1 9 :   [ 0 1 1 3 ]     1.1.11.....     [ 0 2 5 6 ]
2 0 :   [ 0 1 2 0 ]     1.1.1....1..     [ 0 2 4 9 ]
2 1 :   [ 0 1 2 1 ]     1.1.1...1...     [ 0 2 4 8 ]
2 2 :   [ 0 1 2 2 ]     1.1.1..1....     [ 0 2 4 7 ]
2 3 :   [ 0 1 2 3 ]     1.1.1.1.....     [ 0 2 4 6 ]
2 4 :   [ 0 1 2 4 ]     1.1.11......     [ 0 2 4 5 ]
2 5 :   [ 0 1 3 0 ]     1.11.....1..     [ 0 2 3 9 ]
2 6 :   [ 0 1 3 1 ]     1.11....1...     [ 0 2 3 8 ]
2 7 :   [ 0 1 3 2 ]     1.11...1....     [ 0 2 3 7 ]
2 8 :   [ 0 1 3 3 ]     1.11..1.....     [ 0 2 3 6 ]
2 9 :   [ 0 1 3 4 ]     1.11.1......     [ 0 2 3 5 ]
3 0 :   [ 0 1 3 5 ]     1.111.......     [ 0 2 3 4 ]
3 1 :   [ 0 2 0 0 ]     11....1..1..     [ 0 1 6 9 ]
3 2 :   [ 0 2 0 1 ]     11....1.1...     [ 0 1 6 8 ]
3 3 :   [ 0 2 0 2 ]     11....11....     [ 0 1 6 7 ]
3 4 :   [ 0 2 1 0 ]     11...1...1..     [ 0 1 5 9 ]
3 5 :   [ 0 2 1 1 ]     11...1..1...     [ 0 1 5 8 ]
3 6 :   [ 0 2 1 2 ]     11...1.1....     [ 0 1 5 7 ]
3 7 :   [ 0 2 1 3 ]     11...11.....     [ 0 1 5 6 ]
3 8 :   [ 0 2 2 0 ]     11..1....1..     [ 0 1 4 9 ]
3 9 :   [ 0 2 2 1 ]     11..1...1...     [ 0 1 4 8 ]
4 0 :   [ 0 2 2 2 ]     11..1..1....     [ 0 1 4 7 ]
4 1 :   [ 0 2 2 3 ]     11..1.1.....     [ 0 1 4 6 ]
4 2 :   [ 0 2 2 4 ]     11..11......     [ 0 1 4 5 ]
4 3 :   [ 0 2 3 0 ]     11.1.....1..     [ 0 1 3 9 ]
4 4 :   [ 0 2 3 1 ]     11.1....1...     [ 0 1 3 8 ]
4 5 :   [ 0 2 3 2 ]     11.1...1....     [ 0 1 3 7 ]
4 6 :   [ 0 2 3 3 ]     11.1..1.....     [ 0 1 3 6 ]
4 7 :   [ 0 2 3 4 ]     11.1.1......     [ 0 1 3 5 ]
4 8 :   [ 0 2 3 5 ]     11.11.......     [ 0 1 3 4 ]
4 9 :   [ 0 2 4 0 ]     111......1..     [ 0 1 2 9 ]
5 0 :   [ 0 2 4 1 ]     111.....1...     [ 0 1 2 8 ]
5 1 :   [ 0 2 4 2 ]     111....1....     [ 0 1 2 7 ]
5 2 :   [ 0 2 4 3 ]     111...1.....     [ 0 1 2 6 ]
5 3 :   [ 0 2 4 4 ]     111..1......     [ 0 1 2 5 ]
5 4 :   [ 0 2 4 5 ]     111.1.......     [ 0 1 2 4 ]
5 5 :   [ 0 2 4 6 ]     1111........     [ 0 1 2 3 ]
```

Figure 15.5-A: The 55 increment-2 restricted growth strings of length 4 (left), the corresponding 3-ary Dyck words (middle), and positions of ones in the Dyck words (right).

15.5 Increment-i RGS, k-ary Dyck words, and k-ary trees

We generalize the restricted growth strings for paren word by allowing increments at most i: sequences $a_0, a_1, \ldots, a_n$ where $a_0 = 0$ and $a_k \leq a_{k-1} + i$. The case $i = 1$ corresponds to the RGS for paren words.

A k-ary Dyck word is a binary word where each prefix contains at least $k - 1$ times many ones as zeros. The increment-i RGS correspond to k-ary Dyck words where $k = i + 1$, see figure 15.5-A. The positions of the ones in the Dyck words are computed as $c_j = k \cdot j - a_j$ (rightmost column).

The length-n increment-i RGS also correspond to k-ary trees with n internal nodes: start at the root, move out by i positions for every one and follow back by one position for every zero.

15.5.1 Generation in lexicographic order

Figure 15.5-A shows the increment-2 restricted growth strings of length 4. The strings can be generated in lexicographic order via [FXT: class dyck_rgs in comb/dyck-rgs.h]:

```
1    class dyck_rgs
2    {
3    public:
4        ulong *s_;   // restricted growth string
5        ulong n_;    // Length of strings
6        ulong i_;    // s[k] <= s[k-1]+i
7    [--snip--]
8
9        ulong next()
10       // Return index of first changed element in s[],
11       // Return zero if current string is the last
12       {
13           ulong k = n_;
14
15       start:
16           --k;
17           if ( k==0 )  return 0;
18
19           ulong sk = s_[k] + 1;
20           ulong mp = s_[k-1] + i_;
21           if ( sk > mp )  // "carry"
22           {
23               s_[k] = 0;
24               goto start;
25           }
26
27           s_[k] = sk;
28           return k;
29       }
30   [--snip--]
```

The rate of generation is about 168 M/s for $i = 1$, 194 M/s for $i = 2$, and 218 M/s with $i = 3$ [FXT: comb/dyck-rgs-demo.cc].

15.5.2 Gray codes with homogeneous moves

A loopless algorithm for the generation of a Gray code with only homogeneous moves is given in [37]. The RGS used in the algorithm gives the positions (one-based) of the ones in the delta sets, see figure 15.5-B (created with [FXT: comb/dyck-gray-demo.cc]). An implementation is given in [FXT: class dyck_gray in comb/dyck-gray.h].

A Gray code where in addition all transitions are two-close is shown in figure 15.5-C (created with [FXT: comb/dyck-gray2-demo.cc]). Note that the moves are enup-moves, compare to figure 6.6-B on page 189. The underlying algorithm is described in [338] an implementation is given in [FXT: class dyck_gray2 in comb/dyck-gray2.h]:

```
1    class dyck_gray2
2    {
3    public:
4        ulong m, k;   // m ones (and m*(k-1) zeros)
5        bool ptt;     // Parity of Total number of Tories (variable 'Odd' in paper)
```

```
         positions      Dyck word       direction
 1 :   [ 1 4 7 A ]    1..1..1..1..    [ + + + + ]
 2 :   [ 1 4 7 8 ]    1..1..11....    [ + + + - ]
 3 :   [ 1 4 7 9 ]    1..1..1.1...    [ + + + - ]
 4 :   [ 1 4 5 9 ]    1..11...1...    [ + + + - ]
 5 :   [ 1 4 5 8 ]    1..11..1....    [ + + + - ]
 6 :   [ 1 4 5 7 ]    1..11.1.....    [ + + + - ]
 7 :   [ 1 4 5 6 ]    1..111......    [ + + + - ]
 8 :   [ 1 4 5 A ]    1..11....1..    [ + + + + ]
 9 :   [ 1 4 6 A ]    1..1.1...1..    [ + + - + ]
10 :   [ 1 4 6 7 ]    1..1.11.....    [ + + - + ]
11 :   [ 1 4 6 8 ]    1..1.1.1....    [ + + - + ]
12 :   [ 1 4 6 9 ]    1..1.1..1...    [ + + - - ]
13 :   [ 1 2 6 9 ]    11...1..1...    [ + + - - ]
14 :   [ 1 2 6 8 ]    11...1.1....    [ + + - - ]
15 :   [ 1 2 6 7 ]    11...11.....    [ + + - - ]
16 :   [ 1 2 6 A ]    11...1...1..    [ + + - + ]
17 :   [ 1 2 5 A ]    11..1....1..    [ + + - + ]
18 :   [ 1 2 5 6 ]    11..11......    [ + + - + ]
19 :   [ 1 2 5 7 ]    11..1.1.....    [ + + - + ]
20 :   [ 1 2 5 8 ]    11..1..1....    [ + + - + ]
21 :   [ 1 2 5 9 ]    11..1...1...    [ + + - - ]
22 :   [ 1 2 4 9 ]    11.1....1...    [ + + - - ]
23 :   [ 1 2 4 8 ]    11.1...1....    [ + + - - ]
24 :   [ 1 2 4 7 ]    11.1..1.....    [ + + - - ]
25 :   [ 1 2 4 6 ]    11.1.1......    [ + + - - ]
26 :   [ 1 2 4 5 ]    11.11.......    [ + + - - ]
27 :   [ 1 2 4 A ]    11.1.....1..    [ + + - + ]
28 :   [ 1 2 3 A ]    111......1..    [ + + - + ]
29 :   [ 1 2 3 4 ]    1111........    [ + + - + ]
30 :   [ 1 2 3 5 ]    111.1.......    [ + + - + ]
31 :   [ 1 2 3 6 ]    111..1......    [ + + - + ]
32 :   [ 1 2 3 7 ]    111...1.....    [ + + - + ]
33 :   [ 1 2 3 8 ]    111....1....    [ + + - + ]
34 :   [ 1 2 3 9 ]    111.....1...    [ + + - - ]
35 :   [ 1 2 7 9 ]    11....1.1...    [ + + + - ]
36 :   [ 1 2 7 8 ]    11....11....    [ + + + - ]
37 :   [ 1 2 7 A ]    11....1..1..    [ + + + + ]
38 :   [ 1 3 7 A ]    1.1...1..1..    [ + - + + ]
39 :   [ 1 3 7 8 ]    1.1...11....    [ + - + + ]
40 :   [ 1 3 7 9 ]    1.1...1.1...    [ + - + - ]
41 :   [ 1 3 4 9 ]    1.11....1...    [ + - + - ]
42 :   [ 1 3 4 8 ]    1.11...1....    [ + - + - ]
43 :   [ 1 3 4 7 ]    1.11..1.....    [ + - + - ]
44 :   [ 1 3 4 6 ]    1.11.1......    [ + - + - ]
45 :   [ 1 3 4 5 ]    1.111.......    [ + - + - ]
46 :   [ 1 3 4 A ]    1.11.....1..    [ + - + + ]
47 :   [ 1 3 5 A ]    1.1.1....1..    [ + - + + ]
48 :   [ 1 3 5 6 ]    1.1.11......    [ + - + + ]
49 :   [ 1 3 5 7 ]    1.1.1.1.....    [ + - + + ]
50 :   [ 1 3 5 8 ]    1.1.1..1....    [ + - + + ]
51 :   [ 1 3 5 9 ]    1.1.1...1...    [ + - + - ]
52 :   [ 1 3 6 9 ]    1.1..1..1...    [ + - - - ]
53 :   [ 1 3 6 8 ]    1.1..1.1....    [ + - - - ]
54 :   [ 1 3 6 7 ]    1.1..11.....    [ + - - - ]
55 :   [ 1 3 6 A ]    1.1..1...1..    [ + - - + ]
```

Figure 15.5-B: Gray code for 3-ary Dyck words where all changes are homogeneous. The left column shows the vectors of (one-based) positions, the symbol 'A' is used for the number 10.

```
         positions        Dyck word          direction
   1 :  [ 1 2 3 4 ]      1111........    [  .   .   .   .  ]
   2 :  [ 1 2 3 6 ]      111..1......    [  .   .   .  +2  ]
   3 :  [ 1 2 3 8 ]      111....1....    [  .   .   .  +2  ]
   4 :  [ 1 2 3 A ]      111......1..    [  .   .   .  -2  ]
   5 :  [ 1 2 3 9 ]      111.....1...    [  .   .   .  -2  ]
   6 :  [ 1 2 3 7 ]      111...1.....    [  .   .   .  -2  ]
   7 :  [ 1 2 3 5 ]      111.1.......    [  .   .   .   .  ]
   8 :  [ 1 2 4 5 ]      11.11.......    [  .   .  +2   .  ]
   9 :  [ 1 2 4 6 ]      11.1.1......    [  .   .  +2  +2  ]
  10 :  [ 1 2 4 8 ]      11.1...1....    [  .   .  +2  +3  ]
  11 :  [ 1 2 4 A ]      11.1.....1..    [  .   .  +2  -3  ]
  12 :  [ 1 2 4 9 ]      11.1....1...    [  .   .  +2  -3  ]
  13 :  [ 1 2 4 7 ]      11.1..1.....    [  .   .  +2   .  ]
  14 :  [ 1 2 6 7 ]      11...11.....    [  .   .  +3   .  ]
  15 :  [ 1 2 6 8 ]      11...1.1....    [  .   .  +3  +2  ]
  16 :  [ 1 2 6 A ]      11...1...1..    [  .   .  +3  -3  ]
  17 :  [ 1 2 6 9 ]      11...1..1...    [  .   .  +3   .  ]
  18 :  [ 1 2 7 9 ]      11....1.1...    [  .   .  -3   .  ]
  19 :  [ 1 2 7 A ]      11....1..1..    [  .   .  -3  -1  ]
  20 :  [ 1 2 7 8 ]      11....11....    [  .   .  -3   .  ]
  21 :  [ 1 2 5 8 ]      11..1..1....    [  .   .   .   .  ]
  22 :  [ 1 2 5 A ]      11..1....1..    [  .   .   .  -1  ]
  23 :  [ 1 2 5 9 ]      11..1...1...    [  .   .   .  -1  ]
  24 :  [ 1 2 5 7 ]      11..1.1.....    [  .   .   .  -1  ]
  25 :  [ 1 2 5 6 ]      11..11......    [  .   .   .   .  ]
  26 :  [ 1 4 5 6 ]      1..111......    [  .  -2   .   .  ]
  27 :  [ 1 4 5 7 ]      1..11.1.....    [  .  -2   .  +2  ]
  28 :  [ 1 4 5 9 ]      1..11...1...    [  .  -2   .  +3  ]
  29 :  [ 1 4 5 A ]      1..11....1..    [  .  -2   .  -3  ]
  30 :  [ 1 4 5 8 ]      1..11..1....    [  .  -2   .   .  ]
  31 :  [ 1 4 7 8 ]      1..1..11....    [  .  -2  -2   .  ]
  32 :  [ 1 4 7 A ]      1..1..1..1..    [  .  -2  -2  -2  ]
  33 :  [ 1 4 7 9 ]      1..1..1.1...    [  .  -2  -2   .  ]
  34 :  [ 1 4 6 9 ]      1..1.1..1...    [  .  -2   .   .  ]
  35 :  [ 1 4 6 A ]      1..1.1...1..    [  .  -2   .  -1  ]
  36 :  [ 1 4 6 8 ]      1..1.1.1....    [  .  -2   .  -1  ]
  37 :  [ 1 4 6 7 ]      1..1.11.....    [  .  -2   .   .  ]
  38 :  [ 1 3 6 7 ]      1.1..11.....    [  .   .   .   .  ]
  39 :  [ 1 3 6 8 ]      1.1..1.1....    [  .   .   .  +2  ]
  40 :  [ 1 3 6 A ]      1.1..1...1..    [  .   .   .  -3  ]
  41 :  [ 1 3 6 9 ]      1.1..1..1...    [  .   .   .   .  ]
  42 :  [ 1 3 7 9 ]      1.1...1.1...    [  .   .  -1   .  ]
  43 :  [ 1 3 7 A ]      1.1...1..1..    [  .   .  -1  -1  ]
  44 :  [ 1 3 7 8 ]      1.1...11....    [  .   .  -1   .  ]
  45 :  [ 1 3 5 8 ]      1.1.1..1....    [  .   .  -1   .  ]
  46 :  [ 1 3 5 A ]      1.1.1....1..    [  .   .  -1  -1  ]
  47 :  [ 1 3 5 9 ]      1.1.1...1...    [  .   .  -1  -1  ]
  48 :  [ 1 3 5 7 ]      1.1.1.1.....    [  .   .  -1  -1  ]
  49 :  [ 1 3 5 6 ]      1.1.11......    [  .   .  -1   .  ]
  50 :  [ 1 3 4 6 ]      1.11.1......    [  .   .   .   .  ]
  51 :  [ 1 3 4 8 ]      1.11...1....    [  .   .   .  +1  ]
  52 :  [ 1 3 4 A ]      1.11.....1..    [  .   .   .  -1  ]
  53 :  [ 1 3 4 9 ]      1.11....1...    [  .   .   .  -1  ]
  54 :  [ 1 3 4 7 ]      1.11..1.....    [  .   .   .  -1  ]
  55 :  [ 1 3 4 5 ]      1.111.......    [  .   .   .   .  ]
```

Figure 15.5-C: Gray code for 3-ary Dyck words where all changes are both homogeneous and two-close. The left column shows the vectors of (one-based) positions, the symbol 'A' is used for the number 10.

```
6        ulong *c_;    // positions of ones (1-based)
7        ulong *e_;    // Ehrlich array (focus pointers)
8        bool *p_;     // parity (1-based)
9        int *s_;      // directions: whether last/first (==0) or
10       // rising (>0) or falling (<0);  (1-based)
11
12   public:
13       dyck_gray2(ulong tk, ulong tm)
14       // must have tk>=2, tm>=1
15       {
16           k = tk;
17           m = tm;
18           ptt = false;
19           c_ = new ulong[m+2];
20           // sentinels c_[0] (with computing MN) and c_[m+1] (with condition in next())
21
22           e_ = new ulong[m+1];
23           p_ = new bool[m+1];    // p_[0] unused
24           s_ = new int[m+1];     // s_[0] unused
25           first();
26       }
27
28       ~dyck_gray2()
29       [--snip--]
30
31       void first()
32       {
33           for (ulong j=0; j<=m; ++j)  e_[j] = j;       // {e_[j] = j for 0 <= j <= m}
34           for (ulong j=0; j<=m; ++j)  s_[j] = 0;       // {s_[j] = 0 for 1 <= j <= m}
35           for (ulong j=0; j<=m; ++j)  p_[j] = false;   // {p_[j] = 0 for 1 <= j <= m}
36           for (ulong j=0; j<=m; ++j)  c_[j] = j;       // first word == [1, 2, 3, ..., m]
37           c_[m+1] = 0;   // sentinel, c_[0] is also sentinel
38       }
39
```

The following comments in curly braces are from the paper:

```
1        ulong next()
2        // Return zero if current==last, else
3        // position (!=0) in (zero-based) array c_[]
4        // (the first element never changes).
5        {
6            ulong i = e_[m];  // The pivot
7            if ( i==1 )  return 0;  // current is last
8            const ulong MN = c_[i-1] + 1;  // {MN is the minimum value of c_[i]}
9            // can touch sentinel c_[0]
10
11           const ulong MX = (i - 1)*k + 1;  // { MX is the maximum value of c_[i]}
12
13           if ( s_[i] == 0 )  // { c_[i] is at its first value }
14           {
15               p_[i] = ptt;  // { parity of total number of tories }
16               s_[i] = +1;   // {c_[i] starts rising unless it starts at max(i)}
17
18               if ( c_[i] == MX )  // {one of these tories is not to c_[i]'s left}
19               {
20                   p_[i] = 1 - p_[i];
21                   s_[i] = -s_[i];
22               }
23
24               if ( c_[i+1] == MX+k )  // can touch sentinel c_[m+1]==0
25               {
26                   p_[i] = 1 - p_[i];
27               }
28           }
29
30           if ( s_[i] > 0 )  // { c_[i] is rising }
31           {
32               if ( c_[i] == MN )  // {MN is taken and c_[i] can't end there}
33               {
34                   s_[i] = 2;
35               }
36               else
37               {
38                   if ( (c_[i] == MN+1) && (s_[i] == 2) )  // {MN+1 is also taken}
39                   {
40                       s_[i] = 3;
```

```
41              }
42          }
43
44          c_[i] += ( 1 + ( ((c_[i] % 2) == p_[i]) && (c_[i] < MX-1) ) );
45
46          if ( c_[i] == MX )   // {one more tory}
47          {
48              ptt = 1 - ptt;
49              s_[i] = -s_[i];
50          }
51      }
52      else   // { c_[i] is falling }
53      {
54
55          if ( c_[i] == MX ) {  ptt = 1 - ptt; }   // {one fewer tory}
56
57          c_[i] -= ( 1 + ( ((c_[i] % 2) != p_[i] ) && (c_[i] > MN+1) ) );
58      }
59
60      e_[m] = m; // {beginning to update Ehrlich array}
61      if ( c_[i] + s_[i] == MN-1 )   // {c_[i] is at its last value}
62      {
63          s_[i] = 0;   // {c_[i] will be at its first value the next time i is the pivot}
64          e_[i] = e_[i-1];
65          e_[i-1] = i - 1;
66      }
67
68      return  i - 1;   // position in zero-based array c_[]
69  }
70
71  const ulong *data()  const  { return c_+1; }   // zero-based array
72  };
```

15.5.3   The number of increment-i RGS

n:	1	2	3	4	5	6	7	8	9	10	11
i=1:	1	2	5	14	42	132	429	1430	4862	16796	58786
i=2:	1	3	12	55	273	1428	7752	43263	246675	1430715	8414640
i=3:	1	4	22	140	969	7084	53820	420732	3362260	27343888	225568798
i=4:	1	5	35	285	2530	23751	231880	2330445	23950355	250543370	2658968130

Figure 15.5-D: The numbers $C_{n,i}$ of increment-i RGS of length n for $i \leq 4$ and $n \leq 11$.

The number $C_{n,i}$ of length-n increment-i strings equals

$$C_{n,i} \;=\; \frac{\binom{(i+1)\,n}{n}}{i\,n+1} \tag{15.5-1}$$

A recursion generalizing relation 15.4-2 is

$$C_{n+1,i} \;=\; (i+1)\,\frac{\prod_{k=1}^{i}[(i+1)\,n+k]}{\prod_{k=1}^{i}[i\,n+k+1]}\,C_{n,i} \tag{15.5-2}$$

The sequences of numbers of length-n strings for $i = 1, 2, 3, 4$ start as sown in figure 15.5-D. These are respectively the entries A000108, A001764, A002293, A002294 in [312] where combinatorial interpretations are given. We can express the generating function $C_i(x)$ as a hypergeometric series (see chapter 36 on page 685):

$$C_i(x) \;=\; \sum_{n=0}^{\infty} C_{n,i}\, x^n \tag{15.5-3a}$$

$$=\; F\left(\begin{matrix} 1/(i+1),\ 2/(i+1),\ 3/(i+1),\ \ldots,\ (i+1)/(i+1) \\ 2/i,\ 3/i,\ \ldots,\ i/i,\ (i+1)/i \end{matrix} \;\middle|\; \frac{(i+1)^{(i+1)}}{i^i}\,x \right) \tag{15.5-3b}$$

Note that the last upper and second last lower parameter cancel. Now let $f_i(x) := x\,C_i(x^i)$, then

$$f_i(x) - f_i(x)^{i+1} \;=\; x \tag{15.5-4}$$

That is, $f_i(x)$ can be computed as the series reversion of $x - x^{i+1}$. We choose $i = 2$ as an example:

```
? t1=serreverse(x-x^3+O(x^(17)))
   x + x^3 + 3*x^5 + 12*x^7 + 55*x^9 + 273*x^11 + 1428*x^13 + 7752*x^15 + O(x^17)
? t2=hypergeom([1/3,2/3,3/3],[2/2,3/2],3^3/2^2*x)+O(x^17)
   1 + x + 3*x^2 + 12*x^3 + 55*x^4 + 273*x^5 + 1428*x^6 + 7752*x^7 + ... + O(x^17)
? f=x*subst(t2,x,x^2);
? t1-f
   O(x^17)          \\ f is actually the series reversion of x-x^3
? f-f^3
   x + O(x^35)   \\ ... so  f - f^3 == id
```

We further have the following convolution property which generalizes relation 15.4-4:

$$C_{n,i} \quad = \quad \sum_{j_1 + j_2 + \ldots + j_i + j_{(i+1)} = n-1} C_{j_1,i} \, C_{j_2,i} \, C_{j_3,i} \cdots C_{j_i,i} \, C_{j_{(i+1)},i} \qquad (15.5\text{-}5)$$

An explicit expression for the function $C_i(x)$ is

$$C_i(x) \quad = \quad \exp\left(\frac{1}{i+1} \sum_{n=1}^{\infty} \binom{(i+1)\,n}{n} \frac{x^n}{n} \right) \qquad (15.5\text{-}6)$$

The expression generalizes a relation given in [227, rel.6] (set $i = 1$ and take the logarithm on both sides)

$$\sum_{n=1}^{\infty} \frac{1}{n} \binom{2n}{n} x^n \quad = \quad 2 \log\left(\frac{1 - \sqrt{1-4x}}{2x} \right) \qquad (15.5\text{-}7)$$

A curious property of the functions $C_i(x)$ is given in [349, entry "Hypergeometric Function"]:

$$C_i\left(x \, (1-x)^i \right) \quad = \quad \frac{1}{1-x} \qquad (15.5\text{-}8)$$

Chapter 16

Integer partitions

```
 1 :   6 = = 6* 1 + 0    + 0    + 0    + 0    + 0    ==   1 + 1 + 1 + 1 + 1 + 1
 2 :   6 = = 4* 1 + 1 *2 + 0    + 0    + 0    + 0    ==   1 + 1 + 1 + 1 + 2
 3 :   6 = = 2* 1 + 2 *2 + 0    + 0    + 0    + 0    ==   1 + 1 + 2 + 2
 4 :   6 = = 0    + 3* 2 + 0    + 0    + 0    + 0    ==   2 + 2 + 2
 5 :   6 = = 3* 1 + 0    + 1* 3 + 0    + 0    + 0    ==   1 + 1 + 1 + 3
 6 :   6 = = 1* 1 + 1 *2 + 1* 3 + 0    + 0    + 0    ==   1 + 2 + 3
 7 :   6 = = 0    + 0    + 2* 3 + 0    + 0    + 0    ==   3 + 3
 8 :   6 = = 2* 1 + 0    + 0    + 1* 4 + 0    + 0    ==   1 + 1 + 4
 9 :   6 = = 0    + 1* 2 + 0    + 1* 4 + 0    + 0    ==   2 + 4
1 0 :   6 = = 1* 1 + 0    + 0    + 0    + 1* 5 + 0    ==   1 + 5
1 1 :   6 = = 0    + 0    + 0    + 0    + 0    + 1* 6 ==   6
```

Figure 16.0-A: All (eleven) integer partitions of 6.

An integer x is the sum of the positive integers less than or equal to itself in various ways. The decompositions into sums of integers are called the *integer partitions* of the number x. Figure 16.0-A shows all integer partitions of $x = 6$.

16.1 Solution of a generalized problem

We can solve a more general problem and find all partitions of a number x with respect to a set $V = \{v_0, v_1, \ldots, v_{n-1}\}$ where $v_i > 0$, that is all decompositions of the form $x = \sum_{k=0}^{n-1} c_k \cdot v_k$ where $c_i \geq 0$. The integer partitions are the special case $V = \{1, 2, 3, \ldots, n\}$.

To generate the partitions assign to the first bucket r_0 an integer multiple of the first element v_0: $r_0 = c \cdot v_0$. This has to be done for all $c \geq 0$ for which $r_0 \leq x$. Now set $c_0 = c$. If $r_0 = x$, we already found a partition (consisting of c_0 only), else (if $r_0 < x$) solve the remaining problem where $x' := x - c_0 \cdot v_0$ and $V' := \{v_1, v_2, \ldots, v_{n-1}\}$.

A C++ class for the generation of all partitions is [FXT: class `partition_gen` in comb/partition-gen.h]:

```
1    class partition_gen
2    // Integer partitions of x into supplied values pv[0],...,pv[n-1].
3    // pv[] defaults to [1,2,3,...,x]
4    {
5    public:
6        ulong ct_;   // Number of partitions found so far
7        ulong n_;    // Number of values
8        ulong i_;    // level in iterative search
9
10       long *pv_;   // values into which to partition
11       ulong *pc_;  // multipliers for values
12       ulong pci_;  // temporary for pc_[i_]
13       long *r_;    // rest
14       long ri_;    // temporary for r_[i_]
15       long x_;     // value to partition
16
17       partition_gen(ulong x, ulong n=0, const ulong *pv=0)
18       {
19           if ( 0==n )  n = x;
20           n_ = n;
21           pv_ = new long[n_+1];
```

J. Arndt, *Matters Computational: Ideas, Algorithms, Source Code*,
DOI 10.1007/978-3-642-14764-7_16, © Springer-Verlag Berlin Heidelberg 2011

```
22          if ( pv )  for (ulong j=0; j<n_; ++j)  pv_[j] = pv[j];
23          else       for (ulong j=0; j<n_; ++j)  pv_[j] = j + 1;
24          pc_ = new ulong[n_+1];
25          r_  = new long[n_+1];
26          init(x);
27      }
28
29      void init(ulong x)
30      {
31          x_ = x;
32          ct_ = 0;
33          for (ulong k=0; k<n_; ++k)  pc_[k] = 0;
34          for (ulong k=0; k<n_; ++k)  r_[k] = 0;
35          r_[n_-1] = x_;
36          r_[n_] = x_;
37          i_ = n_ - 1;
38          pci_ = 0;
39          ri_ = x_;
40      }
41
42      ~partition_gen()
43      {
44          delete [] pv_;
45          delete [] pc_;
46          delete [] r_;
47      }
48
49      ulong next();  // generate next partition
50      ulong next_func(ulong i);  // aux
51      [--snip--]
52  };
```

The routine to compute the next partition is given in [FXT: comb/partition-gen.cc]:

```
1   ulong
2   partition_gen::next()
3   {
4       if ( i_>=n_ )  return  n_;
5
6       r_[i_] = ri_;
7       pc_[i_] = pci_;
8       i_ = next_func(i_);
9
10      for (ulong j=0; j<i_; ++j)  pc_[j] = r_[j] = 0;
11
12      ++i_;
13      ri_ = r_[i_] - pv_[i_];
14      pci_ = pc_[i_] + 1;
15
16      return  i_ - 1;  // >=0
17  }
```

```
1   ulong
2   partition_gen::next_func(ulong i)
3   {
4    start:
5       if ( 0!=i )
6       {
7           while ( r_[i]>0 )
8           {
9               pc_[i-1] = 0;
10              r_[i-1] = r_[i];
11              --i;  goto start;   // iteration
12          }
13      }
14      else  // iteration end
15      {
16          if ( 0!=r_[i] )
17          {
18              long d = r_[i] / pv_[i];
19              r_[i] -= d * pv_[i];
20              pc_[i] = d;
21          }
22      }
23
24      if ( 0==r_[i] )  // valid partition found
25      {
```

```
26              ++ct_;
27              return i;
28          }
29
30      ++i;
31      if ( i>=n_ )  return n_;  // search finished
32
33      r_[i] -= pv_[i];
34      ++pc_[i];
35
36      goto start;  // iteration
37  }
```

The routines can easily be adapted to the generation of partitions satisfying certain restrictions, for example, partitions into distinct parts (that is, $c_i \leq 1$).

The listing shown in figure 16.0-A can be generated with [FXT: comb/partition-gen-demo.cc]. The $190,569,292$ partitions of 100 are generated at a rate of about 18 M/s.

16.2 Iterative algorithm

An iterative implementation for the generation of the integer partitions is given in [FXT: class partition in comb/partition.h]:

```
1   class partition
2   {
3   public:
4       ulong *c_;   // partition:  c[1]* 1 + c[2]* 2 + ... + c[n]* n == n
5       ulong *s_;   // cumulative sums:  s[j+1] = c[1]* 1 + c[2]* 2 + ... + c[j]* j
6       ulong n_;    // partitions of n
7
8   public:
9       partition(ulong n)
10      {
11          n_ = n;
12          c_ = new ulong[n+1];
13          s_ = new ulong[n+1];
14          s_[0] = 0;   // unused
15          c_[0] = 0;   // unused
16          first();
17      }
18
19      ~partition()
20      {
21          delete [] c_;
22          doloto [] o_;
23      }
24
25      void first()
26      {
27          c_[1] = n_;
28          for (ulong i=2; i<=n_; i++)  { c_[i] = 0; }
29          s_[1] = 0;
30          for (ulong i=2; i<=n_; i++)  { s_[i] = n_; }
31      }
32
33      void last()
34      {
35          for (ulong i=1; i<n_; i++)  { c_[i] = 0; }
36          c_[n_] = 1;
37          for (ulong i=1; i<n_; i++)  { s_[i] = 0; }
38          // s_[n_+1] = n_;  // unused (and out of bounds)
39      }
```

To compute the next partition, find the smallest index $i \geq 2$ so that $[c_1, c_2, \ldots, c_{i-1}, c_i]$ can be replaced by $[z, 0, 0, \ldots, 0, c_i + 1]$ where $z \geq 0$. The index i is determined using cumulative sums. The partitions are generated in the same order as shown in figure 16.0-A. The algorithm was given (2006) by Torsten Finke [priv. comm.].

```
1       bool next()
2       {
3           if ( c_[n_]!=0 )  return false;  // last == 1* n (c[n]==1)
4
```

```
5        // Find first coefficient c[i], i>=2 that can be increased:
6        ulong i = 2;
7        while ( s_[i]<i )  ++i;
8
9        ++c_[i];
10       s_[i] -= i;
11       ulong z = s_[i];
12       // Now set c[1], c[2], ..., c[i-1] to the first partition
13       // of z into i-1 parts, i.e. set to  z, 0, 0, ..., 0:
14       while ( --i > 1 )
15       {
16           s_[i] = z;
17           c_[i] = 0;
18       }
19       c_[1] = z;   // z* 1 == z
20       // s_[1] unused
21
22       return true;
23   }
```

The preceding partition can be computed as follows:

```
1        bool prev()
2        {
3            if ( c_[1]==n_ )  return false;   // first == n* 1 (c[1]==n)
4
5            // Find first nonzero coefficient c[i] where i>=2:
6            ulong i = 2;
7            while ( c_[i]==0 )  ++i;
8
9            --c_[i];
10           s_[i] += i;
11           ulong z = s_[i];
12           // Now set c[1], c[2], ..., c[i-1] to the last partition
13           // of z into i-1 parts:
14           while ( --i > 1  )
15           {
16               ulong q = (z>=i ? z/i : 0);   // == z/i;
17               c_[i] = q;
18               s_[i+1] = z;
19               z -= q*i;
20           }
21           c_[1] = z;
22           s_[2] = z;
23           // s_[1] unused
24
25           return true;
26       }
27   [--snip--]
28 };
```

Divisions which result in $q = 0$ are avoided, leading to a small speedup. The program [FXT:
comb/partition-demo.cc] demonstrates the usage of the class. About 200 million partitions per second
are generated, and about 70 million for the reversed order.

16.3   Partitions into m parts

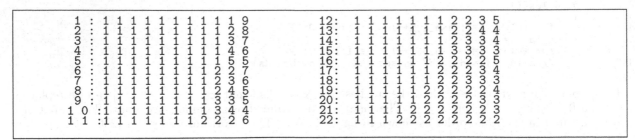

Figure 16.3-A: The 22 partitions of 19 into 11 parts in lexicographic order.

An algorithm for the generation of all partitions of n into m parts is given in [123, vol2, p.106]:

The initial partition contains $m-1$ units and the element $n-m+1$. To obtain a new partition from a given one, pass over the elements of the latter from right to left, stopping at the first element f which is less, by at least two units, than the final element [...]. Without altering any element at the left of f, write $f+1$ in place of f and every element to the right of f with the exception of the final element, in whose place is written the number which when added to all the other new elements gives the sum n. The process to obtain partitions stops when we reach one in which no part is less than the final part by at least two units.

Figure 16.3-A shows the partitions of 19 into 11 parts. The data was generated with the program [FXT: comb/mpartition-demo.cc]. The implementation used is [FXT: class mpartition in comb/mpartition.h]:

```
1    class mpartition
2    // Integer partitions of n into m parts
3    {
4    public:
5        ulong *x_;   // partition: x[1]+x[2]+...+x[m] = n
6        ulong *s_;   // aux: cumulative sums of x[]   (s[0]=0)
7        ulong n_;    // integer partitions of n  (must have n>0)
8        ulong m_;    // ... into m parts   (must have 0<m<=n)
9
10       mpartition(ulong n, ulong m)
11           : n_(n), m_(m)
12       {
13           x_ = new ulong [m_+1];
14           s_ = new ulong [m_+1];
15           init();
16       }
17
18       [--snip--]
19
20       void init()
21       {
22           x_[0] = 0;
23           for (ulong k=1; k<m_; ++k)  x_[k] = 1;
24           x_[m_] = n_ - m_ + 1;
25           ulong s = 0;
26           for (ulong k=0; k<=m_; ++k)  { s+=x_[k]; s_[k]=s; }
27       }
28
```

The successor is computed as follows:

```
1        bool next()
2        {
3            ulong u = x_[m_];  // last element
4            ulong k = m_;
5            while ( --k )  { if ( x_[k]+2<=u ) break; }
6
7            if ( k==0 )  return  false;
8
9            ulong f = x_[k] + 1;
10           ulong s = s_[k-1];
11           while ( k < m_ )
12           {
13               x_[k] = f;
14               s += f;
15               s_[k] = s;
16               ++k;
17           }
18           x_[m_] = n_ - s_[m_-1];
19           // s_[m_] = n_;   // unchanged
20
21           return  true;
22       }
23   };
```

The auxiliary array of cumulative sums allows the recalculation of the final element without rescanning more than the elements just changed. About 134 million partitions per second are generated. A Gray code for integer partitions is described in [279], for algorithmic details see [215, sect.7.2.1.4].

16.4   The number of integer partitions

We give expressions for generating functions for various types of partitions, as, for example, unrestricted partitions, partitions into an even or odd number of parts, partitions into exactly m parts, partitions into distinct parts, and partitions into square-free parts.

The following relations will be useful. The first is found by setting $P_0 = 1$ and $P_N = \prod_{n=1}^{N}(1 + a_n)$ so $P_N = (1 + a_N)\, P_{N-1} = a_N\, P_{N-1} + P_{N-1} = a_N\, P_{N-1} + a_{N-1}\, P_{N-2} + P_{N-2}$ and so on. For the second, replace a_n by $a_n/(1 - a_n)$ (for the other direction replace a_n by $a_n/(1 + a_n)$):

$$\prod_{n=1}^{N}(1 + a_n) \;=\; 1 + \sum_{n=1}^{N} a_n \prod_{k=1}^{n-1}(1 + a_k) \;=\; 1 + \sum_{n=1}^{N} a_n \prod_{k=n+1}^{N}(1 + a_k) \tag{16.4-1a}$$

$$\frac{1}{\prod_{n=1}^{N}(1 - a_n)} \;=\; 1 + \sum_{n=1}^{N} \frac{a_n}{\prod_{k=1}^{n}(1 - a_k)} \;=\; 1 + \sum_{n=1}^{N} \frac{a_n}{\prod_{k=n}^{N}(1 - a_k)} \tag{16.4-1b}$$

The next two are given in [248, p.7, id.7 and id.6]:

$$\prod_{n=0}^{\infty}(1 + x\,q^n) \;=\; \sum_{n=0}^{\infty} \frac{x^n\, q^{n\,(n-1)/2}}{\prod_{k=1}^{n}(1 - q^k)} \tag{16.4-2a}$$

$$\frac{1}{\prod_{n=0}^{\infty}(1 - x\,q^n)} \;=\; \sum_{n=0}^{\infty} \frac{x^n\, q^{n(n-1)}}{\prod_{k=0}^{n-1}(1 - q\,q^k)\,\prod_{k=0}^{n-1}(1 - x\,q^k)} \tag{16.4-2b}$$

The relations are the limits $M \to \infty$ of the following:

$$\prod_{n=0}^{M-1}(1 + x\,q^n) \;=\; \sum_{n=0}^{M} \frac{\prod_{k=0}^{n-1}(1 - q^{M-k})}{\prod_{k=1}^{n}(1 - q^k)}\, x^n\, q^{n\,(n-1)/2} \tag{16.4-3a}$$

$$\frac{1}{\prod_{n=0}^{M-1}(1 - x\,q^n)} \;=\; \sum_{n=0}^{M} \frac{\prod_{k=0}^{n-1}(1 - q^{M-k})}{\prod_{k=0}^{n-1}(1 - q\,q^k)\,\prod_{k=0}^{n-1}(1 - x\,q^k)}\, x^n\, q^{n\,(n-1)} \tag{16.4-3b}$$

These relations are respectively the special cases $(a, b) = (-1, 0)$ and $(a, b) = (0, 1)$ of an identity due to Jacobi [194, p.795]:

$$\prod_{n=0}^{M-1} \frac{(1 - a\,x\,q^n)}{(1 - b\,x\,q^n)} \;=\; \sum_{n=0}^{M} \frac{\prod_{k=0}^{n-1}(1 - q^{M-k})\,\prod_{k=0}^{n-1}(b\,q^k - a)}{\prod_{k=1}^{n}(1 - q^k)\,\prod_{k=0}^{n-1}(1 - b\,x\,q^k)}\, x^n\, q^{n\,(n-1)/2} \tag{16.4-4}$$

In the limit $M \to \infty$ the first product in the numerator on the right is 1, setting $a = -1$ and $b = 0$ gives 16.4-2a, setting $a = 0$ and $b = 1$ gives 16.4-2b. The following identity (given in [99, p.70, rel.1.3] and [15, p.19, rel.2.2.7]) is due to Cauchy, setting $a = -1$ and $b = 0$ gives 16.4-2a:

$$\prod_{n=0}^{\infty} \frac{(1 - a\,x\,q^n)}{(1 - b\,x\,q^n)} \;=\; \sum_{n=0}^{\infty} \frac{\prod_{k=0}^{n-1}(b - a\,q^k)}{\prod_{k=1}^{n}(1 - q^k)}\, x^n \tag{16.4-5}$$

We will use two functions (*eta functions*, or η-*functions*) defined as

$$\eta(x) \;:=\; \prod_{n=1}^{\infty}(1 - x^n) \tag{16.4-6a}$$

$$\eta_+(x) \;:=\; \prod_{n=1}^{\infty}(1 + x^n) \tag{16.4-6b}$$

n :	P_n	n :	P_n	n :	P_n	n :	P_n	n :	P_n
1:	1	11:	56	21:	792	31:	6842	41:	44583
2:	2	12:	77	22:	1002	32:	8349	42:	53174
3:	3	13:	101	23:	1255	33:	10143	43:	63261
4:	5	14:	135	24:	1575	34:	12310	44:	75175
5:	7	15:	176	25:	1958	35:	14883	45:	89134
6:	11	16:	231	26:	2436	36:	17977	46:	105558
7:	15	17:	297	27:	3010	37:	21637	47:	124754
8:	22	18:	385	28:	3718	38:	26015	48:	147273
9:	30	19:	490	29:	4565	39:	31185	49:	173525
10:	42	20:	627	30:	5604	40:	37338	50:	204226

Figure 16.4-A: The number P_n of integer partitions of n for $n \le 50$.

```
 n:       P(n)           P(n,m) for m =
                   1   2   3   4   5   6   7   8   9  10  11  12  13  14  15  16
 1:        1       1
 2:        2       1   1
 3:        3       1   1   1
 4:        5       1   2   1   1
 5:        7       1   2   2   1   1
 6:       11       1   3   3   2   1   1
 7:       15       1   3   4   3   2   1   1
 8:       22       1   4   5   5   3   2   1   1
 9:       30       1   4   7   6   5   3   2   1   1
1 0      :4    2   1   5   8   9   7   5   3   2   1   1
1 1      :5    6   1   5  10  11  10   7   5   3   2   1   1
12:       77       1   6  12  15  13  11   7   5   3   2   1   1
13:      101       1   6  14  18  18  14  11   7   5   3   2   1   1
14:      135       1   7  16  23  23  20  15  11   7   5   3   2   1   1
15:      176       1   7  19  27  30  26  21  15  11   7   5   3   2   1   1
16:      231       1   8  21  34  37  35  28  22  15  11   7   5   3   2   1   1
```

Figure 16.4-B: Numbers $P(n, m)$ of partitions of n into m parts.

16.4.1 Unrestricted partitions and partitions into m parts

The number of integer partitions of n is sequence A000041 in [312], the values for $1 \le x \le 50$ are shown in figure 16.4-A. If we denote the number of partitions of n into exactly m parts by $P(n, m)$, then

$$P(n, m) = P(n-1, m-1) + P(n-m, m) \tag{16.4-7}$$

where we set $P(0,0) = 1$. We obviously have $P_n = \sum_{m=1}^{n} P(n, m)$. Figure 16.4-B shows $P(n, m)$ for $n \le 16$. It was created with the program [FXT: comb/num-partitions-demo.cc]. The number of partitions into m parts equals the number of partitions with maximal part equal to m. This can easily be seen by drawing a *Ferrers diagram* (or *Young diagram*) and its transpose as follows, for the partition $5 + 2 + 2 + 1$ of 10:

```
    43111        5221
5   xxxxx     4  xxxx
2   xx        3  xxx
2   xx        1  x
1   x         1  x
              1  x
```

Any partition with maximal part m (here 5) corresponds to a partition into exactly m parts. The generating function for the partitions into exactly m parts is

$$\sum_{n=1}^{\infty} P(n, m) \, x^n = \frac{x^m}{\prod_{k=1}^{m} (1 - x^k)} \tag{16.4-8}$$

For example, the row for $m = 3$ in figure 16.4-B corresponds to the power series

```
? m=3; (x^m/prod(k=1,m,1-x^k)+O(x^17))
   x^3 + x^4 + 2*x^5 + 3*x^6 + 4*x^7 + 5*x^8 + 7*x^9 + 8*x^10 + \
   10*x^11 + 12*x^12 + 14*x^13 + 16*x^14 + 19*x^15 + 21*x^16 + O(x^17)
```

We have

$$\frac{1}{\prod_{n=1}^{\infty}(1 - u\,x^n)} \;=\; \sum_{n=1}^{\infty}\sum_{m=1}^{\infty} P(n,m)\,x^n\,u^m \tag{16.4-9}$$

The rows of figure 16.4-B correspond to a fixed power of x:

```
? 1/prod(n=1,N,1-u*x^n)
   1  + u*x  + (u^2 + u)*x^2  + (u^3 + u^2 + u)*x^3  + (u^4 + u^3 + 2*u^2 + u)*x^4
   + (u^5 + u^4 + 2*u^3 + 2*u^2 + u)*x^5  + (u^6 + u^5 + 2*u^4 + 3*u^3 + 3*u^2 + u)*x^6 + ...
```

The generating function for the number P_n of integer partitions of n is found by setting $u = 1$:

$$\sum_{n=0}^{\infty} P_n\,x^n \;=\; \frac{1}{\prod_{n=1}^{\infty}(1 - x^n)} \;=\; \frac{1}{\eta(x)} \tag{16.4-10}$$

The partitions are found in the expansion of

$$\frac{1}{\prod_{k=1}^{\infty}(1 - t_k\,x^k)} \tag{16.4-11}$$

```
? N=5; z='x+O('x^(N+1)); 1/prod(k=1,N,1-eval(Str("t"k))*z^k)
   1  + t1*x  + (t1^2 + t2)*x^2  + (t1^3 + t2*t1 + t3)*x^3
   + (t1^4 + t2*t1^2 + t3*t1 + t2^2 + t4)*x^4
   + (t1^5 + t2*t1^3 + t3*t1^2 + (t2^2 + t4)*t1 + t3*t2 + t5)*x^5
```

Summing over m in relation 16.4-8 we find that

$$\frac{1}{\eta(x)} \;=\; \sum_{n=0}^{\infty} \frac{x^n}{\prod_{k=1}^{n}(1 - x^k)} \tag{16.4-12}$$

This relation also is the special case $a_n = x^n$ (and $N \to \infty$) of 16.4-1b on page 344. We also have (setting $x = q$ in 16.4-2b)

$$\frac{1}{\eta(x)} \;=\; \sum_{n=0}^{\infty} \frac{x^{n^2}}{\left[\prod_{k=1}^{n}(1 - x^k)\right]^2} \tag{16.4-13}$$

The expression can also be found by observing that a partition can be decomposed into a square and two partitions whose maximal part does not exceed the length of the side of the square [176, sect.19.7]:

```
      43111
   5  ##xxx
   2  ##
   2  xx
   1  x
```

Let $P(n,m,r)$ be the number of partitions of n into at most m parts with largest part r, then [17, ex.15, p.575]

$$\sum_{n,m,r=0}^{\infty} P(n,m,r)\,q^n\,x^m\,y^r \;=\; \sum_{n=0}^{\infty} \frac{x^n\,y^n\,q^{n^2}}{\prod_{k=0}^{n-1}(1 - x\,q^k)\,\prod_{k=0}^{n-1}(1 - y\,q^k)} \tag{16.4-14}$$

Euler's *pentagonal number theorem* is (see [41] and [16]):

$$\eta(x) \;=\; \sum_{n=-\infty}^{+\infty}(-1)^n\left(x^{n\,(3n-1)/2}\right) = 1 + \sum_{n=1}^{\infty}(-1)^n\,x^{n\,(3n-1)/2}\,(1 + x^n) \tag{16.4-15a}$$

$$=\; 1 - x - x^2 + x^5 + x^7 - x^{12} - x^{15} + x^{22} + x^{26} - x^{35} - x^{40} + x^{51} + x^{57} \pm \ldots \tag{16.4-15b}$$

The sequence of exponents is entry A001318 in [312], the generalized pentagonal numbers.

Further expressions for η are (set $q := x$ and $x := -x$ in relation 16.4-2a for the first equality)

$$\eta(x) = \sum_{n=0}^{\infty} \frac{(-1)^n \, x^{n(n+1)/2}}{\prod_{k=1}^{n}(1-x^k)} = \sum_{n=0}^{\infty} \frac{x^{2n^2+n}\left(1-2\,x^{2n+1}\right)}{\prod_{k=1}^{2n+1}(1-x^k)} \tag{16.4-16a}$$

$$= \sum_{n=0}^{\infty} x^{n^2} \left[\prod_{k=n+1}^{\infty}\left(1-x^k\right)\right]^2 = \sum_{n=0}^{\infty}(-x)^{n^2}\prod_{k=n+1}^{\infty}\left(1-x^{2k}\right) \tag{16.4-16b}$$

Write $\eta(x) = \prod_{j=0}^{\infty} J(x^{2j+1})$ where J is defined by relation 38.1-2a on page 726. Then a divisionless expression for $1/\eta$ is obtained via relation 38.1-11d on page 728:

$$\frac{1}{\eta(x)} = \prod_{k=0}^{\infty}\prod_{j=0}^{\infty}\left(1+x^{(2j+1)\,2^k}\right)^{k+1} = \prod_{k=0}^{\infty}\eta_+\left(x^{2^k}\right) \tag{16.4-17}$$

The sequences of the numbers of partitions into an even/odd number of parts start respectively as

1, 0, 1, 1, 3, 3, 6, 7, 12, 14, 22, 27, 40, 49, 69, 86, 118, 146, 195, 242, ...
0, 1, 1, 2, 2, 4, 5, 8, 10, 16, 20, 29, 37, 52, 66, 90, 113, 151, 190, 248, ...

These are the entries A027193/A027187 in [312]. Their generating functions are found by respectively setting $a_n = x^{2n}$ and $a_n = x^{2n+1}$ in 16.4-1b (see relation 31.3-1c on page 604 for the definition of Θ_4):

$$\sum_{n=0}^{\infty} \frac{x^{2n}}{\prod_{k=1}^{2n}(1-x^k)} = \frac{1}{2}\left[\frac{1}{\eta(x)}+\frac{1}{\eta_+(x)}\right] = \frac{1}{\eta(x)}\cdot\sum_{n=0}^{\infty}(-x)^{n^2} = \frac{1+\Theta_4(x)}{2\,\eta(x)} \tag{16.4-18a}$$

$$\sum_{n=0}^{\infty} \frac{x^{2n+1}}{\prod_{k=1}^{2n+1}(1-x^k)} = \frac{1}{2}\left[\frac{1}{\eta(x)}-\frac{1}{\eta_+(x)}\right] = \frac{-1}{\eta(x)}\cdot\sum_{n=1}^{\infty}(-x)^{n^2} = \frac{1-\Theta_4(x)}{2\,\eta(x)} \tag{16.4-18b}$$

Adding the leftmost sums gives yet another expression for $1/\eta$:

$$\frac{1}{\eta(x)} = \sum_{n=0}^{\infty} \frac{x^{2n}\left(1-x^{2n+1}\right)+x^{2n+1}}{\prod_{k=1}^{2n+1}(1-x^k)} \tag{16.4-19}$$

This relation can be generalized by adding the generating functions for partitions into parts $r+j$ for $j = 0, 1, \ldots, r-1$. For example, for $r = 3$ we have:

$$\frac{1}{\eta(x)} = \sum_{n=0}^{\infty} \frac{x^{3n}\left(1-x^{3n+1}\right)\left(1-x^{3n+2}\right)+x^{3n+1}\left(1-x^{3n+2}\right)+x^{3n+2}}{\prod_{k=1}^{3n+2}(1-x^k)} \tag{16.4-20}$$

The *Rogers-Ramanujan identities* for the numbers of partitions into parts congruent to 1 or 4 (and 2 or 3, respectively) modulo 5 are [176, sec.19.13, p.290]:

$$\prod_{n=0}^{\infty} \frac{1}{(1-x^{5n+1})(1-x^{5n+4})} = \sum_{n=0}^{\infty} \frac{x^{n^2}}{\prod_{k=1}^{n}(1-x^k)} \tag{16.4-21a}$$

$$\prod_{n=0}^{\infty} \frac{1}{(1-x^{5n+2})(1-x^{5n+3})} = \sum_{n=0}^{\infty} \frac{x^{n^2+n}}{\prod_{k=1}^{n}(1-x^k)} \tag{16.4-21b}$$

Many identities of this kind are listed in [311] and [268], a generalization is given in [87]. The sequences of coefficients are entries A003114 and A003106 in [312]:

1, 1, 1, 1, 2, 2, 3, 3, 4, 5, 6, 7, 9, 10, 12, 14, 17, 19, 23, 26, 31, 35, 41, ...
1, 0, 1, 1, 1, 1, 2, 2, 3, 3, 4, 4, 6, 6, 8, 9, 11, 12, 15, 16, 20, 22, 26, ...

$n:$	D_n	$n:$	D_n	$n:$	D_n	$n:$	D_n	$n:$	D_n
1:	1	11:	12	21:	76	31:	340	41:	1260
2:	1	12:	15	22:	89	32:	390	42:	1426
3:	2	13:	18	23:	104	33:	448	43:	1610
4:	2	14:	22	24:	122	34:	512	44:	1816
5:	3	15:	27	25:	142	35:	585	45:	2048
6:	4	16:	32	26:	165	36:	668	46:	2304
7:	5	17:	38	27:	192	37:	760	47:	2590
8:	6	18:	46	28:	222	38:	864	48:	2910
9:	8	19:	54	29:	256	39:	982	49:	3264
10:	10	20:	64	30:	296	40:	1113	50:	3658

Figure 16.4-C: The number D_n of integer partitions into distinct parts of n for $n \leq 50$.

16.4.2 Partitions into distinct parts

The generating function for the number D_n of partitions of n into distinct parts is

$$\sum_{n=0}^{\infty} D_n x^n = \prod_{n=1}^{\infty} (1 + x^n) = \eta_+(x) \tag{16.4-22}$$

The number of partitions into distinct parts equals the number of partitions into odd parts:

$$\eta_+(x) = \frac{\eta(x^2)}{\eta(x)} = \frac{1}{\prod_{k=1}^{\infty} (1 - x^{2k-1})} \tag{16.4-23}$$

The sequence of coefficients D_n is entry A000009 in [312], see figure 16.4-C. The generating function for $D(n,m)$, the number of partitions of n into exactly m distinct parts, is (see [17, p.559])

$$\sum_{n=0}^{\infty} D(n,m) x^n = \frac{x^{m(m+1)/2}}{\prod_{k=1}^{m} (1 - x^k)} \tag{16.4-24}$$

Summing over m (or setting $q = x$ in 16.4-2a) gives

$$\eta_+(x) = \sum_{n=0}^{\infty} \frac{x^{n(n+1)/2}}{\prod_{k=1}^{n} (1 - x^k)} \tag{16.4-25}$$

Equivalently, the Ferrers diagram of a partition into m distinct parts can be decomposed into a triangle of size $m(m+1)/2$ and a partition into at most m elements:

```
#####xxxxx           #####     xxxxx
####xxxx     ==      ####   +  xxxx
###xxxx              ###       xxxx
##x                  ##        x
#x                   #         x
```

The connection between relations 16.4-24 and 16.4-13 can be seen by drawing a diagonal in the diagram of an unrestricted partition:

```
#xxxxxxx           #         xxxxxxx           #         xxxxxxx     xxxx
x#xxxxxx    ==     x#        xxxxxx     ==     #    +    xxxxxx   +   xx
xx#xxxxx           xx#   +   xxxxx             #         xxxxx
xx                 xx
x                  x
```

So each unrestricted partition is decomposed into a diagonal (of, say, m elements) and two partitions into either m or $m-1$ distinct parts. The term corresponding to a diagonal of length m is

$$x^m \left[D(n,m) + D(n,m-1) \right]^2 = \frac{x^{m^2}}{\left[\prod_{k=1}^{m} (1 - x^k) \right]^2} \tag{16.4-26}$$

See [265] for a survey about proving identities using Ferrers diagrams. We also have

$$\prod_{n=1}^{\infty}(1+u\,x^n) \;=\; \sum_{n=1}^{\infty}\sum_{m=1}^{\infty}D(n,m)\,x^n\,u^m \tag{16.4-27}$$

```
? prod(n=1,N,1+u*x^n)
1   + u*x  + u*x^2  + (u^2 + u)*x^3  + (u^2 + u)*x^4  + (2*u^2 + u)*x^5
  + (u^3 + 2*u^2 + u)*x^6  + (u^3 + 3*u^2 + u)*x^7  + (2*u^3 + 3*u^2 + u)*x^8
  + (3*u^3 + 4*u^2 + u)*x^9  + (u^4 + 4*u^3 + 4*u^2 + u)*x^10 + ...
```

The partitions into distinct parts can be computed as the expansion of

$$\prod_{k=1}^{\infty}\left(1+t_k\,x^k\right) \tag{16.4-28}$$

```
? N=9; z='x+O('x^(N+1));
? prod(k=1,N,1+eval(Str("t"k))*z^k)
1   + t1*x  + t2*x^2  + (t2*t1 + t3)*x^3  + (t3*t1 + t4)*x^4
  + (t4*t1 + t3*t2 + t5)*x^5  + ((t3*t2 + t5)*t1 + t4*t2 + t6)*x^6
  + ((t4*t2 + t6)*t1 + t5*t2 + t4*t3 + t7)*x^7
  + ((t5*t2 + t4*t3 + t7)*t1 + t6*t2 + t5*t3 + t8)*x^8
  + ((t6*t2 + t5*t3 + t8)*t1 + (t4*t3 + t7)*t2 + t6*t3 + t5*t4 + t9)*x^9
```

Let $E(n,m)$ be the number of partitions of n into distinct parts with maximal part m, then

$$\sum_{m=0}^{\infty}E(n,m)\,x^n \;=\; x^m\prod_{k=1}^{m-1}\left(1+x^k\right) \tag{16.4-29}$$

Summing over m (or setting $a_n = x^n$ and $N \to \infty$ in relation 16.4-1a on page 344) gives:

$$\eta_+(x) \;=\; 1+\sum_{n=1}^{\infty}x^n\prod_{k=1}^{n-1}\left(1+x^k\right) \tag{16.4-30}$$

For the first of the following equalities, set $q := x^2$ in 16.4-2b, the second is given in [310, p.100]:

$$\eta_+(x) \;=\; \sum_{n=0}^{\infty}\frac{x^{2n^2-n}}{\prod_{k=1}^{2n}\left(1-x^k\right)} \;=\; \sum_{n=0}^{\infty}\frac{x^{2n^2+n}}{\prod_{k=1}^{2n+1}\left(1-x^k\right)} \;=\; \sum_{n=0}^{\infty}\frac{x^n}{\prod_{k=1}^{n}\left(1-x^{2k}\right)} \tag{16.4-31}$$

Set $x := -q$ in relation 16.4-2b to obtain an expression for $1/\eta_+$:

$$\frac{1}{\eta_+(x)} \;=\; \sum_{n=0}^{\infty}\frac{(-x)^{n^2}}{\prod_{k=1}^{n}\left(1-x^{2k}\right)} \tag{16.4-32}$$

The sequences of numbers of partitions into distinct even/odd parts start respectively as (see entries A035457 and A000700 in [312])

```
1, 0, 1, 0, 1, 0, 2, 0, 2, 0, 3, 0, 4, 0, 5, 0, 6, 0, 8, 0, 10, 0, 12, 0, 15, ...
1, 1, 0, 1, 1, 1, 1, 1, 2, 2, 2, 2, 3, 3, 3, 4, 5, 5, 5, 6, 7, 8, 8, 9, 11, ...
```

The generating function for the partitions into distinct even parts is

$$\prod_{n=1}^{\infty}\left(1+x^{2n}\right) \;=\; \eta_+\left(x^2\right) \;=\; \eta_+(-x)\,\eta_+(+x) \;=\; \frac{\eta\left(x^4\right)}{\eta\left(x^2\right)} \;=\; \frac{1}{\prod_{n=0}^{\infty}\left(1-x^{4n+2}\right)} \tag{16.4-33}$$

The last equality tells us that the function also enumerates the partitions into even parts that are not a multiple of 4. Setting $q := x^2$ and $x := 1$ in 16.4-2a gives

$$\prod_{n=1}^{\infty}\left(1+x^{2n}\right) \;=\; \sum_{n=0}^{\infty}\frac{x^{n^2+n}}{\prod_{k=1}^{n}\left(1-x^{2k}\right)} \tag{16.4-34}$$

The generating function for partitions into distinct odd parts is

$$\prod_{n=0}^{\infty}\left(1+x^{2n+1}\right) \;=\; \frac{\eta_+(x)}{\eta_+\left(x^2\right)} \;=\; \frac{1}{\eta_+(-x)} \;=\; \frac{\eta(-x)}{\eta(x^2)} \;=\; \frac{\eta\left(x^2\right)^2}{\eta\left(x\right)\eta\left(x^4\right)} \tag{16.4-35}$$

Also (for the first equality set $q := x^2$ in relation 16.4-2a):

$$\prod_{n=0}^{\infty}\left(1+x^{2n+1}\right) \;=\; \sum_{n=0}^{\infty}\frac{x^{n^2}}{\prod_{k=1}^{n}\left(1-x^{2k}\right)} \;=\; \sum_{n=0}^{\infty}\frac{x^n}{\prod_{k=1}^{n}\left(1-(-x)^k\right)} \tag{16.4-36}$$

The number of partitions where each part is repeated at most $r-1$ times has the generating function

$$\prod_{n=1}^{\infty}\left(1+x^n+x^{2n}+x^{3n}+\ldots+x^{(r-1)\,n}\right) \;=\; \frac{\eta(x^r)}{\eta(x)} \;=\; \frac{1}{\prod_{k\neq 0 \bmod r}\left(1-x^k\right)} \tag{16.4-37}$$

The second equality tells us that the number of such partitions equals the number of partitions into parts not divisible by r, equivalently, partitions into m parts where m is not divisible by r.

Replacing x by x^r and q by x^m in relation 16.4-2b gives an identity for the partitions into parts $\equiv r \bmod m$ (valid for $0 < r < m$, for $r = 0$ replace x by x^m in 16.4-13):

$$\frac{1}{\prod_{n=0}^{\infty}\left(1-x^{m\,n+r}\right)} \;=\; \sum_{n=0}^{\infty}\frac{x^{m\,n^2+(r-m)\,n}}{\prod_{k=0}^{n-1}\left(1-x^{m\,k+m}\right)\prod_{k=0}^{n-1}\left(1-x^{m\,k+r}\right)} \tag{16.4-38}$$

The same replacements (where $0 \le r < m$) in relation 16.4-2a give an identity for the partitions into distinct parts $\equiv r \bmod m$:

$$\prod_{n=0}^{\infty}\left(1+x^{m\,n+r}\right) \;=\; \sum_{n=0}^{\infty}\frac{x^{[m\,n^2+(2r-m)\,n]/2}}{\prod_{k=0}^{n}\left(1-x^{m\,k}\right)} \tag{16.4-39}$$

A generating function for the partitions into distinct parts that differ by at least d is

$$\sum_{n=0}^{\infty}\frac{x^{T(d,n)}}{\prod_{k=1}^{n}\left(1-x^k\right)} \quad \text{where} \quad T(d,n) := d\,\frac{n\,(n+1)}{2}-(d-1)\,n \tag{16.4-40}$$

See sequences A003114 ($d=2$), A025157 ($d=3$), A025158 ($d=4$), A025159 ($d=5$), A025160 ($d=6$), A025161 ($d=7$), and A025162 ($d=8$) in [312]. The relation follows from cutting out a (incomplete) stretched triangle in the Ferrers diagram (here for $d=2$):

```
dist. >= d=2                                 x^(d*(n*(n+1))/2 - (d-1)*n)    * 1/prod(...)
XXXXXXXXXXXXX         #########XXXX          W#########            W            XXXX
XXXXXXXXX      ==     #######XX      ==      W#######          -   W        +   XX
XXXXXX               #####X                  W#####                W            X
XXX                  ###                      W###                 W
X                    #                         W#                  W
```

The sequences of numbers of partitions into an even/odd number of distinct parts are entries A067661 and A067659 in [312], respectively:

$$1,\; 0,\; 0,\; 1,\; 1,\; 2,\; 2,\; 3,\; 3,\; 4,\; 5,\; 6,\; 7,\; 9,\; 11,\; 13,\; 16,\; 19,\; 23,\; 27,\; 32,\; 38,\; 45,\; \ldots$$
$$0,\; 1,\; 1,\; 1,\; 1,\; 1,\; 2,\; 2,\; 3,\; 4,\; 5,\; 6,\; 8,\; 9,\; 11,\; 14,\; 16,\; 19,\; 23,\; 27,\; 32,\; 38,\; 44,\; \ldots$$

The corresponding generating functions are

$$\frac{\eta_+(x)+\eta(x)}{2} \;=\; \sum_{n=0}^{\infty}\frac{x^{2n^2+n}}{\prod_{k=1}^{2n}\left(1-x^k\right)} \tag{16.4-41a}$$

$$\frac{\eta_+(x)-\eta(x)}{2} \;=\; \sum_{n=0}^{\infty}\frac{x^{2n^2+3n+1}}{\prod_{k=1}^{2n+1}\left(1-x^k\right)} \;=\; \sum_{n=0}^{\infty}\frac{x^{2n+1}}{1-x^{2n+1}}\frac{x^{2n^2+n}}{\prod_{k=1}^{2n}\left(1-x^k\right)} \tag{16.4-41b}$$

Adding relations 16.4-41a and 16.4-41b gives the second equality in 16.4-31, subtraction gives the second equality in 16.4-16a.

16.4.3 Partitions into square-free parts ‡

We give relations for the ordinary generating functions for partitions into square-free parts. The Möbius function μ is defined in section 37.1.2 on page 705. The sequence of power series coefficients is given at the end of each relation.

Partitions into square-free parts (entry A073576 in [312]):

$$\prod_{n=1}^{\infty} \frac{1}{1 - \mu(n)^2 \, x^n} = \prod_{n=1}^{\infty} \eta\left(x^{n^2}\right)^{-\mu(n)} \tag{16.4-42}$$

1, 1, 2, 3, 4, 6, 9, 12, 16, 21, 28, 36, 47, 60, 76, 96, 120, 150, ...

Partitions into parts that are not square-free, note the start index on the right side product, (entry A114374):

$$\prod_{n=1}^{\infty} \frac{1}{1 - (1 - \mu(n)^2) \, x^n} = \prod_{n=2}^{\infty} \eta\left(x^{n^2}\right)^{+\mu(n)} \tag{16.4-43}$$

$\frac{1}{11}, \frac{0}{6}, \frac{0}{4}, \frac{0}{3}, \frac{1}{15}, \frac{0}{8}, \frac{0}{6}, \frac{0}{3}, \frac{2}{22}, \frac{1}{13}; \frac{0}{11}, \frac{0}{6}, \frac{3}{34}, \frac{1}{18}, \frac{0}{15}, \frac{5}{15}, \frac{2}{9}, \frac{2}{46}, \frac{0}{27}, \frac{7}{24}, \frac{3}{17}, \frac{2}{}, \frac{0}{}, \setminus$ ...

Partitions into distinct square-free parts (entry A087188):

$$\prod_{n=1}^{\infty} \left(1 + \mu(n)^2 \, x^n\right) = \prod_{n=1}^{\infty} \eta_+\left(x^{n^2}\right)^{+\mu(n)} \tag{16.4-44}$$

1, 1, 1, 2, 1, 2, 3, 3, 4, 4, 5, 6, 6, 8, 9, 10, 13, 14, 16, 18, 20, ...

Partitions into odd square-free parts, also partitions into parts m such that $2m$ is square-free (entry A134345):

$$\prod_{n=1}^{\infty} \frac{1}{1 - \mu(2n-1)^2 \, x^{2n-1}} = \prod_{n=1}^{\infty} \frac{1}{1 - \mu(2n)^2 \, x^n} = \tag{16.4-45a}$$

$$\prod_{n=1}^{\infty} \left[\frac{\eta\left(x^{(2n-1)^2}\right)}{\eta\left(x^{2\,(2n-1)^2}\right)}\right]^{-\mu(2n-1)} = \prod_{n=1}^{\infty} \eta_+\left(x^{(2n-1)^2}\right)^{+\mu(2n-1)} \tag{16.4-45b}$$

1, 1, 1, 2, 2, 3, 4, 5, 6, 7, 9, 11, 13, 16, 19, 23, 27, 32, 38, 44, ...

Partitions into distinct odd square-free parts, also partitions into distinct parts m such that $2m$ is square-free (entry A134337):

$$\prod_{n=1}^{\infty} \left(1 + \mu(2n-1)^2 \, x^{2n-1}\right) = \prod_{n=1}^{\infty} \left(1 + \mu(2n)^2 \, x^n\right) = \prod_{n=1}^{\infty} \left[\frac{\eta_+\left(x^{(2n-1)^2}\right)}{\eta_+\left(x^{2\,(2n-1)^2}\right)}\right]^{+\mu(2n-1)} \tag{16.4-46}$$

1, 1, 0, 1, 1, 1, 1, 1, 2, 1, 1, 2, 2, 2, 2, 3, 4, 3, 4, 5, 5, 6, 6, 7, ...

Partitions into square-free parts $m \not\equiv 0 \bmod p$ where p is prime:

$$\prod_{n=1}^{\infty} \frac{1}{1 - \mu(p\,n)^2 \, x^n} = \prod_{n=1}^{\infty} \prod_{r=1}^{p-1} \left[\frac{\eta\left(x^{(p\,n-r)^2}\right)}{\eta\left(x^{p\,(p\,n-r)^2}\right)}\right]^{-\mu(p\,n-r)} \tag{16.4-47}$$

For example, partitions into square-free parts $m \not\equiv 0 \bmod 3$:

$$\prod_{n=1}^{\infty} \frac{1}{1 - \mu(3\,n)^2\, x^n} \;=\; \prod_{n=1,\; n \not\equiv 0 \bmod 3}^{\infty} \frac{1}{1 - \mu(n)^2\, x^n} \;=\; \tag{16.4-48a}$$

$$= \prod_{n=1}^{\infty} \left[\frac{\eta\left(x^{(3\,n-1)^2}\right)}{\eta\left(x^{3\,(3\,n-1)^2}\right)} \right]^{-\mu(3\,n-1)} \left[\frac{\eta\left(x^{(3\,n-2)^2}\right)}{\eta\left(x^{3\,(3\,n-2)^2}\right)} \right]^{-\mu(3\,n-2)} \tag{16.4-48b}$$

1, 1, 2, 2, 3, 4, 5, 7, 8, 10, 13, 16, 20, 24, 30, 36, 43, 52, 61, 73, 86, ...

Partitions into distinct square-free parts $m \not\equiv 0 \bmod p$ where p is prime:

$$\prod_{n=1}^{\infty} \left(1 + \mu(p\,n)^2\, x^n\right) \;=\; \prod_{n=1}^{\infty} \prod_{r=1}^{p-1} \left[\frac{\eta_+\left(x^{(p\,n-r)^2}\right)}{\eta_+\left(x^{p\,(p\,n-r)^2}\right)} \right]^{+\mu(p\,n-r)} \tag{16.4-49}$$

For example, partitions into distinct square-free parts $m \not\equiv 0 \bmod 3$:

$$\prod_{n=1}^{\infty} \left(1 + \mu(3\,n)^2\, x^n\right) \;=\; \prod_{n=1,\; n \not\equiv 0 \bmod 3}^{\infty} \left(1 + \mu(n)^2\, x^n\right) \;=\; \tag{16.4-50a}$$

$$= \prod_{n=1}^{\infty} \left[\frac{\eta_+\left(x^{(3\,n-1)^2}\right)}{\eta_+\left(x^{3\,(3\,n-1)^2}\right)} \right]^{+\mu(3\,n-1)} \left[\frac{\eta_+\left(x^{(3\,n-2)^2}\right)}{\eta_+\left(x^{3\,(3\,n-2)^2}\right)} \right]^{+\mu(3\,n-2)} \tag{16.4-50b}$$

1, 1, 1, 1, 0, 1, 1, 2, 2, 1, 2, 2, 3, 4, 4, 4, 4, 5, 6, 7, 7, 7, 8, 9, 12, 12, ...

16.4.4　Relations involving sums of divisors ‡

The *logarithmic generating function* (LGF) for objects counted by the sequence c_n has the following form:

$$\sum_{n=1}^{\infty} \frac{c_n\, x^n}{n} \tag{16.4-51}$$

The LGF for $\sigma(n)$, the sum of divisors of n, is connected to the ordinary generating function for the partitions as follows (compare with relation 37.2-15a on page 712):

$$\sum_{n=1}^{\infty} \frac{\sigma(n)\, x^n}{n} \;=\; \log\left(1/\eta(x)\right) \tag{16.4-52}$$

We generate the sequence of the $\sigma(n)$, entry A000203 in [312], using GP:

```
? N=25;  L=ceil(sqrt(N))+1;  x='x+O('x^N);
? s=log(1/eta(x))
  x + 3/2*x^2 + 4/3*x^3 + 7/4*x^4 + 6/5*x^5 + ...
? v=Vec(s);  vector(#v,j,v[j]*j)
  [1, 3, 4, 7, 6, 12, 8, 15, 13, 18, 12, 28, 14, 24, 24, 31, 18, 39, 20, 42, 32, 36, 24, 60]
```

Write $o(n)$ for the sum of odd divisors of n (entry A000593). The LGF is related to the partitions into distinct parts:

$$\sum_{n=1}^{\infty} \frac{o(n)\, x^n}{n} \;=\; \log\left(\eta_+(x)\right) \tag{16.4-53}$$

```
? s=log(eta(x^2)/eta(x))
  x + 1/2*x^2 + 4/3*x^3 + 1/4*x^4 + 6/5*x^5 + ...
? v=Vec(s);  vector(#v,j,v[j]*j)
  [1, 1, 4, 1, 6, 4, 8, 1, 13, 6, 12, 4, 14, 8, 24, 1, 18, 13, 20, 6, 32, 12, 24, 4]
```

Let $s(n)$ be the sum of square-free divisors of n. The LGF for the sums $s(n)$ is the logarithm of the generating function for the partitions into square-free parts:

$$\sum_{n=1}^{\infty} \frac{s(n)\,x^n}{n} \;=\; \log\left(\prod_{n=1}^{\infty} \eta\left(x^{n^2}\right)^{-\mu(n)}\right) \tag{16.4-54}$$

The sequence of the $s(n)$ is entry A048250 in [312]:

```
? s=log(prod(n=1,L,eta(x^(n^2))^(-moebius(n))))
   x + 3/2*x^2 + 4/3*x^3 + 3/4*x^4 + 6/5*x^5 + ...
? v=Vec(s);vector(#v,j,v[j]*j)
   [1, 3, 4, 3, 6, 12, 8, 3, 4, 18, 12, 12, 14, 24, 24, 3, 18, 12, 20, 18, 32, 36, 24, 12]
```

A divisor d of n is called a *unitary divisor* if $\gcd(d, n/d) = 1$. We have the following identity, note the exponent $-\mu(n)/n$ on the right side:

$$\sum_{n=1}^{\infty} \frac{u(n)\,x^n}{n} \;=\; \log\left(\prod_{n=1}^{\infty} \eta\left(x^{n^2}\right)^{-\mu(n)/n}\right) \tag{16.4-55}$$

The sequence of the $u(n)$ is entry A034448:

```
? s=(log(prod(n=1,L,eta(x^(n^2))^(-moebius(n)/n))))
   x + 3/2*x^2 + 4/3*x^3 + 5/4*x^4 + 6/5*x^5 + ...
? v=Vec(s);vector(#v,j,v[j]*j)
   [1, 3, 4, 5, 6, 12, 8, 9, 10, 18, 12, 20, 14, 24, 24, 17, 18, 30, 20, 30, 32, 36, 24, 36]
```

The sums $\overline{u}(n)$ of the divisors of n that are not unitary have a LGF connected to the partitions into distinct square-free parts:

$$\sum_{n=1}^{\infty} \frac{\overline{u}(n)\,x^n}{n} \;=\; \log\left(\prod_{n=1}^{\infty} \eta\left(x^{n^2}\right)^{+\mu(n)/n}\right) \tag{16.4-56}$$

The sequence of the sums $\overline{u}(n)$ is entry A048146:

```
? s=log(prod(n=2,L,eta(x^(n^2))^(+moebius(n)/n)))
   1/2*x^4 + 3/4*x^8 + 1/3*x^9 + 2/3*x^12 + 7/8*x^16 + ...
? v=Vec(s+'x);  v[1]=0;  \\ let vector start with 3 zeros
? vector(#v,j,v[j]*j)
   [0, 0, 0, 2, 0, 0, 0, 6, 3, 0, 0, 8, 0, 0, 0, 14, 0, 9, 0, 12, 0, 0, 0, 24, 5, 0, 12]
```

For the sums $\overline{s}(n)$ of the divisors of n that are not square-free we have the LGF

$$\sum_{n=1}^{\infty} \frac{\overline{s}(n)\,x^n}{n} \;=\; \log\left(\prod_{n=1}^{\infty} \eta\left(x^{n^2}\right)^{+\mu(n)}\right) \tag{16.4-57}$$

The sequence of the sums $\overline{s}(n)$ is entry A162296:

```
? s=log(prod(n=2,L,eta(x^(n^2))^(+moebius(n))))
   x^4 + 3/2*x^8 + x^9 + 4/3*x^12 + 7/4*x^16 + ...
? v=Vec(s+'x);  v[1]=0;  \\ let vector start with 3 zeros
? vector(#v,j,v[j]*j)
   [0, 0, 0, 4, 0, 0, 0, 12, 9, 0, 0, 16, 0, 0, 0, 28, 0, 27, 0, 24, 0, 0, 0, 48, 25, 0, 36]
```

Chapter 17

Set partitions

For a set of n elements, say $S_n := \{1, 2, \ldots, n\}$, a *set partition* is a set $P = \{s_1, s_2, \ldots, s_k\}$ of nonempty subsets s_i of S_n whose intersection is empty and whose union equals S_n.

For example, there are 5 set partitions of the set $S_3 = \{1, 2, 3\}$:

```
1:   { {1, 2, 3} }
2:   { {1, 2}, {3} }
3:   { {1, 3}, {2} }
4:   { {1}, {2, 3} }
5:   { {1}, {2}, {3} }
```

The following sets are not set partitions of S_3:

```
    { {1, 2, 3}, {1} }    // intersection not empty
    { {1}, {3} }          // union does not contain 2
```

As the order of elements in a set does not matter we sort them in ascending order. For a set of sets we order the sets in ascending order of the first elements. The number of set partitions of the n-set is the Bell number B_n, see section 17.2 on page 358.

17.1 Recursive generation

We write Z_n for the list of all set partitions of the n-element set S_n. To generate Z_n we observe that with a complete list Z_{n-1} of partitions of the set S_{n-1} we can generate the elements of Z_n in the following way: For each element (set partition) $P \in Z_{n-1}$, create set partitions of S_n by appending the element n to the first, second, ..., last subset, and one more by appending the set $\{n\}$ as the last subset.

For example, the partition $\{\{1, 2\}, \{3, 4\}\} \in Z_4$ leads to 3 partitions of S_5:

```
P = { {1, 2}, {3, 4} }
      -->   { {1, 2, 5}, {3, 4} }
      -->   { {1, 2}, {3, 4, 5} }
      -->   { {1, 2}, {3, 4}, {5} }
```

Now we start with the only partition $\{\{1\}\}$ of the 1-element set and apply the described step $n-1$ times. The construction (given in [261, p.89]) is shown in the left column of figure 17.1-A, the right column shows all set partitions for $n = 5$.

A modified version of the recursive construction generates the set partitions in a minimal-change order. We can generate the 'incremented' partitions in two ways, forward (left to right)

```
P = { {1, 2}, {3, 4} }
      -->   { {1, 2, 5}, {3, 4} }
      -->   { {1, 2}, {3, 4, 5} }
      -->   { {1, 2}, {3, 4}, {5} }
```

or backward (right to left)

```
P = { {1, 2}, {3, 4} }
      -->   { {1, 2}, {3, 4}, {5} }
      -->   { {1, 2}, {3, 4, 5} }
      -->   { {1, 2, 5}, {3, 4} }
```

J. Arndt, *Matters Computational: Ideas, Algorithms, Source Code,*
DOI 10.1007/978-3-642-14764-7_17, © Springer-Verlag Berlin Heidelberg 2011

```
------------------                        setpart(4) ==
p1={1}                             1:      {1, 2, 3, 4}
   -->  p={1, 2}                   2:      {1, 2, 3}, {4}
   -->  p={1}, {2}                 3:      {1, 2, 4}, {3}
------------------                 4:      {1, 2}, {3, 4}
p1={1, 2}                          5:      {1, 2}, {3}, {4}
   -->  p={1, 2, 3}               6:      {1, 3, 4}, {2}
   -->  p={1, 2}, {3}             7:      {1, 3}, {2, 4}
p1={1}, {2}                        8:      {1, 3}, {2}, {4}
   -->  p={1, 3}, {2}             9:      {1, 4}, {2, 3}
   -->  p={1}, {2, 3}            10:      {1}, {2, 3, 4}
   -->  p={1}, {2}, {3}         11:      {1}, {2, 3}, {4}
------------------               12:      {1, 4}, {2}, {3}
p1={1, 2, 3}                     13:      {1}, {2, 4}, {3}
   -->  p={1, 2, 3, 4}          14:      {1}, {2}, {3, 4}
   -->  p={1, 2, 3}, {4}        15:      {1}, {2}, {3}, {4}
p1={1, 2}, {3}
   -->  p={1, 2, 4}, {3}
   -->  p={1, 2}, {3, 4}
   -->  p={1, 2}, {3}, {4}
p1={1, 3}, {2}
   -->  p={1, 3, 4}, {2}
   -->  p={1, 3}, {2, 4}
   -->  p={1, 3}, {2}, {4}
p1={1}, {2, 3}
   -->  p={1, 4}, {2, 3}
   -->  p={1}, {2, 3, 4}
   -->  p={1}, {2, 3}, {4}
p1={1}, {2}, {3}
   -->  p={1, 4}, {2}, {3}
   -->  p={1}, {2, 4}, {3}
   -->  p={1}, {2}, {3, 4}
   -->  p={1}, {2}, {3}, {4}
------------------
```

Figure 17.1-A: Recursive construction of the set partitions of the 4-element set $S_4 = \{1, 2, 3, 4\}$ (left) and the resulting list of all set partitions of 4 elements (right).

```
------------------       ------------------       setpart(4)==
P={1}                    P={1, 2, 3}              {1, 2, 3, 4}
  --> {1, 2}              --> {1, 2, 3, 4}        {1, 2, 3}, {4}
  --> {1}, {2}           --> {1, 2, 3}, {4}      {1, 2}, {3}, {4}
                                                  {1, 2}, {3, 4}
                         P={1, 2}, {3}            {1, 2, 4}, {3}
                          --> {1, 2}, {3}, {4}    {1, 4}, {2}, {3}
                          --> {1, 2}, {3, 4}      {1}, {2, 4}, {3}
                          --> {1, 2, 4}, {3}      {1}, {2}, {3, 4}
                                                  {1}, {2}, {3}, {4}
------------------       P={1}, {2}, {3}          {1}, {2, 3}, {4}
P={1, 2}                  --> {1, 4}, {2}, {3}    {1}, {2, 3, 4}
  --> {1, 2, 3}           --> {1}, {2, 4}, {3}    {1, 4}, {2, 3}
  --> {1, 2}, {3}         --> {1}, {2}, {3, 4}    {1, 3, 4}, {2}
                          --> {1}, {2}, {3}, {4}  {1, 3}, {2, 4}
P={1}, {2}                                        {1, 3}, {2}, {4}
  -->{1}, {2}, {3}       P={1}, {2, 3}
  -->{1}, {2, 3}          --> {1}, {2, 3}, {4}
  -->{1, 3}, {2}          --> {1}, {2, 3, 4}
                          --> {1, 4}, {2, 3}

                         P={1, 3}, {2}
                          --> {1, 3, 4}, {2}
                          --> {1, 3}, {2, 4}
                          --> {1, 3}, {2}, {4}
```

Figure 17.1-B: Construction of a Gray code for set partitions as an interleaving process.

```
 1:  {1, 2, 3, 4}                    1:  {1}, {2}, {3}, {4}
 2:  {1, 2, 3}, {4}                  2:  {1}, {2}, {3, 4}
 3:  {1, 2}, {3}, {4}                3:  {1}, {2, 4}, {3}
 4:  {1, 2}, {3, 4}                  4:  {1, 4}, {2}, {3}
 5:  {1, 2, 4}, {3}                  5:  {1, 4}, {2, 3}
 6:  {1, 4}, {2}, {3}                6:  {1}, {2, 3, 4}
 7:  {1}, {2, 4}, {3}                7:  {1}, {2, 3}, {4}
 8:  {1}, {2}, {3, 4}                8:  {1, 3}, {2}, {4}
 9:  {1}, {2}, {3}, {4}              9:  {1, 3}, {2, 4}
10:  {1}, {2, 3}, {4}               10:  {1, 3, 4}, {2}
11:  {1}, {2, 3, 4}                 11:  {1, 2, 3, 4}
12:  {1, 4}, {2, 3}                 12:  {1, 2, 3}, {4}
13:  {1, 3, 4}, {2}                 13:  {1, 2}, {3}, {4}
14:  {1, 3}, {2, 4}                 14:  {1, 2}, {3, 4}
15:  {1, 3}, {2}, {4}               15:  {1, 2, 4}, {3}
```

Figure 17.1-C: Set partitions of $S_4 = \{1, 2, 3, 4\}$ in two different minimal-change orders.

The resulting process of interleaving elements is shown in figure 17.1-B. The method is similar to Trotter's construction for permutations, see figure 10.7-B on page 253. If we change the direction with every subset that is to be incremented, we get the minimal-change order shown in figure 17.1-C for $n = 4$. The left column is generated when starting with the forward direction in each step of the recursion, the right when starting with the backward direction. The lists can be computed with [FXT: comb/setpart-demo.cc].

The C++ class [FXT: **class setpart** in comb/setpart.h] stores the list in an array of signed characters. The stored value is negated if the element is the last in the subset. The work involved with the creation of Z_n is proportional to $\sum_{k=1}^{n} k\, B_k$ where B_k is the k-th Bell number.

The parameter **xdr** of the constructor determines the order in which the partitions are being created:

```
1   class setpart
2   // Set partitions of the set {1,2,3,...,n}
3   // By default in minimal-change order
4   {
5   public:
6       ulong n_;     // Number of elements of set (set = {1,2,3,...,n})
7       int *p_;      // p[] contains set partitions of length 1,2,3,...,n
8       int **pp_;    // pp[k] points to start of set partition k
9       int *ns_;     // ns[k] Number of Sets in set partition k
10      int *as_;     // element k attached At Set (0<=as[k]<=k) of set(k-1)
11      int *d_;      // direction with recursion (+1 or -1)
12      int *x_;      // current set partition (==pp[n])
13      bool xdr_;    // whether to change direction in recursion (==> minimal-change order)
14      int dr0;      // dr0: starting direction in each recursive step:
15      //    dr0=+1  ==> start with partition  {{1,2,3,...,n}}
16      //    dr0=-1  ==> start with partition  {{1},{2},{3},...,{n}}}
17
18  public:
19      setpart(ulong n, bool xdr=true, int dr0=+1)
20      {
21          n_ = n;
22          ulong np = (n_*(n_+1))/2;   // == \sum_{k=1}^{n}{k}
23          p_ = new int[np];
24
25          pp_ = new int *[n_+1];
26          pp_[0] = 0;  // unused
27          pp_[1] = p_;
28          for (ulong k=2; k<=n_; ++k)  pp_[k] = pp_[k-1] + (k-1);
29
30          ns_ = new int[n_+1];
31          as_ = new int[n_+1];
32          d_ = new int[n_+1];
33          x_ = pp_[n_];
34
35          init(xdr, dr0);
36      }
37      [--snip--]  // destructor
38
39      bool next()  { return next_rec(n_); }
```

```
40
41        const int* data()  const  { return x_; }
42
43        ulong print()  const
44        // Print current set partition
45        // Return number of chars printed
46        { return print_p(n_); }
47
48        ulong print_p(ulong k)  const;
49        void print_internal()  const;  // print internal state
50
51   protected:
52        [--snip--]  // internal methods
53   };
```

The actual work is done by the methods next_rec() and cp_append() [FXT: comb/setpart.cc]:

```
1    int
2    setpart::cp_append(const int *src, int *dst, ulong k, ulong a)
3    // Copy partition in src[0,...,k-2] to dst[0,...,k-1]
4    // append element k at subset a (a>=0)
5    // Return number of sets in created partition.
6    {
7        ulong ct = 0;
8        for (ulong j=0; j<k-1; ++j)
9        {
10           int e = src[j];
11           if ( e > 0 )  dst[j] = e;
12           else
13           {
14               if ( a==ct )  { dst[j]=-e; ++dst; dst[j]=-k; }
15               else  dst[j] = e;
16               ++ct;
17           }
18       }
19       if ( a>=ct )  { dst[k-1] = -k; ++ct; }
20
21       return ct;
22   }
```

```
1    int
2    setpart::next_rec(ulong k)
3    // Update partition in level k from partition in level k-1  (k<=n)
4    // Return number of sets in created partition
5    {
6        if ( k<=1 )  return 0;  // current is last
7
8        int d = d_[k];
9        int as = as_[k] + d;
10       bool ovq = ( (d>0) ? (as>ns_[k-1]) : (as<0) );
11       if ( ovq )  // have to recurse
12       {
13           ulong ns1 = next_rec(k-1);
14           if ( 0==ns1 )  return 0;
15
16           d = ( xdr_ ? -d : dr0_ );
17           d_[k] = d;
18
19           as = ( (d>0) ? 0 : ns_[k-1] );
20       }
21       as_[k] = as;
22
23       ulong ns = cp_append(pp_[k-1], pp_[k], k, as);
24       ns_[k] = ns;
25       return ns;
26   }
```

The partitions are represented by an array of integers whose absolute value is $\leq n$. A negative value indicates that it is the last of the subset. The set partitions of S_4 together with their 'signed value' representations are shown in figure 17.1-D. The array as[] contains a restricted growth string (RGS) with the condition $a_j \leq 1 + \max_{i<j}(a_i)$. A different sort of RGS is described in section 15.2 on page 325.

The copying is the performance bottleneck of the algorithm. Therefore only about 11 million partitions are generated per second. An $O(1)$ algorithm for the Gray code starting with all elements in one set is given in [201].

```
 1:   as[ 0 0 0 0 ]      x[ +1 +2 +3 -4 ]      {1, 2, 3, 4}
 2:   as[ 0 0 0 1 ]      x[ +1 +2 -3 -4 ]      {1, 2, 3}, {4}
 3:   as[ 0 0 1 0 ]      x[ +1 +2 -4 -3 ]      {1, 2, 4}, {3}
 4:   as[ 0 0 1 1 ]      x[ +1 -2 +3 -4 ]      {1, 2}, {3, 4}
 5:   as[ 0 0 1 2 ]      x[ +1 -2 -3 -4 ]      {1, 2}, {3}, {4}
 6:   as[ 0 1 0 0 ]      x[ +1 +3 -4 -2 ]      {1, 3, 4}, {2}
 7:   as[ 0 1 0 1 ]      x[ +1 -3 +2 -4 ]      {1, 3}, {2, 4}
 8:   as[ 0 1 0 2 ]      x[ +1 -3 -2 -4 ]      {1, 3}, {2}, {4}
 9:   as[ 0 1 1 0 ]      x[ +1 -4 +2 -3 ]      {1, 4}, {2, 3}
1 0 :a s [ 0 1 1 1 ]     x[ - 1+ 2+ 3-4 ]      {1}, {2, 3, 4}
1 1 :a s[ 0 1 1 2 ]      x [-1 +2 -3 -4 ]      {1}, {2, 3}, {4}
12:   as[ 0 1 2 0 ]      x[ +1 -4 -2 -3 ]      {1, 4}, {2}, {3}
1 3 :a s [ 0 1 2 1 ]     x[ - 1+ 2- 4-3 ]      {1}, {2, 4}, {3}
1 4 :a s[ 0 1 2 2 ]      x [-1 -2 +3 -4 ]      {1}, {2}, {3, 4}
1 5 :a s[ 0 1 2 3 ]      x [-1 -2 -3 -4 ]      {1}, {2}, {3}, {4}
```

Figure 17.1-D: The partitions of the set $S_4 = \{1, 2, 3, 4\}$ together with the internal representations: the 'signed value' array x[] and the 'attachment' array as[].

17.2   The number of set partitions: Stirling set numbers and Bell numbers

```
 n:        B(n)   k: 1      2      3      4      5      6      7      8     9    10
 1:          1       1
 2:          2       1      1
 3:          5       1      3      1
 4:    :     1   5   1      7      6      1
 5:         52       1     15     25     10      1
 6:        203       1     31     90     65     15      1
 7:        877       1     63    301    350    140     21      1
 8:       4140       1    127    966   1701   1050    266     28     1
 9:      21147       1    255   3025   7770   6951   2646    462    36     1
10:     115975       1    511   9330  34105  42525  22827   5880   750    45    1
```

Figure 17.2-A: Stirling numbers of the second kind (Stirling set numbers) and Bell numbers.

The numbers $S(n, k)$ of partitions of the n-set into k subsets are called the *Stirling numbers of the second kind* (or *Stirling set numbers*), see entry A008277 in [312]. They can be computed by the relation

$$S(n, k) \;=\; k\, S(n-1, k) + S(n-1, k-1) \tag{17.2-1}$$

which is obtained by counting the partitions in our recursive construction. In the triangular array shown in figure 17.2-A each entry is the sum of its upper left neighbor plus k times its upper neighbor. The figure was generated with the program [FXT: comb/stirling2-demo.cc].

The sum over all elements $S(n, k)$ of row n gives the *Bell number* B_n, the number of set partitions of the n-set. The sequence starts as 1, 2, 5, 15, 52, 203, 877, ..., it is entry A000110 in [312]. The Bell numbers can also be computed by the recursion

$$B_{n+1} \;=\; \sum_{k=0}^{n} \binom{n}{k} B_k \tag{17.2-2}$$

As GP code:

```
? N=11; v=vector(N); v[1]=1;
? for (n=2, N, v[n]=sum(k=1, n-1, binomial(n-2,k-1)*v[k])); v
  [1, 1, 2, 5, 15, 52, 203, 877, 4140, 21147, 115975]
```

Another way of computing the Bell numbers is given in section 3.5.3 on page 151.

17.2.1   Generating functions

The ordinary generating function for the Bell numbers can be given as

$$\sum_{n=0}^{\infty} B_n\, x^n \;=\; \sum_{k=0}^{\infty} \frac{x^k}{\prod_{j=1}^{k}(1-j\,x)} \;=\; 1 + x + 2\,x^2 + 5\,x^3 + 15\,x^4 + 52\,x^5 + \dots \qquad (17.2\text{-}3)$$

The exponential generating function (EGF) is

$$\exp\left[\exp(x) - 1\right] \;=\; \sum_{n=0}^{\infty} B_n \frac{x^n}{n!} \qquad (17.2\text{-}4)$$

```
? sum(k=0,11,x^k/prod(j=1,k,1-j*x))+O(x^8)   \\ OGF
   1 + x + 2*x^2 + 5*x^3 + 15*x^4 + 52*x^5 + 203*x^6 + 877*x^7 + O(x^8)
? serlaplace(exp(exp(x)-1))                  \\ EGF
   1 + x + 2*x^2 + 5*x^3 + 15*x^4 + 52*x^5 + 203*x^6 + 877*x^7 + 4140*x^8 + ...
```

Dobinski's formula for the Bell numbers is [349, entry "Bell Number"]

$$B_n \;=\; \frac{1}{e} \sum_{k=1}^{\infty} \frac{n^k}{k!} \qquad (17.2\text{-}5)$$

The array of Stirling numbers shown in figure 17.2-A can also be computed in polynomial form by setting $B_0(x) = 1$ and

$$B_{n+1}(x) \;=\; x\left[B_n'(x) + B_n(x)\right] \qquad (17.2\text{-}6)$$

The coefficients of $B_n(x)$ are the Stirling numbers and $B_n(1) = B_n$:

```
? B=1; for(k=1,6, B=x*(deriv(B)+B); print(subst(B,x,1),": ",B))
   1:   x
   2:   x^2 + x
   5:   x^3 + 3*x^2 + x
  15:   x^4 + 6*x^3 + 7*x^2 + x
  52:   x^5 + 10*x^4 + 25*x^3 + 15*x^2 + x
 203:   x^6 + 15*x^5 + 65*x^4 + 90*x^3 + 31*x^2 + x
```

The polynomials are called *Bell polynomials*, see [349, entry "Bell Polynomial"].

17.2.2   Set partitions of a given type

We say a set partition of the n-element set is of *type* $C = [c_1, c_2, c_3, \dots, c_n]$ if it has c_1 1-element sets, c_2 2-element sets, c_3 3-element sets, and so on. Define

$$L(z) \;=\; \sum_{k=1}^{\infty} \frac{t_k z^k}{k!} \qquad (17.2\text{-}7a)$$

then we have

$$\exp\left(L(z)\right) \;=\; \sum_{n=0}^{\infty} \left[\sum_{C} \left(Z_{n,C} \prod t_k^{c_k}\right)\right] \frac{z^n}{n!} \qquad (17.2\text{-}7b)$$

where $Z_{n,C}$ is the number of set partitions of the n-element set with type C.

```
? n=8;R=O(z^(n+1));
? L=sum(k=1,n,eval(Str("t"k))*z^k/k!)+R
   t1*z + 1/2*t2*z^2 + 1/6*t3*z^3 + 1/24*t4*z^4 +  [...]  + 1/40320*t8*z^8 + O(z^9)
? serlaplace(exp(L))
   1
 + t1 *z
 + (t1^2 + t2) *z^2
 + (t1^3 + 3*t2*t1 + t3) *z^3
 + (t1^4 + 6*t2*t1^2 + 4*t3*t1 + 3*t2^2 + t4) *z^4
 + (t1^5 + 10*t2*t1^3 + 10*t3*t1^2 + 15*t1*t2^2 + 5*t1*t4 + 10*t3*t2 + t5) *z^5
 + (t1^6 + 15*t2*t1^4 + 20*t3*t1^3 +  [...]  + 15*t4*t2 + 10*t3^2 + t6) *z^6
 + (t1^7 + 21*t2*t1^5 + 35*t3*t1^4 +  [...]  + 105*t3*t2^2 + 21*t5*t2 + 35*t4*t3 + t7) *z^7
 + (t1^8 + 28*t2*t1^6 + 56*t3*t1^5 +  [...]  + 28*t6*t2 + 56*t5*t3 + 35*t4^2 + t8) *z^8
 + O(z^9)
```

Specializations give generating functions for set partitions with certain restrictions. For example, the EGF for the partitions without sets of size one is (set $t_1 = 0$ and $t_k = 1$ for $k \neq 1$) $\exp(\exp(z) - 1 - z)$, see entry A000296 in [312]. Section 11.1.2 on page 278 gives a similar construction for the EGF for permutations of prescribed cycle type.

17.3   Restricted growth strings

For some applications the restricted growth strings (RGS) may suffice. We give algorithms for their generation and describe classes of generalized RGS that contain the RGS for set partitions as a special case.

17.3.1   RGS for set partitions in lexicographic order

The C++ implementation [FXT: class `setpart_rgs_lex` in comb/setpart-rgs-lex.h] generates the RGS for set partitions in lexicographic order:

```
1    class setpart_rgs_lex
2    // Set partitions of the n-set as restricted growth strings (RGS).
3    // Lexicographic order.
4    {
5    public:
6        ulong n_;      // Number of elements of set (set = {1,2,3,...,n})
7        ulong *m_;     // m[k+1] = max(s[0], s[1],..., s[k]) + 1
8        ulong *s_;     // RGS
9
10   public:
11       setpart_rgs_lex(ulong n)
12       {
13           n_ = n;
14           m_ = new ulong[n_+1];
15           m_[0] = ~0UL;     // sentinel m[0] = infinity
16           s_ = new ulong[n_];
17           first();
18       }
19   [--snip--]
```

```
1        void first()
2        {
3            for (ulong k=0; k<n_; ++k)  s_[k] = 0;
4            for (ulong k=1; k<=n_; ++k)  m_[k] = 1;
5        }
6
7        void last()
8        {
9            for (ulong k=0; k<n_; ++k)  s_[k] = k;
10           for (ulong k=1; k<=n_; ++k)  m_[k] = k;
11       }
```

The method to compute the successor resembles the one used with mixed radix counting (see section 9.1 on page 217): find the first digit that can be incremented and increment it, then set all skipped digits to zero and adjust the array of maxima accordingly.

```
1        bool next()
2        {
3            if ( m_[n_] == n_ )  return false;
4
5            ulong k = n_;
6            do  { --k; }  while ( (s_[k] + 1) > m_[k] );
7
8            s_[k] += 1UL;
9            ulong mm = m_[k];
10           mm += (s_[k]>=mm);
11           m_[k+1] = mm;   // == max2(m_[k], s_[k]+1)
12
13           while ( ++k<n_ )
14           {
15               s_[k] = 0;
16               m_[k+1] = mm;
17           }
18
19           return true;
```

```
20          }
21
```

The method for the predecessor is

```
1      bool prev()
2      {
3          if ( m_[n_] == 1 )  return false;
4
5          ulong k = n_;
6          do  { --k; } while ( s_[k]==0 );
7
8          s_[k] -= 1;
9          ulong mm = m_[k+1] = max2(m_[k], s_[k]+1);
10
11         while ( ++k<n_ )
12         {
13             s_[k] = mm;  // == m[k]
14             ++mm;
15             m_[k+1] = mm;
16         }
17
18         return true;
19     }
```

The rate of generation is about 157 M/s with next() and 190 M/s with prev() [FXT: comb/setpart-rgs-lex-demo.cc].

17.3.2   RGS for set partitions into p parts

```
        array of minimal values for m[] is [ 1 1 1 2 3 ]

  1 :   s [. . . 1 2 ]   m [1 1 1 2 3 ]   {1, 2, 3}, {4}, {5}
  2 :   s [. . 1 . 2 ]   m [1 1 2 2 3 ]   {1, 2, 4}, {3}, {5}
  3 :   s [. . 1 1 2 ]   m [1 1 2 2 3 ]   {1, 2}, {3, 4}, {5}
  4 :   s [. . 1 2 . ]   m [1 1 2 3 3 ]   {1, 2, 5}, {3}, {4}
  5 :   s [. . 1 2 1 ]   m [1 1 2 3 3 ]   {1, 2}, {3, 5}, {4}
  6 :   s [. . 1 2 2 ]   m [1 1 2 3 3 ]   {1, 2}, {3}, {4, 5}
  7 :   s [. 1 . . 2 ]   m [1 2 2 2 3 ]   {1, 3, 4}, {2}, {5}
  8 :   s [. 1 . 1 2 ]   m [1 2 2 2 3 ]   {1, 3}, {2, 4}, {5}
  9 :   s [. 1 . 2 . ]   m [1 2 2 3 3 ]   {1, 3, 5}, {2}, {4}
1 0 :   s [. 1 . 2 1 ]   m[ 1 2 2 3 3 ]   {1, 3}, {2, 5}, {4}
1 1 :   s [. 1 . 2 2 ]   m[ 1 2 2 3 3 ]   {1, 3}, {2}, {4, 5}
1 2 :   s [. 1 1 . 2 ]   m[ 1 2 2 2 3 ]   {1, 4}, {2, 3}, {5}
1 3 :   s [. 1 1 1 2 ]   m[ 1 2 2 2 3 ]   {1}, {2, 3, 4}, {5}
1 4 :   s [. 1 1 2 . ]   m[ 1 2 2 3 3 ]   {1, 5}, {2, 3}, {4}
1 5 :   s [. 1 1 2 1 ]   m[ 1 2 2 3 3 ]   {1}, {2, 3, 5}, {4}
1 6 :   s [. 1 1 2 2 ]   m[ 1 2 2 3 3 ]   {1}, {2, 3}, {4, 5}
1 7 :   s [. 1 2 . . ]   m[ 1 2 3 3 3 ]   {1, 4, 5}, {2}, {3}
1 8 :   s [. 1 2 . 1 ]   m[ 1 2 3 3 3 ]   {1, 4}, {2, 5}, {3}
1 9 :   s [. 1 2 . 2 ]   m[ 1 2 3 3 3 ]   {1, 4}, {2}, {3, 5}
2 0 :   s [. 1 2 1 . ]   m[ 1 2 3 3 3 ]   {1, 5}, {2, 4}, {3}
2 1 :   s [. 1 2 1 1 ]   m[ 1 2 3 3 3 ]   {1}, {2, 4, 5}, {3}
2 2 :   s [. 1 2 1 2 ]   m[ 1 2 3 3 3 ]   {1}, {2, 4}, {3, 5}
2 3 :   s [. 1 2 2 . ]   m[ 1 2 3 3 3 ]   {1, 5}, {2}, {3, 4}
2 4 :   s [. 1 2 2 1 ]   m[ 1 2 3 3 3 ]   {1}, {2, 5}, {3, 4}
2 5 :   s [. 1 2 2 2 ]   m[ 1 2 3 3 3 ]   {1}, {2}, {3, 4, 5}
```

Figure 17.3-A: Restricted growth strings in lexicographic order (left, dots for zeros) and array of prefix-maxima (middle) for the set partitions of the 5-set into 3 parts (right).

Figure 17.3-A shows all set partitions of the 5-set into 3 parts, together with their RGSs. The list of RGSs of the partitions of an n-set into p parts contains all length-n *patterns* with p letters. A pattern is a word where the first occurrence of u precedes the first occurrence of v if $u < v$. That is, the list of patterns is the list of words modulo permutations of the letters.

The restricted growth strings corresponding to set partitions into p parts can be generated with [FXT: class setpart_p_rgs_lex in comb/setpart-p-rgs-lex.h]:

```
1   class setpart_p_rgs_lex
```

```
2    {
3    public:
4        ulong n_;        // Number of elements of set (set = {1,2,3,...,n})
5        ulong p_;        // Exactly p subsets
6        ulong *m_;       // m[k+1] = max(s[0], s[1],..., s[k]) + 1
7        ulong *s_;       // RGS
8
9    public:
10       setpart_p_rgs_lex(ulong n, ulong p)
11       {
12           n_ = n;
13           m_ = new ulong[n_+1];
14           m_[0] = ~OUL;     // sentinel m[0] = infinity
15           s_ = new ulong[n_];
16           first(p);
17       }
18   [--snip--]  // destructor
19
20       void first(ulong p)
21       // Must have  2<=p<=n
22       {
23           for (ulong k=0; k<n_; ++k)  s_[k] = 0;
24           for (ulong k=n_-p+1, j=1; k<n_; ++k, ++j)  s_[k] = j;
25
26           for (ulong k=1; k<=n_; ++k)  m_[k] = s_[k-1]+1;
27           p_ = p;
28       }
29
```

The method to compute the successor also checks whether the digit is less than p and has an additional loop to repair the rightmost digits when needed:

```
1    bool next()
2    {
3        // if ( 1==p_ )  return false;  // make things work with p==1
4
5        ulong k = n_;
6        bool q;
7        do
8        {
9            --k;
10           const ulong sk1 = s_[k] + 1;
11           q = (sk1 > m_[k]);    // greater max
12           q |= (sk1 >= p_);     // more than p parts
13       }
14       while ( q );
15
16       if ( k == 0 )  return false;
17
18       s_[k] += 1UL;
19       ulong mm = m_[k];
20       mm += (s_[k]>=mm);
21       m_[k+1] = mm;  // == max2(m_[k], s_[k]+1);
22
23       while ( ++k<n_ )
24       {
25           s_[k] = 0;
26           m_[k+1] = mm;
27       }
28
29       ulong p = p_;
30       if ( mm<p )  // repair tail
31       {
32           do { m_[k] = p; --k; --p; s_[k] = p; }
33           while ( m_[k] < p );
34       }
35
36       return true;
37   }
```

As given the computation will fail for $p = 1$, the line commented out removes this limitation. The rate of generation is about 108 M/s [FXT: comb/setpart-p-rgs-lex-demo.cc].

17.3.3 RGS for set partitions in minimal-change order

For the Gray code we need an additional array of directions, see section 9.2 on page 220 for the equivalent routines with mixed radix numbers. The implementation allows starting either with the partition into one set or the partition into n sets [FXT: class setpart_rgs_gray in comb/setpart-rgs-gray.h]:

```
1    class setpart_rgs_gray
2    {
3    public:
4        ulong n_;       // Number of elements of set (set = {1,2,3,...,n})
5        ulong *m_;      // m[k+1] = max(s[0], s[1],..., s[k]) + 1
6        ulong *s_;      // RGS
7        ulong *d_;      // direction with recursion (+1 or -1)
8
9    public:
10       setpart_rgs_gray(ulong n, int dr0=+1)
11       // dr0=+1  ==> start with partition  {{1,2,3,...,n}}
12       // dr0=-1  ==> start with partition  {{1},{2},{3},...,{n}}}
13       {
14           n_ = n;
15           m_ = new ulong[n_+1];
16           m_[0] = ~0UL;    // sentinel m[0] = infinity
17           s_ = new ulong[n_];
18           d_ = new ulong[n_];
19           first(dr0);
20       }
21   [--snip--]
```

```
1        void first(int dr0)
2        {
3            const ulong n = n_;
4            const ulong dd = (dr0 >= 0 ? +1UL : -1UL);
5            if ( dd==1 )
6            {
7                for (ulong k=0; k<n; ++k)  s_[k] = 0;
8                for (ulong k=1; k<=n; ++k)  m_[k] = 1;
9            }
10           else
11           {
12               for (ulong k=0; k<n; ++k)  s_[k] = k;
13               for (ulong k=1; k<=n; ++k)  m_[k] = k;
14           }
15
16           for (ulong k=0; k<n; ++k)  d_[k] = dd;
17       }
```

The method to compute the successor is

```
1        bool next()
2        {
3            ulong k = n_;
4            do  { --k; } while ( (s_[k] + d_[k]) > m_[k] );  // <0 or >max
5
6            if ( k == 0 )  return false;
7
8            s_[k] += d_[k];
9            m_[k+1] = max2(m_[k], s_[k]+1);
10
11           while ( ++k<n_ )
12           {
13               const ulong d = d_[k] = -d_[k];
14               const ulong mk = m_[k];
15               s_[k] = ( (d==1UL) ? 0 : mk );
16               m_[k+1] = mk + (d!=1UL);   // == max2(mk, s_[k]+1)
17           }
18
19           return true;
20       }
```

The rate of generation is about 154 M/s [FXT: comb/setpart-rgs-gray-demo.cc]. It must be noted that while the corresponding set partitions are in minimal-change order (see figure 17.1-C on page 356) the RGS occasionally changes in more than one digit. A Gray code for the RGS for set partitions into p parts where only one position changes with each update is described in [288].

17.3.4   Max-increment RGS ‡

The generation of RGSs $s = [s_0, s_1, \ldots, s_{n-1}]$ where $s_k \leq i + \max_{j<k}(s_j)$ is a generalization of the RGSs for set partitions (where $i = 1$). Figure 17.3-B show RGSs in lexicographic order for $i = 2$ (left) and $i = 1$ (right). The strings can be generated in lexicographic order using [FXT: class rgs_maxincr in comb/rgs-maxincr.h]:

```
1   class rgs_maxincr
2   {
3   public:
4       ulong *s_;  // restricted growth string
5       ulong *m_;  // m_[k-1] == max possible value for s_[k]
6       ulong n_;   // Length of strings
7       ulong i_;    // s[k] <= max_{j<k}(s[j]+i)
8       // i==1 ==> RGS for set partitions
9
10  public:
11      rgs_maxincr(ulong n, ulong i=1)
12      {
13          n_ = n;
14          m_ = new ulong[n_];
15          s_ = new ulong[n_];
16          i_ = i;
17          first();
18      }
19
20      ~rgs_maxincr()
21      {
22          delete [] m_;
23          delete [] s_;
24      }
25
26      void first()
27      {
28          ulong n = n_;
29          for (ulong k=0; k<n; ++k)  s_[k] = 0;
30          for (ulong k=0; k<n; ++k)  m_[k] = i_;
31      }
32  [--snip--]
```

The computation of the successor returns the index of first (leftmost) changed element in the string. Zero is returned if the current string is the last:

```
1       ulong next()
2       {
3           ulong k = n_;
4       start:
5           --k;
6           if ( k==0 )  return 0;
7
8           ulong sk = s_[k] + 1;
9           ulong m1 = m_[k-1];
10          if ( sk > m1+i_ )  // "carry"
11          {
12              s_[k] = 0;
13              goto start;
14          }
15
16          s_[k] = sk;
17          if ( sk>m1 )  m1 = sk;
18          for (ulong j=k; j<n_; ++j )  m_[j] = m1;
19
20          return k;
21      }
22  [--snip--]
```

About 115 million RGSs per second are generated with the routine. Figure 17.3-B was created with the program [FXT: comb/rgs-maxincr-demo.cc]. The sequence of numbers of max-increment RGSs with increment $i = 1$, 2, 3, and 4, start

n	:0	1	2	3	4	5	6	7	8	9	10
i=1:	1	1	2	5	15	52	203	877	4140	21147	115975
i=2:	1	1	3	12	59	339	2210	16033	127643	1103372	10269643
i=3:	1	1	4	22	150	1200	10922	110844	1236326	14990380	195895202
i=4:	1	1	5	35	305	3125	36479	475295	6811205	106170245	1784531879

```
           RGS(4,2)        max(4,2)              RGS(5,1)        max(5,1)
  1 : [ .  .  .  . ]   [ .  .  .  . ]      1: [ .  .  .  .  . ]   [ .  .  .  .  . ]
  2 : [ .  .  .  1 ]   [ .  .  .  1 ]      2: [ .  .  .  .  1 ]   [ .  .  .  .  1 ]
  3 : [ .  .  .  2 ]   [ .  .  .  2 ]      3: [ .  .  .  1  . ]   [ .  .  .  1  1 ]
  4 : [ .  .  1  . ]   [ .  .  1  1 ]      4: [ .  .  .  1  1 ]   [ .  .  .  1  1 ]
  5 : [ .  .  1  1 ]   [ .  .  1  1 ]      5: [ .  .  .  1  2 ]   [ .  .  .  1  2 ]
  6 : [ .  .  1  2 ]   [ .  .  1  2 ]      6: [ .  .  1  .  . ]   [ .  .  1  1  1 ]
  7 : [ .  .  1  3 ]   [ .  .  1  3 ]      7: [ .  .  1  .  1 ]   [ .  .  1  1  1 ]
  8 : [ .  .  2  . ]   [ .  .  2  2 ]      8: [ .  .  1  .  2 ]   [ .  .  1  1  2 ]
  9 : [ .  .  2  1 ]   [ .  .  2  2 ]      9: [ .  .  1  1  . ]   [ .  .  1  1  1 ]
 10 : [ .  .  2  2 ]   [ .  .  2  2 ]     10: [ .  .  1  1  1 ]   [ .  .  1  1  1 ]
 11 : [ .  .  2  3 ]   [ .  .  2  3 ]     11: [ .  .  1  1  2 ]   [ .  .  1  1  2 ]
 12 : [ .  .  2  4 ]   [ .  .  2  4 ]     12: [ .  .  1  2  . ]   [ .  .  1  2  2 ]
 13 : [ .  1  .  . ]   [ .  1  1  1 ]     13: [ .  .  1  2  1 ]   [ .  .  1  2  2 ]
 14 : [ .  1  .  1 ]   [ .  1  1  1 ]     14: [ .  .  1  2  2 ]   [ .  .  1  2  2 ]
 15 : [ .  1  .  2 ]   [ .  1  1  2 ]     15: [ .  .  1  2  3 ]   [ .  .  1  2  3 ]
 16 : [ .  1  .  3 ]   [ .  1  1  3 ]     16: [ .  1  .  .  . ]   [ .  1  1  1  1 ]
 17 : [ .  1  1  . ]   [ .  1  1  1 ]     17: [ .  1  .  .  1 ]   [ .  1  1  1  1 ]
 18 : [ .  1  1  1 ]   [ .  1  1  1 ]     18: [ .  1  .  .  2 ]   [ .  1  1  1  2 ]
 19 : [ .  1  1  2 ]   [ .  1  1  2 ]     19: [ .  1  .  1  . ]   [ .  1  1  1  1 ]
 20 : [ .  1  1  3 ]   [ .  1  1  3 ]     20: [ .  1  .  1  1 ]   [ .  1  1  1  1 ]
 21 : [ .  1  2  . ]   [ .  1  2  2 ]     21: [ .  1  .  1  2 ]   [ .  1  1  1  2 ]
 22 : [ .  1  2  1 ]   [ .  1  2  2 ]     22: [ .  1  .  2  . ]   [ .  1  1  2  2 ]
 23 : [ .  1  2  2 ]   [ .  1  2  2 ]     23: [ .  1  .  2  1 ]   [ .  1  1  2  2 ]
 24 : [ .  1  2  3 ]   [ .  1  2  3 ]     24: [ .  1  .  2  2 ]   [ .  1  1  2  2 ]
 25 : [ .  1  2  4 ]   [ .  1  2  4 ]     25: [ .  1  .  2  3 ]   [ .  1  1  2  3 ]
 26 : [ .  1  3  . ]   [ .  1  3  3 ]     26: [ .  1  1  .  . ]   [ .  1  1  1  1 ]
 27 : [ .  1  3  1 ]   [ .  1  3  3 ]     27: [ .  1  1  .  1 ]   [ .  1  1  1  1 ]
 28 : [ .  1  3  2 ]   [ .  1  3  3 ]     28: [ .  1  1  .  2 ]   [ .  1  1  1  2 ]
 29 : [ .  1  3  3 ]   [ .  1  3  3 ]     29: [ .  1  1  1  . ]   [ .  1  1  1  1 ]
 30 : [ .  1  3  4 ]   [ .  1  3  4 ]     30: [ .  1  1  1  1 ]   [ .  1  1  1  1 ]
 31 : [ .  1  3  5 ]   [ .  1  3  5 ]     31: [ .  1  1  1  2 ]   [ .  1  1  1  2 ]
 32 : [ .  2  .  . ]   [ .  2  2  2 ]     32: [ .  1  1  2  . ]   [ .  1  1  2  2 ]
 33 : [ .  2  .  1 ]   [ .  2  2  2 ]     33: [ .  1  1  2  1 ]   [ .  1  1  2  2 ]
 34 : [ .  2  .  2 ]   [ .  2  2  2 ]     34: [ .  1  1  2  2 ]   [ .  1  1  2  2 ]
 35 : [ .  2  .  3 ]   [ .  2  2  3 ]     35: [ .  1  1  2  3 ]   [ .  1  1  2  3 ]
 36 : [ .  2  .  4 ]   [ .  2  2  4 ]     36: [ .  1  2  .  . ]   [ .  1  2  2  2 ]
 37 : [ .  2  1  . ]   [ .  2  2  2 ]     37: [ .  1  2  .  1 ]   [ .  1  2  2  2 ]
 38 : [ .  2  1  1 ]   [ .  2  2  2 ]     38: [ .  1  2  .  2 ]   [ .  1  2  2  2 ]
 39 : [ .  2  1  2 ]   [ .  2  2  2 ]     39: [ .  1  2  .  3 ]   [ .  1  2  2  3 ]
 40 : [ .  2  1  3 ]   [ .  2  2  3 ]     40: [ .  1  2  1  . ]   [ .  1  2  2  2 ]
 41 : [ .  2  1  4 ]   [ .  2  2  4 ]     41: [ .  1  2  1  1 ]   [ .  1  2  2  2 ]
 42 : [ .  2  2  . ]   [ .  2  2  2 ]     42: [ .  1  2  1  2 ]   [ .  1  2  2  2 ]
 43 : [ .  2  2  1 ]   [ .  2  2  2 ]     43: [ .  1  2  1  3 ]   [ .  1  2  2  3 ]
 44 : [ .  2  2  2 ]   [ .  2  2  2 ]     44: [ .  1  2  2  . ]   [ .  1  2  2  2 ]
 45 : [ .  2  2  3 ]   [ .  2  2  3 ]     45: [ .  1  2  2  1 ]   [ .  1  2  2  2 ]
 46 : [ .  2  2  4 ]   [ .  2  2  4 ]     46: [ .  1  2  2  2 ]   [ .  1  2  2  2 ]
 47 : [ .  2  3  . ]   [ .  2  3  3 ]     47: [ .  1  2  2  3 ]   [ .  1  2  2  3 ]
 48 : [ .  2  3  1 ]   [ .  2  3  3 ]     48: [ .  1  2  3  . ]   [ .  1  2  3  3 ]
 49 : [ .  2  3  2 ]   [ .  2  3  3 ]     49: [ .  1  2  3  1 ]   [ .  1  2  3  3 ]
 50 : [ .  2  3  3 ]   [ .  2  3  3 ]     50: [ .  1  2  3  2 ]   [ .  1  2  3  3 ]
 51 : [ .  2  3  4 ]   [ .  2  3  4 ]     51: [ .  1  2  3  3 ]   [ .  1  2  3  3 ]
 52 : [ .  2  3  5 ]   [ .  2  3  5 ]     52: [ .  1  2  3  4 ]   [ .  1  2  3  4 ]
 53 : [ .  2  4  . ]   [ .  2  4  4 ]
 54 : [ .  2  4  1 ]   [ .  2  4  4 ]
 55 : [ .  2  4  2 ]   [ .  2  4  4 ]
 56 : [ .  2  4  3 ]   [ .  2  4  4 ]
 57 : [ .  2  4  4 ]   [ .  2  4  4 ]
 58 : [ .  2  4  5 ]   [ .  2  4  5 ]
 59 : [ .  2  4  6 ]   [ .  2  4  6 ]
```

Figure 17.3-B: Length-4 max-increment RGS with $i = 2$ and the corresponding array of maxima (left) and length-5 RGSs with $i = 1$ (right). Dots denote zeros.

The sequence for $i = 2$ is entry A080337 in [312], it has the exponential generating function (EGF)

$$\sum_{n=0}^{\infty} B_{n+1,2} \frac{x^n}{n!} = \exp\left[x + \exp(x) + \frac{\exp(2x)}{2} - \frac{3}{2}\right] \qquad (17.3\text{-}1)$$

The sequence of numbers of increment-3 RGSs has the EGF

$$\sum_{n=0}^{\infty} B_{n+1,3} \frac{x^n}{n!} = \exp\left[x + \exp(x) + \frac{\exp(2x)}{2} + \frac{\exp(3x)}{3} - \frac{11}{6}\right] \qquad (17.3\text{-}2)$$

Omitting the empty set, we restate the EGF for the Bell numbers (relation 17.2-4 on page 359) as

$$\sum_{n=0}^{\infty} B_{n+1,1} \frac{x^n}{n!} = \exp\left[x + \exp(x) - 1\right] = \frac{1}{0!} + \frac{2}{1!}x + \frac{5}{2!}x^2 + \frac{15}{3!}x^3 + \frac{52}{4!}x^4 + \ldots \quad (17.3\text{-}3)$$

The EGF for the increment-i RGS is

$$\sum_{n=0}^{\infty} B_{n+1,i} \frac{x^n}{n!} = \exp\left[x + \sum_{j=1}^{i} \frac{\exp(jx) - 1}{j}\right] \qquad (17.3\text{-}4)$$

17.3.5   F-increment RGS ‡

For a different generalization of the RGS for set partitions, we rewrite the condition $s_k \leq i + \max_{j<k}(s_j)$ for the RGS considered in the previous section:

$$s_k \leq M(k) + i \quad \text{where} \quad M(0) = 0 \quad \text{and} \qquad (17.3\text{-}5\text{a})$$

$$M(k+1) = \begin{cases} s_{k+1} & \text{if } s_{k+1} - s_k > 0 \\ M(k) & \text{otherwise} \end{cases} \qquad (17.3\text{-}5\text{b})$$

The function $M(k)$ is $\max_{j<k}(s_j)$ in notational disguise. We define *F-increment* RGSs with respect to a function F as follows:

$$s_k \leq F(k) + i \quad \text{where} \quad F(0) = 0 \quad \text{and} \qquad (17.3\text{-}6\text{a})$$

$$F(k+1) = \begin{cases} s_{k+1} & \text{if } s_{k+1} - s_k = i \\ F(k) & \text{otherwise} \end{cases} \qquad (17.3\text{-}6\text{b})$$

The function $F(k)$ is a 'maximum' that is increased only if the last increment ($s_k - s_{k-1}$) was maximal. For $i = 1$ we get the RGSs for set partitions. Figure 17.3-C shows all length-4 F-increment RGSs for $i = 2$ (left) and all length-3 RGSs for $i = 5$ (right), together with the arrays of F-values. The listings were created with the program [FXT: comb/rgs-fincr-demo.cc] which uses the implementation [FXT: **class rgs_fincr** in comb/rgs-fincr.h]:

```
1    class rgs_fincr
2    {
3    public:
4        ulong *s_;   // restricted growth string
5        ulong *f_;   // values F(k)
6        ulong n_;    // Length of strings
7        ulong i_;    // s[k] <= f[k]+i
8    [--snip--]
9
10       ulong next()
11       // Return index of first changed element in s[],
12       // Return zero if current string is the last
13       {
14           ulong k = n_;
15
16       start:
17           --k;
18           if ( k==0 )  return 0;
```

```
        RGS(4,2)          F(2)                 RGS(3,5)       F(5)
 1 : [  .  .  .  .  ]   [  .  .  .  .  ]    1: [  .  .  .  ]   [  .  .  .  ]
 2 : [  .  .  .  1  ]   [  .  .  .  .  ]    2: [  .  .  1  ]   [  .  .  .  ]
 3 : [  .  .  .  2  ]   [  .  .  .  2  ]    3: [  .  .  2  ]   [  .  .  .  ]
 4 : [  .  .  1  .  ]   [  .  .  .  .  ]    4: [  .  .  3  ]   [  .  .  .  ]
 5 : [  .  .  1  1  ]   [  .  .  .  .  ]    5: [  .  .  4  ]   [  .  .  .  ]
 6 : [  .  .  1  2  ]   [  .  .  .  2  ]    6: [  .  .  5  ]   [  .  .  5  ]
 7 : [  .  .  2  .  ]   [  .  .  2  2  ]    7: [  .  1  .  ]   [  .  .  .  ]
 8 : [  .  .  2  1  ]   [  .  .  2  2  ]    8: [  .  1  1  ]   [  .  .  .  ]
 9 : [  .  .  2  2  ]   [  .  .  2  2  ]    9: [  .  1  2  ]   [  .  .  .  ]
10 : [  .  .  2  3  ]   [  .  .  2  2  ]   10: [  .  1  3  ]   [  .  .  .  ]
11 : [  .  .  2  4  ]   [  .  .  2  4  ]   11: [  .  1  4  ]   [  .  .  .  ]
12 : [  .  1  .  .  ]   [  .  .  .  .  ]   12: [  .  1  5  ]   [  .  .  5  ]
13 : [  .  1  .  1  ]   [  .  .  .  .  ]   13: [  .  2  .  ]   [  .  .  .  ]
14 : [  .  1  .  2  ]   [  .  .  .  2  ]   14: [  .  2  1  ]   [  .  .  .  ]
15 : [  .  1  1  .  ]   [  .  .  .  .  ]   15: [  .  2  2  ]   [  .  .  .  ]
16 : [  .  1  1  1  ]   [  .  .  .  .  ]   16: [  .  2  3  ]   [  .  .  .  ]
17 : [  .  1  1  2  ]   [  .  .  .  2  ]   17: [  .  2  4  ]   [  .  .  .  ]
18 : [  .  1  2  .  ]   [  .  .  2  2  ]   18: [  .  2  5  ]   [  .  .  5  ]
19 : [  .  1  2  1  ]   [  .  .  2  2  ]   19: [  .  3  .  ]   [  .  .  .  ]
20 : [  .  1  2  2  ]   [  .  .  2  2  ]   20: [  .  3  1  ]   [  .  .  .  ]
21 : [  .  1  2  3  ]   [  .  .  2  2  ]   21: [  .  3  2  ]   [  .  .  .  ]
22 : [  .  1  2  4  ]   [  .  .  2  4  ]   22: [  .  3  3  ]   [  .  .  .  ]
23 : [  .  2  .  .  ]   [  .  2  2  2  ]   23: [  .  3  4  ]   [  .  .  .  ]
24 : [  .  2  .  1  ]   [  .  2  2  2  ]   24: [  .  3  5  ]   [  .  .  5  ]
25 : [  .  2  .  2  ]   [  .  2  2  2  ]   25: [  .  4  .  ]   [  .  .  .  ]
26 : [  .  2  .  3  ]   [  .  2  2  2  ]   26: [  .  4  1  ]   [  .  .  .  ]
27 : [  .  2  .  4  ]   [  .  2  2  4  ]   27: [  .  4  2  ]   [  .  .  .  ]
28 : [  .  2  1  .  ]   [  .  2  2  2  ]   28: [  .  4  3  ]   [  .  .  .  ]
29 : [  .  2  1  1  ]   [  .  2  2  2  ]   29: [  .  4  4  ]   [  .  .  .  ]
30 : [  .  2  1  2  ]   [  .  2  2  2  ]   30: [  .  4  5  ]   [  .  .  5  ]
31 : [  .  2  1  3  ]   [  .  2  2  2  ]   31: [  .  5  .  ]   [  .  5  5  ]
32 : [  .  2  1  4  ]   [  .  2  2  4  ]   32: [  .  5  1  ]   [  .  5  5  ]
33 : [  .  2  2  .  ]   [  .  2  2  2  ]   33: [  .  5  2  ]   [  .  5  5  ]
34 : [  .  2  2  1  ]   [  .  2  2  2  ]   34: [  .  5  3  ]   [  .  5  5  ]
35 : [  .  2  2  2  ]   [  .  2  2  2  ]   35: [  .  5  4  ]   [  .  5  5  ]
36 : [  .  2  2  3  ]   [  .  2  2  2  ]   36: [  .  5  5  ]   [  .  5  5  ]
37 : [  .  2  2  4  ]   [  .  2  2  4  ]   37: [  .  5  6  ]   [  .  5  5  ]
38 : [  .  2  3  .  ]   [  .  2  2  2  ]   38: [  .  5  7  ]   [  .  5  5  ]
39 : [  .  2  3  1  ]   [  .  2  2  2  ]   39: [  .  5  8  ]   [  .  5  5  ]
40 : [  .  2  3  2  ]   [  .  2  2  2  ]   40: [  .  5  9  ]   [  .  5  5  ]
41 : [  .  2  3  3  ]   [  .  2  2  2  ]   41: [  .  5 10  ]   [  .  5 10  ]
42 : [  .  2  3  4  ]   [  .  2  2  4  ]
43 : [  .  2  4  .  ]   [  .  2  4  4  ]
44 : [  .  2  4  1  ]   [  .  2  4  4  ]
45 : [  .  2  4  2  ]   [  .  2  4  4  ]
46 : [  .  2  4  3  ]   [  .  2  4  4  ]
47 : [  .  2  4  4  ]   [  .  2  4  4  ]
48 : [  .  2  4  5  ]   [  .  2  4  4  ]
49 : [  .  2  4  6  ]   [  .  2  4  6  ]
```

Figure 17.3-C: Length-4 F-increment restricted growth strings with maximal increment 2 and the corresponding array of values of F (left) and length-3 RGSs with maximal increment 5 (right). Dots denote zeros.

```
19
20          ulong sk = s_[k] + 1;
21          ulong m1 = f_[k-1];
22          ulong mp = m1 + i_;
23          if ( sk > mp )   // "carry"
24          {
25              s_[k] = 0;
26              goto start;
27          }
28
29          s_[k] = sk;
30          if ( sk==mp )  m1 += i_;
31          for (ulong j=k; j<n_; ++j )  f_[j] = m1;
32
33          return k;
34      }
35  [--snip--]
```

The sequences of numbers of F-increment RGSs with increments $i = 1, 2, 3$, and 4, start

n :	0	1	2	3	4	5	6	7	8	9
i=1:	1	2	5	15	52	203	877	4140	21147	115975
i=2:	1	3	11	49	257	1539	10299	75905	609441	5284451
i=3:	1	4	19	109	742	5815	51193	498118	5296321	60987817
i=4:	1	5	29	201	1657	15821	170389	2032785	26546673	376085653
i=5:	1	6	41	331	3176	35451	447981	6282416	96546231	1611270851

These are respectively entries A000110 (Bell numbers), A004211, A004212, A004213, and A005011 in [312]. The shown array appears in [203]. In general, the number $F_{n,i}$ of F-increment RGSs (length n, with increment i) is

$$F_{n,i} = \sum_{k=0}^{n} i^{n-k} S(n,k) \tag{17.3-7}$$

where $S(n,k)$ are the Stirling numbers of the second kind. The exponential generating functions are

$$\sum_{n=0}^{\infty} F_{n,i} \frac{x^n}{n!} = \exp\left[\frac{\exp(i\,x) - 1}{i}\right] \tag{17.3-8}$$

The ordinary generating functions are

$$\sum_{n=0}^{\infty} F_{n,i}\, x^n = \sum_{n=0}^{\infty} \frac{x^n}{\prod_{k=1}^{n}(1 - i\,k\,x)} \tag{17.3-9}$$

17.3.6 K-increment RGS ‡

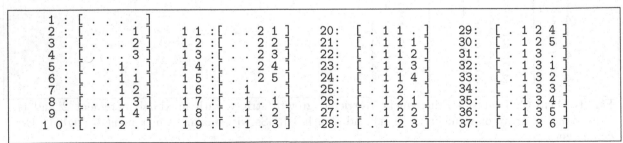

Figure 17.3-D: The 37 K-increment RGS of length 4 in lexicographic order.

We mention yet another type of restricted growth strings, the *K-increment* RGS, which satisfy

$$s_k \leq s_{k-1} + k \tag{17.3-10}$$

An implementation for their generation in lexicographic order is given in [FXT: comb/rgs-kincr.h]:

```
1    class rgs_kincr
2    {
3    public:
4        ulong *s_;   // restricted growth string
5        ulong n_;    // Length of strings
6        [--snip--]
7
8        ulong next()
9        // Return index of first changed element in s[],
10       // Return zero if current string is the last
11       {
12           ulong k = n_;
13
14       start:
15           --k;
16           if ( k==0 )  return 0;
17
18           ulong sk = s_[k] + 1;
19           ulong mp = s_[k-1] + k;
20           if ( sk > mp )  // "carry"
21           {
22               s_[k] = 0;
23               goto start;
24           }
25
26           s_[k] = sk;
27           return k;
28       }
29       [--snip--]
```

The sequence of the numbers of K-increment RGS of length n is entry A107877 in [312]:

n: 0 1 2 3 4 5 6 7 8 9 10
   1 1 2 7 37 268 2496 28612 391189 6230646 113521387

The strings of length 4 are shown in figure 17.3-D. They can be generated with the program [FXT: comb/rgs-kincr-demo.cc].

Chapter 18

Necklaces and Lyndon words

A sequence that is minimal among all its cyclic rotations is called a *necklace* (see section 3.5.2 on page 149 for the definition in terms of equivalence classes). Necklaces with k possible values for each element are called k-ary (or k-bead) necklaces. We restrict our attention to binary necklaces: only two values are allowed and we represent them by 0 and 1.

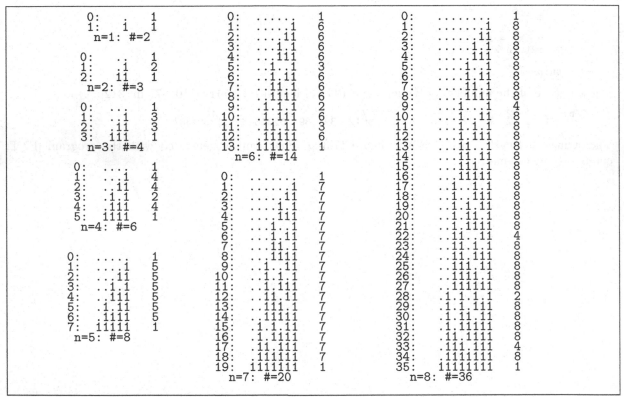

Figure 18.0-A: All binary necklaces of lengths up to 8 and their periods. Dots represent zeros.

To find all length-n necklaces we can, for all binary words of length n, test whether a word is equal to its cyclic minimum (see section 1.13 on page 29). The sequences of binary necklaces for $n \leq 8$ are shown in figure 18.0-A. As 2^n words have to be tested, this approach is inefficient for large n. Luckily there is both a much better algorithm for generating all necklaces and a formula for their number.

Not all necklaces are created equal. Each necklace can be assigned a period that is a divisor of the length. That period is the smallest (nonzero) cyclic shift that transforms the word into itself. The periods are given directly right to each necklace in figure 18.0-A. For n prime the only periodic necklaces are those two that contain all ones or zeros. Aperiodic (or equivalently, period equals length) necklaces are called *Lyndon words*.

J. Arndt, *Matters Computational: Ideas, Algorithms, Source Code*,
DOI 10.1007/978-3-642-14764-7_18, © Springer-Verlag Berlin Heidelberg 2011

For a length-n binary word x the function `bit_cyclic_period(x,n)` from section 1.13 on page 29 returns the period of the word.

18.1 Generating all necklaces

We give several methods to generate all necklaces of a given size. An efficient algorithm for the generation of bracelets (see section 3.5.2.4 on page 150) is given in [299].

18.1.1 The FKM algorithm

```
 1 :  [ . . . . ]   j=1  N            1:  [ . . . . . . ]   j=1  N
 2 :  [ . . . 1 ]   j=4  N L          2:  [ . . . . . 1 ]   j=6  N L
 3 :  [ . . . 2 ]   j=4  N L          3:  [ . . . . 1 . ]   j=5
 4 :  [ . . 1 . ]   j=3               4:  [ . . . . 1 1 ]   j=6  N L
 5 :  [ . . 1 1 ]   j=4  N L          5:  [ . . . 1 . . ]   j=4
 6 :  [ . . 1 2 ]   j=4  N L          6:  [ . . . 1 . 1 ]   j=6  N L
 7 :  [ . . 2 . ]   j=3               7:  [ . . . 1 1 . ]   j=5
 8 :  [ . . 2 1 ]   j=4  N L          8:  [ . . . 1 1 1 ]   j=6  N L
 9 :  [ . . 2 2 ]   j=4  N L          9:  [ . . 1 . . 1 ]   j=3  N
 1 0 :  [ . 1 . 1 ]   j=2  N         10:  [ . . 1 . 1 . ]   j=5
 1 1 :  [ . 1 . 2 ]   j=4  N L       11:  [ . . 1 . 1 1 ]   j=6  N L
 1 2 :  [ . 1 1 . ]   j=3            12:  [ . . 1 1 . . ]   j=4
 1 3 :  [ . 1 1 1 ]   j=4  N L       13:  [ . . 1 1 . 1 ]   j=6  N L
 1 4 :  [ . 1 1 2 ]   j=4  N L       14:  [ . . 1 1 1 . ]   j=5
 1 5 :  [ . 1 2 . ]   j=3            15:  [ . . 1 1 1 1 ]   j=6  N L
 1 6 :  [ . 1 2 1 ]   j=4  N L       16:  [ . 1 . 1 . 1 ]   j=2  N
 1 7 :  [ . 1 2 2 ]   j=4  N L       17:  [ . 1 . 1 1 . ]   j=5
 1 8 :  [ . 2 . 2 ]   j=2  N         18:  [ . 1 . 1 1 1 ]   j=6  N L
 1 9 :  [ . 2 1 . ]   j=3            19:  [ . 1 1 . 1 1 ]   j=3  N
 2 0 :  [ . 2 1 1 ]   j=4  N L       20:  [ . 1 1 1 . 1 ]   j=4
 2 1 :  [ . 2 1 2 ]   j=4  N L       21:  [ . 1 1 1 1 . ]   j=5
 2 2 :  [ . 2 2 . ]   j=3            22:  [ . 1 1 1 1 1 ]   j=6  N L
 2 3 :  [ . 2 2 1 ]   j=4  N L       23:  [ 1 1 1 1 1 1 ]   j=1  N
 24:    [ . 2 2 2 ]   j=4  N L      23 (6, 2) pre-necklaces.
 25:    [ 1 1 1 1 ]   j=1  N        14 necklaces and 9 Lyndon words.
 2 6 :  [ 1 1 1 2 ]   j=4  N L
 2 7 :  [ 1 1 2 1 ]   j=3
 2 8 :  [ 1 1 2 2 ]   j=4  N L
 2 9 :  [ 1 2 1 2 ]   j=2  N
 3 0 :  [ 1 2 2 1 ]   j=3
 3 1 :  [ 1 2 2 2 ]   j=4  N L
 3 2 :  [ 2 2 2 2 ]   j=1  N
32 (4, 3) pre-necklaces.
24 necklaces and 18 Lyndon words.
```

Figure 18.1-A: Ternary length-4 (left) and binary length-6 (right) pre-necklaces as generated by the FKM algorithm. Dots are used for zeros, necklaces are marked with 'N', Lyndon words with 'L'.

The following algorithm for generating all necklaces actually produces *pre-necklaces*, a subset of which are the necklaces. A pre-necklace is a string that is the prefix of some necklace. The *FKM algorithm* (for Fredericksen, Kessler, Maiorana) to generate all k-ary length-n pre-necklaces proceeds as follows:

1. Initialize the word $F = [f_1, f_2, \ldots, f_n]$ to all zeros. Set $j = 1$.

2. (Visit pre-necklace F. If j divides n, then F is a necklace. If j equals n, then F is a Lyndon word.)

3. Find the largest index j so that $f_j < k-1$. If there is no such index (then $F = [k-1, k-1, \ldots, k-1]$, the last necklace), then terminate.

4. Increment f_j. Fill the suffix starting at f_{j+1} with copies of $[f_1, \ldots, f_j]$. Goto step 2.

The crucial steps are [FXT: comb/necklace-fkm-demo.cc]:

```
1        for (ulong i=1; i<=n; ++i)  f[i] = 0;  // Initialize to zero
2        bool nq = 1;   // whether pre-necklace is a necklace
3        bool lq = 0;   // whether pre-necklace is a Lyndon word
4        ulong j = 1;
5        while ( 1 )
6        {
7            // Print necklace:
8            cout << setw(4) << pct << ":";
9            print_vec("    ", f+1, n, true);
10           cout << "    j=" << j;
11           if ( nq )  cout << "  N";
12           if ( lq )  cout << "  L";
13           cout << endl;
14
15           // Find largest index where we can increment:
16           j = n;
17           while ( f[j]==k-1 )  { --j; };
18
19           if ( j==0 )  break;
20
21           ++f[j];
22
23           // Copy periodically:
24           for (ulong i=1,t=j+1; t<=n; ++i,++t)  f[t] = f[i];
25
26           nq = ( (n%j)==0 );  // necklace if j divides n
27           lq = ( j==n );       // Lyndon word if j equals n
28       }
```

Two example runs are shown in figure 18.1-A. An efficient implementation of the algorithm is [FXT: class `necklace` in comb/necklace.h]:

```
1    class necklace
2    {
3    public:
4        ulong *a_;   // the string, NOTE: one-based
5        ulong *dv_;  // delta sequence of divisors of n
6        ulong n_;    // length of strings
7        ulong m1_;   // m-ary strings, m1=m-1
8        ulong j_;    // period of the word (if necklaces)
9
10   public:
11       necklace(ulong m, ulong n)
12       {
13           n_ = ( n ? n : 1 );  // at least 1
14           m1_ = ( m>1 ? m-1 : 1); // at least 2
15           a_ = new ulong[n_+1];
16           dv_ = new ulong[n_+1];
17           for (ulong j=1; j<=n; ++j)  dv_[j] = ( 0==(n_%j ) );  // divisors
18           first();
19       }
20   [--snip--]
21
22       void first()
23       {
24           for (ulong j=0; j<=n_; ++j)  a_[j] = 0;
25           j_ = 1;
26       }
27   [--snip--]
```

The method to compute the next pre-necklace is

```
1        ulong next_pre()  // next pre-necklace
2        // return j (zero when finished)
3        {
4            // Find rightmost digit that can be incremented:
5            ulong j = n_;
6            while ( a_[j] == m1_ )  { --j; }
7
8            // Increment:
9            // if ( 0==j_ )   return 0;  // last
10           ++a_[j];
11
12           // Copy periodically:
```

```
13          for (ulong k=j+1; k<=n_; ++k)  a_[k] = a_[k-j];
14
15          j_ = j;
16          return  j;
17      }
```

Note the commented out return with the last word, this gives a speedup (and no harm is done with the following copying). The array `dv` is used to determine whether the current pre-necklace is also a necklace (or Lyndon word) via simple lookups:

```
1      bool is_necklace()  const
2      {
3          return ( 0!=dv_[j_] );  // whether j divides n
4      }
5
6      bool is_lyn()  const
7      {
8          return ( j_==n_ );  // whether j equals n
9      }
10
```

The methods for the computation of the next necklace or Lyndon word are

```
1      ulong next()  // next necklace
2      {
3          do
4          {
5              next_pre();
6              if ( 0==j_ )  return 0;
7          }
8          while ( 0==dv_[j_] );  // until j divides n
9          return j_;
10     }
11
12     ulong next_lyn()  // next Lyndon word
13     {
14         do
15         {
16             next_pre();
17             if ( 0==j_ )  return 0;
18         }
19         while ( j_==n_ );  // until j equals n
20         return j_;  // == n
21     }
22 };
```

The rate of generation for pre-necklaces is about 98 M/s for base 2, 140 M/s for base 3, and 180 M/s for base 4 [FXT: comb/necklace-demo.cc]. A specialization of the algorithm for binary necklaces is [FXT: **class binary_necklace** in comb/binary-necklace.h]. The rate of generation for pre-necklaces is about 128 M/s [FXT: comb/binary-necklace-demo.cc]. A version of the algorithm that produces the binary necklaces as bits of a word is given in section 1.13.3 on page 30.

The binary necklaces of length n can be used as cycle leaders in the length-2^n zip permutation (and its inverse) that is discussed in section 2.10 on page 125. An algorithm for the generation of all irreducible binary polynomials via Lyndon words is described in section 40.10 on page 856.

18.1.2 Binary Lyndon words with length a Mersenne exponent

The length-n binary Lyndon words for n an exponent of a Mersenne prime $M_n = 2^n - 1$ can be generated efficiently as binary expansions of the powers of a primitive root r of M_n until the second word with just one bit is reached. With $n = 7$, $M_7 = 127$ and the primitive root $r = 3$ we get the sequence shown in figure 18.1-B. The sequence of minimal primitive roots r_n of the first Mersenne primes $M_n = 2^n - 1$ is entry A096393 in [312]:

```
 2:  2      17:  3      107:  3
 3:  3      19:  3      127: 43
 5:  3      31:  7      521:  3
 7:  3      61: 37      607:  5   <--= 5 is a primitive root of 2**607-1
13: 17      89:  3     1279:  5
```

```
           0  :    a=  ......1 =        1    ==  ......1
           1  :    a=  .....11 =        3    ==  .....11
           2  :    a=  ...1..1 =        9    ==  ...1..1
           3  :    a=  ..11.11 =       27    ==  ..11.11
           4  :    a=  1.1...1 =       81    ==  ...11.1
           5  :    a=  111.1.. =      116    ==  ..111.1
           6  :    a=  1.1111. =       94    ==  .1.1111
           7  :    a=  ...111. =       28    ==  ....111
           8  :    a=  1.1.1.. =       84    ==  ..1.1.1
           9  :    a=  11111.1 =      125    ==  .111111
          10  :    a=  1111..1 =      121    ==  ..11111
          11  :    a=  11.11.1 =      109    ==  .11.111
          12  :    a=  1..1..1 =       73    ==  ..1..11
          13  :    a=  1.111.. =       92    ==  ..1.111
          14  :    a=  ..1.11. =       22    ==  ...1.11
          15  :    a=  1....1. =       66    ==  ....1.1
          16  :    a=  1..111 =        71    ==  ...1111
          17  :    a=  1.1.1.. =       86    ==  .1.1.11
          18  :    a=  ....1.. =        4    ==  ......1   <--= sequence restarts
          19  :    a=  ...11.. =       12    ==  ......11
          20  :    a=  .1..1.. =       36    ==  ...1..1
          21  :    a=  11.11.. =      108    ==  ..11.11
          22  :    a=  1...11. =       70    ==  ...11.1
          23  :    a=  1.1..11 =       83    ==  ..111.1
          24  :    a=  1111.1. =      122    ==  .1.1111
          25  :    a=  111.... =      112    ==  ....111
          [--snip--]
```

Figure 18.1-B: Generation of all (18) 7-bit Lyndon words as binary representations of the powers modulo 127 of the primitive root 3. The right column gives the cyclic minima. Dots are used for zeros.

18.1.3   A constant amortized time (CAT) algorithm

A constant amortized time (CAT) algorithm to generate all k-ary length-n pre-necklaces is given in [95]. The crucial part of a recursive algorithm [FXT: comb/necklace-cat-demo.cc] is the function

```
1    ulong K, N;   // K-ary pre-necklaces of length N
2    ulong f[N];
3    void crsms_gen(ulong n, ulong j)
4    {
5        if ( n > N )  visit(j);  // pre-necklace in f[1,...,N]
6        else
7        {
8            f[n] = f[n-j];
9            crsms_gen(n+1, j);
10
11           for (ulong i=f[n-j]+1; i<K; ++i)
12           {
13               f[n] = i;
14               crsms_gen(n+1, n);
15           }
16       }
17   }
```

After initializing the array with zeros the function must be called with both arguments equal to 1. The routine generates about 71 million binary pre-necklaces per second. Ternary and 5-ary pre-necklaces are generated at a rate of about 100 and 113 million per second, respectively.

18.1.4   An order with fewer transitions

The following routine generates the binary pre-necklaces words in the order that would be generated by selecting valid words from the binary Gray code:

```
1    void xgen(ulong n, ulong j, int x=+1)
2    {
3        if ( n > N )  visit(j);
4        else
5        {
6            if ( -1==x )
7            {
8                if ( 0==f[n-j] )  { f[n] = 1;  xgen(n+1, n, -x); }
9                f[n] = f[n-j];  xgen(n+1, j, +x);
10           }
```

```
 1:  .......1       11:  ...11111        21:  ..1.1.11
 2:  ......11       12:  ...111.1        22:  ..1.1111
 3:  .....111       13:  ...1.1.1        23:  ..1.11.1
 4:  .....1.1       14:  ...1..111       24:  ..1...111  <<+1
 5:  ....11.1       15:  ...1...11       25:  ..1...1.1
 6:  ....1111       16:  ..11.111  <<+1  26:  .11.1111   <<+2
 7:  ....1.11       17:  ..11.1.1        27:  .1111111
 8:  ....1..1       18:  ..1111.1        28:  .1.11.11   <<+1
 9:  ...11..1       19:  ..111111        29:  .1.11111
10:  ...11.11       20:  ..111.11        30:  .1.1.111
```

Figure 18.1-C: The 30 binary 8-bit Lyndon words in an order with few changes between successive words. Transitions where more than one bit changes are marked with a '<<'.

$n:$	X_n	$n:$	X_n	$n:$	X_n	$n:$	X_n	$n:$	X_n
1:	0	7:	2	13:	95	19:	2598	25:	85449
2:	0	8:	5	14:	163	20:	4546	26:	155431
3:	0	9:	11	15:	290	21:	8135	27:	284886
4:	0	10:	15	16:	479	22:	14427	28:	522292
5:	1	11:	34	17:	859	23:	26122	29:	963237
6:	1	12:	54	18:	1450	24:	46957	30:	1778145

Figure 18.1-D: Excess (with respect to Gray code) of the number of bits changed.

```
11        else
12        {
13            f[n] = f[n-j];  xgen(n+1, j, +x);
14            if ( 0==f[n-j] )  { f[n] = 1;  xgen(n+1, n, -x); }
15        }
16    }
17  }
```

The program [FXT: comb/necklace-gray-demo.cc] computes the binary Lyndon words with the given routine. The ordering has fewer transitions between successive words but is in general not a Gray code (for up to 6-bit words a Gray code is generated). Figure 18.1-C shows the output with 8-bit Lyndon words. The first $2^{\lfloor n/2 \rfloor} - 1$ Lyndon words of length n are in Gray code order. The number X_n of additional transitions of the length-n Lyndon words is, for $n \leq 30$, shown in figure 18.1-D.

18.1.5 An order with at most three changes per transition

```
 1:  .1111111        13:  ...1...1         25:  ..1.1111
 2:  .111.111        14:  ...1.1.1         26:  ..1.11.1
 3:  .11.1111  <<+1  15:  ...1.111         27:  ..1.1.11   <<+1
 4:  .1.1.111  <<+2  16:  .....111         28:  ..1..1.1   <<+2
 5:  .1.1.1.1        17:  .....1.1         29:  ..1...111
 6:  .1.11.11  <<+2  18:  .......1         30:  ..11.111
 7:  .1.11111        19:  ........         31:  ..11.1.1
 8:  ...11111        20:  ......11   <<+1  32:  ..11..11   <<+1
 9:  ...111.1        21:  .....1.11        33:  ..111.11
10:  ...11..1        22:  .....1..1        34:  ..1111.1   <<+1
11:  ...11.11        23:  .....11.1        35:  ..111111
12:  ...1..11        24:  ....1111         36:  11111111   <<+1
```

Figure 18.1-E: The 30 binary 8-bit necklaces in an order with at most 3 changes per transition. Transitions where more than one bit changes are marked with a '<<'.

An algorithm to generate necklaces in an order such that at most 3 elements change with each update is given in [352]. The recursion can be given as (corrected and shortened) [FXT: comb/necklace-gray3-demo.cc]:

```
1  long *f;  // data in f[1..m],  f[0] = 0
2  long N;   // word length
3  int k;    // k-ary necklaces, k==sigma in the paper
4
5  void gen3(int z, int t, int j)
6  {
7      if ( t > N ) { visit(j); }
```

$n:$	X_n	$n:$	X_n	$n:$	X_n	$n:$	X_n	$n:$	X_n
1:	0	7:	6	13:	200	19:	6462	25:	239008
2:	1	8:	12	14:	360	20:	11722	26:	441370
3:	2	9:	20	15:	628	21:	21234	27:	816604
4:	2	10:	38	16:	1128	22:	38754	28:	1515716
5:	2	11:	64	17:	1998	23:	70770	29:	2818928
6:	4	12:	116	18:	3606	24:	129970	30:	5256628

Figure 18.1-F: Excess (with respect to Gray code) of number of bits changed.

```
 8        else
 9        {
10            if ( (z&1)==0 ) // z (number of elements ==(k-1)) is even?
11            {
12                for (int i=f[t-j]; i<=k-1; ++i)
13                {
14                    f[t] = i;
15                    gen3( z+(i!=k-1), t+1, (i!=f[t-j]?t:j) );
16                }
17            }
18            else
19            {
20                for (int i=k-1; i>=f[t-j]; --i)
21                {
22                    f[t] = i;
23                    gen3( z+(i!=k-1), t+1, (i!=f[t-j]?t:j) );
24                }
25            }
26        }
27    }
```

The variable z counts the number of maximal elements. The output with length-8 binary necklaces is shown in figure 18.1-E. Selecting the necklaces from the reversed list of complemented Gray codes of the n-bit binary words produces the same list.

18.1.6   Binary necklaces of length 2^n via Gray-cycle leaders ‡

```
    16 cycles of length= 8              L=  1..1.11.   [ ...1.11. ]
 L=  1.......   [ 1........ ]           --> 11.111.1   [ ....1.11 ]
 L=  1......1   [ .1111111 ]           --> 1.11..11   [ 1....1.1 ]
 L=  1.....1.   [ ..1.1.1. ]           --> 111.1.1.   [ 11....1. ]
 L=  1.....11   [ 11.1.1.1 ]           --> 1..11111   [ .11....1 ]
 L=  1....1..   [ .1..11.. ]           --> 11.1....   [ 1.11.... ]
 L=  1....1.1   [ 1.11..11 ]           --> 1.111...   [ .1.11... ]
 L=  1....11.   [ 111..11. ]           --> 111..1..   [ ..1.11.. ]
 L=  1....111   [ ...11..1 ]
 L=  1..1....   [ .111.... ]           L=  1..1.111   [ 111.1..1 ]
 L=  1..1...1   [ 1...1111 ]           --> 11.111..   [ 1111.1.. ]
 L=  1..1..1.   [ 11.11.1. ]           --> 1.11..1.   [ .1111.1. ]
 L=  1..1..11   [ ...1.1.1 ]           --> 111.1.11   [ ..1111.1 ]
 L=  1..1.1..   [ 1.1111.. ]           --> 1..1111.   [ 1..1111. ]
 L=  1..1.1.1   [ .1....11 ]           --> 11.1...1   [ .1..1111 ]
 L=  1..1.11.   [ ...1.11. ]           --> 1.111..1   [ 1.1..111 ]
 L=  1..1.111   [ 111.1..1 ]           --> 111..1.1   [ 11.1..11 ]
```

Figure 18.1-G: Left: the cycle leaders (minima) L of the Gray permutation with highest bit at index 7 and their bit-wise Reed-Muller transforms $Y(L)$. Right: the last two cycles and the transforms of their elements.

The algorithm for the generation of cycle leaders for the Gray permutation given section 2.12.1 on page 128 and relation 1.19-10c on page 53, written as

$$S_k\, Y\, x \;=\; Y\, g^k\, x \tag{18.1-1}$$

(Y is the yellow code, the bit-wise Reed-Muller transform) can be used for generating the necklaces of length 2^n: The cyclic shifts of $Y\,x$ are equal to $Y\, g^k\, x$ for $k = 0,\ldots,l-1$ where l is the cycle length.

Figure 18.1-G shows the correspondence between cycles of the Gray permutation and cyclic shifts. It was generated with the program [FXT: comb/necklaces-via-gray-leaders-demo.cc].

If no better algorithm for the cycle leaders of the Gray permutation was known, we could generate them as $Y^{-1}(N) = Y(N)$ where N are the necklaces of length 2^n. The same idea, together with relation 1.19-11b on page 53, give the relation

$$S_k \, B \, x \;=\; B \, e^{-k} \, x \qquad (18.1\text{-}2)$$

where B is the blue code and e the reversed Gray code.

18.1.7 Binary necklaces via cyclic shifts and complements ‡

```
        n = 3           n = 6           n = 7             n = 8          [n=8 cont.]
   1:    ..1       1:  ....,1       1:  .....,1       1:  ......,1     19:  ..11..11
   2:    .11       2:  ....,11      2:  .....,11      2:  ......,11    20:  ....,1.1
   3:    111       3:  ...,111      3:  ....,111      3:  .....,111    21:  ....,1.11
                   4:  ..,1111      4:  ...,1111      4:  ....,1111    22:  ...,1.111
        n = 4      5:  .,11111      5:  ..,11111      5:  ...,11111    23:  ..,1.1111
   1:    ...1      6:  111111       6:  .,111111      6:  ..,111111    24:  .1,11111
   2:    ..11      7:  ..,11.1      7:  1111111       7:  .1111111     25:  ..,1.11.1
   3:    .111      8:  .11.11       8:  ..,111.1      8:  11111111     26:  .1.11.11
   4:    1111      9:  ...,1.1      9:  .,111.1       9:  ..,1111.1    27:  ...,1.1.1
   5:    .1.1      10: ..,1.11      10: ..,11.11      10: ..,111.1     28:  ..,1.1.11
                   11: .1.111       11: .11.111       11: .,1111.1     29:  .1.1.111
        n = 5      12: .1.1.1       12: ...,1.1       12: .111.111     30: .1.1.1.1
   1:    ....,1    13: ..,1..1      13: ..,1.11       13: ....,11.1    31:  ....,1..1
   2:    ...,11                     14: ..,1.111      14: ...,11.11    32:  ...,1..11
   3:    ..,111                     15: .1,1111       15: ..,11.111    33:  ..,1..111
   4:    .,1111                     16: ..,1.1.1      16: .11.1111     34:  ...,1..1.1
   5:    11111                      17: .1.1.11       17: ..,11.1.1    35:  ...,1...1
   6:    ..1.1                      18: ...,1..1      18: ...,11..1
   7:    .1.11                      19: ..,1..11
```

Figure 18.1-H: Nonzero binary necklaces of lengths $n = 3, 4, \ldots, 8$ as generated by the shift and complement algorithm.

A recursive algorithm to generate all nonzero binary necklaces via cyclic shifts and complements of the lowest bit is described in [287]. An implementation of the method is given in [FXT: comb/necklace-sigma-tau-demo.cc]:

```
1    inline ulong sigma(ulong x)  { return bit_rotate_left(x, 1, n); }
2    inline ulong tau(ulong x)  { return  x ^ 1; }
3
4    void search(ulong y)
5    {
6        visit(y);
7        ulong t = y;
8        while ( 1 )
9        {
10           t = sigma(t);
11           ulong x = tau(t);
12           if ( (x&1) && (x == bit_cyclic_min(x, n)) )  search(x);
13           else  break;
14       }
15   }
```

The initial call is `search(1)`. The generated ordering for lengths $n = 3, 4, \ldots, 8$ is shown in figure 18.1-H.

18.2 Lex-min De Bruijn sequence from necklaces

The lexicographically minimal De Bruijn sequence can be obtained from the necklaces in lexicographic order as shown in figure 18.2-A. Let W be a necklace with period p, and define its primitive part $P(W)$ to be the p rightmost digits of W. Then the lex-min De Bruijn sequence is the concatenation of the primitive parts of the necklaces in lex order.

An implementation is [FXT: **class debruijn** in comb/debruijn.h]:

```
           neckl.   period   P(neckl.)
           0000       1           0
           0001       4         0001
           0002       4         0002
           0011       4         0011
           0012       4         0012
           0021       4         0021
           0022       4         0022
           0101       2          01
           0102       4         0102
           0111       4         0111
           0112       4         0112
           0121       4         0121
           0122       4         0122
           0202       2          02
           0211       4         0211
           0212       4         0212
           0221       4         0221
           0222       4         0222
           1111       1           1
           1112       4         1112
           1122       4         1122
           1212       2          12
           1222       4         1222
           2222       1           2

 0 0001 0002 0011 0012 0021 0022 01 0102 0111 0112 [--snip--] 1122 12 1222 2 ==
 00001000200110012002100220101020111011201210122020211021202210222111211221212222
```

Figure 18.2-A: The 3-ary necklaces of length 4 (left) and their primitive parts (right). The concatenation of the primitive parts gives a De Bruijn sequence (bottom).

```
1    class debruijn : public necklace
2    // Lexicographic minimal De Bruijn sequence.
3    {
4    public:
5        ulong i_;   // position of current digit in current string
6
7    public:
8        debruijn(ulong m, ulong n)
9            : necklace(m, n)
10       { first_string(); }
11
12       ~debruijn()  { ; }
13
14       ulong first_string()
15       {
16           necklace::first();
17           i_ = 1;
18           return j_;
19       }
20
21       ulong next_string()  // make new string, return its length
22       {
23           necklace::next();
24           i_ = (j_ != 0);
25           return j_;
26       }
27
28       ulong next_digit()
29       // Return current digit and move to next digit.
30       // Return m if previous was last.
31       {
32           if ( i_ == 0 )  return necklace::m1_ + 1;
33           ulong d = a_[ i_ ];
34           if ( i_ == j_ )  next_string();
35           else  ++i_;
36           return d;
37       }
38
39       ulong first_digit()
40       {
41           first_string();
42           return next_digit();
```

```
43        }
44   };
```

Usage is demonstrated in [FXT: comb/debruijn-demo.cc]:

```
1        ulong m = 3;  //  m-ary De Bruijn sequence
2        ulong n = 4;  //  length = m**n
3        debruijn S(m, n);
4        ulong i = S.first_string();
5        do
6        {
7            cout << " ";
8            for (ulong u=1; u<=i; ++u)  cout << S.a_[u];  // note: one-based array
9            i = S.next_string();
10       }
11       while ( i );
```

For digit by digit generation, use

```
1        ulong i = S.first_digit();
2        do
3        {
4            cout << i;
5            i = S.next_digit();
6        }
7        while ( i!=m );
```

A special version for binary necklaces is [FXT: class binary_debruijn in comb/binary-debruijn.h].

18.3 The number of binary necklaces

$n:$	N_n	$n:$	N_n	$n:$	N_n	$n:$	N_n
1:	2	11:	188	21:	99880	31:	69273668
2:	3	12:	352	22:	190746	32:	134219796
3:	4	13:	632	23:	364724	33:	260301176
4:	6	14:	1182	24:	699252	34:	505294128
5:	8	15:	2192	25:	1342184	35:	981706832
6:	14	16:	4116	26:	2581428	36:	1908881900
7:	20	17:	7712	27:	4971068	37:	3714566312
8:	36	18:	14602	28:	9587580	38:	7233642930
9:	60	19:	27596	29:	18512792	39:	14096303344
10:	108	20:	52488	30:	35792568	40:	27487816992

Figure 18.3-A: The number of binary necklaces for $n \leq 40$.

$n:$	L_n	$n:$	L_n	$n:$	L_n	$n:$	L_n
1:	2	11:	186	21:	99858	31:	69273666
2:	1	12:	335	22:	190557	32:	134215680
3:	2	13:	630	23:	364722	33:	260300986
4:	3	14:	1161	24:	698870	34:	505286415
5:	6	15:	2182	25:	1342176	35:	981706806
6:	9	16:	4080	26:	2580795	36:	1908866960
7:	18	17:	7710	27:	4971008	37:	3714566310
8:	30	18:	14532	28:	9586395	38:	7233615333
9:	56	19:	27594	29:	18512790	39:	14096302710
10:	99	20:	52377	30:	35790267	40:	27487764474

Figure 18.3-B: The number of binary Lyndon words for $n \leq 40$.

The number of binary necklaces of length n equals

$$N_n = \frac{1}{n} \sum_{d \backslash n} \varphi(d)\, 2^{n/d} = \frac{1}{n} \sum_{j=1}^{n} 2^{\gcd(j,n)} \qquad (18.3\text{-}1)$$

The values for $n \leq 40$ are shown in figure 18.3-A. The sequence is entry A000031 in [312].

The number of Lyndon words (aperiodic necklaces) equals

$$L_n = \frac{1}{n} \sum_{d \backslash n} \mu(d)\, 2^{n/d} = \frac{1}{n} \sum_{d \backslash n} \mu(n/d)\, 2^{d} \qquad (18.3\text{-}2)$$

The Möbius function μ is defined in relation 37.1-6 on page 705. The values for $n \leq 40$ are given in figure 18.3-B. The sequence is entry A001037 in [312]. Replacing 2 by k in the formulas for N_n and L_n gives expressions for k-ary necklaces and Lyndon words.

For prime $n = p$ we have $L_p = N_p - 2$ and

$$L_p = \frac{2^p - 2}{p} = \frac{1}{p} \sum_{k=1}^{p-1} \binom{p}{k} \qquad (18.3\text{-}3)$$

The latter form tells us that there are exactly $\binom{p}{k}/p$ Lyndon words with k ones for $1 \leq k \leq p-1$. The difference of 2 is due to the necklaces that consist of all zeros or ones. The number of irreducible binary polynomials (see section 40.6 on page 843) of degree n also equals L_n. For the equivalence between necklaces and irreducible polynomials see section 40.10 on page 856.

Let d be a divisor of n. There are 2^n binary words of length n, each having some period d that divides n. There are d different shifts of the corresponding word, thereby

$$2^n = \sum_{d \backslash n} d\, L_d \qquad (18.3\text{-}4)$$

Möbius inversion gives relation 18.3-2. The necklaces of length n and period d are a concatenation of n/d Lyndon words of length d, so

$$N_n = \sum_{d \backslash n} L_d \qquad (18.3\text{-}5)$$

We note the relations (see section 37.2 on page 709)

$$(1 - 2x) = \prod_{k=1}^{\infty} (1 - x^k)^{L_k} \qquad (18.3\text{-}6\text{a})$$

$$\sum_{k=1}^{\infty} L_k\, x^k = \sum_{k=1}^{\infty} \frac{-\mu(k)}{k} \log\left(1 - 2\,x^k\right) \qquad (18.3\text{-}6\text{b})$$

Defining

$$\eta_B(x) := \prod_{k=1}^{\infty} \left(1 - B\, x^k\right) \qquad (18.3\text{-}7\text{a})$$

we have

$$\eta_2(x) = \prod_{k=1}^{\infty} (1 - x^k)^{N_k} \qquad (18.3\text{-}7\text{b})$$

$$\eta_2(x) = \prod_{k=1}^{\infty} \eta_1(x^k)^{L_k} \qquad (18.3\text{-}7\text{c})$$

n:	N_n	$N_{(n,0)}$	$N_{(n,1)}$	$N_{(n,2)}$	$N_{(n,3)}$	$N_{(n,4)}$	$N_{(n,5)}$	$N_{(n,6)}$	$N_{(n,7)}$	$N_{(n,8)}$	$N_{(n,9)}$	$N_{(n,10)}$
1:	2	1	1									
2:	3	1	1	1								
3:	4	1	1	1	1							
4:	6	1	1	2	1	1						
5:	8	1	1	2	2	1	1					
6:	14	1	1	3	4	3	1	1				
7:	20	1	1	3	5	5	3	1	1			
8:	36	1	1	4	7	10	7	4	1	1		
9:	60	1	1	4	10	14	14	10	4	1	1	
10:	108	1	1	5	12	22	26	22	12	5	1	1
11:	188	1	1	5	15	30	42	42	30	15	5	1
12:	352	1	1	6	19	43	66	80	66	43	19	6
13:	632	1	1	6	22	55	99	132	132	99	55	22
14:	1182	1	1	7	26	73	143	217	246	217	143	73
15:	2192	1	1	7	31	91	201	335	429	429	335	201
16:	4116	1	1	8	35	116	273	504	715	810	715	504
17:	7712	1	1	8	40	140	364	728	1144	1430	1430	1144
18:	14602	1	1	9	46	172	476	1038	1768	2438	2704	2438
19:	27596	1	1	9	51	204	612	1428	2652	3978	4862	4862
20:	52488	1	1	10	57	245	776	1944	3876	6310	8398	9252

Figure 18.3-C: The number $N_{(n,z)}$ of binary necklaces of length n with z zeros.

n:	L_n	$L_{(n,0)}$	$L_{(n,1)}$	$L_{(n,2)}$	$L_{(n,3)}$	$L_{(n,4)}$	$L_{(n,5)}$	$L_{(n,6)}$	$L_{(n,7)}$	$L_{(n,8)}$	$L_{(n,9)}$	$L_{(n,10)}$
1:	2	1	1									
2:	1	0	1	0								
3:	2	0	1	1	0							
4:	3	0	1	1	1	0						
5:	6	0	1	2	2	1	0					
6:	9	0	1	2	3	2	1	0				
7:	18	0	1	3	5	5	3	1	0			
8:	30	0	1	3	7	8	7	3	1	0		
9:	56	0	1	4	9	14	14	9	4	1	0	
10:	99	0	1	4	12	20	25	20	12	4	1	0
11:	186	0	1	5	15	30	42	42	30	15	5	1
12:	335	0	1	5	18	40	66	75	66	40	18	5
13:	630	0	1	6	22	55	99	132	132	99	55	22
14:	1161	0	1	6	26	70	143	212	245	212	143	70
15:	2182	0	1	7	30	91	200	333	429	429	333	200
16:	4080	0	1	7	35	112	273	497	715	800	715	497
17:	7710	0	1	8	40	140	364	728	1144	1430	1430	1144
18:	14532	0	1	8	45	168	476	1026	1768	2424	2700	2424
19:	27594	0	1	9	51	204	612	1428	2652	3978	4862	4862
20:	52377	0	1	9	57	240	775	1932	3876	6288	8398	9225

Figure 18.3-D: The number $L_{(n,z)}$ of binary Lyndon words of length n with z zeros.

18.3.1 Binary necklaces with fixed density

Let $N_{(n,n_0)}$ be the number of binary length-n necklaces with exactly n_0 zeros (and $n_1 = n - n_0$ ones) the *necklaces with fixed density*. We have

$$N_{(n,n_0)} \;=\; \frac{1}{n} \sum_{j \backslash \gcd(n,n_0)} \varphi(j) \binom{n/j}{n_0/j} \tag{18.3-8}$$

Bit-wise complementing gives the symmetry relation $N_{(n,n_0)} = N_{(n,n-n_0)} = N_{(n,n_1)}$. A table of small values is given in figure 18.3-C.

Let $L_{(n,n_0)}$ be the number of binary length-n Lyndon words with exactly n_0 zeros (*Lyndon words with fixed density*), then

$$L_{(n,n_0)} \;=\; \frac{1}{n} \sum_{j \backslash \gcd(n,n_0)} \mu(j) \binom{n/j}{n_0/j} \tag{18.3-9}$$

The symmetry relation is the same as for $N_{(n,n_0)}$. A table of small values is given in figure 18.3-D.

18.3.2 Binary necklaces with even or odd weight

Summing $N_{(n,k)}$ over all even or odd $k \le n$ gives the number of necklaces of even (symbol E_n) or odd (O_n) weight, respectively. The first few values, the differences $E_n - O_n$, and the sums $E_n + O_n = N_n$:

Neckl. n:	1	2	3	4	5	6	7	8	9	10	11	12	13	14	15	16	17
E_n:	1	2	2	4	4	8	10	20	30	56	94	180	316	596	1096	2068	3856
O_n:	1	1	2	2	4	6	10	16	30	52	94	172	316	586	1096	2048	3856
$E_n - O_n$:	0	1	0	2	0	2	0	4	0	4	0	8	0	10	0	20	0
$E_n + O_n$:	2	3	4	6	8	14	20	36	60	108	188	352	632	1182	2192	4116	7712

The number of Lyndon words of even (e_n) and odd (o_n) weight can be computed in the same way:

Lyn. n:	1	2	3	4	5	6	7	8	9	10	11	12	13	14	15	16	17
e_n:	0	0	1	1	3	4	9	14	28	48	93	165	315	576	1091	2032	3855
o_n:	1	1	1	2	3	5	9	16	28	51	93	170	315	585	1091	2048	3855
$e_n - o_n$:	−1	−1	0	−1	0	−1	0	−2	0	−3	0	−5	0	−9	0	−16	0
$e_n + o_n$:	1	1	2	3	6	9	18	30	56	99	186	335	630	1161	2182	4080	7710

The differences between the number of necklaces and Lyndon words are:

n:	1	2	3	4	5	6	7	8	9	10	11	12	13	14	15	16	17
$E_n - e_n$:	1	2	1	3	1	4	1	6	2	8	1	15	1	20	5	36	1
$O_n - o_n$:	0	0	1	0	1	1	1	0	2	1	1	2	1	1	5	0	1
$E_n - o_n$:	0	1	1	2	1	3	1	4	2	5	1	10	1	11	5	20	1
$O_n - e_n$:	1	1	1	1	1	2	1	2	2	4	1	7	1	10	5	16	1

18.3.3 Necklaces with fixed content

Let $N_{(n_0,n_1,\ldots,n_{k-1})}$ be the number of k-symbol length-n necklaces with n_j occurrences of symbol j, the number of such *necklaces with fixed content*, we have ($n = \sum_{j<s} n_j$ and):

$$N_{(n_0,n_1,\ldots,n_{k-1})} \;=\; \frac{1}{n} \sum_{d \backslash g} \varphi(d) \frac{(n/d)!}{(n_0/d)! \cdots (n_{k-1}/d)!} \tag{18.3-10}$$

where $g = \gcd(n_0, n_1, \ldots, n_{k-1})$. The equivalent formula for the *Lyndon words with fixed content* is

$$L_{(n_0,n_1,\ldots,n_{k-1})} \;=\; \frac{1}{n} \sum_{d \backslash g} \mu(d) \frac{(n/d)!}{(n_0/d)! \cdots (n_{k-1}/d)!} \tag{18.3-11}$$

where $g = \gcd(n_0, n_1, \ldots, n_{k-1})$. The relations are taken from [289] and [300], which also give efficient algorithms for the generation of necklaces and Lyndon words with fixed density and content, respectively. The number of strings with fixed content is a *multinomial coefficient*, see relation 13.2-1a on page 296. A method for the generation of all necklaces with forbidden substrings is given in [290].

18.4 Sums of roots of unity that are zero ‡

```
        bitstring       subset
 1:  ............   1    (empty sum)
 2:  .....1.....1   6    0 6
 3:  ....11....11   6    0 1 6 7
 4:  ...1...1...1   4    0 4 8        cyclic shifts are  1 5 9,  2 6 10,  3 7 11
 5:  ...1.1...1.1   6    0 2 6 8
 6:  ...11..1..11  12 L  0 1 4 7 8         Lyndon word
 7:  ...111...111   6    0 1 2 6 7 8
 8:  ..1..1..1..1   3    0 3 6 9
 9:  ..1.11..1.11   6    0 1 3 6 7 9
10:  ..11..11..11   4    0 1 4 5 8 9
11:  ..11.1..11.1   6    0 2 3 6 8 9
12:  ..11.11...111 12 L  0 1 2 5 6 8 9       Lyndon word
13:  ..1111..1111   6    0 1 2 3 6 7 8 9
14:  .1.1.1.1.1.1   2    0 2 4 6 8 10
15:  .1.111.1.111   6    0 1 2 4 6 7 8 10
16:  .11.11.11.11   3    0 1 3 4 6 7 9 10
17:  .111.111.111   4    0 1 2 4 5 6 8 9 10
18:  .1111.11111   6    0 1 2 3 4 6 7 8 9 10
19:  111111111111   1    0 1 2 3 4 5 6 7 8 9 10 11 (all roots of unity)
```

Figure 18.4-A: All subsets of the 12-th roots of unity that add to zero, modulo cyclic shifts.

Let $\omega = \exp(2\pi i/n)$ be a primitive n-th root of unity and S be a subset of the set of n elements. We compute all S such that $\sigma_S = 0$ where $\sigma_S := \sum_{e \in S} \omega^e$ [FXT: comb/root-sums-demo.cc]. If $\sigma_S = 0$ then $\omega^k \sigma_S = 0$ for all k, so we can ignore cyclic shifts, see figure 18.4-A. For n prime only the empty set and all roots of unity add to zero (no proper subset of all roots can add to zero: ω would be a root of a polynomial that has the cyclotomic polynomial $Y_n = 1 + x + \ldots + x^{n-1}$ as divisor which is impossible). All necklaces that are not Lyndon words correspond to a zero sum. The smallest nontrivial cases where Lyndon words lead to zero sums occur for $n = 12$ (marked with 'L' in figure 18.4-A).

Sequence A164896 in [312] gives the number of subsets adding to zero (modulo cyclic shifts), sequence A110981 the number of subsets that are Lyndon words and A103314 the number of subsets where cyclic shifts are considered as different.

Chapter 19

Hadamard and conference matrices

The matrices corresponding to the Walsh transforms (see chapter 23 on page 459) are special cases of Hadamard matrices. Such matrices also exist for certain sizes $N \times N$ for N not a power of 2. We give construction schemes for Hadamard matrices that come from the theory of finite fields.

If we denote the transform matrix for an N-point Walsh transform by $\mathbf{H}$, then

$$\mathbf{H}\,\mathbf{H}^T \;=\; N \,\mathrm{id} \tag{19.0-1}$$

where id is the unit matrix. The matrix $\mathbf{H}$ is orthogonal (up to normalization) and its determinant equals

$$\det(\mathbf{H}) \;=\; \det\left(\mathbf{H}\,\mathbf{H}^T\right)^{1/2} = N^{N/2} \tag{19.0-2}$$

Further, all entries are either $+1$ or -1. An orthogonal matrix with these properties is called a *Hadamard matrix*. We know that for $N = 2^n$ we always can find such a matrix. For $N = 2$ we have

$$\mathbf{H}_2 \;=\; \begin{bmatrix} +1 & +1 \\ +1 & -1 \end{bmatrix} \tag{19.0-3}$$

and we can use the Kronecker product (see section 23.3 on page 462) to construct $\mathbf{H}_{2N}$ from $\mathbf{H}_N$ via

$$\mathbf{H}_n \;=\; \begin{bmatrix} +\mathbf{H}_{N/2} & +\mathbf{H}_{N/2} \\ +\mathbf{H}_{N/2} & -\mathbf{H}_{N/2} \end{bmatrix} = \mathbf{H}_2 \otimes \mathbf{H}_{N/2} \tag{19.0-4}$$

The problem of determining Hadamard matrices (especially for N not a power of 2) comes from combinatorics. Hadamard matrices of size $N \times N$ can only exist if N equals 1, 2, or $4\,k$.

19.1 Hadamard matrices via LFSR

We start with a construction for certain Hadamard matrices for N a power of 2 that uses m-sequences that are created by shift registers (see section 41.1 on page 864). Figure 19.1-A shows three Hadamard matrices that were constructed as follows:

1. Choose $N = 2^n$ and create a maximum length binary shift register sequence S of length $N - 1$.

2. Make S signed, that is, replace all ones by -1 and all zeros by $+1$.

3. The $N \times N$ matrix $\mathbf{H}$ is computed by filling the first row and the first column with ones and filling the remaining entries with cyclic copies of s: for $r = 1, 2, \ldots N - 1$ and $c = 1, 2, \ldots N - 1$ set $\mathbf{H}_{r,c} := S_{c-r+1 \bmod N-1}$.

The matrices in figure 19.1-A were produced with the program [FXT: comb/hadamard-srs-demo.cc].

```
1    #include "bpol/lfsr.h" // class lfsr
2    #include "aux1/copy.h"  // copy_cyclic()
3
4    #include "matrix/matrix.h"  // class matrix
5    typedef matrix<int>  Smat;  // matrix with integer entries
```

J. Arndt, *Matters Computational: Ideas, Algorithms, Source Code*,
DOI 10.1007/978-3-642-14764-7_19, © Springer-Verlag Berlin Heidelberg 2011

```
Signed SRS:                          Signed SRS:                Signed SRS:
- + + - + + - - + - + - - -          - + + - + - -               - + -
Hadamard matrix H:                   Hadamard matrix H:         Hadamard matrix H:
+ + + + + + + + + + + + + + +        + + + + + + + +            + + + +
+ - + + + + - + + - - + - + - -      + - + + + - + - -          + - + -
+ - - + + + - + + - - + - + - -      + - - + + - + -            + - - +
+ - - - + + + - + + - - + - + -      + - - - + + - +            + + - -
+ - - - - + + + - + + - - + - +      + + - - - + + -
+ + - - - - + + + - + + - - + -      + - + - - - + +
+ - + - - - - + + + - + + - - +      + + - + - - - +
+ + - + - - - - + + + - + + - -      + + + - + - - -
+ - + - + - - - - + + + - + + -
+ - - + - + - - - - + + + - + +
+ + - - + - + - - - - + + + - +
+ + + - - + - + - - - - + + + -
+ - + + - + - + - - - - - + + +
+ + - + + - + - + - - - - - + +
+ + + - + + - + - - + - + - - - +
+ + + + - + + - - + - + - - - -
```

Figure 19.1-A: Hadamard matrices created with binary shift register sequences (SRS) of maximum length. Only the sign of the entries is given, all entries are ±1.

```
6
7   [--snip--]
8     ulong n = 5;
9     ulong N = 1UL << n;
10  [--snip--]
11
12    // --- create signed SRS:
13    int vec[N-1];
14    lfsr S(n);
15    for (ulong k=0; k<N-1; ++k)
16    {
17        ulong x = 1UL & S.get_a();
18        vec[k] = ( x ? -1 : +1 );
19        S.next();
20    }
21
22    // --- create Hadamard matrix:
23    Smat H(N,N);
24    for (c=0; c<N; ++c)  H.set(0, c, +1);   // first row = [1,1,1,...,1]
25    for (ulong r=1; r<N; ++r)
26    {
27        H.set(r, 0, +1);   // first column = [1,1,1,...,1]^T
28        copy_cyclic(vec, H.rowp_[r]+1, N-1, N-r);
29    }
30  [--snip--]
```

The function `copy_cyclic()` is defined in [FXT: aux1/copy.h]:

```
1   template <typename Type>
2   inline void copy_cyclic(const Type *src, Type *dst, ulong n, ulong s)
3   // Copy array src[] to dst[]
4   // starting from position s in src[]
5   // wrap around end of src[]  (src[n-1])
6   //
7   // src[] is assumed to be of length n
8   // dst[] must be length n at least
9   //
10  // Equivalent to:  { acopy(src, dst, n); rotate_right(dst, n, s)}
11  {
12      ulong k = 0;
13      while ( s<n )  dst[k++] = src[s++];
14
15      s = 0;
16      while ( k<n )  dst[k++] = src[s++];
17  }
```

If we define the matrix $\mathbf{X}$ to be the $(N-1) \times (N-1)$ block of $\mathbf{H}$ obtained by deleting the first row and column, then we have

$$\mathbf{X}\mathbf{X}^T = \begin{bmatrix} N-1 & -1 & -1 & \cdots & -1 \\ -1 & N-1 & -1 & \cdots & -1 \\ -1 & -1 & N-1 & \cdots & -1 \\ \vdots & \vdots & & \ddots & \vdots \\ -1 & -1 & -1 & \cdots & N-1 \end{bmatrix} \tag{19.1-1}$$

Equivalently, for the (cyclic) auto-correlation of S (see section 41.6 on page 875):

$$\sum_{k=0}^{L-1} S_k \, S_{k+\tau \bmod L} = \begin{cases} +L & \text{if } \tau = 0 \\ -1 & \text{otherwise} \end{cases} \tag{19.1-2}$$

where $L = N - 1$ is the length of the sequence.

An alternative way to find Hadamard matrices of dimension 2^n is to use the signs in the multiplication table for hypercomplex numbers described in section 39.14 on page 815.

19.2   Hadamard matrices via conference matrices

```
Quadratic characters modulo 13:      Quadratic characters modulo 11:
 0 + - + + - - - - + + - +            0 + - + + + - - - + - +
14x14 conference matrix C:           12x12 conference matrix C:
 0 + + + + + + + + + + + +            0 + + + + + + + + + + +
 + 0 + - + + - - - - + + +            - 0 + - + + - - - - + -
 + + 0 + - + + - - - - + + -          - - 0 + - + + - - - - +
 + - + 0 + - + + - - - - + +          - + - 0 + - + + - - - -
 + + - + 0 + - + + - - - - +          - - + - 0 + - + + - - -
 + + + - + 0 + - + + - - - -          - - - + - 0 + - + + - -
 + - + + - + 0 + - + + - - -          - - - - + - 0 + - + + -
 + - - + + - + 0 + - + + - -          - + - - - + - 0 + - + +
 + - - - + + - + 0 + - + + -          - + + - - - + - 0 + - +
 + - - - - + + - + 0 + - + +          - + + + - - - + - 0 + -
 + + - - - - + + - + 0 + - +          - - + + + - - - + - 0 +
 + + + - - - - + + - + 0 + -          - + - + + + - - - + - 0
 + - + + - - - - + + - + 0 +
 + + - + + - - - - + + - + 0
```

Figure 19.2-A: Two Conference matrices, the entries not on the diagonal are ± 1 and only the sign is given. The left is a symmetric 14×14 matrix ($13 \equiv 1 \bmod 4$), the right is an antisymmetric 12×12 matrix ($11 \equiv 3 \bmod 4$). Replacing all diagonal elements of the right matrix with $+1$ gives a 12×12 Hadamard matrix.

```
12x12 Hadamard matrix H:           Quadratic characters modulo 5:
 + + + + + + - + + + + +             0 + - - +
 + + + - - + + - + - - +            6x6 conference matrix C:
 + + + - - + + - + - - -             0 + + + + +
 + - + + + - + - + - + -             + 0 + - - +
 + - - + + + + + - - + +             + + 0 + - -
 + - - - + + + + + - - +             + - + 0 + -
 - + + + + + - - - - - -             + - - + 0 +
 + - + - - + - - - + + -             + + - - + 0
 + + + - + - - - - - + +
 + - + - + - + - - - - +
 + - - + - + - + + - - -
 + + - - + - - - + + - -
```

Figure 19.2-B: A Hadamard matrix (left) created from a symmetric conference matrix (right).

A *conference matrix* $\mathbf{C}_Q$ is a $Q \times Q$ matrix with zero diagonal and all other entries ± 1 so that

$$\mathbf{C}_Q \mathbf{C}_Q^T = (Q-1)\,\mathrm{id} \tag{19.2-1}$$

We give an algorithm for computing a conference matrix $\mathbf{C}_Q$ for $Q = q + 1$ where q is an odd prime:

1. Create a length-q array S with entries $S_k \in \{-1, 0, +1\}$ as follows: set $S_0 = 0$ and, for $1 \leq k < q$ set $S_k = +1$ if k is a square modulo q, $S_k = -1$ else.

2. Set $y = 1$ if $q \equiv 1 \bmod 4$, else $y = -1$ (then $q \equiv 3 \bmod 4$).

3. Set $\mathbf{C}_{0,0} = 0$ and $\mathbf{C}_Q[0, k] = +1$ for $1 \leq k < Q$ (first row). Set $\mathbf{C}_Q[k, 0] = y$ for $1 \leq k < Q$ (first column). Fill the remaining entries with cyclic copies of S: for $1 \leq r < q$ and $1 \leq c < q$ set $\mathbf{C}_Q[r, c] = S_{c-r+1 \bmod q}$.

The quantity y tells us whether $\mathbf{C}_Q$ is symmetric ($y = +1$) or antisymmetric ($y = -1$). If $\mathbf{C}_Q$ is antisymmetric, then

$$\mathbf{H}_Q = \mathbf{C}_Q + \mathrm{id} \tag{19.2-2}$$

is a $Q \times Q$ Hadamard matrix. For example, replacing all zeros in the 12×12 matrix in figure 19.2-A by $+1$ gives a 12×12 Hadamard matrix. If $\mathbf{C}_Q$ is symmetric, then a $2Q \times 2Q$ Hadamard matrix is given by

$$\mathbf{H}_{2Q} := \begin{bmatrix} +\,\mathrm{id} +\mathbf{C}_Q & -\,\mathrm{id} +\mathbf{C}_Q \\ -\,\mathrm{id} +\mathbf{C}_Q & -\,\mathrm{id} -\mathbf{C}_Q \end{bmatrix} \tag{19.2-3}$$

Figure 19.2-B shows a 12×12 Hadamard matrix that was created using this formula. The construction of Hadamard matrices via conference matrices is due to Raymond Paley.

The program [FXT: comb/conference-quadres-demo.cc] outputs for a given q the $Q \times Q$ conference matrix and the corresponding Hadamard matrix:

```
1   #include "mod/numtheory.h" // kronecker()
2   #include "matrix/matrix.h"  // class matrix
3   #include "aux1/copy.h" // copy_cyclic()
4
5     [--snip--]
6     int y = ( 1==q%4 ? +1 : -1 );
7     ulong Q = q+1;
8     [--snip--]
9     // --- create table of quadratic characters modulo q:
10    int vec[q];  fill<int>(vec, q, -1);  vec[0] = 0;
11    for (ulong k=1; k<(q+1)/2; ++k)  vec[(k*k)%q] = +1;
12    [--snip--]
13    // --- create Q x Q conference matrix:
14    Smat C(Q,Q);
15    C.set(0,0, 0);
16    for (ulong c=1; c<Q; ++c)  C.set(0, c, +1);  // first row = [1,1,1,...,1]
17    for (ulong r=1; r<Q; ++r)
18    {
19        C.set(r, 0, y);  // first column = +-[1,1,1,...,1]^T
20        copy_cyclic(vec, C.rowp_[r]+1, q, Q-r);
21    }
22    [--snip--]
23    // --- create a N x N Hadamard matrix:
24    ulong N = ( y<0 ? Q : 2*Q );
25    Smat H(N,N);
26    if ( N==Q )
27    {
28        copy(C, H);
29        H.diag_add_val(1);
30    }
31    else
32    {
33        Smat K2(2,2);  K2.fill(+1); K2.set(1,1, -1);  // K2 = [+1,+1; +1,-1]
34        H.kronecker(K2, C);  // Kronecker product of matrices
35        for (ulong k=0; k<Q; ++k)  // adjust diagonal of sub-matrices
36        {
37            ulong r, c;
38            r=k;    c=k;   H.set(r,c, H.get(r,c)+1);
39            r=k;    c=k+Q; H.set(r,c, H.get(r,c)-1);
40            r=k+Q;  c=k;   H.set(r,c, H.get(r,c)-1);
41            r=k+Q;  c=k+Q; H.set(r,c, H.get(r,c)-1);
42        }
43    }
44    [--snip--]
```

If both $\mathbf{H}_a$ and $\mathbf{H}_b$ are Hadamard matrices (of dimensions a and b, respectively), then their Kronecker product $\mathbf{H}_{ab} = \mathbf{H}_a \otimes \mathbf{H}_b$ is again a Hadamard matrix:

$$\mathbf{H}_{ab}\,\mathbf{H}_{ab}^T \;=\; (\mathbf{H}_a \otimes \mathbf{H}_b)\,(\mathbf{H}_a \otimes \mathbf{H}_b)^T \;=^* \;(\mathbf{H}_a \otimes \mathbf{H}_b)\,(\mathbf{H}_a^T \otimes \mathbf{H}_b^T) \;= \qquad (19.2\text{-}4a)$$

$$=\; (\mathbf{H}_a\,\mathbf{H}_a^T) \otimes (\mathbf{H}_b\,\mathbf{H}_b^T) \;=^* \;(a\,\mathrm{id}) \otimes (b\,\mathrm{id}) \;=\; a\,b\,\mathrm{id} \qquad (19.2\text{-}4b)$$

The starred equalities use relations 23.3-11a and 23.3-10a on page 464, respectively.

19.3 Conference matrices via finite fields

The algorithm for odd primes q can be modified to work also for powers of odd primes. We have to work with the finite fields $\mathrm{GF}(q^n)$. The entries $\mathbf{C}_{r+1,c+1}$ for $r = 0, 1, \ldots, q^n - 1$ and $c = 0, 1, \ldots, q^n - 1$ have to be the quadratic character of $z_r - z_c$ where $z_0, z_1, \ldots, z_{q^n-1}$ are the elements in $\mathrm{GF}(q^n)$ in some (fixed) order.

We give two simple GP routines that map the elements $z_i \in \mathrm{GF}(q^n)$ (represented as polynomials modulo q) to the numbers $0, 1, \ldots, q^n - 1$. The polynomial $p(x) = c_0 + c_1 x + \ldots + c_{n-1} x^{n-1}$ is mapped to $N = c_0 + c_1 q + \ldots + c_{n-1} q^{n-1}$.

```
1    pol2num(p,q)=
2    \\ Return number for polynomial p.
3    {
4        p = lift(p);   \\ remove mods, e.g. p=Mod(2, 3)*x^2 + Mod(1, 3) --> 2*x^2+1
5        return ( subst(p, 'x, q) );
6    }
```

The inverse routine is

```
1    num2pol(n,q)=
2    \\ Return polynomial for number n.
3    {
4        local(p, mq, k);
5        p = Pol(0,'x);
6        k = 0;
7        while ( 0!=n,
8            mq = n % q;
9            p += mq * ('x)^k;
10           n -= mq;
11           n \= q;
12           k++;
13       );
14       return( p );
15   }
```

The quadratic character of an element z can be determined by computing $z^{(q^n-1)/2}$ modulo the field polynomial. The result will be zero for $z = 0$, else ± 1.

For our purpose its is better to precompute a table of the quadratic characters for later lookup:

```
1    quadcharvec(fp, q)=
2    \\ Return a table of quadratic characters in GF(q^n)
3    \\ fp is the field polynomial.
4    {
5        local(n, qn, sv, pl);
6        n=poldegree(fp);
7        qn=q^n-1;
8        sv=vector(qn+1, j, -1);
9        sv[1] = 0;
10       for (k=1, qn,
11           pl = num2pol(k,q);
12           pl = Mod(Mod(1,q)*pl, fp);
13           sq = pl * pl;
14           sq = lift(sq);  \\ remove mod
15           i = pol2num( sq, q );
16           sv[i+1] = +1;
17       );
18       return( sv );
19   }
```

With this table we can compute the quadratic characters of the difference of two elements efficiently:

```
1    getquadchar_v(n1, n2, q, fp, sv)=
2    \\ Return the quadratic character of (n2-n1) in GF(q^n)
3    \\ Table lookup method
4    {
5        local(p1, p2, d, nd, sc);
6        if ( n1==n2, return(0) );
7        p1 = num2pol(n1, q);
8        p2 = num2pol(n2, q);
9        d = (p2-p1) % fp;
10       nd = pol2num(d, q);
11       sc = sv[nd+1];
12       return( sc );
13   }
```

Now we can construct conference matrices:

```
1    matconference(q, fp, sv)=
2    \\ Return a QxQ conference matrix.
3    \\ q  an odd prime.
4    \\ fp an irreducible polynomial modulo q.
5    \\ sv table of quadratic characters in GF(q^n)
6    \\    where n is the degree of fp.
7    {
8        local(y, Q, C, n);
9        n = poldegree(fp);
10       Q=q^n+1;
11       if ( sv[2]==sv[Q-1], y=+1, y=-1 );  \\ symmetry
12
13       C = matrix(Q,Q);
14       for (k=2, Q, C[1,k]=+1);  \\ first row
15       for (k=2, Q, C[k,1]=y);  \\ first column
16       for (r=2, Q,
17           for (c=2, Q,
18               sc = getquadchar_v(r-2, c-2, q, fp, sv);
19               C[r,c] = sc;
20           );
21       );
22       return( C );
23   }
```

```
         q = 3    fp = x^2 + 1    GF(3^2)
         Table of quadratic characters:
             0 + + + - - + - -
         10x10 conference matrix C:
         0 + + + + + + + + +
         - 0 + + + - - + - -
         - + 0 + - + - - + -
         - + + 0 - - + - - +
         - + - - 0 + + + - -
         - - + - + 0 + - + -
         - - - + + + 0 - - +
         - + - - + - - 0 + +
         - - + - - + - + 0 +
         - - - + - - - + + 0
```

Figure 19.3-A: A 10×10 conference matrix for $q = 3$ and the field polynomial $f = x^2 + 1$.

To compute a $Q \times Q$ conference matrix where $Q = q^n + 1$ we need to find a polynomial of degree n that is irreducible modulo q. With $q = 3$ and the field polynomial $f = x^2 + 1$ (so $n = 2$) we get the 10×10 conference matrix shown in figure 19.3-A. A conference matrix for $q = 3$ and $f = x^3 - x + 1$ is given in figure 19.3-B. Hadamard matrices can be created in the same manner as before, the symmetry criterion being whether $q^n \equiv \pm 1 \bmod 4$.

The conference matrices obtained are of size $Q = q^n + 1$ where q is an odd prime. The values $Q \leq 100$ are (see sequence A061344 in [312]):

4, 6, 8, 10, 12, 14, 18, 20, 24, 26, 28, 30, 32, 38, 42, 44, 48,
50, 54, 60, 62, 68, 72, 74, 80, 82, 84, 90, 98

Our construction does not give conference matrices for any odd Q, and these even values $Q \leq 100$:

```
q = 3   f p= x ^ 3 x + 1    GF(3^3)
Table of quadratic characters:
   0 + - - - + + + + - + + + - + + - - - - + - + - - + -
28x28 conference matrix C:
 0 + + + + + + + + + + + + + + + + + + + + + + + + + + +
 - 0 + - - - - + + + + - + + + - + + - - - - + - + - - + -
 - - 0 + - - - + + + + + - - + + - + + + - - - - + - - +
 - + - 0 - - - + + + + + + - - + + - + + + - + - + - + - -
 - + + + 0 + - - - - + + + - + - + + + - + + - - + - + - -
 - + + + - 0 + - - - - + + + + - + + - - + + - - + - + - +
 - + + + + - 0 - - + - + + + + - - + + - + - - + - + - - -
 - - - - + + + 0 + - + + - + + - + + - + - - + - - + + - +
 - - - - + + + + - 0 + - + + - + + - + + - + - - + + - - +
 - - + - + - - + - + 0 + - - - + + + + - + + + - + + + - -
 - + + - + - - + - + - 0 + - - - + + + + - + + + - + + + +
 - - + - + - + - + - + + 0 - - - - + + + - + + + - + + - +
 - - + + + - + - - + - + - 0 - - - + + + - + + + - + + - +
 - + + - + - + - + + + + - 0 - - - - + + + - + + + - + - +
 - - + - + - + - + - + - - + 0 + - + + - + + + - + + + - +
 - + - + - + - + + + - - - - - 0 + + + - - - + + + - + - +
 - + + - + - + + + - - - - + - + - 0 + + - + + - + - + - +
 - + - + + + - + + - - - + - + - - + 0 + - + + - + - + + +
 - + + - + + + + + - - - - + - + - + - 0 + - - - + + + +
 - + - + - + + + - + - + - + - + - + - + - 0 + - - - + - -
 - + - + - + + + + - + - + - + - - + + + + - 0 + - - - -
 - + - + - + + + + - + - + - + - + - + + + + - 0 + - - -
 - + - + - + + + + - + - + - + - + - - + + + + - 0 + - -
 - + - + - + + + + - + - + - + - - + - + + + - + + 0 + -
 - - + + - + + + + - - - + - - + + - - - - + + + - 0 +
 - + - + + - + - + + + + + - - + - - - - + + + + - 0
```

Figure 19.3-B: A 28×28 conference matrix for $q = 3$ and the field polynomial $f = x^3 - x + 1$.

2, 16, 22, 34, 36, 40, 46, 52, 56, 58, 64, 66, 70, 76, 78, 86, 88, 92, 94, 96, 100

For example, $Q = 16 = 15 + 1 = 3 \cdot 5 + 1$ has not the required form.

If a conference matrix of size Q exists, then we can create Hadamard matrices of sizes $N = Q$ whenever $q^n \equiv 3 \bmod 4$ and $N = 2Q$ whenever $q^n \equiv 1 \bmod 4$. Further, if Hadamard matrices of sizes N and M exist, then a $(N \cdot M) \times (N \cdot M)$ the Kronecker product of those matrices is a Hadamard matrix.

The values of $N = 4k \leq 2000$ such that this construction does *not* give an $N \times N$ Hadamard matrix are:

```
92, 116, 156, 172, 184, 188, 232, 236, 260, 268, 292, 324, 356, 372,
376, 404, 412, 428, 436, 452, 472, 476, 508, 520, 532, 536, 584,
596, 604, 612, 652, 668, 712, 716, 732, 756, 764, 772, 808, 836,
852, 856, 872, 876, 892, 904, 932, 940, 944, 952, 956, 964, 980,
988, 996, 1004, 1012, 1016, 1028, 1036, 1068, 1072, 1076, 1100,
1108, 1132, 1148, 1168, 1180, 1192, 1196, 1208, 1212, 1220, 1244,
1268, 1276, 1300, 1316, 1336, 1340, 1364, 1372, 1380, 1388, 1396,
1412, 1432, 1436, 1444, 1464, 1476, 1492, 1508, 1528, 1556, 1564,
1588, 1604, 1612, 1616, 1636, 1652, 1672, 1676, 1692, 1704, 1712,
1732, 1740, 1744, 1752, 1772, 1780, 1796, 1804, 1808, 1820, 1828,
1836, 1844, 1852, 1864, 1888, 1892, 1900, 1912, 1916, 1928, 1940,
1948, 1960, 1964, 1972, 1976, 1992
```

This is sequence A046116 in [312]. It can be computed by starting with a list of all numbers of the form $4k$ and deleting all values $k = 2^a (q + 1)$ where q is a power of an odd prime.

Constructions for Hadamard matrices for numbers of certain forms are known, see [234] and [157]. Whether Hadamard matrices exist for all values $N = 4k$ is an open problem. A readable source about constructions for Hadamard matrices is [316]. Hadamard matrices for all $N \leq 256$ are given in [313].

Chapter 20

Searching paths in directed graphs ‡

We describe how certain combinatorial structures can be represented as paths or cycles in a directed graph. As an example consider Gray codes of n-bit binary words: we are looking for sequences of all 2^n binary words such that only one bit changes between two successive words. A convenient representation of the search space is that of a graph. The nodes are the binary words and an edge is drawn between two nodes if the node's values differ by exactly one bit. Every path that visits all nodes of that graph corresponds to a Gray code. If the path is a cycle, a Gray cycle was found.

Depending on the size of the problem, we can

1. try to find at least one object,

2. generate all objects,

3. show that no such object exists.

The method used is usually called *backtracking*. We will see how to reduce the search space if additional constraints are imposed on the paths. Finally, we show how careful optimization can lead to surprising algorithms for objects of a size where one would hardly expect to obtain a result at all. In fact, Gray cycles through the n-bit binary Lyndon words for all odd $n \leq 37$ are determined.

We use graphs solely as a tool for finding combinatorial structures. For algorithms dealing with the properties of graphs see, for example, [220] and [307].

Terminology and conventions

We will use the terms *node* (instead of *vertex*) and *edge* (sometimes called *arc*). We restrict our attention to *directed graphs* (or *digraphs*) as undirected graphs are just the special case of these: an edge in an undirected graph corresponds to two antiparallel edges (think: 'arrows') in a directed graph.

A length-k *path* is a sequence of nodes where an edge leads from each node to its successor. A path is called *simple* if the nodes are pair-wise distinct. We restrict our attention to simple paths of length N where N is the number of nodes of the graph. We use the term *full path* for a simple path of length N.

If in a simple path there is an edge from the last node of the path to the starting node the path is a *cycle* (or *circuit*). A full path that is a cycle is called a *Hamiltonian cycle*, a graph containing such a cycle is called *Hamiltonian*.

We allow for *loops* (edges that start and point to the same node). Graphs that contain loops are called *pseudo graphs*. The algorithms used will effectively ignore loops. We disallow *multigraphs* (where multiple edges can start and end at the same two nodes), as these would lead to repeated output of identical objects.

The *neighbors* of a node are those nodes to which outgoing edges point. Neighbors can be reached with one step. The neighbors of a node a called *adjacent* to the node. The *adjacency matrix* of a graph with N nodes is an $N \times N$ matrix A where $A_{i,j} = 1$ if there is an edge from node i to node j, else $A_{i,j} = 0$. While easy to implement (and modify later) we will not use this kind of representation as the memory requirement would be prohibitive for large graphs.

J. Arndt, *Matters Computational: Ideas, Algorithms, Source Code*,
DOI 10.1007/978-3-642-14764-7_20, © Springer-Verlag Berlin Heidelberg 2011

20.1   Representation of digraphs

For our purposes a static implementation of the graph as arrays of nodes and (outgoing) edges will suffice. The container class `digraph` merely allocates memory for the nodes and edges. The correct initialization is left to the user [FXT: `class digraph` in graph/digraph.h]:

```
1    class digraph
2    {
3    public:
4        ulong ng_;    // number of Nodes of Graph
5        ulong *ep_;   // e[ep[k]], ..., e[ep[k+1]-1]: outgoing connections of node k
6        ulong *e_;    // outgoing connections (Edges)
7        ulong *vn_;   // optional: sorted values for nodes
8        // if vn is used, then node k must correspond to vn[k]
9
10   public:
11       digraph(ulong ng, ulong ne, ulong *&ep, ulong *&e, bool vnq=false)
12           : ng_(0), ep_(0), e_(0), vn_(0)
13       {
14           ng_ = ng;
15           ep_ = new ulong[ng_+1];
16           e_ = new ulong[ne];
17           ep = ep_;
18           e = e_;
19           if ( vnq )  vn_ = new ulong[ng_];
20       }
21
22       ~digraph()
23       {
24           delete [] ep_;
25           delete [] e_;
26           if ( vn_ )  delete [] vn_;
27       }
28
29   [--snip--]
30
31       void get_edge_idx(ulong p, ulong &fe, ulong &en)  const
32       // Setup fe and en so that the nodes reachable from p are
33       //    e[fe], e[fe+1], ..., e[en-1].
34       // Must have:  0<=p<ng
35       {
36           fe = ep_[p];   // (index of) First Edge
37           en = ep_[p+1]; // (index of) first Edge of Next node
38       }
39
40   [--snip--]
41       void print(const char *bla=0)  const;
42   };
```

The nodes reachable from node p could be listed using

```
// ulong p; // == position
cout << "The nodes reachable from node " << p << " are:" << endl;
ulong fe, en;
g_.get_edge_idx(p, fe, en);
for (ulong ep=fe; ep<en; ++ep)  cout << e_[ep] << endl;
```

With our representation there is no cheap method to find the incoming edges. We will not need this information for our purposes. If the graph is known to be undirected, the same routine obviously lists the incoming edges.

Initialization routines for certain digraphs are declared in [FXT: graph/mk-special-digraphs.h]. A simple example is [FXT: graph/mk-complete-digraph.cc]:

```
1    digraph
2    make_complete_digraph(ulong n)
3    // Initialization for the complete graph.
4    {
5        ulong ng = n, ne = n*(n-1);
6
7        ulong *ep, *e;
8        digraph dg(ng, ne, ep, e);
9
```

```
10        ulong j = 0;
11        for (ulong k=0; k<ng; ++k)  // for all nodes
12        {
13            ep[k] = j;
14            for (ulong i=0; i<n; ++i)  // connect to all nodes
15            {
16                if ( k==i )  continue;  // skip loops
17                e[j++] = i;
18            }
19        }
20        ep[ng] = j;
21        return  dg;
22    }
```

We initialize the *complete graph* (the undirected graph that has edges between any two of its nodes) for $n = 5$ and print it [FXT: graph/graph-perm-demo.cc]:

```
digraph dg = make_complete_digraph(5);
dg.print("Graph =");
```

The output is

```
Graph =
Node: Edge0 Edge1 ...
    0:    1    2    3    4
    1:    0    2    3    4
    2:    0    1    3    4
    3:    0    1    2    4
    4:    0    1    2    3
#nodes=5   #edges=20
```

For many purposes it suffices to implicitly represent the nodes as values p with $0 \le p < N$ where N is the number of nodes. If not, the values of the nodes have to be stored in the array `vn_[]`. One such example is a graph where the value of node p is the p-th (cyclically minimal) Lyndon word that we will meet at the end of this chapter. To make the search for a node by value reasonably fast, the array `vn_[]` should be sorted so that binary search can be used.

20.2 Searching full paths

To search full paths starting from some position p_0 we need two additional arrays for the bookkeeping: A record `rv_[]` of the path so far, its k-th entry is p_k, the node visited at step k. A tag array `qq_[]` that contains a one for nodes already visited, otherwise a zero. The crucial parts of the implementation are [FXT: class `digraph_paths` in graph/digraph-paths.h]:

```
1    class digraph_paths
2    // Find all full paths in a directed graph.
3    {
4    public:
5        digraph &g_;  // the graph
6        ulong *rv_;  // Record of Visits: rv[k] == node visited at step k
7        ulong *qq_;  // qq[k] == whether node k has been visited yet
8    [--snip--]
9        // function to call with each path found with all_paths():
10        ulong (*pfunc_)(digraph_paths &);
11    [--snip--]
12        // function to impose condition with all_cond_paths():
13        bool (*cfunc_)(digraph_paths &, ulong ns);
14
15    public:
16        // graph/digraph.cc:
17        digraph_paths(digraph &g);
18        ~digraph_paths();
19    [--snip--]
20        bool path_is_cycle()  const;
21    [--snip--]
22        void print_path() const;
23    [--snip--]
24
25        // graph/digraphpaths-search.cc:
26        ulong all_paths(ulong (*pfunc)(digraph_paths &),
27                        ulong ns=0, ulong p=0, ulong maxnp=0);
```

```
28    private:
29        void next_path(ulong ns, ulong p);  // called by all_paths()
30    [--snip--]
31    };
```

We could have used a bit-array for the tag values `qq_[]`. It turns out that some additional information can be saved there as we will see in a moment.

To keep matters simple a recursive algorithm is used to search for (full) paths. The search is started via call to `all_paths()` [FXT: graph/digraph-paths.cc]:

```
1    ulong
2    digraph_paths::all_paths(ulong (*pfunc)(const digraph_paths &),
3                             ulong ns/*=0*/, ulong p/*=0*/, ulong maxnp/*=0*/)
4    // pfunc: function to visit (process) paths
5    // ns: start at node index ns (for fixing start of path)
6    // p: start at node value p    (for fixing start of path)
7    // maxnp: stop if maxnp paths were found
8    {
9        pct_ = 0;
10       cct_ = 0;
11       pfct_ = 0;
12       pfunc_ = pfunc;
13       pfdone_ = 0;
14       maxnp_ = maxnp;
15       next_path(ns, p);
16       return pfct_;  // Number of paths where pfunc() returned true
17   }
```

The search is done by the function `next_path()`:

```
1    void
2    digraph_paths::next_path(ulong ns, ulong p)
3    // ns+1 == how many nodes seen
4    // p == position (node we are on)
5    {
6        if ( pfdone_ )  return;
7
8        rv_[ns] = p;  // record position
9        ++ns;
10
11       if ( ns==ng_ )  // all nodes seen ?
12       {
13           pfunc_(*this);
14       }
15       else
16       {
17           qq_[p] = 1;  // mark position as seen (else loops lead to errors)
18           ulong fe, en;
19           g_.get_edge_idx(p, fe, en);
20           ulong fct = 0;  // count free reachable nodes  // FCT
21           for (ulong ep=fe; ep<en; ++ep)
22           {
23               ulong t = g_.e_[ep]; // next node
24               if ( 0==qq_[t] )  // node free?
25               {
26                   ++fct;
27                   qq_[p] = fct; // mark position as seen: record turns  // FCT
28                   next_path(ns, t);
29               }
30           }
31           // if ( 0==fct )  { "dead end: this is a U-turn"; }  // FCT
32
33           qq_[p] = 0; // unmark position
34       }
35   }
```

The lines that are commented with `// FCT` record which among the free nodes is visited. The algorithm still works if these lines are commented out.

```
       Graph =                          0:     1 2 3 4
       Node: Edge0 Edge1 ...            1:     1 2 4 3
          0  : 1   2    3    4          2:     1 3 2 4
          1  : 0   2    3    4          3:     1 3 4 2
          2  : 0   1    3    4          4:     1 4 2 3
          3  : 0   1    2    4          5:     1 4 3 2
          4  : 0   1    2    3          6:     2 1 3 4
       #nodes=5   #edges=20             7:     2 1 4 3
                                        8:     2 3 1 4
                                      [--snip--]
                                       21:     4 2 3 1
                                       22:     4 3 1 2
                                       23:     4 3 2 1
```

Figure 20.2-A: Edges of the complete graph with 5 nodes (left) and full paths starting at node 0 (right). The paths (where 0 is omitted) correspond to the permutations of 4 elements in lexicographic order.

20.2.1   Paths in the complete graph: permutations

The program [FXT: graph/graph-perm-demo.cc] shows the paths in the complete graph from section 20.1 on page 392. We give a slightly simplified version:

```
1   ulong pfunc_perm(digraph_paths &dp)
2   // Function to be called with each path:
3   //   print all but the first node.
4   {
5       const ulong *rv = dp.rv_;
6       ulong ng = dp.ng_;
7
8       cout << setw(4) << dp.pfct_ << ":  ";
9       for (ulong k=1; k<ng; ++k)  cout << " " << rv[k];
10      cout << endl;
11
12      return 1;
13  }
14
15  int
16  main(int argc, char **argv)
17  {
18      ulong n = 5;
19      digraph dg = make_complete_digraph(n);
20      digraph_paths dp(dg);
21
22      dg.print("Graph =");
23      cout << endl;
24
25      dp.all_paths(pfunc_perm, 0, 0, maxnp);
26      return 0;
27  }
```

The output, shown in figure 20.2-A, is a listing of the permutations of the numbers $1, 2, 3, 4$ in lexicographic order (see section 10.2 on page 242).

20.2.2   Paths in the De Bruijn graph: De Bruijn sequences

The graph with $2n$ nodes and two outgoing edges from node k to $2k \bmod 2n$ and $2k+1 \bmod 2n$ is called a (binary) *De Bruijn graph*. For $n = 8$ the graph is (printed horizontally):

```
     Node:  0  1  2  3  4   5   6   7  8  9 10 11 12 13 14 15
  Edge 0:   0  2  4  6  8  10  12  14  0  2  4  6  8 10 12 14
  Edge 1:   1  3  5  7  9  11  13  15  1  3  5  7  9 11 13 15
```

The graph has a loop at each the first and the last node. All paths in the De Bruijn graph are cycles, the graph is Hamiltonian.

With n a power of 2 the paths correspond to the *De Bruijn sequences* (DBS) of length $2n$. The graph has as many full paths as there are DBSs and the zeros/ones in the DBS correspond to even/odd values of the nodes, respectively. This is demonstrated in [FXT: graph/graph-debruijn-demo.cc] (shortened):

```
1   ulong pq = 1; // whether and what to print with each cycle
2
3   ulong pfunc_db(digraph_paths &dp)
```

```
Graph =
    Node:   0   1   2   3   4   5   6   7   8   9  10  11  12  13  14  15
  Edge 0:   0   2   4   6   8   1  02  14   0   2   4   6   8  10  12  14
  Edge 1:   1   3   5   7   9   1      13  15   1   3   5   7   9  11  13  15

     Paths                                                           DBSs
  0   1   2   4   9   3   6   1  30   5  11   7  15  14  12   8      .1..11.1.1111...
  0   1   2   4   9   3   7   1  54  13  10   5  11   6  12   8      .1..1111.1.11...
  0   1   2   5   1  04   9   3   6  13  11   7  15  14  12   8      .1.1..11.1111...
  0   1   2   5   1  04   9   3   7  15  14  13  11   6  12   8      .1.1..1111.11...
  0   1   2   5   1  16  12   9   3   7  15  14  13  10   4   8      .1.11..1111.1...
  0   1   2   5   1  16  13   1  04   9   3   7  15  14  12   8      .1.11.1..1111...
  0   1   2   5   1  17  15   1   4  29   3   6  13  10   4   8      .1.1111..11.1...
  0   1   2   5   1  17  15   1   4  30   4   9   3   6  12   8      .1.1111.1.11.11...
  0   1   3   6   1  29   2   5  11   7  15  14  13  10   4   8      .11..1.1111.1...
  0   1   3   6   1   3  04   9   2   5  11   7  15  14  12   8      .11.1.1..1111...
  0   1   3   6   1   3  05   1  17  15  14  12   9   2   4   8      .11.1.1.1111..1...
  0   1   3   6   1   3  17   1  54  12   9   2   5  10   4   8      .11.1111..1.1...
  0   1   3   7   1   5   4  29   2   5  11   6  13  10   4   8      .1111.1..11.1...
  0   1   3   7   1   5   4  30   4   9   2   5  11   6  12   8      .1111.1..1.11...
  0   1   3   7   1   5   4  30   5  11   6  12   9   2   4   8      .1111.1.11..1...
  0   1   3   7   1   5   4  31   6  12   9   2   5  10   4   8      .1111.11..1.1...

n = 8 (ng=16)   #cycles = 16
```

Figure 20.2-B: Edges of the De Bruijn graph (top) and all paths starting at node 0 together with the corresponding De Bruijn sequences (bottom). Dots denote zeros.

```
 4  // Function to be called with each cycle.
 5  {
 6      switch ( pq )
 7      {
 8      case 0:  break;  // just count
 9      case 1:  // print lowest bits (De Bruijn sequence)
10          {
11              ulong *rv = dp.rv_, ng = dp.ng_;
12              for (ulong k=0; k<ng; ++k)  cout << (rv[k]&1UL ? '1' : '.');
13              cout << endl;
14              break;
15          }
16      [--snip--]
17      }
18      return 1;
19  }
20
21  int main(int argc, char **argv)
22  {
23      ulong n = 8;
24      NXARG(pq, "what to do in pfunc()");
25      ulong maxnp = 0;
26      NXARG(maxnp, "stop after maxnp paths (0: never stop)");
27      ulong p0 = 0;
28      NXARG(p0, "start position <2*n");
29
30      digraph dg = make_debruijn_digraph(n);
31      digraph_paths dp(dg);
32
33      dg.print_horiz("Graph =");
34
35      // call pfunc() with each cycle:
36      dp.all_paths(pfunc_db, 0, p0, maxnp);
37
38      cout << "n = " << n;
39      cout << "  (ng=" << dg.ng_ << ")";
40      cout << "   #cycles = " << dp.cct_;
41      cout << endl;
42
43      return 0;
44  }
45
```

The macro `NXARG()` reads one argument, it is defined in [FXT: nextarg.h]. Figure 20.2-B was created with the shown program.

The algorithm is a very effective way for generating all DBSs of a given length, the 67,108,864 DBSs of length 64 are generated in 140 seconds when printing is disabled (set argument **pq** to zero), corresponding to a rate of more than 450,000 DBSs per second.

```
-#----##---#-#---###--#--#-##--##-#--####-#-#-###-##-######-----
--#----##---#-#---###--#--#-##--##-#--####-#-#-###-##-######----
---#----##---#-#---###--#--#-##--##-#--####-#-#-###-##-######---
----#----##---#-#---###--#--#-##--##-#--####-#-#-###-##-######--
-----#----##---#-#---###--#--#-##--##-#--####-#-#-###-##-######-
------#----##---#-#---###--#--#-##--##-#--####-#-#-###-##-######
```

Figure 20.2-C: A path in the De Bruijn graph with 64 nodes. Each binary word is printed vertically, the symbols '#' and '-' stand for one and zero, respectively.

Setting the argument **pq** to 4 prints the binary values of the successive nodes in the path horizontally, see figure 20.2-C. The graph is constructed in a way that each word is the predecessor shifted by one with either zero or one inserted at position zero (top row of figure 20.2-C).

The number of cycles in the De Bruijn graph equals the number of degree-n normal binary polynomials, see section 42.6.3 on page 904. A closed form for the special case $n = 2^k$ is given in section 41.5 on page 873.

20.2.3 A modified De Bruijn graph: complement-shift sequences

```
------#---#-#-##----##--#--#-###---###-#--##-####--######-##-#-#
-#####-###-#-#--###--##-#-#--#---###---#-##--#-----##------#--#-#
-#------#---#-#-##----##--#--#-###---###-#--##-####--######-##-#
-#-#####-###-#-#--###--##-##-#---###---#-##--#-----##------#--#
-#-#------#---#-#-##----##--#--#-###---###-#--##-####--######-##
-#-#-#####-###-#-#--###--##-##-#---###---#-##--#----##------#-
```

Figure 20.2-D: A path in the modified De Bruijn graph with 64 nodes. Each binary word is printed vertically, the symbols '#' and '-' stand for one and zero, respectively.

A modification of the De Bruijn graph forces the nodes to be the complement of its predecessor shifted by one (again with either zero or one inserted at position zero). The routine to set up the graph is [FXT: graph/mk-debruijn-digraph.cc]:

```
1   digraph
2   make_complement_shift_digraph(ulong n)
3   {
4       ulong ng = 2*n, ne = 2*ng;
5       ulong *ep, *e;
6       digraph dg(ng, ne, ep, e);
7
8       ulong j = 0;
9       for (ulong k=0; k<ng; ++k)  // for all nodes
10      {
11          ep[k] = j;
12          ulong r = (2*k) % ng;
13          e[j++] = r;  // connect node k to node (2*k) mod ng
14          r = (2*k+1) % ng;
15          e[j++] = r;  // connect node k to node (2*k+1) mod ng
16      }
17      ep[ng] = j;
18      // Here we have a De Bruijn graph.
19
20      for (ulong k=0,j=ng-1; k<j; ++k,--j) swap2(e[ep[k]], e[ep[j]]); // end with ones
21      for (ulong k=0,j=ng-1; k<j; ++k,--j) swap2(e[ep[k]+1], e[ep[j]+1]);
22
23      return  dg;
24  }
```

The output of the program [FXT: graph/graph-complementshift-demo.cc] is shown in figure 20.2-D.

For n a power of 2 the sequence of binary words has the interesting property that the changes between successive words depend on their sequency: words with higher sequency change in less positions. Further, if two adjacent bits are set in some word, then the next word never has both bits set again. Out of a run of $k \geq 2$ consecutive set bits in a word only one is contained in the next word.

See section 8.3 on page 208 for the connection with De Bruijn sequences.

20.3 Conditional search

Sometimes one wants to find paths that are subject to certain restrictions. Testing for each path found whether it has the desired property and discarding it if not is the simplest way. However, this will in many cases be extremely ineffective. An upper bound for the number of recursive calls of the search function `next_path()` with a graph with N nodes and a maximal number of v outgoing edges at each node is $u = N^v$.

For example, the graph corresponding to Gray codes of n-bit binary words has $N = 2^n$ nodes and (exactly) $c = n$ outgoing edges at each node. The graph is the n-dimensional hypercube.

$n:$	N	$u = N^c = N^n = 2^{n \cdot n}$
1:	2	2
2:	4	16
3:	8	512
4:	16	65,536
5:	32	33,554,432
6:	64	68,719,476,736
7:	128	562,949,953,421,312
8:	256	18,446,744,073,709,551,616
9:	512	2,417,851,639,229,258,349,412,352
10:	1024	1,267,650,600,228,229,401,496,703,205,376

To reduce the search space we use a function that rejects branches that would lead to a path not satisfying the imposed restrictions. A conditional search can be started via `all_cond_paths()` that has an additional function pointer `cfunc()` as argument. The function must implement the condition. The corresponding method is declared as [FXT: graph/digraph-paths.h]:

```
bool (*cfunc_)(digraph_paths &, ulong ns);
```

Besides the data from the digraph-class it needs the number of nodes seen so far (`ns`) as an argument. A slight modification of the search routine does what we want [FXT: graph/search-digraph-cond.cc]:

```
1    void
2    digraph_paths::next_cond_path(ulong ns, ulong p)
3    {
4        [--snip--]  // same as next_path()
5        if ( ns==ng_ )  // all nodes seen ?
6        [--snip--]  // same as next_path()
7        else
8        {
9            qq_[p] = 1; // mark position as seen (else loops lead to errors)
10           ulong fe, en;
11           g_.get_edge_idx(p, fe, en);
12           ulong fct = 0;   // count free reachable nodes
13           for (ulong ep=fe; ep<en; ++ep)
14           {
15               ulong t = g_.e_[ep]; // next node
16               if ( 0==qq_[t] )  // node free?
17               {
18                   rv_[ns] = t;  // for cfunc()
19                   if ( cfunc_(*this, ns) )
20                   {
21                       ++fct;
22                       qq_[p] = fct; // mark position as seen: record turns
23                       next_cond_path(ns, t);
24                   }
25               }
26           }
27           qq_[p] = 0; // unmark position
```

```
28        }
29    }
```

The free node under consideration is written to the end of the record of visited nodes so `cfunc()` does not need it as an explicit argument.

20.3.1 Modular adjacent changes (MAC) Gray codes

```
 0:  ....  0   0   ...1  0        0:  ....  0   0   ...1  0
 1:  ...1  1   1   ..1.  1        1:  ...1  1   1   ..1.  1
 2:  ..11  2   3   .1..  2        2:  ..11  2   3   .1..  2
 3:  .111  3   7   1...  3        3:  .111  3   7   ..1.  1
 4:  1111  4   15  ...1  0        4:  .1.1  2   5   ...1  0
 5:  111.  3   14  ..1.  1        5:  .1..  1   4   ..1.  1
 6:  11..  2   12  ..1.  0        6:  .11.  2   6   .1..  2
 7:  11.1  3   13  1...  3        7:  ..1.  1   2   1...  3
 8:  .1.1  2   5   ...1  0        8:  1.1.  2   10  .1..  2
 9:  .1..  1   4   ..1.  1        9:  111.  3   14  ..1.  1
10:  .11.  2   6   .1..  2       10:  11..  2   12  ...1  0
11:  ..1.  1   2   1...  3       11:  11.1  3   13  ..1.  1
12:  1.1.  2   10  ...1  0       12:  1111  4   15  .1..  2
13:  1.11  3   11  ..1.  1       13:  1.11  3   11  ..1.  1
14:  1..1  2   9   ...1  0       14:  1..1  2   9   ...1  0
15:  1...  1   8   [1...  3]     15:  1...  1   8   [1...  3]
```

Figure 20.3-A: Two 4-bit modular adjacent changes (MAC) Gray codes. Both are cycles.

We search for Gray codes that have the *modular adjacent changes* (MAC) property: the values of successive elements of the delta sequence can only change by ± 1 modulo n. Two examples are show in figure 20.3-A. The sequence on the right side even has the stated property if the term 'modular' is omitted: It has the *adjacent changes* (AC) property.

As bit-wise cyclic shifts and reflections of MAC Gray codes are again MAC Gray codes we consider paths starting $0 \to 1 \to 2$ as canonical paths.

In the demo [FXT: graph/graph-macgray-demo.cc] the search is done as follows (shortened):

```
1   int main(int argc, char **argv)
2   {
3       ulong n = 5;
4       NXARG(n, "size in bits");
5       cf_nb = n;
6
7       digraph dg = make_gray_digraph(n, 0);
8       digraph_paths dp(dg);
9
10      ulong ns = 0, p = 0;
11      // MAC: canonical paths start as 0-->1-->3
12      {
13          dp.mark(0, ns);
14          dp.mark(1, ns);
15          p = 3;
16      }
17
18      dp.all_cond_paths(pfunc, cfunc_mac, ns, p, maxnp);
19      return 0;
20  }
```

The function used to impose the MAC condition is:

```
1   ulong cf_nb; // number of bits,  set in main()
2   bool cfunc_mac(digraph_paths &dp, ulong ns)
3   // Condition: difference of successive delta values (modulo n) == +-1
4   {
5       // path initialized, we have ns>=2
6       ulong p  = dp.rv_[ns],  p1 = dp.rv_[ns-1], p2 = dp.rv_[ns-2];
7       ulong c = p ^ p1,   c1 = p1 ^ p2;
8       if ( c & bit_rotate_left(c1,1,cf_nb) )  return  true;
9       if ( c1 & bit_rotate_left(c,1,cf_nb) )  return  true;
10      return false;
11  }
```

We find paths for $n \le 7$ ($n = 7$ takes about 15 minutes). Whether MAC Gray codes exist for $n \ge 8$ is unknown (none is found with a 40 hour search).

20.3.2 Adjacent changes (AC) Gray codes

For AC paths we can only discard track-reflected solutions, the canonical paths are those where the delta sequence starts with a value $\le \lceil n/2 \rceil$. A function to impose the AC condition is

```
1   ulong cf_mt; // mid track < cf_mt,  set in main()
2   bool cfunc_ac(digraph_paths &dp, ulong ns)
3   // Condition: difference of successive delta values == +-1
4   {
5       if ( ns<2 )  return  (dp.rv_[1] < cf_mt); // avoid track-reflected solutions
6       ulong p  = dp.rv_[ns],  p1 = dp.rv_[ns-1],  p2 = dp.rv_[ns-2];
7       ulong c = p ^ p1, c1 = p1 ^ p2;
8       if ( c & (c1<<1) )  return  true;
9       if ( c1 & (c<<1) )  return  true;
10      return false;
11  }
```

```
 0:  .....  0    0    ..1..  2       0:  .....  0    0    ...1.  0
 1:  ..1..  1    4    .1...  3       1:  ...1.  1    1    ...1.  1
 2:  .11..  2   12   1....   4       2:  ...11  2    3    ..1..  2
 3: 111..   3   28    .1...  3       3:  ..111  3    7    .1...  3
 4: 1.1..   2   20    ...1.  2       4:  .1111  4   15    ..1..  2
 5: 1....   1   16    ...1.  1       5:  .1.11  3   11    ...1.  1
 6: 1..1.   2   18    .1...  2       6:  .1..1  2    9    ..1..  2
 7: 1.11.   3   22    .1...  3       7:  .11.1  3   13    .1...  3
 8: 1111.   4   30    ...1.  2       8:  ..1.1  2    5   1....   4
 9: 11.1.   3   26    ...1.  1       9: 1.1.1   3   21    .1...  3
10: 11...   2   24    ....1  0      10: 111.1   4   29    ..1..  2
11: 11..1   3   25    ...1.  1      11: 11..1   3   25    ...1.  1
12: 11.11   4   27    .1...  2      12: 11.11   4   27    ..1..  2
13: 11111   5   31    .1...  3      13: 11111   5   31    .1...  3
14: 1.111   4   23    ...1.  2      14: 1.111   4   23    ..1..  2
15: 1..11   3   19    ...1.  1      15: 1..11   3   19    ...1.  1
16: 1...1   2   17    .1...  2      16: 1...1   2   17    ....1  0
17: 1.1.1   3   21   1....   3      17: 1....   1   16    ...1.  1
18: 111.1   4   29   1....   4      18: 1..1.   2   18    .1...  2
19: .11.1   3   13    .1...  3      19: 1.11.   3   22    .1...  3
20: ...1.   2    5    .1...  2      20: 1111.   4   30    .1...  2
21: ...11   1    1    ...1.  1      21: 11.1.   3   26    ...1.  1
22: ..11    2    3    .1...  2      22: 11...   2   24    ..1..  2
23: ..111   3    7    .1...  3      23: 111..   3   28    .1...  3
24: .1111   4   15    ..1..  2      24: 1.1..   2   20   1....   4
25: .1.11   3   11    ...1.  1      25: .1...   1    4    .1...  3
26: .1..1   2    9    ....1  0      26: .11..   2   12    ..1..  2
27: .1...   1    8    ..1..  1      27: .1.1.   1    8    ...1.  1
28: .1.1.   2   10    ..1..  2      28: .1.1.   2   10    ..1..  2
29: .111.   3   14    .1...  3      29: .111.   3   14    .1...  3
30: ..11.   2    6    ..1..  2      30: ..11.   2    6    ..1..  2
31: ...1.   1    2  [...1.  1]      31: ...1.   1    2  [...1.  1]
```

Figure 20.3-B: Two 5-bit adjacent changes (AC) Gray codes that are cycles.

The program [FXT: graph/graph-acgray-demo.cc] allows searches for AC Gray codes. Two cycles for $n = 5$ are shown in figure 20.3-B. It turns out that such paths exist for $n \le 6$ (the only path for $n = 6$ is shown in figure 20.3-C) but there is no AC Gray code for $n = 7$:

```
 time ./bin 7
arg 1: 7 == n  [size in bits]  default=5
arg 2: 0 == maxnp [ stop after maxnp paths (0: never stop)]  default=0
n = 7   #pfct = 0
   #paths = 0    #cycles = 0
./bin 7  20.77s user 0.11s system 98% cpu 21.232 total
```

Nothing is known about the case $n \ge 8$. For $n = 8$ no path is found within 15 days.

By inspection of the AC Gray codes for different values of n we find an ad hoc algorithm. The following routine computes the delta sequence for AC Gray codes for $n \le 6$ [FXT: comb/acgray.cc]:

```
1   void
2   ac_gray_delta(uchar *d, ulong ldn)
3   // Generate a delta sequence for an adjacent-changes (AC) Gray code
4   //   of length n=2**ldn where ldn<=6.
```

```
 0:  ......  0    0    ...1..  2      32:  1.1...  2   40    .1....  4
 1:  ...1..  1    4    ...1.   1      33:  111...  3   56    ..1...  3
 2:  ...11.  2    6    ...1..  2      34:  11....  2   48    ..1...  2
 3:  ....1.  1    2    ..1...  3      35:  11.1..  3   52    ....1.  1
 4:  ..1.1.  2   10    ...1..  2      36:  11.11.  4   54    ...1..  2
 5:  ..111.  3   14    ....1.  1      37:  11..1.  3   50    ..1...  3
 6:  ..11..  2   12    .....1  0      38:  111.1.  4   58    ..1...  2
 7:  ..11.1  3   13    ....1.  1      39:  11111.  5   62    ....1.  1
 8:  ..1111  4   15    ...1..  2      40:  1111..  4   60    .....1  0
 9:  ..1.11  3   11    ..1...  3      41:  1111.1  5   61    ....1.  1
10:  ....11  2    3    ...1..  2      42:  111111  6   63    ..1...  2
11:  ...111  3    7    ....1.  1      43:  111.11  5   59    ..1...  2
12:  ...1.1  2    5    ...1..  2      44:  11..11  4   51    ...1..  2
13:  ....11  1    1    ..1...  3      45:  11.111  5   55    ....1.  1
14:  ..1.1.  2    9    .1....  4      46:  11.1.1  5   53    ...1..  2
15:  .11..1  25   25   ..1...  2      47:  11...1  3   49    ..1...  3
16:  .1...1  2   17    ...1..  2      48:  111..1  4   57    .1....  4
17:  .1.1.1  3   21    ....1.  1      49:  1.1..1  3   41    ..1...  3
18:  .1.111  4   23    ...1..  2      50:  1....1  2   33    ...1..  1
19:  .1..11  3   19    ...1..  3      51:  1...11  3   37    ....1.  1
20:  .11.11  4   27    ...1..  2      52:  1..111  4   39    ...1..  2
21:  .11111  5   31    ....1.  1      53:  1...11  3   35    ..1...  3
22:  .111.1  4   29    .....1  0      54:  1.1.11  4   43    ....1.  2
23:  .111..  3   28    ....1.  1      55:  1.1111  5   47    ....1.  1
24:  .1111.  4   30    ...1..  2      56:  1.11.1  4   45    .....1  0
25:  .11.1.  3   26    ..1...  3      57:  1.11..  3   44    ....1.  1
26:  .1..1.  2   18    ..1...  3      58:  1.111.  4   46    ..1...  2
27:  .1.11.  3   22    ....1.  1      59:  1.1.1.  3   42    ..1...  3
28:  .1.1..  2   20    ...1..  2      60:  1...1.  2   34    ..1...  2
29:  .1....  1   16    .1....  3      61:  1..11.  3   38    ...1..  1
30:  .11...  2   24    .1....  4      62:  1..1..  2   36    ..1...  2
31:  ..1...  1    8    1.....  5      63:  1.....  1   32    [1.....  5]
```

Figure 20.3-C: The (essentially unique) AC Gray code for $n = 6$. While the path is a cycle in the graph, the AC condition does not hold for the transition from the last to the first word.

```
 5    {
 6        if ( ldn<=2 )  // standard Gray code
 7        {
 8            d[0] = 0;
 9            if ( ldn==2 ) { d[1] = 1; d[2] = 0; }
10            return;
11        }
12
13        ac_gray_delta(d, ldn-1);   // recursion
14
15        ulong n = 1UL<<ldn;
16        ulong nh = n/2;
17        if ( 0==(ldn&1) )
18        {
19            if ( ldn>=6 )
20            {
21                reverse(d, nh-1);
22                for (ulong k=0;  k<nh;  ++k)  d[k] = (ldn-2) - d[k];
23            }
24
25            for (ulong k=0,j=n-2;  k<j;  ++k,--j)  d[j] = d[k];
26            d[nh-1] = ldn - 1;
27        }
28        else
29        {
30            for (ulong k=nh-2,j=nh-1;  0!=j;  --k,--j)  d[j] = d[k] + 1;
31            for (ulong k=2,j=n-2;  k<j;  ++k,--j)  d[j] = d[k];
32            d[0] = 0;
33            d[nh] = 0;
34        }
35    }
```

The program [FXT: comb/acgray-demo.cc] can be used to create AC Gray codes for $n \le 6$. For $n \ge 7$ the algorithm produces near-AC Gray codes, where the number of non-AC transitions equals $2^{n-5} - 1$ for odd values of n and $2^{n-5} - 2$ for n even:

```
# non-AC transitions:
 n =0..6    #non-ac = 0
 n =  7     #non-ac = 3
 n =  8     #non-ac = 6
 n =  9     #non-ac = 15
 n = 10     #non-ac = 30
 n = 11     #non-ac = 63
```

```
n = 12    #non-ac = 126
...
```

Near-AC Gray codes with fewer non-AC transitions may exist.

20.4   Edge sorting and lucky paths

The order of the nodes in the representation of the graph does not matter with finding paths as the algorithm at no point refers to it. The order of the outgoing edges, however, *does* matter.

20.4.1   Edge sorting

Consider a large graph that has only a few paths. The calling tree of the recursive function `next_path()` obviously depends on the edge order. Therefore the first path can appear earlier or later in the search. 'Later' may well mean that the path is not found within any reasonable amount of time.

With a bit of luck one might find an ordering of the edges of the graph that will shorten the time until the first path is found. The program [FXT: graph/graph-monotonicgray-demo.cc] searches for monotonic Gray codes and optionally sorts the edges of the graph. The following method sorts the outgoing edges of each node according to a supplied comparison function [FXT: graph/digraph.cc]:

```
1    digraph::sort_edges(int (*cmp)(const ulong &, const ulong &))
2    {
3        if ( 0==vn_ )  // value == index (in e[])
4        {
5            for (ulong k=0; k<ng_; ++k)
6            {
7                ulong x = ep_[k];
8                ulong n = ep_[k+1] - x;
9                selection_sort(e_+x, n, cmp);
10           }
11       }
12       else  // values in vn[]
13       {
14           for (ulong k=0; k<ng_; ++k)
15           {
16               ulong x = ep_[k];
17               ulong n = ep_[k+1] - x;
18               idx_selection_sort(vn_, n, e_+x, cmp);
19           }
20       }
21   }
```

The comparison function actually used imposes the lexicographic order shown in section 1.26 on page 70:

```
1    int my_cmp(const ulong &a, const ulong &b)
2    {
3        if ( a==b )  return  0;
4    #define CODE(x) lexrev2negidx(x);
5        ulong ca = CODE(a);
6        ulong cb = CODE(b);
7        return (ca<cb ? +1 : -1);
8    }
```

The choice was inspired by the observation that the bit-wise difference of successive elements in bit-lex order is either one or three. We search until the first path for 8-bit words is found: for the unsorted graph this task takes 1.14 seconds, for the sorted it takes 0.03 seconds.

20.4.2   Lucky paths

The first Gray code found in the hypercube graph with randomized edge order is shown in figure 20.4-A (left). The corresponding path, as reported by the method `digraph_paths::print_turns` [FXT: graph/digraph-paths.cc], is described in the right column. Here `nn` is the number of neighbors of `node`, `xe` is the index of the neighbor (`next`) in the list of edges of `node`. Finally `xf` is the index among the *free* nodes in the list. The latter corresponds to the value `fct-1` in the function `next_path()` given in section 20.2 on page 393.

```
 0:  .... 0   0    1... 3          step:  node -> next [xf xe / nn]
 1:  1... 1   8    ..1. 1            0:     0  ->    8  [ 0  0 /  4]
 2:  1.1. 2  10    .1.. 2            1:     8  ->   10  [ 0  0 /  4]
 3:  111. 3  14    ...1 0            2:    10  ->   14  [ 0  0 /  4]
 4:  1111 4  15    1... 3            3:    14  ->   15  [ 0  0 /  4]
 5:  .111 3   7    .1.. 2            4:    15  ->    7  [ 0  0 /  4]
 6:  ..11 2   3    ...1 0            5:     7  ->    3  [ 0  1 /  4]
 7:  ..1. 1   2    .1.. 2            6:     3  ->    2  [ 1  2 /  4]
 8:  .11. 2   6    ..1. 1            7:     2  ->    6  [ 0  3 /  4]
 9:  .1.. 1   4    1... 3            8:     6  ->    4  [ 0  0 /  4]
10:  11.. 2  12    ...1 0            9:     4  ->   12  [ 1  3 /  4]
11:  11.1 3  13    1... 3           10:    12  ->   13  [ 0  0 /  4]
12:  .1.1 2   5    .1.. 2           11:    13  ->    5  [ 0  1 /  4]
13:  ...1 1   1    1... 3           12:     5  ->    1  [ 0  3 /  4]
14:  1..1 2   9    ..1. 1           13:     1  ->    9  [ 0  2 /  4]
15:  1.11 3  11   [1.11  -]         14:     9  ->   11  [ 0  0 /  4]
                              Path: #non-first-free turns = 2
```

Figure 20.4-A: A Gray code in the hypercube graph with randomized edge order (left) and the path description (right, see text).

If xf equals zero at some step, the first free neighbor was visited. If xf is nonzero, a dead end was reached in the course of the search and there was at least one U-turn. If the path is not the first found, the U-turn might well correspond to a previous path.

If there was no U-turn, the number of *non-first-free* turns is zero (the number is given as the last line of the report). If it is zero, we call the path found a *lucky path*. For each given ordering of the edges and each starting position of the search there is at most one lucky path and if there is, it is the first path found.

If the first path is a lucky path, the search effectively 'falls through': the number of operations is a constant times the number of edges. That is, if a lucky path exists it is found almost immediately even for huge graphs.

20.5   Gray codes for Lyndon words

We search Gray codes for n-bit binary Lyndon words where n is a prime. Here is a Gray code for the 5-bit Lyndon words that is a cycle:

```
...11
.1.11
.1111
..111
..1.1
```

An important application of such Gray codes is the construction of *single track Gray codes* which can be obtained by appending rotated versions of the block. The following is a single track Gray code based on the block given. At each stage, the block is rotated by two positions (horizontal format):

```
######  --##--  -####-  ------  ---###
-####-  ------  ---###  ######  --##--
---###  ######  --##--  -####-  ------
--##--  -####-  ------  ---###  ######
------  ---###  ######  --##--  -####-
```

The *transition count* (the number of zero-one transitions) is by construction the same for each track. The all-zero and the all-one words are missing in the Gray code, its length equals $2^n - 2$.

20.5.1   Graph search with edge sorting

Gray codes for the 7-bit binary Lyndon words like those shown in figure 20.5-A can easily be found by a graph search. In fact, all of them can be generated in a short time: for $n = 7$ there are 395 Gray codes (starting with the word 0000..001) of which 112 are cycles.

The search for such a path for the next prime, $n = 11$, does not seem to give a result in reasonable time.

```
 0:   ......1     ......1     ......1     ......1     ......1     ......1
 1:   .....11     ...1..1     ...1..1     ...1..1     ....1..1    .....11
 2:   ....111     ..11..1     ..11..1     ..11..1     ..1.11      ....111
 3:   ...1111     ...111.1    ...111.1    ...1..1     .1.11.11    ...1..1
 4:   ..11111     .1.1..1     .111111     .1.1..1     .1.1111     .1.1.1
 5:   ..11.11     ..1.111     .111111     ..111.1     .111111     ..111.1
 6:   ..1...11    .11.111     ..11.111    .11.111     .11.111     ...11..1
 7:   ..1.111     .111111     ..1.111     ..11.11     ..1.111     ...1.11
 8:   .11.111     .1.1111     ..1.1.1     ..1..11     ..1.1.1     ...1.11
 9:   .111111     .1.1.11     ....111     .111.1      .111.1      ....1111
10:   .1.1111     ...1.11     ....111     .11.111     ...11.1     ...11111
11:   .1.1.11     ...1111     ...1111     .111111     ...1.1      ..11.11
12:   ...1.11     ..11111     .1.1111     .1.1111     ....111     ...1..11
13:   ...1..1     .1.1.11     .1.1.11     .1.1.11     ....11      ...1.111
14:   ...11.1     .1..11      ...1.11     ...1.11     ..1.1       .11.111
15:   ..111.1     ....11      ..11.11     ...1111     ..11.11     .111111
16:   ..1.1.1     ....111     .1...11     .....111    ..11111     .1.1111
17:   ....1.1     ....1.1     .....11     .....11     ...1111     .1.1.11
```

Figure 20.5-A: Various Gray codes through the length-7 binary Lyndon words. The first four are cycles.

```
    k :  [ node]  lyn_dec  lyn_bin  #rot  rot(lyn)   diff    delta
    0 : [    0]      1     ......1   0    ......1    ......1   0
    1 : [    1]      3     .....11   0    .....11    .....1.   1
    2 : [    3]      7     ....111   0    ....111    ....1..   2
    3 : [    7]     15     ...1111   0    ...1111    ...1...   3
    4 : [   13]     31     ..11111   0    ..11111    ..1....   4
    5 : [   17]     63     .111111   0    .111111    .1.....   5
    6 : [   15]     47     .1.1111   0    .1.1111    ..1....   4
    7 : [   10]     23     ..1.111   1    .1.111.    ......1   0
    8 : [   16]     55     .11.111   1    11.111.    1......   6
    9 : [   11]     27     ..11.11   2    11.11..    .....1.   1
   10 : [    5]     11     ...1.11   2    .1.11..    1......   6
   11 : [   14]     43     .1.1.11   2    .1.11.1    ......1   0
   12 : [    6]     13     ...11.1   0    ...11.1    .1.....   5
   13 : [   12]     29     ..111.1   0    ..111.1    ..1....   4
   14 : [    8]     19     ..1..11   3    .11..1.    ....1..   2
   15 : [    4]      9     ...1..1   0    ...1..1    ..1....   4
   16 : [    9]     21     ..1.1.1   3    .1.1..1    .1.....   5
   17 : [    2]      5     ....1.1   3    .1.1...    ......1   0
```

Figure 20.5-B: A Gray code through the length-7 binary Lyndon words.

If we do not insist on a Gray code through the cyclic minima, but allow for arbitrary rotations of the Lyndon words, then more Gray codes exist. For that purpose nodes are declared adjacent if there is any cyclic rotation of the second node's value that differs in exactly one bit to the first node's value. The cyclic rotations can be recovered easily after a path is found. This is done in [FXT: graph/graph-lyndon-gray-demo.cc] whose output is shown in figure 20.5-B. Still, already for $n = 11$ we do not get a result. As the corresponding graph has 186 nodes and 1954 edges, this is not a surprise.

Now we sort the edges according to the comparison function [FXT: graph/lyndon-cmp.cc]

```
1    int lyndon_cmp0(const ulong &a, const ulong &b)
2    {
3        int bc = bit_count_cmp(a, b);
4        if ( bc )  return  -bc;  // more bits first
5        else
6        {
7            if ( a==b )  return 0;
8            return  (a>b ?  +1 : -1);  // greater numbers last
9        }
10   }
```

where `bit_count_cmp()` is defined in [FXT: bits/bitcount.h]:

```
1    static inline int bit_count_cmp(const ulong &a, const ulong &b)
2    {
3        ulong ca = bit_count(a);
4        ulong cb = bit_count(b);
5        return ( ca==cb ? 0 : (ca>cb ? +1 : -1) );
6    }
```

We find a Gray code (which also is a cycle) for $n = 11$ immediately. Same for $n = 13$, again a cycle. The

k :	[node]	lyn_dec	lyn_bin	#rot	rot(lyn)	diff	delta
0 :	[0]	1	1	0	1	1	0
1 :	[1]	3	11	0	11	...........1.	1
2 :	[3]	7	111	0	111	..........1..	2
3 :	[7]	15	1111	0	1111	.........1...	3
4 :	[15]	31	11111	0	11111	........1....	4
5 :	[31]	63	111111	0	111111	.......1.....	5
6 :	[63]	127	1111111	0	1111111	......1......	6
7 :	[125]	255	11111111	0	11111111	.....1.......	7
8 :	[239]	511	111111111	0	111111111	....1........	8
9 :	[417]	1023	...1111111111	0	...1111111111	...1.........	9
10 :	[589]	2047	..11111111111	0	..11111111111	..1..........	10
11 :	[629]	4095	.111111111111	0	.111111111111	.1...........	11
12 :	[618]	3071	.1.1111111111	0	.1.1111111111	..1..........	10
13 :	[514]	1535	..1.111111111	1	.1.111111111.	1	0
14 :	[624]	3583	.11.111111111	1	11.111111111.	1...........	12
15 :	[550]	1791	..11.11111111	2	11.11111111..	...........1.	1
16 :	[626]	3839	.111.11111111	2	11.11111111.1	1	0
17 :	[567]	1919	..111.1111111	3	11.1111111..1	..........1..	2
18 :	[627]	3967	.1111.1111111	3	11.1111111.11	...........1.	1
19 :	[576]	1983	..1111.111111	4	11.111111..11	.........1...	3
20 :	[628]	4031	.11111.111111	4	11.111111.111	..........1..	2
21 :	[581]	2015	..11111.11111	5	11.11111..111	........1....	4
22 :	[404]	991	...1111.11111	5	11.11111...11	..........1..	2
23 :	[614]	3039	.1.1111.11111	5	11.11111.1.11	.........1...	3
24 :	[508]	1519	..1.1111.1111	6	11.1111..1.11	.......1.....	5
25 :	[584]	2031	..111111.1111	6	11.1111..1111	..........1..	2
[--snip--]							
615 :	[4]	9	.........1..1	5	....1..1.....	..1..........	10
616 :	[36]	73	......1..1..1	2	....1..1..1..	..........1..	2
617 :	[32]	65	......1.....1	2	....1.....1..	.......1.....	5
618 :	[33]	67	......1....11	2	....1.....11.	.........1...	3
619 :	[153]	323	....1.1....11	2	..1.1.....11.	..1..........	10
620 :	[65]	133	.....1....1.1	8	..1.1.....1..	.........1...	3
621 :	[154]	325	....1.1...1.1	2	..1.1...1.1..	........1....	4
622 :	[79]	161	.....1.1....1	10	..1.....1.1..	....1........	8
623 :	[16]	33	.......1....1	10	..1.......1..	........1....	4
624 :	[126]	265	....1....1..1	2	..1....1..1..	.......1.....	5
625 :	[145]	305	....1..11...1	10	..1....1..11.	...........1.	1
626 :	[130]	273	....1...1...1	10	..1....1...1.	..........1..	2
627 :	[188]	401	....11..1...1	10	..1....11..1.	........1....	4
628 :	[71]	145	.....1..1...1	10	..1.....1..1.	.......1.....	5
629 :	[8]	17	........1...1	10	..1........1.	........1....	4

Figure 20.5-C: Begin and end of a Gray cycle through the 13-bit binary Lyndon words.

graph for $n = 13$ has 630 nodes and 8,056 edges, so finding a path is quite unexpected. The cycle found starts and ends as shown in figure 20.5-C.

For next candidate ($n = 17$) we do not find a Gray code within many hours of search. No surprise for a graph with 7,710 nodes and 130,828 edges. We try another edge sorting scheme, an ordering based on the binary Gray code [FXT: graph/lyndon-cmp.cc]:

```
1    int lyndon_cmp2(const ulong &a, const ulong &b)
2    {
3        if ( a==b )  return 0;
4    #define CODE(x) gray_code(x)
5        ulong ta = CODE(a), tb = CODE(b);
6        return  ( ta<tb ? +1 : -1);
7    }
```

We find a cycle for $n = 17$ and all smaller primes. All are cycles and all paths are lucky paths. The following edge sorting scheme also leads to Gray codes for all prime n where $3 \leq n \leq 17$:

```
1    int lyndon_cmp3(const ulong &a, const ulong &b)
2    {
3        if ( a==b )  return 0;
4    #define CODE(x) inverse_gray_code(x)
5        ulong ta = CODE(a), tb = CODE(b);
6        return  ( ta<tb ? +1 : -1);
7    }
```

Same for $n = 19$, the graph has 27,594 nodes and 523,978 edges. Indeed the sorting scheme leads to cycles for all odd $n \leq 27$. All these paths are lucky paths, a fact that we can exploit.

20.5.2   An optimized algorithm

n	number of nodes	tag-size	time		n	number of nodes	tag-size	time
23	364,722	0.25 MB	1 sec		35	981,706,830	1 GB	1 h
25	1,342,182	1 MB	3 sec		37	3,714,566,310	4 GB	7 h
27	4,971,066	4 MB	12 sec		39	14,096,303,342	16 GB	2 d
29	18,512,790	16 MB	1 min		41	53,634,713,550	64 GB	10 d
31	69,273,666	64 MB	4 min		43	204,560,302,842	256 GB	>40 d
33	260,301,174	256 MB	16 min		45	781,874,934,568	1 TB	>160 d

Figure 20.5-D: Memory and (approximate) time needed for computing Gray codes with n-bit Lyndon words. The number of nodes equals the number of length-n necklaces minus 2. The size of the tag array equals $2^n/4$ bits or $2^n/32$ bytes.

With edge sorting functions that lead to a lucky path we can discard most of the data used with graph searching. We only need to keep track of whether a node has been visited so far. A tag-array ([FXT: ds/bitarray.h], see section 4.6 on page 164) suffices.

With n-bit Lyndon words the amount of tag-bits needed is 2^n. Find an implementation of the algorithm as [FXT: `class lyndon_gray` in graph/lyndon-gray.h].

If only the cyclic minima of the values are tagged, then only $2^n/2$ bits are needed if the access to the single necklace consisting of all ones is treated separately. This variant of the algorithm is activated by uncommenting the line `#define ALT_ALGORITM`. As the lowest bit in a necklace is always one, we need only $2^n/4$ bits: simply shift the words to the right by one position before testing or writing to the tag array. This can be activated by additionally uncommenting the line `#define ALTALT` in the file.

When a node is visited, the algorithm creates a table of neighbors and selects the minimum among the free nodes with respect to the edge sorting function used. Then the table of neighbors is discarded to minimize memory usage.

If no neighbor is found, the number of nodes visited so far is returned. If this number equals the number of n-bit Lyndon words, then a lucky path was found. With composite n a Gray code for n-bit necklaces (with the exception of the all-ones and the all-zeros word) will be searched.

Four variants of the algorithm have been found so far, corresponding to edge sorting with the 3rd, 5th, 21th, and 29th power of the Gray code. We refer to these functions as comparison functions 0, 1, 2, and 3, respectively. All of these lead to cycles for all primes $n \leq 31$. The resources needed with greater values of n are shown in figure 20.5-D.

Using a 64-bit machine equipped with more than 4 Gigabyte of RAM, it can be verified that three of the edge sorting functions lead to a Gray cycle also for $n = 37$, the 3rd power version fails. One of the sorting functions *may* lead to a Gray code for $n = 41$.

A program to compute the Gray codes is [FXT: graph/lyndon-gray-demo.cc], four arguments can be given:

```
arg 1: 13 == n  [ a prime < BITS_PER_LONG ]  default=17
arg 2: 1 == wh  [printing: 0==>none, 1==>delta seq., 2==>full output]  default=1
arg 3: 3 == ncmp  [use comparison function (0,1,2,3)]  default=2
arg 4: 0 == testall  [special: test all odd values <= value]  default=0
```

An example with full output is given in figure 20.5-E. A 64-bit CRC (see section 41.3 on page 868) is computed from the delta sequence (rightmost column) and printed with the last word.

For large n one might want to print only the delta sequence, as shown in figure 20.5-F. The CRC is used to determine whether two delta sequences are different. Different sequences sometimes start identically.

```
% ./bin 7 2 0   # 7 bits, full output, comparison function 0
n = 7   #lyn = 18
      1:   .....1   0   ......1   1   .....1   0
      2:   ...1..1   0   ....1..1   1   ...1...   3
      3:   ..1..11   3   ...11..1   1   ..1...   4
      4:   ..1.111   3   ..111..1   1   .1....   5
      5:   .1.1111   2   .1111..1   1   .....1..   2
      6:   .1.1.11   2   .1.11..1   1   ..1....   4
      7:   .11.111   5   11.11..1   1   1.....   6
      8:   .111111   2   11111..1   1   .1....   4
      9:   ..11111   2   11111...   ......1   0
     10:   ..111.1   2   111.1...   ...1...   3
     11:   .1.1.1   2   1.1.1...   .1....   5
     12:   ...1.1   2   ..1.1...   1.....   6
     13:   ...1.11   1   ..1.11.   ....1.   1
     14:   ..11.11   1   .11.11.   ..1...1.   5
     15:   ...11.1   2   ..1.1...   ....1.   1
     16:   ...1111   2   .1111...   ...1...   3
     17:   ....111   2   ..111...   ..1....   5
     18:   .....11   2   ....11..   ...1..   4
   last = .....11   crc=0b14a5846c41d57f
n = 7   #lyn = 18   #= 18
```

Figure 20.5-E: A Gray code for 7-bit Lyndon words.

```
% ./bin 13 1 2   # 13 bits, delta seq. output, comparison function 2
n = 13   #lyn = 630
06B574583546459625464367340A74684A106C0145120825747A745247AC8564567018A7654647484A756A546457CA1ACBC1C
856BA9A64B974565486456596452194252153153BC82BC75BA0292625635426742462475A3ACB9761560C37412583758CA5624
B8C6A6C6A87A9C20CBA4534042014540523129075697651563160204230A7BA31C1485C6105201510490BCA891BA9B1B9AC0
A9A89B898A565B878574586574784549546702305A412753154587674657478457845470379A8586B0A7698578767976759
A976567686A567656A576B86581305A20AB0ACB0AB5352343823546532524756 3A432532A3723546576435723736246 34642
45323974234325356532364232632352343275323423253969268532342325826424368236323463623584232423832 42327
5232423253234326423242353234 23123
last = ..........11   crc=568dab04b55aa2fb
n = 13   #lyn = 630   #= 630

% ./bin 13 1 3   # 13 bits, delta seq. output, comparison function 3
n = 13   #lyn = 630
06B574583546459625464367353 71CA8B1587BA7610635285A0C2484B9713476B689A897AC98768968B9A106326016261050
1424B8979A78987B97898C98921941315313698314281687BCB9469C489C6210205B050A1A7A4568A9BC5CB79AB647B74812
0AB30BC1A131ACB120B0164CA1CABA121ABACA2B0BACAB18457867849958486764 6A8456191654694745787545865490137
4020103101210427017121650745 7B854606C16BC52380136516413016 4BC7987A09872CBA9A87A20B787AC9B7CBA834C0C1
3C341C1042010C14C01C414587854645A854C95035A6A9570A9756586B9B5969580A0872C3123B0CB316BC6C0B21B2C0C2C0
5301C0530CB1C1530C01CB0BC20CBC0CB1C87565756865A75A65A40898A898B91CA898A8B898A81BC8A9ACA989AB817A9BC1
BA9ABA9CA9AB918A1CACBAC9BCB0BC
last = ..........11   crc=745def277b1fbed0
n = 13   #lyn = 630   #= 630
```

Figure 20.5-F: Delta sequences for two different Gray codes for 13-bit Lyndon words.

```
% ./bin 29 0 0   # 29 bits, output=progress, comparison function 0
n = 29   #lyn = 18512790
................    1048576 (  5.66406 % )   crc=ceabc5f2056be699
................    2097152 ( 11.3281 % )    crc=76dd94f1a554b50d
................    3145728 ( 16.9922 % )    crc=6b39957f1e141f4d
................    4194304 ( 22.6563 % )    crc=53419af1f1185dc0
................    5242880 ( 28.3203 % )    crc=45d45b193f8ee566
...............     6291456 ( 33.9844 % )    crc=95a24c824f56e196
...............     7340032 ( 39.6484 % )    crc=003ee5af5b248e34
..............      8388608 ( 45.3125 % )    crc=23cb74d3ea0c4587
..............      9437184 ( 50.9766 % )    crc=896fd04c87dd0d43
.............       10485760 ( 56.6406 % )   crc=b00d8c899f0fc791
.............       11534336 ( 62.3047 % )   crc=d148f1b95b23eeab
............        12582912 ( 67.9688 % )   crc=82971e2ed4863050
...........         13631488 ( 73.6328 % )   crc=f249ad5b4fed252d
...........         14680064 ( 79.2969 % )   crc=909821d0c7246a98
..........          15728640 ( 84.9609 % )   crc=1c5d68e38e55b3ca
.........           16777216 ( 90.625 % )    crc=0e64f82c67c79cf1
.......             17825792 ( 96.2891 % )   crc=62c17b9f3c644396
last = ..................11                  crc=5736fc9365da927e
n = 29   #lyn = 18512790   #= 18512790
```

Figure 20.5-G: Computation of a Gray code through the 29-bit Lyndon words. Most output is suppressed, only the CRC is printed at certain checkpoints.

For still greater values of n even the delta sequence tends to get huge (for example, with $n = 37$ the sequence would be approximately 3.7 GB). One can suppress all output except for a progress indication, as shown in figure 20.5-G. Here the CRC checksum is updated only with every (cyclically unadjusted) 2^{16}-th Lyndon word.

Sometimes a Gray code through the necklaces (except for the all-zeros and all-ones words) is also found for composite n. Comparison functions 0, 1, and 2 lead to Gray codes (which are cycles) for all odd $n \leq 33$. Gray cycles are also found with comparison function 3, except for $n = 21$, 27, and 33. All functions give Gray cycles also for $n = 4$ and $n = 6$. The values of n for which no Gray code was found are the even values ≥ 8.

20.5.3 No Gray codes for even $n \geq 8$

As the parity of the words in a Gray code sequence alternates between one and zero, the difference between the numbers words of odd and even weight must be zero or one. If it is one, no Gray cycle can exist because the parity of the first and last word is identical.

We use the relations from section 18.3.2 on page 382. For Lyndon words of odd length there are the same number of words for odd and even weight by symmetry, so a Gray code (and also a Gray cycle) can exist.

For even length the sequence of numbers of Lyndon words of odd and even weights start as:

n:	2,	4,	6,	8,	10,	12,	14,	16,	18,	20,	22,	24,	26,	
odd:	1,	2,	5,	16,	51,	170,	585,	2048,	7280,	26214,	95325,	349520,	1290555,	...
even:	0,	1,	4,	14,	48,	165,	576,	2032,	7252,	26163,	95232,	349350,	1290240,	...
diff:	1,	1,	1,	2,	3,	5,	9,	16,	28,	51,	93,	170,	315,	...

The last row gives the differences, entry A000048 in [312]. All entries for $n \geq 8$ are greater than one, so no Gray code exists.

For the number of necklaces we have, for $n = 2, 4, 6, \ldots$:

n:	2,	4,	6,	8,	10,	12,	14,	16,	18,	20,	22,	24,	26,	
odd:	1,	2,	6,	16,	52,	172,	586,	2048,	7286,	26216,	95326,	349536,	1290556,	...
even:	2,	4,	8,	20,	56,	180,	596,	2068,	7316,	26272,	95420,	349716,	1290872,	...
diff:	1,	2,	2,	4,	4,	8,	10,	20,	30,	56,	94,	180,	316,	...

The (absolute) difference of both sequences is entry A000013 in [312]. We see that for $n \geq 4$ the numbers are greater than one, so no Gray code exists.

If we exclude the all-ones and all-zeros words, then the differences are

n:	2,	4,	6,	8,	10,	12,	14,	16,	18,	20,	22,	24,	26,	
diff:	1,	0,	0,	2,	2,	6,	8,	18,	28,	54,	92,	178,	314,	...

And again, no Gray code exists for $n \geq 8$. That is, we have found Gray codes, and even cycles, for all computationally feasible sizes where they can exist.

Part III

Fast transforms

Chapter 21

The Fourier transform

We introduce the discrete Fourier transform and give algorithms for its fast computation. Implementations and optimization considerations for complex and real-valued transforms are given. The fast Fourier transforms are the basis of the algorithms for fast convolution described in chapter 22. These are in turn the core of the fast high precision multiplication routines treated in chapter 28. The number theoretic transforms are treated in chapter 26. Algorithms for Fourier transforms based on fast convolution like Bluestein's algorithm and Rader's algorithm are given in chapter 22.

21.1   The discrete Fourier transform

The *discrete Fourier transform* (DFT) of a complex sequence $a = [a_0, a_1, \ldots, a_{n-1}]$ of length n is the complex sequence $c = [c_0, c_1, \ldots, c_{n-1}]$ defined by

$$c = \mathcal{F}[a] \tag{21.1-1a}$$

$$c_k := \frac{1}{\sqrt{n}} \sum_{x=0}^{n-1} a_x \, z^{+x\,k} \quad \text{where} \quad z = e^{2\pi i/n} \tag{21.1-1b}$$

z is a primitive n-th root of unity: $z^n = 1$ and $z^j \neq 1$ for $0 < j < n$.

The *inverse discrete Fourier transform* is

$$a = \mathcal{F}^{-1}[c] \tag{21.1-2a}$$

$$a_x := \frac{1}{\sqrt{n}} \sum_{k=0}^{n-1} c_k \, z^{-x\,k} \tag{21.1-2b}$$

To see this, consider the element y of the inverse transform of the transform of a:

$$\mathcal{F}^{-1}[\mathcal{F}[a]]_y = \frac{1}{\sqrt{n}} \sum_{k=0}^{n-1} \frac{1}{\sqrt{n}} \sum_{x=0}^{n-1} (a_x \, z^{x\,k}) \, z^{-y\,k} \tag{21.1-3a}$$

$$= \frac{1}{n} \sum_x a_x \sum_k (z^{x-y})^k \tag{21.1-3b}$$

Now $\sum_k (z^{x-y})^k = n$ for $x = y$ and 0 else. This is because z is an n-th primitive root of unity: with $x = y$ the sum consists of n times $z^0 = 1$, with $x \neq y$ the summands lie on the unit circle (on the vertices of an equilateral polygon with center 0) and add up to 0. Therefore the whole expression is equal to

$$\frac{1}{n} n \sum_x a_x \, \delta_{x,y} = a_y \quad \text{where} \quad \delta_{x,y} := \begin{cases} 1 & \text{if } x = y \\ 0 & \text{otherwise} \end{cases} \tag{21.1-4}$$

Here we will call the transform with the plus in the exponent the forward transform. The choice is actually arbitrary, engineers seem to prefer the minus for the forward transform, mathematicians the plus. The sign in the exponent is called the *sign of the transform*.

J. Arndt, *Matters Computational: Ideas, Algorithms, Source Code,*
DOI 10.1007/978-3-642-14764-7_21, © Springer-Verlag Berlin Heidelberg 2011

The Fourier transform is linear: for $\alpha, \beta \in \mathbb{C}$ we have

$$\mathcal{F}[\alpha\, a + \beta\, b] \;\; = \;\; \alpha\,\mathcal{F}[a] + \beta\,\mathcal{F}[b] \tag{21.1-5}$$

Further *Parseval's equation* holds, the sum of squares of the absolute values is identical for a sequence and its Fourier transform:

$$\sum_{x=0}^{n-1} |a_x|^2 \;\; = \;\; \sum_{k=0}^{n-1} |c_k|^2 \tag{21.1-6}$$

A straightforward implementation of the discrete Fourier transform, that is, the computation of n sums each of length n, requires $O(n^2)$ operations [FXT: fft/slowft.cc]:

```
1   void slow_ft(Complex *f, long n, int is)
2   {
3       Complex h[n];
4       const double ph0 = is*2.0*M_PI/n;
5       for (long w=0; w<n; ++w)
6       {
7           Complex t = 0.0;
8           for (long k=0; k<n; ++k)
9           {
10              t +=  f[k] * SinCos(ph0*k*w);
11          }
12          h[w] = t;
13      }
14      acopy(h, f, n);
15  }
```

The variable $\mathtt{is} = \sigma = \pm 1$ is the sign of the transform, the function $\mathtt{SinCos(x)}$ returns the complex number $\cos(x) + i \sin(x)$. Note that the normalization factor $1/\sqrt{n}$ in front of the sums has been left out. The inverse of the transform with sign σ is the transform with sign $-\sigma$ followed by a multiplication of each element by $1/n$. The sum of squares of the original sequence and its transform are equal up to a factor $1/\sqrt{n}$.

A *fast Fourier transform* (FFT) algorithm has complexity $O(n \log(n))$. There are several different FFT algorithms with many variants.

21.2 Radix-2 FFT algorithms

We fix some notation. In what follows let a be a length-n sequence with n a power of 2.

- Let $a^{(even)}$ and $a^{(odd)}$ denote the length-$n/2$ subsequences of those elements of a that have even and odd indices, respectively. That is, $a^{(even)} = [a_0, a_2, a_4, a_6, \ldots, a_{n-2}]$ and $a^{(odd)} = [a_1, a_3, \ldots, a_{n-1}]$.

- Let $a^{(left)}$ and $a^{(right)}$ denote the left and right subsequences, respectively. That is, $a^{(left)} = [a_0, a_1, \ldots, a_{n/2-1}]$ and $a^{(right)} = [a_{n/2}, a_{n/2+1}, \ldots, a_{n-1}]$.

- Let $c = \mathcal{S}^k a$ denote the sequence with elements $c_x = a_x\, e^{\sigma\, 2\pi i k x/n}$ where $\sigma = \pm 1$ is the sign of the transform. The symbol $\mathcal{S}$ shall suggest a shift operator. With radix-2 FFT algorithms only $\mathcal{S}^{1/2}$ is needed. Note that the operator $\mathcal{S}$ depends on the sign of the transform.

- In relations between sequences we sometimes emphasize the length of the sequences on both sides as in $a^{(even)} \stackrel{n/2}{=} b^{(odd)} + c^{(odd)}$. In these relations the operators $+$ and $-$ are element-wise.

21.2.1   Decimation in time (DIT) FFT

The following observation is the key to the (radix-2) *decimation in time* (DIT) FFT algorithm, also called the *Cooley-Tukey* FFT algorithm: For even values of n the k-th element of the Fourier transform is

$$\mathcal{F}[a]_k = \sum_{x=0}^{n-1} a_x z^{xk} = \sum_{x=0}^{n/2-1} a_{2x} z^{2xk} + \sum_{x=0}^{n/2-1} a_{2x+1} z^{(2x+1)k} \tag{21.2-1a}$$

$$= \sum_{x=0}^{n/2-1} a_{2x} z^{2xk} + z^k \sum_{x=0}^{n/2-1} a_{2x+1} z^{2xk} \tag{21.2-1b}$$

where $z = e^{\sigma\, 2\pi i/n}$, $\sigma = \pm 1$ is the sign of the transform, and $k \in \{0, 1, \ldots, n-1\}$.

The identity tells us how to compute the k-th element of the length-n Fourier transform from the length-$n/2$ Fourier transforms of the even and odd indexed subsequences.

To rewrite the length-n transform in terms of length-$n/2$ transforms, we have to distinguish whether $0 \leq k < n/2$ or $n/2 \leq k < n$. In the expressions we rewrite $k \in \{0, 1, 2, \ldots, n-1\}$ as $k = j + \delta\frac{n}{2}$ where $j \in \{0, 1, 2, \ldots, n/2-1\}$ and $\delta \in \{0, 1\}$:

$$\sum_{x=0}^{n-1} a_x z^{x\,(j+\delta\frac{n}{2})} = \sum_{x=0}^{n/2-1} a_x^{(even)} z^{2x\,(j+\delta\frac{n}{2})} + z^{j+\delta\frac{n}{2}} \sum_{x=0}^{n/2-1} a_x^{(odd)} z^{2x\,(j+\delta\frac{n}{2})} \tag{21.2-2a}$$

$$= \begin{cases} \displaystyle\sum_{x=0}^{n/2-1} a_x^{(even)} z^{2xj} + z^j \sum_{x=0}^{n/2-1} a_x^{(odd)} z^{2xj} & \text{for} \quad \delta = 0 \\[2em] \displaystyle\sum_{x=0}^{n/2-1} a_x^{(even)} z^{2xj} - z^j \sum_{x=0}^{n/2-1} a_x^{(odd)} z^{2xj} & \text{for} \quad \delta = 1 \end{cases} \tag{21.2-2b}$$

The minus sign in the relation for $\delta = 1$ is due to the equality $z^{j+1\cdot n/2} = z^j\, z^{n/2} = -z^j$.

Observing that z^2 is just the root of unity that appears in a length-$n/2$ transform we can rewrite the last two equations to obtain the *radix-2 DIT FFT step*:

$$\mathcal{F}[a]^{(left)} \overset{n/2}{=} \mathcal{F}[a^{(even)}] + \mathcal{S}^{1/2} \mathcal{F}[a^{(odd)}] \tag{21.2-3a}$$

$$\mathcal{F}[a]^{(right)} \overset{n/2}{=} \mathcal{F}[a^{(even)}] - \mathcal{S}^{1/2} \mathcal{F}[a^{(odd)}] \tag{21.2-3b}$$

The length-n transform has been replaced by two transforms of length $n/2$. If n is a power of 2, this scheme can be applied recursively until length-one transforms are reached which are identity ('do nothing') operations.

The complexity is $O(n \log_2(n))$: there are $\log_2(n)$ splitting steps, the work in each step is $O(n)$.

21.2.1.1   Recursive implementation

A recursive implementation of radix-2 DIT FFT given as pseudocode (C++ version in [FXT: fft/recfft2.cc]) is

```
1    procedure rec_fft_dit2(a[], n, x[], is)
2    // complex a[0..n-1] input
3    // complex x[0..n-1] result
4    {
5        complex b[0..n/2-1], c[0..n/2-1]    // workspace
6        complex s[0..n/2-1], t[0..n/2-1]    // workspace
7
8        if n == 1 then  // end of recursion
9        {
10           x[0] := a[0]
11           return
```

```
12          }
13
14          nh := n/2
15
16          for k:=0 to nh-1   // copy to workspace
17          {
18              s[k] := a[2*k]     // even indexed elements
19              t[k] := a[2*k+1]   // odd  indexed elements
20          }
21
22          // recursion: call two half-length FFTs:
23          rec_fft_dit2(s[], nh, b[], is)
24          rec_fft_dit2(t[], nh, c[], is)
25
26          fourier_shift(c[], nh, is*1/2)
27
28          for k:=0 to nh-1   // copy back from workspace
29          {
30              x[k]    := b[k] + c[k]
31              x[k+nh] := b[k] - c[k]
32          }
33      }
```

The parameter $\mathtt{is} = \sigma = \pm 1$ is the sign of the transform. The data length $\mathtt{n}$ must be a power of 2. The result is returned in the array $\mathtt{x[]}$. Note that normalization (multiplication of each element of $\mathtt{x[]}$ by $1/\sqrt{n}$) is not included here.

The procedure uses the subroutine $\mathtt{fourier\_shift()}$ which modifies the array $\mathtt{c[]}$ according to the operation $\mathcal{S}^v$: each element $\mathtt{c[k]}$ is multiplied by $e^{v\,2\pi\,ik/n}$. It is called with $v = \pm 1/2$ for the Fourier transform. The pseudocode (C++ equivalent in [FXT: fft/fouriershift.cc]) is

```
1   procedure fourier_shift(c[], n, v)
2   {
3       for k:=0 to n-1
4       {
5           c[k] := c[k] * exp(v*2.0*PI*I*k/n)
6       }
7   }
```

The recursive FFT-procedure involves $O(n)$ function calls to itself, these can be avoided by rewriting it in a iterative way. We can even do all operations *in-place*, no temporary workspace is needed at all. The price is the necessity of an additional data reordering: the procedure $\mathtt{revbin\_permute(a[],n)}$ rearranges the array $\mathtt{a[]}$ in a way that each element a_x is swapped with $a_{\tilde{x}}$, where $\tilde{x}$ is obtained from x by reversing its binary digits. Methods for doing this are discussed in section 2.6 on page 118.

21.2.1.2   Iterative implementation

A non-recursive procedure for the radix-2 DIT FFT is (C++ version in [FXT: fft/fftdit2.cc]):

```
1   procedure fft_depth_first_dit2(a[], ldn, is)
2   // complex a[0..2**ldn-1] input, result
3   {
4       n := 2**ldn  // length of a[] is a power of 2
5
6       revbin_permute(a[], n)
7
8       for ldm:=1 to ldn  // log_2(n) iterations
9       {
10          m  := 2**ldm
11          mh := m/2
12
13          for r:=0 to n-m step m   // n/m iterations
14          {
15              for j:=0 to mh-1   // m/2 iterations
16              {
17                  e := exp(is*2*PI*I*j/m)   // log_2(n)*n/m*m/2 = log_2(n)*n/2 computations
18
19                  u := a[r+j]
20                  v := a[r+j+mh] * e
21
22                  a[r+j]    := u + v
23                  a[r+j+mh] := u - v
24              }
25          }
```

```
26        }
27    }
```

This version of a non-recursive FFT procedure already avoids the calling overhead and it works in-place. But it is a bit wasteful. The (expensive) computation e := exp(is*2*PI*I*j/m) is done $n/2 \cdot \log_2(n)$ times.

21.2.1.3 Saving trigonometric computations

To reduce the number of sine and cosine computations, we can swap the two inner loops, leading to the first 'real world' FFT procedure presented here. A non-recursive procedure for the radix-2 DIT FFT is (C++ version in [FXT: fft/fftdit2.cc]):

```
1    procedure fft_dit2(a[], ldn, is)
2    // complex a[0..2**ldn-1] input, result
3    {
4        n := 2**ldn
5
6        revbin_permute(a[], n)
7
8        for ldm:=1 to ldn  // log_2(n) iterations
9        {
10           m  := 2**ldm
11           mh := m/2
12
13           for j:=0 to mh-1  // m/2 iterations
14           {
15               e := exp(is*2*PI*I*j/m)  // 1 + 2 + ... + n/8 + n/4 + n/2 == n-1 computations
16
17               for r:=0 to n-m step m
18               {
19                   u := a[r+j]
20                   v := a[r+j+mh] * e
21
22                   a[r+j]    := u + v
23                   a[r+j+mh] := u - v
24               }
25           }
26       }
27    }
```

Swapping the two inner loops reduces the number of trigonometric computations to **n** but leads to a feature that many FFT implementations share: memory access is highly non-local. For each recursion stage (value of **ldm**) the array is traversed **mh** times with n/m accesses in strides of **mh**. This memory access pattern can have a very negative performance impact for large **n**. If memory access is very slow compared to the CPU, the naive version can actually be faster.

It is a good idea to extract the **ldm==1** stage of the outermost loop. This avoids complex multiplications with the trivial factors $1 + 0\,i$ and the computations of these quantities as trigonometric functions. Replace the line

```
    for ldm:=1 to ldn
```

by the lines

```
    for r:=0 to n-1 step 2
    {
        { a[r], a[r+1] } := { a[r] + a[r+1], a[r] - a[r+1] }  // parallel assignment
    }
    for ldm:=2 to ldn
```

The parallel assignment would translate into the following C-code:

```
    Complex tmp1 = a[r] + a[r+1],  tmp2 = a[r] - a[r+1];
    a[r] = tmp1;
    a[r+1] = tmp2;
```

21.2.2   Decimation in frequency (DIF) FFT

By splitting the Fourier sum into a left and right half we obtain the *decimation in frequency* (DIF) FFT algorithm, also called *Sande-Tukey* FFT algorithm. For even values of n the k-th element of the Fourier transform is

$$\mathcal{F}\big[a\big]_k = \sum_{x=0}^{n-1} a_x \, z^{x\,k} = \sum_{x=0}^{n/2-1} a_x \, z^{x\,k} + \sum_{x=n/2}^{n-1} a_x \, z^{x\,k} \tag{21.2-4a}$$

$$= \sum_{x=0}^{n/2-1} a_x \, z^{x\,k} + \sum_{x=0}^{n/2-1} a_{x+n/2} \, z^{(x+n/2)\,k} \tag{21.2-4b}$$

$$= \sum_{x=0}^{n/2-1} (a_x^{(left)} + z^{k\,n/2} a_x^{(right)}) \, z^{x\,k} \tag{21.2-4c}$$

where $z = e^{\sigma\,2\,\pi\,i/n}$, $\sigma = \pm 1$ is the sign of the transform, and $k \in \{0, 1, \ldots, n-1\}$.

Here one has to distinguish whether k is even or odd. Therefore we rewrite $k \in \{0, 1, 2, \ldots, n-1\}$ as $k = 2\,j + \delta$ where $j \in \{0, 1, 2, \ldots, n/2-1\}$ and $\delta \in \{0, 1\}$:

$$\sum_{x=0}^{n-1} a_x \, z^{x\,(2\,j+\delta)} = \sum_{x=0}^{n/2-1} (a_x^{(left)} + z^{(2\,j+\delta)\,n/2} a_x^{(right)}) \, z^{x\,(2\,j+\delta)} \tag{21.2-5a}$$

$$= \begin{cases} \displaystyle\sum_{x=0}^{n/2-1} (a_x^{(left)} + a_x^{(right)}) \, z^{2\,x\,j} & \text{for} \quad \delta = 0 \\ \displaystyle\sum_{x=0}^{n/2-1} z^x (a_x^{(left)} - a_x^{(right)}) \, z^{2\,x\,j} & \text{for} \quad \delta - 1 \end{cases} \tag{21.2-5b}$$

Now $z^{(2\,j+\delta)\,n/2} = e^{\pm\pi\,i\,\delta}$ equals $+1$ for $\delta = 0$ (even k) and -1 for $\delta = 1$ (odd k). The last two equations, more compactly written, are the *radix-2 DIF FFT step*:

$$\mathcal{F}\big[a\big]^{(even)} \overset{n/2}{=} \mathcal{F}\big[a^{(left)} + a^{(right)}\big] \tag{21.2-6a}$$

$$\mathcal{F}\big[a\big]^{(odd)} \overset{n/2}{=} \mathcal{F}\big[\mathcal{S}^{1/2}\big(a^{(left)} - a^{(right)}\big)\big] \tag{21.2-6b}$$

A recursive implementation of radix-2 DIF FFT is (C++ version given in [FXT: fft/recfft2.cc]) is

```
1    procedure rec_fft_dif2(a[], n, x[], is)
2    // complex a[0..n-1] input
3    // complex x[0..n-1] result
4    {
5        complex b[0..n/2-1], c[0..n/2-1]    // workspace
6        complex s[0..n/2-1], t[0..n/2-1]    // workspace
7
8        if n == 1 then
9        {
10           x[0]  := a[0]
11           return
12       }
13
14       nh := n/2
15
16       for k:=0 to nh-1
17       {
18           s[k]  := a[k]     // 'left' elements
19           t[k]  := a[k+nh]  // 'right' elements
20       }
21
22       for k:=0 to nh-1
23       {
24           { s[k], t[k] } := { s[k] + t[k], s[k] - t[k] }  // parallel assignment
25       }
26
27       fourier_shift(t[], nh, is*0.5)
28
29       rec_fft_dif2(s[], nh, b[], is)
30       rec_fft_dif2(t[], nh, c[], is)
31
```

```
32        j := 0
33        for k:=0 to nh-1
34        {
35            x[j]   := b[k]
36            x[j+1] := c[k]
37            j := j+2
38        }
39    }
```

The parameter is $= \sigma = \pm 1$ is the sign of the transform. The data length n must be a power of 2. The result is returned in the array x[]. Again, the routine does no normalization.

A non-recursive version is (the C++ equivalent is given in [FXT: fft/fftdif2.cc]):

```
1    procedure fft_dif2(a[],ldn,is)
2    // complex a[0..2**ldn-1] input, result
3    {
4        n := 2**ldn
5
6        for ldm:=ldn to 1 step -1
7        {
8            m  := 2**ldm
9            mh := m/2
10
11           for j:=0 to mh-1
12           {
13               e := exp(is*2*PI*I*j/m)
14
15               for r:=0 to n-m step m
16               {
17                   u := a[r+j]
18                   v := a[r+j+mh]
19
20                   a[r+j]    := (u + v)
21                   a[r+j+mh] := (u - v) * e
22               }
23           }
24       }
25
26       revbin_permute(a[], n)
27   }
```

In DIF FFTs the procedure revbin_permute() is called after the main loop, in the DIT code it is called before the main loop. As in the procedure for the DIT FFT (section 21.2.1.3 on page 414) the inner loops were swapped to save trigonometric computations.

Extracting the ldm==1 stage of the outermost loop is again a good idea. Replace the line

```
    for  ldm:=ldn to 1 step -1
```

by

```
    for  ldm:=ldn to 2 step -1
```

and insert

```
    for r:=0 to n-1 step 2
    {
        { a[r], a[r+1] } := { a[r] + a[r+1], a[r] - a[r+1] }  // parallel assignment
    }
```

before the call of revbin_permute(a[], n).

21.3   Saving trigonometric computations

The sine and cosine computations are an expensive part of any FFT. There are two apparent ways for saving CPU cycles, the use of lookup-tables and recursive methods. The CORDIC algorithms for sine and cosine given in section 33.2.1 on page 646 can be useful when implementing FFTs in hardware.

21.3.1   Using lookup tables

We can precompute and store all necessary values, and later look them up when needed. This is a good idea when computing many FFTs of the same (small) length. For FFTs of long sequences one needs large lookup tables that can introduce a high cache-miss rate. So we may experience little or no speed gain, even a notable slowdown is possible.

However, for a length-n FFT we do not need to store all the (n complex or $2n$ real) sine/cosine values $\exp(2\pi i k/n) = \cos(2\pi k/n) + i\sin(2\pi k/n)$ where $k = 0,1,2,3,\ldots,n-1$. The following symmetry relations reduce the interval from $0\ldots 2\pi$ to $0\ldots \pi$:

$$\cos(\pi + x) = -\cos(x) \tag{21.3-1a}$$
$$\sin(\pi + x) = -\sin(x) \tag{21.3-1b}$$

The next relations further reduce the interval to $0\ldots \pi/2$:

$$\cos(\pi/2 + x) = -\sin(x) \tag{21.3-2a}$$
$$\sin(\pi/2 + x) = +\cos(x) \tag{21.3-2b}$$

Finally, only the table of cosines is needed:

$$\sin(x) = \cos(\pi/2 - x) \tag{21.3-3}$$

That is, already a table of the $n/4$ real values $\cos(2\pi i k/n)$ for $k = 0,1,2,3,\ldots,n/4-1$ suffices for a length-n FFT computation. The size of the table is thereby cut by a factor of 8. Possible cache problems can sometimes be mitigated by simply storing the trigonometric values in reversed order, as this avoids many equidistant memory accesses.

21.3.2 Recursive generation

We write $E(x)$ for $\exp(ix) = \sin(x) + i\cos(x)$. In FFT computations one typically needs the values

$$e_0 = E(\varphi), \; e_1 = E(\varphi + 1\gamma), \; e_2 = E(\varphi + 2\gamma), \; e_3 = E(\varphi + 3\gamma), \; \ldots, \; e_k = E(\varphi + k\gamma), \; \ldots$$

in sequence. We could precompute $g = E(\gamma)$ and $e_0 = E(\varphi)$, and compute the values successively as

$$e_k = g \cdot e_{k-1} \tag{21.3-4}$$

However, the numerical error grows exponentially, rendering the method useless (same for the recursions 35.2-10a and 35.2-10b on page 679). A stable version of a trigonometric recursion for the computation of the sequence can be stated as follows. Precompute

$$c_0 = \cos\varphi, \tag{21.3-5a}$$
$$s_0 = \sin\varphi, \tag{21.3-5b}$$
$$\alpha = 1 - \cos\gamma \qquad \text{[Cancellation!]} \tag{21.3-5c}$$
$$= 2\left(\sin\frac{\gamma}{2}\right)^2 \qquad \text{[OK.]} \tag{21.3-5d}$$
$$\beta = \sin\gamma \tag{21.3-5e}$$

Then compute the next pair (c_{k+1}, s_{k+1}) from (c_k, s_k) via

$$c_{k+1} = c_k - (\alpha c_k + \beta s_k); \tag{21.3-6a}$$
$$s_{k+1} = s_k - (\alpha s_k - \beta c_k); \tag{21.3-6b}$$

Here we use the relation $E(\varphi+\gamma) = E(\varphi) - E(\varphi)\cdot z$, this leads to $z = 1 - \cos\gamma - i\sin\gamma = 2\left(\sin\frac{\gamma}{2}\right)^2 - i\sin\gamma$.

A certain loss of precision still has to be expected, but even for very long FFTs less than 3 bits of precision are lost. When working with the C-type **double** it might be a good idea to use the type **long double** with the trigonometric recursion: the generated values will then always be accurate within the precision of the type **double**, provided **long doubles** are actually more precise than **doubles**. With exact integer convolution this can be mandatory.

We give an example from [FXT: fht/fhtdif.cc], the variable **tt** is γ in relations 21.3-5d and 21.3-5e:

```
1     [--snip--]
2         double tt = M_PI_4/kh;   // the angle increment
3         double s1 = 0.0,  c1 = 1.0;  // start at angle zero
4         double al = sin(0.5*tt);
5         al *= (2.0*al);
6         double be = sin(tt);
7
8         for (ulong i=1; i<kh; i++)
9         {
10            double t1 = c1;
11            c1 -= (al*t1+be*s1);
12            s1 -= (al*s1-be*t1);
13
14            // here c1 = cos(tt*i) and s1 = sin(tt*i)
15        [--snip--]
```

21.4 Higher radix FFT algorithms

Higher radix FFT algorithms save trigonometric computations. The radix-4 FFT algorithms presented in what follows replace all multiplications with complex factors $(0, \pm i)$ by the obvious simpler operations. Radix-8 algorithms also simplify the special cases where the sines and cosines equal $\pm\sqrt{1/2}$.

The bookkeeping overhead is also reduced, due to the more unrolled structure. Moreover, the number of loads and stores is reduced.

We fix more notation. Let a be a length-n sequence where n is a multiple of m.

- Let $a^{(r\%m)}$ denote the subsequence of the elements with index x where $x \equiv r \bmod m$. For example, $a^{(0\%2)} = a^{(even)}$ and $a^{(3\%4)} = [a_3, a_7, a_{11}, a_{15}, \dots]$. The length of $a^{(r\%m)}$ is n/m.

- Let $a^{(r/m)}$ denote the subsequence obtained by splitting a into m parts of length n/m: $a = \left[a^{(0/m)}, a^{(1/m)}, \dots, a^{((m-1)/m)}\right]$. For example $a^{(1/2)} = a^{(right)}$ and $a^{(2/3)}$ is the last third of a.

21.4.1 Decimation in time algorithms

We rewrite the radix-2 DIT step (relations 21.2-3a and 21.2-3b on page 412) in the new notation:

$$\mathcal{F}[a]^{(0/2)} \overset{n/2}{=} \mathcal{S}^{0/2}\mathcal{F}[a^{(0\%2)}] + \mathcal{S}^{1/2}\mathcal{F}[a^{(1\%2)}] \tag{21.4-1a}$$

$$\mathcal{F}[a]^{(1/2)} \overset{n/2}{=} \mathcal{S}^{0/2}\mathcal{F}[a^{(0\%2)}] - \mathcal{S}^{1/2}\mathcal{F}[a^{(1\%2)}] \tag{21.4-1b}$$

The operator $\mathcal{S}$ is defined in section 21.2 on page 411, note that $\mathcal{S}^{0/2} = \mathcal{S}^0$ is the identity operator.

The derivation of the radix-4 step is analogous to the radix-2 step, it just involves more writing and does not give additional insights. So we just state the *radix-4 DIT FFT step* which can be applied when n is divisible by 4:

$$\mathcal{F}[a]^{(0/4)} \overset{n/4}{=} +\mathcal{S}^{0/4}\mathcal{F}[a^{(0\%4)}] + \mathcal{S}^{1/4}\mathcal{F}[a^{(1\%4)}] + \mathcal{S}^{2/4}\mathcal{F}[a^{(2\%4)}] + \mathcal{S}^{3/4}\mathcal{F}[a^{(3\%4)}] \tag{21.4-2a}$$

$$\mathcal{F}[a]^{(1/4)} \overset{n/4}{=} +\mathcal{S}^{0/4}\mathcal{F}[a^{(0\%4)}] + i\sigma\mathcal{S}^{1/4}\mathcal{F}[a^{(1\%4)}] - \mathcal{S}^{2/4}\mathcal{F}[a^{(2\%4)}] - i\sigma\mathcal{S}^{3/4}\mathcal{F}[a^{(3\%4)}] \tag{21.4-2b}$$

$$\mathcal{F}[a]^{(2/4)} \overset{n/4}{=} +\mathcal{S}^{0/4}\mathcal{F}[a^{(0\%4)}] - \mathcal{S}^{1/4}\mathcal{F}[a^{(1\%4)}] + \mathcal{S}^{2/4}\mathcal{F}[a^{(2\%4)}] - \mathcal{S}^{3/4}\mathcal{F}[a^{(3\%4)}] \tag{21.4-2c}$$

$$\mathcal{F}[a]^{(3/4)} \overset{n/4}{=} +\mathcal{S}^{0/4}\mathcal{F}[a^{(0\%4)}] - i\sigma\mathcal{S}^{1/4}\mathcal{F}[a^{(1\%4)}] - \mathcal{S}^{2/4}\mathcal{F}[a^{(2\%4)}] + i\sigma\mathcal{S}^{3/4}\mathcal{F}[a^{(3\%4)}] \tag{21.4-2d}$$

The relations can be written more compactly as

$$\mathcal{F}[a]^{(j/4)} \overset{n/4}{=} +e^{\sigma 2\pi i 0 j/4} \cdot \mathcal{S}^{0/4}\mathcal{F}[a^{(0\%4)}] + e^{\sigma 2\pi i 1 j/4} \cdot \mathcal{S}^{1/4}\mathcal{F}[a^{(1\%4)}]$$
$$+e^{\sigma 2\pi i 2 j/4} \cdot \mathcal{S}^{2/4}\mathcal{F}[a^{(2\%4)}] + e^{\sigma 2\pi i 3 j/4} \cdot \mathcal{S}^{3/4}\mathcal{F}[a^{(3\%4)}] \tag{21.4-3}$$

where $j \in \{0, 1, 2, 3\}$ and n is a multiple of 4. An even more compact form is

$$\mathcal{F}[a]^{(j/4)} \overset{n/4}{=} \sum_{k=0}^{3} e^{\sigma 2\pi i k j/4} \cdot \mathcal{S}^{k/4}\mathcal{F}[a^{(k\%4)}] \qquad j \in \{0, 1, 2, 3\} \tag{21.4-4}$$

where the summation symbol denotes *element-wise* summation of the sequences. The dot indicates multiplication of all elements of the sequence by the exponential.

The general *radix-r DIT FFT step*, applicable when n is a multiple of r, is:

$$\mathcal{F}[a]^{(j/r)} \overset{n/r}{=} \sum_{k=0}^{r-1} e^{\sigma 2\pi i k j/r} \cdot \mathcal{S}^{k/r} \mathcal{F}[a^{(k\%r)}] \qquad j = 0, 1, 2, \ldots, r-1 \qquad (21.4\text{-}5)$$

Our notation turned out to be useful indeed.

21.4.2 Decimation in frequency algorithms

The radix-2 DIF step (relations 21.2-6a and 21.2-6b on page 415), in the new notation, is

$$\mathcal{F}[a]^{(0\%2)} \overset{n/2}{=} \mathcal{F}[\mathcal{S}^{0/2}\big(a^{(0/2)} + a^{(1/2)}\big)] \qquad (21.4\text{-}6a)$$

$$\mathcal{F}[a]^{(1\%2)} \overset{n/2}{=} \mathcal{F}[\mathcal{S}^{1/2}\big(a^{(0/2)} - a^{(1/2)}\big)] \qquad (21.4\text{-}6b)$$

The *radix-4 DIF FFT step*, applicable for n divisible by 4, is

$$\mathcal{F}[a]^{(0\%4)} \overset{n/4}{=} \mathcal{F}[\mathcal{S}^{0/4}\big(a^{(0/4)} + a^{(1/4)} + a^{(2/4)} + a^{(3/4)}\big)] \qquad (21.4\text{-}7a)$$

$$\mathcal{F}[a]^{(1\%4)} \overset{n/4}{=} \mathcal{F}[\mathcal{S}^{1/4}\big(a^{(0/4)} + i\sigma a^{(1/4)} - a^{(2/4)} - i\sigma a^{(3/4)}\big)] \qquad (21.4\text{-}7b)$$

$$\mathcal{F}[a]^{(2\%4)} \overset{n/4}{=} \mathcal{F}[\mathcal{S}^{2/4}\big(a^{(0/4)} - a^{(1/4)} + a^{(2/4)} - a^{(3/4)}\big)] \qquad (21.4\text{-}7c)$$

$$\mathcal{F}[a]^{(3\%4)} \overset{n/4}{=} \mathcal{F}[\mathcal{S}^{3/4}\big(a^{(0/4)} - i\sigma a^{(1/4)} - a^{(2/4)} + i\sigma a^{(3/4)}\big)] \qquad (21.4\text{-}7d)$$

Again, $\sigma = \pm 1$ is the sign of the transform. Written more compactly:

$$\mathcal{F}[a]^{(j\%4)} \overset{n/4}{=} \mathcal{F}[\mathcal{S}^{j/4} \sum_{k=0}^{3} e^{\sigma 2\pi i k j/4} \cdot a^{(k/4)}] \qquad j \in \{0, 1, 2, 3\} \qquad (21.4\text{-}8)$$

The general *radix-r DIF FFT step* is

$$\mathcal{F}[a]^{(j\%r)} \overset{n/r}{=} \mathcal{F}[\mathcal{S}^{j/r} \sum_{k=0}^{r-1} e^{\sigma 2\pi i k j/r} \cdot a^{(k/r)}] \qquad j \in \{0, 1, 2, \ldots, r-1\} \qquad (21.4\text{-}9)$$

21.4.3 Implementation of radix-r FFTs

For the implementation of a radix-r FFT with $r \neq 2$ the `revbin_permute` routine has to be replaced by its radix-r version `radix_permute`. The reordering now swaps elements a_x with $a_{\tilde{x}}$ where $\tilde{x}$ is obtained from x by reversing its radix-r expansion (see section 2.7 on page 121). In most practical cases one considers $r = p^x$ where p is a prime. Pseudocode for a radix $r = p^x$ DIT FFT:

```
1    procedure fftdit_r(a[], n, is)
2    // complex a[0..n-1] input, result.
3    // r == power of p (hard-coded)
4    // n == power of p (not necessarily a power of r)
5    {
6        radix_permute(a[], n, p)
7
8        lx := log(r) / log(p)  // r == p ** lx
9        ln := log(n) / log(p)
10       ldm := (log(n)/log(p)) % lx
11       // lx, ln, abd ldm are all integers
12
13       if ( ldm != 0 )  // n is not a power of p
14       {
```

```
15            xx := p**lx
16            for z:=0 to n-xx step xx
17            {
18                fft_dit_xx(a[z..z+xx-1], is)  // inlined length-xx DIT FFT
19            }
20        }
21
22        for ldm:=ldm+lx to ln step lx
23        {
24            m  := p**ldm
25            mr := m/r
26
27            for j := 0 to mr-1
28            {
29                e := exp(is*2*PI*I*j/m)
30
31                for k:=0 to n-m step m
32                {
33                    // All code in this block should be inlined and unrolled:
34
35                    // temporary  u[0..r-1]
36
37                    for z:=0 to r-1
38                    {
39                        u[z] := a[k+j+mr*z]
40                    }
41
42                    radix_permute(u[], r, p)
43
44                    for z:=1 to r-1   // e**0 == 1
45                    {
46                        u[z] := u[z] * e**z
47                    }
48
49                    r_point_fft(u[], is)
50
51                    for z:=0 to r-1
52                    {
53                        a[k+j+mr*z] := u[z]
54                    }
55                }
56            }
57        }
58    }
```

Of course the loops that use the variable z have to be unrolled, the (length-p^x) array u[] has to be replaced by explicit variables (for example, u0, u1, ...), and the r_point_fft(u[],is) should be an inlined p^x-point FFT.

There is one pitfall: if one uses the radix-p permutation instead of a radix-p^x permutation (for example, the radix-2 revbin_permute() for a radix-4 FFT), then some additional reordering is necessary in the innermost loop. In the given pseudocode this is indicated by the radix_permute(u[],p) just before the p_point_fft(u[],is) line.

21.4.4   Radix-4 DIT FFT

A C++ routine for the radix-4 DIT FFT is given in [FXT: fft/fftdit4l.cc]:

```
1   static const ulong RX = 4;  // == r
2   static const ulong LX = 2;   // == log(r)/log(p) == log_2(r)
3
4   void
5   fft_dit4l(Complex *f, ulong ldn, int is)
6   // Decimation in time radix-4 FFT.
7   {
8       double s2pi = ( is>0 ? 2.0*M_PI : -2.0*M_PI );
9
10      const ulong n = (1UL<<ldn);
11
12      revbin_permute(f, n);
13
14      ulong ldm = (ldn&1);
15
16      if ( ldm!=0 )  // n is not a power of 4, need a radix-2 step
17      {
18          for (ulong r=0; r<n; r+=2)
```

```
19      {
20          Complex a0 = f[r];
21          Complex a1 = f[r+1];
22
23          f[r]   = a0 + a1;
24          f[r+1] = a0 - a1;
25      }
26  }
27
28  ldm += LX;
29
30  for ( ; ldm<=ldn ; ldm+=LX)
31  {
32      ulong m = (1UL<<ldm);
33      ulong m4 = (m>>LX);
34      double ph0 = s2pi/m;
35
36      for (ulong j=0; j<m4; j++)
37      {
38          double phi = j*ph0;
39          Complex e  = SinCos(phi);
40          Complex e2 = SinCos(2.0*phi);
41          Complex e3 = SinCos(3.0*phi);
42
43          for (ulong r=0; r<n; r+=m)
44          {
45              ulong i0 = j + r;
46              ulong i1 = i0 + m4;
47              ulong i2 = i1 + m4;
48              ulong i3 = i2 + m4;
49
50              Complex a0 = f[i0];
51              Complex a1 = f[i2]; // (!)
52              Complex a2 = f[i1]; // (!)
53              Complex a3 = f[i3];
54
55              a1 *= e;
56              a2 *= e2;
57              a3 *= e3;
58
59              Complex t0 = (a0+a2) + (a1+a3);
60              Complex t2 = (a0+a2) - (a1+a3);
61
62              Complex t1 = (a0-a2) + Complex(0,is) * (a1-a3);
63              Complex t3 = (a0-a2) - Complex(0,is) * (a1-a3);
64
65              f[i0] = t0;
66              f[i1] = t1;
67              f[i2] = t2;
68              f[i3] = t3;
69          }
70      }
71  }
72  }
```

An additional radix-2 step has been prepended which is used when n is an odd power of 2. To improve performance, the call to the procedure `radix_permute(u[],p)` of the pseudocode has been replaced by changing indices in the loops where the a[z] are read. The respective lines are marked with the comment '`// (!)`'.

A reasonably optimized radix-4 DIT FFT implementation is given in [FXT: fft/fftdit4.cc]. The transform starts with a radix-2 or radix-8 step for the initial pass. The core routine is hard-coded for $\sigma = +1$ and called with swapped real and imaginary part for the inverse transform as explained in section 21.7 on page 430. The routine uses separate arrays for the real and imaginary parts, which is very problematic with large transforms: the memory access pattern in large skips *will* degrade performance.

Radix-4 FFT routines that use the C++ type `complex` are given in [FXT: fft/cfftdit4.cc]. These should be preferred for large transforms. The core routine is hard-coded for $\sigma = -1$, therefore the name suffix `_m1`:

```
1   void
2   fft_dit4_core_m1(Complex *f, ulong ldn)
3   // Auxiliary routine for fft_dit4().
```

```
 4    // Radix-4 decimation in time (DIT) FFT.
 5    // ldn := base-2 logarithm of the array length.
 6    // Fixed isign = -1.
 7    // Input data must be in revbin_permuted order.
 8    {
 9        const ulong n = (1UL<<ldn);
10
11        if ( n<=2 )
12        {
13            if ( n==2 )  sumdiff(f[0], f[1]);
14            return;
15        }
16
17        ulong ldm = ldn & 1;
18        if ( ldm!=0 )  // n is not a power of 4, need a radix-8 step
19        {
20            for (ulong i0=0; i0<n; i0+=8)  fft8_dit_core_m1(f+i0);  // isign
21        }
22        else
23        {
24            for (ulong i0=0; i0<n; i0+=4)
25            {
26                ulong i1 = i0 + 1;
27                ulong i2 = i1 + 1;
28                ulong i3 = i2 + 1;
29
30                Complex x, y, u, v;
31                sumdiff(f[i0], f[i1], x, u);
32                sumdiff(f[i2], f[i3], y, v);
33                v *= Complex(0, -1);  // isign
34                sumdiff(u, v, f[i1], f[i3]);
35                sumdiff(x, y, f[i0], f[i2]);
36            }
37        }
38        ldm += 2 * LX;
39
40
41        for ( ; ldm<=ldn; ldm+=LX)
42        {
43            ulong m = (1UL<<ldm);
44            ulong m4 = (m>>LX);
45            const double ph0 = -2.0*M_PI/m;  // isign
46
47            for (ulong j=0; j<m4; j++)
48            {
49                double phi = j * ph0;
50                Complex e  = SinCos(phi);
51                Complex e2 = e * e;
52                Complex e3 = e2 * e;
53
54                for (ulong r=0; r<n; r+=m)
55                {
56                    ulong i0 = j + r;
57                    ulong i1 = i0 + m4;
58                    ulong i2 = i1 + m4;
59                    ulong i3 = i2 + m4;
60
61                    Complex x = f[i1] * e2;
62                    Complex u;
63                    sumdiff3_r(x, f[i0], u);
64
65                    Complex v = f[i3] * e3;
66                    Complex y = f[i2] * e;
67                    sumdiff(y, v);
68                    v *= Complex(0, -1);  // isign
69
70                    sumdiff(u, v, f[i1], f[i3]);
71                    sumdiff(x, y, f[i0], f[i2]);
72                }
73            }
74        }
75    }
```

The `sumdiff()` function is defined in [FXT: aux0/sumdiff.h]:

```
1    template <typename Type>
2    static inline void sumdiff(Type &a, Type &b)
```

```
3    // {a, b}  <--| {a+b, a-b}
4    { Type t=a-b; a+=b; b=t; }
```

The routine `fft8_dit_core_m1()` is an unrolled size-8 DIT FFT (hard-coded for $\sigma = -1$) given in [FXT: fft/fft8ditcore.cc]. We further need a version of the routine for the positive sign. It uses a routine `fft8_dit_core_p1()` for the computation of length-8 DIT FFTs with $\sigma = -1$. The following changes need to be made in the core routine [FXT: fft/cfftdit4.cc]:

```
1    void
2    fft_dit4_core_p1(Complex *f, ulong ldn)
3    // Fixed isign = +1
4    {
5        [--snip--]
6            for (ulong i0=0; i0<n; i0+=8)  fft8_dit_core_p1(f+i0);  // isign
7        [--snip--]
8                v *= Complex(0, +1);  // isign
9        [--snip--]
10           const double ph0 = +2.0*M_PI/m;  // isign
11       [--snip--]
12               v *= Complex(0, +1);  // isign
13       [--snip--]
14   }
```

The routine called by the user is

```
1    void
2    fft_dit4(Complex *f, ulong ldn, int is)
3    // Fast Fourier Transform
4    // ldn := base-2 logarithm of the array length
5    // is := sign of the transform (+1 or -1)
6    // Radix-4 decimation in time algorithm
7    {
8        revbin_permute(f, 1UL<<ld);
9        if ( is>0 )  fft_dit4_core_p1(f, ldn);
10       else         fft_dit4_core_m1(f, ldn);
11   }
```

21.4.5 Radix-4 DIF FFT

A routine for the radix-4 DIF FFT is (the C++ equivalent is given in [FXT: fft/fftdif4l.cc])

```
1    procedure fftdif4(a[], ldn, is)
2    // complex a[0..2**ldn-1] input, result
3    {
4        n := 2**ldn
5
6        for ldm := ldn to 2 step -2
7        {
8            m  := 2**ldm
9            mr := m/4
10
11           for j := 0 to mr-1
12           {
13               e  := exp(is*2*PI*I*j/m)
14               e2 := e * e
15               e3 := e2 * e
16
17               for r := 0 to n-m step m
18               {
19                   u0 := a[r+j]
20                   u1 := a[r+j+mr]
21                   u2 := a[r+j+mr*2]
22                   u3 := a[r+j+mr*3]
23
24                   x := u0 + u2
25                   y := u1 + u3
26                   t0 := x + y   // == (u0+u2) + (u1+u3)
27                   t2 := x - y   // == (u0+u2) - (u1+u3)
28
29                   x := u0 - u2
30                   y := (u1 - u3)*I*is
31                   t1 := x + y   // == (u0-u2) + (u1-u3)*I*is
32                   t3 := x - y   // == (u0-u2) - (u1-u3)*I*is
33
34                   t1 := t1 * e
35                   t2 := t2 * e2
```

```
36              t3 := t3 * e3
37
38              a[r+j]      := t0
39              a[r+j+mr]   := t2  // (!)
40              a[r+j+mr*2] := t1  // (!)
41              a[r+j+mr*3] := t3
42          }
43       }
44    }
45
46    if is_odd(ldn) then  // n not a power of 4
47    {
48       for r:=0 to n-2 step 2
49       {
50          {a[r], a[r+1]} := {a[r]+a[r+1], a[r]-a[r+1]}
51       }
52    }
53
54    revbin_permute(a[],n)
55 }
```

A reasonably optimized implementation, hard-coded for $\sigma = +1$, is [FXT: fft/cfftdif4.cc]

```
1  static const ulong RX = 4;
2  static const ulong LX = 2;
3
4  void
5  fft_dif4_core_p1(Complex *f, ulong ldn)
6  // Auxiliary routine for fft_dif4().
7  // Radix-4 decimation in frequency FFT.
8  // Output data is in revbin_permuted order.
9  // ldn := base-2 logarithm of the array length.
10 // Fixed isign = +1
11 {
12     const ulong n = (1UL<<ldn);
13
14     if ( n<=2 )
15     {
16         if ( n==2 )  sumdiff(f[0], f[1]);
17         return;
18     }
19
20     for (ulong ldm=ldn; ldm>=(LX<<1); ldm-=LX)
21     {
22         ulong m = (1UL<<ldm);
23         ulong m4 = (m>>LX);
24
25         const double ph0 = 2.0*M_PI/m;   // isign
26
27         for (ulong j=0; j<m4; j++)
28         {
29             double phi = j * ph0;
30             Complex e  = SinCos(phi);
31             Complex e2 = e * e;
32             Complex e3 = e2 * e;
33
34             for (ulong r=0; r<n; r+=m)
35             {
36                 ulong i0 = j + r;
37                 ulong i1 = i0 + m4;
38                 ulong i2 = i1 + m4;
39                 ulong i3 = i2 + m4;
40
41                 Complex x, y, u, v;
42                 sumdiff(f[i0], f[i2], x, u);
43                 sumdiff(f[i1], f[i3], y, v);
44                 v *= Complex(0, +1);  // isign
45
46                 diffsum3(x, y, f[i0]);
47                 f[i1] = y * e2;
48
49                 sumdiff(u, v, x, y);
50                 f[i3] = y * e3;
51                 f[i2] = x * e;
52             }
53         }
54     }
```

```
55
56
57        if ( ldn & 1 )  // n is not a power of 4, need a radix-8 step
58        {
59            for (ulong i0=0; i0<n; i0+=8)  fft8_dif_core_p1(f+i0);  // isign
60        }
61        else
62        {
63            for (ulong i0=0; i0<n; i0+=4)
64            {
65                ulong i1 = i0 + 1;
66                ulong i2 = i1 + 1;
67                ulong i3 = i2 + 1;
68
69                Complex x, y, u, v;
70                sumdiff(f[i0], f[i2], x, u);
71                sumdiff(f[i1], f[i3], y, v);
72                v *= Complex(0, +1);  // isign
73                sumdiff(x, y, f[i0], f[i1]);
74                sumdiff(u, v, f[i2], f[i3]);
75            }
76        }
77    }
```

The routine for $\sigma = -1$ needs changes where the comment `isign` appears [FXT: fft/cfftdif4.cc]:

```
1     void
2     fft_dif4_core_m1(Complex *f, ulong ldn)
3     // Fixed isign = -1
4     {
5         [--snip--]
6            const double ph0 = -2.0*M_PI/m;  // isign
7         [--snip--]
8                    v *= Complex(0, -1);  // isign
9         [--snip--]
10           for (ulong i0=0; i0<n; i0+=8)  fft8_dif_core_m1(f+i0);  // isign
11        [--snip--]
12                    v *= Complex(0, -1);  // isign
13        [--snip--]
14    }
```

The routine called by the user is

```
1     void
2     fft_dif4(Complex *f, ulong ldn, int is)
3     // Fast Fourier Transform
4     // ldn := base-2 logarithm of the array length
5     // is := sign of the transform (+1 or -1)
6     // radix-4 decimation in frequency algorithm
7     {
8         if ( is>0 )  fft_dif4_core_p1(f, ldn);
9         else         fft_dif4_core_m1(f, ldn);
10        revbin_permute(f, 1UL<<ldn);
11    }
```

A version that uses the separate arrays for real and imaginary part is given in [FXT: fft/fftdif4.cc]. Again, the type `complex` version should be preferred for large transforms. To convert a complex array to and from a pair of real and imaginary arrays, use the zip permutation described in section 2.10 on page 125.

21.5 Split-radix algorithm

The idea underlying the *split-radix FFT algorithm* is to use both radix-2 and radix-4 decompositions at the same time. We use one relation from the radix-2 (DIF) decomposition (relation 21.2-6a on page 415, the one for the even indices) and for the odd indices we use the radix-4 splitting (relations 21.4-7b and 21.4-7d on page 419) in a slightly reordered form. The radix-4 decimation in frequency (DIF) step for the split-radix FFT is

$$\mathcal{F}[a]^{(0\%2)} \overset{n/2}{=} \mathcal{F}\Big[\Big(a^{(0/2)} + a^{(1/2)}\Big)\Big] \tag{21.5-1a}$$

$$\mathcal{F}[a]^{(1\%4)} \overset{n/4}{=} \mathcal{F}\Big[\mathcal{S}^{1/4}\Big(\Big(a^{(0/4)} - a^{(2/4)}\Big) + i\,\sigma\,\Big(a^{(1/4)} - a^{(3/4)}\Big)\Big)\Big] \tag{21.5-1b}$$

$$\mathcal{F}[a]^{(3\%4)} \overset{n/4}{=} \mathcal{F}\Big[\mathcal{S}^{3/4}\Big(\Big(a^{(0/4)} - a^{(2/4)}\Big) - i\,\sigma\,\Big(a^{(1/4)} - a^{(3/4)}\Big)\Big)\Big] \tag{21.5-1c}$$

Now we have expressed the length-$N = 2^n$ FFT as one length-$N/2$ and two length-$N/4$ FFTs. The operation count of the split-radix FFT is actually lower than that of the radix-4 FFT. With the introduced notation it is easy to write down the DIT version of the algorithm. The radix-4 decimation in time (DIT) step for the split-radix FFT is

$$\mathcal{F}[a]^{(0/2)} \overset{n/2}{=} \Big(\mathcal{F}[a^{(0\%2)}] + \mathcal{S}^{1/2}\mathcal{F}[a^{(1\%2)}]\Big) \tag{21.5-2a}$$

$$\mathcal{F}[a]^{(1/4)} \overset{n/4}{=} \Big(\mathcal{F}[a^{(0\%4)}] - \mathcal{S}^{2/4}\mathcal{F}[a^{(2\%4)}]\Big) + i\sigma\mathcal{S}^{1/4}\Big(\mathcal{F}[a^{(1\%4)}] - \mathcal{S}^{2/4}\mathcal{F}[a^{(3\%4)}]\Big) \tag{21.5-2b}$$

$$\mathcal{F}[a]^{(3/4)} \overset{n/4}{=} \Big(\mathcal{F}[a^{(0\%4)}] - \mathcal{S}^{2/4}\mathcal{F}[a^{(2\%4)}]\Big) - i\sigma\mathcal{S}^{1/4}\Big(\mathcal{F}[a^{(1\%4)}] - \mathcal{S}^{2/4}\mathcal{F}[a^{(3\%4)}]\Big) \tag{21.5-2c}$$

The split-radix DIF algorithm can be implemented as

```
1   procedure fft_splitradix_dif(x[], y[], ldn, is)
2   {
3       n := 2**ldn
4       if n<=1  return
5       n2 := 2*n
6
7
8
9       for k:=1 to ldn
10      {
11          n2 := n2 / 2
12          n4 := n2 / 4
13
14          e := 2 * PI / n2
15
16          for j:=0 to n4-1
17          {
18              a := j * e
19              cc1 := cos(a)
20              ss1 := sin(a)
21              cc3 := cos(3*a)   // == 4*cc1*(cc1*cc1-0.75)
22              ss3 := sin(3*a)   // == 4*ss1*(0.75-ss1*ss1)
23
24              ix := j
25              id := 2*n2
26
27              while ix<n-1
28              {
29                  i0 := ix
30                  while i0 < n
31                  {
32                      i1 := i0 + n4
33                      i2 := i1 + n4
34                      i3 := i2 + n4
35
36                      { x[i0], r1 } := { x[i0] + x[i2], x[i0] - x[i2] }
37                      { x[i1], r2 } := { x[i1] + x[i3], x[i1] - x[i3] }
38
39                      { y[i0], s1 } := { y[i0] + y[i2], y[i0] - y[i2] }
40                      { y[i1], s2 } := { y[i1] + y[i3], y[i1] - y[i3] }
41
42                      { r1, s3 } := { r1+s2, r1-s2 }
43                      { r2, s2 } := { r2+s1, r2-s1 }
44
45                      // complex mult: (x[i2],y[i2]) := -(s2,r1) * (ss1,cc1)
46                      x[i2] :=  r1*cc1 - s2*ss1
47                      y[i2] := -s2*cc1 - r1*ss1
48
49                      // complex mult: (y[i3],x[i3]) := (r2,s3) * (cc3,ss3)
50                      x[i3] :=  s3*cc3 + r2*ss3
51                      y[i3] :=  r2*cc3 - s3*ss3
52
53                      i0 := i0 + id
```

```
54            }
55
56                  ix := 2 * id - n2 + j
57                  id := 4 * id
58              }
59          }
60      }
61
62      ix := 1
63      id := 4
64
65      while ix<n
66      {
67          for i0:=ix-1 to n-id step id
68          {
69              i1 := i0 + 1
70              { x[i0], x[i1] } := { x[i0] + x[i1], x[i0] - x[i1] }
71              { y[i0], y[i1] } := { y[i0] + y[i1], y[i0] - y[i1] }
72          }
73
74          ix := 2 * id - 1
75          id := 4 * id
76      }
77
78      revbin_permute(x[],n)
79      revbin_permute(y[],n)
80
81      if is>0
82      {
83          for j:=1 to n/2-1
84          {
85              swap(x[j], x[n-j])
86          }
87
88          for j:=1 to n/2-1
89          {
90              swap(y[j], y[n-j])
91          }
92      }
93  }
```

The C++ implementation given in [FXT: fft/fftsplitradix.cc] uses a DIF core as above which is given in [129]. The C++ type complex version of the split-radix FFT given in [FXT: fft/cfftsplitradix.cc] uses a DIF or DIT core, depending on the sign of the transform. Here we just give the DIF version:

```
1   void
2   split_radix_dif_fft_core(Complex *f, ulong ldn)
3   // Split-radix decimation in frequency (DIF) FFT.
4   // ldn := base-2 logarithm of the array length.
5   // Fixed isign = +1
6   // Output data is in revbin_permuted order.
7   {
8       if ( ldn==0 )  return;
9
10      const ulong n = (1UL<<ldn);
11
12      double s2pi = 2.0*M_PI;   // pi*2*isign
13      ulong n2 = 2*n;
14      for (ulong k=1; k<ldn; k++)
15      {
16          n2 >>= 1;   // == n>>(k-1) == n, n/2, n/4, ..., 4
17          const ulong n4 = n2 >> 2;   // == n/4, n/8, ..., 1
18          const double e = s2pi / n2;
19
20          {  // j==0:
21              const ulong j = 0;
22              ulong ix = j;
23              ulong id = (n2<<1);
24              while ( ix<n )
25              {
26                  for (ulong i0=ix; i0<n; i0+=id)
27                  {
28                      ulong i1 = i0 + n4;
29                      ulong i2 = i1 + n4;
30                      ulong i3 = i2 + n4;
31
32                      Complex t0, t1;
33                      sumdiff3(f[i0], f[i2], t0);
34                      sumdiff3(f[i1], f[i3], t1);
```

```
35
36              // t1 *= Complex(0, 1);   // +isign
37              t1 = Complex(-t1.imag(), t1.real());
38
39              sumdiff(t0, t1);
40              f[i2] = t0; // * Complex(cc1, ss1);
41              f[i3] = t1; // * Complex(cc3, ss3);
42          }
43
44          ix = (id<<1) - n2 + j;
45          id <<= 2;
46      }
47  }
48
49  for (ulong j=1; j<n4; j++)
50  {
51      double a = j * e;
52      double cc1,ss1, cc3,ss3;
53      SinCos(a, &ss1, &cc1);
54      SinCos(3.0*a, &ss3, &cc3);
55
56      ulong ix = j;
57      ulong id = (n2<<1);
58      while ( ix<n )
59      {
60          for (ulong i0=ix; i0<n; i0+=id)
61          {
62              ulong i1 = i0 + n4;
63              ulong i2 = i1 + n4;
64              ulong i3 = i2 + n4;
65
66              Complex t0, t1;
67              sumdiff3(f[i0], f[i2], t0);
68              sumdiff3(f[i1], f[i3], t1);
69
70              t1 = Complex(-t1.imag(), t1.real());
71
72              sumdiff(t0, t1);
73              f[i2] = t0 * Complex(cc1, ss1);
74              f[i3] = t1 * Complex(cc3, ss3);
75          }
76
77          ix = (id<<1) - n2 + j;
78          id <<= 2;
79      }
80  }
81
82
83  for (ulong ix=0, id=4;  ix<n;  id*=4)
84  {
85      for (ulong i0=ix; i0<n; i0+=id)  sumdiff(f[i0], f[i0+1]);
86      ix = 2*(id-1);
87  }
88  }
```

The function `sumdiff3()` is defined in [FXT: aux0/sumdiff.h]:

```
1  template <typename Type>
2  static inline void sumdiff3(Type &a, Type b, Type &d)
3  // {a, b, d} <--| {a+b, b, a-b}  (used in split-radix FFTs)
4  { d=a-b; a+=b; }
```

21.6 Symmetries of the Fourier transform

A bit of notation again. Let $\overline{a}$ be the length-n sequence a reversed around the element with index 0:

$$\overline{a}_0 \quad := \quad a_0 \tag{21.6-1a}$$

$$\overline{a}_{n/2} \quad := \quad a_{n/2} \qquad \text{if } n \text{ even} \tag{21.6-1b}$$

$$\overline{a}_k \quad := \quad a_{n-k} = a_{-k} \tag{21.6-1c}$$

That is, we consider the indices modulo n and $\overline{a}$ is the sequence a with negated indices. Element zero stays in its place and for even n there is also an element with index $n/2$ that stays in place.

Example one, length-4: $a := [0, 1, 2, 3]$, then $\overline{a} = [0, 3, 2, 1]$ (0 and 2 stay).
Example two, length-5: $a := [0, 1, 2, 3, 4]$, then $\overline{a} = [0, 4, 3, 2, 1]$ (only 0 stays).

Let a_S and a_A denote the symmetric and antisymmetric parts of the sequence a, respectively:

$$a_S \; := \; \frac{1}{2} \left(a + \overline{a} \right) \tag{21.6-2a}$$

$$a_A \; := \; \frac{1}{2} \left(a - \overline{a} \right) \tag{21.6-2b}$$

The elements with index 0 (and $n/2$ for even n) of a_A are zero. We have

$$a \; = \; a_S + a_A \tag{21.6-3a}$$

$$\overline{a} \; = \; a_S - a_A \tag{21.6-3b}$$

Let $c + i\, d$ be the transform of the sequence $a + i\, b$, then

$$\mathcal{F}\left[(a_S + a_A) + i\,(b_S + b_A) \right] \; = \; (c_S + c_A) + i\,(d_S + d_A) \quad \text{where} \tag{21.6-4a}$$

$$\mathcal{F}\left[a_S \right] \; = \; c_S \; \in \mathbb{R} \tag{21.6-4b}$$

$$\mathcal{F}\left[a_A \right] \; = \; i\, d_A \; \in i\,\mathbb{R} \tag{21.6-4c}$$

$$\mathcal{F}\left[i\, b_S \right] \; = \; i\, d_S \; \in i\,\mathbb{R} \tag{21.6-4d}$$

$$\mathcal{F}\left[i\, b_A \right] \; = \; c_A \; \in \mathbb{R} \tag{21.6-4e}$$

Here we write $a \in \mathbb{R}$ as a short form for a purely real sequence a. Equivalently, we write $a \in i\,\mathbb{R}$ for a purely imaginary sequence. Thus the transform of a complex symmetric or antisymmetric sequence is symmetric or antisymmetric, respectively:

$$\mathcal{F}\left[a_S + i\, b_S \right] \; = \; c_S + i\, d_S \tag{21.6-5a}$$

$$\mathcal{F}\left[a_A + i\, b_A \right] \; = \; c_A + i\, d_A \tag{21.6-5b}$$

The real and imaginary parts of the transform of a symmetric sequence correspond to the real and imaginary parts of the original sequence. With an antisymmetric sequence the transform of the real and imaginary parts correspond to the imaginary and real parts of the original sequence.

$$\mathcal{F}\left[(a_S + a_A) \right] \; = \; c_S + i\, d_A \tag{21.6-6a}$$

$$\mathcal{F}\left[i\,(b_S + b_A) \right] \; = \; c_A + i\, d_S \tag{21.6-6b}$$

If the sequence a is purely real, then we have

$$\mathcal{F}\left[a_S \right] \; = \; +\overline{\mathcal{F}\left[a_S \right]} \quad \in \mathbb{R} \tag{21.6-7a}$$

$$\mathcal{F}\left[a_A \right] \; = \; -\overline{\mathcal{F}\left[a_A \right]} \quad \in i\,\mathbb{R} \tag{21.6-7b}$$

That is, the transform of a real symmetric sequence is real and symmetric and the transform of a real antisymmetric sequence is purely imaginary and antisymmetric. Thus the transform of a general real sequence is the complex conjugate of its reversal:

$$\mathcal{F}\left[a \right] \; = \; \overline{\mathcal{F}\left[a \right]}^{*} \quad for \quad a \in \mathbb{R} \tag{21.6-8}$$

Similarly, for a purely imaginary sequence $b \in i\,\mathbb{R}$, we have

$$\mathcal{F}\left[b_S \right] \; = \; +\overline{\mathcal{F}\left[b_S \right]} \quad \in i\,\mathbb{R} \tag{21.6-9a}$$

$$\mathcal{F}\left[b_A \right] \; = \; -\overline{\mathcal{F}\left[b_A \right]} \quad \in \mathbb{R} \tag{21.6-9b}$$

We compare the results of the Fourier transform and its inverse (the transform with negated sign σ) by symbolically writing the transforms as a complex multiplication with the trigonometric term (using C for cosine, S for sine):

$$\mathcal{F}[a+ib] \quad : \quad (a+ib)(C+iS) \;=\; (aC-bS)+i(bC+aS) \tag{21.6-10a}$$

$$\mathcal{F}^{-1}[a+ib] \quad : \quad (a+ib)(C-iS) \;=\; (aC+bS)+i(bC-aS) \tag{21.6-10b}$$

The terms on the right side can be identified with those in relation 21.6-4a. Changing the sign of the transform leads to a result where the components due to the antisymmetric parts of the input are negated.

Now write $\mathcal{F}$ for the Fourier transform and R for the reversal. We have $\mathcal{F}^4 = \mathrm{id}$, $\mathcal{F}^3 = \mathcal{F}^{-1}$, and $\mathcal{F}^2 = R$. So the inverse transform can be computed as either

$$\mathcal{F}^{-1} \;=\; R\,\mathcal{F} \;=\; \mathcal{F}\,R \tag{21.6-11}$$

21.7 Inverse FFT for free

Some FFT implementations are hard-coded for a fixed sign of the transform. If we cannot easily modify the implementation into the transform with the other sign (the inverse transform), then how can we compute the inverse FFT?

If the implementation uses separate arrays for the real and imaginary parts of the complex sequences to be transformed, as in

```
1    procedure my_fft(ar[], ai[], ldn)  // only for is==+1 !
2    // real ar[0..2**ldn-1] input, result, real part
3    // real ai[0..2**ldn-1] input, result, imaginary part
4    {
5        // Incredibly complicated code
6        // that you cannot see how to modify
7        // for is==-1
8    }
```

Then do as follows: with the forward transform being

```
    my_fft(ar[], ai[], ldn)  // forward FFT
```

compute the inverse transform as

```
    my_fft(ai[], ar[], ldn)  // inverse FFT
```

Note the swapped real and imaginary parts! The same trick works for a procedure coded for fixed is$= -1$.

To see why this works, we note that

$$\mathcal{F}[a+ib] \;=\; \mathcal{F}[a_S] + i\,\sigma\,\mathcal{F}[a_A] + i\,\mathcal{F}[b_S] + \sigma\,\mathcal{F}[b_A] \tag{21.7-1a}$$

$$=\; \mathcal{F}[a_S] + i\,\mathcal{F}[b_S] + i\,\sigma\,\left(\mathcal{F}[a_A] - i\,\mathcal{F}[b_A]\right) \tag{21.7-1b}$$

For the computation with swapped real and imaginary parts we have

$$\mathcal{F}[b+ia] \;=\; \mathcal{F}[b_S] + i\,\mathcal{F}[a_S] + i\,\sigma\,\left(\mathcal{F}[b_A] - i\,\mathcal{F}[a_A]\right) \tag{21.7-2a}$$

Now the real and imaginary parts are implicitly swapped at the end of the computation, giving

$$\mathcal{F}[a_S] + i\,\mathcal{F}[b_S] - i\,\sigma\,\left(\mathcal{F}[a_A] - i\,\mathcal{F}[b_A]\right) \;=\; \mathcal{F}^{-1}[a+ib] \tag{21.7-2b}$$

When a complex type is used, then the best way to compute the inverse transform may be to reverse the sequence according to the symmetry of the Fourier transform given as relation 21.6-11: the transform with negated sign can be computed by reversing the order of the result (use the routine `reverse_0()` in [FXT: perm/reverse.h]). The reversal can also happen with the input data before the transform, which is advantageous if the data has to be copied anyway (use `copy_reverse_0()` in [FXT: aux1/copy.h]). The additional work will usually not matter.

21.8 Real-valued Fourier transforms

The Fourier transform of a purely real sequence $c = \mathcal{F}[a]$ where $a \in \mathbb{R}$ has a symmetric real part ($\mathfrak{Re}\,\bar{c} = \mathfrak{Re}\,c$, relation 21.6-8) and an antisymmetric imaginary part ($\mathfrak{Im}\,\bar{c} = -\mathfrak{Im}\,c$). The symmetric and antisymmetric parts of the original sequence correspond to the symmetric (and purely real) and antisymmetric (and purely imaginary) parts of the transform, respectively:

$$\mathcal{F}[a] \;=\; \mathcal{F}[a_S] + i\,\sigma\,\mathcal{F}[a_A] \tag{21.8-1}$$

Simply using a complex FFT for real input is a waste by a factor 2 of memory and CPU cycles. There are several alternatives:

- wrapper routines for complex FFTs (section 21.8.3 on the next page),

- usage of the fast Hartley transform (section 25.5 on page 523),

- special versions of the split-radix algorithm (section 21.8.4 on page 434).

All techniques have in common that they store only half of the complex result to avoid the redundancy due to the symmetries of a complex Fourier transform of purely real input. The result of a real to complex FFT (R2CFT) contains the purely real components c_0 (the 'DC-part' of the input signal) and, in case n is even, $c_{n/2}$ (the Nyquist frequency part). The inverse procedure, the complex to real transform (C2RFT) must be compatible to the ordering of the R2CFT.

21.8.1 Sign of the transforms

The sign of the transform can be chosen arbitrarily to be either $+1$ or -1. Note that the transform with the 'other sign' is *not* the inverse transform. The R2CFT and its inverse C2RFT must use the same sign.

Some R2CFT and C2RFT implementations are hard-coded for a fixed sign. For the R2CFT with the other sign, negate the imaginary part after the transform. If we have to copy the data before the transform, then we can exploit the relation

$$\mathcal{F}[\bar{a}] \;=\; \mathcal{F}[a_S] - i\,\sigma\,\mathcal{F}[a_A] \tag{21.8-2}$$

That is, copy the real data in reversed order to get the transform with the other sign. This technique does not involve an extra pass and should be virtually for free.

For the complex to real FFTs (C2RFT) we have to negate the imaginary part before the transform to obtain the transform with the other sign.

21.8.2 Data ordering

Let c be the Fourier transform of the purely real sequence, stored in the array `a[]`. All given procedures use one of the following schemes for storing the transformed sequence.

A scheme that interleaves real and imaginary parts ('complex ordering') is

$$
\begin{aligned}
\mathtt{a[0]} &= \mathfrak{Re}\,c_0 \\
\mathtt{a[1]} &= \mathfrak{Re}\,c_{n/2} \\
\mathtt{a[2]} &= \mathfrak{Re}\,c_1 \\
\mathtt{a[3]} &= \mathfrak{Im}\,c_1 \\
\mathtt{a[4]} &= \mathfrak{Re}\,c_2 \\
\mathtt{a[5]} &= \mathfrak{Im}\,c_2 \\
&\;\;\vdots \\
\mathtt{a[n-2]} &= \mathfrak{Re}\,c_{n/2-1} \\
\mathtt{a[n-1]} &= \mathfrak{Im}\,c_{n/2-1}
\end{aligned}
\tag{21.8-3}
$$

Note the absence of the elements $\Im c_0$ and $\Im c_{n/2}$ which are always zero.

Some routines store the real parts in the lower half and imaginary parts in the upper half. The data in the lower half will always be ordered as follows:

$$
\begin{aligned}
\texttt{a[0]} &= \Re c_0 \\
\texttt{a[1]} &= \Re c_1 \\
\texttt{a[2]} &= \Re c_2 \\
&\vdots \\
\texttt{a[n/2]} &= \Re c_{n/2}
\end{aligned}
\tag{21.8-4}
$$

For the imaginary part of the result there are two schemes:
The 'parallel ordering' is

$$
\begin{aligned}
\texttt{a[n/2 + 1]} &= \Im c_1 \\
\texttt{a[n/2 + 2]} &= \Im c_2 \\
\texttt{a[n/2 + 3]} &= \Im c_3 \\
&\vdots \\
\texttt{a[n - 1]} &= \Im c_{n/2-1}
\end{aligned}
\tag{21.8-5}
$$

The 'antiparallel ordering' is

$$
\begin{aligned}
\texttt{a[n/2 + 1]} &= \Im c_{n/2-1} \\
\texttt{a[n/2 + 2]} &= \Im c_{n/2-2} \\
\texttt{a[n/2 + 3]} &= \Im c_{n/2-3} \\
&\vdots \\
\texttt{a[n - 1]} &= \Im c_1
\end{aligned}
\tag{21.8-6}
$$

21.8.3   Real-valued Fourier transforms via wrapper routines

A complex length-n FFT can be used to compute a real length-$2n$ FFT. For a real sequence a one feeds the (length-n) complex sequence $f = a^{(even)} + i\, a^{(odd)}$ into a complex FFT. Some post-processing is necessary. This is not the most elegant real FFT available, but it is directly usable to turn complex FFTs into real FFTs.

A C++ implementation of the real to complex FFT (R2CFT) is given in [FXT: realfft/realfftwrap.cc], the sign of the transform is hard-coded to $\sigma = +1$:

```
1    void
2    wrap_real_complex_fft(double *f, ulong ldn)
3    // Real to complex FFT (R2CFT)
4    {
5        if ( ldn==0 )  return;
6
7        fht_fft((Complex *)f, ldn-1, +1);  // cast
8
9        const ulong n = 1UL<<ldn;
10       const ulong nh = n/2, n4 = n/4;
11       const double phi0 = M_PI / nh;
12       for(ulong i=1; i<n4; i++)
13       {
14           ulong i1 = 2 * i;   // re low [2, 4, ..., n/2-2]
15           ulong i2 = i1 + 1;  // im low [3, 5, ..., n/2-1]
16
17           ulong i3 = n - i1;  // re hi  [n-2, n-4, ..., n/2+2]
18           ulong i4 = i3 + 1;  // im hi  [n-1, n-3, ..., n/2+3]
19
20           double f1r, f2i;
```

```
21              sumdiff05(f[i3], f[i1], f1r, f2i);
22
23              double f2r, f1i;
24              sumdiff05(f[i2], f[i4], f2r, f1i);
25
26              double c, s;
27              double phi = i*phi0;
28              SinCos(phi, &s, &c);
29
30              double tr, ti;
31              cmult(c, s, f2r, f2i, tr, ti);
32
33              // f[i1] = f1r + tr;  // re low
34              // f[i3] = f1r - tr;  // re hi
35              // =^=
36              sumdiff(f1r, tr, f[i1], f[i3]);
37
38
39              // f[i4] = is * (ti + f1i);  // im hi
40              // f[i2] = is * (ti - f1i);  // im low
41              // =^=
42              sumdiff( ti,  f1i, f[i4], f[i2]);
43          }
44          sumdiff(f[0], f[1]);
45   }
```

The output is ordered according to relations 21.8-3. The same ordering must be used for the input for the inverse routine, the complex to real FFT (C2RFT). Again the sign of the transform is hard-coded to $\sigma = +1$:

```
1    void
2    wrap_complex_real_fft(double *f, ulong ldn)
3    // Complex to real FFT (C2RFT).
4    {
5        if ( ldn==0 )  return;
6
7        const ulong n = 1UL<<ldn;
8        const ulong nh = n/2, n4 = n/4;
9        const double phi0 = -M_PI / nh;
10       for(ulong i=1; i<n4; i++)
11       {
12           ulong i1 = 2 * i;    // re low  [2, 4, ..., n/2-2]
13           ulong i2 = i1 + 1;   // im low  [3, 5, ..., n/2-1]
14
15           ulong i3 = n - i1;   // re hi   [n-2, n-4, ..., n/2+2]
16           ulong i4 = i3 + 1;   // im hi   [n-1, n-3, ..., n/2+3]
17
18           double f1r, f2i;
19           // double f1r =  f[i1] + f[i3];  // re symm
20           // double f2i =  f[i1] - f[i3];  // re asymm
21           // -^-
22           sumdiff(f[i1], f[i3], f1r, f2i);
23
24           double f2r, f1i;
25           // double f2r = -f[i2] - f[i4];  // im symm
26           // double f1i =  f[i2] - f[i4];  // im asymm
27           // =^=
28           sumdiff(-f[i4], f[i2], f1i, f2r);
29
30           double c, s;
31           double phi = i*phi0;
32           SinCos(phi, &s, &c);
33
34           double tr, ti;
35           cmult(c, s, f2r, f2i, tr, ti);
36
37           // f[i1] = f1r + tr;  // re low
38           // f[i3] = f1r - tr;  // re hi
39           // =^=
40           sumdiff(f1r, tr, f[i1], f[i3]);
41
42           // f[i2] = ti - f1i;  // im low
43           // f[i4] = ti + f1i;  // im hi
44           // =^=
45           sumdiff(ti, f1i, f[i4], f[i2]);
46       }
47       sumdiff(f[0], f[1]);
48
49       if ( nh>=2 )  { f[nh] *= 2.0; f[nh+1] *= 2.0; }
```

```
50
51          fht_fft((Complex *)f, ldn-1, -1);  // cast
52   }
```

21.8.4   Real-valued split-radix Fourier transforms

We give pseudocode for the split-radix real to complex FFT and its inverse. The C++ implementations
are given in [FXT: realfft/realfftsplitradix.cc]. The code given here follows [130], see also [318] (erratum
for page 859 of [318]: at the start of the DO 32 loop replace the obvious assignments by CC1=COS(A),
SS1=SIN(A), CC3=COS(A3), SS3=SIN(A3)).

21.8.5   Real to complex split-radix FFT

We give a routine for the split-radix R2CFT algorithm, the sign of the transform is hard-coded to $\sigma = -1$:

```
1    procedure r2cft_splitradix_dit(x[], ldn)
2    {
3        n := 2**ldn
4
5        revbin_permute(x[], n);
6
7        ix := 1;
8        id := 4;
9        do
10       {
11           i0 := ix-1
12           while i0<n
13           {
14               i1 := i0 + 1
15               { x[i0], x[i1] } := { x[i0] + x[i1], x[i0] - x[i1] }  // parallel assignment
16               i0 := i0 + id
17           }
18           ix := 2*id-1
19           id := 4 * id
20       }
21       while ix<n
22
23       n2 := 2
24       nn := n/4
25       while nn!=0
26       {
27           ix := 0
28           n2 := 2*n2
29           id := 2*n2
30           n4 := n2/4
31           n8 := n2/8
32           do  // ix loop
33           {
34               i0 := ix
35               while i0<n
36               {
37                   i1 := i0
38                   i2 := i1 + n4
39                   i3 := i2 + n4
40                   i4 := i3 + n4
41
42                   { t1, x[i4] } := { x[i4] + x[i3], x[i4] - x[i3] }
43                   { x[i1], x[i3] } := { x[i1] + t1, x[i1] - t1 }
44
45                   if  n4!=1
46                   {
47                       i1 := i1 + n8
48                       i2 := i2 + n8
49                       i3 := i3 + n8
50                       i4 := i4 + n8
51
52                       t1 := (x[i3]+x[i4]) * sqrt(1/2)
53                       t2 := (x[i3]-x[i4]) * sqrt(1/2)
54
55                       { x[i4], x[i3] } := { x[i2] - t1, -x[i2] - t1 }
56                       { x[i1], x[i2] } := { x[i1] + t2,  x[i1] - t2 }
57                   }
58
59                   i0 := i0 + id
60               }
61
62               ix := 2*id - n2
63               id := 2*id
64           }
65           while ix<n
66
67           e := 2.0*PI/n2
68           a := e
```

```
69
70          for j:=2 to n8
71          {
72              cc1 := cos(a)
73              ss1 := sin(a)
74              cc3 := cos(3*a)   // == 4*cc1*(cc1*cc1-0.75)
75              ss3 := sin(3*a)   // == 4*ss1*(0.75-ss1*ss1)
76
77              a := j*e
78
79              ix := 0
80              id := 2*n2
81
82              do  // ix-loop
83              {
84                  i0 := ix
85                  while i0<n
86                  {
87                      i1 := i0 + j - 1
88                      i2 := i1 + n4
89                      i3 := i2 + n4
90                      i4 := i3 + n4
91                      i5 := i0 + n4 - j + 1
92                      i6 := i5 + n4
93                      i7 := i6 + n4
94                      i8 := i7 + n4
95
96                      // complex mult: (t2,t1) := (x[i7],x[i3]) * (cc1,ss1)
97                      t1 := cc1 * x[i3] + ss1 * x[i7]
98                      t2 := cc1 * x[i7] - ss1 * x[i3]
99
100                     // complex mult: (t4,t3) := (x[i8],x[i4]) * (cc3,ss3)
101                     t3 := cc3 * x[i4] + ss3 * x[i8]
102                     t4 := cc3 * x[i8] - ss3 * x[i4]
103
104                     t5 := t1 + t3
105                     t6 := t2 + t4
106                     t3 := t1 - t3
107                     t4 := t2 - t4
108
109                     { t2, x[i3] } := { t6 + x[i6], t6 - x[i6] }
110                     x[i8] := t2
111                     { t2, x[i7] } := { x[i2] - t3, -x[i2] - t3 }
112                     x[i4] := t2
113                     { t1, x[i6] } := { x[i1] + t5, x[i1] - t5 }
114                     x[i1] := t1
115                     { t1, x[i5] } := { x[i5] + t4, x[i5] - t4 }
116                     x[i2] := t1
117
118                     i0 := i0 + id
119                 }
120
121                 ix := 2*id - n2
122                 id := 2*id
123
124             }
125             while ix<n
126         }
127         nn := nn/2
128     }
129 }
```

The ordering of the output is given as relations 21.8-4 on page 432 for the real part, and relations 21.8-6 for the imaginary part.

21.8.6   Complex to real split-radix FFT

The following routine is the inverse of `r2cft_splitradix_dit()`. The imaginary part of the input data must be ordered according to relations 21.8-6 on page 432. We give pseudocode for the split-radix C2RFT algorithm, the sign of the transform is hard-coded to $\sigma = -1$:

```
1   procedure c2rft_splitradix_dif(x[], ldn)
2   {
3       n := 2**ldn
4
5       n2 := n/2
6       nn := n/4
7       while nn!=0
8       {
9           ix := 0
10          id := n2
11          n2 := n2/2
12          n4 := n2/4
13          n8 := n2/8
```

```
14          do  // ix loop
15          {
16              i0 := ix
17              while i0<n
18              {
19                  i1 := i0
20                  i2 := i1 + n4
21                  i3 := i2 + n4
22                  i4 := i3 + n4
23
24                  { x[i1], t1 } := { x[i1] + x[i3], x[i1] - x[i3] }
25                  x[i2] := 2*x[i2]
26                  x[i4] := 2*x[i4]
27                  { x[i3], x[i4] } := { t1 + x[i4], t1 - x[i4] }
28
29                  if  n4!=1
30                  {
31                      i1 := i1 + n8
32                      i2 := i2 + n8
33                      i3 := i3 + n8
34                      i4 := i4 + n8
35
36                      { x[i1], t1 } := { x[i2] + x[i1], x[i2] - x[i1] }
37                      { t2, x[i2] } := { x[i4] + x[i3], x[i4] - x[i3] }
38                      x[i3] := -sqrt(2)*(t2+t1)
39                      x[i4] :=  sqrt(2)*(t1-t2)
40                  }
41
42                  i0 := i0 + id
43              }
44
45              ix := 2*id - n2
46              id := 2*id
47          }
48          while ix<n
49
50          e := 2.0*PI/n2
51          a := e
52
53          for j:=2 to n8
54          {
55              cc1 := cos(a)
56              ss1 := sin(a)
57              cc3 := cos(3*a)  // == 4*cc1*(cc1*cc1-0.75)
58              ss3 := sin(3*a)  // == 4*ss1*(0.75-ss1*ss1)
59              a := j*e
60
61              ix := 0
62              id := 2*n2
63              do  // ix-loop
64              {
65                  i0 := ix
66                  while  i0<n
67                  {
68                      i1 := i0 + j - 1
69                      i2 := i1 + n4
70                      i3 := i2 + n4
71                      i4 := i3 + n4
72                      i5 := i0 + n4 - j + 1
73                      i6 := i5 + n4
74                      i7 := i6 + n4
75                      i8 := i7 + n4
76
77                      { x[i1], t1 } := { x[i1] + x[i6], x[i1] - x[i6] }
78                      { x[i5], t2 } := { x[i5] + x[i2], x[i5] - x[i2] }
79                      { t3, x[i6] } := { x[i8] + x[i3], x[i8] - x[i3] }
80                      { t4, x[i2] } := { x[i4] + x[i7], x[i4] - x[i7] }
81                      { t1, t5 } := { t1 + t4, t1 - t4 }
82                      { t2, t4 } := { t2 + t3, t2 - t3 }
83
84                      // complex mult: (x[i7],x[i3]) := (t5,t4)  * (ss1,cc1)
85                      x[i3] :=  cc1 * t5 + ss1 * t4
86                      x[i7] := -cc1 * t4 + ss1 * t5
87
88                      // complex mult: (x[i4],x[i8]) := (t1,t2)  * (cc3,ss3)
89                      x[i4] := cc3 * t1 - ss3 * t2
90                      x[i8] := cc3 * t2 + ss3 * t1
91
92                      i0 := i0 + id
93                  }
94
95                  ix := 2*id - n2
96                  id := 2*id
97              }
98              while ix<n
99          }
100
```

```
101             nn := nn/2
102       }
103
104       ix := 1;
105       id := 4;
106       do
107       {
108           i0 := ix-1
109           while i0<n
110           {
111               i1 := i0 + 1
112               { x[i0], x[i1] } := { x[i0] + x[i1], x[i0] - x[i1] }
113               i0 := i0 + id
114           }
115           ix := 2*id-1
116           id := 4 * id
117       }
118       while ix<n
119
120       revbin_permute(x[], n);
121   }
```

21.9   Multi-dimensional Fourier transforms

Let $a_{x,y}$ ($x = 0, 1, 2, \ldots, C-1$ and $y = 0, 1, 2, \ldots, R-1$) be a 2-dimensional array. That is, an $R \times C$ 'matrix' of R rows (of length C) and C columns (of length R). Its 2-dimensional Fourier transform is defined by:

$$c = \mathcal{F}[a] \tag{21.9-1a}$$

$$c_{k,h} := \frac{1}{\sqrt{n}} \sum_{x=0}^{C-1} \sum_{y=0}^{R-1} a_{x,y} \, z^{+(x\,k/C + y\,h/R)} \quad \text{where} \quad z = e^{\sigma\,2\pi i} \tag{21.9-1b}$$

where $k \in \{0, 1, 2, \ldots, C-1\}$, $h \in \{0, 1, 2, \ldots, R-1\}$, and $n = R \cdot C$. The inverse transform is

$$a = \mathcal{F}^{-1}[c] \tag{21.9-2a}$$

$$a_{x,y} = \frac{1}{\sqrt{n}} \sum_{k=0}^{C-1} \sum_{h=0}^{R-1} c_{k,h} \, z^{-(x\,k/C + y\,h/R)} \tag{21.9-2b}$$

For an m-dimensional array $a_{\vec{x}}$ (where $\vec{x} = (x_1, x_2, x_3, \ldots, x_m)$ and $x_i \in 0, 1, 2, \ldots, S_i$) the m-dimensional Fourier transform $c_{\vec{k}}$ (where $\vec{k} = (k_1, k_2, k_3, \ldots, k_m)$ and $k_i \in 0, 1, 2, \ldots, S_i$) is defined as

$$c_{\vec{k}} := \frac{1}{\sqrt{n}} \sum_{x_1=0}^{S_1-1} \sum_{x_2=0}^{S_2-1} \cdots \sum_{x_m=0}^{S_m-1} a_{\vec{x}} \, z^{(x_1\,k_1/S_1 + x_2\,k_2/S_2 + \ldots + x_m\,k_m/S_m)} \tag{21.9-3a}$$

The inverse transform is, like in the 1-dimensional case, the complex conjugate transform.

21.9.1   The row-column algorithm

The equation of the definition of the 2-dimensional Fourier transform (relation 21.9-1a) can be recast as

$$c_{k,h} = \frac{1}{\sqrt{n}} \sum_{y=0}^{R-1} \left[\exp\left(y\,h/R\right) \sum_{x=0}^{C-1} a_{x,y} \, \exp\left(x\,k/C\right) \right] \tag{21.9-4}$$

This shows that the 2-dimensional transform can be computed by applying 1-dimensional transforms, first on the rows, then on the columns. The same result is obtained when the columns are transformed first and then the rows.

This leads us directly to the *row-column algorithm* for 2-dimensional FFTs. Pseudocode to compute the 2-dimensional FFT of a[][] using the row-column method:

```
1    procedure rowcol_ft(a[][], R, C, is)
2    {
3        complex a[R][C]   // R (length-C) rows, C (length-R) columns
4
5        for r:=0 to R-1   // FFT rows
6        {
7            fft(a[r][], C, is)
8        }
9
10       complex t[R]      // temporary array for columns
11       for c:=0 to C-1   // FFT columns
12       {
13           copy a[0,1,...,R-1][c] to t[]   // get column
14           fft(t[], R, is)
15           copy t[] to a[0,1,...,R-1][c]   // write back column
16       }
17   }
```

Here it is assumed that the rows lie in contiguous memory (as in the C language). The equivalent C++ code is given in [FXT: fft/twodimfft.cc].

Transposing the array before the column pass will, due to a better memory access pattern, improve performance in most cases:

```
1    procedure rowcol_fft2d(a[][], R, C, is)
2    {
3        complex a[R][C]   // R (length-C) rows, C (length-R) columns
4
5        for r:=0 to R-1   // FFT rows
6        {
7            fft(a[r][], C, is)
8        }
9
10       transpose( a[R][C] )   // in-place
11
12       for c:=0 to C-1   // FFT columns (which are rows now)
13       {
14           fft(a[c][], R, is)
15       }
16
17       transpose( a[C][R] )   // transpose back (note swapped R,C)
18   }
```

Transposing back at the end of the routine can be avoided if the inverse transform follows immediately as is typical for a convolution. The inverse transform must then be called with R and C swapped.

21.10   The matrix Fourier algorithm (MFA)

The matrix Fourier algorithm (MFA) is an algorithm for 1-dimensional FFTs that works for data lengths $n = RC$. It is quite similar to the row-column algorithm (relation 21.9-4) for 2-dimensional FFTs. The only differences are n multiplications with trigonometric factors and a final matrix transposition.

Consider the input array as an $R \times C$-matrix (R rows, C columns), with the rows contiguous in memory. Let σ be the sign of the transform. The *matrix Fourier algorithm* (MFA) can be stated as follows:

1. Apply a (length R) FFT on each column.

2. Multiply each matrix element (index r, c) by $\exp(\sigma\, 2\,\pi\, i\, r\, c/n)$.

3. Apply a (length C) FFT on each row.

4. Transpose the matrix.

Note the elegance! A variant of the MFA is called *four step FFT* in [28].

A trivial modification is obtained by executing the steps in reversed order. The *transposed matrix Fourier algorithm* (TMFA) for the FFT:

1. Transpose the matrix.

2. Apply a (length C) FFT on each row of the matrix.

3. Multiply each matrix element (index r, c) by $\exp(\sigma\, 2\,\pi\, i\, r\, c/n)$.

4. Apply a (length R) FFT on each column of the matrix.

A variant of the MFA that, apart from the transpositions, accesses the memory only in consecutive address ranges can be stated as

1. Transpose the matrix.

2. Apply a (length C) FFT on each row of the transposed matrix.

3. Multiply each matrix element (index r, c) by $\exp(\sigma\, 2\,\pi\, i\, r\, c/n)$.

4. Transpose the matrix back.

5. Apply a (length R) FFT on each row of the matrix.

6. Transpose the matrix (if the order of the transformed data matters).

The 'transposed' version of this algorithm is identical. The performance will depend critically on the performance of the transposition routine.

It is usually a good idea to use factors of the data length n that are close to $\sqrt{n}$. Of course we can apply the same algorithm for the row (or column) FFTs again: it can be an improvement to split n into 3 factors (as close to $n^{1/3}$ as possible) if a length-$n^{1/3}$ FFT fits completely into cache. Especially for systems where CPU clock speed is much higher than memory clock speed the performance may increase dramatically. A speedup by a factor of 3 can sometimes be observed, even when compared to otherwise very well optimized FFTs. Another algorithm that is efficient with large arrays is the localized transform described (for the Hartley transform) in section 25.8 on page 529.

Chapter 22

Convolution, correlation, and more FFT algorithms

We give algorithms for fast convolution that are based on the fast Fourier transform. An efficient algorithm for the convolution of arrays that do not fit into the main memory (mass storage convolution) is given for both complex and real data. Further, weighted convolutions and their algorithms are introduced.

We describe how fast convolution can be used for computing the z-transform of sequences of arbitrary length. Another convolution based algorithm for the Fourier transform of arrays of prime length, Rader's algorithm, is described at the end of the chapter.

Convolution algorithms based on the fast Hartley transform are described in section 25.7. The XOR (dyadic) convolution, which is computed via the Walsh transform is treated in section 23.8. The OR-convolution and the AND-convolution are described in section 23.12.

22.1 Convolution

The *cyclic convolution* (or *circular convolution*) of two length-n sequences $a = [a_0, a_1, \ldots, a_{n-1}]$ and $b = [b_0, b1, \ldots, b_{n-1}]$ is defined as the length-n sequence h with elements h_τ as:

$$h \quad = \quad a \circledast b \tag{22.1-1a}$$

$$h_\tau \quad := \quad \sum_{x+y \equiv \tau \pmod n} a_x \, b_y \tag{22.1-1b}$$

The last equation may be rewritten as

$$h_\tau \quad := \quad \sum_{x=0}^{n-1} a_x \, b_{(\tau-x) \mod n} \tag{22.1-2}$$

That is, indices $\tau - x$ wrap around, it is a cyclic convolution. A table illustrating the cyclic convolution of two sequences is shown in figure 22.1-A.

22.1.1 Direct computation

A C++ implementation of the computation by definition is [FXT: convolution/slowcnvl.h]:

```
1    template <typename Type>
2    void slow_convolution(const Type *f, const Type *g, Type *h, ulong n)
3    // (cyclic) convolution:  h[] :=  f[] (*) g[]
4    // n := array length
5    {
6        for (ulong tau=0;  tau<n;  ++tau)
7        {
8            Type s = 0.0;
9            for (ulong k=0; k<n; ++k)
```

J. Arndt, *Matters Computational: Ideas, Algorithms, Source Code*,
DOI 10.1007/978-3-642-14764-7_22, © Springer-Verlag Berlin Heidelberg 2011

```
+   -  0-  1   2   3    4   5   6   7    8   9  10  11   12  13  14  15
|
0 :  0   1   2   3    4   5   6   7    8   9  10  11   12  13  14  15
1 :  1   2   3   4    5   6   7   8    9  10  11  12   13  14  15   0
2 :  2   3   4   5    6   7   8   9   10  11  12  13   14  15   0   1
3 :  3   4   5   6    7   8   9   1   011  12  13  14   15   0   1   2

4 :  4   5   6   7    8   9  10   1   112  13  14  15    0   1   2   3
5 :  5   6   7   8    9  10   1   1   213  14  15   0    1   2   3   4
6 :  6   7   8   9    1  01  12   1   314  15   0   1    2   3   4   5
7 :  7   8   9   1   011  12   1   3   415   0   1   2    3   4   5   6

8 :  8   9   1   0   11  23  14   1   5 0   1   2   3    4   5   6   7
9 :  9   1   0   1   213  14   1   50    1   2   3   4    5   6   7   8
1  0 1: 0   1   2   31  45   0   1   2    3   4   5   6    7   8   9
1  1 1: 1   2   3   41  50   1   2    3   4   5   6    7   8   9  10

12: 12  13  14  15    0   1   2   3    4   5   6   7    8   9  10  11
13: 13  14  15   0    1   2   3   4    5   6   7   8    9  10  11  12
1  4 1: 4   50   1    2   3   4   5    6   7   8   9   10  11  12  13
1  5 1: 50   1   2    3   4   5   6    7   8   9  10   11  12  13  14
```

```
          +   -  0 - 1   2   3   (b)
          |
          0 :  0   1   2   4
(a)       1:   1   3   5  <--= h[5] contains a[1]*b[2]
          2:   4   8   9  <--= h[9] contains a[2]*b[2]
          3:   ...
```

Figure 22.1-A: Semi-symbolic table of the cyclic convolution of two sequences (top). The entries denote where in the convolution the products of the input elements can be found (bottom).

```
10        {
11                ulong k2 = tau - k;
12                if ( (long)k2<0 )  k2 += n;  // modulo n
13                s += (f[k]*g[k2]);
14        }
15        h[tau] = s;
16    }
17  }
```

The following version avoids the `if` statement in the inner loop:

```
1    for (ulong tau=0;  tau<n;  ++tau)
2    {
3        Type s = 0.0;
4        ulong k = 0;
5        for (ulong k2=tau;  k<=tau;  ++k, --k2)  s += (f[k]*g[k2]);
6        for (ulong k2=n-1;  k<n;     ++k, --k2)  s += (f[k]*g[k2]);  // wrapped around
7        h[tau] = s;
8    }
```

For length-n sequences this procedure involves $O(n^2)$ operations, therefore it is slow for large n. For short lengths the algorithm is just fine. Unrolled routines will offer good performance, especially for convolutions of fixed length. For medium length convolutions the splitting schemes given in section 28.1 on page 550 and section 40.2 on page 827 are applicable.

22.1.2 Computation via FFT

The fast Fourier transform provides us with an efficient way to compute convolutions that needs only $O(n \log(n))$ operations. The *convolution property* of the Fourier transform is

$$\mathcal{F}[a \circledast b] = \mathcal{F}[a] \cdot \mathcal{F}[b] \tag{22.1-3}$$

The multiplication indicated by the dot is element-wise. That is, convolution in original space is element-wise multiplication in Fourier space. The statement can be motivated as follows:

$$\mathcal{F}[a]_k \cdot \mathcal{F}[b]_k \;=\; \sum_x a_x\, z^{k\,x} \sum_y b_y\, z^{k\,y} \tag{22.1-4a}$$

$$=\; \sum_x a_x\, z^{k\,x} \sum_{\tau-x} b_{\tau-x}\, z^{k\,(\tau-x)} \quad \text{where} \quad y = \tau - x \tag{22.1-4b}$$

$$=\; \sum_x \sum_{\tau-x} a_x\, z^{k\,x} b_{\tau-x}\, z^{k\,(\tau-x)} \;=\; \sum_\tau \left(\sum_x a_x\, b_{\tau-x} \right) z^{k\,\tau} \tag{22.1-4c}$$

$$=\; \left(\mathcal{F}\Big[\sum_x a_x\, b_{\tau-x} \Big] \right)_k \;=\; \big(\mathcal{F}[a \circledast b] \big)_k \tag{22.1-4d}$$

Rewriting relation 22.1-3 as

$$a \circledast b \;=\; \mathcal{F}^{-1}\big[\mathcal{F}[a] \cdot \mathcal{F}[b] \big] \tag{22.1-5}$$

tells us how to proceed. We give pseudocode for the cyclic convolution of two complex sequences x[] and y[], the result is returned in y[]:

```
1   procedure fft_cyclic_convolution(x[], y[], n)
2   {
3       complex x[0..n-1], y[0..n-1]
4
5       // transform data:
6       fft(x[], n, +1)
7       fft(y[], n, +1)
8
9       // element-wise multiplication in transformed domain:
10      for i:=0 to n-1
11      {
12          y[i] := y[i] * x[i]
13      }
14
15       // transform back:
16      fft(y[], n, -1)
17
18       // normalize:
19      n1 := 1 / n
20      for i:=0 to n-1
21      {
22          y[i] := y[i] * n1
23      }
24  }
```

It is assumed that the procedure fft() does no normalization. For the normalization loop we precompute 1/n and multiply as divisions are usually much slower than multiplications.

22.1.3   Avoiding the revbin permutations

We can save the revbin permutations by observing that any DIF FFT is of the form

```
    DIF_FFT_CORE(f, n);
    revbin_permute(f, n);
```

and any DIT FFT is of the form

```
    revbin_permute(f, n);
    DIT_FFT_CORE(f, n);
```

This way a convolution routine that uses DIF FFTs for the transform and DIT FFTs as inverse transform can omit the revbin permutations. This is demonstrated in the C++ implementation for the cyclic convolution of complex sequences [FXT: convolution/fftcocnvl.cc]:

```
1   #define  DIT_FFT_CORE  fft_dit4_core_m1  // isign = -1
2   #define  DIF_FFT_CORE  fft_dif4_core_p1  // isign = +1
3   void
4   fft_complex_convolution(Complex * restrict f, Complex * restrict g,
```

```
5                          ulong ldn, double v/*=0.0*/)
6    // (complex, cyclic) convolution:  g[] := f[] (*) g[]
7    // (use zero padded data for usual convolution)
8    // ldn := base-2 logarithm of the array length
9    // Supply a value for v for a normalization factor != 1/n
10   {
11       const ulong n = (1UL<<ldn);
12
13       DIF_FFT_CORE(f, ldn);
14       DIF_FFT_CORE(g, ldn);
15       if ( v==0.0 )  v = 1.0/n;
16       for (ulong i=0; i<n; ++i)
17       {
18           Complex t = g[i] * f[i];
19           g[i] = t * v;
20       }
21       DIT_FFT_CORE(g, ldn);
22   }
```

The signs of the two FFTs must be different but are otherwise immaterial.

The *auto-convolution* (or *self-convolution*) of a sequence is defined as the convolution of a sequence with itself: $h = a \circledast a$. The corresponding procedure needs only two instead of three FFTs.

22.1.4   Linear convolution

```
+   - 0- 1  2  3   4  5  6  7   8  9 10 11  12 13 14 15
|
0  : 0  1  2  3   4  5  6  7   8  9 10 11  12 13 14 15
1:   1  2  3  4   5  6  7  8   9 10 11 12  13 14 15 16
2:   2  3  4  5   6  7  8  9  10 11 12 13  14 15 16 17
3:   3  4  5  6   7  8  9 10  11 12 13 14  15 16 17 18

4:   4  5  6  7   8  9 10 11  12 13 14 15  16 17 18 19
5:   5  6  7  8   9 10 11 12  13 14 15 16  17 18 19 20
6:   6  7  8  9  10 11 12 13  14 15 16 17  18 19 20 21
7:   7  8  9 10  11 12 13 14  15 16 17 18  19 20 21 22

8:   8  9 10 11  12 13 14 15  16 17 18 19  20 21 22 23
9:   9 10 11 12  13 14 15 16  17 18 19 20  21 22 23 24
10:  10 11 12 13  14 15 16 17  18 19 20 21  22 23 24 25
11:  11 12 13 14  15 16 17 18  19 20 21 22  23 24 25 26

12:  12 13 14 15  16 17 18 19  20 21 22 23  24 25 26 27
13:  13 14 15 16  17 18 19 20  21 22 23 24  25 26 27 28
14:  14 15 16 17  18 19 20 21  22 23 24 25  26 27 28 29
15:  15 16 17 18  19 20 21 22  23 24 25 26  27 28 29 30
```

Figure 22.1-B: Semi-symbolic table for the linear convolution of two length-16 sequences.

The *linear convolution* of two length-n sequences a and b is the length-$2n$ sequence h defined as

$$h = a \circledast_{lin} b \tag{22.1-6a}$$

$$h_\tau := \sum_{x=0}^{2n-1} a_x b_{\tau-x} \quad \text{where} \quad \tau = 0, 1, 2, \ldots, 2n-1 \tag{22.1-6b}$$

where we set $a_k = 0$ if $k < 0$ or $k \geq n$, and the same for out-of-range elements b_k. The linear convolution is sometimes called *acyclic convolution*, as there is no wrap around of the indices. We note that h_{2n-1}, the last element of the sequence h, is always zero.

The semi-symbolic table for the acyclic convolution is given in figure 22.1-B. The elements in the lower right triangle do not 'wrap around' anymore, they go into extra buckets. Note there are 31 buckets labeled $0, 1, \ldots, 30$.

A routine that computes the linear convolution by the definition is [FXT: convolution/slowcnvl-lin.h]:

```
1    template <typename Type>
2    void slow_linear_convolution(const Type *f, const Type *g, Type *h, ulong n)
3    // Linear (acyclic) convolution.
```

```
4     // n := array length of a[] and b[]
5     // The array h[] must have 2*n elements.
6     {
7         // compute h0 (left half):
8         for (ulong tau=0;  tau<n;  ++tau)
9         {
10            Type s0 = 0;
11            for (ulong k=0, k2=tau;  k<=tau;  ++k, --k2)  s0 += (f[k]*g[k2]);
12            h[tau] = s0;
13        }
14
15        // compute h1 (right half):
16        for (ulong tau=0;  tau<n;  ++tau)
17        {
18            Type s1 = 0;
19            for (ulong k2=n-1, k=tau+1;  k<n;  ++k, --k2)  s1 += (f[k]*g[k2]);
20            h[n+tau] = s1;
21        }
22    }
```

To compute the linear convolution of two length-n sequences a and b, we can use a length-$2n$ cyclic convolution of the *zero padded* sequences A and B where

$$A \quad := \quad [a_0, a_1, a_2, \ldots, a_{n-1}, 0, 0, \ldots, 0] \tag{22.1-7a}$$

$$B \quad := \quad [a_0, a_1, a_2, \ldots, a_{n-1}, 0, 0, \ldots, 0] \tag{22.1-7b}$$

With fast FFT-based algorithms for the cyclic convolution we can compute the linear convolution with the same complexity.

Linear convolution is *polynomial multiplication*: let $A = a_0 + a_1\,x + a_2\,x^2 + \ldots$, $B = b_0 + b_1\,x + b_2\,x^2 + \ldots$, and $C = A\,B = c_0 + c_1\,x + c_2\,x^2 + \ldots$, then

$$c_k \quad = \quad \sum_{i+j=k} a_i\,b_j \tag{22.1-8}$$

This is just another way to write relation 22.1-6a. Chapter 28 on page 550 explains how fast convolution algorithms can be used for fast multiplication of multiprecision numbers.

22.2 Correlation

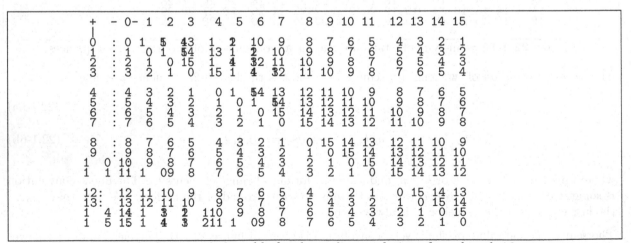

Figure 22.2-A: Semi-symbolic table for the cyclic correlation of two length-16 sequences.

The *cyclic correlation* (or *circular correlation*) of two *real* length-n sequences $a = [a_0, a_1, \ldots, a_{n-1}]$ and $b = [b_0, b_1, \ldots, b_{n-1}]$ can be defined as the length-n sequence h where

$$h_\tau \quad := \quad \sum_{x-y\equiv\tau \bmod n} a_x\,b_y \tag{22.2-1}$$

```
        +   -  0- 1   2   3    4   5   6   7    8   9  10  11   12 13 14 15
        |
        0:  0 31 30 29   28 27 26 25   24 23 22 21   20 19 18 17
        1:  1  0 31 30   29 28 27 26   25 24 23 22   21 20 19 18
        2:  2  1  0 31   30 29 28 27   26 25 24 23   22 21 20 19
        3:  3  2  1  0   31 30 29 28   27 26 25 24   23 22 21 20

        4:  4  3  2  1    0 31 30 29   28 27 26 25   24 23 22 21
        5:  5  4  3  2    1  0 31 30   29 28 27 26   25 24 23 22
        6:  6  5  4  3    2  1  0 31   30 29 28 27   26 25 24 23
        7:  7  6  5  4    3  2  1  0   31 30 29 28   27 26 25 24

        8:  8  7  6  5    4  3  2  1    0 31 30 29   28 27 26 25
        9:  9  8  7  6    5  4  3  2    1  0 31 30   29 28 27 26
       10:  10  9  8  7   6  5  4  3    2  1  0 31   30 29 28 27
       11:  11 10  9  8   7  6  5  4    3  2  1  0   31 30 29 28

       12: 12 11 10  9    8  7  6  5    4  3  2  1    0 31 30 29
       13: 13 12 11 10    9  8  7  6    5  4  3  2    1  0 31 30
       14: 14 13 12 11   10  9  8  7    6  5  4  3    2  1  0 31
       15: 15 14 13 12   11 10  9  8    7  6  5  4    3  2  1  0
```

Figure 22.2-B: Semi-symbolic table for the linear (acyclic) correlation of two length-16 sequences.

The relation can also be written as

$$h_\tau = \sum_{x=0}^{n-1} a_x \, b_{(\tau+x) \bmod n} \tag{22.2-2}$$

The semi-symbolic table for the cyclic correlation is shown in figure 22.2-A. For the computation of the *linear* (or *acyclic*) correlation the sequences have to be zero-padded as in the algorithm for the linear convolution. The corresponding table is shown in figure 22.2-B.

The *auto-correlation* (or *self-correlation*) is the correlation of a sequence with itself, the correlation of two distinct sequences is also called *cross-correlation*. The term *auto-correlation function* (ACF) is often used for the auto-correlation sequence.

22.2.1 Direct computation

A C++ implementation of the computation by the definition is [FXT: correlation/slowcorr.h]:

```cpp
template <typename Type>
void slow_correlation(const Type *f, const Type *g, Type * restrict h, ulong n)
// Cyclic correlation of f[], g[], both real-valued sequences.
// n := array length
{
    for (ulong tau=0;  tau<n;  ++tau)
    {
        Type s = 0.0;
        for (ulong k=0; k<n; ++k)
        {
            ulong k2 = k + tau;
            if ( k2>=n )  k2 -= n;
            s += (g[k]*f[k2]);
        }
        h[tau] = s;
    }
}
```

The `if` statement in the inner loop is avoided by the following version:

```cpp
    for (ulong tau=0;  tau<n;  ++tau)
    {
        Type s = 0.0;
        ulong k = 0;
        for (ulong k2=tau;  k2<n;  ++k, ++k2)  s += (g[k]*f[k2]);
        for (ulong k2=0;     k<n;  ++k, ++k2)  s += (g[k]*f[k2]);
        h[tau] = s;
    }
```

For the linear correlation we avoid zero products:

```
1    template <typename Type>
2    void slow_correlation0(const Type *f, const Type *g, Type * restrict h, ulong n)
3    // Linear correlation of f[], g[], both real-valued sequences.
4    // n := array length
5    // Version for zero padded data:
6    //    f[k],g[k] == 0 for k=n/2 ... n-1
7    // n must be >=2
8    {
9        const ulong nh = n/2;
10       for (ulong tau=0; tau<nh; ++tau)  // k2 == tau + k
11       {
12           Type s = 0;
13           for (ulong k=0, k2=tau;  k2<nh;  ++k, ++k2)  s += (f[k]*g[k2]);
14           h[tau] = s;
15       }
16
17       for (ulong tau=nh; tau<n; ++tau)  // k2 == tau + k - n
18       {
19           Type s = 0;
20           for (ulong k=n-tau, k2=0;  k<nh;  ++k, ++k2)  s += (f[k]*g[k2]);
21           h[tau] = s;
22       }
23   }
```

The algorithm involves $O(n^2)$ operations and is therefore slow with very long arrays.

22.2.2 Computation via FFT

A simple algorithm for fast correlation follows from the relation

$$h_\tau \;=\; \mathcal{F}^{-1}\big[\mathcal{F}[\overline{a}]\cdot\mathcal{F}[b]\big] \tag{22.2-3}$$

That is, use a convolution algorithm with one of the input sequences reversed (indices negated modulo n). For purely real sequences the relation is equivalent to complex conjugation of one of the inner transforms:

$$h_\tau \;=\; \mathcal{F}^{-1}\big[\mathcal{F}[a]^{*}\cdot\mathcal{F}[b]\big] \tag{22.2-4}$$

For the computation of the self-correlation the latter relation is the only reasonable way to go: first transform the input sequence, then multiply each element by its complex conjugate, and finally transform back. A C++ implementation is [FXT: correlation/fftcorr.cc]:

```
1    void
2    fft_correlation(double *f, double *g, ulong ldn)
3    // Cyclic correlation of f[], g[], both real-valued sequences.
4    // Result is written to g[].
5    // ldn := base-2 logarithm of the array length
6    {
7        const ulong n=(1UL<<ldn);
8        const ulong nh=(n>>1);
9
10       fht_real_complex_fft(f, ldn);  // real, imag part in lower, upper half
11       fht_real_complex_fft(g, ldn);
12
13       const double v = 1.0/n;
14       g[0]  *= f[0] * v;
15       g[nh] *= f[nh] * v;
16       for (ulong i=1,j=n-1; i<nh; ++i,--j)  // real at index i, imag at index j
17       {
18           cmult_n(f[i], -f[j], g[i], g[j], v);
19       }
20
21       fht_complex_real_fft(g, ldn);
22   }
```

The function cmult_n() is defined in [FXT: aux0/cmult.h]:

```
1    static inline void
2    cmult_n(double c, double s, double &u, double &v, double dn)
3    // {u,v} <--| {dn*(u*c-v*s), dn*(u*s+v*c)}
4    { double t = u*s+v*c;  u *= c;  u -= v*s;  u *= dn;  v = t*dn; }
```

We note that relation 22.2-4 also holds for complex sequences.

22.2.3 Correlation and difference sets ‡

The linear auto-correlation of a sequence that contains zeros and ones only (a *delta sequence*) is the set of mutual differences of the positions of the ones, including multiplicity. An example:

```
[1, 1, 0, 1, 1, 0, 0, 0, 0, 0, 0]   <--= delta array  R
[4, 2, 1, 2, 1, 0, 0, 1, 2, 1, 2]   <--= linear ACF
 0, 1, 2, 3, 4, 5,-5,-4,-3,-2,-1    <--= index
```

Element zero of the ACF tells us that there are four elements in R (each element has difference zero to just itself). Element one tells us that there are two pairs of consecutive elements, it is identical to the last element (element at index -1). There is just one pair of elements in R whose indices differ by 2 (elements at index 2 and -2 of the ACF), and so on. The ACF does not tell us where the elements with a certain difference are.

The delta array with ones at the seven positions 0, 3, 4, 12, 18, 23, and 25 has the ACF

```
[7, 1, 1, 1, 1, 1, 1, 1, 1, 1, 0, 1, 1, 1, 1, 1, 0, 0, 1, 1, 1, 1, 1, 1, 0, 1, 0, (+symm.)]
 0, 1, 2, 3, 4, 5, 6, 7, 8, 9, 10,        ...                          26, <--= index
```

That is, a ruler of length 26 with marks only at the seven given positions can be used to measure most of the distances up to 26 (the smallest missing distance is 10). Further, no distance appears more than once. Sequences with this property are called *Golomb rulers* and they are very hard to find.

If we allow for two rulers, then the set of mutual differences in positions is the cross-correlation. For this setting analogues of Golomb rulers (that do not have any missing differences) can be found. We use dots for zeros:

```
11..11........11..11.........1....1................  <--= R1
111111111111111111111111111111111111111111111111111  <--= R2 cross-correlation
```

The rulers are binary representations of the evaluations $F(1/2)$ and $F(1/4)$ of a curious function given in section 38.10.1 on page 750.

22.3 Correlation, convolution, and circulant matrices ‡

The cyclic correlation and convolution of two vectors correspond to multiplication with *circulant matrices*. In the following examples we fix the dimension to $n = 4$, the general case will be obvious. Let $a = [a_0, a_1, a_2, a_3]$, $b = [b_0, b_1, b_2, b_3]$, and $r = [r_0, r_1, r_2, r_3]$ the cyclic correlation of a and b (that is, $r_\tau = \sum_{j-k \equiv \tau \bmod n} a_j b_k$):

$$r_0 = b_0 \cdot a_0 + b_1 \cdot a_1 + b_2 \cdot a_2 + b_3 \cdot a_3, \tag{22.3-1a}$$
$$r_1 = b_1 \cdot a_0 + b_2 \cdot a_1 + b_3 \cdot a_2 + b_0 \cdot a_3, \tag{22.3-1b}$$
$$r_2 = b_2 \cdot a_0 + b_3 \cdot a_1 + b_0 \cdot a_2 + b_1 \cdot a_3, \tag{22.3-1c}$$
$$r_3 = b_3 \cdot a_0 + b_0 \cdot a_1 + b_1 \cdot a_2 + b_2 \cdot a_3 \tag{22.3-1d}$$

We have $r^T = R_a b^T$ where R_a is a circulant matrix where row 0 is a and row $k + 1$ is the cyclic right shift of row k:

$$R_a = \begin{bmatrix} a_0 & a_1 & a_2 & a_3 \\ a_3 & a_0 & a_1 & a_2 \\ a_2 & a_3 & a_0 & a_1 \\ a_1 & a_2 & a_3 & a_0 \end{bmatrix} \tag{22.3-2}$$

Now set $c = [c_0, c_1, c_2, c_3]$ to the cyclic convolution of a and b (that is, $r_\tau = \sum_{j+k \equiv \tau \bmod n} a_j b_k$):

$$c_0 = b_0 \cdot a_0 + b_3 \cdot a_1 + b_2 \cdot a_2 + b_1 \cdot a_3, \tag{22.3-3a}$$
$$c_1 = b_1 \cdot a_0 + b_0 \cdot a_1 + b_3 \cdot a_2 + b_2 \cdot a_3, \tag{22.3-3b}$$
$$c_2 = b_2 \cdot a_0 + b_1 \cdot a_1 + b_0 \cdot a_2 + b_3 \cdot a_3, \tag{22.3-3c}$$
$$c_3 = b_3 \cdot a_0 + b_2 \cdot a_1 + b_1 \cdot a_2 + b_0 \cdot a_3 \tag{22.3-3d}$$

We have $c^T = C_a\, b^T$ where $C_a = R_a^T$ is a circulant matrix where column 0 is a^T and column $k+1$ is the cyclic down shift of row k:

$$C_a = \begin{bmatrix} a_0 & a_3 & a_2 & a_1 \\ a_1 & a_0 & a_3 & a_2 \\ a_2 & a_1 & a_0 & a_3 \\ a_3 & a_2 & a_1 & a_0 \end{bmatrix} \tag{22.3-4}$$

Let F be the matrix corresponding to the Fourier transform (either sign, here we choose $\sigma = +1$, so that $\omega = +i$):

$$F = \begin{bmatrix} \omega^0 & \omega^0 & \omega^0 & \omega^0 \\ \omega^0 & \omega^1 & \omega^2 & \omega^3 \\ \omega^0 & \omega^2 & \omega^4 & \omega^6 \\ \omega^0 & \omega^3 & \omega^6 & \omega^9 \end{bmatrix} = \begin{bmatrix} +1 & +1 & +1 & +1 \\ +1 & +i & -1 & -i \\ +1 & -1 & +1 & -1 \\ +1 & -i & -1 & +i \end{bmatrix} \tag{22.3-5}$$

The convolution property of the Fourier transform can now be expressed as

$$C_a\, b^T = F^{-1}\operatorname{diag}\left(F\, a^T\right) F\, b^T \tag{22.3-6}$$

where $\operatorname{diag}(v)$ is the matrix having the components of v on its diagonal:

$$\operatorname{diag}\left([v_0,\, v_1,\, v_2,\, v_3]\right) = \begin{bmatrix} v_0 & 0 & 0 & 0 \\ 0 & v_1 & 0 & 0 \\ 0 & 0 & v_2 & 0 \\ 0 & 0 & 0 & v_3 \end{bmatrix} \tag{22.3-7}$$

The corresponding identity for the correlation is

$$R_a\, b^T = F\operatorname{diag}\left(F\, a^T\right) F^{-1}\, b^T \tag{22.3-8}$$

Relation 22.3-6 restated as

$$F^{-1} C_a\, F = \operatorname{diag}\left(F\, a^T\right) \tag{22.3-9}$$

shows that F diagonalizes a circulant matrix C_a and its eigenvalues are $F\, a^T$, the components of the Fourier transform of a. The determinant of C_a therefore equals the product of the elements of $F\, a^T$:

$$\det C_a = \prod_{j=0}^{n-1}\left(a_0 + a_1\,\omega^{1\,j} + a_1\,\omega^{2\,j} + \ldots + a_{n-1}\,\omega^{(n-1)\,j}\right) \tag{22.3-10}$$

Compare to relation 36.1-23 on page 688 for the multisection of power series.

22.4   Weighted Fourier transforms and convolutions

We introduce the weighted Fourier transform and the weighted convolution which serve as an ingredient for the MFA based convolution algorithm described in section 22.5.

22.4.1   The weighted Fourier transform

We define a new kind of transform by slightly modifying the definition of the Fourier transform (formula 21.1-1a on page 410):

$$c = \mathcal{W}_v\,[a] \tag{22.4-1a}$$

$$c_k := \sum_{x=0}^{n-1} v_x\, a_x\, z^{x\,k} \qquad v_x \neq 0 \;\; \forall x \tag{22.4-1b}$$

where $z := e^{\sigma\, 2\pi i/n}$. The sequence c is called the (discrete) *weighted transform* of the sequence a with the weight sequence v. The weighted transform with $v_x = \frac{1}{\sqrt{n}}\ \forall x$ is just the usual Fourier transform. The inverse transform is

$$a \;=\; \mathcal{W}_v^{-1}[c] \tag{22.4-2a}$$

$$a_x \;=\; \frac{1}{n\,v_x}\sum_{k=0}^{n-1} c_k\, z^{-x\,k} \tag{22.4-2b}$$

This can be seen as follows:

$$\mathcal{W}_v^{-1}\left[\mathcal{W}_v\left[a\right]\right]_y \;=\; \frac{1}{n\,v_y}\sum_{k=0}^{n-1}\sum_{x=0}^{n-1} v_x\, a_x\, z^{x\,k}\, z^{-y\,k} \;=\; \frac{1}{n}\sum_{k=0}^{n-1}\sum_{x=0}^{n-1} v_x\,\frac{1}{v_y}\, a_x\, z^{x\,k}\, z^{-y\,k} \;=\; \tag{22.4-3a}$$

$$=\; \frac{1}{n}\sum_{x=0}^{n-1} v_x\,\frac{1}{v_y}\, a_x\, \delta_{x,y}\, n \;=\; a_y \tag{22.4-3b}$$

Obviously all v_x have to be invertible. That $\mathcal{W}_v\left[\mathcal{W}_v^{-1}[a]\right]$ is also identity is apparent from the definitions.

Given an FFT routine it is easy to set up a weighted Fourier transform. Pseudocode for the discrete weighted Fourier transform:

```
1    procedure weighted_ft(a[], v[], n, is)
2    {
3        for x:=0 to n-1
4        {
5            a[x] := a[x] * v[x]
6        }
7
8        fft(a[], n, is)
9    }
```

The inverse is essentially identical. Pseudocode for the inverse discrete weighted Fourier transform:

```
1    procedure inverse_weighted_ft(a[], v[], n, is)
2    {
3        fft(a[], n, -is)
4
5        for x:=0 to n-1
6        {
7            a[x] := a[x] / v[x]
8        }
9    }
```

The C++ implementations are given in [FXT: fft/weightedfft.cc].

22.4.2 Weighted convolution

In the definition of the cyclic convolution h of two sequences a and b (relations 22.1-1a and 22.1-1b on page 440) we can distinguish between those summands where the index $x+y$ wrapped around ($x+y=n+\tau$) and those where simply $x+y=\tau$ holds. These are, following the notation in [116], denoted by $h^{(1)}$ and $h^{(0)}$, respectively. We have

$$h \;=\; h^{(0)} + h^{(1)} \qquad \text{where} \tag{22.4-4a}$$

$$h^{(0)} \;=\; \sum_{x\le\tau} a_x\, b_{\tau-x} \tag{22.4-4b}$$

$$h^{(1)} \;=\; \sum_{x>\tau} a_x\, b_{n+\tau-x} \tag{22.4-4c}$$

The sequences $h^{(0)}$ and $h^{(1)}$ are the left and right half of the linear convolution sequence $a \circledast_{lin} b$, defined by relation 22.1-6a on page 443. For example, the linear self-convolution of the sequence $[1,1,1,1]$ is the length-8 sequence $[h_0][h_1] = [1,2,3,4][3,2,1,0]$, its cyclic self-convolution is $[h_0 + h_1] = [4,4,4,4]$.

The direct (slow) routine for linear convolution can be modified to compute just one of either $h^{(0)}$ or $h^{(1)}$ [FXT: convolution/slowcnvlhalf.h]:

```
1    template <typename Type>
2    void slow_half_convolution(const Type *f, const Type *g, Type *h, ulong n, int h01)
3    // Half cyclic convolution.
4    // Part determined by h01 which must be 0 or 1.
5    // n := array length
6    {
7        if ( 0==h01 )  // compute h0:
8        {
9            for (ulong tau=0;  tau<n;  ++tau)
10           {
11               Type s0 = 0.0;
12               for (ulong k=0, k2=tau;  k<=tau;  ++k, --k2)  s0 += (f[k]*g[k2]);
13               h[tau] = s0;
14           }
15       }
16       else  // compute h1 (wrapped part):
17       {
18           for (ulong tau=0;  tau<n;  ++tau)
19           {
20               Type s1 = 0.0;
21               for (ulong k2=n-1, k=tau+1;  k<n;  ++k, --k2)  s1 += (f[k]*g[k2]);
22               h[tau] = s1;
23           }
24       }
25   }
```

Define the *weighted (cyclic) convolution* h_v by

$$h_v = a \circledast_{\{v\}} b \tag{22.4-5a}$$

$$= \mathcal{W}_v^{-1} \left[\mathcal{W}_v[a] \cdot \mathcal{W}_v[b] \right] \tag{22.4-5b}$$

where the multiplication indicated by the dot is element-wise. For the special case $v_x = V^x$, we have

$$h_v = h^{(0)} + V^n h^{(1)} \tag{22.4-6}$$

It is not hard to see why this is: Up to the final division by the weight sequence, the weighted convolution is just the cyclic convolution of the two weighted sequences. For the element h_τ we have

$$h_\tau = \sum_{x+y \equiv \tau \mod n} (a_x V^x)(b_y V^y) = \sum_{x \le \tau} a_x b_{\tau-x} V^\tau + \sum_{x > \tau} a_x b_{n+\tau-x} V^{n+\tau} \tag{22.4-7}$$

Final division of this element (by V^τ) gives $h^{(0)} + V^n h^{(1)}$ as stated.

+|	– 0 –	1	2	3	4	5	6	7	8	9	10	11	12	13	14	15
0:	: 0	1	2	3	4	5	6	7	8	9	10	11	12	13	14	15
1:	1	2	3	4	5	6	7	8	9	10	11	12	13	14	15	0–
2:	2	3	4	5	6	7	8	9	10	11	12	13	14	15	0–	1–
3:	3	4	5	6	7	8	9	10	11	12	13	14	15	0–	1–	2–
4:	4	5	6	7	8	9	10	11	12	13	14	15	0–	1–	2–	3–
5:	5	6	7	8	9	10	11	12	13	14	15	0–	1–	2–	3–	4–
6:	6	7	8	9	10	11	12	13	14	15	0–	1–	2–	3–	4–	5–
7:	7	8	9	10	11	12	13	14	15	0–	1–	2–	3–	4–	5–	6–
8:	8	9	10	11	12	13	14	15	0–	1–	2–	3–	4–	5–	6–	7–
9:	9	10	11	12	13	14	15	0–	1–	2–	3–	4–	5–	6–	7–	8–
10:	10	11	12	13	14	15	0–	1–	2–	3–	4–	5–	6–	7–	8–	9–
11:	11	12	13	14	15	0–	1–	2–	3–	4–	5–	6–	7–	8–	9–	10–
12:	12	13	14	15	0–	1–	2–	3–	4–	5–	6–	7–	8–	9–	10–	11–
13:	13	14	15	0–	1–	2–	3–	4–	5–	6–	7–	8–	9–	10–	11–	12–
14:	14	15	0–	1–	2–	3–	4–	5–	6–	7–	8–	9–	10–	11–	12–	13–
15:	15	0–	1–	2–	3–	4–	5–	6–	7–	8–	9–	10–	11–	12–	13–	14–

Figure 22.4-A: Semi-symbolic table for the negacyclic convolution. The products that enter with negative sign are indicated with a postfix minus at the corresponding entry.

The cases when V^n is some root of unity are particularly interesting. For $V^n = \pm i = \pm\sqrt{-1}$ we obtain the *right-angle convolution*:

$$h_v = h^{(0)} \mp i\, h^{(1)} \tag{22.4-8}$$

Choosing $V^n = -1$ leads to the *negacyclic convolution* (or *skew circular convolution*):

$$h_v \;=\; h^{(0)} - h^{(1)} \tag{22.4-9}$$

Cyclic, negacyclic and right-angle convolution can be understood as polynomial products modulo the polynomials $z^n - 1$, $z^n + 1$ and $z^n \pm i$, respectively (see [262]).

The semi-symbolic table for the negacyclic convolution is shown in figure 22.4-A. With right-angle convolution the minuses are replaced by $i = \sqrt{-1}$, so the elements in $h^{(1)}$ go to the imaginary part. With real input one effectively separates $h^{(0)}$ and $h^{(1)}$. Therefore the linear convolution of real sequences can be computed using the complex right-angle convolution.

The parts $h^{(0)}$ and $h^{(1)}$ can be computed as sum and difference of the cyclic and the negacyclic convolution. Thus all expressions of the form $\alpha\, h^{(0)} + \beta\, h^{(1)}$ where $\alpha, \beta \in \mathbb{C}$ can be computed.

The routine for the direct computation has complexity $O(n^2)$ [FXT: convolution/slowweightedcnvl.h]:

```
1    template <typename Type>
2    void slow_weighted_convolution(const Type *f, const Type *g, Type *h, ulong n, Type w)
3    // weighted (cyclic) convolution:  h[] := f[] (*)_w g[]
4    // n := array length
5    {
6        for (ulong tau=0;  tau<n;  ++tau)
7        {
8            ulong k = 0;
9            Type s0 = 0.0;
10           for (ulong k2=tau;  k<=tau;  ++k, --k2)  s0 += (f[k]*g[k2]);
11           Type s1 = 0.0;
12           for (ulong k2=n-1;  k<n;    ++k, --k2)  s1 += (f[k]*g[k2]);  // wrapped around
13           h[tau] = s0 + s1*w;
14       }
15   }
```

Transform-based routines for the negacyclic and right-angle convolution are given in [FXT: convolution/weightedconv.cc]:

```
1    #define  FFTC(f,ldn,is)  fht_fft(f,ldn,is)
2
3    void
4    weighted_complex_auto_convolution(Complex *f, ulong ldn, double w, double v/*=0.0*/)
5    // w = weight:
6    // +0.25 for right angle convolution (-0.25 negates result in fi[])
7    // +0.5  for negacyclic  convolution (also -0.5)
8    // +1.0  for cyclic  convolution (also -1.0)
9    //
10   // v!=0.0 chooses alternative normalization
11   {
12       ulong n = (1UL<<ldn);
13
14       fourier_shift(f, n, w);
15       FFTC(f, ldn, +1);
16
17       if ( v==0.0 )  v = 1.0/n;
18       for (ulong k=0; k<n; k++)
19       {
20           Complex t = f[k];
21           t *= t;
22           t *= v;
23           f[k] = t;
24       }
25
26       FFTC(f, ldn, -1);
27       fourier_shift(f, n, -w);
28   }
```

22.5 Convolution using the MFA

We give an algorithm for convolution that uses the matrix Fourier algorithm (MFA, see section 21.10 on page 438). The MFA is used for the forward transform and the transposed algorithm (TMFA) for the inverse transform. The elements of each row are assumed to be contiguous in memory. In what follows let

R be the total number of rows and C the length of each row (equivalently, the total number of columns). For the sake of simplicity only auto-convolution is considered.

22.5.1   The algorithm

The *MFA convolution* algorithm:

1. Apply a (length R) FFT on each column (*stride-C memory access*).

2. Multiply each matrix element (index r, c) by $\exp(+\sigma\, 2\, \pi\, i\, r\, c/n)$.

3. Apply a (length C) FFT on each row (*stride-1 memory access*).

4. Complex square row (element-wise).

5. Apply a (length C) inverse FFT on each row (*stride-1 memory access*).

6. Multiply each matrix element (index r, c) by $\exp(-\sigma\, 2\, \pi\, i\, r\, c/n)$.

7. Apply a (length R) inverse FFT on each column (*stride-C memory access*).

Note that steps 3, 4, and 5 constitute a length-C convolution on each row.

With the weighted convolutions in mind we reformulate the method as *weighted MFA convolution*:

1. Apply an FFT on each column.

2. For each row $r = 0, 1, \ldots, R-1$, apply the weighted convolution with weight $V^C = e^{2\pi i r/R} = 1^{r/R}$.

3. Apply an inverse FFT on each column.

Implementations of this algorithm for the cyclic and linear convolution are given in [FXT: convolution/matrixfftcnvl.cc], the routines for self-convolution in [FXT: convolution/matrixfftcnvla.cc].

We now consider the special cases of two and three rows and then formulate an MFA-based algorithm for the convolution of real sequences.

22.5.2   The case $R = 2$

Define s and d as the sum and difference of the left and right halves of a given sequence x:

$$s \;:=\; x^{(0/2)} + x^{(1/2)} \tag{22.5-1a}$$
$$d \;:=\; x^{(0/2)} - x^{(1/2)} \tag{22.5-1b}$$

Then the cyclic auto-convolution of the sequence x can be computed by two half-length convolutions of s and d as

$$x \circledast x \;=\; \frac{1}{2} \left[s \circledast s + d \circledast_- d, \quad s \circledast s - d \circledast_- d \right] \tag{22.5-2}$$

where the symbols $\circledast$ and $\circledast_-$ stand for cyclic and negacyclic convolution, respectively (see section 22.4 on page 448). The equivalent formula for the cyclic convolution of two sequences x and y is

$$x \circledast y \;=\; \frac{1}{2} \left[s_x \circledast s_y + d_x \circledast_- d_y, \quad s_x \circledast s_y - d_x \circledast_- d_y \right] \tag{22.5-3}$$

where

$$s_x \;:=\; x^{(0/2)} + x^{(1/2)} \tag{22.5-4a}$$
$$d_x \;:=\; x^{(0/2)} - x^{(1/2)} \tag{22.5-4b}$$
$$s_y \;:=\; y^{(0/2)} + y^{(1/2)} \tag{22.5-4c}$$
$$d_y \;:=\; y^{(0/2)} - y^{(1/2)} \tag{22.5-4d}$$

Now use the fact that a linear convolution can be computed by a cyclic convolution of zero-padded sequences whose upper halves are simply zero, so $s_x = d_x = x$ and $s_y = d_y = y$. Then relation 22.5-3 reads:

$$x \circledast_{lin} y \;=\; \frac{1}{2} \left[x \circledast y + x \circledast_- y, \quad x \circledast y - x \circledast_- y \right] \tag{22.5-5}$$

And for the acyclic auto-convolution:

$$x \circledast_{lin} x \;=\; \frac{1}{2} \left[x \circledast x + x \circledast_- x, \quad x \circledast x - x \circledast_- x \right] \tag{22.5-6}$$

The lower and upper halves of the linear convolution can be computed as the sum and difference of the cyclic and the negacyclic convolution.

22.5.3   The case $R = 3$

Let $\omega = \frac{1}{2}\left(1 + i\sqrt{3}\right)$, a primitive third root of unity, and define

$$A := x^{(0/3)} + x^{(1/3)} + x^{(2/3)} \tag{22.5-7a}$$
$$B := x^{(0/3)} + \omega\, x^{(1/3)} + \omega^2 x^{(2/3)} \tag{22.5-7b}$$
$$C := x^{(0/3)} + \omega^2 x^{(1/3)} + \omega\, x^{(2/3)} \tag{22.5-7c}$$

Let $h := x \circledast x$ and $h^{(0/3)}$, $h^{(1/3)}$, and $h^{(2/3)}$ be the first, second, and last third of h, respectively. We have

$$h^{(0/3)} = A \circledast A + B \circledast_{\{\omega\}} B + C \circledast_{\{\omega^2\}} C \tag{22.5-8a}$$
$$h^{(1/3)} = A \circledast A + \omega^2 B \circledast_{\{\omega\}} B + \omega\, C \circledast_{\{\omega^2\}} C \tag{22.5-8b}$$
$$h^{(2/3)} = A \circledast A + \omega\, B \circledast_{\{\omega\}} B + \omega^2 C \circledast_{\{\omega^2\}} C \tag{22.5-8c}$$

For real-valued data C is the complex conjugate (cc.) of B and (with $\omega^2 = cc.\omega$) $B \circledast_{\{\omega\}} B$ is the cc. of $C \circledast_{\{\omega^2\}} C$ and therefore every $B \circledast_{\{.\}} B$-term is the cc. of the $C \circledast_{\{.\}} C$-term in the same line.

22.5.4   Convolution of real-valued data

Consider the MFA-algorithm for the cyclic convolution (as given in section 22.5.1) with real input data: For row 0, which is real after the column FFTs, the (usual) cyclic convolution is needed. For row $R/2$, which is also real after the column FFTs, a negacyclic convolution (see section 25.7.4 on page 528) is needed (for odd R there is no such row).

All other weighted convolutions involve complex computations, but we can avoid half of the work: as the result must be real, row $R - r$ must be the complex conjugate of row r, due to the symmetries of the real and imaginary part of the Fourier transform of real data. Therefore we use real FFTs (R2CFTs) for all column-transforms in step 1 and half-complex to real FFTs (C2RFTs) in step 3.

For even R we need one cyclic (row 0), one negacyclic (row $R/2$), and $R/2 - 2$ complex weighted convolutions. For odd R we need one cyclic (row 0) and $(R - 1)/2$ complex weighted convolutions. Now the cyclic and the negacyclic real convolutions involve about the same number of computations and that the cost of a weighted complex convolution is about twice as high. So the total work is about half of that for a complex convolution.

For the computation of the linear convolution we can use the right angle convolution (and complex FFTs in the column passes), see section 22.4 on page 448.

22.5.5   Mass storage convolution

Algorithms on data sets which do not fit into physical RAM are called *external*, *out of core*, or *mass storage* algorithms. We give a method for the *mass storage convolution*.

Let the array be organized as an $R \times C = N$ matrix. Assume that the available workspace (RAM) can hold N/α array elements (where α divides N). We consider only self-convolution to keep matters simple.

We rewrite the weighted MFA convolution from section 22.5.1 as a mass storage algorithm.

1. FFTs on columns: for $k = 0, 1, \ldots, \alpha - 1$, do

    1a. read the k-th part of all rows into RAM,

    1b. do the transforms on the columns in RAM,

    1c. and write back to disk.

2. Weighted convolutions on rows: for $r = 0, 1, \ldots R - 1$, do

    2a. read the k-th part of all columns (one or more rows) into RAM,

    2b. do the weighted convolutions on the rows in RAM,

    2c. and write back to disk.

3. Inverse FFTs on columns: (as in step 1, but use inverse transforms)

We want to keep the number S of disk seeks minimal because they are slow. The choice of R determines S: In steps 1a and 1c there are R seeks each, for every value of k; same for steps 3a and 3c; giving $4R\alpha$ seeks. In steps 2a and 2c there are R seeks each; giving $2R$ seeks. We need a total of $S = 2\alpha + 4\alpha R$ seeks for the whole computation.

Therefore we choose R as small as possible and *not* close to $\sqrt{N}$ as done when the array fits into RAM.

The mass storage convolution as described was used for the calculation of the number

$$9^{9^9} \approx 0.4281247 \cdot 10^{369,693,100} \tag{22.5-9}$$

on a 32-bit machine in 1999. The computation used two files of size 2 GB each and took less than eight hours on a system with an AMD K6/2 CPU at 366 MHz with 66 MHz memory. The log-file of the computation is [hfloat: examples/run1-pow999.txt].

A computation of π to 2,700 billion decimal digits on an "inexpensive desktop computer" by Fabrice Bellard finished December 2009, setting the new world record. A mass storage convolution similar to the one described here was used. Technical details of this amazing feat are given in [42].

If multi-threading is available, one can use a *double buffer* technique: split the workspace into halves, one (CPU-intensive) thread does the FFTs in one half and another (hard disk intensive) thread reads and writes in the other half. This keeps the CPU busy during much of the hard disk operations, avoiding the waits during disk activity at least partly.

22.6 The z-transform (ZT)

The discrete z-transform (ZT) of a length-n sequence a is a length-n sequence c defined by

$$c = \mathcal{Z}[a] \tag{22.6-1a}$$

$$c_k := \sum_{x=0}^{n-1} a_x z^{k\,x} \tag{22.6-1b}$$

The z-transform is a linear transformation. It is not an orthogonal transformation unless z is a root of unity. For $z = e^{\pm 2\pi i/n}$ the z-transform specializes to the discrete Fourier transform. An important property is the convolution property:

$$\mathcal{Z}[a \circledast b] = \mathcal{Z}[a] \cdot \mathcal{Z}[b] \tag{22.6-2}$$

Convolution in original space corresponds to element-wise multiplication in z-space. This can be turned into an efficient convolution algorithm for the special case of the Fourier transform but not in general because no efficient algorithm for the inverse transform is known.

22.6.1   Computation via convolution (Bluestein's algorithm)

Using the identity

$$x\,k \;=\; \frac{1}{2}\left(x^2 + k^2 - (k-x)^2\right) \tag{22.6-3}$$

we find the following expression for the element c_k of the Fourier transform of the sequence a:

$$c_k = \sum_{x=0}^{n-1} a_x\, z^{x\,k} \;=\; z^{k^2/2}\left[\sum_{x=0}^{n-1}\left(a_x\, z^{x^2/2}\right) z^{-(k-x)^2/2}\right] \tag{22.6-4}$$

The expression in brackets is a cyclic convolution of the sequence $a_x\, z^{x^2/2}$ with the sequence $z^{-x^2/2}$.

This leads to the algorithm for the *chirp z-transform*:

1. Multiply the sequence a element-wise with $z^{x^2/2}$.

2. Convolve the resulting sequence with the sequence $z^{-x^2/2}$.

3. Multiply element-wise with the sequence $z^{k^2/2}$.

The above algorithm constitutes a fast algorithm for the ZT because fast convolution is possible via FFT. The idea is due to Bluestein [56], a detailed description is given in [328].

22.6.2   Arbitrary length FFT by ZT

The length n of the input sequence a for the fast z-transform is not limited to highly composite values. For values of n where an FFT is not feasible, pad the sequence with zeros up to a length L with $L >= 2\,n$ such that a length-L FFT can be computed (highly composite L, for example a power of 2).

As the Fourier transform is the special case $z = e^{\pm 2\pi i/n}$ of the ZT, the chirp-ZT algorithm constitutes an FFT algorithm for sequences of arbitrary length. An implementation is [FXT: chirpzt/fftarblen.cc]

```
1   void
2   fft_arblen(Complex *x, ulong n, int is)
3   // Arbitrary length FFT.
4   {
5       const ulong ldnn = 1 + ld( (n << 1) - 1 );
6       const ulong nn = (1UL<<ldnn);  // smallest power of 2 >= 2*n
7
8       Complex *f = new Complex[nn];
9       acopy(x, f, n);
10      null(f+n, nn-n);
11
12      Complex *w = new Complex[nn];
13      make_fft_chirp(w, n, nn, is);
14      multiply(f, n, w);
15
16      double *dw = (double *)w;
17      for (ulong k=1; k<2*n; k+=2)  dw[k] = -dw[k];   // =^= make_fft_chirp(w, n, nn, -is);
18
19      fft_complex_convolution(w, f, ldnn);
20
21      if ( n & 1 )  subtract(f, n, f+n);   // odd n:  negacyclic convolution
22      else          add(f, n, f+n);        // even n:  cyclic convolution
23
24      make_fft_chirp(w, n, nn, is);
25      multiply(w, n, f);
26
27      acopy(w, x, n);
28      delete [] w;
29      delete [] f;
30  }
```

The auxiliary routine `make_fft_chirp()` is

```
1   static inline void
2   make_fft_chirp(Complex *w, ulong n, ulong nn, int is)
3   // For k=0..n-1:   w[k] := exp( is * k*k * (i*2*PI/n)/2 )  where i = sqrt(-1)
4   // For k=n..nn-1:  w[k] = 0
5   {
6       double phi = 1.0*is*M_PI/n;   // == (i*2*Pi/n)/2
7       ulong k2 = 0,  n2 = 2*n;
8       for (ulong k=0; k<n; ++k)
9       {
10          w[k] = SinCos(phi*k2);
11          k2 += (2*k+1);
12          if ( k2>n2 )  k2 -= n2;
13          // here:  k2 == (k*k) mod 2*n
14      }
15      null(w+n, nn-n);
16  }
```

The computation of a length-n ZT uses three FFTs with length greater than n. The worst case (if only FFTs for n a power of 2 are available) is $n = 2^p + 1$: we need three FFTs of length $L = 2^{p+1} \approx 2n$ for the computation of the convolution. So the total work is about 6 times the work of an FFT of length n. It is possible to lower this worst case factor to 3 by using highly composite L slightly greater than n.

For multiple computations of z-transforms of the same length one should precompute and store the transform of the sequence $z^{k^2/2}$ as it does not change. Therefore the worst case is a factor 2 with highly composite FFTs and 4 if FFTs are available for powers of 2 only.

22.6.3 Fractional Fourier transform by ZT

The z-transform with $z = e^{\alpha \, 2 \pi \, i/n}$ is called the *fractional Fourier transform* in [29]. The term is usually used for the fractional order transform given as relation 25.11-6 on page 533, see also [274, ch.13].

For $\alpha = \pm 1$ one again obtains the usual Fourier transform. The fractional Fourier transform can be used for the computation of the Fourier transform of sequences with only few nonzero elements and for the exact detection of frequencies that are not integer multiples of the lowest frequency of the DFT.

A C++ implementation of the fractional Fourier transform for sequences of arbitrary length is given in [FXT: chirpzt/fftfract.cc]:

```
1   void
2   fft_fract(Complex *x, ulong n, double v)
3   // Fractional (fast) Fourier transform.
4   {
5       const ulong ldnn = 1 + ld( (n << 1) - 1 );
6       const ulong nn = (1UL<<ldnn);  // smallest power of 2 >= 2*n
7
8       Complex *f = new Complex[nn];
9       acopy(x, f, n);
10      null(f+n, nn-n);
11
12      Complex *w = new Complex[nn];
13      make_fft_fract_chirp(w, v, n, nn);
14
15      for (ulong j=0; j<n; ++j)  f[j] *= w[j];
16      for (ulong j=0; j<nn; ++j)  w[j] = conj(w[j]);
17
18      fft_complex_convolution(w, f, ldnn);
19
20      make_fft_fract_chirp(w, v, n, nn);
21
22      for (ulong j=0; j<n; ++j)  w[j] *= f[j];
23
24      acopy(w+n, x, n);
25      delete [] w;
26      delete [] f;
27  }
```

The auxiliary routine `make_fft_fract_chirp()` is

```
1   static inline void
2   make_fft_fract_chirp(Complex *w, double v, ulong n, ulong nn)
```

```
3    // For k=0..nn-1:    w[k] == exp(v*sqrt(-1)*k*k*2*pi*/n/2)
4    {
5        const double phi = v*2.0*M_PI/n/2;
6        ulong n2 = 2*n;
7        ulong np=0;
8        for (ulong k=0; k<nn; ++k)
9        {
10           w[k] = SinCos(phi*np);
11           np += ((k<<1)+1);   // np == (k*k)%n2
12           if ( np>=n2 )  np -= n2;
13       }
14   }
```

22.7   Prime length FFTs

For the computation of FFTs for sequences whose length is prime we can exploit the existence of primitive roots. We will be able to express the transform of all but the first element as a cyclic convolution of two sequences whose length is reduced by one.

Let p be prime, then an element g exists so that the least positive exponent e so that $g^e \equiv 1 \bmod p$ is $e = p - 1$. The element g is called a *generator* (or *primitive root*) modulo p (see section 39.6 on page 776). Every nonzero element modulo p can be uniquely expressed as a power g^e where $0 \le e < p-1$. For example, a generator modulo $p = 11$ is $g = 2$, its powers are

$$g^0 \equiv 1, \; g^1 \equiv 2, \; g^2 \equiv 4, \; g^3 \equiv 8, \; g^4 \equiv 5, \; g^5 \equiv 10 \equiv -1, \; g^6 \equiv 9, \; g^7 \equiv 7, \; g^8 \equiv 3, \; g^9 \equiv 6, \; g^{p-1} \equiv 1$$

Likewise, we can express any nonzero element as a negative power of g. Let $h = g^{-1}$, then with our example $h \equiv 6$ and

$$h^0 \equiv 1, \; h^1 \equiv 6, \; h^2 \equiv 3, \; h^3 \equiv 7, \; h^4 \equiv 9, \; h^5 \equiv 10 \equiv -1, \; h^6 \equiv 5, \; h^7 \equiv 8, \; h^8 \equiv 4, \; h^9 \equiv 2, \; h^{p-1} \equiv 1$$

This is just the reversed sequence of values. Let C be the Fourier transform of length-p sequence A:

$$C_k = \sum_{x=0}^{p-1} A_x W^{\sigma x k} \tag{22.7-1}$$

where $W = \exp(2\pi i/p)$ and $\sigma = \pm 1$ is the sign of the transform. We split the computation of the Fourier transform into two parts, we compute the first element of the transform as

$$C_0 = \sum_{x=0}^{p-1} A_x \tag{22.7-2}$$

Now it remains to compute C_k for $1 \le k \le p - 1$:

$$C_k = A_0 + \sum_{x=1}^{p-1} A_x W^{\sigma x k} \tag{22.7-3}$$

Note the lower index of the sum. We write $k \equiv g^e$ and $x \equiv g^{-f}$ (modulo p), so

$$C_{(g^e)} - A_0 = \sum_{f=0}^{p-2} A_{(g^{-f})} W^{\sigma (g^{-f})(g^e)} = \sum_{f=0}^{p-2} A_{(g^{-f})} W^{\sigma (g^{e-f})} \tag{22.7-4}$$

The sum is a cyclic convolution of the sequences $W^* := W^{(g^w)}$ and $A^* := A_{(g^{-w})}$ where $0 \le w \le p - 2$. The main algorithm (ignoring the constant terms A_0 and C_0) can be outlined as follows:

1. Compute A^* and W^* by permuting the sequences A and W.

2. Compute C^* as the cyclic convolution of A^* and W^*.

3. Compute W by permuting W^*.

The method is given in [277], it is called *Rader's algorithm*. We implement it in GP:

```
1    ft_rader(a, is=+1)=
2    \\ Fourier transform for prime lengths (Rader's algorithm)
3    {
4        local(n, a0, c0, g, w);
5        local(c, ixp, ixm, pa, pw, t);
6        n = length(a);
7
8        a0 = a[1];  c0 = sum(j=1, n, a[j]);  \\ constant terms
9
10       \\ prepare permutations:
11       g = znprimroot(n);  ixp = vector(n, j, lift( g^(j-1) ) );
12       g = g^(-1);  ixm = vector(n, j, lift( g^(j-1) ) );
13
14       \\ permute sequence W:
15       w = is*2*I*Pi/n;  pw = vector(n-1, j, exp(w*ixp[j]) );
16
17       \\ permute sequence A:
18       pa = vector(n-1);  for (j=1, n-1, pa[j]=a[1+ixp[1+n-j]] );
19
20       \\ cyclic convolution of permuted sequences:
21       t = cconv(pa, pw);  \\ cyclic convolution
22
23       \\ set C_0, and add A_0 to each C_k:
24       c = vector(n);  c[1] = c0;  for (k=1, n-1, c[1+k]=t[k]+a0);
25
26       \\ permute to obtain result:
27       t = vector(n);  t[1] = c[1];  for (k=2, n, t[1+ixp[k-1]]=c[k]);
28       return( t );
29   }
```

With a (slow) implementation of the cyclic convolution and DFT we can check whether the method works by comparing the results:

```
1    cconv(a, b)=
2    /* Cyclic convolution (direct computation, n^2 operations) */
3    /* Example: cconv([a,b],[c,d]) ==> [b*d + c*a, a*d + c*b] */
4    {
5        local(n, f, s, k, k2);
6        n = length(a);  f = vector(n);
7        for (tau=0, n-1,  \\ tau = k + k2
8            s0 = 0;  k = 0;  k2 = tau;
9            while (k<=tau, s0 += (a[k+1]*b[k2+1]);  k++; k2--);
10           s1 = 0;  k2 = n-1; \\ k=tau+1
11           while (k<n,   s1 += (a[k+1]*b[k2+1]);  k++; k2--);
12           f[tau+1] = s0 + s1;
13       );
14       return( f );
15   }
```

```
1    dft(a, is=+1)=
2    /* Complex Fourier transform (direct computation, n^2 operations) */
3    {
4        local(n, f, s, ph0, ph);
5        n = length(a);  f = vector(n);
6        ph0 = is*2*Pi*I/n;
7        for (k=0, n-1,
8            ph = ph0 * k;
9            f[k+1] = sum (x=0, n-1,  a[x+1] * exp(ph*x) );
10       );
11       return( f );
12   }
```

To turn the algorithm into a fast Fourier transform we need to compute the convolution via fast transforms of length $(p-1)$. This is trivially possible when $p-1 = 2^q$, for example when $p = 5$ or $p = 17$. As $p-1$ is always divisible by 2, we can split at least once. For $p = 11$ we have $(p-1)/2 = 5$ so we can again use Rader's algorithm and length-4 transforms. The method can be used to generate code for short (prime) length FFTs. One should precompute the permuted and transformed sequence of the powers of the primitive root W. Therefore only two FFTs of length $(p-1)$ will be needed for a length-p transform. The algorithm is also an ingredient of the so-called *prime factor FFT*, see [131] and [218].

Chapter 23

The Walsh transform and its relatives

We describe several variants of the *Walsh transform*, sometimes called *Walsh-Hadamard transform* or just *Hadamard transform*. The Walsh transform has the same complexity as the Fourier transform but does not involve any multiplications. The XOR (dyadic) convolution that can be computed efficiently by the Walsh transform is introduced. We also give related transforms like the slant transform, the Reed-Muller transform, and the arithmetic transform.

23.1 Transform with Walsh-Kronecker basis

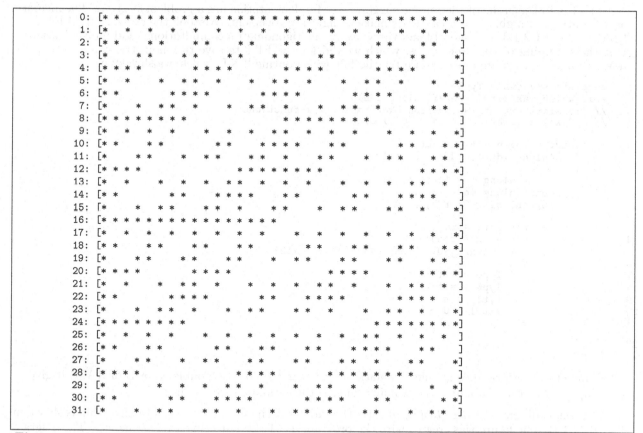

Figure 23.1-A: Basis functions for the Walsh transform (Walsh-Kronecker basis). Asterisks denote the value +1, blank entries denote −1.

A Walsh transform routine can be obtained by removing all multiplications (with sines and cosines) in a

J. Arndt, *Matters Computational: Ideas, Algorithms, Source Code*,
DOI 10.1007/978-3-642-14764-7_23, © Springer-Verlag Berlin Heidelberg 2011

FFT routine. We do so with a radix-2 decimation in time FFT:

```
1    void slow_walsh_wak_dit2(double *f, ulong ldn)
2    // (this routine has a problem)
3    {
4        ulong n = (1UL<<ldn);
5        for (ulong ldm=1; ldm<=ldn; ++ldm)
6        {
7            const ulong m = (1<<ldm);
8            const ulong mh = (m>>1);
9            for (ulong j=0; j<mh; ++j)
10           {
11               for (ulong r=0; r<n; r+=m)
12               {
13                   const ulong t1 = r+j;
14                   const ulong t2 = t1+mh;
15                   double u = f[t1];
16                   double v = f[t2];
17                   f[t1] = u+v;
18                   f[t2] = u-v;
19               }
20           }
21       }
22   }
```

The transform involves $O(n \log_2(n))$ additions (and subtractions) and no multiplication at all. The transform, as given, is its own inverse up to a factor $1/n$. The Walsh transform of integer input is integral.

As the **slow** in the name of the routine suggests, the implementation has a problem as given. The memory access pattern is highly non-local. Let's make a slight improvement. We took the radix-2 DIT FFT code from section 21.2.1.3 on page 414 and threw away all trigonometric computations (and multiplications). But the swapping of the inner loops, which we did for the FFT to save trigonometric computations, is now of no advantage anymore. So we try the following routine [FXT: walsh/walshwak2.h]:

```
1    template <typename Type>
2    void walsh_wak_dit2(Type *f, ulong ldn)
3    // Transform wrt. to Walsh-Kronecker basis (wak-functions).
4    // Radix-2 decimation in time (DIT) algorithm.
5    {
6        const ulong n = (1UL<<ldn);
7        for (ulong ldm=1; ldm<=ldn; ++ldm)
8        {
9            const ulong m = (1UL<<ldm);
10           const ulong mh = (m>>1);
11           for (ulong r=0; r<n; r+=m)
12           {
13               ulong t1 = r;
14               ulong t2 = r+mh;
15               for (ulong j=0;  j<mh;  ++j, ++t1, ++t2)
16               {
17                   Type u = f[t1];
18                   Type v = f[t2];
19                   f[t1] = u + v;
20                   f[t2] = u - v;
21               }
22           }
23       }
24   }
```

The impact on performance is quite dramatic. For $n = 2^{21}$ (and type double, 16 MB of RAM) it gives a speedup by a factor of about 8. For smaller lengths the ratio approaches one.

The data flow diagram (*butterfly diagram*) for the radix-2 decimation in time (DIT) algorithm is shown in figure 23.1-B. The figure was created with the program [FXT: fft/butterfly-texpic-demo.cc]. The diagram for the decimation in frequency (DIF) algorithm is obtained by reversing the order of the steps. In the code, only the outermost loop has to be changed:

```
1    template <typename Type>
2    void walsh_wak_dif2(Type *f, ulong ldn)
3    {
4        const ulong n = (1UL<<ldn);
```

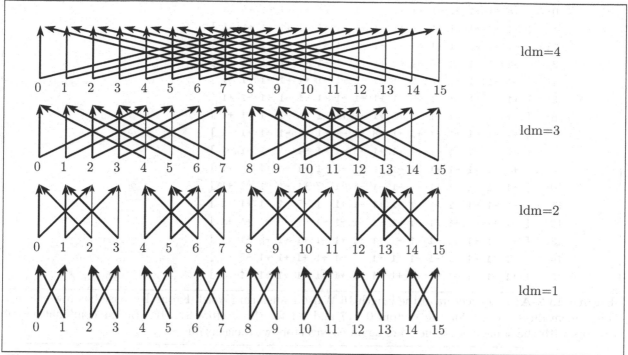

Figure 23.1-B: Data flow for the length-16, radix-2, decimation in time (DIT) transform. The stages are from bottom to top. Thin lines indicate a factor of -1.

```
5       for (ulong ldm=ldn; ldm>=1; --ldm)
6       {
7           [--snip--]   // same block as in DIT routine
8       }
9   }
```

The basis functions are shown in figure 23.1-A. The lowest row is (the signed version of) the *Thue-Morse sequence*, see section 1.16.4 on page 44. A routine that computes the k-th basis function of the transform is [FXT: walsh/walsh-basis.h]:

```
1   template <typename Type>
2   void walsh_wak_basis(Type *f, ulong n, ulong k)
3   {
4       for (ulong i=0; i<n; ++i)
5       {
6           ulong x = i & k;
7           x = parity(x);
8           f[i] = ( 0==x ? +1 : -1 );
9       }
10  }
```

Multi-dimensional Walsh transform

If the row-column algorithm is used (see section 21.9.1 on page 437) to compute a 2-dimensional $n \times m$ Walsh transform, then the result is exactly the same as with a 1-dimensional transform of length $n \cdot m$. That is, a k-dimensional $n_1 \times n_2 \times \ldots \times n_k$ transform is identical to a 1-dimensional transform of length $n_1 \cdot n_2 \cdot \ldots \cdot n_k$. The length-$2^n$ Walsh transform is identical to a n-dimensional length-2 Fourier transform.

23.2 Eigenvectors of the Walsh transform ‡

The Walsh transforms are self-inverse, so their eigenvalues can only be ± 1. Let a be a sequence and let $W(a)$ denote the Walsh transform of a. Set

$$u_+ := W(a) + a \qquad (23.2\text{-}1)$$

```
 0:  [ +5 +1 +1 +1 +1 +1 +1 +1 +1 +1 +1 +1 +1 +1 +1 +1 ]
 1:  [ +1 +3 +1 -1 +1 -1 +1 -1 +1 -1 +1 -1 +1 -1 +1 -1 ]
 2:  [ +1 +1 +3 -1 +1 +1 -1 -1 +1 +1 -1 -1 +1 +1 -1 -1 ]
 3:  [ +1 -1 -1 +5 +1 -1 -1 +1 +1 -1 -1 +1 +1 -1 -1 +1 ]
 4:  [ +1 +1 +1 +1 +3 -1 -1 -1 +1 +1 +1 +1 -1 -1 -1 -1 ]
 5:  [ +1 -1 +1 -1 -1 +5 -1 +1 +1 -1 +1 -1 -1 +1 -1 +1 ]
 6:  [ +1 +1 -1 -1 -1 -1 +5 +1 +1 +1 -1 -1 -1 -1 +1 +1 ]
 7:  [ +1 -1 -1 +1 -1 +1 +1 +3 +1 -1 -1 +1 -1 +1 +1 -1 ]
 8:  [ +1 +1 +1 +1 +1 +1 +1 +1 -5 -1 -1 -1 -1 -1 -1 -1 ]
 9:  [ +1 -1 +1 -1 +1 -1 +1 -1 -1 -3 -1 +1 -1 +1 -1 +1 ]
10:  [ +1 +1 -1 -1 +1 +1 -1 -1 -1 -1 -3 +1 -1 -1 +1 +1 ]
11:  [ +1 -1 -1 +1 +1 -1 -1 +1 -1 +1 +1 -5 -1 +1 +1 -1 ]
12:  [ +1 +1 +1 +1 -1 -1 -1 -1 -1 -1 -1 -1 -3 +1 +1 +1 ]
13:  [ +1 -1 +1 -1 -1 +1 -1 +1 -1 +1 -1 +1 +1 -5 +1 -1 ]
14:  [ +1 +1 -1 -1 -1 -1 +1 +1 -1 -1 +1 +1 +1 +1 -5 -1 ]
15:  [ +1 -1 -1 +1 -1 +1 +1 -1 -1 +1 +1 -1 +1 -1 -1 -3 ]
```

Figure 23.2-A: Eigenvectors of the length-16 Walsh transform (Walsh-Kronecker basis) as row vectors. The eigenvalues are $+1$ for the vectors $0 \ldots 7$ and -1 for the vectors $8 \ldots 16$. Linear combinations of vectors with the same eigenvalue e are again eigenvectors with eigenvalue e.

Then

$$W(u_+) \quad = \quad W(W(a)) + W(a) \quad = \quad a + W(a) \quad = \quad +1 \cdot u_+ \tag{23.2-2}$$

That is, u_+ is an eigenvector of W with eigenvalue $+1$. Equivalently, $u_- := W(a) - a$ is an eigenvector with eigenvalue -1. Thus two eigenvectors can be computed for an arbitrary nonzero sequence. Note that with the unnormalized transforms the eigenvalues are $\pm\sqrt{n}$.

We are interested in a simple routine that for a Walsh transform of length n gives a set of n eigenvectors that span the n-dimensional space. With a routine that computes the k-th basis function of the transform we can obtain an eigenvector by simply adding a delta peak at position k to the basis function. The delta peak has to be scaled according to whether a positive or negative eigenvalue is desired and according to the normalization of the transform.

A suitable routine for the Walsh-Kronecker basis (whose basis functions are given in figure 23.1-A on page 459) is

```
1   void
2   walsh_wak_eigen(double *v, ulong ldn, ulong k)
3   // Eigenvectors of the Walsh transform (walsh_wak).
4   // Eigenvalues are +1 if k<n/2, else -1
5   {
6       ulong n = 1UL << ldn;
7       walsh_wak_basis(v, n, k);
8       double d = sqrt(n);
9       v[k] += (k<n/2 ? +d : -d);
10  }
```

This routine is given in [FXT: walsh/walsheigen.cc]. Figure 23.2-A was created with the program [FXT: fft/walsh-eigenvec-demo.cc].

23.3 The Kronecker product

The length-2 Walsh transform is equivalent to the multiplication of a 2-component vector by the matrix

$$\mathbf{W}_2 \quad = \quad \begin{bmatrix} +1 & +1 \\ +1 & -1 \end{bmatrix} \tag{23.3-1}$$

The length-4 Walsh transform corresponds to

$$\mathbf{W}_4 = \begin{bmatrix} +1 & +1 & +1 & +1 \\ +1 & -1 & +1 & -1 \\ +1 & +1 & -1 & -1 \\ +1 & -1 & -1 & +1 \end{bmatrix} \tag{23.3-2}$$

One might be tempted to write

$$\mathbf{W}_4 = \begin{bmatrix} +\mathbf{W}_2 & +\mathbf{W}_2 \\ +\mathbf{W}_2 & -\mathbf{W}_2 \end{bmatrix} \tag{23.3-3}$$

This idea can indeed be turned into a well-defined notation which is quite powerful when dealing with orthogonal transforms and their fast algorithms. Let $\mathbf{A}$ be an $m \times n$ matrix

$$\mathbf{A} = \begin{bmatrix} a_{0,0} & a_{0,1} & \cdots & a_{0,n-1} \\ a_{1,0} & a_{1,1} & \cdots & a_{1,n-1} \\ \vdots & \vdots & & \vdots \\ a_{m-1,0} & a_{m-1,1} & \cdots & a_{m-1,n-1} \end{bmatrix} \tag{23.3-4}$$

The (right) *Kronecker product* (or *tensor product*) with a matrix $\mathbf{B}$ is

$$\mathbf{A} \otimes \mathbf{B} := \begin{bmatrix} a_{0,0}\mathbf{B} & a_{0,1}\mathbf{B} & \cdots & a_{0,n-1}\mathbf{B} \\ a_{1,0}\mathbf{B} & a_{1,1}\mathbf{B} & \cdots & a_{1,n-1}\mathbf{B} \\ \vdots & \vdots & & \vdots \\ a_{m-1,0}\mathbf{B} & a_{m-1,1}\mathbf{B} & \cdots & a_{m-1,n-1}\mathbf{B} \end{bmatrix} \tag{23.3-5}$$

There is no restriction on the dimensions of $\mathbf{B}$. If $\mathbf{B}$ is an $r \times s$ matrix, then the dimensions of the given Kronecker product are $(mr) \times (ns)$. The entries of the matrix C are $c_{k+ir,l+js} = a_{i,j}\, b_{k,l}$. The Kronecker product is not commutative, that is, $\mathbf{A} \otimes \mathbf{B} \neq \mathbf{B} \otimes \mathbf{A}$ in general.

For a scalar factor α the following relations are immediate:

$$(\alpha\mathbf{A}) \otimes \mathbf{B} = \alpha(\mathbf{A} \otimes \mathbf{B}) \tag{23.3-6a}$$
$$\mathbf{A} \otimes (\alpha\mathbf{B}) = \alpha(\mathbf{A} \otimes \mathbf{B}) \tag{23.3-6b}$$

The next relations are the same as for the ordinary matrix product. Distributivity (the matrices on both sides of a plus sign must be of the same dimensions):

$$(\mathbf{A} + \mathbf{B}) \otimes \mathbf{C} = \mathbf{A} \otimes \mathbf{C} + \mathbf{B} \otimes \mathbf{C} \tag{23.3-7a}$$
$$\mathbf{A} \otimes (\mathbf{B} + \mathbf{C}) = \mathbf{A} \otimes \mathbf{B} + \mathbf{A} \otimes \mathbf{C} \tag{23.3-7b}$$

Associativity:

$$\mathbf{A} \otimes (\mathbf{B} \otimes \mathbf{C}) = (\mathbf{A} \otimes \mathbf{B}) \otimes \mathbf{C} \tag{23.3-8}$$

The matrix product (indicated by a dot) of Kronecker products can be rewritten as

$$(\mathbf{A} \otimes \mathbf{B}) \cdot (\mathbf{C} \otimes \mathbf{D}) = (\mathbf{A} \cdot \mathbf{C}) \otimes (\mathbf{B} \cdot \mathbf{D}) \tag{23.3-9a}$$
$$(\mathbf{L}_1 \otimes \mathbf{R}_1) \cdot (\mathbf{L}_2 \otimes \mathbf{R}_2) \cdot \ldots \cdot (\mathbf{L}_n \otimes \mathbf{R}_n) = (\mathbf{L}_1 \cdot \mathbf{L}_2 \cdot \ldots \cdot \mathbf{L}_n) \otimes (\mathbf{R}_1 \cdot \mathbf{R}_2 \cdot \ldots \cdot \mathbf{R}_n) \tag{23.3-9b}$$

Set $\mathbf{L}_1 = \mathbf{L}_2 = \ldots = \mathbf{L}_n =: \mathbf{L}$ and $\mathbf{R}_1 = \mathbf{R}_2 = \ldots = \mathbf{R}_n =: \mathbf{R}$ in the latter relation to obtain

$$(\mathbf{L} \otimes \mathbf{R})^n = \mathbf{L}^n \otimes \mathbf{R}^n \tag{23.3-9c}$$

The Kronecker product of matrix products can be rewritten as

$$(\mathbf{A} \cdot \mathbf{B}) \otimes (\mathbf{C} \cdot \mathbf{D}) \quad = \quad (\mathbf{A} \otimes \mathbf{C}) \cdot (\mathbf{B} \otimes \mathbf{D}) \tag{23.3-10a}$$

$$(\mathbf{L}_1 \cdot \mathbf{R}_1) \otimes (\mathbf{L}_2 \cdot \mathbf{R}_2) \otimes \ldots \otimes (\mathbf{L}_n \cdot \mathbf{R}_n) \quad = \quad (\mathbf{L}_1 \otimes \mathbf{L}_2 \otimes \ldots \otimes \mathbf{L}_n) \cdot (\mathbf{R}_1 \otimes \mathbf{R}_2 \otimes \ldots \otimes \mathbf{R}_n) \tag{23.3-10b}$$

Here the matrices left and right from a dot must be compatible for ordinary matrix multiplication.

We have

$$(\mathbf{A} \otimes \mathbf{B})^T \quad = \quad \mathbf{A}^T \otimes \mathbf{B}^T \tag{23.3-11a}$$

$$(\mathbf{A} \otimes \mathbf{B})^{-1} \quad = \quad \mathbf{A}^{-1} \otimes \mathbf{B}^{-1} \tag{23.3-11b}$$

If $\mathbf{A}$ and $\mathbf{B}$ are respectively $m \times n$ and $r \times s$ matrices, then

$$\mathbf{A} \otimes \mathbf{B} \quad = \quad (\mathbf{I}_m \otimes \mathbf{B}) \cdot (\mathbf{A} \otimes \mathbf{I}_s) \tag{23.3-12a}$$

$$= \quad (\mathbf{A} \otimes \mathbf{I}_r) \cdot (\mathbf{I}_n \otimes \mathbf{B}) \tag{23.3-12b}$$

where $\mathbf{I}_n$ is the $n \times n$ identity matrix. If $\mathbf{A}$ is $n \times n$ and $\mathbf{B}$ is $t \times t$, then

$$\det (\mathbf{A} \otimes \mathbf{B}) \quad = \quad \det(\mathbf{A})^t \det(\mathbf{B})^n \tag{23.3-13}$$

Back to the Walsh transform, we have $\mathbf{W}_1 = [1]$ and for $n = 2^k$, $n > 1$:

$$\mathbf{W}_n \quad = \quad \begin{bmatrix} +\mathbf{W}_{n/2} & +\mathbf{W}_{n/2} \\ +\mathbf{W}_{n/2} & -\mathbf{W}_{n/2} \end{bmatrix} = \mathbf{W}_2 \otimes \mathbf{W}_{n/2} \tag{23.3-14}$$

To see that this relation is the statement of a fast algorithm, split the (to be transformed) vector x into halves

$$x \quad = \quad \begin{bmatrix} x_0 \\ x_1 \end{bmatrix} \tag{23.3-15}$$

and write out the matrix-vector product

$$\mathbf{W}_n x \quad = \quad \begin{bmatrix} \mathbf{W}_{n/2} x_0 + \mathbf{W}_{n/2} x_1 \\ \mathbf{W}_{n/2} x_0 - \mathbf{W}_{n/2} x_1 \end{bmatrix} = \begin{bmatrix} \mathbf{W}_{n/2} (x_0 + x_1) \\ \mathbf{W}_{n/2} (x_0 - x_1) \end{bmatrix} \tag{23.3-16}$$

That is, a length-n transform can be computed by two length-$n/2$ transforms of the sum and difference of the first and second half of x.

We define a notation equivalent to the product sign,

$$\bigotimes_{k=1}^{n} \mathbf{M}_k \quad := \quad \mathbf{M}_1 \otimes \mathbf{M}_2 \otimes \mathbf{M}_3 \otimes \ldots \otimes \mathbf{M}_n \tag{23.3-17}$$

where the empty product equals a 1×1 matrix with entry 1. If $\mathbf{A} = \mathbf{B}$ in relation 23.3-11b, then we have $(\mathbf{A} \otimes \mathbf{A})^{-1} = \mathbf{A}^{-1} \otimes \mathbf{A}^{-1}$, $(\mathbf{A} \otimes \mathbf{A} \otimes \mathbf{A})^{-1} = \mathbf{A}^{-1} \otimes \mathbf{A}^{-1} \otimes \mathbf{A}^{-1}$ and so on. That is,

$$\left(\bigotimes_{k=1}^{n} \mathbf{A} \right)^{-1} \quad = \quad \bigotimes_{k=1}^{n} \mathbf{A}^{-1} \tag{23.3-18}$$

For the Walsh transform we have

$$\mathbf{W}_n \quad = \quad \bigotimes_{k=1}^{\log_2 (n)} \mathbf{W}_2 \tag{23.3-19}$$

and

$$\mathbf{W}_n^{-1} \;=\; \bigotimes_{k=1}^{\log_2(n)} \mathbf{W}_2^{-1} \tag{23.3-20}$$

The latter relation isn't that exciting as $\mathbf{W}_2^{-1} = \mathbf{W}_2$ for the Walsh transform. However, it also holds if the inverse transform is different from the forward transform. Given a fast algorithm for some transform in the form of a Kronecker product, the fast algorithm for the inverse transform is immediate.

The *direct sum* of two matrices is defined as

$$\mathbf{A} \oplus \mathbf{B} \;:=\; \begin{bmatrix} \mathbf{A} & 0 \\ 0 & \mathbf{B} \end{bmatrix} \tag{23.3-21}$$

In general $\mathbf{A} \oplus \mathbf{B} \neq \mathbf{B} \oplus \mathbf{A}$. As an analogue to the sum sign we have

$$\bigoplus_{k=1}^{n} \mathbf{A} \;:=\; \mathbf{I}_n \otimes \mathbf{A} \tag{23.3-22}$$

where $\mathbf{I}_n$ is the $n \times n$ identity matrix. The matrix $\mathbf{I}_n \otimes \mathbf{A}$ consists of n copies of $\mathbf{A}$ that lie on the diagonal. The Kronecker product can be used to derive properties of unitary transforms, see [282]. In [236] the properties of the Kronecker product are used to develop all well-known algorithms for computing the Fourier transform.

23.4 Higher radix Walsh transforms

23.4.1 Generated transforms

A generator for short-length Walsh (wak) transforms is given as [FXT: fft/gen-walsh-demo.cc]. It can create code for DIF and DIT transforms. For example, the code for the 4-point DIF transform is

```
1   template <typename Type>
2   inline void
3   short_walsh_wak_dif_4(Type *f)
4   {
5       Type t0, t1, t2, t3;
6       t0 = f[0];
7       t1 = f[1];
8       t2 = f[2];
9       t3 = f[3];
10      sumdiff( t0, t2 );
11      sumdiff( t1, t3 );
12      sumdiff( t0, t1 );
13      sumdiff( t2, t3 );
14      f[0] = t0;
15      f[1] = t1;
16      f[2] = t2;
17      f[3] = t3;
18  }
```

To make the code more readable we use the function [FXT: aux0/sumdiff.h]:

```
1   template <typename Type>
2   static inline void sumdiff(Type &a, Type &b)
3   // {a, b}  <--| {a+b, a-b}
4   { Type t=a-b; a+=b; b=t; }
```

We further need a variant that transforms elements which are not contiguous but lie apart by a distance s:

```
1   template <typename Type>
2   inline void
3   short_walsh_wak_dif_4(Type *f, ulong s)
4   {
5       Type t0, t1, t2, t3;
6       {
7       ulong x = 0;
```

```
8          t0 = f[x];   x += s;
9          t1 = f[x];   x += s;
10         t2 = f[x];   x += s;
11         t3 = f[x];
12     }
13     sumdiff( t0, t2 );
14     sumdiff( t1, t3 );
15     sumdiff( t0, t1 );
16     sumdiff( t2, t3 );
17     {
18     ulong x = 0;
19     f[x] = t0;   x += s;
20     f[x] = t1;   x += s;
21     f[x] = t2;   x += s;
22     f[x] = t3;
23     }
24 }
```

The short-length transforms (DIF and DIT variants) are given in [FXT: walsh/shortwalshwakdif.h] and [FXT: walsh/shortwalshwakdit.h], respectively. A radix-4 DIF transform using these as ingredients is [FXT: walsh/walshwak4.h]:

```
1    template <typename Type>
2    void walsh_wak_dif4(Type *f, ulong ldn)
3    // Transform wrt. to Walsh-Kronecker basis (wak-functions).
4    // Radix-4 decimation in frequency (DIF) algorithm.
5    // Self-inverse.
6    {
7        const ulong n = (1UL<<ldn);
8
9        if ( n<=2 )
10       {
11           if ( n==2 )  short_walsh_wak_dif_2(f);
12           return;
13       }
14
15       for (ulong ldm=ldn; ldm>3; ldm-=2)
16       {
17           ulong m = (1UL<<ldm);
18           ulong m4 = (m>>2);
19           for (ulong r=0;  r<n;   r+=m)
20           {
21               for (ulong j=0;  j<m4;  j++)  short_walsh_wak_dif_4(f+j+r, m4);
22           }
23       }
24
25       if ( ldn & 1 )  // n is not a power of 4, need a radix-8 step
26       {
27           for (ulong i0=0; i0<n; i0+=8)  short_walsh_wak_dif_8(f+i0);
28       }
29       else
30       {
31           for (ulong i0=0; i0<n; i0+=4)  short_walsh_wak_dif_4(f+i0);
32       }
33   }
```

With the implementation radix-8 DIF transform some care must be taken to choose the correct final step size [FXT: walsh/walshwak8.h]:

```
1    template <typename Type>
2    void walsh_wak_dif8(Type *f, ulong ldn)
3    // Transform wrt. to Walsh-Kronecker basis (wak-functions).
4    // Radix-8 decimation in frequency (DIF) algorithm.
5    // Self-inverse.
6    {
7        const ulong n = (1UL<<ldn);
8
9        if ( n<=4 )
10       {
11           switch (n )
12           {
13           case 4:  short_walsh_wak_dif_4(f);  break;
14           case 2:  short_walsh_wak_dif_2(f);  break;
15           }
16           return;
17       }
18
```

```
19      const ulong xx = 4;
20      ulong ldm;
21      for (ldm=ldn; ldm>xx; ldm-=3)
22      {
23          ulong m = (1UL<<ldm);
24          ulong m8 = (m>>3);
25          for (ulong r=0;  r<n;  r+=m)
26          {
27              for (ulong j=0;  j<m8;  j++)  short_walsh_wak_dif_8(f+j+r, m8);
28          }
29      }
30
31      switch ( ldm )
32      {
33      case 4:
34          for (ulong i0=0; i0<n; i0+=16)  short_walsh_wak_dif_16(f+i0);
35          break;
36      case 3:
37          for (ulong i0=0; i0<n; i0+=8)   short_walsh_wak_dif_8(f+i0);
38          break;
39      case 2:
40          for (ulong i0=0; i0<n; i0+=4)   short_walsh_wak_dif_4(f+i0);
41          break;
42      }
43  }
```

23.4.2   Performance

For the purpose of performance comparison we include a matrix variant of the Walsh transform [FXT: walsh/walshwakmatrix.h]:

```
1   template <typename Type>
2   void walsh_wak_matrix(Type *f, ulong ldn)
3   {
4       ulong ldc = (ldn>>1);
5       ulong ldr = ldn-ldc;  // ldr>=ldc
6       ulong nc = (1UL<<ldc);
7       ulong nr = (1UL<<ldr);   // nrow >= ncol
8
9       for (ulong r=0;  r<nr;  ++r)  walsh_wak_dif4(f+r*nc, ldc);
10      transpose2(f, nr, nc);
11      for (ulong c=0;  c<nc;  ++c)  walsh_wak_dif4(f+c*nr, ldr);
12      transpose2(f, nc, nr);
13  }
```

The transposition routine is given in [FXT: aux2/transpose2.h]. We only use even powers of 2 so the transposition is that of a square matrix.

As for dyadic convolutions we do not need the data in a particular order so we also include a version of the matrix algorithm that omits the final transposition:

```
1   template <typename Type>
2   void walsh_wak_matrix_1(Type *f, ulong ldn, int is)
3   {
4       ulong ldc = (ldn>>1);
5       ulong ldr = ldn-ldc;  // ldr>=ldc
6       if ( is<0 )  swap2(ldr, ldc);  // inverse
7       ulong nc = (1UL<<ldc);
8       ulong nr = (1UL<<ldr);   // nrow >= ncol
9
10      for (ulong r=0;  r<nr;  ++r)  walsh_wak_dif4(f+r*nc, ldc);
11      transpose2(f, nr, nc);
12      for (ulong c=0;  c<nc;  ++c)  walsh_wak_dif4(f+c*nr, ldr);
13  }
```

The following calls give (up to normalization) the mutually inverse transforms:

```
1       walsh_wak_matrix_1(f, ldn, +1);
2       walsh_wak_matrix_1(f, ldn, -1);
```

We do not consider the range of transform lengths $n < 128$, where unrolled routines and the radix-4 algorithm consistently win. Figure 23.4-A shows a comparison of the routines given so far. There are clearly two regions to distinguish: firstly, the region where the transforms fit into the first-level data cache (which is 64 kilobyte, corresponding to `ldn` = 13). Secondly, the region where `ldn` > 13 and the performance becomes more and more memory bound.

In the first region the radix-4 routine is the fastest. The radix-8 routine comes close but, somewhat surprisingly, never wins.

In the second region the matrix version is the best. However, for very large sizes its performance could be better. Note that with odd `ldn` (not shown) its performance drops significantly due to the more expensive transposition operation. The transposition is clearly the bottleneck. One can use machine-specific optimizations for the transposition to further improve the performance.

In the next section we give an algorithm that avoids the transposition completely and consistently outperforms the matrix algorithm.

23.5   Localized Walsh transforms

A decimation in time (DIT) algorithm combines the halves of the array, then the halves of the halves, the halves of each quarter, and so on. With each step the whole array is accessed which leads to a drop in performance as soon as the array does not fit into the cache.

23.5.1   The method of localization

We can reorganize the algorithm as follows: combine the halves of the array and postpone further processing of the upper half, then combine the halves of the lower half and again postpone processing of its upper half. Repeat until size 2 is reached. Then use the algorithm at the postponed parts, starting with the smallest (last postponed).

For size 16 the scheme can be sketched as follows:

```
hhhhhhhhhhhhhhhh
hhhhhhhh44444444
hhhh333344444444
hh22333344444444
```

The letters 'h' denote places processed before any recursive call. The blocks of twos, threes and fours denote postponed blocks. The Walsh transform is thereby decomposed into a sequence of Haar transforms (see figure 24.6-A on page 508). The algorithm described is most easily implemented via recursion:

```
1    template <typename Type>
2    void walsh_wak_loc_dit2(Type *f, ulong ldn)
3    {
4        if ( ldn<1 )  return;
5
6        // Recursion:
7        for (ulong ldm=1; ldm<ldn; ++ldm)  walsh_wak_loc_dit2(f+(1UL<<ldm), ldm);
8
9        for (ulong ldm=1; ldm<=ldn; ++ldm)
10       {
11           const ulong m = (1UL<<ldm);
12           const ulong mh = (m>>1);
13           for (ulong t1=0, t2=mh;  t1<mh;  ++t1, ++t2)  sumdiff(f[t1], f[t2]);
14       }
15   }
```

23.5.2   Optimizing the routine

Avoiding recursions for small sizes gives a speedup. We use a radix-4 algorithm as soon as the transform fits into cache memory and avoid recursion for tiny transforms [FXT: walsh/walshwakloc2.h]:

```
1    template <typename Type>
2    void walsh_wak_loc_dit2(Type *f, ulong ldn)
3    {
4        if ( ldn<=13 )  // parameter: (2**13)*sizeof(Type) <= L1-cache
5        {
6            walsh_wak_dif4(f,ldn);  // note: DIF version, result is the same
```

```
  8 == ldn;    MemSize ==     2 kB   ==  256 doubles;    rep == 976563
                walsh_wak_dif2(f,ldn);      dt=    2.49551   MB/s= 6114   rel=         1
                walsh_wak_dif4(f,ldn);      dt=    1.56806   MB/s= 9731   rel=  0.628352 *
                walsh_wak_dif8(f,ldn);      dt=    1.57419   MB/s= 9693   rel=  0.63081
                walsh_wak_matrix(f,ldn);    dt=    2.28047   MB/s= 6691   rel=  0.91383
            walsh_wak_matrix_1(f,ldn,+1);   dt=    1.94357   MB/s= 7851   rel=  0.778827

 10 == ldn;    MemSize ==     8 kB   ==  1024 doubles;   rep == 195313
                walsh_wak_dif2(f,ldn);      dt=    2.26683   MB/s= 6731   rel=         1
                walsh_wak_dif4(f,ldn);      dt=    1.47338   MB/s=10356   rel=  0.649977 *
                walsh_wak_dif8(f,ldn);      dt=    1.65262   MB/s= 9233   rel=  0.729044
                walsh_wak_matrix(f,ldn);    dt=    1.91859   MB/s= 7953   rel=  0.846378
            walsh_wak_matrix_1(f,ldn,+1);   dt=    1.69215   MB/s= 9017   rel=  0.746485

 12 == ldn;    MemSize ==    32 kB   ==  4096 doubles;   rep == 20345
                walsh_wak_dif2(f,ldn);      dt=    1.0884    MB/s= 7010   rel=         1
                walsh_wak_dif4(f,ldn);      dt=    0.723136  MB/s=10550   rel=  0.664403 *
                walsh_wak_dif8(f,ldn);      dt=    0.790313  MB/s= 9654   rel=  0.726124
                walsh_wak_matrix(f,ldn);    dt=    1.01233   MB/s= 7536   rel=  0.930112
            walsh_wak_matrix_1(f,ldn,+1);   dt=    0.926387  MB/s= 8236   rel=  0.851146

 14 == ldn;    MemSize ==   128 kB   ==  16384 doubles;  rep == 2180
                walsh_wak_dif2(f,ldn);      dt=    1.17042   MB/s= 3260   rel=         1
                walsh_wak_dif4(f,ldn);      dt=    1.14861   MB/s= 3321   rel=  0.981368
                walsh_wak_dif8(f,ldn);      dt=    1.08501   MB/s= 3516   rel=  0.927026
                walsh_wak_matrix(f,ldn);    dt=    0.669182  MB/s= 5701   rel=  0.571747
            walsh_wak_matrix_1(f,ldn,+1);   dt=    0.552063  MB/s= 6910   rel=  0.471681 *

 16 == ldn;    MemSize ==   512 kB   ==  65536 doubles;  rep == 477
                walsh_wak_dif2(f,ldn);      dt=    1.40004   MB/s= 2726   rel=         1
                walsh_wak_dif4(f,ldn);      dt=    1.70347   MB/s= 2240   rel=  1.21673
                walsh_wak_dif8(f,ldn);      dt=    1.12997   MB/s= 3377   rel=  0.807095
                walsh_wak_matrix(f,ldn);    dt=    0.801902  MB/s= 4759   rel=  0.572769
            walsh_wak_matrix_1(f,ldn,+1);   dt=    0.628073  MB/s= 6076   rel=  0.448609 *

 18 == ldn;    MemSize ==     2 MB   ==  256 K doubles;  rep == 106
                walsh_wak_dif2(f,ldn);      dt=    2.61599   MB/s= 1459   rel=         1
                walsh_wak_dif4(f,ldn);      dt=    2.55153   MB/s= 1496   rel=  0.975359
                walsh_wak_dif8(f,ldn);      dt=    1.9791    MB/s= 1928   rel=  0.756538
                walsh_wak_matrix(f,ldn);    dt=    1.77306   MB/s= 2152   rel=  0.677776
            walsh_wak_matrix_1(f,ldn,+1);   dt=    1.14735   MB/s= 3326   rel=  0.438591 *

 20 == ldn;    MemSize ==     8 MB   ==  1024 K doubles; rep == 24
                walsh_wak_dif2(f,ldn);      dt=    2.64158   MB/s= 1454   rel=         1
                walsh_wak_dif4(f,ldn);      dt=    2.8532    MB/s= 1346   rel=  1.08011
                walsh_wak_dif8(f,ldn);      dt=    2.34867   MB/s= 1635   rel=  0.889113
                walsh_wak_matrix(f,ldn);    dt=    1.88431   MB/s= 2038   rel=  0.713327
            walsh_wak_matrix_1(f,ldn,+1);   dt=    1.21084   MB/s= 3171   rel=  0.458376 *

 22 == ldn;    MemSize ==    32 MB   ==  4096 K doubles; rep == 5
                walsh_wak_dif2(f,ldn);      dt=    2.43537   MB/s= 1445   rel=         1
                walsh_wak_dif4(f,ldn);      dt=    2.82337   MB/s= 1247   rel=  1.15932
                walsh_wak_dif8(f,ldn);      dt=    2.07422   MB/s= 1697   rel=  0.851708
                walsh_wak_matrix(f,ldn);    dt=    1.99251   MB/s= 1767   rel=  0.818155
            walsh_wak_matrix_1(f,ldn,+1);   dt=    1.22719   MB/s= 2868   rel=  0.503901 *

 24 == ldn;    MemSize ==   128 MB   ==  16384 K doubles; rep == 1
                walsh_wak_dif2(f,ldn);      dt=    2.10939   MB/s= 1456   rel=         1
                walsh_wak_dif4(f,ldn);      dt=    2.61517   MB/s= 1175   rel=  1.23977
                walsh_wak_dif8(f,ldn);      dt=    2.11508   MB/s= 1452   rel=  1.0027
                walsh_wak_matrix(f,ldn);    dt=    2.16597   MB/s= 1418   rel=  1.02683
            walsh_wak_matrix_1(f,ldn,+1);   dt=    1.28349   MB/s= 2393   rel=  0.608466 *
```

Figure 23.4-A: Relative speed of different implementations of the Walsh (wak) transform. The transforms were run 'rep' times for each measurement. The quantity 'dt' gives the elapsed time for rep transforms of the given type. The quantity 'MB/s' gives the memory transfer rate as if a radix-2 algorithm were used; it equals 'Memsize' times 'ldn' divided by the time elapsed for a single transform. The 'rel' gives the performance relative to the radix-2 version, smaller values mean better performance.

```
 7          return;
 8      }
 9
10      // Recursion:
11      short_walsh_wak_dit_2(f+2);    // ldm==1
12      short_walsh_wak_dit_4(f+4);    // ldm==2
13      short_walsh_wak_dit_8(f+8);    // ldm==3
14      short_walsh_wak_dit_16(f+16);   // ldm==4
15      for (ulong ldm=5; ldm<ldn; ++ldm)  walsh_wak_loc_dit2(f+(1UL<<ldm), ldm);
16
17      for (ulong ldm=1; ldm<=ldn; ++ldm)
18      {
19          const ulong m = (1UL<<ldm);
20          const ulong mh = (m>>1);
21          for (ulong t1=0, t2=mh;  t1<mh;  ++t1, ++t2)  sumdiff(f[t1], f[t2]);
22      }
23  }
```

A decimation in frequency (DIF) version is obtained by executing the inverse steps in reversed order:

```
 1  template <typename Type>
 2  void walsh_wak_loc_dif2(Type *f, ulong ldn)
 3  {
 4      if ( ldn<=13 )   // parameter: (2**13)*sizeof(Type) <= L1-cache
 5      {
 6          walsh_wak_dif4(f,ldn);
 7          return;
 8      }
 9
10      for (ulong ldm=ldn; ldm>=1; --ldm)
11      {
12          const ulong m = (1UL<<ldm);
13          const ulong mh = (m>>1);
14          for (ulong t1=0, t2=mh;  t1<mh;  ++t1, ++t2)
15          {
16              Type u = f[t1];
17              Type v = f[t2];
18              f[t1] = u + v;
19              f[t2] = u - v;
20          }
21      }
22
23      // Recursion:
24      short_walsh_wak_dif_2(f+2);    // ldm==1
25      short_walsh_wak_dif_4(f+4);    // ldm==2
26      short_walsh_wak_dif_8(f+8);    // ldm==3
27      short_walsh_wak_dif_16(f+16);   // ldm==4
28      for (ulong ldm=5; ldm<ldn; ++ldm)  walsh_wak_loc_dif2(f+(1UL<<ldm), ldm);
29  }
```

The double loop in the algorithm is a reversed Haar transform, see chapter 24 on page 497. The double loop in the DIF algorithm is a transposed reversed Haar transform. The (generated) short-length transforms are given in the files [FXT: walsh/shortwalshwakdif.h] and [FXT: walsh/shortwalshwakdit.h]. For example, the length-8, decimation in frequency routine is

```
 1  template <typename Type>
 2  inline void
 3  short_walsh_wak_dif_8(Type *f)
 4  {
 5    Type t0, t1, t2, t3, t4, t5, t6, t7;
 6    t0 = f[0]; t1 = f[1]; t2 = f[2]; t3 = f[3];
 7    t4 = f[4]; t5 = f[5]; t6 = f[6]; t7 = f[7];
 8    sumdiff( t0, t4 ); sumdiff( t1, t5 ); sumdiff( t2, t6 ); sumdiff( t3, t7 );
 9    sumdiff( t0, t2 ); sumdiff( t1, t3 ); sumdiff( t4, t6 ); sumdiff( t5, t7 );
10    sumdiff( t0, t1 ); sumdiff( t2, t3 ); sumdiff( t4, t5 ); sumdiff( t6, t7 );
11    f[0] = t0; f[1] = t1; f[2] = t2; f[3] = t3;
12    f[4] = t4; f[5] = t5; f[6] = t6; f[7] = t7;
13  }
```

The strategy used leads to a very favorable memory access pattern that results in excellent performance for large transforms. Figure 23.5-A shows a comparison between the localized transforms and the matrix algorithm. Small sizes are omitted because the localized algorithm has the same speed as the radix-4 algorithm it falls back to. The localized algorithms are the clear winners, even against the matrix algorithm with only one transposition. For very large transforms the DIF version is slightly faster, as

```
14 == ldn;    MemSize ==    128 kB   ==   16384 doubles;    rep == 2180
              walsh_wak_matrix(f,ldn);       dt=   0.672327    MB/s= 5674    rel=           1
            walsh_wak_matrix_1(f,ldn,+1);    dt=   0.555851    MB/s= 6863    rel=    0.826756
              walsh_wak_loc_dit2(f,ldn);     dt=   0.498558    MB/s= 7652    rel=    0.741541 *
              walsh_wak_loc_dif2(f,ldn);     dt=   0.533746    MB/s= 7148    rel=    0.793878

16 == ldn;    MemSize ==    512 kB   ==   65536 doubles;    rep == 477
              walsh_wak_matrix(f,ldn);       dt=   0.919579    MB/s= 4150    rel=           1
            walsh_wak_matrix_1(f,ldn,+1);    dt=   0.692488    MB/s= 5511    rel=    0.753049
              walsh_wak_loc_dit2(f,ldn);     dt=   0.653256    MB/s= 5842    rel=    0.710386 *
              walsh_wak_loc_dif2(f,ldn);     dt=   0.670104    MB/s= 5695    rel=    0.728707

18 == ldn;    MemSize ==      2 MB   ==   256 K doubles;    rep == 106
              walsh_wak_matrix(f,ldn);       dt=    2.2111     MB/s= 1726    rel=           1
            walsh_wak_matrix_1(f,ldn,+1);    dt=    1.36827    MB/s= 2789    rel=    0.618819
              walsh_wak_loc_dit2(f,ldn);     dt=   0.938006    MB/s= 4068    rel=    0.424225
              walsh_wak_loc_dif2(f,ldn);     dt=   0.927804    MB/s= 4113    rel=    0.419611 *

20 == ldn;    MemSize ==      8 MB   ==   1024 K doubles;    rep == 24
              walsh_wak_matrix(f,ldn);       dt=    2.31178    MB/s= 1661    rel=           1
            walsh_wak_matrix_1(f,ldn,+1);    dt=    1.42614    MB/s= 2693    rel=    0.616901
              walsh_wak_loc_dit2(f,ldn);     dt=    1.11847    MB/s= 3433    rel=    0.483811
              walsh_wak_loc_dif2(f,ldn);     dt=    1.11142    MB/s= 3455    rel=    0.480765 *

22 == ldn;    MemSize ==     32 MB   ==   4096 K doubles;    rep == 5
              walsh_wak_matrix(f,ldn);       dt=    2.00573    MB/s= 1755    rel=           1
            walsh_wak_matrix_1(f,ldn,+1);    dt=    1.23695    MB/s= 2846    rel=    0.616707
              walsh_wak_loc_dit2(f,ldn);     dt=    1.16461    MB/s= 3022    rel=    0.580644
              walsh_wak_loc_dif2(f,ldn);     dt=    1.16164    MB/s= 3030    rel=    0.579162 *

24 == ldn;    MemSize ==    128 MB   ==   16384 K doubles;    rep == 1
              walsh_wak_matrix(f,ldn);       dt=    2.16536    MB/s= 1419    rel=           1
            walsh_wak_matrix_1(f,ldn,+1);    dt=    1.28455    MB/s= 2392    rel=    0.593226
              walsh_wak_loc_dit2(f,ldn);     dt=    1.10769    MB/s= 2773    rel=    0.511552
              walsh_wak_loc_dif2(f,ldn);     dt=    1.10601    MB/s= 2778    rel=    0.510776 *
```

Figure 23.5-A: Speed comparison between localized and matrix algorithms for the Walsh transform.

it starts with smaller chunks of data and therefore more of the data is in the cache when the larger sub-arrays get accessed.

The localized algorithm can easily be implemented for transforms where a radix-2 step is known. Section 25.8 on page 529 gives the fast Hartley transform variant of the localized algorithm.

Similar routines with higher radix can be developed. However, a radix-4 version was found to be slower than the given routines. A speedup can be achieved by unrolling and prefetching. We use the C-type **double** whose size is 8 bytes. Substitute the double loop in the DIF version (that is, the Haar transform) by

```
1   // machine-specific prefetch instruction:
2   #define PREF(p,o)  asm volatile ("prefetchw " #o "(%0) " : : "r" (p) )
3
4       ulong ldm;
5       for (ldm=ldn; ldm>=6; --ldm)
6       {
7           const ulong m = (1UL<<ldm);
8           const ulong mh = (m>>1);
9           PREF(f, 0);   PREF(f+mh, 0);
10          PREF(f, 64);   PREF(f+mh, 64);
11          PREF(f, 128);   PREF(f+mh, 128);
12          PREF(f, 192);   PREF(f+mh, 192);
13
14          for (ulong t1=0, t2=mh;  t1<mh;  t1+=8, t2+=8)
15          {
16              double *p1 = f + t1, *p2 = f + t2;
17              PREF(p1, 256);   PREF(p2, 256);
18
19              double u0 = f[t1+0], v0 = f[t2+0];
20              double u1 = f[t1+1], v1 = f[t2+1];
21              double u2 = f[t1+2], v2 = f[t2+2];
22              double u3 = f[t1+3], v3 = f[t2+3];
23              sumdiff(u0, v0); f[t1+0] = u0; f[t2+0] = v0;
24              sumdiff(u1, v1); f[t1+1] = u1; f[t2+1] = v1;
25              sumdiff(u2, v2); f[t1+2] = u2; f[t2+2] = v2;
26              sumdiff(u3, v3); f[t1+3] = u3; f[t2+3] = v3;
```

```
27
28            double u4 = f[t1+4], v4 = f[t2+4];
29            double u5 = f[t1+5], v5 = f[t2+5];
30            double u6 = f[t1+6], v6 = f[t2+6];
31            double u7 = f[t1+7], v7 = f[t2+7];
32            sumdiff(u4, v4);  f[t1+4] = u4;  f[t2+4] = v4;
33            sumdiff(u5, v5);  f[t1+5] = u5;  f[t2+5] = v5;
34            sumdiff(u6, v6);  f[t1+6] = u6;  f[t2+6] = v6;
35            sumdiff(u7, v7);  f[t1+7] = u7;  f[t2+7] = v7;
36        }
37    }
38
39    for (  ; ldm>=1; --ldm)
40    {
41        const ulong m = (1UL<<ldm);
42        const ulong mh = (m>>1);
43        for (ulong t1=0, t2=mh;  t1<mh;  ++t1, ++t2)  sumdiff(f[t1], f[t2]);
44    }
```

The following list gives the speed ratio between the optimized and the unoptimized DIF routine:

```
14 == ldn;   MemSize ==   128 kB;   ratio = 1.24252
16 == ldn;   MemSize ==   512 kB;   ratio = 1.43568
18 == ldn;   MemSize ==     2 MB;   ratio = 1.23875
20 == ldn;   MemSize ==     8 MB;   ratio = 1.21012
22 == ldn;   MemSize ==    32 MB;   ratio = 1.19939
24 == ldn;   MemSize ==   128 MB;   ratio = 1.18245
```

For sizes that are out of (level-2) cache most of the speedup is due to the memory prefetch.

23.5.3 Iterative versions of the algorithms

Figure 23.5-B: Binary values of the start index and length of the Haar transforms in the iterative version of the localized DIF (left) and DIT (right) transform. Dots are used for zeros.

In the DIF algorithm the Haar transforms are executed at positions $f+2$, $f+4$, $f+6$, ... and the length of the transform at position $f+s$ is determined by the lowest set bit in s. Additionally, a full-length Haar transform has to be done at the beginning. As C++ code:

```
1     template <typename Type>
2     inline void haar_dif2(Type *f, ulong n)
3     {
4         for (ulong m=n; m>=2; m>>=1)
5         {
6             const ulong mh = (m>>1);
7             for (ulong t1=0, t2=mh;  t1<mh;  ++t1, ++t2)  sumdiff(f[t1], f[t2]);
8         }
9     }
10
11    template <typename Type>
12    void loc_dif2(Type *f, ulong n)
13    {
14        haar_dif2(f, n);
15        for (ulong z=2; z<n; z+=2)  haar_dif2(f+z,  (z&-z));
16    }
```

Note that the routines now take the length of the transform as second argument, not its base-2 logarithm.

With the DIT algorithm matters are slightly more complicated. A pattern can be observed by printing the binary expansions of the starting position and length of the transforms shown in figure 23.5-B (created with [FXT: fft/locrec-demo.cc]). The lengths are again determined by the lowest bit of the start position. And we have also seen the pattern in the left column: the reversed binary words in reversed lexicographic order, see figure 1.26-A on page 70. The implementation is quite concise:

```
1    template <typename Type>
2    inline void haar_dit2(Type *f, ulong n)
3    {
4        for (ulong m=1; m<=n; m<<=1)
5        {
6            const ulong mh = (m>>1);
7            for (ulong t1=0, t2=mh;  t1<mh;  ++t1, ++t2)  sumdiff(f[t1], f[t2]);
8        }
9    }
10
11   template <typename Type>
12   void loc_dit2(Type f, ulong n)
13   {
14       for (ulong z=2, u=1; z<n; z+=2)
15       {
16           ulong s = u<<1;
17           haar_dit2(f+s,  (s&-s));
18           u = prev_lexrev(u);
19       }
20       haar_dit2(f, n);
21   }
```

The routines are slightly slower than the recursive version because they do not fall back to the full Walsh transforms if the transform size is small.

The DIT scheme is a somewhat surprising application of the seemingly esoteric routine **prev_lexrev()** in [FXT: bits/bitlex.h]. Plus we have found a recursive algorithm for the generation of the binary words in lexicographic order [FXT: bits/bitlex-rec-demo.cc]:

```
1    void bitlex_b(ulong f, ulong n)
2    {
3        for (ulong m=1; m<n; m<<=1)  bitlex_b(f+m, m);
4        print_bin(" ", f, ldn);
5    }
```

23.6   Transform with Walsh-Paley basis

A Walsh transform with a different ordering of the basis (see figure 23.6-A) can be computed by [FXT: walsh/walshpal.h]:

```
1    template <typename Type>
2    void walsh_pal(Type *f, ulong ldn)
3    {
4        const ulong n = 1UL<<ldn;
5        revbin_permute(f, n);
6        walsh_wak(f, ldn);
7    // =^=
8    //     walsh_wak(f, ldn);
9    //     revbin_permute(f, n);
10   }
```

Write Z for the zip permutation (see section 2.10 on page 125), and G for the Gray permutation (see section 2.12 on page 128), then we have

$$W_p = G\,W_p\,G = G^{-1}\,W_p\,G^{-1} \tag{23.6-1}$$
$$= Z\,W_p\,Z = Z^{-1}\,W_p\,Z^{-1} \tag{23.6-2}$$

A function to compute the k-th basis function of the transform is [FXT: walsh/walsh-basis.h]:

```
1    template <typename Type>
2    void walsh_pal_basis(Type *f, ulong n, ulong k)
```

```
 0: [ * * * * * * * * * * * * * * * * * * * * * * * * * * * * * * * * ] ( 0)
 1: [ * * * * * * * * * * * * * *                                     ] ( 1)
 2: [ * * * * * * *                           * * * * * * *           ] ( 3)
 3: [ * * * * * * *                               * * * * * * * *     ] ( 2)
 4: [ * * *         * * *           * * *           * * *             ] ( 7)
 5: [ * * *         * * *             * * *             * * *         ] ( 6)
 6: [ * * * *         * * * * * * *                       * * * *     ] ( 4)
 7: [ * * * *           * * * *         * * * * * * *                 ] ( 5)
 8: [ * *     * *     * *     * *     * *     * *     * *     * *     ] (15)
 9: [ * *     * *     * *     * *         * *     * *     * *     * * ] (14)
10: [ * *     * *         * *     * * * *     * *             * *   * * ] (12)
11: [ * *     * *         * *       * *     * *     * * * *     * *   ] (13)
12: [ * *         * * * *         * * * *           * * * *     * *   ] ( 8)
13: [ * *         * * * *           * *     * * * *       * * * *     ] ( 9)
14: [ * *         * *     * * * *     * *             * *     * * * * ] (11)
15: [ * *         * *     * * * *         * * * *     * *         * * ] (10)
16: [ * *   *   *   *   *   *   *   *   *   *   *   *   *   *   *   * ] (31)
17: [ * *   *   *   *   *   *   *   *   *   *   *   *   *   *   *   * ] (30)
18: [ * *   *   *     *   *   * *   *   *   *   *   *     *   *   *   * ] (28)
19: [ * *   *   *     *   *   *   *   *   *     * *   *     *   *   * ] (29)
20: [ * *   *     *   * *   *     * *   *     *   * *   *     *   * * ] (24)
21: [ * *   *     * *   *       * *   *   * *   *     * *   * *   * ] (25)
22: [ * *   *   *   *     * *   *   *     *   *   *     * *   * ] (27)
23: [ * *   *     *   *   * *   *     * *   *   *     *     * * ] (26)
24: [ * *     * *     * *     * *     * *     * *     * *     * * ] (16)
25: [ * *     * *     * *     * *     *   * *     * *     * *   * * ] (17)
26: [ * *     * *     *   * *     * *     *   * *     * *   * * ] (19)
27: [ * *     * *     *   * *     * *     * *   * *   *     * * ] (18)
28: [ * *     * *   * *   *   * *     * *   *   * *     *   * * ] (23)
29: [ * *   *   * *     *   * *   * *   *     *   * *     * ] (22)
30: [ * *   *   * *     * *   *     * *     *   * *     * *   * ] (20)
31: [ * *   *   * *     * *   *     *   * *   *     * *     *   * * ] (21)
```

Figure 23.6-A: Walsh-Paley basis. Asterisks denote the value $+1$, blank entries denote -1.

```
 3   {
 4       k = revbin(k, ld(n));
 5       for (ulong i=0; i<n; ++i)
 6       {
 7           ulong x = i & k;
 8           x = parity(x);
 9           f[i] = ( 0==x ? +1 : -1 );
10       }
11   }
```

23.7 Sequency-ordered Walsh transforms

The term corresponding to the frequency of the Fourier basis functions is the *sequency* of the Walsh functions, the number of the changes of sign of the individual functions. Note that the sequency of a signal with frequency f usually is $2f$.

To order the basis functions by their sequency, use

```
1       const ulong n = (1UL<<ldn);
2       walsh_wak(f, ldn);
3       revbin_permute(f, n);
4       inverse_gray_permute(f, n);
```

That is

$$W_w \;=\; G^{-1} R W_k = W_k R G \tag{23.7-1}$$

A function that computes the k-th basis function of the transform is [FXT: walsh/walsh-basis.h]:

```
1   template <typename Type>
```

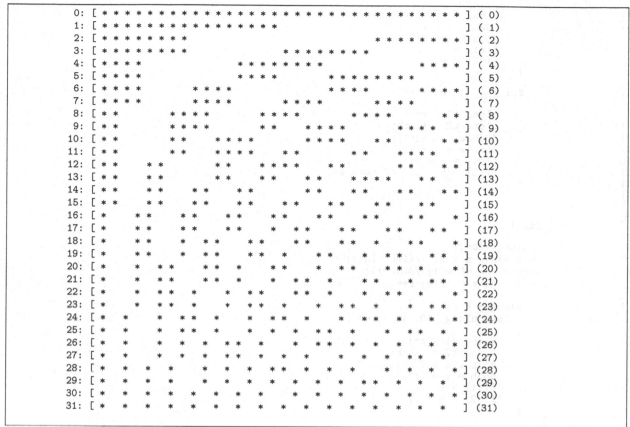

Figure 23.7-A: The Walsh-Kacmarz basis is sequency-ordered. Asterisks denote $+1$, and blanks -1.

```
2    void walsh_wal_basis(Type *f, ulong n, ulong k)
3    {
4        k = revbin(k, ld(n)+1);
5        k = gray_code(k);
6    //    // =^=
7    //    k = revbin(k, ld(n));
8    //    k = rev_gray_code(k);
9        for (ulong i=0; i<n; ++i)
10       {
11           ulong x = i & k;
12           x = parity(x);
13           f[i] = ( 0==x ? +1 : -1 );
14       }
15   }
```

A version of the transform that avoids the Gray permutation is based on [FXT: walsh/walshwal.h]

```
1    template <typename Type>
2    void walsh_wal_dif2_core(Type *f, ulong ldn)
3    // Core routine for sequency-ordered Walsh transform.
4    // Radix-2 decimation in frequency (DIF) algorithm.
5    {
6        const ulong n = (1UL<<ldn);
7        for (ulong ldm=ldn; ldm>=2; --ldm)
8        {
9            const ulong m = (1UL<<ldm);
10           const ulong mh = (m>>1);
11           const ulong m4 = (mh>>1);
12           for (ulong r=0; r<n; r+=m)
13           {
14               ulong j;
15               for (j=0; j<m4; ++j)
16               {
17                   ulong t1 = r+j;
```

```
18                              ulong t2 = t1+mh;
19                              double u = f[t1];
20                              double v = f[t2];
21                              f[t1] = u + v;
22                              f[t2] = u - v;
23                          }
24
25                          for (  ; j<mh; ++j)
26                          {
27                              ulong t1 = r+j;
28                              ulong t2 = t1+mh;
29                              double u = f[t1];
30                              double v = f[t2];
31                              f[t1] = u + v;
32                              f[t2] = v - u;   // reversed
33                          }
34                      }
35                  }
36
37          if ( ldn )
38          {
39              // ulong ldm=1;
40              const ulong m = 2; //(1UL<<ldm);
41              const ulong mh = 1; //(m>>1);
42              for (ulong r=0; r<n; r+=m)
43              {
44                  ulong j = 0;
45  //                  for (ulong j=0; j<mh; ++j)
46                  {
47                      ulong t1 = r+j;
48                      ulong t2 = t1+mh;
49                      double u = f[t1];
50                      double v = f[t2];
51                      f[t1] = u + v;
52                      f[t2] = u - v;
53                  }
54              }
55          }
56  }
```

The transform still needs the revbin permutation:

```
1    template <typename Type>
2    inline void walsh_wal(Type *f, ulong ldn)
3    {
4        revbin_permute(f, (1UL<<ldn));
5        walsh_wal_dif2_core(f, ldn);
6  //   =^=
7  //     walsh_wal_dit2_core(f, ldn);
8  //     revbin_permute(f, (1UL<<ldn));
9    }
```

A decimation in time version of the core-routine is also given in [FXT: walsh/walshwal.h]. The procedure `gray_permute()` is given in section 2.12 on page 128.

23.7.1   Even/odd ordering of sequencies

A transform with an alternative ordering of the basis functions (first even sequencies ascending, then odd sequencies descending) can be computed as follows [FXT: walsh/walshwalrev.h]:

```
1    template <typename Type>
2    inline void walsh_wal_rev(Type *f, ulong ldn)
3    {
4        revbin_permute(f, (1UL<<ldn));
5        walsh_wal_dit2_core(f, ldn);
6        // =^=
7  //     walsh_wal_dif2_core(f, ldn);
8  //     revbin_permute(f, (1UL<<ldn));
9    }
```

This implementation uses the equality

$$\overline{W}_w \;=\; R\,W_w\,R \tag{23.7-2}$$

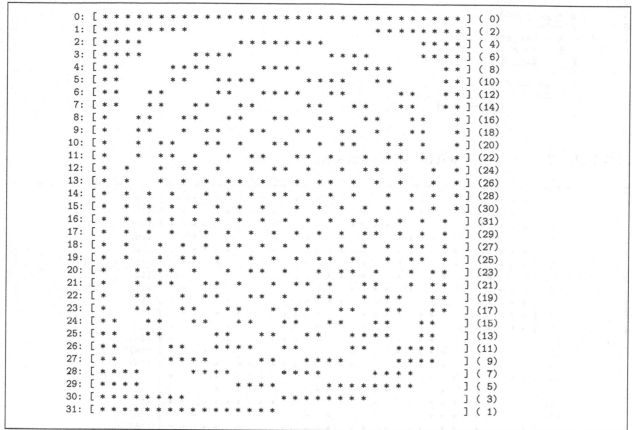

Figure 23.7-B: Basis functions for the reversed sequency-ordered Walsh transform. Asterisks denote the value $+1$, blank entries denote -1.

The same transform can be computed by either of the following sequences of statements (with n=1UL<<ldn):

```
1    { revbin_permute(f, n);  gray_permute(f, n);  walsh_wak(f, ldn); }
2    { walsh_wak(f, ldn);  inverse_gray_permute(f, n);  revbin_permute(f, n); }
3
4    { zip_rev(f, n);  walsh_wal(f, ldn); }
5    { walsh_wal(f, ldn);  unzip_rev(f, n); }
6
```

The corresponding identities are

$$\overline{W}_w \;=\; W_k\,G\,R \;=\; R\,G^{-1}\,W_k \tag{23.7-3a}$$
$$\;=\; W_w\,\overline{Z} \;=\; \overline{Z}^{-1}\,W_w \tag{23.7-3b}$$

Similar relations as for the transform with Walsh-Paley basis (23.6-1 and 23.6-2 on page 473) hold for W_w:

$$W_w \;=\; G\,W_w\,G \;=\; G^{-1}\,W_w\,G^{-1} \tag{23.7-4a}$$
$$\;=\; \overline{Z}\,W_w\,\overline{Z} \;=\; \overline{Z}^{-1}\,W_w\,\overline{Z}^{-1} \tag{23.7-4b}$$

The k-th basis function of the transform can be computed as [FXT: walsh/walsh-basis.h]:

```
1    template <typename Type>
2    void walsh_wal_rev_basis(Type *f, ulong n, ulong k)
3    {
4        k = revbin(k, ld(n));
```

```
5          k = gray_code(k);
6          // =^=
7    //      k = rev_gray_code(k);
8    //      k = revbin(k, ld(n));
9          for (ulong i=0; i<n; ++i)
10         {
11             ulong x = i & k;
12             x = parity(x);
13             f[i] = ( 0==x ? +1 : -1 );
14         }
15   }
```

23.7.2 Transforms with sequencies $n/2$ or $n/2-1$

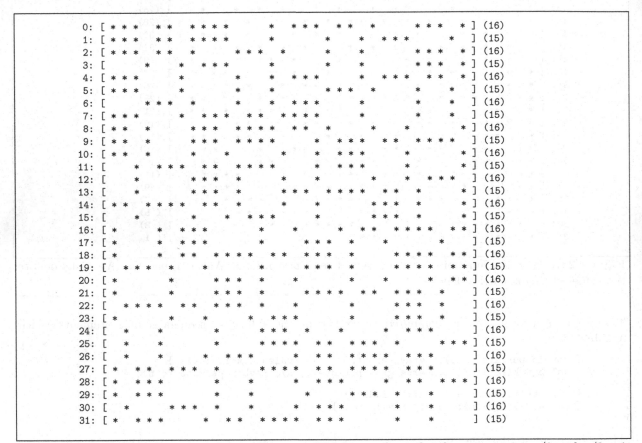

Figure 23.7-C: Basis functions for a self-inverse Walsh transform that has sequencies $n/2$ and $n/2-1$ only. Asterisks denote the value $+1$, blank entries denote -1.

The next variant of the Walsh transform has the interesting feature that the basis functions for a length-n transform have only sequencies $n/2$ and $n/2-1$ at the even and odd indices, respectively. The basis is shown in figure 23.7-C. The transform is self-inverse and can be computed via [FXT: walsh/walshq.h]

```
1    template <typename Type>
2    void walsh_q1(Type *f, ulong ldn)
3    {
4        ulong n = 1UL << ldn;
5        grs_negate(f, n);
6        walsh_gray(f, ldn);
7        revbin_permute(f, n);
8    }
```

The routine `walsh_gray()` is given in [FXT: walsh/walshgray.h]:

```
1    template <typename Type>
2    void walsh_gray(Type *f, ulong ldn)
```

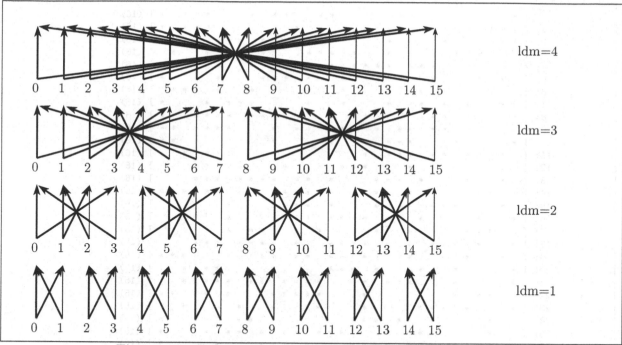

Figure 23.7-D: Data flow for the length-16 Walsh-Gray routine.

```
3    {
4        const ulong n = (1UL<<ldn);
5        for (ulong ldm=ldn; ldm>0; --ldm) // dif
6        {
7            const ulong m = (1UL<<ldm);
8            for (ulong r=0; r<n; r+=m)
9            {
10               ulong t1 = r;
11               ulong t2 = r + m - 1;
12               for (  ;  t1<t2;  ++t1,--t2)
13               {
14                   Type u = f[t1];
15                   Type v = f[t2];
16                   f[t1] = u + v;
17                   f[t2] = u - v;
18               }
19           }
20       }
21   }
```

The data flow is shown in figure 23.7-D, note how the halves of the sub-arrays are accessed in mutually reversed order.

A basis with sequencies $n/2$ for the first half of the functions and sequencies $n/2 - 1$ for the second half is shown in figure 23.7-E. The corresponding transform can be computed by [FXT: walsh/walshq.h]:

```
1    template <typename Type>
2    void walsh_q2(Type *f, ulong ldn)
3    {
4        ulong n = 1UL << ldn;
5        revbin_permute(f, n);
6        grs_negate(f, n);
7        walsh_gray(f, ldn);
8    // =^=
9    //     grs_negate(f, n);
10   //     revbin_permute(f, n);
11   //     walsh_gray(f, ldn);
12   }
```

The transform could be computed by the following statements:

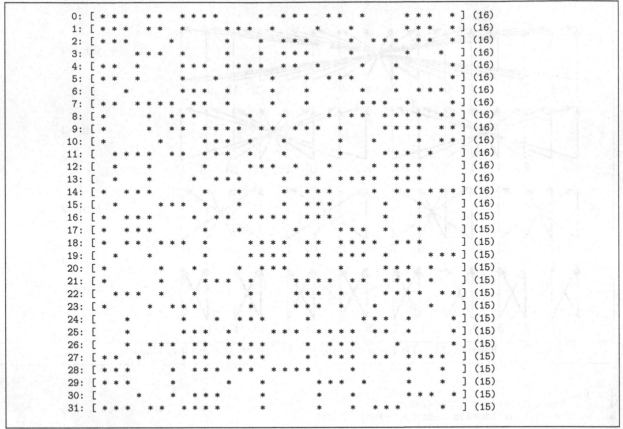

```
 0: [ * * *    * *   * * * *       *   * * *   * *   *       * * *   * ] (16)
 1: [ * * *    * *   *         * * *   *       *     *       * * *   * ] (16)
 2: [ * * *       *         *   *   * * *       *   * * *   * *   * ] (16)
 3: [       * * *   *       *       * * *       *           *     * ] (16)
 4: [ * *   *      * *   * * * *   * *   *     *     *         * ] (16)
 5: [ * *   *      *     *       *     *   * * *       *         * ] (16)
 6: [     *         * * *   *       *     *       *     *   * * * ] (16)
 7: [ * *   * * * *   * *   *       *     *       * * *   *       * ] (16)
 8: [ *         *   * * *       *     *       * *   * * * *   * * ] (16)
 9: [ *         *   * * * * *   * *   * * *   *       * * * *   * * ] (16)
10: [ *         *     * * *   *     *       *     *       *   * * ] (16)
11: [ * * * *   * *   * * *   *     *         *   * * *   * ] (16)
12: [   *     *       * * *   *       *       *   * ] (16)
13: [   *     *       *   * * *   *   * *   * * * *   * * * ] (16)
14: [ *   * * *       *     *       * * *       *   * *   * * * ] (16)
15: [   *       * * *   *     *       *   * * *       *     * ] (16)
16: [ *   * * *       *   * *   * * * *       *       * ] (15)
17: [ *   * * *       *       *       * * *   *     * ] (15)
18: [ *   * *   * * *   *       * * *   *     * * * *   * * * ] (15)
19: [   *     *         *     * * * *   *   * * *   *       * * * ] (15)
20: [ *       *     *       *   * * *       *       * * *   * ] (15)
21: [ *       *       * * *   *       * * * *   * *   * * *   * ] (15)
22: [   * * *   *     *       *   * * *         * * *   * * ] (15)
23: [ *       *   * * *       *     * * *   *       *       * ] (15)
24: [     *     *     *   * * *     *       * * *   *       * ] (15)
25: [     *       * * *   *     * * *   * * * *   * *   *       * ] (15)
26: [     *   * * *   * *   * * * *       *   * * *       *       * ] (15)
27: [ * *   *     * * *   * * * *       *   * * *   * *   * * * * ] (15)
28: [ * * *     *   * * *   * *   * * * *       *         *     * ] (15)
29: [ * * *     *       *     *       * * *   *       *     * ] (15)
30: [     *     *   * * *       *       *     *     * * *   * ] (15)
31: [ * * *   * *   * * * *     *       *     *   * * *       * ] (15)
```

Figure 23.7-E: Basis functions for a self-inverse Walsh transform (second form) that has sequencies $n/2$ and $n/2 - 1$ only. Asterisks denote the value $+1$, blank entries denote -1.

```
ulong n = 1UL << ldn;
revbin_permute(f, n);
walsh_q1(f, ldn);
revbin_permute(f, n);
```

The basis functions of the transforms can be computed as follows [FXT: walsh/walsh-basis.h]:

```
1    template <typename Type>
2    void walsh_q1_basis(Type *f, ulong n, ulong k)
3    {
4        ulong qk = (grs_negative_q(k) ? 1 : 0);
5        k = gray_code(k);
6        k = revbin(k, ld(n));
7        for (ulong i=0; i<n; ++i)
8        {
9            ulong x = i & k;
10           x = parity(x);
11           ulong qi = (grs_negative_q(i) ? 1 : 0);
12           x ^= (qk ^ qi);
13           f[i] = ( 0==x ? +1 : -1 );
14       }
15   }
```

and

```
1    template <typename Type>
2    void walsh_q2_basis(Type *f, ulong n, ulong k)
3    {
4        ulong qk = (grs_negative_q(k) ? 1 : 0);
5        k = revbin(k, ld(n));
6        k = gray_code(k);
7        for (ulong i=0; i<n; ++i)
```

```
8     {
9         ulong x = i & k;
10        x = parity(x);
11        ulong qi = (grs_negative_q(i) ? 1 : 0);
12        x ^= (qk ^ qi);
13        f[i] = ( 0==x ? +1 : -1 );
14    }
15  }
```

The function `grs_negative_q()` is described in section 1.16.5 on page 44.

23.8 XOR (dyadic) convolution

```
       XOR-convolution
    +  - 0- 1   2   3     4   5   6   7     8   9  10  11    12  13  14  15
    |
    0 : 0  1   2   3     4   5   6   7     8   9  10  11    12  13  14  15
    1 : 1  0   3   2     5   4   7   6     9   8  11  10    13  12  15  14
    2 : 2  3   0   1     6   7   4   5    10  11   8   9    14  15  12  13
    3 : 3  2   1   0     7   6   5   4    11  10   9   8    15  14  13  12

    4 : 4  5   6   7     0   1   2   3    12  13  14  15     8   9  10  11
    5 : 5  4   7   6     1   0   3   2    13  12  15  14     9   8  11  10
    6 : 6  7   4   5     2   3   0   1    14  15  12  13    10  11   8   9
    7 : 7  6   5   4     3   2   1   0    15  14  13  12    11  10   9   8

    8 : 8  9  10  11    12  13  14  15     0   1   2   3     4   5   6   7
    9 : 9  8  11  10    13  12  15  14     1   0   3   2     5   4   7   6
   10 :10 11   8   9    14  15  12  13     2   3   0   1     6   7   4   5
   11 :11 10   9   8    15  14  13  12     3   2   1   0     7   6   5   4

   12: 12 13  14  15     8   9  10  11     4   5   6   7     0   1   2   3
   13: 13 12  15  14     9   8  11  10     5   4   7   6     1   0   3   2
   14: 14 15  12  13    10  11   8   9     6   7   4   5     2   3   0   1
   15: 15 14  13  12    11  10   9   8     7   6   5   4     3   2   1   0
```

Figure 23.8-A: Semi-symbolic scheme for the XOR-convolution of two length-16 sequences.

The *dyadic convolution* of the sequences a and b is the sequence h defined by

$$h_\tau := \sum_{i\oplus j=\tau} a_i b_j \tag{23.8-1a}$$

$$= \sum_i a_i b_{i\oplus\tau} \tag{23.8-1b}$$

where the symbol '$\oplus$' stands for bit-wise XOR operator. The dyadic convolution has an XOR where the usual one has a plus, see relations 22.1-1b and 22.1-2 on page 440; it could rightfully be called *XOR-convolution*.

The semi-symbolic scheme of the convolution is shown in figure 23.8-A. The table is equivalent to the one (for cyclic convolution) given in figure 22.1-A on page 441. The dyadic convolution can be used for the multiplication of hypercomplex numbers as shown in section 39.14 on page 815.

A fast algorithm for the computation of the dyadic convolution uses the Walsh transform [FXT: walsh/dyadiccnvl.h]:

```
1   template <typename Type>
2   void dyadic_convolution(Type * restrict f, Type * restrict g, ulong ldn)
3   // Dyadic convolution (XOR-convolution):  h[] of f[] and g[]:
4   //    h[k] = sum( i XOR j == k,  f[i]*g[k] )
5   // Result is written to g[].
6   // ldn := base-2 logarithm of the array length
7   {
8       walsh_wak(f, ldn);
9       walsh_wak(g, ldn);
10      const ulong n = (1UL<<ldn);
11      for (ulong k=0; k<n; ++k)  g[k] *= f[k];
12      walsh_wak(g, ldn);
13  }
```

```
+   - 0- 1  2  3   4  5  6  7   8  9 10 11  12 13 14 15
|
0 :  0  1  2  3   4  5  6  7   8  9 10 11  12 13 14 15
1 :  1  0  3  2   5  4  7  6   9  8 11 10  13 12 15 14
2 :  2  3  0  1   6  7  4  5  10 11  8  9  14 15 12 13
3 :  3  2  1  0   7  6  5  4  11 10  9  8  15 14 13 12

4 :  4  5  6  7   0  1  2  3  12 13 14 15   8  9 10 11
5 :  5  4  7  6   1  0  3  2  13 12 15 14   9  8 11 10
6 :  6  7  4  5   2  3  0  1  14 15 12 13  10 11  8  9
7 :  7  6  5  4   3  2  1  0  15 14 13 12  11 10  9  8

8:   8  9 10 11  12 13 14 15   0- 1- 2- 3-  4- 5- 6- 7-
9:   9  8 11 10  13 12 15 14   1- 0- 3- 2-  5- 4- 7- 6-
10: 10 11  8  9  14 15 12 13   2- 3- 0- 1-  6- 7- 4- 5-
11: 11 10  9  8  15 14 13 12   3- 2- 1- 0-  7- 6- 5- 4-

12: 12 13 14 15   8  9 10 11   4- 5- 6- 7-  0- 1- 2- 3-
13: 13 12 15 14   9  8 11 10   5- 4- 7- 6-  1- 0- 3- 2-
14: 14 15 12 13  10 11  8  9   6- 7- 4- 5-  2- 3- 0- 1-
15: 15 14 13 12  11 10  9  8   7- 6- 5- 4-  3- 2- 1- 0-
```

Figure 23.8-B: Semi-symbolic scheme for the dyadic equivalent of the negacyclic convolution. Negative contributions to a bucket have a minus appended.

A scheme similar to that of the negacyclic convolution is shown in figure 23.8-B. It can be computed via

```
1        walsh_wal_dif2_core(f, ldn);   // note walsh_wal variant used
2        walsh_wal_dif2_core(g, ldn);
3        ulong n = (1UL<<ldn);
4        for (ulong i=0,j=n-1; i<j; --j,++i)  fht_mul(f[i], f[j], g[i], g[j], 0.5);
5        walsh_wal_dit2_core(g, ldn);
```

where `fht_mul()` is the operation used for the convolution with fast Hartley transforms [FXT: convolution/fhtmulsqr.h]:

```
1   template <typename Type>
2   static inline  void
3   fht_mul(Type xi, Type xj, Type &yi, Type &yj, double v)
4   // yi <-- v*( (yi + yj)*xi + (yi - yj)*xj )   == v*( (xi + xj)*yi + (xi - xj)*yj )
5   // yj <-- v*( (-yi + yj)*xi + (yi + yj)*xj )  == v*( (-xi + xj)*yi + (xi + xj)*yj )
6   {
7       Type h1p = xi,   h1m = xj;
8       Type s1 = h1p + h1m,   d1 = h1p - h1m;
9       Type h2p = yi,   h2m = yj;
10      yi = (h2p * s1 + h2m * d1) * v;
11      yj = (h2m * s1 - h2p * d1) * v;
12  }
```

23.9 Slant transform

The *slant transform* can be implemented using a Walsh Transform and just a little pre/post-processing [FXT: walsh/slant.cc]:

```
1   void slant(double *f, ulong ldn)
2   {
3       walsh_wak(f, ldn);
4
5       ulong n = 1UL<<ldn;
6       for (ulong ldm=0; ldm<ldn-1; ++ldm)
7       {
8           ulong m = 1UL<<ldm;  // m = 1, 2, 4, 8, ..., n/4
9           double N = m*2, N2 = N*N;
10          double a = sqrt(3.0*N2/(4.0*N2-1.0));
11          double b = sqrt(1.0-a*a); // == sqrt((N2-1)/(4*N2-1));
12          for (ulong j=m; j<n-1; j+=4*m)
13          {
14              ulong t1 = j;
15              ulong t2 = j + m;
16              double f1 = f[t1],   f2 = f[t2];
17              f[t1] = a * f1 - b * f2;
18              f[t2] = b * f1 + a * f2;
```

```
19              }
20          }
21      }
```

Apart from the Walsh transform only an amount of work linear with the array size has to be done: the inner loop accesses the elements in strides of 4, 8, 16, ..., 2^{n-1}.

The inverse transform is:

```
1    void inverse_slant(double *f, ulong ldn)
2    {
3        ulong n = 1UL<<ldn;
4        ulong ldm=ldn-2;
5        do
6        {
7            ulong m = 1UL<<ldm;   // m = n/4, n/2, ..., 4, 2, 1
8            double N = m*2, N2 = N*N;
9            double a = sqrt(3.0*N2/(4.0*N2-1.0));
10           double b = sqrt(1.0-a*a); // == sqrt((N2-1)/(4*N2-1));
11           for (ulong j=m; j<n-1; j+=4*m)
12           {
13               ulong t1 = j;
14               ulong t2 = j + m;
15               double f1 = f[t1],  f2 = f[t2];
16               f[t1] = b * f2 + a * f1;
17               f[t2] = a * f2 - b * f1;
18           }
19       }
20       while ( ldm-- );
21
22       walsh_wak(f, ldn);
23   }
```

A sequency-ordered version of the transform can be implemented as follows:

```
1    void slant_seq(double *f, ulong ldn)
2    {
3        slant(f, ldn);
4        ulong n = 1UL<<ldn;
5        inverse_gray_permute(f, n);
6        unzip_rev(f, n);
7        revbin_permute(f, n);
8    }
```

This implementation can be optimized by combining the involved permutations, see [345].

The inverse is computed by calling the inverse operations in reversed order:

```
1    void inverse_slant_seq(double *f, ulong ldn)
2    {
3        ulong n = 1UL<<ldn;
4        revbin_permute(f, n);
5        zip_rev(f, n);
6        gray_permute(f, n);
7        inverse_slant(f, ldn);
8    }
```

23.10 Arithmetic transform

There are two (mutually inverse) forms of the *arithmetic transform*, denoted by Y^+ and Y^-. Their basis functions are shown in figure 23.10-A.

A routine for the transforms can be obtained by simple modifications in a Walsh transform:

```
Walsh:    f[t1] = u + v;    f[t2] = u - v;
Y(+):     f[t1] = u;        f[t2] = u + v;
Y(-):     f[t1] = u    ;    f[t2] = v - u;
```

A routine for Y^+ is [FXT: walsh/arithtransform.h]:

```
1    template <typename Type>
2    void arith_transform_plus(Type *f, ulong ldn)
3    // Arithmetic Transform (positive sign).
```

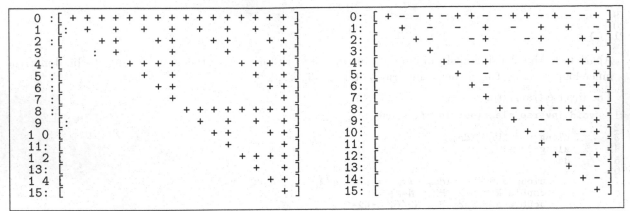

Figure 23.10-A: Basis functions for the transform Y^+ (left) and Y^- (right). The values are ± 1, or 0 (blank entries).

```
4     // Radix-2 decimation In Frequency (DIF) algorithm.
5     {
6         const ulong n = (1UL<<ldn);
7         for (ulong ldm=ldn; ldm>=1; --ldm)
8         {
9             const ulong m = (1UL<<ldm);
10            const ulong mh = (m>>1);
11            for (ulong r=0; r<n; r+=m)
12            {
13                ulong t1 = r;
14                ulong t2 = r+mh;
15                for (ulong j=0;  j<mh;  ++j, ++t1, ++t2)
16                {
17                    Type u = f[t1];
18                    Type v = f[t2];
19                    f[t1] = u;
20                    f[t2] = u + v;
21                }
22            }
23        }
24    }
25
```

The transform Y^- can be computed similarly:

```
1     template <typename Type>
2     void arith_transform_minus(Type *f, ulong ldn)
3     // Arithmetic Transform (negative sign).
4     // Radix-2 decimation In Frequency (DIF) algorithm.
5     // Inverse of arith_transform_plus().
6     {
7         [--snip--]
8                     f[t1] = u;
9                     f[t2] = v - u;
10        [--snip--]
11    }
```

The length-2 transforms can be written as

$$Y_2^+ v \;=\; \begin{bmatrix} +1 & 0 \\ +1 & +1 \end{bmatrix} \begin{bmatrix} a \\ b \end{bmatrix} = \begin{bmatrix} a \\ a+b \end{bmatrix} \tag{23.10-1a}$$

$$Y_2^- v \;=\; \begin{bmatrix} +1 & 0 \\ -1 & +1 \end{bmatrix} \begin{bmatrix} a \\ b \end{bmatrix} = \begin{bmatrix} a \\ b-a \end{bmatrix} \tag{23.10-1b}$$

In Kronecker product notation (see section 23.3 on page 462) the transforms can be written as

$$Y_n^+ = \bigotimes_{k=1}^{\log_2(n)} Y_2^+ \quad \text{where} \quad Y_2^+ = \begin{bmatrix} +1 & 0 \\ +1 & +1 \end{bmatrix} \tag{23.10-2a}$$

$$Y_n^- = \bigotimes_{k=1}^{\log_2(n)} Y_2^- \quad \text{where} \quad Y_2^- = \begin{bmatrix} +1 & 0 \\ -1 & +1 \end{bmatrix} \tag{23.10-2b}$$

The k-th element of the arithmetic transform Y^+ is

$$Y^+[a]_k = \sum_{i \subseteq k} a_i \tag{23.10-3a}$$

where $i \subseteq k$ means that the bits of i are a subset of the bits of k: $i \subseteq k \iff (i \wedge k) = i$. For the transform Y^- we have

$$Y^-[a]_k = (-1)^{p(k)} \sum_{i \subseteq k} (-1)^{p(i)} a_i = \sum_{i \subseteq k} (-1)^{p(k-i)} a_i \tag{23.10-3b}$$

where $p(x)$ is the parity of x.

23.10.1 Reversed arithmetic transform

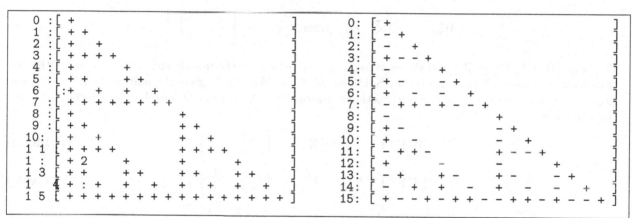

Figure 23.10-B: Basis functions for the transform B^+ (left) and B^- (right).

We define the (mutually inverse) *reversed arithmetic transforms* B^+ and B^- via

$$B_n^+ = \bigotimes_{k=1}^{\log_2(n)} B_2^+ \quad \text{where} \quad B_2^+ = \begin{bmatrix} +1 & +1 \\ 0 & +1 \end{bmatrix}, \tag{23.10-4a}$$

$$B_n^- = \bigotimes_{k=1}^{\log_2(n)} B_2^- \quad \text{where} \quad B_2^- = \begin{bmatrix} +1 & -1 \\ 0 & +1 \end{bmatrix}, \tag{23.10-4b}$$

The k-th element of the transform B^+ is

$$B^+[a]_k = \sum_{\overline{i} \subseteq \overline{k}} a_i = \sum_{k \subseteq i} a_i \tag{23.10-5}$$

where $\overline{k} = n - 1 - k$ is the complement of k: we have $e \subseteq f \iff \overline{f} \subseteq \overline{e}$.

A routine for the transform B^+ is [FXT: walsh/arithtransform.h]

```
1    template <typename Type>
2    void rev_arith_transform_plus(Type *f, ulong ldn)
3    {
4        [--snip--]
5                    f[t1] = u + v;
6                    f[t2] = v;
7        [--snip--]
8    }
```

The omitted lines are identical to the routine for Y^+. The same transform could be computed by the statements:

```
    ulong n=1UL<<ldn;
    reverse(f,n);  arith_transform_plus(f,ldn);  reverse(f,n);
```

The inverse B^- is computed as follows:

```
1    template <typename Type>
2    void rev_arith_transform_minus(Type *f, ulong ldn)
3    // Inverse of rev_arith_transform_plus().
4    {
5        [--snip--]
6                    f[t1] = u - v;
7                    f[t2] = v;
8        [--snip--]
9    }
```

23.10.2   Conversion to and from the Walsh transform ‡

To establish the relation to the Walsh transform recall that its decomposition as a Kronecker product is

$$W_n = \bigotimes_{k=1}^{\log_2(n)} W_2 \quad \text{where} \quad W_2 = \begin{bmatrix} +1 & +1 \\ +1 & -1 \end{bmatrix} \tag{23.10-6}$$

We have $(W\,Y^+)\,Y^- = W$, and the expression in parentheses is the matrix that converts the arithmetic transform Y^- to the Walsh transform. Similarly, $(\frac{1}{2}\,Y^+\,W)\,W = Y^+$, gives the matrix for the conversion from the Walsh transform to the arithmetic transform Y^+. We only need length-2 transforms to obtain the conversions:

$$(W\,Y^+)\,Y^- = W = \begin{bmatrix} +2 & +1 \\ 0 & -1 \end{bmatrix} Y^- \tag{23.10-7a}$$

$$(W\,Y^-)\,Y^+ = W = \begin{bmatrix} 0 & +1 \\ +2 & -1 \end{bmatrix} Y^+ \tag{23.10-7b}$$

$$\left(\frac{1}{2}Y^-\,W\right)W = Y^- = \frac{1}{2}\begin{bmatrix} +1 & +1 \\ 0 & -2 \end{bmatrix} W \tag{23.10-7c}$$

$$\left(\frac{1}{2}Y^+\,W\right)W = Y^+ = \frac{1}{2}\begin{bmatrix} +1 & +1 \\ +2 & 0 \end{bmatrix} W \tag{23.10-7d}$$

The Kronecker product of the given matrices gives the converting transform. For example, using relation 23.10-7a, define

$$T_n := \bigotimes_{k=1}^{\log_2(n)} \begin{bmatrix} +2 & +1 \\ 0 & -1 \end{bmatrix} \tag{23.10-8}$$

Then T_n converts an arithmetic transform Y^- to a Walsh transform: $W_n = T_n\,Y_n^-$. The relations between the arithmetic transform, the Reed-Muller transform, and the Walsh transform are treated in [330].

23.11   Reed-Muller transform

The *Reed-Muller transform* is obtained from the arithmetic transform by working modulo 2: replace all + and − by XOR. The transform is self-inverse, its basis functions are identical to those of the arithmetic transform Y^+, shown in figure 23.10-A on page 484. An implementation is [FXT: walsh/reedmuller.h]:

```
1    template <typename Type>
2    void word_reed_muller_dif2(Type *f, ulong ldn)
3    // Reed-Muller Transform.
4    // Radix-2 decimation in frequency (DIF) algorithm.
5    // Self-inverse.
6    // Type must have the XOR operator.
7    {
8        const ulong n = (1UL<<ldn);
9        for (ulong ldm=ldn; ldm>=1; --ldm)
10       {
11           const ulong m = (1UL<<ldm);
12           const ulong mh = (m>>1);
13           for (ulong r=0; r<n; r+=m)
14           {
15               ulong t1 = r;
16               ulong t2 = r+mh;
17               for (ulong j=0;  j<mh;  ++j, ++t1, ++t2)
18               {
19                   Type u = f[t1];
20                   Type v = f[t2];
21                   f[t1] = u;
22                   f[t2] = u ^ v;
23               }
24           }
25       }
26   }
```

As given, the transforms work word-wise. A version for the bit-wise transform is

```
1    template <typename Type>
2    inline void bit_reed_muller(Type *f, ulong ldn)
3    {
4        word_reed_muller_dif2(f, ldn);
5        ulong n = 1UL << ldn;
6        for (ulong k=0; k<n; ++k)  f[k] = yellow_code(f[k]);
7    }
```

The `yellow_code()` (see section 1.19 on page 49) may also be applied before the main loop. In fact, the yellow code *is* the Reed-Muller transform on a binary word.

The other 'color-transforms' of section 1.19 lead to variants of the Reed-Muller transform, the blue code gives another self-inverse transform, the red code and the green code give transforms R and E so that

$$RRR \;=\; \text{id}, \qquad R^{-1} = RR = E \tag{23.11-1a}$$

$$EEE \;=\; \text{id}, \qquad E^{-1} = EE = R \tag{23.11-1b}$$

$$RE \;=\; ER = \text{id} \tag{23.11-1c}$$

As can be seen from the matrix relations 1.19-12c ... 1.19-12f on page 55, the four transforms are obtained by the following replacements:

```
Walsh:    f[t1] = u + v;     f[t2] = u - v;
    B:    f[t1] = u ^ v;     f[t2] = v;      (reversed Reed-Muller transform)
    Y:    f[t1] = u;         f[t2] = u ^ v;  (Reed-Muller transform)
    R:    f[t1] = v;         f[t2] = u ^ v;
    E:    f[t1] = u ^ v;     f[t2] = u;
```

The basis functions of the transforms are shown in figure 23.11-A.

For example, if we make the following changes in the routines `walsh_wak_dit2()` in the file [FXT: walsh/walshwak2.h], we obtain a Reed-Muller transform:

```
Walsh: f[t1] = u + v;  =-->  Reed-Muller: f[t1] = u;
Walsh: f[t2] = u - v;  =-->  Reed-Muller: f[t2] = u ^ v;
```

For the decimation in time algorithm, make the very same changes in `walsh_wak_dit2()`.

The replacements for the *reversed Reed-Muller transform* are:

```
Walsh: f[t1] = u + v;  =-->  reversed Reed-Muller: f[t1] = u ^ v;
Walsh: f[t2] = u - v;  =-->  reversed Reed-Muller: f[t2] = v;
```

```
        blue              yellow              red               green
   rev. Reed Muller     Reed Muller
1...............     1111111111111111    1111111111111111    ...............1
11..............     .1.1.1.1.1.1.1.1    1.1.1.1.1.1.1.1.    ..............11
1.1.............     ..11..11..11..11    11..11..11..11..    .............1.1
1111............     ....1111....1111    1111....1111....    ............1111
1...1...........     ....1....1....1.1   1111....1111....    ...........1...1
11..11..........     ....1.1....1.1.1    1.1....1.1.1....    ..........11..11
1.1..1.1........     .......11...11..11  11..11..11..        .........1.1..1.1
11111111........     .......1.......1    1.......1.......    ........11111111
1......1........     ........11111111    11111111........    .......1......1
11.....11.......     .........1.1....1.1  1.1.1.1........     ......11.....11
1.1....1.1......     ..........11...11   11..11..........    .....1.1....1.1
1111...1111.....     ...........1...1.1  1111..........      ....1111...1111
11..11..11..11..     ............1...1   1...1...........    ...11..11..11..11
1.1.1.1.1.1.1.1.     ..............1.1   1.1.............     ..1.1.1.1.1.1.1.1
1111111111111111     ...............1    11..............    .1111111111111111
```

Figure 23.11-A: Basis functions of the length-16 blue, yellow, red, and green transforms.

The symbolic powering idea from section 1.19 on page 49 leads to transforms with the following bases (using length-8 arrays and the yellow code):

```
1.......  1...1...  1.1.....  1.1.1.1.  11......  11..11..  1111....  11111111
.1......  .1...1..  .1.1....  .1.1.1.1  .1......  .11..11.  .111....  .1.11.11
..1.....  ..1...1.  ..1.1...  ..1.1.1.  ..11....  ...11..1  ..11....  ...11.11
...1....  ...1...1  ...1.1..  ...1.1.1  ...1....  ....11..  ...1111.  ....1111
....1...  ....1...  ....1.1.  ....1.1.  ....11..  ....1..1  ....1111  ....1.11
.....1..  .....1..  .....1.1  .....1.1  .....1..  .....11.  .....111  .....111
......1.  ......1.  ......1.  ......1.  ......11  ......11  ......11  ......1.11
.......1  .......1  .......1  .......1  .......1  .......1  .......1  .......1
   x=0       x=1       x=2       x=3       x=4       x=5       x=6       x=7
```

The program [FXT: bits/bitxtransforms-demo.cc] gives the matrices for 64-bit words.

A function that computes the k-th basis function of the transform is [FXT: walsh/reedmuller.h]:

```
1    template <typename Type>
2    inline void reed_muller_basis(Type *f, ulong n, ulong k)
3    {
4        for (ulong i=0; i<n; ++i)
5        {
6            f[i] = ( (i & k)==k ? +1 : 0 );  // is k a subset of i (as bitset)?
7        }
8    }
```

Functions that are the word-wise equivalents of the Gray code are given in [FXT: aux1/wordgray.h]:

```
1    template <typename Type>
2    void word_gray(Type *f, ulong n)
3    {
4        for (ulong k=0;  k<n-1;  ++k)  f[k] ^= f[k+1];
5    }
```

and

```
1    void inverse_word_gray(Type *f, ulong n)
2    {
3        ulong x = 0,  k = n;
4        while ( k-- )  { x ^= f[k];  f[k] = x; }
5    }
```

As one might suspect, these are related to the Reed-Muller transform. Writing Y ('yellow') for the Reed-Muller transform, g for the word-wise Gray code and S_k for the cyclic shift by k words (word zero is moved to position k) we have

$$Y\,S_{+1}\,Y \;=\; g \tag{23.11-2a}$$

$$Y\,S_{-1}\,Y \;=\; g^{-1} \tag{23.11-2b}$$

$$Y\,S_k\,Y \;=\; g^k \tag{23.11-2c}$$

These are exactly the relations 1.19-10a ... 1.19-10c on page 53 for the bit-wise transforms.

The power of the word-wise Gray code is equivalent to the bit-wise version:

```
1    template <typename Type>
2    void word_gray_pow(Type *f, ulong n, ulong x)
3    {
4        for (ulong s=1; s<n; s*=2)
5        {
6            if ( x & 1 )
7            {
8                // word_gray ** s:
9                for (ulong k=0, j=k+s;  j<n;  ++k,++j)  f[k] ^= f[j];
10           }
11           x >>= 1;
12       }
13   }
```

Let e be the reversed Gray code operator, then we have for the reversed Reed-Muller transform B:

$$B\,S_{+1}\,B \;=\; e^{-1} \tag{23.11-3a}$$

$$B\,S_{-1}\,B \;=\; e \tag{23.11-3b}$$

$$B\,S_k\,B \;=\; e^{-k} \tag{23.11-3c}$$

Further,

$$E\,S_k\,R \;=\; e^k \tag{23.11-4a}$$

$$E\,e^k\,R \;=\; S_k \tag{23.11-4b}$$

The transforms as Kronecker products (all operations are modulo 2):

$$B_n \;=\; \bigotimes_{k=1}^{\log_2(n)} B_2 \quad \text{where} \quad B_2 = \begin{bmatrix} 1 & 1 \\ 0 & 1 \end{bmatrix} \tag{23.11-5a}$$

$$Y_n \;=\; \bigotimes_{k=1}^{\log_2(n)} Y_2 \quad \text{where} \quad Y_2 = \begin{bmatrix} 1 & 0 \\ 1 & 1 \end{bmatrix} \tag{23.11-5b}$$

$$R_n \;=\; \bigotimes_{k=1}^{\log_2(n)} R_2 \quad \text{where} \quad R_2 = \begin{bmatrix} 0 & 1 \\ 1 & 1 \end{bmatrix} \tag{23.11-5c}$$

$$E_n \;=\; \bigotimes_{k=1}^{\log_2(n)} E_2 \quad \text{where} \quad E_2 = \begin{bmatrix} 1 & 1 \\ 1 & 0 \end{bmatrix} \tag{23.11-5d}$$

23.12 The OR-convolution and the AND-convolution

Let a and b be sequences of length a power of 2. We define the *OR-convolution* h of a and b as

$$h_\tau \;=\; \sum_{i \vee j = \tau} a_i\, b_j \tag{23.12-1}$$

where $\vee$ denotes bit-wise OR. The symbolic table for the OR-convolution is shown in figure 23.12-A (see figure 22.1-A on page 441 for an explanation of the scheme). The OR-convolution can be computed via

```
1    template <typename Type>
2    inline void slow_or_convolution(const Type *f, const Type *g, ulong ldn, Type *h)
3    // Compute the OR-convolution h[] of f[] and g[]:
4    //   h[k] = sum(i | j == k,  f[i]*g[j])
5    // Result written to h[].
6    {
7        const ulong n = 1UL << ldn;
8        for (ulong j=0; j<n; ++j)  h[j] = 0;
9        for (ulong i=0; i<n; ++i)
10           for (ulong j=0; j<n; ++j)
11               h[i|j] += f[i] * g[j];
12   }
```

```
                OR-convolution
        +  - 0- 1  2  3    4  5  6  7    8  9 10 11   12 13 14 15
        |
        0 :  0  1  2  3    4  5  6  7    8  9 10 11   12 13 14 15
        1 :  1  1  3  3    5  5  7  7    9  9 11 11   13 13 15 15
        2:   2  3  2  3    6  7  6  7   10 11 10 11   14 15 14 15
        3:   3  3  3  3    7  7  7  7   11 11 11 11   15 15 15 15

        4:   4  5  6  7    4  5  6  7   12 13 14 15   12 13 14 15
        5:   5  5  7  7    5  5  7  7   13 13 15 15   13 13 15 15
        6:   6  7  6  7    6  7  6  7   14 15 14 15   14 15 14 15
        7:   7  7  7  7    7  7  7  7   15 15 15 15   15 15 15 15

        8:   8  9 10 11   12 13 14 15    8  9 10 11   12 13 14 15
        9:   9  9 11 11   13 13 15 15    9  9 11 11   13 13 15 15
       10:  10 11 10 11   14 15 14 15   10 11 10 11   14 15 14 15
       11:  11 11 11 11   15 15 15 15   11 11 11 11   15 15 15 15

       12:  12 13 14 15   12 13 14 15   12 13 14 15   12 13 14 15
       13:  13 13 15 15   13 13 15 15   13 13 15 15   13 13 15 15
       14:  14 15 14 15   14 15 14 15   14 15 14 15   14 15 14 15
       15:  15 15 15 15   15 15 15 15   15 15 15 15   15 15 15 15


                AND-convolution
        +  - 0- 1  2  3    4  5  6  7    8  9 10 11   12 13 14 15
        |
        0 :  0  0  0  0    0  0  0  0    0  0  0  0    0  0  0  0
        1 :  0  1  0  1    0  1  0  1    0  1  0  1    0  1  0  1
        2 :  0  0  2  2    0  0  2  2    0  0  2  2    0  0  2  2
        3 :  0  1  2  3    0  1  2  3    0  1  2  3    0  1  2  3

        4 :  0  0  0  0    4  4  4  4    0  0  0  0    4  4  4  4
        5 :  0  1  0  1    4  5  4  5    0  1  0  1    4  5  4  5
        6 :  0  0  2  2    4  4  6  6    0  0  2  2    4  4  6  6
        7 :  0  1  2  3    4  5  6  7    0  1  2  3    4  5  6  7

        8 :  0  0  0  0    0  0  0  0    8  8  8  8    8  8  8  8
        9 :  0  1  0  1    0  1  0  1    8  9  8  9    8  9  8  9
       1 0  0  0  2  2    0  0  2  2    8  8 10 10    8  8 10 10
       1 1  0  1  2  3    0  1  2  3    8  9 10 11    8  9 10 11

       1 2  0  0  0  0    4  4  4  4    8  8  8  8   12 12 12 12
       1 3  0  1  0  1    4  5  4  5    8  9  8  9   12 13 12 13
       14:  0  0  2  2    4  4  6  6    8  8 10 10   12 12 14 14
       15:  0  1  2  3    4  5  6  7    8  9 10 11   12 13 14 15
```

Figure 23.12-A: Semi-symbolic scheme for the OR-convolution (top) and the AND-convolution (bottom) of two length-16 sequences.

The following relation is the key to the fast computation of the OR-convolution:

$$h \;=\; Y^{-}\left[\,Y^{+}[a] \cdot Y^{+}[b]\,\right] \tag{23.12-2}$$

Here Y^{+} and Y^{-} denote the arithmetic transforms given in section 23.10 on page 483. An implementation is [FXT: walsh/or-convolution.h]:

```
1    template <typename Type>
2    inline void or_convolution(Type * restrict f, Type * restrict g, ulong ldn)
3    {
4        arith_transform_plus(f, ldn);
5        arith_transform_plus(g, ldn);
6        const ulong n = (1UL<<ldn);
7        for (ulong k=0; k<n; ++k)  g[k] *= f[k];
8        arith_transform_minus(g, ldn);
9    }
```

Define the *AND-convolution* h of two sequences a and b as

$$h_{\tau} \;=\; \sum_{i \wedge j = \tau} a_i \, b_j \tag{23.12-3}$$

where $\wedge$ denotes the bit-wise AND. The symbolic scheme is shown in figure 23.12-A. The AND-convolution can be computed as

```
1    template <typename Type>
2    inline void slow_and_convolution(const Type *f, const Type *g, ulong ldn, Type *h)
3    // Compute the AND-convolution h[] of f[] and g[]:
4    //   h[k] = sum(i & j == k,   f[i]*g[j])
5    // Result written to h[].
6    {
7        const ulong n = 1UL << ldn;
8        for (ulong j=0; j<n; ++j)  h[j] = 0;
9        for (ulong i=0; i<n; ++i)
10           for (ulong j=0; j<n; ++j)
11               h[i&j] += f[i] * g[j];
12   }
```

The key to fast computation is the following relation:

$$h = B^- \left[B^+[a] \cdot B^+[b] \right] \tag{23.12-4}$$

Here B^+ and B^- denote the reversed arithmetic transforms. The implementation of the AND-convolution is [FXT: walsh/and-convolution.h]:

```
1    template <typename Type>
2    inline void and_convolution(Type * restrict f, Type * restrict g, ulong ldn)
3    {
4        rev_arith_transform_plus(f, ldn);
5        rev_arith_transform_plus(g, ldn);
6        const ulong n = (1UL<<ldn);
7        for (ulong k=0; k<n; ++k)  g[k] *= f[k];
8        rev_arith_transform_minus(g, ldn);
9    }
```

23.13 The MAX-convolution ‡

```
+   - 0- 1  2  3   4  5  6  7
|
0  :  0  1  2  3   4  5  6  7
1  :  1  1  2  3   4  5  6  7
2  :  2  2  2  3   4  5  6  7
3  :  3  3  3  3   4  5  6  7

4  :  4  4  4  4   4  5  6  7
5  :  5  5  5  5   5  5  6  7
6  :  6  6  6  6   6  6  6  7
7  :  7  7  7  7   7  7  7  7
```

Figure 23.13-A: Semi-symbolic scheme for the MAX-convolution of two length-8 sequences.

Let a and b be sequences of length n (not necessarily a power of 2). We define the *MAX-convolution* h of a and b as

$$h_\tau = \sum_{\max(i,j)=\tau} a_i b_j \tag{23.13-1}$$

The computation by definition involves $O(n^2)$ operations [FXT: walsh/max-convolution.h]:

```
1    template <typename Type>
2    inline void slow_max_convolution(const Type *f, const Type *g, ulong n, Type *h)
3    // Compute the MAX-convolution h[] of f[] and g[]:
4    //   h[k] = sum( max(i,j) == k,   f[i]*g[j])
5    // Result written to h[].
6    {
7        for (ulong j=0; j<n; ++j)  h[j] = 0;
8        for (ulong i=0; i<n; ++i)
9            for (ulong j=0; j<n; ++j)
10               h[ max2(i,j) ] += f[i] * g[j];
11   }
```

Duraid Madina [priv. comm.] asks whether the MAX-convolution can be computed faster than $O(n^2)$. Indeed, the structure (see figure 23.13-A) is so simple that it can be computed in linear time:

```
1    template <typename Type>
2    inline void max_convolution(const Type *f, const Type *g, ulong n, Type *h)
3    {
4        Type sf=0,  sg=0;   // cumulative sums
5        for (ulong k=0; k<n; ++k)
6        {
7            h[k] = f[k]*g[k] + sf*g[k] + sg*f[k];
8            sf += f[k];
9            sg += g[k];
10       }
11   }
```

23.14 Weighted arithmetic transform and subset convolution

23.14.1 The weighted arithmetic transform

```
[ w^0 w^1 w^1 w^2 w^1 w^2 w^2 w^3 w^1 w^2 w^2 w^3 w^2 w^3 w^3 w^4 ]

[  .  w^1  .  w^2  .  w^2  .  w^3  .  w^2  .  w^3  .  w^3  .  w^4 ]

[  .   .  w^1 w^2  .   .  w^2 w^3  .   .  w^2 w^3  .   .  w^3 w^4 ]

[  .   .   .  w^2  .   .   .  w^3  .   .   .  w^3  .   .   .  w^4 ]

[  .   .   .   .  w^1 w^2 w^2 w^3  .   .   .   .  w^2 w^3 w^3 w^4 ]

[  .   .   .   .   .  w^2  .  w^3  .   .   .   .   .  w^3  .  w^4 ]

[  .   .   .   .   .   .  w   ŵ 3 2.   .   .   .   .   . w^3 w^4 ]

[  .   .   .   .   .   .   .  w 3 ^.   .   .   .   .   .   .  w^4 ]

[  .   .   .   .   .   .   .   .  w^1 w^2 w^2 w^3 w^2 w^3 w^3 w^4 ]

[  .   .   .   .   .   .   .   .   .  w^2  .  w^3  .  w^3  .  w^4 ]

[  .   .   .   .   .   .   .   .   .   .  w^2 w^3  .   .  w^3 w^4 ]

[  .   .   .   .   .   .   .   .   .   .   .  w^3  .   .   .  w^4 ]

[  .   .   .   .   .   .   .   .   .   .   .   .  w^2 w^3 w^3 w^4 ]

[  .   .   .   .   .   .   .   .   .   .   .   .   .  w^3  .  w^4 ]

[  .   .   .   .   .   .   .   .   .   .   .   .   .   .  w^3 w^4 ]

[  .   .   .   .   .   .   .   .   .   .   .   .   .   .   .  w^4 ]
```

Figure 23.14-A: Basis for the weighted arithmetic transform Y^+, dots denote zeros.

We define the *weighted arithmetic transform* Y^+ and its inverse Y^- as

$$Y_n^+ \;=\; \bigotimes_{k=1}^{\log_2(n)} Y_2^+ \quad \text{where} \quad Y_2^+ = \begin{bmatrix} +1 & 0 \\ +1 & +\omega \end{bmatrix} \tag{23.14-1a}$$

$$Y_n^- \;=\; \bigotimes_{k=1}^{\log_2(n)} Y_2^- \quad \text{where} \quad Y_2^- = \begin{bmatrix} +1 & 0 \\ -1/\omega & +1/\omega \end{bmatrix} \tag{23.14-1b}$$

The k-th element of the weighted arithmetic Y^+ transform is

$$Y^+[a]_k \;=\; \sum_{i \subseteq k} \omega^{c(i)} \, a_i \tag{23.14-2a}$$

where $i \subseteq k$ means that the bits of i are a subset of the bits of k, and $c(i)$ is the number of ones in the binary expansion of i. For the transform Y^- we have

$$Y^-[a]_k \;=\; \omega^{-c(k)} \sum_{i \subseteq k} (-1)^{p(k-i)} \, a_i \;=\; (-\omega)^{-c(k)} \sum_{i \subseteq k} (-1)^{p(i)} \, a_i \tag{23.14-2b}$$

where $p(x)$ is the parity of x. The basis functions are shown in figure 23.14-A. Note that the power of ω is identical for each column. The pattern is

```
0   1   1   2   1   2   2   3   1   2   2   3   2   3   3   4 ...
```

This is the sequence of the number of ones in the binary expansions of the natural numbers, entry A000120 in [312]. We can compute the parity transform of f by first multiplying the sequence

```
w^0  w^1  w^1  w^2  w^1  w^2  w^2  w^3  w^1  w^2  w^2  w^3  w^2  w^3  w^3  w^4 ...
```

element-wise to f and then use the (unweighted) transform Y^+ [FXT: walsh/weighted-arithtransform.h]:

```
1   template <typename Type>
2   void arith_transform_plus(Type *f, ulong ldn, Type w)
3   // Weighted arithmetic transform (positive sign).
4   {
5       if ( w!=(Type)1 )  bit_count_weight(f, ldn, w);
6       arith_transform_plus(f, ldn);
7   }
```

The routine for the multiplications with powers of ω is [FXT: walsh/bitcount-weight.h]:

```
1   template <typename Type>
2   void bit_count_weight(Type *f, ulong ldn, Type w)
3   // Multiply f[i] by w**bitcount(i).
4   {
5       ALLOCA(Type, pw, ldn+1);  // powers of w
6       pw[0] = (Type)1;
7       for (ulong j=1; j<=ldn; ++j)  pw[j] = w * pw[j-1];
8       const ulong n = (1UL<<ldn);
9       for (ulong j=1; j<n; ++j)  f[j] *= pw[ bit_count(j) ];
10  }
```

To compute the inverse transform, use

```
1   template <typename Type>
2   void arith_transform_minus(Type *f, ulong ldn, Type w)
3   // Weighted arithmetic transform (negative sign).
4   // Inverse of (weighted) arith_transform_plus().
5   {
6       arith_transform_minus(f, ldn);
7       if ( w!=(Type)1 )  bit_count_weight(f, ldn, 1.0/w);
8   }
```

23.14.2 Subset convolution

We want to compute the *subset convolution* s of the sequences a and b, defined as

$$s_\tau = \sum_{i\vee j=\tau,\ i\wedge j=0} a_i b_j \qquad (23.14\text{-}3)$$

The definition is similar to the OR-convolution, but the condition $i \wedge j = 0$ (no intersecting subsets) makes matters more complicated. Figure 23.14-B shows the symbolic scheme, note that many products $a_i b_j$ do not appear at all in the subset convolution. The total number of products $a_i b_j$ is N^3 for N a power of 2. It may seem that computing fewer products (than N^4, as with the OR-convolution) would allow for a method even cheaper than $O(N \log N)$, but no such scheme is known. We develop a method that is $O(N (\log N)^2)$.

Define the *weighted OR-convolution* $h(\omega)$ of a and b as

$$h(\omega)_\tau = \sum_{i\vee j=\tau} \omega^{c(i\wedge j)} a_i b_j \qquad (23.14\text{-}4)$$

The symbolic table for the convolution with $\omega = -1$ is shown in figure 23.14-C. The positive entries appear where the basis of the Walsh transform is positive, see figure 23.1-A on page 459. We can compute the weighted OR-convolution by definition [FXT: walsh/weighted-or-convolution.h]:

```
template <typename Type>
inline void slow_weighted_or_convolution(const Type *f, const Type *g, ulong ldn,
```

```
[ 0  1  2  3  4  5  6  7  8  9 10 11 12 13 14 15 ]
[ 1  .  3  .  5  .  7  .  9  . 11  . 13  . 15  . ]
[ 2  3  .  .  6  7  .  . 10 11  .  . 14 15  .  . ]
[ 3  .  .  .  7  .  .  . 11  .  .  . 15  .  .  . ]
[ 4  5  6  7  .  .  .  . 12 13 14 15  .  .  .  . ]
[ 5  .  7  .  .  .  .  . 13  . 15  .  .  .  .  . ]
[ 6  7  .  .  .  .  .  . 14 15  .  .  .  .  .  . ]
[ 7  .  .  .  .  .  .  . 15  .  .  .  .  .  .  . ]
[ 8  9  1  0 12 13 1  45  .  .  .  .  .  .  .  . ]
[ 9  . 1  1. 1  3. 15  .  .  .  .  .  .  .  .  . ]
[  1110  .  . 14 15  .  .  .  .  .  .  .  .  .  . ]
[  1 .1  .  . 1  5.  .  .  .  .  .  .  .  .  .  . ]
[  113214 15  .  .  .  .  .  .  .  .  .  .  .  . ]
[  1 .31  5.  .  .  .  .  .  .  .  .  .  .  .  . ]
[  1154  .  .  .  .  .  .  .  .  .  .  .  .  .  . ]
[  1 .5  .  .  .  .  .  .  .  .  .  .  .  .  .  . ]
```

Figure 23.14-B: Semi-symbolic scheme for the subset convolution. Dots denote unused products.

```
    weighted (w=-1) OR-convolution, positive entries:
  +  - 0- 1  2  3  4  5  6  7   8  9 10 11 12 13 14 15
  |
  0  : 0  1  2  3  4  5  6  7   8  9 10 11 12 13 14 15
  1  : 1  .  3  .  5  .  7  .   9  . 11  . 13  . 15  .
  2  : 2  3  .  .  6  7  .  .  10 11  .  . 14 15  .  .
  3  : 3  .  .  3  7  .  .  7  11  .  . 11 15  .  . 15
  4  : 4  5  6  7  .  .  .  .  12 13 14 15  .  .  .  .
  5  : 5  .  7  .  .  5  .  7  13  . 15  .  . 13  . 15
  6  : 6  7  .  .  .  .  6  7  14 15  .  .  .  . 14 15
  7  : 7  .  .  7  .  7  7  .  15  .  . 15  . 15 15  .

  8  : 8  9  1  0 12 13 1  4  5   .  .  9  . 11  . 13  . 15
  9  : 9  .  1  1. 13  . 1  5.   .  9  . 11  . 13  . 15
 10:  10 11  .  . 14 15  .      . 10 11  .  . 14 15
 11:  11  .  . 11 15  .  . 15   . 11 11  .  . 15 15
 12:  12 13 14 15  .  .  .      . 13  . 15 12 13 14 15
 13:  13  . 15  .  . 13  . 15   . 13  . 15 13  . 15  .
 14:  14 15  .  .  . 14 15      . 14 15 14 15  .  . 14 15
 15:  15  .  . 15  . 15 15  .   . 15 15  . 15  .  . 15
```

```
    weighted (w=-1) OR-convolution, negative entries:
  +  - 0- 1  2  3  4  5  6  7   8  9 10 11 12 13 14 15
  |
  0  :  .
  1  :  .  .  1  .  3  .  5  .  7   .  9  . 11  . 13  . 15
  2  :  .  .  3  2  3  .  .  6  7   .  . 10 11  .  . 14 15
  3  :  .  3  3  .  .  7  7  7   . 11 11  .  . 15 15
  4  :  .  .  .  4  5  6  7  .   . 13  . 15 12 13 14 15
  5  :  .  5  .  7  5  .  7  .   . 13  . 15 13  . 15  .
  6  :  .  7  6  7  6  7  .  7   . 14 15 14 15  .  . 15
  7  :  .  7  7  .  7  .  .  7   . 15 15  . 15  .  . 15

  8  :  .                       8  9 10 11 12 13 14 15
  9  :  .  9  .  1  1. 13  . 1  5 9 11  . 13  . 15  .
 10:  .  . 10 11  .  . 14 15 10 11  .  . 14 15
 11:  . 11 11  .  . 15 15 11   .  . 11 15  .  . 15
 12:  .  . 12 13 14 15 12 13 14 15  .  . 13  . 15
 13:  . 13  . 15 13  . 15  . 13  . 15  .  . 13  . 15
 14:  . 14 15 14 15  .  . 14 15  .  .  . 14 15
 15:  . 15 15  . 15  . 15 15  . 15  . 15 15  .
```

Figure 23.14-C: Semi-symbolic scheme for the weighted OR-convolution with $\omega = -1$, separated into positive (top) and negative (bottom) entries.

```
      Type *h, Type w)
// Compute the weighted OR-convolution h[] of f[] and g[]:
//   h[k] = sum(i | j == k,  f[i]*g[j] * (w)**bitcount(i&j))
// Result written to h[].
{
    ALLOCA(Type, pw, ldn+1);   // powers of w
    pw[0] = (Type)1;
    for (ulong j=1; j<=ldn; ++j)  pw[j] = w * pw[j-1];
    const ulong n = 1UL << ldn;
    for (ulong j=0; j<n; ++j)  h[j] = 0;
    for (ulong i=0; i<n; ++i)
        for (ulong j=0; j<n; ++j)
            h[i|j] += f[i] * g[j] * pw[ bit_count( i & j ) ];
}
```

A fast algorithm is based on the relation

$$h(\omega) \;=\; Y^{-}\left[Y^{+}[a] \cdot Y^{+}[b]\right] \tag{23.14-5}$$

Here is the implementation:

```
1    template <typename Type>
2    inline void weighted_or_convolution(Type * restrict f, Type * restrict g, ulong ldn, Type w)
3    {
4        arith_transform_plus(f, ldn, w);
5        arith_transform_plus(g, ldn, w);
6        const ulong n = (1UL<<ldn);
7        for (ulong k=0; k<n; ++k)  g[k] *= f[k];
8        arith_transform_minus(g, ldn, w);
9    }
```

```
[ .   .   .   .   .   .   .   .                 ]
[ .  1  .  1  .  1  .  1  .  1  .  1  .  1  .  1 ]
[ .  .  1  1  .  .  1  1  .  .  1  1  .  .  1  1 ]
[ .  1  1  2  .  1  1  2  .  1  1  2  .  1  1  2 ]
[ .  .  .  .  1  1  1  1  .  .  .  .  1  1  1  1 ]
[ .  1  .  1  1  2  1  2  .  1  .  1  1  2  1  2 ]
[ .  .  1  1  1  1  2  2  .  .  1  1  1  1  2  2 ]
[ .  1  1  2  1  2  2  3  .  1  1  2  1  2  2  3 ]
[ .  .  .  .  .  .  .  .  1  1  1  1  1  1  1  1 ]
[ .  1  .  1  .  1  .  1  1  2  1  2  1  2  1  2 ]
[ .  .  1  1  .  .  1  1  1  1  2  2  1  1  2  2 ]
[ .  1  1  2  .  1  1  2  1  2  2  3  1  2  2  3 ]
[ .  .  .  .  1  1  1  1  1  1  1  1  2  2  2  2 ]
[ .  1  .  1  1  2  1  2  1  2  1  2  2  3  2  3 ]
[ .  .  1  1  1  1  2  2  1  1  2  2  2  2  3  3 ]
[ .  1  1  2  1  2  2  3  1  2  2  3  2  3  3  4 ]
```

Figure 23.14-D: Matrix M where $M_{i,j} = c(i \wedge j)$, the number of bits in the intersection of the bitsets i and j. Dots denote zeros.

The weighted OR-convolution keeps track of the number of bits that overlap. We quantify the overlap by the bit-count of $i \wedge j$, see figure 23.14-D. Only the zero entries give contributions to the subset convolution.

Now set $\omega = \exp\left(2\,\pi\,i/L\right)$ (a primitive L-th root of unity) where $L = 1 + \log_2(N)$ and N is the length of the transforms. We compute the subset convolution s as

$$s \;=\; \frac{1}{L}\sum_{j=0}^{L-1} h\left(\omega^{j}\right) \tag{23.14-6}$$

The implementation uses a unweighted OR-convolution for the case $\omega^0 = 1$ [FXT: walsh/subset-convolution.h]:

```
1    template <typename Type>
2    inline void subset_convolution(Type *f, Type *g, ulong ldn)
3    // Compute the subset convolution h[] of f[] and g[]:
```

```
4      //    h[k] = sum( j subset k,  f[j]*g[k-j] )
5      // Type must allow conversion to and from type Complex.
6      // Result written to g[].
7      {
8          const ulong n = 1UL << ldn;
9          Complex *fc, *gc, *hc;
10         fc = new Complex[n];
11         gc = new Complex[n];
12         hc = new Complex[n];
13
14         // w^0:
15         copy_cast(f, fc, n);
16         copy_cast(g, gc, n);
17         or_convolution(fc, gc, ldn);
18         acopy(gc, hc, n);
19
20         // w^1, w^2, ... , w^(L-1):
21         const ulong L = ldn + 1;
22         const Complex w = SinCos( 2*M_PI/(double)L );
23         Complex wp = 1.0;   // powers of w
24         for (ulong j=1; j<L; ++j)
25         {
26             copy_cast(f, fc, n);
27             copy_cast(g, gc, n);
28             wp *= w;
29             weighted_or_convolution(fc, gc, ldn, wp);
30             for (ulong k=0; k<n; ++k)  hc[k] += gc[k];
31         }
32
33         const double x = 1.0/(double)L;
34         for (ulong k=0; k<n; ++k)  hc[k] *= x;
35         for (ulong k=0; k<n; ++k)  g[k] = (Type)hc[k].real();
36
37         delete [] fc;
38         delete [] gc;
39         delete [] hc;
40     }
```

Relation 23.14-6 is the special case $e = 0$ of

$$s(e) \;=\; \frac{1}{L} \sum_{j=0}^{L-1} \omega^{ej}\, h\left(\omega^j\right) \tag{23.14-7}$$

Where $s(e)$ is the convolution over subsets that share e elements:

$$s(e)_\tau \;=\; \sum_{i \vee j = \tau,\; c(i \wedge j) = e} a_i\, b_j \tag{23.14-8}$$

There are several ways to avoid usage of the complex domain. Relation 23.14-7 is essentially a Fourier sum and we could recast the algorithm in terms of a Hartley transform. This avoids the complex domain but still uses real (inexact) arithmetic.

As L is small we can explicitly represent any number $y = \sum_{j=0}^{L-1} y_j\, \omega^j$ as polynomials modulo $x^L - 1$. The additions are element-wise, and a multiplication by ω is a cyclic shift. This avoids inexact computations but needs space $O\left(n\,log(n)\right)$. Another approach (suggested in [53]) is to compute the L transforms of the subsequences of a and b where the bit-count is constant: let $a^{(e)}$ the sequence defined by

$$a_i^{(e)} \;=\; \begin{cases} a_i & \text{if } c(a_i) = e \\ 0 & \text{otherwise} \end{cases} \tag{23.14-9}$$

then

$$s(e) \;=\; \left(Y^- \left[\sum_{j=0}^{e} Y^+ \left[a^{(j)}\right] \cdot Y^+ \left[b^{(e-j)}\right] \right] \right)^{(e)} \tag{23.14-10}$$

Chapter 24

The Haar transform

Haar transforms are invertible transforms that do not involve trigonometric factors. We present several variants of the transform whose computation involve just $O(n)$ operations. Haar transforms can be used as building blocks of the Walsh transform. We describe the prefix transform and its convolution, and give two non-standard splitting schemes for Haar transforms, based on the Fibonacci and Mersenne numbers.

24.1   The 'standard' Haar transform

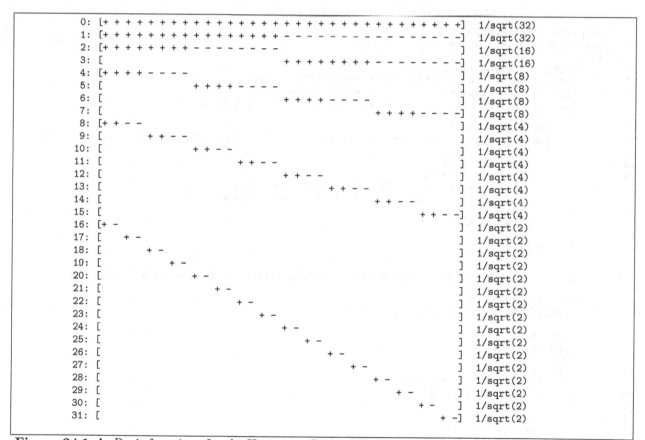

Figure 24.1-A: Basis functions for the Haar transform. Only the signs of the nonzero entries are shown. The absolute value of the nonzero entries in each row is given at the right. The norm of each row is one.

The *Haar transform* of a length-n sequence f consists of $\log_2(n)$ steps where the sums and differences of adjacent pairs of elements f_{2j}, f_{2j+1} are computed. The sums are then written to the lower half of the array f, the differences to the upper half. Ignoring the order (and normalization), each step corresponds

J. Arndt, *Matters Computational: Ideas, Algorithms, Source Code*,
DOI 10.1007/978-3-642-14764-7_24, © Springer-Verlag Berlin Heidelberg 2011

to a matrix multiplication:

$$
\begin{bmatrix}
+1 & +1 & & & & & & & \\
+1 & -1 & & & & & & & \\
& & +1 & +1 & & & & & \\
& & +1 & -1 & & & & & \\
& & & & +1 & +1 & & & \\
& & & & +1 & -1 & & & \\
& & & & & & +1 & +1 & \\
& & & & & & +1 & -1 & \\
& & & & & & & & \ddots
\end{bmatrix}
\cdot
\begin{bmatrix}
f_0 \\ f_1 \\ f_2 \\ f_3 \\ f_4 \\ f_5 \\ f_6 \\ f_7 \\ \vdots
\end{bmatrix}
\qquad (24.1\text{-}1)
$$

The step is applied to the full array, then to the lower half, the lower quarter, ..., the lower four elements, the lowest pair (the array length n must be a power of 2). The computational cost of the transform is proportional to $n + n/2 + n/4 + \ldots + 4 + 2$ which is $O(n)$. The basis functions for the Haar transform are shown in figure 24.1-A.

The following implementation involves $2n$ multiplications by $1/\sqrt{2}$ which make the transform orthogonal, corresponding to a scalar factor of $\sqrt{2}$ in the relation 24.1-1:

```
1    template <typename Type>
2    void haar(Type *f, ulong ldn)
3    {
4        ulong n = (1UL<<ldn);
5        const Type s2 = sqrt(0.5);   // normalization factor
6        Type *g = new Type[n];        // scratch space
7        for (ulong m=n; m>1; m>>=1)   // n, n/2, n/4, n/8, ..., 4, 2
8        {
9            ulong mh = (m>>1);
10           for (ulong j=0, k=0;  j<m;  j+=2, k++)  // sums and differences of adjacent pairs
11           {
12               Type x = f[j];
13               Type y = f[j+1];
14               g[k]    = (x + y) * s2;   // sums to lower half
15               g[mh+k] = (x - y) * s2;   // differences to upper half
16           }
17           acopy(g, f, m);
18       }
19       delete [] g;
20   }
```

We reduce the number of multiplications to n by delaying the multiplications [FXT: haar/haar.h]:

```
1    template <typename Type>
2    void haar(Type *f, ulong ldn, Type *ws=0)
3    {
4        ulong n = (1UL<<ldn);
5        Type s2 = sqrt(0.5);
6        Type v = 1.0;
7        Type *g = ws;
8        if ( !ws )  g = new Type[n];
9        for (ulong m=n; m>1; m>>=1)
10       {
11           v *= s2;
12           ulong mh = (m>>1);
13           for (ulong j=0, k=0;  j<m;  j+=2, k++)
14           {
15               Type x = f[j];
16               Type y = f[j+1];
17               g[k]    =  x + y;
18               g[mh+k] = (x - y) * v;
19           }
20           acopy(g, f, m);
21       }
22       f[0] *= v;  // v == 1.0/sqrt(n);
23       if ( !ws )  delete [] g;
24   }
```

The temporary workspace can be supplied by the caller.

The inverse Haar transform is computed by using the inverse steps in reversed order:

```
1   template <typename Type>
2   void inverse_haar(Type *f, ulong ldn, Type *ws=0)
3   {
4       ulong n = (1UL<<ldn);
5       Type s2 = sqrt(2.0);
6       Type v = 1.0/sqrt(n);
7       Type *g = ws;
8       if ( !ws )  g = new Type[n];
9       f[0] *= v;
10      for (ulong m=2; m<=n; m<<=1)
11      {
12          ulong mh = (m>>1);
13          for (ulong j=0, k=0;  j<m;  j+=2, k++)
14          {
15              Type x = f[k];
16              Type y = f[mh+k] * v;
17              g[j]   = x + y;
18              g[j+1] = x - y;
19          }
20          acopy(g, f, m);
21          v *= s2;
22      }
23      if ( !ws )  delete [] g;
24  }
```

A generalization of the steps used in the Haar transform leads to the wavelet transforms treated in chapter 27 on page 543.

24.2 In-place Haar transform

The 'standard' Haar transform routines are not in-place, they use a temporary storage. A rather simple reordering of the basis functions, however, allows for an in-place algorithm [FXT: haar/haar.h]:

```
1   template <typename Type>
2   void haar_inplace(Type *f, ulong ldn)
3   {
4       ulong n = 1UL<<ldn;
5       Type s2 = sqrt(0.5);
6       Type v = 1.0;
7       for (ulong js=2; js<=n; js<<=1)
8       {
9           v *= s2;
10          for (ulong j=0, t=js>>1;  j<n;  j+=js, t+=js)
11          {
12              Type x = f[j];
13              Type y = f[t];
14              f[j] = x + y;
15              f[t] = (x - y) * v;
16          }
17      }
18      f[0] *= v;  // v==1.0/sqrt(n);
19  }
```

The basis functions of the transform are shown in figure 24.2-A. The routine for the inverse transform is

```
1   template <typename Type>
2   void inverse_haar_inplace(Type *f, ulong ldn)
3   {
4       ulong n = 1UL<<ldn;
5       Type s2 = sqrt(2.0);
6       Type v = 1.0/sqrt(n);
7       f[0] *= v;
8       for (ulong js=n; js>=2; js>>=1)
9       {
10          for (ulong j=0, t=js>>1;  j<n;  j+=js, t+=js)
11          {
12              Type x = f[j];
13              Type y = f[t] * v;
```

```
 0:  [+ + + + + + + + + + + + + + + + + + + + + + + + + + + + + + + +]   1/sqrt(32)
 1:  [+ -                                                           ]   1/sqrt(4)
 2:  [+ + - -                                                       ]   1/sqrt(4)
 3:  [     + -                                                      ]   1/sqrt(4)
 4:  [+ + + - - - -                                                 ]   1/sqrt(8)
 5:  [         + -                                                  ]   1/sqrt(4)
 6:  [         + + - -                                              ]   1/sqrt(4)
 7:  [             + -                                              ]   1/sqrt(4)
 8:  [+ + + + + + + - - - - - - - -                                 ]   1/sqrt(16)
 9:  [                 + -                                          ]   1/sqrt(4)
10:  [                 + + - -                                      ]   1/sqrt(4)
11:  [                     + -                                      ]   1/sqrt(4)
12:  [                 + + + - - - -                                ]   1/sqrt(8)
13:  [                         + -                                  ]   1/sqrt(4)
14:  [                         + + - -                              ]   1/sqrt(4)
15:  [                             + -                              ]   1/sqrt(4)
16:  [+ + + + + + + + + + + + + + + + - - - - - - - - - - - - - - - -]   1/sqrt(32)
17:  [                                 + -                          ]   1/sqrt(4)
18:  [                                 + + - -                      ]   1/sqrt(4)
19:  [                                     + -                      ]   1/sqrt(4)
20:  [                                 + + + - - - -                ]   1/sqrt(8)
21:  [                                         + -                  ]   1/sqrt(4)
22:  [                                         + + - -              ]   1/sqrt(4)
23:  [                                             + -              ]   1/sqrt(4)
24:  [                                 + + + + + + + - - - - - - - -]   1/sqrt(16)
25:  [                                                 + -          ]   1/sqrt(4)
26:  [                                                 + + - -      ]   1/sqrt(4)
27:  [                                                     + -      ]   1/sqrt(4)
28:  [                                                 + + + - - - -]   1/sqrt(8)
29:  [                                                         + -  ]   1/sqrt(4)
30:  [                                                         + + - -]   1/sqrt(4)
31:  [                                                             + -]   1/sqrt(4)
```

Figure 24.2-A: Haar basis functions, in-place order. Only the signs of the nonzero entries are shown. The absolute value of the nonzero entries in each row is given at the right. The norm of each row is one.

```
14                   f[j]  =  x + y;
15                   f[t]  =  x - y;
16              }
17          v *= s2;
18      }
19  }
```

The in-place Haar transform H_i is related to the 'usual' Haar transform H by a permutation P_H via the relations

$$H = P_H \cdot H_i \tag{24.2-1a}$$

$$H^{-1} = H_i^{-1} \cdot P_H^{-1} \tag{24.2-1b}$$

The permutation P_H can be programmed as

```
1   template <typename Type>
2   void haar_permute(Type *f, ulong n)
3   {
4       revbin_permute(f, n);
5       for (ulong m=4; m<=n/2; m*=2)  revbin_permute(f+m, m);
6   }
```

The revbin permutations in the loop do not overlap, so the routine for the inverse Haar permutation is obtained by simply swapping the loop with the full-length revbin permutation [FXT: perm/haarpermute.h]:

```
1   template <typename Type>
2   void inverse_haar_permute(Type *f, ulong n)
3   {
4       for (ulong m=4; m<=n/2; m*=2)  revbin_permute(f+m, m);
5       revbin_permute(f, n);
6   }
```

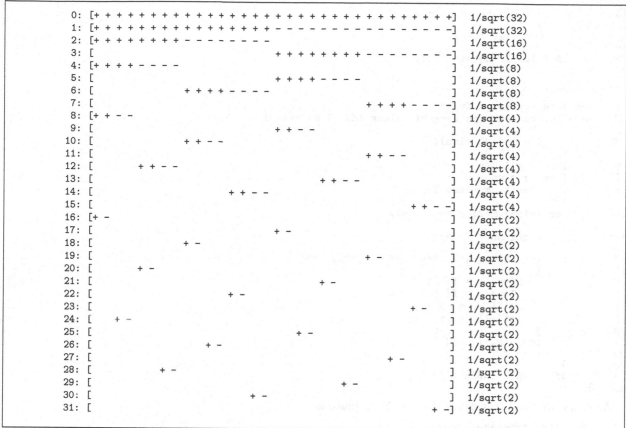

Figure 24.2-B: Basis functions of the in-place order Haar transform followed by a revbin permutation. In this ordering those basis functions which are identical up to a shift appear consecutively.

Relation 24.2-1a tells us that `haar()` is equivalent to the sequence of statements

```
haar_inplace();
haar_permute();
```

and, by relation 24.2-1b, `inverse_haar()` is equivalent to

```
inverse_haar_permute();
inverse_haar_inplace();
```

24.3 Non-normalized Haar transforms

Versions of the Haar transform without normalization are given in [FXT: haar/haarnn.h]. The basis functions are the same as for the normalized versions, only the absolute value of the nonzero entries are different.

```
1    template <typename Type>
2    void haar_nn(Type *f, ulong ldn, Type *ws=0)
3    {
4        ulong n = (1UL<<ldn);
5        Type *g = ws;
6        if ( !ws )  g = new Type[n];
7        for (ulong m=n; m>1; m>>=1)
8        {
9            ulong mh = (m>>1);
10           for (ulong j=0, k=0;  j<m;  j+=2, k++)
11           {
12               Type x = f[j];
13               Type y = f[j+1];
14               g[k]    =  x + y;
```

```
15                    g[mh+k]  =  x - y;
16               }
17               acopy(g, f, m);
18          }
19          if ( !ws )  delete [] g;
20     }
```

The inverse is

```
1     template <typename Type>
2     void inverse_haar_nn(Type *f, ulong ldn, Type *ws=0)
3     {
4          ulong n = (1UL<<ldn);
5          Type s2 = 2.0;
6          Type v = 1.0/n;
7          Type *g = ws;
8          if ( !ws )  g = new Type[n];
9          f[0] *= v;
10         for (ulong m=2; m<=n; m<<=1)
11         {
12              ulong mh = (m>>1);
13
14              for (ulong j=0, k=0;  j<m;  j+=2, k++)
15              {
16                   Type x = f[k];
17                   Type y = f[mh+k] * v;
18                   g[j]   = x + y;
19                   g[j+1] = x - y;
20              }
21              acopy(g, f, m);
22              v *= s2;
23         }
24         if ( !ws )  delete [] g;
25    }
```

An unnormalized transform that works in-place is

```
1     template <typename Type>
2     void haar_inplace_nn(Type *f, ulong ldn)
3     {
4          ulong n = 1UL<<ldn;
5          for (ulong js=2; js<=n; js<<=1)
6          {
7               for (ulong j=0, t=js>>1;  j<n;  j+=js, t+=js)
8               {
9                    Type x = f[j];
10                   Type y = f[t];
11                   f[j]   = x + y;
12                   f[t]   = x - y;
13              }
14         }
15    }
```

The inverse routine is

```
1     template <typename Type>
2     void inverse_haar_inplace_nn(Type *f, ulong ldn)
3     {
4          ulong n = 1UL<<ldn;
5          Type s2 = 2.0;
6          Type v = 1.0/n;
7          f[0] *= v;
8          for (ulong js=n; js>=2; js>>=1)
9          {
10              for (ulong j=0, t=js>>1;  j<n;  j+=js, t+=js)
11              {
12                   Type x = f[j];
13                   Type y = f[t] * v;
14                   f[j]   = x + y;
15                   f[t]   = x - y;
16              }
17              v *= s2;
18         }
19    }
```

The sequence of statements

```
haar_inplace_nn();
haar_permute();
```

is equivalent to `haar_nn()`. The sequence

```
inverse_haar_permute();
inverse_haar_inplace_nn();
```

is equivalent to `inverse_haar_nn()`.

24.4 Transposed Haar transforms ‡

```
 0: [ + + +    +         +               +                          ]
 1: [ + + +    +         +               -                          ]
 2: [ + + +    +         -                    +                     ]
 3: [ + + +    +         -                    -                     ]
 4: [ + + +    -              +                    +                ]
 5: [ + + +    -              +                    -                ]
 6: [ + + +    -              -                         +           ]
 7: [ + + +    -              -                         -           ]
 8: [ + + -    +         +                    +                     ]
 9: [ + + -    +         +                    -                     ]
10: [ + + -    +         -                         +                ]
11: [ + + -    +         -                         -                ]
12: [ + + -    -              +                         +           ]
13: [ + + -    -              +                         -           ]
14: [ + + -    -              -                              +      ]
15: [ + + -    -              -                              -      ]
16: [ + -    +    +         +                    +                  ]
17: [ + -    +    +         +                    -                  ]
18: [ + -    +    +         -                         +             ]
19: [ + -    +    +         -                         -             ]
20: [ + -    +    -              +                         +        ]
21: [ + -    +    -              +                         -        ]
22: [ + -    +    -              -                              +   ]
23: [ + -    +    -              -                              -   ]
24: [ + -    -    +              +                              +   ]
25: [ + -    -    +              +                              -   ]
26: [ + -    -    +         -                              +        ]
27: [ + -    -    +         -                              -        ]
28: [ + -    -    -              +                              +   ]
29: [ + -    -    -              +                              -   ]
30: [ + -    -    -              -                              + ]
31: [ + -    -    -              -                              - ]
```

Figure 24.4-A: Basis functions for the transposed Haar transform. Only the signs of the basis functions are shown. At the blank entries the functions are zero.

Figure 24.4-A shows the basis functions of the transposed Haar transform. The following routine does an unnormalized Haar transform. The result is, up to normalization, the same as with `inverse_haar()`. The implementation uses a temporary array [FXT: haar/transposedhaarnn.h]:

```
1    template <typename Type>
2    void transposed_haar_nn(Type *f, ulong ldn, Type *ws=0)
3    {
4        ulong n = (1UL<<ldn);
5        Type *g = ws;
6        if ( !ws )  g = new Type[n];
7        for (ulong m=2; m<=n; m<<=1)
8        {
9            ulong mh = (m>>1);
10            for (ulong j=0, k=0;  j<m;  j+=2, k++)
11            {
12                Type x = f[k];
13                Type y = f[mh+k];
14                g[j]     =  x + y;
```

```
15              g[j+1]  =  x - y;
16          }
17          acopy(g, f, m);
18      }
19      if ( !ws )  delete [] g;
20  }
```

The inverse transform is

```
1   template <typename Type>
2   void inverse_transposed_haar_nn(Type *f, ulong ldn, Type *ws=0)
3   {
4       ulong n = (1UL<<ldn);
5       Type *g = ws;
6       if ( !ws )  g = new Type[n];
7       for (ulong m=n; m>1; m>>=1)
8       {
9           ulong mh = (m>>1);
10          for (ulong j=0, k=0;  j<m;  j+=2, k++)
11          {
12              Type x = f[j]   * 0.5;
13              Type y = f[j+1] * 0.5;
14              g[k]    = x + y;
15              g[mh+k] = x - y;
16          }
17          acopy(g, f, m);
18      }
19      if ( !ws )  delete [] g;
20  }
```

```
 0: [ + + +   +       +             +                        ]
 1: [ + - +   +       +             +                        ]
 2: [ +   - + +       +             +                        ]
 3: [ +   - - +       +             +                        ]
 4: [ +       - + +   +             +                        ]
 5: [ +       - - +   +             +                        ]
 6: [ +       -   - + +             +                        ]
 7: [ +       -   - - +             +                        ]
 8: [ +           - + +   +         +                        ]
 9: [ +           - - +   +         +                        ]
10: [ +           -   - + +         +                        ]
11: [ +           -   - - +         +                        ]
12: [ +           -       - + +     +                        ]
13: [ +           -       - - +     +                        ]
14: [ +           -       -   - + + +                        ]
15: [ +           -       -   - - + +                        ]
16: [ +                   - + +   +       +                  ]
17: [ +                   - - +   +       +                  ]
18: [ +                   -   - + +       +                  ]
19: [ +                   -   - - +       +                  ]
20: [ +                   -       - + +   +                  ]
21: [ +                   -       - - +   +                  ]
22: [ +                   -       -   - + +                  ]
23: [ +                   -       -   - - +                  ]
24: [ +                   -           - + +   +              ]
25: [ +                   -           - - +   +              ]
26: [ +                   -           -   - + +              ]
27: [ +                   -           -   - - +              ]
28: [ +                   -           -       - + +          ]
29: [ +                   -           -       - - +          ]
30: [ +                   -           -       -   - +        ]
31: [ +                   -           -       -   - -        ]
```

Figure 24.4-B: Basis functions for the transposed in-place Haar transform. Only the signs of the basis functions are shown. At the blank entries the functions are zero.

The following routine does not use a temporary array:

```
1   template <typename Type>
2   void transposed_haar_inplace_nn(Type *f, ulong ldn)
```

```
 3     {
 4         ulong n = 1UL<<ldn;
 5         for (ulong js=n; js>=2; js>>=1)
 6         {
 7             for (ulong j=0, t=js>>1;  j<n;  j+=js, t+=js)
 8             {
 9                 Type x = f[j];
10                 Type y = f[t];
11                 f[j]  =  x + y;
12                 f[t]  =  x - y;
13             }
14         }
15     }
```

The sequence of statements

```
    inverse_haar_permute();
    transposed_haar_inplace_nn();
```

is equivalent to `transposed_haar_nn()`. The routine for the inverse transform is

```
 1     template <typename Type>
 2     void inverse_transposed_haar_inplace_nn(Type *f, ulong ldn)
 3     {
 4         ulong n = 1UL<<ldn;
 5         for (ulong js=2; js<=n; js<<=1)
 6         {
 7             for (ulong j=0, t=js>>1;  j<n;  j+=js, t+=js)
 8             {
 9                 Type x = f[j] * 0.5;
10                 Type y = f[t] * 0.5;
11                 f[j]  =  x + y;
12                 f[t]  =  x - y;
13             }
14         }
15     }
```

24.5 The reversed Haar transform ‡

We give two more variants of the Haar transform, which we call the *reversed Haar transform* and the *transposed reversed Haar transform*. The basis functions of the reversed Haar transform are shown in figure 24.5-A.

Let H_{ni} denote the non-normalized in-place Haar transform (`haar_inplace_nn`), H_{tni} the transposed non-normalized in-place Haar transform (`transposed_haar_inplace_nn`), R the revbin permutation, $\overline{H}$ the reversed Haar transform, and $\overline{H}_t$ the transposed reversed Haar transform. Then

$$\overline{H} = R\,H_{ni}\,R \tag{24.5-1a}$$

$$\overline{H}_t = R\,H_{tni}\,R \tag{24.5-1b}$$

$$\overline{H}^{-1} = R\,H_{ni}^{-1}\,R \tag{24.5-1c}$$

$$\overline{H}_t^{-1} = R\,H_{tni}^{-1}\,R \tag{24.5-1d}$$

Code for the reversed Haar transform [FXT: haar/haarrevnn.h]:

```
 1     template <typename Type>
 2     void haar_rev_nn(Type *f, ulong ldn)
 3     {
 4     //    const ulong n = (1UL<<ldn);
 5         for (ulong ldm=ldn; ldm>=1; --ldm)
 6         {
 7             const ulong m = (1UL<<ldm);
 8             const ulong mh = (m>>1);
 9             ulong r = 0;
10     //        for (ulong r=0; r<n; r+=m)  // almost walsh_wak_dif2()
11             {
12                 ulong t1 = r;
13                 ulong t2 = r + mh;
14                 for (ulong j=0;  j<mh;  ++j, ++t1, ++t2)
```

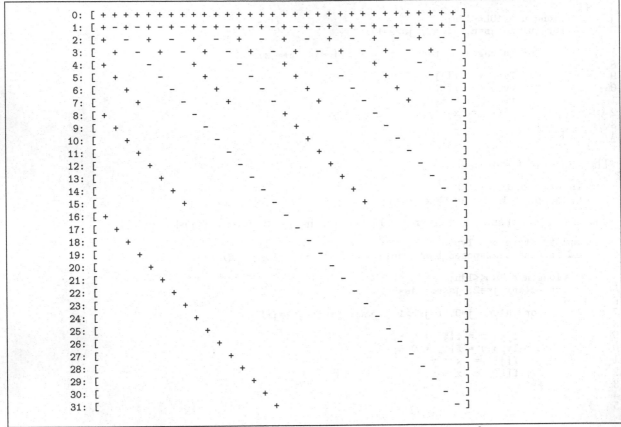

Figure 24.5-A: Basis functions for the reversed Haar transform.

```
15                  {
16                          Type u = f[t1];
17                          Type v = f[t2];
18                          f[t1] = u + v;
19                          f[t2] = u - v;
20                  }
21              }
22          }
23      }
```

This is almost the radix-2 DIF implementation for the Walsh transform. The only change is that the line
`for (ulong r=0; r<n; r+=m)` was replaced by `ulong r = 0`. The transform can also be computed via
the following sequence of statements:
`{ revbin_permute(); haar_inplace_nn(); revbin_permute(); }`.

The inverse transform is obtained by the equivalent modification with the DIT implementation for the
Walsh transform and normalization:

```
1       template <typename Type>
2       void inverse_haar_rev_nn(Type *f, ulong ldn)
3       {
4           for (ulong ldm=1; ldm<=ldn; ++ldm)
5           {
6               const ulong m = (1UL<<ldm);
7               const ulong mh = (m>>1);
8               ulong r = 0;
9       //          for (ulong r=0; r<n; r+=m)  // almost walsh_wak_dit2()
10              {
11                  ulong t1 = r;
12                  ulong t2 = r + mh;
13                  for (ulong j=0;  j<mh;  ++j, ++t1, ++t2)
14                  {
15                          Type u = f[t1] * 0.5;
```

```
16                   Type v = f[t2] * 0.5;
17                   f[t1] = u + v;
18                   f[t2] = u - v;
19               }
20           }
21       }
22   }
```

The reversed transposed Haar transform is, up to normalization, the inverse of `haar_rev_nn()`. It is given in [FXT: haar/transposedhaarrevnn.h]:

```
1    template <typename Type>
2    void transposed_haar_rev_nn(Type *f, ulong ldn)
3    {
4        for (ulong ldm=1; ldm<=ldn; ++ldm)
5        {
6            const ulong m = (1UL<<ldm);
7            const ulong mh = (m>>1);
8            ulong r = 0;
9    //       for (ulong r=0; r<n; r+=m)   // almost walsh_wak_dit2()
10           {
11               ulong t1 = r;
12               ulong t2 = r + mh;
13               for (ulong j=0;  j<mh;  ++j, ++t1, ++t2)
14               {
15                   Type u = f[t1];
16                   Type v = f[t2];
17                   f[t1] = u + v;
18                   f[t2] = u - v;
19               }
20           }
21       }
22   }
```

The same result could be computed with the following sequence of statements:
{ revbin_permute(); transposed_haar_inplace_nn(); revbin_permute(); }.

The inverse transform is

```
1    template <typename Type>
2    void inverse_transposed_haar_rev_nn(Type *f, ulong ldn)
3    {
4    //   const ulong n = (1UL<<ldn);
5        for (ulong ldm=ldn; ldm>=1; --ldm)
6        {
7            const ulong m = (1UL<<ldm);
8            const ulong mh = (m>>1);
9            ulong r = 0;
10   //       for (ulong r=0; r<n; r+=m)   // almost walsh_wak_dif2()
11           {
12               ulong t1 = r;
13               ulong t2 = r + mh;
14               for (ulong j=0;  j<mh;  ++j, ++t1, ++t2)
15               {
16                   Type u = f[t1] * 0.5;
17                   Type v = f[t2] * 0.5;
18                   f[t1] = u + v;
19                   f[t2] = u - v;
20               }
21           }
22       }
23   }
```

24.6   Relations between Walsh and Haar transforms

24.6.1   Computing Walsh transforms via Haar transforms

A length-n Walsh transform can be computed with one length-n Haar transform, one transform of length-$\frac{n}{2}$, two transforms of length-$\frac{n}{4}$, four transforms of length-$\frac{n}{8}$, ..., and $\frac{n}{4}$ transforms of length-2. We implement the Walsh transform W_k (the one with the Walsh Kronecker base) using the reversed Haar transform:

```
        Haar transforms:
           H(16)                          H(8)           H(4)         H(2)
           AAAAAAAAaaaaaaaa               BBBBbbbb        CCcc         Dd
           AAAAaaaa                       BBbb            Cc
           AAaa                           Bb
           Aa


        Walsh(16) =^= 1*H(16) + 1*H(8) + 2*H(4) + 4*H(2)
           AAAAAAAAaaaaaaaa
           AAAAaaaaBBBBbbbb
           AAaaCCccBBbbCCcc
           AaDdCcDdBbDdCcDd
```

Figure 24.6-A: Symbolic description of how to build a Walsh transform from Haar transforms.

```
        Transposed Haar transforms:
           H(16)                          H(8)           H(4)         H(2)
           Aa
           AAaa                           Bb
           AAAAaaaa                       BBbb            Cc
           AAAAAAAAaaaaaaaa               BBBBbbbb        CCcc         Dd


        Walsh(16) =^= 1*H(16) + 1*H(8) + 2*H(4) + 4*H(2)
           AaDdCcDdBbDdCcDd
           AAaaCCccBBbbCCcc
           AAAAaaaaBBBBbbbb
           AAAAAAAAaaaaaaaa
```

Figure 24.6-B: Symbolic description of how to build a Walsh transform from Haar transforms, transposed version.

```
1    // algorithm WH1:
2    ulong n = 1UL<<ldn;
3    haar_rev_nn(f, ldn);
4    for (ulong ldk=ldn-1; ldk>0; --ldk)
5    {
6        ulong k = 1UL << ldk;
7        for (ulong j=k; j<n; j+=2*k)  haar_rev_nn(f+j, ldk);
8    }
```

The idea, as a symbolic scheme, is shown in figure 24.6-A. The scheme obtained by reversing the order of the lines is shown in figure 24.6-B. It corresponds to the computation of W_k using the transposed version of the Haar transform:

```
1    // algorithm WH1T:
2    ulong n = 1UL<<ldn;
3    for (ulong ldk=1; ldk<ldn; ++ldk)
4    {
5        ulong k = 1UL << ldk;
6        for (ulong j=k; j<n; j+=2*k)  transposed_haar_rev_nn(f+j, ldk);
7    }
8    transposed_haar_rev_nn(f, ldn);
```

Two more methods are found by reversing the individual lines of the schemes seen so far, see figure 24.6-C. These correspond to the computation of the inverse Walsh transform ($W_k^{-1} = \frac{1}{n} W_k$) either as

```
1    // algorithm WH2T:
2    ulong n = 1UL<<ldn;
3    inverse_transposed_haar_rev_nn(f, ldn);
4    for (ulong ldk=ldn-1; ldk>0; --ldk)
5    {
```

```
AAAAAAAAaaaaaaaa          aaaaaaaaAAAAAAAA
AAAAaaaaBBBBbbbb          bbbbBBBBBaaaaAAAA
AAaaCCccBBbbCCcc          ccCCbbBBccCCaaAA
AaDdCcDdBbDdCcDd          dDcCdDbBdDcCdDaA


       WH1                       WH2T



AaDdCcDdBbDdCcDd          dDcCdDbBdDcCdDaA
AAaaCCccBBbbCCcc          ccCCbbBBccCCaaAA
AAAAaaaaBBBBbbbb          bbbbBBBBBaaaaAAAA
AAAAAAAAaaaaaaaa          aaaaaaaaAAAAAAAA


       WH1T                      WH2
```

Figure 24.6-C: Symbolic scheme of the four versions of the computation of the Walsh transform via Haar transforms.

```
6          ulong k = 1UL << ldk;
7          for (ulong j=k; j<n; j+=2*k)  inverse_transposed_haar_rev_nn(f+j, ldk);
8      }
```
or as
```
1      // algorithm WH2:
2      ulong n = 1UL<<ldn;
3      for (ulong ldk=1; ldk<ldn; ++ldk)
4      {
5          ulong k = 1UL << ldk;
6          for (ulong j=k; j<n; j+=2*k)  inverse_haar_rev_nn(f+j, ldk);
7      }
8      inverse_haar_rev_nn(f, ldn);
```

24.6.2 Computing Haar transforms via Walsh transforms

The schemes given here are $O(n \log(n))$ and not an efficient method to compute the Haar transform which is $O(n)$. Instead, they can be used to identify the type of Haar transform that is the building block of a given Walsh transform.

The non-normalized transposed reversed Haar transform can (up to normalization) be computed via

```
1      // algorithm HW1:  transposed_haar_rev_nn(f, ldn); =^=
2      for (ulong ldk=1; ldk<ldn; ++ldk)
3      {
4          ulong k = 1UL << ldk;
5          walsh_wak(f+k, ldk);
6      }
7      walsh_wak(f, ldn);
```

and its inverse as

```
1      // algorithm HW1I:  inverse_transposed_haar_rev_nn(f, ldn); =^=
2      walsh_wak(f, ldn);
3      for (ulong ldk=1; ldk<ldn; ++ldk)
4      {
5          ulong k = 1UL << ldk;
6          walsh_wak(f+k, ldk);
7      }
```

The non-normalized transposed Haar transform can (again, up to normalization) be computed via

```
1      // algorithm HW2:  transposed_haar_nn(f, ldn); =^=
2      for (ulong ldk=1; ldk<ldn; ++ldk)
3      {
4          ulong k = 1UL << ldk;
5          walsh_pal(f+k, ldk);
6      }
```

```
    Walsh transform:
          W(16)
        AaDdCcDdBbDdCcDd
        AAaaCCccBBbbCCcc
        AAAAaaaaBBBBbbbb
        AAAAAAAAaaaaaaaa

    Inverse (or transposed) Walsh transforms:
        W(8):              W(4):        W(2):
        BBBBbbbb           CCcc          Dd
        BBbbCCcc           CcDd
        BbDdCcDd


                                    BBBBbbbb
                                  CCccBBbbCCcc
                                  DdCcDdBbDdCcDd
        Aa                        AaDdCcDdBbDdCcDd
        AAaa                      AAaaCCccBBbbCCcc
        AAAAaaaa                  AAAAaaaaBBBBbbbb
        AAAAAAAAaaaaaaaa          AAAAAAAAaaaaaaaa
          Haar(16)      =^=  W(16) + W(8) + W(4) + W(2)
```

Figure 24.6-D: Symbolic description of how to build a Haar transform from Walsh transforms.

```
7        walsh_pal(f, ldn);
```

and its inverse as

```
1        // algorithm HW2I:  inverse_transposed_haar_nn(f, ldn); =^=
2        walsh_pal(f, ldn);  // =^= revbin_permute(f, n); walsh_wak(f, ldn);
3        for (ulong ldk=1; ldk<ldn; ++ldk)
4        {
5            ulong k = 1UL << ldk;
6            walsh_pal(f+k, ldk);
7        }
```

The symbolic scheme is given in figure 24.6-D.

24.7 Prefix transform and prefix convolution

Figure 24.7-A: Basis functions of the prefix transform (left) and its inverse (right).

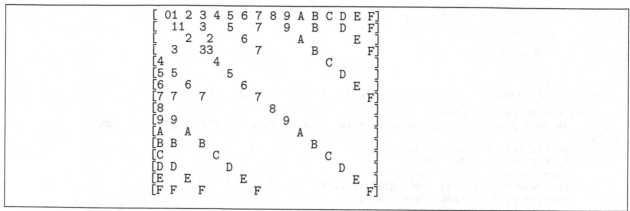

Figure 24.7-B: Scheme for the prefix convolution (hexadecimal).

The set of prefixes $P(k)$ of a binary word k contains (k and) all binary words obtained by successively removing the highest one. For example, $P(22)= P(10110_2)$ contains the words $10110_2 = 22$, $00110_2 = 6$, $00010_2 = 2$, and $00000_2 = 0$. Define the *prefix transform* c of a by setting

$$c_k = \sum_{i \in P(k)} a_i \tag{24.7-1}$$

An algorithm to compute the transform in linear time exploits the fact that $i \in P(k)$ implies $2i \in P(2k)$ [FXT: haar/prefix-transform.h]:

```
1    template <typename Type>
2    void prefix_transform(Type *f, ulong ldn)
3    {
4        for (ulong ldm=1; ldm<=ldn; ++ldm)
5        {
6            const ulong mh = 1UL << (ldm-1);
7            for (ulong i=0; i<mh; ++i)  f[i+mh] += f[i];
8        }
9    }
```

The basis functions of the transform are shown in figure 24.7-A. The inverse transform is

```
1    template <typename Type>
2    void inverse_prefix_transform(Type *f, ulong ldn)
3    {
4        for (ulong ldm=ldn; ldm>=1; --ldm)
5        {
6            const ulong mh = 1UL << (ldm-1);
7            for (ulong i=0; i<mh; ++i)  f[i+mh] -= f[i];
8        }
9    }
```

Define the *prefix convolution* h of two sequences a and b by

$$h_k = -a_k b_k + \sum_{j \in P(k)} (a_j b_k + a_k b_j) \tag{24.7-2}$$

Figure 24.7-B shows the semi-symbolic scheme. The computation by definition costs $O(n \log(n))$ operations:

```
1    template <typename Type>
2    inline void slow_prefix_convolution(const Type *f, const Type *g, ulong ldn, Type *h)
3    {
4        const ulong n = 1UL << ldn;
5        for (ulong k=0; k<n; ++k)  h[k] = f[k] * g[k];
6        for (ulong k=1; k<n; ++k)
7        {
8            ulong j = k;
9            do
10           {
11               j ^= highest_one(j);
```

```
12                h[k] += f[k] * g[j];
13                h[k] += f[j] * g[k];
14            }
15        while ( j );
16        }
17    }
```

The convolution can be computed in linear time via the prefix transform:

```
1    template <typename Type>
2    inline void prefix_convolution(Type * restrict f, Type * restrict g, ulong ldn)
3    {
4        prefix_transform(f, ldn);
5        prefix_transform(g, ldn);
6        const ulong n = (1UL<<ldn);
7        for (ulong k=0; k<n; ++k)  g[k] *= f[k];
8        inverse_prefix_transform(g, ldn);
9    }
```

24.8 Nonstandard splitting schemes ‡

All radix-2 transforms recursively split the length of the array into halves. The size of the transforms is limited to power of 2. In a recursive implementation we use the trivial equality $2^k = 2^{k-1} + 2^{k-1}$. With $N_k := 2^k$ we have $N_0 = 1$, and $N_k = N_{k-1} + N_{k-1}$. We use different recursive schemes to derive nonstandard variants of the Haar and Walsh transforms.

24.8.1 Fibonacci-Haar and Fibonacci-Walsh transform

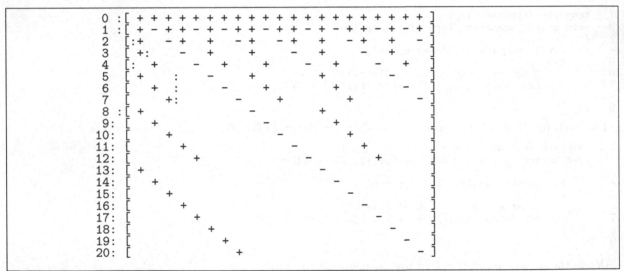

Figure 24.8-A: Basis functions for the non-normalized Fibonacci-Haar transform. Only the signs of the nonzero entries are shown. At the blank entries the functions are zero.

We use the Fibonacci numbers $F_n = F_{n-1} + F_{n-1}$ (where $F_0 = 0$ and $F_1 = 1$) to construct a *Fibonacci-Haar transform* as follows [FXT: haar/fib-haar.h]:

```
1    inline void fibonacci_haar(double *a, ulong f0, ulong f1)
2    // In-place Fibonacci-Haar transform of a[0,...,f0-1].
3    // f0 must be a Fibonacci number, f1 the next smaller Fibonacci number.
4    {
5        if ( f0 < 2 )  return;
6
7        ulong f2 = f0 - f1;
8        for (ulong j=0,k=f1;  j<f2;  ++j,++k)
9        {
10           double u = a[j],  v = a[k];
11           a[j] = (u+v) * SQRT1_2;
12           a[k] = (u-v) * SQRT1_2;
```

```
13          }
14          fibonacci_haar(a, f1, f2);
15     }
```

Omitting the multiplications with $1/\sqrt{2}$ (=SQRT1_2) gives a non-normalized version of the transform. The basis functions for the non-normalized transform with length-21 (= F_8) are shown in figure 24.8-A (compare to figure 24.5-A on page 506). The second row corresponds to the *rabbit sequence* described in section 38.11 on page 753. Figure 24.8-A was created with the program [FXT: fft/fib-haar-demo.cc].

```
 0  : [ + + + + + + + + + + + + + + + + + + + + + ]
 1  : [ + - + + - + - + + - + + - + - + + - + - + ]
 2    [ : +    - +    +    - +    - +    +    - +    +    - ]
 3  : [ + +    - - + +    + +    - - + +    - - + + ]
 4  : [ + -    - + + -    + -    - + + -    - + + - ]
 5  : [ + + +    - - - + + +    + + +    - - - ]
 6  : [ + - +    - + - + +    + - +    - + - ]
 7    [ : +    -    + +    -    + -    - + ]
 8  : [ + + + + +    - - - - + + + + + ]
 9  : [ + - + + -    - + - - + + + - + + - ]
10    [ +    - +    -    + -    + -    + ]
11    [ + +    - -    - -    + + + +    - - ]
12    [ + -    - +    - +    + - + -    - + ]
13    [ + + + + + + + +    - - - - - - - - ]
14    [ + - + + - + - +    - + - - + - + - ]
15    [ + : - +    + -    -    + -    -    + ]
16    [ + +    - - + +    - -    + + - - ]
17    [ + -    - + + -    - +    + - - + ]
18    [ + + +    - - -    - - -    + + + ]
19    [ + - +    - + -    - + -    + - + ]
20    [ + : -    -    +    - +    + - ]
```

Figure 24.8-B: Basis functions for the non-normalized Fibonacci-Walsh transform.

The implementation of the *Fibonacci-Walsh transform* differs by just one line from the code for the Fibonacci-Haar transform [FXT: walsh/fib-walsh.h]:

```
1     inline void fibonacci_walsh(double *a, ulong f0, ulong f1)
2     // In-place Fibonacci-Walsh transform of a[0,...,f0-1].
3     // f0 must be a Fibonacci number, f1 the next smaller Fibonacci number.
4     {
5         if ( f0 < 2 )  return;
6
7         ulong f2 = f0 - f1;
8         for (ulong j=0,k=f1;  j<f2;  ++j,++k)
9         {
10            double u = a[j],   v = a[k];
11            a[j] = (u+v) * SQRT1_2;
12            a[k] = (u-v) * SQRT1_2;
13        }
14        fibonacci_walsh(a, f1, f2);
15        fibonacci_walsh(a+f1, f2, f1-f2);  // <--= omit line to obtain Haar transform
16    }
```

The basis functions for the length 21 transform are shown in figure 24.8-B, which was created with the program [FXT: fft/fib-walsh-demo.cc].

One can find Haar-like and Walsh-like transforms for any linear recursive sequence that is increasing. A construction for recurrences $N_k = N_{k-1} + N_{k-1-p}$ is considered in [136].

24.8.2 Mersenne-Haar and Mersenne-Walsh transform

For the Mersenne numbers $M_k = 2^k - 1$ we have the recursion $M_k = 2 \cdot M_{k-1} + 1$. This gives the splitting scheme in the *Mersenne-Walsh transform* [FXT: walsh/mers-walsh.h]:

```
1     inline void mersenne_walsh(double *a, ulong f0)
2     // In-place Mersenne-Walsh transform of a[0,...,f0-1].
3     // f0 must be a Mersenne number.
4     // Self-inverse.
5     {
```

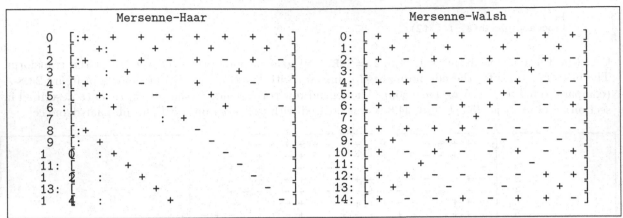

Figure 24.8-C: Basis functions for the non-normalized Mersenne-Haar transform (left) and Mersenne-Walsh transform (right). Only the signs of the nonzero entries are shown. At the blank entries the functions are zero.

```
6        if ( f0 < 2 )  return;
7        ulong f1 = f0 >> 1;  // next smaller Mersenne number
8
9        for (ulong j=0,k=f1+1;  j<f1;  ++j,++k)
10       {
11           double u = a[j],  v = a[k];
12           a[j] = (u+v) * SQRT1_2;
13           a[k] = (u-v) * SQRT1_2;
14       }
15       mersenne_walsh(a, f1);
16       mersenne_walsh(a+f1+1, f1);  // <--= omit line to obtain Mersenne-Haar transform
17   }
```

Figure 24.8-C (right) gives the basis functions for the non-normalized Mersenne-Walsh transform. The Mersenne-Haar transform is obtained by deleting one line as indicated. The implementation is given in [FXT: haar/mers-haar.h], the basis functions of the non-normalized version are shown at the left of figure 24.8-C. The figure was created with the programs [FXT: fft/mers-walsh-demo.cc] and [FXT: fft/mers-haar-demo.cc]. Note that both transforms leave the central element unchanged.

Chapter 25

The Hartley transform

The Hartley transform is a trigonometric transform that maps real data to real data. While the fast algorithms for radix-2 can be found without great difficulty, the higher radix algorithms are not obvious. Therefore it is appropriate to describe the Hartley transform in terms of the Fourier transform. A method for the conversion of FFT algorithms to fast Hartley transform (FHT) algorithms is given.

We give algorithms for the conversion of Hartley transforms to and from Fourier transforms. We further develop FHT-based convolution routines for complex and real-valued data, and for the negacyclic convolution.

25.1 Definition and symmetries

The *discrete Hartley transform* of a length-n sequence a is defined as

$$c \quad = \quad \mathcal{H}[a] \tag{25.1-1a}$$

$$c_k \quad := \quad \frac{1}{\sqrt{n}} \sum_{x=0}^{n-1} a_x \left(\cos\frac{2\pi k x}{n} + \sin\frac{2\pi k x}{n} \right) \tag{25.1-1b}$$

This is almost the discrete Fourier transform, but with 'cos + sin' instead of 'cos $+i \cdot$ sin'. The continuous Hartley transform is treated in [177].

The Hartley transform of a purely real sequence is purely real:

$$\mathcal{H}[a] \quad \in \quad \mathbb{R} \qquad \text{for} \quad a \in \mathbb{R} \tag{25.1-2}$$

The transform is its own inverse:

$$\mathcal{H}[\mathcal{H}[a]] \quad = \quad a \tag{25.1-3}$$

Symmetry is conserved, as with the Fourier transform: the Hartley transform of a symmetric, antisymmetric sequence is symmetric, antisymmetric, respectively. Using the notation from section 21.6 on page 428, we have

$$\mathcal{H}[a_S] \quad = \quad +\overline{\mathcal{H}[a_S]} = +\mathcal{H}[\overline{a_S}] \tag{25.1-4a}$$

$$\mathcal{H}[a_A] \quad = \quad -\overline{\mathcal{H}[a_A]} = -\mathcal{H}[\overline{a_A}] \tag{25.1-4b}$$

An algorithm for the fast $(n \log(n))$ computation of the Hartley transform is called a *fast Hartley transform* (FHT).

25.2 Radix-2 FHT algorithms

25.2.1 Decimation in time (DIT) FHT

For a length-n sequence a of let $\mathcal{X}^{1/2}a$ denote the sequence with elements $a_x \cos\pi x/n + \bar{a}_x \sin\pi x/n$. The operator $\mathcal{X}^{1/2}$ is the equivalent to the operator $\mathcal{S}^{1/2}$ of the Fourier transform algorithms. We use

J. Arndt, *Matters Computational: Ideas, Algorithms, Source Code*,
DOI 10.1007/978-3-642-14764-7_25, © Springer-Verlag Berlin Heidelberg 2011

the notation (*even*) and (*odd*) as introduced in section 21.2 on page 411. The radix-2 decimation in time (DIT) step for the FHT is

$$\mathcal{H}\left[a\right]^{(left)} \overset{n/2}{=} \mathcal{H}\left[a^{(even)}\right] + \mathcal{X}^{1/2}\mathcal{H}\left[a^{(odd)}\right] \tag{25.2-1a}$$

$$\mathcal{H}\left[a\right]^{(right)} \overset{n/2}{=} \mathcal{H}\left[a^{(even)}\right] - \mathcal{X}^{1/2}\mathcal{H}\left[a^{(odd)}\right] \tag{25.2-1b}$$

This is the equivalent to relations 21.2-3a and 21.2-3b on page 412.

Pseudocode for a recursive radix-2 DIT FHT (C++ version in [FXT: fht/recfht2.cc]):

```
1    procedure rec_fht_dit2(a[], n, x[])
2    // real a[0..n-1] input
3    // real x[0..n-1] result
4    {
5        real b[0..n/2-1], c[0..n/2-1]    // workspace
6        real s[0..n/2-1], t[0..n/2-1]    // workspace
7
8        if n == 1 then
9        {
10           x[0] := a[0]
11           return
12       }
13
14       nh := n/2;
15
16       for k:=0 to nh-1
17       {
18           s[k] := a[2*k]      // even indexed elements
19           t[k] := a[2*k+1]  // odd   indexed elements
20       }
21
22       rec_fht_dit2(s[], nh, b[])
23       rec_fht_dit2(t[], nh, c[])
24
25       hartley_shift(c[], nh, 1/2)
26
27       for k:=0 to nh-1
28       {
29           x[k]    := b[k] + c[k];
30           x[k+nh] := b[k] - c[k];
31       }
32   }
```

The result is returned in the array in x[]. The procedure hartley_shift() implements the operator $\mathcal{X}^{1/2}$, it replaces element c_k of the input sequence c by $c_k \cos(\pi k/n) + c_{n-k} \sin(\pi k/n)$. As pseudocode:

```
1    procedure hartley_shift_05(a[], n)
2    // real a[0..n-1] input, result
3    {
4        nh := n/2
5        j  := n-1
6        for k:=1 to nh-1
7        {
8            c := cos( PI*k/n )
9            s := sin( PI*k/n )
10
11           { a[k], a[j] } := { c*a[k] + s*a[j], s*a[k] - c*a[j] }  // parallel assignment
12
13           j := j-1
14       }
15   }
```

C++ implementations are given in [FXT: fht/hartleyshift.h]. A version that exploits the symmetry of the trigonometric factors is

```
1    #define Tdouble long double
2    #define Sin      sinl
3
4    template <typename Type>
5    inline void hartley_shift_05_v2rec(Type *f, ulong n)
6    {
7        const ulong nh = n/2;
8        if ( n>=4 )
9        {
10           ulong im=nh/2, jm=3*im;
```

```
11          Type fi = f[im],   fj = f[jm];
12          double cs = SQRT1_2;
13          f[im] = (fi + fj) * cs;
14          f[jm] = (fi - fj) * cs;
15
16          if ( n>=8 )
17          {
18              const Tdouble phi0 = PI/n;
19              Tdouble be = Sin(phi0),  al = Sin(0.5*phi0);  al *= (2.0*al);
20              Tdouble s = 0.0,  c = 1.0;
21              for (ulong i=1, j=n-1, k=nh-1, l=nh+1;  i<k;   ++i, --j, --k, ++l)
22              {
23                  { Tdouble tt = c;  c -= (al*tt+be*s);  s -= (al*s-be*tt); }
24
25                  fi = f[i];
26                  fj = f[j];
27                  f[i] = fi * (double)c + fj * (double)s;   // jjcast
28                  f[j] = fi * (double)s - fj * (double)c;   // jjcast
29
30                  // l = i + nh;  k = j - nh;
31                  fi = f[k];
32                  fj = f[l];
33                  f[k] = fi * (double)s + fj * (double)c;   // jjcast
34                  f[l] = fi * (double)c - fj * (double)s;   // jjcast
35              }
36          }
37      }
38  }
39
40  #undef Tdouble
41  #undef Sin
```

Pseudocode for a non-recursive radix-2 DIT FHT:

```
1   procedure fht_depth_first_dit2(a[], ldn)
2   // real a[0..n-1] input,result
3   {
4       n := 2**ldn  // length of a[] is a power of 2
5
6       revbin_permute(a[], n)
7
8       for ldm:=1 to ldn
9       {
10          m   := 2**ldm
11          mh  := m/2
12          m4  := m/4
13
14          for r:=0 to n-m step m
15          {
16              for j:=1 to m4-1  // hartley_shift(a+r+mh,mh,1/2)
17              {
18                  k := mh - j
19
20                  u := a[r+mh+j]
21                  v := a[r+mh+k]
22
23                  c := cos(j*PI/mh)
24                  s := sin(j*PI/mh)
25
26                  { u, v } := { c*u + s*v, s*u - c*v }  // parallel assignment
27
28                  a[r+mh+j] := u
29                  a[r+mh+k] := v
30              }
31
32              for j:=0 to mh-1
33              {
34                  u := a[r+j]
35                  v := a[r+j+mh]
36
37                  a[r+j]    := u + v
38                  a[r+j+mh] := u - v
39              }
40          }
41      }
42  }
```

The derivation of the 'usual' DIT2 FHT algorithm starts by combining the Hartley-shift with the sum/diff-operations [FXT: fht/fhtdit2.cc]:

```
1    void fht_depth_first_dit2(double *f, ulong ldn)
2    {
3        const ulong n = 1UL<<ldn;
4
5        revbin_permute(f, n);
6
7        for (ulong ldm=1; ldm<=ldn; ++ldm)
8        {
9            const ulong m = (1UL<<ldm);
10           const ulong mh = (m>>1);
11           const ulong m4 = (mh>>1);
12           const double phi0 = M_PI/mh;
13
14           for (ulong r=0; r<n; r+=m)
15           {
16               {  // j == 0:
17                   ulong t1 = r;
18                   ulong t2 = t1 + mh;
19                   sumdiff(f[t1], f[t2]);
20               }
21
22               if ( m4 )
23               {
24                   ulong t1 = r + m4;
25                   ulong t2 = t1 + mh;
26                   sumdiff(f[t1], f[t2]);
27               }
28
29               for (ulong j=1, k=mh-1; j<k; ++j,--k)
30               {
31                   double s, c;
32                   SinCos(phi0*j, &s, &c);
33
34                   ulong tj = r + mh + j;
35                   ulong tk = r + mh + k;
36                   double fj = f[tj];
37                   double fk = f[tk];
38                   f[tj] = fj * c + fk * s;
39                   f[tk] = fj * s - fk * c;
40
41                   ulong t1 = r + j;
42                   ulong t2 = tj; // == t1 + mh;
43                   sumdiff(f[t1], f[t2]);
44
45                   t1 = r + k;
46                   t2 = tk; // == t1 + mh;
47                   sumdiff(f[t1], f[t2]);
48               }
49           }
50       }
51   }
```

Finally, as with the FFT equivalent (see section 21.2.1.3 on page 414), the number of trigonometric computations can be reduced by swapping the innermost loops [FXT: fht/fhtdit2.cc]:

```
1    void fht_dit2(double *f, ulong ldn)
2    // Radix-2 decimation in time (DIT) FHT.
3    {
4        const ulong n = 1UL<<ldn;
5
6        revbin_permute(f, n);
7
8        for (ulong ldm=1; ldm<=ldn; ++ldm)
9        {
10           const ulong m = (1UL<<ldm);
11           const ulong mh = (m>>1);
12           const ulong m4 = (mh>>1);
13           const double phi0 = M_PI/mh;
14
15           for (ulong r=0; r<n; r+=m)
16           {
17               {  // j == 0:
18                   ulong t1 = r;
19                   ulong t2 = t1 + mh;
20                   sumdiff(f[t1], f[t2]);
21               }
```

```
22
23          if ( m4 )
24          {
25              ulong t1 = r + m4;
26              ulong t2 = t1 + mh;
27              sumdiff(f[t1], f[t2]);
28          }
29      }
30
31      for (ulong j=1, k=mh-1; j<k; ++j,--k)
32      {
33          double s, c;
34          SinCos(phi0*j, &s, &c);
35
36          for (ulong r=0; r<n; r+=m)
37          {
38              ulong tj = r + mh + j;
39              ulong tk = r + mh + k;
40              double fj = f[tj];
41              double fk = f[tk];
42              f[tj] = fj * c + fk * s;
43              f[tk] = fj * s - fk * c;
44
45              ulong t1 = r + j;
46              ulong t2 = tj; // == t1 + mh;
47              sumdiff(f[t1], f[t2]);
48
49              t1 = r + k;
50              t2 = tk; // == t1 + mh;
51              sumdiff(f[t1], f[t2]);
52          }
53      }
54  }
55 }
```

25.2.2 Decimation in frequency (DIF) FHT

The radix-2 decimation in frequency step for the FHT is (compare to relations 21.2-6a and 21.2-6b on page 415):

$$\mathcal{H}[a]^{(even)} \overset{n/2}{=} \mathcal{H}\left[a^{(left)} + a^{(right)}\right] \tag{25.2-2a}$$

$$\mathcal{H}[a]^{(odd)} \overset{n/2}{=} \mathcal{H}\left[\mathcal{X}^{1/2}\left(a^{(left)} - a^{(right)}\right)\right] \tag{25.2-2b}$$

Pseudocode for a recursive radix-2 DIF FHT (the C++ equivalent is given in [FXT: fht/recfht2.cc]):

```
1   procedure rec_fht_dif2(a[], n, x[])
2   // real a[0..n-1] input
3   // real x[0..n-1] result
4   {
5       real b[0..n/2-1], c[0..n/2-1]    // workspace
6       real s[0..n/2-1], t[0..n/2-1]    // workspace
7
8       if n == 1 then
9       {
10          x[0]  := a[0]
11          return
12      }
13
14      nh := n/2;
15
16      for k:=0 to nh-1
17      {
18          s[k]  := a[k]      // 'left'  elements
19          t[k]  := a[k+nh]   // 'right' elements
20      }
21
22      for k:=0 to nh-1
23      {
24          { s[k], t[k] } := { s[k]+t[k], s[k]-t[k] }  // parallel assignment
25      }
26
27      hartley_shift(t[], nh, 1/2)
28
```

```
29        rec_fht_dif2(s[], nh, b[])
30        rec_fht_dif2(t[], nh, c[])
31
32        j := 0
33        for k:=0 to nh-1
34        {
35            x[j]    := b[k]
36            x[j+1]  := c[k]
37            j  := j+2
38        }
39   }
```

Pseudocode for a non-recursive radix-2 DIF FHT (C++ version in [FXT: fht/fhtdif2.cc]):

```
1    procedure fht_depth_first_dif2(a[], ldn)
2    // real a[0..n-1] input,result
3    {
4        n := 2**ldn  // length of a[] is a power of 2
5
6        for ldm:=ldn to 1 step -1
7        {
8            m   := 2**ldm
9            mh  := m/2
10           m4  := m/4
11
12           for r:=0 to n-m step m
13           {
14               for j:=0 to mh-1
15               {
16                   u := a[r+j]
17                   v := a[r+j+mh]
18
19                   a[r+j]    := u + v
20                   a[r+j+mh] := u - v
21               }
22
23               for j:=1 to m4-1
24               {
25                   k := mh - j
26
27                   u := a[r+mh+j]
28                   v := a[r+mh+k]
29
30                   c := cos(j*PI/mh)
31                   s := sin(j*PI/mh)
32
33                   { u, v } := { c * u + s * v, s * u - c * v }  // parallel assignment
34
35                   a[r+mh+j] := u
36                   a[r+mh+k] := v
37               }
38           }
39       }
40
41       revbin_permute(a[], n)
42   }
```

The 'usual' DIF2 FHT algorithm is again obtained by swapping the inner loops, a C++ implementation is [FXT: fht/fhtdif2.cc]:

```
1    void fht_dif2(double *f, ulong ldn)
2    // Radix-2 decimation in frequency (DIF) FHT
3    {
4        const ulong n = (1UL<<ldn);
5        for (ulong ldm=ldn; ldm>=1; --ldm)
6        {
7            const ulong m = (1UL<<ldm);
8            const ulong mh = (m>>1);
9            const ulong m4 = (mh>>1);
10           const double phi0 = M_PI/mh;
11
12           for (ulong r=0; r<n; r+=m)
13           {
14               { // j == 0:
15                   ulong t1 = r;
16                   ulong t2 = t1 + mh;
17                   sumdiff(f[t1], f[t2]);
```

```
18            }
19
20            if ( m4 )
21            {
22                ulong t1 = r + m4;
23                ulong t2 = t1 + mh;
24                sumdiff(f[t1], f[t2]);
25            }
26        }
27
28        for (ulong j=1, k=mh-1; j<k; ++j,--k)
29        {
30            double s, c;
31            SinCos(phi0*j, &s, &c);
32
33            for (ulong r=0; r<n; r+=m)
34            {
35                ulong tj = r + mh + j;
36                ulong tk = r + mh + k;
37
38                ulong t1 = r + j;
39                ulong t2 = tj; // == t1 + mh;
40                sumdiff(f[t1], f[t2]);
41
42                t1 = r + k;
43                t2 = tk; // == t1 + mh;
44                sumdiff(f[t1], f[t2]);
45
46                double fj = f[tj];
47                double fk = f[tk];
48                f[tj] = fj * c + fk * s;
49                f[tk] = fj * s - fk * c;
50            }
51        }
52    }
53
54    revbin_permute(f, n);
55 }
```

25.3 Complex FFT by FHT

The relations between the Hartley and Fourier transforms can be read off directly from their definitions and their symmetry relations. Let σ be the sign of the Fourier transform. The Fourier transform of a complex sequence $d \in \mathbb{C}$ is, in terms of the Hartley transform,

$$\mathcal{F}[d] \;=\; \frac{1}{2}\left(\mathcal{H}[d] + \overline{\mathcal{H}[d]} + \sigma\, i\left(\mathcal{H}[d] - \overline{\mathcal{H}[d]}\right)\right) \tag{25.3-1}$$

Written out for the real and imaginary part of $d = a + ib$ $(a, b \in \mathbb{R})$:

$$\mathfrak{Re}\,\mathcal{F}[a+ib] \;=\; \frac{1}{2}\left(\mathcal{H}[a] + \overline{\mathcal{H}[a]} - \sigma\left(\mathcal{H}[b] - \overline{\mathcal{H}[b]}\right)\right) \tag{25.3-2a}$$

$$\mathfrak{Im}\,\mathcal{F}[a+ib] \;=\; \frac{1}{2}\left(\mathcal{H}[b] + \overline{\mathcal{H}[b]} + \sigma\left(\mathcal{H}[a] - \overline{\mathcal{H}[a]}\right)\right) \tag{25.3-2b}$$

Using the symmetry relations 25.1-4a and 25.1-4b on page 515, we recast the equations as

$$\mathfrak{Re}\,\mathcal{F}[a+ib] \;=\; \frac{1}{2}\mathcal{H}[a_S - \sigma\, b_A] \tag{25.3-3a}$$

$$\mathfrak{Im}\,\mathcal{F}[a+ib] \;=\; \frac{1}{2}\mathcal{H}[b_S + \sigma\, a_A] \tag{25.3-3b}$$

Both formulations lead to the very same conversion procedure:

```
1  procedure fht_fft_conversion(a[], b[], n, is)
2  {
3      for k:=1 to n/2-1
4      {
5          t := n-k
6
```

```
7            as := a[k] + a[t]
8            aa := a[k] - a[t]
9
10           bs := b[k] + b[t]
11           ba := b[k] - b[t]
12
13           aa := is * aa
14           ba := is * ba
15
16           a[k] := 1/2 * (as - ba)
17           a[t] := 1/2 * (as + ba)
18
19           b[k] := 1/2 * (bs + aa)
20           b[t] := 1/2 * (bs - aa)
21        }
22   }
```

The C++ implementations are given in [FXT: fft/fhtfft.cc] for type **double** and [FXT: fft/fhtcfft.cc] for type **complex**. There are two options to compute a complex FFT by two FHTs, we can compute the FHTs either at the beginning of the routine

```
1    procedure fft_by_fht1(a[], b[], n, is)
2    // real a[0..n-1] input,result (real part)
3    // real b[0..n-1] input,result (imaginary part)
4    {
5        fht(a[], n)
6        fht(b[], n)
7        fht_fft_conversion(a[], b[], n, is)
8    }
```

or at the end

```
1    procedure fft_by_fht2(a[], b[], n, is)
2    // real a[0..n-1] input,result (real part)
3    // real b[0..n-1] input,result (imaginary part)
4    {
5        fht_fft_conversion(a[], b[], n, is)
6        fht(a[], n)
7        fht(b[], n)
8    }
```

The real and imaginary parts of the FFT are computed independently by this procedure. This can be very advantageous when the real and imaginary parts of complex data lie in separate arrays. The C++ version is given in [FXT: fft/fhtfft.cc].

25.4   Complex FFT by complex FHT and vice versa

A complex FHT is simply two FHTs (one of the real, one of the imaginary part). So we can use either version from section 25.3 and there is nothing new. Really? If one has a type **complex** version of both the conversion and the FHT routine, then the complex FFT can be computed as either

```
1    procedure fft_by_fht1(c[], n, is)
2    // complex c[0..n-1] input,result
3    {
4        fht(c[], n)
5        fht_fft_conversion(c[], n, is)
6    }
```

or the same with swapped statements. One saves half of the trigonometric computations and book keeping. It is easy to derive a complex FHT from the real version, and with a well optimized FHT you get an even better optimized FFT. C++ implementations of complex FHTs are given in [FXT: fht/cfhtdif.cc] (DIF algorithm), [FXT: fht/cfhtdit.cc] (DIT algorithm), and, for zero padded data, [FXT: fht/cfht0.cc].

The other way round: computation of a complex FHT using FFTs. Let T be the operator corresponding to the **fht_fft_conversion**. The operator is its own inverse: $T = T^{-1}$. We have seen that

$$\mathcal{F} = \mathcal{H} \cdot T \quad \text{and} \quad \mathcal{F} = T \cdot \mathcal{H} \tag{25.4-1}$$

Multiply the relations with T and use $T \cdot T = 1$ to obtain:

$$\mathcal{H} = T \cdot \mathcal{F} \quad \text{and} \quad \mathcal{H} = \mathcal{F} \cdot T \tag{25.4-2}$$

Hence we have either

```
1    procedure fht_by_fft(c[], n, is)
2    // complex c[0..n-1] input,result
3    {
4        fft(c[], n)
5        fht_fft_conversion(c[], n, is)
6    }
```

or the same thing with swapped lines [FXT: fft/fhtcfft.cc]. The same ideas also work for separate real and imaginary parts but in that case one should rather use separate FHTs for the two arrays.

25.5 Real FFT by FHT and vice versa

To express the real and imaginary part of a Fourier transform of a purely real sequence $a \in \mathbb{R}$ by its Hartley transform use relations 25.3-2a and 25.3-2b on page 521 and set $b = 0$:

$$\Re \mathcal{F}[a] = \frac{1}{2}(\mathcal{H}[a] + \overline{\mathcal{H}[a]}) \tag{25.5-1a}$$

$$\Im \mathcal{F}[a] = \sigma \frac{1}{2}(\mathcal{H}[a] - \overline{\mathcal{H}[a]}) \tag{25.5-1b}$$

A C++ implementation is [FXT: realfft/realfftbyfht.cc]

```
1    void
2    fht_real_complex_fft(double *f, ulong ldn, int is/*=+1*/)
3    {
4        fht(f, ldn);
5
6        const ulong n = (1UL<<ldn);
7
8        if ( is>0 )  for (ulong i=1,j=n-1; i<j; i++,j--)  sumdiff05(f[i], f[j]);
9        else         for (ulong i=1,j=n-1; i<j; i++,j--)  sumdiff05_r(f[i], f[j]);
10   }
```

The functions sumdiff05() and sumdiff05_r() are defined as [FXT: aux0/sumdiff.h]

```
1    template <typename Type>
2    static inline void sumdiff05(Type &a, Type &b)
3    // {a, b}  <--| {0.5*(a+b),  0.5*(a-b)}
4    { Type t=(a-b)*0.5; a+=b; a*=0.5; b=t; }
5
6    template <typename Type>
7    static inline void sumdiff05_r(Type &a, Type &b)
8    // {a, b}  <--| {0.5*(a+b), 0.5*(b-a)}
9    { Type t=(b-a)*0.5; a+=b; a*=0.5; b=t; }
```

At the end of the procedure the ordering of the output data $c = \mathcal{F}[a] \in \mathbb{C}$ is

$$\begin{aligned}
a[0] &= \Re c_0 \\
a[1] &= \Re c_1 \\
a[2] &= \Re c_2
\end{aligned} \tag{25.5-2}$$

$$\cdots$$

$$\begin{aligned}
a[n/2] &= \Re c_{n/2} \\
a[n/2+1] &= \Im c_{n/2-1} \\
a[n/2+2] &= \Im c_{n/2-2} \\
a[n/2+3] &= \Im c_{n/2-3}
\end{aligned}$$

$$\cdots$$

$$a[n-1] = \Im c_1$$

The inverse procedure is given in [FXT: realfft/realfftbyfht.cc]:

```
1    void
2    fht_complex_real_fft(double *f, ulong ldn, int is/*=+1*/)
3    {
4        const ulong n = (1UL<<ldn);
5
6        if ( is>0 )  for (ulong i=1,j=n-1; i<j; i++,j--)  sumdiff(f[i], f[j]);
7        else         for (ulong i=1,j=n-1; i<j; i++,j--)  diffsum(f[i], f[j]);
8
9        fht(f,ldn);
10   }
```

The function `sumdiff()` is defined in [FXT: aux0/sumdiff.h]:

```
1    template <typename Type>
2    static inline void sumdiff(Type &a, Type &b)
3    // {a, b}  <--| {a+b, a-b}
4    { Type t=a-b; a+=b; b=t; }
5
6    template <typename Type>
7    static inline void diffsum(Type &a, Type &b)
8    // {a, b}  <--| {a-b, a+b}
9    { Type t=a-b; b+=a; a=t; }
```

The input has to be ordered as given in relations 25.5-2 on the previous page. The sign of the transform (variable `is`) has to be the same as with the forward version.

Computation of an FHT using a real-valued FFT proceeds similarly as for complex versions. Let T_{r2c} be the operator corresponding to the post-processing in `fht_real_complex_fft()`, and T_{c2r} correspond to the preprocessing in `fht_complex_real_fft()`. That is

$$\mathcal{F}_{c2r} = \mathcal{H} \cdot T_{c2r} \qquad \text{and} \qquad \mathcal{F}_{r2c} = T_{r2c} \cdot \mathcal{H} \qquad (25.5\text{-}3)$$

The operators are mutually inverse: $T_{r2c} = T_{c2r}^{-1}$ and $T_{c2r} = T_{r2c}^{-1}$. Multiplying the relations and using $T_{r2c} \cdot T_{c2r} = T_{c2r} \cdot T_{r2c} = 1$ gives

$$\mathcal{H} = T_{c2r} \cdot \mathcal{F}_{r2c} \qquad \text{and} \qquad \mathcal{H} = \mathcal{F}_{c2r} \cdot T_{r2c} \qquad (25.5\text{-}4)$$

25.6   Higher radix FHT algorithms

Higher radix FHT algorithms seem to get complicated due to the structure of the Hartley shift operator. In fact there is a straightforward way to turn any FFT decomposition into an FHT algorithm.

For the moment assume that we want to compute a complex FHT, further assume we want to use a radix-r algorithm. At each step we have r short FHTs and want to combine them to a longer FHT but we do not know how this might be done. In section 25.3 on page 521 we learned how to turn an FHT into an FFT using the T-operator. And we have seen radix-r algorithms for the FFT. The crucial idea is to use the conversion operator T as a wrapper around the FFT-step that combines several short FFTs into a longer one. Turn a radix-r FFT-step into an FHT-step as follows:

1. Convert the r short FHTs into FFTs (use T on the subsequences).

2. Do the radix-r FFT step.

3. Convert the FFT into an FHT (use T on the sequence).

For efficient implementations one obviously wants to combine the computations.

With a radix-r step the scheme always accesses $2r$ elements simultaneously. The symmetry of the trigonometric factors is thereby automatically exploited. Splitting steps for the radix-4 FHT and the split-radix FHT are given in [317].

25.7 Convolution via FHT

The convolution property of the Hartley transform can be stated as

$$\mathcal{H}[a \circledast b] = \frac{1}{2}\left(\mathcal{H}[a]\,\mathcal{H}[b] - \overline{\mathcal{H}[a]}\,\overline{\mathcal{H}[b]} + \mathcal{H}[a]\,\overline{\mathcal{H}[b]} + \overline{\mathcal{H}[a]}\,\mathcal{H}[b]\right) \tag{25.7-1}$$

or, with $c := \mathcal{H}[a]$ and $d := \mathcal{H}[b]$, written element-wise:

$$\mathcal{H}[a \circledast b]_k = \frac{1}{2}\left(c_k\,d_k - \overline{c_k}\,\overline{d_k} + c_k\,\overline{d_k} + \overline{c_k}\,d_k\right) \tag{25.7-2a}$$

$$= \frac{1}{2}\left(c_k\,(d_k + \overline{d_k}) + \overline{c_k}\,(d_k - \overline{d_k})\right) \tag{25.7-2b}$$

$$= \frac{1}{2}\left(d_k\,(c_k + \overline{c_k}) + \overline{d_k}\,(c_k - \overline{c_k})\right) \tag{25.7-2c}$$

The latter forms reduce the number of multiplications. When turning the relation into an algorithm, one has to keep in mind that both elements $y_k = \mathcal{H}[a \circledast b]_k$ and y_{-k} must be computed simultaneously.

For the auto-convolution equation 25.7-2a becomes:

$$\mathcal{H}[a \circledast a]_k = \frac{1}{2}\left(c_k\,(c_k + \overline{c_k}) + \overline{c_k}\,(c_k - \overline{c_k}))\right) \tag{25.7-3a}$$

$$= c_k\,\overline{c_k} + \frac{1}{2}\left(c_k^2 - \overline{c_k}^2\right) \tag{25.7-3b}$$

25.7.1 Algorithms as pseudocode

The following routine computes the cyclic convolution of two real-valued sequences x[] and y[] via the FHT, the array length n must be even:

```
1    procedure fht_cyclic_convolution(x[], y[], n)
2    // real x[0..n-1] input, modified
3    // real y[0..n-1] result
4    {
5        // transform data:
6        fht(x[], n)
7        fht(y[], n)
8
9        // convolution in transformed domain:
10       j := n-1
11       for i:=1 to n/2-1
12       {
13           xi := x[i]
14           xj := x[j]
15
16           yp := y[i] + y[j]    // ==   y[j] + y[i]
17           ym := y[i] - y[j]    // == -(y[j] - y[i])
18
19           y[i] := (xi*yp + xj*ym)/2
20           y[j] := (xj*yp - xi*ym)/2
21
22           j := j-1
23       }
24       y[0] := x[0] * y[0]
25       if n>1 then  y[n/2] := x[n/2] * y[n/2]
26
27       // transform back:
28       fht(y[], n)
29
30       // normalize:
31       for i:=0 to n-1
32       {
33           y[i] := y[i] / n
34       }
35   }
```

It is assumed that the procedure fht() does no normalization. A routine for the cyclic auto-convolution is

```
1    procedure cyclic_self_convolution(x[], n)
2    // real x[0..n-1] input, result
3    {
4        // transform data:
5        fht(x[], n)
6
7        // convolution in transformed domain:
8        j := n-1
9        for i:=1 to n/2-1
10       {
11           ci := x[i]
12           cj := x[j]
13
14           t1 := ci*cj                // == cj*ci
15           t2 := 1/2*(ci*ci-cj*cj)    // == -1/2*(cj*cj-ci*ci)
16
17           x[i] := t1 + t2
18           x[j] := t1 - t2
19
20           j := j-1
21       }
22       x[0]    := x[0] * x[0]
23
24       if n>1 then  x[n/2] := x[n/2] * x[n/2]
25
26       // transform back:
27       fht(x[], n)
28
29       // normalize:
30       for i:=0 to n-1
31       {
32           x[i] := x[i] / n
33       }
34   }
```

For odd n replace the line

```
    for i:=1 to n/2-1
```

by

```
    for i:=1 to (n-1)/2
```

and omit the line

```
    if n>1 then  x[n/2] := x[n/2]*x[n/2]
```

in both procedures above.

25.7.2   C++ implementations

The FHT based routine for the cyclic convolution of two real sequences is [FXT: convolution/fhtcnvl.cc]

```
1    void fht_convolution(double * restrict f, double * restrict g, ulong ldn)
2    {
3        fht(f, ldn);
4        fht(g, ldn);
5        fht_convolution_core(f, g, ldn);
6        fht(g, ldn);
7    }
```

The equivalent of the element-wise multiplication is given in [FXT: convolution/fhtcnvlcore.cc]:

```
1    void
2    fht_convolution_core(const double * restrict f, double * restrict g, ulong ldn,
3                         double v/*=0.0*/)
4    // Auxiliary routine for the computation of convolutions
5    //    via Fast Hartley Transforms.
6    // ldn := base-2 logarithm of the array length.
7    // v!=0.0 chooses alternative normalization.
8    {
9        const ulong n = (1UL<<ldn);
10
11       if ( v==0.0 )  v = 1.0/n;
12
13       g[0]    *=  (v * f[0]);
14       const ulong  nh = n/2;
15
```

```
16        if ( nh>0 )
17        {
18            g[nh] *= (v * f[nh]);
19            v *= 0.5;
20            for (ulong i=1,j=n-1; i<j; i++,j--)  fht_mul(f[i], f[j], g[i], g[j], v);
21        }
22    }
```

The auxiliary function `fht_mul()` is [FXT: convolution/fhtmulsqr.h]

```
1    template <typename Type>
2    static inline  void
3    fht_mul(Type xi, Type xj, Type &yi, Type &yj, double v)
4    // yi <-- v*( (yi + yj)*xi + (yi - yj)*xj )   == v*( (xi + xj)*yi + (xi - xj)*yj )
5    // yj <-- v*( (-yi + yj)*xi + (yi + yj)*xj )  == v*( (-xi + xj)*yi + (xi + xj)*yj )
6    {
7        Type h1p = xi,  h1m = xj;
8        Type s1 = h1p + h1m,  d1 = h1p - h1m;
9        Type h2p = yi,  h2m = yj;
10       yi = (h2p * s1 + h2m * d1) * v;
11       yj = (h2m * s1 - h2p * d1) * v;
12   }
```

A C++ implementation of the FHT based self-convolution is given in [FXT: convolution/fhtcnvla.cc]. It uses the routine [FXT: convolution/fhtcnvlacore.cc]

```
1    void
2    fht_auto_convolution_core(double *f, ulong ldn,
3                               double v/*=0.0*/)
4    // v!=0.0 chooses alternative normalization
5    {
6        const ulong  n  = (1UL<<ldn);
7        if ( v==0.0 )   v = 1.0/n;
8        f[0] *= (v * f[0]);
9        if ( n>=2 )
10       {
11           const ulong  nh = n/2;
12           f[nh] *= (v * f[nh]);
13           v *= 0.5;
14           for (ulong i=1,j=n-1; i<j; i++,j--)  fht_sqr(f[i], f[j], v);
15       }
16   }
```

where [FXT: convolution/fhtmulsqr.h]:

```
1    template <typename Type>
2    static inline  void
3    fht_sqr(Type &xi, Type &xj, double v)
4    // xi <-- v*( 2*xi*xj + xi*xi - xj*xj )
5    // xj <-- v*( 2*xi*xj - xi*xi + xj*xj )
6    {
7        Type a = xi,  b = xj;
8        Type s1 = (a + b) * (a - b);
9        a *= b;
10       a += a;
11       xi = (a+s1) * v;
12       xj = (a-s1) * v;
13   }
```

25.7.3 Avoiding the revbin permutations

The observation that the revbin permutations can be omitted with FFT-based convolutions (see section 22.1.3 on page 442) applies again [FXT: convolution/fhtcnvlcore.cc]:

```
1    void
2    fht_convolution_revbin_permuted_core(const double * restrict f,
3                                          double * restrict g,
4                                          ulong ldn,
5                                          double v/*=0.0*/)
6    // Same as fht_convolution_core() but with data access in revbin order.
7    {
8        const ulong n = (1UL<<ldn);
9
10       if ( v==0.0 )   v = 1.0/n;
11
```

```
12      g[0] *= (v * f[0]);  // 0 == revbin(0)
13      if ( n>=2 )  g[1] *= (v * f[1]); // 1 == revbin(nh)
14
15      if ( n<4 )  return;
16
17      v *= 0.5;
18      const ulong nh = (n>>1);
19
20      ulong r=nh, rm=n-1; // nh == revbin(1),  n1-1 == revbin(n-1)
21      fht_mul(f[r], f[rm], g[r], g[rm], v);
22
23      ulong k=2, km=n-2;
24      while ( k<nh  )
25      {
26          // k even:
27          rm -= nh;
28          ulong tr = r;
29          r^=nh;  for (ulong m=(nh>>1); !((r^=m)&m); m>>=1)  {;}
30          fht_mul(f[r], f[rm], g[r], g[rm], v);
31          --km;
32          ++k;
33
34          // k odd:
35          rm += (tr-r);
36          r += nh;
37          fht_mul(f[r], f[rm], g[r], g[rm], v);
38          --km;
39          ++k;
40      }
41  }
```

The optimized version saving three revbin permutations is [FXT: convolution/fhtcnvl.cc]:

```
1   void fht_convolution(double * restrict f, double * restrict g, ulong ldn)
2   {
3       fht_dif_core(f, ldn);
4       fht_dif_core(g, ldn);
5       fht_convolution_revbin_permuted_core(f, g, ldn);
6       fht_dit_core(g, ldn);
7   }
```

25.7.4 Negacyclic convolution via FHT

Pseudocode for the computation of the negacyclic auto-convolution via FHT:

```
1   procedure negacyclic_self_convolution(x[], n)
2   // real x[0..n-1]  input, result
3   {
4       hartley_shift_05(x, n)     // preprocess
5       fht(x, n)    // transform data
6
7       // convolution in transformed domain:
8       j := n-1
9       for i:=0 to n/2-1  // here i starts from zero
10      {
11          a := x[i]
12          b := x[j]
13
14          x[i] := a*b+(a*a-b*b)/2
15          x[j] := a*b-(a*a-b*b)/2
16          j := j-1
17      }
18
19      fht(x, n)    // transform back
20      hartley_shift_05(x, n)    // postprocess
21  }
```

C++ implementations for the negacyclic convolution and self-convolution are given in [FXT: convolution/fhtnegacnvl.cc]. The negacyclic convolution is used for the computation of weighted transforms, for example in the MFA-based convolution for real input described in section 22.5.4 on page 453.

25.8 Localized FHT algorithms

Localized routines for the FHT can be obtained by slight modifications of the corresponding algorithms for the Walsh transform described in section 23.5 on page 468. The decimation in time (DIT) version is [FXT: fht/fhtloc2.h]:

```
1    template <typename Type>
2    void fht_loc_dit2_core(Type *f, ulong ldn)
3    {
4        if ( ldn<=13 )  // sizeof(Type)*(2**threshold) <= L1_CACHE_BYTES
5        {
6            fht_dit_core(f, ldn);
7            return;
8        }
9
10       // Recursion:
11       fht_dit_core_2(f+2);  // ldm==1
12       fht_dit_core_4(f+4);  // ldm==2
13       fht_dit_core_8(f+8);  // ldm==3
14       for (ulong ldm=4; ldm<ldn; ++ldm)  fht_loc_dit2_core(f+(1UL<<ldm), ldm);
15
16
17       for (ulong ldm=1; ldm<=ldn; ++ldm)
18       {
19           const ulong m = (1UL<<ldm);
20           const ulong mh = (m>>1);
21           hartley_shift_05(f+mh, mh);
22           for (ulong t1=0, t2=mh;  t1<mh;  ++t1, ++t2)  sumdiff(f[t1], f[t2]);
23       }
24   }
```

The routine `hartley_shift_05()` is described in 25.2.1 on page 515. Choose an implementation that uses trigonometric recursion as this improves performance considerably.

The decimation in frequency (DIF) version is:

```
1    template <typename Type>
2    void fht_loc_dif2_core(Type *f, ulong ldn)
3    {
4        if ( ldn<=13 )  // sizeof(Type)*(2**threshold) <= L1_CACHE_BYTES
5        {
6            fht_dif_core(f, ldn);
7            return;
8        }
9
10       for (ulong ldm=ldn; ldm>=1; --ldm)
11       {
12           const ulong m = (1UL<<ldm);
13           const ulong mh = (m>>1);
14           for (ulong t1=0, t2=mh;  t1<mh;  ++t1, ++t2)  sumdiff(f[t1], f[t2]);
15           hartley_shift_05(f+mh, mh);
16       }
17
18       // Recursion:
19       fht_dif_core_2(f+2);  // ldm==1
20       fht_dif_core_4(f+4);  // ldm==2
21       fht_dif_core_8(f+8);  // ldm==3
22       for (ulong ldm=4; ldm<ldn; ++ldm)  fht_loc_dif2_core(f+(1UL<<ldm), ldm);
23   }
```

The (generated) short-length transforms are given in the files [FXT: fht/shortfhtdifcore.h] and [FXT: fht/shortfhtditcore.h]. For example, the length-8 decimation in frequency routine is

```
1    template <typename Type>
2    inline void
3    fht_dif_core_8(Type *f)
4    {
5        Type g0, f0, f1, g1;
6        sumdiff(f[0], f[4], f0, g0);
7        sumdiff(f[2], f[6], f1, g1);
8        sumdiff(f0, f1);
9        sumdiff(g0, g1);
10       Type s1, c1, s2, c2;
11       sumdiff(f[1], f[5], s1, c1);
```

```
12        sumdiff(f[3], f[7], s2, c2);
13        sumdiff(s1, s2);
14        sumdiff(f0, s1, f[0], f[1]);
15        sumdiff(f1, s2, f[2], f[3]);
16        c1 *= SQRT2;
17        c2 *= SQRT2;
18        sumdiff(g0, c1, f[4], f[5]);
19        sumdiff(g1, c2, f[6], f[7]);
20    }
```

An additional revbin permutation is needed if the data is required in order. The FHT can be computed by either

```
fht_loc_dif2_core(f, ldn);
revbin_permute(f, 1UL<<ldn);
```

or

```
revbin_permute(f, 1UL<<ldn);
fht_loc_dit2_core(f, ldn);
```

Performance for large arrays is excellent: the convolutions based on the transforms [FXT: convolution/fhtloccnvl.cc]

```
1    void
2    loc_fht_convolution(double * restrict f, double * restrict g, ulong ldn)
3    {
4        fht_loc_dif2_core(f, ldn);
5        fht_loc_dif2_core(g, ldn);
6        fht_convolution_revbin_permuted_core(f, g, ldn);
7        fht_loc_dit2_core(g, ldn);
8    }
```

and [FXT: convolution/fhtloccnvla.cc]

```
1    void
2    loc_fht_auto_convolution(double *f, ulong ldn)
3    {
4        fht_loc_dif2_core(f, ldn);
5        fht_auto_convolution_revbin_permuted_core(f, ldn);
6        fht_loc_dit2_core(f, ldn);
7    }
```

gave a significant (more than 50 percent) speedup for the high precision multiplication routines (see section 28.2 on page 558) used in the hfloat library [22].

25.9   2-dimensional FHTs

A 2-dimensional FHT can be computed almost as easily as a 2-dimensional FFT, only a simple additional step is needed. Start with the row-column algorithm described in section 21.9.1 on page 437 [FXT: fht/twodimfht.cc]:

```
1    void
2    row_column_fht(double *f, ulong nr, ulong nc)
3    // FHT over rows and columns.
4    // nr := number of rows
5    // nc := number of columns
6    {
7        ulong n = nr * nc;
8
9        // fht over rows:
10       ulong ldc = ld(nc);
11       for (ulong k=0; k<n; k+=nc)  fht(f+k, ldc);
12
13       // fht over columns:
14       double *w = new double[nr];
15       for (ulong k=0; k<nc; k++)  skip_fht(f+k, nr, nc, w);
16       delete [] w;
17    }
```

No attempt has been made to make the routine cache friendly: the routine skip_fht() [FXT: fht/skipfht.cc] simply copies a column into the temporary array, computes the FHT and copies the data back. This is not yet a 2-dimensional FHT, the following post-processing must be made [72]:

```
1    void
2    y_transform(double *f, ulong nr, ulong nc)
3    // Transforms row-column-FHT to 2-dimensional FHT.
4    // Self-inverse.
5    {
6        ulong rh = nr/2;
7        if ( nr&1 )  rh++;
8
9        ulong ch = nc/2;
10       if ( nc&1 )   ch++;
11
12       ulong n = nr*nc;
13       for (ulong tr=1, ctr=nc; tr<rh; tr++,ctr+=nc) // ctr=nc*tr
14       {
15           double *pa = f + ctr;
16           double *pb = pa + nc;
17           double *pc = f + n - ctr;
18           double *pd = pc + nc;
19           for (ulong tc=1; tc<ch; tc++)
20           {
21               pa++;  pb--;  pc++;  pd--;
22               double e = (*pa + *pd - *pb - *pc) * 0.5;
23               *pa -= e;  *pb += e;  *pc += e;  *pd -= e;
24           }
25       }
26   }
```

The canned routine for the 2-dimensional FHT is

```
1    void
2    twodim_fht(double *f, ulong nr, ulong nc)
3    {
4        row_column_fht(f, nr, nc);
5        y_transform(f, nr, nc);
6    }
```

25.10 Automatic generation of transform code

FFT *generators* are programs that output FFT routines, usually for short lengths. The considerations given here are not restricted to FFT codes. However, routines that can be unrolled like those for fast transforms, matrix multiplication, or convolution are prime candidates for automated generation.

Algorithmic knowledge can be built into code generators, but we restrict our attention to a simpler method known as *partial evaluation*. Writing such a program is easy: take an existing FFT and change all computations into print statements that emit the necessary code. The process, however, is less than delightful and very error-prone.

It would be much better to have a program that reads the existing FFT code as input and writes the code for the generator. Let us call this a *meta-generator*. Implementing such a meta-generator is highly nontrivial. It requires writing a parser for the used language, and also data flow analysis. A practical compromise is a program that, while theoretically not even close to a meta-generator, creates output that is a usable generator code.

One should print the current values of the loop variables of the original code as comments at the beginning of a block. That way it is possible to identify the corresponding parts of the generated code and the original file. In addition, one may keep the comments of the original code.

With FFTs it may be necessary to identify the trigonometric values that occur in the process in terms of the corresponding sine and cosine arguments as rational multiples of π. These values should be inlined to some greater precision than actually needed to avoid the generation of multiple copies with differences only due to numeric inaccuracies. Printing the arguments, both as they appear and in lowest terms, inside comments helps to understand and further optimize the generated code:

```
double c1=.98078528040323044912618223613414;  // == cos(Pi*1/16) == cos(Pi*1/16)
double s1=.19509032201612826784828486847614;  // == sin(Pi*1/16) == sin(Pi*1/16)
double c2=.92387953251128675612831838939740;  // == cos(Pi*2/16) == cos(Pi*1/8)
double s2=.38268343236508977172845998402977;  // == sin(Pi*2/16) == sin(Pi*1/8)
```

Automatic verification of the generated codes against the original is a mandatory part of the process.

A level of abstraction for the array indices is of great use: when the print statements in the generator emit some function of the index instead of its plain value, it is easy to generate modified versions of the code for permuted input. That is, instead of

```
cout << "sumdiff(f0, f2, g[" << k0 << "], g[" << k2 << "]);"  << endl;
cout << "sumdiff(f1, f3, g[" << k1 << "], g[" << k3 << "]);"  << endl;
```

use

```
cout << "sumdiff(f0, f2, " << idxf(g,k0) << ", " << idxf(g,k2) << ");"  << endl;
cout << "sumdiff(f1, f3, " << idxf(g,k1) << ", " << idxf(g,k3) << ");"  << endl;
```

where idxf(g, k) can be defined to print a modified (for example, revbin-permuted) index k.

Here is a generated length-8 DIT FHT core as an example [FXT: fht/shortfhtditcore.h]:

```
 1    template <typename Type>
 2    inline void fht_dit_core_8(Type *f)
 3    // unrolled version for length 8
 4    {
 5     { // start initial loop
 6      { // fi = 0  gi = 1
 7       Type g0, f0, f1, g1;
 8       sumdiff(f[0], f[1], f0, g0);
 9       sumdiff(f[2], f[3], f1, g1);
10       sumdiff(f0, f1);
11       sumdiff(g0, g1);
12       Type s1, c1, s2, c2;
13       sumdiff(f[4], f[5], s1, c1);
14       sumdiff(f[6], f[7], s2, c2);
15       sumdiff(s1, s2);
16       sumdiff(f0, s1, f[0], f[4]);
17       sumdiff(f1, s2, f[2], f[6]);
18       c1 *= SQRT2;
19       c2 *= SQRT2;
20       sumdiff(g0, c1, f[1], f[5]);
21       sumdiff(g1, c2, f[3], f[7]);
22      }
23     } // end initial loop
24    }
25    // opcount by generator: #mult=2=0.25/pt    #add=22=2.75/pt
```

Generated DIF FHT codes for lengths up to 64 are given in [FXT: fht/shortfhtdifcore.h].

The generated codes can be useful to spot parts of the original code that allow further optimization. Especially repeated trigonometric values and unused symmetries tend to be apparent in the unrolled code.

It is a good idea to let the generator count the number of operations (multiplications, additions, loads and stores) of the code it emits. Those numbers can be compared to the corresponding values found in the compiled assembler code.

The GCC compiler can produce the assembler code with the original source interlaced. This is a great tool for code optimization. The necessary commands are (include and warning flags omitted)

```
# create assembler code:
c++ -S -fverbose-asm -g -O2  test.cc -o test.s
# create asm interlaced with source lines:
as -alhnd test.s > test.lst
```

For example, the generated length-4 DIT FHT core from [FXT: fht/shortfhtditcore.h] is

```
 1    template <typename Type>
 2    inline void fht_dit_core_4(Type *f)
 3    // unrolled version for length 4
 4    {
 5       Type f0, f1, f2, f3;
 6       sumdiff(f[0], f[1], f0, f1);
 7       sumdiff(f[2], f[3], f2, f3);
 8       sumdiff(f0, f2, f[0], f[2]);
 9       sumdiff(f1, f3, f[1], f[3]);
10    }
```

With Type set to double the generated assembler is, after some editing for readability,

```
1   void fht_dit_core_4(double *f)
2   {
3       double f0, f1, f2, f3;
4       sumdiff(f[0], f[1], f0, f1);
5           movlpd  (%rdi), %xmm1    #* f, tmp63
6           movlpd  8(%rdi), %xmm0   #, tmp64
7       sumdiff(f[2], f[3], f2, f3);
8           movlpd  16(%rdi), %xmm2  #, tmp67
9           movsd   %xmm1, %xmm3     # tmp63, f0
10          subsd   %xmm0, %xmm1     # tmp64, f1
11          movsd   %xmm2, %xmm4     # tmp67, f2
12          addsd   %xmm0, %xmm3     # tmp64, f0
13          movlpd  24(%rdi), %xmm0  #, tmp68
14          addsd   %xmm0, %xmm4     # tmp68, f2
15          subsd   %xmm0, %xmm2     # tmp68, f3
16      sumdiff(f0, f2, f[0], f[2]);
17          movsd   %xmm3, %xmm0     # f0, tmp71
18          addsd   %xmm4, %xmm0     # f2, tmp71
19          subsd   %xmm4, %xmm3     # f2, f0
20          movsd   %xmm0, (%rdi)    # tmp71,* f
21      sumdiff(f1, f3, f[1], f[3]);
22          movsd   %xmm1, %xmm0     # f1, tmp73
23          subsd   %xmm2, %xmm1     # f3, f1
24          movsd   %xmm3, 16(%rdi)  # f0,
25          addsd   %xmm2, %xmm0     # f3, tmp73
26          movsd   %xmm1, 24(%rdi)  # f1,
27          movsd   %xmm0, 8(%rdi)   # tmp73,
28  }
```

Note that the assembler code is not always in sync with the corresponding source lines, especially with higher levels of optimization.

25.11 Eigenvectors of the Fourier and Hartley transform ‡

Let $a_S := a + \overline{a}$ be the symmetric part of a sequence a, then

$$\mathcal{F}[\mathcal{F}[a_S]] = a_S \tag{25.11-1}$$

Now let $u_+ := a_S + \mathcal{F}[a_S]$ and $u_- := a_S - \mathcal{F}[a_S]$, then

$$\mathcal{F}[u_+] = \mathcal{F}[a_S] + a_S = a_S + \mathcal{F}[a_S] = +1 \cdot u_+ \tag{25.11-2a}$$
$$\mathcal{F}[u_-] = \mathcal{F}[a_S] - a_S = -(a_S - \mathcal{F}[a_S]) = -1 \cdot u_- \tag{25.11-2b}$$

Both u_+ and u_- are symmetric. For $a_A := a - \overline{a}$, the antisymmetric part of a, we have

$$\mathcal{F}[\mathcal{F}[a_A]] = -a_A \tag{25.11-3}$$

Therefore with $v_+ := a_A + i\,\mathcal{F}[a_A]$ and $v_- := a_A - i\,\mathcal{F}[a_A]$:

$$\mathcal{F}[v_+] = \mathcal{F}[a_A] - i\,a_A = -i\,(a_A + i\,\mathcal{F}[a_A]) = -i \cdot v_+ \tag{25.11-4a}$$
$$\mathcal{F}[v_-] = \mathcal{F}[a_A] + i\,a_A = +i\,(a_A - i\,\mathcal{F}[a_A]) = +i \cdot v_- \tag{25.11-4b}$$

Both v_+ and v_- are antisymmetric. The sequences u_+, u_-, v_+, and v_- are *eigenvectors* of the Fourier transform, with *eigenvalues* $+1$, -1, $-i$ and $+i$ respectively. The eigenvectors are pair-wise orthogonal. Using the relation

$$a = \frac{1}{2}(u_+ + u_- + v_+ + v_-) \tag{25.11-5}$$

we can, for a given sequence, find a transform that is a 'square root' of the Fourier transform: compute u_+, u_-, v_+, and v_-, and a transform $\mathcal{F}^\lambda[a]$ for $\lambda \in \mathbb{R}$ as

$$\mathcal{F}^\lambda[a] = \frac{1}{2}\Big((+1)^\lambda u_+ + (-1)^\lambda u_- + (-i)^\lambda v_+ + (+i)^\lambda v_-\Big) \tag{25.11-6}$$

This transform is called the *fractional (order) Fourier transform* (but see section 22.6.3 on page 456). Then $\mathcal{F}^0[a]$ is the identity and $\mathcal{F}^1[a]$ is the usual Fourier transform. The transform $\mathcal{F}^{1/2}[a]$ is a transform so that $\mathcal{F}^{1/2}\left[\mathcal{F}^{1/2}[a]\right] = \mathcal{F}[a]$, that is, a 'square root' of the Fourier transform. The transform $\mathcal{F}^{1/2}[a]$ is not unique as the expressions $\pm 1^{1/2}$ and $\pm i^{1/2}$ are not.

A set of eigenvectors (that is, eigenfunctions) of the *continuous* Fourier transform is given by

$$H_n \exp(-x^2/2) \tag{25.11-7}$$

where H_n is the n-th Hermite polynomial, see figure 36.3-A on page 696. The corresponding eigenvalues are i^n. The functions are the eigenstates of the quantum mechanical harmonic oscillator, see [358, entry "Quantum oscillator"].

The eigenvectors of the Hartley transform are

$$u_+ := a + \mathcal{H}[a] \tag{25.11-8a}$$
$$u_- := a - \mathcal{H}[a] \tag{25.11-8b}$$

The eigenvalues are ± 1, we have $\mathcal{H}[u_+] = +1 \cdot u_+$ and $\mathcal{H}[u_-] = -1 \cdot u_-$.

Let M be the $n \times n$ matrix corresponding to the length-n Fourier transform with $\sigma = +1$, that is, $M_{r,c} = 1/\sqrt{n} \exp(2\pi i r c/n)$. Then its characteristic polynomial (see relation 42.5-2 on page 899) is

$$p(x) = (x-1)^{\lfloor (n+4)/4 \rfloor} (x+1)^{\lfloor (n+2)/4 \rfloor} (x-i)^{\lfloor (n+1)/4 \rfloor} (x+i)^{\lfloor (n-1)/4 \rfloor} \tag{25.11-9}$$

We write $p(x) = x^n + c_{n-1} x^{n-1} + \ldots + c_1 x + c_0$. The trace of the matrix M is

$$\mathrm{Tr}(M) = \frac{1}{\sqrt{n}} \sum_{k=0}^{n-1} \exp\left(2\pi i k^2/n\right) \tag{25.11-10}$$

It equals $(-c_{n-1}$, the negated sum of all roots of $p(x)$, and)

$$1+i, \ +1, \ 0, \ +i \tag{25.11-11}$$

for $n \bmod 4 \equiv 0, 1, 2, 3$, respectively. A closed form is $(1 + i^{-n})/(1-i)$. The generating function for the sequence is $((1+i) - x)/\left(1 + (-1+i)x - ix^2\right)$.

The determinant of M equals $((-1)^n c_0$, $(-1)^n$ times the product of all roots of $p(x)$, and)

$$+i, \ +1, \ -1, \ -i, \ -i, \ -1, \ +1, \ +i \tag{25.11-12}$$

for $n \bmod 8 \equiv 0, 1, 2, \ldots, 7$. The generating function for the sequence is $\left(i + x - x^2 - ix^3\right)/\left(1 + x^4\right)$.

Let H be the $n \times n$ matrix corresponding to the length-n Hartley transform, that is, $H_{r,c} = 1/\sqrt{n} \left(\cos(2\pi r c/n) + \sin(2\pi r c/n)\right)$. Then its characteristic polynomial is

$$p(x) = (x-1)^{\lfloor (n+2)/2 \rfloor} (x+1)^{\lfloor (n-1)/2 \rfloor} \tag{25.11-13}$$

Chapter 26

Number theoretic transforms (NTTs)

We introduce the number theoretic transforms (NTTs). The routines for the fast NTTs are rather straightforward translations of the FFT algorithms. Radix-2 and radix-4 routines are given, there should be no difficulty to translate any given complex FFT into the equivalent NTT. For the translation of real-valued FFT (or FHT) routines, we need to express sines and cosines in modular arithmetic, this is presented in sections 39.12.6 and 39.12.7.

As no rounding errors occur with the underlying modular arithmetic, the main application of NTTs is the fast computation of exact convolutions.

26.1 Prime moduli for NTTs

We want to implement FFTs in $\mathbb{Z}/m\mathbb{Z}$ (the ring of integers modulo some integer m) instead of $\mathbb{C}$, the field of complex numbers. These FFTs are called *number theoretic transforms* (NTTs), *mod m FFTs* or (if m is a prime) *prime modulus transforms*.

There is a restriction for the choice of m: for a length-n NTT we need a primitive n-th root of unity. A number r is called an n-th root of unity if $r^n = 1$. It is called a *primitive n-th root* if $r^k \neq 1 \; \forall \, k < n$ (see section 39.5 on page 774).

In $\mathbb{C}$ matters are simple: $e^{\pm 2\pi i/n}$ is a primitive n-th root of unity for arbitrary n. For example, $e^{2\pi i/21}$ is a primitive 21st root of unity. Now $r = e^{2\pi i/3}$ is also 21st root of unity but not a primitive root, because $r^3 = 1$. A primitive n-th root of 1 in $\mathbb{Z}/m\mathbb{Z}$ is also called an *element of order n*. The 'cyclic' property of the elements r of order n lies in the heart of all FFT algorithms: $r^{n+k} = r^k$.

In $\mathbb{Z}/m\mathbb{Z}$ things are not that simple: for a given modulus m primitive n-th roots of unity do not exist for arbitrary n. They only exist for some maximal order R and its divisors d_i: r^{R/d_i} is a d_i-th root of unity because $(r^{R/d_i})^{d_i} = r^R = 1$. Therefore n, the length of the transform, must divide the maximal order R. This is the first condition for NTTs:

$$ n \; \backslash \; R \tag{26.1-1} $$

The operations needed in FFTs are modular addition, subtraction and multiplication, as described in section 39.1 on page 764. Division is not needed, except for the division by n in the final normalization. Division by n is multiplication by the inverse of n, so n must be invertible in $\mathbb{Z}/m\mathbb{Z}$.

Therefore n, the length of the transform, must be *coprime* to the modulus m. This is the second condition for NTTs.

$$ \gcd(n, m) \; = \; 1 \tag{26.1-2} $$

J. Arndt, *Matters Computational: Ideas, Algorithms, Source Code,*
DOI 10.1007/978-3-642-14764-7_26, © Springer-Verlag Berlin Heidelberg 2011

We restrict our attention to prime moduli, though NTTs are also possible with composite moduli. If the modulus is a prime p, then $\mathbb{Z}/p\mathbb{Z}$ is the field $\mathbb{F}_p = \mathrm{GF}(p)$: all elements except 0 have inverses and 'division is possible'. Thus the second condition (relation 26.1-2) is trivially fulfilled for all NTT lengths $n < p$: a prime p is coprime to all integers $n < p$.

Roots of unity are available for the maximal order $R = p - 1$ and its divisors: Therefore the first condition (relation 26.1-1) is that n divides $p - 1$. This restricts the choice for p to primes of the form $p = v\,n + 1$: for length-$n = 2^k$ NTTs one will use primes like $p = 3 \cdot 5 \cdot 2^{27} + 1$ (31 bits), $p = 13 \cdot 2^{28} + 1$ (32 bits), $p = 3 \cdot 29 \cdot 2^{56} + 1$ (63 bits) or $p = 27 \cdot 2^{59} + 1$ (64 bits).

```
arg 1: 62 == wb   [word bits, wb<=63]  default=62
arg 2: 0.01 == deltab   [results are in the range [wb-deltab, wb]]  default=0.01
 minb = 61.99 = wb-0.01
arg 3: 44 == minx   [log_2(min(fftlen))]  default=44

  ---- x = 44: -----
4580495072570638337 = 0x3f91300000000001 = 1 + 2^44 * 83 * 3137            (61.9902 bits)
4581058022524059649 = 0x3f93300000000001 = 1 + 2^44 * 3 * 11 * 13 * 607    (61.9904 bits)
4582113553686724609 = 0x3f96f00000000001 = 1 + 2^44 * 3 * 7 * 79 * 157     (61.9907 bits)
4585702359639785473 = 0x3fa3b00000000001 = 1 + 2^44 * 3^2 * 11 * 2633      (61.9918 bits)
4587039365779161089 = 0x3fa8700000000001 = 1 + 2^44 * 7 * 193^2            (61.9923 bits)
4587391209500049409 = 0x3fa9b00000000001 = 1 + 2^44 * 3 * 17 * 5113        (61.9924 bits)
4588130081313914881 = 0x3fac500000000001 = 1 + 2^44 * 3 * 5 * 17387        (61.9926 bits)
4589572640569556993 = 0x3fb1700000000001 = 1 + 2^44 * 11 * 37 * 641        (61.9931 bits)
[--snip--]
4610999923171655681 = 0x3ffd900000000001 = 1 + 2^44 * 5 * 19 * 31 * 89     (61.9998 bits)
4611105476287922177 = 0x3ffdf00000000001 = 1 + 2^44 * 262111               (61.9998 bits)
  ---- x = 45: -----
4580336742896238593 = 0x3f90a00000000001 = 1 + 2^45 * 29 * 67^2            (61.9902 bits)
4581533011547258881 = 0x3f94e00000000001 = 1 + 2^45 * 3 * 5 * 8681         (61.9905 bits)
4584347761314365441 = 0x3f9ee00000000001 = 1 + 2^45 * 5 * 11 * 23 * 103    (61.9914 bits)
4587655092290715649 = 0x3faaa00000000001 = 1 + 2^45 * 3 * 7^2 * 887        (61.9925 bits)
[--snip--]
  ---- x = 48: -----
4585508845593296897 = 0x3fa3000000000001 = 1 + 2^48 * 11 * 1481            (61.9918 bits)
  ---- x = 49: -----
4582975570802900993 = 0x3f9a000000000001 = 1 + 2^49 * 7 * 1163             (61.991 bits)
4595360469778169857 = 0x3fc6000000000001 = 1 + 2^49 * 3^2 * 907            (61.9949 bits)
  ---- x = 50: -----
4601552919265804289 = 0x3fdc000000000001 = 1 + 2^50 * 61 * 67              (61.9968 bits)
```

Figure 26.1-A: Primes suitable for NTTs of lengths dividing 2^{44}.

modulus (hex)	==	factorization + 1	log(m-1)/log(2)
0x3f40f80000000001	==	2^43.3^2.5^2.7^2.47+1	61.9831
0x3c0eb50000000001	==	2^40.3^3.5^2.7^3.17+1	61.9083
0x3d673d0000000001	==	2^40.3^2.5^3.7^2.73+1	61.9402
0x3fc22b0000000001	==	2^40.3^2.5^2.7^2.379+1	61.9945
0x3bf6190000000001	==	2^40.3^2.5^3.7.499+1	61.906
0x3d1d690000000001	==	2^40.3^2.5^2.7.2543+1	61.9335
0x3d8c270000000001	==	2^40.3^2.5^2.7.13.197+1	61.9436
0x3e8e8d0000000001	==	2^40.3^2.5^2.7.19.137+1	61.9671
0x3ee4af0000000001	==	2^40.3^2.5^2.7.2617+1	61.9748
0x3ed23a0000000001	==	2^41.3^2.5^2.7.1307+1	61.9732
0x3fafb60000000001	==	2^41.3^2.5^4.7.53+1	61.9929
0x3c46140000000001	==	2^42.3^3.5^2.7.11.19+1	61.9135
0x3e32440000000001	==	2^42.3^2.5^2.7.647+1	61.9588
0x3d23900000000001	==	2^44.3^3.5^2.7.53+1	61.934

Figure 26.1-B: Primes suitable for NTTs of lengths dividing $2^{40}\, 3^2\, 5^2\, 7$.

Primes suitable with NTTs (sometimes called *FFT-primes*) can be generated with the program [FXT: mod/fftprimes-demo.cc]. A shortened sample output is shown in figure 26.1-A. A few moduli that allow for transforms of lengths dividing $2^{40} \cdot 3^2 \cdot 5^2 \cdot 7$ are shown in figure 26.1-B, the data is taken from [FXT: mod/moduli.txt]. We note that primality of moduli suitable for NTTs can easily by tested using Proth's theorem, see section 39.11.3.1 on page 795.

26.2   Implementation of NTTs

To implement NTTs (modulo m, length n), we need to implement modular arithmetic and replace $e^{\pm 2\pi i/n}$ by a primitive n-th root r of unity in $\mathbb{Z}/m\mathbb{Z}$ in the code. A C++ class implementing modular arithmetic is [FXT: class mod in mod/mod.h].

For the inverse transform one uses the $(\mathrm{mod}\ m)$ inverse r^{-1} of r that was used for the forward transform. The element r^{-1} is also a primitive n-th root. Methods for the computation of the modular inverse are described in section 39.1.4 on page 767 (GCD algorithm) and in section 39.7.4 on page 781 (powering algorithm).

While the notion of the Fourier transform as a 'decomposition into frequencies' appears to be meaningless for NTTs the algorithms are denoted with 'decimation in time/frequency' in analogy to those in the complex domain.

The nice feature of NTTs is that there is no loss of precision in the transform as with the floating-point FFTs. Using the trigonometric recursion in its most naive form is mandatory, as the computation of roots of unity is expensive.

26.2.1   Radix-2 DIT NTT

Pseudocode for the radix-2 decimation in time (DIT) NTT (to be called with ldn=log2(n)):

```
1    procedure mod_fft_dit2(f[], ldn, is)
2    // mod_type f[0..2**ldn-1]
3    {
4        n := 2**ldn
5
6        rn := element_of_order(n)  // (mod_type)
7
8        if is<0 then  rn := rn**(-1)
9
10       revbin_permute(f[], n)
11
12       for ldm:=1 to ldn
13       {
14           m  := 2**ldm
15           mh := m/2
16
17           dw := rn**(2**(ldn-ldm))   // (mod_type)
18           w  := 1                     // (mod_type)
19
20           for j:=0 to mh-1
21           {
22               for r:=0 to n-m step m
23               {
24                   t1 := r + j
25                   t2 := t1 + mh
26
27                   v := f[t2] * w  // (mod_type)
28                   u := f[t1]      // (mod_type)
29
30                   f[t1] := u + v
31                   f[t2] := u - v
32               }
33
34               w := w * dw  // trig recursion
35           }
36       }
37   }
```

As shown in section 21.2.1 on page 412 it is a good idea to extract the ldm==1 stage of the outermost loop: Replace

```
for ldm:=1 to ldn
{
```

by

```
for r:=0 to n-1 step 2
{
    { f[r], f[r+1] } := { f[r]+f[r+1], f[r]-f[r+1] }  // parallel assignment
}
```

```
for ldm:=2 to ldn
{
```

The C++ implementation is given in [FXT: ntt/nttdit2.cc]:

```
1   void
2   ntt_dit2_core(mod *f, ulong ldn, int is)
3   // Auxiliary routine for ntt_dit2()
4   // Decimation in time (DIT) radix-2 FFT
5   // Input data must be in revbin_permuted order
6   // ldn := base-2 logarithm of the array length
7   // is := sign of the transform
8   {
9       const ulong n = 1UL<<ldn;
10
11      for (ulong i=0; i<n; i+=2)  sumdiff(f[i], f[i+1]);
12
13      for (ulong ldm=2; ldm<=ldn; ++ldm)
14      {
15          const ulong m = (1UL<<ldm);
16          const ulong mh = (m>>1);
17
18          const mod dw = mod::root2pow( is>0 ? ldm : -ldm );
19          mod w = (mod::one);
20
21          for (ulong j=0; j<mh; ++j)
22          {
23              for (ulong r=0; r<n; r+=m)
24              {
25                  const ulong t1 = r + j;
26                  const ulong t2 = t1 + mh;
27
28                  mod v = f[t2] * w;
29                  mod u = f[t1];
30
31                  f[t1] = u + v;
32                  f[t2] = u - v;
33              }
34              w *= dw;
35          }
36      }
37  }
```

```
1   void
2   ntt_dit2(mod *f, ulong ldn, int is)
3   // Radix-2 decimation in time (DIT) NTT
4   {
5       revbin_permute(f, 1UL<<ldn);
6       ntt_dit2_core(f, ldn, is);
7   }
```

The elements of order 2^k are precomputed at initialization of the mod class. The call to mod::root2pow() is a simple table lookup.

26.2.2   Radix-2 DIF NTT

Pseudocode for the radix-2 decimation in frequency (DIF) NTT:

```
1   procedure mod_fft_dif2(f[], ldn, is)
2   // mod_type f[0..2**ldn-1]
3   {
4       n := 2**ldn
5       dw := element_of_order(n)   // (mod_type)
6
7       if is<0 then   dw := rn**(-1)
8
9       for  ldm:=ldn to 1 step -1
10      {
11          m  := 2**ldm
12          mh := m/2
13
14          w := 1  // (mod_type)
15
16          for j:=0 to mh-1
17          {
18              for r:=0 to n-m step m
```

```
19          {
20              t1 := r + j
21              t2 := t1 + mh
22
23              v := f[t2]  // (mod_type)
24              u := f[t1]  // (mod_type)
25
26              f[t1] :=  u + v
27              f[t2] := (u - v) * w
28          }
29
30          w := w * dw  // trig recursion
31      }
32
33      dw := dw * dw
34  }
35
36  revbin_permute(f[], n)
37  }
```

As in section 21.2.2 on page 414 extract the `ldm==1` stage of the outermost loop: replace the line

```
for  ldm:=ldn to 1 step -1
```

by

```
for  ldm:=ldn to 2 step -1
```

and insert

```
for r:=0 to n-1 step 2
{
    { f[r], f[r+1] } := { f[r] + f[r+1], f[r] - f[r+1] }  // parallel assignment
}
```

before the call of `revbin_permute(f[],n)`.

The C++ implementation is given in [FXT: ntt/nttdif2.cc]:

```
1   void
2   ntt_dif2_core(mod *f, ulong ldn, int is)
3   // Auxiliary routine for ntt_dif2().
4   // Decimation in frequency (DIF) radix-2 NTT.
5   // Output data is in revbin_permuted order.
6   // ldn := base-2 logarithm of the array length.
7   // is := sign of the transform
8   {
9       const ulong n = (1UL<<ldn);
10      mod dw = mod::root2pow( is>0 ? ldn : -ldn );
11
12      for (ulong ldm=ldn; ldm>1; --ldm)
13      {
14          const ulong m = (1UL<<ldm);
15          const ulong mh = (m>>1);
16
17          mod w = mod::one;
18
19          for (ulong j=0; j<mh; ++j)
20          {
21              for (ulong r=0; r<n; r+=m)
22              {
23                  const ulong t1 = r + j;
24                  const ulong t2 = t1 + mh;
25
26                  mod v = f[t2];
27                  mod u = f[t1];
28
29                  f[t1] = (u + v);
30                  f[t2] = (u - v) * w;
31              }
32              w *= dw;
33          }
34          dw *= dw;
35      }
36
37      for (ulong i=0; i<n; i+=2)  sumdiff(f[i], f[i+1]);
38  }

1   void
2   ntt_dif2(mod *f, ulong ldn, int is)
```

```
3     // Radix-2 decimation in frequency (DIF) NTT
4     {
5         ntt_dif2_core(f, ldn, is);
6         revbin_permute(f, 1UL<<ldn);
7     }
```

26.2.3   Radix-4 NTTs

The radix-4 versions of the NTT are straightforward translations of the routines that use complex numbers. We simply give the C++ implementations

26.2.3.1   Decimation in time (DIT) algorithm

Code for a radix-4 decimation in time (DIT) NTT [FXT: ntt/nttdit4.cc]:

```
1     static const ulong LX = 2;
2
3     void
4     ntt_dit4_core(mod *f, ulong ldn, int is)
5     // Auxiliary routine for ntt_dit4()
6     // Decimation in time (DIT) radix-4 NTT
7     // Input data must be in revbin_permuted order
8     // ldn := base-2 logarithm of the array length
9     // is := sign of the transform
10    {
11        const ulong n = (1UL<<ldn);
12
13        if ( ldn & 1 )  // n is not a power of 4, need a radix-2 step
14        {
15            for (ulong i=0; i<n; i+=2)  sumdiff(f[i], f[i+1]);
16        }
17
18        const mod imag = mod::root2pow( is>0 ? 2 : -2 );
19
20        ulong ldm = LX + (ldn&1);
21        for ( ; ldm<=ldn ; ldm+=LX)
22        {
23            const ulong m = (1UL<<ldm);
24            const ulong m4 = (m>>LX);
25
26            const mod dw = mod::root2pow( is>0 ? ldm : -ldm );
27            mod w = (mod::one);
28            mod w2 = w;
29            mod w3 = w;
30
31            for (ulong j=0; j<m4; j++)
32            {
33                for (ulong r=0, i0=j+r; r<n; r+=m, i0+=m)
34                {
35                    const ulong i1 = i0 + m4;
36                    const ulong i2 = i1 + m4;
37                    const ulong i3 = i2 + m4;
38
39                    mod a0 = f[i0];
40                    mod a2 = f[i1] * w2;
41                    mod a1 = f[i2] * w;
42                    mod a3 = f[i3] * w3;
43
44                    mod t02 = a0 + a2;
45                    mod t13 = a1 + a3;
46
47                    f[i0] = t02 + t13;
48                    f[i2] = t02 - t13;
49
50                    t02 = a0 - a2;
51                    t13 = a1 - a3;
52                    t13 *= imag;
53
54                    f[i1] = t02 + t13;
55                    f[i3] = t02 - t13;
56                }
57
58                w *= dw;
59                w2 = w * w;
60                w3 = w * w2;
61            }
```

```
62        }
63    }
1     void
2     ntt_dit4(mod *f, ulong ldn, int is)
3     // Radix-4 decimation in time (DIT) NTT
4     {
5         revbin_permute(f, 1UL<<ldn);
6         ntt_dit4_core(f, ldn, is);
7     }
```

26.2.3.2   Decimation in frequency (DIF) algorithm

Code for a radix-4 decimation in frequency (DIT) NTT [FXT: ntt/nttdif4.cc]:

```
1     static const ulong LX = 2;
2
3     void
4     ntt_dif4_core(mod *f, ulong ldn, int is)
5     // Auxiliary routine for ntt_dif4().
6     // Decimation in frequency (DIF) radix-4 NTT.
7     // Output data is in revbin_permuted order.
8     // ldn := base-2 logarithm of the array length.
9     // is := sign of the transform
10    {
11        const ulong n = (1UL<<ldn);
12
13        const mod imag = mod::root2pow( is>0 ? 2 : -2 );
14
15        for (ulong ldm=ldn; ldm>=LX; ldm-=LX)
16        {
17            const ulong m = (1UL<<ldm);
18            const ulong m4 = (m>>LX);
19
20            const mod dw = mod::root2pow( is>0 ? ldm : -ldm );
21            mod w = (mod::one);
22            mod w2 = w;
23            mod w3 = w;
24
25            for (ulong j=0; j<m4; j++)
26            {
27                for (ulong r=0, i0=j+r; r<n; r+=m, i0+=m)
28                {
29                    const ulong i1 = i0 + m4;
30                    const ulong i2 = i1 + m4;
31                    const ulong i3 = i2 + m4;
32
33                    mod a0 = f[i0];
34                    mod a1 = f[i1];
35                    mod a2 = f[i2];
36                    mod a3 = f[i3];
37
38                    mod t02 = a0 + a2;
39                    mod t13 = a1 + a3;
40
41                    f[i0] = (t02 + t13);
42                    f[i1] = (t02 - t13) * w2;
43
44                    t02 = a0 - a2;
45                    t13 = a1 - a3;
46                    t13 *= imag;
47
48                    f[i2] = (t02 + t13) * w;
49                    f[i3] = (t02 - t13) * w3;
50                }
51
52                w *= dw;
53                w2 = w * w;
54                w3 = w * w2;
55            }
56        }
57
58        if ( ldn & 1 )  // n is not a power of 4, need a radix-2 step
59        {
60            for (ulong i=0; i<n; i+=2)  sumdiff(f[i], f[i+1]);
61        }
62    }
```

```
1    void
2    ntt_dif4(mod *f, ulong ldn, int is)
3    // Radix-4 decimation in frequency (DIF) NTT
4    {
5        ntt_dif4_core(f, ldn, is);
6        revbin_permute(f, 1UL<<ldn);
7    }
```

26.3 Convolution with NTTs

The NTTs are natural candidates for the computation of exact integer convolutions, as used in high precision multiplication algorithms. All computations are modulo m, the largest value that can be represented is $m - 1$. Choosing a modulus that is greater than the maximal possible value of the result avoids any truncation.

If m does not fit into a single machine word, the modular arithmetic tends to be expensive. This may slow down the computation unacceptably. It is better to choose m as a product of mutually coprime moduli m_i that are all just below machine word size, compute the convolutions for each modulus m_i, and finally use the Chinese Remainder Theorem (see section 39.4 on page 772) to obtain the result modulo m. In [271] it is suggested to use three primes just below the word size. This method allows computing convolutions (almost) up to lengths that just fit into a machine word.

Routines for the NTT-based exact convolution are given in [FXT: ntt/nttcnvl.cc]. The routines are virtually identical to their complex equivalents given in section 22.1.2 on page 441. For example, the routine for cyclic self-convolution is

```
1    void
2    ntt_auto_convolution(mod *f, ulong ldn)
3    // Cyclic self-convolution.
4    // Use zero padded data for linear convolution.
5    {
6        assert_two_invertible();  // so we can normalize later
7
8        const int is = +1;
9
10       ntt_dif4_core(f, ldn, is);  // transform
11
12       const ulong n = (1UL<<ldn);
13       for (ulong i=0; i<n; ++i)  f[i] *= f[i];  // multiply element-wise
14
15       ntt_dit4_core(f, ldn, -is);  // inverse transform
16
17       multiply_val(f, n, (mod(n)).inv() );  // normalize
18   }
```

The revbin permutations are avoided as explained in section 22.1.3 on page 442.

For further applications of the NTT see the survey article [172] and the references given there.

Chapter 27

Fast wavelet transforms

The discrete wavelet transforms are a class of transforms that can be computed in linear time. We describe wavelet transforms whose basis functions have compact support. These are derived as a generalization of the Haar transform.

27.1 Wavelet filters

We motivate the *wavelet transform* as a generalization of the 'standard' Haar transform given in section 24.1 on page 497. The Haar transform will be reformulated as a sequence of filtering steps.

We consider only (moving average) filters F defined by n coefficients (filter *taps*) $f_0, f_1, \ldots, f_{n-1}$. Let A be the length-N sequence $a_0, a_1, \ldots, a_{N-1}$. Define $F_k(A)$ as the weighted sum

$$F_k(A) := \sum_{j=0}^{n-1} f_j \, a_{k+j \bmod N} \tag{27.1-1}$$

That is, $F_k(A)$ is the result of applying the filter F to the n elements $a_k, a_{k+1}, a_{k+2}, \ldots a_{k+n-1}$, possibly wrapping around.

Now assume that N is a power of 2. Let H be the low-pass filter defined by $h_0 = h_1 = +1/\sqrt{2}$ and G be the high-pass filter defined by $g_0 = +1/\sqrt{2}$, $g_1 = -1/\sqrt{2}$. A single filtering step of the Haar transform consists of

- computing the sums: $s_0 = H_0(A)$, $s_2 = H_2(A)$, $s_4 = H_4(4)$, $\ldots$, $s_{N-2} = H_{N-2}(A)$,

- computing the differences: $d_0 = G_0(A)$, $d_2 = G_2(A)$, $d_4 = G_4(4)$, $\ldots$, $d_{N-2} = G_{N-2}(A)$,

- writing the sums to the left half of A and the differences to the right half:
  $A = [s_0, s_2, s_4, s_6, \ldots, s_{N-2}, d_0, d_2, d_4, d_6, \ldots, d_{N-2}]$.

The Haar transform is computed by applying the filtering step to the whole sequence, then to its left half, then to its left quarter, $\ldots$, the left four elements, the left two elements. With the Haar transform no wrap-around occurs.

The analogous filtering step for the wavelet transform is obtained by defining two length-n filters H (low-pass) and G (high-pass) subject to certain conditions. We consider only filters with an even number n of coefficients.

Define the coefficients of G to be the reversed sequence of the coefficients of H with alternating signs:

$$g_0 = +h_{n-1}, \quad g_1 = -h_{n-2}, \quad g_2 = +h_{n-3}, \quad g_4 = -h_{n-3}, \quad \ldots \tag{27.1-2}$$
$$\ldots, \quad g_{n-3} = -h_2, \quad g_{n-2} = +h_1, \quad g_{n-1} = -h_0$$

We also require that the resulting transform is orthogonal. Let S be the matrix corresponding to one filtering step, ignoring the order:

$$S\,A = [s_0, d_0, \ s_2, d_2, \ s_4, d_4, \ s_6, d_6, \ \ldots, \ s_{N-2}, d_{N-2}] \tag{27.1-3}$$

J. Arndt, *Matters Computational: Ideas, Algorithms, Source Code*,
DOI 10.1007/978-3-642-14764-7_27, © Springer-Verlag Berlin Heidelberg 2011

For example, with length-6 filters and $N = 16$ the matrix S would be

$$
S = \begin{bmatrix}
h_0 & h_1 & h_2 & h_3 & h_4 & h_5 & 0 & 0 & 0 & 0 & 0 & 0 & 0 & 0 & 0 & 0 \\
g_0 & g_1 & g_2 & g_3 & g_4 & g_5 & 0 & 0 & 0 & 0 & 0 & 0 & 0 & 0 & 0 & 0 \\
0 & 0 & h_0 & h_1 & h_2 & h_3 & h_4 & h_5 & 0 & 0 & 0 & 0 & 0 & 0 & 0 & 0 \\
0 & 0 & g_0 & g_1 & g_2 & g_3 & g_4 & g_5 & 0 & 0 & 0 & 0 & 0 & 0 & 0 & 0 \\
0 & 0 & 0 & 0 & h_0 & h_1 & h_2 & h_3 & h_4 & h_5 & 0 & 0 & 0 & 0 & 0 & 0 \\
0 & 0 & 0 & 0 & g_0 & g_1 & g_2 & g_3 & g_4 & g_5 & 0 & 0 & 0 & 0 & 0 & 0 \\
0 & 0 & 0 & 0 & 0 & 0 & h_0 & h_1 & h_2 & h_3 & h_4 & h_5 & 0 & 0 & 0 & 0 \\
0 & 0 & 0 & 0 & 0 & 0 & g_0 & g_1 & g_2 & g_3 & g_4 & g_5 & 0 & 0 & 0 & 0 \\
0 & 0 & 0 & 0 & 0 & 0 & 0 & 0 & h_0 & h_1 & h_2 & h_3 & h_4 & h_5 & 0 & 0 \\
0 & 0 & 0 & 0 & 0 & 0 & 0 & 0 & g_0 & g_1 & g_2 & g_3 & g_4 & g_5 & 0 & 0 \\
0 & 0 & 0 & 0 & 0 & 0 & 0 & 0 & 0 & 0 & h_0 & h_1 & h_2 & h_3 & h_4 & h_5 \\
0 & 0 & 0 & 0 & 0 & 0 & 0 & 0 & 0 & 0 & g_0 & g_1 & g_2 & g_3 & g_4 & g_5 \\
h_4 & h_5 & 0 & 0 & 0 & 0 & 0 & 0 & 0 & 0 & 0 & 0 & h_0 & h_1 & h_2 & h_3 \\
g_4 & g_5 & 0 & 0 & 0 & 0 & 0 & 0 & 0 & 0 & 0 & 0 & g_0 & g_1 & g_2 & g_3 \\
h_2 & h_3 & h_4 & h_5 & 0 & 0 & 0 & 0 & 0 & 0 & 0 & 0 & 0 & 0 & h_0 & h_1 \\
g_2 & g_3 & g_4 & g_5 & 0 & 0 & 0 & 0 & 0 & 0 & 0 & 0 & 0 & 0 & g_0 & g_1
\end{bmatrix}
\tag{27.1-4a}
$$

Using relation 27.1-2 we have:

$$
S = \begin{bmatrix}
+h_0 & +h_1 & +h_2 & +h_3 & +h_4 & +h_5 & 0 & 0 & 0 & 0 & 0 & \cdots & 0 \\
+h_5 & -h_4 & +h_3 & -h_2 & +h_1 & -h_0 & 0 & 0 & 0 & 0 & 0 & \cdots & 0 \\
0 & 0 & +h_0 & +h_1 & +h_2 & +h_3 & +h_4 & +h_5 & 0 & 0 & 0 & \cdots & 0 \\
0 & 0 & +h_5 & -h_4 & +h_3 & -h_2 & +h_1 & -h_0 & 0 & 0 & 0 & \cdots & 0 \\
0 & 0 & 0 & 0 & +h_0 & +h_1 & +h_2 & +h_3 & +h_4 & +h_5 & 0 & \cdots & 0 \\
0 & 0 & 0 & 0 & +h_5 & -h_4 & +h_3 & -h_2 & +h_1 & -h_0 & 0 & \cdots & 0 \\
& & & & & \ddots & & & & & \ddots &
\end{bmatrix}
\tag{27.1-4b}
$$

The orthogonality requires that $S S^T = \text{id}$, that is (setting $h_j = 0$ for $j < 0$ and $j \geq n$)

$$
\sum_j h_j^2 = 1
\tag{27.1-5a}
$$

$$
\sum_j h_j h_{j+2} = 0
\tag{27.1-5b}
$$

$$
\sum_j h_j h_{j+4} = 0
\tag{27.1-5c}
$$

In general, we have the following $n/2$ *wavelet conditions*:

$$
\sum_j h_j^2 = 1
\tag{27.1-6a}
$$

$$
\sum_j h_j h_{j+2i} = 0 \quad \text{where} \quad i = 1, 2, 3, \ldots, n/2 - 1
\tag{27.1-6b}
$$

We call a filter H satisfying these conditions a *wavelet filter*.

For the wavelet transform with $n = 2$ filter taps there is only the condition $h_0^2 + h_1^2 = 1$. It leads to the parametric solution $h_0 = \sin(\phi)$, $h_1 = \cos(\phi)$. Setting $\phi = \pi/4$ we find $h_0 = h_1 = 1/\sqrt{2}$, corresponding to the Haar transform.

27.2 Implementation

A container class for wavelet filters is [FXT: `class wavelet_filter` in wavelet/waveletfilter.h]:

```
1    class wavelet_filter
2    {
3    public:
4        double *h_;   // low-pass filter
5        double *g_;   // high-pass filter
6        ulong n_;     // number of taps
7
8        void ctor_core()
9        {
10           h_ = new double[n_];
11           g_ = new double[n_];
12       }
13
14       wavelet_filter(const double *w, ulong n=0)
15       {
16           if ( 0!=n )  n_ = n;
17           else  // zero terminated array w[]
18           {
19               n_ = 0;
20               while ( w[n_]!=0 )  ++n_;
21           }
22
23           ctor_core();
24
25           for (ulong i=0, j=n_-1;  i<n_;  ++i, --j)
26           {
27               h_[i] = w[i];
28
29               if ( !(i&1) )  g_[j] = -h_[i];  // even indices
30               else           g_[j] = +h_[i];  // odd indices
31           }
32       }
33
34    [--snip--]
```

The wavelet conditions can be checked via

```
1        bool check(double eps=1e-6) const
2        {
3            if ( fabs(norm_sqr(0)-1.0) > eps )  return false;
4
5            for (ulong i=1;  i<n_/2;  ++i)
6                if ( fabs(norm_sqr(i)) > eps )  return false;
7
8            return true;
9        }
```

where `norm_sqr()` computes the sums in the relations 27.1-6a and 27.1-6b:

```
1        static double norm_sqr(const double *h, ulong n, ulong s=0)
2        {
3            s *= 2;  // Note!
4            if ( s>=n )  return 0.0;
5
6            double v = 0;
7            for (ulong k=0,j=s;  j<n;  ++k,++j)  v += (h[k]*h[j]);
8            return  v;
9        }
10
11       double norm_sqr(ulong s=0)  const  { return norm_sqr(h_, n_, s); }
```

A wavelet step can be implemented as [FXT: wavelet/wavelet.cc]:

```
1    void
2    wavelet_step(double *f, ulong n, const wavelet_filter &wf, double *t)
3    {
4        const ulong nh = (n>>1);
5        const ulong m = n-1;  // mask to compute modulo n (n is a power of 2)
6        for (ulong i=0,j=0;  i<n; i+=2,++j) // i \in [0,2,4,..,n-2];  j \in [0,1,2,..,n/2-1]
7        {
8            double s = 0.0,  d = 0.0;
9            for (ulong k=0; k<wf.n_; ++k)
10           {
11               ulong w = (i+k) & m;
12               s += (wf.h_[k] * f[w]);
13               d += (wf.g_[k] * f[w]);
14           }
15           t[j] = s;
```

```
16            t[nh+j] = d;
17        }
18        acopy(t, f, n);  // f[] := t[]
19    }
```

The wavelet transform itself is

```
1    void
2    wavelet(double *f, ulong ldn, const wavelet_filter &wf, ulong minm/*=2*/)
3    {
4        ulong n = (1UL<<ldn);
5        ALLOCA(double, t, n);
6        for (ulong m=n; m>=minm; m>>=1)  wavelet_step(f, m, wf, t);
7    }
```

The step for the inverse transform is [FXT: wavelet/invwavelet.cc]:

```
1    void
2    inverse_wavelet_step(double *f, ulong n, const wavelet_filter &wf, double *t)
3    {
4        const ulong nh = (n>>1);
5        const ulong m = n-1;  // mask to compute modulo n (n is a power of 2)
6        null(t, n);  // t[] := [0,0,...,0]
7        for (ulong i=0, j=0;  i<n;  i+=2, ++j)
8        {
9            const double x = f[j],  y = f[nh+j];
10           for (ulong k=0;  k<wf.n_;  ++k)
11           {
12               ulong w = (i+k) & m;
13               t[w]  += (wf.h_[k] * x);
14               t[w]  += (wf.g_[k] * y);
15           }
16       }
17       acopy(t, f, n);  // f[] := t[]
18   }
```

The inverse transform is

```
1    void
2    inverse_wavelet(double *f, ulong ldn, const wavelet_filter &wf, ulong minm/*=2*/)
3    {
4        ulong n = (1UL<<ldn);
5        ALLOCA(double, t, n);
6        for (ulong m=minm; m<=n; m<<=1)  inverse_wavelet_step(f, m, wf, t);
7    }
```

A readable source about wavelets is [357].

27.3 Moment conditions

As the wavelet conditions do not uniquely define the wavelet filters, we can impose additional properties. We require that the first $n/2$ moments vanish for a $2n$-tap wavelet filter:

$$\sum_j (-1)^j \, h_j \;=\; 0 \tag{27.3-1a}$$

$$\sum_j (-j)^k \, h_j \;=\; 0 \quad \text{where} \quad k = 1, 2, 3, \ldots, n/2 - 1 \tag{27.3-1b}$$

One motivation for these *moment conditions* is that for reasonably smooth signals (for which a polynomial approximation is good) the transform coefficients from the high-pass filter (the d_k) will be close to 0. With compression schemes that simply discard transform coefficients with small values this is a desirable property.

The class [FXT: class wavelet_filter in wavelet/waveletfilter.h] has a method to compute the moments of the filter:

```
1        static double moment(const double *h, ulong n, ulong x=0)
2        {
3            if ( 0==x )
4            {
5                double v = 0.0;
```

```
6            for (ulong k=0; k<n; k+=2)  v += h[k];
7            for (ulong k=1; k<n; k+=2)  v -= h[k];
8            return v;
9        }
10
11       double dk;
12
13       double ve = 0;
14       dk = 2.0;
15       for (ulong k=2;  k<n;  k+=2, dk+=2.0)  ve += (pow(dk,x) * h[k]);
16
17       double vo = 0;
18       dk = 1.0;
19       for (ulong k=1;  k<n;  k+=2, dk+=2.0)  vo += (pow(dk,x) * h[k]);
20       return  ve - vo;
21   }
22
23   double moment(ulong x=0)  const  { return moment(h_, n_, x); }
```

Filter coefficients that satisfy the moment conditions are given in [FXT: wavelet/daubechies.cc]:

```
1    extern const double Daub1[] = {
2    +7.07106781186547524400844362104e-01,
3    +7.07106781186547524400844362104e-01 };
4
5    extern const double Daub2[] = {
6    +4.82962913144534143374871599864e-01,
7    +8.36516303737807905575293780916e-01,
8    +2.24143868042013381025972762240e-01,
9    -1.29409522551260381174449418812e-01 };
10
11   extern const double Daub3[] = {
12   +3.32670552950082615998511589139e-01,
13   +8.06891509311092576494493604088e-01,
14   +4.59877502118491570095151942147e-01,
15   -1.35011020010254588696963899066e-01,
16   -8.54412738820266616928191691817e-02,
17   +3.52262918857095366027406647155e-02 };
18
19   extern const double Daub4[] = {
20   +2.30377813308896500863291183044e-01,
21   +7.14846570552915647089921955273e-01,
22   +6.30880767929858907881716338300e-01,
23   -2.79837694168598542114137471800e-02,
24   -1.87034811719093084079570672789e-01,
25   +3.08413818355607636272193625349e-02,
26   +3.28830116668851997354075135492e-02,
27   -1.05974017850690321048832085240e-02 };
28
29       [--snip--]
30   extern const double Daub38[] = {...}
```

The names reflect the number $n/2$ of vanishing moments. Reversing or negating the sequence of filter coefficients leads to trivial variants which also satisfy the moment conditions.

For the filters of length $n \geq 6$ there are solutions that are essentially different. For $n = 6$ there is one complex solution besides Daub3[]:

```
1    -0.09556007476957763 + 0.0508627772544*I
2    +0.08121662052705924 + 0.1525883317632*I
3    +0.72145023542906591 + 0.1017255545088*I
4    +0.72145023542906591 - 0.1017255545088*I
5    +0.08121662052705924 - 0.1525883317632*I
6    -0.09556007476957763 - 0.0508627772544*I
```

For $n = 8$ there is, besides Daub4[], an additional real solution (left) and a complex one (right):

```
1    -0.07576571478950221          +0.02152475910155493 + 0.0184283603930*I
2    -0.02963552764600249          -0.06571358411493559 + 0.0176792547520*I
3    +0.49761866676277498          -0.19397617446078878 - 0.1319957453155*I
4    +0.80373875180513208          +0.24627664139071534 - 0.2801719341011*I
5    +0.29785779560530605          +0.85723045931761476 - 0.0921418019654*I
6    -0.09921954357663353          +0.59199318785735184 + 0.2064584925288*I
7    -0.01260396726203130          +0.02232773722816661 + 0.2057091868878*I
8    +0.03222310060405146          -0.06544948394658407 + 0.0560343868202*I
```

The number of solutions grows exponentially with n (the minimal polynomial of any tap value has degree 2^n). The filters given in [FXT: wavelet/daubechies.cc] are the filters for the *Daubechies wavelets* (some closed form expressions for the filter coefficients are given in [105]).

Filter coefficients that satisfy the wavelet and the moment conditions can be found by a Newton iteration for zeros of the function $F : \mathbb{R}^n \to \mathbb{R}^n$, $F(\vec{h}) := \vec{w}$ where $w_i = F_i(\vec{h}) = F_i(h_0, h_1, \ldots, h_5)$. For example, with $n = 6$ the F_i are defined by

```
1      F[1]:  h0^2 + h1^2 + h2^2 + h3^2 + h4^2 + h5^2 - 1
2      F[2]:  h2*h0 + h3*h1 + h4*h2 + h5*h3
3      F[3]:  h4*h0 + h5*h1
4      F[4]:  -h0 + h1 + -h2 + h3 + -h4 + h5
5      F[5]:  h1 + -2*h2 + 3*h3 + -4*h4 + 5*h5
6      F[6]:  h1 + -4*h2 + 9*h3 + -16*h4 + 25*h5
```

The derivative is given by the *Jacobi matrix* J. It has the components $J_{r,c} := \dfrac{dF_r}{dh_c}$. For $n = 6$ its rows are

```
1      J[1]= [2*h0, 2*h1, 2*h2, 2*h3, 2*h4, 2*h5]
2      J[2]= [h2, h3, h0 + h4, h1 + h5, h2, h3]
3      J[3]= [h4, h5, 0, 0, h0, h1]
4      J[4]= [-1, 1, -1, 1, -1, 1]
5      J[5]= [0, 1, -2, 3, -4, 5]
6      J[6]= [0, 1, -4, 9, -16, 25]
```

Now iterate (the equivalent to Newton's iteration, $x_{k+1} := x_k - f(x_k)/f'(x_k)$)

$$\vec{h}_{k+1} \quad := \quad \vec{h}_k - J^{-1}(\vec{h}_k)\, F(\vec{h}_k) \tag{27.3-2}$$

The computations have to be carried out with a rather great precision to avoid loss of accuracy.

Part IV
Fast arithmetic

Chapter 28

Fast multiplication and exponentiation

The usual scheme for the multiplication of two N-digit numbers involves $O(N^2)$ operations. We describe multiplication algorithms that are asymptotically better than this, the Karatsuba algorithm, the Toom-Cook algorithms, and multiplication via FFTs. In addition, the left-to-right and right-to-left schemes for binary exponentiation are described.

28.1 Splitting schemes for multiplication

Ordinary multiplication is $O(N^2)$. Assuming the hidden constant equals 1, the computation of the product of two million-digit numbers would require $\approx 10^{12}$ operations. On a machine that does 1 billion operations per second the multiplication would need 1000 seconds. The following schemes lead to algorithms with superior asymptotics.

28.1.1 2-way splitting: the Karatsuba algorithm

The following algorithm is due to A. Karatsuba and Y. Ofman [200].

Split the numbers A and B (assumed to have approximately the same length) into two pieces

$$A = x\,a_1 + a_0, \qquad B = x\,b_1 + b_0 \tag{28.1-1}$$

where x is a power of the radix close to $\sqrt{A}$ (a number with half as many digits as A). The usual multiplication scheme needs four multiplications with half precision for one multiplication with full precision:

$$A\,B = a_0 \cdot b_0 + x\,(a_0 \cdot b_1 + b_0 \cdot a_1) + x^2\,a_1 \cdot b_1 \tag{28.1-2}$$

Only the multiplications $a_i \cdot b_j$ need to be considered. The multiplications by x, a power of the radix, are only shifts. If we use the relation

$$A\,B = (1+x)\,a_0 \cdot b_0 + x\,(a_1 - a_0) \cdot (b_0 - b_1) + (x + x^2)\,a_1 \cdot b_1 \tag{28.1-3}$$

we need three multiplications with half precision for one multiplication with full precision. By applying the scheme recursively until the numbers to multiply are of machine size, we obtain an algorithm which is $O(N^{\log_2(3)}) \approx O(N^{1.585})$. An alternative form of the splitting scheme is

$$A\,B = (1-x)\,a_0 \cdot b_0 + x\,(a_1 + a_0) \cdot (b_0 + b_1) + (x^2 - x)\,a_1 \cdot b_1 \tag{28.1-4}$$

It must be noted that the partial products may produce a carry, so a little bit more than half precision is needed with each splitting step. Also note that partial products in the middle of relation 28.1-3 can be negative.

For squaring use either of the following schemes

$$A^2 = (1+x)\,a_0^2 - x\,(a_1 - a_0)^2 + (x + x^2)\,a_1^2 \tag{28.1-5a}$$

$$A^2 = (1-x)\,a_0^2 + x\,(a_1 + a_0)^2 + (x^2 - x)\,a_1^2 \tag{28.1-5b}$$

J. Arndt, *Matters Computational: Ideas, Algorithms, Source Code*,
DOI 10.1007/978-3-642-14764-7_28, © Springer-Verlag Berlin Heidelberg 2011

We compute $8231^2 = 67749361$ with the first relation (28.1-5a):

```
8231^2  ==  (100*82+31)^2
        ==  (1+100)*31^2  - 100*(82-31)^2 + (100+100^2)*82^2
        ==  (1+100)*[961] - 100*[2601]    + (100+100^2)*[6724]
        ==  961 + 96100   - 260100        + 672400 + 67240000
        ==  67749361
```

Assume that the hidden constant equals 2 as there is more bookkeeping overhead than with the usual algorithm. Computing the product of two million-digit numbers would require $\approx 2 \cdot (10^6)^{1.585} \approx 6.47 \cdot 10^9$ operations, taking about 6.5 seconds on our computer.

The Karatsuba scheme for polynomial multiplication is given in section 40.2 on page 827.

28.1.2   3-way splitting

A method that splits U and V into more than two pieces is called a *Toom-Cook algorithm* (the method is called *Toom algorithm* in [114], and *Cook-Toom algorithm* in [2]).

28.1.2.1   Zimmermann's 3-way multiplication

```
A = a2*x^2 + a1*x + a0
B = b2*x^2 + b1*x + b0

S 0= a 0* b 0
S1 = (a2+a1+a0) * (b2+b1+b0)
S2 = (4*a2+2*a1+a0) * (4*b2+2*b1+b0)
S3 = (a2-a1+a0) * (b2-b1+b0)
S 4= a 2* b 2

T1 = 2*S3 + S2
T1 /= 3   \\ division by 3
T1 += S0
T1 /= 2
T1 -= 2*S4
T2 = (S1 + S3)/2
S1 -= T1
S 2= T 2- S 0- S4
S 3= T 1- T 2

P = S4*x^4 + S3*x^3 + S2*x^2 + S1*x + S0
P - A*B  \\ == zero
```

Figure 28.1-A: Implementation of Zimmermann's 3-way multiplication scheme in GP.

A good scheme for 3-way splitting is due to Paul Zimmermann. We compute the product $C = A \cdot B$ of two numbers, A and B

$$A = a_2 x^2 + a_1 x + a_0 \tag{28.1-6a}$$
$$B = b_2 x^2 + b_1 x + b_0 \tag{28.1-6b}$$
$$C = A \cdot B = c_4 x^4 + c_3 x^3 + c_2 x^2 + c_1 x + c_0 \tag{28.1-6c}$$

by the following scheme (taken from [104]): set

$$S_0 := a_0 \cdot b_0 \tag{28.1-6d}$$
$$S_1 := (a_2 + a_1 + a_0) \cdot (b_2 + b_1 + b_0) \tag{28.1-6e}$$
$$S_2 := (4\,a_2 + 2\,a_1 + a_0) \cdot (4\,b_2 + 2\,b_1 + b_0) \tag{28.1-6f}$$
$$S_3 := (a_2 - a_1 + a_0) \cdot (b_2 - b_1 + b_0) \tag{28.1-6g}$$
$$S_4 := a_2 \cdot b_2 \tag{28.1-6h}$$

This costs 5 multiplications of length $N/3$. We already have found $c_0 = S_0$ and $c_4 = S_4$. We determine

c_1, c_2, and c_3 by the following assignments (in the given order):

$$T_1 \quad := \quad 2\,S_3 + S_2 \quad (= 18\,c_4 + 6\,c_3 + 6\,c_2 + 3\,c_0) \tag{28.1-6i}$$

$$T_1 \quad := \quad T_1/3 \quad (= 6\,c_4 + 2\,c_3 + 2\,c_2 + c_0) \quad \text{exact division by 3} \tag{28.1-6j}$$

$$T_1 \quad := \quad T_1 + S_0 \quad (= 6\,c_4 + 2\,c_3 + 2\,c_2 + 2\,c_0) \tag{28.1-6k}$$

$$T_1 \quad := \quad T_1/2 \quad (= 3\,c_4 + c_3 + c_2 + c_0) \tag{28.1-6l}$$

$$T_1 \quad := \quad T_1 - 2\,S_4 \quad (= c_4 + c_3 + c_2 + c_0) \tag{28.1-6m}$$

$$T_2 \quad := \quad (S_1 + S_3)/2 \quad (= c_4 + c_2 + c_0) \tag{28.1-6n}$$

$$S_1 \quad := \quad S_1 - T_1 \quad (= c_1) \quad \text{wrong in cited paper} \tag{28.1-6o}$$

$$S_2 \quad := \quad T_2 - S_0 - S_4 \quad (= c_2) \tag{28.1-6p}$$

$$S_3 \quad := \quad T_1 - T_2 \quad (= c_3) \tag{28.1-6q}$$

Now we have

$$C \quad = \quad A \cdot B \; = \; S_4\,x^4 + S_3\,x^3 + S_2\,x^2 + S_1\,x + S_0 \tag{28.1-6r}$$

The complexity of recursive multiplication based on this splitting scheme is $N^{\log_3(5)} \approx N^{1.465}$. Assume that the hidden constant again equals 2. Then the computation of the product of two million-digit numbers would require $\approx 2 \cdot (10^6)^{1.465} \approx 1.23 \cdot 10^9$ operations, taking about 1.2 seconds on our computer.

Note the division by 3 in relation 28.1-6j. A division by a constant (that is not a power of 2) cannot be avoided in n-way splitting schemes for multiplication for $n \geq 3$. There are squaring schemes that do not involve such divisions.

28.1.2.2   3-way multiplication by Bodrato and Zanoni

```
A = a2*x^2 + a1*x + a0
B = b2*x^2 + b1*x + b0

S 0= a 0* b 0
S1 = (a2+a1+a0)  *  (b2+b1+b0)
S2 = (4*a2+2*a1+a0) * (4*b2+2*b1+b0)
S3 = (a2-a1+a0) * (b2-b1+b0)
S 4= a 2* b 2

S2 = (S2 - S3)/3   \\ division by 3
S3 = (S1 - S3)/2
S 1= S 1- S 0
S2 = (S2 - S1)/2
S 1= S 1- S 3- S 4
S2 = S2 - 2*S4
S 3= S 3- S 2

P = S4*x^4+ S2*x^3+ S1*x^2+ S3*x + S0

P - A*B \\ == zero
```

Figure 28.1-B: Implementation of the 3-way multiplication scheme of Bodrato and Zanoni.

An alternative algorithm for 3-way splitting is suggested in [60]: setup S_0, S_1, ..., S_4 as in relations 28.1-6d...28.1-6h, then compute, in the given order,

$$S_2 \quad := \quad (S_2 - S_3)/3 \quad (= 5\,c_4 + 3\,c_3 + c_2 + c_1) \quad \text{exact division by 3} \tag{28.1-7a}$$

$$S_3 \quad := \quad (S_1 - S_3)/2 \quad (= c_3 + c_1) \tag{28.1-7b}$$

$$S_1 \quad := \quad S_1 - S_0 \quad (= c_4 + c_3 + c_2 + c_1) \tag{28.1-7c}$$

$$S_2 \quad := \quad (S_2 - S_1)/2 \quad (= 2\,c_4 + c_3) \tag{28.1-7d}$$

$$S_1 \quad := \quad S_1 - S_3 - S_4 \quad (= c_2) \tag{28.1-7e}$$

$$S_2 \quad := \quad S_2 - 2\,S_4 \quad (= c_3) \tag{28.1-7f}$$

$$S_3 \quad := \quad S_3 - S_2 \quad (= c_1) \tag{28.1-7g}$$

Now we have (note the order of the coefficients S_i)

$$C = A \cdot B = S_4 x^4 + S_2 x^3 + S_1 x^2 + S_3 x + S_0 \qquad (28.1\text{-}7\text{h})$$

The scheme requires only one multiplication by 2, while Zimmermann's scheme involves two.

28.1.2.3 3-way squaring

The following scheme is taken from [104]. To compute the square $C = A^2$ of a number A

$$A = a_2 x^2 + a_1 x + a_0 \qquad (28.1\text{-}8\text{a})$$
$$C = A^2 = S_4 x^4 + S_3 x^3 + S_2 x^2 + S_1 x + S_0 \qquad (28.1\text{-}8\text{b})$$

set

$$
\begin{aligned}
S_0 &:= a_0^2 & (28.1\text{-}8\text{c}) \\
S_1 &:= (a_2 + a_1 + a_0)^2 & (28.1\text{-}8\text{d}) \\
S_2 &:= (a_2 - a_1 + a_0)^2 & (28.1\text{-}8\text{e}) \\
S_3 &:= 2\, a_1 \cdot a_2 & (28.1\text{-}8\text{f}) \\
S_4 &:= a_2^2 & (28.1\text{-}8\text{g}) \\
& & (28.1\text{-}8\text{h})
\end{aligned}
$$

This costs four squarings and one multiplication of length $N/3$. The quantities S_0, S_3, and S_4 are already correct. Determine S_1 and S_2 via

$$
\begin{aligned}
T_1 &:= (S_1 + S_2)/2 & (28.1\text{-}8\text{i}) \\
S_1 &:= S_1 - T_1 - S_3 & (28.1\text{-}8\text{j}) \\
S_2 &:= T_1 - S_4 - S_0 & (28.1\text{-}8\text{k})
\end{aligned}
$$

28.1.3 4-way splitting

28.1.3.1 4-way multiplication

An elegant and clean scheme for 4-way splitting of a multiplication is given by Bodrato and Zanoni in [61]. A GP implementation is shown in figure 28.1-C. The algorithm is $O(n^{\log_4(7)}) \approx O(n^{1.403})$. In general, an s-way splitting scheme will be $O(n^{f(s)})$ where $f(s) = \log_s(2s + 1)$.

28.1.3.2 4-way squaring

The following scheme is taken from [104]

$$A = a_3 x^3 + a_2 x^2 + a_1 x + a_0 \qquad (28.1\text{-}9\text{a})$$
$$C = A^2 = c_6 x^6 + c_5 x^5 + c_4 x^4 + c_3 x^3 + c_2 x^2 + c_1 x + c_0 \qquad (28.1\text{-}9\text{b})$$

Set

$$
\begin{aligned}
S_1 &:= a_0^2 & (28.1\text{-}9\text{c}) \\
S_2 &:= 2\, a_0 \cdot a_1 & (28.1\text{-}9\text{d}) \\
S_3 &:= (a_0 + a_1 - a_2 - a_3) \cdot (a_0 - a_1 - a_2 + a_3) & (28.1\text{-}9\text{e}) \\
S_4 &:= (a_0 + a_1 + a_2 + a_3)^2 & (28.1\text{-}9\text{f}) \\
S_5 &:= 2\,(a_0 - a_2) \cdot (a_1 - a_3) & (28.1\text{-}9\text{g}) \\
S_6 &:= 2\, a_3 \cdot a_2 & (28.1\text{-}9\text{h}) \\
S_7 &:= a_3^2 & (28.1\text{-}9\text{i})
\end{aligned}
$$

```
A = a3*x^3 + a2*x^2 + a1*x + a0
B = b3*x^3 + b2*x^2 + b1*x + b0

S1 = a3*b3
S2 = (8*a3+4*a2+2*a1+a0)*(8*b3+4*b2+2*b1+b0)
S3 = (+a3+a2+a1+a0)*(+b3+b2+b1+b0)
S4 = (-a3+a2-a1+a0)*(-b3+b2-b1+b0)
S5 = (+8*a0+4*a1+2*a2+a3)*(+8*b0+4*b1+2*b2+b3)
S6 = (-8*a0+4*a1-2*a2+a3)*(-8*b0+4*b1-2*b2+b3)
S7 = a0*b0

S2 += S5
S4 -= S3
S6 -= S5
S4 /= 2
S5 -= S1
S5 -= (64*S7)
S3 += S4
S5 *= 2
S5 += S6

S2 -= (65*S3)
S3 -= S1
S3 -= S7
S4 = -S4
S6 = -S6
S2 += (45*S3)
S5 -= (8*S3)
S5 /= 24  \\ division by 24

S6 -= S2
S2 -= (16*S4)
S2 /= 18  \\ division by 18
S3 -= S5
S4 -= S2
S6 += (30*S2)
S6 /= 60   \\ division by 60
S2 -= S6

P = S1*x^6 + S2*x^5 + S3*x^4 + S4*x^3 + S5*x^2 + S6*x + S7

P - A*B \\ == zero
```

Figure 28.1-C: Implementation of the 4-way multiplication scheme in GP.

```
A = a3*x^3 + a2*x^2 + a1*x + a0

S1 = a0^2
S2 = 2 *a0 *a1
S 3= ( a + a 1- a 2- a3) * (a0 - a1 - a2 + a3)
S 4= ( a + a 1+ a 2+ a3 )^2
S5 = 2*(a0 - a2)*(a1 - a3)
S6 = 2*a3*a2
S7 = a3^2

T 1= S 3+ S 4
T2 = (T1 + S5)/2
T 3= S 2+ S 6
T 4= T 2- T 3
T 5= T 3- S 5
T 6= T 4- S 3
T 7= T 4- S 1
T 8= T 6- S 7

P = S7 *x^6 + S6 *x^5 + T7 *x^4 + T5 *x^3 + T8 *x^2 + S2 *x + S1
P - A^2  \\ == zero
```

Figure 28.1-D: Implementation of the 4-way squaring scheme in GP.

Then set, in the given order,

$$T_1 := S_3 + S_4 \tag{28.1-9j}$$
$$T_2 := (T_1 + S_5)/2 \tag{28.1-9k}$$
$$T_3 := S_2 + S_6 \tag{28.1-9l}$$
$$T_4 := T_2 - T_3 \tag{28.1-9m}$$
$$T_5 := T_3 - S_5 \tag{28.1-9n}$$
$$T_6 := T_4 - S_3 \tag{28.1-9o}$$
$$T_7 := T_4 - S_1 \tag{28.1-9p}$$
$$T_8 := T_6 - S_7 \tag{28.1-9q}$$

The square then equals

$$C = S_7 x^6 + S_6 x^5 + T_7 x^4 + T_5 x^3 + T_8 x^2 + S_2 x + S_1 \tag{28.1-9r}$$

28.1.4 5-way splitting

28.1.4.1 5-way multiplication

The scheme for 5-way splitting of a multiplication shown in figure 28.1-E is given in [61]. As with the 4-way multiplication scheme, no temporaries are used.

28.1.4.2 5-way squaring

We describe a 5-way squaring scheme given in [60]. Let

$$A = a_4 x^4 + a_3 x^3 + a_2 x^2 + a_1 x + a_0 \tag{28.1-10a}$$
$$C = A^2 = c_8 x^8 + c_7 x^7 + c_6 x^6 + c_5 x^5 + c_4 x^4 + c_3 x^3 + c_2 x^2 + c_1 x + c_0 \tag{28.1-10b}$$

Set

$$S_1 := a_0^2 \tag{28.1-11a}$$
$$S_2 := a_4^2 \tag{28.1-11b}$$
$$S_3 := (a_0 + a_1 + a_2 + a_3 + a_4)^2 \tag{28.1-11c}$$
$$S_4 := (a_0 - a_1 + a_2 - a_3 + a_4)^2 \tag{28.1-11d}$$
$$S_5 := 2(u_0 - u_2 + u_4) \cdot (u_1 - u_3) \tag{28.1-11e}$$
$$S_6 := (a_0 + a_1 - a_2 - a_3 + a_4) \cdot (a_0 - a_1 - a_2 + a_3 + a_4) \tag{28.1-11f}$$
$$S_7 := (a_1 + a_2 - a_4) \cdot (a_1 - a_2 - a_4 + 2(a_0 - a_3)) \tag{28.1-11g}$$
$$S_8 := 2 a_0 \cdot a_1 \tag{28.1-11h}$$
$$S_9 := 2 a_3 \cdot a_4 \tag{28.1-11i}$$

Then do the following assignments, in the order given:

$$S_4 = (S_4 + S_3)/2 \quad (= c_0 + c_2 + c_4 + c_6 + c_8) \tag{28.1-12a}$$
$$S_3 = S_3 - S_4 \quad (= c_1 + c_3 + c_5 + c_7) \tag{28.1-12b}$$
$$S_6 = (S_6 + S_4)/2 \quad (= c_0 + c_4 + c_8) \tag{28.1-12c}$$
$$S_5 = (-S_5 + S_3)/2 \quad (= c_3 + c_7) \tag{28.1-12d}$$
$$S_4 = S_4 - S_6 \quad (= c_2 + c_6) \tag{28.1-12e}$$
$$S_3 = S_3 - S_5 - S_8 \quad (= c_5) \tag{28.1-12f}$$
$$S_6 = S_6 - S_2 - S_1 \quad (= c_4) \tag{28.1-12g}$$
$$S_5 = S_5 - S_9 \quad (= c_3) \tag{28.1-12h}$$
$$S_7 = S_7 - S_2 - S_8 - S_9 + S_6 + S_3 \quad (= c_2) \tag{28.1-12i}$$
$$S_4 = S_4 - S_7 \quad (= c_6) \tag{28.1-12j}$$

```
A = a4*x^4 + a3*x^3 + a2*x^2 + a1*x + a0
B = b4*x^4 + b3*x^3 + b2*x^2 + b1*x + b0


S1 = a4*b4

S2 = (a0-2*a1+4*a2-8*a3+16*a4)*(b0-2*b1+4*b2-8*b3+16*b4)
S5 = (a0+2*a1+4*a2+8*a3+16*a4)*(b0+2*b1+4*b2+8*b3+16*b4)

S3 = (a4+2*a3+4*a2+8*a1+16*a0)*(b4+2*b3+4*b2+8*b1+16*b0)
S8 = (a4-2*a3+4*a2-8*a1+16*a0)*(b4-2*b3+4*b2-8*b1+16*b0)

S4 = (a0+4*a1+16*a2+64*a3+256*a4)*(b0+4*b1+16*b2+64*b3+256*b4)

S6 = (a0-a1+a2-a3+a4)*(b0-b1+b2-b3+b4)
S7 = (a0+a1+a2+a3+a4)*(b0+b1+b2+b3+b4)

S9 = a0*b0


S6 -= S7
S2 -= S5
S4 -= S9
S4 -= (2^16*S1)
S8 -= S3
S6 /= 2
S5 *= 2
S5 += S2
S2 = -S2
S8 = -S8
S7 += S6
S6 = -S6
S3 -= S7
S5 -= (512*S7)
S3 *= 2
S3 -= S8

S7 -= S1
S7 -= S9
S8 += S2
S5 += S3
S8 -= (80*S6)
S3 -= (510*S9)
S4 -= S2
S3 *= 3
S3 += S5
S8 /= 180  \\ division by 180
S5 += (378*S7)
S2 /= 4
S6 -= S2
S5 /= (-72)  \\ division by -72
S3 /= (-360)  \\ division by -360

S2 -= S8
S7 -= S3
S4 -= (256*S5)
S3 -= S5
S4 -= (4096*S3)
S4 -= (16*S7)
S4 += (256*S6)
S6 += S2
S2 *= 180
S2 += S4
S2 /= 11340  \\ division by 11340
S4 += (720*S6)
S4 /= (-2160)  \\ division by -2160
S6 -= S4
S8 -= S2


P = S1*x^8 + S2*x^7 + S3*x^6 + S4*x^5 + S5*x^4 + S6*x^3 + S7*x^2 + S8*x + S9

P - A*B \\ == zero
```

Figure 28.1-E: Implementation of the 5-way multiplication scheme in GP.

```
A = a4*x^4+ a3*x^3 + a2*x^2 + a1*x + a0

S1 = a0^2
S2 = a4^2
S3 = (a0 + a1 + a2 + a3 + a4)^2
S4 = (a0 - a1 + a2 - a3 + a4)^2
S5 = 2* (a0-a2+a4) * (a1-a3)
S 6= ( a + a 1- a 2- a3 + a4) * (a0 - a1 - a2 + a3 + a4)
S7 = (a1 + a2 - a4) * (a1 - a2 - a4 + 2*(a0-a3))
S8 = 2*a0*a1
S9 = 2*a3*a4

S4 = (S4+S3)/2
S3 = S3-S4
S6 = (S6+S4)/2
S5 = (-S5+S3)/2
S4 = S4-S6
S3 = S3-S5-S8
S6 = S6-S2-S1
S5 = S5-S9
S7 = S7-S2-S8-S9+S6+S3
S4 = S4-S7

P = S2*x^8+S9*x^7+S4*x^6+S3*x^5+S6*x^4+S5*x^3+S7*x^2+S8*x+S1
P - A^2  \\ == zero
```

Figure 28.1-F: Implementation of the 5-way squaring scheme.

```
A = a4*x^4+ a3*x^3 + a2*x^2 + a1*x + a0

S1 = a0^2
S2 = a4^2
[ ...S9,  as before]

T1 = S1 + 2*S2 - S7 + 2*S8 + S9
T 2= S 3- S 4
T3 = 2*S5
T 4= T 2+ T 3
T 5= T 2- T 3
T6 = T4/4
T7 = T5/4 - S9
T 8= T 1- T 6- S6
T 9= T 6- S 8
T10 = S3 + S6
T11 = (T10 + S4 + S6)/4
T12 = T11 - S1 - S2
T13 = (T10 + S5)/2
T14 = T13 - T1

P = S2*x^8 + S9*x^7 + T8*x^6 + T9*x^5 +  T12*x^4 + T7*x^3 + T14*x^2 + S8*x + S1
P - A^2 \\ == zero
```

Figure 28.1-G: Implementation of the alternative 5-way squaring scheme in GP. Definition of $S_1,\ldots,S_9$ as in figure 28.1-F.

Now we have (note the order of the coefficients S_i)

$$C \;=\; A^2 \;=\; S_2\,x^8 + S_9\,x^7 + S_4\,x^6 + S_3\,x^5 + S_6\,x^4 + S_5\,x^3 + S_7\,x^2 + S_8\,x + S_1 \qquad (28.1\text{-}12k)$$

The following scheme is taken from [104], with some errors in the paper corrected. Setup $S_1,\ldots,S_9$ as given by relations 28.1-11a...28.1-11i, then compute, in the given order,

$$T_1 := S_1 + 2 S_2 - S_7 + 2 S_8 + S_9 \tag{28.1-13a}$$
$$T_2 := S_3 - S_4 \tag{28.1-13b}$$
$$T_3 := 2 S_5 \tag{28.1-13c}$$
$$T_4 := T_2 + T_3 \tag{28.1-13d}$$
$$T_5 := T_2 - T_3 \tag{28.1-13e}$$
$$T_6 := T_4/4 \tag{28.1-13f}$$
$$T_7 := T_5/4 - S_9 \tag{28.1-13g}$$
$$T_8 := T_1 - T_6 - S_6 \tag{28.1-13h}$$
$$T_9 := T_6 - S_8 \tag{28.1-13i}$$
$$T_{10} := S_3 + S_6 \tag{28.1-13j}$$
$$T_{11} := (T_{10} + S_4 + S_6)/4 \tag{28.1-13k}$$
$$T_{12} := T_{11} - S_1 - S_2 \quad \text{(wrong in cited paper)} \tag{28.1-13l}$$
$$T_{13} := (T_{10} + S_5)/2 \tag{28.1-13m}$$
$$T_{14} := T_{13} - T_1 \tag{28.1-13n}$$

We have (note that the coefficients for x^4 and x^2 are wrong in the cited paper):

$$C = S_2 x^8 + S_9 x^7 + T_8 x^6 + T_9 x^5 + T_{12} x^4 + T_7 x^3 + T_{14} x^2 + S_8 x + S_1 \tag{28.1-13o}$$

28.2   Fast multiplication via FFT

We describe the FFT-based algorithm for multiplication of two numbers. To keep matters simple, we only consider numbers of the same length N.

28.2.1   Numbers are almost polynomials

An N-digit integer A written in radix R as

$$a_{N-1}\, a_{N-2}\, \cdots\, a_2\, a_1\, a_0 \tag{28.2-1}$$

denotes a quantity of

$$\sum_{i=0}^{N-1} a_i \cdot R^i = a_{N-1} \cdot R^{N-1} + a_{N-2} \cdot R^{N-2} + \ldots + a_1 \cdot R + a_0 \tag{28.2-2}$$

The digits can be identified with coefficients of a polynomial in R. For example, with decimal numbers we have $R = 10$ and the number 578 equals $5 \cdot 10^2 + 7 \cdot 10^1 + 8 \cdot 10^0$. The product of two numbers is almost the polynomial product

$$\sum_{k=0}^{2N-2} c_k R^k := \sum_{i=0}^{N-1} a_i R^i \cdot \sum_{j=0}^{N-1} b_j R^j \tag{28.2-3}$$

As the c_k can be greater than $R-1$ (the nine for radix R), the result has to be fixed using *carry* operations: go from right to left, replace c_k by $c_k' = c_k \bmod R$ and add $(c_k - c_k')/R$ to its left neighbor.

An example: usually we would multiply the numbers 82 and 34 as follows:

$$
\begin{array}{rrrr}
 & 82 & \times & 34 \\
\hline
 & 3 & {}^3 2 & 8 \\
2 & {}^2 4 & 6 & \\
\hline
= 2 & 7 & 8 & 8 \\
\end{array}
$$

The carries can be delayed to the end of the computation:

$$
\begin{array}{rrr}
82 & \times & 34 \\
\hline
 & 32 & 8 \\
24 & 6 & \\
\hline
24 & 38 & 8 \\
= 2 & {}^{2}7 \;\; {}^{3}8 & 8
\end{array}
$$

The computation before the carrying is a polynomial multiplication:

$$
\begin{array}{rrr}
(8\,x + 2) & \times & (3\,x + 4) \\
\hline
 & 32\,x & 8 \\
24\,x^2 & 6\,x & \\
\hline
= \quad 24\,x^2 & +38\,x & +8
\end{array}
$$

The value of the polynomial $24\,x^2 + 38\,x + 8$ for $x = 10$ is 2788.

28.2.2 Polynomial multiplication is linear convolution

The c_k in relation 28.2-3 can be found by comparing coefficients: they must satisfy the equation

$$
c_k \;\; := \;\; \sum_{i+j=k} a_i\, b_j \tag{28.2-4}
$$

This is equation 22.1-8 on page 444, a linear convolution: multiplication of two numbers is a linear convolution (polynomial multiplication) of the digit sequences, followed by carries.

In section 22.1.2 on page 441 we have seen that the convolution of two sequences A and B can be computed as follows:

1. Transform: $\widehat{A} :=\mathrm{FFT}(A)$ and $\widehat{B} :=\mathrm{FFT}(B)$.

2. Multiply the transformed sequences element-wise: $\widehat{C} := \widehat{A} \cdot \widehat{B}$.

3. Transform back: $C :=\mathrm{FFT}\!\left(\widehat{C}\right)$.

The scheme is equivalent to the following:

1. Evaluate: evaluate both polynomials A and B at sufficiently many points. Let the sequences of evaluations be $\widehat{A}$ and $\widehat{B}$.

2. Multiply the evaluations element-wise: $\widehat{C} := \widehat{A} \cdot \widehat{B}$. The sequence $\widehat{C}$ contains the values of the polynomial C.

3. Interpolate: find the polynomial C corresponding the sequence of values $\widehat{C}$.

If we use the roots of unity as the points of evaluations, then the FFT can be used to evaluate the polynomials and the inverse FFT for the interpolation, both with complexity $O\left(N \log N\right)$. The FFT is a fast algorithm to evaluate a polynomial of degree n at the n-th roots of unity in parallel. You might be surprised if you thought of the FFT as an algorithm for the decomposition into frequencies. There is no problem with either of these notions.

Re-launching our example ($82 \cdot 34 = 2788$), we use the fourth roots of unity ± 1 and $\pm i = \pm\sqrt{-1}$:

	$A = (8\,x + 2)$	$\times$	$B = (3\,x + 4)$	$C = A\,B$
$+1$	$+10$		$+7$	$+70$
$+i$	$+8i + 2$		$+3i + 4$	$+38i - 16$
-1	-6		$+1$	-6
$-i$	$-8i + 2$		$-3i + 4$	$-38i - 16$
				$C = (24\,x^2 + 38\,x + 8)$

Read this table as follows: First the given polynomials A and B are evaluated at the points given in the left column, thereby the columns below A and B are filled. Then the values are multiplied to fill the column below C, giving sequence $\widehat{C}$ of the values of C at the points. Finally, the actual polynomial C is found from those values, resulting in the lower right entry. We use a GP script that does the Fourier transform by definition:

```
1   C=[+70, +38*I-16, -6,  -38*I-16]
2   \\ Fourier transform by definition:
3   { forstep (k=3, 0, -1,  \\ highest to lowest
4       ck=sum(j=0,3, C[j+1]*exp(-2*Pi*I*k*j/4));   \\ inverse transform: negative sign
5       print( ck/4 );  \\ with normalization
6   ); }
```

The output is

```
-1.88079096131566 E-37 - 4.46687853312469 E-37*I
24.0000000000000 + 0.E-37*I
38.0000000000000 + 0.E-37*I
8.00000000000000 + 0.E-37*I
```

The product of two polynomials of degree n and m has degree $m + n$ and we need at least $m + n$ point of evaluation. An N-digit number corresponds to a polynomial of degree $N - 1$. Therefore, when multiplying two N-digit numbers, we need at least $2N - 2$ points of evaluation (this is why we zero-pad the sequences for linear convolution, see relation 22.1-7a on page 444). In the example above we could have used only three points of evaluation, but the evaluations at the third roots of unity would have given noninteger evaluations, making the table harder to read.

The operation count is dominated by that of the FFTs: the element-wise multiplication is of course $O(N)$, so the whole fast convolution algorithm is $O(N \log(N))$. The following carry operation is also $O(N)$ and can therefore also be neglected.

Assume the hidden constant equals 5. Multiplying our million-digit numbers will need about

$$5 \cdot 10^6 \log_2(10^6) \quad \approx \quad 5 \cdot 10^6 \cdot 20 \; = \; 10^8 \; = \; 0.1 \cdot 10^9$$

operations, taking approximately a tenth of a second on our computer.

We note that the complexity $O(N \log N)$ is not exactly the truth, it has to be $O(N \log(N) f(N))$ for some very slowly growing function f. For example, $f(N) = \log \log N$ with the Schönhage-Strassen multiplication algorithm given in [302], see also [358, entry "Schönhage-Strassen algorithm"]. Several multiplication algorithms are given in [213, ch.4.3.3]. See [224] on how far the idea "polynomials for numbers" can be carried and where it fails.

28.3   Radix/precision considerations with FFT multiplication

Now we look at the dependencies between the radix and the achievable precision with FFT multiplication.

We use unsigned 16-bit words for the digits. So the radix of the numbers can be in the range $2, 3, \ldots, 65536 (= 2^{16})$. If working in base 10, we will actually use 'super-digits' of base 10,000, the largest power of 10 that fits into a 16-bit word. These super-digits are called LIMBs in hfloat.

With very large precision we cannot always use the greatest power of the desired base, since the components of the convolution must be representable as integer numbers with the data type used for the FFTs: the cumulative sums c_k have to be represented precisely enough to distinguish every (integer) quantity from the next greater or smaller value. The highest possible value for a c_k will appear in the middle of the product and if the multiplicand and the multiplier consist of 'nines' (that is $R - 1$) only. For radix R and a precision of N LIMBs the maximal possible value L is

$$L \; = \; N(R - 1)^2 \tag{28.3-1}$$

Note that with FFT-based convolution the *absolute value* of the central term can in fact equal $|L| = N^2 (R - 1)^2$. But there is no need to distinguish that many integers. After dividing by N we are back at relation 28.3-1.

Radix R	max # LIMBs	max # hex digits	max # bits
$2^{10} = 1024$	$1048,576\,k$	$2621,440\,k$	$10240\,M$
$2^{11} = 2048$	$262,144\,k$	$720,896\,k$	$2816\,M$
$2^{12} = 4096$	$65,536\,k$	$196,608\,k$	$768\,M$
$2^{13} = 8192$	$16384\,k$	$53,248\,k$	$208\,M$
$2^{14} = 16384$	$4096\,k$	$14,336\,k$	$56\,M$
$2^{15} = 32768$	$1024\,k$	$3840\,k$	$15\,M$
$2^{16} = 65536$	$256\,k$	$1024\,k$	$4\,M$
$2^{17} = 128\,k$	$64\,k$	$272\,k$	$1062\,k$
$2^{18} = 256\,k$	$16\,k$	$72\,k$	$281\,k$
$2^{19} = 512\,k$	$4\,k$	$19\,k$	$74\,k$
$2^{20} = 1\,M$	$1\,k$	$5\,k$	$19\,k$
$2^{21} = 2\,M$	256	1300	5120

Radix R	max # LIMBs	max # dec digits	max # bits
10^2	$110\,G$	$220\,G$	$730\,G$
10^3	$1100\,M$	$3300\,M$	$11\,G$
10^4	$11\,M$	$44\,M$	$146\,M$
10^5	$110\,k$	$550\,k$	$1826\,k$
10^6	$1\,k$	$6,597$	$22\,k$
10^7	11	77	255

Figure 28.3-A: The maximal number of digits such that FFT multiplication with a mantissa of 53 bits can be used, for hexadecimal (top) and decimal (bottom) numbers.

The number of bits to represent L exactly is the integer greater than or equal to

$$\log_2(N\,(R-1)^2) \;=\; \log_2 N + 2\log_2(R-1) \tag{28.3-2}$$

Due to roundoff errors there must be a few more bits for safety. If computations are made using double-precision floating-point numbers (C-type `double`) one typically has a mantissa (significand) of 53 bits. Then we need to have

$$M \;\geq\; \log_2 N + 2\log_2(R-1) + S \tag{28.3-3}$$

where $M :=$ mantissa-bits and $S :=$ safety-bits. Using $\log_2(R-1) < \log_2(R)$ we obtain

$$N_{max}(R) \;=\; 2^{M-S-2\log_2(R)} \tag{28.3-4}$$

Suppose we have $M = 53$ mantissa-bits and require $S = 3$ safety-bits. With base 2 numbers one could use radix $R = 2^{16}$ for precisions up to a length of $N_{max} = 2^{53-3-2\cdot16} = 256k$ LIMBs. Corresponding are 4096 kilo bits and = 1024 kilo hex digits. For greater lengths smaller radices have to be used according to figure 28.3-A (top, extra horizontal line at the 16 bit limit for LIMBs), the equivalent table for decimal numbers is shown at the bottom of the figure. Summary:

- For decimal digits and precisions up to 11 million LIMBs (44 million decimal digits) use radix 10,000. For even greater precisions choose radix 1,000.

- For hexadecimal digits and precisions up to 256,000 LIMBs (1 million hex digits) use radix 65,536. For even greater precisions choose radix 4,096.

If convolution routines based on number theoretic transforms (NTT) are used (see section 26.3 on page 542), then no loss of precision can occur. However, the creation of a reasonably fast routine is quite nontrivial, see [155] for the implementation of the Schönhage-Strassen algorithm.

28.4 The sum-of-digits test

With high-precision calculations it is mandatory to add a sanity check to the multiplication routines. This way false results due to loss of accuracy should (with high probability) be detected via the *sum-of-digits test* (the radix used is R):

1. Compute the values ('sums of digits') $s_a = a \bmod (R-1)$ and $s_b = b \bmod (R-1)$.

2. Compute the product $c = a \cdot b$.

3. Compute $s_c = c \bmod (R-1)$ and $s_m = s_a \cdot s_b \bmod (R-1)$.

4. If $s_c \neq s_m$, then an error has occurred in the computation of c.

The sum-of-digits function s_a can for a radix-R, length-n number a be computed as [FXT: mult/auxil.cc]:

```
1   ulong
2   sum_of_digits(const LIMB *a, ulong n, ulong nine, ulong s)
3   {
4       for (ulong k=0; k<n; ++k)  s += a[k];
5       s %= nine;
6       return s;
7   }
```

where the variable **nine** has to be set to $R-1$, and **s** to zero.

The computation of $s_m = s_a \cdot s_b$ is done in

```
1   ulong
2   mult_sum_of_digits(const LIMB *a, ulong an,
3                      const LIMB *b, ulong bn,
4                      ulong nine)
5   {
6       ulong qsa = sum_of_digits(a, an, nine, 0);
7       ulong qsb = sum_of_digits(b, bn, nine, 0);
8       ulong qsm = (qsa*qsb) % nine;
9       return  qsm;
10  }
```

The checks in multiplication routine [FXT: mult/fxtmultiply.cc] can be outlined as:

```
1   fxt_multiply(const LIMB *a, ulong an,
2                const LIMB *b, ulong bn,
3                LIMB *c, ulong cn,
4                uint rx)
5   {
6       const ulong nine = rx-1;
7       ulong qsm=0, qsp=0;
8       qsm = mult_sum_of_digits(a, an, b, bn, nine);
9
10      // Multiply: c=a*b
11      // If carrying through c gives an additional (leading) digit,
12      // then set cy to that value,  else set cy=0.
13
14      qsp = sum_of_digits(g, n, nine, cy);
15      if ( qsm!=qsp )  { /* FAILED */ }
16  }
```

If we assume that a failed multiplication produces 'random' digits in c, then the probability that a failed multiplication goes unnoticed equals $1/R$.

Omitting the sum-of-digits test is *not* an option: the situation that some number contains mainly 'nines' in the course of a high-precision calculation is very common. Therefore insufficient precision in the FFTs will almost certainly result in an error.

The simplicity of the sum-of-digits test that uses the modulus $R-1$ can be seen from the polynomial identity

$$\sum_k a_k R^k \equiv \sum_k a_k \qquad \bmod R-1 \tag{28.4-1}$$

One can use other moduli, like

$$\sum_k a_k R^k \;\equiv\; \sum_k (-1)^k a_k \qquad \mod R+1 \tag{28.4-2}$$

Moduli $R^n - 1$ for small n are especially convenient:

$$\sum_k a_k R^k \;\equiv\; \sum_{k\equiv 0 \bmod 2} a_k + R \sum_{k\equiv 1 \bmod 2} a_k \qquad \mod R^2 - 1 \tag{28.4-3a}$$

$$\equiv\; \sum_{k\equiv 0 \bmod 3} a_k + R \sum_{k\equiv 1 \bmod 3} a_k + R^2 \sum_{k\equiv 2 \bmod 3} a_k \qquad \mod R^3 - 1 \tag{28.4-3b}$$

$$\equiv\; \sum_{U=0}^{n-1} R^U \left(\sum_{k\equiv U \bmod n} a_k \right) \qquad \mod R^n - 1 \tag{28.4-3c}$$

The probability of an unrecognized error is reduced to approximately $1/R^n$. The multiplication of the residues involves $O(n^2)$ operations.

28.5 Binary exponentiation

The *binary exponentiation* (or *binary powering*) scheme is a method to compute the e-th power of a number a, using about $\log_2(e)$ multiplications and squarings. The term 'number' can be replaced by about anything one can multiply. That includes integers, floating-point numbers, polynomials, matrices, integer remainders modulo some modulus, polynomials modulo a polynomial and so on. In fact, the given algorithms work for any group: we do not need commutativity but $a^n \cdot a^m = a^{n+m}$ must hold (power-associativity).

28.5.1 Right-to-left powering

This algorithm uses the binary expansion of the exponent: let $e \geq 0$, write e the base 2 as $e = [e_j, e_{j-1}, \ldots, e_1, e_0]$, $e_i \in \{0,1\}$. Then

$$a^e \;=\; a^{1\cdot e_0}\, a^{2\cdot e_1}\, a^{4\cdot e_2}\, a^{8\cdot e_3} \cdots a^{2^j\, e_j} \tag{28.5-1a}$$

$$=\; 1\,(a^1)^{e_0}\,(a^2)^{e_1}\,(a^4)^{e_2} \cdots (a^{2^j})^{e_j} \tag{28.5-1b}$$

We initialize a variable t by 1, generate the powers $s_i = a^{2^i}$ by successive squarings $s_i = s_{i-1}^2 = (a^{2^{i-1}})^2$, and multiply t by s_i if e_i equals 1. The following C++ code computes the e-th power of the (double precision) number a:

```
1   double power_r2l(double a, ulong e)
2   {
3       double t = 1;
4       if ( e )
5       {
6           double s = a;
7           while ( 1 )
8           {
9               if ( e & 1 )  t *= s;
10              e /= 2;
11              if ( 0==e )  break;
12              s *= s;
13          }
14      }
15
16      return t;
17  }
```

An easy optimization is to avoid the multiplication by 1 if the exponent is a power of 2:

```
1   double power_r2l(double a, ulong e)
2   {
3       if ( 0==e )  return 1;
4
```

```
 5        double s = a;
 6        while ( 0==(e&1) )
 7        {
 8            s *= s;
 9            e /= 2;
10        }
11
12        a = s;
13        while ( 0!=(e/=2) )
14        {
15            s *= s;
16            if ( e & 1 )  a *= s;
17        }
18        return a;
19    }
```

The program [FXT: arith/power-r2l-demo.cc] shows the quantities that occur with the computation of $p = 2^{38}$:

```
arg 1: 2 == a [number to exponentiate]  default=2
arg 2: 38 == e [exponent]  default=38
 e = 1..11.
0                                         2                          2
1                                         4                          2
1                                        16                         64
0                                       256                         64
0                                     65536                         64
1                                4294967296          274877906944   64
p=a**e = 274877906944
```

In the right-to-left powering scheme the exponent is scanned starting from the lowest bit.

28.5.2   Left-to-right powering

The left-to-right binary powering algorithm scans the exponent starting from the highest bits. We use the facts that $a^{2k} = (a^k)^2$ and $a^{2k+1} = (a^k)^2 a$. Implementation is simple:

```
 1    double power_l2r(double a, ulong e)
 2    {
 3        if ( 0==e )  return 1;
 4        double s = a;
 5        ulong b = highest_one(e);
 6        while ( b>1 )
 7        {
 8            b >>= 1;
 9            s *= s;
10            if ( e & b )  s *= a;
11        }
12        return s;
13    }
```

The program [FXT: arith/power-l2r-demo.cc] shows the quantities that occur with the computation of $p = 2^{38}$ when the left-to-right scan is used:

```
arg 1: 2 == a [number to exponentiate]  default=2
arg 2: 38 == e [exponent]  default=38
 e = 1..11.
1                                         2                          4
0                                         4                          4
0                                        16                         16
1                                       256                        512
1                                    262144                     524288
0                             274877906944          274877906944
p=a**e = 274877906944
```

All multiplications apart from the squarings happen with the unchanged value of a. This is an advantage if a is a small (integer) value so that the multiplications are cheap. As a slightly extreme example, if one computes $7^{7^7} \approx +0.3759823526783 \cdot 10^{695975}$ to full precision, then the left-to-right powering is about three times faster. If a is a full-precision number (and multiplication is done via FFTs), then the FFT of a only needs to be computed once. Thus all multiplications except for the first count as squarings. This technique is called *FFT caching*.

The given powering algorithms are good enough for most applications. There are schemes that improve further. For repeated power computations, especially for very large exponents the schemes based on *addition chains* lead to better algorithms, see [213] and [44]. The 'flexible window powering method' is described and analyzed in [112]. A readable survey of exponentiation methods is given in [160].

Techniques for accelerating computations of factorials and binomial coefficients are described in [207].

28.5.3 Cost of binary exponentiation of full-precision numbers

With full-precision numbers the cost of binary powering is the same for both the left-to-right and the right-to-left algorithm. As an example, to raise x to the 26-th power, note that $e = 26 = 11010_2$ and we can write

$$x^{26} \quad = \quad x^{16} \cdot x^8 \cdot x^2 \quad = \quad (((x^2)^2)^2)^2 \cdot ((x^2)^2)^2 \cdot (x^2) \qquad (28.5\text{-}2)$$

Here we need four squarings and two multiplications. In general one needs $\lfloor \log_2 e \rfloor$ squarings and $h(e) - 1$ multiplications where $h(e)$ is the number of set bits in the binary expansion of e. Figure 28.5-A lists the cost of the exponentiation for small exponents e in terms of squarings and multiplications and, assuming a squaring costs two FFTs and multiplication three, in terms of FFTs. The table was created with the program [FXT: arith/power-costs-demo.cc].

e :	e (radix 2)	#S	#M	#F	#C		e :	e (radix 2)	#S	#M	#F	#C
1	1	0	0	0			41	.1.1..1	5	2	16	15
2	.....1.	1	0	2			42	.1.1.1.	5	2	16	15
3	11	1	1	5			43	.1.1.11	5	3	19	17
4	....1..	2	0	4			44	.1.11..	5	2	16	15
5	....1.1	2	1	7			45	.1.11.1	5	3	19	17
6	....11.	2	1	7			46	.1.111.	5	3	19	17
7	111	2	2	10	9		47	.1.1111	5	4	22	19
8	...1...	3	0	6			48	.11....	5	1	13	
9	...1..1	3	1	9			49	.11...1	5	2	16	15
10	...1.1.	3	1	9			50	.11..1.	5	2	16	15
11	...1.11	3	2	12	11		51	.11..11	5	3	19	17
12	...11..	3	1	9			52	.11.1..	5	2	16	15
13	...11.1	3	2	12	11		53	.11.1.1	5	3	19	17
14	...111.	3	2	12	11		54	.11.11.	5	3	19	17
15	...1111	3	3	15	13		55	.11.111	5	4	22	19
16	..1....	4	0	8			56	.111...	5	2	16	15
17	..1...1	4	1	11			57	.111..1	5	3	19	17
18	..1..1.	4	1	11			58	.111.1.	5	3	19	17
19	..1..11	4	2	14	13		59	.111.11	5	4	22	19
20	..1.1..	4	1	11			60	.1111..	5	3	19	17
21	..1.1.1	4	2	14	13		61	.1111.1	5	4	22	19
22	..1.11.	4	2	14	13		62	.11111.	5	4	22	19
23	..1.111	4	3	17	15		63	.111111	5	5	25	21
24	..11...	4	1	11			64	1......	6	0	12	
25	..11..1	4	2	14	13		65	1.....1	6	1	15	
26	..11.1.	4	2	14	13		66	1....1.	6	1	15	
27	..11.11	4	3	17	15		67	1....11	6	2	18	17
28	..111..	4	2	14	13		68	1...1..	6	1	15	
29	..111.1	4	3	17	15		69	1...1.1	6	2	18	17
30	..1111.	4	3	17	15		70	1...11.	6	2	18	17
31	..11111	4	4	20	17		71	1...111	6	3	21	19
32	.1.....	5	0	10			72	1..1...	6	1	15	
33	.1....1	5	1	13			73	1..1..1	6	2	18	17
34	.1...1.	5	1	13			74	1..1.1.	6	2	18	17
35	.1...11	5	2	16	15		75	1..1.11	6	3	21	19
36	.1..1..	5	1	13			76	1..11..	6	2	18	17
37	.1..1.1	5	2	16	15		77	1..11.1	6	3	21	19
38	.1..11.	5	2	16	15		78	1..111.	6	3	21	19
39	.1..111	5	3	19	17		79	1..1111	6	4	24	21
40	.1.1...	5	1	13			80	1.1....	6	1	15	

Figure 28.5-A: Cost of binary powering of full-precision numbers for small exponents e in terms of squarings (#S), multiplications (#M) and FFTs (#F). If the left-to-right exponentiation algorithm with FFT caching needs fewer FFTs, then the number is given under (#C).

Chapter 29

Root extraction

We describe methods to compute the inverse, square root, and higher roots of a given number. The computation of any of these costs just the equivalent of a few full-precision multiplications.

29.1 Division, square root and cube root

29.1.1 Inverse and division

The ordinary division algorithm is far too expensive for numbers of extreme precision. Instead one replaces the division $\frac{a}{d}$ by the multiplication of a with the inverse of d. The inverse of d is computed by finding a starting approximation $x_0 \approx \frac{1}{d}$, and then iterating

$$x_{k+1} \;\; = \;\; x_k + x_k \left(1 - d\, x_k\right) \tag{29.1-1}$$

until the desired precision is reached. The convergence is quadratic (second order), which means that the number of correct digits is doubled with each step: if $x_k = \frac{1}{d}(1 + e)$, then $x_{k+1} = \frac{1}{d}\left(1 - e^2\right)$.

Moreover, each step only requires computations with twice the number of digits that were correct at its beginning. Still better: the multiplication $x_k(\dots)$ needs only to be done with half of the current precision as it computes the correcting digits (which alter only the less significant half of the digits). Thus, at each step we have 1.5 multiplications of the current precision: a full precision multiplication for $d\, x_k$ and a half precision multiplication for $x_k(\dots)$. The total work amounts to $1.5 + 1.5/2 + 1.5/4 + \dots = 1.5 \cdot \sum_{n=0}^{N} \frac{1}{2^n}$ which is less than three full precision multiplications. The cost of a multiplication is set to $\sim N$ for the estimates made here, this gives a realistic picture for large N. Together with the final multiplication a division costs as much as four multiplications.

The numerical example given in figure 29.1-A shows the first steps of the computation of an inverse starting from a two-digit initial approximation.

The achieved precision can be determined by the absolute value of $(1 - d\, x_k)$. In hfloat, if the achieved precision is below a certain limit, a third order correction is used to assure maximum precision at the last step:

$$x_{k+1} \;\; = \;\; x_k + x_k \left(1 - d\, x_k\right) + x_k \left(1 - d\, x_k\right)^2 \tag{29.1-2}$$

One should in general *not* use algebraically equivalent forms like $x_{k+1} = 2\, x_k - d\, x_k^2$ (for the second order iteration) because computationally there is a difference: cancellation can occur and the information on the achieved precision is not found easily.

If the divisor has the same precision as the dividend, the division is called a *long division*. If the dividend fits into a machine word the operation can be done in linear time (*short division*). Similarly, a multiplication where both operands have full precision is called a *long multiplication*, and, if one operand fits into a machine word, a *short multiplication*.

J. Arndt, *Matters Computational: Ideas, Algorithms, Source Code*,
DOI 10.1007/978-3-642-14764-7_29, © Springer-Verlag Berlin Heidelberg 2011

$$d \quad := \quad 3.1415926$$

$$x_0 \quad := \quad 0.31 \qquad [\text{initial 2-digit approximation for } 1/d]$$

$$d \cdot x_0 \quad := \quad 3.141 \cdot 0.3100 \; = \; 0.9737$$

$$y_0 \quad := \quad 1.000 - d \cdot x_0 \; = \; 0.02629$$

$$x_0 \cdot y_0 \quad := \quad 0.3100 \cdot 0.02629 \; = \; 0.0081(49)$$

$$x_1 \quad := \quad x_0 + x_0 \cdot y_0 \; = \; 0.3100 + 0.0081 \; = \; 0.3181$$

$$d \cdot x_1 \quad := \quad 3.1415926 \cdot 0.31810000 \; = \; 0.9993406$$

$$y_1 \quad := \quad 1.0000000 - d \cdot x_1 \; = \; 0.0006594$$

$$x_1 \cdot y_1 \quad := \quad 0.31810000 \cdot 0.0006594 \; = \; 0.0002097(5500)$$

$$x_2 \quad := \quad x_1 + x_1 \cdot y_1 \; = \; 0.31810000 + 0.0002097 \; = \; 0.31830975$$

$$d \cdot x_2 \quad := \quad 3.1415926 \cdot 0.31830975 \; = \; 0.99999955$$

$$y_2 \quad := \quad 1.0000000 - d \cdot x_2 \; = \; 0.00000014$$

$$x_2 \cdot y_2 \quad := \quad 0.31830975 \cdot 0.00000014 \; = \; 0.000000044$$

$$x_3 \quad := \quad x_2 + x_2 \cdot y_2 \; = \; 0.31830975 + 0.000000044 \; = \; 0.31830979399$$

Figure 29.1-A: First steps of the computation of the inverse of π.

29.1.2 Inverse square root

Computation of inverse square roots can be done using a similar scheme: find a starting approximation $x_0 \approx \frac{1}{\sqrt{d}}$, then iterate

$$x_{k+1} \quad = \quad x_k + x_k \frac{(1 - d\, x_k^2)}{2} \tag{29.1-3}$$

Convergence is again second order: if $x_k = \frac{1}{\sqrt{d}}(1 + e)$, then

$$x_{k+1} \quad = \quad \frac{1}{\sqrt{d}} \left(1 - \frac{3}{2} e^2 - \frac{1}{2} e^3 \right) \tag{29.1-4}$$

If the achieved precision is below a certain limit, a third order correction should be applied:

$$x_{k+1} \quad = \quad x_k + x_k \frac{(1 - d\, x_k^2)}{2} + x_k \frac{3\,(1 - d\, x_k^2)^2}{8} \tag{29.1-5}$$

To compute the square root, first compute $1/\sqrt{d}$, then a final multiplication with d gives $\sqrt{d}$.

With squaring considered as expensive as multiplication, while FFT multiplication costs about 2/3 of a multiplication, we reach an operation count of four multiplications for computing $1/\sqrt{d}$ and five for $\sqrt{d}$. This algorithm is considerably better than iterating $x_{k+1} := \frac{1}{2}\left(x_k + \frac{d}{x_k}\right)$ because no long divisions are involved.

A unified routine that implements the computation of the inverse a-th roots is given in [hfloat: src/hf/itiroot.cc]. The general form of the divisionless iteration for the a-th root of d is, up to third order:

$$x_{k+1} \quad = \quad x_k \left(1 + \frac{(1 - d\, x_k^a)}{a} + \frac{(1 + a)\,(1 - d\, x_k^a)^2}{2\, a^2} \right) \tag{29.1-6}$$

The initial approximation is computed using ordinary floating-point numbers (type `double`) with special precautions to avoid overflow with exponents that cannot be represented with `doubles`. Third order corrections are made whenever the achieved precision falls below a certain limit.

29.1.3   Cube root extraction

We use the relation $d^{1/3} = d\,(d^2)^{-1/3}$. That is, we compute the inverse third root of d^2 using the iteration

$$x_{k+1} \;=\; x_k + x_k \frac{(1 - d^2\,x_k^3)}{3} \tag{29.1-7}$$

and finally multiply with d. Convergence is second order: if $x_k = \frac{1}{\sqrt[3]{d}}(1 + e)$, then

$$x_{k+1} \;=\; \frac{1}{\sqrt[3]{d}}\left(1 - 2e^2 - \frac{4}{3}e^3 - \frac{1}{3}e^4\right) \tag{29.1-8}$$

29.1.4   Improved iteration for the square root

Actually, the 'simple' version of the square root iteration ($x_{k+1} := \frac{1}{2}\left(x_k + \frac{d}{x_k}\right)$) can be used for practical purposes if rewritten as a *coupled iteration* for both $\sqrt{d}$ and its inverse. For $\sqrt{d}$ we use the iteration

$$x_{k+1} \;=\; x_k - \frac{(x_k^2 - d)}{2\,x_k} \tag{29.1-9}$$

$$\;=\; x_k - v_{k+1}\frac{(x_k^2 - d)}{2} \quad \text{where} \quad v \approx 1/x \tag{29.1-10}$$

For the auxiliary $v \approx 1/\sqrt{d}$ we iterate

$$v_{k+1} = v_k + v_k\,(1 - x_k\,v_k) \tag{29.1-11}$$

We start with approximations

$$x_0 \;\approx\; \sqrt{d} \tag{29.1-12}$$

$$v_0 \;\approx\; 1/x_0 \tag{29.1-13}$$

The v-iteration must precede that for x in each step. If carefully implemented, this method turns out to be significantly more efficient than the computation via the inverse root. An implementation is given in [hfloat: src/hf/itsqrt.cc]. The idea is due to Schönhage.

29.1.5   A different view on the iterations

Let p be a prime and assume you know the inverse x_0 of a given number d modulo p. With (the iteration for the inverse, relation 29.1-1 on page 567) $\Phi(x) := x\,(1 + (1 - d\,x))$ the number $x_1 := \Phi(x_0)$ is the inverse of d modulo p^2. Modulo p^2 we know that $x_0\,d \equiv (1 + k\,p)$ so we can write $x_0 \equiv 1/d\,(1 + k\,p)$, thereby

$$\Phi(x_0) \;=\; \Phi\left(\frac{1}{d}(1 + k\,p)\right) \;=\; \frac{1}{d}\,(1 - k\,p^2) \;\equiv\; \frac{1}{d}\,\bmod p^2 \tag{29.1-14}$$

The very same computation (with $x_1 = 1/d\,(1 + j\,p^2)$) shows that for $x_2 := \Phi(x_1)$ one has $x_2 \equiv 1/d \bmod p^4$. Each application of Φ doubles the exponent of the modulus.

The equivalent scheme works for root extraction. We give an example for the inverse square root. With $p = 17$ and $x_0 = 3$ we have $x_0^2\,2 \equiv 1$. That is, x_0 is the inverse square root of 2 modulo p ($x_0 \equiv 1/\sqrt{d} \bmod p$ where $d = 2$). Now use the iteration $\Phi(x) := x\,(1 + (1 - d\,x)/2)$ to compute $x_1 = \Phi(x_0) = -45/2 \equiv 122 \bmod p$ and observe that $x_1^2\,d \equiv 1 \bmod p^2$. Compute $x_2 = \Phi(x_1) = -1815665 \equiv 21797 \bmod p^2$ and check that $x_2^2\,d \equiv 1 \bmod p^4$. After k steps we have $x_k \equiv 1/\sqrt{d} \bmod p^{2^k}$.

The arithmetic is very similar to the arithmetic of power series. Note that GP allows doing such computations as follows:

```
? 1/sqrt(2+O(17^5))
   3 + 7*17 + 7*17^2 + 4*17^3 + 11*17^4 + O(17^5)
\\ Note that 21797 = 3 + 7*17 + 7*17^2 + 4*17^3 + 11*17^4
\\        and    122 = 3 + 7*17
```

Section 1.21 on page 56 describes the case $p = 2$. The computation of a square root modulo p^e, given a square root modulo p, is described in section 39.9.2 on page 785.

29.2 Root extraction for rationals

We give expressions for the extraction of the a-th root of a rational quantity.

29.2.1 Extraction of the square root

A general formula for a k-th order ($k \geq 2$) iteration for $\sqrt{d}$ is

$$\Phi_k(x) \;=\; \sqrt{d}\,\frac{\left(x+\sqrt{d}\right)^k + \left(x-\sqrt{d}\right)^k}{\left(x+\sqrt{d}\right)^k - \left(x-\sqrt{d}\right)^k} = \sqrt{d}\,\frac{\left(p+q\sqrt{d}\right)^k + \left(p-q\sqrt{d}\right)^k}{\left(p+q\sqrt{d}\right)^k - \left(p-q\sqrt{d}\right)^k} \tag{29.2-1}$$

where $x = p/q$. All $\sqrt{d}$ vanish when expanded:

$$\Phi_2(x) \;=\; \frac{x^2+d}{2\,x} = \frac{p^2+d\,q^2}{2\,p\,q} \tag{29.2-2a}$$

$$\Phi_3(x) \;=\; x\,\frac{x^2+3\,d}{3\,x^2+d} = \frac{p}{q}\,\frac{p^2+3\,d\,q^2}{3\,p^2+d\,q^2} \tag{29.2-2b}$$

$$\Phi_4(x) \;=\; \frac{x^4+6\,d\,x^2+d^2}{4\,x^3+4\,d\,x} = \frac{p^4+6\,d\,p^2\,q^2+d^2\,q^4}{4\,p^3\,q+4\,d\,p\,q^3} \tag{29.2-2c}$$

$$\Phi_5(x) \;=\; x\,\frac{x^4+10\,d\,x^2+5\,d^2}{5\,x^4+10\,d\,x^2+d^2} = \frac{p}{q}\,\frac{p^4+10\,d\,p^2\,q^2+5\,d^2\,q^4}{5\,p^4+10\,d\,p^2\,q^2+d^2\,q^4} \tag{29.2-2d}$$

$$\Phi_k(x) \;=\; x\,\frac{\sum_{j=0}^{\lfloor k/2\rfloor} \binom{k}{2\,j}\,x^{k-2j}\,d^j}{\sum_{j=0}^{\lfloor k/2\rfloor} \binom{k}{2\,j+1}\,x^{k-2j-1}\,d^j} \tag{29.2-2e}$$

The denominators and numerators of Φ_k are terms of the second order recurrence

$$a_k \;=\; 2\,x\,a_{k-1} - \left(x^2-d\right)\,a_{k-2} \tag{29.2-3}$$

with initial terms $a_0 = 1$, $a_1 = x$ for the numerators and $a_0 = 0$, $a_1 = 1$ for the denominators (that is, $\Phi_0 = 1/0$, $\Phi_1 = x/1$). An equivalent form of relation 29.2-1 is

$$\Phi_k(x) \;=\; \sqrt{d}\,\cot\left(k\,\operatorname{arccot}\frac{x}{\sqrt{d}}\right) \tag{29.2-4}$$

Setting $d = -1$ and $x = \cot(z)$ we find

$$\cot(k\,z) \;=\; \Phi_k(\cot(z)) \tag{29.2-5}$$

From this relation we deduce the following composition law:

$$\Phi_m(\Phi_n(x)) \;=\; \Phi_{m\,n}(x) \tag{29.2-6}$$

There is a nice expression for the error behavior of the k-th order iteration:

$$\Phi_k\left(\sqrt{d}\cdot\frac{1+e}{1-e}\right) \;=\; \sqrt{d}\cdot\frac{1+e^k}{1-e^k} \tag{29.2-7}$$

29.2.2   Extraction of the r-th root

A second order iteration for $\sqrt[r]{z}$ is given by

$$\Phi_2(x) \;=\; x + \frac{d - x^r}{r\,x^{r-1}} = \frac{(r-1)\,x^r + d}{r\,x^{r-1}} = \frac{1}{r}\left((r-1)\,x + \frac{d}{x^{r-1}}\right) \qquad (29.2\text{-}8)$$

A third order iteration for $\sqrt[r]{d}$ is

$$\Phi_3(x) \;=\; x\cdot\frac{\alpha\,x^r + \beta\,d}{\beta\,x^r + \alpha\,d} = \frac{p}{q}\cdot\frac{\alpha\,p^r + \beta\,q^r d}{\beta\,p^r + \alpha\,q^r d} \qquad (29.2\text{-}9)$$

where $x = p/q$, $\alpha = r - 1$ and $\beta = r + 1$. An alternative form is

$$\Phi_3(x) \;=\; \frac{d}{x}\cdot\frac{\beta\,x^r + \alpha\,d}{\alpha\,x^r + \beta\,d} \qquad (29.2\text{-}10)$$

where again $\alpha = r - 1$ and $\beta = r + 1$.

29.2.3   Rational iterations for roots ‡

Rational iterations can also be obtained using Padé approximants.

29.2.3.1   Square root

Let $P_{[i,j]}(z)$ be the approximant of $\sqrt{z}$ around $z = 1$ of order $[i,j]$. An iteration of order $i+j+1$ is given by $x\,P_{[i,j]}(\frac{d}{x^2})$. Different combinations of i and j result in alternative iterations:

$$[i,j] \;\longmapsto\; x\,P_{[i,j]}\left(\frac{d}{x^2}\right) \qquad (29.2\text{-}11\text{a})$$

$$[1,0] \;\longmapsto\; \frac{x^2 + d}{2x} \qquad (29.2\text{-}11\text{b})$$

$$[0,1] \;\longmapsto\; \frac{2x^3}{3x^2 - d} \qquad (29.2\text{-}11\text{c})$$

$$[1,1] \;\longmapsto\; x\,\frac{x^2 + 3d}{3x^2 + d} \qquad (29.2\text{-}11\text{d})$$

$$[2,0] \;\longmapsto\; \frac{3x^4 + 6dx^2 - 3d^2}{8x^3} \qquad (29.2\text{-}11\text{e})$$

$$[0,2] \;\longmapsto\; \frac{8x^5}{15x^4 - 10dx^2 + 3d^2} \qquad (29.2\text{-}11\text{f})$$

Still other forms are obtained by using $\frac{d}{x}\,P_{[i,j]}(\frac{x^2}{d})$:

$$[i,j] \;\longmapsto\; \frac{d}{x}\,P_{[i,j]}\left(\frac{x^2}{d}\right) \qquad (29.2\text{-}12\text{a})$$

$$[1,0] \;\longmapsto\; \frac{x^2 + d}{2x} \qquad (29.2\text{-}12\text{b})$$

$$[0,1] \;\longmapsto\; \frac{2d^2}{3dx - x^3} \qquad (29.2\text{-}12\text{c})$$

$$[1,1] \;\longmapsto\; \frac{d\,(d + 3x^3)}{x\,(3d + x^2)} \qquad (29.2\text{-}12\text{d})$$

$$[2,0] \;\longmapsto\; \frac{-x^4 + 6dx^2 + 3d^2}{8xd} \qquad (29.2\text{-}12\text{e})$$

$$[0,2] \;\longmapsto\; \frac{8d^3}{3x^4 - 10dx^2 + 15d^2} \qquad (29.2\text{-}12\text{f})$$

29.2.3.2 r-th root

The Padé approximants for the r-th root can be expressed as ratios of hypergeometric series (using relation 36.2-9 on page 689):

$$F\left(\begin{array}{c} u,\, v \\ u+v+1/r \end{array}\Big|\, z\right) \Big/ F\left(\begin{array}{c} u+1/r,\, v+1/r \\ u+v+1/r \end{array}\Big|\, z\right) \;=\; (1-z)^{1/r} \qquad (29.2\text{-}13)$$

The expression on the left gives the approximant $[i,j]$ if we set $u=-i$ and $v=-j-1/r$ (so both series terminate). The iteration $\Phi_{[i,j]} = x\, P_{[i,j]}\left(\frac{d}{x^r}\right)$ has order $i+j+1$. We compute the third order iteration for the fourth root (relation 29.2-9 with $r=4$):

```
1    ? \r hypergeom.gpi  \\ definition of hypergeom()
2    ? r=4;  \\ r-th root
3    ? i=1;  \\ degree of denominator
4    ? j=1;  \\ degree of numerator
5    ? u=-i;v=-j-1/r;  \\ setup parameters so that series terminate
6    ? N=hypergeom([u,v],[u+v+1/r],x,i)
7       -5/8*x + 1
8    ? D=hypergeom([u+1/r,v+1/r],[u+v+1/r],x,j)
9       -3/8*x + 1
10   ? t=N/D  \\ Pade approximant [i,j]
11      (-5*x + 8)/(-3*x + 8)
12
13   \\ check t == (1-x)^(1/r) + order(i+j+1):
14   ? n=i+j+2;
15   ? t-hypergeom([-1/r],[],x,n)+O(x^(n))
16      5/256*x^3 + O(x^4)
17
18   ? t=subst(t,x,1-x)  \\ Pade approximant in x
19      (5*x + 3)/(3*x + 5)
20   ? it=x*subst(t,x,d/x^r)  \\ iteration for f(x)=x^r-d
21      (3*x^5 + 5*d*x)/(5*x^4 + 3*d)
22   \\ ==   x * (3*x^4 + 5*d)/(5*x^4 + 3*d)
```

Now we check the order of the iteration, we set $d=1$ and compute $f\left(\Phi\left(d^{1/r}(1+e)\right)\right) = f\left(\Phi(1+e)\right)$:

```
1    ? f(x)=x^r-1;  \\ ==x^r-d  for d==1
2    ? it=subst(it,d,1);  \\ d==1
3    ? er=subst(it,x,(1+e));  \\ Phi( d^(1/r))*(1+e) ) = Phi(1+e)
4    ? taylor(f(er),e)  \\ f( Phi(1+e) ) =?= O(e^(i+j+1))
5       5*e^3 - 15/2*e^4 + [...]  \\ OK
```

An alternative expression for iterations of order $i+j+1$ is $\Phi_{[i,j]} = \frac{d}{x}\, P_{[i,j]}\left(\frac{x^r}{d}\right)$. The approximant $P_{[1,1]}$ leads to the third order iteration given as relation 29.2-10.

In section 30.5.2 on page 595 Padé approximants are used to find iterations for arbitrary functions f.

29.3   Divisionless iterations for the inverse a-th root

There is a nice general formula that gives iterations with arbitrary order of convergence for $1/\sqrt[a]{d} = d^{-1/a}$ that involve no long division. We use the identity

$$d^{-1/a} \;=\; x\left(1-(1-x^a d)\right)^{-1/a} \;=\; x\,(1-y)^{-1/a} \quad \text{where} \quad y := (1-x^a d) \qquad (29.3\text{-}1)$$

Expansion as a series in y gives

$$d^{-1/a} \;=\; x\sum_{k=0}^{\infty} (1/a)^{\overline{k}}\, y^k \qquad (29.3\text{-}2)$$

where $z^{\overline{k}} := z\,(z+1)\,(z+2)\ldots(z+k-1)$ (and $z^{\overline{0}} := 1$, $z^{\overline{k}}$ is the rising factorial power), written out:

$$d^{-1/a} \;=\; x\,\frac{1}{\sqrt[a]{1-y}} \;=\; x\left[1 + \frac{y}{a} + \frac{(1+a)\,y^2}{2\,a^2} + \frac{(1+a)(1+2a)\,y^3}{6\,a^3} + \right. \qquad (29.3\text{-}3)$$

$$\left. + \frac{(1+a)(1+2a)(1+3a)\,y^4}{24\,a^4} + \cdots + \frac{\prod_{k=1}^{n-1}(1+k\,a)}{n!\,a^n}\,y^n + \cdots \right]$$

An n-th order iteration for $d^{-1/a}$ is obtained by truncating the above series after the $(n-1)$-th term:

$$x_{k+1} = \Phi_n(x_k) \quad \text{where} \quad \Phi_n(x) = x \sum_{k=0}^{n-1} (1/a)^{\overline{k}} y^k \tag{29.3-4}$$

Convergence is n-th order:

$$\Phi_n\left(d^{-1/a}(1+e)\right) = d^{-1/a}\left(1 + O(e^n)\right) \tag{29.3-5}$$

For example, the second order iteration is

$$\Phi_2(x) := x + x\frac{(1 - d\,x^a)}{a} \tag{29.3-6}$$

Convergence is indeed quadratic: if $x = \frac{1}{\sqrt[a]{d}}(1+e)$, then

$$\Phi_2(x) = \frac{1}{\sqrt[a]{d}}\left((1+e)\left[(1+e)^a - (a+1)\right]\right) = \frac{1}{\sqrt[a]{d}}\left(1 - \frac{a+1}{2}e^2 + O(e^3)\right) \tag{29.3-7}$$

29.3.1 Iterations for the inverse

Set $a = 1$, $y = 1 - d\,x$ to compute the inverse of d.

$$\frac{1}{d} = x\frac{1}{1 - y} \tag{29.3-8a}$$

$$\Phi_k(x) = x\left(1 + y + y^2 + y^3 + y^4 + \cdots + y^{k-1}\right) \tag{29.3-8b}$$

For example, $\Phi_2(x) = x(1+y)$ is the second order iteration 29.1-1 on page 567.

Composition is particularly simple with the iterations for the inverse:

$$\Phi_{n\,m}(x) = \Phi_n\left(\Phi_m(x)\right) \tag{29.3-9}$$

There are simple closed forms for this iteration:

$$\Phi_k = \frac{1 - y^k}{d} = x\frac{1 - y^k}{1 - y} \tag{29.3-10a}$$

$$\Phi_\infty = 1 + x + x^2 + x^3 + x^4 + \ldots \tag{29.3-10b}$$

$$= x(1 + y)(1 + y^2)(1 + y^4)(1 + y^8)\ldots \tag{29.3-10c}$$

$$= x(1 + y + y^2)(1 + y^3 + y^6)(1 + y^9 + y^{18})\ldots \tag{29.3-10d}$$

The expression for the convergence of the k-th order iteration is

$$\Phi_k\left(\frac{1}{d}(1+e)\right) = \frac{1}{d}\left(1 - (-e)^k\right) \tag{29.3-11}$$

The iteration converges if $|e| < 1$ for the start value $x_0 = \frac{1}{d}(1+e)$. That is, the region of attraction is the open disc of radius $r = 1/d$ around the point $1/d$, independent of the order k. For other iterations, the region of attraction usually has a fractal boundary and further depends on the order.

29.3.2 Iterations for the inverse square root

Set $a = 2$, $y = 1 - d\,x^2$ to compute the inverse square root of d.

$$\frac{1}{\sqrt{d}} = x\frac{1}{\sqrt{1 - y}} \tag{29.3-12a}$$

$$= x\left(1 + \frac{y}{2} + \frac{3\,y^2}{8} + \frac{5\,y^3}{16} + \frac{35\,y^4}{128} + \cdots + \frac{\binom{2k}{k}y^k}{4^k} + \ldots\right) \tag{29.3-12b}$$

$$\Phi_{k+1}(x) = x\left(1 + \frac{y}{2} + \frac{3\,y^2}{8} + \ldots + \frac{\binom{2k}{k}y^k}{4^k}\right) \tag{29.3-12c}$$

$\Phi_2(x) = x\,(1 + y/2)$ is the second order iteration 29.1-3 on page 568.

29.3.3   Computation of the a-th root

```
? default(realprecision,55);
? n=5; d=3;
? f=x^n-d
   x^5 - 3
? phi(x)=(x+(x/n-x^(n+1)/(n*d)));
? phi(x)
   -1/15*x^6 + 6/5*x
? y=real(polroots(f)[1])
   1.2457309396155173259666803366403050809393099993068779811
? y*=(1.01); \\ <--= initial approximation within 1%
? for(k=0,7, t=phi(y); print(k,": ",y); y=t; );
0:   1.2581882490116724992263471400067081317487030929999467609
1:   1.2453521998882091612922815042363613525213873439226682049
2:   1.2457305943106651323381267600848321408508336218806673303
3:   1.2457309396152301803405533431627934257835000280138356272
4:   1.2457309396155173259666801380758928589406244031248749620
5:   1.2457309396155173259666803366403050809393099993068684860
6:   1.2457309396155173259666803366403050809393099993068779811
7:   1.2457309396155173259666803366403050809393099993068779811
? y^n
   3.0000000000000000000000000000000000000000000000000000000
```

Figure 29.3-A: Quantities occurring in the iterative computation of $\sqrt[5]{3}$.

The following (second order) iteration computes $\sqrt[a]{d}$ directly:

$$\Phi(x) \;=\; x + \frac{1}{a}\left(x - \frac{x^{a+1}}{d}\right) \tag{29.3-13}$$

Figure 29.3-A shows the quantities occurring in the iterative computation of $\sqrt[5]{3}$. The iteration involves no long division for small (rational) d.

To compute the a-root of a full-precision number d, we can use the iteration for the inverse root and invert afterwards. Another possibility is to compute the inverse a-th root of d^{a-1} and multiply with d afterwards:

$$\left[(d)^{a-1}\right]^{-1/a} d \;=\; d^{(1-a)/a}\, d \;=\; d^{1/a} \tag{29.3-14}$$

If a is small the cost is lower than with the final iteration for the inverse (which costs about three multiplications or nine FFTs). The powering-method is not more expensive than inversion if the rightmost column in figure 28.5-A on page 566 for $e = a - 1 \le 6$. If the iteration for the inverse involves a loss of precision, the method might be preferred even if its cost is higher.

29.3.4   Error expressions for inverse square root iterations ‡

An expression for the error behavior of the n-th order iteration similar to relation 29.2-7 on page 570 is

$$F_n \;:=\; \Phi_n\left(d^{-1/2}\frac{1+e}{1-e}\right)\Big/d^{-1/2} \tag{29.3-15a}$$

$$=\; \frac{\sum_{k=0}^{n}\binom{2n-1}{k}(-e)^k - \sum_{k=n+1}^{2n+1}\binom{2n-1}{k}(-e)^k}{(1-e)^{2n-1}} \tag{29.3-15b}$$

Now define $c := \frac{F_n - 1}{F_n + 1}$, then

$$F_n \;=\; \frac{1+c}{1-c} \quad \text{where} \quad c = e^n\,\frac{\sum_{k=0}^{n}\binom{2n-1}{n-k}(-e)^k}{\sum_{k=0}^{n}\binom{2n-1}{k}(-e)^k} \tag{29.3-15c}$$

For example, with $n = 2$ we have

$$F_2 \quad := \quad \Phi_2\left(d^{-1/2}\frac{1+e}{1-e}\right) / d^{-1/2} \tag{29.3-16a}$$

$$= \quad \frac{1-3\,e-3\,e^2+e^3}{1-3\,e+3\,e^2-e^3} \tag{29.3-16b}$$

$$= \quad 1-6\,e^2-16\,e^3-30\,e^4-48\,e^5-70\,e^6-\cdots \tag{29.3-16c}$$

$$= \quad -1+\frac{6}{(e-1)^2}+\frac{4}{(e-1)^3} \tag{29.3-16d}$$

$$F_2 \quad = \quad \frac{1+c}{1-c} \quad \text{where} \quad c = e^2\,\frac{e-3}{1-3\,e} \tag{29.3-16e}$$

For $n = 4$ we have

$$F_4 \quad := \quad \Phi_4\left(d^{-1/2}\frac{1+e}{1-e}\right) / d^{-1/2} \tag{29.3-17a}$$

$$= \quad \frac{1-7\,e+21\,e^2-35\,e^3-35\,e^4+21\,e^5-7\,e^6+e^7}{1-7\,e+21\,e^2-35\,e^3+35\,e^4-21\,e^5+7\,e^6-e^7} \tag{29.3-17b}$$

$$= \quad 1-70\,e^4-448\,e^5-1680\,e^6-4800\,e^7-11550\,e^8-\cdots \tag{29.3-17c}$$

$$= \quad -1+\frac{70}{(e-1)^4}+\frac{168}{(e-1)^5}+\frac{140}{(e-1)^6}+\frac{40}{(e-1)^7} \tag{29.3-17d}$$

$$F_4 \quad = \quad \frac{1+c}{1-c} \quad \text{where} \quad c = e^4\,\frac{e^3-7\,e^2+21\,e-35}{1-7\,e+21\,e^2-35\,e^3} \tag{29.3-17e}$$

Two curious formulas related to the error behavior of Φ_2 are

$$\Phi_2\left(\frac{1}{\sqrt{d}}\left[e+\frac{1}{e}\right]\right) \quad = \quad \frac{1}{\sqrt{d}}\left[-\frac{1}{2}\cdot\left(e^3+\frac{1}{e^3}\right)\right] \tag{29.3-18}$$

$$\Phi_2\left(\frac{1}{\sqrt{d}}\left[e-\frac{2}{3}\frac{1}{e}\right]\right) \quad = \quad \frac{1}{\sqrt{d}}\left[+\frac{1}{2}\cdot\left(e^3-\frac{2}{3}\frac{1}{e^3}\right)\right] \tag{29.3-19}$$

29.4 Initial approximations for iterations

With the iterative schemes we always need an initial approximation for the value to be computed. Assume we want to compute $f(d)$, for example, $f(d) = \sqrt{d}$ or $f(d) = \exp(d)$. We could convert the high precision number d to a machine floating-point number and use the floating-point unit (FPU) to compute an initial approximation. However, when d cannot be represented with a machine float, the method fails. The method will also fail if the result causes an overflow, which is likely to happen with $f(d) = \exp(d)$. The methods given here avoid this problem.

29.4.1 Inverse roots

With $f(d) = d^{1/a}$ use the following technique. Write d in the form

$$d \quad = \quad M \cdot R^X \tag{29.4-1}$$

where M is the mantissa, R the radix, and X the exponent. We have $0 \le M < 1$ and $X \in \mathbb{Z}$. Now use

$$d^{1/a} \quad = \quad M^{1/a} \cdot R^{X/a} \quad = \quad M^{1/a} \cdot R^{Y/a} \cdot R^Z \tag{29.4-2}$$

where $Z = \lfloor X/a \rfloor$ and $Y = X - a \cdot Z$ (so $X = a \cdot Z + Y$). Compute the three quantities on the right side of relation 29.4-2 separately and finally the product as result. An implementation is [hfloat: src/hf/itiroot.cc]:

```
1   void
2   approx_invpow(const hfloat &d, hfloat &c, long a)
3   {
4       double dd;
5       dt_mantissa_to_double(*(d.data()), dd);
6       dd = pow(dd, 1.0/(double)a);  // M^(1/a)
7
8       long  Z = d.exp() / a;    // Z = X / a
9       long  Y = d.exp() - a*Z;  // Y = X % a
10
11      double tt = pow((double)d.radix(),(double)Y/a);   // R^(Y/a)
12      dd *= tt;              // M^(1/a) * R^(Y/a)
13
14      d2hfloat(dd, c);  // c =  M^(1/a) * R^(Y/a)
15      c.exp( c.exp()+Z );   // c *= R^(Z)
16  }
```

We could also subtract $a \cdot Z$ from the exponent before the iteration and add Z to the exponent afterwards: $\left(R^{X-aZ}\right)^{1/a} = R^{Y/a} = R^{X/a}/R^Z$. In that case the initial approximation can be computed via the straightforward approach.

29.4.2 Exponential function

With $f(d) = \exp(d)$ write

$$\exp(d) \;=\; M \cdot R^X \tag{29.4-3}$$

where $X = \lfloor d/\log(R) \rfloor$ and $M = \exp(d - X \cdot \log R)$. The argument d must fit into a machine float which is not a restriction: for values d that are too big for a machine float $\exp(d)$ will not fit into a `hfloat` type (the exponent of the result would overflow). Compute the initial approximation to $\exp(d)$ as follows [hfloat: src/tz/itexp.cc]:

```
1   void
2   approx_exp(const hfloat &d, hfloat &c)
3   {
4       double dd;
5       hfloat2d(d,dd);
6
7       double lr = log( hfloat::radix() );
8       double X = floor( dd/lr );
9       double M = exp( dd-X*lr );
10
11      d2hfloat(M,c);
12      c.exp( c.exp()+(long)X );
13  }
```

An iteration for the computation of the exponential function is given in section 32.2 on page 627.

29.5   Some applications of the matrix square root

We give applications of the iteration for the (inverse) square root to compute re-orthogonalized matrices, the polar decomposition, the sign decomposition, and the pseudo-inverse of a matrix.

29.5.1   Re-orthogonalization

A task from graphics applications: a rotation matrix A that deviates from being orthogonal (for example, due to cumulative errors resulting from many multiplications with rotation matrices) shall be transformed to the closest orthogonal matrix E. We have (see [295]):

$$E \;=\; A\,(A^T A)^{-\frac{1}{2}} \tag{29.5-1}$$

With the divisionless iteration for the inverse square root

$$\Phi(x) \;=\; x\left(1 + \frac{1}{2}\left(1 - dx^2\right) + \frac{3}{8}\left(1 - dx^2\right)^2 + \frac{5}{16}\left(1 - dx^2\right)^3 + \dots\right) \tag{29.5-2}$$

the given task is easy: as $A^T A$ is close to unity (the identity matrix) we can use the (second order) iteration with $d = A^T A$ and $x = 1$

$$(A^T A)^{-\frac{1}{2}} \approx \left(1 + \frac{1 - A^T A}{2}\right) \tag{29.5-3}$$

and multiply by A to get a 'closer-to-orthogonal' matrix A_+:

$$A_+ = A \left(1 + \frac{1 - A^T A}{2}\right) \approx E \tag{29.5-4}$$

The step can be repeated with A_+ (or higher orders can be used) if necessary. Note that the iteration is the one for the computation of the inverse square root of 1 (relation 29.1-3 on page 568 with $d = 1$):

$$x_+ = x \left(1 + \frac{1 - 1 \cdot x^2}{2}\right) \approx 1 \tag{29.5-5}$$

For scalars sufficiently close to 1 the iteration converges to 1. For matrices not too far from a matrix E such that $E^T E = 1$ (that is, E is orthogonal) the iteration converges to E.

It is instructive to write things down in the *singular value decomposition* (SVD) representation

$$A = U \Omega V^T \tag{29.5-6}$$

where U and V are orthogonal and Ω is a diagonal matrix with non-negative entries, see [367]. We note that the SVD is *not* unique, for example, for the 1×1 matrix $[-2]$ we have $[-2] = [-1][2][1] = [1][2][-1]$. The SVD is a decomposition of the action of the matrix as: rotation – element-wise stretching – rotation. Now

$$A^T A = \left(V \Omega U^T\right) \left(U \Omega V^T\right) = V \Omega^2 V^T \tag{29.5-7}$$

Thus (using the equality $(V \Omega V^T)^n = V \Omega^n V^T$)

$$(A^T A)^{-\frac{1}{2}} = \left(\left(V \Omega U^T\right)\left(U \Omega V^T\right)\right)^{-\frac{1}{2}} = \left(V \Omega^2 V^T\right)^{-\frac{1}{2}} = V \Omega^{-1} V^T \tag{29.5-8}$$

and we have

$$A \left(A^T A\right)^{-\frac{1}{2}} = \left(U \Omega V^T\right) \left(V \Omega^{-1} V^T\right) = U V^T \tag{29.5-9}$$

that is, the 'stretching part' was removed.

A numerical example: for

$$A = \begin{bmatrix} +1.0000000 & +1.0000000 & +0.7500000 \\ -0.5000000 & +1.5000000 & +1.0000000 \\ +0.7500000 & +0.5000000 & -1.0000000 \end{bmatrix} \tag{29.5-10}$$

we have

$$E = \begin{bmatrix} +0.803114165 & +0.291073143 & +0.519888513 \\ -0.486897253 & +0.823533541 & +0.291073143 \\ +0.343422053 & +0.486897252 & -0.803114166 \end{bmatrix} \tag{29.5-11}$$

and $E E^T = 1$.

29.5.2   Polar decomposition

The *polar decomposition* of a matrix A is a representation of the form

$$A \ = \ E R \tag{29.5-12}$$

where the matrix E is orthogonal and $R = R^T$. It is analogous to the representation of a complex number $z \in \mathbb{C}$ as $z = e^{i\phi} r$ (identify $R \sim r$ and $E \sim e^{i\phi}$). The polar decomposition can be defined by

$$A \ = \ E R := \left(A (A^T A)^{-1/2} \right) \left((A^T A)^{1/2} \right) \tag{29.5-13}$$

where $R = (A^T A)^{1/2}$ and $E = A(A^T A)^{-1/2}$. The matrix E is computed as before:

$$E \ = \ A \cdot \left(1 + \frac{1 - A^T A}{2} \right) \cdot \left(1 + \frac{1 - A_+^T A_+}{2} \right) \cdot \ldots \tag{29.5-14}$$

The matrix R equals $E^{-1} A = E^T A$, that is

$$A \ = \ E R = E \left(E^T A \right) \tag{29.5-15}$$
$$= \ U V^T \left(V \Omega V^T \right) \tag{29.5-16}$$

Compute the polar decomposition as

$$E_0 \ = \ A \tag{29.5-17a}$$
$$Y_k \ = \ \left(1 + \frac{1 - E_k^T E_k}{2} \right) \tag{29.5-17b}$$
$$E_{k+1} \ = \ E_k Y_k \quad \to E \tag{29.5-17c}$$
$$R_{k+1} \ = \ E_{k+1}^T A \quad \to R \tag{29.5-17d}$$
$$E_{k+1} R_{k+1} \ \to \ A \tag{29.5-17e}$$

Higher orders can be added in the computation of Y_k. If you prefer $z = r\,e^{i\phi}$ over $e^{i\phi} r$, then iterate as above but set $R' = A\,E^T$ so that

$$A \ = \ R' E = \left(A E^T \right) E \tag{29.5-18}$$
$$= \ \left(U \Omega U^T \right) U V^T \tag{29.5-19}$$

Numerical example: for

$$A \ = \ \begin{bmatrix} +1.00000 & +1.00000 & +0.75000 \\ -0.50000 & +1.50000 & +1.00000 \\ +0.75000 & +0.50000 & -1.00000 \end{bmatrix} \tag{29.5-20}$$

we have

$$A \ = \ E R \tag{29.5-21a}$$

$$= \ \begin{bmatrix} +0.80311 & +0.29107 & +0.51988 \\ -0.48689 & +0.82353 & +0.29107 \\ +0.34342 & +0.48689 & -0.80311 \end{bmatrix} \begin{bmatrix} +1.30412 & +0.24447 & -0.22798 \\ +0.24447 & +1.76982 & +0.55494 \\ -0.22798 & +0.55494 & +1.48410 \end{bmatrix} \tag{29.5-21b}$$

$$A \ = \ R' E \tag{29.5-21c}$$

$$= \ \begin{bmatrix} +1.48410 & +0.55494 & +0.22798 \\ +0.55494 & +1.76982 & -0.24447 \\ +0.22798 & -0.24447 & +1.30412 \end{bmatrix} \begin{bmatrix} +0.80311 & +0.29107 & +0.51988 \\ -0.48689 & +0.82353 & +0.29107 \\ +0.34342 & +0.48689 & -0.80311 \end{bmatrix} \tag{29.5-21d}$$

29.5.3   Sign decomposition

The *sign decomposition* can be defined as

$$A \;=\; S\,N \;=\; \left(A(A^2)^{-1/2}\right)\left((A^2)^{1/2}\right) \tag{29.5-22}$$

where $N = (A^2)^{-1/2}$ and $S = A\,(A^2)^{-1/2}$. The square root has to be chosen such that all its eigenvalues have positive real parts. The sign decomposition is undefined if A has eigenvalues on the imaginary axis. The matrix S is its own inverse (its eigenvalues are ± 1). The matrices A, S and N commute pair-wise: $SN = NS$, $AN = NA$ and $AS = SA$.

Use

$$S_0 \;=\; A \tag{29.5-23a}$$

$$Y_k \;=\; \left(1 + \frac{1 - S_k^2}{2}\right) \tag{29.5-23b}$$

$$S_{k+1} \;=\; S_k\,Y_k \quad \to S \tag{29.5-23c}$$

$$N_{k+1} \;=\; S_{k+1}\,A \quad \to N \tag{29.5-23d}$$

Numerical example: for

$$A \;=\; \begin{bmatrix} +1.00000 & +1.00000 & +0.75000 \\ -0.50000 & +1.50000 & +1.00000 \\ +0.75000 & +0.50000 & -1.00000 \end{bmatrix} \tag{29.5-24}$$

we have

$$A \;=\; S\,N \tag{29.5-25a}$$

$$= \begin{bmatrix} +0.90071 & -0.01706 & +0.29453 \\ -0.24065 & +0.95862 & +0.71389 \\ +0.62679 & +0.10775 & -0.85933 \end{bmatrix} \begin{bmatrix} +1.13014 & +1.02237 & +0.36392 \\ -0.18454 & +1.55423 & +0.06423 \\ -0.07158 & +0.35875 & +1.43718 \end{bmatrix} \tag{29.5-25b}$$

where $S\,S = 1$. See [180] and also [181].

29.5.4   Pseudo-inverse

While we are at it: define a matrix A^+ as

$$A^+ \;:=\; (A\,A^T)^{-1}\,A^T = \left(V\,\Omega^{-2}\,V^T\right)\left(V\,\Omega\,U^T\right) = V\,\Omega^{-1}\,U^T \tag{29.5-26}$$

This looks suspiciously like the inverse of A. In fact, this is the *pseudo-inverse* of A:

$$A^+\,A \;=\; \left(V\,\Omega^{-1}\,U^T\right)\left(U\,\Omega\,V^T\right) = 1 \quad \text{but wait} \tag{29.5-27}$$

A^+ has the nice property to exist even if A^{-1} does not. If A^{-1} exists, it is identical to A^+. If not, $A^+A \neq 1$ but A^+ will give the best possible (in a least-square sense) solution $x^+ = A^+b$ of the equation $A\,x = b$ (see [115, p.770]). To find $(A\,A^T)^{-1}$ use the iteration for the inverse:

$$\Phi(x) = x\left(1 + (1 - dx) + (1 - dx)^2 + \dots\right) \tag{29.5-28}$$

with $d = A\,A^T$ and the start value $x_0 = 2 - n\,(A\,A^T)/\,\|A\,A^T\|^2$ where n is the dimension of A.

A GP implementation of the pseudo-inverse using the SVD:

```
1   matpseudoinv(A)=
2   \\ Return pseudo-inverse of A
3   {
4       local(t, x, U, d, V);
```

```
? A
   [+1.00 +1.00 +0.75 +2.00]
   [-0.50 +1.50 +1.00 +3.00]
   [+0.75 +0.50 -1.00 -3.00]

? t=matSVD(A);  U=t[1];  d=t[2];  V=t[3];
? U
   [+0.644401153492 +0.438818890 +0.6262468643]
   [-0.695372132379 +0.676976586 +0.2411644651]
   [-0.318126941467 -0.590881276 +0.7413869203]

? d
   [+0.95641003 0 0]
   [0 +5.09161169 0]
   [0 0 +1.74234618]

? V
   [+0.787833655771 -0.067332385426 +0.60935354299]
   [-0.583139548860 +0.227598489665 +0.77980313700]
   [+0.110889336609 +0.313647647860 -0.01752654388]
   [+0.164225309908 +0.919396775264 -0.14243646797]

? Ax=matpseudoinv(A)
   [+0.744034618880 -0.497415792829 +0.005046325813]
   [-0.093004327360 +0.562176974103 +0.499369209273]
   [+0.095446097914 -0.041347314730 -0.080741213017]
   [+0.138692567521 -0.016875347613 -0.221929812661]

? A*Ax
   [+1.0000000000000 +3.78653234 E-29 -4.41762106 E-29]
   [+2.52435489 E-29 +1.0000000000000 -2.52435489 E-29]
   [-2.52435489 E-29 -2.52435489 E-29 +1.0000000000000]

? Ax*A
   [+0.9965272596551 +0.0004340925431 +0.0555638455173 -0.0193171181681]
   [+0.0004340925431 +0.9999457384321 -0.0069454806896 +0.0024146397710]
   [+0.0555638455173 -0.0069454806896 +0.1109784717229 +0.3090738906900]
   [-0.0193171181681 +0.0024146397710 +0.3090738906900 +0.8925485301897]
```

Figure 29.5-A: Numerical example for the pseudo-inverse computed by the SVD. We use a 3×4 matrix which is definitely not invertible. A working precision of 25 decimal digits was used, so $A A^+ = 1$ to within that precision. On the other hand, $A^+ A$ is not close to the unit matrix.

```
5        t = matSVD(A);
6        U = t[1];  d = t[2];  V = t[3];
7        for (k=1, matsize(d)[1],
8            x=d[k,k];  if (x>1e-15, d[k,k]=1/x, d[k,k]=0);
9        );
10       return( V*d*U~ );
11   }
```

Where the SVD is computed with the help of a routine (qfjacobi()) that returns the eigenvectors of a real symmetric matrix:

```
1    matSVDcore(A)=
2    \\ Singular value decomposition:
3    \\ Return [U, d, V] so that U*d*V~==A
4    \\ d is a diagonal matrix
5    \\ U, V are orthogonal
6    {
7        local(U, d, V);  \\ returned quantities
8        local(t, R, d1);
9        R = conj(A~)*A;  \\ R==V*d^2*V~
10       t = qfjacobi( R );  \\ fails with eigenvalues==zero
11       V = t[2];
12       d = real(sqrt(t[1]));
13       d1 = d;
14       for (k=1, length(d1), t=d1[k]; if (abs(t)>1e-16, t=1/t, t=0); d1[k]=t );
15       d1 = matdiagonal(d1);
16       d = matdiagonal(d);
17       U = (A*V*d1);
18       return( [U, d, V] );
19   }
```

The core routine is always called with a matrix A whose number of rows is greater than or equal to its number of rows.

```
1   matSVD(A)=
2   {
3       local(tq, t, U, d, V);
4       t = matsize(A);
5       tq=0;  if ( t[1]<t[2],  tq=1; A=A~; );
6       t = matSVDcore(A);
7       d = t[2];
8       if ( tq,
9           U = t[3];   V=t[1];
10      , /* else */
11          U = t[1];   V=t[3];
12      );
13      return( [U, d, V] );
14  }
```

For a numerical example see figure 29.5-A. The connection between the SVD of a matrix a and the eigenvectors of $A^T A$ is described in [198].

29.6 Goldschmidt's algorithm

A framework for the *Goldschmidt algorithm* can be stated as follows. Let A, B, a, and b be integers. Initialize

$$x_0 \;=\; d^A, \qquad E_0 = d^B \tag{29.6-1a}$$

then iterate

$$P_{k+1} \;=\; 1 + \frac{1 - E_k}{a} \tag{29.6-1b}$$

$$x_{k+1} \;=\; x_k \, P_k^b \quad \to d^{A - B\,b/a} \tag{29.6-1c}$$

$$E_{k+1} \;=\; E_k \, P_k^a \quad \to 1 \tag{29.6-1d}$$

The algorithm converges quadratically. The updates for x and E (last two relations) can be computed independently. The iteration is not self-correcting, so the computations have to be carried out with full precision throughout.

An invariant of the algorithm is given by x_k^a / E_k^b:

$$\frac{x_{k+1}^a}{E_{k+1}^b} \;=\; \frac{(x_k \cdot P_k^b)^a}{(E_k \cdot P_k^a)^b} = \frac{x_k^a}{E_k^b} \tag{29.6-2a}$$

We use the relation

$$\frac{x_0^a}{E_0^b} \;=\; \frac{d^{A\,a}}{d^{B\,b}} \;=\; d^{A\,a - B\,b} \tag{29.6-2b}$$

and, as E converges to 1, we find that

$$\frac{x_\infty^a}{E_\infty^b} \;=\; x_\infty^a \;=\; \frac{x_0^a}{E_0^b} \tag{29.6-2c}$$

The quantity computed is $d^{A - B\,b/a}$:

$$x_\infty \;=\; \left(\frac{x_0^a}{E_0^b} \right)^{1/a} \;=\; \frac{x_0}{E_0^{b/a}} \;=\; \frac{d^A}{d^{b\,B/a}} \;=\; d^{A - B\,b/a} \tag{29.6-2d}$$

We consider some interesting special cases in what follows and set $b = 1$.

29.6.1   Algorithm for the a-th root

Solving $A - B/a = 1/a$ gives $B = A\,a - 1$ and especially $A = 0$, $B = 1$. That is, set

$$x_0 \; = \; d, \qquad E_0 \; = \; d^{a-1} \tag{29.6-3a}$$

then iterate, until x close enough to $x_\infty = d^{\frac{1}{a}}$,

$$P_k \; := \; 1 + \frac{1 - E_k}{a} \quad \to 1 \tag{29.6-3b}$$

$$x_{k+1} \; := \; x_k \cdot P_k \tag{29.6-3c}$$

$$E_{k+1} \; := \; E_k \cdot P_k^a \quad \to 1 \tag{29.6-3d}$$

Setting $a = 2$ gives an algorithm for the computation of the square root:

$$\sqrt{d} \; = \; d \prod_{k=0}^{\infty} \frac{3 - E_k}{2} \tag{29.6-4}$$

where $E_0 = d$, $E_{k+1} := E_k \left(\frac{3-E_k}{2}\right)^2$.

An algorithm for the inverse a-th root is obtained by solving $A - B/a = -1/a$: $B = A\,a + 1$ and especially $A = 1$, $B = a - 1$. That is, set $x_0 = 1$ and $E_0 = d$, and iterate as in relations 29.6-3b..29.6-3d until x close enough to $x_\infty = d^{-\frac{1}{a}}$.

Setting $a = 1$ gives an algorithm for the inverse ($P_k = 1 + (1 - E_k) = 2 - E_k$):

$$\frac{1}{d} \; = \; \prod_{k=0}^{\infty} (2 - E_k) \tag{29.6-5}$$

where $E_0 = d$, $E_{k+1} := E_k (2 - E_k)$.

Setting $a = 2$ gives an algorithm for the inverse square root ($P_k = 1 + (1 - E_k)/2 = (3 - E_k)/2$):

$$\frac{1}{\sqrt{d}} \; = \; \prod_{k=0}^{\infty} \frac{3 - E_k}{2} \tag{29.6-6}$$

where $E_0 = d$, $E_{k+1} := E_k \left(\frac{3-E_k}{2}\right)^2$.

29.6.2   Higher order algorithms for the inverse a-th root

Higher order iterations are found by appending higher terms to the expression $\left(1 + \frac{1-E_k}{a}\right)$ in the definitions of P_{k+1}, as suggested by equation 29.3-3 on page 572 and the identification $y = 1 - E$:

$$E_{k+1} \; = \; E_k\, P_k^a \quad \text{where} \tag{29.6-7}$$

$$P_k \; = \; 1 + \frac{1 - E_k}{a} \qquad \text{[second order]} \tag{29.6-8}$$

$$+ \frac{(1 + a)\,(1 - E_k)^2}{2\,a^2} \qquad \text{[third order]}$$

$$+ \frac{(1 + a)\,(1 + 2a)\,(1 - E_k)^3}{6\,a^3} \qquad \text{[fourth order]}$$

$$+ \ldots +$$

$$+ \frac{(1 + a)\,(1 + 2a)\ldots(1 + (n - 1)\,a)\,(1 - E_k)^n}{n!\,a^n} \qquad \text{[order } (n + 1)\text{]}$$

$$
\begin{array}{|l|}
\hline
x_0 = 1 \\
E_0 = 2.0 \\
P_0 = 0.90625 \\
b_0 = 0.0 \\
\hline
x_1 = 0.90625 \\
E_1 = 1.3490314483642578125 \\
P_1 = 0.93177697415069360431516543030738830556640625 \\
b_1 = 1.5185 \\
\hline
x_2 = 0.8444228828240660789106186712160706520008056640625 \\
E_2 = 1.0168806193662645741043332087203920949218854221909296 8 \\
P_2 = 0.9958243694256508418788315054034553239996718905629355821 \\
b_2 = 5.8884 \\
\hline
x_3 = 0.840896884816865852021284660500638771059752871862783095 6 \\
E_3 = 1.0000022336332328355958387702492100757406887968567195 7 \\
P_3 = 0.9999994415924713406977321191709309975809003013470607162 \\
b_3 = 18.772 \\
\hline
x_4 = 0.8408964152537145441292683119973118637849080485731336497 \\
E_4 = 1.0000000000000000052236770943197147970437318824842246 37 \\
P_4 = 0.9999999999999999986940807264200713050026299021477654907 \\
b_4 = 57.409 \\
\hline
x_5 = 0.8408964152537145430311254762332148950400342623567845249 \\
E_5 = 1.0000000000000000000000000000000000000000000000000000000067 \\
P_5 = 0.9999999999999999999999999999999999999999999999999999999833 \\
b_5 = 173.32 \\
\hline
1/\sqrt[4]{2} = 0.8408964152537145430311254762332148950400342623567845108\ldots \\
\hline
\end{array}
$$

Figure 29.6-A: Numerical quantities occurring in the computation of $1/\sqrt[4]{2}$ using a third order Goldschmidt algorithm. The value $\lfloor b_k \rfloor$ gives the number of correct bits after step k.

For example, the inverse fourth root of $d = 2$ can be computed via the third order algorithm

$$
\begin{aligned}
x_0 &= 1 & \text{(29.6-9a)} \\
E_0 &= d = 2 & \text{(29.6-9b)} \\
E_{k+1} &= E_k\, P_k^4 = E_k \left(\frac{45 - 18\, E_k + 5\, E_k^2}{32} \right)^4 & \text{(29.6-9c)} \\
x_{k+1} &= x_k\, P_k & \text{(29.6-9d)}
\end{aligned}
$$

Figure 29.6-A shows the numerical values of x_k, E_k and P_k up to step $k = 6$. The approximate precision in bits of x_k is computed as $b_k = -\log(|1 - E_k|)/\log(2)$.

29.7 Products for the a-th root ‡

Rewrite the well-known product form

$$
\frac{1}{1 - y} = (1 + y)\,(1 + y^2)\,(1 + y^4)\,(1 + y^8) \ldots \tag{29.7-1}
$$

as

$$
\frac{1}{1 - y} = \prod_{k > 0} (1 + Y_k) \quad \text{where} \quad Y_1 := y, \qquad Y_{k+1} := Y_k^2 \tag{29.7-2}
$$

We give product forms for a-th roots and their inverses that generalize the relations above.

29.7.1   Second order products

For the inverse square root use $1/\sqrt{1-y} = (1+y/2)\cdot 1/\sqrt{1-y^2\,(3+y)/4}$, thereby

$$\frac{1}{\sqrt{1-y}} \;=\; \prod_{k>0}(1+Y_k) \quad\text{where}\quad Y_1 := \frac{y}{2}, \qquad Y_{k+1} := Y_k^2\left(\frac{3}{2}+Y_k\right) \tag{29.7-3}$$

For the square root use $\sqrt{1-y} = (1-y/2)\cdot\sqrt{1-(y/(y-2))^2}$, so

$$\sqrt{1-y} \;=\; \prod_{k>0}(1+Y_k) \quad\text{where}\quad Y_1 := -\frac{y}{2}, \qquad Y_{k+1} := -\frac{1}{2}\left(\frac{Y_k}{1+Y_k}\right)^2 \tag{29.7-4}$$

The relation for the inverse a-th root is

$$\frac{1}{\sqrt[a]{1-y}} \;=\; (1-y)^{-1/a} \;=\; \prod_{k>0}(1+Y_k) \quad\text{where} \tag{29.7-5a}$$

$$Y_1 := \frac{y}{a}, \qquad Y_{k+1} := \frac{1}{a}\left(1-(1-a\,Y_k)\,(Y_k+1)^a\right) \tag{29.7-5b}$$

Alternatively,

$$\frac{1}{\sqrt[a]{d}} \;=\; x\,(1-y)^{-1/a} \;=\; x\prod_{k>0}(1+Y_k) \tag{29.7-6}$$

with $y := 1 - d\,x^a$ and the definitions 29.7-5b for Y_k. For the a-th root we get

$$\sqrt[a]{1-y} \;=\; (1-y)^{1/a} \;=\; \prod_{k>0}(1+Y_k) \quad\text{where} \tag{29.7-7a}$$

$$Y_1 := \frac{y}{a}, \qquad Y_{k+1} := \frac{1}{a}\,\frac{(1+a\,Y_k)-(1+Y_k)^a}{(1+Y_k)^a} \tag{29.7-7b}$$

29.7.2   Products of arbitrary order

We want to find an n-th order product for the inverse a-th root

$$\frac{1}{\sqrt[a]{1-y}} \;=\; \prod_{k>0}(1+T(Y_k)) \quad\text{where}\quad Y_1 = y, \qquad Y_{k+1} = N(Y_k) \tag{29.7-8}$$

The functions T and N have to be determined. Set

$$[1-y]^{-\frac{1}{a}} \;=\; (1+T(Y_1))\,[(1+T(Y_1))^a\,(1-y)]^{-\frac{1}{a}} \tag{29.7-9a}$$

$$=:\; (1+T(Y_1))\,[1-Y_2]^{-\frac{1}{a}} \tag{29.7-9b}$$

where $1+T(Y_1)$ is the Taylor expansion

$$[1-y]^{-\frac{1}{a}} \;=\; 1+\frac{y}{a}+\frac{(1+a)\,y^2}{2\,a^2}+\frac{(1+a)(1+2a)\,y^3}{6\,a^3}+\ldots+\frac{\prod_{k=1}^{n-1}(1+k\,a)}{n!\,a^n}\,y^n+\ldots \tag{29.7-10}$$

up to order $n-1$. The Taylor expansion of Y_2 starts with a term $\sim y^n$. Using $Y_{k+1} = N(Y_k)$, as suggested by the relation between Y_2 and Y_1, gives a product with n-th order convergence. For example, for a third order product for $1/\sqrt{1-y}$, set

$$T(Y) \;:=\; \frac{1}{2}Y+\frac{3}{8}Y^2 \tag{29.7-11}$$

Now solve $(1 + T(Y_1))^2 (1 - y) = (1 - Y_2)$ for Y_2 to obtain

$$Y_2 = \frac{5 y^3}{8} + \frac{15 y^4}{64} + \frac{9 y^5}{64} =: N(y) \tag{29.7-12}$$

Then, finally, ($Y_1 := y$ and)

$$\frac{1}{\sqrt{1-y}} = \prod_{k>0} (1 + T(Y_k)) \quad \text{where} \tag{29.7-13a}$$

$$T(Y) := \frac{1}{2} Y + \frac{3}{8} Y^2 \tag{29.7-13b}$$

$$Y_{k+1} = N(Y_k) := \frac{Y_k^3}{64} \left(40 + 15 Y_k + 9 Y_k^2\right) \tag{29.7-13c}$$

Replacing relation 29.7-13c by $Y_{k+1} = 1 - (1 + T(Y_k))^a (1 - Y_k)$ gives the general formula for the inverse a-th root. The second order products lead to expressions that are quite nice:

$$\frac{1}{\sqrt[a]{1-y}} = \prod_{k>0} (1 + T(Y_k)) \quad \text{where} \quad T(y) := +\frac{y}{a} \quad \text{and} \tag{29.7-14a}$$

$$Y_{k+1} = N(Y_k) := 1 - \left(1 + \frac{y}{a}\right)^a (1 - y) \tag{29.7-14b}$$

$$\frac{1}{\sqrt[a]{1+y}} = \prod_{k>0} (1 + T(Y_k)) \quad \text{where} \quad T(y) := -\frac{y}{a} \quad \text{and} \tag{29.7-15a}$$

$$Y_{k+1} = N(Y_k) := \left(1 - \frac{y}{a}\right)^a (1 + y) - 1 \tag{29.7-15b}$$

$$\sqrt[a]{1-y} = \prod_{k>0} (1 + T(Y_k)) \quad \text{where} \quad T(y) := -\frac{y}{a} \quad \text{and} \tag{29.7-16a}$$

$$Y_{k+1} = N(Y_k) := \frac{(a - Y_k)^a - (1 - Y_k) a^a}{(a - Y_k)^a} = 1 - \frac{(1 - Y_k) a^a}{(a - Y_k)^a} \tag{29.7-16b}$$

$$\sqrt[a]{1+y} = \prod_{k>0} (1 + T(Y_k)) \quad \text{where} \quad T(y) := +\frac{y}{a} \quad \text{and} \tag{29.7-17a}$$

$$Y_{k+1} = N(Y_k) := \frac{(1 + Y_k) a^a - (a + Y_k)^a}{(a + Y_k)^a} = \frac{(1 + Y_k) a^a}{(a + Y_k)^a} - 1 \tag{29.7-17b}$$

The third order product for $\frac{1}{\sqrt[a]{1-y}}$ is

$$\frac{1}{\sqrt[a]{1-y}} = \prod_{k>0} (1 + T(Y_k)) \quad \text{where} \quad T(y) = +\frac{y}{a} + \frac{y^2 (1+a)}{2 a^2} \quad \text{and} \tag{29.7-18a}$$

$$Y_{k+1} = N(Y_k) := 1 - \left(1 + \frac{y}{a} + \frac{y^2 (1+a)}{2 a^2}\right)^a (1 - y) \tag{29.7-18b}$$

$$= 1 - (1 + T(y))^a (1 - y) \tag{29.7-18c}$$

29.7.3 Third order product for the a-th root

The third order iteration given as relation 29.2-9 on page 571 gives a simple product for $\sqrt[a]{d}$. Let

$$P_k := \prod_{j=0}^{k} Y_k \tag{29.7-19a}$$

```
? default(realprecision,55);
? a=3;d=2;al=a-1;be=a+1;
? F(x)=(al*x^a+be*d)/(be*x^a+al*d)   \\ == (x^3 + 4)/(2*x^3 + 2)
? p=99.0;   \\ very bad approximation to the root
? for(k=0,25,p*=F(p);print("  ",p););
   49.500153045449860867772853756570132948572606410388539663
   24.750688696322535793295398076760659038190058852964934460
   12.377792780128382599987309228382889563737720225044012905
   6.1986817294679733089803948935359831901917837320165830357
   3.1382160956525775164587135127175212698603091937687217907
   1.7166434303974992394555143292360395395658208028534524867
   1.2833235143227843328303771164010152645995928582804900032
   1.2599262845711532794913599247538658268681639208667671057
   1.2599210498948732250077509793665642207537327503965189867
   1.2599210498948731647672106072782283505702514647015997907
   1.2599210498948731647672106072782283505702514647015079807
   1.2599210498948731647672106072782283505702514647015079807
```

Figure 29.7-A: Computation of $\sqrt[3]{2}$ with a very bad initial approximation.

where Y_0 is sufficiently near to $\sqrt[a]{d}$ and $Y_k = F(P_{k-1})$ where

$$F(x) \;:=\; \frac{\alpha\,x^a + \beta\,d}{\beta\,x^a + \alpha\,d} \qquad (29.7\text{-}19b)$$

with $\alpha = a - 1$ and $\beta = a + 1$. Then $P_\infty = \sqrt[a]{d}$. Figure 29.7-A shows the numerical quantities with the computation of $\sqrt[3]{2}$ with a starting value $Y_0 = 99$ that is not at all close to the root. We have $F(x) = \frac{x^3+4}{2x^3+2}$ which is $\approx \frac{1}{2}$ for large values of x. Therefore the big initial values are repeatedly halved before the third order convergence begins.

29.8 Divisionless iterations for polynomial roots

Let $f(x)$ be a polynomial in x with simple roots only, then

$$\Phi(x) \;:=\; x - p(x)\,f(x) \quad \text{where} \quad p(x) := f'(x)^{-1} \bmod f(x) \qquad (29.8\text{-}1)$$

is a second order iteration for the roots of $f(x)$. The iteration involves no long division if all coefficients are small rationals. Instead of dividing by $f'(x)$ a multiplication by the modular inverse $p(x)$ is used. As $\deg(p) < \deg(f)$ we have $\deg(\Phi) \le 2\deg(f) - 1$.

For example, for $f(x) = a\,x^2 + b\,x + c$ we have

$$\Phi(x) \;=\; x - \frac{2\,a\,x + b}{\Delta}\,f(x) \quad \text{where} \quad \Delta = b^2 - 4\,a\,c \qquad (29.8\text{-}2)$$

The general expressions for polynomials of orders > 2 get complicated. However, for fixed polynomial coefficients the iteration is more manageable. For example, with $f(x) = x^3 + 5\,x + 1$ we find

$$\Phi(x) \;=\; x + \frac{f(x)}{527}\,\left(30\,x^2 - 9\,x + 100\right) \qquad (29.8\text{-}3)$$

For the polynomial $x^n - d$ we have $p = x/(n\,d)$ and the iteration is (relation 29.3-13 on page 574):

$$\Phi(x) \;=\; x - \frac{x}{n\,d}\,(x^n - d) \;=\; x + \frac{1}{n}\left(x - \frac{x^{n+1}}{d}\right) \qquad (29.8\text{-}4)$$

The construction is given in [185] where a method to construct divisionless iterations of arbitrary order is given: let $p\,f' + q\,f \equiv 1$ and

$$\Phi_1 \;:=\; x - p_1\,f, \qquad p_1 := p \qquad (29.8\text{-}5a)$$

$$p_r \;:=\; p\,p'_{r-1} - (r - 1)\,q\,p_{r-1} \qquad (29.8\text{-}5b)$$

$$\Phi_r \;:=\; \Phi_{r-1} + (-1)^r\,p_r\,f^r/r! \qquad (29.8\text{-}5c)$$

then Φ_r is an iteration of order $r + 1$.

Chapter 30

Iterations for the inversion of a function

We study some general expressions for iterations for the zero of a function. Two schemes for one-point iterations of arbitrary order are given: Householder's formula and Schröder's formula. Several methods to construct alternative iterations are described. Moreover, iterations that also converge for multiple roots and a technique to turn a linear iteration into a super-linear one are presented.

30.1 Iterations and their rate of convergence

An *iteration* for a zero r (or root, $f(r) = 0$) of a function $f(x)$ can be given as a function $\Phi(x)$ that, when used like

$$x_{k+1} = \Phi(x_k) \tag{30.1-1}$$

will make x_k converge towards the root: $x_\infty = r$. Convergence is subject to the condition that x_0 is close enough to r. The function $\Phi(x)$ must (and can) be constructed such that it has an attracting fixed point where $f(x)$ has a zero:

$$\Phi(r) = r \quad \text{(fixed point)} \tag{30.1-2}$$

$$|\Phi'(r)| < 1 \quad \text{(attracting)} \tag{30.1-3}$$

This type of iteration is called a *one-point iteration*. There are also *multi-point iterations*, these are of the form $x_{k+1} = \Phi(x_k, x_{k-1}, \ldots, x_{k-j}), j \geq 1$. An example is the two-point iteration known as the *secant method*

$$x_{k+1} = \Phi(x_k, x_{k-1}) = x_k - f(x_k) \frac{x_k - x_{k-1}}{f(x_k) - f(x_{k-1})} \tag{30.1-4}$$

We are mainly concerned with one-point iterations in what follows.

The order of convergence (or simply *order*) of a given iteration can be defined as follows: let $x = r \cdot (1+e)$ with $|e| \ll 1$ and $\Phi(x) = r \cdot (1 + \alpha e^n + O(e^{n+1}))$, then the iteration Φ is called *linear* (or first order) if $n = 1$ (and $|\alpha| < 1$). A linear iteration improves the result by (roughly) adding a constant amount of correct digits with every step.

A *super-linear* iteration does better than that: The number of correct digits grows exponentially (to the base n) at each step. Super-linear convergence of order n should really be called *exponential of order n*. Iterations of second order ($n = 2$) are often called *quadratic* (or *quadratically convergent*), those of third order *cubic* iterations. Fourth, fifth and sixth order iterations are called *quartic*, *quintic* and *sextic* and so on. The two-point iteration relation 30.1-4 has order $(\sqrt{5} + 1)/2 \approx 1.618$, see [186, p.152].

It is conceivable to find iterations that converge better than linear but less than exponential to any base: imagine an iteration that produces proportional to k^2 digits at step k (this is *not* quadratic convergence

J. Arndt, *Matters Computational: Ideas, Algorithms, Source Code*,
DOI 10.1007/978-3-642-14764-7_30, © Springer-Verlag Berlin Heidelberg 2011

which produces proportional to 2^k correct digits at step k). That case is not covered by the 'order-n' notion just introduced. However, those (super-linear but sub-exponential) iterations are not usually encountered. In fact, the constructions used here cannot produce such an iteration. For a more fine-grained definition of the concept of order see [74, p.21].

For $n \geq 2$ the iteration function Φ has a *super-attracting fixed point* at r: $\Phi'(r) = 0$. For an iteration of order n we have

$$\Phi'(r) = 0, \quad \Phi''(r) = 0, \quad \ldots, \quad \Phi^{(n-1)}(r) = 0 \tag{30.1-5}$$

There is no standard term for emphasizing the number of derivatives vanishing at the fixed point: *super-attracting of order n* might be appropriate.

To any iteration of order n for a function f we can add a term $f(x)^n \cdot \varphi(x)$ (where $\varphi(x)$ is an arbitrary function that is analytic in a neighborhood of the root) without changing the order of convergence. Check the statement by verifying that the first $n-1$ derivatives of $\Phi_n(x) + f(x)^n \cdot \varphi(x)$, evaluated at the root r, equal zero.

Any two one-point iterations of the same order n differ by a term $f(x)^n \cdot \varphi(x)$.

Any two iterations of the same order n differ by a term $(x - r)^n \nu(x)$ where $\nu(x)$ is a function that is finite at r [186, p.174, ex.3].

Any one-point iteration of order n must explicitly evaluate $f, f', \ldots, f^{(n-1)}$ [333, p.98]. For methods to find zeros and extrema without evaluating derivatives see [74].

30.2   Schröder's formula

For $n \geq 2$ the expression

$$S_n(x) := x + \sum_{k=1}^{n-1} (-1)^k \frac{f(x)^k}{k!} \left(\frac{1}{f'(x)} \frac{\partial}{\partial x} \right)^{k-1} \frac{1}{f'(x)} \tag{30.2-1}$$

gives an n-th order iteration for a (simple) root r of f [304, p.13]. That is,

$$S := S_\infty(x) = x - \frac{f}{1! \, f'} - \frac{f^2}{2! \, f'^3} \cdot f'' - \frac{f^3}{3! \, f'^5} \cdot \left(3f''^2 - f'f''' \right) \tag{30.2-2}$$

$$- \frac{f^4}{4! \, f'^7} \cdot \left(15f''^3 - 10f'f''f''' + f'^2 f'''' \right)$$

$$- \frac{f^5}{5! \, f'^9} \cdot \left(105f''^4 - 105f'f''^2 f''' + 10f'^2 f'''^2 + 15f'^2 f''f'''' - f'^3 f''''' \right) - \cdots$$

The second order iteration is the Newton iteration. A third order iteration (often referred to as *Householder's method*) is obtained by truncation after the third term on the right side:

$$S_3 = x - \frac{f}{f'} \left(1 + \frac{ff''}{2f'^2} \right) \tag{30.2-3}$$

Approximating the second term on the right gives *Halley's formula*:

$$H_3 = x - \frac{f}{f'} \left(1 - \frac{ff''}{2f'^2} \right)^{-1} \tag{30.2-4}$$

Write

$$S = x - U_1 \frac{f}{1! \, f'} - U_2 \frac{f^2}{2! \, f'^3} - U_3 \frac{f^3}{3! \, f'^5} - \cdots - U_n \frac{f^n}{n! \, f'^{2n-1}} - \cdots \tag{30.2-5}$$

then $U_1 = 1$, $U_2 = f''$, $U_3 = 3f''^2 - f'f'''$, and we have the recursion (see [304, p.16] or [186, p.148])

$$U_n = (2n-3)f''U_{n-1} - f'U'_{n-1} \qquad (30.2\text{-}6)$$

An alternative recursion is given in [333, p.83], write

$$S = x - Y_1\left(\frac{f}{f'}\right) - Y_2\left(\frac{f}{f'}\right)^2 - Y_3\left(\frac{f}{f'}\right)^3 - \ldots - Y_n\left(\frac{f}{f'}\right)^n - \ldots \qquad (30.2\text{-}7)$$

then $Y_1 = 1$ and

$$Y_n = \frac{1}{n}\left(2(n-1)\frac{f''}{2f'}Y_{n-1} - Y'_{n-1}\right) \qquad (30.2\text{-}8)$$

Relation 30.2-1 with $f(x) = 1/x^a - d$ gives the divisionless iteration 29.3-4 on page 573 for arbitrary order. For $f(x) = \log(x) - d$ one finds the iteration 32.2-5 on page 627. For $f(x) = x^2 - d$ we have

$$S(x) = x - \left(\frac{x^2-d}{2x} + \frac{(x^2-d)^2}{8x^3} + \frac{(x^2-d)^3}{16x^5} + \frac{5(x^2-d)^4}{128x^7} + \ldots\right) \qquad (30.2\text{-}9a)$$

$$= x - 2x \cdot \left(Y + Y^2 + 2Y^3 + 5Y^4 + 14Y^5 + 42Y^6 + \ldots\right) \quad \text{where} \quad Y := \frac{x^2-d}{(2x)^2} \qquad (30.2\text{-}9b)$$

The coefficients of the powers of Y are the Catalan numbers, see section 15.4 on page 331.

30.2.1 Schröder's formula and series reversion ‡

We give three ways to derive Schröder's iteration using (implicit or explicit) power series reversion. The *reversion* of the series

$$A(x) = \sum_{k=1}^{\infty} a_k x^k \qquad (30.2\text{-}10)$$

is the series

$$B(x) = \sum_{k=1}^{\infty} b_k x^k \qquad (30.2\text{-}11)$$

such that $A(B(x)) = x$. That is, $B(x) = A^{[-1]}(x)$ is the functional inverse of $A(x)$ (reversion is inversion with respect to composition). Note that $A^{[-1]}(x)$ is *not* the same as $A^{-1}(x) = 1/A(x)$. A useful relation is given in [17, p.634]:

$$A^{[-1]}(x) = \sum_{k=1}^{\infty} \frac{x^k}{k!}\left[\left(\frac{\partial}{\partial x}\right)^{k-1}\left(\frac{x}{f(x)}\right)^k\right]_{x=0} \qquad (30.2\text{-}12)$$

Equivalently, from [213, p.527],

$$k\,b_k = [k-1]\left(\frac{x}{A(x)}\right)^k \qquad (30.2\text{-}13)$$

where $[k-1]\,Q$ denotes the $(k-1)$-st series coefficient of Q. We use the expression to give a few terms of the reversed series explicitly:

```
? n=5; R=O(x^(n+1));
? A=sum(k=1,n,x^k*eval(Str("a"k)))+R
  a1*x + a2*x^2 + a3*x^3 + a4*x^4 + a5*x^5 + O(x^6)
? B=sum(k=1,n,x^k/k*(polcoeff(truncate((x/A)^k),k-1)))+R
 + 1/a1 * x
 + (-a2/a1^3) * x^2
 + ((-a3*a1 + 2*a2^2)/a1^5) * x^3
 + ((-a4*a1^2 + 5*a3*a2*a1 - 5*a2^3)/a1^7) * x^4
 + ((-a5*a1^3 + (6*a4*a2 + 3*a3^2)*a1^2 - 21*a3*a2^2*a1 + 14*a2^4)/a1^9) * x^5 + O(x^6)
```

The same result is computed by the built-in function `serreverse()`. Relation 30.2-13 can be generalized for the n-th power of the reversed series:

$$[k] \, (B(x))^n \;=\; \frac{n}{k} \, [k-n] \left(\frac{x}{A(x)} \right)^k \tag{30.2-14}$$

This is one way to state the *Lagrange inversion formula*.

30.2.1.1   Method of deriving the inverse function

The starting point is the power series of a function f around x_0:

$$f(x) \;=\; \sum_{k=0}^{\infty} \frac{1}{k!} f^{(k)}(x_0) \, (x-x_0)^k \tag{30.2-15a}$$

$$\;=\; f(x_0) + f'(x_0)\,(x-x_0) + \frac{1}{2} f''(x_0)\,(x-x_0)^2 + \frac{1}{6} f'''(x_0)\,(x-x_0)^3 + \ldots \tag{30.2-15b}$$

Now let $f(x_0) = y_0$ and r be the zero of f (that is, $f(r) = 0$). We expand the inverse function $g = f^{-1}$ around y_0:

$$g(0) \;=\; \sum_{k=0}^{\infty} \frac{1}{k!} g^{(k)}(y_0) \, (0-y_0)^k \tag{30.2-16a}$$

$$\;=\; g(y_0) + g'(y_0)\,(0-y_0) + \frac{1}{2} g''(y_0)\,(0-y_0)^2 + \frac{1}{6} g'''(y_0)\,(0-y_0)^3 + \ldots \tag{30.2-16b}$$

Setting $x_0 = g(y_0)$ and $g(0) = r$ we find

$$r \;=\; x_0 - g'(y_0)\,f(x_0) + \frac{1}{2} g''(y_0)\,f(x_0)^2 - \frac{1}{6} g'''(y_0)\,f(x_0)^3 + \ldots \tag{30.2-17}$$

In order to express the derivatives of the inverse g in terms of (derivatives of) f, set

$$f \circ g \;=\; \mathrm{id}\,, \qquad \text{that is:} \quad f(g(x)) \;=\; x \tag{30.2-18}$$

and differentiate the equation (chain rule) to see that $g'(f(x))\, f'(x) = 1$, so $g'(y) = \frac{1}{f'(x)}$. Differentiate $f(g(x)) - x$ multiple times to obtain (arguments y of g and x of f are omitted for readability):

$$1 \;=\; f'g' \tag{30.2-19a}$$
$$0 \;=\; g'f'' + f'^2 g'' \tag{30.2-19b}$$
$$0 \;=\; g'f''' + 3f'f''g'' + f'^3 g''' \tag{30.2-19c}$$
$$0 \;=\; g'f'''' + 4f'g''f''' + 3f''^2 g'' + 6f'^2 f''g''' + f'^4 g'''' \tag{30.2-19d}$$

This system of linear equations in the derivatives of g can be solved successively for g', g'', g''', etc.:

$$g' \;=\; \frac{1}{f'} \tag{30.2-20a}$$

$$g'' \;=\; -\frac{f''}{f'^3} \tag{30.2-20b}$$

$$g''' \;=\; \frac{1}{f'^5} \left(3f''^2 - f'f''' \right) \tag{30.2-20c}$$

$$g'''' \;=\; \frac{1}{f'^7} \left(10f'f''f''' - 15f''^3 - f'^2 f'''' \right) \tag{30.2-20d}$$

$$g''''' \;=\; \frac{1}{f'^9} \left(105f''^4 - f'^3 f''''' - 105f'f''^2 f''' + 15f'^2 f''f'''' + 10f'^2 f'''^2 \right) \tag{30.2-20e}$$

And so equation 30.2-17 can be written as

$$r \;=\; x - \frac{1}{f'}\,f + \frac{1}{2}\left(-\frac{f''}{f'^3}\right)f^2 - \frac{1}{6}\left(\frac{1}{f'^5}\left(3f''^2 - f'f'''\right)\right)f^3 + \dots \qquad (30.2\text{-}21\text{a})$$

$$=\; x - \frac{f}{1!\,f'} - \frac{f^2}{2!\,f'^3}\cdot f'' - \frac{f^3}{3!\,f'^5}\cdot\left(3f''^2 - f'f'''\right) - \dots \qquad (30.2\text{-}21\text{b})$$

which is Schröder's iteration, equation 30.2-2 on page 588.

30.2.1.2 Method of reversing power series

Schröder's formula can be obtained as the reversion of the series

$$E(W) \;:=\; -\sum_{k=1}^{\infty}\frac{f^{(k)}}{k!}\,(-W)^k \;=\; [1 - \exp(-W\,\partial)]\circ f \qquad (30.2\text{-}22)$$

Let $L(W)$ be the reversion of $E(W)$, then $x - L(f)$ is Schröder's iteration:

```
1    ? n=4;  \\ up to order n
2    ? x=W;  \\ kludge for GP's variable ordering
3    ? E=-sum(k=1,n,eval(Str("f"k))*(-x)^k/k!)+O(x^(n+1))
4      f1*W - 1/2*f2*W^2 + 1/6*f3*W^3 - 1/24*f4*W^4 + O(W^5)
5    ? L=serreverse(E)
6      1/f1*W + f2/(2*f1^3)*W^2 + ((-f3*f1 + 3*f2^2)/(6*f1^5))*W^3 + \
7      ((f4*f1^2 - 10*f3*f2*f1 + 15*f2^3)/(24*f1^7))*W^4 + O(W^5)
8    ? L=truncate(L);  \\ make it a polynomial
9    ? for(j=1,n,print(-polcoeff(L,j,x)*(f0)^j))
10     -f0/f1
11     -f0^2*f2/(2*f1^3)
12     (f0^3*f3*f1 - 3*f0^3*f2^2)/(6*f1^5)
13     (-f0^4*f4*f1^2 + 10*f0^4*f3*f2*f1 - 15*f0^4*f2^3)/(24*f1^7)
```

Here we use 'fk' as a symbol for the k-th derivative of f.

30.2.1.3 Method of writing power series as operator functions

Write the power series of the function f symbolically as

$$T(f) \;=\; \sum_{k=0}^{\infty}\frac{f^{(k)}\,x^k}{k!} \;=\; \left[\exp\left(+h\,\frac{\partial}{\partial x}\right)\circ f\right]_{h=x} \qquad (30.2\text{-}23)$$

In this notation Schröder's formula becomes

$$S(x) \;=\; \left[\exp\left(-h\,\frac{\partial}{\partial f}\right)\circ x\right]_{h=f} \qquad (30.2\text{-}24)$$

First expand as a series

$$S(x) \;=\; \left[\sum_{k=0}^{\infty}\frac{\left(-h\,\frac{\partial}{\partial f}\right)^k}{k!}\circ x\right]_{h=f} \;=\; \sum_{k=0}^{\infty}\frac{(-f)^k}{k!}\left[\left(\frac{\partial}{\partial f}\right)^k x\right] \qquad (30.2\text{-}25)$$

Now use

$$\frac{\partial}{\partial f} \;=\; \frac{\partial x}{\partial f}\,\frac{\partial}{\partial x} \;=\; \frac{1}{f'}\,\frac{\partial}{\partial x} \qquad (30.2\text{-}26)$$

and separate the term for $k = 0$ to find

$$S(x) \;=\; x + \sum_{k=1}^{\infty}\frac{(-f)^k}{k!}\left[\left(\frac{1}{f'}\,\frac{\partial}{\partial x}\right)^k x\right] \;=\; x + \sum_{k=1}^{\infty}\frac{(-f)^k}{k!}\left[\left(\frac{1}{f'}\,\frac{\partial}{\partial x}\right)^{k-1}\frac{1}{f'}\right] \qquad (30.2\text{-}27)$$

Truncation gives relation 30.2-1.

30.3   Householder's formula

The following expression gives, for $n \geq 2$, an n-th order iteration for a (simple) root r of f [186, p.169]:

$$H_n(x) \quad := \quad x + (n-1) \frac{\left(\frac{1}{f(x)}\right)^{(n-2)}}{\left(\frac{1}{f(x)}\right)^{(n-1)}} \tag{30.3-1}$$

We refer to iterations of this type as *Householder* iterations, the name *König iteration function* is used in [341]. We have

$$H_2 \;=\; x - \frac{f}{f'} \tag{30.3-2a}$$

$$H_3 \;=\; x - \frac{2ff'}{2f'^2 - ff''} \tag{30.3-2b}$$

$$H_4 \;=\; x - \frac{3f(ff'' - 2f'^2)}{6ff'f'' - 6f'^3 - f^2f'''} \tag{30.3-2c}$$

$$H_5 \;=\; x + \frac{4f\left(6f'^3 - 6ff'f'' + f^2f'''\right)}{f^3f'''' - 24f'^4 + 36ff'^2f'' - 8f^2f'f''' - 6f^2f''^2} \tag{30.3-2d}$$

The second order variant is Newton's formula, the third order iteration is Halley's formula.

Following [196], we give alternative forms of Householder's formula. Define the iteration B_m for $m \geq 2$ as

$$B_m \;=\; x - f \frac{D_{m-2}}{D_{m-1}} \quad \text{where} \quad D_0 = 1, \; D_1 = f', \text{ and} \tag{30.3-3a}$$

$$D_m \;=\; \det \begin{pmatrix} f' & \frac{f''}{2!} & \cdots & \frac{f^{(m-1)}}{(m-1)!} & \frac{f^{(m)}}{m!} \\ f & f' & \ddots & \ddots & \frac{f^{(m-1)}}{(m-1)!} \\ 0 & f & \ddots & \ddots & \vdots \\ \vdots & \vdots & \ddots & \ddots & \frac{f''}{2!} \\ 0 & 0 & \ddots & f & f' \end{pmatrix} \tag{30.3-3b}$$

The iteration is the same as Householder's ($B_n = H_n$). A recursive definition for D_m is given by

$$D_m = \sum_{i=1}^{m} (-1)^{i-1} f^{i-1} \frac{f^{(i)}}{i!} D_{m-i} \tag{30.3-4}$$

The derivation of Halley's formula by applying Newton's formula to $f/\sqrt{f'}$ can be generalized to produce m-order iterations as follows: Let $F_1 = f$ and for $m \geq 2$ let

$$F_m \;=\; \frac{F_{m-1}}{\sqrt[m]{F'_{m-1}}} \tag{30.3-5a}$$

$$H_m \;=\; x - \frac{F_{m-1}}{F'_{m-1}} \tag{30.3-5b}$$

An alternative recursive formulation is

$$Q_2 \;=\; 1 \tag{30.3-6a}$$

$$Q_m \;=\; f' Q_{m-1} - \frac{1}{m-2} f Q'_{m-1} \tag{30.3-6b}$$

$$H_m \;=\; x - f \frac{Q_m}{Q_{m-1}} \tag{30.3-6c}$$

The Taylor series of the k-th order Householder iteration around $f = 0$ up to order $k - 1$ gives the k-th order Schröder iteration.

An *extraneous* fixed point of an iteration for a function f is a fixed point at z such that $f(z) \neq 0$. All extraneous fixed points for the iterations H_n are repelling ($|H(z)'| > 1$), see [197] and [341].

30.4 Dealing with multiple roots

The iterations given so far will not converge at the stated order if f has a multiple root at r. As an example consider the function

$$f(x) \;=\; (x^2 - d)^m \quad \text{where} \quad m \in \mathbb{N}_+, \tag{30.4-1}$$

The iteration $\Phi(x) = x - f/f'$ is

$$\Phi(x) \;=\; x - \frac{x^2 - d}{m2x} \tag{30.4-2}$$

Its convergence is only linear for $m > 1$: $\Phi(\sqrt{d}\,(1+e)) = \sqrt{d}\,(1 + \frac{m-1}{m}\,e + O(e^2))$.

A second order iteration for a root of known multiplicity m is given in [186, p.161, ex.6]

$$\Phi_2(x) = x - m \cdot \frac{f}{f'} \tag{30.4-3}$$

Note that with the example above we obtain a quadratic iteration.

For roots of unknown multiplicity use the general expressions for iterations with $F := f/f'$ instead of f. Both F and f have the same set of roots, but all roots of F are simple. To see this, consider a function f that has a root of multiplicity m at r: $f(x) := (x - r)^m h(x)$ with $h(r) \neq 0$. Then

$$f'(x) \;=\; m\,(x-r)^{m-1}\,h(x) + (x-r)^m\,h'(x) \tag{30.4-4a}$$
$$=\; (x-r)^{m-1}\left(m\,h(x) + (x-r)\,h'(x)\right) \tag{30.4-4b}$$

and

$$F(x) = f(x)/f'(x) \;=\; (x-r)\,\frac{h(x)}{m\,h(x) + (x-r)\,h'(x)} \tag{30.4-5}$$

The fraction on the right side does not vanish at the root r.

Substituting $F = f/f'$ into Householder's formula (relation 30.3-1) gives the following iterations denoted by $H_k^\%$, the iterations H_k are given for comparison:

$$H_2 \;=\; x - \frac{f}{f'} \tag{30.4-6a}$$

$$H_2^\% \;=\; x - \frac{f f'}{f'^2 - f f''} \tag{30.4-6b}$$

$$H_3 \;=\; x - \frac{2 f f'}{2 f'^2 - f f''} \tag{30.4-6c}$$

$$H_3^\% \;=\; x + \frac{2 f^2 f'' - 2 f f'^2}{2 f'^3 - 3 f f' f'' + f^2 f'''} \tag{30.4-6d}$$

$$H_4 \;=\; x + \frac{3 f^2 f'' - 6 f f'^2}{6 f'^3 - 6 f f' f'' + f^2 f'''} \tag{30.4-6e}$$

$$H_4^\% \;=\; x + \frac{6 f f'^3 + 3 f^3 f''' - 9 f^2 f' f''}{f^3 f'''' - 6 f'^4 + 12 f f'^2 f'' - 4 f^2 f' f''' - 3 f^2 f''^2} \tag{30.4-6f}$$

$$H_5 \;=\; x + \frac{24 f f'^3 + 4 f^3 f''' - 24 f^2 f' f''}{f^3 f'''' - 24 f'^4 + 36 f f'^2 f'' - 8 f^2 f' f''' - 6 f^2 f''^2} \tag{30.4-6g}$$

The terms in the numerators and denominators of $H_k^{\%}$ and H_{k+1} are identical up to the integral constants. The iteration $H_k^{\%}$ can also be written as

$$H_k^{\%} \;=\; x + (k-1)\,\frac{(\log(f))^{(k-1)}}{(\log(f))^{(k)}} \tag{30.4-7}$$

Schröder's formula (relation 30.2-1), when inserting f/f', becomes

$$S^{\%} \;=\; x - \frac{f f'}{(f'^2 - f f'')} - \frac{f^2 f'\left(f f' f''' - 2 f f''^2 + f'^2 f''\right)}{2\left(f f'' - f'^2\right)^3} - \dots - \frac{f^k f'\,P(k)}{k!\left(f f'' - f'^2\right)^{2k-1}} \tag{30.4-8}$$

where $P(k)$ contains derivatives up to $f^{(2k-1)}$.

We check the convergence with our example (relation 30.4-1), the second order iteration is

$$\Phi_2^{\%}(x) \;=\; S_2 = H_2 = x + x\frac{d - x^2}{d + x^2} = \frac{2\,d\,x}{x^2 + d} \tag{30.4-9}$$

Convergence is indeed second order, as we have (compare to relation 29.2-7 on page 570)

$$\Phi_2^{\%}\left(\sqrt{d}\cdot\frac{1-e}{1+e}\right) \;=\; \sqrt{d}\cdot\frac{1-e^2}{1+e^2} \tag{30.4-10}$$

which holds independent of m. In general we have

$$\Phi_k^{\%}\left(\sqrt{d}\cdot\frac{1-e}{1+e}\right) \;=\; \sqrt{d}\cdot\frac{1-e^k}{1+e^k} \tag{30.4-11}$$

Schröder's third order formula for f/f' with f as in relation 30.4-1 gives a *fourth* order iteration for $\sqrt{d}$:

$$S_3^{\%}(x) \;=\; x + x\frac{d - x^2}{d + x^2} + x\,d\,\frac{(d - x^2)^2}{(d + x^2)^3} \tag{30.4-12a}$$

$$S_3^{\%}\left(\sqrt{d}\,\frac{1-e}{1+e}\right) \;=\; \sqrt{d}\,\frac{1 + 3e^2 - 3e^4 - e^6}{1 + 3e^2 + 3e^4 + e^6} \tag{30.4-12b}$$

$$\;=\; \sqrt{d}\,\frac{1-c}{1+c} \quad\text{where}\quad c = e^4\,\frac{e^2 + 3}{3e^2 + 1} \tag{30.4-12c}$$

In general, the $(1 + a\,k)$-th order Schröder iteration for $1/\sqrt[a]{d}$ with f/f' has an order of convergence that exceeds the expected order by one. The third order Schröder iteration for $f(x) = 1 - d\,x^2$ is

$$S_3^{\%}(x) \;=\; x + x\frac{1 - dx^2}{1 + dx^2} + x\,\frac{(1 - dx^2)^2}{(1 + dx^2)^3} \tag{30.4-13}$$

The iteration also has fourth order convergence and the error expression $S_3^{\%}\left(\frac{1}{\sqrt{d}}\,\frac{1-e}{1+e}\right)$ is obtained by replacing $\sqrt{d}$ with $1/\sqrt{d}$ in relation 30.4-12b.

30.5 More iterations

We give expressions for iterations via Padé approximants, radicals, and show how iterations can be obtained from given ones. Finally we give one form of a multi-point iteration.

```
exp(x) =~= 1/24*x^4 + 1/6*x^3 + 1/2*x^2 + x + 1

P[4,0] =    (1/24*x^4 + 1/6*x^3 + 1/2*x^2 + x + 1) / (1)
P[3,1] =    (4*x^3 + 24*x^2 + 72*x + 96) / (-24*x + 96)
P[2,2] =    (1/4*x^2 + 3/2*x + 3) / (1/4*x^2 - 3/2*x + 3)
P[1,3] =    (24*x + 96) / (-4*x^3 + 24*x^2 - 72*x + 96)
P[0,4] =    (1) / (1/24*x^4 - 1/6*x^3 + 1/2*x^2 - x + 1)
```

Figure 30.5-A: Padé approximants $P_{[i,j]}$ where $i + j = 4$ for the exponential function.

30.5.1   Padé approximants

Let $S = \sum_{k=0}^{\infty} a_k x^k$ be a power series. A *Padé approximant* $P_{[i,j]}$ of S is a ratio A/B of polynomials A and B with $\deg(A) = i$ and $\deg(B) = j$ such that $A/B = S + O\left(x^{n+1}\right)$ where $n = i + j$. Figure 30.5-A shows the approximants $P_{[i,j]}$ where $i + j = 4$ for the exponential function.

Let S_n be a polynomial that coincides with a power series S up to (and including) the n-th power and assume that the constant term a_0 is nonzero. Then the approximant $P_{[n-d,d]}$ can be computed with the extended GCD algorithm given in section 39.1.4 on page 767. For convenience we rewrite the EGCD implementation in GP:

```
1    egcd(u, v)=
2    \\ Same as the built-in bezout(u, v)
3    {
4        local(t, q);
5        u = [1, 0, u];
6        v = [0, 1, v];
7        t = [0, 0, 0];
8        while ( v[3]!=0,
9            q = (u[3] \ v[3]);  \\ division without remainder
10           t = u - v*q;  u = v;  v = t;
11       );
12       return( [u[1], u[2], u[3]] );
13   }
```

Now, following [213, ex.13, p.534], we can compute $P_{[n-d,d]}$ with the EGCD routine with arguments S (up to the n-th term) and x^{n+1}, terminated after d steps:

```
1    pade(s, d)=
2    /*
3    Compute Pade approximant A/B (of the power series S)
4    such that deg(A)=deg(S)-d.
5    Must have: d < deg(S);
6    S must have a nonzero constant term.
7    */
8    {
9        local(n, t, q);
10       s = truncate(s);  \\ remove O(x^(n+1)) term if present
11       n = poldegree(s);
12       u = [1, 0, x^(n+1)];
13       v = [0, 1, s];
14       t = [0, 0, 0];
15       \\ PRINT  v[3] / v[2]  ( == s / 1 )
16       for ( j=1, d,
17           q = (u[3] \ v[3]);  \\ division without remainder
18           t = u - v*q;  u = v;  v = t;
19           \\ PRINT  v[3] / v[2]
20       );
21       return( v[3]/v[2] );
22   }
```

If the first nonzero coefficient of S is a_k, then $P_{[i,j]} = x^k Q_{[i-k,j]}$ where Q is the approximant for S/x^k.

30.5.2   Rational iterations from Padé approximants

The $[i,j]$-th Padé approximant of Φ_n in f gives an iteration of order $p = i + j + 1$ (if $n \geq p$). Write $\Phi_{[i,j]}$ for an iteration (of order $i + j + 1$) that is obtained using the approximant $[i,j]$. For the second order (where the Newton iteration is $\Phi_{[1,0]}(x) = x - \frac{f}{f'}$) this method gives one alternative form, namely

$$\Phi_{[0,1]}(x) \;=\; x^2\,\frac{f'}{f + x f'} \;=\; x - \frac{x f}{f + x f'} \;=\; x - \frac{x f}{(x f)'} \;=\; x\left(1 + \frac{f}{x f'}\right)^{-1} \tag{30.5-1}$$

For the third order we find $\Phi_{[2,0]}(x) = S_3(x)$, $\Phi_{[1,1]}(x) = H_3(x)$, and

$$\Phi_{[0,2]}(x) \;=\; \frac{2x^3 f'^3}{2f^2 f' + 2x f f'^2 + x f^2 f'' + 2x^2 f'^3} \tag{30.5-2a}$$

$$=\; x - \frac{x f\left(2 f f' + x f f'' + 2x f'^2\right)}{\left(2f^2 f' + 2x f f'^2 + x f^2 f'' + 2x^2 f'^3\right)} \tag{30.5-2b}$$

$$=\; x\left(1 + \frac{f}{x f'} + \frac{f^2}{x^2 f'^2} + \frac{f^2 f''}{2x f'^3}\right)^{-1} \tag{30.5-2c}$$

$$=\; x\left(1 + \frac{f}{(x f')} + \frac{f^2 (x^2 f'')}{2(x f')^3} + \frac{f^2}{(x f')^2}\right)^{-1} \tag{30.5-2d}$$

Alternatively we can use the Padé approximant $A_{[i,j]}$ of $(\Phi(x) - x)/f$ in f where $\Phi(x)$ is a given iteration of order $\ge i + j + 2$. Then $\Phi^+_{[i,j]} := x + f \cdot A_{[i,j]}$ is an iteration which has order $n = i + j + 2$.

$$\Phi^+_{[0,1]}(x) \;=\; x - \frac{2 f f'}{2 f'^2 - f f''} \;=\; H_3(x) \tag{30.5-3a}$$

$$\Phi^+_{[1,0]}(x) \;=\; x - \frac{f\left(f f'' + 2 f'^2\right)}{2 f'^3} \;=\; S_3(x) \tag{30.5-3b}$$

The iterations Φ^+ of order n are expressions in $x, f, f', \ldots, f^{(n-1)}$. Fourth order iterations are

$$\Phi^+_{[2,0]}(x) \;=\; x - \frac{f\left(6 f'^4 + 3 f f'^2 f'' - f^2 f' f''' + 3 f^2 f''^2\right)}{6 f'^5} \tag{30.5-4a}$$

$$=\; x - \frac{f}{f'} - \frac{f^2}{2 f'^3}\cdot f'' - \frac{f^3}{6 f'^5}\cdot\left(3 f''^2 - f' f'''\right) \;=\; S_4(x) \tag{30.5-4b}$$

$$=\; x - \frac{f^2}{f'^2}\left(\frac{f'}{f} + \frac{f''}{2 f'} + \frac{f\left(3 f''^2 - f' f'''\right)}{6 f'^3}\right) \tag{30.5-4c}$$

$$\Phi^+_{[1,1]}(x) \;=\; x - \frac{f\left(2 f f' f''' - 3 f f''^2 + 6 f'^2 f''\right)}{f'\left(2 f f' f''' - 6 f f''^2 + 6 f'^2 f''\right)} \tag{30.5-4d}$$

$$\Phi^+_{[0,2]}(x) \;=\; x - \frac{12 f f'^3}{\left(12 f'^4 - 6 f f'^2 f'' + 2 f^2 f' f''' - 3 f^2 f''^2\right)} \tag{30.5-4e}$$

$$=\; x - \left(\frac{f'}{f} - \frac{f''}{2 f'} - \frac{f\left(3 f''^2 - 2 f' f'''\right)}{12 f'^3}\right)^{-1} \tag{30.5-4f}$$

The iteration $\Phi^+_{[n,0]}$ always coincides with Schröder's iteration. In general one finds $n-1$ additional forms of iterations using the approximants $[0, n-2]$, $[1, n-3]$, $\ldots$, $[n-3, 1]$.

Neglecting terms that contain the third derivative in relation 30.5-4d we find the third order iteration

$$\Phi_3 \;=\; x - \frac{f\left(2 f'^2 - f f''\right)}{f'\left(2 f'^2 - 2 f f''\right)} \tag{30.5-5}$$

A closed form for the Padé approximants of the r-th root is given in relation 29.2-13 on page 572.

30.5.3 An iteration involving radicals

By directly solving the truncated Taylor expansion

$$f(r) = f(x) + f'(x)(r-x) + \frac{1}{2}f''(x)(r-x)^2 \tag{30.5-6}$$

of $f(r) = 0$ around x we find the following third order iteration:

$$\Phi_3 = x - \frac{1}{f''}\left(f' \pm \sqrt{f'^2 - 2ff''}\right) = x - \frac{f'}{f''}\left(1 \pm \sqrt{1 - 2\frac{ff''}{f'^2}}\right) \tag{30.5-7}$$

For $f(x) = ax^2 + bx + c$ this gives the two solutions of the quadratic equation $f(x) = 0$; for other functions we find iterated square root expression for the roots.

The following form, given in [333, p.94], avoids possible cancellation:

$$\Phi_3 = x - \frac{2u}{1 + \sqrt{1 - 4Au}} \quad \text{where} \quad u = f/f' \quad \text{and} \quad A = f''/(2f) \tag{30.5-8}$$

It can be found by observing that

$$\frac{-b + \sqrt{b^2 - 4ac}}{2a} = \frac{-2c}{b + \sqrt{b^2 - 4ac}} \tag{30.5-9}$$

30.5.4 Iterations from iterations

Alternative rational forms can also be obtained in a way that generalizes the method used for multiple roots. We emphasize the so far notationally omitted dependency on the function f as $\Phi\{f\}$. The iteration $\Phi\{f\}$ has fixed points where f has a root r, so $x - \Phi\{f\}$ again has a root at r. Hence we can build more iterations that will converge to those roots as $\Phi\{x - \Phi\{f\}\}$. For dealing with multiple roots we used $\Phi\{x - \Phi_2\{f\}\}_k = \Phi\{f/f'\}$. An iteration $\Phi_k\{x - \Phi_j\{f\}\}$ can only be expected to have a k-th order convergence.

30.5.5 A multi-point iteration

A multi-point iteration of order r can be given [333, p.165] as

$$\Phi_r(x) = \Phi_{r-1}(x) - \frac{f(\Phi_{r-1}(x))}{f'(x)} \tag{30.5-10}$$

where $\Phi_{r-1}(x)$ is an iteration of order $r - 1$. For example, choose $\Phi_2(x) = x - f(x)/f'(x)$ to find the third order iteration

$$\Phi_3(x) = \Phi_2(x) - \frac{f(\Phi_2(x))}{f'(x)} \tag{30.5-11}$$

Apply the method again to find

$$\Phi_4(x) = \Phi_3(x) - \frac{f(\Phi_3(x))}{f'(x)} = \Phi_2(x) - \frac{f(\Phi_2(x))}{f'(x)} - \frac{f(\Phi_3(x))}{f'(x)} \tag{30.5-12}$$

The r-th order iteration is

$$\Phi_r(x) = \Phi_2(x) - \sum_{k=2}^{r-1} \frac{f(\Phi_k(x))}{f'(x)} \tag{30.5-13a}$$

$$= x - \frac{1}{f'(x)}\left[f(x) + \sum_{k=2}^{r-1} f(\Phi_k(x))\right] \tag{30.5-13b}$$

The function f is evaluated at $r - 1$ points but the derivative is only evaluated at x. The iteration also involves only one inversion.

30.6   Convergence improvement by the delta squared process

Given a sequence of partial sums x_k the *delta squared process* computes a new sequence x_k^* of extrapolated sums:

$$x_k^* \;=\; x_{k+2} - \frac{(x_{k+2} - x_{k+1})^2}{x_{k+2} - 2\,x_{k+1} + x_k} \tag{30.6-1}$$

The method is due to Aitken. The name 'delta squared process' is due to the alternative form

$$x^* = x - \frac{(\Delta x)^2}{(\Delta^2 x)} \tag{30.6-2}$$

where Δ is the difference operator. Note that the algebraically equivalent form

$$x_k^* \;=\; \frac{x_k\, x_{k+2} - x_{k+1}^2}{x_{k+2} - 2\,x_{k+1} + x_k} \tag{30.6-3}$$

should be avoided in numerical computations due to possible cancellation.

If $x_k = \sum_{i=0}^{k} a_i$ and the ratio of consecutive summands a_i is approximately constant (that is, a is close to a geometric series), then x^* converges significantly faster to x_∞ than x. Rewrite relation 30.6-1 with $a_k := x_k - x_{k-1}$:

$$x_k^* \;=\; x_{k+2} - \frac{(a_{k+2})^2}{a_{k+2} - a_{k+1}} \tag{30.6-4}$$

For a geometric series (where $a_{k+1}/a_k = q$) we have

$$x_k^* \;=\; x_{k+2} - \frac{(a_{k+2})^2}{a_{k+2} - a_{k+1}} = x_{k+2} - \frac{\left(a_0\, q^{k+2}\right)^2}{a_0\,(q^{k+2} - q^{k+1})} \tag{30.6-5a}$$

$$= \; a_0\,\frac{1 - q^{k+3}}{1 - q} + a_0\, q^{k+2} \cdot \frac{q^{k+2}}{q^{k+1} - q^{k+2}} = \frac{a_0}{1 - q}\left(1 - q^{k+3} + q^{k+3}\right) = \frac{a_0}{1 - q} \tag{30.6-5b}$$

which is the exact sum. Now consider the sequence of successively better approximations to some root r of a function f:

$$x_0, \quad x_1 = \Phi(x_0), \quad x_2 = \Phi(x_1) = \Phi\left(\Phi(x_0)\right), \quad \ldots, \quad x_k = \Phi^{[k]}(x_0), \quad \ldots \tag{30.6-6}$$

Think of the x_k as partial sums of a series whose sum is the root r. Apply the idea to define an improved iteration Φ^* from a given one Φ:

$$\Phi^*(x) \;=\; \Phi(\Phi(x)) - \frac{[\Phi(\Phi(x)) - \Phi(x)]^2}{\Phi(\Phi(x)) - 2\,\Phi(x) + x} \tag{30.6-7}$$

The good news is that $\Phi*$ will give quadratic convergence even if Φ only has linear convergence. For example, take $f(x) = (x^2 - d)^2$, forget that its root $\sqrt{d}$ is a double root, and happily define $\Phi(x) = x - f(x)/f'(x) = x - (x^2 - d)/(4x)$. Convergence is only linear:

$$\Phi(\sqrt{d} \cdot (1 + e)) \;=\; \sqrt{d} \cdot \left(1 + \frac{e}{2} + \frac{e^2}{4} + O(e^3)\right) \tag{30.6-8}$$

Then try

$$\Phi^*(x) \;=\; \frac{d\,(7\,x^2 + d)}{x\,(3\,x^2 + 5\,d)} \tag{30.6-9}$$

and find that it has quadratic convergence

$$\Phi^*\left(\sqrt{d} \cdot (1 + e)\right) \;=\; \sqrt{d} \cdot \left(1 - \frac{e^2}{4} + \frac{e^3}{16} + O(e^4)\right) \tag{30.6-10}$$

In general, if Φ_n has convergence of order $n > 1$, then Φ_n^* will be of order $2n - 1$, but linear convergence ($n = 1$) is turned into second order, see [186, p.165].

Chapter 31

The AGM, elliptic integrals, and algorithms for computing π

The arithmetic-geometric mean (AGM) is the basis for fast algorithms for the computation of π to high precision. We give several relations between the elliptic integrals that are special cases of hypergeometric transformations and AGM-based algorithms for the computation of certain hypergeometric functions. AGM-based algorithms for the computation of the logarithm are given in section 32.1.1 on page 622 and for the exponential function in section 32.2.1 on page 627.

31.1 The arithmetic-geometric mean (AGM)

The *arithmetic-geometric mean* (AGM) plays a central role in the high precision computation of logarithms and π. The $\mathrm{AGM}(a, b)$ is defined as the limit of the iteration

$$a_{k+1} \;=\; \frac{a_k + b_k}{2} \tag{31.1-1a}$$

$$b_{k+1} \;=\; \sqrt{a_k\, b_k} \tag{31.1-1b}$$

starting with $a_0 = a$ and $b_0 = b$. Both of the values converge quadratically to a common limit. The related quantity c_k used in many AGM-based computations is defined as

$$c_k^2 \;=\; a_k^2 - b_k^2 \;=\; (a_{k-1} - a_k)^2 \tag{31.1-2}$$

We also have $c_{k+1} = c_k^2 / (4\, a_{k+1})$ which is numerically stable but involves a long division. The quantity

$$R'(k) \;:=\; 1 - \frac{1}{2} \sum_{n=0}^{\infty} 2^n\, c_n^2 \tag{31.1-3}$$

will be used in the computation of the elliptic integral of the second kind.

Another way for computing the AGM is the iteration

$$a_{k+1} \;=\; \frac{a_k + b_k}{2} \tag{31.1-4a}$$

$$c_{k+1} \;=\; \frac{a_k - b_k}{2} \tag{31.1-4b}$$

$$b_{k+1} \;=\; \sqrt{a_{k+1}^2 - c_{k+1}^2} \;=\; \sqrt{[a_{k+1} + c_{k+1}]\,[a_{k+1} - c_{k+1}]} \tag{31.1-4c}$$

31.1.1 Schönhage's variant

Schönhage gives the most economic variant of the AGM, which, apart from the square root, only needs one squaring per step: initialize

$$A_0 \;=\; a_0^2, \qquad B_0 = b_0^2, \qquad t_0 = 1 - (A_0 - B_0) \tag{31.1-5a}$$

J. Arndt, *Matters Computational: Ideas, Algorithms, Source Code*,
DOI 10.1007/978-3-642-14764-7_31, © Springer-Verlag Berlin Heidelberg 2011

and iterate

(31.1-5b)

$$S_k = \frac{A_k + B_k}{4} \tag{31.1-5c}$$

$$b_k = \sqrt{B_k} \quad \text{[square root]} \tag{31.1-5d}$$

$$a_{k+1} = \frac{a_k + b_k}{2} \tag{31.1-5e}$$

$$A_{k+1} = a_{k+1}^2 \quad \text{[squaring]} \tag{31.1-5f}$$

$$= \left(\frac{\sqrt{A_k} + \sqrt{B_k}}{2}\right)^2 = \frac{A_k + B_k}{4} + \frac{\sqrt{A_k B_k}}{2} \tag{31.1-5g}$$

$$B_{k+1} = 2\,(A_{k+1} - S_k) = b_{k+1}^2 \tag{31.1-5h}$$

$$c_{k+1}^2 = A_{k+1} - B_{k+1} = a_{k+1}^2 - b_{k+1}^2 \tag{31.1-5i}$$

$$t_{k+1} = t_k - 2^{k+1}\, c_{k+1}^2 \tag{31.1-5j}$$

Starting with $a_0 = A_0 = 1$, $B_0 = 1/2$ one has $\pi \approx (2\,a_n^2)/t_n$.

31.1.2 Fourth order iteration for the AGM

Combining two steps of the AGM iteration leads to the fourth order AGM iteration:

$$\alpha_0 = \sqrt{a_0}, \qquad \beta_0 = \sqrt{b_0} \tag{31.1-6a}$$

$$\alpha_{k+1} = \frac{\alpha_k + \beta_k}{2} \tag{31.1-6b}$$

$$\beta_{k+1} = \sqrt[4]{\frac{\alpha_k\,\beta_k\,(\alpha_k^2 + \beta_k^2)}{2}} \tag{31.1-6c}$$

$$\gamma_k^4 = \alpha_k^4 - \beta_k^4 \quad = c_{2k}^2 \tag{31.1-6d}$$

We have $\alpha_k = \sqrt{a_{2k}}$, $\beta_k = \sqrt{b_{2k}}$, and $\gamma_k = \sqrt{c_{2k}}$. Writing $\mathrm{AGM}_4(a, b)$ for the common mean we have $\mathrm{AGM}(a, b) = \left[\mathrm{AGM}_4(\sqrt{a}, \sqrt{b})\right]^2$. Another form of the iteration is:

$$\gamma_{k+1} = \frac{\alpha_k - \beta_k}{2} \tag{31.1-7a}$$

$$\alpha_{k+1} = \frac{\alpha_k + \beta_k}{2} \tag{31.1-7b}$$

$$\beta_{k+1} = \sqrt[4]{\alpha_{k+1}^4 - \gamma_{k+1}^4} = \sqrt[4]{[\alpha_{k+1}^2 + \gamma_{k+1}^2]\,[\alpha_{k+1}^2 - \gamma_{k+1}^2]} \tag{31.1-7c}$$

$$c_{2k}^2 + 2\,c_{2k+1}^2 = \alpha_{k-1}^4 - (\alpha_k^2 - \gamma_k^2)^2 \tag{31.1-7d}$$

The second identity for β_{k+1} replaces the computation of two fourth powers by two squarings and a multiplication. Compute R' via

$$R'(k) = 1 - \sum_{n=0}^{\infty} 4^n \left(\alpha_n^4 - \left(\frac{\alpha_n^2 + \beta_n^2}{2}\right)^2\right) \tag{31.1-8}$$

31.2 The elliptic integrals K and E

The elliptic integrals $K(k)$ and $E(k)$ can be computed via the AGM which gives super-linear convergence. The logarithmic singularity of $K(k)$ at the point $k = 1$ (relation 31.2-6, see also relation 32.1-1a on page 622) is the key to the fast computation of the logarithm. The exponential function could be computed by inverting the logarithm but also as described in section 32.2.1 on page 627. For computations with very high precision the algorithms based on the elliptic integrals are among the fastest known today for the logarithm, the number π, and the exponential function.

31.2.1 Elliptic K

The *complete elliptic integral of the first kind* can be defined as

$$K(k) = \int_0^{\pi/2} \frac{d\vartheta}{\sqrt{1 - k^2 \sin^2 \vartheta}} = \int_0^1 \frac{dt}{\sqrt{(1 - t^2)(1 - k^2 t^2)}} \tag{31.2-1}$$

Special values are $K(0) = \frac{\pi}{2}$ and $\lim_{k \to 1-} K(k) = +\infty$, and we have

$$K(k) = \frac{\pi}{2} F\left(\begin{matrix} \frac{1}{2}, \frac{1}{2} \\ 1 \end{matrix} \,\middle|\, k^2 \right) \tag{31.2-2a}$$

$$= \frac{\pi}{2} \sum_{i=0}^{\infty} \left(\frac{(2i-1)!!}{2^i i!} \right)^2 k^{2i} = \frac{\pi}{2} \sum_{i=0}^{\infty} \left(\frac{\binom{2i}{i}}{4^i} \right)^2 k^{2i} \tag{31.2-2b}$$

$$= \frac{\pi}{2} \left(1 + \left(\frac{1}{2} \right)^2 k^2 + \left(\frac{1 \cdot 3}{2 \cdot 4} \right)^2 k^4 + \left(\frac{1 \cdot 3 \cdot 5}{2 \cdot 4 \cdot 6} \right)^2 k^6 + \dots \right) \tag{31.2-2c}$$

$$= \frac{\pi}{2} \left(1 + \frac{1}{4} k^2 + \frac{9}{64} k^4 + \frac{25}{256} k^6 + \frac{1225}{16384} k^8 + \frac{3969}{65536} k^{10} + \dots \right) \tag{31.2-2d}$$

31.2.1.1 Computation via the AGM

The connection to the AGM is

$$F\left(\begin{matrix} \frac{1}{2}, \frac{1}{2} \\ 1 \end{matrix} \,\middle|\, k \right) = \frac{1}{\mathrm{AGM}(1, \sqrt{1 - k})} \tag{31.2-3}$$

This relation can also be written as

$$F\left(\begin{matrix} \frac{1}{2}, \frac{1}{2} \\ 1 \end{matrix} \,\middle|\, 1 - \frac{b^2}{a^2} \right) = \frac{a}{\mathrm{AGM}(a, b)} = \frac{1}{\mathrm{AGM}(1, b/a)} \tag{31.2-4}$$

or, in terms of $K(k)$ as

$$K(k) = \frac{\pi}{2\,\mathrm{AGM}(1, k')} = \frac{\pi}{2\,\mathrm{AGM}(1, \sqrt{1 - k^2})} \tag{31.2-5a}$$

A C++ implementation of the AGM-based computation is given in [hfloat: src/tz/elliptic-k.cc]. We define $k' = \sqrt{1 - k^2}$ and $K'(k)$ as $K(k')$:

$$K'(k) := K\left(\sqrt{1 - k^2} \right) = \frac{\pi}{2\,\mathrm{AGM}(1, k)} \tag{31.2-5b}$$

For k close to 1 we have

$$K(k) \approx \log \frac{4}{\sqrt{1 - k^2}} \tag{31.2-6}$$

The following estimate is given in [66, p.11]:

$$\left| K'(k) - \log \frac{4}{k} \right| \leq 4k^2 (8 + \log k) \quad \text{where} \quad 0 < k \leq 1 \tag{31.2-7}$$

31.2.1.2   Product forms

Product forms for K and K' that are also candidates for fast computations are, for $0 < k_0 \leq 1$,

$$\frac{2}{\pi} K'(k_0) \;=\; \prod_{n=0}^{\infty} \frac{2}{1+k_n} \;=\; \prod_{n=1}^{\infty} (1+k'_n) \quad \text{where} \quad k_{n+1} := \frac{2\sqrt{k_n}}{1+k_n}, \quad k_\infty = 1 \qquad (31.2\text{-}8a)$$

$$\frac{2}{\pi} K'(k_0) \;=\; \prod_{n=0}^{\infty} \frac{1}{\sqrt{k_n}} \quad \text{where} \quad k_{n+1} := \frac{1+k_n}{2\sqrt{k_n}}, \quad k_\infty = 1 \qquad (31.2\text{-}8b)$$

The second form is computationally especially attractive since, apart from the multiplication with the main product, only an inverse square root needs to be computed per step. The product formulas follow directly from relation 31.2-5b (and $\mathrm{AGM}(a,b) = a\,\mathrm{AGM}(1,b/a) = b\,\mathrm{AGM}(a/b,1)$):

$$\frac{1}{\mathrm{AGM}(1,k)} \;=\; \left[\mathrm{AGM}\left(\frac{1+k}{2}, \sqrt{k} \right) \right]^{-1} \qquad (31.2\text{-}9a)$$

$$=\; \left[\frac{1+k}{2}\, \mathrm{AGM}\left(1, \frac{2\sqrt{k}}{1+k} \right) \right]^{-1} \quad \text{(first form)} \qquad (31.2\text{-}9b)$$

$$=\; \left[\sqrt{k}\, \mathrm{AGM}\left(\frac{1+k}{2\sqrt{k}}, 1 \right) \right]^{-1} \quad \text{(second form)} \qquad (31.2\text{-}9c)$$

Similarly, for $0 < k_0 \leq 1$,

$$\frac{2}{\pi} K(k_0) \;=\; \prod_{n=0}^{\infty} \frac{2}{1+k'_n} \;=\; \prod_{n=1}^{\infty} (1+k_n) \quad \text{where} \quad k_{n+1} := \frac{1-k'_n}{1+k'_n}, \quad k_\infty = 0 \qquad (31.2\text{-}10a)$$

$$\frac{2}{\pi} K(k_0) \;=\; \prod_{n=0}^{\infty} \frac{1}{\sqrt{k'_n}} \quad \text{where} \quad k_{n+1} := i\,\frac{1-k'_n}{2\sqrt{k'_n}}, \quad k_\infty = 0 \qquad (31.2\text{-}10b)$$

31.2.1.3   Higher order products

A product of order 4 follows from relation 36.4-6 on page 701:

$$F\left(\begin{matrix} \tfrac{1}{2}, \tfrac{1}{2} \\ 1 \end{matrix} \,\middle|\, k \right) \;=\; \left[\prod_{n=0}^{\infty} P_n \right]^2 \quad \text{where} \quad P_n = \frac{2}{1+\sqrt[4]{1-k_n}}, \quad M_n = \frac{1-\sqrt[4]{1-k_n}}{2}, \qquad (31.2\text{-}11a)$$

$$k_0 = k, \quad k_{n+1} = [M_n\, P_n]^4, \quad k_\infty = 0 \qquad (31.2\text{-}11b)$$

Another quartic product is

$$F\left(\begin{matrix} \tfrac{1}{2}, \tfrac{1}{2} \\ 1 \end{matrix} \,\middle|\, k \right) \;=\; \left[\prod_{n=0}^{\infty} R_n \right]^{1/2} \quad \text{where} \quad W_n = \sqrt{1-k_n}, \quad Q_n = \sqrt[4]{1-k_n} = \sqrt{W_n}, \qquad (31.2\text{-}12a)$$

$$R_n = \frac{2}{Q_n\,(1+W_n)}, \quad k_0 = k, \quad k_{n+1} = -R_n\,(1-Q_n)^4, \quad k_\infty = 0 \qquad (31.2\text{-}12b)$$

This can be obtained by setting $a = 1/2$ in the following relation [222, rel.22, p.130]:

$$F\left(\begin{matrix} a, \frac{4a+1}{6} \\ \frac{4a+1}{3} \end{matrix} \,\middle|\, z \right) \;=\; \left(\frac{Q\,(1+W)}{2} \right)^{-a} F\left(\begin{matrix} a, \frac{2-a}{3} \\ \frac{2a+5}{6} \end{matrix} \,\middle|\, \frac{-(1-Q)^4}{8\,Q\,(1+W)} \right) \quad \text{where} \qquad (31.2\text{-}13a)$$

$$W = \sqrt{1-z}, \quad Q = \sqrt[4]{1-z} \qquad (31.2\text{-}13b)$$

Here is a product of order 16 for $\frac{2}{\pi} K(\sqrt{k}) = \mathrm{AGM}\left(1, \sqrt{1-k}\right)$, compare to relations 31.3-25a and 31.3-25b on page 607:

$$F\left(\begin{array}{c}\frac{1}{2}, \frac{1}{2} \\ 1\end{array}\middle|\, k\right) \;=\; \left[\prod_{n=0}^{\infty} \frac{2}{P_n + R_n}\right]^2 \quad \text{where} \quad R_n = \left(P_n^4 - M_n^4\right)^{1/4}, \tag{31.2-14a}$$

$$s_n = (1 - k_n)^{1/4}, \quad P_n = \frac{1 + s_n}{2}, \quad M_n = \frac{1 - s_n}{2}, \tag{31.2-14b}$$

$$k_0 = k, \quad k_{n+1} = \left[\frac{P_n - R_n}{P_n + R_n}\right]^4 \tag{31.2-14c}$$

Some operations can be saved as follows:

$$F\left(\begin{array}{c}\frac{1}{2}, \frac{1}{2} \\ 1\end{array}\middle|\, k\right) \;=\; \left[\prod_{n=0}^{\infty} 2 X_n\right]^2 \quad \text{where} \quad R_n = \left(\frac{s_n\left(1 + s_n^2\right)}{2}\right)^{1/4}, \tag{31.2-15a}$$

$$s_n = (1 - k_n)^{1/4}, \quad P_n = \frac{1 + s_n}{2}, \quad X_n = \frac{1}{P_n + R_n}, \tag{31.2-15b}$$

$$k_0 = k, \quad k_{n+1} = \left[(P_n - R_n)\, X_n\right]^4 \tag{31.2-15c}$$

31.2.2 Elliptic E

The *complete elliptic integral of the second kind* can be defined as

$$E(k) \;=\; \int_0^{\pi/2} \sqrt{1 - k^2 \sin^2 \vartheta}\, d\vartheta \;=\; \int_0^1 \frac{\sqrt{1 - k^2 t^2}}{\sqrt{1 - t^2}}\, dt \tag{31.2-16}$$

We have

$$E(k) \;=\; \frac{\pi}{2} F\left(\begin{array}{c}-\frac{1}{2}, \frac{1}{2} \\ 1\end{array}\middle|\, k^2\right) \tag{31.2-17a}$$

$$= \frac{\pi}{2}\left(-\sum_{i=0}^{\infty}\left(\frac{(2i-1)!!}{2^i\, i!}\right)^2 \frac{k^{2i}}{2i-1}\right) = \frac{\pi}{2}\sum_{i=0}^{\infty}\left(\frac{\binom{2i}{i}}{4^i}\right)^2 \frac{k^{2i}}{2i-1} \tag{31.2-17b}$$

$$= \frac{\pi}{2}\left(1 - \left(\frac{1}{2}\right)^2 k^2 - \left(\frac{1\cdot 3}{2\cdot 4}\right)^2 \frac{k^4}{3} - \left(\frac{1\cdot 3\cdot 5}{2\cdot 4\cdot 6}\right)^2 \frac{k^6}{5} - \cdots\right) \tag{31.2-17c}$$

$$= \frac{\pi}{2}\left(1 - \frac{1}{4} k^2 - \frac{3}{64} k^4 - \frac{5}{256} k^6 - \frac{175}{16384} k^8 - \frac{441}{65536} k^{10} - \cdots\right) \tag{31.2-17d}$$

Special values are $E(0) = \frac{\pi}{2}$ and $E(1) = 1$. The latter leads to a (slowly converging) series for $2/\pi$:

$$\frac{2}{\pi} \;=\; F\left(\begin{array}{c}-\frac{1}{2}, \frac{1}{2} \\ 1\end{array}\middle|\, 1\right) \tag{31.2-18}$$

Similarly as for K', one defines E' as

$$E'(k) \;:=\; E(k') = E\left(\sqrt{1 - k^2}\right) \tag{31.2-19}$$

The key to fast computation of E is the relation

$$\frac{E}{K} \;=\; 1 - \frac{1}{2}\sum_{n=0}^{\infty} 2^n c_n'^2 \tag{31.2-20}$$

The terms c' in the sum occur naturally during the computation of the AGM, see relation 31.1-2 on page 599. One defines

$$R := \frac{E}{K}, \qquad R' := \frac{E'}{K'} \tag{31.2-21}$$

Then E can be computed via

$$E(k) \;=\; R(k)\,K(k) \;=\; \frac{\pi}{2\,\mathrm{AGM}(1,\sqrt{1-k^2})} \cdot \left(1 - \sum_{n=0}^{\infty} 2^{n-1} c_n'^2\right) \tag{31.2-22}$$

Legendre's relation between K and E is (arguments omitted for readability, choose your favorite form):

$$\frac{E}{K} + \frac{E'}{K'} - 1 \;=\; \frac{\pi}{2\,K\,K'}, \qquad E\,K' + E'\,K - K\,K' \;=\; \frac{\pi}{2} \tag{31.2-23}$$

Equivalently,

$$\mathrm{AGM}(1,k) \;=\; \frac{E/K}{(1 - E'/K')} \;=\; \frac{R}{(1 - R')} \tag{31.2-24}$$

For $k = \frac{1}{\sqrt{2}} =: s$ we have $k = k'$, thereby $K = K'$ and $E = E'$, so

$$\frac{K(s)}{\pi}\left(\frac{2\,E(s)}{\pi} - \frac{K(s)}{\pi}\right) \;=\; \frac{1}{2\pi} \tag{31.2-25}$$

As expressions 31.2-5a and 31.2-22 provide a fast AGM-based computation of $\frac{K}{\pi}$ and $\frac{E}{\pi}$ the above formula can be used to compute π.

The following expressions for the derivatives of K, K', E, and E' allow fast computation (see [124, p.75]):

$$\frac{dK}{dk} \;=\; \frac{E - k'^2\,K}{k\,k'^2}, \qquad \frac{dK'}{dk} \;=\; \frac{k^2\,K' - E'}{k\,k'^2} \tag{31.2-26a}$$

$$\frac{dE}{dk} \;=\; \frac{E - K}{k}, \qquad \frac{dE'}{dk} \;=\; \frac{k\,(K' - E')}{k'^2} \tag{31.2-26b}$$

31.3　Theta functions, eta functions, and singular values

The *theta functions* Θ_2, Θ_3, and Θ_4 are defined as

$$\Theta_2(q) \;=\; \sum_{n=-\infty}^{\infty} q^{(n+1/2)^2} \;=\; 2\sum_{n=0}^{\infty} q^{(n+1/2)^2} \;=\; 2\,q^{1/4}\sum_{n=0}^{\infty} q^{n^2+n} \tag{31.3-1a}$$

$$\Theta_3(q) \;=\; \sum_{n=-\infty}^{\infty} q^{n^2} \;=\; 1 + 2\sum_{n=0}^{\infty} q^{n^2} \tag{31.3-1b}$$

$$\Theta_4(q) \;=\; \sum_{n=-\infty}^{\infty} (-1)^n\, q^{n^2} \;=\; 1 + 2\sum_{n=0}^{\infty} (-1)^n\, q^{n^2} \tag{31.3-1c}$$

These are the expressions for $z = 0$ of the more general form in two variables, see [1, sect.16.27, p.576]. The following relations hold for the theta functions:

$$\Theta_3^2(q^2) \;=\; \frac{\Theta_3^2(q) + \Theta_4^2(q)}{2} \tag{31.3-2a}$$

$$\Theta_4^2(q^2) \;=\; \sqrt{\Theta_3^2(q)\,\Theta_4^2(q)} \;=\; \Theta_3(q)\,\Theta_4(q) \tag{31.3-2b}$$

$$\Theta_2^2(q^2) \;=\; \frac{\Theta_3^2(q) - \Theta_4^2(q)}{2} \tag{31.3-2c}$$

Using the first two relations (and $\lim_{n \to \infty} \Theta_3(q^n) = \lim_{n \to \infty} \Theta_4(q^n) = 1$ for $|q| < 1$) we see that
$\text{AGM}\left(\Theta_3^2(q), \Theta_4^2(q)\right) = \text{AGM}\left(\Theta_3^2(q^2), \Theta_4^2(q^2)\right) = \text{AGM}\left(\Theta_3^2(q^4), \Theta_4^2(q^4)\right) = \text{AGM}\left(\Theta_3^2(q^8), \Theta_4^2(q^8)\right) = \ldots$

$$1 = \text{AGM}\left(\Theta_3^2(q), \Theta_4^2(q)\right) \tag{31.3-3}$$

By the linearity of the AGM in both arguments we have

$$\frac{1}{\Theta_3^2(q)} = \text{AGM}\left(1, \frac{\Theta_4^2(q)}{\Theta_3^2(q)}\right) \tag{31.3-4}$$

The relation can be identified with $\frac{\pi}{2K} = \text{AGM}(1, k')$ if k and q are connected via

$$q = \exp\left(-\pi \frac{K'}{K}\right) \tag{31.3-5}$$

The relations between the theta functions and K, k, k' are

$$\Theta_2^2(q) = \frac{2kK}{\pi}, \qquad \Theta_3^2(q) = \frac{2K}{\pi}, \qquad \Theta_4^2(q) = \frac{2k'K}{\pi} \tag{31.3-6a}$$

We also have $\log(1/q) = -\log q = \pi K'/K$, so

$$\frac{\pi}{\log(1/q)} = -\frac{\pi}{\log(q)} = \text{AGM}\left(\Theta_3^2(q), \Theta_2^2(q)\right) = \frac{\text{AGM}(1, k)}{\text{AGM}(1, k')} \tag{31.3-7}$$

Identifying $a_k = \Theta_3^2(q)$ and $b_k = \Theta_4^2(q)$ in relations 31.1-1a and 31.1-1b on page 599 we see that $a_{k+1} = \Theta_3^2(q^2)$ (via relation 31.3-2a) and $b_{k+1} = \Theta_4^2(q^2)$ (via relation 31.3-2b). That is, the AGM sends q to q^2. We can also identify $c_k = \Theta_2^2(q)$, then $c_{k+1} = \Theta_2^2\left(q^2\right)$.

31.3.1 Relations for the theta functions

We give identities involving fourth powers, the first is *Jacobi's identity*, it follows from 31.1-2:

$$\Theta_3^4(q) = \Theta_4^4(q) + \Theta_2^4(q) \tag{31.3-8a}$$
$$\frac{\Theta_3^4(q) + \Theta_4^4(q)}{2} = \Theta_3^4(q^2) + \Theta_2^4(q^2) = 2\,\Theta_3^4(q^2) - \Theta_4^4(q^2) = \Theta_4^4(q^2) + 2\,\Theta_2^4(q^2) \tag{31.3-8b}$$

Now identify $\alpha_k = \Theta_3(q)$ and $\alpha_{k+1} = \Theta_3(q^4)$ in relation 31.1-6b on page 600 and $\beta_k = \Theta_4(q)$ and $\beta_{k+1} = \Theta_4(q^4)$ in 31.1-6c. The 4th order variant of the AGM sends the pair $(\Theta_3(q), \Theta_4(q))$ to $(\Theta_3(q^4), \Theta_4(q^4))$:

$$\Theta_3(q^4) = \frac{\Theta_3(q) + \Theta_4(q)}{2} = \sqrt{\frac{\Theta_3^2(q^2) + \Theta_4^2(q^2)}{2}} \tag{31.3-9a}$$

$$\Theta_4(q^4) = \sqrt[4]{\Theta_3(q)\,\Theta_4(q)\,\frac{\Theta_3^2(q) + \Theta_4^2(q)}{2}} = \sqrt{\Theta_3(q^2)\,\Theta_4(q^2)} \tag{31.3-9b}$$

We also have $\gamma_k = \Theta_2(q)$, $\gamma_{k+1} = \Theta_2(q^4)$, and

$$\Theta_2(q^4) = \frac{\Theta_3(q) - \Theta_4(q)}{2} \tag{31.3-10}$$

The following expressions can be verified using relations 31.3-2a, 31.3-2b, and 31.3-9a.

$$32\,\Theta_1^8(q^8) = [\Theta_3(q) + \Theta_4(q)]^4 \left[\Theta_3^2(q) + \Theta_4^2(q)\right] \Theta_3(q)\,\Theta_4(q) \tag{31.3-11a}$$
$$16\,\Theta_4^8(q^4) = 16\,\Theta_3^8(q^2) - \Theta_2^8(q) \tag{31.3-11b}$$

Repeated application of the identities

$$\Theta_3(q) = \Theta_3(q^4) + \Theta_2(q^4) \tag{31.3-12a}$$
$$\Theta_4(q) = \Theta_3(q^4) - \Theta_2(q^4) \tag{31.3-12b}$$

gives

$$\Theta_3(q) = +\Theta_2(q^4) + \Theta_2(q^{16}) + \Theta_2(q^{64}) + \ldots + \Theta_2(q^{4^N}) + \Theta_3(q^{4^N}) \tag{31.3-13a}$$
$$\Theta_4(q) = -\Theta_2(q^4) + \Theta_2(q^{16}) + \Theta_2(q^{64}) + \ldots + \Theta_2(q^{4^N}) + \Theta_3(q^{4^N}) \tag{31.3-13b}$$

These are also valid in the limit $N \to \infty$ ($\lim_{n\to\infty} \Theta_3(q^n) = 1$, so):

$$\Theta_3(q) = 1 + \Theta_2(q^4) + \Theta_2(q^{16}) + \Theta_2(q^{64}) + \Theta_2(q^{256}) + \ldots \tag{31.3-14a}$$
$$\Theta_4(q) = 1 - \Theta_2(q^4) + \Theta_2(q^{16}) + \Theta_2(q^{64}) + \Theta_2(q^{256}) + \ldots \tag{31.3-14b}$$

From [206, p.35, ex.6], attributed to Gauss:

$$\Theta_3^4(q) = 1 + \frac{1}{2}\Theta_2^4(q) + \frac{3}{2}\left[\Theta_2^4(q^2) + \Theta_2^4(q^4) + \Theta_2^4(q^8) + \Theta_2^4(q^{16}) + \ldots\right] \tag{31.3-15a}$$
$$\Theta_4^4(q) = 1 - \frac{1}{2}\Theta_2^4(q) + \frac{3}{2}\left[\Theta_2^4(q^2) + \Theta_2^4(q^4) + \Theta_2^4(q^8) + \Theta_2^4(q^{16}) + \ldots\right] \tag{31.3-15b}$$

These can be obtained from the following:

$$\left[2\,\Theta_3^4(q) - \Theta_2^4(q)\right] = \left[2\,\Theta_3^4(q^2) - \Theta_2^4(q^2)\right] + 3\,\Theta_2^4(q^2) \tag{31.3-16a}$$
$$\left[2\,\Theta_4^4(q) + \Theta_2^4(q)\right] = \left[2\,\Theta_4^4(q^2) + \Theta_2^4(q^2)\right] + 3\,\Theta_2^4(q^2) \tag{31.3-16b}$$

The following relations are a consequences of 31.3-9a and 31.3-2a, they are valid only for finite N:

$$\Theta_3(q) = 2^N \Theta_3(q^{4^N}) - \left[\Theta_4(q) + 2\,\Theta_4(q^4) + 4\,\Theta_4(q^{16}) + \ldots + 2^{N-1}\Theta_4(q^{4^{N-1}})\right] \tag{31.3-17a}$$
$$\Theta_3^2(q) = 2^N \Theta_3^2(q^{2^N}) - \left[\Theta_4^2(q) + 2\,\Theta_4^2(q^2) + 4\,\Theta_4^2(q^4) + \ldots + 2^{N-1}\Theta_4^2(q^{2^{N-1}})\right] \tag{31.3-17b}$$

From (a factorization of 31.3-8a)

$$\Theta_3^2(q) = \Theta_3^2(q^2) + \Theta_2^2(q^2) \tag{31.3-18a}$$
$$\Theta_4^2(q) = \Theta_3^2(q^2) - \Theta_2^2(q^2) \tag{31.3-18b}$$

we obtain

$$\Theta_3^2(q) = \Theta_3^2(q^{2^N}) + \left[+\Theta_2^2(q^2) + \Theta_2^2(q^4) + \Theta_2^2(q^8) + \ldots + \Theta_2^2(q^{2^N})\right] \tag{31.3-19a}$$
$$= 1 + \Theta_2^2(q^2) + \Theta_2^2(q^4) + \Theta_2^2(q^8) + \Theta_2^2(q^{16}) + \ldots \tag{31.3-19b}$$
$$\Theta_4^2(q) = \Theta_3^2(q^{2^N}) + \left[-\Theta_2^2(q^2) + \Theta_2^2(q^4) + \Theta_2^2(q^8) + \ldots + \Theta_2^2(q^{2^N})\right] \tag{31.3-19c}$$
$$= 1 - \Theta_2^2(q^2) + \Theta_2^2(q^4) + \Theta_2^2(q^8) + \Theta_2^2(q^{16}) + \ldots \tag{31.3-19d}$$

We give two relations from [66, pp.110-112]:

$$\Theta_4(q)\,\Theta_4(q^3) + \Theta_2(q)\,\Theta_2(q^3) = \Theta_3(q)\,\Theta_3(q^3) \tag{31.3-20a}$$
$$\sqrt{\Theta_4(q)\,\Theta_4(q^7)} + \sqrt{\Theta_2(q)\,\Theta_2(q^7)} = \sqrt{\Theta_3(q)\,\Theta_3(q^7)} \tag{31.3-20b}$$

31.3.2 Corresponding transformations of q and k

The map $q \mapsto -q$ swaps Θ_3 with Θ_4 and sends $k' \mapsto 1/k'$ and $k \mapsto \pm i\,k/k'$. The map $q \mapsto q^2$ corresponds to the maps (compare with relations 31.2-10a and 31.2-9a on page 602)

$$k(q) \;\mapsto\; k(q^2) = \frac{1-k'}{1+k'}, \qquad k'(q) \;\mapsto\; k'(q^2) = \frac{2\sqrt{k'}}{1+k'} \tag{31.3-21}$$

For the map $q \mapsto q^4$ we have

$$\sqrt{k} \;\mapsto\; \frac{1-\sqrt{k'}}{1+\sqrt{k'}}, \qquad \sqrt{k'} \;\mapsto\; \sqrt[4]{1 - \left[\frac{1-\sqrt{k'}}{1+\sqrt{k'}}\right]^4} = \frac{\sqrt[4]{8\sqrt{k'}\,(1+k')}}{1+\sqrt{k'}} \tag{31.3-22}$$

the map $q \mapsto q^{16}$ is obtained by applying $q \mapsto q^4$ twice. Define

$$P \;=\; \frac{\Theta_3(q) + \Theta_4(q)}{2}, \qquad M = \frac{\Theta_3(q) - \Theta_4(q)}{2}, \tag{31.3-23a}$$

$$R \;=\; \sqrt[4]{P^4 - M^4} = \sqrt[4]{\frac{\Theta_3(q)\,\Theta_4(q)\,[\Theta_3^2(q) + \Theta_4^2(q)]}{2}} \tag{31.3-23b}$$

Then we have, in terms of the theta functions,

$$\Theta_2(q^{16}) \;=\; \frac{P - R}{2} \tag{31.3-24a}$$

$$\Theta_3(q^{16}) \;=\; \frac{P + R}{2} \tag{31.3-24b}$$

$$\Theta_4(q^{16}) \;=\; \sqrt[4]{\frac{P\,R\,[P^2 + R^2]}{2}} \tag{31.3-24c}$$

Adding the first two relations gives $\Theta_3(q^{16}) + \Theta_2(q^{16}) = \frac{1}{2}\left[\Theta_3(q) + \Theta_4(q)\right]$. The maps for k and k' are

$$\sqrt{k} \;\mapsto\; \frac{P - \sqrt[4]{P^4 - M^4}}{P + \sqrt[4]{P^4 - M^4}} \quad \text{where} \quad P = 1 + \sqrt{k'}, \quad M = 1 - \sqrt{k'} \tag{31.3-25a}$$

$$\sqrt{k'} \;\mapsto\; \frac{\sqrt[4]{8\,P\,R\,(P^2 + R^2)}}{P + R} \quad \text{where} \quad R = \sqrt[4]{P^4 - M^4} \tag{31.3\ 25b}$$

31.3.3 Relations for the eta functions

We define the eta functions η and η_+ as

$$\eta(q) := \prod_{j=1}^{\infty} \left(1 - q^j\right), \qquad \eta_+(q) := \prod_{j=1}^{\infty} \left(1 + q^j\right) = \frac{\eta\left(q^2\right)}{\eta\left(q\right)} \tag{31.3-26}$$

Note that η is not the *Dedekind eta function*, which is $q^{1/24} \prod_{j=1}^{\infty} \left(1 - q^j\right)$, see [358, entry "Dedekind eta function"]. We write E_k for $\eta(q^k)$ where convenient. Expressions for the theta functions are

$$\Theta_2(q) \;=\; 2\,\sqrt[4]{q}\,\frac{E_4^2}{E_2} = 2\,\sqrt[4]{q}\,\eta_+(q^2)\,\eta(q^4) = 2\,\sqrt[4]{q}\,\eta_+^2(q^2)\,\eta(q^2) \tag{31.3-27a}$$

$$\Theta_3(q) \;=\; \frac{E_2^5}{E_1^2\,E_4^2} = \frac{\eta^2(-q)}{\eta(q^2)} = \frac{\eta(-q)}{\eta_+(-q)} = \frac{\eta(q^2)}{\eta_+^2(-q)} \tag{31.3-27b}$$

$$\Theta_4(q) \;=\; \frac{E_1^2}{E_2} = \frac{\eta^2(q)}{\eta(q^2)} = \frac{\eta(q)}{\eta_+(q)} = \frac{\eta(q^2)}{\eta_+^2(q)} = \Theta_3(-q) \tag{31.3-27c}$$

$$2\,\sqrt[4]{q}\,\eta^3(q^2) \;=\; \Theta_2(q)\,\Theta_3(q)\,\Theta_4(q) = \Theta_2(q)\,\Theta_4^2(q^2) \tag{31.3-27d}$$

Expressions for K, k, and $k' = \sqrt{1-k^2}$ are

$$\frac{2K}{\pi} = \Theta_3^2(q) = \frac{E_2^{10}}{E_1^4 E_4^4}, \qquad \frac{2kK}{\pi} = \Theta_2^2(q) = \frac{2\sqrt{q}\,E_4^4}{E_2^2}, \qquad \frac{2k'K}{\pi} = \Theta_4^2(q) = \frac{E_1^4}{E_2^2} \qquad \text{(31.3-28a)}$$

$$k = \frac{\Theta_2^2(q)}{\Theta_3^2(q)} = 4\sqrt{q}\left[\frac{E_1 E_4^2}{E_2^3}\right]^4 = 4\sqrt{q}\,\frac{E_1^4 E_4^8}{E_2^{12}} = 4\sqrt{q}\left[\frac{\eta_+^2(q^2)}{\eta_+(q)}\right]^4 \qquad \text{(31.3-28b)}$$

$$k' = \frac{\Theta_4^2(q)}{\Theta_3^2(q)} = \left[\frac{E_1^2 E_4}{E_2^3}\right]^4 = \frac{E_1^8 E_4^4}{E_2^{12}} = \left[\frac{\eta(q)}{\eta(-q)}\right]^4 = \left[\frac{\eta_+(q^2)}{\eta_+^2(q)}\right]^4 \qquad \text{(31.3-28c)}$$

The first equalities of the following six relations are taken from [356, p.488]:

$$\prod_{n=1}^{\infty}(1-q^n)^{24} = \frac{256\,k^2\,k'^8\,K^{12}}{q\,\pi^{12}} = \eta^{24}(q) = E_1^{24} \qquad \text{(31.3-29a)}$$

$$\prod_{n=1}^{\infty}(1-q^{2n-1})^{24} = \frac{16\,q\,k'^4}{k^2} = \frac{1}{\eta_+^{24}(q)} = \frac{\eta^{24}(q)}{\eta^{24}(q^2)} = \left[\frac{E_1}{E_2}\right]^{24} \qquad \text{(31.3-29b)}$$

$$\prod_{n=1}^{\infty}(1-q^{2n})^{24} = \frac{16\,k^4\,k'^4\,K^{12}}{q^2\,\pi^{12}} = \eta^{24}(q^2) = E_2^{24} \qquad \text{(31.3-29c)}$$

$$\prod_{n=1}^{\infty}(1+q^n)^{24} = \frac{k^2}{16\,q\,k'^4} = \eta_+^{24}(q) = \frac{\eta^{24}(q^2)}{\eta^{24}(q)} = \left[\frac{E_2}{E_1}\right]^{24} \qquad \text{(31.3-29d)}$$

$$\prod_{n=1}^{\infty}(1+q^{2n-1})^{24} = \frac{16\,q}{k^2\,k'^2} = \frac{\eta_+^{24}(q)}{\eta_+^{24}(q^2)} = \left[\frac{E_2^2}{E_1 E_4}\right]^{24} \qquad \text{(31.3-29e)}$$

$$\prod_{n=1}^{\infty}(1+q^{2n})^{24} = \frac{k^4}{256\,q^2\,k'^2} = \eta_+^{24}(q^2) = \left[\frac{E_4}{E_2}\right]^{24} \qquad \text{(31.3-29f)}$$

Replacing $q \mapsto -q$, $k'^2 \mapsto 1/k'^2$, and $k^2 \mapsto -k^2/k'^2$ in 31.3-29d gives

$$\prod_{n=1}^{\infty}(1+(-q)^n)^{24} = \frac{k^2\,k'^2}{16\,q} = \eta_+^{24}(-q) = \frac{\eta_+^{24}(q^2)}{\eta_+^{24}(q)} = \frac{\eta^{24}(q)\,\eta^{24}(q^4)}{\eta^{48}(q^2)} = \left[\frac{E_1 E_4}{E_2^2}\right]^{24} \qquad \text{(31.3-29g)}$$

Multiplying 31.3-29c and 31.3-29f gives

$$\prod_{n=1}^{\infty}(1-q^{4n})^{24} = \frac{k^8\,k'^2\,K^{12}}{16\,q\,\pi^{12}} = \eta^{24}(q^4) = E_4^{24} \qquad \text{(31.3-29h)}$$

Most of the following identities can be found by rewriting other relations (typically involving the theta functions or k) in terms of the eta function.

$$k = \frac{4\sqrt{q}\,E_2^2\,E_4^6\,E_8^4}{E_4^{12} + 4\,q\,E_2^4\,E_8^8} \qquad \text{(31.3-30a)}$$

$$k' = \frac{E_4^{12} - 4\,q\,E_2^4\,E_8^8}{E_4^{12} + 4\,q\,E_2^4\,E_8^8} \qquad \text{(31.3-30b)}$$

$$\sqrt{k'} = \frac{E_8^6 - 2\,q\,E_4^2\,E_{16}^4}{E_8^6 + 2\,q\,E_4^2\,E_{16}^4} \qquad \text{(31.3-30c)}$$

For the numerators and denominators in the last two equations we have (see section 37.2.4 on page 714 for more relations of this type)

$$E_4^{12} - 4\,q\,E_2^4\,E_8^8 = E_1^4\,E_2^2\,E_4^2\,E_8^4, \qquad E_4^{12} + 4\,q\,E_2^4\,E_8^8 = \frac{E_2^{14}\,E_8^4}{E_1^4\,E_4^2} \qquad \text{(31.3-31a)}$$

$$E_8^6 - 2\,q\,E_4^2\,E_{16}^4 = \frac{E_1^2\,E_4^2\,E_8\,E_{16}^2}{E_2}, \qquad E_8^6 + 2\,q\,E_4^2\,E_{16}^4 = \frac{E_2^5\,E_8\,E_{16}^2}{E_1^2} \qquad \text{(31.3-31b)}$$

The first identity can be obtained by multiplying the last two and replacing q^2 by q. Multiplying the first two relations gives a relation equivalent to $k^2 + k'^2 = 1$, we give several forms:

$$E_2^{24} - 16\,q\,E_1^8\,E_4^{16} \;=\; E_1^{16}\,E_4^8 \tag{31.3-32a}$$

$$\eta^8(-q) - \eta^8(q) \;=\; 16\,q\,\eta^8\,(q^4) \tag{31.3-32b}$$

$$\eta_+^8(q) - \eta_+^8(-q) \;=\; 16\,q\,\eta_+^{16}\,(q^2) \;=\; 16\,q\,\eta_+^{16}\,(q)\,\eta_+^{16}\,(-q) \tag{31.3-32c}$$

$$\eta_+^8\,(q^2) + 16\,q\,\eta_+^{16}\,(q^2)\,\eta_+^8\,(q) \;=\; \eta_+^{16}\,(q) \tag{31.3-32d}$$

The identity is also the product of the following two relations:

$$E_2^{12} - E_1^8\,E_4^4 \;=\; 8\,q\,E_1^4\,E_2^2\,E_4^2\,E_8^4, \qquad E_2^{12} + E_1^8\,E_4^4 \;=\; \frac{2\,E_1^4\,E_4^{14}}{E_2^2\,E_8^4} \tag{31.3-33}$$

Their ratio is

$$\frac{E_2^{12} - E_1^8\,E_4^4}{E_2^{12} + E_1^8\,E_4^4} \;=\; \frac{4\,q\,E_2^4\,E_8^8}{E_4^{12}} \;=\; k(q^2) \tag{31.3-34}$$

The numerator is the product of the first two of the following identities:

$$E_2^6 + E_1^4\,E_4^2 \;=\; \frac{2\,E_1^2\,E_2\,E_8^5}{E_{16}^2}, \qquad E_2^6 - E_1^4\,E_4^2 \;=\; \frac{4\,q\,E_1^2\,E_2\,E_4^2\,E_{16}^2}{E_8} \tag{31.3-35a}$$

$$\frac{E_2^6 - E_1^4\,E_4^2}{E_2^6 + E_1^4\,E_4^2} \;=\; \frac{2\,q\,E_4^2\,E_{16}^4}{E_8^6} \;=\; \sqrt{k(q^4)} \tag{31.3-35b}$$

We rewrite the first two relations, and multiply to obtain an expression for $k'(q^2)$:

$$\frac{2\,E_1^2\,E_2^3\,E_4}{E_2^6 + E_1^4\,E_4^2} \;=\; \frac{E_2^2\,E_4\,E_{16}^2}{E_8^5}, \qquad \frac{4\,q\,E_1^2\,E_2^3\,E_4}{E_2^6 - E_1^4\,E_4^2} \;=\; \frac{E_2^2\,E_8}{E_4\,E_{16}^2} \tag{31.3-36a}$$

$$\frac{2\,E_1^4\,E_2^6\,E_4^2}{E_2^{12} + E_1^8\,E_4^4} \;=\; \frac{E_2^8\,E_8^4}{E_4^{12}} \;=\; k'(q^2) \tag{31.3-36b}$$

31.3.4 Singular values

```
n:    kn                              minpoly( kn^2 )
1: 0.70710678118654752244008444      2*x - 1
2: 0.41421356237309504880016887      x^2 - 6*x + 1

3: 0.25881904510252076234889988      16*x^2 - 16*x + 1
4: 0.17157287525380990239966226      x^2 - 34*x + 1

5: 0.11887694580260010119927468      16*x^4 - 32*x^3 + 88*x^2 - 72*x + 1
6: 0.08516423317474258764887993      x^4 - 140*x^3 + 294*x^2 - 140*x + 1

7: 0.06262291254316797010266646      256*x^2 - 256*x + 1
8: 0.04702189950099110167091430      x^4 - 452*x^3 - 122*x^2 - 452*x + 1

9: 0.03592156820388989341106255      16*x^4 - 32*x^3 + 792*x^2 - 776*x + 1
10: 0.02784244474454950317011183     x^4 - 1292*x^3 + 2598*x^2 - 1292*x + 1
```

Figure 31.3-A: Singular values k_n for $n \le 10$ and minimal polynomials of k_n^2.

For every $n \in \mathbb{N}_+$ there is a unique k_n $(0 < k_n < 1)$ such that

$$\frac{K'(k_n)}{K(k_n)} \;=\; \sqrt{n} \tag{31.3-37}$$

The value of k_n can be computed by setting $q = \exp\left(-\pi\,\sqrt{n}\right)$ in relation 31.3-28b, or by solving $\mathrm{AGM}(1, \sqrt{1 - k_n^2})/\mathrm{AGM}(1, k_n) = \sqrt{n}$. The values k_n are algebraic (over $\mathbb{Q}$). A few examples are (find more values in [349, entry "Elliptic Lambda Function"]):

$$k_1 = \frac{1}{\sqrt{2}} \tag{31.3-38a}$$

$$k_2 = \sqrt{2} - 1 \tag{31.3-38b}$$

$$k_3 = \frac{\sqrt{3} - 1}{2\sqrt{2}} = \frac{1}{2}\sqrt{2 - \sqrt{3}} \tag{31.3-38c}$$

$$k_4 = 3 - 2\sqrt{2} \tag{31.3-38d}$$

$$k_5 = \sqrt{\frac{1}{2} - \sqrt{\sqrt{5} - 2}} = \frac{1}{2}\left(\sqrt{\sqrt{5} - 1} - \sqrt{3 - \sqrt{5}}\right) \tag{31.3-38e}$$

$$k_6 = \left(2 - \sqrt{3}\right)\left(\sqrt{3} - \sqrt{2}\right) \tag{31.3-38f}$$

$$k_7 = \frac{1}{8}\sqrt{2}\left(3 - \sqrt{7}\right) = \frac{1}{4}\sqrt{8 - 3\sqrt{7}} \tag{31.3-38g}$$

The degree of the minimal polynomial of k_n^2 can (for $n \geq 2$) be computed in the GP language as `2*qfbclassno(-4*n)`. The sequence of the degrees of the minimal polynomials for k_n^2 starts as

n:	2	3	4	5	6	7	8	9	10	11	12	13	14	15	16	17	18	19	20	21	22	23	24	25	26	27	28	29	30
deg:	2	2	2	4	4	2	4	4	4	6	4	4	8	4	4	8	4	6	8	8	4	6	8	4	12	6	4	12	8

This is twice entry A000003 in [312]. The first few minimal polynomials are shown in figure 31.3-A. If the degree of the minimal polynomial is small, one sometimes can solve it in radicals even for large n. For example, with $n = 163$ we have

$$k_{163} = \frac{1}{2}\sqrt{2 - \sqrt{3 + UT - \frac{2U^2}{3T}}} \qquad \text{where} \tag{31.3-39}$$

$$U = 80040, \qquad T = \sqrt[3]{1 + 557403\sqrt{3 \cdot 163}}$$

and $k_{163} \approx 7.80664428497433 \cdot 10^{-9}$. The quantity

$$P_n := \frac{-1}{\sqrt{n}}\log\left(\frac{k_n^2}{16}\right) \tag{31.3-40}$$

is an approximation for π. For example, $\pi - P_{163} \approx -2.38 \cdot 10^{-18}$. Better approximations are given by

$$P_{n,i} := \frac{-1}{\sqrt{n}}\log\left(w_n + 8w_n^2 + 84w_n^3 + 992w_n^4 + \ldots + c_i w_n^i\right) \tag{31.3-41}$$

where $w_n = k_n^2/16$ and the coefficients c_i are given as entry A005797 in [312]:

1, 8, 84, 992, 12514, 164688, 2232200, 30920128, 435506703, 6215660600, 89668182220, ...

For example, $\pi - P_{2,11} \approx -2.15 \cdot 10^{-10}$ and $\pi - P_{163,4} \approx -2.06 \cdot 10^{-67}$.

Certain values of the gamma function can be expressed in terms of evaluations of K at singular values (taken from [339, p.12]):

$$\Gamma(1/3) = \pi^{1/3}\, 2^{7/9}\, 3^{-1/12}\, K(k_3)^{1/3} \tag{31.3-42a}$$

$$\Gamma(1/4) = \pi^{1/4}\, 2\, K(k_1)^{1/2} \tag{31.3-42b}$$

$$\Gamma(1/8) = \pi^{1/8}\, 2^{17/8}\, K(k_1)^{1/4}\, K(k_2)^{1/2} \tag{31.3-42c}$$

$$\Gamma(1/24) = \pi^{1/24}\, 2^{89/36}\, 3^{25/48}\, \sqrt{\sqrt{2} + 1}\, \left(\sqrt{3} - 1\right)^{1/4}\, K(k_1)^{1/4}\, K(k_3)^{1/3}\, K(k_6)^{1/2} \tag{31.3-42d}$$

31.4 AGM-type algorithms for hypergeometric functions

We give AGM-based algorithms for the hypergeometric functions

$$F\left(\begin{matrix}\frac{1}{2}-s,\,\frac{1}{2}+s\\1\end{matrix}\middle|z\right) \qquad \text{where} \quad s\in\left\{0,\frac{1}{6},\frac{1}{4},\frac{1}{3}\right\} \tag{31.4-1a}$$

$$F\left(\begin{matrix}\frac{1}{4}-t,\,\frac{1}{4}+t\\1\end{matrix}\middle|z\right) \qquad \text{where} \quad t\in\left\{\frac{1}{12},\frac{1}{6}\right\} \tag{31.4-1b}$$

These are taken from [69] and [151], both papers are recommended for further studies. See also [241], [68], [97], and [96]. The limit of a three-term iteration as a generalized hypergeometric function is determined in [217]. A four-term iteration is considered in [67].

The following transformations can be applied to the functions, these are special cases of relations 36.2-12a and 36.2-12b on page 690:

$$F\left(\begin{matrix}\frac{1}{2}+s,\,\frac{1}{2}-s\\1\end{matrix}\middle|z\right) = F\left(\begin{matrix}\frac{1}{4}+\frac{s}{2},\,\frac{1}{4}-\frac{s}{2}\\1\end{matrix}\middle|4z(1-z)\right) \quad \text{where} \quad |z|<\frac{1}{2} \tag{31.4-2a}$$

$$F\left(\begin{matrix}\frac{1}{4}+t,\,\frac{1}{4}-t\\1\end{matrix}\middle|z\right) = F\left(\begin{matrix}\frac{1}{2}+2t,\,\frac{1}{2}-2t\\1\end{matrix}\middle|\frac{1-\sqrt{1-z}}{2}\right). \tag{31.4-2b}$$

31.4.1 Algorithms for $F\left(\begin{matrix}1/2,\,1/2\\1\end{matrix}\middle|z\right)$ $[1/2\pm 0]$

The following is relation 31.2-5a on page 601, the classical AGM algorithm which has quadratic convergence:

$$F\left(\begin{matrix}\frac{1}{2},\,\frac{1}{2}\\1\end{matrix}\middle|z\right) = 1/M\left(1,\sqrt{1-z}\right) \quad \text{where} \tag{31.4-3a}$$

$$M(a,b) := \left[(a+b)/2,\sqrt{a\,b}\right] \tag{31.4-3b}$$

We write the AGM as $M := [f(a,b),\,g(a,b)]$ in the obvious way.

Compare to the following hypergeometric transformation

$$F\left(\begin{matrix}\frac{1}{2},\,\frac{1}{2}\\1\end{matrix}\middle|z'\right) = (1+z)\,F\left(\begin{matrix}\frac{1}{2},\,\frac{1}{2}\\1\end{matrix}\middle|z^2\right) \tag{31.4-4a}$$

where

$$z = \frac{1-(1-z')^{1/2}}{1+(1-z')^{1/2}}, \qquad z' = 1-\left(\frac{1-z}{1+z}\right)^2 \tag{31.4-4b}$$

It is the special case $a=1/2$ and $b=1/2$ of the transformation

$$F\left(\begin{matrix}a,\,b\\2b\end{matrix}\middle|\frac{4z}{(1+z)^2}\right) = F\left(\begin{matrix}a,\,b\\2b\end{matrix}\middle|1-\left(\frac{1-z}{1+z}\right)^2\right) = (1+z)^{2a}\,F\left(\begin{matrix}a,\,a-b+\frac{1}{2}\\b+\frac{1}{2}\end{matrix}\middle|z^2\right) \tag{31.4-5}$$

A fourth order algorithm is found by combining two steps of the classical AGM:

$$F\left(\begin{matrix}\frac{1}{2},\,\frac{1}{2}\\1\end{matrix}\middle|z\right) = 1/M\left(1,\sqrt[4]{1-z}\right)^2 \quad \text{where} \tag{31.4-6a}$$

$$M(a,b) := \left[(a+b)/2,\sqrt{a\,b\,(a^2+b^2)/2}\right] \tag{31.4-6b}$$

31.4.2   Algorithms for $F\left(\begin{smallmatrix} 1/3,\, 2/3 \\ 1 \end{smallmatrix} \middle| z\right)$ [1/2 ± 1/6]

A third order algorithm:

$$F\left(\begin{matrix} \frac{1}{3},\, \frac{1}{3} \\ 1 \end{matrix} \middle| z\right) \;=\; 1/M\left(\sqrt[3]{1-z},\, 1\right) \;=\; \sqrt[3]{1-z}\, F\left(\begin{matrix} \frac{2}{3},\, \frac{2}{3} \\ 1 \end{matrix} \middle| z\right) \quad \text{where} \tag{31.4-7a}$$

$$M(a,b) \;:=\; \left[(a+2\,b)/3,\; \sqrt[3]{b\,(a^2+a\,b+b^2)\,/3}\,\right] \tag{31.4-7b}$$

We further have

$$F\left(\begin{matrix} \frac{1}{3},\, \frac{2}{3} \\ 1 \end{matrix} \middle| z\right) \;=\; 1/M\left(1,\, \sqrt[3]{1-z}\right) \tag{31.4-8}$$

A quadratic algorithm:

$$F\left(\begin{matrix} \frac{1}{3},\, \frac{2}{3} \\ 1 \end{matrix} \middle| z\right) \;=\; 1/M\left(1,\, \sqrt[3]{1-z}\right) \quad \text{where} \tag{31.4-9a}$$

$$M(a,b) \;:=\; \left[\frac{1}{2}\left(\sqrt[3]{2p-a^3} + \sqrt[3]{2m-a^3}\right),\; \frac{1}{2}\left(\sqrt[3]{p} + \sqrt[3]{m}\right)\right] \quad \text{and} \tag{31.4-9b}$$

$$p \;:=\; b^3+t, \qquad m \;:=\; b^3-t, \qquad t \;:=\; \sqrt{b^6 - a^3\,b^3} \tag{31.4-9c}$$

And again (see relation 31.4-7a):

$$F\left(\begin{matrix} \frac{1}{3},\, \frac{1}{3} \\ 1 \end{matrix} \middle| z\right) \;=\; 1/M\left(\sqrt[3]{1-z},\, 1\right) \;=\; \sqrt[3]{1-z}\, F\left(\begin{matrix} \frac{2}{3},\, \frac{2}{3} \\ 1 \end{matrix} \middle| z\right) \tag{31.4-10}$$

We note the following hypergeometric transformation due to Ramanujan:

$$F\left(\begin{matrix} \frac{1}{3},\, \frac{2}{3} \\ 1 \end{matrix} \middle| z'\right) \;=\; (1+2\,z)\, F\left(\begin{matrix} \frac{1}{3},\, \frac{2}{3} \\ 1 \end{matrix} \middle| z^3\right) \tag{31.4-11a}$$

where

$$z \;=\; \frac{1-(1-z')^{1/3}}{1+2\,(1-z')^{1/3}}, \qquad z' \;=\; 1-\left(\frac{1-z}{1+2z}\right)^3 \tag{31.4-11b}$$

The general form is given in [48]:

$$F\left(\begin{matrix} c,\, c+\frac{1}{3} \\ \frac{3c+1}{2} \end{matrix} \middle| 1-\left(\frac{1-z}{1+2z}\right)^3\right) \;=\; (1+2z)^{3c}\, F\left(\begin{matrix} c,\, c+\frac{1}{3} \\ \frac{3c+5}{6} \end{matrix} \middle| z^3\right) \tag{31.4-12}$$

For $c = 1/3$ we obtain relation 31.4-11a. A computer algebra proof that relation 31.4-12 is the only possible generalization of relation 31.4-11a is given in [216].

An alternative quadratic algorithm is

$$F\left(\begin{matrix} \frac{1}{3},\, \frac{2}{3} \\ 1 \end{matrix} \middle| z\right) \;=\; 1/M\left(1,\, W\right) \quad \text{where} \tag{31.4-13a}$$

$$M(a,b) \;:=\; \left[(a+b)/2,\; \left(3\,\sqrt{b\,(b+2a)/3} - b\right)/2\right] \quad \text{and} \tag{31.4-13b}$$

$$W \;:=\; \frac{1-R+R^2}{R}, \qquad R \;:=\; \left[\sqrt{u^2-1} + u\right]^{1/3}, \qquad u \;:=\; 1-2z \tag{31.4-13c}$$

It is given in the form

$$F\left(\begin{matrix} \frac{1}{3},\, \frac{2}{3} \\ 1 \end{matrix} \middle| (1-x)\,(1+x/2)^2\right) \;=\; 1/M\left(1,\, x\right) \tag{31.4-14}$$

A product form can be derived from [47, Theorem 6.1]: let

$$\alpha(z) \quad := \quad \frac{z\,(3+z)^2}{2\,(1+z)^3} \tag{31.4-15a}$$

$$p(z) \quad := \quad \frac{r^2 - r + 1}{r} \quad \text{where} \quad r := \left[2z + 2\sqrt{z^2 - z} - 1\right]^{1/3} \tag{31.4-15b}$$

then, with $t_0 := 1 - z$ and $t_{k+1} := \alpha(p(t_k))$,

$$F\left(\begin{matrix} \frac{1}{3}, \frac{2}{3} \\ 1 \end{matrix} \middle| z\right) \quad = \quad \left[\prod_{k=0}^{\infty} \frac{1 + p(t_k)}{2}\right]^{-1} \tag{31.4-15c}$$

The function $p(z)$ is the real solution of $p(\beta(z)) = z$ where $\beta(z) := (z^2(3+z))/4$.

31.4.3 Algorithms for $F\left(\begin{matrix} 1/4, 3/4 \\ 1 \end{matrix} \middle| z\right)$ $[1/2 \pm 1/4]$

A quadratic algorithm:

$$F\left(\begin{matrix} \frac{1}{4}, \frac{3}{4} \\ 1 \end{matrix} \middle| z\right) \quad = \quad 1/M\left(1, \sqrt{1-z}\right)^{1/2} \quad \text{where} \tag{31.4-16a}$$

$$M(a,b) \quad := \quad \left[(a + 3b)/4, \sqrt{b\,(a+b)/2}\right] \tag{31.4-16b}$$

We further have (note the swapped arguments in the mean)

$$F\left(\begin{matrix} \frac{1}{4}, \frac{1}{4} \\ 1 \end{matrix} \middle| z\right) \quad = \quad 1/M\left(\sqrt{1-z}, 1\right)^{1/2} = \sqrt{1-z}\, F\left(\begin{matrix} \frac{3}{4}, \frac{3}{4} \\ 1 \end{matrix} \middle| z\right) \tag{31.4-17}$$

Now set $A_k := \sqrt{(a_k + b_k)/2}$ and $B_k := \sqrt{b_k}$, then

$$A_{k+1} \quad = \quad \frac{1}{2}\,(A_k + B_k) \tag{31.4-18a}$$

$$B_{k+1} \quad = \quad \sqrt{A_k\,B_k} \tag{31.4-18b}$$

This is the iteration of the classical AGM:

$$M(a,b)^{1/2} \quad = \quad \text{AGM}\left(\sqrt{\frac{a+b}{2}}, \sqrt{b}\right) \tag{31.4-19}$$

Equivalently, we have

$$F\left(\begin{matrix} \frac{1}{4}, \frac{3}{4} \\ 1 \end{matrix} \middle| z\right) \quad = \quad 1/\text{AGM}\left(\sqrt{\frac{1 + \sqrt{1-z}}{2}}, \sqrt[4]{1-z}\right) \tag{31.4-20a}$$

$$F\left(\begin{matrix} \frac{1}{4}, \frac{1}{4} \\ 1 \end{matrix} \middle| z\right) \quad = \quad 1/\text{AGM}\left(\sqrt{\frac{1 + \sqrt{1-z}}{2}}, 1\right) \tag{31.4-20b}$$

Compare to the hypergeometric transformation

$$F\left(\begin{matrix} \frac{1}{4}, \frac{3}{4} \\ 1 \end{matrix} \middle| z'\right) \quad = \quad \sqrt{1 + 3z}\, F\left(\begin{matrix} \frac{1}{4}, \frac{3}{4} \\ 1 \end{matrix} \middle| z^2\right) \tag{31.4-21a}$$

where

$$z \quad = \quad \frac{1 - (1 - z')^{1/2}}{1 + 3\,(1 - z')^{1/2}} \tag{31.4-21b}$$

$$z' \quad = \quad 1 - \left(\frac{1-z}{1+3z}\right)^2 \tag{31.4-21c}$$

It is the special case $d = 1/4$ of the transformation

$$F\left(\begin{matrix} d,\, d+\frac{1}{2} \\ \frac{4d+2}{3} \end{matrix} \middle| z'\right) \;=\; (1+3z)^{2d}\, F\left(\begin{matrix} d,\, d+\frac{1}{2} \\ \frac{4d+5}{6} \end{matrix} \middle| z^2\right) \tag{31.4-22}$$

Various such transformations and their generalizations are given in [152].

31.4.4 Algorithm for $F\left(\begin{matrix} 1/6,\, 1/3 \\ 1 \end{matrix} \middle| z\right)$ $[1/4 \pm 1/12]$

A quadratic algorithm is

$$F\left(\begin{matrix} \frac{1}{6},\, \frac{1}{3} \\ 1 \end{matrix} \middle| z\right) \;=\; 1/M\,(1,\, W)^{1/2} \quad \text{where} \tag{31.4-23a}$$

$$M\,(a,b) \;:=\; \left[(a+3b)/4,\, \left(\sqrt{ab}+b\right)/2\right] \quad \text{and} \tag{31.4-23b}$$

$$W \;:=\; \frac{1+R+R^2}{3\,R}, \quad R \;:=\; \left[2\left(z^2-z\right)^{1/2} - 2z + 1\right]^{1/3} \tag{31.4-23c}$$

It is given [69, p.515] as

$$\left[F\left(\begin{matrix} \frac{1}{6},\, \frac{1}{3} \\ 1 \end{matrix} \middle| 27\,x^2\,(1-x)/4\right)\right]^2 \;=\; 1/M\,(1,\, x) \tag{31.4-24}$$

Note that R in general has a nonzero imaginary part, but W is real for real z.

31.4.5 Algorithm for $F\left(\begin{matrix} 1/12,\, 5/12 \\ 1 \end{matrix} \middle| z\right)$ $[1/4 \pm 1/6]$

The following algorithm has quadratic convergence, W is defined by relation 31.4-23c:

$$F\left(\begin{matrix} \frac{1}{12},\, \frac{5}{12} \\ 1 \end{matrix} \middle| z\right) \;=\; 1/M\,(1,\, W)^{1/4} \quad \text{where} \tag{31.4-25a}$$

$$M\,(a,b) \;:=\; \left[(a+15b)/16,\, \left(\sqrt{b\,(a+3b)/4}+b\right)/2\right] \tag{31.4-25b}$$

The next relation is the special case $a = 1/6$ of relation 36.2-20e on page 691:

$$F\left(\begin{matrix} \frac{1}{6},\, \frac{1}{6} \\ 1 \end{matrix} \middle| z\right) \;=\; (1-z)^{-1/6}\, F\left(\begin{matrix} \frac{1}{12},\, \frac{5}{12} \\ 1 \end{matrix} \middle| \frac{-4z}{(1-z)^2}\right) \tag{31.4-26}$$

The following relations are given in [241, p.17]:

$$F\left(\begin{matrix} \frac{1}{4},\, \frac{1}{4} \\ 1 \end{matrix} \middle| -\frac{z}{64}\right) \;=\; \left[\frac{1}{16^3}\,(z+16)^3\right]^{-1/12} F\left(\begin{matrix} \frac{1}{12},\, \frac{5}{12} \\ 1 \end{matrix} \middle| \frac{1728\,z}{(z+16)^3}\right) \tag{31.4-27a}$$

$$F\left(\begin{matrix} \frac{1}{3},\, \frac{1}{3} \\ 1 \end{matrix} \middle| -\frac{z}{27}\right) \;=\; \left[\frac{1}{3^6}\,(z+3)^3\,(z+27)\right]^{-1/12} F\left(\begin{matrix} \frac{1}{12},\, \frac{5}{12} \\ 1 \end{matrix} \middle| \frac{1728\,z}{(z+3)^3\,(z+27)}\right) \tag{31.4-27b}$$

$$F\left(\begin{matrix} \frac{1}{2},\, \frac{1}{2} \\ 1 \end{matrix} \middle| -\frac{z}{16}\right) \;=\; \left[\frac{1}{16^3}\,(z^2+16z+16)^3\right]^{-1/12} F\left(\begin{matrix} \frac{1}{12},\, \frac{5}{12} \\ 1 \end{matrix} \middle| \frac{1728\,z\,(z+16)}{(z^2+16z+16)^3}\right) \tag{31.4-27c}$$

We finally give a curious transformation which follows from [242] (entry $N = 5$ of table 12 on p.32, together with entry $N = 2$, $M = 5$ of table 17 on p.43):

$$M_L^{1/4}\, F\left(\begin{matrix} \frac{1}{12},\, \frac{5}{12} \\ 1 \end{matrix} \middle| A_L\right) \;=\; 2\,M_R^{1/4}\, F\left(\begin{matrix} \frac{1}{12},\, \frac{5}{12} \\ 1 \end{matrix} \middle| A_R\right) \quad \text{where} \tag{31.4-28a}$$

$$M_L \;=\; z^6 - 4\,z^5 + 256\,z + 256, \qquad M_R \;=\; z^6 - 4\,z^5 + 16\,z + 16 \tag{31.4-28b}$$

$$A_L \;=\; 1728\,\frac{(z-4)\,z^5\,(z+1)^2}{M_R^3}, \qquad A_R \;=\; 1728\,\frac{(z-4)^2\,z^{10}\,(z+1)}{M_L^3} \tag{31.4-28c}$$

31.5 Computation of π

We give various iterations for computing π with super-linear convergence. The number of full precision multiplications (FPM) is an indication of the efficiency of the algorithm. The approximate number of FPMs with a computation of π to 4 million decimal digits (using radix $10,000$ and 1 million LIMBs) is indicated as, for example #FPM=123.4.

31.5.1 Super-linear iterations for π

AGM implemented in [hfloat: src/pi/piagm.cc], #FPM=98.4:

$$a_0 = 1, \qquad b_0 = \frac{1}{\sqrt{2}} \tag{31.5-1a}$$

$$a_{k+1} = \frac{a_k + b_k}{2} \tag{31.5-1b}$$

$$b_{k+1} = \sqrt{a_k b_k} \tag{31.5-1c}$$

$$p_n = \frac{2 a_{n+1}^2}{1 - \sum_{k=0}^n 2^k c_k^2} \quad \to \pi \tag{31.5-1d}$$

$$\pi - p_n = \frac{\pi^2 2^{n+4} e^{-\pi 2^{n+1}}}{\mathrm{AGM}^2(a_0, b_0)} \tag{31.5-1e}$$

Convergence is second order. Computing π based on the fourth order AGM (relations 31.1-6a... 31.1-6d on page 600) is possible by setting the second argument of the routine (#FPM=149.3 for the quartic variant). Schönhage's variant of the AGM computation (relations 31.1-5a... 31.1-5j on page 600) is implemented in [hfloat: src/pi/piagmsch.cc] (#FPM=78.424).

The AGM method goes back to Gauss, a facsimile of the entry in his 1809 handbook 6 is given in [19, p.101]. The entry states that

$$\pi = \frac{\mathrm{AGM}(1, k)\, \mathrm{AGM}(1, k')}{1 - \sum_{k=0}^\infty 2^{k-1}(c_k^2 + c_k'^2)} \tag{31.5-2}$$

where $k' = b_0/a_0$ and $k = \sqrt{1 - b_0^2/a_0^2} = c_0/a_0$. For $k = k' = 1/\sqrt{2}$ one obtains relation 31.5-1d. The formula appeared also 1924 in [206, p.39]. The algorithm was rediscovered 1976 independently by Brent [75] (reprinted in [45, p.424]) and Salamin [294] (reprinted in [45, p.418]).

AGM variant given in [64], [hfloat: src/pi/piagm3.cc], #FPM=99.5 (#FPM=155.3 for the quartic variant):

$$a_0 = 1, \qquad b_0 = \frac{\sqrt{6} + \sqrt{2}}{4} \tag{31.5-3a}$$

$$p_n = \frac{2 a_{n+1}^2}{\sqrt{3}\,(1 - \sum_{k=0}^n 2^k c_k^2) - 1} \quad \to \pi \tag{31.5-3b}$$

$$\pi - p_n < \frac{\sqrt{3}\,\pi^2 2^{n+4} e^{-\sqrt{3}\,\pi 2^{n+1}}}{\mathrm{AGM}^2(a_0, b_0)} \tag{31.5-3c}$$

AGM variant given in [64], [hfloat: src/pi/piagm3.cc], #FPM=108.2 (#FPM=169.5 for the quartic variant):

$$a_0 = 1, \qquad b_0 = \frac{\sqrt{6} - \sqrt{2}}{4} \tag{31.5-4a}$$

$$p_n = \frac{6 a_{n+1}^2}{\sqrt{3}\,(1 - \sum_{k=0}^n 2^k c_k^2) + 1} \quad \to \pi \tag{31.5-4b}$$

$$\pi - p_n < \frac{\frac{1}{\sqrt{3}}\pi^2 2^{n+4} e^{-\frac{1}{\sqrt{3}}\pi 2^{n+1}}}{\mathrm{AGM}(a_0, b_0)^2} \tag{31.5-4c}$$

Second order iteration from [66, p.170], [hfloat: src/pi/pi2nd.cc], #FPM=255.7:

$$y_0 = \frac{1}{\sqrt{2}}, \qquad a_0 = \frac{1}{2} \tag{31.5-5a}$$

$$y_{k+1} = \frac{1 - (1 - y_k^2)^{1/2}}{1 + (1 - y_k^2)^{1/2}} \quad \to 0+ \tag{31.5-5b}$$

$$= \frac{(1 - y_k^2)^{-1/2} - 1}{(1 - y_k^2)^{-1/2} + 1} \tag{31.5-5c}$$

$$a_{k+1} = a_k (1 + y_{k+1})^2 - 2^{k+1} y_{k+1} \quad \to \frac{1}{\pi} \tag{31.5-5d}$$

$$a_k - \pi^{-1} \leq 16 \cdot 2^{k+1} e^{-2^{k+1} \pi} \tag{31.5-5e}$$

Relation 31.5-5c shows how to save 1 multiplication per step (see section 29.1 on page 567). A simple proof of this iteration is given in [173].

Borwein's quartic (fourth order) iteration from [66, p.170], variant $r = 4$, implemented in [hfloat: src/pi/pi4th.cc], #FPM=170.5:

$$y_0 = \sqrt{2} - 1, \qquad a_0 = 6 - 4\sqrt{2} \tag{31.5-6a}$$

$$y_{k+1} = \frac{1 - (1 - y_k^4)^{1/4}}{1 + (1 - y_k^4)^{1/4}} \quad \to 0+ \tag{31.5-6b}$$

$$= \frac{(1 - y_k^4)^{-1/4} - 1}{(1 - y_k^4)^{-1/4} + 1} \tag{31.5-6c}$$

$$a_{k+1} = a_k (1 + y_{k+1})^4 - 2^{2k+3} y_{k+1} (1 + y_{k+1} + y_{k+1}^2) \quad \to \frac{1}{\pi} \tag{31.5-6d}$$

$$= a_k ((1 + y_{k+1})^2)^2 - 2^{2k+3} y_{k+1} ((1 + y_{k+1})^2 - y_{k+1}) \tag{31.5-6e}$$

$$0 < a_k - \pi^{-1} \leq 16 \cdot 4^n 2 e^{-4^n 2 \pi} \tag{31.5-6f}$$

Identities 31.5-6c and 31.5-6e show how to save operations.

Borwein's quartic (fourth order) iteration, variant $r = 16$, implemented in [hfloat: src/pi/pi4th.cc], #FPM=164.4:

$$y_0 = \frac{1 - 2^{-1/4}}{1 + 2^{-1/4}}, \qquad a_0 = \frac{8/\sqrt{2} - 2}{(2^{-1/4} + 1)^4} \tag{31.5-7a}$$

$$y_{k+1} = \frac{(1 - y_k^4)^{-1/4} - 1}{(1 - y_k^4)^{-1/4} + 1} \quad \to 0+ \tag{31.5-7b}$$

$$a_{k+1} = a_k (1 + y_{k+1})^4 - 2^{2k+4} y_{k+1} (1 + y_{k+1} + y_{k+1}^2) \quad \to \frac{1}{\pi} \tag{31.5-7c}$$

$$0 < a_k - \pi^{-1} \leq 16 \cdot 4^n 4 e^{-4^n 4 \pi} \tag{31.5-7d}$$

The operation count is unchanged, but this variant gives approximately twice as much precision after the same number of steps. The general form of the quartic iterations (relations 31.5-6a..., and 31.5-7a...) is given in [66, pp.170ff]:

$$y_0 = \sqrt{\lambda^*(r)}, \qquad a_0 = \alpha(r) \tag{31.5-8a}$$

$$y_{k+1} = \frac{(1 - y_k^4)^{-1/4} - 1}{(1 - y_k^4)^{-1/4} + 1} \quad \to 0+ \tag{31.5-8b}$$

$$a_{k+1} = a_k (1 + y_{k+1})^4 - 2^{2k+2} \sqrt{r} \, y_k (1 + y_{k+1} + y_{k+1}^2) \quad \to \frac{1}{\pi} \tag{31.5-8c}$$

$$0 < a_k - \pi^{-1} \leq 16 \cdot 4^n \sqrt{r} \, e^{-4^n \sqrt{r} \pi} \tag{31.5-8d}$$

Derived AGM iteration (second order, from [66, pp.46ff]), implemented in [hfloat: src/pi/pideriv.cc], #FPM=276.2:

$$x_0 = \sqrt{2}, \qquad p_0 = 2 + \sqrt{2}, \qquad y_1 = 2^{1/4} \tag{31.5-9a}$$

$$x_{k+1} = \frac{1}{2}\left(\sqrt{x_k} + \frac{1}{\sqrt{x_k}}\right) \quad (k \geq 0) \quad \to 1+ \tag{31.5-9b}$$

$$y_{k+1} = \frac{y_k \sqrt{x_k} + \dfrac{1}{\sqrt{x_k}}}{y_k + 1} \quad (k \geq 1) \quad \to 1+ \tag{31.5-9c}$$

$$p_{k+1} = p_k \frac{x_k + 1}{y_k + 1} \quad (k \geq 1) \quad \to \pi+ \tag{31.5-9d}$$

$$p_k - \pi < 10^{-2^{k+1}} \tag{31.5-9e}$$

Cubic AGM iteration (third order) from [70], implemented in [hfloat: src/pi/picubagm.cc], #FPM=182.7:

$$a_0 = 1, \qquad b_0 = \frac{\sqrt{3} - 1}{2} \tag{31.5-10a}$$

$$a_{n+1} = \frac{a_n + 2\,b_n}{3} \tag{31.5-10b}$$

$$b_{n+1} = \sqrt[3]{\frac{b_n\,(a_n^2 + a_n\,b_n + b_n^2)}{3}} \tag{31.5-10c}$$

$$p_n = \frac{3\,a_n^2}{1 - \sum_{k=0}^{n} 3^k\,(a_k^2 - a_{k+1}^2)} \to \pi \tag{31.5-10d}$$

Quintic (fifth order) iteration from [66, p.310], [hfloat: src/pi/pi5th.cc], #FPM=353.2:

$$s_0 = 5(\sqrt{5} - 2), \qquad a_0 = \frac{1}{2} \tag{31.5-11a}$$

$$x = \frac{5}{s_n} - 1 \quad \to 4 \tag{31.5-11b}$$

$$y = (x - 1)^2 + 7 \quad \to 16 \tag{31.5-11c}$$

$$z = \left(\frac{x}{2}\left(y + \sqrt{y^2 - 4x^3}\right)\right)^{1/5} \quad \to 2 \tag{31.5-11d}$$

$$s_{n+1} = \frac{25}{s_n(z + x/z + 1)^2} \quad \to 1 \tag{31.5-11e}$$

$$a_{n+1} = s_n^2 a_n - 5^n\left(\frac{s_n^2 - 5}{2} + \sqrt{s_n\,(s_n^2 - 2s_n + 5)}\right) \quad \to \frac{1}{\pi} \tag{31.5-11f}$$

$$a_n - \frac{1}{\pi} < 16 \cdot 5^n\,e^{-\pi\,5^n} \tag{31.5-11g}$$

Cubic (third order) iteration from [30], implemented in [hfloat: src/pi/pi3rd.cc], #FPM=200.3:

$$a_0 = \frac{1}{3}, \qquad s_0 = \frac{\sqrt{3} - 1}{2} \tag{31.5-12a}$$

$$r_{k+1} = \frac{3}{1 + 2\,(1 - s_k^3)^{1/3}} \tag{31.5-12b}$$

$$s_{k+1} = \frac{r_{k+1} - 1}{2} \tag{31.5-12c}$$

$$a_{k+1} = r_{k+1}^2\,a_k - 3^k\,(r_{k+1}^2 - 1) \quad \to \frac{1}{\pi} \tag{31.5-12d}$$

Nonic (9th order) iteration from [30], implemented in [hfloat: src/pi/pi9th.cc], #FPM=273.7:

$$a_0 = \frac{1}{3}, \qquad r_0 = \frac{\sqrt{3}-1}{2}, \qquad s_0 = (1 - r_0^3)^{1/3} \tag{31.5-13a}$$

$$t = 1 + 2\,r_k \tag{31.5-13b}$$

$$u = \left(9\,r_k\left(1 + r_k + r_k^2\right)\right)^{1/3} \tag{31.5-13c}$$

$$v = t^2 + t\,u + u^2 \tag{31.5-13d}$$

$$m = \frac{27\left(1 + s_k + s_k^2\right)}{v} \tag{31.5-13e}$$

$$a_{k+1} = m\,a_k + 3^{2\,k-1}\left(1 - m\right) \;\rightarrow\; \frac{1}{\pi} \tag{31.5-13f}$$

$$s_{k+1} = \frac{(1 - r_k)^3}{(t + 2\,u)\,v} \tag{31.5-13g}$$

$$r_{k+1} = (1 - s_k^3)^{1/3} \tag{31.5-13h}$$

31.5.2　Measured timings and operation counts

```
     #FPM    - order -  routine in hfloat             -    time
    -----------------------------------------------------------------
    78.424   -   2   -  pi_agm_sch()                  -     76 sec
    98.424   -   2   -  pi_agm()                      -     93 sec
    99.510   -   2   -  pi_agm3(fast variant)         -     94 sec
   108.241   -   2   -  pi_agm3(slow variant)         -    103 sec
   149.324   -   4   -  pi_agm(quartic)               -    139 sec
   155.265   -   4   -  pi_agm3(quartic, fast variant) -   145 sec
   164.359   -   4   -  pi_4th_order(r=16 variant)    -    154 sec
   169.544   -   4   -  pi_agm3(quartic, slow variant) -   159 sec
   170.519   -   4   -  pi_4th_order(r=4 variant)     -    160 sec
   182.710   -   3   -  pi_cubic_agm()                -    173 sec
   200.261   -   3   -  pi_3rd_order()                -    189 sec
   255.699   -   2   -  pi_2nd_order()                -    240 sec
   273.763   -   9   -  pi_9th_order()                -    256 sec
   276.221   -   2   -  pi_derived_agm()              -    259 sec
   353.202   -   5   -  pi_5th_order()                -    329 sec
```

Figure 31.5-A: Measured operations counts and timings for various iterations for the computation of π to 4 million decimal digits.

The operation counts and timings for the algorithms given so far when computing π to 4 million decimal digits (using 1 million LIMBs and radix 10,000) are shown in figure 31.5-A. In view of these figures it seems surprising that the quartic algorithms pi_4th_order() and the quartic AGM pi_agm(quartic) are usually considered close competitors to the second order AGM schemes.

Apart from the operation count the number of variables used has to be taken into account. The algorithms using more variables (like pi_5th_order()) cannot be used to compute as many digits as those using only a few (notably the AGM-schemes) given a fixed amount of RAM. Higher order algorithms tend to require more variables.

A further disadvantage of the algorithms of higher order is the more discontinuous growth of the work: if just a few more digits are to be computed than are available after step k, then an additional step is required. Consider an extreme case where an algorithm T of order $1,000$ would compute 1 million digits after the second step, at a slightly lower cost than the most effective competitor. Then algorithm T would likely be the 'best' one only for small ranges in the number of digits around the values 10^3, 10^6, 10^9, $\ldots$.

Finally, it is much easier to find special arithmetical optimizations for the 'simple' (low order) algorithms, Schönhage's AGM variant being the prime example.

31.5.3 More iterations for π

The following iterations are not implemented in hfloat.

Second order algorithm from [71]:

$$\alpha_0 \;=\; 1/3, \qquad m_0 \;=\; 2 \tag{31.5-14a}$$

$$m_{n+1} \;=\; \frac{4}{1 + \sqrt{(4 - m_n)(2 + m_n)}} \tag{31.5-14b}$$

$$\alpha_{n+1} \;=\; m_n\,\alpha_n + \frac{2^n}{3}(1 - m_n) \quad \to \frac{1}{\pi} \tag{31.5-14c}$$

Implicit second order algorithm from [71] (also in [68, p.700]):

$$\alpha_0 \;=\; 1/3, \qquad s_1 \;=\; 1/3 \tag{31.5-15a}$$

$$(s_n)^2 + (s_n^*)^2 \;=\; 1 \tag{31.5-15b}$$

$$(1 + 3\,s_{n+1})(1 + 3\,s_n^*) \;=\; 4 \tag{31.5-15c}$$

$$\alpha_{n+1} \;=\; (1 + 3\,s_{n+1})\,\alpha_n - 2^n\,s_{n+1} \quad \to \frac{1}{\pi} \tag{31.5-15d}$$

It is easy to turn this algorithm into an explicit form as with the next algorithm. However, there exist iterations that cannot be turned into explicit forms.

Implicit fourth order algorithm from [71] (also in [68, p.700]):

$$\alpha_0 \;=\; 1/3 \qquad s_1 \;=\; \sqrt{2} - 1 \tag{31.5-16a}$$

$$(s_n)^4 + (s_n^*)^4 \;=\; 1 \tag{31.5-16b}$$

$$(1 + 3\,s_{n+1})(1 + 3\,s_n^*) \;=\; 2 \tag{31.5-16c}$$

$$\alpha_{n+1} \;=\; (1 + s_{n+1})^4 \alpha_n + \frac{4^{n+1}}{3}\left[1 - (1 + s_{n+1})^4\right] \quad \to \frac{1}{\pi} \tag{31.5-16d}$$

Third order algorithm from [63]:

$$v_0 \;=\; 2^{-1/8}, \qquad v_1 \;=\; 2^{-7/8}\left((1 - 3^{1/2})\,2^{-1/2} + 3^{1/4}\right) \tag{31.5-17a}$$

$$w_0 \;=\; 1, \qquad \alpha_0 \;=\; 1, \qquad \beta_0 \;=\; 0 \tag{31.5-17b}$$

$$v_{n+1} \;=\; v_n^3 - \left\{v_n^6 + \left[4v_n^2(1 - v_n^8)\right]^{1/3}\right\}^{1/2} + v_{n-1} \tag{31.5-17c}$$

$$w_{n+1} \;=\; \frac{2v_n^3 + v_{n+1}\left(3v_{n+1}^2 v_n^2 - 1\right)}{2v_{n+1}^3 - v_n\left(3v_{n+1}^2 v_n^2 - 1\right)}\,w_n \tag{31.5-17d}$$

$$\alpha_{n+1} \;=\; \left(\frac{2v_{n+1}^3}{v_n} + 1\right)\alpha_n \tag{31.5-17e}$$

$$\beta_{n+1} \;=\; \left(\frac{2v_{n+1}^3}{v_n} + 1\right)\beta_n + (6w_{n+1}v_n - 2v_{n+1}w_n)\,\frac{v_{n+1}^2\alpha_n}{v_n^2} \tag{31.5-17f}$$

$$\pi_n \;=\; \frac{8 \cdot 2^{1/8}}{\alpha_n\,\beta_n} \quad \to \pi \tag{31.5-17g}$$

Combining two steps of the fourth order iteration leads to an algorithm of order 16, from [71, p.108]:

$$\alpha_0 = 1/3, \qquad s_1 = \sqrt{2} - 1 \tag{31.5-18a}$$

$$s_n^* = \left(1 - s_n^4\right)^{1/4} \tag{31.5-18b}$$

$$x_n = 1/\left(1 + s_n^*\right)^4 \tag{31.5-18c}$$

$$y_n = x_n \left(1 + s_n\right)^4 \tag{31.5-18d}$$

$$\alpha_n = 16\, y_n\, \alpha_{n-1} + \frac{4^{2n-1}}{3}\left[1 - 12\, x_n - 4\, y_n\right] \quad \to \frac{1}{\pi} \tag{31.5-18e}$$

$$t_n = 1 + s_n^* \tag{31.5-18f}$$

$$u_n = \left[8\, s_n^* \left(1 + s_n^{*\,2}\right)\right]^{1/4} \tag{31.5-18g}$$

$$s_{n+1} = \frac{(1 - s_n^*)^4}{(t + u)^2\,(t^2 + u^2)} \tag{31.5-18h}$$

Quadratic iteration by Christian Hoffmann, given in [184, p.5]:

$$a_0 = \sqrt{2}, \qquad b_0 = 0, \qquad p_0 = 2 + \sqrt{2} \tag{31.5-19a}$$

$$a_{n+1} = \frac{1}{2}\left(\sqrt{a_n} + 1/\sqrt{a_n}\right) \quad \to 1+ \tag{31.5-19b}$$

$$b_{n+1} = \sqrt{a_n}\,\frac{b_n + 1}{b_n + a_n} \quad \to 1- \tag{31.5-19c}$$

$$p_{n+1} = p_n\, b_{n+1}\,\frac{1 + a_{n+1}}{1 + b_{n+1}} \quad \to \pi \tag{31.5-19d}$$

Note that relation 31.5-19b deviates from the one given in the cited paper which seems to be incorrect. This is a variant of the iteration given as relations 31.5-9a... 31.5-9e on page 617. The values p_k are identical in both iterations.

Cubic iteration given in [65, p.125]:

$$s_0 = \sqrt{3 + 2\sqrt{3}}, \qquad a_0 = 1/2 \tag{31.5-20a}$$

$$m_n = 3/s_n \tag{31.5-20b}$$

$$a_{n+1} = \left[\left(s_n^2 - 1\right)^{1/3} + 2\right]^2 / s_n \tag{31.5-20c}$$

$$a_{n+1} = m_n^2\, a_n - 3^n\left(m_n^2 + 2m_n - 3\right)/2 \quad \to \frac{1}{\pi} \tag{31.5-20d}$$

The cited paper actually gives a more general form, here we take $N = 1$ for simplicity.

Cubic iteration given in [97, p.1506, it-1.2]:

$$t_0 = 1/3, \qquad s_0 = \left(\sqrt{3} - 1\right)/2 \tag{31.5-21a}$$

$$s_n = \frac{1 - \left(1 - s_{n-1}^3\right)^{1/3}}{1 + 2\left(1 - s_{n-1}^3\right)^{1/3}} \tag{31.5-21b}$$

$$= \frac{\left(1 - s_{n-1}^3\right)^{-1/3} - 1}{\left(1 - s_{n-1}^3\right)^{-1/3} + 2} \tag{31.5-21c}$$

$$t_n = (1 + 2s_n)^2\, t_{n-1} - 3^{n-1}\left((1 + 2s_n)^2 - 1\right) \quad \to \frac{1}{\pi} \tag{31.5-21d}$$

Note the corrected denominator in relation 31.5-21b (exponent of s_{n-1} is wrongly given as 2).

Quadratic iteration given in [97, p.1507, it-1.3]:

$$k_0 = 0, \qquad s_0 = 1/\sqrt{2} \tag{31.5-22a}$$

$$s_n = \frac{1 - \sqrt{1 - s_{n-1}^2}}{1 + \sqrt{1 - s_{n-1}^2}} \tag{31.5-22b}$$

$$k_n = (1 + s_n)^2 \, k_{n-1} + 2^n \, (1 - s_n) \, s_n \quad \rightarrow \frac{1}{\pi} \tag{31.5-22c}$$

Cubic iteration given in [97, p.1507, it-1.4]:

$$k_0 = 0, \qquad s_0 = 1/\sqrt[3]{2} \tag{31.5-23a}$$

$$s_n = \frac{1 - \sqrt[3]{1 - s_{n-1}^3}}{1 + 2\sqrt[3]{1 - s_{n-1}^3}} \tag{31.5-23b}$$

$$k_n = (1 + 2\,s_n)^2 \, k_{n-1} + 8 \cdot 3^{n-2} \sqrt{3}\, s_n \frac{1 - s_n^3}{1 + 2\,s_n} \quad \rightarrow \frac{1}{\pi} \tag{31.5-23c}$$

Quadratic iteration given in [97, p.1508, it-1.5]:

$$k_0 = 0, \qquad y_0 = 8/9 \tag{31.5-24a}$$

$$y_n = 2\frac{6\,y_{n-1}^2 - 5\,y_{n-1} + \sqrt{y_{n-1}(4 - y_{n-1})}}{9\,y_{n-1}^2 - 6\,y_{n-1} + 1} \tag{31.5-24b}$$

$$k_n = 2^n \sqrt{3} \frac{y_{n-1}(1 - y_{n-1})}{\sqrt{4 - 3\,y_{n-1}}} + (4 - 3\,y_{n-1})\,k_{n-1} \quad \rightarrow \frac{1}{\pi} \tag{31.5-24c}$$

Quadratic iteration given in [97, p.1508, it-1.6]:

$$k_0 = 0, \qquad y_0 = 4/5 \tag{31.5-25a}$$

$$y_n = \frac{2\,y_{n-1}^2 - y_{n-1} + \sqrt{4\,y_{n-1} - 3\,y_{n-1}^2}}{1 + y_{n-1}^2} \tag{31.5-25b}$$

$$Q_n = \sqrt{(y_{n-1} + 1)(4 - 3\,y_{n-1})(y_{n-1}^2 - 3\,y_{n-1} + 4)} \tag{31.5-25c}$$

$$k_n = \frac{2^n}{\sqrt{7}} \frac{y_{n-1}(1 - y_{n-1})}{2 - y_{n-1}} Q_n + (2 - y_{n-1})^2\,k_{n-1} \quad \rightarrow \frac{1}{\pi} \tag{31.5-25d}$$

Quadratic iteration (as product, two forms) given in [67, p.324]:

$$x_1 = \frac{2}{9}\left(\sqrt{6} + 2\right), \qquad y_1 = \frac{1}{6}\left(\sqrt{6} + 4\right) \tag{31.5-26a}$$

$$x_{n+1} = \frac{2\left(\sqrt{x_n} + x_n\right)}{1 + 3\,x_n} \tag{31.5-26b}$$

$$y_{n+1} = \frac{2y_n + y_n/\sqrt{x_n} + \sqrt{x_n}}{1 + 3\,y_n} \tag{31.5-26c}$$

$$\pi = \frac{27}{8} \prod_{n=1}^{\infty} \frac{(1 + 3\,x_n)^2}{(1 + 3\,y_n)/4} \tag{31.5-26d}$$

$$\pi = \frac{5 + 2\sqrt{6}}{3} \prod_{n=1}^{\infty} \frac{(1 + 1/\sqrt{x_n})^2}{1 + 3\,y_n} \tag{31.5-26e}$$

The definitive source for iterations to compute π and the underlying mathematics is [66].

Chapter 32

Logarithm and exponential function

We describe algorithms for the computation of the exponential function (and hyperbolic cosine) and the logarithm (and inverse tangent). Constructions of super-linear iterations to compute the functions from their inverses are given. We also present argument reduction schemes and methods for the fast computation of the exponential and logarithm of power series.

32.1 Logarithm

32.1.1 AGM-based computation

The (natural) logarithm can be computed using the relation (see [66, p.221])

$$\left| \log(d) - R'(10^{-n}) + R'(10^{-n} d) \right| \;\leq\; \frac{n}{10^{2(n-1)}} \tag{32.1-1a}$$

$$\log(d) \;\approx\; R'(10^{-n}) - R'(10^{-n} d) \tag{32.1-1b}$$

which holds for $n \geq 3$ and $d \in]\frac{1}{2}, 1[$. The first term on the right side is constant and can be saved for subsequent computations of the logarithm. We use the relation

$$\log(M\, r^X) \;=\; \log(M) + X \log(r) \tag{32.1-2}$$

where M is the mantissa, r the radix, and X the exponent of the floating-point representation. The value $\log(r)$ is computed only once. If M is not in the interval $[1/2,\, 3/2]$ an argument reduction is done via

$$\log(M) \;=\; \log\left(M\, s^f\right) - f \log(s) \tag{32.1-3}$$

Where $0 < M < 1$ for the mantissa M, $s = \sqrt{2}$, and $f \in \mathbb{Z}$ so that $M\, s^f \in [1/2, 3/2]$. The quantity $\log(s) = \log(\sqrt{2})$ can be precomputed directly via the AGM. A C++ implementation is given in [hfloat: src/tz/log.cc].

There is a nice way to compute the $\log(r)$, the logarithm of the radix, if the value of π has been precomputed. We need to compute $\Theta_3(q)$ and $\Theta_2(q)$ where $q = 1/r$ (see section 31.3 on page 604):

$$\Theta_3(q) \;=\; 1 + 2 \sum_{n=1}^{\infty} q^{n^2} \tag{32.1-4}$$

For the computation of $\Theta_2(q)$ we choose $q = 1/r^4 =: b^4$:

$$\Theta_2(q) \;=\; 0 + 2 \sum_{n=0}^{\infty} q^{(n+1/2)^2} \;=\; 2 \sum_{n=0}^{\infty} b^{4n^2+4n+1} \quad \text{where} \quad q = b^4 \tag{32.1-5a}$$

$$=\; 2\, b \sum_{n=0}^{\infty} q^{n^2+n} \;=\; 2\, b \left(1 + \sum_{n=1}^{\infty} q^{n^2+n} \right) \tag{32.1-5b}$$

J. Arndt, *Matters Computational: Ideas, Algorithms, Source Code,*
DOI 10.1007/978-3-642-14764-7_32, © Springer-Verlag Berlin Heidelberg 2011

Set $q = 1/r$, then relation 31.3-7 on page 605 becomes

$$\frac{\pi}{\log(1/q)} = \frac{\pi}{\log(r)} = 4 \, \text{AGM} \left(\Theta_3 \left(q^4 \right)^2, \Theta_2 \left(q^4 \right)^2 \right) \tag{32.1-6}$$

Functions to compute $\Theta_2(b^4)$, $\Theta_3(b^4)$ where b is the inverse fourth power of the used radix r and $\pi / \log(r)$ are given in [hfloat: src/tz/pilogq.cc].

32.1.2 Computation by inverting the exponential function

32.1.2.1 Iterations from the power series

With an efficient algorithm for the exponential function, we can compute the logarithm using

$$
\begin{align}
y &:= 1 - d\,e^{-x} \tag{32.1-7a} \\
\log(d) &= x + \log(1 - y) \tag{32.1-7b} \\
&= x + \log\left(1 - (1 - d\,e^{-x})\right) = x + \log\left(e^{-x}d\right) = x + (-x + \log(d)) \tag{32.1-7c}
\end{align}
$$

Expansion of $\log(1 - y)$ as power series in y yields

$$\log(d) = x + \log(1 - y) = x - \left(y + \frac{y^2}{2} + \frac{y^3}{3} + \frac{y^4}{4} + \cdots \right) \tag{32.1-8}$$

Truncation of the series before the n-th power of y gives an iteration of order n:

$$x_{k+1} = \Phi_n(x_k) := x - \left(y + \frac{y^2}{2} + \frac{y^3}{3} + \cdots + \frac{y^{n-1}}{n-1} \right) \tag{32.1-9}$$

32.1.2.2 Iterations from Padé approximants

$$
\begin{align}
1 &\mapsto P_{[1,0]} = \frac{z}{1} \\[4pt]
2 &\mapsto P_{[1,1]} = \frac{2z}{2+z} \\[4pt]
3 &\mapsto P_{[2,1]} = \frac{6z + z^2}{6 + 4z} \\[4pt]
4 &\mapsto P_{[2,2]} = \frac{6z + 3z^2}{6 + 6z + z^2} \\[4pt]
5 &\mapsto P_{[3,2]} = \frac{30z + 21z^2 + z^3}{30 + 36z + 9z^2} \\[4pt]
6 &\mapsto P_{[3,3]} = \frac{60z + 60z^2 + 11z^3}{60 + 90z + 36z^2 + 3z^3}
\end{align}
$$

Figure 32.1-A: Padé approximants for $\log(1 + z)$.

The Padé approximants $P_{[i,j]}(z)$ of $\log(1 - z)$ at $z = 0$ produce iterations of order $i + j + 1$. Compared to the power series based iteration one needs one additional long division but saves half of the exponentiations. This can be a substantial saving for high order iterations.

The approximants can be computed via the continued fraction expansion of $\log(1 + z)$:

$$\log(1 + z) = 0 + \cfrac{c_1 z}{1 + \cfrac{c_2 z}{1 + \cfrac{c_3 z}{1 + \cfrac{c_4 z}{1 + \cdots}}}} \tag{32.1-10}$$

where $c_1 = 1$ and

$$c_k = \frac{k}{4(k-1)} \quad \text{if } k \text{ even}, \qquad c_k = \frac{k-1}{4k} \quad \text{else} \tag{32.1-11}$$

Using recurrence relations 37.3-7a and 37.3-7b on page 719 with $a_0 = 0$, $a_k = 1$ and $b_k = c_k \cdot z$ we find what is shown in figure 32.1-A. The expressions are Padé approximants correct up to order k. For even k these are the diagonal approximants $[k/2, k/2]$ which satisfy the functional equation $\log(1/z) = -\log(z)$: $P(1/z - 1) = -P(z - 1)$. Further information like the error term of the diagonal approximants is given in [239].

The diagonal approximants can be computed by setting $P_0 = 0$, $Q_0 = 1$, $P_2 = z$, $Q_2 = 1 + z/2$, and computing, for $k = 4, 6, \ldots, 2n$,

$$P_k = A_k P_{k-2} + B_k P_{k-4} \tag{32.1-12a}$$

$$Q_k = A_k Q_{k-2} + B_k Q_{k-4} \tag{32.1-12b}$$

(these are relations 37.3-14a and 37.3-14b on page 722). The A_k and B_k are defined as

$$A_k = 1 + z/2 \tag{32.1-12c}$$

$$B_k = \frac{z^2}{16} \frac{(k-2)^2}{1 - (k-2)^2} \tag{32.1-12d}$$

Then P_{2n}/Q_{2n} is the Padé approximant $P_{[n,n]}$ of $\log(1+z)$ which is correct up to order $2n$. The following GP function implements the algorithm:

```
1    log_pade(n, z='z)=
2    { /* Return Pade approximant [n,n] of log(1+z) */
3        local(P0,Q0,P2,Q2,tp,tq, t);
4        if ( n<1, return(0) );
5        P0=0;  Q0=1;
6        P2=z;  Q2=1+z/2;
7        forstep (k=4, 2*n, 2,
8            Ak = 1+z/2;  \\ == +z*C(k-1)+z*C(k)+1;
9            t = (k-2)^2;
10           Bk = z^2/16*t/(1-t);  \\ == -z^2*C(k-1)*C(k-2);
11           tp = Ak*P2 + Bk*P0;
12           tq = Ak*Q2 + Bk*Q0;
13           P0=P2; P2=tp;
14           Q0=Q2; Q2=tq;
15       );
16       return( P2/Q2 );
17   }
```

32.1.2.3   Padé approximants for arctan ‡

A continued fraction for the inverse tangent is (given in [238, p.569])

$$\arctan(z) = z \cfrac{1}{1 + \cfrac{z^2/(1 \cdot 3)}{1 + \cfrac{2^2 z^2/(3 \cdot 5)}{1 + \cfrac{3^2 z^2/(5 \cdot 7)}{1 + \cdots}}}} \tag{32.1-13}$$

The Padé approximants P_k/Q_k for arctan are computed by setting $P_0 = 0$, $P_1 = z$, $Q_0 = 1$, $Q_1 = 1$, and the recurrences

$$P_{k+1} = P_k + P_{k-1} \frac{k^2 z^2}{4k^2 - 1} \tag{32.1-14a}$$

$$Q_{k+1} = Q_k + P_{k-1} \frac{k^2 z^2}{4k^2 - 1} \tag{32.1-14b}$$

The first few approximants are shown in figure 32.1-B.

$$2 \quad \mapsto \quad P_{[1,2]} \; = \; \frac{3\,x}{3+x^2}$$

$$3 \quad \mapsto \quad P_{[3,2]} \; = \; \frac{15\,x+4\,x^3}{15+9\,x^2}$$

$$4 \quad \mapsto \quad P_{[3,4]} \; = \; \frac{105\,x+55\,x^3}{105+90\,x^2+9\,x^4}$$

$$5 \quad \mapsto \quad P_{[5,4]} \; = \; \frac{945\,x+735\,x^3+64\,x^5}{945+1050\,x^2+225\,x^4}$$

$$6 \quad \mapsto \quad P_{[5,6]} \; = \; \frac{1155\,x+1190\,x^3+231\,x^5}{1155+1575\,x^2+525\,x^4+25\,x^6}$$

$$k \quad \mapsto \quad P_{[i,j]} \; = \; \arctan(z)+O(z^{2k+1})$$

Figure 32.1-B: Padé approximants for $\arctan(z)$.

32.1.3   Argument reduction for the logarithm

If the logarithm is computed for moderate precision (up to several hundred decimal digits or so), the following scheme can beat the AGM algorithm. Use the functional equation for the logarithm

$$\log(z^a) \;=\; a\,\log(z) \tag{32.1-15}$$

to reduce the argument by setting $a=1/N$. Now with N big enough $z^{1/N}$ will be close to 1: $r := z^{1/N} = 1+e$ where e is small. Then a few terms of the power series of $\log(1+e)=e-e^2/2+e^3/3\pm\ldots$ suffice to compute the logarithm. Compute the logarithm of z as follows

1. Set $r = z^{1/N}$ and $e = r-1$.

2. Compute $l := \log(1+e)$ to the desired precision using the power series.

3. Return $L := N\,l$.

We can also use a Padé approximant in step 2. With argument $z = 2.0$, $N = 2^{32}$, and four terms of the series we obtain:

```
? z=2.0;    \\ argument for log()
? n=32; N=2^n;
? r=z^(1/N)  \\ compute by 32 sqrt extractions
  1.0000000001613859042096597612039766311019850327446120l6
? e=r-1; \\ small
  1.6138590420965976120397663110198503274461201650532657B5 E-10
? l=e-1/2*e^2+1/3*e^3-1/4*e^4  \\ approx log(1+e)
  1.6138590419663705616659301367080224865940541336931405S0 E-10
? L=N*l    \\ final result
  0.69314718055994530941723212145817656807540609322656503S5
? log(z)   \\ check with built-in log
  0.69314718055994530941723212145817656807550013436025525A1
```

We may also use the following reduction for $L(z) := \log(1+z)$, which avoids loss of precision for small values of z:

$$L(z) \;=\; 2\,L\!\left(\frac{z}{1+\sqrt{1+z}}\right) \tag{32.1-16}$$

32.1.4   Argument reduction for arctan

We use the equation

$$\arctan(z) \;=\; 2\,\arctan\!\left(\frac{z}{1+\sqrt{1+z^2}}\right) \tag{32.1-17}$$

Compute the inverse tangent of z as follows

1. set $r := z$

2. repeat n times: $r = r/(1 + \sqrt{1 + r^2})$ (for n big enough)

3. compute $a := \arctan(r)$ to the desired precision using the power series

4. return $A := 2^n a$

We compute $\arctan(1.0)$ using $n = 16$ and four terms of the series:

```
? z=1.0;
? n=16;
? r=z;for(k=1,n,r=r/(1+sqrt(1+r^2)));r
  0.000011984224905930303478511634794650661319585128744025261 89
? a=r-1/3*r^3+1/5*r^5-1/7*r^7
  0.00001198422490535657210717255929290581849745567656967660263
? A=2^n*a
  0.78539816339744830961566084581987572104925521967 03258299
? atan(z)   \\ check with built-in atan
  0.78539816339744830961566084581987572104929232349843 7764552
```

All divisions in the reduction phase can be saved by using

$$\arctan(1/z) \quad = \quad 2\arctan\left(\frac{1}{1 + \sqrt{1 + z^2}}\right) \tag{32.1-18}$$

The inverse sine and cosine can be computed as

$$\arcsin(z) \quad = \quad \arctan\left(\frac{z}{\sqrt{1 - z^2}}\right) \tag{32.1-19a}$$

$$\arccos(z) \quad = \quad \arctan\left(\frac{\sqrt{1 - z^2}}{z}\right) \tag{32.1-19b}$$

32.1.5   Curious series for the logarithm ‡

We note two relations resembling the well-known series

$$\frac{1}{2}\log\left(\frac{1+x}{1-x}\right) \quad = \quad x + \frac{1}{3}x^3 + \frac{1}{5}x^5 + \ldots + \frac{1}{2k+1}x^{2k+1} + \ldots \tag{32.1-20}$$

The first is

$$\frac{1}{6}\log\left(\frac{1 + 3x + 3x^2}{1 - 3x + 3x^2}\right) \quad = \quad x - \frac{3^2}{5}x^5 - \frac{3^3}{7}x^7 + \frac{3^5}{11}x^{11} + \frac{3^6}{13}x^{13} \pm \ldots = \tag{32.1-21a}$$

$$= \quad \sum_{k=0}^{\infty}\left(+\frac{3^{6k+0}}{12k+1}x^{12k+1} - \frac{3^{6k+2}}{12k+5}x^{12k+5} - \frac{3^{6k+3}}{12k+7}x^{12k+7} + \frac{3^{6k+5}}{12k+11}x^{12k+11}\right) \tag{32.1-21b}$$

The second, given in [31], is

$$\frac{1}{3}\log\left(\frac{1 + x + x^2}{1 - 2x + x^2}\right) \quad = \quad x + \frac{x^2}{2} + \frac{x^4}{4} + \frac{x^5}{5} + \ldots = \sum_{k=0}^{\infty}\left(+\frac{x^{3k+1}}{3k+1} + \frac{x^{3k+2}}{3k+2}\right) \tag{32.1-22}$$

Relation 32.1-21a can be brought into a similar form:

$$\frac{1}{2\sqrt{3}}\log\left(\frac{1 + \sqrt{3}\,x + x^2}{1 - \sqrt{3}\,x + x^2}\right) \quad = \quad x - \frac{x^5}{5} - \frac{x^7}{7} + \frac{x^{11}}{11} + \frac{x^{13}}{13} \pm \ldots = \tag{32.1-23a}$$

$$= \quad \sum_{k=0}^{\infty}\left(+\frac{x^{12k+1}}{12k+1} - \frac{x^{12k+5}}{12k+5} - \frac{x^{12k+7}}{12k+7} + \frac{x^{12k+11}}{12k+11}\right) \tag{32.1-23b}$$

Let F_k be the Fibonacci numbers and P_k the Pell numbers (respectively entries A000045 and A000129 in [312]), then

$$\frac{1}{5} \log \left(\frac{1 + 2x + x^2}{1 - 3x + x^2} \right) = \sum_{k=1}^{\infty} \frac{F_k^2}{k} x^k = x + \frac{1^2}{2} x^2 + \frac{2^2}{3} x^3 + \frac{3^2}{4} x^4 + \frac{5^2}{5} x^5 + \dots \quad (32.1\text{-}24a)$$

$$\frac{1}{8} \log \left(\frac{1 + 2x + x^2}{1 - 6x + x^2} \right) = \sum_{k=1}^{\infty} \frac{P_k^2}{k} x^k = x + \frac{1^2}{2} x^2 + \frac{2^2}{3} x^3 + \frac{5^2}{4} x^4 + \frac{12^2}{5} x^5 + \dots \quad (32.1\text{-}24b)$$

The relations are special cases of the following identity. Fix u and let $V_0 = 0$, $V_1 = 1$, and $V_k = u V_{k-1} + V_{k-2}$, set $a = u^2 + 4$, then

$$\frac{1}{a} \log \left(\frac{1 + 2x + x^2}{1 + (2 - a)x + x^2} \right) = \sum_{k=1}^{\infty} \frac{V_k^2}{k} x^k \quad (32.1\text{-}24c)$$

32.2 Exponential function

32.2.1 AGM-based computation of the exponential function

We use $q = \exp\left(-\pi \frac{K'}{K} \right)$ (relation 31.3-5 on page 605) and write

$$\frac{K'}{K} = \frac{\text{AGM}(1, k')}{\text{AGM}(1, k)} = \frac{\text{AGM}(1, b_0)}{\text{AGM}(1, b'_0)} \quad (32.2\text{-}1)$$

where $k' = b_0$ and $k = b'_0 = \sqrt{1 - b_0^2}$ and use [206, p.38]

$$\frac{\pi}{2} \frac{\text{AGM}(1, b_0)}{\text{AGM}(1, b'_0)} = \lim_{n \to \infty} \frac{1}{2^n} \log \frac{4 a_n}{c_n} \quad (32.2\text{-}2)$$

thereby

$$q = \exp\left(-2 \lim_{n \to \infty} \frac{1}{2^n} \log \frac{4 a_n}{c_n} \right) = \lim_{n \to \infty} \exp\left(-\frac{1}{2^{n-1}} \log \frac{4 a_n}{c_n} \right) \quad (32.2\text{-}3a)$$

$$= \lim_{n \to \infty} \left(\exp \log \frac{4 a_n}{c_n} \right)^{-1/2^{n-1}} = \lim_{n \to \infty} \left(\frac{4 a_n}{c_n} \right)^{-1/(2^{n-1})} \quad (32.2\text{-}3b)$$

This gives

$$q = \lim_{n \to \infty} \left(\frac{c_n}{4 a_n} \right)^{1/(2^{n-1})} \quad (32.2\text{-}4)$$

One obtains an algorithm for $\exp(-x)$ by first solving for k, k' such that $x = \pi K'/K$ (precomputed π) and applying the last relation that implies the computation of a 2^{n-1}-th root. Note that c_{n+1} should be computed as $c_{n+1} = \frac{c_n^2}{4 a_{n+1}}$ throughout the AGM computation to preserve its accuracy.

For $k = 1/\sqrt{2} =: s$ we have $k = k'$ and so $q = \exp(-\pi)$. Thus the calculation of $\exp(-\pi) = 0.0432139182637\dots$ can directly be done via a single AGM computation as $(c_n/(4 a_n))^N$ where $N = 1/2^{(n-1)}$. The quantity $i^i = \exp(-\pi/2) = 0.2078795763507\dots$ can be computed using $N = 1/2^n$.

32.2.2 Computation by inverting the logarithm

32.2.2.1 Iterations from the power series

The exponential function can be computed using the n-th order iteration

$$x_{k+1} = \Phi_n(x_k) := x_k \left(1 + y + \frac{y^2}{2} + \frac{y^3}{3!} + \dots + \frac{y^{n-1}}{(n-1)!} \right) \quad (32.2\text{-}5)$$

The iteration can be derived as follows:

$$\exp(d) \;=\; x \exp\left(d - \log(x)\right) = x \exp(y) \quad \text{where} \quad y := d - \log(x) \tag{32.2-6a}$$

$$=\; x \left(1 + y + \frac{y^2}{2} + \frac{y^3}{3!} + \frac{y^4}{4!} + \cdots\right) \tag{32.2-6b}$$

As the computation of logarithms is expensive one should use an iteration of high order. The C++ implementation given in [hfloat: src/tz/itexp.cc] uses the iteration of order 20.

32.2.2.2 Iterations from Padé approximants

$$P_{[1,1]} \;=\; \frac{2 + z}{2 - z}$$

$$P_{[2,2]} \;=\; \frac{12 + 6z + z^2}{12 - 6z + z^2}$$

$$P_{[3,3]} \;=\; \frac{120 + 60z + 12z^2 + z^3}{120 - 60z + 12z^2 - z^3}$$

$$P_{[4,4]} \;=\; \frac{1680 + 840z + 180z^2 + 20z^3 + z^4}{1680 - 840z + 180z^2 - 20z^3 + z^4}$$

Figure 32.2-A: Diagonal Padé approximants for the exponential function.

The Padé approximants $P_{[i,j]}(z)$ of $\exp(z)$ give iterations of order $i + j + 1$. The first few approximants for $i = j$ are shown in figure 32.2-A. The functional equation $\exp(-z) = \frac{1}{\exp(z)}$ holds for the diagonal approximants. In general, we have $P_{[i,j]}(-z) = 1/P_{[j,i]}(z)$. This can be seen from the following closed form

$$P_{[i,j]}(z) \;=\; \left[\sum_{k=0}^{i} \frac{\binom{i}{k}}{\binom{i+j}{k}} \frac{z^k}{k!}\right] \Big/ \left[\sum_{k=0}^{j} \frac{\binom{j}{k}}{\binom{i+j}{k}} \frac{(-z)^k}{k!}\right] \tag{32.2-7}$$

The numerator for $i = j$, multiplied by $(2i)!/i!$ to avoid rational coefficients, equals

$$=\; \frac{(2i)!}{i!} \cdot \sum_{k=0}^{i} \frac{\binom{i}{k}}{\binom{2i}{k}} \frac{z^k}{k!} \tag{32.2-8}$$

The coefficients of the numerator and denominator in the diagonal approximant

$$P_{[i,i]} \;=\; \frac{\sum_{k=0}^{i} c_k \, z^k}{\sum_{k=0}^{i} c_k \, (-z)^k} \tag{32.2-9}$$

can be computed using $c_i = 1$ (the coefficient of the highest power of z) and the recurrence

$$c_k \;=\; c_{k+1} \frac{(k+1)\,(2i-k)}{(i-k)} \tag{32.2-10}$$

It is usually preferable to generate the coefficients in the other direction. Compute the constant c_0

$$c_0 \;=\; \prod_{w=1}^{i} (4\,w - 2) \;=\; 2,\, 12,\, 120,\, 1680,\, 30240,\, \ldots \tag{32.2-11}$$

and use the recurrence

$$c_k \;=\; c_{k-1} \frac{(i-k)}{(2i-k)\,(k+1)} \tag{32.2-12}$$

We generate the coefficients for $1 \le i \le 8$:

```
? c0(i)=prod(w=1,i,4*w-2)
? qq(i,k)=(i-k)/((2*i-k)*(k+1))
? for (i=1, 8, c=c0(i); print1(["i,",",i,"]:   "); \
?    for (k=0, i, print1("  ", c); c*=qq(i,k)); print();)
  [1,1]:     2  1
  [2,2]:     12   6   1
  [3,3]:     120   60   12   1
  [4,4]:     1680   840   180   20   1
  [5,5]:     30240   15120   3360   420   30   1
  [6,6]:     665280   332640   75600   10080   840   42   1
  [7,7]:     17297280   8648640   1995840   277200   25200   1512   56  1
  [8,8]:     518918400   259459200   60540480   8648640   831600   55440   2520   72   1
```

Finally, the approximant $P_{[i,j]}$ can be expressed as ratio of hypergeometric series:

$$P_{[i,j]} \;=\; F\left(\begin{matrix} -i \\ -i-j \end{matrix}\bigg| z\right) \bigg/ F\left(\begin{matrix} -j \\ -i-j \end{matrix}\bigg| -z\right) \tag{32.2-13}$$

This is relation 36.2-33 on page 693 with $a = -i$ and $b = -j$ where i and j are positive integers.

32.2.3 Argument reduction for the exponential function and cosine

As for the logarithm an argument reduction technique can be useful with moderate precisions. We do not use the functional equation for the exponential function $(\exp(2z) = \exp(z)^2)$ because of the loss of precision when adding up the terms of the power series (1 plus a tiny quantity). Instead we use the functional equation for $E(z) := \exp(z) - 1$:

$$E(2z) \;=\; 2\,E(z) + E^2(z) \tag{32.2-14}$$

Compute the exponential function of z as follows

1. Set $r = z/2^n$ (for n big enough).

2. Compute $E := \exp(r) - 1$ to the desired precision using the power series.

3. Repeat n times: $E = 2\,E + E^2$.

4. Return $E + 1$.

We compute $\exp(1.0)$ using $n = 16$ and eight terms of the series:

```
? z=1.0;
? n=16;
? r=z/2^n
  0.000015258789062500000000000000000000000000000000000000000000000
? E=r*(1+r/2*(1+r/3*(1+r/4*(1+r/5*(1+r/6*(1+r/7*(1+r/8)))))))
  0.000015258905478413948140042622480661730187012348455116225 83
? for(k=1,n,E=2*E+E^2);E=E+1
  2.7182818284590452353602874713526624977572470716866614582
? exp(1.0)    \\ check with built-in exp()
  2.7182818284590452353602874713526624977572470933699959575
```

We can also compute the exponential function via the hyperbolic cosine or sine:

$$\exp(z) \;=\; \cosh(z) + \sinh(z) \;=\; \cosh(z) + \sqrt{\cosh^2(z) - 1} \tag{32.2-15a}$$
$$\;=\; \sinh(z) + \sqrt{\sinh(z)^2 + 1} \tag{32.2-15b}$$

The advantage is that half of the coefficients of the power series are zero. Again we do not use the functional equation for the hyperbolic cosine $(\cosh(2z) = 2\cosh^2(z) - 1)$ but that for $C(z) := \cosh(z) - 1$:

$$C(2z) \;=\; 2\,(C(z) + 1)^2 - 2 \;=\; 2\,C(z)^2 + 4\,C(z) \tag{32.2-16}$$

Compute the hyperbolic cosine as follows

1. set $r = z/2^n$ (for n big enough)

2. compute $C := \cosh(r) - 1$ to the desired precision using the power series

3. repeat n times: $C = 2\,[C+1]^2 - 2$

4. return $C + 1$

We compute $\cosh(1.5)$ using $n = 16$ and four terms of the series:

```
? z=1.50;
? n=16;
? r=z/2^n
  0.000022888183593750000000000000000000000000000000000000000000000
? C=1/2*r^2+1/24*r^4+1/720*r^6+1/40320*r^8
  0.00000000026193447412203827730766398499405829034331005424264555923
? for(k=1,n,C=2*(C+1)^2-2);C
  1.3524096152432473257676679654416441701739606825748392216
? C+1
  2.3524096152432473257676679654416441701739606825748392216
? cosh(z) \\ check with built-in cosh
  2.3524096152432473257676679654416441701739600748865373192
```

If the series for $\cos(z) - 1$ is used, then the cosine can be computed by the identical algorithm:

```
? z=1.50;
? n=16;
? r=z/2^n
  0.000022888183593750000000000000000000000000000000000000000000000
? C=-1/2*r^2+1/24*r^4-1/720*r^6+1/40320*r^8
  -0.0000000002619344740991683877317978758392098468831796333435288181
? for(k=1,n,C=2*(C+1)^2-2);C
  -0.929262798332297089911810148565731290914908941381793162 3
? C+1
  0.070737201667702910088189851434268709085091058618206837 69
? cos(z) \\ check with built-in cos
  0.0707372016677029100881898514342687090850910275633468694 2
```

Compute the sine as $\sin(z) = \sqrt{1 - \cos^2(z)} = \sqrt{-2C - C^2}$ and the tangent as $\tan(z) = \sin(z)/\cos(z)$.

32.3   Logarithm and exponential function of power series

The computation of the logarithm, the exponential function, and the inverse trigonometric functions turns out to be surprisingly simple with power series.

32.3.1   Logarithm

Let $f(x)$ be a power series in x and $g(x) = \log(f(x))$. Then we have $\frac{d\,g(x)}{dx} = \frac{f'(x)}{f(x)}$, and

$$g(x) \;=\; \log(f(x)) \;=\; \int \frac{f'(x)}{f(x)}\,dx \tag{32.3-1}$$

A few lines of GP demonstrate this:

```
? sp=8;default(seriesprecision,sp+1);
? f=taylor((1)/(1-x-x^2),x) /* shifted Fibonacci (with constant term) */
  1 + x + 2*x^2 + 3*x^3 + 5*x^4 + 8*x^5 + 13*x^6 + 21*x^7 + 34*x^8 + O(x^9)
? d=deriv(f,x)
  1 + 4*x + 9*x^2 + 20*x^3 + 40*x^4 + 78*x^5 + 147*x^6 + 272*x^7 + O(x^8)
? q=d/f   /* the only nontrivial computation */
  1 + 3*x + 4*x^2 + 7*x^3 + 11*x^4 + 18*x^5 + 29*x^6 + 47*x^7 + O(x^8)
? lf=intformal(q)
  x + 3/2*x^2 + 4/3*x^3 + 7/4*x^4 + 11/5*x^5 + 3*x^6 + 29/7*x^7 + 47/8*x^8 + O(x^9)
? f-exp(lf)  /* check with built-in exp() */
  O(x^9)
```

32.3.2   Inverse trigonometric functions

Now let $a(x) = \arctan(f(x))$. Then, symbolically,

$$a(x) \;=\; \int \frac{f'(x)}{1 + f(x)^2}\,dx \tag{32.3-2}$$

Verification for the trivial case $f(x) = x$:

```
? sp=13;default(seriesprecision,sp+1);
? f=taylor(x,x)
 x + O(x^14)
? d=deriv(f,x)
 1 + O(x^13)
? q=d/(1+f^2)
 1 - x^2 + x^4 - x^6 + x^8 - x^10 + x^12 + O(x^13)
? af=intformal(q,x)
 x - 1/3*x^3 + 1/5*x^5 - 1/7*x^7 + 1/9*x^9 - 1/11*x^11 + 1/13*x^13 + O(x^14)
? f-tan(af)  /* check with built-in tan() */
 O(x^14)
```

For $s(x) = \arcsin(f(x))$ use

$$s(x) = \int \frac{f'(x)}{\sqrt{1 - f(x)^2}} \, dx \qquad (32.3\text{-}3)$$

32.3.3 Exponential function

With $e(x) = \exp(f(x))$ we can use a scheme similar to those shown in section 29.7 on page 583. We express a function $g(y)$ as

$$g(y) = \prod_{k=1}^{\infty} [1 + T(Y_k)] \qquad (32.3\text{-}4)$$

where $Y_1 = y$, $Y_{k+1} = N(Y_k)$ and $1 + T(y)$ is the truncated power series of g. A second order product is obtained by taking $1 + T(y) = 1 + y$ (the series of $\exp(y)$ truncated before the second term) and

$$N(y) = f^{-1}\left(\frac{f(y)}{1 + T(y)}\right) \qquad (32.3\text{-}5)$$

For $g(y) = \exp(y)$ we have $N(y) = y - \log(1 + y)$ and

$$\exp(y) = \prod_{k=1}^{\infty} [1 + Y_k] \qquad (32.3\text{-}6)$$

where $Y_1 = y = f(x)$ and $Y_{k+1} = Y_k - \log(1 + Y_k)$. The product $\prod_{k=1}^{N}$ is correct up to order $y^{2^N - 1}$. The computation involves $N - 2$ logarithms and $N - 1$ multiplications. Implementation in GP:

```
1    texp(y, N=5)=
2    {
3        local(Y, e, t);
4        Y = y;   e = 1 + Y;
5        for (k=2, N,
6            t = deriv(1+Y,x)/(1+Y);
7            t = intformal(t);   \\ here: t = log(1+Y);
8            Y -= t;
9            e *= (1+Y);
10       );
11       return( e );
12   }
```

Check:

```
? f=taylor((x)/(1-x-x^2),x)
 x + x^2 + 2*x^3 + 3*x^4 + 5*x^5 + 8*x^6 + 13*x^7 + 21*x^8 + ...
? e=exp(f)  /* built-in exp() */
 1 + x + 3/2*x^2 + 19/6*x^3 + 145/24*x^4 + 467/40*x^5 + 16051/720*x^6 + ...
? t=texp(f,4);
? t-e
 -1/32768*x^16 - 35/98304*x^17 - ...
```

The a-th power of a power series S can be computed as

$$S^a = \exp[a \log(S)] \qquad (32.3\text{-}7)$$

32.4   Simultaneous computation of logarithms of small primes

We describe a method to compute the logarithms of a given set of (small) primes simultaneously. We define

$$L(z) := 2 \operatorname{arccoth}(z) = 2 \sum_{k=0}^{\infty} \frac{1}{(2k+1)\, z^{2k+1}} \tag{32.4-1}$$

and note that (relation 36.3-23d on page 699)

$$\log(z) = 2 \operatorname{arccoth} \frac{z+1}{z-1} \tag{32.4-2}$$

We will determine a set of relations that express the logarithm of a prime as linear combination of terms $L(X_i)$ where the X_i are large integers so that the series for L converges quickly.

```
S = { 51744295, 170918749, 265326335, 287080366, 362074049, 587270881,
      617831551, 740512499, 831409151, 1752438401, 2151548801, 2470954914, 3222617399 }

 2:  [ -1595639,  -17569128,  -8662593,  -31112926,  -13108464,  -11209640,
       -12907342, +9745611,  -1705229,  -12058985, +4580610,  +4775383,  -12972664 ]

 3:  [ -2529028,  -27846409,  -13729885,  -49312821,  -20776424,  -17766859,
       -20457653, +15446428,  -2702724,  -19113039, +7260095,  +7568803,  -20561186 ]

 5:  [ -3704959,  -40794252,  -20113918,  -72241977,  -30436911,  -26027978,
       -29969920, +22628608,  -3959419,  -28000096, +10635847, +11088096,  -30121593 ]

 7:  [ -4479525,  -49322778,  -24318973,  -87345026,  -36800111,  -31469438,
       -36235490, +27359389,  -4787183,  -33853851, +12859398, +13406195,  -36418872 ]

11:  [ -5520004,  -60779197,  -29967648,  -107633040,  -45347835,  -38778983,
       -44652067, +33714275,  -5899123,  -41717234, +15846307, +16520111,  -44878044 ]

13:  [ -5904566,  -65013499,  -32055403,  -115131507,  -48507081,  -41480597,
       -47762841, +36063046,  -6310097,  -44623547, +16950271, +17671017,  -48004561 ]

17:  [ -6522115,  -71813158,  -35408027,  -127172929,  -53580360,  -45818987,
       -52758281, +39834823,  -6970060,  -49290653, +18723073, +19519201,  -53025282 ]

19:  [ -6778159,  -74632382,  -36798067,  -132165454,  -55683805,  -47617738,
       -54829453, +41398649,  -7243689,  -51225694, +19458099, +20285481,  -55106936 ]

23:  [ -7217972,  -79475039,  -39185776,  -140741248,  -59296949,  -50707501,
       -58387161, +44084875,  -7713709,  -54549566, +20720673, +21601741,  -58682649 ]

29:  [ -7751584,  -85350490,  -42082712,  -151146003,  -63680669,  -54456218,
       -62703622, +47343993,  -8283970,  -58582320, +22252516, +23198720,  -63020955 ]

31:  [ -7905109,  -87040909,  -42916186,  -154139543,  -64941904,  -55534757,
       -63945506, +48281670,  -8448039,  -59742579, +22693241, +23658185,  -64269124 ]

37:  [ -8312407,  -91525553,  -45127374,  -162081337,  -68287932,  -58396097,
       -67240196, +50769306,  -8883311,  -62820720, +23862474, +24877135,  -67580488 ]

41:  [ -8548719,  -94127517,  -46410292,  -166689119,  -70229278,  -60056229,
       -69151756, +52212618,  -9135853,  -64606639, +24540856, +25584363,  -69501722 ]
```

Figure 32.4-A: Relations for the fast computation of the logarithms of the primes up to 41.

Compute $\log(p_i)$ for the primes p_i in a predefined set P of n primes as follows:

1. Find a set S of numbers $X \in \mathbb{Z}$ so that $X^2 - 1$ factor completely into the primes in P.

2. Select a subset of n (large) numbers X_k so that all $L(X_k)$ are linearly independent.

3. Try to find, for each prime p_i, a relation $\log(p_i) = \sum_{j=1}^{n} m_j L(X_j)$. If this fails return to step 2.

For example, with the first 13 primes ($P = \{2, 3, 5, 7, 11, \ldots, 41\}$) we find

$$S = \{X_1, X_2, \ldots, X_{13}\} = \tag{32.4-3}$$

$$\{51744295, 170918749, 265326335, 287080366, 362074049, 587270881,$$

$$617831551, 740512499, 831409151, 1752438401, 2151548801, 2470954914, 3222617399\}$$

We use the short form   p: [m1, m2, m3, ..., m13]   to denote a relation

$$\log(p) \;=\; \sum_{j=1}^{13} m_j\, L(X_j) \tag{32.4-4}$$

Now we have the relations given in figure 32.4-A, the first is

$$\log(2) \;=\; -1595639\, L(51,744,295) - 17569128\, L(170,918,749) \pm \ldots - 12972664\, L(3,222,617,399)$$

The series with slowest convergence (with argument $X_1 = 51,744,295$) already gives more than 15 digits per term: we have $\log_{10}\left(X_1^2\right) \approx 15.4$. The last series gives 19 digits per term.

```
                2,  3,  5,  7, 11, 13, 17, 19, 23, 29, 31, 37, 41
   51744295:  [ -2, +2,  0, +3,  0,  0, +2, -3, -1, +1,  0,  0, -1 ]
  170918749:  [ +1, +4, -5, +1, +1, +1, +1,  0, -1, -1, +1,  0, -1 ]
  265326335:  [ -7, -2,  0, +1, -1, +1,  0, -2,  0, -1, +2, +1, +1 ]

  287080366:  [  0, +1, +1, -5, +2, +1,  0, -1, +3, -1, -1,  0,  0 ]
  362074049:  [ +5, -4, -2, +1,  0, -2,  0,  0, -2, +2, +2,  0,  0 ]
  587270881:  [ +4, +2, +1, +3, -1,  0, -1,  0,  0, +1, -1, -3, +1 ]

  617831551:  [ -6, +4, +2, +1,  0, -6,  0, +1,  0,  0, +1, +1,  0 ]
  740512499:  [ -1, -1, -5, -2, +7, -1,  0, +1,  0,  0, -1,  0,  0 ]
  831409151:  [ -9, -1, +2, -1, +3, +1,  0,  0, -1,  0, +2,  0, -2 ]

 1752438401:  [ +6, -4, +2,  0, -2, -2,  0, +2, -2,  0,  0, +1, +1 ]
 2151548801:  [ +6, -2, +2,  0,  0, -2,  0,  0, +2, -4, +1,  0, +1 ]
 2470954914:  [  0,  0, -1, +1, -3, -5, +2,  0,  0,  0, +3,  0, +1 ]
 3222617399:  [ -2, -6, -2, +4, +1, +2,  0, +2, -1,  0, -2,  0,  0 ]
```

Figure 32.4-B: Values $L(x)$ as linear combinations of logarithms of small primes.

Figure 32.4-B shows the linear combinations of logarithms of small primes that give the values $L(x)$. The first row is the relation

$$L(51,744,295) \;=\; -2\log(2) + 2\log(3) + 3\log(7) \pm \ldots - 1\log(41) \tag{32.4-5}$$

The shown values, as a matrix, are the inverse of the values in figure 32.4-A.

Precomputed logarithms of small primes can be used for the computation of the logarithms of integers k if one can determine a smooth number near k. For example, the logarithm of 65537 (a prime) can be computed as

$$\log(65537) \;=\; \log\left(65537 \cdot \frac{65536}{65536}\right) = \log\left(\frac{65537}{65536}\right) + \log(65536) \tag{32.4-6a}$$

$$\;=\; \log\left(1 + \frac{1}{65536}\right) + 16\log(2) \tag{32.4-6b}$$

The series of the first logarithm converges fast and $\log(2)$ is precomputed. Jim White suggested this approach [priv. comm.]. If k is not near a smooth number but $u \cdot k$ is smooth where u factors into the chosen prime set, use the relation

$$\log(k) \;=\; \log(u\,k) - \log(u) \tag{32.4-7}$$

Here $\log(u)$ is the sum of precomputed logarithms and with $\log(u\,k)$ we proceed as above.

32.5   Arctangent relations for π ‡

We consider relations of the form

$$k\,\frac{\pi}{4} \;=\; m_1 \arctan\frac{1}{x_1} + m_2 \arctan\frac{1}{x_2} + \ldots + m_n \arctan\frac{1}{x_n} \tag{32.5-1}$$

```
+4[5]  -1[239]    == 1 * Pi/4

+12[18] +8[57] -5[239]   == 1 * Pi/4

+44[57] +7[239] -12[682] +24[12943]   == 1 * Pi/4

+88[192] +39[239] +100[515] -32[1068] -56[173932]   == 1 * Pi/4

+322[577] +76[682] +139[1393] +156[12943] +132[32807] +44[1049433]   == 1 * Pi/4

+1587[2852] +295[4193] +593[4246] +359[39307]
 +481[55603] +625[211050] -708[390112]   == 1 * Pi/4

+2192[5357] +2097[5507] -227[9466] +832[12943]
 +537[34522] -2287[39307] -171[106007] -708[1115618]   == 1 * Pi/4

+3286[34208] +9852[39307] +5280[41688] +7794[44179]
 +7608[60443] +4357[275807] -1484[390112] -1882[619858] +776[976283]   == 1 * Pi/4

+1106[54193] -30569[78629] -28687[88733] -13882[173932]
 +9127[390112] -9852[478707] -24840[1131527] +4357[3014557]
 +21852[5982670] +23407[201229582]   == -1 * Pi/4

+36462[390112] +135908[485298] +274509[683982] -39581[1984933]
 +178477[2478328] -114569[3449051] -146571[18975991] +61914[22709274]
 -69044[24208144] -89431[201229582] -43938[2189376182]   == 1 * Pi/4

+893758[1049433] +655711[1264557] +310971[1706203] +503625[1984933]
 -192064[2478328] -229138[3449051] -875929[18975991] -616556[21638297]
 -187143[22709274] -171857[24208144] -251786[201229582] -432616[2189376182]   == 2 * Pi/4
```

Figure 32.5-A: Best n-term arctan relations currently known for $2 \leq n \leq 12$.

```
13: +1126917[3449051] +1337518[4417548] ... -216308[2189376182]   == 1 * Pi/4

14: +446879[6826318] +5624457[8082212] ... +483341[17249711432]   == 1 * Pi/4

15: +5034126[20942043] +1546003[22709274] ... +1337518[250645741818]   == 1 * Pi/4

16: +14215326[53141564] +6973645[54610269] ... +8735690[34840696582]   == 1 * Pi/4

17: +12872838[201229582] +27205340[203420807] ... +35839320[134520516108]   == 1 * Pi/4

18: +2859494[299252491] -41068896[321390012] ... -89623108[18004873694818]   == -1 * Pi/4

19: +270619381[778401733] -138919506[1012047353] ... +146407224[30038155625330]   == 1 * Pi/4

20: +807092487[2674664693] +479094776[2701984943] ... +214188292[564340076432]   == 1 * Pi/4

21: +598245178[5513160193] -115804626[7622130953] ... -1521437626[38057255532937]   == 1 * Pi/4
```

Figure 32.5-B: The best n-term arctan relations (shortened) currently known for $13 \leq n \leq 21$.

where k, $m_1,\ldots,m_n$, $x_1,\ldots,x_n \in \mathbb{Z}$ (in fact, $k = 1$ almost always). This is an n-term relation. For example, a 4-term relation, found 1896 by Størmer [326], is

$$\frac{\pi}{4} = +44 \arctan\frac{1}{57} + 7\arctan\frac{1}{239} - 12\arctan\frac{1}{682} + 24\arctan\frac{1}{12943} \qquad (32.5\text{-}2)$$

We use the following compact notation

```
m1[x1] +m2[x2] + ... +mn[xn]  == k * Pi/4
```

for relation 32.5-1 on the previous page. For example, Størmer's relation 32.5-2 would be written as

```
+44[57] +7[239] -12[682] +24[12943]   == 1 * Pi/4
```

We write the relations so that the arguments x_j are strictly increasing. Further, n-term relations are sorted so that the first arguments x_1 are in decreasing order (if $x_1 \ldots x_j$ coincide with two relations, then the arguments x_{j+1} are used for sorting). For example, a few 6-term relations are

```
+322[577]  +76[682] +139[1393] +156[12943] +132[32807] +44[1049433]   == 1 * Pi/4
+122[319]  +61[378] +115[557]   +29[1068]   +22[3458]  +44[27493]   == 1 * Pi/4
+100[319] +127[378]  +71[557]   -15[1068]   +66[2943]  +44[478707]   == 1 * Pi/4
+337[307] -193[463] +151[4193] +305[4246] -122[39307] -83[390112]   == 1 * Pi/4
+183[268]  +32[682]  +95[1568]  +44[4662] -166[12943] -51[32807]   == 1 * Pi/4
```

Note that the second and third relation are sorted according to their fifth arguments (3458 and 2943). Among all n-term relations we consider a relation *better* than another if it precedes it. The first one is the *best* relation. Our goal is to find the best n-term relation for n small. For example, the relation

```
    +322[577]   +76[682]  +139[1393]  +156[12943]  +132[32807]  +44[1049433]    == 1 * Pi/4
```

is the best (known!) 6-term relation. The best n-term relations for $2 \leq n \leq 12$ currently known are shown in figure 32.5-A. Note that $k = -1$ in the 10-term relation and $k = 2$ in the 12-term relation. The best relations for $13 \leq n \leq 21$ (shortened to save space) are shown in figure 32.5-B. Figure 32.5-C gives just the first argument (x_1) of the best relations for $2 \leq n \leq 27$.

```
    n-terms         min-arg
       2               5     Machin (1706)     +4[5]  -1[239]    == 1 * Pi/4
       3              18     Gauss (YY?)       +12[18] +8[57] -5[239]   == 1 * Pi/4
       4              57     Stormer (1896)
       5             192     JJ (1993), prev: Stormer (1896) 172
       6             577     JJ (1993)
       7           2,852     JJ (1993)
       8           5,357     JJ (2006), prev: JJ (1993) 4,246
       9          34,208     JJ (2006), prev: JJ (1993) 12,943, prev: Gauss (Y?) 5,257
      10          54,193     JJ (2006), prev: JJ (1993) 51,387
      11         390,112     JJ (1993)
      12       1,049,433     JJ (2006), prev: JJ (1993) 683,982
      13       3,449,051     JJ (2006), prev: JJ (1993) 1,984,933
      14       6,826,318     JJ (2006)
      15      20,942,043     HCL (1997), prev: MRW (1997) 18.975,991
      16      53,141,564     JJ (2006)
      17     201,229,582     JJ (2006)
      18     299,252,491     JJ (2006)
      19     778,401,733     JJ (2006)
      20   2,674,664,693     JJ (2006)
      21   5,513,160,193     JJ (2006)
      22  17,249,711,432     JJ (2006), prev: 16,077,395,443 MRW (27-Jan-2003)
      23  58,482,499,557     JJ (2006)
      24 102,416,588,812     JJ (2006)
      25 160,422,360,532     JJ (2006)
      26 392,943,720,343     JJ (2006)
      27 970,522,492,753     JJ (2006)

    MRW := Michael Roby Wetherfield
    HCL := Hwang Chien-Lih
    JJ  := Joerg Arndt
```

Figure 32.5-C: First arguments of the best n-term arctan relation known today, for $2 \leq n \leq 27$.

32.5.1 How to find one relation

In the 5-term relation

```
    +88[192] +39[239] +100[515] -32[1068] -56[173932]    == 1 * Pi/4
```

factor $x_j^2 + 1$ for all (inverse) arguments x_j:

```
192^2+1 == 36865 == 5 73 101
239^2+1 == 57122 == 2 13 13 13 13
515^2+1 == 265226 == 2 13 101 101
1068^2+1 == 1140625 == 5 5 5 5 5 73
173932^2+1 == 30252340625 == 5 5 5 5 5 13 73 101 101
```

Note that all odd prime factors are the four primes $5, 13, 73, 101$. The coefficients m_j can be computed as follows. Write (for all arguments x_j)

$$x_j^2 + 1 \quad = \quad 2^{e(j,0)}\, 5^{e(j,1)}\, 13^{e(j,2)}\, 73^{e(j,3)}\, 101^{e(j,4)} \tag{32.5-3}$$

Now define a matrix M using the exponents $e(j,u)$ (ignoring the prime 2):

$$M_{j,i}^T \quad := \quad \pm e(j,i) \tag{32.5-4}$$

The sign of $M_{j,i}$ is minus if $(x_j \bmod p_i) < p_i/2$. With our example we find

```
transpose(M) :=
  [-5, -1, +1, -2]  //   173932^2+1  ==   5^5 *13^1 *73^1 *101^2
  [+6,  0, +1,  0]  //    1068^2+1   ==   5^6       *73^1
  [ 0, +1,  0, -2]  //     515^2+1   ==        13^1       *101^2  (*2)
  [ 0, -4,  0,  0]  //     239^2+1   ==        13^4                (*2)
  [-1,  0, +1, +1]  //     192^2+1   ==   5^1       *73^1 *101^1
  //  5, 13, 73, 101  <--= primes
```

For the signs of the upper left 3×2 sub-matrix, note that $(173932 \bmod 5) = 2 < 5/2$, $(173932 \bmod 13) = 5 < 13/2$, $(1068 \bmod 5) = 3 > 5/2$, and $(515 \bmod 13) = 8 > 13/2$. The nullspace of M consists of one vector:

```
[-56,   -32,   100,   39,   88]
```

This tells us that

```
+88[192] +39[239] +100[515] -32[1068] -56[173932]   == k * Pi/4
```

We determine that $k = 1$ by a floating-point computation of the left side. Quite often one finds a relation where $k = 0$, but we are not interested in those. For example, the candidates 12943, 1068, 682, 538, 239 lead to factorizations into (2 and) the odd primes 5, 13, 61, 73. The matrix M is

```
transpose(M) =
  [+4, +3, -1,  0]  //   12943^2+1  ==   5^4 *13^3 *61^1          (*2)
  [+6,  0,  0, +1]  //    1068^2+1  ==   5^6             *73^1
  [-3,  0, -2,  0]  //     682^2+1  ==   5^3       *61^2
  [+1, -1, +1, -1]  //     538^2+1  ==   5^1 *13^1 *61^1 *73^1
  [ 0, -4,  0,  0]  //     239^2+1  ==        13^4                 (*2)
  //  5, 13, 61, 73  <--= primes
```

The nullspace of M is `[1, -1, -1, -1, 1]` and the relation is

```
+1[239] -1[538] -1[682] -1[1068] +1[12943]   ==   0
```

32.5.2   Searching for sets of candidate arguments

A set of candidate arguments x_j will give a relation only if the $x_j^2 + 1$ factor into a common set of primes. Apart from the factor 2, all prime factors are of the form $4\,i+1$. One can choose a subset of those primes $S := \{p_1, \ldots, p_u\}$ and test which of the products $P = 2^{e_0} \cdot p_1^{e_1} \cdots p_u^{e_u}$ are of the form $P = x^2 + 1$. The test is to determine whether $P - 1$ is a perfect square. The GP function `issquare()` does this in an efficient way (as described in [110]). A recursive implementation of the search is

```
 1   \\ global variables:
 2   ct=0;  \\ count solutions
 3   av=vector(1000);  \\ vector containing solutions
 4   \\ pv = [...]; \\ vector of primes of the form 4*i+1
 5   m=10^20;  \\ search max := sqrt(m)
 6
 7   check(t)=
 8   {
 9       local(a);
10       if ( issquare(t-1, &a),  ct++; av[ct] = a; );
11       if ( issquare(t+t-1, &a),  ct++; av[ct] = a; );
12   }
13
14   gen_rec(d, p)=
15   {
16       local(g, gg, t);
17       if ( d>length(pv),  return() );
18       g = pv[d];
19       gg = 1;
20       while ( 1,
21           t = p * gg;
22           if ( t>m,  return() );
23           if ( gg!=1,  check(t) );
24           gen_rec(d+1, t);
25           gg *= g;
26       );
27       return();
28   }
```

We do the search using the four primes 5, 13, 61, and 73:

```
pv=[5, 13, 61, 73]; \\ vector of primes
gen_rec(1, 1); \\ do the search
```

The candidates found are

    12943, 1068, 682, 538, 239, 57, 27, 18, 11, 8, 7, 5, 3, 2

The following relations are found:

```
+1[239] -1[538] -1[682] -1[1068] +1[12943]    ==   NULL
+44[57] +7[538] -5[682] +7[1068] +17[12943]   == 1 * Pi/4  (5-term)
+1[27] +42[57] +6[538] -5[682] +7[1068] +16[12943]  == 1 * Pi/4  (6-term)
+1[18] +41[57] +6[538] -5[682] +6[1068] +16[12943]  == 1 * Pi/4  (6-term)
+1[11] +39[57] +6[538] -5[682] +6[1068] +15[12943]  == 1 * Pi/4  (6-term)
[--snip--]
+1[3] +26[57] +4[538] -3[682] +4[1068] +10[12943]  == 1 * Pi/4  (6-term)
+1[2] +18[57] +3[538] -2[682] +3[1068] +7[12943]  == 1 * Pi/4  (6-term)
```

The search is reasonably fast for up to about 12 primes. However, one needs to guess which prime set may lead to a good arctan relation. The particular set of primes

$$\{5, 13, 17, 29, 37, 53, 61, 89, 97, 101\} \tag{32.5-5}$$

led me (1993) to the relation

```
+36462[390112] +135908[485298] +274509[683982] -39581[1984933]
+178477[2478328] -114569[3449051] -146571[18975991] +61914[22709274]
-69044[24208144] -89431[201229582] -43938[2189376182]  == 1 * Pi/4
```

which is still the best 11-term relation known today.

The April-2006 computations were done with a more exhaustive search described in the next section.

32.5.3   Exhaustive search for sets of candidate arguments

We want to find all x where $x^2 + 1$ factors into (2 and) the first 64 primes of the form $4i + 1$ ($S = \{5, 13, 17, 29, \ldots, 761\}$). Call the resulting set of candidates A. We will later try (for small n) all $(n-1)$-subsets of S and test whether the corresponding subset of A leads to an arctan relation.

The simplest approach is to factor (for x up to a practical maximum) all $x^2 + 1$ and add x to the set A if all odd prime factors of $x^2 + 1$ are in S. This method, however, is rather slow: about 11,000 CPU cycles are needed for each test.

A much faster approach is the following sieving method. We can determine x such that a given prime p divides $x^2 + 1$ by solving $x^2 \equiv -1 \pmod{p}$ as shown in section 39.9 on page 784. We can further solve $x^2 \equiv -1 \pmod{p^h}$ for all h as shown in the cited section. Initialize an array with the value 1 for even indices, else with 2 ($x^2 + 1$ is even if and only if x is odd). For each prime $p \in S$ do, for all powers p^h, as follows: multiply the array entries with indices $s, s + p^h, s + 2p^h, s + 3p^h, \ldots$ where $s^2 \equiv -1 \pmod{p^h}$ by p. Finally find the entries with index x that are equal to $x^2 + 1$, these are the candidates.

We can use the logarithm of a prime and add it instead of multiplying by the prime, then we need to test whether entry x is (approximately) equal to $\log(x^2 + 1)$.

The array can be avoided altogether by using priority queues (see section 4.5.3 on page 162). An event scheduled for index x corresponding to a prime power p^h will trigger addition of $\log(p)$ to bucket x. The event must then be rescheduled to $x + p^h$.

Almost all computations of the logarithm can be avoided by observing that both $x^2 + 1$ and the logarithm are strictly increasing functions. We call a number x so that $x^2 + 1$ has all odd prime factors in S a *candidate*. The sum of logarithms (of primes) for candidates x are equal to $\log(x^2 + 1)$. If a was the last candidate, then for the next candidate b the sum of logarithms must be strictly greater than that for a. Therefore we only need to compute $\log(x^2 + 1)$ if a new sum of logarithms is greater than the one for the candidate found most recently. It turns out that a logarithm is computed *exactly* whenever a new candidate is found.

The search costs about 250 cycles per test, which is a good improvement over the first attempt. Analysis of the machine code shows that most of the time is spent in the reschedule operations.

The final improvement comes from the separation of the frequent events (small prime powers) from the rare events (big prime powers). Again we need an array, but only a small one that fits into level-1 cache. A segmented search has to be used.

Now we need to find the threshold beyond which an event is considered rare. Very surprisingly, it turns out that the search is fastest if *all* events are considered frequent! This means that we can forget about the priority queues. A better suited algorithm (and implementation) for a priority queue might give different results.

The resulting routine is remarkably fast, it uses just slightly more than 11 cycles per test. It was used to determine all candidates $x \leq 10^{14}$. The search took about eight days. The last entries in the list of candidates are

```
99205431802196^2+1 = [13.29.37.53.89.157.241.257.337.373.401^2.761]
99238108604548^2+1 = [5.29.37.61^2.101.349.397^2.433.557^2.661]
99311314035643^2+1 = [2.5^2.13.29.73.113.233.241.269.281.293.317.349.461]
99395767528881^2+1 = [2.13.29.37.53.149.173.181.193.313.353.373.401.449]
99501239756693^2+1 = [2.5^4.13.29.37^2.61.233.277.313^3.317.401]
99627378461772^2+1 = [5.13^2.37.41.73^2.137.277.281.521.557.617.761]
99759820688082^2+1 = [5^2.17.29.37.109.181.257.269.337.389.409.457.653]
99849755159917^2+1 = [2.5.89.101.181.233.257.293.389.457.521.557.677]
99950583525307^2+1 = [2.5^3.13.173.181.193.241^3.257.457^2.677]
99955223464153^2+1 = [2.5.13.61^2.101^2.109.373.421.433.509.709.757]
```

The search produced 43,936 candidates (including 0 and 1). Exactly that many logarithms were computed. This means that on average one logarithm was computed for one in $10^{14}/43{,}936 > 2 \cdot 10^9$ values tested.

We can extend the list by testing (for each element x found so far) whether $x + d$ or $x + (x^2 + 1)/d$ are new candidates:

```
[x] == [x+d] + [x+(x^2+1)/d]   where d divides x^2+1
```

Additionally we can try the arguments on the right side of relations like

```
[x] == 2[2*x] - [4*x^3+3*x]
[x] == [2*x-1] + [2*x+1] - [2*x^3+x]
[x] == 3[3*x] - [(9*x^3+7*x)/2] - [(27*x^3+9*x)/2]
```

Michael Roby Wetherfield has developed a more sophisticated approach for extending the list and sent me a big set of candidates beyond 10^{14}. His methods are described in [353] (see also [354], [331], [43], and [226]). We note that a single value, $x = 276{,}914{,}859{,}479{,}857{,}813{,}947$ where

```
x^2+1 = [2.5.13.17.29^3.41.53^2.73^2.101.157.181.229.241.313.397.401.509.577]
```

was discarded because it is greater than $2^{64} = 18{,}446{,}744{,}073{,}709{,}551{,}616$.

We note the curious relation

$$[k\,a] \;=\; [(k+1)\,a] + [(k+1)\,k\,a] - [(k^4 + 2\,k^3 + k^2)\,a^3 + (k^2 + k + 1)\,a] \qquad (32.5\text{-}6)$$

Set $f(a, k) := (k^4 + 2\,k^3 + k^2)\,a^3 + (k^2 + k + 1)\,a$, then we have

$$f(a,k)^2 + 1 \;=\; \left((k\,a)^2 + 1\right) \cdot \left(((k+1)\,a)^2 + 1\right) \cdot \left(((k+1)\,k\,a)^2 + 1\right) \qquad (32.5\text{-}7)$$

32.5.4   Searching for all n-term relations

To find all n-term relations whose arguments are a subset of our just determined list of candidates, we have to test all subsets of $(n-1)$ (out of 64) odd primes, select the corresponding values x, and compute the nullspace as described. Let A_j be the j-th candidate. An array M of 64-bit auxiliary values is used. Its j-th entry M_j is a bit-mask corresponding to the odd primes in the factorization of $A_j^2 + 1$: bit i of M_j is set if the i-th odd prime divides $A_j^2 + 1$.

To find n-term relations, we must try all $\binom{64}{n-1}$ subsets of size $n - 1$ out of the 64 odd primes in our scope. The bit-combination routine from section 1.24 on page 62 was used for this task. The selection of the entries that factor completely in the subset of $n-1$ primes under consideration can be done with a single bit-AND and a branch. The candidates with more than $n-1$ odd primes in their factorization should be discarded before the search.

While the search is very fast for small n, it does not finish in reasonable time for $n > 8$. A considerable speedup is obtained by splitting our $N = 64$ odd primes into a group of the 20 smallest and $b = 64 - 20 = 44$ 'big' primes. Write ($q = n - 1$ and)

$$\binom{N}{q} = \binom{b}{0}\binom{N-b}{q} + \binom{b}{1}\binom{N-b}{q-1} + \binom{b}{2}\binom{N-b}{q-2} + \ldots \qquad (32.5\text{-}8a)$$

$$= \sum_{j=0}^{q} \binom{b}{j}\binom{N-b}{q-j} \qquad (32.5\text{-}8b)$$

This means, we first select the $j = 0, 1, 2, \ldots$-subsets of the big primes. We copy the corresponding candidates whose big prime factors are in the current subset into a new array B. The size of B will be significantly smaller than the size of A. From this array we select the arguments according to subsets of the small primes (leaving the subset of big primes fixed). This results in a much improved memory locality and accelerates the search by a factor of about 25.

```
 n    prime set of best relation
 2    {13}
 3    {5, 13}
 4    {5, 13, 61}
 5    {5, 13, 73, 101}
 6    {5, 13, 61, 89, 197}
 7    {5, 13, 17, 29, 97, 433}
 8    {5, 13, 29, 37, 61, 97, 337}
 9    {5, 13, 17, 29, 41, 53, 97, 269}
10    {5, 13, 17, 41, 53, 73, 97, 101, 157}
11    {5, 13, 17, 29, 37, 53, 61, 89, 97, 101}
12    {5, 13, 17, 29, 37, 53, 61, 89, 97, 101, 197}
13    {5, 13, 17, 29, 37, 53, 61, 89, 97, 101, 181, 281}
14    {5, 13, 17, 29, 37, 53, 61, 89, 97, 101, 181, 269, 457}
15    {5, 13, 17, 29, 37, 41, 53, 61, 89, 97, 101, 181, 337, 389}
```

Figure 32.5-D: Primes with the best n-term relations known.

Still, the limit for n so that an exhaustive search can be done has only been moved a little. But if we look at the prime sets that lead to the best relations, shown in figure 32.5-D, we observe that small primes are much 'preferred'.

The data suggests that the best possible relation is found long before the search space is exhausted. Therefore we stop after the number of big primes in the subset is greater than, say, 4. Both parameters, the number b of primes considered big and the maximum number of primes taken from that set, should be chosen depending on n.

Another important improvement is to discard small candidates before the search. This spares us a huge amount of uninteresting relations with small first arguments x_1. Obviously, the amount of nullspace computation is also reduced significantly.

The results of the searches can be found in [20]. While the searches for the n-term relations with $n > 11$ did not even exhaust the table of candidates (which in turn is incomplete!), we can be reasonably sure that we found the best relations within our scope (of the first 64 odd primes $4i + 1$). Indeed I do not expect to see a better relation for any $n \leq 15$.

To improve on the results, one may use the first 128 odd primes $4i + 1$, sieve up to 10^{16} (distributed on 100 machines) and a 3-phase subset selection instead of the described 2-phase selection. The selection (a nullspace computation) stage should also be done in a distributed fashion to reasonably exhaust the table of candidates. Such a computation will likely improve on some of the relations with more than 17 terms and produce up to 35-term relations that are in the vicinity of the best possible.

A method for the simultaneous computation of logarithms of small primes that uses a similar method to the one given here is described in section 32.4 on page 632.

32.5.5   Checking pairs

```
+12[18]  +8[57]  -5[239]      == 1 * Pi/4
+8[10]  -1[239]  -4[515]      == 1 * Pi/4

+44[57]  +7[239]  -12[682]  +24[12943]      == 1 * Pi/4
+20[57]  +24[68]  +12[117]  -5[239]         == 1 * Pi/4

+44[57]  +7[239]  -12[682]  +24[12943]      == 1 * Pi/4
+24[53]  +20[57]  -5[239]  +12[4443]        == 1 * Pi/4

+68[99]  +27[239]   -4[307]  -12[12238]  -24[58911]   == 1 * Pi/4
+56[99]  +39[239]  +20[307]  -24[2332]   +12[6948]    == 1 * Pi/4

+68[99]  +27[239]   -4[307]  -12[12238]  -24[58911]   == 1 * Pi/4
+44[99]  +51[239]  +44[307]  -12[682]    +24[12943]   == 1 * Pi/4

+44[99]  +51[239]  +44[307]  -12[682]    +24[12943]   == 1 * Pi/4
+56[99]  +27[239]  +20[307]  +24[568]    -12[19703]   == 1 * Pi/4

+122[319]   +61[378]  +115[557]  +29[1068]  +22[3458]  +44[27493]    == 1 * Pi/4
+100[319]  +127[378]   +71[557]  -15[1068]  +66[2943]  +44[478707]   == 1 * Pi/4

+39[239]  +188[307]   +32[2332]  -44[6948]   +112[32318]  -56[55368]   == 1 * Pi/4
+95[239]  +132[307]  -136[2332]  +68[6948]    +56[12238]  +112[58911]  == 1 * Pi/4

+95[239]  +132[307]  -34[682]  +90[12943]  +22[34522]  +22[106007]   == 1 * Pi/4
+139[239]   +88[307]  -56[682]  -44[5357]   +68[12943]  +88[39307]   == 1 * Pi/4

+27[239]  +132[307]  +80[568]  +112[1123]  +44[19703]  -56[160590]    == 1 * Pi/4
+83[239]   +76[307]  +80[568]   +56[1113]  -12[19703]  +56[4180652]   == 1 * Pi/4

+776[4193]  +593[4246]  +2212[5701]  +481[34208]  +1321[39307] \
   +962[44179]  +1106[219602]  -708[390112]    == 1 * Pi/4
-330[4193]  +1699[4246]  +2212[5648]  +1587[34208]  +215[39307] \
   -144[44179]  +1106[48737]  +398[390112]    == 1 * Pi/4

+625[4052]  +295[4193]  +1555[4246]  +1587[9210]  +481[37107] \
   +359[39307]  +962[299655]  -1189[390112]    == 1 * Pi/4
+1106[4052]  +776[4193]  +593[4246]  +1106[9210]  +481[34208] \
   +1321[39307]  +962[44179]  -708[390112]    == 1 * Pi/4

+6056[10842]  +4062[34208]  +3796[39307]  +962[44179]  +776[139693] \
   -2475[275807]  -1484[390112]  -1882[619858]  -776[201229582]    == 1 * Pi/4
+5280[10842]  +4838[34208]  +776[38280]  +4572[39307]  +1738[44179] \
   -3251[275807]  -708[390112]  -2658[619858]  -1552[1460857]    == 1 * Pi/4

+6056[10842]  +4062[34208]  +3796[39307]  +962[44179]  +776[139693]  -2475[275807] \
   -1484[390112]  -1882[619858]  -776[201229582]    == 1 * Pi/4
+5280[10842]  +4838[34208]  +776[38280]  +4572[39307]  +1738[44179]  -3251[275807] \
   -708[390112]  -2658[619858]  -1552[1460857]    == 1 * Pi/4
```

Figure 32.5-E: Checking pairs of arctan relations for the computation of π.

When computing π via arctan relations one should make reasonably sure that no error occurred. To minimize the extra work, a *checking pair* of relations should be used. The checking pair

```
+12[49]  +32[57]  -5[239]  +12[110443]     == 1 * Pi/4
+44[57]  +7[239]  -12[682]  +24[12943]      == 1 * Pi/4
```

is given in [32]. The values $\arctan(1/57)$ and $\arctan(1/239)$ occur in both relations. Figure 32.5-E shows some checking pairs where the differing terms tend to be rapidly convergent.

In a checking pair the multipliers must be different for a shared argument of the arctan, the following two relations are *not* a checking pair:

```
+56[99]  +27[239]  +32[307]  +12[4193]  -12[39307]    == 1 * Pi/4
+56[99]  +39[239]  +20[307]  -24[2332]  +12[6948]      == 1 * Pi/4
```

The term $\arctan(1/99)$ has the same multiplier 56 in both relations, so an error in the computation of this term would go undetected.

Chapter 33

Computing the elementary functions with limited resources

This chapter presents two types of algorithms for computations with limited resources, the shift-and-add and the CORDIC algorithms. The algorithms allow the computation of elementary functions such as the logarithm, exponential function, sine, cosine and their inverses with only shifts, adds, comparisons and table lookups. Some early floating-point units (FPUs) used CORDIC algorithms and your pocket calculator surely does.

33.1 Shift-and-add algorithms for $\log_b(x)$ and b^x

Shift-and-add algorithms use only additions, multiplications by a power of 2 ('shifts'), and comparisons. A precomputed lookup table with as many entries as the desired accuracy in bits is required. The algorithms are especially useful with limited hardware capabilities.

The implementations given in this section use floating-point numbers. They can be rewritten to use scaled integer arithmetic without difficultly.

33.1.1 Computing the base-b logarithm

We will use a table that contains the values $A_k = \log_b\left(1 + \frac{1}{2^k}\right)$, it is created as follows:

```
1    double *shiftadd_ltab;   // element [0] unused
2    ulong ltab_n;
3
4    void
5    make_shiftadd_ltab(double b)
6    {
7        double l1b = 1.0 / log(b);
8        double s = 1.0;
9        for (ulong k=0; k<ltab_n; ++k)
10       {
11           shiftadd_ltab[k] = log(1.0+s) * l1b;   // == log_b(1+1/2^k)
12           s *= 0.5;
13       }
14   }
```

The algorithm takes as input the argument $x \geq 1$ and the number of iterations n and computes $\log_b(x)$:

1. Initialize: set $t_0 = 0$, $e_0 = 1$, and $k = 1$.

2. Compute $u_k = e_k \cdot \left(1 + 2^{-k}\right)$. If $u_k \leq x$ then set $d_k = 1$, else set $d_k = 0$.

3. If $d_k \neq 0$, then set $t_{k+1} = t_k + A_k$ and $e_{k+1} = u_k$ and repeat the last step. Else set $t_{k+1} = t_k$ and $e_{k+1} = e_k$.

4. Increment k. If $k = n$ return t_k, else goto step 2.

A C++ implementation is given in [FXT: arith/shiftadd-log-demo.cc]:

J. Arndt, *Matters Computational: Ideas, Algorithms, Source Code*,
DOI 10.1007/978-3-642-14764-7_33, © Springer-Verlag Berlin Heidelberg 2011

$k:$	u_k	t_k	e_k	A_k
init	–	0.00000000	+1.00000000	+1.00000000
1:	1.50000000	0.00000000	+1.00000000	+0.58496250
2:	1.25000000	0.00000000	+1.00000000	+0.32192809
2:	1.56250000	0.32192809	+1.25000000	+0.32192809
3:	1.40625000	0.32192809	+1.25000000	+0.16992500
3:	1.58203125	0.49185309	+1.40625000	+0.16992500
4:	1.49414062	0.49185309	+1.40625000	+0.08746284
5:	1.45019531	0.49185309	+1.40625000	+0.04439411
6:	1.42822265	0.49185309	+1.40625000	+0.02236781
7:	1.41723632	0.49185309	+1.40625000	+0.01122725
8:	1.41174316	0.49185309	+1.40625000	+0.00562454
8:	1.41725778	0.49747764	+1.41174316	+0.00562454
9:	1.41450047	0.49747764	+1.41174316	+0.00281501
10:	1.41312181	0.49747764	+1.41174316	+0.00140819
10:	1.41450182	0.49888583	+1.41312181	+0.00140819
11:	1.41381182	0.49888583	+1.41312181	+0.00070426
11:	1.41450215	0.49959010	+1.41381182	+0.00070426
12:	1.41415698	0.49959010	+1.41381182	+0.00035217
12:	1.41450224	0.49994228	+1.41415698	+0.00035217
13:	1.41432961	0.49994228	+1.41415698	+0.00017609
14:	1.41424330	0.49994228	+1.41415698	+0.00008805
15:	1.41420014	0.49994228	+1.41415698	+0.00004402
15:	1.41424330	0.49998631	+1.41420014	+0.00004402
$\infty:$	1.41421356	0.50000000	+1.41421356	+0.00000000
	$= x$	$= \log_2(\sqrt{2})$	$= x$	$= 0$

Figure 33.1-A: Numerical values occurring in the shift-and-add computation of $\log_2(\sqrt{2}) = 1/2$. The computation of $\log_{1/2}(\sqrt{2}) = -1/2$ corresponds to the same values but opposite signs for all entries A_k and y_k. Note that certain steps are repeated (for $k = 2, 3, 8, 10, 11, 12, 15$).

```
1    double
2    shiftadd_log(double x, ulong n)
3    {
4        if ( n>=ltab_n )  n = ltab_n;
5        double t = 0.0;
6        double e = 1.0;
7        double v = 1.0;
8        // [PRINT]
9        for (ulong k=1; k<n; ++k)
10       {
11           v *= 0.5;   // v == (1>>k)
12
13           double u;
14           bool d;
15           while ( 1 )
16           {
17               u = e + e * v;  // u=e;  u+=(e>>k);
18               d = ( u<=x );
19               // [PRINT]
20               if ( d==false )  break;
21               t += shiftadd_ltab[k];
22               e = u;
23           }
24       }
25       return  t;
26   }
```

The variable v is a power of $1/2$, therefore all multiplications by it can, with scaled integer arithmetic, be replaced by shifts as indicated in the comments. The values for the first steps of the computation for the argument $x_0 = \sqrt{2}$ are given in figure 33.1-A. The columns of the figure correspond to the variables u($= u_k$), t($= t_k$), e($= e_k$), and shiftadd_ltab[k]($= A_k$).

The algorithm has been adapted from [256] (chapter 5) where the correction is made only once for each

$k:$	u_k	t_k	e_k	A_k
init	–	0.00000000	+1.00000000	+1.00000000
1:	1.50000000	0.00000000	+1.00000000	+0.58496250
1:	2.25000000	0.58496250	+1.50000000	+0.58496250
1:	3.37500000	1.16992500	+2.25000000	+0.58496250
1:	5.06250000	1.75488750	+3.37500000	+0.58496250
1:	7.59375000	2.33985000	+5.06250000	+0.58496250
1:	11.3906250	2.92481250	+7.59375000	+0.58496250
2:	9.49218750	2.92481250	+7.59375000	+0.32192809
3:	8.54296875	2.92481250	+7.59375000	+0.16992500
4:	8.06835937	2.92481250	+7.59375000	+0.08746284
5:	7.83105468	2.92481250	+7.59375000	+0.04439411
5:	8.07577514	2.96920662	+7.83105468	+0.04439411
6:	7.95341491	2.96920662	+7.83105468	+0.02236781
6:	8.07768702	2.99157443	+7.95341491	+0.02236781
$\infty:$	8.00000000	2.99999999	+8.00000000	+0.00000000
	$= x$	$= \log_2(8)$	$= x$	$= 0$

Figure 33.1-B: Values occurring in the first few steps of a shift-and-add computation of $\log_2(8) = 3$.

value A_k limiting the range of convergence to $x < X$ where

$$ X = \prod_{k=0}^{\infty}\left(1 + \frac{1}{2^k}\right) = 4.768462058062743448299798577356794477543\ldots \qquad (33.1\text{-}1) $$

As given, the algorithm converges for any $x > 0$, $x \neq 1$. A numerical example for the argument $x = 8$ is given in figure 33.1-B. The base b must satisfy $b > 0$ and $b \neq 1$.

33.1.2 Computing b^x

We can use the same precomputed table as with the computation of $\log_b(x)$.

The algorithm takes as input the argument x and the number of iterations n and computes b^x for $b > 1$, $x \in \mathbb{R}$. It proceeds as follows:

1. Initialize: set $t_0 = 0$, $e_0 = 1$, and $k = 1$.

2. Compute $u_k = l_k + A_k$. If $u_k \leq x$ the set $d_k = 1$, else set $d_k = 0$.

3. If $d_k \neq 0$, then set $t_{k+1} = u_k$ and $e_{k+1} = e_k \cdot \left(1 + 2^{-k}\right)$ and repeat the last step. Else set $t_{k+1} = t_k$ and $e_{k+1} = e_k$.

4. Increment k. If $k = n$ return e_k, else goto step 2.

A C++ implementation is given in [FXT: arith/shiftadd-exp-demo.cc]:

```
1    double
2    shiftadd_exp(double x, ulong n)
3    {
4        if ( n>=ltab_n )  n = ltab_n;
5        double t = 0.0;
6        double e = 1.0;
7        double v = 1.0;
8        // [PRINT]
9        for (ulong k=1; k<n; ++k)
10       {
11           v *= 0.5;   // v == (1>>k)
12
13           double u;
14           bool d;
15           while ( 1 )
16           {
17               u = t + shiftadd_ltab[k];
18               d = ( u<=x );
19               // [PRINT]
```

k :	u_k	t_k	e_k	A_k
init	0.00000000	0.00000000	+1.00000000	+0.00000000
1:	0.58496250	0.00000000	+1.00000000	+0.58496250
2:	0.32192809	0.00000000	+1.00000000	+0.32192809
2:	0.64385618	0.32192809	+1.25000000	+0.32192809
3:	0.49185309	0.32192809	+1.25000000	+0.16992500
3:	0.66177809	0.49185309	+1.40625000	+0.16992500
4:	0.57931593	0.49185309	+1.40625000	+0.08746284
5:	0.53624721	0.49185309	+1.40625000	+0.04439411
6:	0.51422090	0.49185309	+1.40625000	+0.02236781
7:	0.50308035	0.49185309	+1.40625000	+0.01122725
8:	0.49747764	0.49185309	+1.40625000	+0.00562454
8:	0.50310219	0.49747764	+1.41174316	+0.00562454
9:	0.50029266	0.49747764	+1.41174316	+0.00281501
10:	0.49888583	0.49747764	+1.41174316	+0.00140819
10:	0.50029403	0.49888583	+1.41312181	+0.00140819
11:	0.49959010	0.49888583	+1.41312181	+0.00070426
11:	0.50029437	0.49959010	+1.41381182	+0.00070426
12:	0.49994228	0.49959010	+1.41381182	+0.00035217
12:	0.50029446	0.49994228	+1.41415698	+0.00035217
13:	0.50011838	0.49994228	+1.41415698	+0.00017609
14:	0.50003033	0.49994228	+1.41415698	+0.00008805
15:	0.49998631	0.49994228	+1.41415698	+0.00004402
15:	0.50003034	0.49998631	+1.41420014	+0.00004402
∞:	0.50000000	0.50000000	+1.41421356	+0.00000000
	$= x$	$= x$	$= 2^{1/2}$	$= 0$

Figure 33.1-C: Numerical values occurring in the shift-and-add computation of $b^x = 2^{1/2} = \sqrt{2}$. The values are printed at points where a comment [PRINT] appears in the code.

```
20                    if ( d==false )  break;
21                    t = u;
22                    e += e * v;  // e+=(e>>k);
23                }
24            }
25            return  e;
26        }
```

33.1.3 An alternative algorithm for the logarithm

A slightly different method for the computation of the base-b logarithm ($b > 0$, $b \neq 1$) is given in [212, ex.25, sect.1.2.2, p.26]. Here the table used has to contain the values $A_k = \log_b\left(\frac{2^k}{2^k-1}\right)$:

```
1     double *briggs_ltab;
2     ulong  ltab_len;
3
4     void
5     make_briggs_ltab(ulong na, double b)
6     {
7         double l1b = 1.0 / log(b);
8         double s = 2.0; // == 2^k
9         briggs_ltab[0] = -1.0; // unused
10        for (ulong k=1; k<na; ++k)
11        {
12            briggs_ltab[k] = log(s/(s-1.0)) * l1b;
13            s *= 2.0;
14        }
15    }
```

The algorithm works for $x > 1$ and terminates when a given precision (eps) is reached [FXT: arith/briggs-log-demo.cc]:

```
1     double
2     briggs_log(double x, double eps)
```

k :	x_k	y_k	z_k	A_k
init	1.41421356	0.00000000	+0.70710678	+0.00000000
2:	1.41421356	0.00000000	+0.35355339	+0.41503749
2:	1.06066017	0.41503749	+0.26516504	+0.41503749
3:	1.06066017	0.41503749	+0.13258252	+0.19264507
4:	1.06066017	0.41503749	+0.06629126	+0.09310940
5:	1.06066017	0.41503749	+0.03314563	+0.04580368
5:	1.02751454	0.46084118	+0.03210982	+0.04580368
6:	1.02751454	0.46084118	+0.01605491	+0.02272007
6:	1.01145962	0.48356126	+0.01580405	+0.02272007
7:	1.01145962	0.48356126	+0.00790202	+0.01131531
7:	1.00355759	0.49487657	+0.00784029	+0.01131531
8:	1.00355759	0.49487657	+0.00392014	+0.00564656
9:	1.00355759	0.49487657	+0.00196007	+0.00282051
9:	1.00159752	0.49769709	+0.00195624	+0.00282051
10:	1.00159752	0.49769709	+0.00097812	+0.00140957
10:	1.00061940	0.49910666	+0.00097716	+0.00140957
11:	1.00061940	0.49910666	+0.00048858	+0.00070461
11:	1.00013081	0.49981128	+0.00048834	+0.00070461
12:	1.00013081	0.49981128	+0.00024417	+0.00035226
13:	1.00013081	0.49981128	+0.00012208	+0.00017612
13:	1.00000873	0.49998740	+0.00012207	+0.00017612
∞:	1.00000000	0.50000000	+0.00000000	+0.00000000
	$= 1$	$= \log_2(\sqrt{2})$	$= 0$	$= 0$

Figure 33.1-D: Numerical values occurring in the computation of $\log_2(\sqrt{2}) = 1/2$. The value of k is incremented in the inner loop (comment [PRINT1] in the code, the value of z changes). The values of x and y change just before the location of the comment [PRINT2], corresponding to consecutive rows with same value of k. The computation of $\log_{1/2}(\sqrt{2}) = -1/2$ corresponds to the same values but opposite signs for all entries A_k and y_k.

```
3    {
4        double y = 0;
5        double z = x * 0.5;
6        // [PRINT]
7
8        ulong k = 1;
9        double v = 0.5;  // v == 2^(-k)
10       while ( fabs(x-1.0)>=eps )
11       {
12           while ( fabs(x-z)<1.0 )
13           {
14               z *= 0.5;
15               ++k;  v *= 0.5;
16               if ( k >= ltab_len )  goto done;  // no more table entries
17               // [PRINT1]
18           }
19
20           x -= z;
21           y += briggs_ltab[k];
22           z = x * v;  // z=(x>>k)
23           // invariant:  y_k + log_b(x_k) == log_b(x_0)
24
25           // [PRINT2]
26       }
27
28   done:
29       return y;
30   }
```

The values for first steps of the computation for the argument $x_0 = \sqrt{2}$ are given in figure 33.1-D.

33.2   CORDIC algorithms

The *CORDIC algorithms* can be used for the computation of functions like sine, cosine, exp and log. The acronym CORDIC stands for **Co**ordinate **R**otation **D**igital **C**omputer. Similar to the shift-and-add algorithms only multiplications by powers of 2 (shifts), additions, subtractions and comparisons are used. Again, a precomputed lookup table with as many entries as the desired accuracy in bits is required.

33.2.1   The circular case: sine and cosine

$k:$	x_k	y_k	z_k	$-d \cdot A_k$
init	0.60725293	0.00000000	+1.04719755	+0.00000000
0:	0.60725293	0.60725293	+0.26179938	−0.78539816
1:	0.30362646	0.91087940	−0.20184822	−0.46364760
2:	0.53134631	0.83497278	+0.04313044	+0.24497866
3:	0.42697471	0.90139107	−0.08122455	−0.12435499
4:	0.48331166	0.87470515	−0.01880574	+0.06241880
5:	0.51064619	0.85960166	+0.01243409	+0.03123983
6:	0.49721492	0.86758051	−0.00318963	−0.01562372
7:	0.50399289	0.86369602	+0.00462270	+0.00781234
8:	0.50061908	0.86566474	+0.00071647	−0.00390623
9:	0.49892833	0.86664251	−0.00123664	−0.00195312
10:	0.49977466	0.86615528	−0.00026008	+0.00097656
11:	0.50019758	0.86591124	+0.00022819	+0.00048828
12:	0.49998618	0.86603336	−0.00001594	−0.00024414
13:	0.50009190	0.86597233	+0.00010612	+0.00012207
14:	0.50003904	0.86600285	+0.00004508	−0.00006103
15:	0.50001261	0.86601811	+0.00001457	−0.00003051
∞:	0.50000000	0.86602540	+0.00000000	+0.00000000
	$= \cos(\pi/3)$	$= \sin(\pi/3)$	$= 0$	$= 0$

Figure 33.2-A: Numerical values occurring in the CORDIC computation of $\cos(\pi/3)$ and $\sin(\pi/3)$.

We start with a CORDIC routine for the computation of the sine and cosine. The lookup table has to contain the values $\arctan(2^{-k})$ for $k = 0, 1, 2, 3, \ldots$, these are stored in the array `cordic_ctab[]`. An implementation of the function is given in [FXT: arith/cordic-circ-demo.cc]:

```
1   void
2   cordic_circ(double theta, double &s, double &c, ulong n)
3   {
4       double x = cordic_1K;
5       double y = 0;
6       double z = theta;
7       double v = 1.0;
8       // [PRINT]
9       for (ulong k=0; k<n; ++k)
10      {
11          double d = ( z>=0 ? +1 : -1 );
12          double tx = x - d * v * y;
13          double ty = y + d * v * x;
14          double tz = z - d * cordic_ctab[k];
15          x = tx;  y = ty;  z = tz;
16          v *= 0.5;
17          // [PRINT]
18      }
19      c = x;
20      s = y;
21  }
```

For the sake of clarity floating-point types are used. All operations can easily be converted to integer arithmetic. The multiplications by `d` are sign changes and should be replaced by an `if`-construct. The multiplications by `v` are shifts.

The values for the first 16 steps of the computation for the argument $z_0 = \theta = \pi/3 = 1.04719755\ldots$ are given in figure 33.2-A. While z gets closer to 0 (however, the magnitude of z does not necessarily decrease with every step) the values of x and y approach $\sin(\pi/3) = 1/2$ and $\cos(\pi/3) = \sqrt{3}/2 = 0.86602540\ldots$, respectively.

More formally, one initializes

$$
\begin{aligned}
x_0 &= 1/K = 0.607252935008881\ldots & \text{(33.2-1a)} \\
y_0 &= 0 & \text{(33.2-1b)} \\
z_0 &= \theta & \text{(33.2-1c)}
\end{aligned}
$$

and iterates (starting with $k = 0$)

$$
\begin{aligned}
A_k &= \arctan\left(2^{-k}\right) & \text{(precomputed)} & \quad \text{(33.2-1d)} \\
v_k &= 2^{-k} & & \quad \text{(33.2-1e)} \\
d_k &= \operatorname{sign}(z_k) & & \quad \text{(33.2-1f)} \\
x_{k+1} &= x_k - d_k\,v_k\,y_k & \to \cos(\theta) & \quad \text{(33.2-1g)} \\
y_{k+1} &= y_k + d_k\,v_k\,x_k & \to \sin(\theta) & \quad \text{(33.2-1h)} \\
z_{k+1} &= z_k - d_k\,A_k & \to 0 & \quad \text{(33.2-1i)}
\end{aligned}
$$

The scaling constant K is

$$
K = \prod_{k=0}^{\infty} \sqrt{1 + 2^{-2k}} \tag{33.2-2a}
$$

$$
K = 1.6467602581210656483660512222822984356523767257010274 09\ldots \tag{33.2-2b}
$$

$$
\frac{1}{K} = 0.60725293500888125616944675250492826311239085215008977 24\ldots \tag{33.2-2c}
$$

We note that K can be computed more efficiently as $K = \sqrt{2\,F(1/4)}$ where $F(z)$ is defined as

$$
F(z) = \prod_{k=1}^{\infty} \left(1 + z^k\right) \tag{33.2-3}
$$

We use relation 16.4-23 on page 348 and relation 16.4-15a: $F(z) = P(z^2)/P(z)$ where

$$
P(z) = 1 + \sum_{k=1}^{\infty} (-1)^k \left(z^{k(3k-1)/2} + z^{k(3k+1)/2} \right) \tag{33.2-4}
$$

Using n terms of the sum gives a precision of about $3\,(n-1)^2$ bits:

```
? pent(z, n)= 1+sum(k=1,n, (-1)^k*(z^(k*(3*k-1)/2) + z^(k*(3*k+1)/2)));
? n=30; u=0.25; K=sqrt( 2 * pent(u^2,n)/pent(u,n) )
  1.6467602581210656483660512222822984356523767257010274 09
```

The CORDIC algorithm converges if $-r \le z_0 \le r$ where

$$
r = \sum_{k=0}^{\infty} \arctan(2^{-k}) \tag{33.2-5a}
$$

$$
r = 1.7432866204723400035043376561364162858138311854282065 23\ldots \tag{33.2-5b}
$$

$$
r > \frac{\pi}{2} = 1.57079632\ldots \tag{33.2-5c}
$$

With arguments x_0, y_0, z_0 one has

$$
\begin{aligned}
x &\to K\left(x_0\cos(z_0) - y_0\sin(z_0)\right) & \text{(33.2-6a)} \\
y &\to K\left(y_0\cos(z_0) + x_0\sin(z_0)\right) & \text{(33.2-6b)} \\
z &\to 0 & \text{(33.2-6c)}
\end{aligned}
$$

which for $x_0 = 1/K, y_0 = 0, z_0 = \theta$ specializes to the computation as above.

A nice feature of the algorithm is that it also works backwards: initialize as above and use the same iteration with the slight modification that $d_k := -\,\mathrm{sign}\,(y_k)$, then

$$x \;\rightarrow\; K\sqrt{x_0^2 + y_0^2} \tag{33.2-7a}$$

$$y \;\rightarrow\; 0 \tag{33.2-7b}$$

$$z \;\rightarrow\; z_0 - \arctan\left(\frac{y_0}{x_0}\right) \tag{33.2-7c}$$

The algorithm can be derived by writing

$$\begin{bmatrix} x_{k+1} \\ y_{k+1} \end{bmatrix} = \begin{bmatrix} +\cos(d_k A_k) & -\sin(d_k A_k) \\ +\sin(d_k A_k) & +\cos(d_k A_k) \end{bmatrix} \begin{bmatrix} x_k \\ y_k \end{bmatrix} \tag{33.2-8}$$

and noting that (using $d_k = \pm 1$, so $\cos(d_k A_k) = \cos(A_k)$ and $\sin(d_k A_k) = d_k \sin(A_k)$)

$$\begin{bmatrix} x_{k+1} \\ y_{k+1} \end{bmatrix} = \cos(A_k) \begin{bmatrix} +1 & -d_k v_k \\ +d_k v_k & +1 \end{bmatrix} \begin{bmatrix} x_k \\ y_k \end{bmatrix} \tag{33.2-9}$$

where $v_k = 2^{-k}$. The CORDIC algorithm postpones the multiplications by $\cos(A_k)$. We have

$$\cos(A_k) = \cos\left(\arctan(2^{-k})\right) = \frac{1}{\sqrt{1 + 2^{-2k}}} \tag{33.2-10}$$

and

$$K = 1/\prod_{k=0}^{\infty} \cos(A_k) = \prod_{k=0}^{\infty} \sqrt{1 + 2^{-2k}} \tag{33.2-11}$$

33.2.2 The linear case: multiplication and division

A slight variation gives a base-2 multiply-add algorithm:

$$A_k = 2^{-k} \tag{33.2-12a}$$

$$v_k = 2^{-k} \tag{33.2-12b}$$

$$d_k = \mathrm{sign}(z_k) \tag{33.2-12c}$$

$$x_{k+1} = x_k \tag{33.2-12d}$$

$$y_{k+1} = y_k + d_k v_k x_k \tag{33.2-12e}$$

$$z_{k+1} = z_k - d_k A_k \tag{33.2-12f}$$

We have

$$x \;\rightarrow\; x_0 \tag{33.2-13a}$$

$$y \;\rightarrow\; y_0 + x_0 z_0 \tag{33.2-13b}$$

$$z \;\rightarrow\; 0 \tag{33.2-13c}$$

Going backwards (replace relation 33.2-12c by $d_k := -\,\mathrm{sign}\,(y_k)$) gives an algorithm for division:

$$x \;\rightarrow\; x_0 \tag{33.2-14a}$$

$$y \;\rightarrow\; 0 \tag{33.2-14b}$$

$$z \;\rightarrow\; z_0 - \frac{y_0}{x_0} \tag{33.2-14c}$$

k :	x_k	y_k	z_k	A_k
init	1.20749706	0.00000000	+1.00000000	+0.00000000
1:	1.20749706	0.60374853	+0.45069385	-0.54930614
2:	1.35843420	0.90562280	+0.19528104	-0.25541281
3:	1.47163705	1.07542707	+0.06962382	-0.12565721
4:	1.53885124	1.16740439	+0.00704225	-0.06258157
+4:	1.61181401	1.26358259	-0.05553931	-0.06258157
5:	1.57232706	1.21321340	-0.02427913	+0.03126017
6:	1.55337060	1.18864579	-0.00865286	+0.01562627
7:	1.54408430	1.17651008	-0.00084020	+0.00781265
8:	1.53948856	1.17047850	+0.00306606	+0.00390626
9:	1.54177465	1.17348532	+0.00111293	-0.00195312
10:	1.54292063	1.17499096	+0.00013637	-0.00097656
11:	1.54349436	1.17574434	-0.00035190	-0.00048828
12:	1.54320731	1.17536751	-0.00010776	+0.00024414
13:	1.54306383	1.17517913	+0.00001430	+0.00012207
+13:	1.54320729	1.17536749	-0.00010776	-0.00012207
14:	1.54313555	1.17527330	-0.00004673	+0.00006103
15:	1.54309968	1.17522621	-0.00001621	+0.00003051
∞:	1.54308063	1.17520119	+0.00000000	+0.00000000
	$= \cosh(1)$	$= \sinh(1)$	$= 0$	$= 0$

Figure 33.2-B: Numerical values occurring in the CORDIC computation of cosh(1) and sinh(1). Note that steps 4 and 13 are executed twice.

33.2.3 The hyperbolic case: *sinh* and *cosh*

The versions presented so far can be unified as

$$v_k = 2^{-k} \tag{33.2-15a}$$

$$x_{k+1} = x_k - m\,d_k\,v_k\,y_k \tag{33.2-15b}$$

$$y_{k+1} = y_k + d_k\,v_k\,x_k \tag{33.2-15c}$$

$$z_{k+1} = z_k - d_k\,A_k \tag{33.2-15d}$$

where the linear case corresponds to $m = 0$ and $A_k = 2^{-k}$, the circular case to $m = 1$ and $A_k = \arctan(2^{-k})$. The forward direction ('rotation mode') is obtained by setting $d_k = \text{sign}(z_k)$, the backward direction ('vectoring mode') by setting $d_k = -\text{sign}(y_k)$.

Setting $m = -1$ gives a CORDIC algorithm for the computation of the hyperbolic sine and cosine or their inverses. The lookup table has to contain the values $\text{arctanh}(2^{-k})$ for $k = 1, 2, 3, \ldots$, stored in the array `cordic_htab[]`. The algorithm needs a modification: the iteration starts with index one and some steps have to be executed twice. The sequence of the indices that need to be processed twice is $4, 13, 40, 121, \ldots$ ($i_0 = 4$, $i_{k+1} = 3\,i_k + 1$, entry A003462 in [312]).

A sample implementation is given in [FXT: arith/cordic-hyp-demo.cc]:

```
1    void
2    cordic_hyp(double theta, double &s, double &c, ulong n)
3    {
4        double x = cordic_1Kp;
5        double y = 0;
6        double z = theta;
7        double v = 1.0;
8        // [PRINT]
9        ulong i = 4;
10       for (ulong k=1; k<n; ++k)
11       {
12           v *= 0.5;
13       again:
14           double d = ( z>=0 ? +1 : -1 );
15           double tx = x + d * v * y;
16           double ty = y + d * v * x;
```

```
17              double tz = z - d * cordic_htab[k];
18              x = tx;   y = ty;   z = tz;
19              // [PRINT]
20              if ( k==i )   { i=3*i+1; goto again; }
21          }
22          c = x;
23          s = y;
24      }
```

The values for the first steps of the computation for the argument $\theta = z_1 = 1.0$ are given in figure 33.2-B. The scaling constant K' can be computed as

$$K' = \prod_{k=1}^{\infty} \sqrt{1 - 2^{-2k}} \cdot \prod_{k=0}^{\infty} \sqrt{1 - 2^{-2i_k}} \tag{33.2-16a}$$

$$K' = 0.8281593609602156270761983277591751468694538376908425291\ldots \tag{33.2-16b}$$

$$\frac{1}{K'} = 1.2074970677630721288777210113109158368127832217769813422\ldots \tag{33.2-16c}$$

The duplicated indices appear twice in the product. The algorithm can be used for the computation of the exponential function using $\exp(x) = \sinh(x) + \cosh(x)$. The algorithm converges if $-r' \leq z_1 \leq r'$ where

$$r' = \sum_{k=1}^{\infty} \operatorname{arctanh}(2^{-k}) + \sum_{k=0}^{\infty} \operatorname{arctanh}(2^{-i_k}) \tag{33.2-17a}$$

$$r' = 1.1181730155265038036106275567830924518065729429295361 06\ldots \tag{33.2-17b}$$

With arguments x_1, y_1, z_1 we have

$$x \;\rightarrow\; K' \big(x_1 \cosh(z_1) + y_1 \sinh(z_1) \big) \tag{33.2-18a}$$

$$y \;\rightarrow\; K' \big(y_1 \cosh(z_1) + x_1 \sinh(z_1) \big) \tag{33.2-18b}$$

$$z \;\rightarrow\; 0 \tag{33.2-18c}$$

The backward version $(d_k := -\operatorname{sign}(y_k))$ computes

$$x \;\rightarrow\; K' \sqrt{x_1^2 - y_1^2} \tag{33.2-19a}$$

$$y \;\rightarrow\; 0 \tag{33.2-19b}$$

$$z \;\rightarrow\; z_1 - \operatorname{arctanh}\left(\frac{y_1}{x_1}\right) \tag{33.2-19c}$$

For the computation of the natural logarithm use $\log(w) = 2 \operatorname{arctanh} \frac{w-1}{w+1}$. That is, start with $x_1 = w+1$ and $y_1 = w - 1$, then $z \to \frac{1}{2} \log(w)$.

The square root $\sqrt{w}$ can be computed by starting with $x_1 = w + 1/4$ and $y_1 = w - 1/4$, then $z \to K' \sqrt{w}$.

For further information see [14], [179], and [256, chap.6]. An algorithm working with complex numbers is given in [36].

Chapter 34

Numerical evaluation of power series

We give algorithms for the numerical evaluation of power series. If the series coefficients are rational, the binary splitting (binsplit) algorithm can be applied for rational arguments and the rectangular schemes for real (full-precision) arguments. As a special case of the binary splitting algorithm, a method for fast radix conversion is described. Finally we describe a technique for the summation of series with alternating coefficients.

34.1 The binary splitting algorithm for rational series

The straightforward computation of a series for which each term adds a constant amount of precision (for example, the arc-cotangent series with arguments > 1) to a precision of N digits involves the summation of $O(N)$ terms. To get N bits of precision one has to add $O(N)$ terms of the sum, each term involves one (length-N) short division (and one addition). Therefore the total work is $O(N^2)$, which makes it impossible to compute billions of digits from linearly convergent series even if they are as 'good' as Chudnovsky's famous series for π (given in [102]):

$$\frac{1}{\pi} = \frac{6541681608}{\sqrt{640320}^3} \sum_{k=0}^{\infty} \left(\frac{13591409}{545140134} + k \right) \left(\frac{(6k)!}{(k!)^3 (3k)!} \frac{(-1)^k}{640320^{3k}} \right) \tag{34.1-1a}$$

$$= \frac{12}{\sqrt{640320}^3} \sum_{k=0}^{\infty} (-1)^k \frac{(6k)!}{(k!)^3 (3k)!} \frac{13591409 + 545140134 \cdot k}{(640320)^{3k}} \tag{34.1-1b}$$

34.1.1 Binary splitting scheme for products

34.1.1.1 Computation of the factorial

We motivate the binsplit algorithm by giving the analogue for the fast computation of the factorial. Define $f_{m,n} := m \cdot (m+1) \cdot (m+2) \cdots (n-1) \cdot n$, then $n! = f_{1,n}$. We compute $n!$ by recursively using the relation $f_{m,n} = f_{m,x} \cdot f_{x+1,n}$ where $x = \lfloor (m+n)/2 \rfloor$:

```
1    indent(i)=for(k=1,8*i,print1(" "));  \\ aux: print 8*i spaces
2
3    F(m, n, i=0)=
4    { /* Factorial, self-documenting */
5        local(x, ret);
6        indent(i);  print( "F(", m, ", ", n, ")");
7        if ( m==n, /* then: */
8            ret = m;  \\ == F(m,m)
9        , /* else: */
10           x = floor( (m+n)/2 );
11           ret = F(m, x, i+1) * F(x+1, n, i+1);
12       );
13       indent(i);  print( "^== ", ret);
14       return( ret );
15   }
```

The function prints the intermediate values occurring in the computation. The additional parameter i keeps track of the calling depth, used with the auxiliary function indent(). Figure 34.1-A shows the output with the computation of 8! =F(1,8). A fragment like

J. Arndt, *Matters Computational: Ideas, Algorithms, Source Code*,
DOI 10.1007/978-3-642-14764-7_34, © Springer-Verlag Berlin Heidelberg 2011

```
        F(1, 8)
           F(1, 4)
              F(1, 2)
                 F(1, 1)
                 ^== 1
                 F(2, 2)
                 ^== 2
              ^== 2
              F(3, 4)
                 F(3, 3)
                 ^== 3
                 F(4, 4)
                 ^== 4
              ^== 12
           ^== 24
           F(5, 8)
              F(5, 6)
                 F(5, 5)
                 ^== 5
                 F(6, 6)
                 ^== 6
              ^== 30
              F(7, 8)
                 F(7, 7)
                 ^== 7
                 F(8, 8)
                 ^== 8
              ^== 56
           ^== 1680
        ^== 40320
```

Figure 34.1-A: Quantities with the computation of 8!.

```
        F(5, 6)
           F(5, 5)
           ^== 5
           F(6, 6)
           ^== 6
        ^== 30
```

says "F(5,6) called F(5,5) [which returned 5], then called F(6,6) [which returned 6]. Then F(5,6) returned 30." For the computation of other products modify the line ret=m; as indicated in the code.

Note that we compute the product in a depth-first fashion to obtain a localized memory access. An implementation of the scheme by computing products of pairs, pairs of pairs, etc., gives the identical result but is likely to suffer from cache problems.

34.1.1.2   Computation of a polynomial from its roots

Given the n roots a_i of a polynomial $C = \sum_{j=0}^{n} c_j x^j$ we can compute C by a trivial modification of the routine above:

```
1    F(m, n, i=0)=
2    { /* Polynomial by roots, self-documenting */
3       [--snip--]
4    \\          ret = m;   \\ == F(m,m)
5               ret = 'x - m;  \\ == F(m,m)   :=  (x - a_i) where a_i is the i-th root
6       [--snip--]
7    }
```

Here we choose the roots to be $a_i = i$. The quantities with the computation of $C = \prod_{i=1}^{8} (x - i)$ are shown in figure 34.1-B. The coefficient of this particular polynomial are the (signed) Stirling numbers of the first kind, see figure 11.1-A on page 277.

34.1.2   Binary splitting scheme for sums

For the evaluation of a sum $\sum_{k=0}^{N-1} a_k$ we use the ratios R_k of consecutive terms:

$$R_k \quad := \quad \frac{a_k}{a_{k-1}} \tag{34.1-2}$$

```
F(1, 8)
     F(1, 4)
          F(1, 2)
               F(1, 1)
               ^== x - 1
               F(2, 2)
               ^== x - 2
          ^== x^2 - 3*x + 2
          F(3, 4)
               F(3, 3)
               ^== x - 3
               F(4, 4)
               ^== x - 4
          ^== x^2 - 7*x + 12
     ^== x^4 - 10*x^3 + 35*x^2 - 50*x + 24
     F(5, 8)
          F(5, 6)
               F(5, 5)
               ^== x - 5
               F(6, 6)
               ^== x - 6
          ^== x^2 - 11*x + 30
          F(7, 8)
               F(7, 7)
               ^== x - 7
               F(8, 8)
               ^== x - 8
          ^== x^2 - 15*x + 56
     ^== x^4 - 26*x^3 + 251*x^2 - 1066*x + 1680
^== x^8 - 36*x^7 + 546*x^6 - 4536*x^5 + 22449*x^4 - 67284*x^3 + 118124*x^2 - 109584*x + 40320
```

Figure 34.1-B: Computation of the polynomial $\prod_{i=1}^{8}(x-i)$.

Set $a_{-1} := 1$ to avoid a special case for $k = 0$. We have

$$\sum_{k=0}^{N-1} a_k \;=:\; R_0\left(1 + R_1\left(1 + R_2\left(1 + R_3\left(1 + \dots(1+R_{N-1})\dots\right)\right)\right)\right) \tag{34.1-3}$$

Now define

$$R_{m,n} \;:=\; R_m\left(1 + R_{m+1}\left(\dots(1+R_n)\dots\right)\right) \quad \text{where} \quad m < n \tag{34.1-4a}$$
$$R_{m,m} \;:=\; R_m \tag{34.1-4b}$$

Then we have

$$R_{m,n} \;=\; \frac{1}{a_{m-1}}\sum_{k=m}^{n} a_k \tag{34.1-5}$$

and especially

$$R_{0,n} \;=\; \sum_{k=0}^{n} a_k \tag{34.1-6}$$

We have

$$R_{m,n} \;=\; R_m + R_m \cdot R_{m+1} + R_m \cdot R_{m+1} \cdot R_{m+2} + \dots \tag{34.1-7a}$$
$$\dots + R_m \cdot \dots \cdot R_x + R_m \cdot \dots \cdot R_x \cdot \left[R_{x+1} + \dots + R_{x+1} \cdot \dots \cdot R_n\right]$$
$$=\; R_{m,x} + \prod_{k=m}^{x} R_k \cdot R_{x+1,n} \tag{34.1-7b}$$

The product telescopes, one gets (for $m \le x < n$)

$$R_{m,n} \;=\; R_{m,x} + \frac{a_x}{a_{m-1}} \cdot R_{x+1,n} \tag{34.1-8}$$

```
      R(0, 6)
            R(0, 3)
                   R(0, 1)
                          R(0, 0)
                          ^== 1/2
                          R(1, 1)
                          ^== 1/2
                   ^== 3/4
                   R(2, 3)
                          R(2, 2)
                          ^== 1/2
                          R(3, 3)
                          ^== 1/2
                   ^== 3/4
            ^== 15/16
            R(4, 6)
                   R(4, 5)
                          R(4, 4)
                          ^== 1/2
                          R(5, 5)
                          ^== 1/2
                   ^== 3/4
                   R(6, 6)
                   ^== 1/2
            ^== 7/8
      ^== 127/128
```

Figure 34.1-C: Quantities with the binsplit computation of $\sum_{k=0}^{6} 2^{-(k+1)} = 127/128$.

34.1.3   Implementation using rationals

Now we can formulate the binary splitting algorithm by giving a binsplit function using GP:

```
1    R(m, n)=
2    { /* Rational binsplit */
3        local(x, ret);
4        if ( m==n, /* then: */
5            ret = A(m)/A(m-1);
6        , /* else: */
7            x = floor( (m+n)/2 );
8            ret = R(m, x) + A(x) / A(m-1) * R(x+1, n);
9        );
10       return( ret );
11   }
```

Here `A(k)` must be a function that returns the k-th term of the series we wish to compute, in addition one must have `a(-1)=1`. For example, to compute arctan(1/10) one would use

```
A(k)=if(k<0, 1, (-1)^(k)/((2*k+1)*10^(2*k+1)));
```

Figure 34.1-C shows the intermediate values with the computation of $\sum_{k=0}^{6} 2^{-(k+1)}$.

34.1.4   Implementation using integers

In case the programming language used does not provide rational numbers, rewrite formula 34.1-8 in separate parts for the denominator and numerator. With $a_i = p_i/q_i$, $p_{-1} = q_{-1} = 1$ and $R_{m,n} =: U_{m,n}/V_{m,n}$ one gets

$$U_{m,n} = p_{m-1}\, q_x\, U_{m,x}\, V_{x+1,n} + p_x\, q_{m-1}\, U_{x+1,n}\, V_{m,x} \tag{34.1-9a}$$

$$V_{m,n} = p_{m-1}\, q_x\, V_{m,x}\, V_{x+1,n} \tag{34.1-9b}$$

The following implementation also contains code for reduction to lowest terms:

```
1    Q(m, n)=
2    { /* Integer binsplit */
3        local(x, ret, bm, bx, tm, tx);
4        if ( m==n, /* then: */
5            bm = B(m);  bx = B(m-1);
6            ret = [ bm[1]*bx[2] , bx[1]*bm[2] ]; \\ == B(m)/B(m-1);
7            x = gcd(ret[1], ret[2]);  /* Reduction */
```

```
        Q(0, 6)
            Q(0, 3)
                Q(0, 1)
                    Q(0, 0)
                    ^== [1, 10]
                    Q(1, 1)
                    ^== [-10, 3000]
                ^== [29900, 300000]
                Q(2, 3)
                    Q(2, 2)
                    ^== [3000, -500000]
                    Q(3, 3)
                    ^== [-500000, 70000000]
                ^== [-104250000000000000, 175000000000000000000]
            ^== [156978127500000000000000000, 1575000000000000000000000000000]
        [--snip--]
```

Figure 34.1-D: Explosive growth of intermediate quantities with computing arctan(1/10).

```
 8          ret = [ret[1]/x, ret[2]/x];  /* Reduction */
 9      , /* else: */
10          x = floor( (m+n)/2 );
11          tm = Q(m, x);       \\ [U_{m,x}, V_{m,x}]
12          tx = Q(x+1, n);     \\ [U_{x+1,n}, V_{m,n}]
13          bm = B(m-1);        \\ [p_{m-1}, q_{m-1}]
14          bx = B(x);          \\ [p_{x}, q_{x}]
15          \\ ret == Q(m, x) + B(x) / B(m-1) * Q(x+1, n);
16          ret = [ (bm[1]*bx[2]*tm[1]*tx[2] + bx[1]*bm[2]*tx[1]*tm[2])/10,
17                  (bm[1]*bx[2]*tm[2]*tx[2])/10 ];
18          x = gcd(ret[1], ret[2]);  /* Reduction */
19          ret = [ret[1]/x, ret[2]/x];  /* Reduction */
20      );
21      return( ret );
22  }
```

Whether the reduction should be used depends on the terms of the sum. If $\arctan(1/10)$ is computed *without* the reduction, the intermediate quantities grow exponentially, as shown in figure 34.1-D. The square brackets are the quantities $[U_{m,n}, V_{m,n}]$. Such explosive growth will occur with all power series unless the function argument is 1.

34.1.5 Performance

We compute the sum for $\arctan(1/10)$ up to the 5,000th term with the direct method, the rational binsplit and the integer binsplit with and without reduction. The timings for the computation are:

```
A(k)=if(k<0,1, (-1)^(k)/((2*k+1)*10^(2*k+1)));  \\ for rational binsplit
B(k)=if(k<0, [1,1], [(-1)^(k), ((2*k+1)*10^(2*k+1))] ); \\ for integer binsplit
N=5000;
sum(k=0,N,A(k)); \\ direct method:  69,385 ms.
R(0,N); \\ rational binsplit: 2,532 ms.
Q(0,N); \\ integer binsplit with gcd reduction: 4,152 ms.
Q(0,N); \\ integer binsplit without gcd reduction: >8min, "forever"
```

Things look quite different when computing the sum $\sum_{k=0}^{50,000} (-1)^k/(2k+1)^2$. The intermediate quantities U and V have only small common factors, so it is better to omit the reduction step:

```
B(k)=if(k<0, [1,1], [(-1)^k, (2*k+1)^2] );
A(k)=if(k<0,1, (-1)^(k)/(2*k+1)^2);
N=50000;
sum(k=0,N,A(k)); \\ direct method:  32,396 ms.
R(0,N); \\ rational binsplit:  6,826 ms.
Q(0,N); \\ integer binsplit with gcd reduction:  27,485 ms.
Q(0,N); \\ integer binsplit without gcd reduction:  6,251 ms.
```

Built-in routines for binsplit summation would likely be faster than these figures suggest.

The reason why summation via binary splitting is better than the straightforward way is that its complexity is only $O(\log N \cdot M(N))$, where $M(N)$ is the complexity of one N-bit multiplication (see [175]). If an FFT-based multiplication algorithm is used ($M(N) \approx N \cdot \log N$), the work is $\approx O((\log N)^2 N)$. This means that sums of linear but sufficient convergence are again candidates for high precision computations. The algorithm should be implemented in the 'depth first' manner presented, and *not* via the naive pairs, pairs of pairs, etc. (breadth first) way. The reasons are better locality and less memory consumption. The naive way needs the most memory after the first pass, when pairs have been multiplied.

34.1.6   Extending prior computations

To evaluate the sum to a higher precision, reuse $R_{0,N-1}$, the sum of the first N terms. For example, the sum of the first $2N$ terms can be computed as

$$R_{0,2N-1} \;=\; R_{0,N-1} + a_{N-1} \cdot R_{N,2N-1} \tag{34.1-10}$$

This is formula 34.1-8 with $m = 0$, $x = N - 1$, and $n = 2N - 1$. The same relation with explicit rational arithmetic is

$$U_{0,2N-1} \;=\; q_{N-1}\,U_{0,N-1}\,V_{N,2N-1} + p_{N-1}\,U_{N,2N-1}\,V_{0,N-1} \tag{34.1-11a}$$
$$V_{0,2N-1} \;=\; q_{N-1}\,V_{0,N-1}\,V_{N,2N-1} \tag{34.1-11b}$$

With the appearance of some new computer that can multiply two length $2N$ numbers (assuming the old model could multiply length-N numbers) we only need to combine the ratios $R_{0,N-1}$ and $R_{N,2N-1}$ that had been precomputed by the last generation of computers. This costs only a few full-size multiplications, so we can improve on prior computations cheaply.

34.1.7   Computation of π: binary splitting versus AGM-type iterations

The binary splitting scheme for the computation of π (for example, with the series 34.1-1a on page 651) can outperform the AGM-based iterations given in section 31.5 on page 615.

This is due to the more favorable memory access pattern with binary splitting. When computing N digits of π the AGM iterations compute $O\left(\log_2 N\right)$ roots (and or inverses) to full precision. At the last phase of each root computation full-length multiplications that access all of the memory have to be performed. In contrast, the binary splitting involves full-precision multiplications only at the very last phase.

The drawback of the binary splitting scheme is that it may need significantly more memory than two full words. This may happen if the numerator and denominator grow fast which is more likely if no series so favorable as 34.1-1a can be used for the quantity to be computed. The problem can be mitigated by computing the floating-point value whenever the integer values become too large (as pointed out by Richard Kreckel [priv. comm.], see [219] and [100]). This technique is used in the CLN library [174].

34.1.8   Fast radix conversion

A binary splitting scheme for radix conversion of a radix-z integer $[a_N a_{N-1} \ldots a_2 a_1 a_0]_z$ into the radix used is obtained via recursive application of the scheme

$$\sum_{k=M}^{N} a_k\, z^k \;=\; \sum_{k=M}^{M+X-1} a_k\, z^k + z^X \sum_{k=M+X}^{N} a_k\, z^k \tag{34.1-12}$$

where X is chosen to be the largest power of 2 that is less than $d := N - M$.

In the following we pretend that the computations with GP are done in decimal. While this is not true (the radix used internally is binary and the numbers are converted to decimal only with printing), nothing in the output would appear different with decimal calculations.

We define an auxiliary function that computes (for $d > 1$) the largest exponent s so that $2^s < d$:

```
1   ex2le(d)=
2   { /* return largest s so that 2^s < d */
3       local(s, t);
4       t=1;   s=0;
5       while ( d>t,   t<<=1;  s+=1; );
```

```
           R(0, 15)
               R(0, 7)
                   R(0, 3)
                           R(0, 1)
                           ^== 67
                           R(2, 3)
                           ^== 101
                       ^== 25923
                   R(4, 7)
                           R(4, 5)
                           ^== 7
                           R(6, 7)
                           ^== 33
                       ^== 8455
                   ^== 554132803
               R(8, 15)
                   R(8, 11)
                           R(8, 9)
                           ^== 67
                           R(10, 11)
                           ^== 101
                       ^== 25923
                   R(12, 15)
                           R(12, 13)
                           ^== 7
                           R(14, 15)
                           ^== 33
                       ^== 8455
                   ^== 554132803
           ^== 2379982267079943491
```

Figure 34.1-E: Intermediate results when converting the number 2107654321076543_{16} to decimal.

```
6        t >>= 1;  s--;
7        return(s);
8    }
```

We precompute $z^2, z^4, z^8, \ldots, z^{2^w}$ where $2^w < N$:

```
1    z=16;  \\ radix
2    N=15;  \\ number of digits in radix z
3    vz=vector(ceil(log(N)/log(2)));
4    vz[1]=z;  for (k=2, length(vz), vz[k]=vz[k-1]^2);  //  O(N) space
```

Now the conversion function can be defined as

```
1    Ri(m, n, i=0)=
2    { /* Radix conversion, self-documenting */
3        local(x, d, ret, t);
4        indent(i);  print( "R(", m, ", ", n, ")");
5        d = n-m;
6        if ( d <= 1, /* then: */
7            if ( d==0, ret = A(m); , ret = A(m) + z*A(n); );
8        , /* else: */
9            t = ex2le(d);
10           x = 1<<t;
11           ret = Ri(m, m+x-1, i+1) +  vz[t+1] * Ri(m+x, n, i+1);
12       );
13       indent(i);  print( "^== ", ret);
14       return( ret );
15   }
```

We convert the 16-digit, radix-16 number

$$A = 2107654321076543_{16} = [a_{15}\,a_{14}\,\ldots\,a_2\,a_1\,a_0]_{16} \qquad (34.1\text{-}13)$$

The intermediate results are shown in figure 34.1-E. The k-th digit of A is $a_k = (k+3) \bmod 8$, it is supplied as the function A(k)=(k+3)%8.

34.2   Rectangular schemes for evaluation of power series

The *rectangular scheme* for the evaluation of polynomials was given in [267] and later in [314]. We use it for the evaluation of truncated power series up to a given power $N-1$ of the series variable. We look at two variants, one for series whose coefficients are small rationals (as for the logarithm) and another for series where the ratios of successive coefficients are small rationals (as for the exponential function). If the numbers of rows and columns in the schemes are identical, a method involving $O(\sqrt{N})$ full-precision multiplications is obtained. The schemes are very competitive up to very high precision in practice, even compared with AGM-based methods.

34.2.1   Rectangular scheme for arctan and logarithm

Computing the sum of the first N terms of a power series as

$$S_N \ := \ \sum_{k=0}^{N-1} A_k \, z^k \ = \ A_0 + z\left(A_1 + z\left(A_2 + z\left(A_3 + \ldots z\left(A_{N-1}\right)\ldots\right)\right)\right) \tag{34.2-1}$$

costs N long (full-precision) multiplications if z is a full-precision number. If the A_k are small rational values and $N = R \cdot C$, then we can rewrite S_N as

$$
\begin{aligned}
S_N \ = \ \ & A_{0C} + A_{0C+1}\,z + A_{0C+2}\,z^2 + \ldots + A_{1C-1}\,z^{C-1} + \qquad\qquad\qquad\qquad\;\; (34.2\text{-}2)\\
& +z^C \left[A_{1C} + A_{1C+1}\,z + A_{1C+2}\,z^2 + \ldots + A_{2C-1}\,z^{C-1} + \right.\\
& +z^C \left[A_{2C} + A_{2C+1}\,z + A_{2C+2}\,z^2 + \ldots + A_{3C-1}\,z^{C-1} + \right.\\
& +z^C \left[A_{3C} + A_{3C+1}\,z + A_{3C+2}\,z^2 + \ldots + A_{4C-1}\,z^{C-1} + \right.\\
& + \quad\ \ \ldots \quad\ \ +\\
& +z^C \left[A_{(R-1)C} + A_{(R-1)C+1}\,z + A_{(R-1)C+2}\,z^2 + \ldots + A_{RC-1}\,z^{C-1} \ \ \right]\ldots]]]
\end{aligned}
$$

We compute S_N as

$$\left[\left[\left[\ldots\left[U_{R-1}\right] z^C + \ldots + U_3\right] z^C + U_2\right] z^C + U_1\right] z^C + U_0 \tag{34.2-3}$$

where $U_r := \sum_{k=0}^{C-1} A_{rC+k}\, z^k$ is the sum in one row of relation 34.2-2.

Precomputing the quantities z^2, z^3, $z^4, \ldots z^C$ involves $C-1$ long multiplications. The sums in each row of expression 34.2-2 involve only short multiplications with series coefficients A_i. The multiplication by z^C for each but the first row involves further $R-1$ long multiplications. The computation uses C temporaries (z, z^2, $\ldots$, z^C) and $O(R+C)$ long multiplications. Choosing $R = C = \sqrt{N}$ leads to a complexity of $O(2\sqrt{N})$ long multiplications and also involves $\sqrt{N}$ temporaries. With argument reduction the complexity can be improved to $O(\sqrt[3]{N})$ multiplications, see [83, p.25].

34.2.1.1   Implementation for arctan

We implement the scheme for the arctan in GP:

```
1    fa(n) =   \\ inverse of series coefficient
2    {  /* fa(n) := (-1)^n/(2n+1) */
3        local(an);
4        an = (2*n+1);
5        if ( bitand(n,1), an=-an);
6        return( an );
7    }
```

```
1    atan_rect(z, R, C)=
2    {  /* compute atan(z) as z*(1-z^2/3+z^4/5-z^6/7+-... +-z^(2*(R*C-1))/(2*R*C-1) */
3        local(S, vz, s, ur, k);
4        vz = vector(C);  \\ vz == [z^2,z^4,z^6,...,z^(2*C)]
5        vz[1] = z*z;  \\ 1 long multiplication (special for arctan)
6        for (k=2, C, vz[k]=vz[1]*vz[k-1]);  \\ C-1 long multiplications
7        k = R*C;  \\ index of current coefficient
8        s = 0;  \\ sum
```

```
9        forstep (r=R-1, 0, -1,
10           ur = 0;  \\ sum of this row
11           forstep (c=C-1, 1, -1,  k-=1;  ur+=vz[c]/fa(k); );
12           k -= 1;  ur += 1/fa(k);
13           if ( r!=R-1, s*=vz[C]; );  \\ R-1 long multiplications
14           s += ur;
15        );
16        s *= z;  \\ 1 long multiplication (special for arctan)
17        return( s );
18    }
```

We compute $\pi/16$ as $\arctan(z)$ where $z = \sqrt{2\sqrt{2}+4} - \sqrt{2} - 1 \approx 0.19891236$ (using relation 32.1-18 on page 626 twice on $z=1$), using a precision of 30,000 decimal digits. We use $R = C = \sqrt{N} =: S$:

```
? ? z=1;z=z+sqrt(z^2+1);z=z+sqrt(z^2+1);z=1/z;  \\ ==> Pi/16
? a=atan(z);  \\ built-in arctan:  computed in 1,123 ms.
? r=atan_rect(z,S,S);  \\ computed in 2,377 ms.
  \\ using S=147, and N=S^2=21609
? a-r
0.E-30017  \\ result OK
```

The given implementation is about half as fast as the built-in routine. Argument reduction makes the method much more competitive:

```
? a=atan(z);  \\ computed in 1,123 ms.
? z=1/z;
? for(k=1,32,z=z+sqrt(z^2+1))  \\ computed in 204 ms.
? z=1/z
4.5716189977098740032886154873 E-11
? S=ceil(sqrt(-1/2*rp*log(10)/log(z)))
39  \\ N=S^2=1521
? r=atan_rect(z,S,S);  \\ computed in 284 ms.
? r*=2^32
? a-r
-1.3690050398194919519 E-30016  \\ OK
```

With 100,000 decimal digits the performance ratio is roughly the same. Note that one has to limit the number C of temporaries according to the available memory.

Compute the inverse sine and cosine as

$$\arcsin(z) = \arctan \frac{z}{\sqrt{1-z^2}} \qquad (34.2\text{-}4a)$$

$$\arccos(z) = \frac{\pi}{2} - \arcsin(z) \qquad (34.2\text{-}4b)$$

34.2.1.2 Implementation for the logarithm

A routine for $\log(1-z)$ is

```
1    log_rect(z, R, C)=
2    { /* compute log(1-z) as 1+x/2+x^2/3+...+x^(R*C-1)/(R*C) */
3        local(S, vz, s, ur, k);
4        vz = vector(C);  \\ vz == [z^2,z^4,z^6,...,z^(2*C)]
5        vz[1] = z;
6        for (k=2, C, vz[k]=z*vz[k-1]);  \\ C-1 long multiplications
7        k = R*C;  \\ index of current coefficient
8        s = 0;  \\ sum
9        forstep (r=R-1, 0, -1,
10           ur = 0;  \\ sum of this row
11           forstep (c=C-1, 1, -1,  k-=1;  ur+=vz[c]/(k+1); );
12           k -= 1;  ur += 1/(k+1);
13           if ( r!=R-1, s*=vz[C]; );  \\ R-1 long multiplications
14           s += ur;
15        );
16        s *= z;  \\ 1 long multiplication (special for arctan)
17        return( -s );
18    }
```

However, using a precision of 30,000 decimal digits and argument $z = 1/5$ the routine is slower than the built-in one (using the AGM) by a factor of about 1/7. With argument reduction (relation 32.1-15 on page 625) and $R = C = \sqrt{N} =: S$ we get a more competitive performance:

```
? e=log(1-z)  \\ computed in 621 ms.
-0.22314355131420975575766295090310
? z=1-z;
? for(k=1,32,z=sqrt(z));  \\ computed in 132 ms.
? z=1-z;  \\ == 5.1954656678348100387255273834 E-11
? S=ceil(sqrt(-rp*log(10)/log(z)))
55  \\ N=S^2=3025
? r=log_rect(z,N);  \\ computed in 461 ms.
? r*=2^32
-0.22314355131420975575766295090310
? e-r
-6.0716131297620509 E-30008  \\ OK
```

We note that with both the logarithm and the arctan, subsequent computations with the built-in routine are faster as some constants that are computed with the first call are reused.

Compute the inverse hyperbolic sine and cosine as

$$\operatorname{arcsinh}(z) \;=\; \log(z + \sqrt{z^2 + 1}) \tag{34.2-5a}$$

$$\operatorname{arccosh}(z) \;=\; \log(z + \sqrt{z^2 - 1}) \quad \text{where} \quad z \geq 1 \tag{34.2-5b}$$

34.2.2   Rectangular scheme for exp, sin, and cos

We rewrite the sum of the first N terms of a power series

$$S_N \;:=\; \sum_{k=0}^{N-1} A_k\, z^k \tag{34.2-6}$$

as

$$
\begin{aligned}
S_N \;=\; & 1 \left[A_{0C+0} + A_{1C+0}\, z^{1C} + A_{2C+0}\, z^{2C} + \ldots + A_{(R-1)C+0} z^{(R-1)C} \right] + \\
& z^1 \left[A_{0C+1} + A_{1C+1}\, z^{1C} + A_{2C+1}\, z^{2C} + \ldots + A_{(R-1)C+1} z^{(R-1)C} \right] + \\
& z^2 \left[A_{0C+2} + A_{1C+2}\, z^{1C} + A_{2C+2}\, z^{2C} + \ldots + A_{(R-1)C+2} z^{(R-1)C} \right] + \\
& z^3 \left[A_{0C+3} + A_{1C+3}\, z^{1C} + A_{2C+3}\, z^{2C} + \ldots + A_{(R-1)C+3} z^{(R-1)C} \right] + \\
& + \quad \ldots \quad + \\
& z^{C-2} \left[A_{1C-2} + A_{2C-2}\, z^{1C} + A_{3C-2}\, z^{2C} + \ldots + A_{RC-2} z^{(R-1)C} \right] + \\
& z^{C-1} \left[A_{1C-1} + A_{2C-1}\, z^{1C} + A_{3C-1}\, z^{2C} + \ldots + A_{RC-1} z^{(R-1)C} \right]
\end{aligned}
\tag{34.2-7}
$$

Compute the sum as (the transposed version of relation 34.2-2 on page 658)

$$S_N \;=\; [[[\ldots[[U_{C-1}]\, z + U_{C-2}]\, z + \ldots + U_3]\, z + U_2]\, z + U_1]\, z + U_0 \tag{34.2-8}$$

where $U_c = \sum_{k=0}^{R-1} A_{kC+c}\, z^{kC}$ (C temporary sums are computed). If proceeding colum-wise, the update $A_i \to A_{i+1}$ involves only a short multiplication by the ratio A_{i+1}/A_i. Only when going to the next column a long multiplication by z^C is required ($R-1$ long multiplications). Finally, there are $C-1$ long multiplications by z.

34.2.2.1   Implementation for the exponential function

A routine for the computation of $\exp(z) - 1$ can be given as follows:

```
1    exp_rect(z, R, C)=
2    { /* compute exp(z)-1 as z*[ 1+z/2!+z^2/3! +...+z^(R*C-1)/((R*C)!) ] */
3        local(ur, zc, k, t);
4        zc = z^C;  \\ proportional log(C) long multiplications
5        ur = vector(C);
6        k = 1;  \\ ratio of series coefficients  /* set to zero for plain exp */
7        t = 1.0;
```

```
 8      for (r=1, R,   \\ number of columns (!)
 9          for (c=1, C,  ur[c] += t;  k++;  t /= (k); );
10          if ( r!=R,  t *= zc; );  \\ R-1 long multiplications
11      );
12      t = ur[C];
13      forstep (c=C-1, 1, -1,  t*=z; t+=ur[c]);  \\ C-1 long multiplications
14      t *= z;  /* omit for plain exp */
15      return( t );
16  }
```

We use the argument reduction given as relation 32.2-14 on page 629 and compute $\exp(1/5)$ to a precision of 30,000 decimal digits. We use $R = C = \sqrt{N} =: S$:

```
? z=0.2;
? e=exp(z)  \\ computed in 855 ms.
1.22140275816016983392107199464
? nred=32;
? z/=2^nred
4.65661287307739257812500000000 E-11
? S=48;  \\ N=S^2=2304
? r=exp_rect(z,S,S)  \\ computed in 395 ms.
4.65661287318581279537523334667 E-11
? for(k=1,nred,r=r+r+r^2);  \\ computed in 68 ms.
? r+=1
1.22140275816016983392107199464
? e-r
7.965120231677044083 E-30016  \\ OK
```

The timings for 100,000 digits, `nred=112`, and `S=52` are:

```
? e=exp(z);               \\ computed in 8,601 ms.
? r=exp_rect(z,S,S);      \\ computed in 2,345 ms.
? for(k=1,nred,r=r+r+r^2); \\ computed in 1,640 ms.
```

34.2.2.2 Implementation for the cosine

A routine for computing $\cos(z) - 1$ can be given as

```
 1   cos_rect(z, R, C)=
 2   { /* compute cos(z)-1 as z^2*[ -1/2!+z^2/4! - z^4/6! +- ... ] */
 3       local(ur, zc, k, t);
 4       z *= z;
 5       zc = z^C; \\ proportional log(C) long multiplications
 6       ur = vector(C);
 7       k = 2;  \\ ratio of series coefficients
 8       t = -0.5;
 9       for (r=1, R,  \\ number of columns (!)
10           for (c=1, C,  ur[c] += t;  k++;  t /= (k); k++;  t /= -(k); );
11           if ( r!=R,  t *= zc; );  \\ R-1 long multiplications
12       );
13       t = ur[C];
14       forstep (c=C-1, 1, -1,  t*=z; t+=ur[c]);  \\ C-1 long multiplications
15       t *= z;  /* omit for plain exp */
16       return( t );
17   }
```

We use the argument reduction as in relation 32.2-16 on page 629 and compute $\cos(1/5)$ to 30,000 decimal digits:

```
? z=0.2;
? e=cos(z)  \\ computed in 788 ms.
0.980066577841241631124196516748
? nred=32;
? z/=2^nred;
? S=34;  \\ N=S^2=1156
? r=cos_rect(z,S,S);  \\ computed in 318 ms.
? for(k=1,nred,r=2*(r+1)^2-2);  \\ computed in 70 ms.
? r+=1
0.980066577841241631124196516748
? e-r
-3.646143951667310362 E-30017  \\ OK
```

The sine and tangent can be computed as

$$\sin(z) \;=\; \sqrt{1 - \cos(z)^2} \qquad\qquad (34.2\text{-}9a)$$

$$\tan(z) \;=\; \frac{\sin(z)}{\cos(z)} \qquad\qquad (34.2\text{-}9b)$$

The routine is easily converted to compute the hyperbolic cosine. The following relation gives an alternative way to compute the exponential function:

$$\exp(z) \;=\; \cosh(z) - \sqrt{\cosh(z)^2 - 1} \qquad\qquad (34.2\text{-}10)$$

34.3 The magic sumalt algorithm for alternating series

The following convergence acceleration algorithm for alternating series is due to Cohen, Villegas and Zagier, see [111]. As remarked in the cited paper, the algorithm often gives meaningful results also for non-alternating and even divergent series.

The algorithm computes an estimate of the sum $s = \sum_{k=0}^{\infty} x_k$ as

$$s_n \;=\; \sum_{k=0}^{n-1} c_{n,k}\, x_k \qquad\qquad (34.3\text{-}1)$$

The weights $c_{n,k}$ do not depend on the values x_j. With the following pseudocode the summands x_k have to be supplied in the array x[0,1,...,n-1]:

```
1    function sumalt(x[], n)
2    {
3        d := (3+sqrt(8))^n
4        d := (d+1/d)/2
5        b := 1
6        c := d
7        s := 0
8        for k:=0 to n-1
9        {
10           c := c - b
11           s := s + c * x[k]
12           b := b * (2*(n+k)*(n-k)) / ((2*k+1)*(k+1))
13       }
14       return s/d
15   }
```

With alternating sums the accuracy of the estimate will be $(3 + \sqrt{8})^{-n} \approx 5.82^{-n}$. For example, the estimate for $4 \cdot \arctan(1)$ using the first 8 terms is

$$\pi \;\approx\; 4 \cdot \left(\frac{1}{1} - \frac{1}{3} + \frac{1}{5} - \frac{1}{7} + \frac{1}{9} - \frac{1}{11} + \frac{1}{13} - \frac{1}{15} \right) = 3.017\ldots \qquad (34.3\text{-}2)$$

The sumalt-massaged estimate with 8 terms is

$$\pi \;\approx\; 4 \cdot \left(\frac{665856}{1} - \frac{665728}{3} + \frac{663040}{5} - \frac{641536}{7} + \frac{557056}{9} - \frac{376832}{11} + \frac{163840}{13} - \frac{32768}{15} \right) / 665857 \qquad (34.3\text{-}3)$$

$$= \; 4 \cdot 3365266048/4284789795 \;=\; 3.141592665\ldots$$

and already gives seven correct digits of π. The linear but impressive growth of the accuracy of successive sumalt estimates with n, the number of terms used, is illustrated in figure 34.3-A.

n:	sumalt(n)	sumalt(n)$-\pi$
1:	2.6666666666666666666	0.4749259869231265717957
2:	3.1372549019607843137	0.0043377516290089247370
3:	3.1407407407407407407	0.0008519128490524977215
4:	3.1416357184121482215	$-$0.0000430648223549830441
5:	3.1415865464036739683	0.0000061071861192701145
6:	3.1415933442156594036	$-$0.0000006906258661651970
7:	3.1415925649375401220	0.0000000886522531164470
8:	3.1415926652243158640	$-$0.0000000116345226255550
9:	3.1415926520088119516	0.0000000015809812868435
10:	3.1415926538097315693	$-$0.0000000002199383308560
11:	3.1415926535585787555	0.0000000000312144829485
12:	3.1415926535942963384	$-$0.0000000000045031000073
13:	3.1415926535891345805	0.0000000000006586579445
14:	3.1415926535898907186	$-$0.0000000000000974801637
15:	3.1415926535897786643	0.0000000000000145740876
16:	3.1415926535897954367	$-$0.0000000000000021983122
17:	3.1415926535897929042	0.0000000000000003341779
18:	3.1415926535897932896	$-$0.0000000000000000511518
19:	3.1415926535897932305	0.0000000000000000078774
20:	3.1415926535897932396	$-$0.0000000000000000012209

Figure 34.3-A: Sumalt-estimates of $\pi = 4 \cdot \arctan(1)$ using $n = 1, 2, \ldots, 20$ terms.

Therefore even slowly converging series like

$$\pi = 4 \cdot \sum_{k=0}^{\infty} \frac{(-1)^k}{2\,k+1} = 4 \cdot \arctan(1) \tag{34.3-4a}$$

$$C = \sum_{k=0}^{\infty} \frac{(-1)^k}{(2\,k+1)^2} = 0.9159655941772190\ldots \tag{34.3-4b}$$

$$\log(2) = \sum_{k=0}^{\infty} \frac{(-1)^k}{k+1} = 0.6931471805599453\ldots \tag{34.3-4c}$$

$$\zeta(s) = \frac{1}{1-2^{1-s}} \sum_{k=1}^{\infty} \frac{(-1)^k}{k^s} \tag{34.3-4d}$$

can be used to compute estimates that are correct up to thousands of digits. The algorithm scales like n^2 if the series terms in the array x[] are small rational values and like $n^3 \cdot \log(n)$ if they are full precision (rational or float) values.

In fact, GP has a built-in sumalt routine, we use it to compute the *Catalan constant*:

```
? default(realprecision,1000); sumalt(k=0,(-1)^k/(2*k+1)^2);   \\ takes    60 ms.
? default(realprecision,2000); sumalt(k=0,(-1)^k/(2*k+1)^2);   \\ takes   376 ms.
? default(realprecision,4000); sumalt(k=0,(-1)^k/(2*k+1)^2);   \\ takes 2,730 ms.
```

The time scales roughly with the third power of the precision used.

The values c_k and b_k occurring in the computation are integers. In fact, the b_k in the computation with n terms are the coefficients of the expanded n-th Chebyshev polynomial of the first kind with argument $1 + 2x$ (see section 35.2 on page 676):

k :	b_k	c_k
0:	1	665857
1:	128	665856
2:	2688	665728
3:	21504	663040
4:	84480	641536
5:	180224	557056
6:	212992	376832
7:	131072	163840
8:	32768	32768

$$
\begin{aligned}
T_8(1+2x) &= 1 + 128x + 2688x^2 + 21504x^3 + 84480x^4 + \\
&\quad + 180224x^5 + 212992x^6 + 131072x^7 + 32768x^8 = T_{16}(\sqrt{1+x})
\end{aligned} \tag{34.3-5a}
$$

$$
\begin{aligned}
T_{16}(x) &= 1 - 128x^2 + 2688x^4 - 21504x^6 + 84480x^8 - \\
&\quad - 180224x^{10} + 212992x^{12} - 131072x^{14} + 32768x^{16}
\end{aligned} \tag{34.3-5b}
$$

Now observe that one has always $c_n = b_n = 2^{2n-1}$ in a length-n sumalt computation. The computation of $(3 + \sqrt{8})^n$ can be avoided by the following variant:

```
1    function sumalt(x[], n)
2    {
3        b := 2**(2*n-1)
4        c := b
5        s := 0
6        for k:=n-1 to 0 step -1
7        {
8            s := s + c * x[k]
9            b := b * ((2*k+1)*(k+1)) / (2*(n+k)*(n-k))
10           c := c + b
11       }
12       return s/c
13   }
```

The b_k and c_k occurring in a length-n sumalt computation can be given explicitly as

$$
b_k = \frac{n}{n+k}\binom{n+k}{2k}2^{2k} \tag{34.3-6a}
$$

$$
c_k = \sum_{i=k}^{n}\frac{n}{n+i}\binom{n+i}{2i}2^{2i} \tag{34.3-6b}
$$

To compute an estimate of $\sum_{k=0}^{\infty} x_k$ using the first n partial sums use the following pseudocode (the partial sums $p_k = \sum_{j=0}^{k} x_j$ are expected in p[0,1,...,n-1]):

```
1    function sumalt_partial(p[], n)
2    {
3        d := (3+sqrt(8))^n
4        d := (d+1/d)/2
5        b := 1
6        c := d
7        s := 0
8        for k:=0 to n-1
9        {
10           s := s + b * p[k]
11           b := b * (2*(n+k)*(n-k)) / ((2*k+1)*(k+1))
12       }
13       return s/d
14   }
```

The backward variant is:

```
1    function sumalt_partial(p[], n)
2    {
3        b := 2**(2*n-1)
4        c := b
5        s := 0
6        for k:=n-1 to 0 step -1
```

```
7        {
8            s := s + b * p[k]
9            b := b * ((2*k+1)*(k+1)) / (2*(n+k)*(n-k))
10           c := c + b
11       }
12       return s/c
13   }
```

Implementations of the sumalt algorithm and the variant for partial sums are given in [hfloat: src/hf/sumalt.cc].

For series of already geometrical rate of convergence (where $|a_k/a_{k+1}| \approx e$) it is better to use

```
1    function sumalt_partial(p[], n, e)
2    {
3        d := ( 2*e + 1 + 2*sqrt(e*(e+1)) )^n
4        d := (d+1/d)/2
5        b := 1
6        c := d
7        s := 0
8        for k:=0 to n-1
9        {
10           s := s + b * p[k]
11           b := b * (2*(n+k)*(n-k)) / ((2*k+1)*(k+1)) * e
12       }
13       return s/d
14   }
```

Convergence is improved from $\sim e^{-n}$ to $\sim \left(2e + 1 + 2\sqrt{e(e+1)}\right)^{-n} \approx (4e+2)^{-n}$. The special case $e = 1$ gives the original sumalt algorithm. For a survey of methods for convergence acceleration see [351].

Chapter 35

Recurrences and Chebyshev polynomials

We look at several algorithms for recurrences, mostly for the case of constant coefficients. The Chebyshev polynomials are described as an important special case of a recurrence.

35.1 Recurrences

A sequence $[a_0, a_1, a_2, \ldots]$ so that a *recurrence relation*

$$a_n = \sum_{j=1}^{k} m_j \, a_{n-j} \tag{35.1-1}$$

with given m_j holds for all a_j is called a k-th order *recurrence*. The recurrence is linear, homogeneous, with constant coefficients. The sequence is defined by both the recurrence relation and the first k elements.

For example, the second order recurrence relation $a_n = 1\,a_{n-1} + 1\,a_{n-2}$ together with $a_0 = 0$ and $a_1 = 1$ gives the Fibonacci numbers F_n, starting with $a_0 = 2$ and $a_1 = 1$ gives the Lucas numbers L_n:

```
  n : 0   1   2   3   4   5   6   7   8    9   10   11   12   13   14
F(n): 0   1   1   2   3   5   8  13  21   34   55   89  144  233  377
L(n): 2   1   3   4   7  11  18  29  47   76  123  199  322  521  843
```

The *characteristic polynomial* of the recurrence relation 35.1-1 is given by

$$p(x) = x^k - \sum_{j=1}^{k} m_j \, x^{k-j} \tag{35.1-2}$$

The definition can be motivated by writing down the recurrence relation for the element with index $n = k$:

$$0 = a_k - \left(\sum_{j=1}^{k} m_j \, a_{k-j} \right) \tag{35.1-3}$$

35.1.1 Fast computation using matrix powers

To compute the recurrence defined by the recurrence relation

$$a_n := m_1 \, a_{n-1} + m_2 \, a_{n-2} \tag{35.1-4}$$

and the initial values a_0, a_1, use

$$[a_0, \ a_1] \begin{bmatrix} 0 & m_2 \\ 1 & m_1 \end{bmatrix}^k = [a_k, \ a_{k+1}] \tag{35.1-5}$$

The algorithm is fast when powering algorithms (see section 28.5) are used.

J. Arndt, *Matters Computational: Ideas, Algorithms, Source Code*,
DOI 10.1007/978-3-642-14764-7_35, © Springer-Verlag Berlin Heidelberg 2011

Note that two consecutive terms of the sequence are computed, so the following terms a_{k+1}, a_{k+2}, ... can easily be computed by the original recurrence relation.

The generalization is straightforward. For example, a recurrence $a_n = m_1 a_{n-1} + m_2 a_{n-2} + m_3 a_{n-3}$ corresponds to

$$[a_0, \ a_1, \ a_2] \begin{bmatrix} 0 & 0 & m_3 \\ 1 & 0 & m_2 \\ 0 & 1 & m_1 \end{bmatrix}^k = [a_k, \ a_{k+1}, \ a_{k+2}] \qquad (35.1\text{-}6)$$

The matrix is the companion matrix of the characteristic polynomial $x^3 - (m_1 x^2 + m_2 x^1 + m_3 x^0)$, see relation 42.5-1 on page 899. Note that the indexing of the m_k is different here.

Performance

The computations are fast. As an example we give the timing of the computation of a few sequence terms with large indices. The following calculations were carried out with exact arithmetic, the post-multiply with the float 1.0 renders the output readable:

```
? M=[0,1;1,1]  \\ Fibonacci sequence
? #
   timer = 1 (on)
? ([0,1]*M^10000)[1]*1.0
time = 1 ms.
3.364476487643 E2089
? ([0,1]*M^100000)[1]*1.0
time = 10 ms.
2.597406934722 E20898
? ([0,1]*M^1000000)[1]*1.0
time = 458 ms.
1.953282128707 E208987
```

The powering algorithm can also be used for polynomial recurrences such as for the Chebyshev polynomials $T_n(x)$:

```
? M=[0,-1;1,2*x]
  [0 -1]
  [1 2*x]
? for(n=0,5,print(n,": ",([1,x]*M^n)[1]))
0: 1
1: x
2: 2*x^2 - 1
3: 4*x^3 - 3*x
4: 8*x^4 - 8*x^2 + 1
5: 16*x^5 - 20*x^3 + 5*x
? p=([1,x]*M^1000)[1];
time = 1,027 ms.
? poldegree(p)
1000
? log(polcoeff(p,poldegree(p)))/log(10)
300.728965668317  \\ The coefficient of x^1000 is a 301-digit number
```

With modular arithmetic the quantities remain bounded and the computations can be carried out for extreme large values of n. We use the modulus $m = 2^{1279} - 1$ and compute the $n = (m+1)/4$ element of the sequence $2, 4, 14, 52, \ldots$ where $a_n = 4 a_{n-1} - a_{n-2}$:

```
? m=2^1279-1;  \\ a 1279-bit number
? log(m)/log(10)
385.0173 \\ 306 decimal digits
? M=Mod([0,-1;1,4],m);  \\ all entries modulo m
? lift( ([2,4]*M^((m+1)/4))[1] )
time = 118 ms.
0
```

The result is zero which proves that m is prime, see section 39.11.4. Here is a one-liner that prints all exponents $e < 1000$ of Mersenne primes:

```
? forprime(e=3,1000,m=2^e-1;M=Mod([0,-1;1,4],m);if(0==(([2,4]*M^((m+1)/4))[1]),print1(" ", e)))
 3 5 7 13 17 19 31 61 89 107 127 521 607
```

The computation takes a few seconds only.

The connection of recurrences and matrix powers is investigated in [40].

35.1.2 Faster computation using polynomial arithmetic

The matrix power algorithm for computing the k-th element of an n-th order recursion involves $O(\log k)$ multiplications of $n \times n$ matrices. As matrix multiplication (with the straightforward algorithm) is $O(n^3)$ the algorithm is not optimal for recursions of high order. Note that the matrix entries grow exponentially, so the asymptotics as given is valid only for computations with bounded values such as with modular arithmetic. We will see that the involved work can be brought down from $\log k \cdot n^3$ to $\log k \cdot n^2$ and even to $\log k \cdot n \cdot \log n$.

The characteristic polynomial for the recursion $a_n := 3\,a_{n-1} + 1\,a_{n-2} + 2\,a_{n-3}$ is

$$p(x) \;=\; x^3 - 3\,x^2 - 1\,x - 2 \tag{35.1-7}$$

We list the first few powers of the companion matrix M of $p(x)$:

$$M^0 = \begin{bmatrix} 1 & 0 & 0 \\ 0 & 1 & 0 \\ 0 & 0 & 1 \end{bmatrix} \quad M^1 = \begin{bmatrix} 0 & 0 & 2 \\ 1 & 0 & 1 \\ 0 & 1 & 3 \end{bmatrix} \quad M^2 = \begin{bmatrix} 0 & 2 & 6 \\ 0 & 1 & 5 \\ 1 & 3 & 10 \end{bmatrix} \quad M^3 = \begin{bmatrix} 2 & 6 & 20 \\ 1 & 5 & 16 \\ 3 & 10 & 35 \end{bmatrix} \tag{35.1-8}$$

Each power is a left shifted version of its predecessor, only the rightmost colum is 'new'. Now compare the columns of the matrix powers to the first few values x^k modulo $p(x)$:

$$x^0 \bmod p(x) \;=\; 0\,x^2 + 0\,x + 1 \tag{35.1-9a}$$
$$x^1 \bmod p(x) \;=\; 0\,x^2 + 1\,x + 0 \tag{35.1-9b}$$
$$x^2 \bmod p(x) \;=\; 1\,x^2 + 0\,x + 0 \tag{35.1-9c}$$
$$x^3 \bmod p(x) \;=\; 3\,x^2 + 1\,x + 2 \tag{35.1-9d}$$
$$x^4 \bmod p(x) \;=\; 10\,x^2 + 5\,x + 6 \tag{35.1-9e}$$
$$x^5 \bmod p(x) \;=\; 35\,x^2 + 16\,x + 20 \tag{35.1-9f}$$

Observe that $x^k \bmod p(x)$ corresponds to the leftmost column of M^k.

We now turn the observation into an efficient algorithm. The main routines in this section take as arguments a vector v of initial values, a vector m of recursion coefficients and an index k. The vector $r = [a_k, a_{k+1}, \ldots, a_{k+n}]$ is returned. We compute the leftmost column of M^k as $z := x^k \bmod p(x)$ and compute a_k as the scalar product of z (as a vector) and v. Our main routine is:

```
1    frec(v, m, k)=
2    {
3        local(n, pc, pv, pp, px, r, t);
4        n = length(m);
5        if ( k<=n, return( recstep(v, m, k) ) );  \\ small indices by definition
6        pc = vec2charpol(m);
7        pp = Mod( x, pc );
8        px = pp^(k);
9        r = vector(n);
10       for (i=1, n,
11           t = lift(px);
12           r[i] = sum(j=1,n, v[j]*polcoeff(t,j-1,x));
13           px *= pp;
14       );
15       return( r );
16   }
```

If only the value a_k is of interest, skip the computations in the final `for` loop for the values i> 1.

For small indices k the result is computed directly by definition, using the following auxiliary routine:

```
1    recstep(v, m, k)=
2    { /* update v by k steps according to the recursion coefficients in m */
3        local(n,r);
4        if ( k<=0, return(v) );  \\ negative k is forbidden
5        n = length(m);
6        r = vector(n);
7        for (i=1, k,
```

```
8              for (j=1, n-1, r[j]=v[j+1] ); \\ shift left
9              r[n] = sum(j=1,n, m[n+1-j]*v[j]);  \\ new element (convolution)
10             v = r;
11          );
12          return( r );
13      }
```

The auxiliary routine used to compute the characteristic polynomial corresponding to the vector m is:

```
1   vec2charpol(m)=
2   { /* return characteristic polynomial for the recursion coefficients in m */
3       local(d,p);
4       d = length(m);
5       p = x^d - Pol(m,x);
6       return( p );
7   }
```

The computation of the k-th element of an n-term recurrence involves $O(\log k)$ modular polynomial multiplications. Thus the total cost is $O(\log k \cdot M(n))$ where $M(n)$ is the cost of the multiplication of two polynomials of degree n. That is, the method is $O(\log k \cdot n^2)$ when usual polynomial multiplication is used and $O(\log k \cdot n \cdot \log n)$ if an FFT scheme is applied. The computational advantage of powering modulo the characteristic polynomial versus matrix powering is pointed out in [77, p.392] (page 4 of the preprint).

The matrix power algorithm, restated for the argument structure defined above, can be implemented as:

```
1   mrec(v, m, k)=
2   {
3       local(p,M);
4       p = vec2charpol(m);
5       M = matcompanion(p);
6       M = M^k;
7       return ( v * M );
8   }
```

All main routines can be used with symbolic values:

```
? frec([a0,a1],[m1,m2],3)
   [m2*m1*a0 + (m1^2 + m2)*a1, (m2*m1^2 + m2^2)*a0 + (m1^3 + 2*m2*m1)*a1]
? mrec([a0,a1],[m1,m2],3)    \\ same result
? recstep([a0,a1],[m1,m2],3)  \\ same result
```

Performance

We check the performance of our routines (suppressing output):

```
? k=10^5;
? recstep([0,1],[1,1],k);
   time = 2,811 ms.  \\ time linear in k
? mrec([0,1],[1,1],k);
   time = 10 ms. \\ time linear in log(k)
? frec([0,1],[1,1],k);
   time = 4 ms. \\ time linear in log(k)
```

The relative performance of the routine `frec()` and `mrec()` differs more with higher orders n of the recurrence, we use $n = 10$:

```
? n=10; v=vector(n); v[n]=1; m=vector(n,j,1); k=10^5;  \\ tenth order recurrence
? mrec(v,m,k);
   time = 2,813 ms.
? f=frec(v,m,k);
   time =  159 ms.
? log(f)/log(10.0)
   [30078.67, 30078.97, 30079.27, 30079.58, 30079.88, 30080.18, \
   30080.48, 30080.78, 30081.08, 30081.38] \\ about 30k decimal digits each
```

We see a performance gain of $2813/159 \approx 17.7$, which is even greater than n. Finally, we repeat the computations modulo $p = 2^{521} - 1$ for $k = 10^{30}$:

```
?  n=10; v=vector(n); v[n]=1; m=vector(n,j,1); k=10^30;
?  p=2^521-1; v=Mod(v,p); m=Mod(m,p);
?  mrec(v,m,k);
   time = 312 ms.
```

```
? frec(v,m,k);
  time = 14 ms.
```

Here the performance gain is $312/14 \approx 22.3$.

35.1.3   Inhomogeneous recurrences

The fast algorithms for the computation of recurrences only work with *homogeneous* recurrences as defined by relation 35.1-1 on page 666. An *inhomogeneous* recurrence is defined by a relation

$$a_n = \sum_{j=1}^{k} m_j \, a_{n-j} + P(n) \qquad\qquad (35.1\text{-}10)$$

where $P(n)$ is a nonzero polynomial in n. We will show how to transform an inhomogeneous recurrence into a homogeneous recurrence of greater order.

35.1.3.1   Recurrence relations with a constant

Let the (k-th order) recurrence relation be

$$a_n = m_1 \, a_{n-1} + m_2 \, a_{n-2} + \ldots + m_k \, a_{n-k} + C \qquad\qquad (35.1\text{-}11)$$

Now subtract a shifted version

$$a_{n-1} = m_1 \, a_{n-2} + m_2 \, a_{n-3} + \ldots + m_k \, a_{n-k-1} + C \qquad\qquad (35.1\text{-}12)$$

to obtain a recurrence of order $k + 1$:

$$a_n = (m_1 + 1) \, a_{n-1} + (m_2 - m_1) \, a_{n-2} + \ldots + (m_k - m_{k-1}) \, a_{n-k} \qquad\qquad (35.1\text{-}13)$$

An example should make the idea clear: with $a_n = 34 \, a_{n-1} - a_{n-2} + 2$ subtract the shifted version $a_{n-1} = 34 \, a_{n-2} - a_{n-3} + 2$ to get $a_n = 35 \, a_{n-1} - 35 \, a_{n-2} + a_{n-3}$. For $a_0 = 1$, $a_1 = 36$ we computed the sequence with the original relation:

```
? n=7;
? ts=vector(n); ts[1]=1; ts[2]=36;
? for(k=3,n,ts[k]=34*ts[k-1]-ts[k-2]+2);
? ts
  [1, 36, 1225, 41616, 1413721, 48024900, 1631432881]
```

The same sequence can be computed with the relation without constant:

```
? ts=vector(n); ts[1]=1; ts[2]=36; ts[3]=34*ts[2]-ts[1]+2;
? for(k=4,n,ts[k]=35*ts[k-1]-35*ts[k-2]+ts[k-3]);
? ts
  [1, 36, 1225, 41616, 1413721, 48024900, 1631432881]
```

35.1.3.2   The general case

If the recurrence is of the form

$$a_n = m_1 \, a_{n-1} + m_2 \, a_{n-2} + \ldots + m_k \, a_{n-k} + P(n) \qquad\qquad (35.1\text{-}14)$$

where $P(n)$ is a polynomial of degree d in n, then a homogeneous recurrence of order $k + d + 1$

$$a_n = M_1 \, a_{n-1} + M_2 \, a_{n-2} + \ldots + M_{k+d+1} \, a_{n-k-d-1} \qquad\qquad (35.1\text{-}15)$$

can be found by repeatedly subtracting a shifted relation.

The following GP routine takes as input a vector of the multipliers m_i ($i = 1, \ldots, k$) and a polynomial of degree d in n. It returns a homogeneous recurrence relation as a vector $[M_1, \ldots, M_{k+d+1}]$:

```
1    ihom2hom(m, p)=
2    {
3        local(d, M, k);
4        if ( p==0, return(m) );
5        d = poldegree(p, 'n);
6        k = length(m);
7        M = vector(k+d+1);
8        for (j=1, k, M[j]=m[j]);
9        for (s=1, d+1,
10           M[1] += 1;  \\ left side
11           for (j=2, k+s, M[j] -= m[j-1]; );
12           m = M;
13       );
14       return(M);
15   }
```

To verify the output, we use a (slow) routine that directly computes the values of an inhomogeneous recurrence:

```
1    ihom(v, m, k, p)=
2    {
3        local(n, r);
4        if ( k<=0, return(v[1]) );
5        n = length(m);
6        r = vector(n);
7        for (i=1, k,
8            for (j=1, n-1, r[j]=v[j+1] ); \\ shift left
9            r[n] = sum(j=1,n, m[n+1-j]*v[j]);  \\ new element (convolution)
10           r[n] += subst(p, 'n, i+n-1);  \\ add inhomogeneous term
11           v = r;
12       );
13       return( r[1] );
14   }
```

We use the recurrence relation $a_n = 3\,a_{n-1} + 2a_{n-2} + (n^3 - n^2 - 7)$. We compute the homogeneous equivalent (intermediate values of M added):

```
? m=[3,+2];p=n^3-n^2-7;
? M=ihom2hom(m,p)
     [3, 2, 0, 0, 0, 0]
     [4, -1, -2, 0, 0, 0]
     [5, -5, -1, 2, 0, 0]
     [6, -10, 4, 3, -2, 0]
     [7, -16, 14, -1, -5, 2]
   [7, -16, 14, -1, -5, 2]  \\ a_n = 7*a_{n-1} - 16*a_{n-2} + 14*a_{n-3} +- ...
```

We can compute the first few values for the sequence starting with $a_0 = 2$, $a_1 = 5$ by the direct method:

```
? v=[2,5];
? for(k=0,9,print(k,":   ",ihom(v,m,k,p)));
   0:  2
   1:  5
   2:  16
   3:  69
   4:  280
   5:  1071
   6:  3946
   7:  14267
   8:  51134
   9:  182577
```

A vector of start values and the homogeneous equivalent allow the fast computation using the powering algorithms:

```
? V=vector(length(M),j,ihom(v,m,j-1,p))
   [2, 5, 16, 69, 280, 1071]
? for(k=0,9,print(k,":   ",frec(V,M,k)[1]));
   [- same output as with direct computation -]
```

The computation of $a_{10,000}$ now takes less than a second:

```
? z=frec(V,M,10^5)[1];  \\ result computed in 156 ms.
? 1.0*z
   1.72279531330182 E55164
? z=ihom(v,m,10^5,p);  \\ result computed in 6,768 ms.
```

35.1.4   Recurrence relations for subsequences

35.1.4.1   Two-term recurrences

The recurrence for the subsequence of every k-th element of a two-term recurrence $a_n = \alpha\, a_{n-1} + \beta\, a_{n-2}$ can be found as follows. Write

$$
\begin{aligned}
a_{n+0} &= A_0\, a_n + B_0\, a_{n-0} = 2\, a_n - 1\, a_{n-0} & \text{(35.1-16a)}\\
a_{n+1} &= A_1\, a_n + B_1\, a_{n-1} = \alpha\, a_n + \beta\, a_{n-1} & \text{(35.1-16b)}\\
a_{n+2} &= A_2\, a_n + B_2\, a_{n-2} = (\alpha^2 + 2\beta)\, a_n - \beta^2\, a_{n-2} & \text{(35.1-16c)}\\
a_{n+3} &= A_3\, a_n + B_3\, a_{n-3} = (\alpha^3 + 3\alpha\beta)\, a_n + \beta^3\, a_{n-3} & \text{(35.1-16d)}\\
a_{n+4} &= A_4\, a_n + B_4\, a_{n-4} = (\alpha^4 + 4\alpha^2\beta + 2\beta^2)\, a_n - \beta^4\, a_{n-4} & \text{(35.1-16e)}\\
a_{n+k} &= A_k\, a_n + B_k\, a_{n-k} & \text{(35.1-16f)}
\end{aligned}
$$

We have $a_n = A_k\, a_{n-k} + B_k\, a_{n-2k}$ where $A_0 = 2$, $A_1 = \alpha$ and $A_{k+1} = \alpha\, A_k + \beta\, A_{k-1}$ (and $B_k = -(-\beta)^k$). That is, the first coefficient A_k of the recursion relations for the subsequences can be computed by the original recurrence relation. For efficient computation use

$$
[A_k,\ A_{k+1}] = [2,\ \alpha]\begin{bmatrix} 0 & \beta \\ 1 & \alpha \end{bmatrix}^k \tag{35.1-17}
$$

A closed form for A_k in terms of Chebyshev polynomials is given in [39, item 14]:

$$
A_k = 2\,(-\beta)^{k/2}\, T_k\left(\alpha/\sqrt{-4\beta}\right) \tag{35.1-18}
$$

A simple example, let F_n and L_n denote the n-th Fibonacci and Lucas number, respectively. Then $\alpha = \beta = 1$ and

$$
[A_k,\ A_{k+1}] = [2,\ 1]\begin{bmatrix} 0 & 1 \\ 1 & 1 \end{bmatrix}^k = [L_k,\ L_{k+1}] \tag{35.1-19}
$$

That is

$$
F_{k\,n+e} = L_k\, F_{k\,(n-1)+e} - (-1)^k\, F_{k\,(n-2)+e} \tag{35.1-20}
$$

where $k \in \mathbb{Z}$ and $e \in \mathbb{Z}$. The variable e expresses the shift invariance of the relation.

35.1.4.2   Recurrences of order n

For the stride-s recurrence relations of order n the following may be the most straightforward algorithm. Let $p(x)$ be the characteristic polynomial of the recurrence and M its companion matrix. Then the characteristic polynomial of M^s corresponds to the recurrence relation of the stride-s subsequence.

```
1    recsubseq(n, s, m=0)=
2    { /* Return vector coefficients of the stride-s subsequence
3      * of the n-th order linear recurrence.
4      */
5      local(p, M, z, r);
6      if ( 0==m,
7          m = vector(n,j,eval(Str("m" j)));   \\ use symbols m_j
8          , /* else */
9          n = length(m);   \\ m given
10       );
11       p = vec2charpol(m);
12       M = matcompanion(p);
13       z = x^n-charpoly(M^s);
14       r = vector(n,j,polcoeff(z,n-j,x));
15       return( r );
16    }
```

For the second order recurrence we find what we have already seen for $s = 0, \dots, 4$:

```
? m=[a,b];
? for(s=-2,5,print(s,": ",recsubseq(0,s,m)););
  -2:  [1/b^2*a^2 + 2/b,   -1/b^2]
  -1:  [-1/b*a,    1/b]
   0:  [2,    -1]
   1:  [a,    b]
   2:  [a^2 + 2*b,    -b^2]
   3:  [a^3 + 3*b*a,    b^3]
   4:  [a^4 + 4*b*a^2 + 2*b^2,    -b^4]
   5:  [a^5 + 5*b*a^3 + 5*b^2*a,    b^5]
```

For the third order recurrence we find:

```
? m=[a,b,c];
? for(s=-2,5,print(s,": ",recsubseq(0,s,m)););
  -2:  [2/-c*a - 1/-c^2*b^2,   1/-c^2*a^2 + 2/-c^2*b,   1/c^2]
  -1:  [-1/c*b,   1/-c*a,   1/c]
   0:  [3,   -3,   1]
   1:  [a,   b,   c]
   2:  [a^2 + 2*b,   2*c*a - b^2,   c^2]
   3:  [a^3 + 3*b*a + 3*c,   -3*c*b*a + (b^3 - 3*c^2),   c^3]
   4:  [a^4 + 4*b*a^2 + 4*c*a + 2*b^2, \
       -2*c^2*a^2 + 4*c*b^2*a + (-b^4 + 4*c^2*b), \
       c^4]
   5:  [a^5 + 5*b*a^3 + 5*c*a^2 + 5*b^2*a + 5*c*b, \
       5*c^2*b*a^2 + (-5*c*b^3 + 5*c^3)*a + (b^5 - 5*c^2*b^2), \
       c^5]
```

35.1.5 Generating functions for recurrences

A generating function for a recurrence has a power series where the k-th coefficient equals the k-th term of the recurrence. For example, for the Fibonacci and Lucas numbers:

$$\frac{x}{1-x-x^2} \; = \; 0 + x + x^2 + 2x^3 + 3x^4 + 5x^5 + 8x^6 + 13x^7 + \dots \; = \; \sum_{k=0}^{\infty} F_k \, x^k \qquad (35.1\text{-}21\text{a})$$

$$\frac{2-x}{1-x-x^2} \; = \; 2 + x + 3x^2 + 4x^3 + 7x^4 + 11x^5 + 18x^6 + 29x^7 + \dots \; = \; \sum_{k=0}^{\infty} L_k \, x^k \qquad (35.1\text{-}21\text{b})$$

In general, for a recurrence $a_n = \sum_{k=1}^{K} m_k \, a_{n-k}$ with given $a_0, a_1, \dots, a_K$ we have

$$\frac{\sum_{j=0}^{K-1} b_j \, x^j}{1 - \sum_{j=1}^{K} m_j \, x^j} \; = \; \sum_{j=0}^{\infty} a_j \, x^j \qquad (35.1\text{-}22\text{a})$$

where the denominator is the reciprocal polynomial of the characteristic polynomial and

$$b_0 \; = \; a_0 \qquad\qquad\qquad\qquad\qquad\qquad (35.1\text{-}23\text{a})$$

$$b_1 \; = \; a_1 - (a_0 \, m_1) \qquad\qquad\qquad\qquad (35.1\text{-}23\text{b})$$

$$b_2 \; = \; a_2 - (a_0 \, m_2 + a_1 \, m_1) \qquad\qquad (35.1\text{-}23\text{c})$$

$$b_3 \; = \; a_3 - (a_0 \, m_3 + a_1 \, m_2 + a_2 \, m_1) \qquad (35.1\text{-}23\text{d})$$

$$b_k \; = \; a_k - \sum_{j=0}^{k-1} a_j \, m_{k-j} \qquad\qquad\qquad (35.1\text{-}23\text{e})$$

As an example we choose the sequence

$$[0, 0, 1, 1, 2, 4, 7, 13, 24, 44, 81, 149, 274, \dots] \qquad (35.1\text{-}24)$$

with the recurrence relation $a_n = a_{n-1} + a_{n-2} + a_{n-2}$:

```
? a=[0,0,1];  m=[1,1,1];  K=length(m);
? b=vector(K, k, a[k]-sum(j=0,k-2, a[j+1]*m[k-j-1]))
  [0, 0, 1]
? pb=sum(j=0,K-1,b[j+1]*x^j)
  x^2
? pr=1-sum(k=1,K,m[k]*x^k) \\ reciprocal of charpoly
  -x^3 - x^2 - x + 1
? gen=pb/pr  \\ the generating function
  x^2/(-x^3 - x^2 - x + 1)
? t=taylor(gen, x)
  x^2 + x^3 + 2*x^4 + 4*x^5 + 7*x^6 + 13*x^7 + 24*x^8 + 44*x^9 + 81*x^10
  + 149*x^11 + 274*x^12 + 504*x^13 + 927*x^14 + 1705*x^15 + 3136*x^16 + O(x^17)
? t=truncate(t);  for(j=0,poldegree(t),print1("  ",polcoeff(t,j)))
  0  0  1  1  2  4  7  13  24  44  81  149  274  504  927  1705  3136
```

Note that the denominator is the reciprocal of the characteristic polynomial. The general form of the expressions for a two-term linear recurrence can be computed using symbols:

```
? a=[a0,a1];  m=[m1,m2];  K=length(m);
? b=vector(K,k,a[k]-sum(j=0,k-2,a[j+1]*m[k-j-1]))
  [a0, -m1*a0 + a1]
? pb=sum(j=0,K-1,b[j+1]*x^j)
  (-m1*a0 + a1)*x + a0
? pr=1-sum(k=1,K,m[k]*x^k)
  -m2*x^2 - m1*x + 1
? gen=pb/pr  \\ the generating function
  ((-m1*a0 + a1)*x + a0)/(-m2*x^2 - m1*x + 1)
? t=taylor(gen,x);
? t=truncate(t);  for(j=0,poldegree(t),print(j,":  ",polcoeff(t,j)))
  0:  a0
  1:  a1
  2:  m2*a0 + m1*a1
  3:  m2*m1*a0 + (m1^2 + m2)*a1
  4:  (m2*m1^2 + m2^2)*a0 + (m1^3 + 2*m2*m1)*a1
  5:  (m2*m1^3 + 2*m2^2*m1)*a0 + (m1^4 + 3*m2*m1^2 + m2^2)*a1
  6:  (m2*m1^4 + 3*m2^2*m1^2 + m2^3)*a0 + (m1^5 + 4*m2*m1^3 + 3*m2^2*m1)*a1
  7:  (m2*m1^5 + 4*m2^2*m1^3 + 3*m2^3*m1)*a0 + (m1^6 + 5*m2*m1^4 + 6*m2^2*m1^2 + m2^3)*a1
```

35.1.6   Binet forms for recurrences

A closed form expression for the Fibonacci numbers is

$$F_n = \frac{1}{\sqrt{5}}\left[\left(\frac{1+\sqrt{5}}{2}\right)^n - \left(\frac{1-\sqrt{5}}{2}\right)^n\right] \tag{35.1-25}$$

A closed form solution for the two-term recurrence $a_n = m_1\,a_{n-1} + m_2\,a_{n-2}$ is given by

$$a_n = \frac{1}{w}\left[(a_1 - a_0\,r_1)\,r_0^n - (a_1 - a_0\,r_0)\,r_1^n\right] \tag{35.1-26a}$$

where $w = \sqrt{m_1^2 + 4\,m_2}$, $r_0 = (m_1 + w)/2$, and $r_1 = (m_1 - w)/2$ (the relation is valid only if $r_0 \neq r_1$). For $a_0 = 0$ we have

$$a_n = \frac{a_1}{w}\left[r_0^n - r_1^n\right] \tag{35.1-27a}$$

If $a_0 = 0$, $a_1 = 1$, $\gcd(m_1, m_2) = 1$, and $a_n > 0$ for $n > 0$, then (compare with 39.11-3a on page 797)

$$\gcd(a_i, a_j) = a_{\gcd(i,j)} \tag{35.1-28}$$

With integer $m_1 = k > 0$ the a_n are positive for all $n > 0$ if $m_2 \geq -e_k$ where $[e_1, e_2, \ldots, e_8] = [0, 1, 2, 3, 6, 7, 12, 15]$ and $e_k = +2\,e_{k-1} - e_{k-2} + e_{k-4} - 2\,e_{k-5} + e_{k-6}$ for $k \geq 9$. The sequence of values e_k starts as

```
m1=k:  1,  2,  3,  4,  5,  6,   7,   8,   9,  10,  11,  12,  13,  14,  15,  16,  17,  18,  19,  20,   21,  ...
  ek:  0,  1,  2,  3,  6,  7,  12,  15,  20,  23,  30,  35,  42,  47,  56,  63,  72,  79,  90,  99,  110,  ...
```

With $a_0 = 0$, $a_1 = 1$, $\gcd(m_1, m_2) = 1$, but m_1 and m_2 are otherwise arbitrary, we have

$$\gcd(|a_i|, |a_j|) = |a_{\gcd(i,j)}| \tag{35.1-29}$$

35.1.6.1 Binet form for n-term recurrences

We use a three-term recurrence to exemplify how expressions like 35.1-26a can be found in general: Let $a_n = m_1 a_{n-1} + m_2 a_{n-2} + m_3 a_{n-3}$, its characteristic polynomial is $p(x) = x^3 - (m_1 x^2 + m_2 x + m_3)$. Let r_0, r_1, r_2 be the roots of $p(x)$. The *Binet form* of the recurrence is

$$a_n = c_0 r_0^n + c_1 r_1^n + c_2 r_2^n \tag{35.1-30}$$

The coefficients c_0, c_1, and c_2 have to satisfy

$$
\begin{aligned}
a_0 &= c_0 + c_1 + c_2 & \text{(35.1-31a)}\\
a_1 &= r_0 c_0 + r_1 c_1 + r_2 c_2 & \text{(35.1-31b)}\\
a_2 &= r_0^2 c_0 + r_1^2 c_1 + r_2^2 c_2 & \text{(35.1-31c)}
\end{aligned}
$$

We have to solve the equation $Z \cdot c = a$ for the vector c where a is the vector of starting values and

$$Z = \begin{bmatrix} 1 & 1 & 1 \\ r_0 & r_1 & r_2 \\ r_0^2 & r_1^2 & r_2^2 \end{bmatrix} \tag{35.1-32}$$

Verification with the recurrence $a_n = a_{n-1} + a_{n-2} + a_{n-2}$ starting with $a_0 = a_1 = 0$ and $a_2 = 1$:

```
? a=[0,0,1]~;  m=[1,1,1]~;  K=length(m);
? p=x^K-sum(k=1,K,m[k]*x^(K-k)) \\ characteristic polynomial
  x^3 - x^2 - x - 1
? r=(polroots(p))
  [1.8392867,   -0.419643 - 0.606290*I,  -0.419643 + 0.6062907*I]~
? Z=matrix(K,K,ri,ci,r[ci]^(ri-1))
  [1 1 1]
  [1.839286   -0.4196433 - 0.6062907*I   -0.4196433 + 0.6062907*I]
  [3.382975   -0.1914878 + 0.5088517*I   -0.1914878 - 0.5088517*I]
? c=matsolve(Z,a)
  [0.1828035 + 1.8947 E-20*I,  -0.09140176 - 0.3405465*I,  -0.0914017 + 0.3405465*I]~
? norm(Z*c-a) \\ check solution
  [1.147 E-39,   6.795 E-39,   3.673 E-39]~
? seq(n)=sum(k=0,K-1,c[k+1]*r[k+1]^n)
? for(n=0,20,print1(" ",round(seq(n))))
  0 0 1 1 2 4 7 13 24 44 81 149 274 504 927 1705 3136 5768 10609 19513 35890
```

The method fails if the characteristic polynomial has multiple roots because then the matrix Z is singular.

35.1.6.2 Binet form with multiple roots of the characteristic polynomial

If the characteristic polynomial has multiple roots, the Binet form has coefficients that are polynomials in n. For example, for the characteristic polynomials $p(x) = (x - r_0)^3 (x - r_1)$ the Binet form would be $a_n = (c_0 + n d_0 + n^2 e_0) r_0^n + c_1 r_1^n$. With $n = 0$, 1, and 2 we obtain the system of equations

$$
\begin{aligned}
a_0 &= (c_0 + 0 d_0 + 0^2 e_0) + c_1 & \text{(35.1-33a)}\\
a_1 &= r_0 (c_0 + 1 d_0 + 1^2 e_0) + r_1 c_1 & \text{(35.1-33b)}\\
a_2 &= r_0^2 (c_0 + 2 d_0 + 2^2 e_0) + r_1^2 c_1 & \text{(35.1-33c)}
\end{aligned}
$$

In general, the coefficient of the power of the k-th root r_k in the Binet form must be a polynomial of degree $m_k - 1$ where m_k is the multiplicity of r_k.

35.1.6.3 The special case $c_k = 1$ for all k

Let $p(x)$ be the characteristic polynomial of a recurrence, with roots r_i: $p(x) = \prod_k (x - r_k)$. We want to determine the generating function for the recurrence such that $a_j = \sum_k r_k^j$ (that is, all constants c_k are one). For the reciprocal polynomial h of p we have $h(x) = \prod_k (1 - r_k x_k)$ and (using the product rule for differentiation)

$$h'(x) = h(x) \sum_k \frac{-r_k}{1 - r_k x} \tag{35.1-34}$$

With $r/(1 - r\,x) = \sum_{j\geq 0} r^{j+1}\,x^j$ we find that

$$-\frac{h'(x)}{h(x)} \;=\; \sum_{j\geq 0}\left(\sum_k r_k^{j+1}\right) x^j \tag{35.1-35}$$

That is, $a_j = \sum_k r_k^{j+1}$ and $c_k = 1$ for all k. The relation is the key to the fast computation of the trace vector in finite fields, see relation 42.3-6 on page 896.

35.1.7   Logarithms of generating functions ‡

A seemingly mysterious relation for the generating function of the Fibonacci numbers

$$f(x) \;:=\; \frac{1}{1 - x - x^2} \;=\; 1 + x + 2x^2 + 3x^3 + 5x^4 + 8x^5 + \ldots \;=\; \sum_{k=0}^{\infty} F_{k+1}\,x^k \tag{35.1-36a}$$

is

$$\log(f(x)) \;=\; x + \frac{1}{2}\,3\,x^2 + \frac{1}{3}\,4\,x^3 + \frac{1}{4}\,7\,x^4 + \frac{1}{5}\,11\,x^5 + \ldots \;=\; \sum_{k=1}^{\infty} \frac{1}{k}\,L_k\,x^k \tag{35.1-36b}$$

where L_k are the Lucas numbers. Similarly,

$$g(x) \;:=\; \frac{1}{1 - 2\,x - x^2} \;=\; 1 + 2x + 5x^2 + 12x^3 + 29x^4 + 70x^5 + 169x^6 + \ldots \tag{35.1-37a}$$

$$\log(g(x)) \;=\; 2\left[x + \frac{1}{2}\,3\,x^2 + \frac{1}{3}\,7\,x^3 + \frac{1}{4}\,17\,x^4 + \frac{1}{5}\,41\,x^5 + \frac{1}{6}\,99\,x^6 + \ldots\right] \tag{35.1-37b}$$

Now set $f(x) =: \frac{1}{h(x)}$, then

$$\frac{d}{d\,x}\log(f(x)) \;=\; \frac{d}{d\,x}\log\left(\frac{1}{h(x)}\right) = -\frac{h'(x)}{h(x)} \tag{35.1-38}$$

The expression $\frac{h'(x)}{h(x)}$ is again the generating function of a recurrence and formal integration of the power series gives the factors $\frac{1}{k}$. This is a special case of the algorithm for the computation of the logarithm for powers series given in section 32.3 on page 630.

35.2   Chebyshev polynomials

The *Chebyshev polynomials* of the first (T) and second (U) kind can be defined by the functions

$$T_n(x) \;=\; \cos\left[n\,\arccos(x)\right] \tag{35.2-1a}$$

$$U_n(x) \;=\; \frac{\sin\left[(n+1)\,\arccos(x)\right]}{\sqrt{1 - x^2}} \tag{35.2-1b}$$

For integral n both of them are polynomials. The first few polynomials are given in figure 35.2-A (first kind) and figure 35.2-B (second kind).

Expressions as hypergeometric series are given as relations 36.3-7b and 36.3-7c on page 695. Explicit

$$
\begin{aligned}
T_{-n}(x) &= T_n(x) \\
T_{-1}(x) &= x \\
T_0(x) &= 1 \\
T_1(x) &= x \\
T_2(x) &= 2\,x^2 - 1 \\
T_3(x) &= 4\,x^3 - 3\,x \\
T_4(x) &= 8\,x^4 - 8\,x^2 + 1 \\
T_5(x) &= 16\,x^5 - 20\,x^3 + 5\,x \\
T_6(x) &= 32\,x^6 - 48\,x^4 + 18\,x^2 - 1 \\
T_7(x) &= 64\,x^7 - 112\,x^5 + 56\,x^3 - 7\,x \\
T_8(x) &= 128\,x^8 - 256\,x^6 + 160\,x^4 - 32\,x^2 + 1 \\
T_9(x) &= 256\,x^9 - 576\,x^7 + 432\,x^5 - 120\,x^3 + 9\,x \\
T_{10}(x) &= 512\,x^{10} - 1280\,x^8 + 1120\,x^6 - 400\,x^4 + 50\,x^2 - 1 \\
T_{11}(x) &= 1024\,x^{11} - 2816\,x^9 + 2816\,x^7 - 1232\,x^5 + 220\,x^3 - 11\,x
\end{aligned}
$$

Figure 35.2-A: The first few Chebyshev polynomials of the first kind.

$$
\begin{aligned}
U_{-n}(x) &= -U_{n-2}(x) \\
U_{-2}(x) &= -1 \\
U_{-1}(x) &= 0 \\
U_0(x) &= 1 \\
U_1(x) &= 2\,x \\
U_2(x) &= 4\,x^2 - 1 \\
U_3(x) &= 8\,x^3 - 4\,x \\
U_4(x) &= 16\,x^4 - 12\,x^2 + 1 \\
U_5(x) &= 32\,x^5 - 32\,x^3 + 6\,x \\
U_6(x) &= 64\,x^6 - 80\,x^4 + 24\,x^2 - 1 \\
U_7(x) &= 128\,x^7 - 192\,x^5 + 80\,x^3 - 8\,x \\
U_8(x) &= 256\,x^8 - 448\,x^6 + 240\,x^4 - 40\,x^2 + 1 \\
U_9(x) &= 512\,x^9 - 1024\,x^7 + 672\,x^5 - 160\,x^3 + 10\,x \\
U_{10}(x) &= 1024\,x^{10} - 2304\,x^8 + 1792\,x^6 - 560\,x^4 + 60\,x^2 - 1 \\
U_{11}(x) &= 2048\,x^{11} - 5120\,x^9 + 4608\,x^7 - 1792\,x^5 + 280\,x^3 - 12\,x
\end{aligned}
$$

Figure 35.2-B: The first few Chebyshev polynomials of the second kind.

expressions are

$$
T_n(x) = \frac{n}{2} \sum_{k=0}^{\lfloor n/2 \rfloor} (-1)^k \frac{(n-k-1)!}{k!\,(n-2k)!} (2x)^{n-2k} \tag{35.2-2a}
$$

$$
= \frac{n}{2} \sum_{k=0}^{\lfloor n/2 \rfloor} (-1)^k \frac{1}{n-k} \binom{n-k}{k} (2x)^{n-2k} \tag{35.2-2b}
$$

$$
= \sum_{k=0}^{\lfloor n/2 \rfloor} \binom{n}{2k} x^{n-2k} (x^2 - 1)^k \tag{35.2-2c}
$$

and

$$U_n(x) \quad = \quad \sum_{k=0}^{\lfloor n/2 \rfloor} (-1)^k \frac{(n-k)!}{k!\,(n-2k)!} \,(2x)^{n-2k} \tag{35.2-3a}$$

$$= \quad \sum_{k=0}^{\lfloor n/2 \rfloor} (-1)^k \binom{n-k}{k} (2x)^{n-2k} \tag{35.2-3b}$$

$$= \quad \sum_{k=0}^{\lfloor n/2+1 \rfloor} \binom{n+1}{2\,k+1} x^{n-2k} \,(x^2-1)^k \tag{35.2-3c}$$

The indexing of U seems to be slightly unfortunate, having $U_0 = 0$ would render many of the relations for the Chebyshev polynomials more symmetric.

The $n+1$ extrema of $T_n(x)$ are located at the points $x_k = \cos \frac{k\pi}{n}$ where $k = 0, 1, 2, \ldots, n$ and $-1 \leq x_k \leq +1$, which can be seen from the definition. The values at those points are ± 1. The n zeros lie at $x_k = \cos \frac{(k-1/2)\,\pi}{n}$ where $k = 1, 2, 3, \ldots, n$.

The expansion of x^n in terms of Chebyshev polynomials of the first kind is, for n even,

$$x^n \quad = \quad \frac{1}{2^n} \binom{n}{n/2} + \frac{1}{2^{n-1}} \sum_{k=0}^{n/2-1} \binom{n}{k} T_{n-2k}(x) \tag{35.2-4a}$$

and, for odd n,

$$x^n \quad = \quad \frac{1}{2^{n-1}} \sum_{k=0}^{(n-1)/2} \binom{n}{k} T_{n-2k}(x) \tag{35.2-4b}$$

For the Chebyshev polynomials of the first kind we have

$$T_n\left(\frac{x+1/x}{2}\right) \quad = \quad \frac{x^n + 1/x^n}{2} \tag{35.2-5}$$

This relation can be used to find a solution of $T_n(x) = z$ directly. Indeed

$$x \quad = \quad \frac{R_n + 1/R_n}{2} \quad \text{where} \quad R_n := \left(z + \sqrt{z^2-1}\right)^{1/n} \tag{35.2-6}$$

is a solution which can be chosen to be real if $z \in \mathbb{R}$ and $z > 1$. Thus we have the closed form expression

$$T_n(z) \quad = \quad \frac{r^n + r^{-n}}{2} \quad \text{where} \quad r := \left(z + \sqrt{z^2-1}\right) \tag{35.2-7}$$

35.2.1   Recurrence relation, generating functions, and the composition law

Both types of Chebyshev polynomials obey the same recurrence (omitting the argument x)

$$N_n \quad = \quad 2\,x\,N_{n-1} - N_{n-2} \tag{35.2-8}$$

where N can be either symbol, T or U. Recurrence relations for subsequences are:

$$N_{n+1} \quad = \quad [2\,x] \cdot N_n - N_{n-1} \tag{35.2-9a}$$
$$N_{n+2} \quad = \quad \left[2\,(2x^2 - 1)\right] \cdot N_n - N_{n-2} \tag{35.2-9b}$$
$$N_{n+3} \quad = \quad \left[2\,(4x^3 - 3x)\right] \cdot N_n - N_{n-3} \tag{35.2-9c}$$
$$N_{n+4} \quad = \quad \left[2\,(8x^4 - 8x^2 + 1]\right] \cdot N_n - N_{n-4} \tag{35.2-9d}$$
$$N_{n+5} \quad = \quad \left[2\,(16x^5 - 20x^3 + 5x)\right] \cdot N_n - N_{n-5} \tag{35.2-9e}$$
$$N_{n+s} \quad = \quad [2\,T_s(x)] \cdot N_n - N_{n-s} \tag{35.2-9f}$$

The identities are equivalent to

$$\cos(\varphi + \gamma) = 2\cos(\gamma)\cos(\varphi) - \cos(\varphi - \gamma) \qquad (35.2\text{-}10a)$$
$$\sin(\varphi + \gamma) = 2\cos(\gamma)\sin(\varphi) - \sin(\varphi - \gamma) \qquad (35.2\text{-}10b)$$

The generating functions are

$$\frac{1 - xt}{1 - 2xt + t^2} = \sum_{n=0}^{\infty} t^n T_n(x) \qquad (35.2\text{-}11a)$$

$$\frac{1}{1 - 2xt + t^2} = \sum_{n=0}^{\infty} t^n U_n(x) \qquad (35.2\text{-}11b)$$

Quick check of relation 35.2-11a using GP:

```
? gen=truncate(taylor((1-t*x)/(1-2*x*t+t^2),t));
? for(k=0,5,print(k,":  ",polcoeff(gen,k,t)));
0:  1
1:  x
2:  2*x^2 - 1
3:  4*x^3 - 3*x
4:  8*x^4 - 8*x^2 + 1
5:  16*x^5 - 20*x^3 + 5*x
```

Binet forms for T (compare with relation 35.2-7) and U are

$$T_n(x) = \frac{1}{2}\left[\left(x + \sqrt{x^2 - 1}\right)^n + \left(x - \sqrt{x^2 - 1}\right)^n\right] \qquad (35.2\text{-}12a)$$

$$U_n(x) = \frac{1}{2\sqrt{x^2 - 1}}\left[\left(x + \sqrt{x^2 - 1}\right)^{n+1} - \left(x - \sqrt{x^2 - 1}\right)^{n+1}\right] \qquad (35.2\text{-}12b)$$

We have (compare to relation 35.1-28 on page 674)

$$\gcd(U_{n-1}, U_{m-1}) = U_{\gcd(n-1, m-1)} \qquad (35.2\text{-}13)$$

Composition is multiplication of indices as can be seen by the definition (relation 35.2-1a):

$$T_n(T_m(x)) = T_{nm}(x) \qquad (35.2\text{-}14)$$

For example,

$$T_{2n}(x) = T_2(T_n(x)) = 2T_n^2(x) - 1 \qquad (35.2\text{-}15a)$$
$$= T_n(T_2(x)) = T_n(2x^2 - 1) \qquad (35.2\text{-}15b)$$

35.2.2 Index-doubling and relations between T and U

Index-doubling relations for the polynomials of the first kind are

$$T_{2n} = 2T_n^2 - 1 \qquad (35.2\text{-}16a)$$
$$T_{2n+1} = 2T_{n+1}T_n - x \qquad (35.2\text{-}16b)$$
$$T_{2n-1} = 2T_n T_{n-1} - x \qquad (35.2\text{-}16c)$$

Similar relations for the polynomials of the second kind are

$$U_{2n} = U_n^2 - U_{n-1}^2 = (U_n + U_{n-1})(U_n - U_{n-1}) \qquad (35.2\text{-}17a)$$
$$= U_n(U_n - U_{n-2}) - 1 = U_{n-1}(U_{n+1} - U_{n-1}) + 1 \qquad (35.2\text{-}17b)$$
$$U_{2n+1} = U_n(U_{n+1} - U_{n-1}) \qquad (35.2\text{-}17c)$$
$$= 2U_n(U_{n+1} - xU_n) = 2U_n(xU_n - U_{n-1}) \qquad (35.2\text{-}17d)$$
$$U_{2n-1} = U_{n-1}(U_n - U_{n-2}) \qquad (35.2\text{-}17e)$$
$$= 2U_{n-1}(U_n - xU_{n-1}) = 2U_{n-1}(xU_{n-1} - U_{n-2}) \qquad (35.2\text{-}17f)$$

Some relations between T and U are

$$T_n \;=\; U_n - x\,U_{n-1} \;=\; x\,U_{n-1} - U_{n-2} \;=\; \frac{1}{2}\,(U_n - U_{n-2}) \tag{35.2-18a}$$

$$T_{n+1} \;=\; x\,T_n - (1 - x^2)\,U_{n-1} \tag{35.2-18b}$$

$$U_{2n} \;=\; 2\,T_n\,U_n - 1 \tag{35.2-18c}$$

$$U_{2n-1} \;=\; 2\,T_n\,U_{n-1} \;=\; 2\,(T_{n+1}\,U_n + x) \tag{35.2-18d}$$

$$U_{2n+1} \;=\; 2\,T_{n+1}\,U_n \;=\; 2\,(T_{n+2}\,U_{n-1} + x) \tag{35.2-18e}$$

$$U_{2^n - 1} \;=\; 2^n \prod_{k=0}^{n-1} T_{2^k} \tag{35.2-18f}$$

Relation 35.2-18b, written as

$$U_n \;=\; \frac{x\,T_{n+1} - T_{n+2}}{1 - x^2} \;=\; \frac{T_n - x\,T_{n+1}}{1 - x^2} \tag{35.2-19}$$

can be used to compute the polynomials of the second kind from those of the first kind. One further has:

$$T_{n+m} + T_{n-m} \;=\; 2\,T_n\,T_m \tag{35.2-20a}$$

$$T_{n+m} - T_{n-m} \;=\; 2\,(x^2 + 1)\,U_{n-1}\,U_{m-1} \tag{35.2-20b}$$

$$U_{n+m-1} + U_{n-m-1} \;=\; 2\,U_{n-1}\,T_m \tag{35.2-20c}$$

$$U_{n+m-1} - U_{n-m-1} \;=\; 2\,T_n\,U_{m-1} \tag{35.2-20d}$$

Expressions for certain sums:

$$\sum_{k=0}^{n} T_{2k} \;=\; \frac{1}{2}\,(1 + U_{2n}) \tag{35.2-21a}$$

$$\sum_{k=0}^{n-1} T_{2k+1} \;=\; \frac{1}{2}\,U_{2n-1} \tag{35.2-21b}$$

$$\sum_{k=0}^{n} U_{2k} \;=\; \frac{1 - T_{2n+2}}{2\,(1 - x^2)} \tag{35.2-21c}$$

$$\sum_{k=0}^{n-1} U_{2k+1} \;=\; \frac{x - T_{2n+1}}{2\,(1 - x^2)} \tag{35.2-21d}$$

From the relation $\partial_x \cos(n\,\arccos(x)) = n\,\sin(n\,\arccos(x))/\sqrt{1 - x^2}$ we obtain

$$\partial_x T_n(x) \;=\; n\,U_{n-1}(x) \tag{35.2-22}$$

35.2.3   Fast computation of the Chebyshev polynomials

We give algorithms that improve on both the matrix power and the polynomial-based algorithms.

35.2.3.1   Chebyshev polynomials of the first kind

For even index use relation 35.2-16a ($T_{2n} = 2\,T_n^2 - 1$). For odd index we use relations 35.2-16c and 35.2-16b. We compute the pair $[T_{n-1}, T_n]$ recursively via

$$[T_{n-1},\, T_n] \;=\; [2\,T_{q-1}\,T_q - x,\; 2\,T_q^2 - 1] \quad \text{where} \quad q = n/2, \quad \text{if } n \text{ even} \tag{35.2-23a}$$

$$[T_{n-1},\, T_n] \;=\; [2\,T_{q-1}^2 - 1,\; 2\,T_{q-1}\,T_q - x] \quad \text{where} \quad q = (n+1)/2, \quad \text{if } n \text{ odd} \tag{35.2-23b}$$

No multiplication with x occurs, therefore the computation is efficient also for floating-point arguments. With integer x the cost of the computation of $T_n(x)$ is $O(M(n))$ where $M(n)$ is the cost of a multiplication of numbers with the precision of the result. If x is a floating-point number, then the cost is $O(\log_2(n) M(n))$ where $M(n)$ is the cost of a multiplication with the precision used.

The code for the pair computations is

```
1    fvT(n, x)=
2    { /* return  [ T(n-1,x), T(n,x) ]  */
3        local(nr, t, t1, t2);
4        if ( n<=1,
5            if ( 1==n, return( [1, x] ) );
6            if ( 0==n, return( [x, 1] ) );
7            if ( -1==n, return( [2*x^2-1, x] ) );
8            return( 0 );  \\ disallow negative index < -1
9        );
10
11        nr = (n+1) >> 1;  \\   if ( "n even",  nr = n/2 , nr = (n+1)/2; );
12        vr = fvT(nr, x);  \\ recursion
13        t1 = vr[1];   t2 = vr[2];
14        if ( !bitand(n,1),  \\ n is even
15            t = [2*t1*t2-x, 2*t2^2-1];
16            ,
17            t = [2*t1^2-1, 2*t1*t2-x];
18        );
19        return( t );
20    }
```

The function called by the user is

```
1    fT(n, x)=
2    {
3        local(q, t, v, T);
4        n = abs(n);
5        if ( n<=1,
6            if (n>=0,  return(if(0==n,1,x)));
7            return( fT(-n, x) );
8        );
9        t = 0;   q = n;
10       while ( 0==bitand(q, 1), q>>=1; t+=1; );
11       \\ here: n==q*2^t
12       T = fvT(q, x)[2];
13       while ( t,   T=2*T*T-1; t-=1; );
14       return( T );
15   }
```

We check the speedup by comparing with the matrix-power computation that gives identical results. We compute $T_{4,545,967}(2)$, a number with more than 2,600,000 decimal digits:

```
vT(n,x)= return( ([1, x]*[0,-1; 1,2*x]^n) );
x=2;  \\ want integer calculations
n=4545967;
vT(n,x);    \\ computed in 9,800 ms.
fvT(n,x);   \\ computed in 2,241 ms.
```

C++ implementations for the computation of $T_n(2)$ and $T_n(x)$ modulo m are given in [FXT: mod/chebyshev1.cc]. Methods similar to the one shown here for the computation of Fibonacci and Lucas numbers are given in [158, sect.16.7.4-16.7.5, p.106-107].

35.2.3.2   Chebyshev polynomials of the second kind

We can use the fast algorithm for the polynomials of the first kind and relation 35.2-19 on the preceding page ($U_n = (T_n - x\,T_{n+1})/(1 - x^2)$), this involves a division:

```
1    fU(n, x)=
2    {
3        local(v);
4        if ( 1==x, return(n+1) );  \\ avoid division by zero
5        if ( -1==x, return ( if ( bitand(n,1), -(n+1), (n+1) ) ) );  \\ avoid division by zero
6        v = fvT(n+1, x);
7        return( (v[1]-x*v[2])/(1-x^2) );
8    }
```

We give an additional algorithm that involves three multiplications for each reduction of the index n. One multiplication is by the variable x. We compute the pair $[U_{n-1}, U_n]$ recursively via

$$M_q := (U_q + U_{q-1})(U_q - U_{q-1}) \tag{35.2-24a}$$

$$[U_{n-1}, U_n] = [2U_{q-1}(U_q - xU_{q-1}), M_q] \quad \text{where} \quad q = n/2, \quad \text{if } n \text{ even} \tag{35.2-24b}$$

$$[U_{n-1}, U_n] = [M_q, 2U_q(xU_q - U_{q-1})] \quad \text{where} \quad q = (n-1)/2, \quad \text{if } n \text{ odd} \tag{35.2-24c}$$

The code for the pair computations is

```
1    fvU(n, x)=
2    { /* return  [ U(n-1,x), U(n,x) ] */
3        local(nr, u1, u0, ue, t, u);
4        if ( n<=1,
5            if ( 1==n, return( [1, (2*x)] ) );
6            if ( 0==n, return( [0, 1] ) );
7            if ( -1==n, return( [-1, 0] ) );
8            if ( -2==n, return( [-(2*x), -1] ) );
9            return( 0 );  \\ disallow negative index < -2
10       );
11
12       nr = n >> 1;  \\ if ( "n even",  nr = n/2 , nr = (n-1)/2; );
13       vr = fvU(nr, x);  \\ recursion
14       u1 = vr[1];   u0 = vr[2];
15       ue = (u0+u1) * (u0-u1);
16       if ( !bitand(n,1),  \\ n is even
17           t = u1*(u0-x*u1);   t+=t;
18           u = [t,  ue];
19           ,
20           t = u0*(x*u0-u1);   t+=t;
21           u = [ue, t];
22       );
23       return( u );
24   }
```

The function called by the user is

```
1    fU(n, x)= return( fvU(n,x)[2] );
```

The comparison with the matrix-power computation shows almost the same speedup as for the polynomials of the first kind:

```
vU(n,x)= return( [0, 1]*[0,-1; 1,2*x]^n );
x=2;  \\ want integer calculations
n=4545967;
vU(n,x);    \\ computed in 9,783 ms.
fvU(n,x);   \\ computed in 2,704 ms.
```

C++ implementations for the computation of $U_n(2)$ and $U_n(x)$ modulo m are given in [FXT: mod/chebyshev2.cc].

35.2.3.3 Symbolic computation

For symbolic computations the explicit power series as in 35.2-2a or 35.2-3a on page 678 should be preferred. The following routine computes T_n as a polynomial in x:

```
1    chebyTsym(n, x)=
2    {
3        local(b, s);
4        if ( n<0,  n = -n );  \\ symmetry
5        if ( n==1, return( x ) );  \\ avoid division by zero
6        b = 2^(n-1);
7        if ( 0==n%2, if ( 0==n%4, s=+1, s=-1 ), s=0 );
8        forstep (k=n, 1, -2,
9            s += b*x^(k);
10           b *= -(k*(k-1))/((n+k-2)*(n-k+2));
11       );
12       return( s );
13   }
```

To compute U_n, use

```
1    chebyUsym(n, x)=
```

```
2    {
3        local(b, s);
4        if ( n<=0,
5            if ( n>=-2, return( n+1 ) );
6            return( -chebyUsym( -n-2, x ) );    \\ use symmetry
7        );
8        n += 1;
9        b = 2^(n-1) / n;
10       s = 0;
11       forstep (k=n, 1, -2,
12           s += (k)*b*x^(k-1);
13           b *= -(k*(k-1))/((n+k-2)*(n-k+2));
14       );
15       return( s );
16   }
```

35.2.4 Relations to approximations of the square root ‡

35.2.4.1 Padé approximants for $\sqrt{x^2 \pm 1}$

k:	$R_k(2)$	$R_k(x)$
1:	2/1	$(x)/(1)$
2:	7/4	$\left(2x^2 - 1\right)/(2x)$
3:	26/15	$\left(4x^3 - 3x\right)/\left(4x^2 - 1\right)$
4:	97/56	$\left(8x^4 - 8x^2 + 1\right)/\left(8x^3 - 4x\right)$
5:	362/209	$\left(16x^5 - 20x^3 + 5x\right)/\left(16x^4 - 12x^2 + 1\right)$
∞:	$\sqrt{3}$	$\sqrt{x^2 - 1}$

Figure 35.2-C: The first few values of $R_k(2)$ and $R_k(x)$.

k:	$R_k^+(1)$	$R_k^+(x)$
1:	1/1	$(x)/(1)$
2:	3/2	$\left(2x^2 + 1\right)/(2x)$
3:	7/5	$\left(4x^3 + 3x\right)/\left(4x^2 + 1\right)$
4:	17/12	$\left(8x^4 + 8x^2 + 1\right)/\left(8x^3 + 4x\right)$
5:	41/29	$\left(16x^5 + 20x^3 + 5x\right)/\left(16x^4 + 12x^2 + 1\right)$
∞:	$\sqrt{2}$	$\sqrt{x^2 + 1}$

Figure 35.2-D: The first few values of $R_k^+(1)$ and $R_k^+(x)$.

We start with the relation (from the definitions 35.2-1a and 35.2-1b on page 676 and $\sin^2 + \cos^2 = 1$)

$$T_n^2 - \left(x^2 - 1\right) U_{n-1}^2 = 1 \tag{35.2-25}$$

Now rewrite the equation as

$$\sqrt{x^2 - 1} = \sqrt{\frac{T_n^2 - 1}{U_{n-1}^2}} \tag{35.2-26}$$

If we define $R_n = T_n/U_{n-1}$, then

$$R_n(x) = \frac{T_n}{U_{n-1}} \approx \sqrt{x^2 - 1} \tag{35.2-27}$$

A composition law holds for R:

$$R_{mn}(x) = R_m(R_n(x)) \tag{35.2-28}$$

The first few values of $R_k(2)$ and $R_k(x)$ are shown in figure 35.2-C.

If we define $T_n^+(x) := T(ix)/i^n$ and $U_n^+(x) := U(ix)/i^n$, then

$$T_n^{+2} - (x^2+1)\,U_{n-1}^{+2} = (-1)^n \tag{35.2-29}$$

Defining $R_n^+ := T_n^+/U_{n-1}^+$ we have

$$R_{mn}^+(x) = R_m^+\left(R_n^+(x)\right) \tag{35.2-30}$$

and

$$\sqrt{x^2+1} = \sqrt{\frac{T_n^{+2}-1}{U_{n-1}^{+2}}} \approx \frac{T_n^+}{U_{n-1}^+} = R_n^+(x) \tag{35.2-31}$$

The first few values of $R_k^+(1)$ and $R_k^+(x)$ are shown in figure 35.2-D. Relations 35.2-29 and 35.2-25 can be used to power solutions of Pell's Diophantine equation, see relation 39.13-13a on page 815.

35.2.4.2   Two products for the square root

For those fond of products: for $d > 0$, $d \neq 1$

$$\sqrt{d} = \prod_{k=0}^{\infty}\left(1+\frac{1}{q_k}\right) \quad \text{where} \quad q_0 = \frac{d+1}{d-1}, \quad q_{k+1} = 2\,q_k^2 - 1 \tag{35.2-32}$$

(convergence is quadratic) and

$$\sqrt{d} = \prod_{k=0}^{\infty}\left(1+\frac{2}{h_k}\right) \quad \text{where} \quad h_0 = \frac{d+3}{d-1}, \quad h_{k+1} = (h_k+2)^2\,(h_k-1) + 1 \tag{35.2-33}$$

(convergence is cubic). These are given in [38] and also in [142], more expressions can be found in [133]. The paper gives $h_{k+1} = \frac{4d}{d-1}\prod_{i=0}^{k}\left(h_i^2\right) - 3$. For q_k in relation 35.2-32 we have

$$q_k = T_{2^k}(q_0) \tag{35.2-34}$$

$$\frac{1}{q_k} = \frac{(d-1)^N}{\sum_{i=0}^{N}\binom{2N}{2i}d^i} = \frac{2\,(1-d)^N}{(1+\sqrt{d})^{2N}+(1-\sqrt{d})^{2N}} \quad \text{where} \quad N = 2^k \tag{35.2-35}$$

We have

$$q_k = T_{2^k}(1/c) \quad \text{where} \quad c = \frac{1-d}{1+d}, \quad c < 1 \tag{35.2-36}$$

and

$$\sqrt{\frac{1-c}{1+c}} \approx \frac{1-c}{c}\,\frac{U_{2^k-1}(1/c)}{T_{2^k}(1/c)} \tag{35.2-37}$$

which can be expressed in $d = \frac{1-c}{1+c}$ as

$$\sqrt{d} \approx \frac{2d}{1-d}\,\frac{U_{2^k-1}\left(\frac{1+d}{1-d}\right)}{T_{2^k}\left(\frac{1+d}{1-d}\right)} \quad \text{where} \quad d > 1 \tag{35.2-38}$$

We have $U_{2^k-1}(x) = 2^k \prod_{i=0}^{k-1} T_{2^i}(x)$. Successively compute $T_{2^i} = 2\,T_{2^{i-1}}^2 - 1$ and accumulate the product $U_{2^i-1} = 2\,U_{2^{i-1}-1}\,T_{2^{i-1}}$ until U_{2^k-1} and T_{2^k} are obtained. Alternatively use the relation $U_k(x) = \frac{1}{k+1}\,\partial_x T_{k+1}(x)$ and use the recursion for the coefficients of T as shown in section 35.2.3.3 on page 682.

A systematic approach to find product expressions for roots is given in section 29.7 on page 583.

Chapter 36

Hypergeometric series

We describe the hypergeometric functions which contain most of the 'useful' functions such as the logarithm and the sine as special cases. The transformation formulas for hypergeometric series often give series transformations that are non-obvious. The computation of certain hypergeometric functions by AGM-type algorithms is described in section 31.4 on page 611.

36.1   Definition and basic operations

The *hypergeometric series* $F\left(\begin{smallmatrix} a,\, b \\ c \end{smallmatrix}\middle| z\right)$ is defined as

$$F\left(\begin{matrix} a,\, b \\ c \end{matrix}\middle|\, z\right) \;:=\; \sum_{k=0}^{\infty} \frac{a^{\overline{k}}\, b^{\overline{k}}}{c^{\overline{k}}} \frac{z^k}{k!} \tag{36.1-1}$$

where $z^{\overline{k}} := z\,(z+1)\,(z+2)\,\ldots\,(z+k-1)$ is the *rising factorial power* ($z^{\overline{0}} := 1$). Some sources use the *Pochhammer symbol* $(x)_k$ which is the same thing: $(x)_k = x^{\overline{k}}$. We'll stick to the factorial notation.

The variable z is called the *argument*, a, b and c are the *parameters*. Parameters in the upper and lower row are called upper and lower parameters, respectively.

Note the $k! = 1^{\overline{k}}$ in the denominator of relation 36.1-1. Keep the hidden lower parameter 1 in mind:

$$F\left(\begin{matrix} 2,\, 2 \\ 1 \end{matrix}\middle|\, z\right) \;=\; \text{``}F\left(\begin{matrix} 2,\, 2 \\ 1,\, 1 \end{matrix}\middle|\, z\right)\text{''} \tag{36.1-2}$$

The previous expression is a sum of perfect squares if z is a square.

When a hypergeometric series converges it corresponds to a *hypergeometric function*. We have

$$F\left(\begin{matrix} a,\, b \\ c \end{matrix}\middle|\, z\right) \;=\; 1 + \frac{a}{1}\frac{b}{c} z\left(1 + \frac{a+1}{2}\frac{b+1}{c+1} z\left(1 + \frac{a+2}{3}\frac{b+2}{c+2} z\,(1 + \ldots)\right)\right) \tag{36.1-3}$$

Therefore hypergeometric functions with rational arguments can be computed with the binary splitting method described in section 34.1.2 on page 652.

Hypergeometric series can have any number of parameters:

$$F\left(\begin{matrix} a_1, \ldots, a_m \\ b_1, \ldots, b_n \end{matrix}\middle|\, z\right) \;=\; \sum_{k=0}^{\infty} \frac{a_1^{\overline{k}} \ldots a_m^{\overline{k}}}{b_1^{\overline{k}} \ldots b_n^{\overline{k}}} \frac{z^k}{k!} \tag{36.1-4}$$

These are sometimes called *generalized hypergeometric functions*. The number of upper and lower parameters are often emphasized as subscripts left and right to the symbol F. For example, $_mF_n$ for the series in the last relation.

J. Arndt, *Matters Computational: Ideas, Algorithms, Source Code*,
DOI 10.1007/978-3-642-14764-7_36, © Springer-Verlag Berlin Heidelberg 2011

The functions $F\left(\begin{smallmatrix} a \\ b \end{smallmatrix}\middle| z\right)$ (of type $_1F_1$) are sometimes written as $M(a, b, z)$ or $\Phi(a; b; z)$. *Kummer's function* $U(a, b, z)$ (or $\Psi(a; b; z)$) is related to hypergeometric functions of type $_2F_0$:

$$U(a, b, z) \;=\; z^{-a} F\left(\begin{matrix} a,\, 1 + a - b \\ \end{matrix}\middle| -1/z\right) \tag{36.1-5}$$

Note that series $_2F_0$ are not convergent. Still, they can be used as asymptotic series for large values of z. The *Whittaker functions* are related to hypergeometric functions as follows:

$$M_{a,b}(z) \;=\; e^{-z/2} z^{b+1/2} F\left(\begin{matrix} \tfrac{1}{2} + b - a \\ 1 + 2b \end{matrix}\middle| z\right) \tag{36.1-6a}$$

$$W_{a,b}(z) \;=\; e^{-z/2} z^{b+1/2} U\left(\tfrac{1}{2} + b - a,\, 1 + 2b,\, z\right) \tag{36.1-6b}$$

$$\;=\; e^{-z/2} z^{a} F\left(\begin{matrix} \tfrac{1}{2} + b - a,\, \tfrac{1}{2} - b - a \\ \end{matrix}\middle| -1/z\right) \tag{36.1-6c}$$

Negative integer parameters in the upper row lead to polynomials:

$$F\left(\begin{matrix} -3,\, 3 \\ 1 \end{matrix}\middle| z\right) \;=\; 1 - 9z + 18z^2 - 10z^3 \tag{36.1-7}$$

The lower parameter must not be zero or a negative integer unless there is a negative upper parameter with smaller absolute value.

Sometimes one finds the notational convention omitting an argument $z = 1$:

$$F\left(\begin{matrix} a_1,\, \ldots,\, a_m \\ b_1,\, \ldots,\, b_n \end{matrix}\right) \;:=\; F\left(\begin{matrix} a_1,\, \ldots,\, a_m \\ b_1,\, \ldots,\, b_n \end{matrix}\middle| 1\right) \tag{36.1-8}$$

In the following we never omit the argument.

In-depth treatments of hypergeometric functions are [17] and [356]. Many relations for hypergeometric functions are given in [1] and [139, vol.1].

36.1.1   Derivative and differential equation

The n-th derivative of a hypergeometric function $f(z) = F\left(\begin{smallmatrix} a,\, b,\, \ldots \\ c,\, d,\, \ldots \end{smallmatrix}\middle| z\right)$ is

$$\frac{d}{dz^n} F\left(\begin{matrix} a,\, b\, \ldots \\ c,\, d,\, \ldots \end{matrix}\middle| z\right) \;=\; \frac{a^{\overline{n}}\, b^{\overline{n}}\, \ldots}{c^{\overline{n}}\, d^{\overline{n}}\, \ldots} F\left(\begin{matrix} a+n,\, b+n\, \ldots \\ c+n,\, d+n,\, \ldots \end{matrix}\middle| z\right) \tag{36.1-9}$$

The function $f(z) = F\left(\begin{smallmatrix} a,\, b \\ c \end{smallmatrix}\middle| z\right)$ is a solution of the differential equation

$$z(1-z)\frac{d^2 f}{dz^2} + [c - (1 + a + b)z]\frac{df}{dz} - a b f \;=\; 0 \tag{36.1-10}$$

A general form of the differential equation satisfied by $F\left(\begin{smallmatrix} a,\, b,\, c,\, \ldots \\ u,\, v,\, w,\, \ldots \end{smallmatrix}\middle| z\right)$ is

$$z(\vartheta + a)(\vartheta + b)(\vartheta + c) \ldots f(z) \;=\; \vartheta(\vartheta + u - 1)(\vartheta + v - 1)(\vartheta + w - 1) \ldots f(z) \tag{36.1-11}$$

where ϑ is the operator $z\frac{d}{dz}$. The leftmost ϑ on the right side of the equation takes care of the hidden lower parameter 1: $\vartheta = (\vartheta + 1 - 1)$. See [166] for a beautiful derivation. Use relation 11.1-3a on page 278 to rewrite powers of ϑ as polynomials in $\frac{d}{dz}$.

36.1.2 Evaluations for fixed argument ‡

A closed form (in terms of the gamma function) evaluation at $z = 1$ can be given for $_2F_1$:

$$F\left(\begin{matrix} a, b \\ c \end{matrix} \middle| 1\right) = \frac{\Gamma(c)\,\Gamma(c - a - b)}{\Gamma(c - a)\,\Gamma(c - b)} \quad \text{if} \quad \mathfrak{Re}(c - a - b) > 0 \quad \text{or} \quad b \in \mathbb{N}, b < 0 \quad (36.1\text{-}12)$$

If $c - a - b < 0$, then we have [356, ex.18, p.299]

$$\lim_{z \to 1-} F\left(\begin{matrix} a, b \\ c \end{matrix} \middle| z\right) \bigg/ \left(\frac{\Gamma(c)\,\Gamma(a + b - c)}{\Gamma(a)\,\Gamma(b)} (1 - z)^{c - a - b}\right) = 1 \quad (36.1\text{-}13a)$$

and, for $c - a - b = 0$,

$$\lim_{z \to 1-} F\left(\begin{matrix} a, b \\ c \end{matrix} \middle| z\right) \bigg/ \left(\frac{\Gamma(a + b)}{\Gamma(a)\,\Gamma(b)} \log\frac{1}{1 - z}\right) = 1 \quad (36.1\text{-}13b)$$

For $z = -1$ there is an evaluation due to Kummer:

$$F\left(\begin{matrix} a, b \\ 1 + a - b \end{matrix} \middle| -1\right) = \frac{\Gamma(1 - a + b)\,\Gamma(1 + a/2)}{\Gamma(1 + a)\,\Gamma(1 + a/2 - b)} \quad (36.1\text{-}14a)$$

$$= 2^{-a}\,\pi\,\frac{\Gamma(1 - a + b)}{\Gamma(1/2 + a/2)\,\Gamma(1 + a/2 - b)} \quad (36.1\text{-}14b)$$

Several evaluations at $z = \frac{1}{2}$ are given in [1], we just give one:

$$F\left(\begin{matrix} a, b \\ \frac{1}{2} + \frac{1}{2}a + \frac{1}{2}b \end{matrix} \middle| \frac{1}{2}\right) = \sqrt{\pi}\,\frac{\Gamma(\frac{1}{2} + \frac{1}{2}a + \frac{1}{2}b)}{\Gamma(\frac{1}{2} + \frac{1}{2}a)\,\Gamma(\frac{1}{2} + \frac{1}{2}b)} \quad (36.1\text{-}15)$$

For further information see [1, chap.15], [349, entry "Hypergeometric Function"], and [273]. Various evaluations of $F\left(\begin{matrix} -an, bn + b_1 \\ cn + c_1 \end{matrix} \middle| z\right)$ for integer a, b, c can be found in [138].

36.1.3 Extraction of even and odd part

Let $E[f(z)] = (f(z) + f(z))/2$ (the even powers of the series of $f(z)$) and $O[f(z)] = (f(z) - f(-z))/2$ (the odd powers). We express the even and odd parts of a hypergeometric series as follows:

$$E\left[F\left(\begin{matrix} a, b \\ c \end{matrix} \middle| z\right)\right] = F\left(\begin{matrix} \frac{a}{2}, \frac{a+1}{2}, \frac{b}{2}, \frac{b+1}{2} \\ \frac{c}{2}, \frac{c+1}{2}, \frac{1}{2} \end{matrix} \middle| z^2\right) \quad (36.1\text{-}16a)$$

$$O\left[F\left(\begin{matrix} a, b \\ c \end{matrix} \middle| z\right)\right] = \frac{a\,b}{c}\,z\,F\left(\begin{matrix} \frac{a+1}{2}, \frac{a+2}{2}, \frac{b+1}{2}, \frac{b+2}{2} \\ \frac{c+1}{2}, \frac{c+2}{2}, \frac{3}{2} \end{matrix} \middle| z^2\right) \quad (36.1\text{-}16b)$$

The lower parameters 1/2 and 3/2 are due to the hidden lower parameter 1. The general case for

$$H(z) := F\left(\begin{matrix} a_1, \ldots, a_m \\ b_1, \ldots, b_n \end{matrix} \middle| z\right) \quad (36.1\text{-}17a)$$

is

$$E\left[H(z)\right] = F\left(\begin{matrix} \frac{a_1}{2}, \frac{a_1+1}{2}, \ldots, \frac{a_m}{2}, \frac{a_m+1}{2} \\ \frac{b_1}{2}, \frac{b_1+1}{2}, \ldots, \frac{b_n}{2}, \frac{b_n+1}{2}, \frac{1}{2} \end{matrix} \middle| X\,z^2\right) \quad (36.1\text{-}17b)$$

$$O\left[H(z)\right] = \frac{a_1 \cdots a_m}{b_1 \cdots b_n}\,z\,F\left(\begin{matrix} \frac{a_1+1}{2}, \frac{a_1+2}{2}, \ldots, \frac{a_m+1}{2}, \frac{a_m+2}{2} \\ \frac{b_1+1}{2}, \frac{b_1+2}{2}, \ldots, \frac{b_n+1}{2}, \frac{b_n+2}{2}, \frac{3}{2} \end{matrix} \middle| X\,z^2\right) \quad (36.1\text{-}17c)$$

where $X = 4^{m - n - 1}$. For example,

$$E\left[F\left(\begin{matrix} \frac{1}{2} \\ \end{matrix} \middle| z\right)\right] = F\left(\begin{matrix} \frac{1}{2}, 1 \\ 1, \frac{3}{2}, \frac{1}{2} \end{matrix} \middle| \frac{z^2}{4}\right) = F\left(\begin{matrix} \\ \frac{3}{2} \end{matrix} \middle| \frac{z^2}{4}\right) = \frac{\sinh z}{z} \quad (36.1\text{-}18)$$

36.1.4   Multisection by selecting terms with exponents $s \bmod M$

Let $H(z)$ be any power series. If we write $H_{[s,M]}(z)$ for the series obtained by selecting only the terms whose exponent of z is congruent to s modulo M (that is, exponents s, $s + M$, $s + 2M$, and so on), then

$$H_{[s,M]}(z) \;=\; \frac{1}{M} \sum_{k=0}^{M-1} \omega^{-s\,k}\, H\!\left(\omega^k\, z\right) \quad \text{where} \quad \omega := \exp\left(2\,\pi\, i/M\right) \tag{36.1-19}$$

For a hypergeometric function $H(z)$ replace every upper and lower parameter A by the M parameters $(A + s)/M$, $(A + s + 1)/M$, $(A + s + 2)/M$, $\ldots$, $(A + s + M - 1)/M$, the argument z by $X\, z^M$ where $X = (M^M)^{m-n-1}$, and multiply by

$$z^s\, \frac{a_1^{\overline{s}}, \,\ldots, \, a_m^{\overline{s}}}{b_1^{\overline{s}}, \,\ldots, \, b_n^{\overline{s}}} \tag{36.1-20}$$

For example, the following two forms give $H_{[0,3]}(z)$, the extraction of all terms of $H(z)$ where the exponent of z is divisible by 3 ($s = 0$):

$$\frac{H(z) + H(\omega\, z) + H(\omega^2\, z)}{3} \;=\; F\!\left(\begin{matrix} \frac{a_1}{3}, \frac{a_1+1}{3}, \frac{a_1+2}{3} \cdots \frac{a_m}{3}, \frac{a_m+1}{3}, \frac{a_m+2}{3} \\ \frac{b_1}{3}, \frac{b_1+1}{3}, \frac{b_1+2}{3}, \ldots, \frac{b_n}{3}, \frac{b_n+1}{3}, \frac{b_n+2}{3}, \frac{1}{3}, \frac{2}{3} \end{matrix} \,\middle|\, X\, z^3 \right) \tag{36.1-21}$$

where $\omega = \exp(2\,\pi\, i/3)$ and $X = 27^{m-n-1}$. With $H(z) = \exp(z) = F\!\left(\,\middle|\,z\right)$ we find

$$H_{[0,3]}(z) \;=\; F\!\left(\begin{matrix} \\ \frac{1}{3}, \frac{2}{3} \end{matrix} \,\middle|\, \frac{z^3}{27} \right) \;=\; \sum_{k=0}^{\infty} \frac{z^{3k}}{(3k)!} \;=\; \frac{1}{3}\left[e^z + e^{\omega\, z} + e^{\omega^2\, z} \right] \tag{36.1-22a}$$

The remaining two functions from the 3-section of $\exp(z)$ are

$$H_{[1,3]}(z) \;=\; z\, F\!\left(\begin{matrix} \\ \frac{2}{3}, \frac{4}{3} \end{matrix} \,\middle|\, \frac{z^3}{27} \right) \;=\; \sum_{k=0}^{\infty} \frac{z^{3k+1}}{(3k+1)!} \;=\; \frac{1}{3}\left[e^z + \Omega\, e^{\omega\, z} + \Omega^2\, e^{\omega^2\, z} \right] \tag{36.1-22b}$$

$$H_{[2,3]}(z) \;=\; z^2\, \frac{1}{2}\, F\!\left(\begin{matrix} \\ \frac{4}{3}, \frac{5}{3} \end{matrix} \,\middle|\, \frac{z^3}{27} \right) \;=\; \sum_{k=0}^{\infty} \frac{z^{3k+2}}{(3k+2)!} \;=\; \frac{1}{3}\left[e^z + \Omega^2\, e^{\omega\, z} + \Omega\, e^{\omega^2\, z} \right] \tag{36.1-22c}$$

where $\Omega = \omega^{-1} = \omega^2$. Now write $C_s = H_{[s,3]}(z)$ for $s \in \{0,1,2\}$, then we have (omitting arguments)

$$\det \begin{bmatrix} C_0 & C_1 & C_2 \\ C_2 & C_0 & C_1 \\ C_1 & C_2 & C_0 \end{bmatrix} \;=\; C_0^3 + C_1^3 + C_2^3 - 3\, C_0\, C_1\, C_2 \;=\; 1 \;=\; e^z\, e^{\omega\, z}\, e^{\omega^2\, z} \tag{36.1-23}$$

which is a three power series analogue of the relation $\cosh^2 - \sinh^2 = 1$, see [336].

36.2   Transformations of hypergeometric series

As is obvious from the definition, parameters in the upper row can be swapped (capitalized symbols for readability):

$$F\!\left(\begin{matrix} A, B, c \\ e, f, g \end{matrix} \,\middle|\, z \right) \;=\; F\!\left(\begin{matrix} B, A, c \\ e, f, g \end{matrix} \,\middle|\, z \right) \tag{36.2-1}$$

The same is true for the lower row. Usually one writes the parameters in ascending order. Identical elements in the lower and upper row can be canceled:

$$F\!\left(\begin{matrix} a, b, C \\ e, f, C \end{matrix} \,\middle|\, z \right) \;=\; F\!\left(\begin{matrix} a, b \\ e, f \end{matrix} \,\middle|\, z \right) \tag{36.2-2}$$

These trivial transformations are true for any number of elements. The following transformations are only valid for the given structure, unless the list of parameters contain an ellipsis '$\ldots$'.

36.2.1 Elementary and contiguous relations

By definition we have

$$F\left(\begin{array}{c} a,\,b,\,\dots \\ c,\,\dots \end{array}\middle|\,z\right) \;=\; 1+z\,\frac{a\,b\,\dots}{c\,\dots}\,F\left(\begin{array}{c} a+1,\,b+1,\,\dots,\,1 \\ c+1,\,\dots,\,2 \end{array}\middle|\,z\right) \tag{36.2-3}$$

Identities of the following type are called *contiguous relations*:

$$(a-b)\,F\left(\begin{array}{c} a,\,b,\,\dots \\ c,\,\dots \end{array}\middle|\,z\right) \;=\; a\,F\left(\begin{array}{c} a+1,\,b,\,\dots \\ c,\,\dots \end{array}\middle|\,z\right) - b\,F\left(\begin{array}{c} a,\,b+1,\,\dots \\ c,\,\dots \end{array}\middle|\,z\right) \tag{36.2-4}$$

$$(a-c)\,F\left(\begin{array}{c} a,\,b,\,\dots \\ c+1,\,\dots \end{array}\middle|\,z\right) \;=\; a\,F\left(\begin{array}{c} a+1,\,b,\,\dots \\ c+1,\,\dots \end{array}\middle|\,z\right) - c\,F\left(\begin{array}{c} a,\,b,\,\dots \\ c,\,\dots \end{array}\middle|\,z\right) \tag{36.2-5}$$

These are given in [166], the following is taken from [356].

$$F\left(\begin{array}{c} a,\,b \\ c \end{array}\middle|\,z\right) \;=\; F\left(\begin{array}{c} a,\,b+1 \\ c \end{array}\middle|\,z\right) - \frac{a\,z}{c}\,F\left(\begin{array}{c} a+1,\,b+1 \\ c+1 \end{array}\middle|\,z\right) \tag{36.2-6}$$

More relations of this type are given in [1].

36.2.2 Pfaff's reflection law and Euler's identity

Pfaff's reflection law can be given as either of:

$$\frac{1}{(1-z)^a}\,F\left(\begin{array}{c} a,\,b \\ c \end{array}\middle|\,\frac{-z}{1-z}\right) \;=\; F\left(\begin{array}{c} a,\,c-b \\ c \end{array}\middle|\,z\right) \tag{36.2-7a}$$

$$F\left(\begin{array}{c} a,\,b \\ c \end{array}\middle|\,z\right) \;=\; \frac{1}{(1-z)^a}\,F\left(\begin{array}{c} a,\,c-b \\ c \end{array}\middle|\,\frac{-z}{1-z}\right) \tag{36.2-7b}$$

$$\;=\; \frac{1}{(1-z)^b}\,F\left(\begin{array}{c} c-a,\,b \\ c \end{array}\middle|\,\frac{-z}{1-z}\right) \tag{36.2-7c}$$

Applying the Pfaff reflection on both upper parameters gives *Euler's identity*:

$$F\left(\begin{array}{c} a,\,b \\ c \end{array}\middle|\,z\right) \;=\; (1-z)^{(c-a-b)}\,F\left(\begin{array}{cc} c & a,\,c-b \\ & c \end{array}\middle|\,z\right) \tag{36.2-8}$$

Now write Euler's transform as

$$F\left(\begin{array}{c} a,\,b \\ a+b+1/r \end{array}\middle|\,z\right) \Big/ F\left(\begin{array}{c} a+1/r,\,b+1/r \\ a+b+1/r \end{array}\middle|\,z\right) \;=\; (1-z)^{1/r} \tag{36.2-9}$$

If both hypergeometric series terminate, then the expression on the left is a Padé approximant for the r-th root, see section 29.2.3.2 on page 572.

Euler's transformation can be generalized for hypergeometric functions $_{r+1}F_r$, see [240]. We give two transforms for hypergeometric functions $_3F_2$ where one upper parameter exceeds a lower parameter by 1, taken from [243, p.17]. The first is reminiscent of the Pfaff reflection, for $f = e\,(b-a_2-1)/(e-a_2)$,

$$F\left(\begin{array}{c} a_1,\,a_2,\,e+1 \\ b,\,e \end{array}\middle|\,z\right) \;=\; (1-z)^{-a_1}\,F\left(\begin{array}{c} a_1,\,b-a_2-1,\,f+1 \\ b,\,f \end{array}\middle|\,\frac{-z}{1-z}\right) \tag{36.2-10}$$

The second is similar to Euler's identity, for $g = \left[(b-a_1-1)\,(b-a_2-1)\,e\right] / \left[(b-a_1-a_2-1)\,e + a_1\,a_2\right]$,

$$F\left(\begin{array}{c} a_1,\,a_2,\,e+1 \\ b,\,e \end{array}\middle|\,z\right) \;=\; (1-z)^{b-a_1-a_2-1}\,F\left(\begin{array}{c} b-a_1-1,\,b-a_2-1,\,g+1 \\ b,\,g \end{array}\middle|\,z\right) \tag{36.2-11}$$

36.2.3   Quadratic transformations and Whipple's identity

The following transformations are due to Gauss:

$$F\left(\begin{matrix} 2a,\, 2b \\ a+b+\frac{1}{2} \end{matrix}\,\middle|\, z\right) \;=\; F\left(\begin{matrix} a,\, b \\ a+b+\frac{1}{2} \end{matrix}\,\middle|\, 4z(1-z)\right) \quad \text{where} \quad |z| < \frac{1}{2} \tag{36.2-12a}$$

$$F\left(\begin{matrix} a,\, b \\ a+b+\frac{1}{2} \end{matrix}\,\middle|\, z\right) \;=\; F\left(\begin{matrix} 2a,\, 2b \\ a+b+\frac{1}{2} \end{matrix}\,\middle|\, \frac{1-\sqrt{1-z}}{2}\right) \tag{36.2-12b}$$

Rewriting relation 36.2-12a for the argument $\frac{1-z}{2}$ we find

$$F\left(\begin{matrix} 2a,\, 2b \\ a+b+\frac{1}{2} \end{matrix}\,\middle|\, \frac{1-z}{2}\right) \;=\; F\left(\begin{matrix} a,\, b \\ a+b+\frac{1}{2} \end{matrix}\,\middle|\, 1-z^2\right) \tag{36.2-13}$$

Whipple's identity connects two hypergeometric functions $_3F_2$:

$$F\left(\begin{matrix} \frac{1}{2}a,\, \frac{1}{2}a+\frac{1}{2},\, 1-a-b-c \\ 1+a-b,\, 1+a-c \end{matrix}\,\middle|\, \frac{-4z}{(1-z)^2}\right) \;=\; (1-z)^a\, F\left(\begin{matrix} a,\, b,\, c \\ 1+a-b,\, 1+a-c \end{matrix}\,\middle|\, z\right) \tag{36.2-14}$$

Specializing 36.2-14 for $c = (a+1)/2$ (note the symmetry between b and c so specializing for $c = (b+1)/2$ produces the identical relation) gives

$$F\left(\begin{matrix} a,\, b \\ 1+a-b \end{matrix}\,\middle|\, z\right) \;=\; \frac{1}{(1-z)^a}\, F\left(\begin{matrix} \frac{1}{2}a,\, \frac{1}{2}a+\frac{1}{2}-b \\ 1+a-b \end{matrix}\,\middle|\, \frac{-4z}{(1-z)^2}\right) \tag{36.2-15}$$

$$F\left(\begin{matrix} a,\, b \\ a+b+\frac{1}{2} \end{matrix}\,\middle|\, z\right) \;=\; \left(\frac{2\left(1-\sqrt{1-z}\right)}{z}\right)^{2a}\, F\left(\begin{matrix} 2a,\, a-b+\frac{1}{2} \\ a+b+\frac{1}{2} \end{matrix}\,\middle|\, -\frac{\left(1-\sqrt{1-z}\right)^2}{z}\right) \tag{36.2-16}$$

By setting $c := a - b$ in 36.2-15 we find

$$F\left(\begin{matrix} a,\, a-c \\ 1+c \end{matrix}\,\middle|\, z\right) \;=\; \frac{1}{(1-z)^a}\, F\left(\begin{matrix} \frac{1}{2}a,\, \frac{1}{2}-\frac{1}{2}a+c \\ 1+c \end{matrix}\,\middle|\, \frac{-4z}{(1-z)^2}\right) \tag{36.2-17}$$

Similar to the relations by Gauss, from equations 36.2-15 and 36.2-16 we have:

$$F\left(\begin{matrix} a,\, b \\ 1+a-b \end{matrix}\,\middle|\, -\frac{1-z}{1+z}\right) \;=\; \left(\frac{1+z}{2}\right)^a\, F\left(\begin{matrix} \frac{1}{2}a,\, \frac{1}{2}a+\frac{1}{2}-b \\ 1+a-b \end{matrix}\,\middle|\, 1-z^2\right) \tag{36.2-18a}$$

$$F\left(\begin{matrix} a,\, b \\ 1+a-b \end{matrix}\,\middle|\, -\frac{1-\sqrt{1-z^2}}{1+\sqrt{1-z^2}}\right) \;=\; \left(\frac{1+\sqrt{1-z^2}}{2}\right)^a\, F\left(\begin{matrix} \frac{1}{2}a,\, \frac{1}{2}a+\frac{1}{2}-b \\ 1+a-b \end{matrix}\,\middle|\, z^2\right) \tag{36.2-18b}$$

Relation 36.2-18b is found by setting $x = \sqrt{1-z^2}$ (and replacing x by z) in 36.2-18a. The same is true for the next pair of relations:

$$F\left(\begin{matrix} a,\, b \\ a+b+\frac{1}{2} \end{matrix}\,\middle|\, 1-z^2\right) \;=\; \left(\frac{2}{1+z}\right)^{2a}\, F\left(\begin{matrix} 2a,\, a-b+\frac{1}{2} \\ a+b+\frac{1}{2} \end{matrix}\,\middle|\, -\frac{1-z}{1+z}\right) \tag{36.2-19a}$$

$$F\left(\begin{matrix} a,\, b \\ a+b+\frac{1}{2} \end{matrix}\,\middle|\, z^2\right) \;=\; \left(\frac{2}{1+\sqrt{1-z^2}}\right)^{2a}\, F\left(\begin{matrix} 2a,\, a-b+\frac{1}{2} \\ a+b+\frac{1}{2} \end{matrix}\,\middle|\, -\frac{1-\sqrt{1-z^2}}{1+\sqrt{1-z^2}}\right) \tag{36.2-19b}$$

The transformations

$$F\left(\begin{matrix} a,\, b \\ a-b+1 \end{matrix}\,\middle|\, z\right) \;=\; (1+z)^{-a}\, F\left(\begin{matrix} \frac{1}{2}a,\, \frac{1}{2}a+\frac{1}{2} \\ a-b+1 \end{matrix}\,\middle|\, \frac{4z}{(1+z)^2}\right) \tag{36.2-20a}$$

$$=\; (1-z)^{-a}\, F\left(\begin{matrix} \frac{1}{2}a,\, \frac{1}{2}a-b+\frac{1}{2} \\ a-b+1 \end{matrix}\,\middle|\, \frac{-4z}{(1-z)^2}\right) \tag{36.2-20b}$$

$$=\; (1\pm\sqrt{z})^{-2a}\, F\left(\begin{matrix} a,\, a-b+\frac{1}{2} \\ 2a-2b+1 \end{matrix}\,\middle|\, \frac{\pm 4\sqrt{z}}{(1\pm\sqrt{z})^2}\right) \tag{36.2-20c}$$

are given in [1, rel.15.3.26, p.561]. Specializing for $a = b$ gives

$$F \left(\begin{matrix} a, \ a \\ 1 \end{matrix} \middle| z \right) = (1+z)^{-a} F \left(\begin{matrix} \frac{1}{2}a, \ \frac{1}{2} + \frac{1}{2}a \\ 1 \end{matrix} \middle| \frac{4z}{(1+z)^2} \right) \tag{36.2-20d}$$

$$= (1-z)^{-a} F \left(\begin{matrix} \frac{1}{2}a, \ \frac{1}{2} - \frac{1}{2}a \\ 1 \end{matrix} \middle| \frac{-4z}{(1-z)^2} \right) \tag{36.2-20e}$$

$$= (1 \pm \sqrt{z})^{-2a} F \left(\begin{matrix} a, \ \frac{1}{2} \\ 1 \end{matrix} \middle| \frac{\pm 4\sqrt{z}}{(1 \pm \sqrt{z})^2} \right) \tag{36.2-20f}$$

Relation 36.2-20e is found by setting $c = 0$ in relation 36.2-15. Observe that the hypergeometric function on the right side of relation 36.2-20e does not change when replacing a by $1 - a$. The next $({}_3F_2)$ transformation is given in [240]:

$$(1-z)^{-1} F \left(\begin{matrix} a, \ b, \ 1 \\ \frac{1}{2} + \frac{1}{2}a + \frac{1}{2}b, \ 2 \end{matrix} \middle| z \right) = F \left(\begin{matrix} \frac{1}{2} + \frac{1}{2}a, \ \frac{1}{2} + \frac{1}{2}b, \ 1 \\ \frac{1}{2} + \frac{1}{2}a + \frac{1}{2}b, \ 2 \end{matrix} \middle| 4z(1-z) \right) \tag{36.2-21}$$

The following are special cases of this transformation:

$$(1-z)^{-1} F \left(\begin{matrix} a, \ 1-a \\ 2 \end{matrix} \middle| z \right) = F \left(\begin{matrix} \frac{1}{2} + \frac{1}{2}a, \ 1 - \frac{1}{2}a \\ 2 \end{matrix} \middle| 4z(1-z) \right) \tag{36.2-22a}$$

$$(1-z)^{-1} F \left(\begin{matrix} a, \ 1 \\ 2 \end{matrix} \middle| z \right) = F \left(\begin{matrix} \frac{1}{2} + \frac{1}{2}a, \ 1 + \frac{1}{2}a, \ 1 \\ 1 + a, \ 2 \end{matrix} \middle| 4z(1-z) \right) \tag{36.2-22b}$$

$$(1-z)^{-1} F \left(\begin{matrix} a, \ 1 \\ \frac{3}{2} + \frac{1}{2}a \end{matrix} \middle| z \right) = F \left(\begin{matrix} \frac{1}{2} + \frac{1}{2}a, \ \frac{3}{2}, \ 1 \\ \frac{3}{2} + \frac{1}{2}a, \ 2 \end{matrix} \middle| 4z(1-z) \right) \tag{36.2-22c}$$

More quadratic (and cubic) transformations are given in [139, vol.1, pp.110-114] and [222], see also [163]. The nonlinear transformation (given in [273, p.21])

$$F \left(\begin{matrix} a, \ b \\ c \end{matrix} \middle| z \right) = (1-\omega)^{2a} \sum_{n=0}^{\infty} d_n \, \omega^n \tag{36.2-23a}$$

where

$$\omega = \frac{-4z}{(1-z)^2}, \qquad z = \frac{\sqrt{1-\omega} - 1}{\sqrt{1-\omega} + 1} \tag{36.2-23b}$$

and

$$d_0 = 1 \tag{36.2-23c}$$

$$d_1 = \frac{2a \, (c - 2b)}{c} \tag{36.2-23d}$$

$$d_{n+2} = \frac{2 \, (c - 2b) \, (n + 1 + a) \, d_{n+1} + (n + 2a) \, (n + 2a + 1 - c) \, d_n}{(n+2) \, (n+1+c)} \tag{36.2-23e}$$

maps the complex z-plane onto the unit disc. Therefore the ω-form of the series converges for all $z \neq 1$.

36.2.4 Clausen's product formula

Clausen's product formula [108] connects hypergeometric functions of type ${}_2F_1$ and ${}_3F_2$:

$$\left[F \left(\begin{matrix} a, \ b \\ a + b + \frac{1}{2} \end{matrix} \middle| z \right) \right]^2 = F \left(\begin{matrix} 2a, \ a + b, \ 2b \\ a + b + \frac{1}{2}, \ 2a + 2b \end{matrix} \middle| z \right) \tag{36.2-24}$$

A relation due to Goursat [164, p.416] is:

$$\left[F\left(\begin{matrix} a+1,\, b+1 \\ a+b+\frac{3}{2} \end{matrix}\,\middle|\, z\right)\right]^2 \;=\; (1-z)^{-1}\, F\left(\begin{matrix} 2a+1,\, a+b+1,\, 2b+1 \\ a+b+\frac{3}{2},\, 2a+2b+2 \end{matrix}\,\middle|\, z\right) \qquad (36.2\text{-}25)$$

Two transforms from [98, p.266], the second form is found by setting $(a,\, b) \mapsto (a-1/4,\, b-1/4)$:

$$F\left(\begin{matrix} a,\, b \\ a+b+\frac{1}{2} \end{matrix}\,\middle|\, z\right) F\left(\begin{matrix} \frac{1}{2}-a,\, \frac{1}{2}-b \\ \frac{3}{2}-a-b \end{matrix}\,\middle|\, z\right) \;=\; F\left(\begin{matrix} \frac{1}{2},\, \frac{1}{2}+a-b,\, \frac{1}{2}-a+b \\ \frac{1}{2}+a+b,\, \frac{3}{2}-a-b \end{matrix}\,\middle|\, z\right) \qquad (36.2\text{-}26a)$$

$$F\left(\begin{matrix} \frac{1}{4}+a,\, \frac{1}{4}+b \\ 1+a+b \end{matrix}\,\middle|\, z\right) F\left(\begin{matrix} \frac{1}{4}-a,\, \frac{1}{4}-b \\ 1-a-b \end{matrix}\,\middle|\, z\right) \;=\; F\left(\begin{matrix} \frac{1}{2},\, \frac{1}{2}+a-b,\, \frac{1}{2}-a+b \\ 1+a+b,\, 1-a-b \end{matrix}\,\middle|\, z\right) \qquad (36.2\text{-}26b)$$

The following relations are given in [17, p.184]:

$$F\left(\begin{matrix} a,\, b \\ a+b-\frac{1}{2} \end{matrix}\,\middle|\, z\right) F\left(\begin{matrix} a,\, b \\ a+b+\frac{1}{2} \end{matrix}\,\middle|\, z\right) \;=\; F\left(\begin{matrix} 2a,\, 2b,\, a+b \\ 2a+2b-1,\, a+b+\frac{1}{2} \end{matrix}\,\middle|\, z\right) \qquad (36.2\text{-}27a)$$

$$F\left(\begin{matrix} a,\, b \\ a+b-\frac{1}{2} \end{matrix}\,\middle|\, z\right) F\left(\begin{matrix} a,\, b-1 \\ a+b-\frac{1}{2} \end{matrix}\,\middle|\, z\right) \;=\; F\left(\begin{matrix} 2a,\, 2b-1,\, a+b-1 \\ 2a+2b-2,\, a+b-\frac{1}{2} \end{matrix}\,\middle|\, z\right) \qquad (36.2\text{-}27b)$$

We note that relation 36.2-24 is the special case $c = a+b$ of the identity [356, ex.16, p.298]:

$$F\left(\begin{matrix} a,\, b \\ c+\frac{1}{2} \end{matrix}\,\middle|\, z\right) F\left(\begin{matrix} c-a,\, c-b \\ c+\frac{1}{2} \end{matrix}\,\middle|\, z\right) \;=\; \sum_{k=0}^{\infty} A_k\, \frac{c^{\overline{k}}}{\left(c+\frac{1}{2}\right)^{\overline{k}}}\, z^k \qquad (36.2\text{-}28a)$$

where the A_k are defined by

$$(1-z)^{a+b-c}\, F\left(\begin{matrix} 2a,\, 2b \\ 2c \end{matrix}\,\middle|\, z\right) \;=\; \sum_{k=0}^{\infty} A_k\, z^k \qquad (36.2\text{-}28b)$$

For more relations of this type see [34, p.84-87]. If $a = b + \frac{1}{2}$ in relation 36.2-24, then (two parameters on the right side cancel)

$$\left[F\left(\begin{matrix} b+\frac{1}{2},\, b \\ 2b+1 \end{matrix}\,\middle|\, z\right)\right]^2 \;=\; F\left(\begin{matrix} 2b+\frac{1}{2},\, 2b \\ 4b+1 \end{matrix}\,\middle|\, z\right) \qquad (36.2\text{-}29)$$

and the right side again matches the structure on the left. The corresponding function can be identified (see [66, p.190]) as $G_b(z) := F\left(\begin{matrix} b+\frac{1}{2},\, b \\ 2b+1 \end{matrix}\,\middle|\, z\right) = \left(\frac{1+\sqrt{1-z}}{2}\right)^{-2b}$. We have $G_{n\,m}(z) = [G_n(z)]^m$.

Specializing relation 36.2-26b for $b = -a$ we find

$$\left[F\left(\begin{matrix} \frac{1}{4}+a,\, \frac{1}{4}-a \\ 1 \end{matrix}\,\middle|\, z\right)\right]^2 \;=\; F\left(\begin{matrix} \frac{1}{2}+2a,\, \frac{1}{2},\, \frac{1}{2}-2a \\ 1,\, 1 \end{matrix}\,\middle|\, z\right) \qquad (36.2\text{-}30)$$

For $a = 0$, $z = 1$ (or z a sixth power) this relation is an identity between the square of a sum of squares and a sum of cubes:

$$\left[\sum_{n=0}^{\infty}\left[\prod_{j=1}^{n} \frac{1/4+j-1}{j}\right]^2\right]^2 \;=\; \sum_{n=0}^{\infty}\left[\prod_{j=1}^{n} \frac{1/2+j-1}{j}\right]^3 \;=\; 1.39320392968\ldots \qquad (36.2\text{-}31)$$

The relation can be found by setting $\alpha = \beta = 1/4$ and $\gamma = 1/2$ in exercise 16 in [356, p.298]. Setting $a = 1/2$ in exercise 28 in [356, p.301] we find that the quantity equals $\pi/\Gamma(3/4)^4 = \Gamma(1/4)^4/(4\pi^3)$. For the square root of the expressions ($\sqrt{1.39320\ldots} = 1.180340\ldots$) we have [140, p.34]:

$$F\left(\begin{matrix} \frac{1}{2},\, \frac{1}{2} \\ 1 \end{matrix}\,\middle|\, \frac{1}{2}\right) \;=\; \left[\sum_{n=-\infty}^{\infty} e^{-n^2\pi}\right]^2 \;=\; 1.180340599016\ldots \qquad (36.2\text{-}32)$$

36.2.5 The Kummer transformation

The *Kummer transformation* connects two hypergeometric functions of type $_1F_1$:

$$\exp(z)\, F \left(\begin{matrix} a \\ a+b \end{matrix} \middle| -z \right) = F \left(\begin{matrix} b \\ a+b \end{matrix} \middle| z \right) \tag{36.2-33}$$

The relation is not valid if both a and b are negative integers. In that case one obtains the Padé approximants of $\exp(z)$, see relation 32.2-13 on page 629.

We give more transformations where the number of the lower parameters is greater than or equal to the number of upper parameters. A transformation from $_1F_1$ to $_2F_3$ is given by

$$F \left(\begin{matrix} a \\ b \end{matrix} \middle| z \right) F \left(\begin{matrix} a \\ b \end{matrix} \middle| -z \right) = F \left(\begin{matrix} a,\, b-a \\ b,\, \frac{1}{2}b,\, \frac{1}{2}(b+1) \end{matrix} \middle| \frac{z^2}{4} \right) \tag{36.2-34}$$

Setting $b = 2a$ and using relation 36.2-33 gives

$$\left[F \left(\begin{matrix} a \\ 2a \end{matrix} \middle| z \right) \right]^2 = \exp(z)\, F \left(\begin{matrix} a \\ a+\frac{1}{2},\, 2a \end{matrix} \middle| \frac{z^2}{4} \right) \tag{36.2-35}$$

This relation (attributed to Preece) and also the following transformation are given in [355].

$$F \left(\begin{matrix} \frac{1}{2}+a \\ 1+2a \end{matrix} \middle| z \right) F \left(\begin{matrix} \frac{1}{2}-a \\ 1-2a \end{matrix} \middle| z \right) = \exp(z)\, F \left(\begin{matrix} \frac{1}{2} \\ \frac{1}{2}+a,\, \frac{1}{2}-a \end{matrix} \middle| \frac{z^2}{4} \right) \tag{36.2-36}$$

The relation

$$F \left(\begin{matrix} a \\ 2a \end{matrix} \middle| z \right) F \left(\begin{matrix} b \\ 2b \end{matrix} \middle| -z \right) = F \left(\begin{matrix} \frac{1}{2}(a+b),\, \frac{1}{2}(a+b+1) \\ a+\frac{1}{2},\, b+\frac{1}{2},\, a+b \end{matrix} \middle| \frac{z^2}{4} \right) \tag{36.2-37}$$

is given in [33, rel.2.11, p.246]. Setting $b = a$ gives

$$F \left(\begin{matrix} a \\ 2a \end{matrix} \middle| z \right) F \left(\begin{matrix} a \\ 2a \end{matrix} \middle| -z \right) = F \left(\begin{matrix} a \\ a+\frac{1}{2},\, 2a \end{matrix} \middle| \frac{z^2}{4} \right) \tag{36.2-38}$$

A generalization is [204]

$$F \left(\begin{matrix} a \\ k\,a \end{matrix} \middle| z \right) F \left(\begin{matrix} a \\ k\,a \end{matrix} \middle| -z \right) = F \left(\begin{matrix} a,\, (k-1)a \\ ka,\, \frac{1}{2}ka,\, \frac{1}{2}ka+\frac{1}{2} \end{matrix} \middle| \frac{z^2}{4} \right) \tag{36.2-39}$$

The following transformation [33, rel.2.03, p.245] connects functions $_0F_1$ and $_2F_3$:

$$F \left(\begin{matrix} \\ a \end{matrix} \middle| z \right) F \left(\begin{matrix} \\ b \end{matrix} \middle| z \right) = F \left(\begin{matrix} \frac{1}{2}(a+b),\, \frac{1}{2}(a+b-1) \\ a,\, b,\, a+b-1 \end{matrix} \middle| 4z \right) \tag{36.2-40}$$

The relation is given in [139, vol.1, p.186] and also

$$F \left(\begin{matrix} \\ a \end{matrix} \middle| z \right) F \left(\begin{matrix} \\ a \end{matrix} \middle| -z \right) = F \left(\begin{matrix} \\ a,\, \frac{1}{2}a,\, \frac{1}{2}(a+1) \end{matrix} \middle| \frac{-z^2}{4} \right) \tag{36.2-41}$$

Splitting into even and odd parts gives

$$F \left(\begin{matrix} \\ a \end{matrix} \middle| z \right) = F \left(\begin{matrix} \\ \frac{1}{2},\, \frac{a}{2},\, \frac{a+1}{2} \end{matrix} \middle| \frac{z^2}{16} \right) + \frac{z}{a} F \left(\begin{matrix} \\ \frac{3}{2},\, \frac{a+1}{2},\, \frac{a+2}{2} \end{matrix} \middle| \frac{z^2}{16} \right) \tag{36.2-42}$$

Setting $b = a$ in relation 36.2-40 gives (cancellation of parameters on the right side)

$$\left[F\left(\begin{matrix} \\ a \end{matrix} \middle| z \right) \right]^2 = F\left(\begin{matrix} a - \frac{1}{2} \\ a, \, 2a - 1 \end{matrix} \middle| 4z \right) \tag{36.2-43}$$

This relation together with 36.2-35 gives

$$\exp(z)\, F\left(\begin{matrix} \\ a \end{matrix} \middle| \frac{z^2}{4} \right) = F\left(\begin{matrix} a - \frac{1}{2} \\ 2a - 1 \end{matrix} \middle| 2z \right) \tag{36.2-44}$$

The following relations are derived from the preceding ones:

$$F\left(\begin{matrix} a - \frac{1}{2} \\ a, \, 2a - 1 \end{matrix} \middle| z \right) F\left(\begin{matrix} b - \frac{1}{2} \\ b, \, 2b - 1 \end{matrix} \middle| z \right) = \left[F\left(\begin{matrix} \frac{1}{2}(a+b), \, \frac{1}{2}(a+b-1) \\ a, \, b, \, a+b-1 \end{matrix} \middle| z \right) \right]^2 \tag{36.2-45}$$

$$F\left(\begin{matrix} a - \frac{1}{2} \\ a, \, 2a - 1 \end{matrix} \middle| z \right) F\left(\begin{matrix} a - \frac{1}{2} \\ a, \, 2a - 1 \end{matrix} \middle| -z \right) = \left[F\left(\begin{matrix} \\ a, \, \frac{1}{2}a, \, \frac{1}{2}(a+1) \end{matrix} \middle| \frac{-z^2}{64} \right) \right]^2. \tag{36.2-46}$$

$$F\left(\begin{matrix} a \\ 2a \end{matrix} \middle| z \right) F\left(\begin{matrix} a \\ 2a \end{matrix} \middle| -z \right) = \left[F\left(\begin{matrix} \\ a + \frac{1}{2} \end{matrix} \middle| \frac{z^2}{16} \right) \right]^2 \tag{36.2-47a}$$

$$F\left(\begin{matrix} a \\ 2a + 1 \end{matrix} \middle| z \right) F\left(\begin{matrix} a \\ 2a + 1 \end{matrix} \middle| -z \right) = F\left(\begin{matrix} a \\ 2a + 1, \, a + \frac{1}{2} \end{matrix} \middle| \frac{z^2}{4} \right) \tag{36.2-47b}$$

$$F\left(\begin{matrix} \\ a \end{matrix} \middle| z \right) F\left(\begin{matrix} \\ 1 - a \end{matrix} \middle| z \right) = \frac{1}{2}\left[1 + F\left(\begin{matrix} \frac{1}{2} \\ a, \, 1 - a \end{matrix} \middle| 4z \right) \right] \tag{36.2-48a}$$

$$F\left(\begin{matrix} \\ a \end{matrix} \middle| z \right) F\left(\begin{matrix} \\ a + 1 \end{matrix} \middle| z \right) = F\left(\begin{matrix} a + \frac{1}{2} \\ a + 1, \, 2a \end{matrix} \middle| 4z \right) \tag{36.2-48b}$$

36.3   Examples: elementary functions

The 'well-known' functions like exp, log and sin are expressed as hypergeometric functions. In some cases a transformation is applied to obtain alternative series.

36.3.1   Powers, roots, and binomial series

$$\frac{1}{(1-z)^a} = F\left(\begin{matrix} a \\ \end{matrix} \middle| z \right) = \sum_{k=0}^{\infty} \binom{a+k-1}{k} z^k = F\left(\begin{matrix} -a \\ \end{matrix} \middle| \frac{-z}{1-z} \right) \tag{36.3-1a}$$

$$(1+z)^a = F\left(\begin{matrix} -a \\ \end{matrix} \middle| -z \right) = \sum_{k=0}^{\infty} \binom{a}{k} z^k = F\left(\begin{matrix} a \\ \end{matrix} \middle| \frac{z}{1+z} \right) \tag{36.3-1b}$$

An important special case of relation 36.3-1a is

$$\frac{1}{1-z} = F\left(\begin{matrix} 1 \\ \end{matrix} \middle| z \right) = \sum_{k=0}^{\infty} z^k \tag{36.3-2}$$

Further identities are

$$F\left(\begin{matrix} -n,\, n+1 \\ n \end{matrix}\,\middle|\, z\right) = (1-2z)\,(1-z)^{n-1} \tag{36.3-3a}$$

$$F\left(\begin{matrix} \frac{n}{2},\, \frac{n+1}{2} \\ n+1 \end{matrix}\,\middle|\, z\right) = \left(\frac{2}{1+\sqrt{1-z}}\right)^{n} \tag{36.3-3b}$$

$$F\left(\begin{matrix} \frac{n}{2},\, \frac{n+1}{2} \\ n \end{matrix}\,\middle|\, z\right) = \frac{1}{\sqrt{1-z}}\left(\frac{2}{1+\sqrt{1-z}}\right)^{n-1} \tag{36.3-3c}$$

$$F\left(\begin{matrix} \frac{n}{2},\, \frac{n+1}{2} \\ \frac{1}{2} \end{matrix}\,\middle|\, z\right) = \frac{(1-\sqrt{z})^{-n} + (1+\sqrt{z})^{-n}}{2} \tag{36.3-4a}$$

$$F\left(\begin{matrix} \frac{n+1}{2},\, \frac{n+2}{2} \\ \frac{3}{2} \end{matrix}\,\middle|\, z\right) = \frac{(1-\sqrt{z})^{-n} - (1+\sqrt{z})^{-n}}{2\,n\,\sqrt{z}} \quad \text{if } n \neq 0 \tag{36.3-4b}$$

$$F\left(\begin{matrix} \frac{1}{2},\, 1 \\ \frac{3}{2} \end{matrix}\,\middle|\, z\right) = \frac{1}{2\sqrt{z}}\,\log\left(\frac{1+\sqrt{z}}{1-\sqrt{z}}\right) \tag{36.3-4c}$$

The following identities are found by dividing relations 36.3-4b and 36.3-4a:

$$\frac{(1+z)^n - (1-z)^n}{(1+z)^n + (1-z)^n} = n\,z\,F\left(\begin{matrix} \frac{1}{2}-\frac{n}{2},\, 1-\frac{n}{2} \\ \frac{3}{2} \end{matrix}\,\middle|\, z^2\right)\Big/F\left(\begin{matrix} \frac{1}{2}-\frac{n}{2},\, -\frac{n}{2} \\ \frac{1}{2} \end{matrix}\,\middle|\, z^2\right) \tag{36.3-5a}$$

$$= n\,z\,F\left(\begin{matrix} \frac{1}{2}-\frac{n}{2},\, \frac{1}{2}+\frac{n}{2} \\ \frac{3}{2} \end{matrix}\,\middle|\, \frac{z^2}{z^2-1}\right)\Big/F\left(\begin{matrix} \frac{1}{2}-\frac{n}{2},\, \frac{1}{2}+\frac{n}{2} \\ \frac{1}{2} \end{matrix}\,\middle|\, \frac{z^2}{z^2-1}\right) \tag{36.3-5b}$$

Set in 36.3-3b to obtain the first of the following identities. The second, given by Michael Somos [priv. comm.], can be found by swapping the lower and upper parameters and replacing $4z$ by $z/4$. The C_k denote the Catalan numbers, see section 15.4 on page 331:

$$F\left(\begin{matrix} \frac{1}{2},\, 1 \\ 2 \end{matrix}\,\middle|\, 4z\right) = \sum_{k=0}^{\infty} C_k\, z^k = \frac{1-\sqrt{1-4z}}{2z} = \frac{2}{1+\sqrt{1-4z}} \tag{36.3-6a}$$

$$F\left(\begin{matrix} 1,\, 2 \\ \frac{1}{2} \end{matrix}\,\middle|\, \frac{z}{4}\right) = \sum_{k=0}^{\infty} \frac{1}{C_k}\, z^k \tag{36.3-6b}$$

36.3.2 Chebyshev polynomials

The Chebyshev polynomials are treated in section 35.2 on page 676, we have

$$T_n(1-2z) = F\left(\begin{matrix} n,\, -n \\ \frac{1}{2} \end{matrix}\,\middle|\, z\right) \tag{36.3-7a}$$

$$T_n(z) = F\left(\begin{matrix} n,\, -n \\ \frac{1}{2} \end{matrix}\,\middle|\, \frac{1-z}{2}\right) \tag{36.3-7b}$$

$$U_n(z) = (n+1)\,F\left(\begin{matrix} -n,\, n+2 \\ \frac{3}{2} \end{matrix}\,\middle|\, \frac{1-z}{2}\right) \tag{36.3-7c}$$

Relation 35.2-14 on page 679, written as $T_n(T_{1/n}(z)) = z = \mathrm{id}(z)$, shows that

$$F\left(\begin{matrix} n,\, -n \\ \frac{1}{2} \end{matrix}\,\middle|\, \frac{1-z}{2}\right)^{[-1]} = F\left(\begin{matrix} \frac{1}{n},\, -\frac{1}{n} \\ \frac{1}{2} \end{matrix}\,\middle|\, \frac{1-z}{2}\right) \tag{36.3-8}$$

near $z = 1$ (here $F^{[-1]}$ denotes the inverse function).

$$
\begin{aligned}
H_0 &= 1 \\
H_1 &= 2z \\
H_2 &= 4z^2 - 2 \\
H_3 &= 8z^3 - 12z \\
H_4 &= 16z^4 - 48z^2 + 12 \\
H_5 &= 32z^5 - 160z^3 + 120z \\
H_6 &= 64z^6 - 480z^4 + 720z^2 - 120 \\
H_7 &= 128z^7 - 1344z^5 + 3360z^3 - 1680z \\
H_8 &= 256z^8 - 3584z^6 + 13440z^4 - 13440z^2 + 1680 \\
H_9 &= 512z^9 - 9216z^7 + 48384z^5 - 80640z^3 + 30240z \\
H_{10} &= 1024z^{10} - 23040z^8 + 161280z^6 - 403200z^4 + 302400z^2 - 30240
\end{aligned}
$$

Figure 36.3-A: The first few Hermite polynomials.

36.3.3 Hermite polynomials

The Hermite polynomials $H_n(z)$ can be defined by the recurrence

$$
H_{n+1}(z) = 2z\, H_n(z) - 2n\, H_{n-1}(x) \tag{36.3-9}
$$

where $H_0(z) = 1$ and $H_1(z) = 2z$. The first few are shown in figure 36.3-A. For nonnegative integer n we have

$$
H_n(z) = (2z)^n\, F\left(\left. \begin{array}{c} -\frac{1}{2}\,n,\ -\frac{1}{2}\,(n-1) \end{array} \right| -\frac{1}{z^2} \right) \tag{36.3-10}
$$

36.3.4 Exponential function and logarithm

The exponential function is the hypergeometric with empty argument lists:

$$
\exp(z) = F\left(\left. \right| z \right) = \sum_{k=0}^{\infty} \frac{z^k}{k!} \tag{36.3-11}
$$

For the logarithm we have

$$
\log(1+z) = z\, F\left(\left. \begin{array}{c} 1,1 \\ 2 \end{array} \right| -z \right) = \sum_{k=0}^{\infty} \frac{(-1)^k\, z^{k+1}}{k+1} \tag{36.3-12a}
$$

$$
\log\left(\frac{1+z}{1-z} \right) = 2z\, F\left(\left. \begin{array}{c} \frac{1}{2},1 \\ \frac{3}{2} \end{array} \right| z^2 \right) = \log\left(1 + \frac{2}{1-z} \right) \tag{36.3-12b}
$$

For large arguments the following relation can be useful [1, p.68]. Set $w = \frac{z}{2a+z}$, then

$$
\log(z+a) = \log(z) + \log\left(\frac{z+a}{a} \right) = \log(a) + 2w\left[1 + \frac{w^3}{3} + \frac{w^5}{5} + \ldots \right] \tag{36.3-13a}
$$

$$
= \log(a) + 2w\, F\left(\left. \begin{array}{c} \frac{1}{2},1 \\ \frac{3}{2} \end{array} \right| w^2 \right) \tag{36.3-13b}
$$

36.3.5   Bessel functions and error function

The Bessel functions J_n of the first kind and the modified Bessel functions I_n (as given in [1]):

$$J_n(z) \;=\; \frac{(z/2)^n}{n!}\, F\left(\begin{array}{c} \\ n+1 \end{array}\middle|\, \frac{-z^2}{4}\right) \tag{36.3-14a}$$

$$I_n(z) \;=\; \frac{(z/2)^n}{n!}\, F\left(\begin{array}{c} \\ n+1 \end{array}\middle|\, \frac{z^2}{4}\right) \tag{36.3-14b}$$

$$F\left(\begin{array}{c} \\ n \end{array}\middle|\, z\right) \;=\; \frac{(n-1)!}{z^{(n-1)/2}}\, I_{n-1}(2\sqrt{z}) \tag{36.3-14c}$$

$$F\left(\begin{array}{c} \\ 1 \end{array}\middle|\, z\right) \;=\; I_0(2\sqrt{z}) = \sum_{k=0}^{\infty} \frac{z^k}{k!^2} \tag{36.3-14d}$$

Error function (the Kummer transformation, relation 36.2-33 on page 693, gives relation 36.3-15b):

$$\frac{\sqrt{\pi}}{2}\, \operatorname{erf}(z) \;:=\; \int_{t=0}^{z} e^{-t^2}\, dt \;=\; z\, F\left(\begin{array}{c} \frac{1}{2} \\ \frac{3}{2} \end{array}\middle|\, -z^2\right) \tag{36.3-15a}$$

$$=\; z\, e^{-z^2}\, F\left(\begin{array}{c} 1 \\ \frac{3}{2} \end{array}\middle|\, z^2\right) = z\, e^{-z^2} \sum_{k=0}^{\infty} \frac{(2z^2)^k}{1\cdot 3\cdot 5 \cdots (2k+1)} \tag{36.3-15b}$$

$$=\; \frac{1}{2z}\left[F\left(\begin{array}{c} -\frac{1}{2} \\ \frac{1}{2} \end{array}\middle|\, -z^2\right) - e^{-z^2} \right] \tag{36.3-15c}$$

36.3.6   Trigonometric and hyperbolic functions

Series for sine and hyperbolic sine are

$$\sin(z) \;=\; z\, F\left(\begin{array}{c} \\ \frac{3}{2} \end{array}\middle|\, \frac{-z^2}{4}\right) = \sum_{k=0}^{\infty} \frac{(-1)^k z^{2k+1}}{(2k+1)!} \tag{36.3-16a}$$

$$\sinh(z) \;=\; z\, F\left(\begin{array}{c} \\ \frac{3}{2} \end{array}\middle|\, \frac{z^2}{4}\right) = \sum_{k=0}^{\infty} \frac{z^{2k+1}}{(2k+1)!} \tag{36.3-16b}$$

Applying the transformation 36.2-43 on page 694 to relation 36.3-16a gives

$$[\sin(z)]^2 \;=\; z^2\, F\left(\begin{array}{c} 1 \\ \frac{3}{2},\, 2 \end{array}\middle|\, -z^2\right) \tag{36.3-17}$$

For the cosine and hyperbolic cosine we have

$$\cos(z) \;=\; F\left(\begin{array}{c} \\ \frac{1}{2} \end{array}\middle|\, \frac{-z^2}{4}\right) = \sum_{k=0}^{\infty} \frac{(-1)^k z^{2k}}{(2k)!} \tag{36.3-18a}$$

$$\cosh(z) \;=\; F\left(\begin{array}{c} \\ \frac{1}{2} \end{array}\middle|\, \frac{z^2}{4}\right) = \sum_{k=0}^{\infty} \frac{z^{2k}}{(2k)!} \tag{36.3-18b}$$

$$\exp(z)\, \frac{\sinh(z)}{z} \;=\; F\left(\begin{array}{c} 1 \\ 2 \end{array}\middle|\, 2z\right) \tag{36.3-19a}$$

$$\exp(-iz)\, \frac{\sin(z)}{z} \;=\; F\left(\begin{array}{c} 1 \\ 2 \end{array}\middle|\, -2iz\right) \tag{36.3-19b}$$

Further expressions for the sine and cosine are

$$\frac{\sin(a\,z)}{a\,\sin(z)} = F\left(\begin{array}{c} \frac{1+a}{2}, \frac{1-a}{2} \\ \frac{3}{2} \end{array}\middle|\; \sin(z)^2\right) \tag{36.3-20a}$$

$$\cos(a\,z) = F\left(\begin{array}{c} +\frac{a}{2}, -\frac{a}{2} \\ \frac{1}{2} \end{array}\middle|\; \sin(z)^2\right) \tag{36.3-20b}$$

$$\frac{\cos(a\,z)}{\cos(z)} = F\left(\begin{array}{c} \frac{1+a}{2}, \frac{1-a}{2} \\ \frac{1}{2} \end{array}\middle|\; \sin(z)^2\right) \tag{36.3-20c}$$

$$\frac{\sin(a\,z)}{a\,\sin(z)\,\cos(z)} = \frac{2\,\sin(a\,z)}{a\,\sin(2\,z)} = F\left(\begin{array}{c} 1+\frac{a}{2}, 1-\frac{a}{2} \\ \frac{3}{2} \end{array}\middle|\; \sin(z)^2\right) \tag{36.3-20d}$$

Relations for the hyperbolic sine and cosine are obtained by replacing $\sin \mapsto \sinh$, $\cos \mapsto \cosh$, and negating the sign of the argument of the hypergeometric function. For example, relation 36.3-20b gives

$$\cosh(a\,z) = F\left(\begin{array}{c} +\frac{a}{2}, -\frac{a}{2} \\ \frac{1}{2} \end{array}\middle|\; -\sinh(z)^2\right) \tag{36.3-20e}$$

The transformation 36.2-41 on page 693 (with $a = 1/2$ and $a = 3/2$, respectively) gives

$$\cos(z)\,\cosh(z) = F\left(\begin{array}{c} \\ \frac{1}{4}, \frac{2}{4}, \frac{3}{4} \end{array}\middle|\; \frac{-z^4}{64}\right) = \sum_{n=0}^{\infty} \frac{(-1)^n\,z^{4n}}{(4n)!/4^n} \tag{36.3-21a}$$

$$= 1 - \frac{1}{6}z^4 + \frac{1}{2520}z^8 - \frac{1}{7484400}z^{12} \pm \ldots \tag{36.3-21b}$$

$$\sin(z)\,\sinh(z) = z^2\,F\left(\begin{array}{c} \\ \frac{3}{4}, \frac{5}{4}, \frac{6}{4} \end{array}\middle|\; \frac{-z^4}{64}\right) = 2\sum_{n=0}^{\infty} \frac{(-1)^n\,z^{4n+2}}{(4n+2)!/4^n} \tag{36.3-21c}$$

$$= z^2 - \frac{1}{90}z^6 + \frac{1}{113400}z^{10} - \frac{1}{681080400}z^{14} \pm \ldots \tag{36.3-21d}$$

36.3.7   Inverse trigonometric and hyperbolic functions

Series for the inverse tangent and cotangent:

$$\arctan(z) = -\frac{i}{2}\log\frac{1+iz}{1-iz} = \mathfrak{Im}\log(1+iz) \tag{36.3-22a}$$

$$= z\,F\left(\begin{array}{c} \frac{1}{2}, 1 \\ \frac{3}{2} \end{array}\middle|\; -z^2\right) = \sum_{k=0}^{\infty} \frac{(-1)^k\,z^{2k+1}}{2k+1} \tag{36.3-22b}$$

Pfaff's reflection (relation 36.2-7b) leads to

$$\arctan(z) = \frac{z}{\sqrt{1+z^2}}\,F\left(\begin{array}{c} \frac{1}{2}, \frac{1}{2} \\ \frac{3}{2} \end{array}\middle|\; \frac{z^2}{1+z^2}\right) = \arccos\frac{1}{\sqrt{1+z^2}} \tag{36.3-22c}$$

$$= \frac{z}{1+z^2}\,F\left(\begin{array}{c} 1, 1 \\ \frac{3}{2} \end{array}\middle|\; \frac{z^2}{1+z^2}\right) \quad \text{by 36.2-7b} \tag{36.3-22d}$$

$$\text{arctanh}(z) \;=\; \frac{1}{2}\,\log\frac{1+z}{1-z} \tag{36.3-23a}$$

$$=\; z\,F\left(\genfrac{}{}{0pt}{}{\tfrac{1}{2},\,1}{\tfrac{3}{2}}\,\Big|\,z^2\right) = \sum_{k=0}^{\infty}\frac{z^{2k+1}}{2k+1} \tag{36.3-23b}$$

$$\text{arccoth}(z) \;=\; \frac{1}{2}\,\log\frac{z+1}{z-1} = \sum_{k=0}^{\infty}\frac{1}{(2k+1)\,z^{2k+1}} \tag{36.3-23c}$$

$$\log(z) \;=\; 2\,\text{arctanh}\frac{z-1}{z+1} = 2\,\text{arccoth}\frac{z+1}{z-1} \tag{36.3-23d}$$

$$\text{arccot}(z) \;=\; \arctan\left(\frac{1}{z}\right) = -\frac{i}{2}\,\log\frac{z+i}{z-i} \tag{36.3-24a}$$

$$=\; \frac{1}{z}\,F\left(\genfrac{}{}{0pt}{}{\tfrac{1}{2},\,1}{\tfrac{3}{2}}\,\Big|\,-\frac{1}{z^2}\right) = \sum_{k=0}^{\infty}\frac{(-1)^k}{(2k+1)\,z^{2k+1}} \tag{36.3-24b}$$

$$=\; \frac{1}{\sqrt{1+z^2}}\,F\left(\genfrac{}{}{0pt}{}{\tfrac{1}{2},\,\tfrac{1}{2}}{\tfrac{3}{2}}\,\Big|\,\frac{1}{1+z^2}\right) = \arcsin\frac{1}{\sqrt{1+z^2}} \tag{36.3-24c}$$

$$=\; \frac{z}{1+z^2}\,F\left(\genfrac{}{}{0pt}{}{1,\,1}{\tfrac{3}{2}}\,\Big|\,\frac{1}{1+z^2}\right) \tag{36.3-24d}$$

Series for the inverse sine and cosine are

$$\arcsin(z) \;=\; z\,F\left(\genfrac{}{}{0pt}{}{\tfrac{1}{2},\,\tfrac{1}{2}}{\tfrac{3}{2}}\,\Big|\,z^2\right) = \arctan\frac{z}{\sqrt{1-z^2}} \tag{36.3-25a}$$

$$=\; z\,F\left(\genfrac{}{}{0pt}{}{1,\,1}{\tfrac{3}{2}}\,\Big|\,\frac{1-\sqrt{1-z^2}}{2}\right) \quad \text{by 36.2-12b} \tag{36.3-25b}$$

$$=\; z\,\sqrt{1-z^2}\,F\left(\genfrac{}{}{0pt}{}{1,\,1}{\tfrac{3}{2}}\,\Big|\,z^2\right) \tag{36.3-25c}$$

The two latter relations suggest the following argument reduction applicable for the inverse sine (and tangent). Let $G(z) = (1-\sqrt{1-z})/2$, then

$$F\left(\genfrac{}{}{0pt}{}{1,\,1}{\tfrac{3}{2}}\,\Big|\,z\right) \;=\; \frac{1}{\sqrt{1-z}}\,F\left(\genfrac{}{}{0pt}{}{1,\,1}{\tfrac{3}{2}}\,\Big|\,G(z)\right) \tag{36.3-26a}$$

$$=\; \frac{1}{\sqrt{1-z}}\,\frac{1}{\sqrt{1-G(z)}}\,F\left(\genfrac{}{}{0pt}{}{1,\,1}{\tfrac{3}{2}}\,\Big|\,G(G(z))\right) = \ldots \tag{36.3-26b}$$

$$F\left(\genfrac{}{}{0pt}{}{1,\,1}{\tfrac{3}{2}}\,\Big|\,z\right) \;=\; \left[\prod_{k=0}^{\infty}1-z_k\right]^{-1/2} \quad \text{where} \quad z_0 = z, \quad z_{k+1} = G(z_k) \tag{36.3-26c}$$

$$\arccos(z) \;=\; \frac{\pi}{2} - \arcsin(z) = \text{arccot}\frac{z}{\sqrt{1-z^2}} \tag{36.3-27}$$

For the inverse hyperbolic sine we have

$$\operatorname{arcsinh}(z) \quad = \quad \log(z + \sqrt{1+z^2}) \quad = \quad z\,F\left(\begin{matrix}\frac{1}{2}, \frac{1}{2}\\ \frac{3}{2}\end{matrix}\,\middle|\, -z^2\right) \tag{36.3-28a}$$

$$= \quad \frac{z}{\sqrt{1+z^2}}\,F\left(\begin{matrix}\frac{1}{2}, 1\\ \frac{3}{2}\end{matrix}\,\middle|\, \frac{z^2}{1+z^2}\right) \quad \text{by 36.2-7b} \tag{36.3-28b}$$

$$= \quad z\,F\left(\begin{matrix}1, 1\\ \frac{3}{2}\end{matrix}\,\middle|\, \frac{1-\sqrt{1+z^2}}{2}\right) \quad \text{by 36.2-12b} \tag{36.3-28c}$$

The following relations follow from Clausen's product formula (relation 36.2-24 on page 691):

$$[\arctan(z)]^2 \quad = \quad \frac{z^2}{1+z^2}\,F\left(\begin{matrix}1, 1, 1\\ \frac{3}{2}, 2\end{matrix}\,\middle|\, \frac{z^2}{1+z^2}\right) \tag{36.3-29a}$$

$$[\operatorname{arccot}(z)]^2 \quad = \quad \frac{1}{1+z^2}\,F\left(\begin{matrix}1, 1, 1\\ \frac{3}{2}, 2\end{matrix}\,\middle|\, \frac{1}{1+z^2}\right) \tag{36.3-29b}$$

$$[\arcsin(z)]^2 \quad = \quad z^2\,F\left(\begin{matrix}1, 1, 1\\ \frac{3}{2}, 2\end{matrix}\,\middle|\, z^2\right) \tag{36.3-29c}$$

36.4   Transformations for elliptic integrals ‡

We give relations between elliptic integrals defined in section 31.2 on page 600 in terms of hypergeometric functions. To avoid the factor $\frac{\pi}{2}$, define $\tilde{K} := \frac{2K}{\pi}$ and $\tilde{E} := \frac{2E}{\pi}$. Then we have

$$\tilde{K}(k) \quad = \quad F\left(\begin{matrix}\frac{1}{2}, \frac{1}{2}\\ 1\end{matrix}\,\middle|\, k^2\right), \qquad \tilde{E}(k) \quad = \quad F\left(\begin{matrix}-\frac{1}{2}, \frac{1}{2}\\ 1\end{matrix}\,\middle|\, k^2\right) \tag{36.4-1}$$

The product form given as relation 31.2-10a on page 602 is the transformation

$$\tilde{K}(k) \quad = \quad \frac{2}{1+k'}\,F\left(\begin{matrix}\frac{1}{2}, \frac{1}{2}\\ 1\end{matrix}\,\middle|\, \left(\frac{1-k'}{1+k'}\right)^2\right) \tag{36.4-2a}$$

The relation can be written as

$$\tilde{K}(k) \quad = \quad (1+z(k))\,\tilde{K}\left(z(k)\right) \quad \text{where} \quad z(k) := \frac{1-k'}{1+k'} \tag{36.4-2b}$$

Relation 36.2-20f on page 691 with $a = \frac{1}{2}$ gives

$$\tilde{K}(k) \quad = \quad \frac{1}{1+k}\,\tilde{K}\left(\frac{2\sqrt{k}}{1+k}\right) \tag{36.4-3}$$

From relations 36.2-12a on page 690 and 36.2-30 on page 692 we find

$$\tilde{K}(k) \quad = \quad F\left(\begin{matrix}\frac{1}{4}, \frac{1}{4}\\ 1\end{matrix}\,\middle|\, (2\,k\,k')^2\right) \quad = \quad \left[F\left(\begin{matrix}\frac{1}{2}, \frac{1}{2}, \frac{1}{2}\\ 1, 1\end{matrix}\,\middle|\, (2\,k\,k')^2\right)\right]^{1/2} \tag{36.4-4}$$

The following transformation is due to Kummer [222, rel.13, p.129]:

$$F\left(\begin{matrix}a, \frac{4a+1}{6}\\ \frac{4a+3}{3}\end{matrix}\,\middle|\, z\right) \quad = \quad \left(\frac{1+\sqrt[4]{1-z}}{2}\right)^{-4a}\,F\left(\begin{matrix}a, \frac{4a+1}{6}\\ \frac{2a+5}{6}\end{matrix}\,\middle|\, \left[\frac{1-\sqrt[4]{1-z}}{1+\sqrt[4]{1-z}}\right]^4\right) \tag{36.4-5}$$

Setting $a = 1/2$ gives

$$\tilde{K}(k) = \frac{4}{\left(1 + \sqrt[4]{1 - k^2}\right)^2} \, \tilde{K}\left(\left[\frac{1 - \sqrt[4]{1 - k^2}}{1 + \sqrt[4]{1 - k^2}}\right]^2\right) \tag{36.4-6}$$

We further set

$$\tilde{N}(k) = F\left(\begin{matrix} -\frac{1}{2}, \, -\frac{1}{2} \\ 1 \end{matrix} \,\middle|\, k^2\right) \tag{36.4-7}$$

$$= 1 + \frac{1}{4}k^2 + \frac{1}{64}k^4 + \frac{1}{256}k^6 + \frac{25}{16384}k^8 + \frac{49}{65536}k^{10} + \frac{441}{1048576}k^{10} + \cdots \tag{36.4-8}$$

A special value is $\tilde{N}(1) = 4/\pi$. We have

$$\tilde{E}(k) = \frac{(1 + \sqrt{1 - k^2})}{2} \, F\left(\begin{matrix} -\frac{1}{2}, \, -\frac{1}{2} \\ 1 \end{matrix} \,\middle|\, \left(\frac{1 - \sqrt{1 - k^2}}{1 + \sqrt{1 - k^2}}\right)^2\right) \tag{36.4-9a}$$

$$= \frac{1 + k'}{2} \, F\left(\begin{matrix} -\frac{1}{2}, \, -\frac{1}{2} \\ 1 \end{matrix} \,\middle|\, \left(\frac{1 - k'}{1 + k'}\right)^2\right) \tag{36.4-9b}$$

$$= (1 + z(k))^{-1} \, \tilde{N}(z(k)) \quad \text{where} \quad z(k) := \frac{1 - k'}{1 + k'} \tag{36.4-9c}$$

Compare the last equality to relation 36.4-2b: Relations 36.2-20e on page 691 and 36.2-7b on page 689 give

$$\tilde{N}(k) = \sqrt{1 - k^2} \, F\left(\begin{matrix} -\frac{1}{4}, \, \frac{3}{4} \\ 1 \end{matrix} \,\middle|\, \frac{-4\,k^2}{(1 - k^2)^2}\right) \tag{36.4-10a}$$

$$= k' \, F\left(\begin{matrix} -\frac{1}{4}, \, \frac{3}{4} \\ 1 \end{matrix} \,\middle|\, -\left(\frac{2k}{k'^2}\right)^2\right) \tag{36.4-10b}$$

$$= \sqrt{1 + k^2} \, F\left(\begin{matrix} -\frac{1}{4}, \, \frac{1}{4} \\ 1 \end{matrix} \,\middle|\, \left(\frac{2k}{k^2 + 1}\right)^2\right) \tag{36.4-10c}$$

More such transformations are given in [222, pp.145-148].

Applying the transformation 36.2-20f on page 691 on the defining relation for $\tilde{N}(k)$ gives the key to fast computation of this function:

$$\tilde{N}(k) = (1 + k) \, \tilde{E}\left(\frac{2\sqrt{k}}{1 + k}\right) \tag{36.4-11}$$

The relation

$$2\,\tilde{E}(k) - k'^2 \, \tilde{K}(k) = \tilde{N}(k) \tag{36.4-12}$$

can be used to rewrite Legendre's relation (equation 31.2-23 on page 604) as either of the following (set $N := \pi/2 \, \tilde{N}$ in the second identity):

$$\frac{4}{\pi} = \tilde{N}\,\tilde{K}' + \tilde{K}\,\tilde{N}' - \tilde{K}\,\tilde{K}', \qquad \pi = N\,K' + K\,N' - K\,K' \tag{36.4-13}$$

We note the following generalization of Legendre's relation given in [139, vol.1, p.85] (and [17, p.138]):

$$\frac{\Gamma\left(1+a+b\right)\Gamma\left(1+c+b\right)}{\Gamma\left(\frac{3}{2}+a+b+c\right)\Gamma\left(\frac{1}{2}+b\right)} = \tag{36.4-14}$$

$$+F\left(\begin{matrix} +\frac{1}{2}+a, \ -\frac{1}{2}-c \\ 1+a+b \end{matrix}\middle| z\right) F\left(\begin{matrix} +\frac{1}{2}-a, \ +\frac{1}{2}+c \\ 1+c+b \end{matrix}\middle| 1-z\right) +$$

$$+F\left(\begin{matrix} +\frac{1}{2}+a, \ +\frac{1}{2}-c \\ 1+a+b \end{matrix}\middle| z\right) F\left(\begin{matrix} -\frac{1}{2}-a, \ +\frac{1}{2}+c \\ 1+c+b \end{matrix}\middle| 1-z\right) -$$

$$-F\left(\begin{matrix} +\frac{1}{2}-a, \ +\frac{1}{2}-c \\ 1+a+b \end{matrix}\middle| z\right) F\left(\begin{matrix} +\frac{1}{2}-a, \ +\frac{1}{2}+c \\ 1+c+b \end{matrix}\middle| 1-z\right)$$

Setting $a = b = c = 0$ gives Legendre's relation. Setting $c = a$ and $b = -a$ gives [66, rel.5.5.6, p.178]:

$$\frac{1}{\Gamma\left(\frac{3}{2}+a\right)\Gamma\left(\frac{1}{2}-1\right)} = \frac{2}{\pi}\frac{\cos(a\pi)}{1+2a} = \tag{36.4-15}$$

$$+F\left(\begin{matrix} +\frac{1}{2}+a, \ -\frac{1}{2}-a \\ 1 \end{matrix}\middle| z\right) F\left(\begin{matrix} +\frac{1}{2}-a, \ +\frac{1}{2}+a \\ 1 \end{matrix}\middle| 1-z\right) +$$

$$+F\left(\begin{matrix} +\frac{1}{2}+a, \ +\frac{1}{2}-a \\ 1 \end{matrix}\middle| z\right) F\left(\begin{matrix} -\frac{1}{2}-a, \ +\frac{1}{2}+a \\ 1 \end{matrix}\middle| 1-z\right) -$$

$$-F\left(\begin{matrix} +\frac{1}{2}-a, \ +\frac{1}{2}-a \\ 1 \end{matrix}\middle| z\right) F\left(\begin{matrix} +\frac{1}{2}-a, \ +\frac{1}{2}+a \\ 1 \end{matrix}\middle| 1-z\right)$$

36.5   The function x^x ‡

Boldly setting $a = 1 + z$ in $(1+z)^a = F\left(\begin{matrix} -a \\ \end{matrix}\middle| -z\right)$ (relation 36.3-1b on page 694) gives

$$(1+z)^{(1+z)} \;=\; F\left(\begin{matrix} -1-z \\ \end{matrix}\middle| -z\right) \;=\; \exp\left[(1+z)\log(1+z)\right] \tag{36.5-1a}$$

$$=\; 1+\frac{(z+1)}{1}z\left[1+\frac{(z+0)}{2}z\left[1+\frac{(z-1)}{3}z\left[1+\frac{(z-2)}{4}z\left[1+\ldots \right]\right]\right]\right] \tag{36.5-1b}$$

$$=\; 1+z+z^2+\frac{1}{2}z^3+\frac{1}{3}z^4+\frac{1}{12}z^5+\frac{3}{40}z^6-\frac{1}{120}z^7+\frac{59}{2520}z^8-\frac{71}{5040}z^9\pm\ldots \tag{36.5-1c}$$

This somewhat surprising expression allows the computation of x^x without computing $\exp()$ or $\log()$. The series converges for real $z > 0$ so we can compute x^x (where $x = 1+z$) for real $x > +1$ as

$$x^x \;=\; F\left(\begin{matrix} -x \\ \end{matrix}\middle| -x+1\right) \tag{36.5-2a}$$

$$=\; 1+\frac{x-0}{1}(x-1)\left[1+\frac{x-1}{2}(x-1)\left[1+\frac{x-2}{3}(x-1)\left[1+\ldots \right]\right]\right] \tag{36.5-2b}$$

We denote the series obtained by truncating after the n-th term of the hypergeometric series by $g_n(x)$. For example, with $n = 2$ and $n = 4$ we find

$$g_2(x) \;=\; \frac{1}{2}x^4-\frac{3}{2}x^3+\frac{5}{2}x^2-\frac{3}{2}x+1 \tag{36.5-3a}$$

$$=\; \frac{1}{2}z^4+\frac{1}{2}z^3+z^2+z+1 \tag{36.5-3b}$$

$$g_4(x) \;=\; \frac{1}{24}x^8-\frac{5}{12}x^7+\frac{15}{8}x^6-\frac{19}{4}x^5+\frac{61}{8}x^4-\frac{31}{4}x^3+\frac{131}{24}x^2-\frac{25}{12}x+1 \tag{36.5-3c}$$

$$=\; \frac{1}{24}z^8-\frac{1}{12}z^7+\frac{1}{8}z^6+\frac{1}{12}z^5+\frac{1}{3}z^4+\frac{1}{2}z^3+z^2+z+1 \tag{36.5-3d}$$

We have $g_n(n) = n^n$ and further $g_n(k) = k^k$ for all integer $k \leq n$. Thus we have just invented a curious way to find polynomials of degree $2n$ that interpolate k^k for $0 \leq k \leq n$ (setting $0^0 := 1$ for our purposes).

The polynomials actually give acceptable estimates for x^x also for non-integer x, especially for x near 1. The (unique) degree-n polynomials $i_n(x)$ that are obtained by interpolating the values k^k have much greater coefficients and give values far away from x^x for non-integer arguments x.

For $0 < x < n$ the interpolating polynomials $i_n(x)$ give an estimate that is consistently worse than $g_n(x)$ for non-integer values of x. The same is true even for the polynomials $i_{2n}(x)$ that interpolate k^k for $0 \leq k \leq 2n$ (so that $\deg(i_{2n}) = \deg(g_n) = 2n$). In fact, the $i_{2n}(x)$ approximate consistently worse than $i_n(x)$ for non-integer x.

Finally, the Padé approximants $P_{[n,n]}(x)$ for $g_n(x)$ give estimates that are worse than with both $i_n(x)$ or $g_n(x)$. Further, $g_n(x) \neq x^x$ even for integer x and the $P_{[n,n]}(x)$ have a pole on the real axis near $x = 1$. That is, we found a surprisingly good and compact polynomial approximation for the function x^x.

The sequence of the n-th derivatives of $(1 + z)^{(1+z)}$ at $z = 0$ is entry A005727 in [312]:

```
? Vec(serlaplace(exp((1+z)*log(1+z))))
   [1, 1, 2, 3, 8, 10, 54, -42, 944, -5112, 47160, -419760, 4297512, ... ]
```

Many other expressions for the function x^x can be given, we note just one: set $n = 2+z$ in relation 36.3-3a on page 695 to obtain

$$(1+z)^{(1+z)} \;=\; \frac{1}{1+2z} F\left(\begin{array}{c} -z-2,\, z+3 \\ z+2 \end{array} \middle| -z \right) \tag{36.5-4}$$

Chapter 37

Cyclotomic polynomials, product forms, and continued fractions

We describe the cyclotomic polynomials and some of their properties, together with the Möbius inversion principle. We also give algorithms to convert power series into Lambert series and infinite products. Continued fractions are described together with algorithms for their computation.

37.1 Cyclotomic polynomials, Möbius inversion, Lambert series

37.1.1 Cyclotomic polynomials

The roots (over $\mathbb{C}$) of the polynomial $x^n - 1$ are the n-th roots of unity:

$$x^n - 1 \;=\; \prod_{k=0}^{n-1} \left[x - \exp\left(\frac{2\pi i k}{n} \right) \right] \tag{37.1-1}$$

The n-th *cyclotomic polynomial* Y_n can be defined as the (monic) polynomial whose roots are the primitive n-th roots of unity:

$$Y_n(x) \;:=\; \prod_{\substack{k=0\,\ldots\,n-1 \\ \gcd(k,n)=1}} \left[x - \exp\left(\frac{2\pi i k}{n} \right) \right] \tag{37.1-2}$$

Most sources use $\Phi_n(x)$ for the cyclotomic polynomials, we use Y because Φ is overused. The degree of Y_n equals the number of primitive n-th roots, that is

$$\deg(Y_n) \;=\; \varphi(n) \tag{37.1-3}$$

The coefficients are integers, for example,

$$Y_{63}(x) \;=\; x^{36} - x^{33} + x^{27} - x^{24} + x^{18} - x^{12} + x^9 - x^3 + 1 \tag{37.1-4}$$

The first 30 cyclotomic polynomials are shown in figure 37.1-A. The first cyclotomic polynomial with a coefficient not in the set $\{0, \pm 1\}$ is Y_{105}:

$$Y_{105}(x) \;=\; x^{48} + x^{47} + x^{46} - x^{43} - x^{42} - 2 \cdot x^{41} - x^{40} - x^{39} + \ldots \tag{37.1-5}$$

The cyclotomic polynomials are irreducible over $\mathbb{Z}$. All except Y_1 are self-reciprocal.

For n prime the cyclotomic polynomial $Y_n(x)$ equals $(x^n - 1)/(x - 1) = x^{n-1} + x^{n-2} + \ldots + x + 1$. For $n = 2k$ and odd $k \geq 3$ we have $Y_n(x) = Y_k(-x)$. For $n = pk$ where p is a prime that does not divide k we have $Y_n(x) = Y_k(x^p)/Y_p(x)$. The following algorithm for the computation of $Y_n(x)$ is given in [154, p.403]:

J. Arndt, *Matters Computational: Ideas, Algorithms, Source Code*,
DOI 10.1007/978-3-642-14764-7_37, © Springer-Verlag Berlin Heidelberg 2011

```
n:      Yn(x)
1 :     x - 1
2 :     x + 1
3 :     x ^ 2 x + 1
4:      x^2 + 1
5 :     x ^ 4 x ^ 3 x ^ 2 x + 1
6 :     x ^ 2 x + 1
7 :     x ^ 6 x ^ 5 x ^ 4 x ^ 3 x 2 + x + 1
8:      x^4 + 1
9:      x^6 + x^3 + 1
10:     x^4 - x^3 + x^2 - x + 1
11:     x^10 + ... + 1   <--= all coefficients are one for prime n
12:     x^4 - x^2 + 1
13:     x^12 + ... + 1
14:     x^6 - x^5 + x^4 - x^3 + x^2 - x + 1
15:     x^8 - x^7 + x^5 - x^4 + x^3 - x + 1
16:     x^8 + 1
17:     x^16 + ... + 1
18:     x^6 - x^3 + 1
19:     x^18 + ... + 1
20:     x^8 - x^6 + x^4 - x^2 + 1
21:     x^12 - x^11 + x^9 - x^8 + x^6 - x^4 + x^3 - x + 1
22:     x^10 - x^9 + x^8 - x^7 + x^6 - x^5 + x^4 - x^3 + x^2 - x + 1
23:     x^22 + ... + 1
24:     x^8 - x^4 + 1
25:     x^20 + x^15 + x^10 + x^5 + 1
26:     x^12 - x^11 + x^10 - x^9 + x^8 - x^7 + x^6 - x^5 + x^4 - x^3 + x^2 - x + 1
27:     x^18 + x^9 + 1
28:     x^12 - x^10 + x^8 - x^6 + x^4 - x^2 + 1
29:     x^28 + ... + 1
30:     x^8 + x^7 - x^5 - x^4 - x^3 + x + 1
```

Figure 37.1-A: The first 30 cyclotomic polynomials.

1. Let $[p_1, p_2, \ldots, p_r]$ the distinct prime divisors of n. Set $y_0(x) = x - 1$.

2. For $j = 1, 2, \ldots, r$ set $y_j(x) = y_j(x^{p_j})/y_j(x)$ (the division is exact).

3. Return $y_r(x^{n/(p_1 p_2 \cdots p_r)})$

The last statement uses the fact that for $n = k t$ where all prime factors of k divide t we have $Y_n(x) = Y_t(x^k)$. An implementation is

```
1    polcyclo2(n, z='x)=
2    {
3        local(fc, y);
4        fc = factor(n)[,1];   \\ prime divisors
5        y = z - 1;
6        for (j=1, #fc,  y=subst(y,z,z^fc[j])\y;  n\=fc[j]; );
7        y = subst(y, z, z^n);
8        return( y );
9    }
```

Note that the routine will only work when the argument z is a symbol.

37.1.2   The Möbius inversion principle

The *Möbius function* $\mu(n)$ is defined for positive integer arguments n as

$$
\mu(n) \quad := \quad \begin{cases} 0 & \text{if} \quad n \text{ has a square factor} \\ (-1)^k & \text{if} \quad n \text{ is a product of } k \text{ distinct primes} \\ +1 & \text{if} \quad n = 1 \end{cases} \tag{37.1-6}
$$

The function satisfies

$$
\sum_{d \backslash n} \mu(d) \quad = \quad \begin{cases} 1 & \text{if } n = 1 \\ 0 & \text{otherwise} \end{cases} \tag{37.1-7}
$$

The Möbius function can be expressed as a sum of the primitive n-th roots of unity [139, vol.3, p.173]:

$$
\mu(n) \quad = \sum_{\substack{k=0 \ldots n-1 \\ \gcd(k,n)=1}} \exp\left(2\pi i k/n\right) \tag{37.1-8}
$$

$n :\mu(n)$	$n :\mu(n)$	$n :\mu(n)$	$n :\mu(n)$	$n :\mu(n)$	$n :\mu(n)$	$n :\mu(n)$	$n :\mu(n)$
1: +1	11: −1	21: +1	31: −1	41: −1	51: +1	61: −1	71: −1
2: −1	12: 0	22: +1	32: 0	42: −1	52: 0	62: +1	72: 0
3: −1	13: −1	23: −1	33: +1	43: −1	53: −1	63: 0	73: −1
4: 0	14: +1	24: 0	34: +1	44: 0	54: 0	64: 0	74: 1
5: −1	15: +1	25: 0	35: +1	45: 0	55: +1	65: +1	75: 0
6: +1	16: 0	26: +1	36: 0	46: +1	56: 0	66: −1	76: 0
7: −1	17: −1	27: 0	37: −1	47: −1	57: +1	67: −1	77: 1
8: 0	18: 0	28: 0	38: +1	48: 0	58: +1	68: 0	78: −1
9: 0	19: −1	29: −1	39: +1	49: 0	59: −1	69: +1	79: −1
10: +1	20: 0	30: −1	40: 0	50: 0	60: 0	70: −1	80: 0

Figure 37.1-B: Values of the Möbius function $\mu(n)$ for $n \leq 80$.

The sequence of the values of the Möbius function (see figure 37.1-B) is entry A008683 in [312].

A function $f(n)$ is called *multiplicative* if $f(1) = 1$ and f satisfies

$$f(n \cdot m) = f(n) \cdot f(n) \quad \text{if } \gcd(n, m) = 1 \tag{37.1-9}$$

For a multiplicative function one always has $f(n) = f(p_1^{e_1}) \cdot f(p_2^{e_2}) \cdot \ldots \cdot f(p_k^{e_k})$ where $n = p_1^{e_1} \cdot p_2^{e_2} \cdot \ldots \cdot p_k^{e_k}$ is the factorization of n into prime powers $p_i^{e_i}$. If the equality holds also for $\gcd(n, m) \neq 1$ the function is called *completely multiplicative*. Such a function satisfies $f(n) = f(p_1)^{e_1} \cdot f(p_2)^{e_2} \cdot \ldots \cdot f(p_k)^{e_k}$. For a multiplicative function f we have (subject to convergence, see [139, vol.3, p.169])

$$\sum_{n=1}^{\infty} f(n) = \prod_{p} \left[1 + f(p) + f\left(p^2\right) + f\left(p^3\right) + \ldots \right] \tag{37.1-10}$$

where the product on the right side is over all primes. If f is completely multiplicative, then $f\left(p^k\right) = f\left(p\right)^k$ and

$$\sum_{n=1}^{\infty} f(n) = \prod_{p} \frac{1}{1 - f(p)} \tag{37.1-11}$$

The Möbius function is multiplicative:

$$\mu(n)\,\mu(m) = \begin{cases} \mu(n \cdot m) & \text{if } \gcd(n, m) = 1 \\ 0 & \text{otherwise} \end{cases} \tag{37.1-12}$$

We now state the multiplicative version of the *Möbius inversion principle*:

$$g(n) = \prod_{d \backslash n} f(d) \quad \Longleftrightarrow \quad f(n) = \prod_{d \backslash n} g(d)^{\mu(n/d)} \tag{37.1-13}$$

For example, for the cyclotomic polynomials we have

$$x^n - 1 = \prod_{d \backslash n} Y_d(x) \tag{37.1-14}$$

Möbius inversion gives

$$Y_n(x) = \prod_{d \backslash n} \left(x^d - 1\right)^{\mu(n/d)} \tag{37.1-15}$$

The relation implies a reasonably efficient algorithm for the computation of the cyclotomic polynomials. The method also works when the argument x is not a symbol (x must be different from the n-th roots of unity).

Relation 37.1-14 implies (considering the polynomial degrees only and using relation 37.1-3)

$$n = \sum_{d\backslash n} \varphi(d) \tag{37.1-16}$$

while relation 37.1-15 corresponds to the equality

$$\varphi(n) = \sum_{d\backslash n} d\,\mu(n/d) \tag{37.1-17}$$

Relations 37.1-16 and 37.1-17 are a special case of the additive version of the Möbius inversion principle:

$$g(n) = \sum_{d\backslash n} f(d) \iff f(n) = \sum_{d\backslash n} g(d)\,\mu(n/d) \tag{37.1-18}$$

More general, if h is completely multiplicative (see [123, vol.1, p.447]), then

$$g(n) = \sum_{d\backslash n} f(d)\,h(n/d) \iff f(n) = \sum_{d\backslash n} g(d)\,h(n/d)\,\mu(n/d) \tag{37.1-19}$$

Setting $h(n) = 1$ gives relation 37.1-18.

We note two relations that are valid for multiplicative functions f (see [285, sect.4.6.4, facts.4+5]):

$$\sum_{d\backslash n} \mu(d)\,f(d) = \prod_{d\backslash n,\ d\ \text{prime}} (1 - f(d)) \tag{37.1-20a}$$

$$\sum_{d\backslash n} \mu(d)^2\,f(d) = \prod_{d\backslash n,\ d\ \text{prime}} (1 + f(d)) \tag{37.1-20b}$$

Relation 37.1-20a with $f(n) = 1/n$ gives relation 37.1-16 and also

$$\varphi(n) = n \prod_{d\backslash n,\ d\ \text{prime}} \left(1 - \frac{1}{d}\right) \tag{37.1-21}$$

We give two more inversion principles, taken from [176, p.237, thm.268-270]. For $x > 0$

$$g(x) = \sum_{n=1}^{\lfloor x\rfloor} f(x/n) \iff f(x) = \sum_{n=1}^{\lfloor x\rfloor} \mu(n)\,g(x/n) \tag{37.1-22}$$

$$g(n) = \sum_{k=1}^{\infty} f(k\,n) \iff f(n) = \sum_{k=1}^{\infty} g(k\,n)\,\mu(k) \tag{37.1-23}$$

A much more general version of the Möbius inversion principle is described in [86], see also [286].

37.1.3 Lambert series

A *Lambert series* is an expansion of the form

$$L(x) = \sum_{k>0} \frac{a_k\,x^k}{1 - x^k} = \sum_{k>0}\sum_{j>0} a_k\,x^{kj} \tag{37.1-24}$$

It can be converted to a power series

$$L(x) \;=\; \sum_{k>0} b_k\, x^k \quad \text{where} \quad b_k = \sum_{d\backslash k} a_d \tag{37.1-25}$$

The inversion principle can be used to transform a power series to a Lambert series:

$$a_k = \sum_{d\backslash k} b_d\, \mu(k/d) \tag{37.1-26}$$

The conversion can be implemented as

```
ser2lambert(t)=
{
/* Let t=[a1,a2,a3, ...], n=length(v), where t(x)=sum_{k=1}^{n}{a_k*x^k};
 * Return  L=[l1,l2,l3,...] so that (up to order n)
 * t(x)=\sum_{j=1}^{n}{l_j*x^j/(1-x^j)}
 */
    local(n, L);
    n = length(t);
    L = vector(n);
    for (k=1, n,  fordiv(k, d, L[k]+=moebius(k/d)*t[d]); );
    return( L );
}
```

The conversion in the other direction is

```
lambert2ser(L)=
{ /* inverse of ser2lambert() */
    local(n, t);
    n = length(L);
    t = sum(k=1, length(L), O('x^(n+1))+L[k]*'x^k/(1-'x^k) );
    t = Vec(t);
    return( t );
}
```

For the Lambert series with $a_k = 1$ for all k we have [109, p.95]

$$\sum_{k>0} d(k)\, x^k \;=\; \sum_{k>0} \frac{x^k}{1-x^k} = \sum_{k>0}\sum_{j>0} x^{kj} = \sum_{k>0} \frac{1+x^k}{1-x^k}\, x^{k^2} \tag{37.1-27}$$

where $d(k)$ is the number of the divisors of k, entry A000005 in [312]. More generally, we have

$$\sum_{k>0} \frac{k^e\, x^k}{1-x^k} \;=\; \sum_{k>0} \sigma_e(k)\, x^k \tag{37.1-28}$$

where $\sigma_e(n)$ is the sum of the e-th powers of the divisors of n. Let $o(n)$ denote the numbers of odd divisors of n (sequence A001227 in [312]), then

$$\sum_{k>0} o(k)\, x^k \;=\; \sum_{k>0} \frac{x^{2k-1}}{1-x^{2k-1}} = \sum_{k>0} \frac{x^k}{1-x^{2k}} = \sum_{k>0} \frac{x^{k(k+1)/2}}{1-x^k} \tag{37.1-29}$$

The first of the following relations is given in [214, p.644, ex.27]:

$$\sum_{k>0} \frac{x^k}{1-x^k} \;=\; \sum_{k>0} \left[k\, x^k \prod_{j\geq k+1} (1-x^j) \right] = \sum_{k>0} \left[1 - \prod_{j\geq k} (1-x^j) \right] \tag{37.1-30a}$$

For the Lambert series with $a_k = \mu(k)$ we have

$$x \;=\; \sum_{k>0} \frac{\mu(k)\, x^k}{1-x^k} \tag{37.1-31}$$

For $a_k = \alpha^k$ we have

$$\sum_{k>0} \frac{\alpha^k\, x^k}{1 - x^k} \;=\; \sum_{k>0} \frac{\alpha\, x^k}{1 - \alpha\, x^k} \tag{37.1-32}$$

This is given in [209, p.468], also the following:

$$\text{if} \quad \sum_{k>0} \left(a_k\, x^k\right) / \left(1 - x^k\right) = f(x) \quad \text{and} \quad \sum_{k>0} a_k\, x^k = g(x) \quad \text{then} \quad f(x) = \sum_{k>0} g\left(x^k\right) \tag{37.1-33}$$

We note a relation that is useful for the computation of the sum, it is given in [214, p.644, ex.27]:

$$L(x) \;=\; \sum_{k>0} x^{k^2} \left[a_k + \sum_{j>0} \left(a_k + a_{k+j}\right) x^{k\,j} \right] \tag{37.1-34}$$

For the related series

$$P(x) \;=\; \sum_{k>0} \frac{a_k\, x^k}{1 + x^k} \;=\; -\sum_{k>0}\sum_{j>0} (-1)^j\, a_k\, x^{k\,j} \tag{37.1-35}$$

we find (by computing the k-th term on both sides: $a_k\, x^k/(1+x^k) = a_k\, x^k/(1-x^k) - 2\, a_k\, x^{2k}/(1-x^{2k})$)

$$P(x) \;=\; L(x) - 2\, L(x^2) \tag{37.1-36}$$

The other direction is obtained by repeatedly using $L(x) = P(x) + 2\, L(x^2)$:

$$L(x) \;=\; \sum_{k=0}^{\infty} 2^k\, P(x^{2^k}) \tag{37.1-37}$$

Use relations 37.1-34 and 37.1-36 to find

$$P(x) \;=\; \sum_{k>0} x^{k^2} \left[a_k \left(1 - 2\, x^{k^2}\right) + \sum_{j>0} \left(a_k + a_{k+j}\right) \left(x^{k\,j} - 2\, x^{(k+j)^2 - j^2} \right) \right] \tag{37.1-38}$$

37.2 Conversion of power series to infinite products

37.2.1 Products of the form $\prod_{k>0} \left(1 - x^k\right)^{b_k}$

Given a series with constant term one,

$$f(x) \;=\; 1 + \sum_{k>0} a_k\, x^k \tag{37.2-1}$$

we want to find an infinite product such that

$$f(x) \;=\; \prod_{k>0} \left(1 - x^k\right)^{b_k} \tag{37.2-2}$$

We take the logarithm, differentiate, and multiply by x:

$$x\, \frac{f'(x)}{f(x)} \;=\; \sum_{k>0} \frac{(-k\, b_k)\, x^k}{1 - x^k} \tag{37.2-3}$$

The expression on the right side is a Lambert series with coefficients $-k\,b_k$, the expression on the left is easily computable as a power series, and we know how to compute a Lambert series from a power series. We have

$$b_k \;=\; -\frac{1}{k}\sum_{d\backslash k} a_k\,\mu(k/d) \tag{37.2-4}$$

where the a_k are the coefficients of the power series for $x\,f'(x)/f(x)$. The conversion to a product can be implemented as

```
1   ser2prod(t)=
2   {
3   /* Let t=[1,a1,a2,a3, ...], n=length(v), where t(x)=1+sum_{k=1}^{n}{a_k*x^k};
4    * Return  p=[p1,p2,p3,...] so that (up to order n)
5    * t(x)=\prod_{j=1}^{n}{(1-x^j)^{p_j}}
6    */
7       local(v);
8       v = Ser(t);
9       v = v'/v;
10      v = vector(#t-1, j, polcoeff(v, j-1));
11      v = ser2lambert(v);
12      v = vector(#v, j, -v[j]/j);
13      return( v );
14  }
```

A simple example is $f(x)=\exp(x)$, so $x\,f'/f=x$, and

$$\exp(x) \;=\; \prod_{k>0}\left(1-x^k\right)^{-\mu(k)/k} \;=\; \frac{\left(1-x^2\right)^{1/2}\left(1-x^3\right)^{1/3}\left(1-x^5\right)^{1/5}\cdots}{\left(1-x^1\right)^{1/1}\left(1-x^6\right)^{1/6}\left(1-x^{10}\right)^{1/10}\cdots} \tag{37.2-5}$$

Taking the logarithm, we find

$$x \;=\; -\sum_{k>0}\frac{\mu(k)}{k}\,\log\left(1-x^k\right) \tag{37.2-6}$$

Setting $f(x)=1-2\,x$ gives relation 18.3-6a on page 380 (number of binary Lyndon words):

```
? ser2prod(Vec(1-2*x+O(x^20)))
   [2, 1, 2, 3, 6, 9, 18, 30, 56, 99, 186, 335, 630, 1161, 2182, 4080, 7710, 14532, 27594]
```

Setting $f(x)=1-x-x^2$ gives the number of binary Lyndon words without the subsequence 00 (entry A006206 in [312]):

```
? ser2prod(Vec(1-x-x^2+O(x^20)))
   [1, 1, 1, 1, 2, 2, 4, 5, 8, 11, 18, 25, 40, 58, 90, 135, 210, 316, 492]
```

The ordinary generating function for the e_k corresponding to the product form $f(x)=\prod\left(1-x^k\right)^{e_k}$ is

$$\sum_{k=1}^{\infty} e_k\,x^k \;=\; -\sum_{k=1}^{\infty}\frac{\mu(k)}{k}\,\log\left(f\left(x^k\right)\right) \tag{37.2-7}$$

This can be seen by using the product form for f on the right side, using the power series $\log(1-x)=-(x+x^2/2+x^3/3+\ldots)$ and using the defining property of the Möbius function (relation 37.1-7 on page 705). An example is relation 18.3-6b on page 380. For the cyclotomic polynomials we find (via relation 37.1-15 on page 706):

$$-\sum_{k=1}^{\infty}\frac{\mu(k)}{k}\,\log\left(Y_n\left(x^k\right)\right) \;=\; \sum_{d\backslash n}\mu(d)\,x^{n/d} \tag{37.2-8}$$

For example, by setting $n=2$ we get

$$x^2-x \;=\; -\sum_{k=1}^{\infty}\frac{\mu(k)}{k}\,\log\left(1+x^k\right) \tag{37.2-9}$$

37.2.2   Products of the form $\prod_{k>0}(1+x^k)^{c_k}$

For the transformation into products of the form $\prod(1+x^k)^{c_k}$ we set

$$f(x) = \prod_{k>0}(1+x^k)^{c_k} \tag{37.2-10}$$

and note that

$$x\,\frac{f'(x)}{f(x)} = \sum_{k>0}\frac{(+k\,c_k)\,x^k}{1+x^k} \tag{37.2-11}$$

So we need a transformation into series of this type. As the Möbius transform is not (easily) applicable we use a greedy algorithm:

```
1   ser2lambertplus(t)=
2   {
3   /* Let t=[a1,a2,a3, ...], n=length(v), where t(x)=sum_{k=1}^{n}{a_k*x^k};
4    * Return  L=[l1,l2,l3,...] so that (up to order n)
5    * t(x)=\sum_{j=1}^{n}{l_j*x^j/(1+x^j)}
6    */
7       local(n, L, k4);
8       n = length(t);
9       L = vector(n);
10      for (k=1, n,
11          tk = t[k];
12          L[k] = tk;
13          \\ subtract tk * x^k/(1+x^k):
14          forstep(j=k, n, 2*k, t[j] -= tk);
15          forstep(j=k+k, n, 2*k, t[j] += tk);
16      );
17      return( L );
18  }
```

Now we can compute the product form via

```
1   ser2prodplus(t)=
2   {
3   /* Let t=[1,a1,a2,a3, ...], n=length(v), where t(x)=1+sum_{k=1}^{n}{a_k*x^k};
4    * Return  p=[p1,p2,p3,...] so that (up to order n)
5    * t(x)=\prod_{j=1}^{n}{(1+x^j)^{p_j}}
6    */
7       local(v);
8       v = Ser(t);
9       v = v'/v;
10      v = vector(#t-1, j, polcoeff(v, j-1));
11      v = ser2lambertplus(v);
12      v = vector(#v, j, v[j]/j);
13      return( v );
14  }
```

A product $\prod_{k>0}(1-x^k)^{b_k}$ can be converted into a product $\prod_{k>0}(1+x^k)^{c_k}$ via the relation $(1-x)=\prod_{k\geq0}(1+x^{2^k})^{-1}$.

37.2.3   Conversion to eta-products

Define the *eta function* (or *η-function*) via

$$\eta(x) := \prod_{j=1}^{\infty}(1-x^j) \tag{37.2-12}$$

The conversion of a power series to a product of the form (*eta-product*, or *η-product*)

$$\prod_{k=1}^{\infty}\eta\left(x^k\right)^{u_k} \tag{37.2-13}$$

can be done as follows:

```
1   ser2etaprod(v)=
2   {
3   /* Let t=[1,a1,a2,a3, ...], n=length(v), where t(x)=1+sum_{k=1}^{n}{a_k*x^k};
4    * Return  p=[p1,p2,p3,...] so that (up to order n)
5    * t(x)=\prod_{j=1}^{n}{eta(x^j)^{p_j}}
6    * where eta(x) = prod(k>0, (1-x^k))
7    */
8       local(n, t);
9       v = ser2prod(v);
10      n = length(v);
11      for (k=1, n,
12          t = v[k];
13          forstep (j=k+k, n, k, v[j]-=t; );
14      );
15      return( v );
16  }
```

Similarly, to convert into a product of the form

$$\prod_{k=1}^{\infty} \eta_+ \left(x^k \right)^{u_k} \quad \text{where} \quad \eta_+(x) := \prod_{j=1}^{\infty} \left(1 + x^j \right) = \frac{\eta(x^2)}{\eta(x)} \tag{37.2-14}$$

use

```
1   ser2etaprodplus(v)=
2   {
3   /* Let t=[1,a1,a2,a3, ...], n=length(v), where t(x)=1+sum_{k=1}^{n}{a_k*x^k};
4    * Return  p=[p1,p2,p3,...] so that (up to order n)
5    * t(x)=\prod_{j=1}^{n}{eta_+(x^j)^{p_j}}
6    * where eta_+(x) = prod(k>0, (1+x^k))
7    */
8       local(n, t);
9       v = ser2prodplus(v);
10      n = length(v);
11      for (k=1, n,
12          t = v[k];
13          forstep (j=k+k, n, k, v[j]-=t; );
14      );
15      return( v );
16  }
```

The routines are useful for computations with the generating functions of integer partitions of certain types, see section 16.4 on page 344.

We note two relations with Lambert series taken from [209, p.468]:

$$\eta(x) \;=\; \exp\left(-\sum_{k=1}^{\infty} \frac{1}{k} \frac{x^k}{1-x^k} \right) \;=\; \exp\left(-\sum_{k=1}^{\infty} x^k \sum_{d\backslash k} \frac{1}{d} \right) \;=\; \exp\left(-\sum_{k=1}^{\infty} \frac{x^k}{n} \sum_{d\backslash k} d \right) \tag{37.2-15a}$$

$$\eta_+(x) \;=\; \exp\left(-\sum_{k=1}^{\infty} \frac{(-1)^k}{k} \frac{x^k}{1-x^k} \right) \;=\; \exp\left(+\sum_{k=1}^{\infty} x^k \left(1-x^k\right) \sum_{d\backslash k} \frac{1}{d} \right) \tag{37.2-15b}$$

Further expressions for η and η_+ are (special cases of relation 16.4-1a on page 344)

$$\eta(x) \;=\; 1 - \sum_{k=1}^{\infty} x^k \prod_{j=1}^{k-1} \left(1 - x^j\right) \;=\; 1 - \sum_{k=1}^{\infty} x^k \prod_{j=k+1}^{\infty} \left(1 - x^j\right) \tag{37.2-16a}$$

$$\eta_+(x) \;=\; 1 + \sum_{k=1}^{\infty} x^k \prod_{j=1}^{k-1} \left(1 + x^j\right) \;=\; 1 + \sum_{k=1}^{\infty} x^k \prod_{j=k+1}^{\infty} \left(1 + x^j\right) \tag{37.2-16b}$$

```
 2:  ( E2^3 ) / ( E4 )
 3:  ( E3^4 ) / ( E9 )
 4:  ( E4^7 ) / ( E8^3 )
 5:  ( E5^6 ) / ( E25 )
 6:  ( E6^12 E36 ) / ( E12^4 E18^3 )
 7:  ( E7^8 ) / ( E49 )
 8:  ( E8^15 ) / ( E16^7 )
 9:  ( E9^13 ) / ( E27^4 )
10:  ( E10^18 E100 ) / ( E20^6 E50^3 )
11:  ( E11^12 ) / ( E121 )
12:  ( E12^28 E72^3 ) / ( E24^12 E36^7 )
13:  ( E13^14 ) / ( E169 )
14:  ( E14^24 E196 ) / ( E28^8 E98^3 )
15:  ( E15^24 E225 ) / ( E45^6 E75^4 )
16:  ( E16^31 ) / ( E32^15 )
17:  ( E17^18 ) / ( E289 )
18:  ( E18^39 E108^4 ) / ( E36^13 E54^12 )
19:  ( E19^20 ) / ( E361 )
20:  ( E20^42 E200^3 ) / ( E40^18 E100^7 )
21:  ( E21^32 E441 ) / ( E63^8 E147^4 )
22:  ( E22^36 E484 ) / ( E44^12 E242^3 )
23:  ( E23^24 ) / ( E529 )
24:  ( E24^60 E144^7 ) / ( E48^28 E72^15 )
25:  ( E25^31 ) / ( E125^6 )
26:  ( E26^42 E676 ) / ( E52^14 E338^3 )
27:  ( E27^40 ) / ( E81^13 )
28:  ( E28^56 E392^3 ) / ( E56^24 E196^7 )
29:  ( E29^30 ) / ( E841 )
30:  ( E30^72 E180^6 E300^4 E450^3 ) / ( E60^24 E90^18 E150^12 E900 )
31:  ( E31^32 ) / ( E961 )
32:  ( E32^63 ) / ( E64^31 )
33:  ( E33^48 E1089 ) / ( E99^12 E363^4 )
34:  ( E34^54 E1156 ) / ( E68^18 E578^3 )
35:  ( E35^48 E1225 ) / ( E175^8 E245^6 )
36:  ( E36^91 E216^12 ) / ( E72^39 E108^28 )
37:  ( E37^38 ) / ( E1369 )
38:  ( E38^60 E1444 ) / ( E76^20 E722^3 )
39:  ( E39^56 E1521 ) / ( E117^14 E507^4 )
40:  ( E40^90 E400^7 ) / ( E80^42 E200^15 )
41:  ( E41^42 ) / ( E1681 )
42:  ( E42^96 E252^8 E588^4 E882^3 ) / ( E84^32 E126^24 E294^12 E1764 )
```

Figure 37.2-A: Expressions for $\prod_{j=1}^{n} \eta(\omega^j q)$ as products of η-functions, Ek denotes $\eta(q^k)$.

```
 2:  ( E2^3 ) / ( E1 E4 )
 3:  ( E3^4 ) / ( E1 E9 )
 4:  ( E4^8 ) / ( E2^3 E8^3 )
 5:  ( E5^6 ) / ( E1 E25 )
 6:  ( E1 E4 E6^12 E9 E36 ) / ( E2^3 E3^4 E12^4 E18^3 )
 7:  ( E7^8 ) / ( E1 E49 )
 8:  ( E8^18 ) / ( E4^7 E16^7 )
 9:  ( E9^14 ) / ( E3^4 E27^4 )
10:  ( E1 E4 E10^18 E25 E100 ) / ( E2^3 E5^6 E20^6 E50^3 )
11:  ( E11^12 ) / ( E1 E121 )
12:  ( E2^3 E8^3 E12^32 E18^3 E72^3 ) / ( E4^8 E6^12 E24^12 E36^8 )
13:  ( E13^14 ) / ( E1 E169 )
14:  ( E1 E4 E14^24 E49 E196 ) / ( E2^3 E7^8 E28^8 E98^3 )
15:  ( E1 E9 E15^24 E25 E225 ) / ( E3^4 E5^6 E45^6 E75^4 )
16:  ( E16^38 ) / ( E8^15 E32^15 )
17:  ( E17^18 ) / ( E1 E289 )
18:  ( E3^4 E12^4 E18^42 E27^4 E108^4 ) / ( E6^12 E9^14 E36^14 E54^12 )
19:  ( E19^20 ) / ( E1 E361 )
20:  ( E2^3 E8^3 E20^48 E50^3 E200^3 ) / ( E4^8 E10^18 E40^18 E100^8 )
21:  ( E1 E9 E21^32 E49 E441 ) / ( E3^4 E7^8 E63^8 E147^4 )
22:  ( E1 E4 E22^36 E121 E484 ) / ( E2^3 E11^12 E44^12 E242^3 )
23:  ( E23^24 ) / ( E1 E529 )
24:  ( E4^7 E16^7 E24^72 E36^7 E144^7 ) / ( E8^18 E12^28 E48^28 E72^18 )
```

Figure 37.2-B: Expressions for $\prod_{j=1,\ \gcd(j,n)=1}^{n} \eta(\omega^j q)$ as products of η-functions, Ek denotes $\eta(q^k)$.

37.2.4   Some identities for the eta function ‡

The given routines let us discover identities like the following: let $\omega = \exp{(2\,\pi\,i/n)}$, $\sigma(n)$ the sum of the divisors of n, and μ the Möbius function, then

$$P_n(q) := \prod_{j=1}^{n} \eta\left(\omega^j\,q\right) \;=\; \prod_{d\backslash n} \eta\left(q^{d\,n}\right)^{\sigma(n/d)\,\mu(d)} \tag{37.2-17}$$

See figure 37.2-A for such identities with small n. Special cases are

$$P_n(q) \;=\; \frac{\eta\left(q^n\right)^{2n-1}}{\eta\left(q^{2n}\right)^{n-1}} \qquad \text{for } n \text{ a power of 2} \tag{37.2-18a}$$

$$P_p(q) \;=\; \frac{\eta\left(q^p\right)^{p+1}}{\eta\left(q^{p^2}\right)} \qquad \text{for } p \text{ prime} \tag{37.2-18b}$$

We further have

$$T_n(q) := \prod_{j=1,\,\gcd(j,n)=1}^{n} \eta\left(\omega^j\,q\right) \;=\; \prod_{d\backslash n} P_d(q)^{\mu(n/d)} \tag{37.2-19}$$

and by Möbius inversion, $P_n(q) = \prod_{d\backslash n} T_d(q)$. From the first few such relations (see figure 37.2-B) we get, writing E_k for $\eta(q^k)$ where convenient:

$$\eta\left(-q\right) \;=\; \frac{E_2^3}{E_1\,E_4} \tag{37.2-20a}$$

$$\eta_+\left(-q\right) \;=\; \frac{E_1\,E_4}{E_2^2} \;=\; \frac{\eta_+\left(q^2\right)}{\eta_+\left(q\right)} \tag{37.2-20b}$$

$$\eta(-q)\,\eta_+(-q) \;=\; E_2 \;=\; \eta(q)\,\eta_+(q) \tag{37.2-20c}$$

$$\eta\left(+i\,q\right)\,\eta\left(-i\,q\right) \;=\; \frac{E_4^8}{E_2^3\,E_8^3} \tag{37.2-20d}$$

Product expansions of the real and imaginary parts of $\eta(i\,q)$ and $\eta^{-1}(i\,q)$ are

$$\eta\left(i\,q\right) \;=\; \prod_{n=1}^{\infty} \frac{\left(1-q^{16n}\right)\left(1-q^{16n-4}\right)\left(1-q^{16n-12}\right)}{\left(1-q^{16n-2}\right)\left(1-q^{16n-14}\right)} \tag{37.2-21a}$$

$$-i\,q\prod_{n=1}^{\infty} \frac{\left(1-q^{16n}\right)\left(1-q^{16n-4}\right)\left(1-q^{16n-12}\right)}{\left(1-q^{16n-6}\right)\left(1-q^{16n-10}\right)}$$

$$\eta^{-1}\left(i\,q\right) \;=\; \prod_{n=1}^{\infty} \frac{\left(1-q^{16n-2}\right)^2\left(1-q^{16n-6}\right)^3\left(1-q^{16n-10}\right)^3\left(1-q^{16n-14}\right)^2}{\left(1-q^{16n}\right)\left(1-q^{16n-4}\right)^4\left(1-q^{16n-8}\right)^2\left(1-q^{16n-12}\right)^4} \tag{37.2-21b}$$

$$+i\,q\prod_{n=1}^{\infty} \frac{\left(1-q^{16n-2}\right)^3\left(1-q^{16n-6}\right)^2\left(1-q^{16n-10}\right)^2\left(1-q^{16n-14}\right)^3}{\left(1-q^{16n}\right)\left(1-q^{16n-4}\right)^4\left(1-q^{16n-8}\right)^2\left(1-q^{16n-12}\right)^4}$$

Many identities from section 31.3.3 on page 607 can be rediscovered (without the need of elliptic functions) by determining the η-products for the absolute value and the real and imaginary parts of certain expressions. The relation for the eta function then follows from $|a|^2 = \Re^2 a + \Im^2 a$. For example, for $a := \eta^2(i\,q)$ we find

$$\eta^2(i\,q) \;=\; \frac{E_4\,E_8^4}{E_2\,E_{16}^2} - 2\,i\,q\,\frac{E_4^3\,E_{16}^2}{E_2\,E_8^2}, \qquad \left|\eta^2(i\,q)\right|^2 \;=\; \frac{E_4^{16}}{E_2^6\,E_8^6} \tag{37.2-22}$$

Writing $|a|^2 = \mathfrak{Re}^2 a + \mathfrak{Im}^2(a)$ in terms of the η-products gives

$$\left[\frac{E_4^{16}}{E_2^6 E_8^6}\right] = \left[\frac{E_4 E_8^4}{E_2 E_{16}^2}\right]^2 + 4 q^2 \left[\frac{E_4^3 E_{16}^2}{E_2 E_8^2}\right]^2 \tag{37.2-23}$$

We substitute q^2 by q and give the resulting relation in two forms:

$$E_2^{14} E_8^4 = E_1^4 E_4^{14} + 4 q E_1^4 E_2^4 E_4^2 E_8^8 \tag{37.2-24a}$$

$$\left[\frac{E_2}{E_1^2 E_4 E_8^2}\right]^6 = \left[\frac{E_4}{E_1 E_2 E_8^2}\right]^8 + 4 q \left[\frac{1}{E_1^2 E_2 E_4 E_8^2}\right]^4 \tag{37.2-24b}$$

For $a := \eta^4(i q)$ we find

$$a = \frac{E_2^2 E_4^4}{E_8^2} - 4 i q \frac{E_4^4 E_8^2}{E_2^2}, \qquad |a|^2 = \frac{E_4^{32}}{E_2^{12} E_8^{12}} \tag{37.2-25}$$

This gives identity 31.3-32a on page 609:

$$E_2^{24} = E_1^{16} E_4^8 + 16 q E_1^8 E_4^{16} \tag{37.2-26a}$$

$$Z^{24} = X^{16} Y^8 + 16 q X^8 Y^{16} \quad \text{where} \tag{37.2-26b}$$

$$Z = E_2, \quad X = E_1, \quad Y = E_4 \tag{37.2-26c}$$

For $a := \eta(i q)/\eta(i q^3)$ we find

$$a = \frac{E_4 E_6^4 E_8 E_{24}^2}{E_2 E_{12}^7} - i q \frac{E_2 E_4 E_6^2 E_{24}^4}{E_8 E_{12}^7}, \qquad |a|^2 = \frac{E_4^8 E_6^3 E_{24}^3}{E_2^3 E_8^3 E_{12}^8} \tag{37.2-27}$$

This gives

$$E_2^6 E_6^6 = E_1 E_3^5 E_4^5 E_{12} + q E_1^5 E_3 E_4 E_{12}^5 \tag{37.2-28a}$$

$$\left[\frac{E_2^2 E_6^2}{E_1 E_3 E_4 E_{12}}\right]^3 = \left[\frac{E_3 E_4}{E_1 E_{12}}\right]^2 + q \left[\frac{E_1 E_{12}}{E_3 E_4}\right]^2 \tag{37.2-28b}$$

$$Z^6 = X Y^5 + q Y X^5 \quad \text{where} \tag{37.2-28c}$$

$$Z = E_2 E_6, \quad X = F_1 E_{12}, \quad Y = E_3 E_4 \tag{37.2-28d}$$

Using $a := \eta^3(i q)/\eta((i q)^3) = \eta^3(i q)/\eta(-i q^3)$ we find

$$a = \frac{E_4^3}{E_{12}} + 3 i q^2 \frac{E_4^5 E_6^2 E_{24}^2}{E_2^2 E_8^2 E_{12}^3}, \qquad |a|^2 = \frac{E_4^{24} E_6^3 E_{24}^3}{E_2^9 E_8^9 E_{12}^8} \tag{37.2-29}$$

This gives

$$E_2^{18} E_3^3 E_{12}^3 = E_1^9 E_4^9 E_6^6 + 9 q E_1^5 E_2^4 E_3^4 E_4^5 E_6^2 E_{12}^4 \tag{37.2-30a}$$

$$\left[\frac{E_3 E_{12}}{E_1 E_4}\right]^9 = \left[\frac{E_2 E_3 E_6 E_{12}}{E_2^4}\right]^6 + 9 q \left[\frac{E_2^5 E_3^5 E_6 E_{12}^5}{E_1^2 E_2^{12} E_4^2}\right]^2 \tag{37.2-30b}$$

For $a := \eta(i q)/\eta(i q^9)$ we find

$$a = \frac{E_4^2 E_6 E_{18}^2 E_{24} E_{72}^2}{E_2 E_8 E_{36}^6} - i q \frac{E_4 E_{12}^2 E_{18}^3 E_{72}^3}{E_6 E_{24} E_{36}^7}, \qquad |a|^2 = \frac{E_4^8 E_{18}^3 E_{72}^3}{E_2^3 E_8^3 E_{36}^8} \tag{37.2-31}$$

This gives

$$E_2^6 E_3^2 E_{12}^2 E_{18}^6 = E_1 E_2^2 E_3^4 E_4 E_9 E_{12}^4 E_{18}^2 E_{36} + q E_1^3 E_4^3 E_6^4 E_9^3 E_{36}^3 \tag{37.2-32}$$

For $a := \eta(i\,q)/\eta(i\,q^5)$ we obtain

$$a \;=\; \frac{E_4^2\,E_{10}^3\,E_{40}^2}{E_2\,E_{20}^6} - i\,q\,\frac{E_4^2\,E_{10}^2\,E_{40}^3}{E_8\,E_{20}^6}, \qquad |a|^2 \;=\; \frac{E_4^8\,E_{10}^3\,E_{40}^3}{E_2^3\,E_8^3\,E_{20}^8} \tag{37.2-33}$$

This gives

$$E_2^4\,E_{10}^4 \;=\; q\,E_1^3\,E_4\,E_5\,E_{20}^3 + E_1\,E_4^3\,E_5^3\,E_{20} \tag{37.2-34a}$$

$$\left[\frac{E_5\,E_{20}}{E_1\,E_4}\right]^3 \;=\; \left[\frac{E_5^3\,E_{20}^2}{E_1\,E_2^2\,E_{10}^2}\right]^2 + q\left[\frac{E_5^2\,E_{20}^3}{E_4\,E_2^2\,E_{10}^2}\right]^2 \tag{37.2-34b}$$

$$Z^4 \;=\; X\,Y^3 + q\,Y\,X^3 \quad\text{where} \tag{37.2-34c}$$

$$Z \;=\; E_2\,E_{10}, \qquad X \;=\; E_1\,E_{20}, \qquad Y \;=\; E_4\,E_5 \tag{37.2-34d}$$

By replacing q by q/i in relation 37.2-22 and using identity 37.2-20a we get

$$E_2\,E_8^6 \;=\; E_1^2\,E_4^2\,E_8\,E_{16}^2 + 2\,q\,E_2\,E_4^2\,E_{16}^4 \tag{37.2-35}$$

The same can be done for all a considered so far. For example, the second of the following identities is obtained from the first:

$$\eta^{-2}(i\,q) \;=\; \frac{E_2^5\,E_8^{10}}{E_4^{15}\,E_{16}^2} + 2\,i\,q\,\frac{E_2^5\,E_8^4\,E_{16}^2}{E_4^{13}} \tag{37.2-36a}$$

$$E_2^5\,E_8\,E_{16}^2 \;=\; E_1^2\,E_8^6 + 2\,q\,E_1^2\,E_4^2\,E_{16}^4 \tag{37.2-36b}$$

No identities are obtained for $a = \eta(i\,q)/\eta(i\,q^p)$ for (apparently) any odd prime $p \geq 7$. We use relation 31.3-20b on page 606 for $p = 7$:

$$E_2^3\,E_{14}^3 \;=\; E_1^2\,E_4\,E_7^2\,E_{28} + 2\,q\,E_1\,E_4^2\,E_7\,E_{28}^2 \tag{37.2-37a}$$

$$Z^3 \;=\; X^2\,Y + 2\,q\,Y^2\,X \quad\text{where} \tag{37.2-37b}$$

$$Z \;=\; E_2\,E_{14}, \qquad X \;=\; E_1\,E_7, \qquad Y \;=\; E_4\,E_{28} \tag{37.2-37c}$$

37.3   Continued fractions

A *continued fraction* is an expression of the form:

$$K(a,b) \;=\; a_0 + \cfrac{b_1}{a_1 + \cfrac{b_2}{a_2 + \cfrac{b_3}{a_3 + \cfrac{b_4}{a_4 + \cdots}}}} \tag{37.3-1}$$

Continued fractions are sometimes expressed in the following form:

$$K(a,b) \;=\; a_0 + \frac{b_1}{a_1+} \; \frac{b_2}{a_2+} \; \frac{b_3}{a_3+} \; \frac{b_4}{a_4+} \; \cdots \tag{37.3-2}$$

The b_k and a_k are respectively called the k-th *partial numerators* and *denominators*.

For $k > 0$ let P_k/Q_k be the value of the above fraction if b_{k+1} is set to zero (that is, the continued fraction terminates at index k). The ratio is called the k-th *convergent* of the continued fraction:

$$\frac{P_k}{Q_k} \;=\; a_0 + \frac{b_1}{a_1+} \; \frac{b_2}{a_2+} \; \frac{b_3}{a_3+} \; \frac{b_4}{a_4+} \; \cdots \; \frac{b_{k-1}}{a_{k-1}+} \; \frac{b_k}{a_k} \tag{37.3-3}$$

Simultaneous multiplication of a_i, b_i, b_{i+1} by some nonzero value does not change the value of the continued fraction: we have

$$a_0 + \frac{b_1}{a_1+} \; \frac{b_2}{a_2+} \; \frac{b_3}{a_3+} \; \frac{b_4}{a_4+} \; \cdots \;=\; a_0 + \frac{c_1\,b_1}{c_1\,a_1+} \; \frac{c_2\,c_1\,b_2}{c_2\,a_2+} \; \frac{c_3\,c_2\,b_3}{c_3\,a_3+} \; \frac{c_4\,c_3\,b_4}{c_4\,a_4+} \; \cdots \tag{37.3-4}$$

where all c_i are arbitrary nonzero constants.

37.3.1 Simple continued fractions

Continued fractions where all b_k are equal to 1 (and all the a_k are positive) are called *simple continued fractions*. Rational numbers have terminating continued fractions. Note that the expression of a rational number as simple continued fraction is not unique:

$$[a_0, \ldots, a_{n-1}, a_n] \ = \ [a_0, \ldots, a_{n-1}, a_n - 1, 1] \quad \text{if } a_n > 1 \qquad (37.3\text{-}5a)$$

$$[a_0, \ldots, a_{n-1}, 1] \ = \ [a_0, \ldots, a_{n-1} + 1] \qquad \text{if } a_n = 1 \qquad (37.3\text{-}5b)$$

Solutions of the quadratic equation $\alpha x^2 + \beta x + \gamma = 0$ that are not rational ($\Delta := \beta^2 - 4\alpha\gamma$ not a square) have simple continued fractions that are eventually periodic. For example:

```
? contfrac(sqrt(5))
  [2, 4, 4, 4, 4, 4, ...]
? contfrac(2+sqrt(3))
  [3, 1,2, 1,2, 1,2, ...]
? contfrac(sqrt(19))
  [4, 2,1,3,1,2,8, 2,1,3,1,2,8, 2,1,3,1,2,8, ...]
```

Write P_k/Q_k for the k-th convergent (in lowest terms) of the simple continued fraction expansion of the number x. Then the convergent is the *best approximation* in the following sense: if p/q is any better rational approximation to x (that is, $\left|\frac{p}{q} - x\right| < \left|\frac{P_k}{Q_k} - x\right|$), then one must have $q > Q_k$.

For the simple continued fraction of x we have

$$\left| x - \frac{P_n}{Q_n} \right| \ \leq \ \frac{1}{Q_n Q_{n-1}} \ < \ \frac{1}{Q_n^2} \qquad (37.3\text{-}6)$$

and equality can only occur with terminating continued fractions.

Use relation 37.3-4 to convert a continued fraction into a simple continued fraction:

```
1   cf2simple(A,B)=
2   {
3       local(c);   c=1;
4       for (j=2, #A-1,
5           c = 1/(B[j]);
6           B[j] *= c;   \\ B[j]==1
7           B[j+1] *= c;
8           A[j] *= c;
9       );
10      \\ note last term of B[] != 1 in general
11      return([A,B]);
12  }
```

The terms a_j where $j > 0$ can be set to 1 by the next routine:

```
1   cf2simpleB(A,B)=
2   {
3       local(c);   c=1;
4       for (j=2, #B-1,   \\ leave a0 as it is
5           c = 1/(A[j]);
6           A[j] *= c;   \\ A[j]==1
7           B[j] *= c;
8           B[j+1] *= c;
9       );
10      \\ note first and last term of A[] != 1 in general
11      return([A,B]);
12  }
```

37.3.1.1 Computing the simple continued fraction of a real number

Compute the simple continued fraction of a real number x as follows:

```
1   procedure number_to_scf(x, n, a[0..n-1])
2   {
3       for k:=0 to n-1
4       {
```

```
5        xi := floor(x)
6        a[k] := xi
7        /* if (x-xi)==0 then terminate */
8        x := 1 / (x-xi)
9      }
10  }
```

Here **n** is the number of requested terms a_k. Some check has to be inserted to avoid possible division by zero (indicating a terminating continued fraction, as will occur for rational x).

37.3.1.2 Continued fractions of polynomial roots

```
r = RootOf(z^3 - 2) == 1.2599210...
contfrac(r) == [1, 3, 1, 5, 1, 1, 4, 1, 1, 8, 1, 14, 1, 10, 2, ...]

f=z^3 - 2       r=1.25992104989487   ==> 1
f=z^3 - 3*z^2 - 3*z - 1       r=3.84732210186307   ==> 3
f=10*z^3 - 6*z^2 - 6*z - 1       r=1.18018873554841   ==> 1
f=3*z^3 - 12*z^2 - 24*z - 10       r=5.54973648578239   ==> 5
f=55*z^3 - 81*z^2 - 33*z - 3       r=1.81905335713127   ==> 1
f=62*z^3 + 30*z^2 - 84*z - 55       r=1.22092167902528   ==> 1
f=47*z^3 - 162*z^2 - 216*z - 62       r=4.52649103705930   ==> 4
f=510*z^3 - 744*z^2 - 402*z - 47       r=1.89936756679748   ==> 1
f=683*z^3 + 360*z^2 - 786*z - 510       r=1.11189244188653   ==> 1
f=253*z^3 - 1983*z^2 - 2409*z - 683       r=8.93715413784671   ==> 8
f=17331*z^3 - 14439*z^2 - 4089*z - 253       r=1.06706032616757   ==> 1
f=1450*z^3 - 19026*z^2 - 37554*z - 17331       r=14.9119465584038   ==> 14
```

Figure 37.3-A: Computation of the continued fraction of the positive real root of the polynomial $z^3 - 2$.

```
r = RootOf(z^2 - 29) == 5.38516480...
contfrac(r) ==[5,    2, 1, 1, 2, 10,    2, 1, 1, 2, 10,   ...]

f=z^2 - 29       r=5.38516480713450   ==> 5
f=4*z^2 - 10*z - 1       r=2.59629120178363   ==> 2
f=5*z^2 - 6*z - 4       r=1.67703296142690   ==> 1
f=5*z^2 - 4*z - 5       r=1.47703296142690   ==> 1
f=4*z^2 - 6*z - 5       r=2.09629120178363   ==> 2
f=z^2 - 10*z - 4       r=10.3851648071345   ==> 10

f=4*z^2 - 10*z - 1       r=2.59629120178363   ==> 2   <--= restart period
f=5*z^2 - 6*z - 4       r=1.67703296142690   ==> 1
```

Figure 37.3-B: Computation of the continued fraction of the positive real root of the polynomial $z^2 - 29$.

Let $r > 1$ be the only real positive root of a polynomial $F(x)$ with integer coefficients and positive leading coefficient. Then the (simple) continued fraction $[a_0, a_1, \ldots, a_n]$ of r can be computed as follows (taken from [221, p.261]):

1. Set $k = 0$, $F_0(x) = F(x)$, and $d = \deg(F)$.

2. Find the (unique) real positive root r_k of $F_k(x)$, set $a_k = \lfloor r \rfloor$. If $k = n$, then stop.

3. Set $G(x) = F_k(x + a_k)$, set $F_{k+1} = -G^*(x) = -x^d G(1/x)$.

4. Set $k = k + 1$ and goto step 2.

A simple demonstration is

```
1    f = z^3 - 2
2    ff(y)=subst(f, z, y)  \\ for solve() function
3
4    { for (k=1, 12,
5        print1("  f=", f);
6        r = solve(x=0.9, 1e9, ff(x));  \\ lazy implementation
7        print1("     r=", r);
8        ak = floor( r );
9        print1("  ==> ", ak);
10       g = subst(f, z, z+ak);  \\ shifted polynomial
11       f = -polrecip( g );       \\ negated reciprocal of g
12       print();
13   ); }
```

The output with $F(x) = x^3 - 2$ is shown in figure 37.3-A. With quadratic equations one obtains periodic continued fractions, figure 37.3-B shows the computation for $F(x) = x^2 - 29$. For a comparison of methods for the computation of continued fractions for algebraic numbers see [79].

37.3.2 Computation of the convergents (evaluation)

The computation of the sequence of convergents uses the recurrence

$$P_k \;=\; a_k\,P_{k-1} + b_k\,P_{k-2} \tag{37.3-7a}$$

$$Q_k \;=\; a_k\,Q_{k-1} + b_k\,Q_{k-2} \tag{37.3-7b}$$

Set $P_{-1}/Q_{-1} := 1/0$ and $P_0/Q_0 := a_0/1$ to initialize. The following procedure computes the sequences of values P_k and Q_k for $k = -1 \ldots n$ for a given continued fraction:

```
1    procedure ratios_from_cf(a[0..n], b[0..n], n, P[-1..n], Q[-1..n])
2    {
3        P[-1]  := 1
4        Q[-1]  := 0
5
6        P[0]  := a[0]
7        Q[0]  := 1
8
9        for k:=1 to n
10       {
11           P[k]  := a[k] * P[k-1] + b[k] * P[k-2]
12           Q[k]  := a[k] * Q[k-1] + b[k] * Q[k-2]
13       }
14   }
```

A function to compute the numerical value x from the first n terms of a simple continued fraction is

```
1    function ratio_from_cf(a[0..n-1], n)
2    {
3        x := a[n-1]
4        for k:=n-2 to 0 step -1
5        {
6            x := 1/x + a[k]
7        }
8
9        return x
10   }
```

With rational arithmetic and a general (non-simple) continued fraction, the algorithm becomes:

```
1    function ratio_from_cf(a[0..n-1], b[0..n-1], n)
2    {
3        P  := a[n-1]
4        Q  := b[n-1]
5        for k:=n-2 to 0 step -1
6        {
7            { P, Q } := { a[k] * P + b[k] * Q,  P }   // x := b[k] / x + a[k]
8        }
9
10       return P/Q
11   }
```

37.3.2.1 Implementation

Converting a number to a simple continued fraction can be done with GP's built-in function `contfrac()`. The final convergent can be computed with `contfracpnqn()`:

```
? default(realprecision,23)
     realprecision = 28 significant digits (23 digits displayed)
? Pi
     3.1415926535897932384626
? cf=contfrac(Pi)
     [3, 7, 15, 1, 292, 1, 1, 1, 2, 1, 3, 1, 14, 2, 1, 1, 2, 2, 2, 2, 1, 84, 2, 1, 1, 15, 3]
? ?contfracpnqn
     contfracpnqn(x): [p_n,p_{n-1}; q_n,q_{n-1}] corresponding to the continued fraction x.
? m=contfracpnqn(cf)
     [428224593349304 139755218526789]
     [136308121570117 44485467702853]
? 1.0*m[1,1]/m[2,1]
     3.1415926535897932384626
```

The number of terms of the continued fraction depends on the precision used, with greater precision more terms can be computed. The computation of the m-th convergent of a continued fraction given as two vectors a[] and b[] can be implemented as (backward variant):

```
1    cfab2r(a,b, m=-2)=
2    {
3        local(n, r);
4        n = length(a);
5        if ( m>-2, m = min(n, m) );  \\ default: m=n
6        if ( m>=n,  m=n-1 );
7        if ( m<0, return( 0 ) );  \\ infinity
8        r = 0;
9        m += 1;
10       forstep (k=m, 2, -1,  r = b[k]/(a[k]+r); );
11       r += a[1];  \\ b[1] unused
12       return( r );
13   }
```

We can also use the recursion relations 37.3-7a and 37.3-7b. We do not store all pairs P_n, Q_n but only return the final pair P_m, Q_m:

```
1    cfab2pq(a,b,m=-2)=
2    {
3        local(n, p, p1, p2, q, q1, q2, i);
4        n = length(a)-1;
5        if ( m>-2, m = min(n, m) );  \\ default: m=n
6        if ( m<0, return( [1, 0] ) );  \\ infinity
7        p1 = 1;
8        q1 = 0;
9        p = a[1];
10       q = 1;  \\ b[1] unused
11       for (k=1, m,
12           i = k+1;
13           p2 = p1;  p1 = p;
14           q2 = q1;  q1 = q;
15           p = a[i]*p1 + b[i]*p2;
16           q = a[i]*q1 + b[i]*q2;
17       );
18       return( [p,q] );
19   }
```

We use our routines to compute the convergents of the continued fraction for $4/\pi$ given 1658 by Brouncker:

$$\frac{4}{\pi} = 1 + \cfrac{1^2}{2 + \cfrac{3^2}{2 + \cfrac{5^2}{2 + \cfrac{7^2}{2 + \cdots}}}} = a_0 + \cfrac{b_1}{a_1 + \cfrac{b_2}{a_2 + \cfrac{b_3}{a_3 + \cfrac{b_4}{a_4 + \cdots}}}} \qquad (37.3\text{-}8)$$

Figure 37.3-C shows how to set up the vectors containing the a_k and b_k and check the convergents.

37.3.2.2   Fast evaluation as matrix product

For the evaluation of a continued fraction with a large number of terms rewrite relations 37.3-7a and 37.3-7b as a matrix product:

$$\begin{bmatrix} P_k & Q_k \\ P_{k-1} & Q_{k-1} \end{bmatrix} = \begin{bmatrix} a_k & b_k \\ 1 & 0 \end{bmatrix} \begin{bmatrix} P_{k-1} & Q_{k-1} \\ P_{k-2} & Q_{k-2} \end{bmatrix} = \prod_{j=0}^{k} \begin{bmatrix} a_j & b_j \\ 1 & 0 \end{bmatrix} = \begin{bmatrix} a_k & b_k \\ 1 & 0 \end{bmatrix} \prod_{j=0}^{k-1} \begin{bmatrix} a_j & b_j \\ 1 & 0 \end{bmatrix} \qquad (37.3\text{-}9)$$

The last equality shows that the next term in the product has to be multiplied at the left. An example, compare to figure 37.3-C:

```
? a=[1, 2, 2, 2, 2, 2, 2, 2, 2, 2, 2, 2, 2, 2, 2];
? b=[1, 1, 9, 25, 49, 81, 121, 169, 225, 289, 361, 441, 529, 625, 729];
? m=matid(2);for(n=1,5,m=[a[n],b[n];1,0]*m);m
   [945 789]
   [105  76]
? P=m[1,1];   \\ == 945
```

```
         default(realprecision, 55);  \\ use enough precision
         default(format, "g.11"); \\ print with moderate precision
         default(echo, 0);
         \r contfrac.gpi  \\ functions cfab2pq and cfab2r

         x=4.0/Pi
         n=15
         /* set up the continued fraction: */
         a=vector(n, j, 2);  a[1]=1;
         b=vector(n, j, (2*j-3)^2);

         /* print convergents and their error: */
         { for(k=0, n-1,
             t=cfab2pq(a,b, k);
             p=t[1]; q=t[2];
             print1(k, ":  ",p, " / ", q);
             print1("\n  d=", x-p/q);
             print();
           ); }
```
```
         15  /* =n */
         [1, 2, 2, 2, 2, 2, 2, 2, 2, 2, 2, 2, 2, 2, 2]  /* =a */
         [1, 1, 9, 25, 49, 81, 121, 169, 225, 289, 361, 441, 529, 625, 729]  /* =b */
         1.2732395447 /* = 4/Pi */

         0:  1 / 1
           d=0.27323954473
         1:  3 / 2
           d=-0.22676045526
         2:  15 / 13
           d=0.11939339088
         3:  105 / 76        /* =p3/q3 */
           d=-0.10833940263  /* =p3/q3-4/Pi */
         4:  945 / 789
           d=0.075520913556
         5:  10395 / 7734
           d=-0.070825622061
         [--snip--]
         13:  213458046676875 / 163842638377950
           d=-0.029583998575
         14:  6190283353629375 / 4964894559637425
           d=0.026428906710
```

Figure 37.3-C: A GP script demonstrating the function `cfab2pq()` which computes the convergents of a continued fraction (top) and its output (bottom, comments added). Here convergence is rather slow.

```
? Q=m[1,2];   \\ == 789
? P/Q
  315/263
? 4/Pi-P/Q
  0.075520913556
```

Use the binary splitting algorithm (section 34.1 on page 651) for the efficient computation of the matrix product.

37.3.3 Determinantal expressions

The numerators and denominators of successive convergents can be expressed as a determinant:

$$\det \begin{bmatrix} P_k & Q_k \\ P_{k-1} & Q_{k-1} \end{bmatrix} \;=\; P_k\,Q_{k-1} - P_{k-1}\,Q_k \;=\; (-1)^{k-1}\prod_{j=1}^{k} b_j \tag{37.3-10}$$

The relation is obtained by taking determinants on both sides of equation 37.3-9. The relation can also be written as

$$\frac{P_k}{Q_k} - \frac{P_{k-1}}{Q_{k-1}} \;=\; \frac{(-1)^{k-1}\prod_{j=1}^{k} b_j}{Q_{k-1}\,Q_k} \tag{37.3-11}$$

For simple continued fractions we have $b_j = 1$ so the product in the numerator equals 1. Further, by inserting $P_{k-1} = (P_k - b_k\,P_{k-2})/a_k$ (relation 37.3-7a) and the equivalent expression for Q_{k-1} into relation 37.3-10, we get

$$\det \begin{bmatrix} P_k & Q_k \\ P_{k-2} & Q_{k-2} \end{bmatrix} = P_k Q_{k-2} - P_{k-2} Q_k = (-1)^k a_k \prod_{j=1}^{k-1} b_j \tag{37.3-12}$$

Equivalently,

$$\frac{P_k}{Q_k} - \frac{P_{k-2}}{Q_{k-2}} = \frac{(-1)^k a_k \prod_{j=1}^{k-1} b_j}{Q_{k-2} Q_k} \tag{37.3-13}$$

This relation tells us (provided all a_j and b_j are positive) that the sequence of even convergents is increasing and the sequence of odd convergents is decreasing. As both converge to a common limit we have $P_o/Q_o \geq P_e/Q_e$ for all even e and odd o. Equality can occur only for terminating continued fractions.

37.3.4   Subsequences of convergents

Sometimes the terms a_k, b_k of the continued fraction are given in the form "$a_k = u(k)$ *if k even,* $a_k = v(k)$ *else*" (and b_k equivalently). Then one may want to compute the $x = K(a, b)$ in a stride-2 manner to regularize the involved expressions:

$$P_k = A_k P_{k-2} + B_k P_{k-4} \tag{37.3-14a}$$
$$Q_k = A_k Q_{k-2} + B_k Q_{k-4} \tag{37.3-14b}$$

We write the recurrence relation three times

$$P_k = a_k P_{k-1} + b_k P_{k-2} \tag{37.3-15a}$$
$$P_{k-1} = a_{k-1} P_{k-2} + b_{k-1} P_{k-3} \tag{37.3-15b}$$
$$P_{k-2} = a_{k-2} P_{k-3} + b_{k-2} P_{k-4} \tag{37.3-15c}$$

and eliminate the terms P_{k-1} and P_{k-3}. This gives

$$A_k = \frac{a_k b_{k-1} + b_k a_{k-2} + a_k a_{k-1} a_{k-2}}{a_{k-2}} = \frac{a_k b_{k-1}}{a_{k-2}} + b_k + a_k a_{k-1} \tag{37.3-16a}$$

$$B_k = \frac{-a_k b_{k-1} b_{k-2}}{a_{k-2}} \tag{37.3-16b}$$

The stride-3 version

$$P_k = A_k P_{k-3} + B_k P_{k-6} \tag{37.3-17a}$$
$$Q_k = A_k Q_{k-3} + B_k Q_{k-6} \tag{37.3-17b}$$

leads to the expressions (writing a_n for a_{k-n} to reduce line width):

$$A_k = \frac{a_0 b_1 b_3 + b_0 a_2 b_3 + b_0 b_2 a_4 + a_0 a_1 a_2 b_3 + a_0 a_1 b_2 a_4 + a_0 b_1 a_3 a_4 + b_0 a_2 a_3 a_4 + a_0 a_1 a_2 a_3 a_4}{b_3 + a_3 a_4} \tag{37.3-18a}$$

$$B_k = \frac{b_0 b_2 b_3 b_4 + a_0 a_1 b_2 b_3 b_4}{b_3 + a_3 a_4} \tag{37.3-18b}$$

When setting $a_k := \alpha$, $b_k := \beta$ the expressions for A_k and B_k simplify to the coefficients in relations 35.1-16c on page 672 (stride-2) and 35.1-16d (stride-3) for recurrences.

37.3.5   Relation to alternating series

With relation 37.3-11 it is possible to rewrite a continued fraction $x = K(a, b)$ with positive a_k, b_k as an alternating series

$$x = a_0 + \frac{b_1}{Q_0 Q_1} - \frac{b_1 b_2}{Q_1 Q_2} + \frac{b_1 b_2 b_3}{Q_2 Q_3} \pm \ldots + (-1)^{k+1} \frac{\prod_{i=1}^{k} b_i}{Q_k Q_{k+1}} \pm \ldots \tag{37.3-19}$$

Thus the algorithm for the accelerated summation of alternating series from section 34.3 can be applied to compute x.

37.3.6 Continued fractions for infinite products

A continued fraction for the product

$$P \; := \; \prod_{k=0}^{\infty} (1 + Y_k) \tag{37.3-20a}$$

in terms of $a = [a_0, a_1, \ldots]$ and $b = [b_0, b_1, \ldots]$ is

$$a \;=\; [1, \quad 1, \quad +Y_1 + (1 + Y_1) \cdot Y_0, \quad +Y_2 + (1 + Y_2) \cdot Y_1, \quad +Y_3 + (1 + Y_3) \cdot Y_2, \ldots] \tag{37.3-20b}$$

$$b \;=\; [1, \quad +Y_0, \quad -1 \cdot Y_1 \cdot (1 + Y_0), \quad -Y_0 \cdot Y_2 \cdot (1 + Y_1), \quad -Y_1 \cdot Y_3 \cdot (1 + Y_2), \ldots] \tag{37.3-20c}$$

```
Y(k) = eval(Str("Y" k))  \\ return symbol Yk
yprod(n)= if (n<=0, 1, prod(j=0, n-1, (1+Y(j))))
n=3
pr = yprod(n)
     ((Y2 + 1)*Y1 + (Y2 + 1))*Y0 + ((Y2 + 1)*Y1 + (Y2 + 1))
yv = vector(n, j, Y(j-1) )
     [Y0, Y1, Y2]
t = cfprod(yv);
a=t[1]
     [1, 1, (Y1 + 1)*Y0 + Y1, (Y2 + 1)*Y1 + Y2]
b=t[2]
     [1, Y0, -Y1*Y0 - Y1, (-Y2*Y1 - Y2)*Y0]

{ for(k=0, n,
    t=cfab2pq(a,b, k);
    p=t[1]; q=t[2];
    print1(k, ":  (",p, ") / (", q,")");
    yp = yprod(k);
    print1("\n    == ", simplify(p/q));
    print();
  ); }
     0:  (1) / (1)
         == 1
     1:  (Y0 + 1) / (1)   \\  (p1) / (q1)
         == Y0 + 1        \\  == yprod(1)
     2:  ((Y1 + 1)*Y0^2 + (Y1 + 1)*Y0) / (Y0)   \\  (p2) / (q2)
         == (Y1 + 1)*Y0 + (Y1 + 1)              \\ == yprod(2) == (1+Y0)*(1+Y1)
     3:  (((Y2 + 1)*Y1^2 + (Y2 + 1)*Y1)*Y0^2 + ((Y2 + 1)*Y1^2 + (Y2 + 1)*Y1)*Y0) / (Y1*Y0)
         == ((Y2 + 1)*Y1 + (Y2 + 1))*Y0 + ((Y2 + 1)*Y1 + (Y2 + 1))
```

Figure 37.3-D: Verification of relations 37.3-20b and 37.3-20c using GP.

For a given vector $y = [Y_0, Y_1, \ldots]$ the computation of individual values a_k and b_k can be implemented as:

```
1   cfproda(yv, n)=
2   {
3       local( y2, y3, d );
4       if ( n<=1, return(1) );
5       y3 = yv[n];
6       y2 = yv[n-1];
7       return( (y2+y3*(1+y2)) );
8
9   }
```

```
1   cfprodb(yv, n)=
2   {
3       local( y1, y2, y3 );
4       if (0==n, return(1) );  \\ unused
5       if (1==n, return(+yv[1+0]) );
6       y3 = yv[n];
7       y2 = yv[n-1];
8       y1 = if ( n==2, 1, yv[n-2] );
9       return( -y1*y3*(1+y2) );
10
11  }
```

The routine `cfprod()` generates the vectors a and b with $n + 1$ terms where n is the length of y:

```
1    cfprod(yv)=
2    {
3        local(n, a, b);
4        n = length(yv);
5        n += 1;   \\ n+1 terms in continued fraction
6        a = vector(n);
7        b = vector(n);
8        for (k=0, n-1,
9            a[k+1] = cfproda(yv, k);
10           b[k+1] = cfprodb(yv, k);
11       );
12       return( [a, b] );
13   }
```

Relations 37.3-20b and 37.3-20c can be verified using GP as shown in figure 37.3-D.

37.3.7　An expression for a sum of products

Define Z_n as

$$Z_n \quad := \quad z_1 + z_1 z_2 + z_1 z_2 z_3 + z_1 z_2 z_3 z_4 + \ldots = \sum_{k=1}^{n} \prod_{i=1}^{k} z_i \tag{37.3-21a}$$

$$= \quad z_1 \left[1 + z_2 \left[1 + z_3 \left[1 + z_4 \left[\ldots\right]\right]\right]\right] \tag{37.3-21b}$$

Then Z_∞ has the continued fraction

$$Z_\infty \quad = \quad \cfrac{z_1}{1 - \cfrac{z_2}{1 + z_2 - \cfrac{z_3}{1 + z_3 - \cfrac{z_4}{1 + z_4 - \cfrac{z_5}{1 + z_5 - \ldots}}}}} \tag{37.3-22}$$

That is, $Z_\infty = K(a, b)$ where

$$a \quad = \quad [0, \ 1, \ z_2 + 1, \ z_3 + 1, \ z_4 + 1, \ z_5 + 1, \ z_6 + 1, \ \ldots] \tag{37.3-23a}$$

$$b \quad = \quad [1, \ z_1, \ -z_2, \quad -z_3, \quad -z_4, \quad -z_5, \quad -z_6, \quad \ldots] \tag{37.3-23b}$$

For the n-th convergent P_n/Q_n one has $Q_n = 1$ and $P_n = Z_n$. The corresponding simple continued fraction is

$$a \quad = \quad \left[0, \ \frac{1}{z_1}, \ \frac{-(z_2+1)z_1}{z_2}, \ \frac{(z_3+1)z_2}{z_3 z_1}, \ \frac{-(z_4+1)z_3 z_1}{z_4 z_2}, \ \frac{(z_5+1)z_4 z_2}{z_5 z_3 z_1}, \right. \tag{37.3-24}$$

$$\left. \frac{-(z_6+1)z_5 z_3 z_1}{z_6 z_4 z_2}, \ \frac{(z_7+1)z_6 z_4 z_2}{z_7 z_5 z_3 z_1}, \ \frac{-(z_8+1)z_7 z_5 z_3 z_1}{z_8 z_6 z_4 z_2}, \ \ldots \right]$$

With $a_0 = 0$ and $a_n = 1$ for $n > 0$ we have

$$b \quad = \quad \left[0, \ z_1, \ \frac{-z_2}{z_2+1}, \ \frac{-z_3}{(z_3+1)(z_2+1)}, \ \frac{-z_4}{(z_4+1)(z_3+1)}, \ \frac{-z_5}{(z_5+1)(z_4+1)}, \ \ldots \right] \tag{37.3-25}$$

To convert a hypergeometric series (see chapter 36 on page 685)

$$F\left(\begin{array}{c} a_1, a_2, \ldots, a_u \\ b_1, b_2, \ldots, b_v \end{array} \middle| z \right) \tag{37.3-26}$$

into a continued fraction, set $z_1 = 1$ and for $k \geq 1$ set

$$z_{k+1} \quad = \quad \frac{z \prod_{j=1}^{u}(a_j + k)}{k \prod_{j=1}^{v}(b_j + k)} \tag{37.3-27}$$

An implementation is

```
1    hyper2cf(va, vb, n, z='z)=
2    \\ convert hypergeom(va,vb,z) into a continued fraction
3    {
4        local(cfa, cfb, m);
5        n += 2;
6        cfa = vector(n);
7        cfb = vector(n);
8        cfa[1] = 0;     cfa[2] = 1;
9        cfb[1] = 1;     cfb[2] = 1;
10       for (k=3, n,
11           m = 1/(k-2);  \\ hidden lower parameter 1:  (n-2) == 1+(n-3)
12           m *= prod(j=1, #va, va[j]+(k-3));  \\ upper parameters
13           m /= prod(j=1, #vb, vb[j]+(k-3));  \\ lower parameters
14           m *= z;  \\ argument
15           cfa[k]=(m+1);
16           cfb[k]=-m;
17       );
18       return( [cfa, cfb] );
19   }
```

We convert $\log(1-z)/z = F\left(\begin{smallmatrix}1,1\\2\end{smallmatrix}\middle|\, z\right)$ to a continued fraction and check the result:

```
? N=7;
? va=[1,1];vb=[2];
? t=hyper2cf(va,vb,N);
? cfa=t[1]
   [0, 1, 1/2*z + 1, 2/3*z + 1, 3/4*z + 1, 4/5*z + 1, 5/6*z + 1, 6/7*z + 1, 7/8*z + 1]
? cfb=t[2]
   [1, 1, -1/2*z, -2/3*z, -3/4*z, -4/5*z, -5/6*z, -6/7*z, -7/8*z]
? t=cfab2pq(cfa,cfb)
   [1/8*z^7 + 1/7*z^6 + 1/6*z^5 + 1/5*z^4 + 1/4*z^3 + 1/3*z^2 + 1/2*z + 1, 1]
? s1=t[1]/t[2]+O(z^N)
   1 + 1/2*z + 1/3*z^2 + 1/4*z^3 + 1/5*z^4 + 1/6*z^5 + 1/7*z^6 + O(z^7)
? s2=hypergeom(va,vb,z,N)+O(z^N)
   1 + 1/2*z + 1/3*z^2 + 1/4*z^3 + 1/5*z^4 + 1/6*z^5 + 1/7*z^6 + O(z^7)
```

For further information on continued fractions see [263] and [166]. An in-depth treatment is [238].

Chapter 38

Synthetic Iterations ‡

It is easy to construct arbitrary many iterations that converge super-linearly. Guided by some special constants that in base 2 can be obtained by recursive constructions we build iterations that allow the computation of the constant in a base independent manner. The iterations lead to functions that typically cannot be identified in terms of known (named) functions. Some of the functions can be expressed as infinite sums or products.

38.1   A variation of the iteration for the inverse

We start with the product form for the simplest iteration, the one for $1/(1-y)$:

$$I(y) \quad := \quad \frac{1}{1-y} \tag{38.1-1a}$$

$$= \quad 1 + y + y^2 + y^3 + y^4 + \dots \tag{38.1-1b}$$

$$= \quad (1+y)\,(1+y^2)\,(1+y^4)\,(1+y^8) \dots (1+y^{2^k}) \dots \tag{38.1-1c}$$

$$= \quad (1+Y_0)\,(1+Y_1)\,(1+Y_2)\,(1+Y_3) \dots (1+Y_k) \dots \tag{38.1-1d}$$

$$\text{where} \quad Y_0 = y, \quad Y_{k+1} = Y_k^2$$

We now modify the signs in the infinite product:

$$J(y) \quad := \quad (1-y)\,(1-y^2)\,(1-y^4)\,(1-y^8) \dots (1-y^{2^k}) \dots \tag{38.1-2a}$$

$$= \quad 1 - y - y^2 + y^3 - y^4 + y^5 + y^6 - y^7 - y^8 \pm \dots \tag{38.1-2b}$$

$$= \quad (1-Y_0)\,(1-Y_1)\,(1-Y_2)\,(1-Y_3) \dots (1-Y_k) \dots \tag{38.1-2c}$$

$$\text{where} \quad Y_0 = y, \quad Y_{k+1} = Y_k^2$$

The value of the n-th coefficient equals $+1$ if the parity of n is zero, else -1 (sequence A106400 in [312], the *Thue-Morse sequence*). The function J can be implemented as

```
1   fj(y,N=5)=
2   {
3       local(r);
4       r = 1;
5       for (k=1, N,
6           r -= r*y;
7           y *= y;
8       );
9       return(r);
10  }
```

Replacing the minus by a plus gives the implementation for the function I.

A related constant is the *parity number* (or *Prouhet-Thue-Morse constant*):

$$P \quad = \quad 0.4124540336401075977833613682584552830894783744557695575\dots \tag{38.1-3}$$

$$[\text{base 2}] \quad = \quad 0.0110, 1001, 1001, 0110, 1001, 0110, 0110, 1001, 1001, 0110, 0110, 1001, \dots$$

$$[\text{base 16}] \quad = \quad 0.6996, 9669, 9669, 6996, 9669, 6996, 6996, 9669, 9669, 6996, 6996, 9669, \dots$$

$$[\text{CF}] \quad = \quad [0, 2, 2, 2, 1, 4, 3, 5, 2, 1, 4, 2, 1, 5, 44, 1, 4, 1, 2, 4, 1, 1, 1, 5, 14, 1, 50, 15, 5, 1, 1, 1, 4, 2, 1, \dots]$$

J. Arndt, *Matters Computational: Ideas, Algorithms, Source Code,*
DOI 10.1007/978-3-642-14764-7_38, © Springer-Verlag Berlin Heidelberg 2011

```
Start: 0
Rules:
  0 --> 01
  1 --> 10

P0 =  0
P1 =  01
P2 =  0110
P3 =  01101001
P4 =  0110100110010110
P5 =  0110100110010110100101100110100 1

P --> 0110100110010110100101100110100110010110011010010110100110010110 ...
```

Figure 38.1-A: Computation of the Thue-Morse sequence by string substitution.

The sequence of zeros and ones in the binary expansions is entry A010060 in [312]. The constant P can be computed defining

$$K(y) \;=\; \frac{[I(y) - J(y)]}{2} \;=\; y + y^2 + y^4 + y^7 + y^8 + y^{11} + y^{13} + y^{14} + y^{16} + \dots \tag{38.1-4}$$

We have

$$P \;=\; \frac{1}{2} K\left(\frac{1}{2}\right) \;=\; \frac{1}{2} \frac{[I(\frac{1}{2}) - J(\frac{1}{2})]}{2} \;=\; \frac{1}{2} - \frac{1}{4} J\left(\frac{1}{2}\right) \tag{38.1-5}$$

and [39, item 125]

$$2 - 4P \;=\; J\left(\frac{1}{2}\right) \;=\; \prod_{k=0}^{\infty}\left(1 - \frac{1}{2^{2^k}}\right) \;=\; 0.3501838654395696088665545269661 78\dots \tag{38.1-6}$$

The sequence of bits of the parity number can also be computed by the string substitution shown in figure 38.1-A (which was created with the program [FXT: ds/stringsubst-demo.cc]).

The following relations are direct consequences of the definitions of the functions I and J:

$$I(y)\,I(-y) \;=\; I(y^2) \;=\; \frac{I(y) + I(-y)}{2} \tag{38.1-7a}$$

$$I(y) \;=\; \frac{J(y^2)}{J(y)} \tag{38.1-7b}$$

$$I(-y) \;=\; \frac{1-y}{1+y} I(y) \tag{38.1-7c}$$

$$J(-y) \;=\; \frac{1+y}{1-y} J(y) \tag{38.1-7d}$$

We have (from relation 16.4-1a on page 344):

$$I(y) \;=\; 1 + \sum_{k=0}^{\infty}\left[y^{2^k} \prod_{j=0}^{k-1}\left(1 + y^{2^j}\right) \right] \tag{38.1-8a}$$

$$J(y) \;=\; 1 - \sum_{k=0}^{\infty}\left[y^{2^k} \prod_{j=0}^{k-1}\left(1 - y^{2^j}\right) \right] \tag{38.1-8b}$$

A functional equation for K is

$$K(y) \;=\; (1-y)\,K(y^2) + \frac{y}{1-y^2} \tag{38.1-9}$$

It is solved by

$$K(y) = \sum_{k=0}^{\infty} \left[\frac{y^{2^k}}{1 - y^{2^{k+1}}} \prod_{j=0}^{k-1} \left(1 - y^{2^j}\right) \right] \tag{38.1-10}$$

For the inverse of J we have

$$\frac{1}{J(y)} = 1 + y + 2y^2 + 2y^3 + 4y^4 + 4y^5 + 6y^6 + 6y^7 + 10y^8 + 10y^9 + 14y^{10} + \ldots \tag{38.1-11a}$$

$$= \left[(1-y)(1-y^2)(1-y^4)(1-y^8) \ldots \right]^{-1} = \prod_{k=0}^{\infty} I(y^{2^k}) \tag{38.1-11b}$$

$$= (1-y) \prod_{k=0}^{\infty} \frac{1 + y^{2^k}}{1 - y^{2^k}} \tag{38.1-11c}$$

$$= (1+y)(1+y^2)^2(1+y^4)^3(1+y^8)^4(1+y^{16})^5 \ldots (1+y^{2^k})^{k+1} \ldots \tag{38.1-11d}$$

Relation 38.1-11d can be used for a divisionless algorithm for the computation of $1/J$:

```
1    binpart(y,N=5)=
2    {
3        local(r);
4        r = 1;
5        for (k=1, N,
6            for (j=1, k,   r += r*y; );
7            y *= y;
8        );
9        return(r);
10   }
```

The sequence of coefficients of the even powers of x in relation 38.1-11a is

$$1, \ 2, \ 4, \ 6, \ 10, \ 14, \ 20, \ 26, \ 36, \ 46, \ 60, \ 74, \ 94, \ 114, \ 140, \ 166, \ 202, \ \ldots$$

This is entry A000123 in [312], the number of binary partitions of the even numbers. The sequence $\frac{1}{2}[2, 4, 6, 10, 14, \ldots]$ modulo 2 equals the period-doubling sequence, see section 38.5 on page 734. The generating function $1 + 2y + 4y^2 + 6y^3 + 10y^4 + 14y^5 + 20y^6 + \ldots$ equals

$$\frac{I(y)}{J(y)} = (1+y)^2(1+y^2)^3(1+y^4)^4(1+y^8)^5(1+y^{16})^6 \ldots (1+y^{2^k})^{k+2} \ldots \tag{38.1-12}$$

It can be computed via (note the change in the inner loop)

```
1    binpart2(y,N=5)=
2    {
3        local(r);
4        r = 1;
5        for (k=1, N,
6            for (j=1, k+1,   r += r*y; );   \\ 1 ... k+1
7            y *= y;
8        );
9        return(r);
10   }
```

For the function I we have

$$I(y) = \sum_{k=0}^{\infty} \frac{y^{2^k - 1}}{1 - y^{2^{k+1}}} = \sum_{k=0}^{\infty} \frac{2^k \, y^{2^k - 1}}{1 + y^{2^k}} \tag{38.1-13a}$$

Integration gives

$$-\log(1-y) = \sum_{k=0}^{\infty} \frac{1}{2^{k+1}} \log\left(\frac{1 + y^{2^k}}{1 - y^{2^k}}\right) = \sum_{k=0}^{\infty} \log\left(1 + y^{2^k}\right) \tag{38.1-14a}$$

For the derivative of J we have

$$J'(y) = -J(y) \sum_{k=0}^{\infty} \frac{2^k y^{2^k-1}}{1-y^{2^k}} \tag{38.1-15}$$

The following functional equations hold for $I(y)$:

$$0 = B - 2AB + A^2 \quad \text{where} \quad A = I(y), \quad B = I(y^2) \tag{38.1-16a}$$
$$0 = B - 2AB - A^2 + 2A^2B \quad \text{where} \quad A = I(-y), \quad B = I(-y^2) \tag{38.1-16b}$$
$$0 = B - 3AB + 3A^2B - A^3 \quad \text{where} \quad A = I(y), \quad B = I(y^3) \tag{38.1-16c}$$
$$0 = B - 5AB + 10A^2B - 10A^3B + 5A^4B - A^5 \quad \text{where} \tag{38.1-16d}$$
$$A = I(y), \quad B = I(y^5)$$
$$0 = B\left[(1-A)^k - (-A)^k\right] + (-A)^k \quad \text{where} \quad A = I(y), \quad B = I(y^k) \tag{38.1-16e}$$

The following relation for $J(y)$ can be derived from the functional equation for $K(y)$ (relation 38.1-9), the definition of $K(y)$, and relation 38.1-7b:

$$0 = J_2^3 - 2J_4J_2J_1 + J_4J_1^2 \quad \text{where} \quad J_1 = J(y), \quad J_2 = J(y^2), \quad J_4 = J(y^4) \tag{38.1-17}$$

This relation is given with entry A106400 in [312], together with

$$0 = J_6J_1^3 - 3J_6J_2J_1^2 + 3J_6J_2^2J_1 - J_3J_2^3 \tag{38.1-18}$$

where $J_k = J(y^k)$. Relations between J_1, J_2, J_k, and J_{2k} can be derived from relation 38.1-16e by replacing $I(y)$ by $J(y^2)/J(y)$. For example, $k = 5$ gives

$$0 = J_{10}J_1^5 - 5J_{10}J_2J_1^4 + 10J_{10}J_2^2J_1^3 - 10J_{10}J_2^3J_1^2 + 5J_{10}J_2^4J_1 - J_5J_2^5 \tag{38.1-19}$$

Relations 37.2-20a ... 37.2-20d on page 714 hold when replacing $\eta(x)$ with $J(x)$ and $\eta_+(x)$ with $I(x)$, as well as relation 37.2-18a on page 714.

38.1.1 The Komornik-Loreti constant

We have $K(1/\beta) = 1$ for

$$\frac{1}{\beta} = 0.559524558496726525132209765157432285831076478968660 3076\ldots \tag{38.1-20a}$$
$$[\text{base 2}] = 0.10001111001111010000000001100000000011010110001000 10110\ldots$$
$$\beta = 1.787231650182965933013274890337008385337931402961810997\ldots \tag{38.1-20b}$$
$$[\text{base 2}] = 1.110010011000100000000011011011111110100101110101101 0000\ldots$$
$$[\text{CF}] = [1, 1, 3, 1, 2, 3, 188, 1, 12, 1, 1, 22, 33, 1, 10, 1, 1, 7, 1, 9, 1, 1, 20, 2, 15, 1, \ldots]$$

The constant β is the smallest real number in the interval $(1, 2)$ so that 1 has a unique expansion of the form $\sum_{n=1}^{\infty} \delta_n \beta^{-n}$ where $\delta_n \in \{0, 1\}$. It is called the *Komornik-Loreti constant* (see [8]). We have $\delta_n = 1$ where the Thue-Morse sequence equals 1. This was used for the computation of β: one solves $K(y) = 1$ for y. The transcendence of β is proved (using that $J(y)$ is transcendental for algebraic y) in [9].

38.1.2 Third order variants

Variations of the third order iteration for $1/(1-y)$

$$I(y) := \frac{1}{1-y} = 1 + y + y^2 + y^3 + y^4 + \ldots \tag{38.1-21a}$$
$$= \left(1 + y + y^2\right)\left(1 + y^3 + y^6\right)\left(1 + y^9 + y^{18}\right) \ldots \left(1 + y^{3^k} + y^{2 \cdot 3^k}\right) \ldots \tag{38.1-21b}$$
$$= \left(1 + Y_0 + Y_0^2\right)\left(1 + Y_1 + Y_1^2\right)\left(1 + Y_2 + Y_2^2\right) \ldots \left(1 + Y_k + Y_k^2\right) \ldots \tag{38.1-21c}$$
$$\text{where} \quad Y_0 = y, \quad Y_{k+1} = Y_k^3$$

```
Start:  0
Rules:
  0 --> 001
  1 --> 110
--------------
0: 0
1: 001
2: 001001110
3: 001001110001001110110110001
4: 001001110001001110110110001001001110001001110110110001110110001110110001001001110
```

Figure 38.1-B: Computation of the Mephisto Waltz sequence via string substitution.

lead to series related to the base-3 analogue of the parity. The simplest example may be

$$T(y) = \left(1 + Y_0 - Y_0^2\right)\left(1 + Y_1 - Y_1^2\right)\left(1 + Y_2 - Y_2^2\right)\ldots\left(1 + Y_k - Y_k^2\right)\ldots \tag{38.1-22a}$$

$$= 1 + y - y^2 + y^3 + y^4 - y^5 - y^6 - y^7 + y^8 + y^9 + y^{10} - y^{11} + y^{12} \pm \ldots \tag{38.1-22b}$$

The sign of the n-th coefficient is the parity of the number of twos in the radix-3 expansion of n. We have

$$\frac{1}{2}\left[I(y) - T(y)\right] = y^2 + y^5 + y^6 + y^7 + y^{11} + y^{14} + y^{15} + y^{16} + y^{18} + y^{19} + y^{21} + \ldots \tag{38.1-23}$$

$$\frac{1}{4}\left[I\left(\frac{1}{2}\right) - T\left(\frac{1}{2}\right)\right] = 0.1526445236254075825319249214757916793115045148714892548\ldots \tag{38.1-24}$$

$$[\text{base 2}] = 0.0010011100010011101101100010010011100010011101101100011\ldots$$

$$[\text{CF}] = [0, 6, 1, 1, 4, 2, 1, 1, 2, 4, 1, 1, 4, 1, 4, 2, 1, 1, 1, 2, 1, 18, 3, 24, 1, 6, 1, 3, \ldots]$$

The sequence of zeros and ones in the binary expansion is entry A064990 in [312], the *Mephisto Waltz sequence*. Its computation via string substitution is shown in figure 38.1-B.

38.2   An iteration related to the Thue constant

```
T0 =  0

T1 =  111

T2 =  110110110
   == 3 times 11.0

T3 =  110110111110110111110110111
   == 3 times 110110.111

T4 =  110110111110110111110110111110110111110110111110110110110111110110111110110110
   == 3 times 110110111110110111.110110110

T --> 110110111110110111110110111110110111110110111110110110110111110110111110110111...
```

Figure 38.2-A: Computation of the Thue constant in binary.

We construct a sequence of zeros and ones that can be generated by starting with a single 0 and repeated application of the substitution rules $0 \mapsto 111$ and $1 \mapsto 110$. The evolution starting with a single zero is shown in figure 38.2-A. The crucial observation is that $T_n = U.U.U$ where $U = T'_{n-1}.T_{n-2}$ and T'_k consists of the first and second third of T_k. The length of the n-th string is 3^n. Let $T(y)$ be the function whose power series corresponds to the string T_∞:

$$T(y) = 1 + y + y^3 + y^4 + y^6 + y^7 + y^8 + y^9 + y^{10} + y^{12} + y^{13} + y^{15} + y^{16} + y^{17} + y^{18} + \ldots \tag{38.2-1}$$

It can be computed by the iteration

$$L_0 = 0, \quad A_0 = 1 + y, \quad B_0 = y^2, \quad Y_0 = y \tag{38.2-2a}$$

$$R_n = A_n + y^2 L_n \tag{38.2-2b}$$

$$L_{n+1} = A_n + B_n \tag{38.2-2c}$$

$$Y_{n+1} = Y_n^3 \tag{38.2-2d}$$

$$A_{n+1} = R_n \left(1 + Y_{n+1}\right) \quad \to T(y) \tag{38.2-2e}$$

$$B_{n+1} = R_n Y_{n+1}^2 \tag{38.2-2f}$$

The implementation is slightly tricky:

```
1    th(y, N=5)=
2    {
3        local(L, R, A, B, y2, y3, t);
4        /* correct up to order 3^(N+1)-1 */
5        L=0;
6        A=1+y;  B=y^2; /* R = A.B */
7        for(k=1, N,
8            /* (L, A.B) --> (A.B,  A.L.A.L . A.L) */
9            y2 = y^2;
10           R = A + y2*L; /* A.L */
11           L = A + B;    /* next L = A.B */
12           y3 = y * y2;
13           B = R * (y3*y3);
14           A = R * (1+y3);     /* next A = A.L.A.L */
15           y = y3;
16       );
17       return( A + B )
18   }
```

The *Thue constant* (which should be called *Roth's constant*, see entries A014578 and A074071 in [312]) can be computed as

$$\frac{1}{2} T\left(\frac{1}{2}\right) = 0.85909979685470310490357250284197420261423995555594390874\ldots \tag{38.2-3}$$

[base 2] $= 0.110, 110, 111, 110, 110, 111, 110, 110, 110, 110, 110, 111, 110, 110, 111, 110, 110, \ldots$

[base 8] $= 0.667, 667, 666, 667, 667, 666, 667, 667, 667, 667, 667, 666, 667, 667, 666, 667, 667, \ldots$

[CF] $= [0, 1, 6, 10, 3, 2, 513, 1, 1, 2, 1, 4, 2, 6576668769, 1, 1, 4,$

$\qquad 1, 2, 2, 256, 1, 1, 2, 1, 2, 3, 1, 3, 3, 241785163922925834941235\overline{3},$

$\qquad 1, 2, 3, 1, 3, 2, 1, 2, 1, 1, 256, 2, 2, 1, 4, 2, 3288334384,$

$\qquad 1, 1, 4, 1, 2, 2, 146, 2, 3, 3, 2, 1, 2, 1, 12, X, \ldots]$

The term X in the continued fraction has 74 decimal digits. By construction the bits at positions n not divisible by 3 are one and otherwise the complement of the bit at position $n/3$. As a functional equation (see also section 38.5 on page 734):

$$y\, T(y) + y^3\, T(y^3) = \frac{y}{1-y} \tag{38.2-4}$$

From this relation we can obtain a series for $T(y)$:

$$T(y) = \sum_{n=0}^{\infty} (-1)^n \frac{y^{3^n-1}}{1-y^{3^n}} \tag{38.2-5}$$

38.3 An iteration related to the Golay-Rudin-Shapiro sequence

We define the function $Q(y)$ by the iteration

$$L_0 = 1, \qquad R_0 = y, \qquad Y_0 = y \tag{38.3-1a}$$
$$L_{n+1} = L_n + R_n \quad \to Q(y) \tag{38.3-1b}$$
$$Y_{n+1} = Y_n^2 \tag{38.3-1c}$$
$$R_{n+1} = Y_{n+1}\,(L_n - R_n) \tag{38.3-1d}$$

The power series for $Q(y)$ is

$$Q(y) = 1 + y + y^2 - y^3 + y^4 + y^5 - y^6 + y^7 + y^8 + y^9 + y^{10} - y^{11} - y^{12} - y^{13} + y^{14} - y^{15} + \ldots \tag{38.3-2}$$

```
Number of symbols = 4
Start: e
Rules:
  e --> ed
  d --> e2
  2 --> 1d
  1 --> 12

Q0 =  e
Q1 =  ed
Q2 =  ede2
Q3 =  ede2ed1d
Q4 =  ede2ed1dede212e2
Q5 =  ede2ed1dede212e2ede2ed1d121ded1d
Q --> ede2ed1dede212e2ede2ed1d121ded1dede2ed1dede212e2121d12e2ede212e2 ...
```

Figure 38.3-A: Computation of the GRS constant in hexadecimal.

The sequence of coefficients is the *Golay-Rudin-Shapiro sequence* (or *GRS sequence*, entry A020985 in [312], see also section 1.16.5 on page 44).

We define the *Golay-Rudin-Shapiro constant* (or *GRS-constant*)

$$Q \;=\; 0.9292438695973788532539766447220507644128755395243255222\ldots \qquad (38.3\text{-}3)$$

$$[\text{base 2}] \;=\; 0.1110, 1101, 1110, 0010, 1110, 1101, 0001, 1101, 1110, 1101, 1110, 0010, \ldots$$

$$[\text{base 16}] \;=\; 0.ede2, ed1d, ede2, 12e2, ede2, ed1d, 121d, ed1d, ede2, ed1d, ede2, 12e2, \ldots$$

$$[\text{CF}] \;=\; [0, 1, 13, 7, 1, 1, 15, 4, 1, 3, 1, 2, 2, 1000, 12, 2, 1, 6, 1, 1, 1, 1, 1, 1, 8, 2, 1, 1, 2, 4, 1, 1, 3, \ldots]$$

as the evaluation

$$Q \;=\; \frac{1 + \frac{1}{2}Q(\frac{1}{2})}{2} \qquad (38.3\text{-}4)$$

An implementation using GP is

```
1  qq(y, N=8)=
2  {
3      local(L, R, Lp, Rp);
4      /* correct up to order 2**(N+1) */
5      L=1;  R=y;
6      for(k=0,N, Lp=L+R; y*=y; Rp=y*(L-R); L=Lp; R=Rp);
7      return( L + R )
8  }
```

The hexadecimal expansion can also be computed with a string substitution shown in figure 38.3-A (which was created with the program [FXT: ds/stringsubst-demo.cc]).

The following functional equations hold for Q:

$$Q(y^2) \;=\; \frac{Q(y) + Q(-y)}{2} \qquad (38.3\text{-}5\text{a})$$

$$Q(y) \;=\; Q(y^2) + y\,Q(-y^2) \qquad (38.3\text{-}5\text{b})$$

$$Q(-y) \;=\; Q(y^2) - y\,Q(-y^2) \qquad (38.3\text{-}5\text{c})$$

Combining the latter two relations gives

$$Q(y) \;=\; (1 + y)\,Q(y^4) + (y^2 - y^3)\,Q(-y^4) \qquad (38.3\text{-}6)$$

Michael Somos [priv. comm.] gives

$$Q(y) \;=\; (1 - y)\,Q(y^2) + 2\,y\,Q(y^4) \qquad (38.3\text{-}7)$$

Counting zeros and ones in the binary expansion of Q

The number of ones and zeros in the first 4^k bits of the constant Q can be computed as follows:

```
1    /*   e --> ed  ;  d --> e2  ;  2 --> 1d  ;  1 --> 12   */
2    /*   e   d     ;  e    2    ;  d    1;      2  1; */
3    mg= [1, 1, 0, 0;  1, 0, 1, 0;  0, 1, 0, 1;  0, 0, 1, 1];
4    mg=mattranspose(mg)
5    { for (k=0, 40,
6        print1( k, ":  " );
7        mm=mg^k;
8        mv = mm*[1,0,0,0]~;
9        t = sum(i=1,4, mv[i]);
10       /* e and d have three ones and one zero */
11       /* 1 and 2 have one one and three zeros */
12       n0 = 3*(mv[3]+mv[4]) + (mv[1]+mv[1]); /* # of zeros */
13       n1 = 3*(mv[1]+mv[2]) + (mv[3]+mv[4]); /* # of ones  */
14       print( t, "   ", mv~,
15       "   #0=",  n0, " #1=", n1, "  diff=", n1-n0, "  #1/#0=", 1.0*n1/n0 );
16   ) }
```

```
           #e   #d   #2   #1
0:       1  [  1,   0,   0,   0]   #0=    2  #1=    3  diff= 1  #1/#0=1.5000000
1:       2  [  1,   1,   0,   0]   #0=    2  #1=    6  diff= 4  #1/#0=3.0000000
2:       4  [  2,   1,   1,   0]   #0=    7  #1=   10  diff= 3  #1/#0=1.4285714
3:       8  [  3,   3,   1,   1]   #0=   12  #1=   20  diff= 8  #1/#0=1.6666666
4:      16  [  6,   4,   4,   2]   #0=   30  #1=   36  diff= 6  #1/#0=1.2000000
5:      32  [ 10,  10,   6,   6]   #0=   56  #1=   72  diff=16  #1/#0=1.2857142
6:      64  [ 20,  16,  16,  12]   #0=  124  #1=  136  diff=12  #1/#0=1.0967741
7:     128  [ 36,  36,  28,  28]   #0=  240  #1=  272  diff=32  #1/#0=1.1333333
8:     256  [ 72,  64,  64,  56]   #0=  504  #1=  528  diff=24  #1/#0=1.0476190
9:     512  [136, 136, 120, 120]   #0= 992  #1=1056  diff=64  #1/#0=1.0645161
10:   1024  [272, 256, 256, 240]   #0=2032  #1=2080  diff=48  #1/#0=1.0236220
      [--snip--]
40: 1099511627776    [274878431232, 274877906944, 274877906944, 274877382656]  \
         #0=2199022731264 #1=2199024304128  diff=1572864  #1/#0=1.00000071525
```

Figure 38.3-B: Number of symbols, zeros and ones with the n-th step of the string substitution engine for the GRS sequence. For long strings the ratio of the number of zeros and ones approaches one.

The data is shown in figure 38.3-B. The sequence of the numbers of ones is entry A005418 in [312]. It is identical to the sequence of numbers of equivalence classes obtained by identifying bit-strings that are mutual reverses or complements, see section 3.5.2.5 on page 151.

38.4 Iteration related to the ruler function

```
R 0= 0
R 1= 0 1
R 2= 0 1 2 1
R 3= 0 1 2 1 3 1 2 1
R 4= 0 1 2 1 3 1 2 1 4 1 2 1 3 1 2 1
R 5= 0 1 2 1 3 1 2 1 4 1 2 1 3 1 2 1 5 1 2 1 3 1 2 1 4 1 2 1 3 1 2 1
R 6= 0 1 2 1 3 1 2 1 4 1 2 1 3 1 2 1 5 1 2 1 3 1 2 1 4 1 2 1 3 1 2 1 6 1 ...
```

Figure 38.4-A: Computation of the power series of the ruler function via a (generalized) string substitution engine.

The *ruler function* $r(n)$ is defined to be the highest exponent e so that 2^e divides n. Here we consider the function that equals $r(n) + 1$ for $n \neq 0$ and zero for $n = 0$. The partial sequences up to indices $2^n - 1$ are shown in figure 38.4-A. Observe that $R_n = R_{n-1}.(R_{n-1} + [n, 0, 0, \ldots, 0])$. The limiting sequence is entry A001511 in [312]. Define the function $R(y)$ as the limit of the iteration

$$R_1 = y, \qquad Y_1 = y \tag{38.4-1a}$$

$$Y_{n+1} = Y_n^2 \tag{38.4-1b}$$

$$R_{n+1} = R_n + Y_{n+1}[R_n + (1+n)] \quad \to R(y) \tag{38.4-1c}$$

Implementation in GP:

```
1    r2(y, N=11)=
2    { /* correct to order = 2^N-1 */
3        local(A);  A=y;
4        for(k=2, N,  y *= y;  A += y*(A + k); );
5        return( A );
6    }
```

To compute $\frac{y}{1-y}$, replace the statement `A += y*(A + k);` by `A += y*(A + 1);` For the function R we have

$$R\left(\frac{1}{q^2}\right) \;=\; \frac{1}{2q}\left[(q-1)\,R\left(\frac{1}{q}\right) + (q+1)\,R\left(-\frac{1}{q}\right)\right] \tag{38.4-2a}$$

$$R\left(\frac{1}{q}\right) \;=\; R\left(\frac{1}{q^2}\right) + \frac{1}{q-1} \tag{38.4-2b}$$

$$R(y) \;=\; R(y^2) + \frac{y}{1-y} \;=\; R(y^4) + \frac{y}{1-y} + \frac{y^2}{1-y^2} \;=\; \ldots \tag{38.4-2c}$$

and so

$$R(y) \;=\; \sum_{n=0}^{\infty} \frac{y^{2^n}}{1-y^{2^n}} \tag{38.4-3}$$

We further have

$$R(y) \;=\; \sum_{n=0}^{\infty} (1+n)\,\frac{y^{2^n}}{1-y^{2^{n+1}}} \tag{38.4-4}$$

Michael Somos [priv. comm.] gives

$$R(y) - 3\,R(y^2) + 2\,R(y^4) \;=\; \frac{R(y^2) - R(y^4)}{R(y) - R(y^2)} \tag{38.4-5}$$

Define the *ruler constant* as $R := R(1/2)/2$, then

$$
\begin{aligned}
R \;&=\; 0.7019684139410891602881030370686046772688193807609450337\ldots \tag{38.4-6}\\
[\text{base 2}] \;&=\; 0.10110011101101000011001110110100101100111011010000110011\ldots\\
[\text{CF}] \;&=\; [0,1,2,2,1,4,2,1,1,1,2,2,1,3,3,4,5,6,1,5,1,1,9,49,1,8,1,1,5,1,\\
&\qquad 6,5,1,3,3,1,2,4,3,1,2,4,2,1,1,3,1,9,1,11,18,2,4,5,1,3,2,25,9,\\
&\qquad 2,3,1,2,3,1,9,1,2,8,1,3,4,1,1,1,1,31,1,1,6,1,13,1,1,14,1,6,1,\ldots]
\end{aligned}
$$

38.5   An iteration related to the period-doubling sequence

```
      Start: 0
      Rules:
         0 --> 11
         1 --> 10

  T0 =  0
  T 1=  1 1
  T 2=  1 0 1 0
  T 3=  1 0 1 1 1 0 1 1
  T 4=  1 0 1 1 1 0 1 0 1 0 1 1 1 0 1 0
  T 5=  1 0 1 1 1 0 1 0 1 0 1 1 1 0 1 1 1 0 1 1 1 0 1 0 1 0 1 1 1 0 1 1
  T 6=  1 0 1 1 1 0 1 0 1 0 1 1 1 0 1 1 1 0 1 1 1 0 1 0 1 0 1 1 1 0 1 0 1 0 1 1 1 0 1 0 1 0 1 1 ...
```

Figure 38.5-A: Computation of the period-doubling sequence via string substitution.

Define the function $T(y)$ as

$$T(y) = \sum_{n=0}^{\infty} \frac{y^{2^n}}{1+(-1)^n y^{2^n}} = \sum_{n=0}^{\infty} (-1)^n \frac{y^{2^n}}{1-y^{2^n}} \tag{38.5-1a}$$

$$= y + y^3 + y^4 + y^5 + y^7 + y^9 + y^{11} + y^{12} + y^{13} + y^{15} + y^{16} + y^{17} + \ldots \tag{38.5-1b}$$

The function can be computed by the iteration

$$A_1 = 0, \quad L_1 = y, \quad R_1 = y, \quad Y_1 = y \tag{38.5-2a}$$
$$A_{n+1} = L_n + Y_n R_n \quad \to T(y) \tag{38.5-2b}$$
$$L_{n+1} = L_n + Y_n A_n \tag{38.5-2c}$$
$$R_{n+1} = R_n + Y_n A_n \tag{38.5-2d}$$
$$Y_{n+1} = Y_n^2 \tag{38.5-2e}$$

Implementation in GP:

```
1    t2(y, N=11)=
2    { /* correct to order = 2^N-1 */
3        local(A, L, R, t);
4        A=0;   L=y;   R=y;
5        for(k=2, N,
6            t = y*A;
7            A = L + y*R;
8            L += t;   R += t;
9            y *= y;
10       );
11       return( A );
12   }
```

The power series can be computed by starting with a single zero and applying the substitution rules $0 \mapsto 11$ and $1 \mapsto 10$. The evolution is shown in figure 38.5-A. Observe that $T_n = L(T_{n-1}).T_{n-2}.R(T_{n-1}).T_{n-2}$ where L and R denote the left and right half of their arguments. The limiting sequence is the *period-doubling sequence*. It is entry A035263 in [312] where it is called the *first Feigenbaum symbolic sequence*. Define the *period-doubling constant* as $T := T(1/2)$, then

$$T = 0.72942702349494840570906620689405261706002694446658547417\ldots \tag{38.5-3}$$

$$[\text{base 2}] = 0.101110101011101110111010101110101011101010111011101110110\ldots$$

$$[\text{CF}] = [0, 1, 2, 1, 2, 3, 2, 8, 1, 1, 1, 2, 1, 8, 6, 1, 2, 1, 2, 8, 1, 2, 2, 1, 1, 24, 2, 2, 2, 1,$$
$$8, 2, 1, 2, 1, 8, 6, 1, 2, 1, 2, 2, 1, 1, 1, 13, 1, 1, 8, 2, 13, 1, 1, 1, 2, 2, 1, 2, 1,$$
$$6, 8, 1, 2, 1, 2, 8, 1, 2, 2, 1, 1, 24, 2, 2, 2, 1, 8, 2, 1, 2, 1, 11, 1, 9, 2, 1, 116, \ldots]$$

The transcendence of this constant is proved in [199]. A functional equation for $T(y)$ is

$$T(y) + T(y^2) = \frac{y}{1-y} \tag{38.5-4}$$

The power series of $T(y^2)$ has coefficients one where the series of $T(y)$ has coefficients zero. Michael Somos [priv. comm.] gives

$$\left[T(y) - T(y^4)\right]^2 = \left[1 + T(y^2) + T(y^4)\right]\left[T(y^2) + T(y^4)\right] \tag{38.5-5}$$

38.5.1   Connection to the towers of Hanoi puzzle

The *towers of Hanoi* puzzle consists of three piles and n disks of different size. In the initial configuration all disks are on the leftmost pile, ordered by size (smallest on top). The task is to move all disks to the rightmost pile by moving only one disk at a time and never putting a bigger disk on top of a smaller one.

The puzzle with n disks can be solved in $2^n - 1$ steps. Figure 38.5-B shows the solution for $n = 4$ [FXT: bits/hanoi-demo.cc]. Here the piles are represented as binary words. Note that with each move the lowest bit in one of the three words is moved to another word where it is again the lowest bit.

	pile_0	pile_+	pile_-	moved disk	summary	direction of move
0:	1111	....	....	....	0 0 0 0	
1:	111.	...1.	...1	...1	0 0 0 -	1
2:	11..	...1.	...1	...1	0 0 + -	0
3:	11..	..11	...1	...1	0 0 + +	1
4:	1..1	..11	.1..	.1..	0 - + 0	1
5:	1..1	...1.	.1..	...1	0 - + -	1
6:	1..1	....	.11.	.1..	0 - - 0	0
7:	1...	....	.111	...1	0 - - -	1
8:	....	1...	.111	1...	+ - - -	0
9:	....	1..1	.11.	...1	+ - - +	1
10:	..1.	1..1	.1..	...1	+ - 0 +	0
11:	..11	1..1	.1..	...1	+ - 0 0	1
12:	..11	11..	....	.1..	+ + 0 0	1
13:	..1.	11..	...1	...1	+ + 0 -	1
14:	....	111.	...1	..1.	+ + + -	0
15:	....	1111	....	...1	+ + + +	1

Figure 38.5-B: Solution of the towers of Hanoi puzzle for 4 disks. The rightmost column corresponds to the direction of the move, it is the period-doubling sequence.

For a simple solution, we observe that the disk moved with step $k = 1, \ldots, 2^n - 1$ corresponds to the lowest set bit in the binary representation of k and the index of the untouched pile changes by $+1$ mod 3 for n even and -1 mod 3 for n odd. The essential part of the implementation is

```
void
hanoi(ulong n)
{
    ulong f[3];
    f[0] = first_comb(n);  f[1] = 0;  f[2] = 0;  // Initial configuration

    const int dr = (n&1 ? -1 : +1);  // == +1 (if n even), else  == -1

    // PRINT configuration
    int u;  // index of tower untouched in current move
    if ( dr<0 ) u=2;  else u=1;

    ulong n2 = 1UL<<n;
    for (ulong k=1; k<n2; ++k)
    {
        ulong s = lowest_one(k);

        ulong j = 3;  while ( j-- ) f[j] ^= s;  // change all piles
        f[u] ^= s;  // undo change for untouched pile

        u += dr;
        if ( u<0 ) u=2;  else if ( u>2 ) u=0;  // modulo 3

        // PRINT configuration
    }
}
```

Now with each step the transferred disk is moved by $+1$ or -1 position (modulo 3). The rightmost column in figure 38.5-B consists of zeros and ones corresponding to the direction of the move. It is the period-doubling sequence. A recursive algorithm for the towers of Hanoi puzzle is [FXT: comb/hanoi-rec-demo.cc]

```
ulong f[3];  // the three piles
void hanoi(int k, ulong A, ulong B, ulong C)
// Move k disks from pile A to pile C
{
    if ( k==0 ) return;

    // 1. move k-1 disks from pile A to pile B:
    hanoi(k-1, A, C, B);

    // 2. move disk k from pile A to pile C:
    ulong b = 1UL << (k-1);
    f[A] ^= b;
    f[C] ^= b;

    print_hanoi(b); // visit state

    // 3. move k-1 disks from pile B to pile C:
```

```
18        hanoi(k-1, B, A, C);
19    }
```

The piles are represented by the binary words `f[A]`, `f[B]`, and `f[C]`, the variable `k` is the number of the disk moved. The routine is called as follows

```
1       ulong n = 5;
2       // Initial configuration:
3       f[0] = first_comb(n);   // n ones as lowest bits
4       f[1] = 0;  f[2] = 0;    // empty
5
6       // visit initial state
7
8       hanoi(n-1, 0, 1, 2);  // solve
```

More about the computation of the moves is given in [342], an extensive bibliography is [325].

38.5.2 Generalizations of the period-doubling sequence

```
? default(realprecision,85);
? tm(y,m,N=8)=sum(n=0,N,(-1)^n*(y^(m^n)/(1-y^(m^(n)))))
? for(m=2,9,print(m,": ",tm(1.0/10,m,4));print("    ",tm(1.0/10^m,m,4)))
   2: 1,111,1,1,111,111,111,1,1,111,111,111,1,1,1,111,111,111,1,1,111,111,111,1,1,1,111,111,111
      .1..1.1....1...1...1.1.1....1...1.1.1....1...1.1.1....1...1.1.1....1...1.1.1....1...1.1.1...
   3: 11,11,11111,11,11111,11,11,11,11,11111,11,11111,11,11,11,11,11111,11,11111,11,11111,11,1
      ..1..1.....1...1.....1...1...1.1.....1...1.....1...1...1.1.....1...1.....1...1.....1...1.
   4: 111,111,111,1111111,111,111,1111111,111,111,1111111,111,111,111,111,111,111,1111111,1
      ...1...1...1.......1...1...1.......1...1...1.......1...1...1...1...1...1...1.......1.
   5: 1111,1111,1111,1111,111111111,1111,1111,1111,111111111,1111,1111,1111,111111111,1111,
      ....1...1....1...1.........1....1...1...1.........1....1...1...1.........1....1
   6: 11111,11111,11111,11111,11111,11111111111,11111,11111,11111,11111,11111111111,11111,1
      .....1.....1.....1.....1.....1...........1.....1.....1.....1.....1...........1.....1.
   7: 111111,111111,111111,111111,111111,111111,1111111111111,111111,111111,111111,111111,1
      ......1.....1......1......1......1......1.............1......1......1......1......1.
   8: 1111111,1111111,1111111,1111111,1111111,1111111,1111111,111111111111111,1111111,11111
      .......1.......1.......1.......1.......1.......1.......1...............1.......1.....
   9: 11111111,11111111,11111111,11111111,11111111,11111111,11111111,11111111,1111111111111111
      ........1........1........1........1........1........1........1........1.....
```

Figure 38.5-C: Visual verification of the higher order analogues of the period-doubling sequence. In the output lines the leading '0.' was removed and all zeros were replaced by dots.

The functional equation for the period-doubling sequence, relation 38.5-4 can be generalized in several ways. For example, one can look for a function for which $F_3(y) + F_3(y^3) = y/(1-y)$. It is given by

$$F(y) = \sum_{k=0}^{\infty} (-1)^n \frac{y^{3^n}}{1-y^{3^n}} \tag{38.5-6a}$$

$$= z + z^2 + z^4 + z^5 + z^7 + z^8 + z^9 + z^{10} + z^{11} + z^{13} + z^{14} + z^{16} + z^{17} + \ldots \tag{38.5-6b}$$

We can compute the constant

$$F_3(1/2) = 0.85909979685470310490357250284197420261423995555594390874\ldots \tag{38.5-7}$$

But this is just the Thue constant, see section 38.2 on page 730. Large terms occur in the continued fraction expansion of this constant. Even greater terms occur in the continued fractions of $F_m(1/2)$ for $m > 3$ (replace 3 by m in relation 38.5-6a). For example, the 45-th term of $F_5(1/2)$ has 565 digits. In contrast, the greatest of the first 1630 terms of the continued fraction of $F_2(1/2) = T(1/2)$ equals 288. Some sequences corresponding to the higher order analogues of the period-doubling sequence are shown in figure 38.5-C.

A different way to generalize is to search functions for which, for example, the following functional equation holds:

$$F(y) + F(y^2) + F(y^3) = \frac{y}{1-y} \tag{38.5-8}$$

The equation can be solved by writing $F(y) = y/(1 - y) - F(y^2) - F(y^3)$ and using recursions that terminate when a prescribed order is reached.

```
1   F(z, R)=
2   {/* solve F(y) + F(y^2) + F(y^3) = y/(1-y) */
3       local(s, y);
4       y = z + R;
5       s = y/(1-y);
6       if ( y^2!=R,  s -= F(z^2, R) );
7       if ( y^3!=R,  s -= F(z^3, R) );
8       return(s);
9   }
```

To verify that the function F does satisfy the given functional equation, we show the sequences of coefficients of the power series of $F(y)$, $F(y^2)$, $F(y^3)$ and their sum:

```
F(y)=   [0, 1, 0, 0, 1, 1, 1, 1, 0, 1, 0, 1,-1, 1, 0, 0, 1, 1,-1, 1, 1, 0, 0, 1, 2, 1, ...]
F(y^2)= [0, 0, 1, 0, 0, 0, 0, 0, 1, 0, 1, 0, 1, 0, 1, 0, 0, 0, 1, 0, 0, 0, 1, 0,-1, 0, ...]
F(y^3)= [0, 0, 0, 1, 0, 0, 0, 0, 0, 0, 0, 0, 1, 0, 0, 1, 0, 0, 1, 0, 0, 1, 0, 0, 0, 0, ...]
sum=    [0, 1, 1, 1, 1, 1, 1, 1, 1, 1, 1, 1, 1, 1, 1, 1, 1, 1, 1, 1, 1, 1, 1, 1, 1, 1, ...]
```

```
F(y) = y + y^4 + y^5 + y^7 + y^9 + y^11 + y^13 + y^16 + y^17 + y^19 + y^20 + y^23 + y^25 + y^28 + y^29 + ...
F(y)=    .1..11.1.1.1.1..11.11..1.1..11.1...111...1.111.1.1..11.1...1.1.111.11..1.1
F(y^2)= ..1.....1.1...1...1...1...1.....1.1...1.1.....1...1.....1.1...1.......1.1.
F(y^3)= ...1........1.1.....1....1.....1.....1.........1..1.....1..1........1....
F(y^6)= ......1................1...1.............1........1.............1.........
sum=    .1111111111111111111111111111111111111111111111111111111111111111111111111111
```

Figure 38.5-D: Visual demonstration that $F(y)$ satisfies the functional equation $F(y) + F(y^2) + F(y^3) + F(y^6) = y/(1 - y)$. Dots are used for zeros.

The power series of $F(y)$ where $F(y) + F(y^2) + F(y^3) + F(y^6) = y/(1 - y)$ contains only ones and zeros. We have

$$F(y) = \sum_{k=1}^{\infty} R(k) \frac{x^k}{1 - x^k} \quad \text{where} \quad R(k) = \begin{cases} (-1)^{e_2 + e_3} & \text{if } k = 2^{e_2} 3^{e_3} \\ 0 & \text{otherwise} \end{cases} \tag{38.5-9}$$

This is a Lambert series, it can be converted into a power series by relation 37.1-25 on page 708. It turns out that with $k = u \, 2^{e_2} 3^{e_3}$ (where neither 2 nor 3 divides u), we have

$$r(k) = \begin{cases} 0 & \text{if either of } e_2 \text{ or } e_3 \text{ is odd} \\ 1 & \text{otherwise (i.e. both } e_2 \text{ and } e_3 \text{ are even)} \end{cases} \tag{38.5-10}$$

38.6   An iteration from substitution rules with sign

```
Start: 1
Rules:
   0 --> L1
   1 --> 10
   L --> L0

D0 =  1
D1 =  10
D2 =  10L1
D3 =  10L1L010
D4 =  10L1L010L01L10L1
D5 =  10L1L010L01L10L1L01L10L010L1L010

D --> 10L1L010L01L10L1L01L10L010L1L010L01L10L010L1L01L10L1L010L01L...
```

Figure 38.6-A: String substitution used to define the function $D(y)$.

Let D be the fixed point (limit) of the string substitution shown in figure 38.6-A. Now identify L with

−1 and observe that for $n > 1$ we have $D_n = D_{n-1}.(-D_{n-2}).D_{n-2}$. Define $D(y)$ by the iteration

$$
\begin{aligned}
L_0 &= 1, &\qquad R_0 &= 1(+0\,y), &\qquad Y_0 &= y & \text{(38.6-1a)} \\
L_{n+1} &= R_n & & & & & \text{(38.6-1b)} \\
R_{n+1} &= R_n + Y_n^2\,(-L_n + Y_n\,L_n) &\quad &\to D(y) & & & \text{(38.6-1c)} \\
Y_{n+1} &= Y_n^2 & & & & & \text{(38.6-1d)}
\end{aligned}
$$

Implementation in GP:

```
1    dd(y, N=7)=
2    {
3        local(R, L, y2, t);
4        /* correct up to order 2^(N) */
5        L = 1;
6        R = 1 + 0*y;
7        for(k=1, N,
8           /* (L, R) --> (R,  R.(-L).L) */
9           y2 = y^2;
10          t = R;
11          R = R + y2*(-L + y*L);   /* R.(-L).L */
12          L = t;
13          y = y2;
14       );
15       return( R )
16   }
```

The power series is

$$
D(y) \;=\; 1 - y^2 + y^3 - y^4 + y^6 - y^8 + y^{10} - y^{11} + y^{12} - y^{14} + y^{15} - y^{16} + y^{18} \pm \ldots \quad \text{(38.6-2)}
$$

The coefficients are sequence A029883 in [312] where the following functional equation is given: set $T_1 = y\,D(y)$, $T_2 = y^2\,D(y^2)$, and $T_4 = y^4\,D(y^4)$, then

$$
T_2 - T_4 - T_1^2 - T_2^2 + 2\,T_1\,T_4 \;=\; 0 \qquad \text{(38.6-3)}
$$

We further have (see relation 38.1-4 on page 727)

$$
\frac{y}{1-y}\,D(y) \;=\; K(y) \;=\; y + y^2 + y^4 + y^7 + y^8 + y^{11} + \ldots \qquad \text{(38.6-4)}
$$

The coefficients are 1 where the Thue-Morse sequence equals −1. Thus the parity number can be computed as $P = \frac{1}{2} D\left(\frac{1}{2}\right)$. A functional equation for D is

$$
D(y) \;=\; y\,\frac{1-y}{1+y}\,D\left(y^2\right) + \frac{1}{1+y} \qquad \text{(38.6-5)}
$$

38.7 Iterations related to the sum of digits

```
S0 =   0
S1 =   0 1
S2 =   0 1 1 2
S3 =   0 1 1 2 1 2 2 3
S4 =   0 1 1 2 1 2 2 3 1 2 2 3 2 3 3 4
S -> 0 1 1 2 1 2 2 3 1 2 2 3 2 3 3 4 1 2 2 3 2 3 3 4 2 3 3 4 3 4 4 5 ...
```

Figure 38.7-A: Generalized string substitution leading to the 1's-counting sequence.

The sequence of the sum of binary digits of the natural numbers starting with zero can be constructed as shown in figure 38.7-A. The sequence (entry A000120 in [312]) is called the *1's-counting sequence*. Observe that $S_n = S_{n-1}.(S_{n-1} + I_{n-1})$ where I_n is a sequence of n ones and addition is element-wise.

Define the function $S(y)$ by

$$I_1 \; = \; 1, \qquad A_1 \; = \; y, \qquad Y_1 \; = \; y \tag{38.7-1a}$$

$$I_{n+1} \; = \; I_n \, (1 + Y_n) \; = \; \sum_{k=0}^{2^n-1} y^k \tag{38.7-1b}$$

$$Y_{n+1} \; = \; Y_n^2 \tag{38.7-1c}$$

$$A_{n+1} \; = \; A_n + Y_{n+1} \, (I_{n+1} + A_n) \quad \to S(y) \tag{38.7-1d}$$

Implementation in GP:

```
1   s2(y, N=7)=
2   {
3       local(in, A);
4       /* correct to order = 2^N-1 */
5       in = 1; /* 1+y+y^2+y^3+...+y^(2^k-1) */
6       A = y;
7       for(k=2, N,
8           in *= (1+y);
9           y *= y;
10          A += y*(in + A);
11      );
12      return( A );
13  }
```

The power series is

$$S(y) \; = \; 0 + y + y^2 + 2y^3 + y^4 + 2y^5 + 2y^6 + 3y^7 + y^8 + 2y^9 + 2y^{10} + 3y^{11} + 2y^{12} + 3y^{13} + \ldots \tag{38.7-2}$$

Define the *sum-of-digits constant* as $S := S(1/2)/2$, then

$$S \; = \; 0.5960631721178216794237939258627906454623612384781099326\ldots \tag{38.7-3}$$

$$[\text{base } 2] \; = \; 0.1001100010010111100110001001011010011000100101111001100011\ldots$$

$$[\text{CF}] \; = \; [0, 1, 1, 2, 9, 1, 3, 5, 1, 2, 1, 1, 1, 1, 8, 2, 1, 1, 2, 1, 12, 19, 24, 1, 18, 12, 1, \ldots]$$

The sequence of decimal digits is entry A051158 in [312]. We have (see [324])

$$S(y) \; = \; \frac{1}{1-y} \sum_{k=0}^{\infty} \frac{y^{2^k}}{1 + y^{2^k}} \tag{38.7-4}$$

and also

$$S(y) \; = \; \sum_{k=0}^{\infty} \left[\frac{y^{2^k}}{1 - y^{2^k}} \prod_{j=0}^{k-1} \left[1 + y^{2^j} \right] \right] \tag{38.7-5}$$

The last relation follows from the functional equation for S,

$$S(y) \; = \; (1 + y) \, S(y^2) + \frac{y}{1 - y^2} \tag{38.7-6}$$

It is of the form $F(y) = A(y) \, F(y^2) + B(y)$ where $A(y) = 1 + y$ and $B(y) = y/(1 - y^2)$ and has the solution

$$F(y) \; = \; \sum_{k=0}^{\infty} \left[B(y^{2^k}) \prod_{j=0}^{k-1} \left[A(y^{2^j}) \right] \right] \tag{38.7-7}$$

This can be seen by applying the functional equation several times:

$$F(y) \; = \; A(y) \, F(y^2) + B(y) \tag{38.7-8a}$$

$$= \; A(y) \left[A(y^2) \, F(y^4) + B(y^2) \right] + B(y) \tag{38.7-8b}$$

$$= \; A(y) \left[A(y^2) \left[A(y^4) \, F(y^8) + B(y^4) \right] + B(y^2) \right] + B(y) \; = \; \ldots \tag{38.7-8c}$$

$$= \; B(y) + A(y) \, B(y^2) + A(y) \, A(y^2) \, B(y^4) + \ldots \tag{38.7-8d}$$

Weighted sum of digits

Define $W(y)$ by

$$I_1 \;=\; \frac{1}{2}, \qquad A_1 \;=\; 1, \qquad Y_1 \;=\; y \tag{38.7-9a}$$

$$l_{n+1} \;=\; I_n \, \frac{(1+Y_n)}{2} \;=\; \frac{1}{2^n} \sum_{k=0}^{2^n-1} y^k \tag{38.7-9b}$$

$$Y_{n+1} \;=\; Y_n^2 \tag{38.7-9c}$$

$$A_{n+1} \;=\; A_n + Y_{n+1}\,(I_{n+1} + A_n) \quad \to W(y) \tag{38.7-9d}$$

Implementation in GP:

```
1   w2(y, N=7)=
2   {
3       local(in, y2, A);
4       /* correct to order = 2^N-1 */
5       in = 1/2; /* 1/2^k * (1+y+y^2+y^3+...+y^(2^k-1)) */
6       A = y/2;
7       for(k=2, N,
8           in *= (1+y)/2;
9           y *= y;
10          A += y*(in + A);
11      );
12      return( A );
13  }
```

In the power series

$$
\begin{aligned}
W(y) \;=\;& 0 + \frac{1}{2}y + \frac{1}{4}y^2 + \frac{3}{4}y^3 + \frac{1}{8}y^4 + \frac{5}{8}y^5 + \frac{3}{8}y^6 + \frac{7}{8}y^7 + \\[4pt]
&+ \frac{1}{16}y^8 + \frac{9}{16}y^9 + \frac{5}{16}y^{10} + \frac{13}{16}y^{11} + \frac{3}{16}y^{12} + \frac{11}{16}y^{13} + \frac{7}{16}y^{14} + \frac{15}{16}y^{15} + \\[4pt]
&+ \frac{1}{32}y^{16} + \frac{17}{32}y^{17} + \frac{9}{32}y^{18} + \frac{25}{32}y^{19} + \frac{5}{32}y^{20} + \frac{21}{32}y^{21} + \frac{13}{32}y^{22} + \frac{29}{32}y^{23} + \\[4pt]
&+ \frac{3}{32}y^{24} + \frac{19}{32}y^{25} + \frac{11}{32}y^{26} + \frac{27}{32}y^{27} + \frac{7}{32}y^{28} + \frac{23}{32}y^{29} + \frac{15}{32}y^{30} + \frac{31}{32}y^{31} + \frac{1}{64}y^{32} + \dots
\end{aligned}
\tag{38.7-10}
$$

the coefficient of the y^n is the weighted sum of digits $w(n) = \sum_{i=0}^{\infty} 2^{-(i+1)} b_i$ where $b_0, b_1, \dots$ is the base-2 representation of n. The numerator in the n-th coefficient is the reversed binary expansion of n.

The corresponding *weighted sum-of-digits constant* or *revbin constant* is $W := W(1/2)$. Then

$$W \;=\; 0.44852655067627237892368772125452609761627881353844481336\dots \tag{38.7-11}$$

$$\text{[base 2]} \;=\; 0.01110010110100101010001011010010100010101101001010101\dots$$

$$\text{[CF]} \;=\; [0, 2, 4, 2, 1, 4, 18, 1, 2, 6, 5, 17, 2, 14, 1, 1, 1, 2, 1, 1, 2, 1, 3, 1, 29, 4, 1, \dots]$$

For the function W we have the following functional equation:

$$W\left(\frac{1}{q}\right) \;=\; \frac{1}{2}\left[\frac{1+q}{q}\,W\left(\frac{1}{q^2}\right) + \frac{q}{q^2-1}\right] \tag{38.7-12}$$

38.8   Iterations related to the binary Gray code

38.8.1   Series where the coefficients are the Gray code of exponents

We construct a function with power series coefficients that are the binary Gray code of the exponent of y. A list of the Gray codes is given below (see section 1.16 on page 41):

```
k ==
0  1  2  3  4  5  6  7   8  9 10 11 12 13 14 15 16 17 18 19 20 21 22 23 24 25 26 27 28 29 30 31
0  1  3  2  6  7  5  4  12 13 15 14 10 11  9  8 24 25 27 26 30 31 29 28 20 21 23 22 18 19 17 16
== graycode(k)
```

The sequence of Gray codes is entry A003188 in [312]. Define the function $G(y)$ as the limit of the iteration

$$
\begin{aligned}
F_1 &= y, \qquad B_1 = 1, \qquad Y_1 = y, \qquad I_1 = 1 + y & \text{(38.8-1a)} \\
Y_n &= Y_{n-1}^2 & \text{(38.8-1b)} \\
F_n &= (F_{n-1} \qquad\quad) + Y_n\,(B_{n-1} + 2\,I_{n-1}) \quad \to G(y) & \text{(38.8-1c)} \\
B_n &= (F_{n-1} + 2\,I_{n-1}) + Y_n\,(B_{n-1} \qquad\quad) & \text{(38.8-1d)} \\
I_n &= I_{n-1}\,(1 + Y_n) & \text{(38.8-1e)}
\end{aligned}
$$

Implementation in GP:

```
1    gg(y, N=15)=
2    {
3        local(t, ii, F, B, Fp, Bp);
4        /* correct up to order 2^N-1 */
5        F=0+y;  B=1+0;  ii=1+y;
6        for(k=2,N,
7           y *= y;
8           ii *= 2;  /* remove line for sum of digits */
9           Fp = (F     ) + y * (B + ii);
10          Bp = (F + ii) + y * (B     );
11          F = Fp;  B = Bp;
12          ii *= (1+y);
13        );
14        return( F )
15   }
```

In the algorithm F contains the approximation so far and B contains the reversed polynomial:

```
    ---- k = 1 :
F = (y)
B = (1)
    ---- k = 2 :
F = (2y^3+3y^2+y)
B = (y^2+3y+2)
    ---- k = 3 :
F = (4y^7+5y^6+7y^5+6y^4+2y^3+3y^2+y)
B = (y^6+3y^5+2y^4+6y^3+7y^2+5y+4)
    ---- k = 4 :
F = (8y^15+9y^14+11y^13+10y^12+14y^11+15y^10+13y^9+12y^8+4y^7+5y^6+7y^5+6y^4+2y^3+3y^2+y)
B = (y^14+3y^13+2y^12+6y^11+7y^10+5y^9+4y^8+12y^7+13y^6+15y^5+14y^4+10y^3+11^2+9y+8)
```

We obtain the series

$$
\begin{aligned}
G(y) \;=\; & 0 + 1y + 3y^2 + 2y^3 + 6y^4 + 7y^5 + 5y^6 + 4y^7 + & \text{(38.8-2)} \\
& + 12y^8 + 13y^9 + 15y^{10} + 14y^{11} + 10y^{12} + 11y^{13} + 9y^{14} + 8y^{15} + \\
& + 24y^{16} + 25y^{17} + 27y^{18} + 26y^{19} + 30y^{20} + 31y^{21} + 29y^{22} + 28y^{23} + \\
& + 20y^{24} + 21y^{25} + 23y^{26} + 22y^{27} + 18y^{28} + 19y^{29} + 17y^{30} + 16y^{31} + \cdots
\end{aligned}
$$

We define the *Gray code constant* as $G := G(1/2)$:

$$
\begin{aligned}
G \;&=\; 2.3022182877876893012293330063913107610004310777704369505\ldots & \text{(38.8-3)} \\
[\text{base 2}] \;&=\; 10.0100110101011110001011010111111001001101000111100101\ldots \\
[\text{CF}] \;&=\; [2,3,3,4,4,1,4,4,1,2,1,1,1,2,24,205,1,4,2,2,1,1,4,10,8,1,9,1,\ldots]
\end{aligned}
$$

For the function G we have

$$G\left(\frac{1}{q^2}\right) = \frac{1}{4}\left[\frac{q}{q+1}G\left(\frac{1}{q}\right) + \frac{q}{q-1}G\left(-\frac{1}{q}\right)\right] \tag{38.8-4a}$$

$$G\left(\frac{1}{q}\right) = \frac{2(q+1)}{q}G\left(\frac{1}{q^2}\right) + \frac{q^2}{(q-1)(q^2+1)} \tag{38.8-4b}$$

$$G(y) = 2(1+y)G(y^2) + \frac{y}{(1-y)(1+y^2)} \tag{38.8-4c}$$

$$G\left(-\frac{1}{q}\right) = \frac{2(q-1)}{q}G\left(\frac{1}{q^2}\right) - \frac{q^2}{(q+1)(q^2+1)} \tag{38.8-4d}$$

$$G\left(\frac{1}{q}\right) = \frac{2(q^2+1)}{q(q-1)}G\left(-\frac{1}{q^2}\right) + \frac{q^2(q^4+4q^3+4q+1)}{(q^4+1)(q^2+1)(q-1)} \tag{38.8-4e}$$

$$G\left(\frac{1}{q}\right) = \frac{1}{2q^2}\left[\frac{(q+1)(q^4+4q^3+4q+1)}{(q^2+1)}G\left(\frac{1}{q^2}\right) - \frac{(q^4+1)}{(q-1)}G\left(-\frac{1}{q^2}\right)\right] \tag{38.8-4f}$$

The function $G(y)$ can be expressed as

$$G(y) = \frac{1}{1-y}\sum_{k=0}^{\infty}\frac{2^k\,y^{2^k}}{1+y^{2^{k+1}}} \tag{38.8-5}$$

38.8.2 Differences of the Gray code

We define $F(y) = (1-y)\,G(y)$ to obtain the power series whose coefficients are the successive differences of the Gray code. The coefficients are powers of 2 in magnitude:

$$F(y) = 0 + y + 2y^2 - y^3 + 4y^4 + y^5 - 2y^6 - y^7 + 8y^8 + y^9 + 2y^{10} - y^{11} - 4y^{12} + y^{13} \pm \ldots \tag{38.8-6}$$

We have

$$F(y) = 2F(y^2) + \frac{y}{1+y^2} \tag{38.8-7}$$

Now, as $y/(1+y) = q/(1+q)$ for $q = 1/y$,

$$F(y) = F\left(\frac{1}{y}\right) = \sum_{k=0}^{\infty}2^k\frac{y^{2^k}}{1+y^{2^{k+1}}} \tag{38.8-8}$$

Thus $F(y)$ can be computed everywhere except on the unit circle. The sum

$$\sum_{k=0}^{\infty}2^k\frac{y^{2^k}}{1-y^{2^{k+1}}} \tag{38.8-9}$$

leads to a series with coefficients

0 1 2 1 4 1 2 1 8 1 2 1 4 1 2 1 16 1 2 1 4 1 2 1 8 1 2 1 4 1 2 1 32 1 ...

corresponding to the (exponential) version of the ruler function which is defined as the highest power of 2 that divides n. The ruler function (see section 38.4 on page 733)

. 0 1 0 2 0 1 0 3 0 1 0 2 0 1 0 4 0 1 0 2 0 1 0 3 0 1 0 2 0 1 0 5 0 1 ...

is the base-2 logarithm of that series.

38.8.3   Sum of Gray code digits

The sequence of the sum of digits of the Gray code of $k \geq 0$ is (entry A005811 in [312]):

0 1 2 1 2 3 2 1 2 3 4 3 2 3 2 1 2 3 4 3 4 5 4 3 2 3 4 3 2 3 2 1 2 3 ...

Omit the factor 2 in relations 38.8-1c and 38.8-1d on page 742. That is, in the implementation simply remove the line

```
ii *= 2;  /* remove line for sum of digits */
```

Let $R(y)$ be the corresponding function and define the *sum of Gray code digits constant* as $R := R(1/2)/2$, then

$$
\begin{aligned}
R &= 0.7014723764037345207355955210641332088227989861654212954\ldots & (38.8\text{-}10)\\
[\text{base 2}] &= 0.1011001110010011101100011001001110110011100100011011000\ldots\\
[\text{CF}] &= [0,1,2,2,1,6,10,1,9,53,1,1,3,10,1,2,1,3,2,14,2,1,2,1,3,4,2,\\
&\quad\ \ 1,34,1,1,3,1,1,109,1,1,4,2,9,1,642,51,4,3,2,2,2,2,1,2,3,\ldots]
\end{aligned}
$$

One finds:

$$
R\left(\frac{1}{q^2}\right) = \frac{1}{2}\left[\frac{q}{q+1}R\left(\frac{1}{q}\right) + \frac{q}{q-1}R\left(-\frac{1}{q}\right)\right] \tag{38.8-11a}
$$

$$
R\left(\frac{1}{q}\right) = \frac{q+1}{q}R\left(\frac{1}{q^2}\right) + \frac{q^2}{q^3-q^2+q-1} \tag{38.8-11b}
$$

$$
R\left(-\frac{1}{q}\right) = \frac{q-1}{q}R\left(\frac{1}{q^2}\right) - \frac{q^2}{q^3+q^2+q+1} \tag{38.8-11c}
$$

The function $R(y)$ can be expressed as

$$
R(y) = \frac{1}{1-y}\sum_{k=0}^{\infty}\frac{y^{2^k}}{1+y^{2^{k+1}}} \tag{38.8-12}
$$

Define the *paper-folding constant* P as $P = (R+1)/2$

$$
\begin{aligned}
P &= 0.8507361882018672603677977605320660441139949308271064 77\ldots & (38.8\text{-}13)\\
[\text{base 2}] &= 0.1101100111001001110110001100100111011001110010001101100\ldots\\
[\text{CF}] &= [0,1,5,1,2,3,21,1,4,107,7,5,2,1,2,1,1,2,1,6,1,2,6,1,1,8,1,\\
&\quad\ \ 2,17,3,1,1,3,1,54,3,1,1,1,2,1,4,2,321,102,2,6,1,4,1,5,2,\ldots]
\end{aligned}
$$

The decimal expansion is sequence A143347 in [312]. The following relation is given in [140, p.440]:

$$
P = \sum_{k=0}^{\infty}\frac{1}{2^{2^k}}\left(1-\frac{1}{2^{2^{k+2}}}\right)^{-1} \tag{38.8-14}
$$

The binary expansion of P is the *paper-folding sequence*, entry A014577 in [312]. A bit-level algorithm to generate the sequence is given in section 1.31.3 on page 88.

38.8.4   Differences of the sum of Gray code digits

Now define $E(y) = (1-y)R(y)$ to obtain the differences of the sum of Gray code digits. From this definition and relation 38.8-12 we see that

$$
E(y) = \sum_{k=0}^{\infty}\frac{y^{2^k}}{1+y^{2^{k+1}}} \tag{38.8-15}
$$

```
L = 0
R = +

L = 0 +
R = + -

L = 0++-
R = ++--

L = 0++-++--
R = +++--+--

L = 0++-++--+++--+--
R = +++-++---++--+--

L = 0++-++--+++--+--+++-++---++--+--
R = +++-++--+++--+--++-++---++--+--

L = 0++-++--+++--+--+++-++---++--+--+++-++--+++--+---++-++---++--+--
R = +++-++--+++--+--+++-++---++--+--++-++--+++--+---++-++---++--+--
```

Figure 38.8-A: String substitution for sum of Gray code digits.

All power series coefficients except for the constant term are ± 1:

$$E(y) \;=\; 0 + y + y^2 - y^3 + y^4 + y^5 - y^6 - y^7 + y^8 + y^9 + y^{10} - y^{11} - y^{12} + y^{13} \pm \ldots \qquad (38.8\text{-}16)$$

We have

$$E\left(\frac{1}{q}\right) \;=\; E\left(\frac{1}{q^2}\right) + \frac{q}{q^2+1} \qquad (38.8\text{-}17a)$$

$$E\left(y\right) \;=\; E\left(y^2\right) + \frac{y}{y^2+1} \qquad (38.8\text{-}17b)$$

(use $\frac{y}{y^2+1} = \frac{q}{q^2+1}$ where $q = \frac{1}{y}$ for the latter relation), thereby

$$E\left(y\right) \;=\; E\left(\frac{1}{y}\right) \qquad (38.8\text{-}18)$$

So we can compute $E(y)$ everywhere except on the unit circle. For $y < 1$ compute $E(y)$ by the iteration

$$
\begin{aligned}
L_0 &= 0, & R_0 &= 1, & Y_0 &= y & (38.8\text{-}19a)\\
L_{n+1} &= L_n + Y_n R_n & &\to E(y) & & & (38.8\text{-}19b)\\
R_{n+1} &= (L_n + 1) + Y_n (R_n - 2) & & & & & (38.8\text{-}19c)\\
Y_{n+1} &= Y_n^2 & & & & & (38.8\text{-}19d)
\end{aligned}
$$

Implementation in GP:

```
1    ge(y, N=7)=
2    {
3        local(L, R, Lp, Rp);
4        /* correct up to order 2^N-1 */
5        L=0;  R=1;
6        for(k=2, N,
7          Lp = (L    ) +  y * (R    );
8          Rp = (L + 1) +  y * (R - 2);
9          L = Lp;  R = Rp;
10         y *= y;
11       );
12       return( L + y*R )
13   }
```

The symbolic representations of the polynomials L and R are shown in figure 38.8-A. The limit of the sequence L is entry A034947 in [312]. It is a signed version of the *paper-folding sequence*. The sequence after the initial zero is identical to the sequence of the $\left(\frac{-1}{n}\right)$ for $n = 0, 1, 2, 3, \ldots$ where $\left(\frac{a}{b}\right)$ denotes the Kronecker symbol, see section 39.8 on page 781. Quick verification:

```
? for(n=1,88,print1(if(-1==kronecker(-1,n),"-","+")))
++-++--+++--+--+++-++--++-+--+++-++--+++--+---++-++---++--+--+++-++--+++--+--+++-++---
```

The algorithm is divisionless and fast in practice, we compute $R = E(1/2)$ to more than 600,000 decimal digits:

```
? N=21 ; \\ number of iterations
? B=2^N-1  \\ precision in bits
2097151
? D=ceil(B * log(2)/log(10)) + 1  \\ precision in decimal digits
631307
? default(realprecision,D);

? r=ge(1.0/2, N)
0.70147237640373452073559552106...4 [... + > 600k digits]
? ##
***    last result computed in 2,726 ms.

? r-ge(1.0/2, N+2)  \\ checking precison
-3.744192708419695540526787319381583798...4 E-631306

? p=(1+r)/2  \\ paper folding constant
0.85073618820186726036779776053...2 [... + > 600k digits]
```

38.8.5 Weighted sum of Gray code digits

Define $H(y)$ by its power series $H(y) = \sum_{k=1}^{\infty} h(k)y^k$ where $h(k)$ is the weighted sum of digits of the Gray code:

```
1    wgs(k)=
2    {
3        local(g,t,s);   s=0;  g=gray(k);
4        for(n=0,33, s+=if(bittest(g,n),1/2^(n+1),0));
5        return(s);
6    }

? for(k=1,33,  print1(" ",wgs(k)))
  1/2
  3/4 1/4
  3/8 7/8 5/8 1/8
  3/16 11/16 15/16 7/16 5/16 13/16 9/16 1/16
  3/32 19/32 27/32 11/32 15/32 31/32 23/32 7/32 5/32 21/32 29/32 13/32 9/32 25/32 17/32 1/32
  3/64 35/64 ...
```

An iteration for the computation of $H(y)$ is:

$$F_1 = y/2, \qquad B_1 = 1/2, \qquad Y_1 = y, \qquad I_1 = (1+y)/2 \tag{38.8-20a}$$

$$Y_n = Y_{n-1}^2 \tag{38.8-20b}$$

$$K_n = I_{n-1}/2 \tag{38.8-20c}$$

$$F_n = (F_{n-1} \quad) + Y_n (B_{n-1} + K_n) \quad \to H(y) \tag{38.8-20d}$$

$$B_n = (F_{n-1} + K_n) + Y_n (B_{n-1} \quad) \tag{38.8-20e}$$

$$I_n = K_n (1 + Y_n) \tag{38.8-20f}$$

Implementation in GP:

```
1    gw(y, N=11)=
2    {
3        local(t, ii, F, B, Fp, Bp);
4        /* correct up to order 2^N-1 */
5        F=0+y;  B=1+0;  ii=1+y;
6        ii /= 2;  F /= 2;  B /= 2;
7        for(k=2,N,
8          y *= y;
9          ii /= 2;
10         Fp = (F      ) +  y * (B + ii);
11         Bp = (F + ii) +  y * (B      );
12         F = Fp;  B = Bp;
13         ii *= (1+y);
14       );
15       return( F )
16    }
```

We define the *weighted sum of Gray code digits constant* as $H := H(1/2)$, then

$$H \;=\; 0.53370048863928499195888048148212428585491932254561189911\ldots \quad (38.8\text{-}21)$$

$$[\text{base 2}] \;=\; 0.1000100010100000100110000110000010010000101000000111100\ldots$$

$$[\text{CF}] \;=\; [0,1,1,6,1,11,4,5,6,1,13,1,3,1,18,5,77,1,2,2,3,1,2,1,1,\ldots]$$

We have:

$$H\left(\frac{1}{q^2}\right) \;=\; \frac{q}{q+1}\,H\left(\frac{1}{q}\right) + \frac{q}{q-1}\,H\left(-\frac{1}{q}\right) \qquad (38.8\text{-}22\text{a})$$

$$H\left(\frac{1}{q}\right) \;=\; \frac{1}{2}\left[\frac{q+1}{q}\,H\left(\frac{1}{q^2}\right) + \frac{q^2}{q^3 - q^2 + q - 1}\right] \qquad (38.8\text{-}22\text{b})$$

$$H\left(-\frac{1}{q}\right) \;=\; \frac{1}{2}\left[\frac{q-1}{q}\,H\left(\frac{1}{q^2}\right) - \frac{q^2}{q^3 + q^2 + q + 1}\right] \qquad (38.8\text{-}22\text{c})$$

38.9 A function encoding the Hilbert curve

We define a function $H(y)$ by the following iteration:

$$H_1 \;=\; +i\,y + 1\,y^2 - i\,y^3 \qquad (38.9\text{-}1\text{a})$$
$$R_1 \;=\; +i\,y - 1\,y^2 - i\,y^3 \qquad (38.9\text{-}1\text{b})$$
$$Y_1 \;=\; y \qquad (38.9\text{-}1\text{c})$$
$$Y_{n+1} \;=\; Y_n^4 \qquad (38.9\text{-}1\text{d})$$
$$H_{n+1} \;=\; -i\,R_n + Y_n\left(+i + H_n + Y_n\left(+1 + H_n + Y_n\left(-i + i\,R_n\right)\right)\right) \qquad (38.9\text{-}1\text{e})$$
$$R_{n+1} \;=\; +i\,H_n + Y_n\left(+i + R_n + Y_n\left(-1 + R_n + Y_n\left(-i - i\,H_n\right)\right)\right) \qquad (38.9\text{-}1\text{f})$$
$$H_{2n} \;\rightarrow\; H(y) \qquad (38.9\text{-}1\text{g})$$

As the real and imaginary parts are swapped with each step we agree on iterating an even number of times. The resulting function $H(y)$ is

$$H(y) \;=\; 0 + y + i\,y^2 - y^3 + i\,y^4 + i\,y^5 + y^6 - i\,y^7 + y^8 + i\,y^9 + y^{10} - i\,y^{11} \pm \ldots \quad (38.9\text{-}2)$$

The coefficients of the series are ± 1 and $\pm i$, except for the constant term which is zero. If the sequence of coefficients is interpreted as follows:

```
 0  :=  goto start   '0'
+1  :=  move right    '>'
-1  :=  move left     '<'
+i  :=  move up       '^'
-i  :=  move down     'v'
```

Then, symbolically:

```
H = 0>^<^^>v>^>vv<v>>^>v>>^<^>^<<v<^^^>v>>^<^>^<<v<^<<v>vv<^<v<^^>^< ...
```

Follow the signs to walk along the Hilbert curve, see figure 1.31-A on page 84. An implementation is

```
1   hh(y, N=4)=
2   {
3       /* correct to order = 4^N-1 */
4       local(H, R, tH, tR);
5       H= +I*y + 1*y^2 -I*y^3;   R= +I*y - 1*y^2 -I*y^3;
6       for(k=2, N,
7           y=y^4;
8           tH = -I*R + y*(+I + H + y*(+1 + H + y*(-I + I*R)));
9           tR = +I*H + y*(+I + R + y*(-1 + R + y*(-I - I*H)));
10          H=tH;   R=tR;
11      );
12      return( H );
13  }
```

The value of $H(y)$ for $y < 1$ gives the limiting point in the complex plane when the walk according to the coefficients is done with decreasing step lengths: step number k has step length y^k. The least positive y where the real and imaginary part of the endpoint are equal is $y_1 = 0.5436890126920\ldots$. It turns out that y_1 is the real solution of the polynomial $y^3 + y^2 + y - 1$. One might suspect that $M(y) := \Re H(y) - \Im H(y)$, the difference between the real and the imaginary part of $H(y)$, has the factor $y^3 + y^2 + y - 1$. Indeed we have $M(y) = y\,(y^3 + y^2 + y - 1)\,(y^{12} + y^8 + y^4 - 1)\cdots$ and a similar statement is true for the $P(y) := \Re H(y) + \Im H(y)$. We use this observation for the construction of a simplified and quite elegant algorithm for the computation of $H(y)$.

38.9.1 A simplified algorithm

Define the function $P(y)$ as the result of the iteration

$$Y_1 \;=\; y, \qquad P_1 = 1 \tag{38.9-3a}$$

$$P_{n+1} \;=\; P_n\left(+1 + Y_n + Y_n^2 - Y_n^3\right) \tag{38.9-3b}$$

$$Y_{n+1} \;=\; Y_n^4 \tag{38.9-3c}$$

$$P_n - 1 \;\rightarrow\; P(y) \tag{38.9-3d}$$

and the function $M(y)$ by

$$Y_1 \;=\; y, \qquad M_1 = 1 \tag{38.9-4a}$$

$$M_{n+1} \;=\; M_n\left(-1 + Y_n + Y_n^2 + Y_n^3\right) \tag{38.9-4b}$$

$$Y_{n+1} \;=\; Y_n^4 \tag{38.9-4c}$$

$$y\,M_n \;\rightarrow\; M(y) \tag{38.9-4d}$$

Now the function $H(y)$ can be computed as

$$H(y) \;=\; \frac{1}{2}\Big[(P(y) + M(y)) + i\,(P(y) - M(y))\Big] \tag{38.9-5}$$

The following implementations compute the series up to order $4^N - 1$:

```
1    fpp(y, N=4)=
2    {
3        local( t, Y );
4        t = 1;  Y=y;
5        for (k=1, N,  t *= (+1+Y+Y^2-Y^3);  Y=Y^4; );
6        return( t-1 );
7    }
8
9    fmm(y, N=4)=
10   {
11       local( t, Y );
12       t = 1;  Y=y;
13       for (k=1, N,  t*= (-1+Y+Y^2+Y^3);  Y=Y^4; );
14       return( t*y-Y );
15   }
16
17   hhpm(y, N=4)=
18   {
19       local( tp, tm );
20       tp = fpp(y);
21       tm = fmm(y);
22       return( ((tp+tm) + I*(tp-tm))/2 );
23   }
```

With a routine `tdir()` that prints a power series with coefficients $\in \{-1, 0, +1\}$ symbolically we obtain:

```
? N=4;
? tdir(fpp(y));tdir(fmm(y));
0++-+++-+++----++++-+++-+++----++++-+++-+++----+---+---+---++++-++
0+----+++-+++-+++-++++---+---+----++++---+---+----++++---+---+----

? tdir((fpp(y)+fmm(y))/2);tdir((fpp(y)-fmm(y))/2);
0+0-00+0+0+00-0++0+0++0-0+0--0-000+0++0-0+0--0-0--0+00-0-0-00+0-00
00+0++0-0+0--0-00+0-00+0+0+00-0+++0-00+0+0+00-0+00-0--0+0-0++0+0++
```

```
Number of symbols = 2
Start: +
Rules:
    + --> +++-
    - --> ---+
    -------------
0:    (#=1)
    +
1:    (#=4)
    +++-
2:    (#=16)
    +++-+++-+++----+
3:    (#=64)
    +++-+++-+++----+++-+++-+++---+++----+++-+++-+++----+---+---+---+++-
4:    (#=256)
    +++-+++-+++---+++-+++-+++---+++-+++-+++----+---+---+---+++-+++-+++-++ ...

0++-+++-+++---+++-+++-+++---+++-+++-+++----+---+---+---+++-++ == fpp()
```

```
Number of symbols = 2
Start: +
Rules:
    + --> -+++
    - --> +---
    -------------
0:    (#=1)
    +
1:    (#=4)
    -+++
2:    (#=16)
    +---+++-+++-+++
3:    (#=64)
    -+++---+---+---+---+++-+++-+++---+++-+++-+++---+++-+++-+++
4:    (#=256)
    +---+++-+++-+++-+++---+---+---+++-+++---+---+---+++-+++---+---+---+++-+++---+- ...

0+---+++-+++-+++-+++---+---+---+++-+++---+---+---+++-+++---+---+--- == fmm()
```

Figure 38.9-A: Computation of the power series of the functions P (top) and M (bottom) with a string substitution engine.

The n-th coefficient of the power series of $P(y)$ equals the parity of the number of threes in the radix-4 representation of n. This can be used for an efficient bit level algorithm, see section 1.31.1 on page 83.

The coefficients of the power series of the functions P and M can be computed with a string substitution engine, see figure 38.9-A.

38.9.2   The turns of the Hilbert curve

We compute a function with series coefficients $\in \{-1, 0, +1\}$ that correspond to the turns of the Hilbert curve. We use $+1$ for a right turn, -1 for a left turn and zero for no turn. The sequences of turns starts as

```
0--+0++--++0+--0-++-0--++--0-++00++-0--++--0-++-0--+0++--++0+--+ \
0++-0--++--0-++0+--+0++--++0+--00--+0++--++0+--+0++-0--++--0-++- \
-++-0--++--0-++0+--+0++--++0+--00--+0++--++0+--+0++-0--++--0-++0 \
+--+0++--++0+--0-++-0--++--0-++00++-0--++--0-++-0--+0++--++0+--  ...
```

The computation is slightly tricky:

```
1    hht(y, N=4)=
2    {
3        /* correct to order = 4^N-1 */
4        local( t, Y, F, s, p );
5        t = 1;   Y=y;  p = 1;
6        F = y + y^2;
7        for(k=2, N,
8            Y = Y^4;
9            t = -F + Y*F + Y^2*F  - Y^3*F;
10           p *= 4;
11           if ( 0==(k%2),
12               t +=   y^(1*p-1);
13               t +=   y^(3*p);
14               t -=   (y+1)*y^(2*p-1);
15               , /* else */
16               t +=   y^(1*p);
17               t +=   y^(3*p-1);
18           );
19           F = t;
```

```
20      );
21      if ( 1==N%2,   F = -F );   \\ same result for even and odd N
22      return( F );
23   }
```

38.10 Sparse power series

We give modifications of the iteration for $1/(1-y)$ where the power series are sparse.

38.10.1 A fourth order iteration

Define the function $F(y)$ as the result of the iteration

$$F_0 = 1, \qquad Y_0 = y \tag{38.10-1a}$$

$$F_{n+1} = F_n\,(1+Y_n) \quad \to F(y) \tag{38.10-1b}$$

$$Y_{n+1} = Y_n^4 \tag{38.10-1c}$$

We have

$$F(y) = 1 + y + y^4 + y^5 + y^{16} + y^{17} + y^{20} + y^{21} + y^{64} + y^{65} + y^{68} + y^{69} + \ldots \tag{38.10-2}$$

The sequence of exponents is the *Moser – De Bruijn sequence*, entry A000695 in [312]. Let $[t_0, t_1, t_2, \ldots]$ be the continued fraction of $F(1/q)$, then

$$t_0 = 1 \tag{38.10-3a}$$

$$t_1 = q - 1 \tag{38.10-3b}$$

$$t_2 = 1 \tag{38.10-3c}$$

$$t_3 = q^2 - q \tag{38.10-3d}$$

$$t_4 = q^2 + q \tag{38.10-3e}$$

$$t_5 = q^6 - q^5 + q^4 - q^3 \tag{38.10-3f}$$

$$t_6 = q^{10} + q^9 + q^6 + q^5 \tag{38.10-3g}$$

$$t_7 = q^{22} - q^{21} + q^{20} - q^{19} + q^{14} - q^{13} + q^{12} - q^{11} \tag{38.10-3h}$$

$$t_8 = q^{42} + q^{41} + q^{38} + q^{37} + q^{26} + q^{25} + q^{22} + q^{21} \tag{38.10-3i}$$

$$t_9 = q^{86} - q^{85} + q^{84} - q^{83} + q^{78} - q^{77} + q^{76} - q^{75} + \tag{38.10-3j}$$
$$+ q^{54} - q^{53} + q^{52} - q^{51} + q^{46} - q^{45} + q^{44} - q^{43}$$

For $j \geq 4$ we have

$$\frac{t_j}{t_{j-2}} = q^{2J} + q^J = q^J\,(q^J + 1) \quad \text{where} \quad J = 2^{j-4} \tag{38.10-4}$$

A functional equation for F is given by

$$F(y)\,F(y^2) = \frac{1}{1-y} \tag{38.10-5}$$

The relation is (mutatis mutandis) also true for the truncated product. The binary expansions of $F(y)$, $F(y^2)$ and their product for $y = 1/2$ are (dots for zeros):

```
11..11.........11..11.............................................. F(y)
1.1.....1.1.....................1.1.....1.1........................ F(y^2)
11111111111111111111111111111111111111111111111111111111111111.... 1/(1-y)
```

Since the expansions are palindromes, their correlation is also a sequence of ones. The decimal expansions of the corresponding constants $A = F(1/2)/2$ and $B = F(1/4)/2$ (so that $A \cdot B = 1/2$) start as

$$A = 0.79688715934753417973069933946951994548641286068846632333\ldots \quad (38.10\text{-}6a)$$

$$B = 0.62744140639608758647227659821510314941590638457172648011\ldots \quad (38.10\text{-}6b)$$

Now define $F_k := F(y^k)$. Then, by relations 38.10-5 and 38.1-16e on page 729 (for $k = 2$, 3, and 5), we have

$$0 = F_1^2 F_2 - 2 F_1 F_2 F_4 + F_4 \quad (38.10\text{-}7a)$$

$$0 = F_1^3 F_2^3 - F_3 F_6 \left(3 F_1^2 F_2^2 - 3 F_1 F_2 + 1 \right) \quad (38.10\text{-}7b)$$

$$0 = F_1^5 F_2^5 - F_{10} F_5 \left(5 F_1^4 F_2^4 - 10 F_1^3 F_2^3 + 10 F_1^2 F_2^2 - 5 F_1 F_2 + 1 \right) \quad (38.10\text{-}7c)$$

For power series over GF(2) relation 38.10-5 becomes $F(y)^3 = 1/(1 - y)$. That is, $F(y) = \sqrt[3]{1 - y}$. In general, an iteration for the inverse $(2^w - 1)$-st root is obtained by replacing relation 38.10-1c with $Y_{k+1} = Y_k^e$ where $e = 2^w$.

38.10.2   A different fourth order iteration

The third order iteration for $\frac{1}{1+y}$ can be implemented as

```
1    inv3m(y, N=6)=  /* third order --> 1/(1+y) */
2    { /* correct to order 3^N */
3        local(T);
4        T = 1;
5        for(k=1, N,
6            T *= ( 1 - y + y^2 );
7            y = y^3;
8        );
9        return( T );
10   }
```

To define the function $F(y)$, we modify the routine to obtain a fourth-order iteration:

```
1    f43(y, N=6)=
2    { /* correct to order 4^N */
3        local(T, yt);
4        T = 1;
5        for(k=1, N,
6            T *= ( 1 - y + y^2 );
7            y = y^4;  /* Note fourth power */
8        );
9        return( T );
10   }
```

That is,

$$F_0 = 1, \quad Y_0 = y \quad (38.10\text{-}8a)$$

$$F_{n+1} = F_n \left(1 - Y_n + Y_n^2 \right) \quad \to F(y) \quad (38.10\text{-}8b)$$

$$Y_{n+1} = Y_n^4 \quad (38.10\text{-}8c)$$

The first few terms of the power series are

$$F(y) = 1 - y + y^2 - y^4 + y^5 - y^6 + y^8 - y^9 + y^{10} - y^{16} + y^{17} - y^{18} + y^{20} - y^{21} \pm \ldots \quad (38.10\text{-}9)$$

Let $[t_0, t_1, t_2, \ldots]$ be the continued fraction of $F(1/q)$, then

$$t_0 \;=\; 0 \tag{38.10-10a}$$
$$t_1 \;=\; 1 \tag{38.10-10b}$$
$$t_2 \;=\; q \tag{38.10-10c}$$
$$t_3 \;=\; q \tag{38.10-10d}$$
$$t_4 \;=\; q^2 - q \tag{38.10-10e}$$
$$t_5 \;=\; q^4 + q^3 - q - 1 \tag{38.10-10f}$$
$$t_6 \;=\; q^8 - q^7 + q^6 - q^4 + q^3 - q^2 \tag{38.10-10g}$$
$$t_7 \;=\; q^{16} + q^{15} - q^{13} + q^{11} + q^{10} - q^8 - q^7 + q^5 - q^3 - q^2 \tag{38.10-10h}$$

For $j \geq 6$ we have

$$\frac{t_j}{t_{j-2}} \;=\; q^{6J} + q^{4J} + q^{3J} + q^J \;=\; q^J \left(q^J + 1\right)\left(q^{2J} - q^J + 1\right)\left(q^{2J} + 1\right) \tag{38.10-11}$$

where $J = 2^{j-6}$. The terms of the continued fraction of $F(1/q)$ for integer q grow doubly exponentially:

```
? contfrac(f43(0.5))
  [0, 1, 2, 2, 2, 21, 180, 92820, 3032435520, 26126907554432455680,
   240254294248527099500117907463345274880,
   16400125675021534706794412973442019102853751066678216639025390799096507269120,
   ... ]
/* number of decimal digits of the terms in the CF: */
  [-, 1, 1, 1, 1, 2, 3, 5, 10, 20, 39, 78, 154, 309, ... ]
```

By construction,

$$F(y) \;=\; \left(1 - y + y^2\right) F\left(y^4\right) \tag{38.10-12a}$$
$$F(-y) \;=\; \left(1 + y + y^2\right) F\left(y^4\right) \tag{38.10-12b}$$

The equivalent forms with $y = 1/q$ are

$$F\left(\frac{1}{q}\right) \;=\; \frac{q^2 - q + 1}{q^2}\, F\left(\frac{1}{q^4}\right) \tag{38.10-13a}$$
$$F\left(-\frac{1}{q}\right) \;=\; \frac{q^2 + q + 1}{q^2}\, F\left(\frac{1}{q^4}\right) \tag{38.10-13b}$$

Now $q^2 - q + 1 = p^2 - p + 1$ if $p = 1 - q$, so

$$F\left(1 - \frac{1}{q}\right) \;=\; \frac{q^2 - q + 1}{q^2}\, F\left(\left(1 - \frac{1}{q}\right)^4\right) \quad \text{where} \quad q > 1 \tag{38.10-14a}$$

$$F\left(1 + \frac{1}{q}\right) \;=\; \frac{q^2 + q + 1}{q^2}\, F\left(\left(1 + \frac{1}{q}\right)^4\right) \quad \text{where} \quad q < -1 \tag{38.10-14b}$$

Adding relations $\alpha \times$ (38.10-13a) and $\beta \times$ (38.10-14a) and simplifying gives

$$\frac{\alpha\, F(y) + \beta\, F(1 - y)}{\alpha\, F(y^4) + \beta\, F((1-y)^4)} \;=\; y^2 - y + 1 \quad \text{where} \quad \alpha, \beta \in \mathbb{C} \tag{38.10-15}$$

38.10.3   A sixth order iteration

Define the function $F(y)$ by the iteration

$$F_0 \;=\; 1, \qquad Y_0 = y \tag{38.10-16a}$$
$$F_{n+1} \;=\; F_n \left(1 + Y_n + Y_n^2\right) \quad \to F(y) \tag{38.10-16b}$$
$$Y_{n+1} \;=\; Y_n^6 \tag{38.10-16c}$$

Let $[t_0, t_1, t_2, \ldots]$ be the continued fraction of $F(1/q)$, then

$$t_0 = 1 \tag{38.10-17a}$$
$$t_1 = q - 1 \tag{38.10-17b}$$
$$t_2 = q + 1 \tag{38.10-17c}$$
$$t_3 = q^2 - q \tag{38.10-17d}$$
$$t_4 = q^{10} + q^9 + q^8 + q^4 + q^3 + q^2 \tag{38.10-17e}$$
$$t_5 = q^8 - q^7 + q^5 - q^4 \tag{38.10-17f}$$
$$t_6 = q^{64} + q^{63} + q^{62} + q^{58} + q^{57} + q^{56} + q^{52} + q^{51} + q^{50} + \tag{38.10-17g}$$
$$+ q^{28} + q^{27} + q^{26} + q^{22} + q^{21} + q^{20} + q^{16} + q^{15} + q^{14}$$
$$t_7 = q^{44} - q^{43} + q^{41} - q^{40} + q^{26} - q^{25} + q^{23} - q^{22} \tag{38.10-17h}$$
$$t_8 = q^{388} + q^{387} + \ldots + q^{87} + q^{86} \tag{38.10-17i}$$

For $j \geq 4$ we have

$$\frac{t_j}{t_{j-2}} = \begin{cases} q^J + q^{J/2} & \text{if } j \text{ odd} \\ \left(q^{10J} + q^{9J} + q^{8J} + q^{4J} + q^{3J} + q^{2J} \right) / \left(q^J + 1 \right) & \text{otherwise} \end{cases} \tag{38.10-18}$$

where $J = 6^{j-4}$.

38.11 An iteration related to the Fibonacci numbers

```
Rules:
  0 --> 1
  1 --> 10

A 0= 0
A 1= 1
A2 = 10
A3 = 101
A4 = 10110
A5 = 10110101
A6 = 1011010110110
A7 = 10110101101101011010110101

A -->1011010110110101101011011010110101101101101011010110101...
```

Figure 38.11-A: String substitution to compute the rabbit constant.

The *rabbit constant* is

$$A = 0.7098034428612913146417873994445755970125022057678605169\ldots \tag{38.11-1}$$
$$[\text{base 2}] = 0.1011010110110101101011011010110110101101011011010110101\ldots$$
$$[\text{CF}] = [0, 1, 2, 2, 4, 8, 32, 256, 8192, 2097152, 17179869184,$$
$$36028797018963968, 618970019642690137449562112, \ldots]$$
$$= [0, 2^0, 2^1, 2^1, 2^2, 2^3, 2^5, 2^8, 2^{13}, \ldots, 2^{F_n}, \ldots]$$

The sequence of zeros and ones after the decimal point in the binary expansion is referred to as *rabbit sequence* or *infinite Fibonacci word*, entry A005614 in [312], the sequence of decimal digits is entry A014565. The rabbit sequence can be computed by starting with a single zero and repeated application of the following substitution rules: simultaneously replace all zeros by one ($0 \mapsto 1$, 'young rabbit gets old') and all ones by one-zero ($1 \mapsto 10$, 'old rabbit gets child'). No sex, no death. The evolution is shown in figure 38.11-A.

The crucial observation is that each element A_n can be obtained by appending A_{n-2} to A_{n-1}, that is $A_n = A_{n-1}.A_{n-2}$. To compute the value of the rabbit constant in base 2 to N bits precision, the whole process requires only copying N bits of data is the minimal conceivable work for a (non-sparse) computation.

We define a function $A(y)$ that has the special value

$$A \;=\; \frac{1}{2} A\left(\frac{1}{2}\right) \tag{38.11-2}$$

by the equivalent operation for power series. The function can be computed by the following iteration:

$$L_0 \;=\; 0, \qquad R_0 \;=\; 1, \qquad l_0 \;=\; 1, \qquad r_0 \;=\; y \tag{38.11-3a}$$
$$l_{n+1} \;=\; r_n \;=\; y^{F_n} \tag{38.11-3b}$$
$$r_{n+1} \;=\; r_n l_n \;=\; y^{F_{n+1}} \tag{38.11-3c}$$
$$L_{n+1} \;=\; R_n \tag{38.11-3d}$$
$$R_{n+1} \;=\; R_n + r_{n+1} L_n \;=\; R_n + y^{F_{n+1}} L_n \;=\; R_n + y^{F_{n+1}} R_{n-1} \quad \to A(y) \tag{38.11-3e}$$

Here F_n denotes the n-th Fibonacci number (sequence A000045 in [312]):

n	0	1	2	3	4	5	6	7	8	9	10	11	12	13	14	15	...
Fn	0	1	1	2	3	5	8	13	21	34	55	89	144	233	377	610	...

A GP implementation of the iteration is

```
1    fa(y, N=10)=
2    {
3        local(t, yl, yr, L, R, Lp, Rp);
4        /* correct up to order fib(N+2)-1 */
5        L=0;  R=1;   yl=1;  yr=y;
6        for(k=1, N,
7          t=yr;  yr*=yl;  yl=t;
8          Lp=R;  Rp=R+yr*L;  L=Lp;  R=Rp;
9        );
10       return( R )
11   }
```

After the n-th step the series in y is correct up to order $F_{n+2} - 1$. That is, the order of convergence equals $\frac{\sqrt{5}+1}{2} \approx 1.6180$. The function $A(y)$ has the power series

$$A(y) \;=\; 1 + y^2 + y^3 + y^5 + y^7 + y^8 + y^{10} + y^{11} + y^{13} + y^{15} + y^{16} + y^{18} + y^{20} + y^{21} \cdots \tag{38.11-4}$$

The sequence of exponents of y in the series is entry A022342 in [312], the Fibonacci-even numbers. The Fibonacci-odd numbers are entry A003622.

The following continued fraction for $(1 - 1/q)\, A\,(1/q)$ is from [166, p.294]:

$$\left[\, 0,\, 1,\, q,\, q,\, q^2,\, q^3,\, q^5,\, q^8,\, q^{13},\, \ldots,\, q^{F_k},\, \ldots \right] \tag{38.11-5}$$

38.11.1   Fibonacci representation

The greedy algorithm to compute the *Fibonacci representation* (or *Zeckendorf representation*) of an integer repeatedly subtracts the largest Fibonacci number that is greater than or equal to it until the number is zero. The Fibonacci representations of the numbers $0 \ldots 80$ are shown in figure 38.11-B.

The sequence of lowest Fibonacci bits (entry A003849 in [312]) is

0,1,0,0,1,0,1,0,0,1,0,0,1,0,1,0,0,1,0,1,0,0,1,0,0,1,0,1,0,0,1,0,0,1,0,1,0,0,1,0,1,0,0, ...

The string, interpreted as the binary number $x = 0.1001010010010_2 \ldots$ gives the decimal constant $x = 0.5803931\ldots$. It turns out that $A = 1 - x/2$ (that is, $x = 2 - A(1/2)$).

The sequence of numbers of digits in the Fibonacci representations (second lowest row in figure 38.11-B) is entry A007895 in [312]. This sequence modulo 2 gives the *Fibonacci parity* (entry A095076). It can be computed by initializing $L_0 = 1$ and changing relation 38.11-3e to

$$R_{n+1} \;=\; R_n - r_{n+1} L_n \;=\; R_n - y^{F_{n+1}} L_n \quad \to A_p(y) \tag{38.11-6}$$

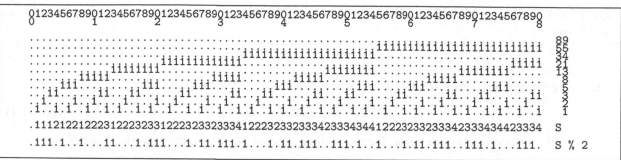

Figure 38.11-B: Fibonacci representations of the numbers $0 \ldots 80$. A dot is used for zero. The two lower lines are the sum of digits and the sum of digits modulo 2, the *Fibonacci parity*.

Let $A_p(y)$ be the corresponding function. We define the *Fibonacci parity constant* A_p as

$$A_p = 1 - A_p(1/2)/2 \tag{38.11-7a}$$

$$= 0.9105334708635617638046868867710980073445812290069376454\ldots \tag{38.11-7b}$$

$$[\text{base 2}] = 0.1110100100011000101110001011011101000101101110011101001 0\ldots$$

$$[\text{CF}] = [0, 1, 10, 5, 1, 1, 1, 3, 4, 2, 6, 25, 4, 5, 1, 1, 3, 5, 1, 3, 2, 1, 1, 1, 3, 1, 3, 22, 1,$$
$$10, 1, 2, 3, 2, 73, 1, 111, 46, 1, 51, 2, 1, 1, 5, 1, 65, 3, 1, 3, 2, 5, 6, 1, 4, 1, 2, \ldots]$$

The sequence of the Fibonacci representations interpreted as binary numbers is

$$0, 1, 2, 4, 5, 8, 9, 10, 16, 17, 18, 20, 21, 32, 33, 34, 36, 37, 40,$$
$$41, 42, 64, 65, 66, 68, 69, 72, 73, 74, 80, 81, 82, 84, 85, 128, 129, \ldots$$

This is entry A003714 in [312], where the numbers are called *Fibbinary numbers*. Define $F_2(y)$ to be the function with the same sequence of power series coefficients:

$$F(y) = 0 + 1\,y + 2\,y^2 + 4\,y^3 + 5\,y^4 + 8\,y^5 + 9\,y^6 + 10\,y^7 + 16\,y^8 + 17\,y^9 + 18\,y^{10} + \ldots \tag{38.11-8}$$

A slightly more general function $F_b(y)$ (which for $b = 2$ gives the power series above) can be computed by the iteration

$$L_0 = 0, \quad R_0 = y, \quad l_0 = y, \quad r_0 = y \tag{38.11-9a}$$

$$A_0 = 1, \quad B_0 = 1, \quad b = 2 \tag{38.11-9b}$$

$$A_{n+1} = b\,B_n \tag{38.11-9c}$$

$$B_{n+1} = b\,[B_n + r_n\,A_n] \tag{38.11-9d}$$

$$l_{n+1} = r_n = y^{F_{n+1}} \tag{38.11-9e}$$

$$r_{n+1} = r_n l_n = y^{F_{n+2}} \tag{38.11-9f}$$

$$L_{n+1} = R_n \tag{38.11-9g}$$

$$R_{n+1} = R_n + r_{n+1}\,[L_n + A_{n+1}] \quad \to F_b(y) \tag{38.11-9h}$$

A GP implementation is

```
1    ffb(y, b=2, N=13)=
2    { /* correct up to order fib(N+3)-1 */
3        local(t, yl, yr, L, R, Lp, Rp, Ri, Li);
4        L=0;  R=0+1*y;
5        Li=1;  Ri=1;
6        yl=y;  yr=y;
7        for (k=1, N,
8            Li*=b;  Ri*=b;
9            Lp=Ri;  Rp=Ri+yr*Li;  Li=Lp;  Ri=Rp;
10           t=yr;  yr*=yl;  yl=t;
11           Lp=R;  Rp=R+yr*(L+Li);  L=Lp;  R=Rp;
12       );
13       return( R )
14   }
```

Let $B(x)$ be the function with power series coefficients equal to 1 if the exponent is a Fibbinary number and zero else:

$$B(x) \quad := \quad 1 + x + x^2 + x^4 + x^5 + x^8 + x^9 + x^{10} + x^{16} + x^{17} + x^{18} + x^{20} + \dots \quad (38.11\text{-}10)$$

Then a functional equation for $B(x)$ is (see entry A003714 in [312])

$$B(x) \quad = \quad x\,B(x^4) + B(x^2) \qquad\qquad (38.11\text{-}11)$$

We turn the relation into a recursion for the computation of $B(x)$ correct up to the term x^N:

```
1    fibbi(z, R)=
2    {
3        if ( z+R==0, return( 1+R ) );
4        return( z*fibbi(z^4,R) + fibbi(z^2,R) );
5    }
```

We check the functional equation:

```
? N=30; R=O(x^(N+1));  \\ R is used to truncate terms of order >N
? t=fibbi(x,R)
   1 + x + x^2 + x^4 + x^5 + x^8 + x^9 + x^10 + x^16 + x^17 + x^18 + x^20 + x^21 + O(x^31)
? t2=fibbi(x^2,R)
   1 + x^2 + x^4 + x^8 + x^10 + x^16 + x^18 + x^20 + O(x^31)
? t4=x*fibbi(x^4,R)
   x + x^5 + x^9 + x^17 + x^21 + O(x^32)
? t-(t4+t2)
   O(x^31)
```

38.11.2 Digit extract algorithms for the rabbit constant

The *spectrum* of a real number x is the sequence of integers $\lfloor k \cdot x \rfloor$ where $k \in \mathbb{N}_+$ (the sequence $\lfloor k \cdot x \rfloor$ where x is irrational is called a *Beatty sequence*). The spectrum of the golden ratio $g = (\sqrt{5}+1)/2 \approx 1.61803$ gives the exponents of y where the series for $y\,A(y)$ has coefficient one:

```
1    bt(x, n=25)=
2    {
3        local(v);
4        v = vector(n);
5        for (k=1, n, v[k]=floor(x*k));
6        return ( v );
7    }
```

```
g=(sqrt(5)+1)/2
  1.6180339887498948482045868343656381177203091798057628621
```

```
n=40;
bt(g, n)
   [1, 3, 4, 6, 8, 9, 11, 12, 14, 16, 17, 19, 21, 22, 24, 25, 27, 29,
   30, 32, 33, 35, 37, 38, 40, 42, 43, 45, 46, 48, 50, 51, 53, 55, 56,
   58, 59, 61, 63, 64]
```

```
t=taylor(y*fa(y),y)
   y + y^3 + y^4 + y^6 + y^8 + y^9 + y^11 + y^12 + y^14 + y^16 + y^17 +
   y^19 + y^21 + y^22 + y^24 + y^25 + y^27 + y^29 + y^30 + y^32 + y^33 +
   y^35 + y^37 + y^38 + y^40 + y^42 + y^43 + y^45 + y^46 + y^48 + y^50 +
   y^51 + y^53 + y^55 + y^56 + y^58 + y^59 + y^61 + y^63 + y^64 + O(y^66)
```

The sequence $[1, 3, 4, 6, \dots]$ of exponents where the coefficient equals 1 is sequence A000201 in [312]. There is a digit extract algorithm for the binary expansion of the rabbit constant. We use a binary search algorithm:

```
1    bts(x, k)=
2    { /* return 0 if k is not in the spectrum of x, else return index >=1 */
3        local(nlo, nhi, t);
4        if ( 0==k, return(0) );
5        t = 1 + ceil(k/x);  \\ floor(t*x)>=k
6        nlo = 1;  nhi = t;
7        while ( nlo!=nhi,
8            t = floor( (nlo+nhi)/2 );
9            if ( floor(t*x) < k,  nlo=t+1,  nhi=t);
10       );
11       if ( floor(nhi*x) == k,  return(nhi),  return (0));
12   }
```

```
g=(sqrt(5)+1)/2
for(k=1,65,if(bts(g,k),print1("1"),print1("0")));print();
    10110101101101011010110110101101101011010110110101101011011010110
```

The algorithm is very fast, we compute 1000 bits starting from position 1,000,000,000,000:

```
g=(sqrt(5)+1)/2
dd=10^12;  /* digits starting at position dd... */
for(k=dd,dd+1000,if(bts(g,k),print1("1"),print1("0")));print();
    11011010110110101101011011010110110101101011011010110101101101 0110
    [--snip--]
***    last result computed in 236 ms.
```

An even faster method for computing individual bits of the sequence proceeds by subtracting the Fibonacci numbers > 1 until zero or one is reached. This gives the complement of the rabbit sequence:

```
1   fpn=999;
2   vpv=vector(fpn, j, fibonacci(j+2)); /* vpv=[2,3,5,8,...] */
3   t=vpv[length(vpv)];  /* log(t)/log(10)== 208.8471.  OK for range up to >10^200 (!) */
4
5   flb(x)=
6   { /* return the lowest bit of the Fibonacci representation */
7       local(k, t);
8       k=bsearchgeq(x, vpv);
9       while ( k>0,
10          t = vpv[k];
11          if (x>=t,  x-=t);
12          k-- );
13      return ( x );
14  }
```

```
dd=0;
for(k=dd,dd+40,t=flb(k);print1(1-t))
    10110101101101011010110110101101101011010
/* 0.10110101101101011010110110101101101011010  rabbit constant */
```

The routine bsearchgeq() does a binary search (see section 3.2 on page 141) for the first element that is greater than or equal to the element sought:

```
1   bsearchgeq(x, v)=
2   { /* return index of first element in v[] that is >=x, return 0 if x>max(v[])  */
3       local(nlo, nhi, t);
4       nlo = 1;  nhi = length(v);
5       while ( nlo!=nhi,
6           t = floor( (nlo+nhi)/2 );
7           if ( v[t] < x,  nlo=t+1,  nhi=t);
8       );
9       if ( v[nhi] >= x,  return(nhi),  return (0));
10  }
```

We compute the first 1000 bits starting from position 10^{100}:

```
dd=10^100-1;
for (k=dd, dd+1000, t=flb(k); print1(1-t))
    110101101101011010110110101101101011010110110 10
    [--snip--]
***    last result computed in 1,305 ms.
```

38.12   Iterations related to the Pell numbers

```
    Start: 0
    Rules:
       0 --> 1
       1 --> 110

    B0 =   0
    B1 =   1
    B2 =   110
    B3 =   1101101
    B4 =   1101101110110 110
    B5 =   1101101110110111011011011101101101101

    B --> 1101101110110111011011011101101101101101110110110111011... 
```

Figure 38.12-A: Evolution for the string substitution rules $0 \mapsto 1$ and $1 \mapsto 110$.

We use the string substitution shown in figure 38.12-A. The length of the n-th string is

$$p_n \;=\; 1, 1, 3, 7, 17, 41, 99, 239, \ldots \qquad p_k \;=\; 2p_{k-1} + p_{k-2}$$

This sequence is entry A001333 in [312], the numerators of the continued fraction of $\sqrt{2}$. The Pell numbers are the first differences (and the denominators of the continued fraction of $\sqrt{2}$), sequence A000129:

$$0, 1, 2, 5, 12, 29, 70, 169, 408, 985, 2378, 5741, \ldots$$

Observe that $B_n = B_{n-1}.B_{n-1}.B_{n-2}$. Define the function $B(y)$ by the iteration

$$L_0 \;=\; 1, \qquad R_0 = 1+y, \qquad l_0 = y, \qquad r_0 = y \tag{38.12-1a}$$
$$l_{n+1} \;=\; r_n \tag{38.12-1b}$$
$$r_{n+1} \;=\; r_n^2 \, l_n \tag{38.12-1c}$$
$$L_{n+1} \;=\; R_n \tag{38.12-1d}$$
$$R_{n+1} \;=\; R_n + r_{n+1} R_n + r_{n+1}^2 L_n \quad \to B(y) \tag{38.12-1e}$$

After the n-th step the series in y is correct up to order p_n. That is, the order of convergence is $\sqrt{2}+1$ ≈ 2.4142. We implement the function $B(y)$ in GP:

```
1   fb(y, N=8)=
2   {
3       local(t, yr, yl, L, R, Lp, Rp);
4       L=1;  R=1+y;  yl=y;  yr=y;
5       for(k=1,N,
6           t=yr; yr*=yr*yl; yl=t;
7           Lp=R; Rp=R+yr*R+yr^2*L; L=Lp; R=Rp;
8       );
9       return( R )
10  }
```

We obtain the series

$$B(y) \;=\; 1 + y + y^3 + y^4 + y^6 + y^7 + y^8 + y^{10} + y^{11} + y^{13} + y^{14} + y^{15} + y^{17} + y^{18} + y^{20} + \cdots \tag{38.12-2}$$

Define the *Pell constant* B as $B = \tfrac{1}{2} B(\tfrac{1}{2})$, then

$$B \;=\; 0.85826765646100205579226030843337514866490519008350067786\ldots \tag{38.12-3}$$
$$[\text{base 2}] \;=\; 0.11011011101101011011011011101101011011011011101101101111011011\ldots$$
$$[\text{CF}] \;=\; [0, 1, 6, 18, 1032, 16777344, 288230376151842816,$$
$$13937965749081639463459823920427216173793328, \ldots]$$

The sequence of zeros and ones in the binary expansion is entry A080764 in [312]. For the terms of the continued fraction we note

$$6 \;=\; 2^{2\cdot1} + 2^1 \tag{38.12-4a}$$
$$18 \;=\; 2^{2\cdot2} + 2^1 \tag{38.12-4b}$$
$$1032 \;=\; 2^{2\cdot5} + 2^3 \tag{38.12-4c}$$
$$16777344 \;=\; 2^{2\cdot12} + 2^7 \tag{38.12-4d}$$
$$288230376151842816 \;=\; 2^{2\cdot29} + 2^{17} \tag{38.12-4e}$$
$$13937965749081639463459823920427216173793328 \;=\; 2^{2\cdot70} + 2^{41} \tag{38.12-4f}$$

38.12.1 Pell palindromes

Define the function $P(y)$ by

$$L_0 = 1, \qquad R_0 = 1 + y^2, \qquad l_0 = y, \qquad r_0 = y \tag{38.12-5a}$$
$$l_{n+1} = r_n \tag{38.12-5b}$$
$$r_{n+1} = r_n^2 l_n \tag{38.12-5c}$$
$$L_{n+1} = R_n \tag{38.12-5d}$$
$$R_{n+1} = R_n + r_{n+1} L_n + r_{n+1} l_{n+1} R_n \quad \to P(y) \tag{38.12-5e}$$

Note that R_0 is a palindrome and in relation 38.12-5e the combination of the parts gives a palindrome. For $R_0 = 1 + y + y^2$ the iteration computes $\frac{1}{1-y}$.

Define the *Pell palindromic constant* as $P = P(1/2)/2$, then

$$P = 0.73216043306353283716459018717730446572729865896041112390\ldots \tag{38.12-6}$$
$$[\text{base } 2] = 0.1011101101101110110110110110110110110110110110110111011011011\ldots$$
$$[\text{CF}] = [0, 1, 2, 1, 2, 1, 3, 17, 1, 7, 2063, 1, 63, 268437503, 1, 8191, 590295810358974087167,$$
$$1, 1073741823, 37414441915671114706014331717595874884227743665356 7, 1, \ldots]$$

By construction, the binary expansion is a palindrome up to lengths $1, 3, 7, 17, 41, 99, 239, \ldots$.

```
Start: 0
Rules:
  0 --> 1
  1 --> 101

P0 =  0
P1 =  1
P2 =  101
P3 =  1011101
P4 =  10111011011011101
P5 =  1011101101101110110110110110111011011011101

P --> 10111011011011101101101101101101101101101101101110110110111 01101...
```

Figure 38.12-B: String substitution for the Pell palindromic constant.

The sequence of zeros and ones in the binary expansion of P is entry A104521 in [312]. It can be computed by the replacement rules $0 \mapsto 1$ and $1 \mapsto 101$ shown in figure 38.12-B.

38.12.2 Pell representation

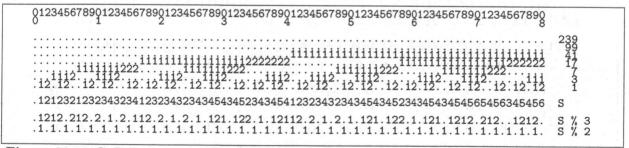

Figure 38.12-C: Pell representations of the numbers $0 \ldots 80$ (dots for zeros). The three lower lines are the sum of digits and the sum of digits modulo 3 and 2.

To compute the Pell representation of a given number n, set $t = n$ repeatedly subtract from t the largest number $p_k \in \{1, 3, 7, 17, 41, 99, 239, \ldots\}$ that is not greater than t. Stop when $t = 0$. The number of times that p_k has been subtracted gives the k-th digit of the representation. The resulting digits are 0, 1, or 2. If the k-th digit equals 2, then the $(k-1)$-th digit will be zero.

The power series of the function $S(y)$ has the sums of Pell digits as coefficients:

$$S(y) \quad = \quad 0 + 1y + 2y^2 + 1y^3 + 2y^4 + 3y^5 + 2y^6 + 1y^7 + 2y^8 + 3y^9 + 2y^{10} + 3y^{11} + 4y^{12} + \dots \quad (38.12\text{-}7)$$

can be computed via the iteration (see section 38.7 on page 739)

$$L_0 \;\; = \;\; 0, \qquad R_0 \;\; = \;\; 0 + y + 2\,y^2, \qquad l_0 \;\; = \;\; y, \qquad r_0 \;\; = \;\; y \qquad (38.12\text{-}8\text{a})$$

$$A_0 \;\; = \;\; 1, \qquad B_0 \;\; = \;\; 1 + y + y^2 \qquad\qquad\qquad\qquad\qquad\qquad (38.12\text{-}8\text{b})$$

$$l_{n+1} \;\; = \;\; r_n \qquad\qquad\qquad\qquad\qquad\qquad\qquad\qquad\qquad\qquad (38.12\text{-}8\text{c})$$

$$r_{n+1} \;\; = \;\; r_n^2\,l_n \qquad\qquad\qquad\qquad\qquad\qquad\qquad\qquad\qquad (38.12\text{-}8\text{d})$$

$$L_{n+1} \;\; = \;\; R_n \qquad\qquad\qquad\qquad\qquad\qquad\qquad\qquad\qquad\quad (38.12\text{-}8\text{e})$$

$$R_{n+1} \;\; = \;\; R_n + r_{n+1}\,(R_n + B_n) + r_{n+1}^2\,(L_n + 2\,A_n) \quad \to S(y) \quad (38.12\text{-}8\text{f})$$

$$A_{n+1} \;\; = \;\; B_n \qquad\qquad\qquad\qquad\qquad\qquad\qquad\qquad\qquad\quad (38.12\text{-}8\text{g})$$

$$B_{n+1} \;\; = \;\; B_n + r_{n+1}\,B_n + r_{n+1}^2\,A_n \qquad\qquad\qquad\qquad\qquad (38.12\text{-}8\text{h})$$

Implementation in GP:

```
1   fs(y, N=8)=
2   {
3       local(t, yr, yl, L, R, Lp, Rp, Li, Ri);
4       L =  0;  R = 0+y+2*y^2;
5       Li = 1;  Ri = 1+y+y^2;
6       yl = y;  yr = y;
7       for(k=1,N,
8          t=yr; yr*=yr*yl; yl=t;
9          Lp=R;  Rp=R+yr*(R+Ri)+yr^2*(L+2*Li);   L=Lp; R=Rp;
10         Lp=Ri; Rp=Ri+yr*Ri+yr^2*Li;   Li=Lp; Ri=Rp;
11      );
12      return( R )
13  }
```

The series coefficients grow slowly, so the first few of them can nicely be displayed as

$$S\left(\frac{1}{10}\right) \quad = \quad 0.12123212323432341232343234345434523434541232343234343... \quad (38.12\text{-}9)$$

38.12.3   Pell Gray code

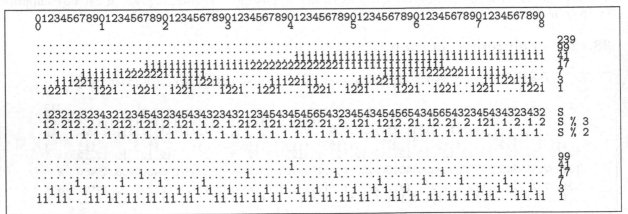

Figure 38.12-D: A Gray code for Pell representations. A dot is used for zero. The three following lines are the sum of digits and the sum of digits modulo 3 and 2. The sequence is $0, 1, 2, 5, 4, 3, 6, 13, 10, 11, 12, 9, 8, 7, 14\dots$, the difference between successive elements is a Pell number. The lowest block gives the Pell representations of the (absolute) differences, the *Pell ruler function*.

Figure 38.12-D gives a Gray code for the Pell representations (see also section 14.6.1 on page 313). The Gray code can be constructed recursively as shown in figure 38.12-E. In the algorithm each block is split

```
  . _12

  ..._ 1112
  .12_21..

  ......_..._ 1111111222
  ...1112 2111......_..
  .1221.._...1221..12

  ............_.........._ 1111111111111111112222222
  ...1111111222 2221111111..._........._
  ...11122111........_...._...11122111...._...1112
  .1221....1221..12_21..1221....1221..1221..
```

Figure 38.12-E: Construction for a Gray code for Pell representations.

into a left and a right part. The next block is created by appending to the current block its reverse with ones on top and appending the left part with twos on top. The iteration can actually be started with a block of a single zero (the left part being also a single zero), as in the following algorithm:

$$F_0 = 0, \quad F_0' = 0, \quad B_0 = 0, \quad B_0' = 0 \tag{38.12-10a}$$

$$I_0 = 1, \quad I_0' = 1, \quad Y_0 = y, \quad Y_0' = y \tag{38.12-10b}$$

$$b_n = 4^{n-1}, \quad c_n = 2\,b_n \tag{38.12-10c}$$

$$F_{n+1} = (F_n \quad) + Y_n\,(B_n + b_n\,I_n) + \ Y_n^2\,(F_n' + c_n\,I_n') \quad \rightarrow G_b(y) \tag{38.12-10d}$$

$$B_{n+1} = (B_n' + c_n\,I_n') + Y_n'\,(F_n + b_n\,I_n) + Y_n'\,Y_n\,(B_n \quad) \tag{38.12-10e}$$

$$I_{n+1} = I_n + Y_n\,I_n + Y_n^2\,I_n' \tag{38.12-10f}$$

$$Y_{n+1} = Y_n^2\,Y_n' \tag{38.12-10g}$$

$$F_{n+1}' = F_n, \quad B_{n+1}' = B_n \tag{38.12-10h}$$

$$I_{n+1}' = I_n, \quad Y_{n+1}' = Y_n \tag{38.12-10i}$$

```
      ----- k = 0
yl = (y)   yr = (y)
iir = 1
iil = 1
F = 0
B = 0
      ----- k = 1    b=1
yl = (y)   yr = (y^3)
iir = (y^2 + y + 1)
iil = 1
F = (2 y^2 + y)
B = (y + 2)
      ----- k = 2    b=4
yl = (y^3)   yr = (y^7)
iir = (y^6 + y^5 + y^4 + y^3 + y^2 + y + 1)
iil = (y^2 + y + 1)
F = (8 y^6 + 4 y^5 + 5 y^4 + 6 y^3 + 2 y^2 + y)
B = (y^5 + 2 y^4 + 6 y^3 + 5 y^2 + 4 y + 8)
      ----- k = 3    b=16
yl = (y^7)   yr = (y^17)
iir = (y^16 + y^15 + y^14 + y^13 + y^12 + y^11 + y^10 + y^9
    + y^8 + y^7 + y^6 + y^5 + y^4 + y^3 + y^2 + y + 1)
iil = (y^6 + y^5 + y^4 + y^3 + y^2 + y + 1)
F = (34 y^16 + 33 y^15 + 32 y^14
    + 16 y^13 + 17 y^12 + 18 y^11 + 22 y^10 + 21 y^9 + 20 y^8 + 24 y^7
    + 8 y^6 + 4 y^5 + 5 y^4 + 6 y^3 + 2 y^2 + y)
B = (y^15 + 2 y^14 + 6 y^13 + 5 y^12 + 4 y^11 + 8 y^10
    + 24 y^9 + 20 y^8 + 21 y^7 + 22 y^6 + 18 y^5 + 17 y^4 + 16 y^3
    + 32 y^2 + 33 y + 34)
```

Figure 38.12-F: Quantities with the computation of the series related to the Pell Gray code.

Implementation in GP:

```
1  pgr(y, N=11)= /* Pell Gray code */
2  {
```

```
3      local(iir, iil, yl, yr, Fl, F, Bl, B, b, c);
4      local(t, tf, tb);
5      /* correct up to order pell(N+1)-1 */
6      F=0;  Fl=0;   B=0;  Bl=0;
7      iil=1;  iir=1;  yl=y;  yr=y;
8      for(k=1, N,
9          b = 4^(k-1);   c = 2*b;  /* b = pell(k);*/
10         tf = (F          ) + yr * (B + b*iir) + yr*yr * (Fl + c*iil);
11         tb = (Bl + c*iil) + yl * (F + b*iir) + yl*yr * (B          );
12         Fl = F;   Bl = B;
13         F = tf;   B = tb;
14         t = iir;  iir += yr*(iir + yr*iil);  iil = t;
15         t = yr;  yr *= (yr*yl);  yl = t;
16     );
17     return( F )
18  }
```

It is instructive to look at the variables in the first few steps of the iteration, see figure 38.12-F.

The power series for $G_2(y)$ is

$$G_2(y) = 0 + 1y + 2y^2 + 6y^3 + 5y^4 + 4y^5 + 8y^6 + 24y^7 + 20y^8 + 21y^9 + 22y^{10} + 18y^{11} + \qquad (38.12\text{-}11)$$
$$+17y^{12} + 16y^{13} + 32y^{14} + 33y^{15} + 34y^{16} + 98y^{17} + 97y^{18} + 96y^{19} + 80y^{20} + 81y^{21} +$$
$$+82y^{22} + 86y^{23} + 85y^{24} + 84y^{25} + 88y^{26} + 72y^{27} + 68y^{28} + 69y^{29} + 70y^{30} + 66y^{31} + \dots$$

The coefficients corresponds to the Pell representations interpreted as binary numbers, each Pell-digit occupying two bits (figure 38.12-D).

If relation 38.12-10c is changed to $b_n = P_n$ (indicated in the code, the function can be defined as `pell(k)=if(k<=1, 1, return(2*pell(k-1)+pell(k-2)));`), then the function $G_P(y)$ which has the Pell Gray code sequence as coefficients is computed:

$$G_P(y) = 0 + 1y + 2y^2 + 5y^3 + 4y^4 + 3y^5 + 6y^6 + 13y^7 + 10y^8 + 11y^9 + 12y^{10} + 9y^{11} + \qquad (38.12\text{-}12)$$
$$+8y^{12} + 7y^{13} + 14y^{14} + 15y^{15} + 16y^{16} + 33y^{17} + 32y^{18} + 31y^{19} + 24y^{20} + 25y^{21} +$$
$$+26y^{22} + 29y^{23} + 28y^{24} + 27y^{25} + 30y^{26} + 23y^{27} + 20y^{28} + 21y^{29} + 22y^{30} + 19y^{31} + \dots$$

Section 14.6 on page 313 gives a recursive algorithm to compute the words of the Pell Gray code.

Define the *Pell Gray code constant* as

$$G_P = G_P\left(\frac{1}{2}\right) \qquad (38.12\text{-}13\text{a})$$

$$= 2.245567348365072195720956572438998819867495229140192012\dots \qquad (38.12\text{-}13\text{b})$$

$$[\text{base 2}] = 10.0011111011011101100000000111001000110001100001000111\dots \qquad (38.12\text{-}13\text{c})$$

$$[\text{CF}] = [2, 4, 13, 1, 5, 1, 1, 1, 27, 1, 9, 1, 3, 8, 1, 2, 1, 1, 3, 14, 1, 8, 1, 1, 6, 3, 1,$$
$$1, 1, 2, 1, 7, 210, 1, 1, 3, 2, 1, 1, 10, 1, 1, 6, 1, 1, 2, 1, 2, 1, 4, 6, 12, 1, \dots]$$

Setting $b_n = 1$ and $c_n = 2$ in the algorithm gives a function whose series coefficients are the sum of Pell Gray code digits. The coefficients coincide with the start of the decimal expansion $G_{[1,2]}(1/10)$ (until the first count > 9 appears):

$$G_{[1,2]}\left(\frac{1}{10}\right) = 0.12321232343212345432345434323432123454345456543234543 45\dots \qquad (38.12\text{-}14)$$

Set $b_n = 1$ and $c_n = 0$ to count the ones in the Pell Gray code:

$$G_{[1,0]}\left(\frac{1}{10}\right) = 0.10121012321210101212323432123212101012101232123234323\dots \qquad (38.12\text{-}15)$$

With $b_n = 0$ and $c_n = 1$ we count the twos:

$$G_{[0,1]}\left(\frac{1}{10}\right) = 0.01100110011001122110011001100110011221122112211001100110\dots \qquad (38.12\text{-}16)$$

Part V

Algorithms for finite fields

Chapter 39

Modular arithmetic and some number theory

We implement the arithmetical operations modulo m, such as addition, subtraction, multiplication, and division. Basic concepts of number theory, like the order of an element, quadratic residues, and primitive roots are developed. Selected algorithms such as the Rabin-Miller compositeness test and several primality tests are presented. Finally we give the Cayley-Dickson construction for hypercomplex numbers and compute their multiplication tables.

Modular arithmetic and the concepts of number theory are fundamental to many areas like cryptography, error correcting codes, and digital signal processing.

39.1 Implementation of the arithmetic operations

We implement the basic operations of modular arithmetic: addition, subtraction, multiplication, powering, inversion and division. The representatives modulo m are chosen to be $0, 1, \ldots, m-1$.

39.1.1 Addition and subtraction

Addition and subtraction modulo m can easily be implemented as [FXT: mod/modarith.h]:

```
1    inline umod_t sub_mod(umod_t a, umod_t b, umod_t m)
2    {
3        if ( a>=b )  return  a - b;
4        else         return  m - b + a;
5    }
6
7    inline umod_t add_mod(umod_t a, umod_t b, umod_t m)
8    {
9        if ( 0==b )  return  a;
10       // return sub_mod(a, m-b, m);
11       b = m - b;
12       if ( a>=b )  return  a - b;
13       else         return  m - b + a;
14   }
```

The type `umod_t` is an unsigned 64-bit integer. Care has been taken to avoid any overflow of intermediate results. The routines for assignment, increment, decrement and negation are:

```
1    inline umod_t incr_mod(umod_t a, umod_t m)
2    { a++; if ( a==m )  a = 0;   return a; }
3
4    inline umod_t decr_mod(umod_t a, umod_t m)
5    { if ( a==0 )  a = m - 1;  else a--;  return a; }
6
7    inline umod_t neg_mod(umod_t b, umod_t m)
8    { if ( 0==b )  return 0;  else  return m - b; }
```

The addition tables for the moduli 13 and 9 are shown in figure 39.1-A

J. Arndt, *Matters Computational: Ideas, Algorithms, Source Code,*
DOI 10.1007/978-3-642-14764-7_39, © Springer-Verlag Berlin Heidelberg 2011

```
        0  1  2  3  4  5  6  7  8  9 10 11 12                  0  1  2  3  4  5  6  7  8
     --------------------------------------------           ----------------------------
   0    0  1  2  3  4  5  6  7  8  9 10 11 12            0    0  1  2  3  4  5  6  7  8
   1    1  2  3  4  5  6  7  8  9 10 11 12  0            1    1  2  3  4  5  6  7  8  0
   2    2  3  4  5  6  7  8  9 10 11 12  0  1            2    2  3  4  5  6  7  8  0  1
   3    3  4  5  6  7  8  9 10 11 12  0  1  2            3    3  4  5  6  7  8  0  1  2
   4    4  5  6  7  8  9 10 11 12  0  1  2  3            4    4  5  6  7  8  0  1  2  3
   5    5  6  7  8  9 10 11 12  0  1  2  3  4            5    5  6  7  8  0  1  2  3  4
   6    6  7  8  9 10 11 12  0  1  2  3  4  5            6    6  7  8  0  1  2  3  4  5
   7    7  8  9 10 11 12  0  1  2  3  4  5  6            7    7  8  0  1  2  3  4  5  6
   8    8  9 10 11 12  0  1  2  3  4  5  6  7            8    8  0  1  2  3  4  5  6  7
   9    9 10 11 12  0  1  2  3  4  5  6  7  8
  10   10 11 12  0  1  2  3  4  5  6  7  8  9
  11   11 12  0  1  2  3  4  5  6  7  8  9 10
  12   12  0  1  2  3  4  5  6  7  8  9 10 11
```

Figure 39.1-A: Addition modulo 13 (left) and modulo 9 (right).

39.1.2 Multiplication

Multiplication is a bit harder: with something like

```
1    inline umod_t mul_mod(umod_t a, umod_t b, umod_t m)
2    {
3        return  (a * b) % m;
4    }
```

the modulus would be restricted to half of the word size. Almost all bits can be used for the modulus with the following trick. Let $\langle x \rangle_y$ denote x modulo y, let $\lfloor x \rfloor$ denote the integer part of x. For $0 \leq a, b < m$ we have

$$a \cdot b \;=\; \left\lfloor \frac{a \cdot b}{m} \right\rfloor \cdot m + \langle a \cdot b \rangle_m \tag{39.1-1}$$

Rearranging and taking both sides modulo $z > m$ (where $z = 2^k$ on a k-bit machine):

$$\left\langle a \cdot b - \left\lfloor \frac{a \cdot b}{m} \right\rfloor \cdot m \right\rangle_z \;=\; \langle \langle a \cdot b \rangle_m \rangle_z \tag{39.1-2}$$

The right side equals $\langle a \cdot b \rangle_m$ because $m < z$.

$$\langle a \cdot b \rangle_m \;=\; \left\langle \langle a \cdot b \rangle_z - \left\langle \left\lfloor \frac{a \cdot b}{m} \right\rfloor \cdot m \right\rangle_z \right\rangle_z \tag{39.1-3}$$

The expression on the right can be translated into a few lines of C-code. For the following implementation we require 64-bit integer types `int64` (signed) and `uint64` (unsigned) and a floating-point type with 64-bit mantissa, `float64` (typically `long double`).

```
1    uint64 mul_mod(uint64 a, uint64 b, uint64 m)
2    {
3        uint64 y = (uint64)((float64)a*(float64)b/m+(float64)1/2);  // floor(a*b/m)
4        y = y * m;             // m*floor(a*b/m) mod z
5        uint64 x = a * b;      // a*b mod z
6        uint64 r = x - y;      // a*b mod z - m*floor(a*b/m) mod z
7        if ( (int64)r < 0 )    // normalization needed ?
8        {
9            r = r + m;
10           y = y - 1;         // (a*b)/m  quotient, omit line if not needed
11       }
12       return  r;             // (a*b)%m  residue
13   }
```

The technique uses the fact that integer multiplication computes the least significant bits of the result $\langle a \cdot b \rangle_z$, whereas float multiplication computes the most significant bits of the result. The above routine works if $0 \leq a,\, b < m < 2^{63} = \frac{z}{2}$. The normalization is not necessary if $m < 2^{62} = \frac{z}{4}$.

When working with a fixed modulus the division by p may be replaced by a multiplication with the inverse modulus, that only needs to be computed once:

precompute: `float64 i = (float64)1/m;`

and replace the line   `uint64 y = (uint64)((float64)a*(float64)b/m+(float64)1/2);`

by   `uint64 y = (uint64)((float64)a*(float64)b*i+(float64)1/2);`

so any division inside the routine is avoided. Beware that the routine cannot be used for $m >= 2^{62}$: it very rarely fails for moduli of more than 62 bits, due to the additional error when inverting and multiplying as compared to dividing alone. An implementation is [FXT: mod/modarith.h]:

```
1    inline umod_t mul_mod(umod_t a, umod_t b, umod_t m)
2    {
3        umod_t x = a * b;
4        umod_t y = m * (umod_t)( (ldouble)a * (ldouble)b/m + (ldouble)1/2 );
5        umod_t r = x - y;
6        if ( (smod_t)r < 0 )  r += m;
7        return  r;
8    }
```

```
        0  1  2  3  4  5  6  7  8  9 10 11 12              0  1  2  3  4  5  6  7  8
   ------------------------------------------         -------------------------------
    0   0  0  0  0  0  0  0  0  0  0  0  0  0         0   0  0  0  0  0  0  0  0  0
    1   0  1  2  3  4  5  6  7  8  9 10 11 12         1   0  1  2  3  4  5  6  7  8
    2   0  2  4  6  8 10 12  1  3  5  7  9 11         2   0  2  4  6  8  1  3  5  7
    3   0  3  6  9 12  2  5  8 11  1  4  7 10         3   0  3  6  0  3  6  0  3  6
    4   0  4  8 12  3  7 11  2  6 10  1  5  9         4   0  4  8  3  7  2  6  1  5
    5   0  5 10  2  7 12  4  9  1  6 11  3  8         5   0  5  1  6  2  7  3  8  4
    6   0  6 12  5 11  4 10  3  9  2  8  1  7         6   0  6  3  0  6  3  0  6  3
    7   0  7  1  8  2  9  3 10  4 11  5 12  6         7   0  7  5  3  1  8  6  4  2
    8   0  8  3 11  6  1  9  4 12  7  2 10  5         8   0  8  7  6  5  4  3  2  1
    9   0  9  5  1 10  6  2 11  7  3 12  8  4
   10   0 10  7  4  1 11  8  5  2 12  9  6  3
   11   0 11  9  7  5  3  1 12 10  8  6  4  2
   12   0 12 11 10  9  8  7  6  5  4  3  2  1
```

Figure 39.1-B: Multiplication modulo 13 (left) and modulo 9 (right).

Two multiplication tables for the moduli 13 and 9 are shown in figure 39.1-B. Note that for the modulus 9 some products $a \cdot b$ are zero though neither of a or b is zero. The tables were computed with the program [FXT: mod/modarithtables-demo.cc].

For alternative multiplication (and reduction) techniques see [250, ch.14]. One method of great practical importance is the Montgomery multiplication described in [252].

39.1.3 Exponentiation

The algorithm used for exponentiation (powering) is the binary exponentiation algorithm shown in section 28.5 on page 563:

```
1    inline umod_t pow_mod(umod_t a, umod_t e, umod_t m)
2    // Right-to-left scan
3    {
4        if ( 0==e )  { return 1; }
5        else
6        {
7            umod_t z = a;
8            umod_t y = 1;
9            while ( 1 )
```

```
10       {
11           if ( e&1 )  y = mul_mod(y, z, m);   // y *= z;
12           e >>= 1;
13           if ( 0==e )  break;
14           z = sqr_mod(z, m);   // z *= z;
15       }
16       return  y;
17   }
18 }
```

39.1.4 Division and modular inversion

Subtraction is the inverse of addition. To subtract b from a, we add $-b := m - b$ to a. The element $-b$ is the *additive inverse* of b. Every element has an additive inverse.

Division is the inverse of multiplication. To divide a by b, we multiply a by b^{-1}, the *multiplicative inverse* of b. However, not all elements have a multiplicative inverse, only those b that are coprime to the modulus m (that is, $\gcd(b, m) = 1$). These elements are called *invertible* modulo m, or *units*. For a prime modulus all elements except zero are invertible.

The computation of the GCD uses the *Euclidean algorithm* [FXT: mod/gcd.h]:

```
1  template <typename Type>
2  Type gcd(Type a, Type b)
3  // Return greatest common divisor of a and b.
4  {
5      if ( a < b )  swap2(a, b);
6      if ( b==0 )  return a;
7      Type r;
8      do
9      {
10         r = a % b;
11         a = b;
12         b = r;
13     }
14     while ( r!=0 );
15     return a;
16 }
```

A variant of the algorithm that avoids most of the (expensive) computations a%b is called the *binary GCD algorithm* [FXT: mod/binarygcd.h]:

```
1  template <typename Type>
2  Type binary_ugcd(Type a, Type b)
3  // Return greatest common divisor of a and b.
4  // Version for unsigned types.
5  {
6      if ( a < b )  swap2(a, b);
7      if ( b==0 )  return a;
8
9      Type r = a % b;
10     a = b;
11     b = r;
12     if ( b==0 )  return a;
13
14     ulong k = 0;
15     while ( !((a|b)&1) )  // both even
16     {
17         k++;
18         a >>= 1;
19         b >>= 1;
20     }
21
22     while ( !(a&1) )  a >>= 1;
23     while ( !(b&1) )  b >>= 1;
24
25     while ( 1 )
26     {
27         if ( a==b )  return  a << k;
28
29         if ( a < b )  swap2(a, b);
30         Type t = (a-b) >> 1;  // t>0
31
32         while ( !(t&1) )  t >>= 1;
```

```
33          a = t;
34      }
35  }
```

The complexity of this algorithm for N-bit numbers is $O(N^2)$, an $O(N \log(N))$ algorithm is given in [322].

The *least common multiple* (LCM) of two numbers is

$$\text{lcm}(a,\, b) \;=\; \frac{a \cdot b}{\gcd(a,\, b)} \;=\; \left(\frac{a}{\gcd(a,\, b)} \right) \cdot b \tag{39.1-4}$$

The latter form avoids overflow when using integer types of fixed size.

For modular inversion we can use the extended Euclidean algorithm to compute the *extended GCD* (EGCD), which for two integers a and b finds $d = \gcd(a, b)$ and u, v such that $a\,u + b\,v = d$. The following code implements the EGCD algorithm as given in [213, alg.X, p.342]:

```
1   template <typename Type>
2   Type egcd(Type u, Type v, Type &tu1, Type &tu2)
3   // Return u3 and set u1,v1 so that
4   //    gcd(u,v) == u3 == u*u1 + v*u2
5   // Type must be a signed type.
6   {
7       Type u1 = 1,   u2 = 0;
8       Type v1 = 0,   v3 = v;
9       Type u3 = u,   v2 = 1;
10      while ( v3!=0 )
11      {
12          Type q = u3 / v3;
13
14          Type t1 = u1 - v1 * q;
15          u1 = v1;   v1 = t1;
16
17          Type t3 = u3 - v3 * q;
18          u3 = v3;   v3 = t3;
19
20          Type t2 = u2 - v2 * q;
21          u2 = v2;   v2 = t2;
22      }
23      tu1 = u1;   tu2 = u2;
24      return u3;
25  }
```

To invert b modulo m, we must have $\gcd(b, m) = 1$. With the EGCD of b and m we compute u and v such that $m\,u + b\,v = 1$. Reduce modulo m to see that $b\,v \equiv 1 \pmod{m}$. That is, v is the inverse of b modulo m and $a/b := a\,b^{-1} = a\,v$.

Another algorithm for the computation of the modular inversion uses exponentiation. It is given only after the concept of the *order* of an element has been introduced (section 39.5 on page 774).

39.2 Modular reduction with structured primes

The modular reduction with Mersenne primes $M = 2^k - 1$ is especially easy: let u and v be in the range $0 \leq u, v < M = 2^k - 1$, then with the non-reduced product written as $u\,v = 2^k\,r + s$ (where $0 \leq r, s < M = 2^k - 1$) the reduction is simply $u\,v \equiv r + s \pmod{M}$.

A modular reduction algorithm that uses only shifts, additions and subtractions can also be found for *structured primes* (called *generalized Mersenne primes* in [315]). Let the modulus M be of the form

$$M \;=\; \sum_{i=0}^{n} m_i\, x^i \tag{39.2-1}$$

where $x = 2^k$ and $m_n = 1$. We further assume that $m_i = \pm 1$ and $m_{n-1} = -1$ (so that the numbers fit into n bits). The reduction algorithm can be found using polynomial arithmetic. Write the non-reduced

```
2^64-2^32+1  == 2^(32*2)-2^(32*1)+1      2^80-2^48+1   == 2^(16*5)-2^(16*3)+1
2^96-2^32+1  == 2^(32*3)-2^(32*1)+1      2^176-2^48+1  == 2^(16*11)-2^(16*3)+1
2^224-2^96+1 == 2^(32*7)-2^(32*3)+1      2^176-2^80+1  == 2^(16*11)-2^(16*5)+1
2^320-2^288+1 == 2^(32*10)-2^(32*9)+1    2^368-2^336+1 == 2^(16*23)-2^(16*21)+1
2^512-2^32+1  == 2^(32*16)-2^(32*1)+1    2^384-2^80+1  == 2^(16*24)-2^(16*5)+1
2^512-2^288+1 == 2^(32*16)-2^(32*9)+1    2^400-2^160+1 == 2^(16*25)-2^(16*10)+1
2^544-2^32+1  == 2^(32*17)-2^(32*1)+1    2^528-2^336+1 == 2^(16*33)-2^(16*21)+1
2^544-2^96+1  == 2^(32*17)-2^(32*3)+1    2^544-2^304+1 == 2^(16*34)-2^(16*19)+1
2^576-2^512+1 == 2^(64*9)-2^(64*8)+1     2^560-2^112+1 == 2^(16*35)-2^(16*7)+1
2^672-2^192+1 == 2^(32*21)-2^(32*6)+1    2^576-2^240+1 == 2^(16*36)-2^(16*15)+1
2^832-2^448+1 == 2^(64*13)-2^(64*7)+1    2^672-2^560+1 == 2^(16*42)-2^(16*35)+1
2^992-2^832+1 == 2^(32*31)-2^(32*26)+1   2^688-2^96+1  == 2^(16*43)-2^(16*6)+1
2^1088-2^608+1 == 2^(32*34)-2^(32*19)+1  2^784-2^48+1  == 2^(16*49)-2^(16*3)+1
2^1184-2^768+1 == 2^(32*37)-2^(32*24)+1  2^832-2^432+1 == 2^(16*52)-2^(16*27)+1
2^1376-2^32+1  == 2^(32*43)-2^(32*1)+1   2^880-2^368+1 == 2^(16*55)-2^(16*23)+1
2^1664-2^256+1 == 2^(128*13)-2^(128*2)+1 2^912-2^32+1  == 2^(16*57)-2^(16*2)+1
2^1856-2^1056+1 == 2^(32*58)-2^(32*33)+1 2^944-2^784+1 == 2^(16*59)-2^(16*49)+1
2^1920-2^384+1 == 2^(128*15)-2^(128*3)+1 2^1008-2^144+1 == 2^(16*63)-2^(16*9)+1
2^1984-2^544+1 == 2^(32*62)-2^(32*17)+1  2^1024-2^880+1 == 2^(16*64)-2^(16*55)+1
```

Figure 39.2-A: The complete list of primes of the form $p = x^k - x^j + 1$ where $x = 2^G$, $G = 2^i$, $G \geq 32$ and p up to 2048 bits (left) and the equivalent list for $x = 2^{16}$ and p up to 1024 bits (right).

```
? M=x^20-x^15+x^10-x^5+1;
? n=poldegree(M);
? P=sum(i=0,2*n-1,eval(Str("p_"i))*x^i)
  p_39*x^39 + p_38*x^38 + [--snip--] + p_3*x^3 + p_2*x^2 + p_1*x + p_0
? R=P%M;
? for(i=0,n-1,print("  ",eval(Str("r_"i))," = ",polcoeff(R,i)))
  r_0 = p_0 + (-p_20 - p_25)
  r_1 = p_1 + (-p_21 - p_26)
  r_2 = p_2 + (-p_22 - p_27)
  r_3 = p_3 + (-p_23 - p_28)
  r_4 = p_4 + (-p_24 - p_29)
  r_5 = p_5 + (p_20 - p_30)
  r_6 = p_6 + (p_21 - p_31)
  r_7 = p_7 + (p_22 - p_32)
  r_8 = p_8 + (p_23 - p_33)
  r_9 = p_9 + (p_24 - p_34)
  r_10 = p_10 + (-p_20 - p_35)
  r_11 = p_11 + (-p_21 - p_36)
  r_12 = p_12 + (-p_22 - p_37)
  r_13 = p_13 + (-p_23 - p_38)
  r_14 = p_14 + (-p_24 - p_39)
  r_15 = p_15 + p_20
  r_16 = p_16 + p_21
  r_17 = p_17 + p_22
  r_18 = p_18 + p_23
  r_19 = p_19 + p_24
```

Figure 39.2-B: Computation of the reduction rule for the 640-bit prime $Y_{50}(2^{32})$.

product P as

$$P = \sum_{i=0}^{2n-1} p_i\, x^i \qquad\qquad (39.2\text{-}2)$$

where $0 \le p_i < x$. Write the reduced product R as

$$R = \sum_{i=0}^{n-1} r_i\, x^i := P \pmod{M} \qquad\qquad (39.2\text{-}3)$$

where $0 \le r_i < x$. We determine the reduction rules for moduli of the form $x^k - x^j + 1$ (for $k = 3$ and $j = 2$, the rules are the last three lines):

```
? k=3;j=2;
? M=x^k-x^j+1
  x^3 - x^2 + 1
? n=poldegree(M);
? P=sum(i=0,2*n-1,eval(Str("p_"i))*x^i) \\ unreduced product
  p_5*x^5 + p_4*x^4 + p_3*x^3 + p_2*x^2 + p_1*x + p_0
? R=P%M;  \\ reduced product
? for(i=0,n-1,print("  ",eval(Str("r_"i))," = ",polcoeff(R,i)))
  r_0 = p_0 + (-p_3 + (-p_4 - p_5))
  r_1 = p_1 + (-p_4 - p_5)
  r_2 = p_2 + (p_3 + p_4)
```

A list of primes of the form $p = x^k - x^j + 1$ where $x = 2^G$, G a power of 2 and $G \ge 16$ is shown in figure 39.2-A. The equivalent list with i a multiple of 8 is given in [FXT: data/structured-primes-2k2j1.txt]. The primes allow radix-2 number theoretic transforms up to a length of x^j.

Structured primes that are evaluations of cyclotomic polynomials are given in section 39.11.4.7 on page 802. The reduction rule for the 640-bit prime $M = Y_{50}(2^{32})$ is shown in figure 39.2-B. There is a choice for the 'granularity' of the rule: the modulus also equals $Y_{10}(2^{5 \cdot 32})$, so we can obtain the reduction rule for groups of five 32-bit words

```
? M=x^4-x^3+x^2-x^1+1;
  [--snip--]
? for(i=0,n-1,print("  ",eval(Str("r_"i))," = ",polcoeff(R,i)))
  r_0 = p_0 + (-p_4 - p_5)
  r_1 = p_1 + (p_4 - p_6)
  r_2 = p_2 + (-p_4 - p_7)
  r_3 = p_3 + p_4
```

The rule in terms of single words seems to be more appropriate as it allows for easier code generation.

39.3 The sieve of Eratosthenes

Several number theoretic algorithms can take advantage of a precomputed list of primes. A simple and quite efficient algorithm, called the *sieve of Eratosthenes* computes all primes up to a given limit. It uses a tag-array where all entries ≥ 2 are initially marked as potential primes. The algorithm proceeds by searching for the next marked entry and removing all multiples of it.

An implementation that uses the `bitarray` class (see section 4.6 on page 164) is given in [FXT: mod/eratosthenes-demo.cc]:

```
1   void
2   eratosthenes(bitarray &ba)
3   {
4       ba.set_all();
5       ba.clear(0);
6       ba.clear(1);
7       ulong n = ba.n_;
8       ulong k = 0;
9       while ( (k=ba.next_set(k+1)) < n )
10      {
11          for (ulong j=2, i=j*k;  i<n;  ++j, i=j*k)  ba.clear(i);
12      }
13  }
```

The program prints the resulting list of primes (code slightly simplified):

```
int
main(int argc, char **argv)
{
    ulong n = 100;
    bitarray ba(n);
    eratosthenes(ba);

    ulong k = 0;
    ulong ct = 0;
    while ( (k=ba.next_set(k+1)) < n )
    {
        ++ct;
        cout << " " << k;
    }
    cout << endl;
    cout << "Found " << ct << " primes below " << n << "." << endl;
    return 0;
}
```

The output is:

```
 2 3 5 7 1 11 31 71 92 32 93 13 74 14 34 753 59 61 67 71 73 79 83 89 97
Found 25 primes below 100.
```

A little thought leads to a faster variant: when removing the multiples $k \cdot p$ of the prime p from the list we only need to care about the values of k that are greater than all primes found so far. Further, values $k \cdot p$ containing only prime factors less than p have already been removed. That is, we only need to remove the values $\{p^2, p^2 + p, p^2 + 2p, p^2 + 3p, \ldots\}$. This algorithmic improvement can be deduced from the series acceleration of the Lambert series given as relation 37.1-27 on page 708. If we further extract the loop for the prime 2, then for the odd primes, we need to remove only the values $\{p^2, p^2 + 2p, p^2 + 4p, p^2 + 6p, \ldots\}$.

The implementation is [FXT: mod/eratosthenes-demo.cc]:

```
1    void
2    eratosthenes_opt(bitarray &ba)
3    {
4        ba.set_all();
5        ba.clear(0);
6        ba.clear(1);
7        ulong n = ba.n_;
8        for (ulong k=4; k<n; k+=2)  ba.clear(k);
9        ulong r = isqrt(n);
10       ulong k = 0;
11       while ( (k=ba.next_set(k+1)) < n )
12       {
13           if ( k > r )  break;
14           for (ulong j=k*k; j<n; j+=k*2)  ba.clear(j);
15       }
16   }
```

When computing the primes up to a limit N, about N/p values are removed after finding the prime p. If we slightly overestimate the computational work W by

$$W \approx N \sum_{p<N,\,prime} \frac{1}{p} \tag{39.3-1}$$

then we have $W \approx N \log(\log(N))$, which is almost linear. Practically, much of the time used with greater values of N is spent waiting for memory access. Therefore further improvements should rather address machine-specific optimizations than additional algorithmic refinements.

We can save half of the space by recording only the odd primes. A C++ implementation of the modified algorithm is [FXT: mod/eratosthenes.cc]

```
1    bitarray *
2    make_oddprime_bitarray(ulong n, bitarray *ba/*=0*/)
3    {
4        if ( 0!=ba )  delete ba;
5        ba = new bitarray( n/2 );
6
7        ba->set_all();
```

```
8       const ulong m = ba->n_;
9
10      ba->clear(0);
11      ulong r = isqrt(n);
12      ulong i = 3;
13      ulong ih = i/2;
14      while ( i <= r )
15      {
16          if ( ba->test( ih ) )
17          {
18              for (ulong kh=(i*i)/2;  kh<m;  kh+=i)  ba->clear( kh );
19          }
20          ih = ba->next_set( ih+1 );
21          i = 2*ih + 1;
22      }
23
24      return ba;
25  }
```

The corresponding table is created at the startup of programs linking the FXT-library. Now we can verify the primality of small numbers [FXT: mod/primes.cc]:

```
1   bool
2   is_small_prime(ulong n, const bitarray *ba/*=0*/)
3   // Return if n is a small prime.
4   // Return false if table of primes is not big enough.
5   {
6       if ( 0==(n&1) )  return  (2==n); // n even: 2 is prime, else composite
7       if ( n<=1 )  return  0;  // zero or one
8
9       if ( 0==ba )  ba = oddprime_bitarray;
10      ulong nh = n/2;
11      if ( nh >= ba->n_ )  return false;
12      return  ba->test( nh );
13  }
```

The data can also be used to compute the next prime greater than or equal to a given value:

```
1   ulong
2   next_small_prime(ulong n, const bitarray *ba/*=0*/)
3   // Return next prime >= n.
4   // Return zero if table of primes is not big enough.
5   {
6       if ( n<=2 )  return 2;
7
8       if ( 0==ba )  ba = oddprime_bitarray;
9       ulong nh = n/2;
10
11      n = ba->next_set( nh );
12      if ( n==(ba->n_) )  return 0;
13      return  2 * n + 1;
14  }
```

39.4   The Chinese Remainder Theorem (CRT)

Let $m_1, m_2, \ldots, m_f$ be pair-wise coprime (that is, $\gcd(m_i, m_j) = 1$ for all $i \neq j$). If $x \equiv x_i \pmod{m_i}$ for $i = 1, 2, \ldots, f$ then x is unique modulo the product $M = m_1 \cdot m_2 \cdots m_f$. This is the *Chinese remainder theorem* (CRT). Note that it is not assumed that any of the m_i is prime.

The theorem tells us that a computation modulo a composite number M can be split into separate computations modulo the coprime factors of M. To evaluate a function $y := F(x) \bmod M$ where $M = m_1 \cdot m_2 \cdot \ldots \cdot m_f$ (with $\gcd(m_i, m_j) = 1$ for all $i \neq j$), proceed as follows

1. Splitting: compute $x_1 = x \bmod m_1$, $x_2 = x \bmod m_2$, ..., $x_f = x \bmod m_f$.

2. Separate computations: compute $y_1 := F(x_1) \bmod m_1$, $y_2 := F(x_2) \bmod m_2$, ..., $F(x_f) = F(x_f) \bmod m_f$.

3. Recombination: compute y from $y_1, y_2, \ldots, y_f$ using the CRT.

For example, when computing the exact convolution of a long sequence via number theoretic transforms (see section 26.3 on page 542) the largest term of the result must be less than the modulus. Assume that (efficient) modular arithmetic is available for moduli of at most word size. Now choose several coprime moduli that fit into a word and whose product M is greater than the largest element of the result. Compute the transforms separately and only at the very end compute, via the CRT, the result modulo M. Note that only the result needs to be less than M, we do not need to worry about intermediate quantities.

39.4.1 Efficient computation

For two moduli m_1, m_2 compute x with $x \equiv x_1 \pmod{m_1}$ and $x \equiv x_2 \pmod{m_2}$ as suggested by the following pseudocode:

```
1    function crt2(x1, m1, x2, m2)
2    {
3        c := m1**(-1) mod m2    // inverse of m1 modulo m2
4
5        s := ((x2-x1)*c) mod m2
6
7        return  x1 + s * m1
8    }
```

For repeated CRT calculations with the same modulus one should precompute and store $c = m_1^{-1} \bmod m_2$. With more than two moduli use the above algorithm repeatedly. As pseudocode:

```
1    function crt(x[0,...,f-1], m[0,...,f-1], f)
2    {
3        x1 := x[0]
4        m1 := m[0]
5        i := 1
6        do
7        {
8            x2 := x[i]
9            m2 := m[i]
10           x1 := crt2(x1, m1, x2, m2)
11           m1 := m1 * m2
12           i := i + 1
13       }
14       while i < f
15       return x1
16   }
```

A C++ implementation is given in [FXT: mod/chinese.cc]:

```
1    umod_t
2    chinese(const umod_t *x, const factorization &f)
3    // Return R modulo M where:
4    //    f[] is the factorization of M,
5    //    x[] := R modulo the prime powers of f[].
6    {
7        const int n = f.nprimes();
8        // (omitted test that gcd(m_0,...,m_{n-1})=1 )
9
10       const umod_t M = f.product();
11       umod_t R = 0;
12       for (int i=0; i<n; ++i)
13       {
14           // Ti = prod(mk)  (where k!=i);  Ti==M/mi:
15           const umod_t Ti = M / f.primepow(i);  // exact division
16
17           // ci = 1 / Ti:
18           umod_t ci = inv_modpp(Ti, f.prime(i), f.exponent(i));
19           // here:   0 <= ci < mi
20
21           // Xi = x[i] * ci * Ti:
22           umod_t Xi = ci * Ti;  // 0 <= Xi < M
23           Xi = mul_mod(Xi, x[i], M);
24
25           // add Xi to result:
26           R = add_mod(R, Xi, M);
27       }
28
29       return R;
30   }
```

39.4.2   The underlying construction ‡

We derive the algorithm for CRT recombination from a construction for k coprime moduli. Define T_i as

$$T_i \ := \ \prod_{k \neq i} m_k \qquad\qquad (39.4\text{-}1)$$

and c_i as

$$c_i \ := \ T_i^{-1} \ \ \mathrm{mod} \ m_i \qquad\qquad (39.4\text{-}2)$$

Then for X_i defined as

$$X_i \ := \ x_i \, c_i \, T_i \qquad\qquad (39.4\text{-}3)$$

one has

$$X_i \ \ \mathrm{mod} \ m_j \ = \ \begin{cases} x_i & \text{if } j = i \\ 0 & \text{otherwise} \end{cases} \qquad\qquad (39.4\text{-}4)$$

Therefore

$$x \ := \ \sum_k X_k \ = \ x_i \ \mathrm{mod} \ m_i \qquad\qquad (39.4\text{-}5)$$

For the special case of two moduli m_1, m_2 one has

$$T_1 \ = \ m_2, \qquad T_2 \ = \ m_1 \qquad\qquad (39.4\text{-}6\text{a})$$
$$c_1 \ = \ m_2^{-1} \ \ \mathrm{mod} \ m_1, \qquad c_2 \ = \ m_1^{-1} \ \ \mathrm{mod} \ m_2 \qquad\qquad (39.4\text{-}6\text{b})$$

The quantities are related by

$$c_1 \, m_2 + c_2 \, m_1 \ = \ 1 \qquad\qquad (39.4\text{-}7)$$

and

$$x \ = \ \sum_k X_k \ = \ x_1 \, c_1 \, T_1 + x_2 \, c_2 \, T_2 \qquad\qquad (39.4\text{-}8\text{a})$$
$$= \ x_1 \, c_1 \, m_2 + x_2 \, c_2 \, m_1 \qquad\qquad (39.4\text{-}8\text{b})$$
$$= \ x_1 \, (1 - c_2 \, m_1) + x_2 \, c_2 \, m_1 \qquad\qquad (39.4\text{-}8\text{c})$$
$$= \ x_1 + (x_2 - x_1) \, (m_1^{-1} \ \ \mathrm{mod} \ m_2) \, m_1 \qquad\qquad (39.4\text{-}8\text{d})$$

The last equality is used in the code.

39.5   The order of an element

The (multiplicative) *order* $r = \mathrm{ord}(a)$ of an element a is the smallest positive exponent so that $a^r = 1$. For elements that are not invertible ($\gcd(a, m) \neq 1$) the order is not defined. Figure 39.5-A shows the powers of all elements modulo the prime 13. The rightmost column gives the order of those elements that are invertible.

An element a whose r-th power equals 1 is called an *r-th root of unity*: $a^r = 1$. Modulo 9 both elements 2 and 4 are 6th roots of unity, see figure 39.5-B.

If $a^r = 1$ but $a^x \neq 1$ for all $x < r$, then a is called a *primitive r-th root of unity*. Modulo 9 the element 2 is a primitive 6th root of unity; the element 4 is not, it is a primitive 3rd root of unity. An element of order r is an r-th primitive root of unity.

```
          0  1  2  3  4  5  6  7  8  9 10 11 12 <--= exponent
         ----------------------------------------- [order]
     0    1  0  0  0  0  0  0  0  0  0  0  0  0   [ --]
     1    1  1  1  1  1  1  1  1  1  1  1  1  1   [  1]
     2    1  2  4  8  3  6 12 11  9  5 10  7  1   [ 12]
     3    1  3  9  1  3  9  1  3  9  1  3  9  1   [  3]
     4    1  4  3 12  9 10  1  4  3 12  9 10  1   [  6]
     5    1  5 12  8  1  5 12  8  1  5 12  8  1   [  4]
     6    1  6 10  8  9  2 12  7  3  5  4 11  1   [ 12]
     7    1  7 10  5  9 11 12  6  3  8  4  2  1   [ 12]
     8    1  8 12  5  1  8 12  5  1  8 12  5  1   [  4]
     9    1  9  3  1  9  3  1  9  3  1  9  3  1   [  3]
    10    1 10  9 12  3  4  1 10  9 12  3  4  1   [  6]
    11    1 11  4  5  3  7 12  2  9  8 10  6  1   [ 12]
    12    1 12  1 12  1 12  1 12  1 12  1 12  1   [  2]
```

Figure 39.5-A: Powers and orders modulo 13, the maximal order is $R(13) = 12 = \varphi(13)$.

```
      0 1 2 3 4 5 6 7 8 <--= exponent              0 1 2 3 4 5 6 <--= exponent
     ------------------- [order]                  --------------- [order]
   0  1 0 0 0 0 0 0 0 0  [ --]                  1  1 1 1 1 1 1 1  [ 1]
   1  1 1 1 1 1 1 1 1 1  [  1]                  2  1 2 4 8 7 5 1  [ 6]
   2  1 2 4 8 7 5 1 2 4  [  6]                  4  1 4 7 1 4 7 1  [ 3]
   3  1 3 0 0 0 0 0 0 0  [ --]                  5  1 5 7 8 4 2 1  [ 6]
   4  1 4 7 1 4 7 1 4 7  [  3]                  7  1 7 4 1 7 4 1  [ 3]
   5  1 5 7 8 4 2 1 5 7  [  6]                  8  1 8 1 8 1 8 1  [ 2]
   6  1 6 0 0 0 0 0 0 0  [ --]
   7  1 7 4 1 7 4 1 7 4  [  3]
   8  1 8 1 8 1 8 1 8 1  [  2]
```

Figure 39.5-B: Powers and orders modulo 9 (left), the maximal order is $R(9) = 6 = \varphi(9)$. The order modulo m is defined only for elements a where $\gcd(a, m) = 1$. The table of powers for the group of units $(\mathbb{Z}/9\mathbb{Z})^*$ (right) is obtained by dropping all elements for which the order is undefined.

The *maximal order* $R(m)$ is simply the maximum of the orders of all elements for a fixed modulus m. For prime modulus p the maximal order equals $R(p) = p - 1$. We omit the argument p of the maximal order where it cannot cause confusion.

An element of maximal order is an R-th primitive root of unity. Roots of unity of an order different from R are available only for the divisors d_i of R: if g is an element of maximal order R, then g^{R/d_i} has order d_i (it is a primitive d_i-th root of unity):

$$\mathrm{ord}\left(g^{R/d_i}\right) = d_i \tag{39.5-1}$$

This is because $(g^{R/d_i})^{d_i} = g^R = 1$ and $(g^{R/d_i})^k \neq 1$ for $k < d_i$.

The factor by which the order of an element falls short of the maximal order is sometimes called the *index* of the element. Let i be the index and r the order, then $i \cdot r = R$.

The concept of the order comes from group theory. The invertible elements modulo m with multiplication form a group: the *multiplicative group*. The neutral element is 1. The (multiplicative) order defined above is the order in this group, it tells us how often we have to multiply the element to 1 to get 1. We restrict orders to positive values, else every element would have order zero.

With addition things are simpler, all elements with addition form a group with 0 as neutral element: the *additive group*. The additive order of an element in this group tells us how often we have to add the element to 0 to get 0. The additive order of the element a modulo m is simply $m/\gcd(a, m)$. All elements coprime to m (and especially 1 and -1) are generators of the additive group.

The maximal order R of all elements of a group is sometimes called the *exponent of the group*. With certain moduli the powers of the elements of maximal order generate the whole multiplicative group. Such elements are called *primitive elements*, *primitive roots*, or *generators* of the group. In what follows we describe under which conditions the multiplicative group has generators.

39.6 Prime modulus: the field $\mathbb{Z}/p\mathbb{Z} = \mathbb{F}_p = \mathrm{GF}(p)$

If the modulus is a prime p, then $\mathbb{Z}/p\mathbb{Z}$ is the finite field $\mathbb{F}_p = \mathrm{GF}(p)$: all elements except 0 have inverses and thereby division is possible in $\mathrm{GF}(p)$. The maximal order R equals $p - 1$. Elements of order R are called *primitive roots modulo p* or *generators modulo p*.

If g is a generator, then every element in $\mathrm{GF}(p)$ different from 0 is equal to some power g^e ($1 \leq e < p$) of g and its order is R/e. To test whether g is a primitive root we only need to check whether

$$g^{(p-1)/q_i} \neq 1 \bmod p \tag{39.6-1}$$

for all prime divisors of q_i of $p - 1$. To find a primitive root, use a simple search:

```
1   function primroot(p)
2   {
3       if p==2 then  return 1
4       f[] := distinct_prime_factors(p-1)
5       for r:=2 to p-1
6       {
7           x := TRUE
8           foreach q in f[]
9           {
10              if r**((p-1)/q)==1 then x:=FALSE
11          }
12          if x==TRUE then  return r
13      }
14      error("no primitive root found")  // p cannot be prime !
15  }
```

In practice the root is found after only a few tries. Note that the factorization of $p - 1$ must be known. An element of order n in $\mathrm{GF}(p)$ is returned by the following function, n must divide $p - 1$:

```
1   function element_of_order(n, p)
2   {
3       R := p-1  // maxorder
4       r := primroot(p)
5       x := r**(R/n)
6       return x
7   }
```

39.7 Composite modulus: the ring $\mathbb{Z}/m\mathbb{Z}$

In what follows we will need the function φ, the *totient function* (or *Euler's totient function*). The function $\varphi(m)$ counts the number of integers coprime to and less than m:

$$\varphi(m) \quad := \quad \sum_{\substack{1 \leq k < m \\ \gcd(k,m)=1}} 1 \tag{39.7-1}$$

The sequence of values $\varphi(n)$ is entry A000010 in [312]. The values of $\varphi(n)$ for $n \leq 96$ are shown in figure 39.7-A. For $m = p$ prime we have

$$\varphi(p) = p - 1 \tag{39.7-2}$$

For m composite $\varphi(m)$ is always less than $m - 1$. For $m = p^k$ a prime power we have

$$\varphi(p^k) = p^k - p^{k-1} = p^{k-1}(p - 1) \tag{39.7-3}$$

$n\!:\!\varphi(n)$	$n\!:\!\varphi(n)$	$n\!:\!\varphi(n)$	$n\!:\!\varphi(n)$	$n\!:\!\varphi(n)$	$n\!:\!\varphi(n)$	$n\!:\!\varphi(n)$	$n\!:\!\varphi(n)$
1: 1	13: 12	25: 20	37: 36	49: 42	61: 60	73: 72	85: 64
2: 1	14: 6	26: 12	38: 18	50: 20	62: 30	74: 36	86: 42
3: 2	15: 8	27: 18	39: 24	51: 32	63: 36	75: 40	87: 56
4: 2	16: 8	28: 12	40: 16	52: 24	64: 32	76: 36	88: 40
5: 4	17: 16	29: 28	41: 40	53: 52	65: 48	77: 60	89: 88
6: 2	18: 6	30: 8	42: 12	54: 18	66: 20	78: 24	90: 24
7: 6	19: 18	31: 30	43: 42	55: 40	67: 66	79: 78	91: 72
8: 4	20: 8	32: 16	44: 20	56: 24	68: 32	80: 32	92: 44
9: 6	21: 12	33: 20	45: 24	57: 36	69: 44	81: 54	93: 60
10: 4	22: 10	34: 16	46: 22	58: 28	70: 24	82: 40	94: 46
11: 10	23: 22	35: 24	47: 46	59: 58	71: 70	83: 82	95: 72
12: 4	24: 8	36: 12	48: 16	60: 16	72: 24	84: 24	96: 32

Figure 39.7-A: Values of $\varphi(n)$, the number of integers less than n and coprime to n, for $n \leq 96$.

The totient function is a *multiplicative* function: one has $\varphi(x_1\,x_2) = \varphi(x_1)\,\varphi(x_2)$ for coprime x_1, x_2, that is, $\gcd(x_1, x_2) = 1$ (but x_1 and x_2 are not required to be primes). Thus, if p_i are the distinct primes in the factorization of n, then

$$\varphi(n) \;=\; \prod_i \varphi(p_i^{e_i}) \qquad \text{where} \quad n = \prod_i p_k^{e_i} \tag{39.7-4}$$

An alternative expression for $\varphi(n)$ is

$$\varphi(n) \;=\; n \prod_{p_i}\left(1 - \frac{1}{p_i}\right) \qquad \text{where} \quad n = \prod_i p_k^{e_i} \tag{39.7-5}$$

We note a generalization: the number of s-element sets of numbers $\leq n$ whose greatest common divisor is coprime to n equals

$$\varphi_s(n) \;=\; n^s \prod_{p_i}\left(1 - \frac{1}{p_i^s}\right) \qquad \text{where} \quad n = \prod_i p_i^{e_i} \tag{39.7-6}$$

Pseudocode to compute $\varphi(m)$ for arbitrary m:

```
1    function euler_phi(m)
2    {
3        { n, p[], x[] } := factorization(m)   // m==product(i=0..n-1, p[i]**x[i])
4        ph := 1
5        for i:=0 to n-1
6        {
7            k = := x[i]   // exponent
8            ph := ph * (p[i]**(k-1)) * (p[i]-1)   // ==ph * euler_phi(p[i]**x[i])
9        }
10   }
```

The *multiplicative group* consists of the invertible elements (or *units*) and is denoted by $(\mathbb{Z}/m\mathbb{Z})^*$. The size of the group $(\mathbb{Z}/m\mathbb{Z})^*$ equals the number of units:

$$\left|(\mathbb{Z}/m\mathbb{Z})^*\right| \;=\; \varphi(m) \tag{39.7-7}$$

If m factorizes as $m = 2^{e_0} \cdot p_1^{e_1} \cdot \ldots \cdot p_q^{e_q}$ where p_i are pair-wise distinct primes, then

$$\left|(\mathbb{Z}/m\mathbb{Z})^*\right| \;=\; \varphi\left(2^{e_0}\right) \cdot \varphi\left(p_1^{e_1}\right) \cdot \ldots \cdot \varphi\left(p_q^{e_q}\right) \tag{39.7-8}$$

Further, the group $(\mathbb{Z}/m\mathbb{Z})^*$ is isomorphic to the direct product of the multiplicative groups modulo the prime powers:

$$(\mathbb{Z}/m\mathbb{Z})^* \;\simeq\; (\mathbb{Z}/2^{e_0}\mathbb{Z})^* \times (\mathbb{Z}/p_1^{e_1}\mathbb{Z})^* \times \cdots \times (\mathbb{Z}/p_q^{e_q}\mathbb{Z})^* \tag{39.7-9}$$

The relation suggests that we can, instead of working modulo m, do computations modulo all prime powers in parallel. The Chinese remainder theorem (section 39.4 on page 772) tells us how to find the element modulo m, given the results modulo the prime powers. The other direction is simply modular reduction.

39.7.1 Cyclic and noncyclic multiplicative groups

```
       0  1  2  3  4  5  6  7  8  9 10 11 12 13 14                    0  1  2  3  4
     ---------------------------------------------              --------------------
 0   1  0  0  0  0  0  0  0  0  0  0  0  0  0  0  [ --]      1   1  1  1  1  1   [ 1]
 1   1  1  1  1  1  1  1  1  1  1  1  1  1  1  1  [  1]      2   1  2  4  8  1   [ 4]
 2   1  2  4  8  1  2  4  8  1  2  4  8  1  2  4  [  4]      4   1  4  1  4  1   [ 2]
 3   1  3  9 12  6  3  9 12  6  3  9 12  6  3  9  [ --]      7   1  7  4 13  1   [ 4]
 4   1  4  1  4  1  4  1  4  1  4  1  4  1  4  1  [  2]      8   1  8  4  2  1   [ 4]
 5   1  5 10  5 10  5 10  5 10  5 10  5 10  5 10  [ --]     11   1 11  1 11  1   [ 2]
 6   1  6  6  6  6  6  6  6  6  6  6  6  6  6  6  [ --]     13   1 13  4  7  1   [ 4]
 7   1  7  4 13  1  7  4 13  1  7  4 13  1  7  4  [  4]     14   1 14  1 14  1   [ 2]
 8   1  8  4  2  1  8  4  2  1  8  4  2  1  8  4  [  4]
 9   1  9  6  9  6  9  6  9  6  9  6  9  6  9  6  [ --]
10   1 10 10 10 10 10 10 10 10 10 10 10 10 10 10  [ --]
11   1 11  1 11  1 11  1 11  1 11  1 11  1 11  1  [  2]
12   1 12  9  3  6 12  9  3  6 12  9  3  6 12  9  [ --]
13   1 13  4  7  1 13  4  7  1 13  4  7  1 13  4  [  4]
14   1 14  1 14  1 14  1 14  1 14  1 14  1 14  1  [  2]
```

Figure 39.7-B: Powers and orders modulo 15 (left). The group $(\mathbb{Z}/15\mathbb{Z})^*$ is noncyclic: there are $\varphi(15) = 8$ invertible elements but no element generates all of them as the maximal order is $R(15) = 4 < \varphi(15)$. The table of powers for the group $(\mathbb{Z}/15\mathbb{Z})^*$ (right) is obtained by dropping all non-invertible elements.

If the maximal order $R(m)$ is equal to $|(\mathbb{Z}/m\mathbb{Z})^*| = \varphi(m)$, then the multiplicative group $(\mathbb{Z}/m\mathbb{Z})^*$ is called *cyclic*, else we call it *noncyclic*. The term cyclic reflects that the powers of any element of maximal order 'cycle through' all elements of $(\mathbb{Z}/m\mathbb{Z})^*$. An element of maximal order in a cyclic group is also called a *generator* as its powers 'generate' all elements.

Figure 39.7-B shows the powers and orders of the noncyclic group $(\mathbb{Z}/15\mathbb{Z})^*$ where no element generates all units. The groups $(\mathbb{Z}/13\mathbb{Z})^*$ and $(\mathbb{Z}/9\mathbb{Z})^*$ are cyclic, see figure 39.5-A on page 775 and figure 39.5-B.

For prime modulus m the group $(\mathbb{Z}/m\mathbb{Z})^*$ contains all nonzero elements and any element of maximal order is a generator of the group.

For m a power p^k of an odd prime p the maximal order R in $(\mathbb{Z}/m\mathbb{Z})^*$ is

$$R\left(p^k\right) \;=\; \varphi\left(p^k\right) \tag{39.7-10}$$

For m a power of 2 an irregularity occurs:

$$R(2^k) \;=\; \begin{cases} 1 & \text{for } k = 1 \\ 2 & \text{for } k = 2 \\ 2^{k-2} & \text{for } k \geq 3 \end{cases} \tag{39.7-11}$$

That is, for powers of 2 greater than 4 the maximal order falls short from $\varphi(2^k) = 2^{k-1}$ by a factor of 2. For the general modulus $m = 2^{k_0} \cdot p_1^{k_1} \cdot \ldots \cdot p_q^{k_q}$ the maximal order is

$$R(m) \;=\; \mathrm{lcm}\left(R\left(2^{k_0}\right), R\left(p_1^{k_1}\right), \ldots, R\left(p_q^{k_q}\right)\right) \tag{39.7-12}$$

39.7.1.1   Computation of the maximal order

The maximal order $R(m)$ of an element in $(\mathbb{Z}/m\mathbb{Z})^*$ can be computed as follows:

```
1  function maxorder(m)
2  {
3      {n, p[], k[]} := factorization(m)   // m==product(i=0..n-1,p[i]**k[i])
4
5      R := 1
6      for i:=0 to n-1
7      {
8          t := euler_phi_pp(p[i], k[i])   // ==euler_phi(p[i]**k[i])
9          if p[i]==2 AND k[i]>=3 then  t := t / 2
10         R := lcm(R, t)
11     }
12
13     return R
14 }
```

Now we can see for which moduli m the multiplicative group $(\mathbb{Z}/m\mathbb{Z})^*$ will be cyclic:

$$(\mathbb{Z}/m\mathbb{Z})^* \quad \text{is cyclic for} \quad m = 2,\, 4,\, p^k,\, 2 \cdot p^k \qquad \text{where } p \text{ is an odd prime} \qquad (39.7\text{-}13)$$

If the factorization of m contains two different odd primes p_a and p_b, then

$$R(m) \;=\; \text{lcm}(\ldots, \varphi(p_a), \ldots, \varphi(p_b), \ldots)$$

is at least by a factor of 2 smaller than

$$\varphi(m) \;=\; \ldots \cdot \varphi(p_a) \cdot \ldots \cdot \varphi(p_b) \cdot \ldots$$

because both $\varphi(p_a)$ and $\varphi(p_b)$ are even. So $(\mathbb{Z}/m\mathbb{Z})^*$ cannot be cyclic in that case. The same argument holds for $m = 2^{k_0} \cdot p^k$ if $k_0 > 1$. For $m = 2^k$ the group $(\mathbb{Z}/m\mathbb{Z})^*$ is cyclic only for $k = 1$ and $k = 2$ because of the mentioned irregularity of power of 2 (relation 39.7-11).

39.7.1.2   Computation of the order of an element

Pseudocode for a function that returns the order of a given element x in $(\mathbb{Z}/m\mathbb{Z})^*$:

```
1  function order(x, m)
2  {
3      if gcd(x,m)!=1 then  return 0  // x not a unit
4      h := euler_phi(m)  // number of units
5      e := h
6      { n, p[], k[] } := factorization(h)  // h==product(i=0..n-1,p[i]**k[i])
7
8      for i:=0 to n-1
9      {
10         f := p[i]**k[i]
11         e := e / f
12         g1 := x**e mod m
13         while g1!=1
14         {
15             g1 := g1**p[i] mod m
16             e := e * p[i]
17         }
18     }
19
20     return e
21 }
```

Pseudocode for a function that returns an element x in $(\mathbb{Z}/m\mathbb{Z})^*$ of maximal order:

```
1  function maxorder_element(m)
2  {
3      R := maxorder(m)
4      for x:=1 to m-1
5      {
6          if order(x, m)==R then  return x
7      }
8      // never reached
9  }
```

Again, while the function does a simple search it is efficient in practice. For prime m the function returns a primitive root. A C++ implementation is given in [FXT: mod/maxorder.cc]. Note that for noncyclic groups the returned element does not necessarily have maximal order modulo all factors of the modulus. We list all elements of $(\mathbb{Z}/15\mathbb{Z})^*$ together with their orders modulo 15, 3, and 5:

```
 1:   r=1   r3=1   r5=1
 2:   r=4   r3=2   r5=4
 4:   r=2   r3=1   r5=2
 7:   r=4   r3=1   r5=4   <--=
 8:   r=4   r3=2   r5=4
11:   r=2   r3=2   r5=1
13:   r=4   r3=1   r5=4   <--=
14:   r=2   r3=2   r5=2
```

The two elements marked with an arrow have maximal order modulo 15, but not modulo 3. An element of maximal order modulo all factors of a composite modulus (equivalently, maximal order in all subgroups) can be found by computing a generator for all cyclic subgroups and applying the Chinese remainder algorithm given in section 39.4 on page 772.

39.7.2 Generators in cyclic groups

Let G be the set of all generators in a cyclic group modulo n. Then the number of generators is given by

$$|G| \;=\; \varphi\,(\varphi(n)) \tag{39.7-14}$$

Let g be a generator, then g^k is a generator if and only if $\gcd(k, \varphi(n)) = 1$. There are $\varphi\,(\varphi(n))$ numbers k that are coprime to $\varphi(n)$.

Let g be a generator modulo a prime p. Then g is a generator modulo $2\,p^k$ for all $k \geq 1$ if g is odd. If g is even, then $g + p^k$ is a generator modulo $2\,p^k$.

Further, g is a generator modulo p^k if $g^{p-1} \bmod p^2 \neq 1$. The only primes below $2^{36} \approx 68 \cdot 10^9$ for which the smallest primitive root is not a generator modulo p^2 are 2, 40487 and 6692367337. Such primes are called *non-generous primes*, see entry A055578 in [312].

The only known primes p below $32 \cdot 10^{12}$ where $2^{p-1} = 1$ modulo p^2 are 1093 and 3511 (such primes are called *Wieferich primes*, see entry A001220 in [312]). Now 2 is not a generator modulo either of the two. Thus, whenever 2 is a generator modulo a prime $p < 32 \cdot 10^{12}$, it is also a generator modulo p^k for all $k > 1$.

39.7.3 Generators in noncyclic groups

If the group is cyclic, an element of maximal order generates all invertible elements. With noncyclic groups one needs more than one generator. GP's function `znstar()` gives the complete information about the multiplicative group of units. The help text reads:

```
znstar(n): 3-component vector v, giving the structure of (Z/nZ)^*.
 v[1] is the order (i.e. eulerphi(n)),
 v[2] is a vector of cyclic components, and
 v[3] is a vector giving the corresponding  generators.
```

Its output for $2 \leq n \leq 25$ is shown in figure 39.7-C.

The group is cyclic if there is just one generator. In general, when `znstar(n)` returns

$$[\varphi, \; [r_1, r_2, \ldots, r_k], \; [g_1, g_2, \ldots, g_k]] \tag{39.7-15}$$

then the φ invertible elements u are of the form

$$u \;=\; g_1^{e_1}\, g_2^{e_2}\, \cdots\, g_k^{e_k} \tag{39.7-16}$$

where $0 \leq e_i < r_i$ for $1 \leq i \leq k$. For example, with $n = 15$:

```
? for(n=2,25,print(n," ",znstar(n)))
    2 [1,   [],     []]      /* read:  [1, [1], [Mod(1,2)]] */
    3 [2,   [2],    [Mod(2, 3)]]
    4 [2,   [2],    [Mod(3, 4)]]
    5 [4,   [4],    [Mod(2, 5)]]
    6 [2,   [2],    [Mod(5, 6)]]
    7 [6,   [6],    [Mod(3, 7)]]
    8 [4,   [2, 2], [Mod(5, 8), Mod(3, 8)]]
    9 [6,   [6],    [Mod(2, 9)]]
   10 [4,   [4],    [Mod(7, 10)]]
   11 [10,  [10],   [Mod(2, 11)]]
   12 [4,   [2, 2], [Mod(7, 12), Mod(5, 12)]]
   13 [12,  [12],   [Mod(2, 13)]]
   14 [6,   [6],    [Mod(3, 14)]]
   15 [8,   [4, 2], [Mod(8, 15), Mod(11, 15)]]
   16 [8,   [4, 2], [Mod(5, 16), Mod(7, 16)]]
   17 [16,  [16],   [Mod(3, 17)]]
   18 [6,   [6],    [Mod(11, 18)]]
   19 [18,  [18],   [Mod(2, 19)]]
   20 [8,   [4, 2], [Mod(3, 20), Mod(11, 20)]]
   21 [12,  [6, 2], [Mod(5, 21), Mod(8, 21)]]
   22 [10,  [10],   [Mod(13, 22)]]
   23 [22,  [22],   [Mod(5, 23)]]
   24 [8,   [2, 2, 2], [Mod(13, 24), Mod(19, 24), Mod(17, 24)]]
   25 [20,  [20],   [Mod(2, 25)]]
```

Figure 39.7-C: Structure of the multiplicative groups modulo n for $2 \leq n \leq 25$.

```
? znstar(15)
 [8, [4, 2], [Mod(8, 15), Mod(11, 15)]]
? g1=Mod(8, 15); g2=Mod(11,15);
? for(e1=0,4-1,for(e2=0,2-1,print(e1," ",e2,"  ",g1^e1*g2^e2)))
  0 0  Mod(1, 15)
  0 1  Mod(11, 15)
  1 0  Mod(8, 15)
  1 1  Mod(13, 15)
  2 0  Mod(4, 15)
  2 1  Mod(14, 15)
  3 0  Mod(2, 15)
  3 1  Mod(7, 15)
```

The multiplicative group modulo $n = 2^k$ is cyclic only for $k \leq 2$:

```
? for(i=1,6,print(i,": ",znstar(2^i)))
  1: [1, [], []]
  2: [2, [2], [Mod(3, 4)]]
  3: [4, [2, 2], [Mod(5, 8), Mod(3, 8)]]
  4: [8, [4, 2], [Mod(5, 16), Mod(7, 16)]]
  5: [16, [8, 2], [Mod(5, 32), Mod(15, 32)]]
  6: [32, [16, 2], [Mod(5, 64), Mod(31, 64)]]
```

For $k \geq 3$ the multiplicative group is generated by the two elements 5 and -1.

39.7.4 Inversion by exponentiation

For a unit u of order $r = \text{ord}(u)$ one has $u^r = 1$. As r divides the maximal order R also $u^R = 1$ holds and so $u^{R-1} \cdot u = 1$. That is, the inverse of any invertible element u equals u to the $(R-1)$-st power:

$$u^{-1} \;=\; u^{R-1} \tag{39.7-17}$$

In fact, one has also $u^{-1} = u^{\varphi(m)-1}$ which may involve slightly more work if the group is noncyclic.

39.8 Quadratic residues

Let p be a prime. The *quadratic residues modulo* p are those values a so that the equation

$$x^2 \;\equiv\; a \pmod{p} \tag{39.8-1}$$

has a solution. If the equation has no solution, then a is called a *quadratic non-residue modulo p* or simply a *non-residue*. A quadratic residue is a square (modulo p) of some number, so we can safely just call it a *square modulo p*. Another short form is simply *residue*.

Let g be a primitive root (the particular choice does not matter), then every nonzero element x can uniquely be written as $x = g^e$ where $0 < e < p$. Rewriting equation 39.8-1 as $x^2 = (g^e)^2 = g^{2e} = a$ makes it apparent that the quadratic residues are the even powers of g. The non-residues are the odd powers of g. All generators are non-residues: $g = g^1$.

Let us compute $f(x) := x^{(p-1)/2}$ for both residues and non-residues: With a quadratic residue g^{2e} we get $f(g^{2e}) = g^{2e(p-1)/2} = 1^e = 1$ where we used $g^{p-1} = 1$. With a non-residue $a = g^k$, k odd, we get $f(a) = f(g^k) = g^{k(p-1)/2} = -1$ where we used $g^{(p-1)/2} = -1$ (the only square root of 1 apart from 1 is -1) and $-1^k = -1$ for k odd.

Apparently we just found a function that can tell residues from non-residues. In fact, we rediscovered the *Legendre symbol* usually written as $\left(\dfrac{a}{p}\right)$. A surprising property of the Legendre symbol is the *law of quadratic reciprocity*: Let p and q be distinct odd primes, then

$$\left(\frac{p}{q}\right) = (-1)^{\frac{p-1}{2}\frac{q-1}{2}}\left(\frac{q}{p}\right) \tag{39.8-2}$$

Also the following relations hold:

$$\left(\frac{-1}{p}\right) = (-1)^{\frac{p-1}{2}} = \begin{cases} +1 & \text{if } p \equiv 1 \pmod 4 \\ -1 & \text{if } p \equiv 3 \pmod 4 \end{cases} \tag{39.8-3a}$$

$$\left(\frac{2}{p}\right) = (-1)^{\frac{p^2-1}{8}} = \begin{cases} +1 & \text{if } p \equiv \pm 1 \pmod 8 \\ -1 & \text{if } p \equiv \pm 3 \pmod 8 \end{cases} \tag{39.8-3b}$$

$$\left(\frac{3}{p}\right) = 1 \iff p \equiv \pm 1 \bmod 12 \tag{39.8-3c}$$

$$\left(\frac{-3}{p}\right) = 1 \iff p = 2,\ p = 3,\ \text{or } p \equiv 1 \bmod 3 \tag{39.8-3d}$$

If a is a square modulo p, then the polynomial $x^2 - a$ (with coefficients modulo p) factors as $(x - r_1)(x - r_2)$ where $r_1^2 \equiv a$ and $r_2^2 \equiv a$. The number -1 is a square modulo $41 = 4 \cdot 10 + 1$ and we have $x^2 + 1 = (x - 9)(x - 32)$. The polynomial $x^2 + 1$ with coefficients modulo $43 = 4 \cdot 10 + 3$ is irreducible, -1 is not a square modulo 43.

The relation between the Legendre symbols of positive and negative arguments is

$$\left(\frac{-a}{p}\right) = (-1)^{\frac{p-1}{2}}\left(\frac{a}{p}\right) = \begin{cases} +\left(\frac{a}{p}\right) & \text{if } p = 4k + 1 \\ -\left(\frac{a}{p}\right) & \text{if } p = 4k + 3 \end{cases} \tag{39.8-4}$$

Modulo a prime $p = 4k + 3$, if $+a$ is a square, then $-a$ is not a square. The orders of any two elements $+a$ and $-a$ differ by a factor of 2. Non-residues can easily be found: $-(b^2)$ is a non-residue for all b.

Modulo a prime $p = 4k + 1$, if $+a$ is a square, then $-a$ is also a square. The orders of two non-residues $+a$ and $-a$ are identical. The orders of two residues $+a$ and $-a$ can be identical or differ by a factor of 2.

A special case are primes of the form $p = 2^x + 1$, the *Fermat primes*. Only five Fermat primes are known today: $2^1 + 1 = 3$, $2^2 + 1 = 5$, $2^4 + 1 = 17$, $2^8 + 1 = 257$ and $2^{16} + 1 = 65537$. To be prime the exponent x must be a power of 2. The primitive roots are exactly the non-residues: the maximal order equals $R = \varphi(p) = 2^x$. There are $\varphi(\varphi(p)) = 2^{x-1}$ primitive roots. There are $(p-1)/2 = 2^{x-1}$ squares which all have order at most $R/2$. The remaining 2^{x-1} non-residues must all be primitive roots.

We will not pursue the issue, but it should be noted that there are more efficient ways than powering to determine the Legendre symbol. A generalization of the Legendre symbol for composite moduli is the *Kronecker symbol*. An efficient implementation for its computation (following [110, p.29]) is given in [FXT: mod/kronecker.cc]:

```
 b\a  0  2  4  6  8 10 12 14 16 18 20 22 24 26 28 30 32 34 36
  0 : 0 + 0 0 0 0 0 0 0 0 0 0 0 0 0 0 0 0 0 0 0 0 0 0 0 0 0 0 0 0 0 0 0 0 0 0 0 0
  1 :: + + + + + + + + + + + + + + + + + + + + + + + + + + + + + + + + + + + + + +
  2 : 0 + 0 - 0 - 0 + 0 + 0 - 0 - 0 + 0 + 0 - 0 - 0 + 0 + 0 - 0 - 0 + 0 + 0 - 0 - 0 -
  3 : 0 + - 0 + - 0 + - 0 + - 0 + - 0 + - 0 + - 0 + - 0 + - 0 + - 0 + - 0 + - 0 +
  4 : 0 + 0 + 0 + 0 + 0 + 0 + 0 + 0 + 0 + 0 + 0 + 0 + 0 + 0 + 0 + 0 + 0 + 0 + 0 +
  5 : 0 + - - + 0 + - - + 0 + - - + 0 + - - + 0 + - - + 0 + - - + 0 + - - + 0 + -
  6 : 0 + 0 0 0 + 0 + 0 0 0 + 0 - 0 0 0 - 0 - 0 0 0 - 0 + 0 0 0 + 0 + 0 0 0 + 0 -
  7 : 0 + + - + - - 0 + + - + - - 0 + + - + - - 0 + + - + - - 0 + + - + - - 0 + +
  8 : 0 + 0 - 0 - 0 + 0 + 0 - 0 - 0 + 0 + 0 - 0 - 0 + 0 + 0 - 0 - 0 + 0 + 0 - 0 - 0 -
  9 : 0 + + 0 + + 0 + + 0 + + 0 + + 0 + + 0 + + 0 + + 0 + + 0 + + 0 + + 0 + + 0 +
 10 : 0 + 0 + 0 0 0 - 0 + 0 - 0 + 0 0 0 - 0 - 0 - 0 - 0 0 0 + 0 - 0 + 0 - 0 0 0 +
 11 : 0 + - + + + - - - + - 0 + - + + + - - - + - 0 + - + + + - - - + - 0 + - + +
 12 : 0 + 0 0 0 - 0 + 0 0 0 - 0 + 0 0 0 - 0 + 0 0 0 - 0 + 0 0 0 - 0 + 0 0 0 - 0 +
 13 : 0 + - + + - - - - + + - + 0 + - + + - - - - + + - + 0 + - + + - - - - + + -
 14 : 0 + 0 + 0 + 0 0 0 + 0 - 0 + 0 + 0 - 0 + 0 0 0 + 0 + 0 + 0 - 0 - 0 - 0 0 0 -
 15 : 0 + + 0 + 0 0 - + 0 0 - 0 - - 0 + + 0 + 0 0 - + 0 0 - 0 - - 0 + + 0 + 0 0 -
 16 : 0 + 0 + 0 + 0 + 0 + 0 + 0 + 0 + 0 + 0 + 0 + 0 + 0 + 0 + 0 + 0 + 0 + 0 + 0 +
 17 : 0 + + - + - - - + + - - - + - + + 0 + + - + - - - + + - - - + - + + 0 + + -
 18 : 0 + 0 0 0 - 0 + 0 0 0 - 0 - 0 0 0 + 0 - 0 0 0 + 0 + 0 0 0 - 0 + 0 0 0 - 0 -
 19 : 0 + - - + + + + - + - + - - - - + + - 0 + - - + + + + - + - + - - - - + + -
 20 : 0 + 0 - 0 0 0 - 0 + 0 + 0 - 0 0 0 - 0 + 0 + 0 - 0 0 0 - 0 + 0 + 0 - 0 0 0 -
```

Figure 39.8-A: Kronecker symbols $\left(\frac{a}{b}\right)$ for small positive a and b.

```
int
kronecker(umod_t a, umod_t b)
// Return Kronecker symbol (a/b).
// Equal to Legendre symbol (a/b) if b is an odd prime.
{
    static const int  tab2[] = {0, 1, 0, -1, 0, -1, 0, 1};
    // tab2[ a & 7 ] := (-1)^((a^2-1)/8)

    if ( 0==b )  return (1==a);
    if ( 0==((a|b)&1) )  return 0;  // a and b both even ?

    int v = 0;
    while ( 0==(b&1) )  { ++v;  b>>=1; }

    int k;
    if ( 0==(v&1) )  k = 1;
    else             k = tab2[ a & 7 ];

    while ( 1 )
    {
        if ( 0==a )  return ( b>1 ? 0 : k );

        v = 0;
        while ( 0==(a&1) )  { ++v;  a>>=1; }

        if ( 1==(v&1) )  k *= tab2[ b & 7 ];  // k *= (-1)**((b*b-1)/8)

        if ( a & b & 2 )  k = -k;  // k = k*(-1)**((a-1)*(b-1)/4)

        umod_t r = a; // signed:  r = abs(a)
        a = b % r;
        b = r;
    }
}
```

A table of Kronecker symbols $\left(\frac{a}{b}\right)$ for small a and b is shown in figure 39.8-A. It was created with the program [FXT: mod/kronecker-demo.cc].

The following relations hold for the Kronecker symbol:

$$\left(\frac{ab}{n}\right) = \left(\frac{a}{n}\right)\left(\frac{b}{n}\right) \tag{39.8-5a}$$

$$\left(\frac{a}{mn}\right) = \left(\frac{a}{m}\right)\left(\frac{a}{n}\right) \tag{39.8-5b}$$

Note we may have $\left(\frac{a}{mn}\right) = +1$ while a is *not* a square modulo mn: If $\left(\frac{a}{m}\right) = \left(\frac{a}{n}\right) = -1$ (a is a non-square modulo both m and n), then (by relation 39.8-5b) $\left(\frac{a}{mn}\right) = +1$. But a is not a square mod mn, as a square mod mn must be a square both mod m and mod n. For example, $\left(\frac{2}{143}\right) = +1$ but 2 is not a square modulo $143 = 11 \cdot 13$, we have $\left(\frac{2}{11}\right) = -1$ and $\left(\frac{2}{13}\right) = -1$, so 2 is a non-square modulo both primes and so modulo their product.

For a square $b = a^2$ the Kronecker symbol will always be $+1$: $\left(\frac{b}{n}\right) = \left(\frac{a}{n}\right) \cdot \left(\frac{a}{n}\right) = +1$ (by relation 39.8-5a).

Whether a given number a is a square modulo 2^x can be determined via the simple routine [FXT: mod/quadresidue.cc]:

```
1    bool is_quadratic_residue_2ex(umod_t a, ulong x)
2    // Return whether a is quadratic residue mod 2**x
3    {
4        if ( x==1 )  return true;
5        if ( (x>=3 ) && (1==(a&7)) )  return true;
6        if ( (x==2 ) && (1==(a&3)) )  return true;
7        return false;
8    }
```

A curious observation regarding quadratic residues is that exactly for the 29 moduli

> 2, 3, 4, 5, 8, 12, 15, 16, 24, 28, 40, 48, 56, 60, 72, 88, 112, 120,
> 168, 232, 240, 280, 312, 408, 520, 760, 840, 1320, 1848

all quadratic residues are non-prime. This sequence is entry A065428 in [312]. It can be generated using the program [FXT: mod/mod-residues-demo.cc].

See any textbook on number theory for the details of the theory of quadratic residues and [110], [221], [323], and [309] for the corresponding algorithms. A method for watermarking that uses quadratic residues is discussed in [25]. An algorithm to compute conference matrices via quadratic residues is given in section 19.2 on page 386.

39.9 Computation of a square root modulo m

We give algorithms for computing square roots modulo primes, prime powers, and composites.

39.9.1 Square roots modulo a prime

The square roots of a square a modulo a prime $p = 4k + 3$ can be computed as

$$\sqrt{a} \;=\; \pm a^{(p+1)/4} \tag{39.9-1}$$

Observe that $(a^{(p+1)/4})^2 = a^{(p+1)/2} = a^{(p-1)/2+1} = \pm 1 \cdot a = \pm a$. If a is not a square, then a square root of $-a$ is obtained. Similar expressions for square roots modulo p are developed in [3]. An algorithm for the computation of a square root modulo a prime p (without restriction on the form of p) is given in [110, p.32]. We just give a C++ implementation [FXT: mod/sqrtmod.cc]:

```
1    umod_t
2    sqrt_modp(umod_t a, umod_t p)
3    // Return x such that x*x==a (mod p)
4    // p must be an odd prime.
5    // If a is not a square mod p then return 0.
6    {
7        if ( 1!=kronecker(a,p) )  return 0;  // not a square mod p
8
9        // initialize q,t so that  p == q * 2^t + 1
10       umod_t q;  int t;
11       n2qt(p, q, t);
12
13       umod_t z = 0,  n = 0;
14       for (n=1; n<p; ++n)
15       {
16           if ( -1==kronecker(n, p) )
17           {
18               z = pow_mod(n, q, p);
19               break;
20           }
21       }
22
```

```
23        if ( n>=p )  return 0;
24
25        umod_t y = z;
26        uint r = t;
27        umod_t x = pow_mod(a, (q-1)/2, p);
28        umod_t b = x;
29        x = mul_mod(x, a, p);
30        b = mul_mod(b, x, p);
31
32        while ( 1 )
33        {
34            if ( 1==b )  return x;
35
36            uint m;
37            for (m=1; m<r; ++m)
38            {
39                if ( 1==pow_mod(b, 1ULL<<m, p) )  break;
40            }
41
42            if ( m==r )  return  0;  // a is not a square mod p
43
44            umod_t v = pow_mod(y, 1ULL<<(r-m-1), p);
45            y = sqr_mod(v, p);
46            r = m;
47            x = mul_mod(x, v, p);
48            b = mul_mod(b, y, p);
49        }
50  }
```

39.9.2   Square roots modulo a prime power

For the computation of a square root modulo a prime power p^e the Newton iteration can be used (see section 29.1.5 on page 569). The case $p = 2$ has to be treated separately [FXT: mod/sqrtmod.cc]:

```
1   umod_t
2   sqrt_modpp(umod_t a, umod_t p, long ex)
3   // Return r so that r^2 == a (mod p^ex)
4   // return 0 if there is no such r
5   {
6       umod_t r;
7
8       if ( 2==p )  // case p==2
9       {
10          if ( false==is_quadratic_residue_2ex(a, ex) )  return 0;  // no sqrt exists
11          else  r = 1;  // (1/r)^2  = a mod 2
12      }
13      else         // case p odd
14      {
15          umod_t z = a % p;
16          r = sqrt_modp(z, p);
17          if ( r==0 )  return  0;  // no sqrt exists
18      }
19      // here r^2 == a (mod p)
20
21      if ( 1==ex )  return  r;
```

Here r is a square root of a modulo p, Newton steps are used to compute $\sqrt{a}$ modulo powers of p:

```
1   const umod_t m = ipow(p, ex);
2   if ( 2==p )  // case p==2
3   {
4       long x = 1;
5       while ( x<ex )  // Newton iteration for inverse sqrt, 2-adic case
6       {
7           umod_t z = a;
8           z = mul_mod(z, r, m);   // a*r
9           z = mul_mod(z, r, m);   // a*r*r
10          z = sub_mod(3, z, m);   // 3 - a*r*r
11          r = mul_mod(r, z/2, m); // r*(3 - a*r*r)/2 = r*(1 + (1-a*r*r)/2)
12          x *= 2;  //   (1/r)^2 == a mod 2^x
13      }
14      r = mul_mod(r, a, m);
15  }
16  else   // case p odd
17  {
```

```
18              const umod_t h = inv_modpp(2, p, ex);   // 1/2
19              long x = 1;
20              while ( x<ex )  // Newton iteration for square root
21              {
22                  umod_t ri = inv_modpp(r, p, ex);    // 1/r
23                  umod_t ar = mul_mod(a, ri, m);      // a/r
24                  r = add_mod(r, ar, m);              // r+a/r
25                  r = mul_mod(r, h, m);               // (r+a/r)/2
26                  x *= 2;  //  r^2 == a mod p^x
27              }
28          }
29          return  r;
30      }
```

39.9.3 Square roots modulo an arbitrary number

Square roots modulo an arbitrary number can be computed from the square roots of its prime power factors using the Chinese remainder theorem (see section 39.4 on page 772) [FXT: mod/sqrtmod.cc]:

```
1   umod_t
2   sqrt_modf(umod_t a, const factorization &mf)
3   // Return sqrt(a) mod m, given the factorization mf of m
4   {
5       ALLOCA(umod_t, x, mf.nprimes() );
6       for (int i=0; i<mf.nprimes(); ++i)
7       {
8           // x[i]=sqrt(a) modulo i-th prime power:
9           x[i] = sqrt_modpp( a, mf.prime(i), mf.exponent(i) );
10          if ( x[i]==0 )  return 0;  // no sqrt exists
11      }
12      return  chinese(x, mf);  // combine via CRT
13  }
```

39.10 The Rabin-Miller test for compositeness

We describe a probabilistic method to prove compositeness of an integer.

39.10.1 Pseudoprimes and strong pseudoprimes

For a prime p the maximal order of an element equals $p - 1$. That is, for all $a \neq 0$

$$a^{p-1} \equiv 1 \mod p \qquad\qquad (39.10\text{-}1)$$

If for a given number n one finds an $a > 1$ so that $a^{n-1} \neq 1 \mod n$, then the compositeness of n has been proved. Composite numbers n for which $a^{n-1} = 1 \mod n$ are called *pseudoprime to base a* (or a-pseudoprime). For example, for $n = 15$ we find

a :	2	3	4	5	6	7	8	9	10	11	12	13	14
a^{14}:	4	9	1	10	6	4	4	6	10	1	9	4	1

We found that 15 is pseudoprime to the bases 4, 11 and 14 which we also could have read off the rightmost column of figure 39.7-B on page 778.

The bad news is that some composite numbers are pseudoprime to very many bases. The smallest such number is 561 which is pseudoprime to all bases a with $\gcd(a, n) = 1$. Numbers with this property are called *Carmichael numbers*. The first few are 561, 1105, 1729, 2465, 2821, 6601, 8911, ..., this is sequence A002997 in [312]. There are infinitely many Carmichael numbers as proved in [7]. Finding a base that proves a Carmichael number composite is as difficult as finding a factor.

A significantly better algorithm can be found by a rather simple modification. Write $n - 1 =: q \cdot 2^t$ where q is odd, we examine the sequence $b := a^q$, b^2, b^4, ..., $b^{2^{t-1}} = a^{(n-1)/2}$. We say that n is a *strong pseudoprime to base a* if either $b \equiv 1$ or $b^{2^e} \equiv -1 \equiv n - 1$ for some e where $0 \leq e < t$. We abbreviate strong pseudoprime as SPP. If neither of the conditions holds, then n is proved composite. Then n is either not a pseudoprime to base a or we found a square root of 1 that is not equal to $n - 1$.

With two different square roots s_1, s_2 modulo n of a number z (here $z = 1$) we have

$$s_1^2 - z \equiv 0 \mod n \tag{39.10-2a}$$
$$s_2^2 - z \equiv 0 \mod n \tag{39.10-2b}$$
$$s_1^2 - s_2^2 = (s_1 + s_2)(s_1 - s_2) \equiv 0 \mod n \tag{39.10-2c}$$

So both $s_1 + s_2$ and $s_1 - s_2$ are nontrivial factors of n if $s_1 \neq n - s_2$. Thus a square root $s \neq -1$ of 1 proves compositeness because both $\gcd(s + 1, n)$ and $\gcd(s - 1, n)$ are nontrivial factors of n.

Let $B = \left[b, b^2, b^4, \ldots, b^{2^t}\right]$, then for n prime the sequence B must have one of the following forms: either

$$B = [1, 1, 1, \ldots, 1] \quad \text{or} \tag{39.10-3a}$$
$$B = [*, \ldots, *, -1, 1, \ldots, 1] \tag{39.10-3b}$$

where an asterisk denotes any number not equal to $\pm 1 \mod n$ (notation as in [221]). For n composite the sequence B can also be of the form

$$B = [*, \ldots, *] \quad (a^{n-1} \neq 1, \text{not a pseudoprime to base } a) \quad \text{or} \tag{39.10-4a}$$
$$B = [*, \ldots, *, 1, \ldots, 1] \quad \text{(found square root of 1 not equal to } -1) \tag{39.10-4b}$$

If one of the latter two forms is encountered, then n must be composite.

With our example $n = 15$ we have $n - 1 = 7 \cdot 2^1$, thereby $q = 7$ and $t = 1$. We only have to examine the value of b. Values of a for which b is not equal to either $+1$ or -1 prove the compositeness of 15.

a:	2	3	4	5	6	7	8	9	10	11	12	13	14
b:	8	12	4	5	6	13	2	9	10	11	3	7	−1

In our example all bases $\neq 14$ prove 15 composite. As n is always an SPP to base $a = n - 1 \equiv -1$, we restrict our attention to values $2 \leq a \leq n - 2$.

A GP implementation of the test whether n is an SPP to base a:

```
1    sppq(n, a)=
2    { /* Return whether n is a strong pseudoprime to base a */
3        local(q, t, b, e);
4        q = n-1;
5        t = 0;
6        while ( 0==bitand(q,1), q/=2; t+=1 );
7        /* here  n==2^t*q+1 */
8
9        b = Mod(a, n)^q;
10       if ( 1==b, return(1) );
11       e = 1;
12       while ( e<t,
13           if( (b==1) || (b==n-1), break(); );
14           b *= b;
15           e++;
16       );
17       return( if ( b!=(n-1), 0, 1 ) );
18   }
```

The Carmichael number 561 ($561 - 1 = 35 \cdot 2^4$, so $q = 35$ and $t = 4$) is an SPP to only 8 out of the 558 interesting bases and not an SPP for any $2 \leq a \leq 20$, as shown in figure 39.10-A. Note that with $a = 4$ we found $s = 67$ where $s^2 \equiv 1 \mod 561$ and thereby the factors $\gcd(67 + 1, 561) = 17$ and $\gcd(67 - 1, 561) = 33$ of 561.

39.10.2 The Rabin-Miller test

The *Rabin-Miller test* is an algorithm to prove compositeness of a number n by testing strong pseudoprimality with several bases:

```
a=2:       b=263     b^2=166    b^4= 67
a=3:       b= 78     b^2=474    b^4=276
a=4:       b=166     b^2= 67    b^4=  1
a=5:       b= 23     b^2=529    b^4=463                all SPP bases:
a=6:       b=318     b^2=144    b^4=540        a=50:              b=560
a=7:       b=241     b^2=298    b^4=166        a=101:             b=560
a=8:       b=461     b^2=463    b^4= 67        a=103:             b=  1
a=9:       b=474     b^2=276    b^4=441        a=256:             b=  1
a=10:      b=439     b^2=298    b^4=166        a=305:             b=560
a=11:      b=209     b^2=484    b^4=319        a=458:             b=560
a=12:      b= 45     b^2=342    b^4=276        a=460:             b=  1
a=13:      b=208     b^2= 67    b^4=  1        a=511:             b=  1
a=14:      b=551     b^2=100    b^4=463
a=15:      b=111     b^2=540    b^4=441
a=16:      b= 67     b^2=  1
a=17:      b=527     b^2= 34    b^4= 34
a=18:      b=120     b^2=375    b^4=375
a=19:      b= 76     b^2=166    b^4= 67
a=20:      b=452     b^2=100    b^4=463
```

Figure 39.10-A: The Carmichael number $561 = 35 \cdot 2^4 + 1$ is a strong pseudoprime to 8 out of 558 bases a (right) and no base $2 \le a \le 20$ (left).

```
1    rm(n, na=20)=
2    { /* Rabin Miller test */
3        local(a);
4        for (a=2, na+2,
5            if ( a>n-2,  break() );
6            if ( 0==sppq(n, a), return(0) );   /* proven composite */
7        );
8        return(1); /* composite with probability less than 0.25^na */
9    }
```

For a composite number the probability of being a SPP to a 'random' base is at most $1/4$. So the compositeness of a number can quickly be proved in practice. While the algorithm does *not* prove primality, it can be used to rule out compositeness with a very high probability.

Bases tested:	2	3	5	6	7	10	11	12	13	14	15	17
91: [3]						10		12				17
133: [2]							11	12				
145: [2]								12				17
276: [2]							11		13			
286: [2]		3										17
703: [2]		3			7							
742: [2]											15	17
781: [2]			5									17
946: [2]					7						15	
1111: [2]				6								17
1729: [2]						10		12				
2047: [2]	2						11					
2806: [2]			5						13			
2821: [2]								12				17
3277: [3]	2									14	15	
4033: [2]	2											17
4187: [2]						10						17
5662: [2]			5									17
5713: [2]				6						14		
6533: [2]				6		10						
6541: [2]										14	15	
7171: [2]										14		17
8401: [2]		3				10						
8911: [3]		3						12	13			
9073: [2]								12		14		

Figure 39.10-B: All numbers $\le 10{,}000$ that are strong pseudoprimes to more than one base $a \le 17$ (omitting bases a that are prime powers).

A list (created with the program [FXT: mod/rabinmiller-demo.cc]) of composites $n \le 10{,}000$ that are SPP to more than one base $a \le 17$ is shown in figure 39.10-B. The table indicates how effective the Rabin-Miller algorithm actually is: it does not contain a single number pseudoprime to both 2 and 3. The first few odd composite numbers that are SPP to both bases $a = 2$ and $a = 3$ are shown in figure 39.10-C. There are 104 such composite $n < 2^{32}$, given in [FXT: data/pseudo-spp23.txt]. This sequence of numbers is entry A072276 in [312], entry A001262 gives the base-2 SPPs, and entry A020229 gives the base-3

```
1,373,653  ==  1 + 2^2 * 3^3 * 7 * 23 * 79
           ==  829 * 1657  == (1 + 2^2 *3^2 *23) * (1 + 2^3 *3^2 *23)
1,530,787  ==  1 + 2 * 3 * 103 * 2477
           ==  619 * 2473  == (1 + 2 *3 *103)    * (1 + 2^3 *3 *103)
1,987,021  ==  1 + 2^2 * 3^2 * 5 * 7 * 19 * 83
           ==  997 * 1993  == (1 + 2^2 *3 *83)   * (1 + 2^3 *3 *83)
2,284,453  ==  1 + 2^2 * 3^2 * 23 * 31 * 89
           == 1069 * 2137  == (1 + 2^2 *3 *89)   * (1 + 2^3 *3 *89)
3,116,107  ==  1 + 2 * 3^2 * 7^2 * 3533
           ==  883 * 3529  == (1 + 2 *3^2 *7^2)  * (1 + 2^3 *3^2 *7^2)
5,173,601  ==  1 + 2^5 * 5^2 * 29 * 223
           ==  929 * 5569  == (1 + 2^5 *29)      * (1 + 2^6 *3 *29)
6,787,327  ==  1 + 2 * 3 * 7 * 13 * 31 * 401
           == 1303 * 5209  == (1 + 2 *3 *7 *31)  * (1 + 2^3 *3 *7 *31)
11,541,307 ==  1 + 2 * 3 * 7 * 283 * 971
           == 1699 * 6793  == (1 + 2 *3 *283)    * (1 + 2^3 *3 *283)
13,694,761 ==  1 + 2^3 * 3^2 * 5 * 109 * 349
           == 2617 * 5233  == (1 + 2^3 *3 *109)  * (1 + 2^4 *3 *109)
```

Figure 39.10-C: The first composite numbers that are SPP to both bases 2 and 3.

```
  25,326,001  ==  1 + 2^4 * 3^3 * 5^3 * 7 * 67
              ==  2251 * 11251  == (1 + 2 *3^2 *5^3) * (1 + 2 *3^2 *5^4)
 161,304,001  ==  1 + 2^6 * 3 * 5^3 * 11 * 13 * 47
              ==  7333 * 21997  == (1 + 2^2 *3 *13 *47) * (1 + 2^2 *3^2 *13 *47)
 960,946,321  ==  1 + 2^4 * 3 * 5 * 29 * 101 * 1367
              == 11717 * 82013  == (1 + 2^2 *29 *101) * (1 + 2^2 *7 *29 *101)
1,157,839,381 ==  1 + 2^2 * 3^3 * 5 * 401 * 5347
              == 24061 * 48121  == (1 + 2^2 *3 *5 *401) * (1 + 2^3 *3 *5 *401)
3,215,031,751 ==  1 + 2 * 3^4 * 5^3 * 7 * 37 * 613
              == 151 * 751 * 28351
              == (1 + 2 *3 *5^2)  * (1 + 2 *3 *5^3) * (1 + 2 *3^4 *5^2 *7)
3,697,278,427 ==  1 + 2 * 3^3 * 31 * 563 * 3923
              == 30403 * 121609  == (1 + 2 *3^3 *563) * (1 + 2^3 *3^3 *563)
```

Figure 39.10-D: All composite numbers $n \leq 2^{32}$ that are SPP to the three bases 2, 3 and 5.

SPPs. We note the uneven distribution modulo 12:

(n%12: num)   (1: 75)   (5: 9)   (7: 18)   (11: 2)

Composites that are SPP to the three bases 2, 3 and 5 are quite rare, figure 39.10-D shows all 6 such composite numbers $< 2^{32}$ (values taken from [272] which lists all such numbers $< 25 \cdot 10^9$). Thus we can speed up the Rabin-Miller test for small values of n (say, $n < 2^{32}$) by only testing the bases $a = 2, 3, 5$ and, if n is a SPP to these bases, look up the composites in the table. The smallest odd composites that are SPP to the first k prime bases up to $k = 8$ are determined in [191], they are given as sequence A006945 in [312].

```
composite           SPP to base
         2047       2
      1373653       2, 3
     25326001       2, 3, 5
   3215031751       2, 3, 5, 7
 2152302898747      2, 3, 5, 7, 11
 3474749660383      2, 3, 5, 7, 11, 13
341550071728321     2, 3, 5, 7, 11, 13, 17 [and 19]
341550071728321     2, 3, 5, 7, 11, 13, 17, 19
```

Note that if the probability of a base not proving compositeness was exactly $1/4$ we would find *much* more entries in figure 39.10-D. Slightly overestimating the number of composites below N as N, there should be about $(1/4)^3 N = N/64$ entries, that is $2^{26} \approx 6 \cdot 10^7$ for $N = 2^{32}$, but we have only six entries. So the Rabin-Miller test is in practice significantly more efficient than one may initially assume. Let $p_{k,t}$ be the probability that a k-bit composite 'survives' t passes of the Rabin-Miller test. Then we have, as shown in [121],

$$p_{k,1} \;<\; k^2\, 4^{2-\sqrt{k}} \qquad \text{for} \quad k > 2 \tag{39.10-5}$$

For large numbers, the bound on the left side is much smaller than $1/4$: for example, $p_{1000,1} < 2^{-39}$. Other bounds given in the cited paper are

$$p_{100,10} \;<\; 2^{-44} \tag{39.10-6a}$$

$$p_{300,5} \;<\; 2^{-60} \tag{39.10-6b}$$

$$p_{600,1} \;<\; 2^{-75} \tag{39.10-6c}$$

The last bound is stronger than that of relation 39.10-5. Still stronger bounds are given in [91], also the relation $p_{k,t} < 4^{-t}$ for all $k \geq 2$ and $t \geq 1$.

```
Bases tested:  2   3  5  6   7 10 11 12 13 14  15 17
      11476:       3  5                         15 17
      88831:                 7      11 12       15 17
     188191:       3         7 10               17
     597871:                   10 11 12 13
     736291:                 7 10      12 13
     765703:                   10 11 12       14
    1024651:       3  5       7         12          15
    1056331:                 7 10      12 13
    1152271:       3         7      11 12 13
    1314631:          5       7      11 12 13
    1373653:  2    3     6              12            17
    1530787:  2    3     6              12
    1627921:       3  5                       14 15
    1857241:          5             11 12      14
    1987021:  2    3     6              12            17
    2030341:                       11 12      14 15
    2284453:  2    3     6 7         11 12      14 15
    2741311:                       11 12      14 15
    3116107:  2    3     6              12
    4181921:  2       5         10            13
    4224533:             6              11      14 15 17  <--=
    5122133:             6 7 10 11
    5173601:  2    3     6              12
    5481451:       3  5                12              15
    6594901:          5                12 13 14
    6787327:  2    3     6              12 13
    8086231:          5                12      14      17
    9504191:                       11 12 13      15
    9863461:  2       5  6   10                       17
```

Figure 39.10-E: Composites $\leq 10^7$ that are SPP to at least four bases.

The composites $\leq 10^7$ that are SPP to four or more bases $a < 17$ are shown in figure 39.10-E. We omit values of a that are perfect powers because if n is a base-a SPP, then it is also a base-a^k SPP for all $k > 1$. The entry for $n = 4224533$ (marked with an arrow) shows that a number that is not an SPP to two bases a_1 and a_2 may still be a SPP to the base $a_1 \cdot a_2$ (here $a_1 = 2$, $a_2 = 3$). This indicates that one might want to restrict the tested bases to primes. All odd composite numbers $\leq 10^7$ that are SPP to four or more prime bases $a \leq 17$ are

```
Bases tested:   2  3  5   7 11 13 17
1152271:  [4]      3       7 11 13
1314631:  [4]         5    7 11 13
2284453:  [4]   2  3       7 11
```

Note that a number that is an SPP to bases a_1 and a_2 is *not* necessarily SPP to the base $a_1 \cdot a_2$. An example is $n = 9,006,401$ which is an SPP to bases 2 and 5 but not to base 10:

```
9006401:   2    4  5       8              16    18
```

All composites $\leq 10^7$ that are SPP to bases 2 and 3 are also SPP to base 6, same for bases 2 and 5. Out of six composites $\leq 10^7$ that are SPP to bases 2 and 7 three are not SPP to base 14:

```
 314821:   2     4    6 7 8 9              16    18
2269093:   2     4      7 8            14  16
2284453:   2  3  4    6 7 8 9    11 12     16    18
3539101:   2     4      7 8         13
5489641:   2     4      7 8            14  16
6386993:   2     4      7 8            14  16
```

Numbers which are SPP to several chosen bases are constructed in [18] where a composite 337-digit number is given that is SPP to all prime bases $a < 200$. See also [365] and [366].

39.10.3 Implementation of the Rabin-Miller test

A C++ implementation of the test for pseudoprimality is given in [FXT: mod/rabinmiller.cc]:

```
bool
is_strong_pseudo_prime(const umod_t n, const umod_t a, const umod_t q, const int t)
// Return whether n is a strong pseudoprime to base a.
// q and t must be set so that   n == q * 2^t + 1
{
    umod_t b = pow_mod(a, q, n);

    if ( 1==b )  return true;  // passed
    // if ( n-1==b )  return true;  // passed

    int e = 1;
    while ( (b!=1) && (b!=(n-1)) && (e<t) )
    {
        b = mul_mod(b, b, n);
        e++;
    }

    if ( b!=(n-1) )  return false;  // =--> composite

    return  true;  // passed
}
```

It uses the routine

```
void
n2qt(const umod_t n, umod_t &q, int &t)
// Set q,t so that  n == q * 2^t + 1
// n must not equal 1, else routine loops.
{
    q = n - 1;  t = 0;
    while ( 0==(q & 1) )  { q >>= 1; ++t; }
}
```

Now the Rabin-Miller test can be implemented as

```
bool
rabin_miller(umod_t n, uint cm/*=0*/)
// Rabin-Miller compositeness test.
// Return true of none of the bases <=cm prove compositeness.
// If false is returned, then n is proven composite (also for n=1 or n=0).
// If true is returned the probability
//    that n is composite is less than (1/4)^cm
{
    if ( n<=1 )  return false;
    if ( n < small_prime_limit )  return  is_small_prime( (ulong)n );

    umod_t q;
    int t;
    n2qt(n, q, t);

    if ( 0==cm )  cm = 20;  // default
    uint c = 0;
    while ( ++c<=cm )
    {
        umod_t a = c + 1;

        // if n is a c-SPP, then it also is a c**k (k>1) SPP.
        // That is, powers of a non-witness are non-witnesses.
        // So we skip perfect powers:
        if ( is_small_perfpow(a) )  continue;

        if ( a >= n )  return  true;
        if ( !is_strong_pseudo_prime(n, a, q, t) )  return false;  // proven composite
    }

    return true;  // strong pseudoprime for all tested bases
}
```

The function `is_small_perfpow()` [FXT: mod/perfpow.cc] returns `true` if its argument is a (small) perfect power. It uses a lookup in a precomputed bit-array.

A generalization of the Rabin-Miller test applicable when more factors (apart from 2) of $n-1$ are known is given in [49]. The *Frobenius test* is described in [118, p.145], see also [237]. Another generalization (named extended quadratic Frobenius primality test) is suggested in [122].

39.11   Proving primality

We describe several methods to prove primality. Only the first, Pratt's certificate of primality, is applicable for numbers of arbitrary form but not practical in general because it relies on the factorization of $n-1$. The Pocklington-Lehmer test only needs a partial factorization of $n-1$. We give further tests applicable for numbers of special forms: Pepin's test, the Lucas-Lehmer test, and the Lucas test.

As already said, the Rabin-Miller test can only prove compositeness. Even if a candidate 'survives' many passes, we only know that it is prime with a high probability.

39.11.1   Pratt's certificate of primality

Only with a prime modulus p the maximal order equals $R = p-1$. To determine the order of an element modulo p one needs the factorization of $p-1$. If the factorization of $p-1$ is known and we can find a primitive root, then we do know that p is prime. Thus it is quite easy to prove primality for numbers of certain special forms. For example, let $p := 2 \cdot 3^{30} + 1 = 411,782,264,189,299$. One finds that 3 is a primitive root and so we know that p is prime.

```
[314159311, [3], [2, 3, 5, 199, 1949]]
    [2, "--"]
    [3, [2], [2]]
        [2, "--"]
    [5, [2], [2]]
        [2, "--"]
    [199, [3], [2, 3, 11]]
        [2, "--"]
        [3, [2], [2]]
            [2, "--"]
        [11, [2], [2, 5]]
            [2, "--"]
            [5, [2], [2]]
                [2, "--"]
    [1949, [2], [2, 487]]
        [2, "--"]
        [487, [3], [2, 3]]
            [2, "--"]
            [3, [2], [2]]
                [2, "--"]
```

Figure 39.11-A: A certificate for the primality of $p = 314,159,311$.

In general, the factorization of $p-1$ can contain large factors whose primality needs to be proven. Recursion leads to a primality certificate in the form of a tree which is called *Pratt's certificate of primality*.

A certificate for the primality of $p = 314,159,311$ is shown in figure 39.11-A. The first line says that 3 is a primitive root of $p = 314159311$ and $p-1$ has the prime factors $2, 3, 5, 199, 1949$ (actually, $p-1 = 2 \cdot 3^4 \cdot 5 \cdot 199 \cdot 1949$, but we can ignore exponents). The second level, indented by 4 characters, gives the prime factors just determined together with their primality certificates: the prime 2 is trivially accepted, all other primes are followed by their (further indented) certificates.

The certificate was produced with the following GP code:

```
1   indprint(x, ind)=
2   { /* print x, indented by ind characters */
3       for (k=1, ind, print1(" ") );
```

```
        [3141592653589793238462643383279502884197169399375311, [3], \
         [2, 3, 5, 67, 89, 151, 39829177707048956693, 2920017949296038456621939]]

        [151, [6], [2, 3, 5]]
        [39829177707048956693, [2], [2, 9957294426762239173]]
            [9957294426762239173, [6], [2, 3, 7, 11, 14153, 385109, 1977139]]
                [14153, [3], [2, 29, 61]]
                [385109, [2], [2, 43, 2239]]
                    [2239, [3], [2, 3, 373]]
                        [373, [2], [2, 3, 31]]
                [1977139, [3], [2, 3, 109841]]
                    [109841, [3], [2, 5, 1373]]
                        [1373, [2], [2, 7]]
        [2920017949296038456621939, [2], [2, 13, 3157127, 3557296955910619]]
            [3157127, [7], [2, 7, 225509]]
                [225509, [2], [2, 56377]]
                    [56377, [5], [2, 3, 29]]
            [3557296955910619, [3], [2, 3, 47, 673, 6247908971]]
                [673, [5], [2, 3, 7]]
                [6247908971, [2], [2, 5, 624790897]]
                    [624790897, [5], [2, 3, 13016477]]
                        [13016477, [2], [2, 11, 29, 101]]
                            [101, [2], [2, 5]]
```

Figure 39.11-B: A shortened certificate for the primality of first prime greater than $\pi \cdot 10^{50}$. Here all primes less than 100 are considered trivially verifiable and not listed.

```
4          print(x);
5      }
6
7      pratt(p, ind=0)=
8      {
9          local( a, p1, f, nf, t );
10         if ( p<=2,    \\ 2 is trivially prime
11             indprint([p, "--"], ind);
12             return();
13         );
14         \\ p-1 is factored here:
15         a = lift( znprimroot(p) );
16         \\ but we cannot access the factorization, so we do it "manually":
17         p1 = p-1;
18         f = factor(p1);
19         nf = matsize(f)[1];
20         t = vector(nf,j, f[j,1] );  f = t;  \\ prime factors only
21         indprint([p, [a], t], ind);
22         \\ recurse on prime factors of p-1:
23         for (k=1, nf, pratt(f[k], ind+4));
24         return();
25     }
? p=nextprime(Pi*10^8);
? pratt(p)
```

The routine has to be taken with a grain of salt as we rely on `znprimroot(p)` failing for composite p:

```
? pratt(1000)
  ***    primitive root does not exist in gener
```

The routine has an additional parameter `ind` determining the indentation used with printing. This parameter is incremented with the recursion level, resulting in the tree-like structure of the output. This little trick is often useful with recursive procedures.

With a precomputed table of small primes (see section 39.3 on page 770) the line

```
    if ( p<=2,    \\ 2 is trivially prime
```

can be changed to something like

```
    if ( (p<=ptable_max) && (ptable[p]==1),    \\ trivial to verify
```

which will shorten the certificate significantly. A certificate for the smallest prime p greater than $\pi \cdot 10^{50}$ and `ptable_max=100` is shown in figure 39.11-B, the output of 'trivial' primes is suppressed. We note that $p = \lceil \pi \cdot 10^{50} \rceil + 20$.

Once a certificate is computed it can be verified very quickly. As this type of primality certificate needs the factorization of $p - 1$ its computation is in general not feasible for large values of p.

39.11.2   The Pocklington-Lehmer test

Let $p - 1 = F \cdot U$ where $F > U$ and the complete factorization of F is known. If, for each prime factor q of F, we can find a_q such that $a_q^{p-1} \equiv 1 \bmod p$ and $\gcd\left(a_q^{(p-1)/q} - 1, p\right) = 1$, then p is prime.

The corresponding algorithm is called the *Pocklington-Lehmer test* for primality. The following implementation removes entries from the list of prime factors q of F until the list is empty:

```
1    pocklington_lehmer(F, u, c=10000)=
2    { /* Pocklington-Lehmer test for the primality of p=f*u+1.
3       * Return last successful base, else zero.
4       * F must be the factorization of f.
5       * Test bases a=2...c
6       * Must have u<f.
7       */
8       local(n, f, C, p, t, ct);
9       n = matsize(F)[1];
10      f = prod(j=1, n, F[j,1]^F[j,2]);
11      if ( f<=u, return(0) );
12      p = f*u + 1;
13      C = vector(n, j, (p-1)/F[j,1]);
14      ct = n;   \\ number remaining prime divisors of f
15      for (a=2, c,
16          if ( 1==Mod(a,p)^(p-1),
17              for (j=1, n,
18                  if ( C[j]!=0,  \\ skip entries already removed
19                      t = lift( Mod(a,p)^C[j] );
20                      if( 1==gcd(t-1, p),
21                          C[j] = 0;  \\ remove entry
22                          ct -= 1;   \\ number of remaining entries
23                      );
24                  );
25              );
26              if ( ct==0, return(a) );
27          );
28      );
29      return( 0 );
30   }
```

We search all primes of the form $p = F \cdot U + 1$ where $F = 100!$, $U = F - d$, and d lies in the range $1, \ldots, 1000$. Only candidates that are strong pseudoprimes to both bases 2 and 3 are tested:

```
f=100!;
F=factor(f);
{ for (d=1, 1000,
    u = f - d;
    p = f*u+1;
    if ( sppq(p, 2) && sppq(p,3),
        q2 = pocklington_lehmer(F, u);
        print1(d, ":  ");
        print1("  ", q2);
        print();
    );
) }
```

We find five such primes $\approx 8.70978248908948 \cdot 10^{315}$ (in about ten seconds):

```
   d:     last a
   45:      103
   778:     101
   818:     101
   880:     101
   884:     103
```

The returned value a_q is the one that did lead to the removal of the last entry in `C[]`. The value is smaller with less prime factors of F. Setting $F = 2^{500}$ we find primes ($\approx 1.07150860718626 \cdot 10^{301}$) of the form $p = F \cdot U + 1$ where $U = F - d$ and $1 \leq d \leq 3000$ for the following d and maximal a_q:

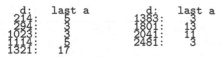

d:	last a	d:	last a
214:	5	1383:	3
254:	7	1801:	13
294:	3	2041:	11
1023:	3	2481:	3
1114:	5		
1321:	17		

The search takes about 20 seconds. Discarding candidates that have small prime factors ($p < 1,000$) gives a four-fold speedup. The prime $2^{3340}\,(2^{3340} - 1633) + 1 \approx 7.59225935 \cdot 10^{2010}$ is found within five minutes. A further refinement of the test is given in [110], see also [88].

39.11.3 Tests for $n = k\,2^t + 1$

39.11.3.1 Proth's theorem and Pepin's test

For numbers of the form $p = q \cdot 2^t + 1$ with q odd and $2^t > q$ primality can be proven as follows: If there is an integer a such that $a^{(p-1)/2} \equiv -1$, then p must be prime. This is *Proth's theorem*.

The 'FFT-primes' (see section 26.1 on page 535) are natural candidates for Proth's theorem. For example, with $p := 2^{57} \cdot 29 + 1 = 4,179,340,454,199,820,289$ one finds that $a^{(p-1)/2} \equiv -1$ for $a = 3$, so p must be prime. Note that Proth's theorem is the special case $F = 2^t > k = U$ of the Pocklington-Lehmer test.

Numbers of the form $2^t + 1$ are composite unless t is a power of 2. The candidates are therefore restricted to the *Fermat numbers* $F_n := 2^{2^n} + 1$. Here it suffices to test whether $3^x \equiv -1 \bmod F_n$ where $x = 2^{t-1}$:

```
1    pepin(tx)=
2    {
3        local(t, F, x);
4        t = 2^tx;
5        F = 2^t+1;
6        x = 2^(t-1);
7        return(  (-1==Mod(3,F)^x) );
8    }
```

This test is known as *Pepin's test*. As shown in section 39.8 on page 781 all non-residues are primitive roots modulo prime F_n. Three is just the smallest non-residue.

```
for (tx=1,12, print(tx," ", pepin(tx)))
   1  1   \\ F_1 = 5
   2  1   \\ F_2 = 17
   3  1   \\ F_3 = 257
   4  1   \\ F_4 = 65537
   5  0
   0
  12  0
```

No Fermat prime greater than $F_4 = 65537$ is known today and all F_n where $5 \leq n \leq 32$ are known to be composite.

Note that F_{n+1} has (about) twice as many bits as F_n. Also the number of squarings $(t - 1)$ involved in the test is (about) doubled. If we underestimate the cost of multiplying N-bit numbers as N operations, we get a lower bound 4 for the ratio of the costs of testing F_{n+1} and F_n. Assuming the computer power doubles every 18 month and Pepin's test of F_n is just feasible today we'd have to wait three years (36 month) before we can test F_{n+1}. The computation that proved F_{24} composite is described in [117].

39.11.3.2 What to consider before doing Pepin's test

As $2^t \equiv -1 \bmod F_n = 2^t + 1$ we see that the order of 2 equals $2\,t = 2^{n+1}$. The same is true for factors of composite Fermat numbers. When searching factors of F_n we only need to consider candidates of the form $1 + k\,2^{n+2}$. A routine that searches for small factors of F_n can be implemented as:

```
1    ord2pow2(p)=
2    \\ Return the base-2 logarithm of the order of 2 modulo p
3    \\ Must have: ord(2)==2^k for some k
4    {
5        local(m, rx);
6        rx = 0;
7        m = Mod(2,p);
8        while ( m!=1, m*=m; rx++; );
```

```
 9        return( rx );
10    }

 1    ftrialx(n, mm=10^5, brn=0)=
 2    \\ Try to find small factors of the Fermat number F_n=2^(2^n)+1
 3    \\ Try factors 1+ps, 1+2*ps, ..., 1+mm*ps  where ps=2^(n+2)
 4    \\ Stop if brn factors were found (zero: do not stop)
 5    {
 6        local(p,ps,ttx,fct);
 7        ps = 2^(n+2);    \\ factors are of the form 1+k*ps
 8        p = ps+1;        \\ trial factor
 9        ttx = 2^(n+1); \\ will test whether Mod(2,p)^ttx==1
10        fct = 0;  \\ how many factors were found so far
11        for (ct=1, mm,
12            if ( (Mod(2,p)^(ttx)==1)  \\ order condition
13                && ( (rx=ord2pow2(p)) == n+1 ) \\ avoid factors of smaller Fermat numbers
14            , /* then */
15                print1(n, ": ");
16                print1(p);
17                print1("    p-1=",factor(p-1));
18                print();
19                fct++;
20                if ( fct==brn,  break() );
21            );
22            p += ps;
23        );
24        return(fct);
25    }
```

We create a list of small prime factors of F_n for $5 \le n \le 32$ where the search is restricted to factors $f \le 1 + 10^5\, 2^{n+2}$ and stopped when a factor was found:

```
for(n=5,32, ftrialx(n, 10^5, 1); );
   5:  641      p-1=[2, 7; 5, 1]
   6:  274177    p-1=[2, 8; 3, 2; 7, 1; 17, 1]
   9:  2424833     p-1=[2, 16; 37, 1]
  10:  45592577     p-1=[2, 12; 11131, 1]
  11:  319489      p-1=[2, 13; 3, 1; 13, 1]
  12:  114689      p-1=[2, 14; 7, 1]
  15:  1214251009     p-1=[2, 21; 3, 1; 193, 1]
  16:  825753601    p-1=[2, 19; 3, 2; 5, 2; 7, 1]
  18:  13631489    p-1=[2, 20; 13, 1]
  19:  70525124609     p-1=[2, 21; 33629, 1]
  23:  167772161    p-1=[2, 25; 5, 1]
  32:  25409026523137     p-1=[2, 34; 3, 1; 17, 1; 29, 1]
```

A list for $5 \le n \le 300$ is given in [FXT: data/small-fermat-factors.txt]. Note that an entry

```
 201:  12456983719095692616001290139828692494752117607804210059256266 7521 \
        p-1=[2, 204; 3, 1; 5, 1; 17, 1; 19, 1]
```

asserts the compositeness of the number F_{201} where Pepin's test is out of reach by far. Indeed, its binary representation could not be stored in all existing computer memory combined: F_{201} is a $\log_2(F_{201}) \approx 2^{201} = 3.2138 \cdot 10^{60}$ -bit number.

The currently known (partial) factorizations of Fermat numbers are given in [202].

39.11.4 Tests for $n = k\, 2^t - 1$

39.11.4.1 The Lucas-Lehmer test for Mersenne numbers

Define the sequence H by $H_0 = 1$, $H_1 := 2$ and $H_i = 4\,H_{i-1} - H_{i-2}$. The Mersenne number $n = 2^e - 1$ is prime if and only if $H_{2^{e-2}} \equiv 0 \bmod n$. The first few terms of the sequence H are

k:	0	1	2	3	4	5	6	7	8	9	10	11	12
H_k:	1	2	7	26	97	362	1351	5042	18817	70226	262087	978122	3650401 ...

The numbers H_k can be computed efficiently via the index doubling formula $H_{2k} = 2\,H_k^2 - 1$. Starting with the value $H_1 = 2$ and computing modulo n the implementation is as simple as

```
 1    LL(e)=
 2    {
```

```
3        local(n, h);
4        n = 2^e-1;
5        h = Mod(2,n);
6        for (k=1, e-2, h=2*h*h-1);
7        return( 0==h );
8   }
? LL(521)
   1  \\  2^521-1 is prime
? LL(239)
   0  \\  2^239-1 is composite
? LL(9941)
   1 \\ 2^9941-1 is prime
? ##
   ***    last result computed in 4,296 ms.
```

The algorithm is called the *Lucas-Lehmer test*. Note that most sources use the sequence $V = 2, 4, 14, 52, 194, 724, 2702, \ldots$ that satisfies the same recurrence relation. We have $H_k = \frac{1}{2} V_k$ (H is *half* of V). The index doubling relation becomes $V_{2k} = V_k^2 - 2$. The sequence of values H_{2^k} starts as

  2, 7, 97, 18817, 708158977, 1002978273411373057, 20119308333870518011412817828051050497, ...

This is entry A002812 in [312]; entry A003010 gives the values V_{2^k}:

  4, 14, 194, 37634, 1416317954, 2005956546822746114, 4023861667741036022825635656102100994, ...

The sequence of (currently known) exponents e such that $n = 2^e - 1$ is entry A000043 in [312]:

  2, 3, 5, 7, 13, 17, 19, 31, 61, 89, 107, 127, 521, 607, 1279, 2203, 2281, 3217,
  4253, 4423, 9689, 9941, 11213, 19937, 21701, 23209, 44497, 86243, 110503,
  132049, 216091, 756839, 859433, 1257787, 1398269, 2976221, 3021377, 6972593, 13466917

A few more exponents for Mersenne primes are known:

  20996011, 24036583, 25964951, 30402457, 32582657, 37156667, 42643801, 43112609

They are not included in the sequence as they might be preceded by currently unknown values. The list of exponents is also given in [FXT: mod/mersenne-exponents.cc].

39.11.4.2   What to consider before doing the Lucas-Lehmer test

The exponent e of a Mersenne prime must be prime, else n factors algebraically as

$$2^e - 1 \;=\; \prod_{d \backslash e} Y_d(2) \tag{39.11-1}$$

where $Y_k(x)$ is the k-th cyclotomic polynomial (see section 37.1.1 on page 704). For example, with $2^{21} - 1 = 2097151$ the following factors are found:

```
? m=1; fordiv(21,d, y2=subst(polcyclo(d,x),x,2); m*=y2;print(d,": ",y2)); m
   1: 1
   3: 7
   7: 127
  21: 2359
  2097151   \\ == 2^21-1
```

These factors are not necessarily prime: here 2359 factors further into $7 \cdot 337$. More information on the multiplicative structure of $b^e \pm 1$ can be found in [89]. We note the relation

$$\gcd\left(2^n - 1, 2^m - 1\right) \;=\; 2^g - 1 = \prod_{d \backslash g} Y_d(2) \quad \text{where} \quad g = \gcd(n, m) \tag{39.11-2}$$

It is the special case $x = 2$, $y = 1$ of

$$\gcd\left(x^n - y^n, x^m - y^m\right) \;=\; x^g - y^g \tag{39.11-3a}$$

$$= \; y^g \prod_{d \backslash g} \left[Y_d(x/y)\right] = \prod_{d \backslash g} \left[y^{\varphi(d)} Y_d(x/y)\right] \tag{39.11-3b}$$

The relation follows from 37.1-14 on page 706 and the fact that the cyclotomic polynomials Y_n and Y_m are coprime for $n \neq m$.

Before doing the Lucas-Lehmer test one should do a special version of trial division based on the following observation: any factor f of $m = 2^e - 1$ has the property that $2^e \equiv 1 \bmod f$. That is, $2^e - 1 \equiv 0 \bmod f$, so $m \equiv 0 \bmod f$ and f divides m. We further exploit that possible factors f are of the form $2ek+1$ and that $f \equiv \pm 1 \bmod 8$. The following routine does not try to assert the primality of a candidate factor as this would render the computation considerably slower.

```
1    mers_trial(e, mct=10^7, bnf=0)=
2    \\  try to discover small factors of the Mersenne number 2^e-1
3    \\  e : exponent of the Mersenne number
4    \\  mct : how many factors are tried
5    \\  pfq : stop with the factor found (zero: do not stop)
6    {
7        local(f, fi, ct, fct, m8);
8        print("exponent e=",e);
9        print("trying up to ", mct, " factors");
10       fi=2*e; \\ factors are of the form 2*e*k+1
11       f=1;
12       ct=0;
13       fct=0;  \\ how many factors where found so far
14       while (ct < mct,
15           f += fi;
16           m8 = bitand(f, 7);  \\ factor modulo 8
17           if ( (1!=m8) && (7!=m8), next(); );  \\ must equal +1 or -1
18           if ( Mod(2, f)^e == Mod(1, f),
19               print(f, " ", isprime(f));  \\ give factor and tell whether it is prime
20               fct++;
21               if ( fct==bnf , break(); );
22           );
23           ct++;
24       );
25   }
```

For $m = 2^{10007} - 1$ (3013 decimal digits) we find three factors of which all are prime:

```
? e=10007; mers_trial(e,,3);
exponent e=10007
trying up to 10000000 factors
   240169   1
   60282169  1
   136255313  1
? ##
***    last result computed in 44 ms.
? ceil((e*log(2.0)/log(10.0)))
   3013  \\ m=2^e-1 has 3,013 decimal digits
```

Sometimes one is lucky with truly huge numbers:

```
? e=2^31-1; mers_trial(e,,1);
exponent e=2147483647
trying up to 10000000 factors
   295257526626031   1
? ##
***    last result computed in 583 ms.
? ceil((e*log(2.0)/log(10.0)))
   646456993   \\  m=2^e-1 has 646,456,993 decimal digits
```

Note that we found that $m = 2^e - 1$ is prime if and only if there is no prime $f < m$ where the order of 2 equals e. A special case is sometimes given as follows: if both $p = 4k + 3$ and $q = 2p + 1$ are prime, then q divides $2^p - 1$ (because the order of 2 modulo q equals p).

By the way, if both $p = 4k + 1$ and $q = 2p + 1$ are prime, then q divides $2^p + 1$ (because the order of 2 modulo q equals $2p$ and $2^{2p} - 1 = (2^p + 1)(2^p - 1)$).

39.11.4.3   Lucas-Lehmer test with floats ‡

The Binet form (see section 35.1.6 on page 674) of the sequence H_n is

$$H_n = \frac{1}{2}\left[\left(2 + \sqrt{3}\right)^n + \left(2 + \sqrt{3}\right)^{-n}\right] \tag{39.11-4}$$

We can rewrite the expression in the form

$$H_n = \frac{1}{2}\left[\exp(x)^n + \exp(x)^{-n}\right] = \frac{1}{2}\left[\exp(nx) + \exp(-nx)\right] \tag{39.11-5}$$

where $x = \log(2 + \sqrt{3})$. The hyperbolic cosine can be defined as

$$\cosh(z) \;=\; \frac{1}{2}\left[\exp(z) + \exp(-z)\right] \tag{39.11-6}$$

and the expression equals H_n for $z = n \log(2 + \sqrt{3})$. Now we can give a criterion equivalent to the Lucas-Lehmer condition as follows:

$$\cosh\left(2^{m-2} \log\left(2 + \sqrt{3}\right)\right) \;\equiv\; 0 \quad \mod M_m \qquad \Longrightarrow \qquad M_m \text{ is prime} \tag{39.11-7}$$

The relation is computationally useless because the quantity to be computed grows doubly-exponential with m: the number of digits grows exponentially with m. Already for $m = 17$ the calculation has to be carried out with more than $18,741$ decimal digits:

```
? cosh(2^(17-2)*log(2+sqrt(3)))
 1.8888939581139837726097538478056602 E18741
```

The program [hfloat: examples/ex8.cc] does the computations in the obvious (insane) way. Using a precision of 32,768 decimal digits we obtain:

```
cosh(...)=
 +.18888939581139837726097538478056602859465844315551 \
  [... about 18,000 digits ...]
   ... 557975003980068028417000000000000000 ...
                     ^[decimal point after 7]
 00000000000000000000000000000000000000000000000000000 \
 [...]
 0000000000000000015496957204461401504275889854001854472*10^18742
                 [nonzero due to numerical imprecision]
```

After rounding and computing the modulus, the program declares $M_{17} = 2^{17} - 1$ prime. All this using just 4 MB of memory and computations equivalent to about 35 FFTs of length 1 million, taking about four seconds. This is many many million times the work needed by the original (sane) version of the test. Even trial division would have been significantly faster.

The number M_{31} would need a bigger machine as the computations needs a precision of more than 300 million digits:

```
? (2^(31-2)*log(2+sqrt(3)))/log(10)   /* approx decimal digits */
 307062001.46039800926268312190009204
```

Apart from being insane the computation can be used to test high precision floating-point libraries.

39.11.4.4 The Lucas test

The Lucas-Lehmer test can be generalized for a less restricted set of candidates. The *Lucas test* can be stated as follows (taken from [284, p.131]):

Let $n = k\,2^t - 1$ where k is odd, $2^t > k$, $n \neq 0 \mod 3$ and $k \neq 0 \mod 3$ (so we must have $n \equiv 1 \mod 3$). Then n is prime if and only if $H_{(n+1)/4} \equiv 0 \mod n$ where H is as given above.

To turn this into an efficient algorithm use the relation $(n+1)/4 = k\,2^{t-2}$. Compute H_k as described in section 35.1.1 on page 666:

$$[H_k,\ H_{k+1}] \;=\; [H_0,\ H_1]\begin{bmatrix} 0 & -1 \\ 1 & 4 \end{bmatrix}^k \tag{39.11-8}$$

This is a one-liner in GP:

```
? H(k)= return( ([1,2] * [0, -1; 1, 4]^k)[1] );
? for(k=0,10,print(k,": ",H(k)," = 1/2 * ",2*H(k)))
  0: 1    = 1/2 * 2
  1: 2    = 1/2 * 4
  2: 7    = 1/2 * 14
  3: 26   = 1/2 * 52
  4: 97   = 1/2 * 194          /* = 2*7^2-1 = (14^2-2)/2 */
  5: 362  = 1/2 * 724
  6: 1351 = 1/2 * 2702         /* = 2*26^2-1 = (52^2-2)/2 */
  7: 5042 = 1/2 * 10084
```

```
 8: 18817   = 1/2 * 37634
 9: 70226   = 1/2 * 140452
10: 262087  = 1/2 * 524174
```

To compute $H_{k\,2^{t-2}}$ from H_k use ($t-2$ times) the index doubling relation $H_{2k} = 2\,H_k^2 - 1$. The test can be implemented as

```
1    H(k, n)= return( (Mod([1,2],n) * Mod([0,-1; 1,4], n)^k)[1] );
2
3    lucas(k, t)=
4    {
5        local(n, h);
6        /* check preconditions: */
7        if ( 0==bitand(k,1), return(0) );   \\ k must be odd
8        if ( k>=2^t, return(0) );
9        n = k*2^t-1;
10       if ( n%3!=1, return(0) );   \\ gcd(3,k)!=0 && gcd(3,n)!=0
11
12       /* main loop: */
13       h = H(k, n);
14       for (j=1,t-2, h*=h; h+=h; h-=1; );   \\ index doubling
15       return ( 0==h );
16   }
```

Note that the routine returns 'false' even for primes if the preconditions are not met. With $n = 5 \cdot 2^{12} - 1 = 20479$ we obtain

```
n=20479   k=5   t=12
  j  H_{k*2^j} modulo n
  0       362
  1     16339
  2     17832
  3      5581
  4     18482
  5      9686
  6      8593
  7      5228
  8      5516
  9      9402
 10         0
```

which shows that 20479 is prime. Proving $n = 5 \cdot 2^{1340} - 1$ prime takes about ten milliseconds. The following code finds the first value $t \geq 2500$ so that $n = 5 \cdot 2^t - 1$ is prime:

```
k=5;  t=2500;  while ( 0==lucas(k,t), t+=1; );  t
```

Within one second we get the result $t = 2548$.

39.11.4.5   Numbers of the form $n = 24\,j + 7$ and $n = 24\,j + 19$ ‡

```
         n:    SPP bases a<100,000 (max 5 given)
   1037623:   67191 67192                                    [--snip--]
   2211631:   6333 7260 8160 16793 21219 21580          2946282799:
   4196191:   9104 26498 93477                          3075304399:
   7076623:                                             3145717759:
   9100783:                                             3299597407:
  11418991:   44936                                     3554502799:
  15219559:                                             3554889199:
  21148399:                                             4091977039:
    [--snip--]                                          4207009999:
 829577839:
 887557999:   4899 33982 46674 62180
 961315183:
1192222639:
    [--snip--]
```

Figure 39.11-C: Composite numbers $n < 2^{32}$ of the form $n = 24\,j + 7$ that pass the Lucas-type test. Five of them are strong pseudoprime to some base $a < 100,000$.

Numbers of the form $n = 24\,j + 7$ satisfy the preconditions of the Lucas test *except* for the condition that $2^t > k$ where $n = k\,2^t - 1$. We test whether $H_{(n+1)/4} \equiv 0 \bmod n$, as in the Lucas test. Note that $H_n = T_n(2)$ where $T_n(x)$ is the n-th Chebyshev polynomial of the first kind. We use the fast algorithm for its computation described in section 35.2.3 on page 680 for the test routine:

```
1    bool test_7mod24(ulong n)
2    {
3        ulong nu = (n+1) >> 2;
```

```
4       umod_t t = chebyT2(nu, n);    // == chebyT(nu, 2, n);
5       return  (0==u1);
6   }
```

The function `chebyT2()` is given in [FXT: mod/chebyshev1.cc]. Figure 39.11-C gives composite numbers $n < 2^{32}$ that pass the test. The complete list of such numbers is given in [FXT: data/pseudo-7mod24.txt], there are just 64 entries. Only five entries are strong pseudoprimes to any base $a < 100,000$, all shown in figure 39.11-C.

The data suggests that composites of the form $n = 24j + 7$ that pass the test and are pseudoprime to a small base are extremely rare. The implied test would cover $1/8$ of all candidates (that are not divisible by 2 or 3), as eight numbers (1, 5, 7, 11, 13, 17, 19, and 23) are coprime to 24.

```
        n:   SPP bases a<100,000
    30739:                                          [--snip--]
   153931:                                       97917619:
   249331:                                      100079611:    4820
  1575859:                                      124134067:
  1960243:                                          [--snip--]
  2557627:   36814 49266 49267 86080            2946282799:
  3444403:                                      3075304399:
  3767347:   26452 79860 94736                  3145717759:
  3881179:   47489 67676 72825 73841 84995 87856  3299597407:
  3882283:                                      3554502799:
 14324491:                                      3554889199:
 14970499:                                      4091977039:
 15894163:                                      4207009999:
```

Figure 39.11-D: Composite numbers $n < 2^{32}$ of the form $n = 24k + 19$ that pass the Lucas-type test. Four of them are strong pseudoprimes to some base $a < 100,000$.

For numbers of the form $n = 24j + 19$ we use a different test: here we check whether $U_{(n+1)/4-1} \equiv 0 \bmod n$ where $U_0 = 0$, $U_1 = 1$, and $U_k = 4U_{k-1} - U_{k-2}$ (the Chebyshev polynomial of the second kind, $U_n(x)$, evaluated at $x = 2$). The function for testing is

```
1   bool test_19mod24(ulong n)
2   {
3       ulong nu = ((n+1) >> 2) - 1;
4       umod_t t = chebyU2(nu, n);  // == chebyU(nu, 2, n);
5       return  (0==t);
6   }
```

where the function `chebyU2()` is given in [FXT: mod/chebyshev2.cc]. The list [FXT: data/pseudo-19mod24.txt] contains all (155) composites $n < 2^{32}$ that pass the test. An extract is shown in figure 39.11-D. Just four numbers $n < 2^{32}$ are also strong pseudoprimes to any base $a < 100,000$.

The application of second order recurrent sequences to primality testing is described in [35]: define the sequence W_k by

$$W_k = PW_{k-1} - QW_{k-2}, \qquad W_0 = 0, \quad W_1 = 1 \qquad (39.11\text{-}9)$$

Then n is a *Lucas pseudoprime* (with parameters P and Q) if $W_{n\pm1} \equiv 0 \bmod n$, where the sign depends on whether $D = P^2 - 4Q$ is a square modulo n. For both cases considered here we have $n = 12j + 7$, $D = 16 - 4 = 12 = 4 \cdot 3$, and 3 is not a square modulo n. The test would be (note that $W_n = U_{n-1}(2)$)

```
1   bool lucas_7mod12(ulong n)
2   {
3       ulong nu = n;
4       umod_t t = chebyU2(nu, n);
5       return  (0==t);
6   }
```

This test is passed by far more composites than the two tests considered before. A primality test combining a Lucas-type test and a test for strong pseudoprimality has been suggested in [272]. No composite that passes the test has been found so far.

39.11.4.6   An observation regarding Mersenne numbers

An interesting observation is that the following *seems* to be true:

$$M = 2^e - 1 \quad \text{prime} \quad \Longleftrightarrow \quad 3^{2^{e-1}} \equiv -3 \bmod M \tag{39.11-10}$$

Note that for odd e the condition is equivalent to $3^{(M-1)/2} \equiv -1 \bmod n$ and 3 is a non-residue. For prime exponents e we can see that we are very unlikely to find a composite M_e where $3^{(M-1)/2} \equiv -1 \bmod n$: the number m is a strong pseudoprime (SPP) to base 2 by construction and the right side of condition 39.11-10 says that m is an SPP to base 3. Given the rarity of composites that are SPP to both bases (see section 39.10.2 on page 787) the chances of finding such a number among the exponentially growing Mersenne numbers are very small. Tony Reix, who observed the statement of relation 39.11-10, independently verified it for prime exponents up to 132,499.

39.11.4.7   Primes that are evaluations of cyclotomic polynomials

The Mersenne numbers and Fermat numbers are special cases of evaluations of cyclotomic polynomials Y_n (see section 37.1.1 on page 704). The first numbers $Y_n(2)$ are shown in figure 39.11-E, the sequence is entry A019320 in [312]. The sequence of values n such that $Y_n(2)$ is prime is entry A072226 in [312]:

2, 3, 4, 5, 6, 7, 8, 9, 10, 12, 13, 14, 15, 16, 17, 19, 22, 24, 26, 27, 30, 31, 32, 33, 34, 38, 40, 42, 46, 49, 56, 61, 62, 65, 69, 77, 78, 80, 85, 86, 89, 90, 93, 98, 107, 120, 122, 126, 127, 129, 133, 145, 150, 158, 165, 170, 174, 184, 192, 195, 202, 208, 234, 254, 261, ...

The powers of two correspond to the Fermat primes. The prime numbers correspond to Mersenne primes. The sequence of numbers n such that $Y_n(3)$ is prime is entry A138933:

1, 3, 6, 7, 9, 10, 12, 13, 14, 15, 21, 24, 26, 33, 36, 40, 46, 60, 63, 70, 71, 72, 86, 103, 108, 130, 132, 143, 145, 154, 161, 236, 255, 261, 276, 279, 287, ...

Now set $N := Y_n(2)$, testing whether N is a base-3 SPP seems to determine primality for all values of $n \notin \{2, 6\}$. Note that for n a power of 2 the test is Pepin's test. Information about the primality of $Y_n(2)$ is given in [148]. Theorems about factorizations of $Y_n(x)$ where x is an integer are given in [159], see also [78] and [76]. The factorization into Gaussian primes is discussed in [128].

The primes $Y_n(2)$ are also of interest for number theoretic transforms (see section 26.1 on page 535) because of their special structure allowing for very efficient modular reduction (see section 39.2 on page 768). A prominent example is $Y_{192}(2) = 2^{64} - 2^{32} + 1$. Note that the order of 2 modulo $Y_n(2)$ equals n.

The structure of the primes becomes (in base 10) visible if we check evaluations at 10, the first primes of the form $Y_n(10)$ are

```
n:    Yn(10)
2:    11
4:    101
10:   9091
12:   9901
14:   909091
19:   1111111111111111111
23:   11111111111111111111111
24:   99990001
36:   999999000001
38:   909090909090909091
39:   900900900900990990990991
48:   9999999900000001
```

Finally, we do a silly thing: the factors of $Y_{2^7-1}(x)$ over GF(2) are the irreducible binary polynomials of degree 7. If we evaluate them as polynomials over $\mathbb{Z}$ at $x = 10$ and select the prime numbers we find the following 8-digit primes consisting of only zero and ones:

10011101   10111001   11100101   11110111   11111101

The same procedure, with $Y_{3^5-1}(x)$ and factoring over GF(3) gives the primes

101221   102101   111121   111211   112111   120011   122021

The list is created via

```
n=3^5-1;  f=lift(factor(polcyclo(n)*Mod(1,3)));  f=f[,1];
for(k=1, #f, v=subst(f[k],x,10); if(isprime(v), print(v)));
```

```
 n:  s=Yn(2)                                 n:  s=Yn(3)
 2:  3                                        2:  2 * 2
 3:  7                                        3:  13
 4:  5                                        4:  2 * 5
 5:  31                                       5:  11 * 11
 6:  3                                        6:  7
 7:  127                                      7:  1093
 8:  17                                       8:  2 * 41
 9:  73                                       9:  757
10:  11                                      10:  61
11:  23 * 89       <--= SPP [11]            11:  23 * 3851
12:  13                                      12:  73
13:  8191                                    13:  797161
14:  43                                      14:  547
15:  151                                     15:  4561
16:  257                                     16:  2 * 17 * 193
17:  131071                                  17:  1871 * 34511
18:  3 * 19                                  18:  19 * 37           <--= SPP [7]
19:  524287                                  19:  1597 * 363889
20:  5 * 41                                  20:  5 * 1181
21:  7 * 337                                 21:  368089
22:  683                                     22:  67 * 661
23:  47 * 178481                             23:  47 * 1001523179
24:  241                                     24:  6481
25:  601 * 1801    <--= SPP [29]            25:  8951 * 391151
26:  2731                                    26:  398581
27:  262657                                  27:  109 * 433 * 8209
28:  29 * 113                                28:  29 * 16493
29:  233 * 1103 * 2089                       29:  59 * 28537 * 20381027
30:  331                                     30:  31 * 271          <--= SPP [29]
31:  2147483647                              31:  683 * 102673 * 4404047
32:  65537                                   32:  2 * 21523361
33:  599479                                  33:  2413941289
34:  43691                                   34:  103 * 307 * 1021
35:  71 * 122921                             35:  71 * 2664097031
36:  37 * 109   <--= SPP [17, 19, 23]       36:  530713
37:  223 * 616318177                         37:  13097927 * 17189128703
38:  174763                                  38:  2851 * 101917
39:  79 * 121369                             39:  13 * 313 * 6553 * 7333
40:  61681                                   40:  42521761
41:  13367 * 164511353                       41:  83 * 2526913 * 86950696619
42:  5419                                    42:  7 * 43 * 2269
43:  431 * 9719 * 2099863                    43:  431 * 380808546861411923
44:  397 * 2113                              44:  5501 * 570461
45:  631 * 23311       <--= SPP [5]         45:  181 * 1621 * 927001
46:  2796203                                 46:  23535794707
47:  2351 * 4513 * 13264529                  47:  1223 * 21997 * 5112661 * 96656723
48:  97 * 673                                48:  97 * 577 * 769
49:  4432676798593                           49:  491 * 4019 * 8233 * 51157 * 131713
50:  251 * 4051                              50:  151 * 22996651
51:  103 * 2143 * 11119                      51:  12853 * 99810171997
52:  53 * 157 * 1613                         52:  53 * 4795973261
53:  6361 * 69431 * 20394401                 53:  107 * 24169 * 3747607031112307667
54:  3 * 87211                               54:  19441 * 19927
55:  881 * 3191 * 201961                     55:  11 * 1321 * 560088668384411
56:  15790321                                56:  430697 * 647753
57:  32377 * 1212847                         57:  229 * 248749 * 1824179209
58:  59 * 3033169                            58:  523 * 6091 * 5385997
59:  179951 * 3203431780337                  59:  14425532687 * 489769993189671059
60:  61 * 1321                               60:  47763361
61:  2305843009213693951                     61:  603901 * 10529331366039186 1035901
62:  715827883                               62:  6883 * 22434744889
63:  92737 * 649657                          63:  144542918285300809
64:  641 * 6700417                           64:  2 * 926510094425921
65:  145295143558111                         65:  131 * 3701101 * 110133112994711
```

Figure 39.11-E: Evaluations s of the first cyclotomic polynomials at 2 (left). Entries at prime n are Mersenne numbers M_n, entries at $n = 2^k$ are Fermat numbers F_k. Composites that are strong pseudoprimes to prime bases other than 2 are marked with 'SPP'. The right side shows the corresponding data for evaluations at 3.

39.11.4.8   Further reading

Excellent introductions into topics related to prime numbers and methods of factorization are [284], [361], [283], and [118]. Primality tests and factorization algorithms are also described in [154]. Some of the newer factorization algorithms can be found in [110], readable surveys are [230] and [253]. Tables of factorizations of numbers of the form $b^e \pm 1$ are given in [89] which also contains much historical information.

A deterministic polynomial-time algorithm for proving primality was published by Agrawal, Kayal and Saxena in August 2002 [4]. While this is a major breakthrough in mathematics it does not render the Rabin-Miller test worthless. Indeed, 'industrial grade' primes are still produced with it, see [81] (but see [270] for 'counter examples'). Good introductions into the ideas behind the *AKS algorithm* and its improvements are [170] and [118, p.200ff].

39.12   Complex modulus: the field $\mathrm{GF}(p^2)$

With real numbers the equation $x^2 = -1$ has no solution, there is no real square root of -1. The construction of complex numbers proceeds by taking pairs of real numbers $(a, b) = a + ib$ together with component-wise addition $(a, b) + (c, d) = (a + c, b + d)$ and multiplication defined by $(a, b)(c, d) = (ac - bd, ad + bc)$. Indeed the pairs of real numbers together with addition and multiplication as given constitute a field.

We will now rephrase the construction in a way that shows how to construct an *extension field* from a given *ground field* (or *base field*). In the example above the real numbers are the ground field and the complex numbers are the extension field.

39.12.1   The construction of complex numbers

There is no real square root of -1, that is, the polynomial $x^2 + 1$ has no real root. The construction of the complex numbers proceeds by taking numbers of the form $a + bi$ where i is boldly defined to be a root of the polynomial $x^2 + 1$. Now observe that if we identify $a + bi = bi + a$ with the polynomial $bx + a$ and use polynomial addition and multiplication modulo the polynomial $x^2 + 1$, then we obtain the arithmetic of complex numbers. Addition is component-wise, no modular reduction occurs. Now we determine the multiplication rule:

$$
\begin{array}{rcll}
(bx + a)(dx + c) & = & (bd)x^2 + (ad + bc)x + (ac) & \text{(39.12-1a)} \\
& \equiv & (ad + bc)x + (ac - bd) \quad (\bmod\ x^2 + 1) & \text{(39.12-1b)}
\end{array}
$$

We used the relation $x^2 = -1$, so $u x^2 \equiv -u \pmod{x^2 + 1}$. Identify x with i in the relations to see that the complex arithmetic is the polynomial arithmetic of real polynomials modulo the polynomial $x^2 + 1$.

If the ground field is the real numbers, the story comes to an end: every polynomial of arbitrary degree n with complex coefficients has exactly n complex roots (including multiplicity). That is, we cannot use the given construction to extend the field $\mathbb{C}$: all roots of every polynomial $p(x)$ with coefficients in $\mathbb{C}$ lie in $\mathbb{C}$. The field $\mathbb{C}$ is *algebraically closed*.

If we choose the ground field to be $\mathbb{F}_p = \mathrm{GF}(p)$, the integers modulo a prime p, and an irreducible polynomial $c(x)$ of degree n whose coefficients are in $\mathbb{F}_p$, then we obtain an extension field $\mathbb{F}_{p^n} = \mathrm{GF}(p^n)$, a *finite field* with p^n elements. The special case of the *binary finite fields* $\mathrm{GF}(2^n)$ is treated in chapter 42 on page 886.

39.12.2   Complex finite fields

With primes of the form $p = 4k + 3$ it is possible to construct a field of complex numbers as -1 is a quadratic non-residue and so the polynomial $x^2 + 1$ is irreducible. The field is denoted by $\mathrm{GF}(p^2)$.

```
a= 1+1*i
a^1  = 1+1*i
a^2  = 0+2*i  // (1+x)*(1+x)   = x^2+2*x+1   == 2*x+1 - 1 = 2*x+0 == 0+2*x
a^3  = 1+2*i  // (1+x)*(0+2*x) = 2*x^2+2*x   == 2*x   - 2 = 2*x-2 == 1+2*x
a^4  = 2+0*i  // (1+x)*(1+2*x) = 2*x^2+3*x+1 == 3*x+1 - 2 = 3*x-1 == 2+0*x
a^5  = 2+2*i  //                                ^^                   ^^
a^6  = 0+1*i  //                        mod(x^2+1)           mod(3)
a^7  = 2+1*i == a^(-1)= 2+1*i
a^8  = 1+0*i == one
a^9  = 1+1*i

R=maxord==8 == Mat([2, 3])
r=ord(a)==8
R/r=1
```

Figure 39.12-A: The powers of the element $1 + 1\,x$ modulo $x^2 + 1$ and $p = 3$.

The rules for complex addition, subtraction and multiplication are the 'usual' ones. The field has p^2 elements of which $R = p^2 - 1$ are invertible. The maximal order equals R, so the inverse of an element a can be computed as $a^{-1} = a^{R-1} = a^{p^2-2}$.

For example, the powers of $a = 1 + x = 1 + i$ modulo $c = x^2 + 1 = 0 = 3 + 3i$ are shown in figure 39.12-A Note that the modular reduction happens with both the polynomial $x^2 + 1$ and the prime $p = 3$. The polynomial reduction uses $x^2 = -1$.

```
a^1  = 1 + 3*x
a^2  = 2 + 2*x  // (1+3*x)*(1+3*x) = 9*x^2+6*x+1 == 6*x+1 - (9*x+9) =-3*x-8 == 2+2*x
a^3  = 1 + 2*x  // (1+3*x)*(2+2*x) = 6*x^2+8*x+2 == 8*x+2 - (6*x+6) = 2*x-4 == 1+2*x
a^4  = 0 + 4*x  // (1+3*x)*(1+2*x) = 6*x^2+5*x+1 == 5*x+1 - (6*x+6) =  -x-5 == 0+4*x
a^5  = 3 + 2*x  //                                  ^^                         ^^
a^6  = 2 + 0*x  //                          mod(x^2+x+1)              mod(5)
a^7  = 2 + 1*x
a^8  = 4 + 4*x
a^9  = 2 + 4*x
a^10 = 0 + 3*x
a^11 = 1 + 4*x
a^12 = 4 + 0*x
a^13 = 4 + 2*x
a^14 = 3 + 3*x
a^15 = 4 + 3*x
a^16 = 0 + 1*x
a^17 = 2 + 3*x
a^18 = 3 + 0*x
a^19 = 3 + 4*x
a^20 = 1 + 1*x
a^21 = 3 + 1*x
a^22 = 0 + 2*x
a^23 = 4 + 1*x
a^24 = 1 + 0*x
```

Figure 39.12-B: The powers of the element $1 + 3\,x$ modulo $x^2 + x + 1$ and $p = 5$.

With primes of the form $p = 4k + 1$ it is also possible to construct a field GF(p^2). But we have to use a different polynomial as $x^2 + 1$ is reducible modulo p and thereby the multiplication rule is different. For example, with $p = 5$ we find that $x^2 + x + 1$ is irreducible:

```
? p=5;  m=Mod(1,p)*(1+x+x^2);  polisirreducible(m)
 1
? a=Mod(1,p)*(1+3*x)
? for(k=1,p^2-1,print("a^",k," = ",lift(Mod(a,m)^k)))
  a^1 = Mod(3, 5)*x + Mod(1, 5)
  a^2 = Mod(2, 5)*x + Mod(2, 5)
  a^3 = Mod(2, 5)*x + Mod(1, 5)
  [--snip--]
```

The complete list of powers is shown in figure 39.12-B. We see that $a = 1 + 3x$ has the maximal order (24), it is a primitive root. The polynomial reduction uses the relation $x^2 = -(x + 1)$.

The values of the powers of the primitive root can be used to 'randomly' fill a $p \times p$ array. With $a^k = u + x\,v$ we mark the entry at row v, column u with k:

```
[ 4 11  9 19  8]
[10  1 17 14 15]
[22  3  2  5 13]
[16 20  7 21 23]
[-- 24  6 18 12]
```

The position $0, 0$ (lower left) is not visited. Note row zero is the lowest row.

As described, the procedure fills a $p \times p$ array where p is a prime. With an irreducible polynomial of degree n we can fill a $p^e \times p^f \times p^g \times \ldots \times p^k$ array if $e + f + g + \ldots + k = n$: For exponents equal to 1 choose an arbitrary polynomial coefficient. For exponents $h > 1$, combine h polynomial coefficients c_0, c_1, $\ldots$, c_{h-1} as $z_h = c_0 + c_1 p + c_2 p^2 + \ldots c_{h-1} p^{h-1}$.

39.12.3   Efficient reduction modulo certain quadratic polynomials

The polynomial $C = x^2 + 1$ is irreducible for primes of the form $4k + 3$ (-1 is not a square)

$$
\begin{aligned}
(a x + b)(A x + B) &= (a A) x^2 + (a B + b A) x + (b B) & \text{(39.12-2a)} \\
&\equiv (a B + b A) x + (-a A + b B) \quad \bmod x^2 + 1 & \text{(39.12-2b)} \\
&= ((a + b)(A + B) - a A - b B) x + (-a A + b B) & \text{(39.12-2c)}
\end{aligned}
$$

The last equality shows how to multiply two complex numbers at the cost of three real multiplications and five real additions instead of four multiplications and two additions.

The polynomial $C = x^2 + d$ is irreducible if $-d$ is not a square. We have

$$
\begin{aligned}
(a x + b)(A x + B) &\equiv (a B + b A) x + (-d a A + b B) \quad \bmod x^2 + d & \text{(39.12-3a)} \\
&= ((a + b)(A + B) - a A - b B) x + (-d a A + b B) & \text{(39.12-3b)}
\end{aligned}
$$

If the multiplication by d is cheap (for example, if $d = 2$) the implied technique can be a gain.

The polynomial $C := x^2 + x + 1$ has the roots $\left(-1 \pm \sqrt{-3}\right)/2$ so it is irreducible modulo p if -3 is not a square modulo p. The first few such primes p are

2 5 11 17 23 29 41 47 53 59 71 83 89 101 107 113 131 137 149 167 173 179 191 197 227 233 239

Multiplication modulo C costs only three scalar multiplications:

$$
\begin{aligned}
(a x + b)(A x + B) &= (a A) x^2 + (a B + b A) x + (b B) & \text{(39.12-4a)} \\
&\equiv (-a A + a B + b A) x + (-a A + b B) \quad \bmod x^2 + x + 1 & \text{(39.12-4b)} \\
&= ((a - b)(B - A) + b B) x + (-a A + b B) & \text{(39.12-4c)}
\end{aligned}
$$

For the polynomial $C = x^2 + x + d$ use

$$
\begin{aligned}
(a x + b)(A x + B) &\equiv (-a A + a B + b A) x + (-d a A + b B) \quad \bmod x^2 + x + d & \text{(39.12-5a)} \\
&= ((a - b)(B - A) + b B) x + (-d a A + b B) & \text{(39.12-5b)}
\end{aligned}
$$

The polynomial $C = x^2 - x - 1$ has the roots $\left(1 \pm \sqrt{5}\right)/2$, so it is irreducible modulo p if 5 is not a square modulo p. The first few such primes are:

2 3 7 13 17 23 37 43 47 53 67 73 83 97 103 107 113 127 137 157 163 167 173 193 197 223 227 233

Again, multiplication modulo C costs only three scalar multiplications:

$$
\begin{aligned}
(a x + b)(A x + B) &= (a A) x^2 + (a B + b A) x + (b B) & \text{(39.12-6a)} \\
&\equiv (a A + a B + b A) x + (a A + b B) \quad \bmod x^2 - x - 1 & \text{(39.12-6b)} \\
&= ((a + b)(A + B) - b B) x + (a A + b B) & \text{(39.12-6c)}
\end{aligned}
$$

With the polynomial $C = x^2 - x - d$ use

$$
\begin{aligned}
(a x + b)(A x + B) &\equiv (a A + a B + b A) x + (d a A + b B) \quad \bmod x^2 - x - d & \text{(39.12-7a)} \\
&= ((a + b)(A + B) - b B) x + (d a A + b B) & \text{(39.12-7b)}
\end{aligned}
$$

For polynomials of the form $C = x^2 - e\,x - d$ we have

$$
\begin{aligned}
(a\,x + b)\,(A\,x + B) &= (a\,A)\,x^2 + (a\,B + b\,A)\,x + (b\,B) &\text{(39.12-8a)}\\
&\equiv (e\,a\,A + a\,B + b\,A)\,x + (d\,a\,A + b\,B) \quad \bmod x^2 - e\,x - d &\text{(39.12-8b)}\\
&= ((a + b)\,(A + B) - [e - 1]\,a\,A - b\,B)\,x + (d\,a\,A + b\,B) &\text{(39.12-8c)}
\end{aligned}
$$

If the multiplications by $e - 1$ and d are cheap, then the last equality can be useful. For example, with the polynomial $C = x^2 - 2\,x - 1$ use

$$
\begin{aligned}
(a\,x + b)\,(A\,x + B) &\equiv (2\,a\,A + a\,B + b\,A)\,x + (a\,A + b\,B) \quad \bmod x^2 - 2\,x - 1 &\text{(39.12-9a)}\\
&= ((a + b)\,(A + B) - b\,B + a\,A)\,x + (a\,A + b\,B) &\text{(39.12-9b)}
\end{aligned}
$$

With $C = x^2 - 3\,x \pm 1$ use

$$
\begin{aligned}
(a\,x + b)\,(A\,x + B) &\equiv (3\,a\,A + a\,B + b\,A)\,x + (\mp a\,A + b\,B) \quad \bmod x^2 - 3\,x \pm 1 &\text{(39.12-10a)}\\
&= ((a + b)\,(A + B) - b\,B + 2\,a\,A)\,x + (\mp a\,A + b\,B) &\text{(39.12-10b)}
\end{aligned}
$$

39.12.4 An algorithm for primitive 2^j-th roots

For primes with the lowest k bits set ($p \equiv (2^k - 1) \pmod{2^k}$) the largest power of 2 dividing the maximal order in GF(p^2) equals $N = 2^{k+1}$: $p = j\,2^k - 1$ with j odd, so $p + 1 = j\,2^k$ and $p - 1 = j\,2^k - 2 = 2\,(j\,2^{k-1} - 1)$, thereby $p^2 - 1 = 2^{k+1}\,[j\,(j\,2^k - 1)]$ where the term in square brackets is odd.

An algorithm for the construction of primitive 2^j-th roots in GF(p^2) for $j = 2, 3, \ldots, a$ where 2^a is the largest power of 2 dividing $p^2 - 1$ is given in [149] (and also in [54]):

Let $u_2 := 0$ and for $j > 2$ define

$$
u_j := \begin{cases}
\left((u_{j-1} + 1)/2 \right)^{(p+1)/4} & \text{if } j < a \\
\left((u_{j-1} - 1)/2 \right)^{(p+1)/4} & \text{if } j = a
\end{cases}
\tag{39.12-11}
$$

and (for $j = 2, 3, \ldots, a$)

$$
v_j := \begin{cases}
(+1 - u_j^2)^{(p+1)/4} & \text{if } j < a \\
(-1 - u_j^2)^{(p+1)/4} & \text{if } j = a
\end{cases}
\tag{39.12-12}
$$

where all operations are modulo p. Then $u_j + i\,v_j$ is a primitive 2^j-th root of unity in GF(p^2).

For example, with $p = 127$ (and field polynomial $x^2 + 1$) we compute

```
j:      u_j  v_j
2:      ord(0 + i*1) = 4
3:      ord(8 + i*8) = 8
4:      ord(103 + i*21) = 16
5:      ord(68 + i*87) = 32
6:      ord(15 + i*41) = 64
7:      ord(32 + i*82) = 128
8:      ord(98 + i*38) = 256
```

For Mersenne primes $p = 2^e - 1$ one has $p^2 - 1 = (p + 1)\,(p - 1) = 2^e\,(2^e - 2) = 2^{e+1}\,(2^{e-1} - 1) =: 2^a\,k$ where k is odd. The highest power of 2 for which a primitive root exists is 2^a where $a = e + 1$. This checks with our example where $p = 127 = 2^7 - 1$.

39.12.5 Primitive 2^j-th roots with Mersenne primes

For Mersenne primes $p = 2^e - 1$ an element of order 2^{e+1} (in GF(p^2) with field polynomial $x^2 + 1$) can be constructed more directly: first compute $\sqrt{-3} = 3^{(p+1)/4} = 3^{2^{e-2}}$ by squaring $e - 2$ times, then compute $1/\sqrt{2} = 2^{(e-1)/2}$ which does not require modular reduction. Now an element of order 2^{e+1} is

$$
z := \frac{1}{\sqrt{2}}\,(1 + \sqrt{3}) = \frac{1}{\sqrt{2}}\,(1 + i\,\sqrt{-3})
\tag{39.12-13}
$$

```
    p =   131071  = 2^17-1
    r3 =    43811      r3^2 =  -3

    k:      h + i*w =    z^(2^k)           =   h + i*r3*  u
    0:      h + i*w =   +256 + i*  -56490  =   h + i*r3*    +256    ord(.) = 2^18
    1:      h + i*w =     +2 + i*  +43811  =   h + i*r3*      +1    ord(.) = 2^17
    2:      h + i*w =     +7 + i*  +44173  =   h + i*r3*      +4    ord(.) = 2^16
    3:      h + i*w =    +97 + i*  -36933  =   h + i*r3*     +56    ord(.) = 2^15
    4:      h + i*w = +18817 + i*  +43903  =   h + i*r3*  +10864    ord(.) = 2^14
    5:      h + i*w = -17636 + i*  -35524  =   h + i*r3*  +45327    ord(.) = 2^13
    6:      h + i*w =  -5975 + i*  -36232  =   h + i*r3*  +30114    ord(.) = 2^12
    7:      h + i*w = -32446 + i*  +44887  =   h + i*r3*  +58666    ord(.) = 2^11
    8:      h + i*w = -38713 + i*  -16371  =   h + i*r3*   +3123    ord(.) = 2^10
    9:      h + i*w = +61109 + i*  -46595  =   h + i*r3*  +24597    ord(.) = 2^9
   10:      h + i*w = +63110 + i*  +25098  =   h + i*r3*  -48310    ord(.) = 2^8
   11:      h + i*w = +35245 + i*  +14561  =   h + i*r3*   -3138    ord(.) = 2^7
   12:      h + i*w = -30756 + i*  -12111  =   h + i*r3*  +50228    ord(.) = 2^6
   13:      h + i*w = -15743 + i*  -35732  =   h + i*r3*  -19124    ord(.) = 2^5
   14:      h + i*w = -26425 + i*  -55712  =   h + i*r3*   -1910    ord(.) = 2^4
   15:      h + i*w =   -256 + i*    +256  =   h + i*r3*  +18830    ord(.) = 2^3
   16:      h + i*w =      0 + i*      -1  =   h + i*r3*  +58294    ord(.) = 2^2
   17:      h + i*w =     -1 + i*       0  =   h + i*r3*       0    ord(.) = 2^1
   18:      h + i*w =     +1 + i*       0  =   h + i*r3*       0    ord(.) = 2^0
```

Figure 39.12-C: Elements of order 2^j in $\mathrm{GF}(p^2)$ where $p = 2^{17} - 1$ is a Mersenne prime.

The result is given in [280] (where a different element $z' = \sqrt{2} + \sqrt{3}$ of the same order is used; note that $\sqrt{2} = 2^{2^{e-2}} = 2^{(e+1)/2}$). The number z' is sometimes called the *Creutzburg-Tasche primitive root* as the construction is also described in [119, p.200]. We have $z^2 = 2 + \sqrt{3} = 2 + i\sqrt{-3} = H_1 + i\sqrt{-3}\,U_1$, and

$$z^{2^k} = H_{2^{k-1}} + i\sqrt{-3}\,U_{2^{k-1}} \qquad \text{for } (k \geq 1) \tag{39.12-14}$$

Figure 39.12-C shows the values of the successive 2^k-th powers of z in $\mathrm{GF}(p^2)$ where $p = 2^{17} - 1$.

The sequences $H = 2, 7, 97, 18817, \ldots$ and $U = 1, 4, 56, 10864, \ldots$ are those which appear in the Lucas-Lehmer test (see section 39.11.4.1 on page 796). The order of z^{2^k} is 2^{e+1-k}. We have $H_{2j} = 2\,H_j^2 - 1$, $H_j^2 - 3\,U_j^2 = 1$, and the index doubling formulas for the convergents of the continued fraction of $\sqrt{3}$:

$$H_{2j} = H_j^2 + 3\,U_j^2 \tag{39.12-15a}$$
$$U_{2j} = 2\,H_j U_j \tag{39.12-15b}$$

A method to compute a primitive root is described in [281]: Let c be a primitive root in $\mathrm{GF}(p)$, then $a + bi$ is a primitive root in $\mathrm{GF}(p^2)$ if $a^2 + b^2 \equiv c \bmod p$ (this can always be solved for any c). For $c = 3$ a solution is given by $a = 2^{(e-1)/2} + 1$ and $b = 2^{(e-1)/2} - 1$.

39.12.6 Cosine and sine in $\mathrm{GF}(p^2)$

```
   j:      elem. of order 2^j      cosine       sine
   0:      u+i*v=    1 + i* 0      cos=   1      i*sin=  0
   1:      u+i*v=  126 + i* 0      cos= 126      i*sin=  0
   2:      u+i*v=    0 + i* 1      cos=   0      i*sin=  1*i
   3:      u+i*v=    8 + i* 8      cos=   8      i*sin=  8*i
   4:      u+i*v=  103 + i*21      cos= 103      i*sin= 21*i
   5:      u+i*v=   68 + i*87      cos=  68      i*sin= 87*i
   6:      u+i*v=   15 + i*41      cos=  15      i*sin= 41*i
   7:      u+i*v=   32 + i*82      cos=  32      i*sin= 82*i
   8:      u+i*v=   98 + i*38      cos= 38*i     i*sin= 98
```

Figure 39.12-D: Elements of order 2^j and the corresponding sines and cosines in $\mathrm{GF}\left(127^2\right)$.

Let z be an element of order n in $\mathrm{GF}(p^2)$, we would like to identify z with $\exp(2\pi i/n)$ and determine the values equivalent to $\cos(2\pi/n)$ and $\sin(2\pi/n)$. We set

$$\cos\frac{2\pi}{n} \;:=\; \frac{z^2+1}{2z} \tag{39.12-16a}$$

$$i\sin\frac{2\pi}{n} \;:=\; \frac{z^2-1}{2z} \tag{39.12-16b}$$

For this choice of sine and cosine following relations hold:

$$\exp(x) \;=\; \cos(x) + i\sin(x) \tag{39.12-17a}$$

$$\sin(x)^2 + \cos(x)^2 \;=\; 1 \tag{39.12-17b}$$

The first relation is trivial: $\frac{z^2+1}{2z} + \frac{z^2-1}{2z} = z$. The second can be verified by writing i for some element that is the square root of -1: $(\frac{z^2+1}{2z})^2 + (\frac{z^2-1}{2zi})^2 = \frac{(z^2+1)^2 - (z^2-1)^2}{4z^2} = 1$.

The quantities corresponding to the 2^j-th roots in GF(127^2) are shown in figure 39.12-D. Note how the i swaps side with the element of highest order 2^a.

The construction shows how to mechanically convert fast Fourier (and Hartley) transforms with explicit trigonometric constants into the corresponding number theoretic transforms. The idea of expressing cosines and sines in terms of primitive roots was taken from [332].

39.12.7   Cosine and sine in GF(p)

What about primes of the form $p = 4k+1$ that are used anyway for NTTs? The same construction works. The polynomial x^2+1 is reducible modulo $p = 4k+1$, so -1 is a quadratic residue and its square root lies in GF(p). We could say: i is real modulo p if p is of the form $4k+1$.

```
modulus= 257 == 0x101
modulus is cyclic
modulus is prime
bits(modulus)= 8.0056245  == 9 - 0.99437545
euler_phi(modulus)= 256 == 0x100 == 2^8
maxorder= 256 == 0x100
maxordelem= 3 == 0x3
max2pow= 8    (max FFT length = 2**8 == 256)
root2pow(max2pow)=3   root2pow(-max2pow)=86
sqrt(-1) =: i = 2 4 1

  8:     z=    3 = ( 173  +   87) = ( 173  + 107*i)
  7:     z=    9 = ( 233  +   33) = ( 233  +  14*i)
  6:     z=   81 = ( 123  +  215) = ( 123  +  99*i)
  5:     z=  136 = ( 188  +  205) = ( 188  + 196*i)
  4:     z=  249 = (  12  +  237) = (  12  + 194*i)
  3:     z=   64 = (  30  +   34) = (  30  +  30*i)
  2:     z=  241 = (   0  +  241) = (   0  +   1*i)
  1:     z=  256 = ( 256  +    0) = ( 256  +   0*i)
  0:   : z   =1 = (   1  +    0) ⇒ (   1  +   0*i)
 -1:     z=  256 = ( 256  +    0) = ( 256  +   0*i)
 -2:     z=   16 = (   0  +   16) = (   0  + 256*i)
 -3:     z=  253 = (  30  +  223) = (  30  + 227*i)
 -4:     z=   32 = (  12  +   20) = (  12  +  63*i)
 -5:     z=  240 = ( 188  +   52) = ( 188  +  61*i)
 -6:     z=  165 = ( 123  +   42) = ( 123  + 158*i)
 -7:     z=  200 = ( 233  +  224) = ( 233  + 243*i)
 -8:     z=   86 = ( 173  +  170) = ( 173  + 150*i)
```

Figure 39.12-E: Roots of order 2^j modulo $p = 257 = 2^8 + 1$.

In the implementation [FXT: class mod in mod/mod.h] the cosine and sine values are computed from the primitive roots of order 2^j. The program [FXT: mod/modsincos-demo.cc] generates the list of 2^j-th roots and inverse roots shown in figure 39.12-E.

Again we can translate a routine for the fast Fourier (or Hartley) transform in a mechanical way.

An element modulo a prime $p = k \cdot 2^t + 1$ whose order equals 2^t can be found by the following algorithm even if the factorization of k is not known: Choose a random a where $1 < a < p - 1$ and compute $s = a^k$, if $-1 = s^{2^{t-1}}$, then return s, else try another a.

The algorithm terminates when the first element a is encountered whose order has the factor 2^t. An implementation that tests $a = 2, 3, \ldots, p - 2$ sequentially is

```
1    el2(k, t)=
2    {
3        local(p, s);
4        p = k*2^t+1;
5        for(a=2, p-2,  s = Mod(a,p)^k;  if( Mod(-1,p)==s^(2^(t-1)), return( s ); ); );
6    }
```

With $p = 314151729239163 \cdot 2^{26} + 1$ the algorithm terminates after testing $a = 5$ (of order $(p-1)/3$) and returning $s = 18583781386455525528042$ whose order is indeed 2^{26}.

In general, if $p = u \cdot f + 1$, $\gcd(f, u) = 1$ and $f = \prod p_i^{e_i}$ is fully factored, then an element of order f can be determined by testing random values a:

1. Take a random a and set $s = a^u$.

2. If $s^{f/p_i} \neq 1$ for all prime factors p_i of f, then return s (an element of order f).

3. Go to step 1.

39.12.8 Decomposing $p = 4k + 1$ as sum of two squares

We give algorithms to decompose a prime $p = 4k + 1$ as a sum of two squares.

39.12.8.1 Direct computation

The direct way to determine u and v with $n = u^2 + v^2$ is to check, for $v = 0, 1, 2, \ldots, \lfloor \sqrt{n} \rfloor$, whether $n - v^2$ is a perfect square. If so, return $u = \sqrt{n - v^2}$ and v:

```
1    sumofsquares_naive(n)=
2    { /* return [u,v] such that u^2+v^2==n */
3        local(w);
4        for (v=0, sqrtint(n),  \\ search until n-v^2 is a square
5            w = n-v^2;
6            if ( issquare(w), return( [sqrtint(w), v] ) );
7        );
8        return ( 0 );  \\ not the sum of two squares
9    }
```

The routine needs at most $\lfloor \sqrt{n} \rfloor$ steps which renders it rather useless for n large. With the prime $n = 314151729239163 \cdot 2^{26} + 1 \approx 2 \cdot 10^{22}$ we have $n = u^2 + v^2$ where $u = 132599472793$ and $v = 59158646772$ and the routine would need v steps to find the solution. The method described next finds the solution immediately.

39.12.8.2 Computation using continued fractions

The square root i of -1 can be used to find the representation of a prime $p = 4k + 1$ as a sum of two squares, $p = u^2 + v^2$, as follows:

1. Determine i where $i^2 = -1$ modulo p. If $i \geq p/2$, then set $i = p - i$.

2. Compute the continued fraction of p/i, it has the form $[a_0, a_1, \ldots, a_n, a_n, \ldots, a_1, a_0]$.

3. Compute the numerators of the $(n-1)$-st and the n-th convergent, P_{n-1} and P_n. Return $u = P_{n-1}$ and $v = P_n$.

Assume that $p = k \cdot 2^t + 1$ where $t \geq 2$. Use an element of order 2^t to find a square root of -1:

```
1    imag4k1(k, t)=
2    { /* determine s such that s^2=-1 modulo p=k*2^t+1 */
3        local(s);
4        s = el2(k, t);
```

```
5      s = s^(2^(t-2));
6      return( s );
7    }
```

Now the decomposition as a sum of two squares can be found with

```
1    sumofsquares(k, t)=
2    { /* return [u,v] such that u^2+v^2==p =k*2^t+1 */
3        local(i, s, p, cf, q, u, v);
4        i = lift( imag4k1(k, t) );
5        p = k*2^t+1;
6        if ( i>=p/2, i = p-i );
7        cf = contfrac(p/i);
8        cf = vector(length(cf)/2, j, cf[j]);
9        q = contfracpnqn(cf);
10       u = q[1, 1];  v = q[1, 2];
11       return( [u, v] );
12   }
```

For example, the relevant quantities with $p = 2281$ are

```
i = 1571   \\ square root of -1
i =  710   \\ choose smaller square root
cf = [3, 4, 1, 2, 2, 1, 4, 3]   \\ == contfrac(2281/710)
cf = [3, 4, 1, 2]   \\ first half on contfrac

q = contfracpnqn(cf) =
  [45 16]   \\ == [P_4, P_3]
  [14 5]    \\ == [Q_4, Q_3] (unused)

u=45;  v=16;   \\ u^2 + v^2 = 2025 + 256 = 2281
```

39.12.8.3   A memory saving version

An algorithm that avoids storing the continued fraction comes from the observation that u and v appear in the calculation of $\gcd(p, i)$. We use the routine

```
1    gcd_print(p, i)=
2    {
3        local( t, s );
4        if ( p<i,   t=p; p=i; i=t; );
5        s = sqrtint(p);
6        while ( i,
7            print ("  ", p, "  ", i);
8            t = p % i;  p = i;  i = t;
9        );
10   }
```

For $p = 2281$ (where $i = 710$) the following list is produced:

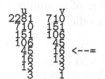

```
   u    v
2281  710
 710  151
 151  106
 106   45
  45   16  <--=
  16   13
  13    3
   3    1
```

The marked pair is the first where $u^2 < p$. The routine for the decomposition into two squares is

```
1    sumofsquares_gcd(k, t)=
2    { /* return [u,v] such that u^2+v^2==p =k*2^t+1 */
3        local(s, p, i, w);
4        i = lift( imag4k1(k, t) );
5        p = k*2^t+1;
6        if ( i>=p/2, i = p-i );
7        w = sqrtint(p);
8        while ( i,
9            if ( p<=w, return( [p,i] ) );
10           t = p % i;  p = i;  i = t;
11       );
12       return( [0,0] ); \\ failure
13   }
```

Using the relation $a^2+b^2 = (a+i\,b)\,(a-i\,b)$ we can use the decomposition into two squares to compute the factorization of a number over the complex integers. For example, we have $3141592653 = 3 \cdot 107 \cdot 9786893$

(over $\mathbb{Z}$) where the greatest prime factor is of the form $4k + 1$. For $9786893 = 2317^2 + 2102^2$ we find $3141592653 = -i \cdot 3 \cdot 107 \cdot (2317 + 2102i) \cdot (2102 + 2317i)$. GP has a built-in routine for this task:

```
? factor( 3141592653 + 0*I )
   [-I 1]    [3 1]    [107 1]    [2317 + 2102*I 1]    [2102 + 2317*I 1]
```

If a decomposition $n = x^2 + y^2$ of n is known, then the square roots of -1 can be computed as $i = \pm x/y \bmod n$. For $n = x^2 + dy^2$ we have $\sqrt{-d} = x/y \bmod n$, and for $n = x^k + dy^k$ we have $\sqrt[k]{-d} = x/y \bmod n$. For example, for $n = 2^k + 1$ we know that $\sqrt[k]{-1} = 2/1 = 2 \bmod n$, and for $n = 2^7 + 3 \cdot 5^7 = 234503$ we have $\sqrt[7]{-3} = 2/5 = 46901 \bmod n$. For $n = a\,x^k + b\,y^k$ we have $\sqrt[k]{-b/a} = x/y \bmod n$.

39.13   Solving the Pell equation

Simple continued fractions (see section 37.3 on page 716) can be used to find integer solutions of the equations

$$x^2 - d\,y^2 = +1 \tag{39.13-1a}$$
$$x^2 - d\,y^2 = -1 \tag{39.13-1b}$$

Equation 39.13-1a is usually called the *Pell equation*. The name *Bhaskara equation* (or *Brahmagupta-Bhaskara equation*, used in [221]) has been suggested because Brahmagupta (ca. 600 AD) and Bhaskara (ca. 1100 AD) were the first to study and solve this equation.

39.13.1   Solution via continued fractions

The convergents P_k/Q_k of the continued fraction of $\sqrt{d}$ are close to $\sqrt{d}$: $(P_k/Q_k)^2 \approx d$. If we define $e_k := P_k^2 - d\,Q_k^2$, then solutions of relation 39.13-1a correspond to $e_k = +1$, solutions of 39.13-1b to $e_k = -1$.

As an example we set $d = 53$. The continued fraction of $\sqrt{53}$ is

$$\mathrm{CF}(\sqrt{53}) = [7,\ 3,1,1,3,14,\ 3,1,1,3,14,\ 3,1,1,3,14,\ \ldots] \tag{39.13-2a}$$
$$= [7,\ \overline{3,1,1,3,14}] \tag{39.13-2b}$$

We observe that the sequence is periodic after the initial term and the last term of the period is twice the initial term. Moreover, disregarding the term 14, the terms in the period form a palindrome. These properties actually hold for all simple continued fractions of square roots $\sqrt{d}$ with d not a perfect square, for the proofs see [263] or [221]. For the computation of the continued fraction of a square root a specialized version of the algorithm from section 37.3.1.2 on page 718 will be most efficient.

The table shown in figure 39.13-A gives the first convergents P_k/Q_k together with $e_k := P_k^2 - 53\,Q_k^2$. The entry for $k = 4$ corresponds to the smallest solution (x, y) of $x^2 - 53\,y^2 = -1$: $182^2 - 53 \cdot 25^2 = -1$. Entry $k = 9$ corresponds to $66249^2 - 53 \cdot 9100^2 = +1$, the smallest nontrivial solution to $x^2 - 53\,y^2 = +1$ (the trivial solution is $(P_{-1}, Q_{-1}) = (1, 0)$).

The continued fraction for $\sqrt{19}$ is

$$\mathrm{CF}(\sqrt{19}) = [4,\ 2,1,3,1,2,8,\ 2,1,3,1,2,8,\ 2,1,3,1,2,8,\ \ldots] \tag{39.13-3a}$$
$$= [4,\ \overline{2,1,3,1,2,8}] \tag{39.13-3b}$$

Its period is $l = 6$. Figure 39.13-B shows the corresponding table, it contains solutions with $e_k = +1$ but none with $e_k = -1$.

Let e correspond the minimal nontrivial solution of $x^2 - d\,y^2 = \pm 1$. If $e = +1$, then no solution for $x^2 - d\,y^2 = -1$ exists. Nontrivial solutions with $e = +1$ always exist, solutions with $e = -1$ only exist when the period l of the continued fraction of $\sqrt{d}$ is odd. The period is always odd for primes of the form $p = 4\,k + 1$ and never for numbers of the form $n = 4\,k + 3$ or $4\,k$. If any factor f_i of d is of the form

$k:$	a_k	P_k	Q_k	$e_k := $ $P_k^2 - d\,Q_k^2$
−1:	−	0	1	+1
0:	7	7	1	−4
1:	3	22	3	+7
2:	1	29	4	−7
3:	1	51	7	+4
4:	3	182	25	−1
5:	14	2599	357	+4
6:	3	7979	1096	−7
7:	1	10578	1453	+7
8:	1	18557	2549	−4
9:	3	66249	9100	+1
10:	14	946043	129949	−4
11:	3	2904378	398947	+7
12:	1	3850421	528896	−7
13:	1	6754799	927843	+4
14:	3	24114818	3312425	−1
15:	14	344362251	47301793	+4

Figure 39.13-A: The first convergents P_k/Q_k of the continued fraction of $\sqrt{53}$.

$k:$	a_k	P_k	Q_k	$e_k := $ $P_k^2 - d\,Q_k^2$
−1:	−	0	1	+1
0:	4	4	1	−3
1:	2	9	2	+5
2:	1	13	3	−2
3:	3	48	11	+5
4:	1	61	14	−3
5:	2	170	39	+1
6:	8	1421	326	−3
7:	2	3012	691	+5
8:	1	4433	1017	−2
9:	3	16311	3742	+5
10:	1	20744	4759	−3
11:	2	57799	13260	+1
12:	8	483136	110839	−3

Figure 39.13-B: The first convergents P_k/Q_k of the continued fraction of $\sqrt{19}$.

$f_i = 4\,k + 3$, then no solution with $e = -1$ exists, because this would imply $x^2 \equiv -1 \bmod f_i$ but -1 is never a quadratic residue modulo $f_i = 4\,k + 3$ by relation 39.8-3a on page 782.

However, all prime factors being of the form $4\,k+1$ does not guarantee that $e = -1$, the smallest examples are $205 = 5 \cdot 41$, $221 = 13 \cdot 17$, $305 = 5 \cdot 61$, and $377 = 13 \cdot 29$. The list of such numbers up to 2500 is

205, 221, 305, 377, 505, 545, 689, 725, 745, 793, 905, 1205, 1345, 1405, 1469, 1513, 1517, 1537, 1717, 1885, 1945, 1961, 2005, 2041, 2045, 2105, 2225, 2245, 2329, 2353

The sequence of numbers d with no factor of the form $4\,k + 3$ such that $x^2 - d\,y^2 = -1$ has no solution is entry A031399 in [312]:

4, 8, 16, 20, 25, 32, 34, 40, 52, 64, 68, 80, 100, 104, 116, 128, 136, 146, 148, 160, 164, 169, 178, 194, 200, 205, 208, 212, 221, 232, 244, 256, 260, 272, 289, 292, 296, . . .

An algorithm for computing solutions (x, y) of the equation $A\,x^2 - B\,y^2 = N$ is given in [246].

39.13.2   Multiplying and powering solutions

Consider two solutions (x, y) and (r, s) of the Pell equation

$$x^2 - dy^2 = e \qquad (39.13\text{-}4a)$$
$$r^2 - ds^2 = f \qquad (39.13\text{-}4b)$$

where $e = \pm 1$ and $f = \pm 1$. Now write

$$x^2 - Dy^2 = \left(x + \sqrt{d}\, y\right)\left(x - \sqrt{d}\, y\right) \qquad (39.13\text{-}5)$$

and the same for (r, s). We compute the products

$$\left(x + \sqrt{d}\, y\right)\left(r + \sqrt{d}\, y\right) = (xr + dys) + \sqrt{d}\,(xs + yr) \qquad (39.13\text{-}6a)$$
$$\left(x - \sqrt{d}\, y\right)\left(r - \sqrt{d}\, y\right) = (xr + dys) - \sqrt{d}\,(xs + yr) \qquad (39.13\text{-}6b)$$

By multiplying both relations we see that $(U, V) := (xr + dys,\ xs + yr)$ is also a solution:

$$U^2 - dV^2 = ef \qquad (39.13\text{-}7)$$

Now let (r, s) be the smallest nontrivial solution and define (x_k, y_k) by

$$\begin{bmatrix} x_k \\ y_k \end{bmatrix} := \begin{bmatrix} r & ds \\ s & r \end{bmatrix}^k \begin{bmatrix} 1 \\ 0 \end{bmatrix} \qquad (39.13\text{-}8)$$

Then (x_k, y_k) is the k-th solution of the Pell equation.

Let $r^2 - ds^2 = e$, then we have $x_k^2 - dy_k^2 = e^k$. Therefore, if $r^2 - ds^2 = +1$, then there is no solution (x, y) such that $x^2 - dy^2 = -1$. If $r^2 - ds^2 = -1$, then $x_k^2 - dy_k^2 = -1$ for all odd k.

As we can multiply solutions, we can also raise them to any power. Let (x, y) be such that $x^2 - dy^2 = e$ where $e = \pm 1$ and define the matrix M by

$$M := \begin{bmatrix} x & dy \\ y & x \end{bmatrix} \qquad (39.13\text{-}9)$$

The k-th power of the solution (x, y) is

$$(x, y)^k = M^k \begin{bmatrix} 1 \\ 0 \end{bmatrix} \qquad (39.13\text{-}10)$$

Now write (X_k, Y_K) for the k-th power of (x, y). We have, for the squared solution,

$$X_2 = x^2 + dy^2 = 2x^2 - e = 2dy^2 + e \qquad (39.13\text{-}11a)$$
$$Y_2 = 2xy \qquad (39.13\text{-}11b)$$

And for the third power

$$X_3 = x\left(x^2 + 3dy^2\right) = x\left(4x^2 - 3e\right) \qquad (39.13\text{-}12a)$$
$$Y_3 = y\left(3x^2 + dy^2\right) = y\left(4x^2 - e\right) = y\left(4dy^2 + 3e\right) \qquad (39.13\text{-}12b)$$

Note that the last equality in the first relation expresses X_3 solely in terms of x, d, and e, and the last equality in the second relation expresses Y_3 solely in terms of y, d, and e. Therefore X_{3^k} and Y_{3^k} can be computed independently.

Relations 39.13-11a and 39.13-11b are the numerator and denominator of the second order iteration for $\sqrt{d}$, relation 29.2-2a on page 570. Relations 39.13-12a and 39.13-12b correspond to the third order iteration, relation 29.2-2b.

If the pair (x, y) is a solution with $e = +1$, then $(T_n(x),\, y\, U_{n-1}(x))$ is also a solution, where T_n and U_n are the Chebyshev polynomials of the first and second kind:

$$T_n^2(x) - d\,(y\, U_{n-1}(x))^2 \;=\; T_n^2(x) - d\, y^2\, U_{n-1}^2(x) \;= \tag{39.13-13a}$$
$$T_n^2(x) - (x^2 - 1)\, U_{n-1}^2(x) \;=\; 1 \tag{39.13-13b}$$

The last equality is relation 35.2-25 on page 683. Similarly, if (x, y) is a solution with $e = -1$, then $\big(T_n^+(x),\, y\, U_{n-1}^+(x)\big)$ is also a solution if n is odd, by equation 35.2-29 on page 684. See [190] for much more information about Pell's equation.

39.14   Multiplication of hypercomplex numbers ‡

An n-dimensional vector space (over a field) together with component-wise addition and a *multiplication table* that defines the product of any two (vector) components defines an *algebra*.

The product of two elements $x = \sum_k \alpha_k\, e_k$ and $y = \sum_j \beta_j\, e_j$ of the algebra is defined as

$$x \cdot y \;=\; \sum_{k,j=0}^{n-1} \left[(\alpha_k \cdot \beta_j)\, m_{k,j}\right] \tag{39.14-1}$$

The quantities $m_{k,j} = e_k\, e_j$ are given in the multiplication table of the algebra. These can be arbitrary elements of the algebra, that is, linear combinations of the components e_i. For example, a 2-dimensional algebra over the real numbers could have the following multiplication table:

```
            e0                    e1
  e0:   (5*e1 + 3*e0)      (239*e0 + 3.1415*e1)
  e1:       (0)            (17*e1 + 2.71828*e0)
```

Note that there is no neutral element of multiplication ('one'). Further, the algebra has *zero divisors*: the equation $x \cdot y = 0$ has a solution where neither element is zero, namely $x = e_1$ and $y = e_0$. As almost all randomly defined algebras, it is completely uninteresting.

In what follows we will only consider algebras over the real numbers where the product of two components equals ± 1 times another component. For example, the complex numbers are a 2-dimensional algebra (over the real numbers) with the multiplication table

```
        e0    e1

  e0:   +e0   +e1
  e1:   +e1   -e0
```

Which is, using the symbols '1' and 'i',

```
        1    i

  1:   +1   +i
  i:   +i   -1
```

We will denote the components of an n-dimensional algebra by the numbers $0, 1, \ldots, n-1$. The multiplication table for the complex numbers would thus be written as

```
        0    1

  0:   +0   +1
  1:   +1   -0
```

39.14.1   The Cayley-Dickson construction

The *Cayley-Dickson construction* recursively defines multiplication tables for certain algebras where the dimension is a power of 2. Let a, A, b and B be elements of a 2^{n-1}-dimensional algebra U. Define the multiplication rule for an algebra V (of dimension 2^n), written as pairs of elements of U, via

$$(a,\, b) \cdot (A,\, B) \;:=\; (a \cdot A - B \cdot b^*,\; a^* \cdot B + A \cdot b) \tag{39.14-2}$$

where the *conjugate* C^* of an element $C = (a, b)$ is defined as

$$(a, b)^* := (a^*, -b) \tag{39.14-3}$$

and the conjugate of a real number a equals a (unmodified). The construction leads to multiplication tables where the product of two units always equals ± 1 times some unit: $e_i \cdot e_j = \pm e_k$.

	0	1	2	3	4	5	6	7	8	9	a	b	c	d	e	f
0:	+0	+1	+2	+3	+4	+5	+6	+7	+8	+9	+a	+b	+c	+d	+e	+f
1:	+1	-0	-3	+2	-5	+4	+7	-6	-9	+8	+b	-a	+d	-c	-f	+e
2:	+2	+3	-0	-1	-6	-7	+4	+5	-a	-b	+8	+9	+e	+f	-c	-d
3:	+3	-2	+1	-0	-7	+6	-5	+4	-b	+a	-9	+8	+f	-e	+d	-c
4:	+4	+5	+6	+7	-0	-1	-2	-3	-c	-d	-e	-f	+8	+9	+a	+b
5:	+5	-4	+7	-6	+1	-0	+3	-2	-d	+c	-f	+e	-9	+8	-b	+a
6:	+6	-7	-4	+5	+2	-3	-0	+1	-e	+f	+c	-d	-a	+b	+8	-9
7:	+7	+6	-5	-4	+3	+2	-1	-0	-f	-e	+d	+c	-b	-a	+9	+8
8:	+8	+9	+a	+b	+c	+d	+e	+f	-0	-1	-2	-3	-4	-5	-6	-7
9:	+9	-8	+b	-a	+d	-c	-f	+e	+1	-0	+3	-2	+5	-4	-7	+6
a:	+a	-b	-8	+9	+e	+f	-c	-d	+2	-3	-0	+1	+6	+7	-4	-5
b:	+b	+a	-9	-8	+f	-e	+d	-c	+3	+2	-1	-0	+7	-6	+5	-4
c:	+c	-d	-e	-f	-8	+9	+a	+b	+4	-5	-6	-7	-0	+1	+2	+3
d:	+d	+c	-f	+e	-9	-8	-b	+a	+5	+4	-7	+6	-1	-0	-3	+2
e:	+e	+f	+c	-d	-a	+b	-8	-9	+6	+7	+4	-5	-2	+3	-0	-1
f:	+f	-e	+d	+c	-b	-a	+9	-8	+7	-6	+5	+4	-3	-2	+1	-0

Figure 39.14-A: Multiplication table for the sedenions. The entry in row R, column C gives the product $R \cdot C$ of the components R and C (hexadecimal notation).

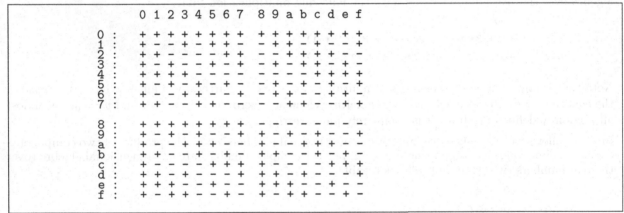

Figure 39.14-B: Signs in the multiplication table for sedenions.

Figure 39.14-A gives the multiplication table for a 16-dimensional algebra, the *sedenions*. The upper left 8×8 square gives the multiplication rule for the *octonions* (or *Cayley numbers*), the upper left 4×4 square gives the rule for the *quaternions* and the upper left 2×2 square corresponds to the complex numbers. Note that multiplication is in general neither commutative (only up to dimension 2) nor associative (only up to dimension 4).

The 2^n-dimensional algebras are (for $n > 1$) referred to as *hypercomplex numbers*. There is no generally accepted naming scheme for the algebras beyond dimension 16. We will use the names 2^n-*ions*.

The form (relation 39.14-2) of the construction is given in [27], an alternative form is used in [135]:

$$(a, b) \cdot (A, B) := (a \cdot A - B^* \cdot b, \; b \cdot A^* + B \cdot a) \tag{39.14-4}$$

It leads to a table that is the transpose of figure 39.14-A.

By construction, $e_0^2 = e_0$, $e_k^2 = -e_0$ for $k \neq 0$, $e_0 e_k = e_k e_0 = e_k$, and $e_k e_j = -e_j e_k$ whenever both of k and j are nonzero (and $k \neq j$). Further,

$$e_k e_j = \pm e_x \quad \text{where} \quad x = k \, \text{XOR} \, j \tag{39.14-5}$$

where the sign is to be determined. Figure 39.14-B shows the pattern of the signs of the sedenion algebra. The lower left quarter is the transpose of the upper left quarter, so is the lower right quarter, except for its top row. The upper right quarter is (except for its first row) the negated upper left quarter. These observations, together with the partial antisymmetry can be cast into an algorithm to compute the signs [FXT: aux0/cayley-dickson-mult.h]:

```
1    int CD_sign_rec(ulong r, ulong c, ulong n)
2    // Signs in the multiplication table for the
3    //    algebra of n-ions (where n is a power of 2)
4    //    that is obtained by the Cayley-Dickson construction:
5    // If component r is multiplied with component c, then the
6    //    result is CD_sign_rec(r,c,n) * (r XOR c).
7    {
8        if ( (r==0) || (c==0) )  return +1;
9        if ( c>=r )
10       {
11           if ( c>r )   return  -CD_sign_rec(c, r, n);
12           else  return -1;  // r==c
13       }
14       // here r>c (triangle below diagonal)
15
16       ulong h = n>>1;
17       if ( c>=h )  // right
18       {
19           // (upper right not reached)
20           return   CD_sign_rec(c-h, r-h, h); // lower right
21       }
22       else  // left
23       {
24           if ( r>=h ) return    CD_sign_rec(c, r-h, h); // lower left
25           else        return    CD_sign_rec(r, c, h); // upper left
26       }
27   }
```

The function uses at most $2 \cdot \log_2(n)$ steps. Note that the second row in the table is (the signed version of) the Thue-Morse sequence, see section 1.16.4 on page 44. The matrix filled with entries ± 1 according to figure 39.14-B is a Hadamard matrix, see chapter 19 on page 384. The sequence of signs, read by anti-diagonals, and setting $0 := +$ and $1 := -$, is entry A118685 in [312].

An iterative version of the function is [FXT: aux0/cayley-dickson-mult.h]:

```
1    inline void cp2(ulong a, ulong b, ulong &u, ulong &v)  { u=a; v=b; }
2    //
3    inline int CD_sign_it(ulong r, ulong c, ulong n)
4    {
5        int s = +1;
6        while ( true )
7        {
8            if ( (r==0) || (c==0) )  return s;
9            if ( c==r )  return -s;
10           if ( c>r )   { swap2(r,c); s=-s; }
11           n >>= 1;
12           if ( c>=n )  cp2(c-n, r-n, r, c);
13           else if ( r>=n ) cp2(c, r-n, r, c);
14       }
15   }
```

The rate of generation with the computation of all 2^{24} signs in the multiplication table for the '2^{12}-ions' is about 12 million per second with both routines [FXT: arith/cayley-dickson-demo.cc].

```
        0  1  2  3  4  5  6  7

0  :  +  0+ 1+ 2+3 +  4+5 +6 +7        +  +  +  +  +  +  +  +
1  :  +  1- 0+ 6+4 -  3+7 -2 -5        +  -  +  +  -  +  -  -
2  :  +  2- 6- 0+7 +  5-4 +1 -3        +  -  -  +  +  -  +  -
3  :  +  3- 4- 7-0 +  1+6 -5 +2        +  -  -  -  +  +  -  +
4  :  +  4+ 3- 5-1 -  0+2 +7 -6        +  +  -  -  -  +  +  -
5  :  +  5- 7+ 4-6 -  2-0 +3 +1        +  -  +  -  -  -  +  +
6  :  +  6+ 2- 1+5 -  7-3 -0 +4        +  +  -  +  -  -  -  +
7  :  +  7+ 5+ 3-2 +  6-1 -4 -0        +  +  +  -  +  -  -  -
```

Figure 39.14-C: Alternative multiplication table for the octonions (left) and its sign pattern (right).

An alternative multiplication table for the octonions is given in figure 39.14-C. Its sign pattern is the 8×8 Hadamard matrix shown in figure 19.1-A on page 385. Properties of this representation and the relation to shift register sequences are given in [125].

39.14.2   Fast multiplication of quaternions

```
+   -0 -1  2  3      +   -0 -1  2  3      +--  0  1  2  3
|                    |                    |
0  :0  1  2  3       0  ÷  01  2  3      0 0:  0*  1   2   3
1  :1  0  3  2       1  :1  -  03  2     i 1:  1  -0   3  -2*
2  :2  3  0  1       2  :2  3  -0  1     j 2:  2  -3* -0   1
3  :3  2  1  0       3  :3  2  1  -0     k 3:  3   2  -1* -0
```

Figure 39.14-D: Scheme for the length-4 dyadic convolution (left), same with bucket zero negated (middle) and the multiplication table for the units of the quaternions (right). The asterisks mark those entries where the sign is different from the scheme in the middle.

```
-  01  2  3  4  5  6  7      0  1  2  3  4  5  6  7      #0  1  2  3  4  5  6  7
1  -  03  2  5  4  7  6      1  -  03 -2  5 -4 -7  6      1  0  3 #2  5 #4 #7  6
2  3  -  01  6  7  4  5      2  -  3  01  6  7 -4 -5      2 #3  0  1  6  7 #4 #5
3  2  1  -  0  7  6  5  4    3  2  -  ±0  7 -6  5 -4      3  2 #1  0  7 #6  5 #4

4  5  6  7  -  01  2  3      4  -  5  67 -0  1  2  3      4 #5 #6 #7  0  1  2  3
5  4  7  6  1  -  03  2      5  4  -  76 -1 -0 -3  2      5  4 #7  6 #1  0 #3  2
6  7  4  5  2  3  -  01      6  7  4 -5 -2  3 -0 -1      6  7  4 #5 #2  3  0 #1
7  6  5  4  3  2  1  -  0    7  -  65  4 -3 -2  1 -0      7 #6  5  4 #3 #2  1  0
```

Figure 39.14-E: Scheme for the length-8 dyadic convolution with bucket zero negated (left) and multiplication table for the octonions (middle, taken from [135]). There are 22 places where the signs differ (right, marked with '#'). This leads to an algorithm involving $8 + 22 = 30$ multiplications.

Quaternion multiplication can be done with eight real multiplications using the dyadic convolution (see section 23.8 on page 481). The scheme in figure 39.14-D suggests using the dyadic convolution with bucket zero negated as a starting point which costs four multiplications. Some entries have to be corrected which costs four more multiplications.

```
1    // f[] == [ re1, i1, j1, k1 ]
2    // g[] == [ re2, i2, j2, k2 ]
3    c0 := f[0] * g[0]
4    c1 := f[3] * g[2]
5    c2 := f[1] * g[3]
6    c3 := f[2] * g[1]
7
8    // length-4 dyadic convolution:
9    walsh(f[])
10   walsh(g[])
11   for i:=0 to 3  g[i] := (f[i] * g[i])
12   walsh(g[])
13
14   // normalization and correction:
15   g[0] :=   2 * c0 - g[0] / 4
16   g[1] := - 2 * c1 + g[1] / 4
17   g[2] := - 2 * c2 + g[2] / 4
18   g[3] := - 2 * c3 + g[3] / 4
```

The algorithm is taken from [187] which also gives a second variant.

The complex multiplication by three real multiplications (relation 39.12-2c on page 806) corresponds to one length-2 Walsh dyadic convolution and the correction for the product of the imaginary units:

```
1    // f[] == [ re1, im1 ]
2    // g[] == [ re2, im2 ]
3    c0 := f[1] * g[1]  // == im1 * im2
4    // length-2 dyadic convolution:
5    { f[0], f[1] } := { f[0] + f[1], f[0] - f[1] }
```

```
6      { g[0], g[1] } := { g[0] + g[1], g[0] - g[1] }
7      g[0] := f[0] * g[0]
8      g[1] := f[1] * g[1]
9      { g[0], g[1] } := { g[0] + g[1], g[0] - g[1] }
10     // normalization:
11     f[0] := f[0] / 2
12     g[0] := g[0] / 2
13     // correction:
14     g[0] := -2 * c0 + g[0]
15     // here:  g[] == [ re1 * re2 - im1 * im2,  re1 * im2 + im1 * re2 ]
```

For complex numbers of high precision multiplication is asymptotically equivalent to two real multiplications as one FFT-based (complex linear) convolution can be used for the computation. Similarly, high precision quaternion multiplication is as expensive as four real multiplications. Figure 39.14-E shows an equivalent construction for the octonions leading to an algorithm with 30 multiplications.

39.14.3   Eight-square identity ‡

```
{C=[
+B0, +B1, +B2, +B3, +B4, +B5, +B6, +B7;
+B1, -B0, -B3, +B2, -B5, +B4, +B7, -B6;
+B2, +B3, -B0, -B1, -B6, -B7, +B4, +B5;
+B3, -B2, +B1, -B0, -B7, +B6, -B5, +B4;
+B4, +B5, +B6, +B7, -B0, -B1, -B2, -B3;
+B5, -B4, +B7, -B6, +B1, -B0, +B3, -B2;
+B6, -B7, -B4, +B5, +B2, -B3, -B0, +B1;
+B7, +B6, -B5, -B4, +B3, +B2, -B1, -B0
]; }

A=[ +A0, +A1, +A2, +A3, +A4, +A5, +A6, +A7 ]
B=[ +B0, +B1, +B2, +B3, +B4, +B5, +B6, +B7 ]
```

Figure 39.14-F: Symbolic matrix and vectors used with four and eight squares theorems.

Define the matrix C and vectors A and B as shown in figure 39.14-F (compare to figure 39.14-A). With $P := C\,A$ we have the following *eight-square identity*

$$\sum_{k=0}^{n-1} A_k^2 \cdot \sum_{k=0}^{n-1} B_k^2 \;=\; \sum_{k=0}^{n-1} P_k^2 \tag{39.14-6}$$

The components of P are

```
P0 =  + A7*B7 + A6*B6 + A5*B5 + A4*B4 + A3*B3 + A2*B2 + A1*B1 + A0*B0
P1 =  + A6*B7 - A7*B6 - A4*B5 + A5*B4 - A2*B3 + A3*B2 + A0*B1 - A1*B0
P2 =  - A5*B7 - A4*B6 + A7*B5 + A6*B4 + A1*B3 + A0*B2 - A3*B1 - A2*B0
P3 =  - A4*B7 + A5*B6 - A6*B5 + A7*B4 + A0*B3 - A1*B2 + A2*B1 - A3*B0
P4 =  + A3*B7 + A2*B6 + A1*B5 + A0*B4 - A7*B3 - A6*B2 - A5*B1 - A4*B0
P5 =  + A2*B7 - A3*B6 + A0*B5 - A1*B4 + A6*B3 - A7*B2 + A4*B1 - A5*B0
P6 =  - A1*B7 + A0*B6 + A3*B5 - A2*B4 - A5*B3 + A4*B2 + A7*B1 - A6*B0
P7 =  + A0*B7 + A1*B6 - A2*B5 - A3*B4 + A4*B3 + A5*B2 - A6*B1 - A7*B0
```

The given equality also holds if matrix and vectors are truncated to length 4 (*four-square identity*), 2, or 1 (trivially):

```
? n=4; An=vector(n,k,A[k]);  Bn=vector(n,k,B[k]);  Cn=matrix(n,n,r,c,C[r,c]);
? Pn=Cn*An~;
? t1=sum(k=1,n,Pn[k]^2);
? t2=sum(k=1,n,An[k]^2) * sum(k=1,n,Bn[k]^2);
? z=t1-t2
  0  \\ OK
```

With length 16 the difference of the left and right side of 39.14-6 has 168 terms:

```
4*(
+A01*A10*B04*B15 +A01*A10*B06*B12 +A01*A10*B06*B13 +A01*A10*B07*B13
+A01*A12*B03*B14 +A01*A12*B07*B10 +A01*A13*B02*B14 +A01*A13*B03*B15
+A01*A14*B04*B11 +A01*A14*B05*B10 +A01*A15*B02*B12 +A01*A15*B05*B11
+A02*A09*B05*B14
+ ...
-A01*A10*B04*B14 -A01*A10*B05*B14 -A01*A10*B05*B15 -A01*A10*B07*B12
-A01*A12*B02*B15 -A01*A12*B06*B11 -A01*A13*B06*B10 -A01*A13*B07*B11
-A01*A14*B02*B13 -A01*A14*B03*B12 -A01*A15*B03*B13 -A01*A15*B04*B10
-A02*A09*B04*B15 -A02*A09*B06*B13
- ... )
```

39.14.4 Simple zero-divisors of the sedenions ‡

```
 1: ( 1 + 10 ) * ( 4 - 15 )    29: ( 2 + 11 ) * ( 4 - 13 )    57: ( 3 + 14 ) * ( 4 +  9 )
 2: ( 1 + 10 ) * ( 5 + 14 )    30: ( 2 + 11 ) * ( 5 + 12 )    58: ( 3 + 14 ) * ( 7 - 10 )
 3: ( 1 + 10 ) * ( 6 - 13 )    31: ( 2 + 11 ) * ( 6 + 15 )    59: ( 3 + 15 ) * ( 5 +  9 )
 4: ( 1 + 10 ) * ( 7 + 12 )    32: ( 2 + 11 ) * ( 7 - 14 )    60: ( 3 + 15 ) * ( 6 + 10 )
 5: ( 1 + 11 ) * ( 4 + 14 )    33: ( 2 + 12 ) * ( 3 + 13 )    61: ( 4 +  9 ) * ( 6 - 11 )
 6: ( 1 + 11 ) * ( 5 + 15 )    34: ( 2 + 12 ) * ( 5 - 11 )    62: ( 4 +  9 ) * ( 7 + 10 )
 7: ( 1 + 11 ) * ( 6 - 12 )    35: ( 2 + 12 ) * ( 7 +  9 )    63: ( 4 + 10 ) * ( 5 + 11 )
 8: ( 1 + 11 ) * ( 7 - 13 )    36: ( 2 + 13 ) * ( 3 - 12 )    64: ( 4 + 10 ) * ( 7 -  9 )
 9: ( 1 + 12 ) * ( 2 + 15 )    37: ( 2 + 13 ) * ( 4 + 11 )    65: ( 4 + 11 ) * ( 5 - 10 )
10: ( 1 + 12 ) * ( 3 - 14 )    38: ( 2 + 13 ) * ( 6 -  9 )    66: ( 4 + 11 ) * ( 6 +  9 )
11: ( 1 + 12 ) * ( 6 + 11 )    39: ( 2 + 14 ) * ( 3 - 15 )    67: ( 4 + 13 ) * ( 6 + 15 )
12: ( 1 + 12 ) * ( 7 - 10 )    40: ( 2 + 14 ) * ( 5 +  9 )    68: ( 4 + 13 ) * ( 7 - 14 )
13: ( 1 + 13 ) * ( 2 - 14 )    41: ( 2 + 14 ) * ( 7 + 11 )    69: ( 4 + 14 ) * ( 5 - 15 )
14: ( 1 + 13 ) * ( 3 - 15 )    42: ( 2 + 15 ) * ( 3 + 14 )    70: ( 4 + 14 ) * ( 7 + 13 )
15: ( 1 + 13 ) * ( 6 + 10 )    43: ( 2 + 15 ) * ( 4 -  9 )    71: ( 4 + 15 ) * ( 5 + 14 )
16: ( 1 + 13 ) * ( 7 + 11 )    44: ( 2 + 15 ) * ( 6 - 11 )    72: ( 4 + 15 ) * ( 6 - 13 )
17: ( 1 + 14 ) * ( 2 + 13 )    45: ( 3 +  9 ) * ( 4 - 14 )    73: ( 5 +  9 ) * ( 6 - 10 )
18: ( 1 + 14 ) * ( 3 + 12 )    46: ( 3 +  9 ) * ( 5 - 15 )    74: ( 5 +  9 ) * ( 7 - 11 )
19: ( 1 + 14 ) * ( 4 - 11 )    47: ( 3 +  9 ) * ( 6 + 12 )    75: ( 5 + 10 ) * ( 6 +  9 )
20: ( 1 + 14 ) * ( 5 - 10 )    48: ( 3 +  9 ) * ( 7 + 13 )    76: ( 5 + 11 ) * ( 7 +  9 )
21: ( 1 + 15 ) * ( 2 - 12 )    49: ( 3 + 10 ) * ( 4 + 13 )    77: ( 5 + 12 ) * ( 6 - 15 )
22: ( 1 + 15 ) * ( 3 + 13 )    50: ( 3 + 10 ) * ( 5 - 12 )    78: ( 5 + 12 ) * ( 7 + 14 )
23: ( 1 + 15 ) * ( 4 + 10 )    51: ( 3 + 10 ) * ( 6 - 15 )    79: ( 5 + 14 ) * ( 7 - 12 )
24: ( 1 + 15 ) * ( 5 - 11 )    52: ( 3 + 10 ) * ( 7 + 14 )    80: ( 5 + 15 ) * ( 6 + 12 )
25: ( 2 +  9 ) * ( 4 + 15 )    53: ( 3 + 12 ) * ( 5 + 10 )    81: ( 6 + 10 ) * ( 7 - 11 )
26: ( 2 +  9 ) * ( 5 - 14 )    54: ( 3 + 12 ) * ( 6 -  9 )    82: ( 6 + 11 ) * ( 7 + 10 )
27: ( 2 +  9 ) * ( 6 + 13 )    55: ( 3 + 13 ) * ( 4 - 10 )    83: ( 6 + 12 ) * ( 7 - 13 )
28: ( 2 +  9 ) * ( 7 - 12 )    56: ( 3 + 13 ) * ( 7 -  9 )    84: ( 6 + 13 ) * ( 7 + 12 )
```

Figure 39.14-G: Products of simple zero-divisors of the sedenions.

An element $U \neq 0$ such that there is an element $V \neq 0$ and either $UV = 0$ or $VU = 0$ is called a *zero-divisor*. The simplest zero-divisors of the sedenions are sums or differences of two units, we call these *simple zero-divisors*. Figure 39.14-G gives products of simple zero-divisors where the first factor is a sum of units in symbolic form. For every entry $(a + b)(c \pm d)$ there is another product $(a - b)(c \mp d)$. All products remain zero when the factors are swapped. The list was created with the program [FXT: arith/zero-divisors-demo.cc], see also [FXT: data/sedenion-zero-products.txt].

Let (a, b) be a pair of indices such that neither a nor b have all three lowest bits zero, the highest bits of a and b are different, and a and b do not coincide in all three lowest bits. Then all elements $U = (\pm a \pm b)$ are zero divisors and both equations $UV = 0$ and $WU = 0$ have a solution where V and W are elements of the same type.

If $(\pm a \pm b)(\pm c \pm d) = 0$ then $(a \text{ XOR } b) = (c \text{ XOR } d)$. The converse is not true.

There are 42 zero-divisors that are sums of two units, appearing as either left or right factor in figure 39.14-G (they are listed in [FXT: data/sedenion-zero-divisors.txt]). If $(+a + b)$ is a zero-divisor then all 4 of $(\pm a \pm b)$ are zero-divisors, so there are 168 simple zero-divisors.

There are zero-divisors for all Cayley-Dickson algebras with at least $2^n = 16$ elements (and none for less than 16 elements). The sequence of numbers of zero-divisors of the form $(a + b)$ is entry A167654 in [312]:

```
n:  0, 1, 2, 3,  4,   5,    6,     7,      8,
zd: 0, 0, 0, 0, 42, 294, 1518, 6942, 29886,
```

The sequence can be computed as follows:

```
? v=vector(14); v[4]=42; for(k=5,#v, v[k]=2*v[k-1]+(2^(k-1)-1)*(2^(k-1)-2) ); v
   [0, 0, 0, 42, 294, 1518, 6942, 29886, 124542, 509694, 2064894, 8317950, 33400830, 133885950]
```

The pairs of units leading to zero-divisors of the 64-ions are shown in figure 39.14-H. The upper left 8×8 entries are zero as there are no zero-divisors for the octonions. The simple zero-divisors of the sedenions appear in the upper left 16×16 matrix. The matrix is from [FXT: data/zero-divisor-structure.txt].

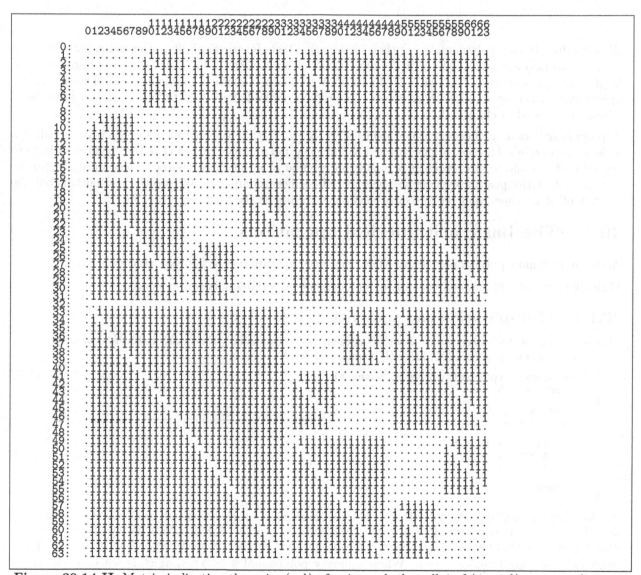

Figure 39.14-H: Matrix indicating the pairs (a, b) of units such that all 4 of $(\pm a \pm b)$ are zero-divisors.

Chapter 40

Binary polynomials

We introduce binary polynomials and their arithmetic. Tests for irreducibility, primitivity, and a method for factorization are given. Many of the algorithms shown can easily be implemented in hardware. An important application is the linear feedback shift registers, described in chapter 41. The arithmetic operations with binary polynomials are the underlying methods for computations in binary finite fields which are treated in chapter 42.

A polynomial with coefficients in the field $GF(2) = \mathbb{Z}/2\mathbb{Z}$ (that is, 'coefficients modulo 2') is called a *binary polynomial*. The operations proceed as for usual polynomials except that the coefficients have to be reduced modulo 2. To represent a binary polynomial in a binary computer we use words where the bits are set at the positions where the polynomial coefficients are one. We use the convention that the coefficient of x^k appears at bit k, so the constant term lies at the least significant bit.

40.1 The basic arithmetical operations

Addition of binary polynomials is the XOR operation. Subtraction is the very same operation.

Multiplication of a binary polynomial by its independent variable x is simply a shift to the left.

40.1.1 Multiplication and squaring

Multiplication of two polynomials A and B is identical to the usual (binary algorithm for) multiplication, except that no carry occurs [FXT: bpol/bitpol-arith.h]:

```
1    inline ulong bitpol_mult(ulong a, ulong b)
2    // Return  A * B
3    {
4        ulong t = 0;
5        while ( b )
6        {
7            if ( b & 1 )  t ^= a;
8            b >>= 1;
9            a <<= 1;
10       }
11       return  t;
12   }
```

As for integer multiplication with the C-type `unsigned long`, the result will silently overflow if $\deg(A) + \deg(B)$ is equal to or greater than the word length (`BITS_PER_LONG`). If the operation `t^=a;` was replaced with `t+=a;` the ordinary (integer) product would be returned [FXT: gf2n/bitpolmult-demo.cc], see figure 40.1-A (top). When a binary polynomial $p = \sum_{k=0}^{d} a_k x^k$ is squared, the result equals $p^2 = \sum_{k=0}^{d} a_k x^{2k}$, figure 40.1-A (bottom). So we just have to move the bits from position k to position $2k$:

```
1    inline ulong bitpol_square(ulong a)
2    // Return A * A
3    {
4        ulong t = 0,  m = 1UL;
5        while ( a )
6        {
7            if ( a&1 )  t ^= m;
```

```
           1..11.111 * 11.1.1
                              product as bitpol        ordinary product
                1..11.111  1   t= .....1..11.111   c= ......1..11.111
                           0
                 1..11.111..  1   t= ...1.1111.1.11   c= ....11....1..11
                              0
              1..11.111....  1   t= .1.11.1..11.11   c= ..11..11.....11
              1..11.111....  1   t= 11.....1111.11   c= 1.......11...11
```

```
           1..11.111 * 1..11.111
                              product as bitpol        ordinary product
                1..11.111  1   t= .......1..11.111  c= .........1..11.111
                 1..11.111. 1   t= ......11.1.11..1  c= .......111.1..1.1
                 1..11.111..  1   t= ......1111....1.1 c= ......1...1......1
                              0
              1..11.111....  1   t= ...1.1..1111.1.1  c= .....11.111111...1
              1..11.111....  1   t= ...11..1...1.1.1  c= ...1....1.11.1...1
                              0
                              0
             1..11.111.......  1   t= 1.....1.1...1.1.1  c= .1.1111..111.1...1
```

Figure 40.1-A: Multiplication (top) and squaring (bottom) of binary polynomials and numbers.

```
8              m <<= 2;
9              a >>= 1;
10         }
11         return t;  // == bitpol_mult(a, a);
12     }
```

40.1.2   Optimization of the squaring and multiplication routines

The routines for multiplication and squaring can be optimized by partially unrolling which avoids branches. As given, the function is compiled to:

```
0:    31 c9                    xor    %ecx,%ecx  // t = 0
2:    48 85 ff                 test   %rdi,%rdi  // a
5:    ba 01 00 00 00           mov    $0x1,%edx  // m = 1
a:    74 1b                    je     27 <_Z13bitpol_squarem+0x27>  // a==0 ?

10:   48 89 c8                 mov    %rcx,%rax  // tmp = t
13:   48 31 d0                 xor    %rdx,%rax  // tmp ^= m
16:   40 f6 c7 01              test   $0x1,%dil  // if ( a&1 )
1a:   48 0f 45 c8              cmovne %rax,%rcx  // then t = tmp
1e:   48 c1 e2 02              shl    $0x2,%rdx  // m <<= 2
22:   48 d1 ef                 shr    %rdi       // a >>= 1
25:   75 e9                    jne    10 <_Z13bitpol_squarem+0x10>  // a!=0 ?

27:   48 89 c8                 mov    %rcx,%rax
2a:   c3                       retq
```

The if-statement does not cause a branch so we unroll the contents of the loop 4-fold. We also move the `while()` statement to the end of the loop to avoid the initial branch:

```
1    inline ulong bitpol_square(ulong a)
2    {
3        ulong t = 0,  m = 1UL;
4        do
5        {
6            if ( a&1 )  t ^= m;
7            m <<= 2;  a >>= 1;
8            if ( a&1 )  t ^= m;
9            m <<= 2;  a >>= 1;
10           if ( a&1 )  t ^= m;
11           m <<= 2;  a >>= 1;
12           if ( a&1 )  t ^= m;
13           m <<= 2;  a >>= 1;
14       }
15       while ( a );
16       return t;
17   }
```

Now we obtain machine code that executes much faster:

```
0:    31 c9                    xor    %ecx,%ecx  // t = 0
```

```
 2:    ba 01 00 00 00          mov     $0x1,%edx   // m = 1

 7:    48 89 c8                mov     %rcx,%rax   // tmp = t
 a:    48 31 d0                xor     %rdx,%rax   // tmp ^= m
 d:    40 f6 c7 01             test    $0x1,%dil   // if ( a&1 )
11:    48 0f 45 c8             cmovne  %rax,%rcx   // then t = tmp
15:    48 c1 e2 02             shl     $0x2,%rdx   // m <<= 2
19:    48 d1 ef                shr     %rdi        // a >>= 1

1c:    48 89 c8                mov     %rcx,%rax
1f:    48 31 d0                xor     %rdx,%rax
22:    40 f6 c7 01             test    $0x1,%dil
26:    48 0f 45 c8             cmovne  %rax,%rcx
2a:    48 c1 e2 02             shl     $0x2,%rdx
2e:    48 d1 ef                shr     %rdi

31:    48 89 c8                mov     %rcx,%rax
[--snip--]
43:    48 d1 ef                shr     %rdi

46:    48 89 c8                mov     %rcx,%rax
[--snip--]
58:    48 d1 ef                shr     %rdi

5b:    75 aa                   jne     7 <_Z13bitpol_squarem+0x7>  // a!=0 ?
5d:    48 89 c8                mov     %rcx,%rax
60:    c3                      retq
```

The multiplication algorithm is optimized in the same way. For squaring we can also use the bit-zip function given in section 1.15 on page 39:

```
1   inline ulong bitpol_square(ulong a)  { return bit_zip0( a ); }
```

The upper half of the bits of the argument must be zero.

40.1.3 Exponentiation

With a multiplication (and squaring) function at hand, it is straightforward (see section 28.5 on page 563) to implement the algorithm for binary exponentiation [FXT: bpol/bitpol-arith.h]:

```
 1   inline ulong bitpol_power(ulong a, ulong e)
 2   // Return A ** e
 3   {
 4       if ( 0==e )  return 1;
 5
 6       ulong s = a;
 7       while ( 0==(e&1) )
 8       {
 9           s = bitpol_square(s);
10           e >>= 1;
11       }
12
13       a = s;
14       while ( 0!=(e>>=1) )
15       {
16           s = bitpol_square(s);
17           if ( e & 1 )  a = bitpol_mult(a, s);
18       }
19       return  a;
20   }
```

Note that overflow will occur even for moderate exponents.

40.1.4 Quotient and remainder

The remainder a modulo b can be computed by initializing $A = a$ and subtracting $B = x^j \cdot b$ with $\deg(B) = \deg(A)$ from A at each step. The computation is finished as soon as $\deg b > \deg A$. As C-code [FXT: bpol/bitpol-arith.h]:

```
1   inline ulong bitpol_rem(ulong a, ulong b)
2   // Return  R = A % B = A - (A/B)*B
3   // Must have: B!=0
4   {
5       const ulong db = highest_one_idx(b);
6       ulong da;
```

```
7        while ( db <= (da=highest_one_idx(a)) )
8        {
9            if ( 0==a )  break;   // needed because highest_one_idx(0)==highest_one_idx(1)
10           a ^= (b<<(da-db));
11       }
12       return  a;
13   }
```

The function `highest_one_idx()` is given in section 1.6 on page 14. The following version may be superior if the degree of a is small or if no fast version of the function `highest_one_idx()` is available:

```
1        while ( b <= a )
2        {
3            ulong t = b;
4            while ( (a^t) > t )   t <<= 1;
5            // =^= while ( highest_one(a) > highest_one(t) )  t <<= 1;
6            a ^= t;
7        }
8        return  a;
```

The quotient and remainder of two polynomials is computed as follows:

```
1    inline void bitpol_divrem(ulong a, ulong b, ulong &q, ulong &r)
2    // Set R, Q so that   A == Q * B + R.
3    // Must have B!=0.
4    {
5        const ulong db = highest_one_idx(b);
6        q = 0;  // quotient
7        ulong da;
8        while ( db <= (da=highest_one_idx(a)) )
9        {
10           if ( 0==a )  break;   // needed because highest_one_idx(0)==highest_one_idx(1)
11           a ^= (b<<(da-db));
12           q ^= (1UL<<(da-db));
13       }
14       r = a;
15   }
```

The division routine does the same computation but discards the remainder:

```
1    inline ulong bitpol_div(ulong a, ulong b)
2    // Return  Q = A / B
3    // Must have B!=0.
4    {
5        [--snip--]  // identical code
6        return  q;
7    }
```

40.1.5   Greatest common divisor (GCD)

The polynomial greatest common divisor (GCD) can be computed with the Euclidean algorithm [FXT: bpol/bitpol-gcd.h]:

```
1    inline ulong bitpol_gcd(ulong a, ulong b)
2    // Return  polynomial gcd(A, B)
3    {
4        if ( a<b )  { ulong t=a; a=b; b=t; }   // swap if deg(A)<deg(B)
5        // here: b<=a
6        while ( 0!=b )
7        {
8            ulong c = bitpol_rem(a, b);
9            a = b;
10           b = c;
11       }
12       return  a;
13   }
```

Note that the comment

```
if ( a < b )  { ulong t=a; a=b; b=t; };   // swap if deg(A)<deg(B)
```

is not strictly correct as the swap can also happen with $\deg(a) = \deg(b)$ but that does no harm.

The binary GCD algorithm can be implemented as follows:

```
1   inline ulong bitpol_binary_gcd(ulong a, ulong b)
2   {
3       if ( a < b )  { ulong t=a; a=b; b=t; };  // swap if deg(A)<deg(B)
4       if ( b==0 )  return a;
5
6       ulong k = 0;
7       while ( !((a|b)&1) )  // both divisible by x
8       {
9           k++;
10          a >>= 1;
11          b >>= 1;
12      }
13      while ( !(a&1) )  a >>= 1;
14      while ( !(b&1) )  b >>= 1;
15
16      while ( a!=b )
17      {
18          if ( a < b )  { ulong t=a; a=b; b=t; };  // swap if deg(A)<deg(B)
19          ulong t = (a^b) >> 1;
20          while ( !(t&1) )  t >>= 1;
21          a = t;
22      }
23
24      return  a << k;
25  }
```

With a fast bit-scan instruction we can optimize the function:

```
1   inline ulong bitpol_binary_gcd(ulong a, ulong b)
2   {
3       if ( (a==0) || (b==0) )  return a|b; // one (or both) of a, b zero?
4
5       ulong ka = lowest_one_idx(a);
6       a >>= ka;
7       ulong kb = lowest_one_idx(b);
8       b >>= kb;
9       ulong k = ( ka<kb ? ka : kb );
10
11      while ( a!=b )
12      {
13          if ( a < b )  { ulong t=a; a=b; b=t; } // swap if deg(A)<deg(B)
14          ulong t = (a^b) >> 1;
15          a = (t >> lowest_one_idx(t));
16      }
17      return  a << k;
18  }
```

40.1.6 Exact division

Let C be a binary polynomial in x with constant term 1. We use the relation (for power series)

$$\frac{1}{C} \;=\; \frac{1}{1-Y} = (1+Y)\,(1+Y^2)\,(1+Y^4)\,(1+Y^8)\,\dots\,(1+Y^{2^n}) \quad \bmod x^{2^{n+1}} \qquad (40.1\text{-}1)$$

where $Y = 1 - C$. Now let $Y = x^{e_1} + x^{e_2} + \dots + x^{e_k}$ where $e_i \geq 1$ and $e_{i+1} > e_i$. Then $Y^q = x^{qe_1} + x^{qe_2} + \dots + x^{qe_k}$ whenever q is a power of 2, and the multiplication by $(1 - Y^q)$ is done by shifts and subtractions. If A is an exact multiple of C, then $R = A/C$ is a polynomial that can be computed as follows. We assume that arrays of N bits are used for the polynomials.

1. Set $R := A$ and let e_i (for $i = 1, 2, \dots, k$) be the (ordered) positions of the nonzero coefficients of C. Set $q := 1$.

2. If $qe_1 \geq N$, then return R.

3. Set $T := 0$. For $j = 1, 2, \dots, k$, set $T := T + R\,x^{qe_j}$. The multiplications with x^{qe_j} are left shifts by qe_j positions. Set $R := T$.

4. Set $q := 2\,q$ and goto step 2.

The method is most efficient if k, the number of nonzero coefficients of $C - 1$, is small. Sometimes we can reduce the work by dividing by $C\,D$ and finally multiplying by D for some appropriate D. For example, with all-ones polynomials $C = 1 + x + x^2 + \ldots + x^k$ and $D = 1 + x$, then $C D = 1 + x^{k+1}$. If C is of the form $x^u (1 + \ldots + x^k)$, then A/C can be computed as $(A/x^u)/(C/x^u)$.

The simplest example is $C = 1 + x$ where the above procedure reduces to the inverse reversed Gray code given in section 1.16.6 on page 45:

```
1    inline ulong bitpol_div_xp1(ulong a)
2    // Return power series  A / (x+1)
3    // If A is a multiple of x+1, then the returned value
4    //   is the exact division by x+1
5    {
6        a ^= a<<1;   // rev_gray ** 1
7        a ^= a<<2;   // rev_gray ** 2
8        a ^= a<<4;   // rev_gray ** 4
9        a ^= a<<8;   // rev_gray ** 8
10       a ^= a<<16;  // rev_gray ** 16
11   #if  BITS_PER_LONG >= 64
12       a ^= a<<32;   // for 64bit words
13   #endif
14       return a;
15   }
```

For the division by $x^2 + 1$ use the function

```
1    inline ulong bitpol_div_x2p1(ulong a)
2    // Return power series  A / (x^2+1)
3    // If A is a multiple of x^2+1, then the returned value
4    //   is the exact division by x^2+1
5    {
6        a ^= a<<2;   // rev_gray ** 2
7        a ^= a<<4;   // rev_gray ** 4
8        a ^= a<<8;   // rev_gray ** 8
9        a ^= a<<16;  // rev_gray ** 16
10   #if  BITS_PER_LONG >= 64
11       a ^= a<<32;   // for 64bit words
12   #endif
13       return a;
14   }
```

An algorithm for the exact division by $C = 2^k \pm 1$ (over $\mathbb{Z}$) is given in section 1.21.2 on page 57.

40.2 Multiplying binary polynomials of high degree

We used the straightforward multiplication scheme which is $O(N^2)$ for polynomials of degree N. This is fine when working with polynomials of small degree. However, when working with polynomials of high degree, the following splitting schemes should be used.

40.2.1 Karatsuba method: 2-way splitting

Let U and V be binary polynomials of (even) degree N. Write $U = U_0 + U_1 x^{N/2}$, $V = V_0 + V_1 x^{N/2}$ and use the scheme

$$U V \quad = \quad U_0 \cdot V_0 (1 + x^{N/2}) + (U_1 - U_0) \cdot (V_0 - V_1) x^{N/2} + U_1 \cdot V_1 (x^{N/2} + x^N) \qquad (40.2\text{-}1)$$

Only the three multiplications indicated by a dot are expensive, the multiplications by a power of x are just shifts. The resulting scheme is the *Karatsuba multiplication for polynomials*, relation 28.1-3 on page 550 interpreted for polynomials (set $x^{N/2} = B$). Recursive application of the scheme leads to the asymptotic cost $O(N^{\log_2(3)}) \approx O(N^{1.585})$.

40.2.2 Splitting schemes that do not involve constants ‡

A generalization of the Karatsuba scheme is given in [347] (see also [348]). It does not lead to schemes asymptotically better than $O(N^{\log_2(3)})$ but has a simple structure and avoids all multiplications by constants. As with 2-way splitting the method works for polynomials over any field.

For the 3-way splitting scheme set

$$
\begin{align*}
A &= a_2\, x^2 + a_1\, x + a_0 \tag{40.2-2a}\\
B &= b_2\, x^2 + b_1\, x + b_0 \tag{40.2-2b}\\
C &= A\,B = c_4\, x^4 + c_3\, x^3 + c_2\, x^2 + c_1\, x + c_0 \tag{40.2-2c}
\end{align*}
$$

Then the c_k are

$$
\begin{align*}
c_0 &= d_{0,0} \tag{40.2-3a}\\
c_1 &= d_{0,1} - d_{0,0} - d_{1,1} \tag{40.2-3b}\\
c_2 &= d_{0,2} - d_{0,0} - d_{2,2} + d_{1,1} \tag{40.2-3c}\\
c_3 &= d_{1,2} - d_{1,1} - d_{2,2} \tag{40.2-3d}\\
c_4 &= d_{2,2} \tag{40.2-3e}
\end{align*}
$$

where

$$
\begin{align*}
d_{0,0} &= a_0\, b_0 \tag{40.2-4a}\\
d_{1,1} &= a_1\, b_1 \tag{40.2-4b}\\
d_{2,2} &= a_2\, b_2 \tag{40.2-4c}\\
d_{0,1} &= (a_0 + a_1)\,(b_0 + b_1) \tag{40.2-4d}\\
d_{0,2} &= (a_0 + a_2)\,(b_0 + b_2) \tag{40.2-4e}\\
d_{1,2} &= (a_1 + a_2)\,(b_1 + b_2) \tag{40.2-4f}
\end{align*}
$$

The scheme involves 6 multiplications and 13 additions. Recursive application leads to the asymptotic cost $(N^{\log_3(6)}) \approx O(N^{1.6309})$ which is slightly worse than for the 2-term scheme. However, applying this scheme first for a polynomial with $N = 3 \cdot 2^n$ terms and then using the Karatsuba scheme recursively can be advantageous.

We generalize the method for n-term polynomials and denote the scheme by KA-n. The 2-term scheme KA-2 is the Karatsuba algorithm. With

$$
A = \sum_{k=0}^{n-1} a_k\, x^k \tag{40.2-5a}
$$

$$
B = \sum_{k=0}^{n-1} b_k\, x^k \tag{40.2-5b}
$$

$$
C = A\,B =: \sum_{k=0}^{2n-2} c_k\, x^k \tag{40.2-5c}
$$

define

$$
\begin{align*}
d_{s,s} &:= a_s\, b_s \quad \text{for } s = 0, 1, \ldots, n-1 \tag{40.2-6a}\\
d_{s,t} &:= (a_s + b_s)\,(a_t + b_t) \quad \text{for } s+t = i,\ t > s \geq 0,\ 1 \leq i \leq 2n-3 \tag{40.2-6b}\\
c_i^{*} &= \sum_{\substack{s+t=i\\0 \leq s < t}} d_{s,t} - \sum_{\substack{s+t=i\\0 \leq s < n-1}} (d_{s,s} + d_{t,t}) \tag{40.2-6c}
\end{align*}
$$

Then

$$
\begin{align*}
c_0 &= d_{0,0} \tag{40.2-7a}\\
c_{2n-2} &= d_{n-1,n-1} \tag{40.2-7b}
\end{align*}
$$

and for $0 < i < 2n - 2$:

$$c_i \;=\; \begin{cases} c_i^* & \text{if } i \text{ odd} \\ c_i^* + d_{i/2,i/2} & \text{otherwise} \end{cases} \tag{40.2-7c}$$

The Karatsuba scheme is obtained for $n = 2$.

We give GP code whose output is the KA-n algorithm for given n. We need to create symbols 'ak' (for a_k), 'bk', and so on:

```
1    fa(k)=eval(Str("a" k))
2    fb(k)=eval(Str("b" k))
3    fc(k)=eval(Str("c" k))
4    fd(k,j)=eval(Str("d" k "" j))
```

For example, we can create a symbolic polynomial of degree 3:

```
? sum(k=0,3, fa(k) * x^k)
   a3*x^3 + a2*x^2 + a1*x + a0
```

The next routine generates the definitions of all $d_{s,t}$. It returns the number of multiplications involved:

```
1    D(n)=
2    {
3        local(mct);
4        mct = 0; \\ count multiplications
5        for (i=0, n-1, mct+=1; print(fd(i,i), " = ", fa(i), " * ", fb(i) ) );
6        for (t=1, n-1,
7            for (s=0, t-1,
8                mct += 1;
9                print(fd(s,t), " = (", fa(s)+fa(t), ") * (", fb(s)+fb(t), ")" ) ;
10           );
11       );
12       return(mct);
13   }
```

For $n = 3$ the output is

```
d00 = a0 * b0
d11 = a1 * b1
d22 = a2 * b2
d01 = (a0 + a1) * (b0 + b1)
d02 = (a0 + a2) * (b0 + b2)
d12 = (a1 + a2) * (b1 + b2)
```

The following routine prints c_i, the coefficient of the product, in terms of several $d_{s,t}$. It returns the number of additions involved:

```
1    C(i, n)=
2    {
3        local(N, s, act);
4        act = -1; \\ count additions
5        print1(fc(i), " = ");
6        for (s=0, i-1,
7            t = i - s;
8            if ( (t>s) && (t<n),
9                act += 3;
10               print1(" + ", fd(s,t));
11               print1(" - ", fd(s,s));
12               print1(" - ", fd(t,t));
13           );
14       );
15       if ( 0==i%2, act+=1; print1(" + ", fd(i/2,i/2)) );
16       print();
17       return( act );
18   }
```

It has to be called for all i where $0 \le i \le 2n - 2$. The algorithm is generated by the following routine:

```
1    KA(n)=
2    {
3        local(mct, act);
4        act = 0; \\ count additions
5        mct = 0; \\ count multiplications
6        mct = D(n);  \\ generate definitions for the d_{s,t}
7        \\ generate rules for computation of c_i in terms of d_{s,t}:
8        for (i=0, 2*n-2, act+=C(i,n) );
```

```
9       act += n*(n-1); \\ additions when setting up d(i,j) for i!=j
10      return( [mct, act] );
11    }
```

With $n = 3$ we find the relations 40.2-3a ... 40.2-3e:

```
c0 =  + d00
c1 =  + d01 - d00 - d11
c2 =  + d02 - d00 - d22 + d11
c3 =  + d12 - d11 - d22
c4 =  + d22
```

```
d00 = a0 * b0
d11 = a1 * b1
d22 = a2 * b2
d33 = a3 * b3
d44 = a4 * b4
d01 = (a0 + a1) * (b0 + b1)
d02 = (a0 + a2) * (b0 + b2)
d12 = (a1 + a2) * (b1 + b2)
d03 = (a0 + a3) * (b0 + b3)
d13 = (a1 + a3) * (b1 + b3)
d23 = (a2 + a3) * (b2 + b3)
d04 = (a0 + a4) * (b0 + b4)
d14 = (a1 + a4) * (b1 + b4)
d24 = (a2 + a4) * (b2 + b4)
d34 = (a3 + a4) * (b3 + b4)

c0 =  + d00
c1 =  + d01 - d00 - d11
c2 =  + d02 - d00 - d22 + d11
c3 =  + d03 - d00 - d33 + d12 - d11 - d22
c4 =  + d04 - d00 - d44 + d13 - d11 - d33 + d22
c5 =  + d14 - d11 - d44 + d23 - d22 - d33
c6 =  + d24 - d22 - d44 + d33
c7 =  + d34 - d33 - d44
c8 =  + d44
```

Figure 40.2-A: Code for the algorithm KA-5.

Now we generate the definitions for the KA-5 algorithm:

```
n=5 /* n terms, degree=n-1 */
default(echo, 0);
KA(n);
```

We obtain the algorithm KA-5 shown in figure 40.2-A. The format is valid GP input, so we add a few
lines that print code to check the algorithm:

```
1     print("A=",sum(k=0,n-1, fa(k) * x^k))
2     print("B=",sum(k=0,n-1, fb(k) * x^k))
3     print("/* direct computation of the product: */")
4     print("C=A*B")
5     print("/* Karatsuba computation of the product: */")
6     print("K=",sum(k=0,2*n-2, fc(k) * x^k))
7     print("qq=K-C")
8     print("print( if(0==qq, \"OK.\", \" **** OUCH!\") )")
```

This gives for $n = 5$:

```
A=a4*x^4 + a3*x^3 + a2*x^2 + a1*x + a0
B=b4*x^4 + b3*x^3 + b2*x^2 + b1*x + b0
/* direct computation of the product: */
C=A*B
/* Karatsuba computation of the product: */
K=c8*x^8 + c7*x^7 + c6*x^6 + c5*x^5 + c4*x^4 + c3*x^3 + c2*x^2 + c1*x + c0
qq=K-C
print( if(0==qq, "OK.", " **** OUCH!") )
```

We can feed the output into another GP session to verify the algorithm:

```
gp -f -q < karatsuba-n.gp | gp
```

The output is (shortened and comments added)

```
/* definitions of d(s,t): */
b0*a0
b1*a1
b2*a2
b3*a3
```

```
b4*a4
(b0 + b1)*a0 + (a1*b0 + b1*a1)
(b0 + b2)*a0 + (a2*b0 + b2*a2)
[--snip--]
(b3 + b4)*a3 + (a4*b3 + b4*a4)

/* the c_i in terms of d(s,t), evaluated: */
b0*a0
b1*a0 + a1*b0
b2*a0 + (a2*b0 + b1*a1)
b3*a0 + (a3*b0 + (b2*a1 + a2*b1))
b4*a0 + (a4*b0 + (b3*a1 + (a3*b1 + b2*a2)))
b4*a1 + (a4*b1 + (b3*a2 + a3*b2))
b4*a2 + (a4*b2 + b3*a3)
b4*a3 + a4*b3
b4*a4

/* polynomials: */
a4*x^4 + a3*x^3 + a2*x^2 + a1*x + a0
b4*x^4 + b3*x^3 + b2*x^2 + b1*x + b0

/* direct computation of product: */
b4*a4*x^8 + (b4*a3 + a4*b3)*x^7 + (b4*a2 + (a4*b2 + b3*a3))*x^6 + [...]

/* Karatsuba computation of product: */
b4*a4*x^8 + (b4*a3 + a4*b3)*x^7 + (b4*a2 + (a4*b2 + b3*a3))*x^6 + [...]

/* difference: */
0

OK.  /* looks good */
```

The number of multiplications with the KA-n splitting scheme is $(n^2 + n)/2$ which is suboptimal except for $n = 2$. However, recursive application can be worthwhile. One should start with the biggest prime factors as the number of additions is then minimized. The number of multiplications does not depend on the order of recursion (see [347] which also tabulates the number of additions and multiplications for $n \leq 128$).

With n just below a highly composite number one may append zeros as 'dummy' terms and recursively use KA-n algorithms for small n. For example, for polynomials of degree 63 the recursion with KA-2 (and $n = 64$) will beat the scheme "KA-7, then KA-3".

One can write code generators that create expanded versions of the recursions for n the product of small primes. If the cost of multiplication is much higher than for addition (as for binary polynomial multiplication on general purpose CPUs), then substantial savings can be expected.

40.2.3 Toom-Cook algorithms for binary polynomials

The 3-way and 4-way splitting schemes described in section 28.1 on page 550 cannot be used with binary polynomials because constants other than 0 and 1 are used. We now give splitting schemes that use the constants 0 and 1 only, they are given in [59]. The schemes are valid only for binary polynomials.

40.2.3.1 3-way splitting

For the multiplication of two polynomials A and B both of degree $3N$ write

$$A = a_0 + a_1\,x^N + a_2\,x^{2N} =: a_0 + a_1\,Y + a_2\,Y^2 \tag{40.2-8}$$

and identically for B. A 3-way splitting scheme for multiplication is shown in figure 40.2-B. The multiplications and divisions by x are shifts and the exact divisions are linear operations if we use the method of section 40.1.6 on page 826.

40.2.3.2 4-way splitting

For the multiplication of two polynomials A and B both of degree $4N$ write

$$A = a_0 + a_1\,Y + a_2\,Y^2 + a_3\,Y^3 \tag{40.2-9}$$

where $Y := x^N$ and identically for B. The 4-way splitting multiplication scheme is shown in figure 40.2-C.

```
      A = a2*Y^2 + a1*Y + a0
      B = b2*Y^2 + b1*Y + b0

      S 3= a 2+ a 1+ a 0 ;
      S 2= b 2+ b 1+ b 0 ;
      S1 = S3 * S2;             \\ Mult (1)
      S0 = a2*x^2 + a1*x;
      S4 = b2*x^2 + b1*x;
      S3 += S0;
      S2 += S4;
      S0 += a0;
      S4 += b0;
      S3 *= S2;                 \\ Mult (2)
      S2 = S0 * S4;             \\ Mult (3)
      S4 = a2 * b2;             \\ Mult (4)
      S0 = a0 * b0;             \\ Mult (5)

      S3 += S2;

      S2 += S0;  S2 /= x;   S2 += S3;
      T = S4;   T *= (x^3+1);  \\ temporary variable
      S2 += T;   S2 /= (x+1);  \\ exact division

      S1 += S0;
      S3 += S1;   S3 /= x;   S3 /= (x+1);   \\ exact division
      S1 += S4;   S1 += S2;
      S2 += S3;

      P = S4*Y^4 + S3*Y^3 + S2*Y^2 + S1*Y + S0;
      Mod(1,2)* (P - A*B) \\ == zero
      (P - A*B) \\ NOT zero, the scheme only works over GF(2)
```

Figure 40.2-B: Implementation of the 3-way multiplication scheme for binary polynomials. The five expensive multiplications are commented with 'Mult (n)'.

40.2.4 FFT based methods

For polynomials of very high degree FFT-based algorithms can be used. The simplest method is to use integer multiplication without the carry phase (which is polynomial multiplication!). We give an example using decimal digits. The carry phase of the integer multiplication is replaced by a reduction modulo 2:

```
    100110111 * 110101
 == 11022223331211  // integer multiplication
 == 11000001111011  // parity of digits
```

The scheme will work for polynomials of degree less than nine only. When using an FFT multiplication scheme (see section 28.2 on page 558), we can multiply polynomials up to degree N as long as the integer values $0, 1, 2 \ldots N + 1$ can be distinguished after computing the FFT. This is hardly a limitation at all: with the C-type `float` (24 bit mantissa) polynomials up to degree one million can be multiplied assuming at least 20 bits are correct after the FFT. With type `double` (53-bit mantissa) there is no practical limit. While the algorithm is very easy to implement it is not competitive to well implemented splitting schemes and the FFT method described in [303] or the multiplication algorithm given in [92]. An excellent source for multiplication algorithms for binary polynomials is [85].

40.3 Modular arithmetic with binary polynomials

Here we consider arithmetic of binary polynomials modulo a binary polynomial. Addition and subtraction are again the XOR operation and no modular reduction is required.

40.3.1 Multiplication and squaring

Multiplication of a polynomial A by x modulo (a polynomial) C can be done by shifting left and subtracting C if the coefficient shifted out is one [FXT: bpol/bitpolmod-arith.h]:

```
1    static inline ulong bitpolmod_times_x(ulong a, ulong c, ulong h)
2    // Return  (A * x) mod C
3    // where A and C represent polynomials over Z/2Z:
```

```
A = a3*Y^3 + a2*Y^2 + a1*Y + a0;
B = b3*Y^3 + b2*Y^2 + b1*Y + b0;

S 1= a 3+ a 2+ a1 + a0;
S 2= b 3+ b 2+ b1 + b0;
S3 = S1 * S2;                      \\ Mult (1)
S0 = a1 + x*(a2 + x*a3);
S6 = b1 + x*(b2 + x*b3);
S4 = (S0 + a3*(x+1))*x + S1;
S5 = (S6 + b3*(x+1))*x + S2;
S0 = S0*x + a0;
S6 = S6*x + b0;
S5 = S5 * S4;                      \\ Mult (2)
S4 = S0 * S6;                      \\ Mult (3)
S0 = a0*x^3 + a1*x^2 + a2*x;
S6 = b0*x^3 + b1*x^2 + b2*x;
S1 = S1 + S0 + a0*(x^2+x);
S2 = S2 + S6 + b0*(x^2+x);
S0 = S0 + a3;
S6 = S6 + b3;
S1 = S1 * S2;                      \\ Mult (4)
S2 = S0 * S6;                      \\ Mult (5)
S6 = a3 * b3;                      \\ Mult (6)
S0 = a0 * b0;                      \\ Mult (7)

S1 = S1 + S2 + S0*(x^4+x^2+1);
S5 = (S5 + S4 + S6*(x^4+x^2+1) + S1) \ (x^4+x);
S2 = S2 + S6 + S0*x^6;
S4 = S4 + S2 + S6*x^6 + S0;
S4 = (S4 + S5*(x^5+x)) \ (x^4+x^2);
S 3= S 3+ S 0+ S6 ;
S1 = S1 + S3;
S2 = S2 + S1*x + S3*x^2;
S 3= S 3+ S 4+ S5 ;
S1 = (S1 + S3*(x^2+x)) \ (x^4+x);
S5 = S5 + S1;
S2 = (S2 + S5*(x^2+x)) \ (x^4+x^2);
S4 = S4 + S2;

P = S6*Y^6 + S5*Y^5 + S4*Y^4 + S3*Y^3 + S2*Y^2 + S1*Y + S0;
Mod(1,2)*(P - A*B)  \\ == zero
(P - A*B) \\ NOT zero, the scheme only works over GF(2)
```

Figure 40.2-C: Implementation of the 4-way multiplication scheme for binary polynomials. The seven expensive multiplications are commented with 'Mult (n)'.

```
4     //   W - pol(w) =: \sum_k{ [bit_k(w)] * x^k}
5     //
6     // h needs to be a mask with one bit set:
7     //   h == highest_one(c) >> 1   == 1UL << (degree(C)-1)
8     {
9         ulong s = a & h;
10        a <<= 1;
11        if ( s )  a ^= c;
12        return  a;
13    }
```

To avoid the repeated computation of the highest set bit, we introduced the auxiliary variable h that has to be initialized as described in the comment. Section 1.6 on page 14 gives algorithms for the function `highest_one()`. Note that h needs to be recomputed only if the degree of the modulus C changes, which is usually only once for a series of calculations. By using the variable h we can use the routine even if the degree of C equals the number of bits in a word in which case C does not fit into a word.

The routine for the multiplication of two polynomials a and b modulo C is obtained by adding a reduction step to the binary multiplication routine:

```
1     inline ulong bitpolmod_mult(ulong a, ulong b, ulong c, ulong h)
2     // Return  (A * B) mod C
3     {
4         ulong t = 0;
5         while ( b )
6         {
```

```
7              if ( b & 1 )  t ^= a;
8              b >>= 1;
9
10             ulong s = a & h;
11             a <<= 1;
12             if ( s )  a ^= c;
13         }
14         return  t;
15  }
```

40.3.2 Optimization of the squaring and multiplication routines

Squaring a can be done by the multiplication $a \cdot a$. If many squarings have to be done with a fixed modulus, then the optimization using a precomputed table of the residues $x^{2k} \bmod C$ shown in section 42.1 on page 886 can be useful. Squaring of the polynomial $\sum_{k=0}^{d} a_k x^k$ is the computation of the sum $\sum_{k=0}^{d} a_k x^{2k}$ modulo C. We use the auxiliary function

```
1   static inline ulong bitpolmod_times_x2(ulong a, ulong c, ulong h)
2   // Return  (A * x * x) mod C
3   {
4       { ulong s=a&h;  a<<=1;  if (s) a^=c; }
5       { ulong s=a&h;  a<<=1;  if (s) a^=c; }
6       return  a;
7   }
```

The squaring function, with a 4-fold unrolled loop, is

```
1   static inline ulong bitpolmod_square(ulong a, ulong c, ulong h)
2   // Return A*A mod C
3   {
4       ulong t = 0, s = 1;
5       do
6       {
7           if (a&1) t^=s;  a>>=1;  s=bitpolmod_times_x2(s, c, h);
8           if (a&1) t^=s;  a>>=1;  s=bitpolmod_times_x2(s, c, h);
9           if (a&1) t^=s;  a>>=1;  s=bitpolmod_times_x2(s, c, h);
10          if (a&1) t^=s;  a>>=1;  s=bitpolmod_times_x2(s, c, h);
11      }
12      while ( a );
13      return t;
14  }
```

Whether the unrolled code is used can be specified via the line

```
#define  MULT_UNROLL  // define to unroll loops 4-fold
```

The optimization used for the multiplication routine is also unrolling as described in section 40.1.2 on page 823:

```
1   static inline ulong bitpolmod_mult(ulong a, ulong b, ulong c, ulong h)
2   {
3       ulong t = 0;
4       do
5       {
6           { if(b&1) t^=a;  b>>=1;  ulong s=a&h;  a<<=1;  if(s) a^=c; }
7           { if(b&1) t^=a;  b>>=1;  ulong s=a&h;  a<<=1;  if(s) a^=c; }
8           { if(b&1) t^=a;  b>>=1;  ulong s=a&h;  a<<=1;  if(s) a^=c; }
9           { if(b&1) t^=a;  b>>=1;  ulong s=a&h;  a<<=1;  if(s) a^=c; }
10      }
11      while ( b );
12      return  t;
13  }
```

It turns out that squaring via multiplication is slightly faster than via the described sum computation.

40.3.3 Exponentiation

The following routine for modular exponentiation uses the right-to-left powering algorithm from section 28.5.1 on page 563 [FXT: bpol/bitpolmod-arith.h]:

```
1   inline ulong bitpolmod_power(ulong a, ulong e, ulong c, ulong h)
2   // Return (A ** e)  mod C
3   {
4       if ( 0==e )  return 1;  // avoid hang with e==0 in next while()
```

```
5
6       ulong s = a;
7       while ( 0==(e&1) )
8       {
9           s = bitpolmod_square(s, c, h);
10          e >>= 1;
11      }
12
13      a = s;
14      while ( 0!=(e>>=1) )
15      {
16          s = bitpolmod_square(s, c, h);
17          if ( e & 1 )  a = bitpolmod_mult(a, s, c, h);
18      }
19      return  a;
20  }
```

The left-to-right powering algorithm given in section 28.5.2 on page 564 can be implemented as:

```
1   inline ulong bitpolmod_power(ulong a, ulong e, ulong c, ulong h)
2   {
3       ulong s = a;
4       ulong b = highest_one(e);
5       while ( b>1 )
6       {
7           b >>= 1;
8           s = bitpolmod_square(s, c, h); // s *= s;
9           if ( e & b )  s = bitpolmod_mult(s, a, c, h);    // s *= a;
10      }
11      return s;
12  }
```

Computing a power of x can be optimized with this scheme:

```
1   inline ulong bitpolmod_xpower(ulong e, ulong c, ulong h)
2   // Return (x ** e)  mod C
3   {
4       ulong s = 2;  // 'x'
5       ulong b = highest_one(e);
6       while ( b>1 )
7       {
8           b >>= 1;
9           s = bitpolmod_square(s, c, h); // s *= s;
10          if ( e & b )  s = bitpolmod_times_x(s, c, h);    // s *= x;
11      }
12      return s;
13  }
```

40.3.4 Division by x

Division by x is possible if the modulus has a nonzero constant term (that is, $\gcd(C, x) = 1$). The routine is quite simple [FXT: bpol/bitpolmod-arith.h]:

```
1   static inline ulong bitpolmod_div_x(ulong a, ulong c, ulong h)
2   // Return  (A / x) mod C
3   // C must have nonzero constant term: (c&1)==1
4   {
5       ulong s = a & 1;
6       a >>= 1;
7       if ( s )
8       {
9           a ^= (c>>1);
10          a |= h;  // so it also works for  n == BITS_PER_LONG
11      }
12      return  a;
13  }
```

If we do not insist on correct results for the case that the degree of C equals the number of bits in a word, we could simply use the following two-liner:

```
        if ( a & 1 )  a ^= c;
        a >> 1;
```

The operation needs only about two CPU cycles. The inverse of x can be computed with:

```
1   static inline ulong bitpolmod_inv_x(ulong c, ulong h)
2   // Return  (1 / x) mod C
```

```
3    // C must have nonzero constant term: (c&1)==1
4    {
5        ulong a = (c>>1);
6        a |= h;  // so it also works for  n == BITS_PER_LONG
7        return  a;
8    }
```

40.3.5   Inversion and division

The method to compute the extended GCD (EGCD) is the same as given in section 39.1.4 on page 767 [FXT: bpol/bitpol-gcd.h]:

```
1    inline ulong bitpol_egcd(ulong u, ulong v, ulong &iu, ulong &iv)
2    // Return u3 and set u1,v1 so that   gcd(u,v) == u3 == u*u1 + v*u2
3    {
4        ulong u1 = 1,   u2 = 0;
5        ulong v1 = 0,   v3 = v;
6        ulong u3 = u,   v2 = 1;
7        while ( v3!=0 )
8        {
9            ulong q = bitpol_div(u3, v3);   // == u3 / v3;
10
11           ulong t1 = u1 ^ bitpol_mult(v1, q);  // == u1 - v1 * q;
12           u1 = v1;  v1 = t1;
13
14           ulong t3 = u3 ^ bitpol_mult(v3, q);  // == u3 - v3 * q;
15           u3 = v3;  v3 = t3;
16
17           ulong t2 = u2 ^ bitpol_mult(v2, q);  // == u2 - v2 * q;
18           u2 = v2;  v2 = t2;
19       }
20
21       iu = u1;  iv = u2;
22       return u3;
23   }
```

The routine can be optimized using `bitpol_divrem()`: remove the lines

```
    ulong q = bitpol_div(u3, v3);  // == u3 / v3;
[--snip--]
    ulong t3 = u3 ^ bitpol_mult(v3, q);  // == u3 - v3 * q;
```

and insert at the beginning of the body of the loop:

```
    ulong q, t3;
    bitpol_divrem(u3, v3, q, t3);
```

The routine computes the GCD g and two additional quantities i_u and i_v so that

$$g = u \cdot i_u + v \cdot i_v \tag{40.3-1}$$

If $g = 1$, we have

$$1 \equiv u \cdot i_u \bmod v \tag{40.3-2}$$

That is, i_u is the inverse of u modulo v. The implementation is [FXT: bpol/bitpolmod-arith.h]

```
1    inline ulong bitpolmod_inverse(ulong a, ulong c)
2    // Returns the inverse of A modulo C if it exists, else zero.
3    // Must have deg(A) < deg(C)
4    {
5        ulong i, t;  // t unused
6        ulong g = bitpol_egcd(a, c, i, t);
7        if ( g!=1 )  i = 0;
8        return i;
9    }
```

Modular division is done by multiplication with the inverse:

```
1    inline ulong bitpolmod_divide(ulong a, ulong b, ulong c, ulong h)
2    // Return a/b modulo c.
3    // Must have: gcd(b,c)==1
4    {
5        ulong i = bitpolmod_inverse(b, c);
```

```
6        a = bitpolmod_mult(a, i, c, h);
7        return a;
8    }
```

The inverse of a number a modulo a prime m can be computed as $a^{-1} = a^{m-2}$ ($m - 1$ is the maximal order of an element in $\mathbb{Z}/m\mathbb{Z}$). With an irreducible (see section 40.4) polynomial C of degree n the inverse modulo C of a polynomial A can be computed as $A^{-1} = A^{2^n - 2}$ ($2^n - 1$ is the maximal order modulo C, see section 40.5 on page 841):

```
1    inline ulong bitpolmod_inverse_irred(ulong a, ulong c, ulong h)
2    // Return (A ** -1)  mod C
3    // Must have: C irreducible.
4    {
5        ulong r1 = (h<<1) - 2;  // max order minus one
6        ulong i = bitpolmod_power(a, r1, c, h);
7        return  i;
8    }
```

40.4   Irreducible polynomials

A polynomial is called *irreducible* if it has no nontrivial factors (trivial factors are the constant polynomial '1' and the polynomial itself). A polynomial that has a nontrivial factorization is called *reducible*. The irreducible polynomials are the 'primes' among the polynomials.

The factorization of a polynomial depends on its coefficient field: The polynomial $x^2 + 1$ over $\mathbb{R}$ (or $\mathbb{Z}$) is irreducible. Over $\mathbb{C}$ it factors as $(x^2 + 1) = (x + i)(x - i)$. As a binary polynomial, the factorization is $(x^2 + 1) = (x + 1)^2$.

All polynomials with zero constant coefficient (except x) are reducible because they have the factor x. A binary polynomial that is irreducible has at least one nonzero coefficient of odd degree (else it would be a square). All binary polynomials except for $x + 1$ that have an even number of nonzero coefficients are reducible because they have the factor $x + 1$.

40.4.1   Testing for irreducibility

Irreducibility tests for binary polynomials use the fact that the polynomial $x^{2^n} - x = x^{2^n} + x$ has all irreducible polynomials whose degrees divide n as factors. For example, with $n = 6$ we get

$$
\begin{aligned}
x^{2^6} + x \; &= \; x^{64} + x &\text{(40.4-1a)}\\
&= \; (x) \cdot (x + 1) \cdot &\text{(40.4-1b)}\\
&\quad \cdot \left(x^2 + x + 1\right) \cdot \\
&\quad \cdot \left(x^3 + x + 1\right) \cdot \left(x^3 + x^2 + 1\right) \cdot \\
&\quad \cdot \left(x^6 + x + 1\right) \cdot \left(x^6 + x^3 + 1\right) \cdot \left(x^6 + x^4 + x^2 + x + 1\right) \cdot \\
&\quad \cdot \left(x^6 + x^4 + x^3 + x + 1\right) \cdot \left(x^6 + x^5 + 1\right) \cdot \left(x^6 + x^5 + x^2 + x + 1\right) \cdot \\
&\quad \cdot \left(x^6 + x^5 + x^3 + x^2 + 1\right) \cdot \left(x^6 + x^5 + x^4 + x + 1\right) \cdot \left(x^6 + x^5 + x^4 + x^2 + 1\right)
\end{aligned}
$$

40.4.1.1   The Ben-Or test for irreducibility

A binary polynomial C of degree d is reducible if $\gcd(x^{2^k} - x \bmod C, C) \neq 1$ for any $k < d$. We compute $u_k = x^{2^k}$ (modulo C) for each $k < d$ by successive squarings and test whether $\gcd(u_k + x, C) = 1$ for all k. But as a factor of degree f implies another one of degree $d - f$ it suffices to do the first $\lfloor d/2 \rfloor$ of the tests. The algorithm is called the *Ben-Or irreducibility test*. A C++ implementation is given in [FXT: bpol/bitpol-irred-ben-or.cc]:

```
1    bool bitpol_irreducible_q(ulong c, ulong h)
2    // Return whether C is irreducible (via the Ben-Or irreducibility test_;
3    // h needs to be a mask with one bit set:
4    //   h == highest_one(C) >> 1   == 1UL << (degree(C)-1)
5    {
```

```
6      if ( c<4 )
7      {
8          if ( c>=2 )  return true;    // x, and 1+x are irreducible
9          else         return false;   // constant polynomials are reducible
10     }
11
12     if ( 0==(1&c) )  return false;   // x is a factor
13
14     // if ( 0==(c & 0xaaaaaaaaUL) )  return 0; // at least one odd degree term
15     // if ( 0==parity(c) )  return 0; // need odd number of nonzero coeff.
16     // if ( 0!=bitpol_test_squarefree(c) )  return 0; // must be square-free
17
18     ulong d = h >> 1;
19     ulong u = 2;  // =^= x
20     while ( 0 != d )  // floor( degree/2 ) times
21     {
22         // Square r-times for coefficients of c in GF(2^r).
23         // We have r==1:
24         u = bitpolmod_square(u, c, h);
25
26         ulong upx = u ^ 2;  // =^= u+x
27
28         ulong g = bitpol_binary_gcd(upx, c);
29
30         if ( 1!=g )  return false;   // reducible
31
32         d >>= 2;
33     }
34     return  true;   // irreducible
35  }
```

Commented out at the beginning are a few tests for some necessary conditions for irreducibility. For the
test `bitpol_test_squarefree()` (for a square factor) see section 40.12.2 on page 860. The routine will
fail if $\deg c = $ `BITS_PER_LONG`, because the gcd-computation fails in this case.

40.4.1.2 Rabin's test for irreducibility

A binary polynomial C of degree d is irreducible if and only if

$$x^{2^d} \equiv x \bmod C \tag{40.4-2a}$$

and, for all prime divisors p_i of d

$$\gcd\left(x^{2^{d/p_i}} - x \bmod C, C\right) = 1 \tag{40.4-2b}$$

The implied test is called *Rabin's algorithm* for irreducibility testing, see [276, p.7]. The number of GCD
computations equals the number of prime divisors of d.

If the prime divisors are processed in decreasing order, the successive exponents are increasing and the
power of x can be updated via squarings. The total number of squarings equals d which is minimal.

A C++ implementation of Rabin's test is given in [FXT: bpol/bitpol-irred-rabin.cc]. A table of auxiliary
bit-masks gives the number of squarings between the GCD computations:

```
1   static const ulong rabin_tab[] =
2   {
3    0UL,   // x = 0  (bits: ...........)  OPS:
4    0UL,   // x = 1  (bits: ...........)  OPS:  finally sqr 1 times
5    0UL,   // x = 2  (bits: ...........)  OPS:  finally sqr 2 times
6    0UL,   // x = 3  (bits: ...........)  OPS:  finally sqr 3 times
7    4UL,   // x = 4  (bits: ........1..)  OPS:  sqr 2 times,    finally sqr 2 times
8    0UL,   // x = 5  (bits: ...........)  OPS:  finally sqr 5 times
9    12UL,  // x = 6  (bits: ......11..)  OPS:  sqr 2 times,  sqr 1 times,   finally sqr 3 times
10   0UL,   // x = 7  (bits: ...........)  OPS:  finally sqr 7 times
11   16UL,  // x = 8  (bits: ......1....)  OPS:  sqr 4 times,    finally sqr 4 times
12   8UL,   // x = 9  (bits: .......1...)  OPS:  sqr 3 times,    finally sqr 6 times
13   36UL,  // x = 10  (bits: .....1..1..)  OPS:  sqr 2 times,  sqr 3 times,   finally sqr 5 times
14   [--snip--]
```

The GCD computation for the divisor 1 can be avoided by noting that only the polynomial $x^2 + x = (x+1)\,x$ would wrongly pass the test, so we exclude the factor x explicitly. The testing routine is

```
1   inline bool bitpol_irreducible_rabin_q(ulong c, ulong h)
2   // Return whether C is irreducible (via Rabin's irreducibility test).
3   // h needs to be a mask with one bit set:
4   //   h == highest_one(C) >> 1  == 1UL << (degree(C)-1)
5   {
6       if ( c<4 )  // C is one of 0, 1, x, 1+x
7       {
8           if ( c>=2 )  return true; // x, and 1+x are irreducible
9           else         return false; // constant polynomials are reducible
10      }
11
12      if ( 0==(1&c) )  return false; // x is a factor
13
14      ulong d = 1 + lowest_one_idx(h);  // degree
15      ulong rt = rabin_tab[d];
16      ulong m = 2; // =^= 'x'
17
18      while ( rt > 1 )
19      {
20          do
21          {
22              --d;
23              m = bitpolmod_square(m, c, h);
24              rt >>= 1;
25          }
26          while ( 0 == (rt & 1) );
27
28          ulong g = bitpol_binary_gcd( m ^ 2UL, c );
29          if ( g!=1 )  return false;
30      }
31
32      do  { m = bitpolmod_square(m, c, h); }  while ( --d );
33      if ( m ^ 2UL )  return false;
34
35      return true;
36  }
```

Rabin's test will be faster than the Ben-Or test if the polynomial is irreducible. If the polynomial is reducible and has small factors (as often the case with 'random' polynomials), then the Ben-Or test will be faster. A comparison of the tests is given in [150].

40.4.1.3   Testing for irreducibility without GCD computations

Call a binary polynomial C of degree d that has no linear factors and for which

$$x^{2^d} \equiv x \bmod C \tag{40.4-3}$$

and, for all $l < d$,

$$x^{2^l} \equiv x \bmod C \tag{40.4-4}$$

a *strong pseudo irreducible* (SPI). The test whether a polynomial is SPI does not involve any GCD computation. The test for a polynomial C of degree d can be given as

1. If C has a linear factor (x or $x + 1$), then return false.

2. For $k = 1, \ldots, d$ compute $s_k := x^{2^k} \bmod C$ by successive squarings.

3. If $s_k = x$ for any $k < d$, then return false.

4. If $s_d \neq x$, then return false.

5. Return true.

If d is a prime, the power of a prime, or the product of two primes, then strong pseudo irreducibility implies irreducibility (see [23]). We list the degrees $1 < d < 63$ where strong pseudo irreducibility does not imply irreducibility (and GCDs are needed for irreducibility testing):

12, 18, 20, 24, 28, 30, 36, 40, 42, 44, 45, 48, 50, 52, 54, 56, 60, 63

The sequence is entry A102467 in [312]. For the degrees $44 = 4 \cdot 11$ and $52 = 4 \cdot 13$ no GCDs are needed because (see [23]) if $d = r^e s$ where r and s are distinct primes and $s > (2^{r^e} - 2)/r$. We have $r^e = 4$ so we need $s > (2^4 - 2)/2 = 7$ which holds for primes $s \geq 11$.

In the implementation of the SPI test an extra branch is needed if the polynomial C does not fit into a word. In that case the parity must be even [FXT: bpol/bitpol-spi.cc]:

```
1   bool
2   bitpol_spi_q(ulong c, ulong h)
3   // Return whether C is a strong pseudo irreducible (SPI).
4   // A polynomial C of degree d is an SPI if
5   //    it has no linear factors, x^(2^k)!=x for 0<k<d, and x^(2^d)==x.
6   // h needs to be a mask with one bit set:
7   //    h == highest_one(C) >> 1   == 1UL << (degree(C)-1)
8   {
9       const bool md = (bool)((h<<1)==0);  // whether degree == BITS_PER_LONG
10
11      if ( md )
12      {
13          if ( (c&1)==0 ) return false;        // factor x
14          if ( 0 != parity(c) )  return false;  // factor x+1
15      }
16      else
17      {
18          if ( c<4 )  // C is one of 0, 1, x, 1+x
19          {
20              if ( c>=2 )  return true;   // x, and 1+x are irreducible
21              else         return false;  // constant polynomials are reducible
22          }
23
24          if ( (c&1)==0 )  return false;        // factor x
25          if ( 0 == parity(c) )  return false;  // factor x+1
26      }
27
28      ulong t = 1;
29      ulong m = 2;  // x
30      m = bitpolmod_square(m, c, h);
31      do
32      {
33          if ( m==2 )  return false;
34          m = bitpolmod_square(m, c, h);
35          t <<= 1;
36      }
37      while ( t!=h );
38
39      if ( m!=2 )  return false;
40
41      return true;
42  }
```

An auxiliary function returns whether GCDs are needed with the irreducibility test (64-bit version):

```
1   bool bitpol_need_gcd(ulong h)
2   // Return whether GCDs are needed for irreducibility test.
3   {
4       // degrees where GCDs are needed:
5       // 12, 18, 20, 24, 28, 30, 36, 40, 42,    45, 48, 50,    54, 56, 60, 63
6       const ulong gn =
7           (1UL<<12)|(1UL<<18)|(1UL<<20)|(1UL<<24)|(1UL<<28)|(1UL<<30)|
8           (1UL<<36)|(1UL<<40)|(1UL<<42)|(1UL<<45)|(1UL<<48)|(1UL<<50)|
9           (1UL<<54)|(1UL<<56)|(1UL<<60)|(1UL<<63);
10      return  0 != ( h & (gn>>1) );
11  }
```

Now the irreducibility test can be implemented as follows:

```
1   inline bool bitpol_irreducible_q(ulong c, ulong h)
2   {
3       if ( bitpol_need_gcd(h) )  return bitpol_irreducible_ben_or_q(c, h);
4       else                       return bitpol_spi_q(c, h);
5   }
```

As the SPI test also works for polynomials not fitting into a word we can test those for irreducibility.

40.5 Primitive polynomials

Let C be an irreducible polynomial. Then the sequence $p_k = x^k \bmod (C)$, $k = 1, 2, \ldots$ is periodic and the (smallest) period m of the sequence is the order of x modulo C. We call m the *period* (or *order*) of the polynomial C. For a binary polynomial of degree n the maximal period equals $2^n - 1$.

For the period m of C we have $x^m = 1 \bmod C$, so $x^m - 1 = 0 \bmod C$. That is, C divides $x^m - 1$ but no polynomial $x^k - 1$ with $k < m$.

A polynomial is called *primitive* if its period is maximal. Then the powers of x generate all nonzero binary polynomials of degree $\leq n - 1$. The polynomial x is a generator ('primitive root') modulo C. Primitivity implies irreducibility, the converse is not true.

The situation is somewhat parallel to the operations modulo an integer:

- Among those integers m that are prime some have the primitive root 2: the sequence 2^k for $k = 1, 2, \ldots, m - 1$ contains all nonzero numbers modulo m (see chapter 26 on page 535).

- Among those polynomials C that are irreducible some are primitive: the sequence x^k for $k = 1, 2, \ldots, 2^n - 1$ contains all nonzero polynomials modulo C.

Note that there is another notion of the term 'primitive', that of a polynomial for which the greatest common divisor of all coefficients is one.

40.5.1 Roots of primitive polynomials have maximal order

A different characterization of primitivity is as follows. Suppose you want to do computations with linear combinations $A = \sum_{k=0}^{n-1} a_k \, \alpha^k$ (where $a_k \in \mathrm{GF}(2)$) of the powers of an (unknown!) root α of an irreducible polynomial $C = x^n + \sum_{k=0}^{n-1} c_k \, x^k$.

When multiplying A with the root α we get a term α^n which we want to get rid of. But we have

$$\alpha^n = -\sum_{k=0}^{n-1} c_k \, \alpha^k \tag{40.5-1}$$

as α is a root of the polynomial C. Therefore we can use exactly the same modular reduction as with polynomial computation modulo C. The same is true for the multiplication of two linear combinations (of the powers of the same root α).

We see that the order of a polynomial p is the order of its root α modulo p and that a polynomial is primitive if and only if its root has maximal order. An irreducible polynomial C of degree n has n distinct roots, they are equal to $\alpha^{2^k} \bmod C$ for $0 \leq k < n$. The orders of all roots are identical.

40.5.2 Testing for primitivity

Checking a degree-d binary polynomial for primitivity by directly using the definition has complexity $O(2^d)$ which is prohibitive except for tiny d. A much better solution is a modification of the algorithm to determine the order in a finite field given in section 39.7.1.2 on page 779. The implementation given here uses the GP language:

```
1   polorder(p) =
2   /* Order of x modulo p (p irreducible over GF(2)) */
3   {
4       local(g, g1, te, tp, tf, tx);
5       g = 'x;
6       p *= Mod(1,2);
7       te = nn_;
8       for(i=1, np_,
9           tf = vf_[i];  tp = vp_[i];  tx = vx_[i];
10          te = te / tf;
11          g1 = Mod(g, p)^te;
12          while ( 1!=g1,
```

```
13                  g1 = g1^tp;
14                  te = te * tp;
15              );
16          );
17          return( te );
18  }
```

The function uses the following global variables that must be set up before call:

```
1   nn_ = 0;   /* max order  = 2^n-1 */
2   np_ = 0;   /* number of primes in factorization */
3   vp_ = [];  /* vector of primes */
4   vf_ = [];  /* vector of factors (prime powers) */
5   vx_ = [];  /* vector of exponents */
```

As given, the algorithm will do n_p exponentiations modulo p where n_p is the number of different primes in the factorization in m. A C++ implementation of the algorithm is given in [FXT: bpol/bitpol-order.cc].

A shortcut that makes the algorithm terminate as soon as the computed order drops below maximum is

```
1   polmaxorder_q(p) =
2   /* Whether order of x modulo p is maximal  (p irreducible over GF(2)) */
3   /* Early-out variant */
4   {
5       local(g1, te, tp, tf, tx, ct);
6       p *= Mod(1,2);
7       te = nn_;
8       for(i=1, np_,
9           tf = vf_[i];  tp = vp_[i];  tx = vx_[i];
10          te = te / tf;
11          g1 = Mod(g, p)^te;
12          ct = 0;
13          while ( 1!=g1,
14              g1 = g1^tp;
15              te = te * tp;
16              ct = ct + 1;
17          );
18          if ( ct<tx,  return(0) );
19      );
20      return(1);
21  }
```

With `polmaxorder_q()` and GP's built-in `polisirreducible()` the search for the lexicographically minimal primitive polynomials up to degree $n = 100$ is a matter of about ten seconds. Extending the list up to $n = 200$ takes three minutes. The computation of all polynomials up to degree $n = 400$ takes less than an hour.

Again, the algorithm depends on precomputed factorizations. The table [FXT: data/mersenne-factors.txt] taken from [89] was used to save computation time.

For prime $m = 2^n - 1$ (that is, m is a Mersenne prime) irreducibility suffices for primality: The one-liner

```
n=607;  for(k=1,n-1,if(polisirreducible(Mod(1,2)*(1+t^k+t^n)),print1(" ",k)))
```

finds all primitive trinomials $x^n + x^k + 1$ whose degree is the Mersenne exponent $n = 607$. The computation of the following list takes about two minutes.

```
 89:  38 51
127:  1 7 15 30 63 64 97 112 120 126
521:  32 48 158 168 353 363 473 489
607:  105 147 273 334 460 502
```

Note we did not exploit the symmetry (reversed polynomials are also primitive). Techniques to find primitive trinomials whose degrees are very big Mersenne exponents are described in [80] and [84].

Here is a surprising theorem: Let $p(x) = \sum_{k=0}^{d} c_k x^k$ be an irreducible binary polynomial and $L_p(x) := \sum_{k=0}^{d} c_k x^{2^k}$. Then all irreducible factors of $L_p(x)/x$ (a polynomial of degree $2^d - 1$) are of degree equal to $\text{ord}(p)$ (the order of x modulo $p(x)$). Especially, if $p(x)$ is primitive, then $L_p(x)/x$ is irreducible. The theorem is proved in [368] and also in [233, p.110]. An example: $x^7 + x + 1$ is primitive, so $x^{127} + x + 1$

is irreducible. But, as $2^{127} - 1$ is prime, $x^{127} + x + 1$ is also primitive. Therefore $x^{2^{127}-1} + x + 1$ is irreducible.

40.6 The number of irreducible and primitive polynomials

$n:$	I_n	$n:$	I_n	$n:$	I_n	$n:$	I_n
1:	2	11:	186	21:	99858	31:	69273666
2:	1	12:	335	22:	190557	32:	134215680
3:	2	13:	630	23:	364722	33:	260300986
4:	3	14:	1161	24:	698870	34:	505286415
5:	6	15:	2182	25:	1342176	35:	981706806
6:	9	16:	4080	26:	2580795	36:	1908866960
7:	18	17:	7710	27:	4971008	37:	3714566310
8:	30	18:	14532	28:	9586395	38:	7233615333
9:	56	19:	27594	29:	18512790	39:	14096302710
10:	99	20:	52377	30:	35790267	40:	27487764474

Figure 40.6-A: The number of irreducible binary polynomials for degrees $n \leq 40$.

$n:$	P_n	$n:$	P_n	$n:$	P_n	$n:$	P_n
1:	1	11:	176	21:	84672	31:	69273666
2:	1	12:	144	22:	120032	32:	67108864
3:	2	13:	630	23:	356960	33:	211016256
4:	2	14:	756	24:	276480	34:	336849900
5:	6	15:	1800	25:	1296000	35:	929275200
6:	6	16:	2048	26:	1719900	36:	725594112
7:	18	17:	7710	27:	4202496	37:	3697909056
8:	16	18:	7776	28:	4741632	38:	4822382628
9:	48	19:	27594	29:	18407808	39:	11928047040
10:	60	20:	24000	30:	17820000	40:	11842560000

Figure 40.6-B: The number of primitive binary polynomials for degrees $n \leq 40$.

The number of irreducible binary polynomials of degree n is

$$I_n = \frac{1}{n} \sum_{d \backslash n} \mu(d) \, 2^{n/d} = \frac{1}{n} \sum_{d \backslash n} \mu(n/d) \, 2^d \qquad (40.6\text{-}1)$$

The Möbius function μ is defined by relation 37.1-6 on page 705. The expression is identical to the formula for the number of Lyndon words (relation 18.3-2 on page 380). If n is prime, then $I_n = \frac{2^n - 2}{n}$. Figure 40.6-A gives I_n for $n \leq 40$, the sequence is entry A001037 in [312]. The list of all irreducible polynomials up to degree 11 is given in [FXT: data/all-irredpoly.txt].

For large degrees n the probability that a randomly chosen polynomial is irreducible is about $1/n$. With polynomials in two or more variables the situation is very different: the probability that a random polynomial is irreducible tends to 1 for large n, see [58].

The number of primitive binary polynomials of degree n equals

$$P_n = \frac{\varphi(2^n - 1)}{n} \qquad (40.6\text{-}2)$$

If n is the exponent of a Mersenne prime we have $P_n = \frac{2^n - 2}{n} = I_n$. The values of P_n for $n \leq 40$ are shown in figure 40.6-B. The sequence is entry A011260 in [312]. The list of all primitive polynomials up to degree 11 is given in [FXT: data/all-primpoly.txt].

$n:$	D_n	$n:$	D_n	$n:$	D_n	$n:$	D_n
1:	1	11:	10	21:	15186	31:	0
2:	0	12:	191	22:	70525	32:	67106816
3:	0	13:	0	23:	7762	33:	49284730
4:	1	14:	405	24:	422390	34:	168436515
5:	0	15:	382	25:	46176	35:	52431606
6:	3	16:	2032	26:	860895	36:	1183272848
7:	0	17:	0	27:	768512	37:	16657254
8:	14	18:	6756	28:	4844763	38:	2411232705
9:	8	19:	0	29:	104982	39:	2168255670
10:	39	20:	28377	30:	17970267	40:	15645204474

Figure 40.6-C: The number of irreducible non-primitive binary polynomials for degrees $n \leq 40$.

$n:$	P_n/I_n	$n:$	P_n/I_n	$n:$	P_n/I_n	$n:$	P_n/I_n
1:	0.50000000	26:	0.66642256	51:	0.84834222	76:	0.52983738
2:	1.0	27:	0.84540117	52:	0.51936149	77:	0.93832726
3:	1.0	28:	0.49462097	53:	0.99982834	78:	0.56391518
4:	0.66666667	29:	0.99432922	54:	0.53392943	79:	0.99962783
5:	1.0	30:	0.49790073	55:	0.91393553	80:	0.42915344
6:	0.66666667	31:	1.0	56:	0.46549716	81:	0.84506003
7:	1.0	32:	0.50000763	57:	0.85711404	82:	0.65858526
8:	0.53333333	33:	0.81066253	58:	0.65165057	83:	0.99401198
9:	0.85714286	34:	0.66665141	59:	0.99999444	84:	0.38979140
10:	0.60606061	35:	0.94659138	60:	0.35255399	85:	0.96773455
11:	0.94623656	36:	0.38011770	61:	1.0	86:	0.66505112
12:	0.42985075	37:	0.99551569	62:	0.66666667	87:	0.85207814
13:	1.0	38:	0.66666285	63:	0.83624531	88:	0.47128978
14:	0.65116279	39:	0.84618267	64:	0.49921989	89:	1.0
15:	0.82493126	40:	0.43083023	65:	0.96762379	90:	0.46446197
16:	0.50196078	41:	0.99992518	66:	0.53157031	91:	0.99091593
17:	1.0	42:	0.55199996	67:	0.99999999	92:	0.51925414
18:	0.53509496	43:	0.99757669	68:	0.52884860	93:	0.85714286
19:	1.0	44:	0.50216809	69:	0.83890107	94:	0.66388120
20:	0.45821639	45:	0.81138931	70:	0.55834947	95:	0.96267339
21:	0.84792405	46:	0.65247846	71:	0.99999560	96:	0.38730483
22:	0.62990076	47:	0.99935309	72:	0.35544000	97:	0.99991264
23:	0.97871804	48:	0.38932803	73:	0.99772166	98:	0.64603552
24:	0.39561006	49:	0.99212598	74:	0.66330362	99:	0.79553432
25:	0.96559617	50:	0.58273388	75:	0.82216371	100:	0.45025627

Figure 40.6-D: Ratios P_n/I_n for degrees $n \leq 100$: a random irreducible binary polynomial of prime degree n is likely primitive even if n is not a Mersenne exponent.

The difference $D_n := I_n - P_n$ is the number of irreducible non-primitive polynomials (see figure 40.6-C). If n is the exponent of a Mersenne prime, we have $D_n = 0$. The complete list of these polynomials up to degree 12 inclusive is given in [FXT: data/all-nonprim-irredpoly.txt].

Figure 40.6-D gives the probability that a randomly chosen irreducible polynomial of degree n is primitive. A polynomial of prime degree is very likely primitive, so any conjecture suggesting that polynomials of a certain type are always primitive for prime degree is dubious: if we take one random irreducible polynomial for each prime degree n, then chances are that all of them are primitive.

40.7 Transformations that preserve irreducibility

40.7.1 The reciprocal polynomial

The *reciprocal* of a polynomial $F(x)$ is the polynomial

$$F^*(x) = x^{\deg F} F(1/x) \tag{40.7-1}$$

The roots of $F^*(x)$ are the inverses of the roots of $F(x)$. The reciprocal of a binary polynomial is the reversed binary word:

```
1    inline ulong bitpol_recip(ulong c)
2    // Return x^deg(C) * C(1/x)  (the reciprocal polynomial)
3    {
4        ulong t = 0;
5        while ( c )
6        {
7            t <<= 1;
8            t |= (c & 1);
9            c >>= 1;
10       }
11       return  t;
12   }
```

Alternatively, we can use the bit-reversal routines given in section 1.14 on page 33. The reciprocal of an irreducible polynomial is again irreducible. The order of the polynomial is preserved under the transformation.

40.7.2 The polynomial $p(x + 1)$

If a polynomial $p(x)$ is irreducible, then $p(x + 1)$, the composition with $x + 1$, is also irreducible. The composition with $x+1$ does not in general preserve order: the simplest example is the primitive polynomial $p(x) = x^4 + x^3 + 1$ where $p(x+1) = x^4 + x^3 + x^2 + x + 1$ has the order 5. The order of x modulo $p(x)$ equals the order of $x + 1$ modulo $p(x + 1)$. The composition with $x + 1$ can be computed by [FXT: bpol/bitpol-irred.h]:

```
1    inline ulong bitpol_compose_xp1(ulong c)
2    // Return C(x+1).
3    // Self-inverse.
4    {
5        ulong z = 1;
6        ulong r = 0;
7        while ( c )
8        {
9            if ( c & 1 )  r ^= z;
10           c >>= 1;
11           z ^= (z<<1);
12       }
13       return  r;
14   }
```

A faster routine that finishes in time $\log_2(b)$ (where b = bits per word) is the `blue_code()` from section 1.19 on page 49.

In general the sequence of successive 'compose' and 'reverse' operations leads to six different polynomials:

```
C= [11, 10, 4, 3, 0]

     [11, 10, 4, 3, 0]               -- recip (C=bitpol_recip(C)) -->
```

```
[11,  8, 7, 1, 0]               -- compose (C=bitpol_compose_xp1(C)) -->
[11, 10, 9, 7, 6, 5, 4, 1, 0]   -- recip -->
[11, 10, 7, 6, 5, 4, 2, 1, 0]   -- compose -->
[11,  9, 7, 2, 0]               -- recip -->
[11,  9, 4, 2, 0]               -- compose -->
[11, 10, 4, 3, 0]               == initial value
```

40.8   Self-reciprocal polynomials

```
              irred. poly      irred. SRP
        1:    11...1..11       111..1..111..1...111
        2:    1..111.111       1.11111.111.11111.1
        3:    1.11.11.11       1..111.11111.111..1
        4:    11111....11       11.1..1..1.1..1..1.11
        5:    1.....1.111       1..1..1.11111.1..1.1
        6:    11.11.1.11       11111..1.1.1..11111
        7:    111...1111       11..1..11111..1..11
        8:    1.....11.11       1.1..11..1.11..1.1
        9:    11.111..11       111111111111111111111
       10:    1..11.111       1.111..1...1..111.1
       11:    11..1.11111      1.11.11..1..11.11.1
       12:    1111...1.11      11.11..11111..11.11
       13:    1.11....111      1.1...111...11..1
       14:    11..11...11      1111.111..1.111.1111
       15:    1111111.11       11.1.111111111.1.11
       16:    1111...111       11.11.1..1..1.11.11
       17:    1.1.11.111       1....1.1.1.1..1..1
       18:    11.1...1111      1111..1..1...1..1111
       19:    11.1111111       111111...11...111111
       20:    1.1.1.1111       1.....1111111.....1
       21:    1.1.1...11       1..1..1....1...1..1
       22:    1..1..1.11       1.11..11.1.11..11.1
       23:    1.1.....111      1...1.11.1.11.1...1
       24:    1.....1..11      1.1....111....1.1
       25:    11...11111       111..111.1.111..111
       26:    11..111.11       111.11.1...11.111
       27:    1...11..11       1.1.111.111.111.1.1
       28:    11..1...11       111.1.1.111.1.1.111
```

Figure 40.8-A: All irreducible self-reciprocal binary polynomials of degree 18 (right) and the corresponding irreducible polynomials of degree 9 with constant linear coefficient (left).

A polynomial is called *self-reciprocal* if it is its own reciprocal. The irreducible self-reciprocal polynomials (SRPs), except for $1 + x$, are of even degree $2\,d$. They can be computed from the irreducible polynomials of degree d with nonzero linear coefficient. Let $F(x) = \sum_{j=0}^{d} f_j\, x^j$ and $S_F(x)$ the corresponding SRP, then

$$S_F(x) = x^d\, F(x + 1/x) = \sum_{j=0}^{d} F_j\, x^{d-j}\, (1 + x^2)^j \tag{40.8-1}$$

The irreducible SRPs of degree 18 and their corresponding polynomials are shown in figure 40.8-A [FXT: gf2n/bitpol-srp-demo.cc]. The conversion can be implemented as [FXT: bpol/bitpol-srp.h]:

```
1    inline ulong bitpol_pol2srp(ulong f, ulong d)
2    // Return  the self-reciprocal polynomial S=x^d*F(x+1/x) where d=deg(f).
3    // W = sum(j=0, d,   F(j)*x^(d-j)*(1+x^2)^j ) where
4    //    F(j) is the j-th coefficient of F.
5    // Must have: d==degree(F)
6    {
7        ulong w = 1;   // == (x^2+1)^j
8        ulong s = 0;
9        do  // for j = 0 ... d:
10       {
11           if ( f & 1 )  s ^= (w << d);  // S += F(j)*x^(d-j)*(1+x^2)^j
12           w ^= (w<<2);                  // w *= (1+x^2)
13           f >>= 1;                      // next coefficient to low end
14       }
15       while ( d-- );
16       return s;
17   }
```

The inverse function is given in [244]:

1. Set $F := 0$ and $j := 0$.

2. If $S \bmod (x^2 + 1) \equiv 0$, then set $f_j := 0$, else set $f_j := 1$.

3. Set $S := (S - f_j \, x^{d-j})/(x^2 + 1)$ [the division is exact].

4. Set $j := j + 1$. If $j \leq d$ goto step 2.

5. Return F $(= \sum_{j=0}^{d} f_j \, x^j)$.

The computation of $S \bmod (x^2 + 1)$ can be omitted because the quantity is 0 if and only if the central coefficient of S equals 0. The assignment $S := (S - f_j \, x^{d-j})/(x^2 + 1)$ can be replaced by $S := S/(x^2 + 1)$ (as power series) because no coefficient beyond the position $d - j$ is needed by the following steps. We use the power series division shown in section 40.1.6 on page 826 for this computation:

```
1    inline ulong bitpol_srp2pol(ulong s, ulong hd)
2    // Inverse of bitpol_pol2srp().
3    // Must have: hd = degree(s)/2 (note: _half_ of the degree).
4    // Only the lower half coefficients are accessed, i.e.
5    //    the routine works for degree(S) <= 2*BITS_PER_LONG-2.
6    {
7        ulong f = 0;
8        ulong mh = 1UL << hd;
9        ulong ml = 1;
10       do
11       {
12           ulong b = s & mh;  // central coefficient
13   //        s ^= b;  // set central coefficient to zero (not needed)
14           if ( b )  f |= ml;  // positions 0,1,...,hd
15           ml <<= 1;
16           s = bitpol_div_x2p1(s);  // exact division by (x^2+1)
17       }
18       while ( (mh>>=1) );
19       return f;
20   }
```

The self-reciprocal polynomials of degree $2n$ are factors of the polynomial $x^{2^n+1} - 1$ (see [251]). For example, for $n = 5$ we find

```
? lift(factormod(x^(2^5+1)-1,2))
 [x + 1  1]
 [x^2 + x + 1  1]
 [x^10 + x^7 + x^5 + x^3 + 1  1]
 [x^10 + x^9 + x^5 + x + 1  1]
 [x^10 + x^9 + x^8 + x^7 + x^6 + x^5 + x^4 + x^3 + x^2 + x + 1  1]
```

The order of a self-reciprocal polynomial of degree $2n$ is a divisor of $2^n + 1$. The list of all irreducible SRP up to degree 22 is given in [FXT: data/all-irred-srp.txt].

$n:$	S_n	$n:$	S_n	$n:$	S_n	$n:$	S_n
1:	1	11:	93	21:	49929	31:	34636833
2:	1	12:	170	22:	95325	32:	67108864
3:	1	13:	315	23:	182361	33:	130150493
4:	2	14:	585	24:	349520	34:	252645135
5:	3	15:	1091	25:	671088	35:	490853403
6:	5	16:	2048	26:	1290555	36:	954437120
7:	9	17:	3855	27:	2485504	37:	1857283155
8:	16	18:	7280	28:	4793490	38:	3616814565
9:	28	19:	13797	29:	9256395	39:	7048151355
10:	51	20:	26214	30:	17895679	40:	13743895344

Figure 40.8-B: Number of irreducible self-reciprocal polynomials of degree $2n$.

$n:$	T_n	$n:$	T_n	$n:$	T_n	$n:$	T_n
1:	1	11:	62	21:	32508	31:	23091222
2:	1	12:	160	22:	76032	32:	67004160
3:	1	13:	210	23:	121574	33:	85342752
4:	2	14:	448	24:	344064	34:	200422656
5:	2	15:	660	25:	405000	35:	289531200
6:	4	16:	2048	26:	1005888	36:	892477440
7:	6	17:	2570	27:	1569780	37:	1237491936
8:	16	18:	5184	28:	4511520	38:	2874507264
9:	18	19:	9198	29:	6066336	39:	4697046900
10:	40	20:	24672	30:	12672000	40:	13690417152

Figure 40.8-C: Number of primitive self-reciprocal polynomials of degree $2n$.

The number S_n of irreducible SRPs of degree $2n$ is

$$S_n \;=\; \frac{1}{2n} \sum_{d\backslash n,\ d\ \text{odd}} \mu(d)\, 2^{n/d} \tag{40.8-2}$$

Values of S_n for $n \leq 40$ are shown in figure 40.8-B. The sequence of values S_n is entry A000048 in [312]. The number of irreducible polynomials of degree n with linear coefficient one is also S_n.

The number $\tilde{S}_n$ of irreducible SRPs of degree n is

$$\tilde{S}_n \;=\; \frac{-1}{n} \sum_{d\backslash n,\ d\ \text{even}} \mu(d)\, 2^{n/d} \tag{40.8-3}$$

We have $\tilde{S}_n = 0$ for n odd and $\tilde{S}_n = S_{n/2}$ for n even. The number T_n of primitive SRPs of degree $2n$ is

$$T_n \;=\; \frac{\varphi\left(2^n + 1\right)}{2\,n} \tag{40.8-4}$$

The sequence of values T_n is entry A069925 in [312], values for $n \leq 40$ are shown in figure 40.8-C.

40.9 Irreducible and primitive polynomials of special forms ‡

We give lists of irreducible and primitive polynomials of special forms. The abbreviation 'PP' is used for 'primitive polynomial' in what follows. The *weight* of a binary polynomial is the sum of its coefficients. Polynomials of low weight allow for cheap modular reduction.

40.9.1 All irreducible and primitive polynomials for low degrees

For degrees $n \leq 8$ the complete list of irreducible polynomials is shown in figure 40.9-A. The list up to degree $n = 11$ is given in [FXT: data/all-irredpoly.txt]. The list of PPs for $n \leq 11$ is given in [FXT: data/all-primpoly.txt]. The list of all irreducible polynomials that are *not* primitive for $n \leq 12$ is given in [FXT: data/all-nonprim-irredpoly.txt].

40.9.2 All irreducible and primitive trinomials for low degrees

A *trinomial* is a polynomial with exactly three nonzero coefficients. The irreducible binary trinomials for degrees $n \leq 49$ are shown in figure 40.9-B (there are no irreducible trinomials for degrees 50 and 51). A list of all irreducible trinomials up to degree $n = 400$ is given in [FXT: data/all-trinomial-irredpoly.txt]. A more compact form of the list can is given in [FXT: data/all-trinomial-irredpoly-short.txt]:

```
2:   1
3:   1   2
4:   1
5:   2   3
```

```
2,1,0                7,1,0                8,4,3,2,0
                     7,3,0                8,5,3,1,0
3,1,0                7,3,2,1,0            8,5,3,2,0
3,2,0                7,4,0                8,6,3,2,0
                     7,4,3,2,0            8,6,4,3,2,1,0
4,1,0                7,5,2,1,0            8,6,5,1,0
4,3,0                7,5,3,1,0            8,6,5,2,0
# non-primitive:     7,5,4,3,0            8,6,5,3,0
4,3,2,1,0            7,5,4,3,2,1,0        8,6,5,4,0
                     7,6,0                8,7,2,1,0
5,2,0                7,6,3,1,0            8,7,3,2,0
5,3,0                7,6,4,1,0            8,7,5,3,0
5,3,2,1,0            7,6,4,2,0            8,7,6,1,0
5,4,2,1,0            7,6,5,2,0            8,7,6,3,2,1,0
5,4,3,1,0            7,6,5,3,2,1,0        8,7,6,5,2,1,0
5,4,3,2,0            7,6,5,4,0            8,7,6,5,4,2,0
                     7,6,5,4,2,1,0        # non-primitive:
6,1,0                7,6,5,4,3,2,0        8,4,3,1,0
6,4,3,1,0                                 8,5,4,3,0
6,5,0                                     8,5,4,3,2,1,0
6,5,2,1,0                                 8,6,5,4,2,1,0
6,5,3,2,0                                 8,6,5,4,3,1,0
6,5,4,1,0                                 8,7,3,1,0
# non-primitive:                          8,7,4,3,2,1,0
6,3,0                                     8,7,5,1,0
6,4,2,1,0                                 8,7,5,4,0
6,5,4,2,0                                 8,7,5,4,3,2,0
                                          8,7,6,4,2,1,0
                                          8,7,6,4,3,2,0
                                          8,7,6,5,4,1,0
                                          8,7,6,5,4,3,0
```

Figure 40.9-A: All binary irreducible polynomials up to degree 8.

```
2,1     10,3     17,3     22,1     -30,1    35,2     -42,7
3,1     10,7     17,5     22,21    -30,9    35,33    -42,35
3,2     11,2     17,6     23,5     -30,21   -36,9    -44,5
4,1     11,9     17,11    23,9     -30,29   36,11    -44,39
4,3    -12,3     17,12    23,14    31,3     -36,15   -46,1
5,2    -12,5     17,14    23,18    31,6     -36,21   -46,45
5,3    -12,7    -18,3     25,3     31,7     36,25    47,5
6,1    -12,9     18,7     25,7     31,13    -36,27   47,14
-6,3   -14,5    -18,9     25,18    31,18    39,4     47,20
6,5    -14,9     18,11    25,22    31,24    39,8     47,21
7,1     15,1    -18,15   -28,1     31,25    39,14    47,26
7,3     15,4     20,3     28,3     31,28    39,25    47,27
7,4     15,7    -20,5     28,9     -33,10   39,31    47,33
7,6     15,8    -20,15    28,13    33,13    39,35    47,42
-9,1    15,11    20,17    28,15    33,20    41,3     49,9
9,4     15,14    21,2     28,19    -33,23   41,20    49,12
9,5             -21,7     28,25    -34,7    41,21    49,15
-9,8            -21,14   -28,27    -34,27   41,38    49,22
                 21,19    29,2                       49,27
                          29,27                      49,34
                                                     49,37
                                                     49,40
```

Figure 40.9-B: All irreducible trinomials $x^n + x^k + 1$ for degrees $n \leq 49$. The format of the entries is n,k for primitive trinomials and -n,k for non-primitive trinomials.

```
 6:  1 3
 7:  1 3 4 6
 9:  4 5
10:  3 7
11:  2 9
15:  1 4 7 8 11 14
```

A line starts with the entry for the degree followed by all possible positions of the middle coefficient. The corresponding files giving primitive trinomials only are [FXT: data/all-trinomial-primpoly.txt] and [FXT: data/all-trinomial-primpoly-short.txt]. A list of irreducible trinomials that are *not* primitive is [FXT: data/all-trinomial-nonprimpoly.txt].

Values of n such that an irreducible trinomial of degree n exists are given in sequence A073571 in [312]. Values such that at least one primitive trinomial exists are given in entry A073726. The values n, k for primitive polynomials of the form $(x+1)^n + (x+1)^k + 1$ are listed in [FXT: data/all-t1-primpoly.txt].

Polynomials of that form are irreducible whenever $x^n + x^k + 1$ is irreducible. The list is not the same as for primitive trinomials as the transformation $p(x) \mapsto p(x+1)$ does in general not preserve the order. The sequence of degrees n such that there is a primitive polynomial $(x+1)^n + (x+1)^k + 1$ where $0 < k < n$ is entry A136416 in [312].

Regarding trinomials, there is a theorem by Swan (given in [327]): The trinomial $x^n + x^k + 1$ over GF(2) has an even number of irreducible factors (and therefore is reducible) if

1. n is even, k is odd, $n \neq 2k$, and either $nk/2 \equiv 0 \bmod 4$ or $nk/2 \equiv 1 \bmod 4$,

2. n is odd, k is even and does not divide $2n$, and $n \equiv \pm 3 \bmod 8$,

3. n is even, k is odd and does divide $2n$, and $n \equiv \pm 1 \bmod 8$,

4. any of the above holds for k replaced by $n - k$ (that is, for the reciprocal trinomial).

The first condition implies that no irreducible trinomial for n a multiple of 8 exists (as n is even, k must be odd, else the trinomial is a perfect square; and $nk/2 \equiv 0 \bmod 4$). Further, if n is a prime with $n \equiv \pm 3 \bmod 8$, then the trinomial can be irreducible only if $k = 2$ (or $n - k = 2$). In the note [106] it is shown that no irreducible trinomial exists for n a prime such that $n \equiv 13 \bmod 24$ or $n \equiv 19 \bmod 24$.

For some applications one may want to use reducible trinomials whose period is close to that of a primitive one. For example, the trinomial

$$
x^{32} + x^{15} + 1 = \tag{40.9-1}
$$
$$
(x^{11} + x^9 + x^7 + x^2 + 1) \cdot (x^{21} + x^{19} + x^{15} + x^{13} + x^{12} + x^{10} + x^9 + x^8 + x^7 + x^6 + x^4 + x^2 + 1)
$$

has the period $p = 4{,}292{,}868{,}097$ which is very close to $2^{32} - 1 = 4{,}294{,}967{,}295$. Note that the degree is a multiple of 8, so no irreducible trinomial of that degree exists. See [82], [126], and [107].

40.9.3 Irreducible trinomials of the form $1 + \mathbf{x}^k + \mathbf{x}^d$

With each sequence, we give its number as entry in [312].

k=1: The trinomial $p = 1 + x + x^d$ is irreducible for the following $2 \leq d \leq 34353$ (sequence A002475):

2, 3, 4, 6, 7, 9, 15, 22, 28, 30, 46, 60, 63,
127, 153, 172, 303, 471, 532, 865, 900,
1366, 2380, 3310, 4495, 6321, 7447,
10198, 11425, 21846, 24369, 27286, 28713, 32767, 34353

The trinomials are primitive for the following $d \leq 4400$ (sequence A073639):

2, 3, 4, 6, 7, 15, 22, 60, 63, 127, 153, 471, 532, 865, 900, 1366

k=2: $p = 1 + x^2 + x^d$ is irreducible for the following $3 \leq d \leq 57341$ (sequence A057460):

3, 5, 11, 21, 29, 35, 93, 123, 333, 845, 4125,
10437, 10469, 14211, 20307, 34115, 47283, 50621, 57341

The trinomials are primitive for all $n \leq 845$ (sequence A074710).

k=3: $p = 1 + x^3 + x^d$ is irreducible for the following $4 \leq d \leq 1000$ (sequence A057461):

4, 5, 6, 7, 10, 12, 17, 18, 20, 25, 28, 31, 41, 52, 66,
130, 151, 180, 196, 503, 650, 761, 986

The trinomials are primitive for the following $n \leq 400$:

4, 5, 7, 10, 17, 20, 25, 28, 31, 41, 52, 130, 151,

k=4: $p = 1 + x^4 + x^d$ is irreducible for the following $5 \leq d \leq 1000$ (sequence A057463):

7, 9, 15, 39, 57, 81, 105

The trinomials are primitive for the following $n \leq 400$: 7, 9, 15, 39, 81.

k=5: $p = 1 + x^5 + x^d$ is irreducible for the following $6 \leq d \leq 1000$ (sequence A057474):

6, 9, 12, 14, 17, 20, 23, 44, 47, 63, 84,
129, 236, 278, 279, 297, 300, 647, 726, 737,

The trinomials are primitive for the following $n \leq 400$:

6, 9, 17, 23, 47, 63, 129, 236, 278, 279, 297

40.9.4 Irreducible trinomials of the form $1 + x^d + x^{kd}$

The trinomial $p = 1 + x^d + x^{2d}$ is irreducible whenever d is a power of 3:

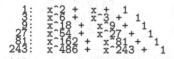

```
  1:   x^2  +  x  +  1
  3:   x^6  +  x^3  +  1
  9:   x^18 +  x^9  +  1
 27:   x^54 +  x^27 +  1
 81:   x^162 +  x^81 +  1
243:   x^486 +  x^243 +  1
...
```

The trinomial $p = 1 + x^d + x^{3d}$ is irreducible whenever d is a power of 7, and $p = 1 + x^d + x^{4d}$ is irreducible whenever $d = 3^i \, 5^j$, $i, j \in \mathbb{N}$. Similar regularities can be observed for other forms, see [55].

40.9.5 Primitive pentanomials

	15,4,2,1,0	30,6,4,1,0	45,4,3,1,0	60,5,4,2,0	75,6,3,1,0
	16,5,3,2,0	31,3,2,1,0	46,8,7,6,0	61,5,2,1,0	76,5,4,2,0
	17,3,2,1,0	32,7,6,2,0	47,5,4,1,0	62,6,5,3,0	77,6,5,2,0
	18,5,2,1,0	33,6,4,1,0	48,9,7,4,0	63,5,4,1,0	78,7,2,1,0
	19,5,2,1,0	34,8,4,3,0	49,6,5,4,0	64,4,3,1,0	79,4,3,2,0
5,3,2,1,0	20,6,4,1,0	35,8,7,1,0	50,4,3,2,0	65,4,3,1,0	80,9,4,2,0
6,4,3,1,0	21,5,2,1,0	36,8,7,1,0	51,6,3,1,0	66,9,8,6,0	81,6,3,2,0
7,3,2,1,0	22,5,4,3,0	37,6,4,1,0	52,6,2,1,0	67,5,2,1,0	82,9,6,4,0
8,4,3,2,0	23,5,3,1,0	38,6,5,1,0	53,6,2,1,0	68,7,5,1,0	83,7,4,2,0
9,4,3,1,0	24,4,3,1,0	39,7,4,1,0	54,8,6,3,0	69,6,5,2,0	84,9,7,1,0
10,4,3,1,0	25,3,2,1,0	40,5,4,3,0	55,6,2,1,0	70,5,3,1,0	85,8,2,1,0
11,4,2,1,0	26,6,2,1,0	41,3,2,1,0	56,7,4,2,0	71,5,3,1,0	86,6,5,2,0
12,6,4,1,0	27,5,2,1,0	42,7,4,3,0	57,5,3,2,0	72,10,9,3,0	87,7,5,1,0
13,4,3,1,0	28,6,4,1,0	43,6,4,3,0	58,6,5,1,0	73,4,3,2,0	88,11,9,8,0
14,5,3,1,0	29,4,2,1,0	44,6,5,2,0	59,7,4,2,0	74,7,4,3,0	89,6,5,3,0

Figure 40.9-C: The first (in lexicographic order) primitive pentanomials for $n \leq 89$.

A *pentanomial* is a polynomial that has exactly five nonzero coefficients. PPs that are pentanomials are given in [FXT: data/pentanomial-primpoly.txt]. For all degrees $n \geq 5$ an irreducible (and primitive) pentanomial seems to exist, but this has not been proved so far. Pentanomials of the form $x^n + x^3 + x^2 + x + 1$ are primitive for $n \in \{5, 7, 17, 25, 31, 41, 151\}$ (and $n \leq 400$), and irreducible for

5, 7, 10, 17, 20, 25, 28, 31, 41, 52, 130, 151, 196, 503, 650, 761, 986, 1391, 2047,
6172, 6431, 6730, 8425, 10162, 11410, 12071, 13151, 14636, 17377, 18023, 32770, ...

This is sequence A057496 in [312].

40.9.6 Primitive minimum-weight and low-bit polynomials

[1,0]	17,3,0	33,13,0	49,9,0
2,1,0	18,7,0	34,8,4,3,0	50,4,3,2,0
3,1,0	19,5,2,1,0	35,2,0	51,6,3,1,0
4,1,0	20,3,0	36,11,0	52,3,0
5,2,0	21,2,0	37,6,4,1,0	53,6,2,1,0
6,1,0	22,1,0	38,6,5,1,0	54,8,6,3,0
7,1,0	23,5,0	39,4,0	55,24,0
8,4,3,2,0	24,4,3,1,0	40,5,4,3,0	56,7,4,2,0
9,4,0	25,3,0	41,3,0	57,7,0
10,3,0	26,6,2,1,0	42,7,4,3,0	58,19,0
11,2,0	27,5,2,1,0	43,6,4,3,0	59,7,4,2,0
12,6,4,1,0	28,3,0	44,6,5,2,0	60,1,0
13,4,3,1,0	29,2,0	45,4,3,1,0	61,5,2,1,0
14,5,3,1,0	30,6,4,1,0	46,8,7,6,0	62,6,5,3,0
15,1,0	31,3,0	47,5,0	63,1,0
16,5,3,2,0	32,7,6,2,0	48,9,7,4,0	64,4,3,1,0

Figure 40.9-D: Binary primitive polynomials of minimum weight.

```
    [1,0]                17,3,0              33,6,4,1,0          49,6,5,4,0
   2,1,0                 18,5,2,1,0          34,7,6,5,2,1,0      50,4,3,2,0
   3,1,0                 19,5,2,1,0          35,2,0              51,6,3,1,0
   4,1,0                 20,3,0              36,6,5,4,2,1,0      52,3,0
   5,2,0                 21,2,0              37,5,4,3,2,1,0      53,6,2,1,0
   6,1,0                 22,1,0              38,6,5,1,0          54,6,5,4,3,2,0
   7,1,0                 23,5,0              39,4,0              55,6,2,1,0
   8,4,3,2,0             24,4,3,1,0          40,5,4,3,0          56,7,4,2,0
   9,4,0                 25,3,0              41,3,0              57,5,3,2,0
  10,3,0                 26,6,2,1,0          42,5,4,3,2,1,0      58,6,5,1,0
  11,2,0                 27,5,2,1,0          43,6,4,3,0          59,6,5,4,3,1,0
  12,6,4,1,0             28,3,0              44,6,5,2,0          60,1,0
  13,4,3,1,0             29,2,0              45,4,3,1,0          61,5,2,1,0
  14,5,3,1,0             30,6,4,1,0          46,8,5,3,2,1,0      62,6,5,3,0
  15,1,0                 31,3,0              47,5,0              63,1,0
  16,5,3,2,0             32,7,5,3,2,1,0      48,7,5,4,2,1,0      64,4,3,1,0
```

Figure 40.9-E: Binary primitive polynomials of small weight and nonzero coefficient at low indices.

The data in [FXT: data/minweight-primpoly.txt] lists minimal-weight PPs where in addition the coefficients are as close to the low end as possible. The first entries are shown in figure 40.9-D A list of minimal-weight PPs that fit into a machine word is given in [FXT: bpol/primpoly-minweight.cc].

By choosing those PPs where the highest nonzero coefficient is as low as possible one obtains the list in [FXT: data/lowbit-primpoly.txt]. It starts as shown in figure 40.9-E. The corresponding extract for small degrees is given in [FXT: bpol/primpoly-lowbit.cc]. The index (position) of the second highest nonzero coefficient (the *subdegree* of the polynomial) grows slowly with n and is ≤ 12 for all $n \leq 400$. So we can store the list compactly as an array of 16-bit words.

40.9.7 All primitive low-bit polynomials for certain degrees

A list of all PPs $x^n + \sum_{j=0}^k c_j x^j$ for degree $n = 256$ with the second-highest order $k \leq 15$ (and the first few polynomials for $k = 16$) is given in [FXT: data/lowbit256-primpoly.txt]. The first few are

```
256,10,5,2,0
256,10,8,5,4,1,0
256,10,9,8,7,4,2,1,0
256,11,8,4,3,2,0
256,11,8,6,4,3,0
256,11,10,9,4,2,0
256,11,10,9,7,4,0
256,12,7,5,4,2,0
256,12,8,7,6,3,0
```

Equivalent tables for degrees DEG= 63, 64, 127, 128, 256, 512, 521, 607, 1000, and 1024, can be found in the files `data/lowbitDEG-primpoly.txt` (where DEG has to be replaced by the number).

40.9.8 Primitive low-block polynomials

A low-block polynomial has the special form $x^n + \sum_{j=0}^k x^j$. Such PPs exist for 218 degrees $n \leq 400$. These are especially easy to store in an array (saving the index of the second highest nonzero coefficient in array element n). A complete list of all low-block PPs with degree $n \leq 400$ is given in [FXT: data/all-lowblock-primpoly.txt]. A short form of the list is [FXT: data/all-lowblock-primpoly-short.txt]. Among the low-block PPs are a few where just one bit (the coefficient after the leading coefficient) is not set. For $n \leq 400$ this is for the following degrees:

    3, 5, 7, 13, 15, 23, 37, 47, 85, 127, 183, 365, 383

The PPs listed in [FXT: data/lowblock-primpoly.txt] have the smallest possible block of set bits.

40.9.9 Irreducible all-ones polynomials

Irreducible polynomials of the form $x^n + x^{n-1} + x^{n-2} + \ldots + x + 1$ (*all-ones polynomials*) exist whenever $n + 1$ is a prime number for which 2 is a primitive root. The list of such primes up to 2000 is shown in figure 41.7-B on page 878. The all-ones polynomials are irreducible for the following $s < 400$:

    1, 2, 4, 10, 12, 18, 28, 36, 52, 58, 60, 66, 82, 100, 106, 130, 138, 148,

162, 172, 178, 180, 196, 210, 226, 268, 292, 316, 346, 348, 372, 378, 388

The sequence is entry A071642 in [312].

With the exception of $x^2 + x + 1$, none of the all-ones polynomials is primitive. In fact, the order of x equals $n+1$, which is immediate when printing the powers of x (example using $n+1 = 5$, $p = x^4 + x^3 + x^2 + x + 1$):

```
k     x^k
0     ...1
1     ..1.
2     .1..
3     1...
4     1111
5     ...1  == x^5 == 1
```

For computations modulo all-ones polynomials it is advisable to use the redundant polynomial $x^{n+1} + 1$ during the calculations:

$$\left(1 + x + x^2 + x^3 + \ldots + x^n\right) \cdot (1 + x) \;=\; 1 + x^{n+1} \tag{40.9-2}$$

One does all computations modulo the product (with cheap reductions) and only reduces the final result modulo the all-ones polynomial.

The all-ones polynomials are a special case for the factorization of cyclotomic polynomials, see section 40.11 on page 857. Irreducible polynomials of high weight are considered in [6] where irreducible polynomials of the form $(x^{n+1} + 1)/(x + 1) + x^k$ up to degree 340 are given.

40.9.10   Irreducible alternating polynomials

The 'alternating' polynomial $1 + \sum_{k=0}^{d} x^{2k+1} = 1 + x + x^3 + x^5 \ldots + x^{2d+1}$ can be irreducible only if d is odd:

```
d:    (irred. poly.)
1:    x^3 + x + 1
3:    x^7 + x^5 + x^3 + x + 1
5:    x^11 + x^9 + x^7 + x^5 + x^3 + x + 1
```

The list up to $d = 1000$ (sequence A107220 in [312]) is

1, 3, 5, 7, 9, 13, 23, 27, 31, 37, 63, 69, 117, 119, 173, 219, 223,
247, 307, 363, 383, 495, 695, 987,

It can be computed (within about ten minutes) via

```
for(d=1,1000, p=(1+sum(t=0,d,x^(2*t+1))); if(polisirreducible(Mod(1,2)*p),print1(d,", ")))
```

Similar to the all-ones polynomials, a speedup can be achieved by using the redundant modulus

$$\left(1 + x + x^3 + x^5 + \ldots + x^n\right) \cdot \left(1 + x^2\right) \;=\; 1 + x + x^2 + x^{n+2} \tag{40.9-3}$$

40.9.11   Primitive polynomials with uniformly distributed coefficients

Primitive polynomials with (roughly) equally spaced coefficients are given in [278] for degrees from 9 to 660. Polynomials with weight 5 (pentanomials) are given in [FXT: data/eq-primpoly-w5.txt], the polynomials around degree 500 are

```
498 372 247 124 0;    499 380 253 125 0,    500 378 250 127 0,
501 375 255 125 0;    502 370 240 121 0
```

The polynomials with weight 7 are given in [FXT: data/eq-primpoly-w7.txt], the list for weight 9 is [FXT: data/eq-primpoly-w9.txt].

40.9.12   Irreducible self-reciprocal polynomials

A list of all irreducible self-reciprocal polynomials (see section 40.8 on page 846) up to degree 22 is given in [FXT: data/all-irred-srp.txt]. These polynomials have even degree and none of them (with the exception of $x^2 + x + 1$) is primitive. The number after the percent sign with each entry in figure 40.9-F equals $(2^{n/2} + 1)/r$ where r is the order of the polynomial with degree n.

```
2,1,0    % 1                         14,9,7,5,0      % 1
                                     14,10,8,7,6,4,0      % 1
                                     14,11,10,9,8,7,6,5,4,3,0      % 3
4,3,2,1,0      % 1                   14,12,10,7,4,2,0      % 3
                                     14,12,9,8,7,6,5,2,0      % 1
                                     14,13,10,8,7,6,4,1,0      % 1
6,3,0    % 1                         14,13,11,7,3,1,0      % 3
                                     14,13,12,11,10,9,7,5,4,3,2,1,0      % 1
                                     14,13,12,9,8,7,6,5,2,1,0      % 1
8,5,4,3,0      % 1
8,7,6,4,2,1,0      % 1               16,15,8,1,0      % 1
                                     16,12,11,8,5,4,0      % 1
                                     16,13,12,10,8,6,4,3,0      % 1
10,7,5,3,0      % 1                  16,13,8,3,0      % 1
10,9,5,1,0      % 1                  16,14,12,11,8,5,4,2,0      % 1
10,9,8,7,6,5,4,3,2,1,0      % 3      16,14,13,11,10,9,8,7,6,5,3,2,0      % 1
                                     16,14,13,12,10,8,6,4,3,2,0      % 1
                                     16,14,13,12,11,9,8,7,5,4,3,2,0      % 1
12,10,7,6,5,2,0      % 1             16,15,13,11,10,8,6,5,3,1,0      % 1
12,10,9,8,6,4,3,2,0      % 1         16,15,13,12,10,9,8,7,6,4,3,1,0      % 1
12,11,10,9,8,7,6,5,4,3,2,1,0      % 5   16,15,13,9,8,7,3,1,0      % 1
12,11,9,7,6,5,3,1,0      % 1         16,15,14,12,10,8,6,4,2,1,0      % 1
12,8,7,6,5,4,0      % 1              16,15,14,13,11,10,8,6,5,3,2,1,0      % 1
                                     16,15,14,13,12,11,8,5,4,3,2,1,0      % 1
                                     16,15,14,13,9,8,7,3,2,1,0      % 1
                                     16,15,14,8,2,1,0      % 1
```

Figure 40.9-F: Irreducible self-reciprocal polynomials up to degree 16.

```
m:   deg    polynomial fm
0:   1      11                        == x + 1
1:   2      111                       == x^2 + x + 1
2:   4      11111                     == x^4 + x^3 + x^2 + x + 1
3:   8      111.1.111                 == x^8 + x^7 + x^6 + x^4 + x^2 + x + 1
4:   16     1111111.1..111111
5:   32     1111.111.1..1...111....1.1.111.111
6:   64     11111....1.1.11..11...11.1.1....1111111...1.1.11...11...11.1.1...11111
7:   128    111.1.1111...1...11..1...1111.1.11.11.1.1111...1...11..1...1111.1.1 \
              .1.1111...1...11..1...1111.1.11.11.1.1111...1...11..1...1111.1.111
```

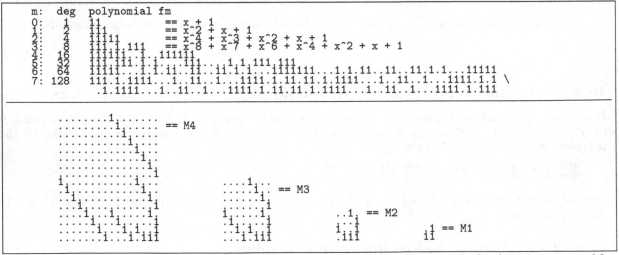

Figure 40.9-G: A family f_m of irreducible self-reciprocal binary polynomials (top) and matrices M_m whose characteristic polynomials are f_m (bottom).

Given an irreducible polynomial $f_0(x) = \sum_{k=0}^{n} c_k x^k$ where $c_1 = 1$ and $c_{n-1} = 1$ an infinite family of irreducible polynomials $f_m(x)$ of degrees $n\,2^m$ can be given as follows [113]: for $m > 0$ set $f_m(x) = S(f_{m-1}(x))$ where $S(p(x)) = x^d\,p(x + 1/x)$ and d is the degree of p (relation 40.8-1 on page 846). The polynomials f_m are self-reciprocal for $m \geq 1$. A formula for the number of degree-n polynomials suitable as f_0 is given in [260], see sequence A175390 in [312].

Starting with $f_0 = x + 1$ we obtain the polynomials shown in figure 40.9-G. The matrices M_m whose characteristic polynomials are f_m have a simple structure.

The polynomials f_m can be computed in a different way [149, p.63]: set $a_0 = x$, $b_0 = 1$, $a_{m+1} = a_m\,b_m$, and $b_{m+1} = a_m^2 + b_m^2 = (a_m + b_m)^2$, then $f_m = a_m + b_m$.

40.9.13 Irreducible normal polynomials

```
   2,1,0                      8,7,2,1,0                 -9,8,0
                             -8,7,3,1,0                  9,8,4,1,0
   3,2,0                      8,7,3,2,0                  9,8,4,2,0
                             -8,7,4,3,2,1,0              9,8,4,3,2,1,0
   4,3,0                     -8,7,5,1,0                  9,8,5,4,0
  -4,3,2,1,0                  8,7,5,3,0                  9,8,5,4,3,1,0
                             -8,7,5,4,0                 -9,8,6,3,0
   5,4,2,1,0                 -8,7,5,4,3,2,0              9,8,6,3,2,1,0
   5,4,3,1,0                  8,7,6,1,0                  9,8,6,4,3,1,0
   5,4,3,2,0                  8,7,6,3,2,1,0              9,8,6,5,3,1,0
                            -8,7,6,4,2,1,0               9,8,6,5,3,2,0
   6,5,0                     -8,7,6,4,3,2,0              9,8,6,5,4,1,0
   6,5,2,1,0                  8,7,6,5,2,1,0              9,8,7,2,0
   6,5,4,1,0                  8,7,6,5,4,1,0              9,8,7,3,2,1,0
  -6,5,4,2,0                  8,7,6,5,4,2,0              9,8,7,5,4,3,0
                            -8,7,6,5,4,3,0               9,8,7,6,2,1,0
   7,6,0                                                 9,8,7,6,3,1,0
   7,6,3,1,0                                             9,8,7,6,4,2,0
   7,6,4,1,0                                             9,8,7,6,4,3,0
   7,6,4,2,0                                             9,8,7,6,5,1,0
   7,6,5,2,0                                             9,8,7,6,5,4,3,1,0
   7,6,5,3,2,1,0
   7,6,5,4,2,1,0
```

Figure 40.9-H: All normal irreducible polynomials up to degree $n = 9$.

```
   2,1,0                      9,8,6,5,4,1,0             13,12,10,6,0
                            -9,8,6,3,0                  13,12,10,7,4,3,0
   3,2,0                      9,8,6,3,2,1,0             13,12,10,9,8,3,2,1,0
                                                        13,12,10,9,8,6,4,1,0
   5,4,2,1,0                 10,9,8,6,3,2,0             13,12,10,9,8,7,6,4,3,2,0
                             10,9,8,5,4,3,0
  -6,5,4,2,0                -10,9,8,5,3,1,0             14,13,12,10,6,3,2,1,0
   6,5,4,1,0                 10,9,8,6,4,3,0            -14,13,12,9,7,5,3,2,0
                                                       -14,13,12,9,8,6,5,2,0
   7,6,4,1,0                 11,10,8,7,6,5,0            14,13,12,10,8,6,5,4,2,1,0
                             11,10,8,5,2,1,0           -14,13,12,9,5,3,2,1,0
                             11,10,8,4,3,2,0            14,13,12,10,7,5,4,1,0
                                                      -14,13,12,10,8,4,2,1,0
                                                       14,13,12,9,8,1,0
```

Figure 40.9-I: All normal polynomials whose roots form a self-dual basis up to degree $n = 14$.

The *normal* irreducible polynomials are those whose roots are linearly independent (see section 42.6 on page 900). A complete list up to degree $n = 13$ is given in [FXT: data/all-normalpoly.txt], figure 40.9-H shows the polynomials up to degree $n = 9$ (polynomials that are not primitive are marked with a '-').

Normal polynomials must have subdegree $n - 1$, that is, they are of the form $x^n + x^{n-1} + \ldots$. The condition is necessary but not sufficient: not all irreducible polynomials of subdegree $n - 1$ are normal. A list of primitive normal polynomials $x^n + x^{n-1} + \ldots + x^w + 1$ with w as big as possible is given in [FXT: data/highbit-normalpoly.txt]. Primitive normal polynomials $x^n + x^{n-1} + x^w + \ldots + 1$ where w is as small as possible are given in [FXT: data/lowbit-normalprimpoly.txt]. Every irreducible all-ones polynomial is normal.

The polynomials f_m (see figure 40.9-G) are normal for all m, they are primitve only for $m = 0$ and $m = 1$.

All normal polynomials whose roots form a self-dual basis (see section 42.6.4 on page 908) up to degree $n = 19$ are given in [FXT: data/all-irred-self-dual.txt]. The list, up to degree $n = 14$ is shown in figure 40.9-I. No such polynomials exist for n a multiple of 4.

40.10   Generating irreducible polynomials from Lyndon words

It is not a coincidence that the number of length-n Lyndon words (see section 18.3 on page 379) is equal to the number of degree-n irreducible polynomials. Indeed, [95] gives an algorithm that, given one primitive polynomial, generates an irreducible polynomial from a Lyndon word: Let b be a Lyndon word, c an irreducible polynomial of degree n and a an element of maximal order modulo c. Set $e = a^b$ and compute the polynomial $p_e(x)$ over $GF(2^n)$, defined as

$$p_e(x) \quad := \quad (x - e)\,(x - e^2)\,(x - e^4)\,(x - e^8)\,\cdots\,(x - e^{2^{n-1}}) \tag{40.10-1}$$

Then all coefficients of $p_e(x)$ are either zero or one and the polynomial is irreducible over $GF(2)$.

```
     b           e         p               b           e         p
....1 4 m    ...1.    .11..1 P         ...1 4 m    ...1.    .11..1 P
...1. 4      ..1...   .11..1 P         ..11 4 m    .1...    .11111
..11 4 m     .1...    .11111           ..1.1 2 m   .1.11    .1.1.1 red.
.1... 4      .1...1   .11..1 P         ..111 4 m   ..111    .1..11 P
.1.1 2 m     .1.11    .1.1.1 red.      .1111 1 m   ....1    .1...1 red.
..11. 4      .1111    .11111
..111 4 m    ..111    .1..11 P
.1... 4      .111.    .11..1 P
.1..1 4      ..1.1    .11111
.1.1. 2      .1.1.    .1.1.1 red.
.1.11 4      .11.1    .1..11 P
.11.. 4      ...11    .11111
.11.1 4      ..11.    .1..11 P
.111. 4      .11..    .1..11 P
.1111 1 m    ....1    .1...1 red.
```

Figure 40.10-A: Polynomials $p_e(x)$ for the powers $e = x^b$ of the primitive element x modulo $c = x^4 + x^3 + 1$ (left). If only necklaces are used as exponents b, each polynomial is found only once (right). Irreducible polynomials are obtained for aperiodic necklaces.

An implementation in C++ is given in [FXT: class `necklace2bitpol` in bpol/necklace2bitpol.h]:

```cpp
1    class necklace2bitpol
2    {
3    public:
4        ulong p_[BITS_PER_LONG+1];  // polynomial over GF(2**n_)
5        ulong n_;  // degree of c_
6        ulong c_;  // modulus (irreducible polynomial)
7        ulong h_;  // mask used for computation
8        ulong a_;  // generator modulo c
9        ulong e_;  // a^b
10
11   public:
12       necklace2bitpol(ulong n, ulong c=0, ulong a=0)
13           : n_(n), c_(c), a_(a)
14       {
15           if ( 0==c )  c_ = lowbit_primpoly[n];
16           if ( 0==a )  a_ = 2UL;  // 'x'
17           h_ = (highest_one(c_) >> 1);
18       }
19
20       ~necklace2bitpol()  { ; }
21
22       ulong poly(ulong b)
23       {
24           const ulong e = bitpolmod_power(a_, b, c_, h_);
25           e_ = e;
26           const ulong x = 2;  // a root of the C
27           ulong s = e;
28           ulong m = 1;  // minpoly
29           for (ulong j=0; j<n_; ++j)
```

```
30      {
31          ulong t = x ^ s;
32          m = bitpolmod_mult(m, t, c_, h_);
33          s = bitpolmod_square(s, c_, h_);
34      }
35      bp_ = m ^ c_;
36      return bp_;
37   }
38  };
```

The computation of the polynomials is a variant of the second algorithm in section 42.2 on page 892. Figure 40.10-A (left) shows all polynomials that are generated with $c = x^4 + x^3 + 1$ and the generator $a = x$. This is the output of [FXT: gf2n/necklace2irred-demo.cc]. The columns are: b and its cyclic period (symbol 'm' appended if the word is the cyclic minimum), e and p where a 'P' indicates that p is primitive. Observe that cyclic shifts of the same word give identical polynomials p. Further, if the period is not maximal, then p is reducible. Restricting our attention to the necklaces b we obtain each polynomial just once (right of figure 40.10-A). The Lyndon words b give all degree-n irreducible polynomials. The primitive polynomials are exactly those where $\gcd(b, 2^n - 1) = 1$.

degree:	necklaces	search
24:	276 k/sec	147 k/sec
35:	124 k/sec	64 k/sec
45:	73 k/sec	36 k/sec
63:	38 k/sec	18 k/sec

Figure 40.10-B: Rate of generation of irreducible polynomials via necklaces and with exhaustive search.

To generate all irreducible binary polynomials of fixed degree use [FXT: `class all_irredpoly` in bpol/all-irredpoly.h]. The usage is shown in [FXT: gf2n/all-irredpoly-demo.cc]. It turns out that the generation via exhaustive search [FXT: gf2n/bitpol-search-irred-demo.cc] is not much slower, figure 40.10-B gives the rates of generation for various degrees and both methods.

40.11 Irreducible and cyclotomic polynomials ‡

The primitive binary polynomials of degree n can be obtained by factoring the cyclotomic polynomial (see section 37.1.1 on page 704) Y_N over GF(2) where $N = 2^n - 1$. For example, with $n = 6$,

```
? n=6; N=2^n-1; lift( factormod(polcyclo(N),2) )
    [x^6 + x + 1   1]
    [x^6 + x^4 + x^3 + x + 1   1]
    [x^6 + x^5 + 1   1]
    [x^6 + x^5 + x^2 + x + 1   1]
    [x^6 + x^5 + x^3 + x^2 + 1   1]
    [x^6 + x^5 + x^4 + x + 1   1]
```

We use a routine (`pcfprint(N)`) that prints the N-th cyclotomic polynomial and its factors in symbolic form. With $n = 6$, $N = 2^n - 1 = 63$ we obtain

```
? n=6; N=2^n-1;
? pcfprint(N)
    63: [ 36 33 27 24 18 12 9 3 0 ]
        [ 6 1 0 ]
        [ 6 4 3 1 0 ]
        [ 6 5 0 ]
        [ 6 5 2 1 0 ]
        [ 6 5 3 2 0 ]
        [ 6 5 4 1 0 ]
```

The irreducible but non-primitive binary polynomials are factors of cyclotomic polynomials Y_d where $d \backslash N$, $d < N$ and the order of 2 modulo d equals n:

```
? fordiv(N,d,if(n==znorder(Mod(2,d)) && (d<N), pcfprint(d) ));
     9: [ 6 3 0 ]
        [ 6 3 0 ]
    21: [ 12 11 9 8 6 4 3 1 0 ]
        [ 6 4 2 1 0 ]
        [ 6 5 4 2 0 ]
```

The number of factors of Y_d equals $\varphi(d)/n$ so we can count how many degree-n irreducible polynomials correspond to which divisor of $N = 2^n - 1$:

```
 1:  [1:1]     1
 2:  [3:1]     1
 3:  [7:2]     2
 4:  [5:1]   [15:2]      3
 5:  [31:6]     6
 6:  [9:1]   [21:2]    [63:6]      9
 7:  [127:18]      18
 8:  [17:2]   [51:4]    [85:8]    [255:16]      30
 9:  [73:8]   [511:48]      56
10:  [11:1]   [33:2]    [93:6]    [341:30]   [1023:60]      99
11:  [23:2]   [89:8]    [2047:176]      186
```

Line 6 tells us that one irreducible polynomial of degree 6 is due to the factor 9, two are due to the factor 21, and the 6 primitive polynomials correspond to $N = 63$ itself, which we have verified a moment ago. Further, the a polynomials corresponding to an entry [d:a] all have order d. The list was produced using

```
1   { for (n=1, 11,
2       print1(n,": ");
3       s = 0;
4       N = 2^n-1;
5       fordiv (N, d,
6           if ( n==znorder(Mod(2,d)) ,
7               a = eulerphi(d)/n;
8               print1(" [",d,":",a,"] ");
9               s += a;
10          );
11      );
12      print("   ",s);
13  ); }
```

40.12 Factorization of binary polynomials

We give a method for the factorization of binary polynomials. The first part describes how to factorize polynomials that do not contain a square factor. The second part gives algorithms to detect and remove square factors. Finally, an algorithm to factorize arbitrary binary polynomials is given.

40.12.1 Factorization of square-free polynomials

A polynomial that does not contain a nontrivial square factor is called *square-free*. To factorize a square-free polynomial, we will use *Berlekamp's Q-matrix algorithm* described in [46]. The algorithm consists of two main steps: the computation of the nullspace of a matrix and a refinement phase that finds the distinct irreducible factors.

Let c be a binary polynomial of degree d. The Q-matrix is a $d \times d$ matrix whose n-th column can be computed as the binary polynomial $x^{2n} \pmod{c}$. The algorithm will use the nullspace of $Q - \text{id}$.

The routine to compute the Q-matrix is [FXT: bpol/berlekamp.cc]:

```
1   void
2   setup_q_matrix(ulong c, ulong d, ulong *ss)
3   // Compute the Q-matrix for the degree-d polynomial c.
4   // Used in Berlekamp's factorization algorithm.
5   {
6       ulong h = 1UL << (d-1);
7       {
8           ulong x2 = 2UL;   // == 'x'
9           ulong q = 1UL;
10          x2 = bitpolmod_mult(x2, x2, c, h);
11          for (ulong k=0;  k<d;  ++k)
12          {
13              ss[k] = q;
14              q = bitpolmod_mult(q, x2, c, h);
15          }
16          bitmat_transpose(ss, d, ss);
17      }
18  }
```

```
    c = x⁷ + x + 1 (irreducible):
         Q=               Q-id=           nullspace=
         1......          .......         1......
         ....1..          .1...1..        .
         .1..1..          .11.1..         .
         ....1..          ...1.1.         .
         ...1.1.          ..1.11.         .
         .....1           ....11          .
         ...1..1          ...1...
```

```
    c = x⁷ + x³ + x + 1 = (x + 1)(x² + x + 1)(x⁴ + x + 1) (reducible but square-free):
         Q=               Q-id=           nullspace=
         1......          .......         1......
         ....1.1          .1...1.1        .1...1.
         .1..1.1          .11.1.1         .1.1.11
         ....1.           ...1.1.         .
         ..1.111          ..1..11         .
         .....1           .....11         .
         ...1.11          ...1.1.
```

```
    c = (1 + x)⁷ = x⁷ + x⁶ + x⁵ + x⁴ + x³ + x² + x + 1 (not square-free):
         Q=               Q-id=
         1...1..          ....1..         nullspace=
         .1...1.          .1....         1......
         ..1...1.         .11..1.         .
         ..1...1          ..1.1.1         .
         ...1...          ...1..1
```

Figure 40.12-A: The Q-matrices for three binary polynomials and the nullspaces of $Q - \mathrm{id}$.

The Q-matrix and nullspace of $Q - \mathrm{id}$ for the irreducible binary polynomial $c = x^7 + x + 1$ are shown at the top of figure 40.12-A. The vector $n_0 = [1, 0, \ldots, 0]$ lies in the nullspace of $Q - \mathrm{id}$ for every polynomial. For $c = x^7 + x^3 + x + 1 = (x + 1)(x^2 + x + 1)(x^4 + x + 1)$ the nullspace has rank three (middle of figure 40.12-A). the rank of the nullspace equals the number of distinct irreducible factors if c is square-free. For polynomials containing a square factor we do not get the total number of factors, the data for $c = (1 + x)^7 = x^7 + x^6 + x^5 + x^4 + x^3 + x^2 + x + 1$ is shown at the bottom of figure 40.12-A. The figure was created with the program [FXT: gf2n/qmatrix-demo.cc].

To find the irreducible factors of c, the vectors spanning the nullspace must be post-processed. The algorithm can be described as follows: let F be a set of binary polynomials whose product equals c, the refinement step R_i proceeds as follows:

Let t be the i-th element of the nullspace. For each element $f \in F$ do the following: if the degree of f equals 1, keep it in the set, else remove f from the set and add from the set $X = \{\gcd(f, t), \gcd(f, t+1)\}$ those elements whose degrees are greater than or equal to 1.

One starts with $F = \{c\}$ and does the refinement steps $R_0, R_1, \ldots R_{r-1}$ corresponding to the vectors of the nullspace. Afterwards the set F will contain exactly the distinct irreducible factors of c. This is done in the following routine [FXT: bpol/berlekamp.cc]:

```
1    ulong
2    bitpol_refine_factors(ulong *f, ulong nf, const ulong *nn, ulong r)
3    // Given the nullspace nn[0,...,r-1] of (Q-id)
4    // and nf factors f[0,...,nf-1] whose product equals c
5    // (typically nf=1 and f[0]==c)
6    // then get all r irreducible factors of c.
7    {
8        ulong ss[r];
9        for (ulong j=0; j<r; ++j) // for all elements t in nullspace
10       {
11           ulong t = nn[j];
12
13           // skip trivial elements in nullspace:
14           if ( bitpol_deg(t)==0 )  continue;
15
16           ulong sc = 0;
```

```
17            for (ulong b=0; b<nf; ++b)  // for all elements bv in set
18            {
19                ulong bv = f[b];
20                ulong db = bitpol_deg(bv);
21                if ( db <= 1 )  // bv cannot be reduced
22                {
23                    ss[sc++] = bv;
24                }
25                else
26                {
27                    for (ulong s=0; s<2; ++s)  // for all elements in GF(2)
28                    {
29                        ulong ti = t ^ s;
30                        ulong g = bitpol_gcd(bv, ti);
31                        if ( bitpol_deg(g) >= 1 )  ss[sc++] = g;
32                    }
33                }
34            }
35
36            nf = sc;
37            for (ulong k=0; k<nf; ++k)  f[k] = ss[k];
38
39            if ( nf>=r )  break;  // done
40        }
41
42        return nf;
43    }
```

We skip elements corresponding to constant polynomials. Further, as soon as the set F contains r elements, all factors are found and the algorithm terminates.

Now Berlekamp's algorithm can be implemented as

```
1   ulong
2   bitpol_factor_squarefree(ulong c, ulong *f)
3   // Fill irreducible factors of square-free polynomial c into f[]
4   // Return number of factors.
5   {
6       ulong d = bitpol_deg(c);
7
8       if ( d<=1 )  // trivial cases:  0, 1, x, x+1
9       {
10          f[0] = c;
11          if ( 0==c )  d = 1;  // 0==0^1
12          return d;
13      }
14
15      ulong ss[d];
16      setup_q_matrix(c, d, ss);
17      bitmat_add_unit(ss, d);
18
19      ulong nn[d];
20      ulong r = bitmat_nullspace(ss, d, nn);
21
22
23      f[0] = c;
24      ulong nf = 1;
25      if ( r>1 )  nf = bitpol_refine_factors(f, nf, nn, r);
26
27      return r;
28  }
```

The algorithm for the computation of the nullspace was taken from [213], find the implementation in [FXT: bmat/bitmat-nullspace.cc].

Berlekamp's algorithm is given in [110] in a more general form: to factorize a polynomial with coefficients in the finite field $GF(q)$, set up the Q-matrix with columns x^{qi} and set $X = \{\gcd(f, t+0), \gcd(f, t+1), \ldots, \gcd(f, t+(q-1))\}$ in the refinement step. The algorithm is efficient only if q is small.

40.12.2   Extracting the square-free part of a polynomial

To test whether a polynomial c has a square factor one computes $g = \gcd(c, c')$ where c' is the derivative. If $g \neq 1$, then c has the square factor g: let $c = a \cdot b^2$, then $c' = a' b^2 + a\, 2\, b\, b' = a' b^2$, so $\gcd(c, c') = b^2$. The corresponding routine for binary polynomials is given in [FXT: bpol/bitpol-squarefree.h]:

```
1    inline ulong bitpol_test_squarefree(ulong c)
2    // Return  0 if polynomial is square-free
3    // else return square factor != 0
4    {
5        ulong d = bitpol_deriv(c);
6        if ( 0==d )  return  (1==c ? 0 : c);
7        ulong g = bitpol_gcd(c, d);
8        return  (1==g ? 0 : g);
9    }
```

The derivative of a binary polynomial can be computed easily [FXT: bpol/bitpol-deriv.h] (64-bit version):

```
1    inline ulong bitpol_deriv(ulong c)
2    // Return derivative of polynomial c
3    {
4        c &= 0xaaaaaaaaaaaaaaaaUL;
5        return  (c>>1);
6    }
```

The coefficients at the even powers have to be cleared because derivation multiplies them with an even factor which equals 0 modulo 2.

If the derivative of a binary polynomial is zero, then it is a perfect square or a constant polynomial:

```
1    inline ulong bitpol_pure_square_q(ulong c)
2    // Return whether polynomial is a pure square != 1
3    {
4        if ( 1UL==c )  return 0;
5        c &= 0xaaaaaaaaaaaaaaaaUL;
6        return  (0==c);
7    }
```

The following routine returns zero if c is square-free. If c is has a square factor $s \neq 1$, then s is returned:

```
1    inline ulong bitpol_test_squarefree(ulong c)
2    {
3        ulong d = bitpol_deriv(c);
4        if ( 0==d )  return  (1==c ? 0 : c);
5        ulong g = bitpol_gcd(c, d);
6        return  (1==g ? 0 : g);
7    }
```

If a polynomial is a perfect square, then its square root can be computed as

```
1    inline ulong bitpol_pure_sqrt(ulong c)
2    {
3        ulong t = 0;
4        for (ulong mc=1,mt=1;  mc;  mc<<=2,mt<<=1)
5        {
6            if ( mc & c )  t |= mt;
7        }
8        return  t;
9    }
```

A faster way to do the computation is to use the function `bit_unzip0()` from section 1.15 on page 38. For the factorization algorithm for general polynomials we have to extract the product of all distinct irreducible factors (the square-free part) from a polynomial. The following routine returns a polynomial where the even exponents in the factorization are reduced [FXT: bpol/bitpol-squarefree.cc]:

```
1    ulong
2    bitpol_sreduce(ulong c)
3    {
4        ulong s = bitpol_test_squarefree(c);
5        if ( 0==s )  return c;  // c is square-free
6
7        ulong f = bitpol_div(c, s);
8
9        do  // here s is a pure square and s>1
10       {
11           s = bitpol_pure_sqrt(s);
12       }
13       while ( bitpol_pure_square_q(s) );
14
15       ulong g = bitpol_gcd(s, f);
16       s = bitpol_div(s, g);
```

```
17        f = bitpol_mult(f, s);
18
19        return f;
20  }
```

With $c = f \cdot s^{k\,2^t}$ (k odd, the factors of f and s not necessarily distinct) the returned polynomial equals $f \cdot s^k$. Some examples:

$$a^2 \;\mapsto\; a \tag{40.12-1a}$$

$$a^4 \;\mapsto\; a \tag{40.12-1b}$$

$$a^3 = a\,a^2 \;\mapsto\; a\,a \tag{40.12-1c}$$

$$a^5 = a\,a^4 \;\mapsto\; a\,a \tag{40.12-1d}$$

$$a\,b^2 \;\mapsto\; a\,b \tag{40.12-1e}$$

$$a\,b\,b^2 \;\mapsto\; a\,b\,b = a\,b^2 \;\mapsto\; a\,b \tag{40.12-1f}$$

$$f \cdot s^{k\,2^t} \;\mapsto\; f \cdot s^k \tag{40.12-1g}$$

To extract the square-free part of a polynomial call the routine repeatedly until the returned polynomial equals the input:

```
1   inline ulong bitpol_make_squarefree(ulong c)
2   {
3       ulong z = c, t;
4       while ( z!=(t=bitpol_sreduce(z)) )  z = t;
5       return z;
6   }
```

The reduction routine will be called at most $\log_2(n)$ times for a polynomial of degree n: the worst case is a perfect power $p = a^{2^k-1}$ where $2^k - 1 \le n$. Observe that $(2^k - 1) = 1 + 2\,(2^{k-1} - 1)$, so the reduction routine will split p as $p = a\,s^2 \mapsto a\,s$ where $s = a^{2^{k-1}-1}$ is of the same form.

40.12.3 Factorization of arbitrary polynomials

The factorization routine for arbitrary binary polynomials extracts the square-free part f of its input c, uses Berlekamp's algorithm to factor f and updates the exponents according to the polynomial $s = c/f$. There is just one call to the routine that computes a nullspace [FXT: bpol/bitpol-factor.cc]:

```
1   ulong
2   bitpol_factor(ulong c, ulong *f, ulong *e)
3   // Factorize the binary polynomial c:
4   // c = \prod_{i=0}^{fct-1}{f[i]^e[i]}
5   // The number of factors (fct) is returned.
6   {
7       ulong d = bitpol_deg(c);
8       if ( d<=1 )  // trivial cases:  0, 1, x, x+1
9       {
10          f[0] = c;
11          if ( 0==c )  d = 1;  // 0==0^1
12          return d;
13      }
14
15      // get square-free part:
16      ulong cf = bitpol_make_squarefree(c);
17
18      // ... and factor it:
19      ulong fct = bitpol_factor_squarefree(cf, f);
20
21      // All exponents are one:
22      for (ulong j=0; j<fct; ++j)  { e[j] = 1; }
23
24      // Here f[],e[] is a valid factorization of the square-free part cf
25
26      // Update exponents with square part:
27      ulong cs = bitpol_div(c, cf);
28      for (ulong j=0; j<fct; ++j)
29      {
30          if ( 1==cs )  break;
```

```
31          ulong fj = f[j];
32          ulong g = bitpol_gcd(cs, fj);
33          while ( 1!=g )
34          {
35              ++e[j];
36              cs = bitpol_div(cs, fj);
37              if ( 1==cs )  break;
38              g = bitpol_gcd(cs, fj);
39          }
40      }
41
42      return fct;
43  }
```

```
  0:  x^5                    ==   (x)^5
  1:  x^5              +1     ==   (x+1) * (x^4+x^3+x^2+x+1)
  2:  x^5            +x       ==   (x) * (x+1)^4
  3:  x^5            +x+1     ==   (x^2+x+1) * (x^3+x^2+1)
  4:  x^5       +x^2          ==   (x)^2 * (x+1) * (x^2+x+1)
  5:  x^5       +x^2 +1       ==   (x^5+x^2+1)
  6:  x^5       +x^2+x        ==   (x) * (x^4+x+1)
  7:  x^5       +x^2+x+1      ==   (x+1)^2 * (x^3+x+1)
  8:  x^5  +x^3               ==   (x)^3 * (x+1)^2
  9:  x^5  +x^3         +1    ==   (x^5+x^3+1)
 10:  x^5  +x^3       +x      ==   (x) * (x^2+x+1)^2
 11:  x^5  +x^3       +x+1    ==   (x+1) * (x^4+x^3+1)
 12:  x^5  +x^3+x^2           ==   (x)^2 * (x^3+x+1)
 13:  x^5  +x^3+x^2     +1    ==   (x+1)^3 * (x^2+x+1)
 14:  x^5  +x^3+x^2+x         ==   (x) * (x+1) * (x^3+x^2+1)
 15:  x^5  +x^3+x^2+x+1       ==   (x^5+x^3+x^2+x+1)
 16:  x^5+x^4                 ==   (x)^4 * (x+1)
 17:  x^5+x^4            +1   ==   (x^2+x+1) * (x^3+x+1)
 18:  x^5+x^4          +x     ==   (x) * (x^4+x^3+1)
 19:  x^5+x^4          +x+1   ==   (x+1)^5
 20:  x^5+x^4     +x^2        ==   (x)^2 * (x^3+x^2+1)
 21:  x^5+x^4     +x^2 +1     ==   (x+1) * (x^4+x+1)
 22:  x^5+x^4     +x^2+x      ==   (x) * (x+1)^2 * (x^2+x+1)
 23:  x^5+x^4     +x^2+x+1    ==   (x^5+x^4+x^2+x+1)
 24:  x^5+x^4+x^3             ==   (x)^3 * (x^2+x+1)
 25:  x^5+x^4+x^3       +1    ==   (x+1)^2 * (x^3+x^2+1)
 26:  x^5+x^4+x^3     +x      ==   (x) * (x+1) * (x^3+x+1)
 27:  x^5+x^4+x^3     +x+1    ==   (x^5+x^4+x^3+x+1)
 28:  x^5+x^4+x^3+x^2         ==   (x)^2 * (x+1)^3
 29:  x^5+x^4+x^3+x^2   +1    ==   (x^5+x^4+x^3+x^2+1)
 30:  x^5+x^4+x^3+x^2+x       ==   (x) * (x^4+x^3+x^2+x+1)
 31:  x^5+x^4+x^3+x^2+x+1     ==   (x+1) * (x^2+x+1)^2
```

Figure 40.12-B: Factorizations of the binary polynomials of degree 5.

Figure 40.12-B shows the factorizations of the binary polynomials of degree 5. It was created with the program [FXT: gf2n/bitpolfactor-demo.cc]. Factoring the first million polynomials of degrees 20, 30, 40 and 60 takes about 5, 10, 15 and 30 seconds, respectively.

A variant of the factorization algorithm often given uses the *square-free factorization* $c = \prod_i a_i^i$ where the polynomials a_i are square-free and pair-wise coprime. Given the square-free factorization one has to call the core routine for each nontrivial a_i.

As noted, the refinement step becomes expensive if the coefficients are in a field GF(q) where q is not small because q computations of the polynomial gcd are involved. For an algorithm that is efficient also for large values of q see [110] or [154, ch.14]. A 'baby step/giant step' method is given in [308].

Chapter 41

Shift registers

We describe shift register sequences (SRS) and their generation via linear feedback shift registers (LFSR). The underlying mechanism is the modular arithmetic of binary polynomials treated in section 40.3. We give an expression for the number of shift registers sequences of maximal length, the m-sequences. We look at two related mechanisms, feedback carry shift registers (FCSR) and linear hybrid cellular automata (LHCA). Most of these algorithms given can easily be implemented in hardware. Among the many applications for shift registers are random number generators, the computation of CRCs, spectrum spreading with communication protocols, and hardware testing.

41.1 Linear feedback shift registers (LFSR)

```
      c = 1..11 == 0x13 == 19   (deg = 4)
       0    w =    15  = 1111  1  ...1 =    1 = a
       1    w =    14  = 111.  .  ..1. =    2 = a
       2    w =    12  = 11..  .  .1.. =    4 = a
       3    w =     8  = 1...  .  1... =    8 = a
       4    w =     1  = ...1  1  ..11 =    3 = a
       5    w =     2  = ..1.  .  .11. =    6 = a
       6    w =     4  = .1..  .  11.. =   12 = a
       7    w =     9  = 1..1  1  1.11 =   11 = a
       8    w =     3  = ..11  1  .1.1 =    5 = a
       9    w =     6  = .11.  .  1.1. =   10 = a
      10    w =    13  = 11.1  1  .111 =    7 = a
      11    w =    10  = 1.1.  .  111. =   14 = a
      12    w =     5  = .1.1  1  1111 =   15 = a
      13    w =    11  = 1.11  1  11.1 =   13 = a
      14    w =     7  = .111  1  1..1 =    9 = a

   >>  0    w =    15  = 1111  1  ...1 =    1 = a   << new period starts
       1    w =    14  = 111.  .  ..1. =    2 = a
       2    w =    12  = 11..  .  .1.. =    4 = a
       3    w =     8  = 1...  .  1... =    8 = a
       4    w =     1  = ...1  1  ..11 =    3 = a
       5    w =     2  = ..1.  .  .11. =    6 = a
```

Figure 41.1-A: Linear feedback shift register using the primitive polynomial $C = x^4 + x + 1$.

Multiplication of a binary polynomial A by x modulo a polynomial C is particularly easy as shown near the beginning of section 40.3 on page 832: shift the input to the left (multiplication); if the result $A \cdot x$ has the same degree as C, then subtract (XOR) the polynomial C (modular reduction).

The underlying mechanism of shifting and conditionally feeding back certain bits is called a *linear feedback shift register* (LFSR). A *shift register sequence* (SRS) can be generated by computing $A_k = x^k$, $k = 0, 1, \ldots, 2^n - 1$ modulo C and setting bit k of the SRS to the least significant bit of A_k. In the context of LFSRs the polynomial C is sometimes called the *connection polynomial* of the shift register.

If the modulus C is a primitive polynomial (see section 40.5 on page 841) of degree n, then the SRS is a sequence of zeros and ones that contains all nonzero words of length n. Further, if a word W is updated at each step by left shifting and adding the bit of the SRS, this sequence also contains all nonzero words.

This is demonstrated in [FXT: gf2n/lfsr-demo.cc], which for $n = 4$ uses the primitive polynomial $C =$

J. Arndt, *Matters Computational: Ideas, Algorithms, Source Code*,
DOI 10.1007/978-3-642-14764-7_41, © Springer-Verlag Berlin Heidelberg 2011

$x^4 + x + 1$ and gives the output shown in figure 41.1-A. Here we pasted the first few lines after the end of the actual output to emphasize the periodicity of the sequences. The corresponding SRS of period 15 is (extra spaces mark start of new periods):

     1 0 0 0 1 0 0 1 1 0 1 0 1 1 1   1 0 0 0 1 0 0 1 1 0 1 0 1 1 1   1 0 ...

In fact any of the bits of the words $A_k = x^k \bmod C$ (or linear combination of two or more bits) could be used, each producing a cyclically shifted version of the SRS.

An efficient way to generate an SRS is to compute the powers x^{-k} modulo C, that is, to repeatedly divide by x:

```
1        ulong c = /* a primitive polynomial */;
2        ulong n = /* degree of C */;
3        ulong a = 1;
4        for (ulong k=0; k<n; ++k)
5        {
6            ulong s = a & 1;
7            // Use s here.
8            if ( s )  a ^= c;
9            a >> 1;
10        }
```

The routine will work for $\deg(C) < n$ where n is the number of bits in a machine word. A version that also works for $\deg(C) = n$ is given in section 40.3 on page 832.

A C++ implementation of an LFSR is [FXT: **class lfsr** in bpol/lfsr.h]:

```
1    class lfsr
2    // (binary) Linear Feedback Shift Register
3    // Produces a shift register sequence (SRS)
4    // generated by  a_k=x^k (mod c) where
5    // c is a primitive polynomial of degree n.
6    // The period of SRS is 2^n - 1
7    // (non-primitive c lead to smaller periods)
8    {
9    public:
10        ulong a_;  // internal state (polynomial modulo c)
11        ulong w_;  // word of the shift_register_sequence (SRS)
12        ulong c_;  // (mod 2) poly  e.g. x^4+x+1 == 0x13 == 1..11
13        ulong h_;  // highest bit in SRS word  e.g. (above) == 16 = 1...
14        ulong mask_;  // mask  e.g. (above) == 15 == 1111
15        ulong n_;  // degree of polynomial  e.g. (above) == 4
16
17    public:
18        lfsr(ulong n, ulong c=0)
19        // n: degree of polynomial c
20        // c: polynomial (defaults to minimum weight primitive polynomial)
21        {
22    [--snip--]
```

The crucial computation is implemented as

```
1        ulong next()
2        {
3            ulong s = a_ & h_;
4            a_ <<= 1;
5            w_ <<= 1;
6            if ( 0!=s )
7            {
8                a_ ^= c_;
9                w_ |= 1;
10            }
11            w_ &= mask_;
12            return w_;
13        }
```

Up to the lines that update the word w_ this function is identical to **bitpolmod_times_x()** given in section 40.3 on page 832.

The method **next_w()** skips to the next word by calling **next()** n times:

```
1        ulong next_w()
```

```
2        {
3            for (ulong k=0; k<n_; ++k)  next();
4            return w_;
5        }
```

Let a and w a pair of values that correspond to each other. The following two methods directly set one of these two while keeping the pair consistent. This routine sets a to a given value:

```
1        void set_a(ulong a)
2        {
3            a_ = a;
4            w_ = 0;
5            ulong b = 1;
6            for (ulong j=0; j<n_; ++j)
7            {
8                if ( a & 1 )
9                {
10                   w_ |= b;
11                   a ^= c_;
12               }
13               b <<= 1;
14               a >>= 1;
15           }
16       }
```

The loop executes n times where n is the degree of the modulus. This routine sets w to a given value:

```
1        void set_w(ulong w)
2        {
3            w_ = w;
4            a_ = 0;
5            ulong c = c_;
6            while ( w )
7            {
8                if ( w & 1 )  a_ ^= c;
9                c <<= 1;
10               w >>= 1;
11           }
12           a_ &= mask_;
13       }
```

The supplied value must be nonzero for both methods.

Going back one step is possible via the method `prev()`

```
1    public:
2        ulong prev()
3        {
4            prev_a();
5            set_a(a_);
6            return w_;
7        }
```

which calls `prev_a()`:

```
1    private:
2        void prev_a()
3        {
4            ulong s = a_ & 1;
5            a_ >>= 1;
6            if ( s )
7            {
8                a_ ^= (c_>>1);
9                a_ |= h_;  // so it works for  n_ == BITS_PER_LONG
10           }
11       }
```

The method `prev_a()` leaves the value of w inconsistent with a and therefore cannot be called directly. Note that stepping back is more expensive than stepping forward because `set_a()` is rather expensive.

It is also possible to go backwards word-wise:

```
1        ulong prev_w()
2        {
3            for (ulong k=0; k<n_; ++k)  prev_a();
4            set_a(a_);
5            return w_;
```

```
6        }
```

As this routine involves only one call to `set_a()` it is about as expensive as stepping one word forward using `next_w()`.

41.2 Galois and Fibonacci setup

```
    c = .11..1 == 0x19 == 25   (deg = 4)
    r = .1..11 == 0x13 == 19   (deg = 4)

          -------- Galois --------------      --------- Fibonacci ---------
    k:     Lc      Lr      Rc      Rr          Lc      Lr      Rc      Rr
    1:    ....1   ....1   ...,1   .,..1       ....1   ....1   ...,1   .,..1
    2:    ...1.   ...1.   .11..   .1..1       ...1.   ...11   .1...   .1...
    3:    ..1..   ..1..   ..11.   .11.1       ..1..   ..111   .11..   ...1.
    4:    .1...   .1...   ...11   .1111       .1..1   .1111   .111.   ..1..
    5:    .1..1   ...11   .11.1   .111.       ...11   .111.   .1111   .1..1
    6:    .1..1   ..11.   .1..1   ..111       ..11.   ..11.1  ..111   .11..
    7:    .1111   ..11.   ..1.1   .1..1       .11.1   .1..1   .11.11  ..11.
    8:    ..111   .1.11   .111.   .1..1       .1.1.   ..1..1  ..1.1   .1.11
    9:    .111.   ..1.1   .111.   .1.11       .1.1.   .1.1.   .1.1.   ..1.1
    10:   ..1.1   .1.1.   .1111   .11..       .1.11   ...11.  .11.1   .1.1.
    11:   .1.1.   ...111  .1.11   ..11.       ...111  ..11..  ...11.  .11.1
    12:   .11.1   ...111  .1..1   ...11       .1111   .1..1   ...11   .111.
    13:   ...11   ..1111  .1...   .1...       .111.   ...1.   .1..1   .1111
    14:   ..11.   .11.1   ..1..   ..1..       .11..   ..1..   ..1..   ..111
    15:   .11..   .1..1   ...1.   ...1,       .1...   .1...   ...1.   ...11
    16:   ....1   ....1   ....1   ....1       ....1   ....1   ....1   ....1
```

Figure 41.2-A: Sequences of words generated with the Galois and Fibonacci mechanisms, either with the left or the right shift (capital letters 'L' and 'R' on top of columns) and primitive polynomial 'c' or its reciprocal 'r'. Each track of any sequence is a shift register sequence.

The type of shift registers considered so far is the *Galois setup* of a binary shift register. The mechanism is to detect whether a one is being shifted out and, if so, subtract the polynomial modulus. The auxiliary variable h must be the word where only bit $n-1$ is set where n is the degree of the polynomial c. The left and right shift operations can be implemented as

```
1    ulong galois_left(ulong x, ulong c, ulong h)
2    {
3        ulong s = x & h;
4        x <<= 1;
5        if ( 0!=s )  x ^= c;
6        return x;
7    }
```

and

```
1    ulong galois_right(ulong x, ulong c)
2    {
3        ulong s =  ( x & 1UL );
4        x >>= 1;
5        if ( s )  x ^= (c>>1);
6        return x;
7    }
```

Four sequences of binary words that are generated with either the left or right shift and a primitive polynomial or its reciprocal (reversed word) are shown in figure 41.2-A. A different set of sequences shown in the same figure is obtained with the *Fibonacci setup*. In the Fibonacci setup the sum (modulo 2) of bits determined by the used polynomial is shifted in at each step.

The left and right shift operations can be implemented as

```
1    ulong fibonacci_left(ulong x, ulong c, ulong h)
2    {
3        x <<= 1;
4        ulong s = parity( x & c );
5        if ( 0!=s )  x ^= 1;
6        x &= ~(h<<1);  // remove excess bit at high end
7        return x;
8    }
```

and

```
1    ulong fibonacci_right(ulong x, ulong c, ulong h)
2    {
3        ulong s = parity( x & c );
4        x >>= 1;
5        if ( s )  x ^= h;
6        return x;
7    }
```

As the parity computation is expensive on most machines (see section 1.16.1 on page 42), the Galois setup should usually be preferred. The programs [FXT: gf2n/lfsr-fibonacci-demo.cc] and [FXT: gf2n/lfsr-galois-demo.cc] can be used to create the binary patterns shown in figure 41.2-A. With both programs the polynomial modulus can be specified.

41.3 Error detection by hashing: the CRC

A *hash value* is an element from a set H that is computed via a *hash function* f that maps any (finite) sequence of input data to H:

$$f : S \to H, \qquad s \mapsto h \tag{41.3-1}$$

where $s \in S$ and $h \in H$. For the sake of simplicity we now consider input sequences of fixed size, so they are in a fixed set S. We further assume that the set S is (much) bigger than H.

Input sequences with different hash values are necessarily different. But, as the hash function maps a bigger set to a smaller one, there are different input sequences with identical hash values.

A trivial example is the set $H = \{0, 1\}$ together with a function that counts binary digits modulo 2, the parity function. Another example is the sum-of-digits test (see section 28.4 on page 562), that is used to check the multiplication of large numbers. In the test we compute the value of a multi-digit decimal number modulo 9, so $H = \{0, 1, 2, \ldots, 9\}$. The crucial additional property of this hash is that with $f(A) = a$, $f(B) = b$, $f(C) = c$ (where A, B, and C are decimal numbers), $A \cdot B = C$ implies $a \cdot b = c$.

To be useful, a hash function f should have the *mixing* property: it should map the elements $s \in S$ 'randomly' to H. With the sum-of-digits test we could have used rather arbitrary moduli for the hash function. With one exception: the value modulo 10 as hash would be rather useless as no change in any digit except for the last could ever be detected.

The *cyclic redundancy check* (CRC) is a hash where the hash values are binary words of fixed length. The hash function (basically) computes $h = s \bmod c$ where s is the binary polynomial corresponding to the input sequence and c is a binary polynomial that is primitive (see chapter 40 on page 822). We will use polynomials c of degree 64 so the hash values (CRCs) are 64-bit words.

A C++ implementation is given as [FXT: class crc64 in bits/crc64.h]:

```
1    class crc64
2    // 64-bit CRC (cyclic redundancy check)
3    {
4    public:
5        uint64 a_;  // internal state (polynomial modulo c)
6        uint64 c_;  // a binary primitive polynomial
7        // (non-primitive c lead to smaller periods)
8        // The leading coefficient needs not be present.
9        uint64 h_;  // auxiliary
10
11       static const uint64 cc[];   // 16 "random" 64-bit primitive polynomials
12
13   public:
14       crc64(uint64 c=0)
15       {
16           if ( 0==c )  c = 0x1bULL; // =^= 64,4,3,1,0 (default)
17           init(c);
18       }
19
20       ~crc64()  {;}
```

```
21
22        void init(uint64 c)
23        {
24            c_ = c;
25            c_ >>= 1;
26            h_ = 1ULL<<63;
27            c_ |= h_;  // leading coefficient
28            reset();
29        }
30
31        void reset()  { set_a(~0ULL); }  // all ones
32        void set_a(uint64 a)  { a_=a; }
33
34        uint64 get_a()  const  { return a_; }
35        [--snip--]
```

Note that a nonzero initial state (member variable a) is used: starting with zero will only go to a nonzero state with the first nonzero bit in the input sequence. That is, input sequences differing only by initial runs of zeros would get the same CRC.

Individual bits can be fed into a CRC using the method bit_in(b), the lowest bit of the argument b is used:

```
1        [--snip--]
2        void shift()
3        {
4            bool s = (a_ & 1);
5            a_ >>= 1;
6            if ( 0!=s )  a_ ^= c_;
7        }
8
9        uint64 bit_in(unsigned char b)
10       {
11           a_ ^= (b&1);
12           shift();
13           return  a_;
14       }
15       [--snip--]
```

For checksumming a byte, we can do better than just feeding in the bits one by one:

```
1        [--snip--]
2        uint64 byte_in(unsigned char b)
3        {
4   #if 1
5            a_ ^= b;
6            shift();   shift();   shift();   shift();
7            shift();   shift();   shift();   shift();
8   #else  // identical but slower:
9            bit_in(b);  b>>=1;  // bit 0
10           bit_in(b);  b>>=1;  // bit 1
11           bit_in(b);  b>>=1;  // bit 2
12           bit_in(b);  b>>=1;  // bit 3
13           bit_in(b);  b>>=1;  // bit 4
14           bit_in(b);  b>>=1;  // bit 5
15           bit_in(b);  b>>=1;  // bit 6
16           bit_in(b);  b>>=1;  // bit 7
17   #endif
18           return  a_;
19       }
20       [--snip--]
```

The lower block implements the straightforward idea. The program [FXT: bits/crc64-demo.cc] computes the 64-bit CRC of a single byte in both ways.

Binary words are fed in byte by byte, starting from the lower end:

```
1        uint64 word_in(uint64 w)
2        {
3            ulong k = BYTES_PER_LONG_LONG;
4            while ( k-- )  { byte_in( (uchar)w );  w>>=8; }
5            return  a_;
6        }
```

To feed in a given number of bits of a word, use the following method:

```
1        uint64 bits_in(uint64 w, uchar k)
```

```
2      // Feed in the k lowest bits of w
3      {
4          if ( k&1 )  { a_ ^= (w&1);   w >>= 1;  shift(); }
5          k >>= 1;
6
7          if ( k&1 )  { a_ ^= (w&3);   w >>= 2;  shift();  shift(); }
8          k >>= 1;
9
10         if ( k&1 )  { a_ ^= (w&15);  w >>= 4;  shift();  shift();  shift();  shift(); }
11         k >>= 1;
12
13         while ( k-- )  { byte_in( (uchar)w );  w>>=8; }
14
15         return  a_;
16     }
```

The operation is the optimized equivalent to

```
while ( k-- )  { bit_in( (uchar)w );  w>>=1; }
```

If two sequences differ in a single block of up to 64 bits, their CRCs will be different. The probability that different sequences have the same CRC equals $2^{-64} \approx 5.42 \cdot 10^{-20}$. If that is not enough (and one does not want to write a CRC with more than 64 bits), then we can use two (or more) instances where different polynomials are used. Sixteen 'random' primitive polynomials are given [FXT: bits/crc64.cc] as static class member:

```
1      const uint64 crc64::cc[] = {
2          0x5a0127dd34af1e81ULL,   // [0]
3          0x4ef12e145d0e3ccdULL,   // [1]
4          0x16503f45acce9345ULL,   // [2]
5          0x24e8034491298b3fULL,   // [3]
6          0x9e4a8ad2261db8b1ULL,   // [4]
7          0xb199aecfbb17a13fULL,   // [5]
8          0x3f1fa2cc0dfbbf51ULL,   // [6]
9          0xfb6e45b2f694fb1fULL,   // [7]
10         0xd4597140a01d32edULL,   // [8]
11         0xbd08ba1a2d621bffULL,   // [9]
12         0xae2b680542730db1ULL,   // [10]
13         0x8ec06ec4a8fe8f6dULL,   // [11]
14         0xb89a2ecea2233001ULL,   // [12]
15         0x8b996e790b615ad1ULL,   // [13]
16         0x7eaef8397265e1f9ULL,   // [14]
17         0xf368ae22deecc7c3ULL,   // [15]
18     };
```

These are taken from the list [FXT: data/rand64-hex-primpoly.txt]. Initialize multiple CRCs as follows:

```
crc64 crca( crc64::cc[0] );
crc64 crcb( crc64::cc[1] );
```

A class for 32-bit CRCs is given in [FXT: `class crc32` in bits/crc32.h]. Its usage is completely equivalent.

The CRC can easily be implemented in hardware and is, for example, used to detect errors in hard disk blocks. When a block is written its CRC is computed and stored in an extra word. When the block is read, the CRC is computed from the data and compared to the stored CRC. A mismatch indicates an error.

One property that the CRC does not have is cryptographic security. It is possible to intentionally create a data set with a prescribed CRC. With *secure hashes* (like MD5 and SHA) it is (practically) not possible to do so. Secure hashes can be used to 'sign' data. Imagine you distribute a file (for example, a binary executable) over the Internet. You have to make sure that someone downloading the file (from any source) can verify that it is not an altered version (like, in the case of an executable, a malicious program). You create a (secure!) hash value which you publish on your web site. Any person can verify the authenticity of the file by computing the hash and comparing it to the published version.

The cryptographic security of hash functions like MD5 and SHA is the object of ongoing research, see [344], [50], and [51].

41.3.1 Optimization via lookup tables

To feed an n-bit word w into the CRC in one step (instead of n steps), do as follows: Add w to (the CRC word) a. Save the lowest n bits of the result to a variable x. Right shift a by n bits. Add to a the entry x of an auxiliary table t. For $n = 8$ the operation can be implemented as [FXT: class `tcrc64` in bits/tcrc64.h]:

```
1    uint64 byte_in(uchar b)
2    {
3        a_ ^= b;
4        uint64 x =  t_[a_ & 255];
5        a_ >>= 8;
6        a_ ^= x;
7        return  a_;
8    }
```

The size of the table t is $2^n = 256$ words. For $n = 1$ the table would have only two entries, 0 and c, the polynomial used. Then the implementation reduces to

```
1    uint64 bit_in(uchar b)
2    {
3        a_ ^= (b&1);
4        bool s = (a_ & 1);
5        a_ >>= 1;
6        if ( 0!=s )  a_ ^= c_;  // t[0]=0; t[1]=c_;
7        return  a_;
8    }
```

which is equivalent to the `bit_in()` routine of the unoptimized CRC.

The lookup table is computed with initialization:

```
1        for (ulong w=0; w<256; ++w)
2        {
3            set_a(0);
4            for (ulong k = 0; k<8; ++k)  bit_in( (uchar)w>>k );
5            t_[w] = a_;
6        }
```

The class can use tables of either 16 or 256 words. If a table of size 16 is used, the computation is about six times faster than with the non-optimized routine. A table of size 256 gives a speedup by a factor of twelve. Optimization techniques based on lookup tables are often used in practical applications, both in hardware and in software, see [73].

41.3.2 Parallel CRCs

A very fast method for checksumming is to compute the CRCs for each bit of the fed-in words in parallel. An array of 64 words is used [FXT: class `pcrc64` in bits/pcrc64.h]:

```
1    template <typename Type>
2    class pcrc64
3    // Parallel computation of 64-bit CRCs for each bit of the input words.
4    // Primitive polynomial used is x^64 + x^4 + x^3 + x^2 + 1
5    {
6    public:
7        Type x_[64];     // CRC data
8        // bit(i) of x_[0], x_[1], ..., x_[63] is a 64-bit CRC
9        //    of bit(i) of all input words
10       uint pos_;       // position of constant polynomial term
11       const uint m_;   // mask to compute mod 64
12
```

At initialization all words are set to all ones:

```
1    public:
2        pcrc64()
3            : m_(63)
4        {
5            reset();
6        }
7
8        ~pcrc64()  { ; }
9
```

```
10        void reset()
11        {
12            pos_ = 0;
13            Type ff = 0;  ff = ~ff;
14            for (uint k=0; k<64; ++k)  x_[k] = ff;
15        }
```

The cyclic shift of the array is avoided by working modulo 64 when feeding in words:

```
1         void word_in(Type w)
2         {
3             uint p = pos_;
4             pos_ = (p+1) & m_;
5             uint h = (p-1) & m_;
6             Type a = x_[p & m_];  // 0
7             p += 2;
8             a ^= x_[p & m_];  // 2
9             ++p;
10            a ^= x_[p & m_];  // 3
11            ++p;
12            a ^= x_[p & m_];  // 4
13            x_[h] = a ^ w;
14        }
```

The algorithm corresponds to the Fibonacci setup of the linear feedback shift registers (see section 41.2 on page 867). There is no primitive trinomial with degree a multiple of 8, so we use the pentanomial $x^{64} + x^4 + x^3 + x^2 + 1$. With an array size where a primitive trinomial exists the modulo computations would be more expensive. An unrolled routine can be used to feed in multiple words:

```
1         void words_in(Type *w, ulong n)
2         {
3             if ( n&1 )  { word_in(w[0]); ++w; }
4             n >>= 1;
5
6             if ( n&1 )  { word_in(w[0]); word_in(w[1]); w+=2; }
7             n >>= 1;
8
9             for (ulong k=0; k<n; ++k)
10            {
11                word_in(w[0]);
12                word_in(w[1]);
13                word_in(w[2]);
14                word_in(w[3]);
15                w += 4;
16            }
17        }
```

The program [FXT: bits/pcrc64-demo.cc] feeds the numbers up to a given value into a pcrc64<uint>:

```
int main()
{
    Type n = 32768;
    pcrc64<Type> P;
    for (Type k=0; k<n; ++k)  P.word_in(k);

    // print array P.x_[] here
}
```

This rather untypical type of input data illustrates the independence of the bits in the array x_[]:

The implementation can process about 2 GB of data per second when 64-bit types are used, 1 GB/s with 32-bit types, 500 MB/sec with 16-bit types, and about 230 MB/sec with 8-bit types.

41.4 Generating all revbin pairs

```
polynomial:  c       cr              c       cr
           1.1111  1111.1          1.1111  1111.1

      k:     x       xr       k:     x       xr
      1:  ....1   1....      17:  11...   ...11
      2:  1.111   111.1      18:  .11..   ..11.
      3:  111..   ..111      19:  ..11.   .11..
      4:  .111.   .111.      20:  ...11   11...
      5:  ..111   111..      21:  1.11.   .11.1
      6:  1.1..   ..1.1      22:  .1.11   11.1.
      7:  .1.1.   .1.1.      23:  1..1.   .1..1
      8:  ..1.1   1.1..      24:  .1..1   1..1.
      9:  1.1.1   1.1.1      25:  1..11   11..1
     10:  111.1   1.111      26:  1111.   .1111
     11:  11.1.   1..11      27:  .1111   1111.
     12:  11.11   11.11      28:  1....   ....1
     13:  11.1.   .1.11      29:  .1...   ...1.
     14:  .11.1   1.11.      30:  ..1..   ..1..
     15:  1...1   1...1      31:  ...1.   .1...
     16:  11111   11111      32:  ....1   1....  <--= initial pair
```

Figure 41.4-A: All nonzero 5-bit revbin pairs generated by an LFSR.

With a primitive polynomial of degree n and its reverse we can generate all nonzero pairs x and revbin(x,n) as follows [FXT: gf2n/lfsr-revbin-demo.cc]:

```
1    inline void revbin_next(ulong &x, ulong c, ulong &xr, ulong cr)
2    // if x and xr are (nonzero) n-bit words that are a revbin pair
3    // compute the next revbin pair.
4    // c must be a primitive polynomial, cr its reverse (the reciprocal polynomial).
5    {
6        ulong s =  ( x & 1UL );
7        x >>= 1;
8        xr <<= 1;
9        if ( s )
10       {
11           x  ^= (c>>1);
12           xr ^= (cr);
13       }
14   }
```

An equivalent technique for computing the revbin permutation (see section 2.6 on page 118) has been proposed in [264]. Figure 41.4-A shows all nonzero 5-bit revbin pairs generated with the primitive polynomial $c = x^5 + x^3 + x^2 + x + 1$ and its reverse.

41.5 The number of m-sequences and De Bruijn sequences

The shift register sequences generated with a polynomial of degree n is of maximal length if the polynomial is primitive. The corresponding shift register sequences are called *m-sequences*.

We now consider all sequences that are cyclic shifts of each other as the same sequence. For given n there are as many m-sequences as primitive polynomials ($P_n = \varphi(2^n - 1)/n$, see section 40.6 on page 843). These can be generated using the linear feedback shift registers described in section 41.1 on page 864.

One might suspect that using the powers of other elements than x might lead to additional m-sequences, but this is not the case. Further, the powers of elements of maximal order modulo irreducible non-primitive polynomials do not give additional m-sequences.

The program [FXT: gf2n/all-primpoly-srs-demo.cc] computes all m-sequences for a given n. The output for $n = 2, 3, 4, 5, 6$ is shown in figure 41.5-A.

```
degree = 2
c=111 :   .11

degree = 3
c=1.11 :   ..1.111
c=11.1 :   ..111.1

degree = 4
c=1..11 :   ...1..11.1.1111
c=11..1 :   ...1111.1.11..1

degree = 5
c=1..1.1 :   ....1..1.11..11111...11.111.1.1
c=1111.1 :   ....11..1..11111.111...1.1.11.1
c=11.111 :   ....111..11.11111.1...1..1.1.11
c=1.1111 :   ....1.11.1.1...111.11111.1..11
c=111.11 :   ....11.1.1...1.11111.11..111
c=1.1..1 :   ....1.1.111.11...11111..11.1..1

degree = 6
c=1....11 :   .....1....11...1.1..1111.1...111..1..1.11.111.11..11.1.1.111111
c=11..111 :   .....1111..1..1.1.1..11.1...1...1.11.111111.1.111../11..111.11
c=1.11.11 :   .....1.111111..1.1.1...1.11.111.1.11.1...1..1.....111
c=11.11.1 :   .....111....1..1..11.11..1.11.1.111.1111..11...1.1.1..111111.1
c=111..11 :   .....11.111...11...111.1.111111.11.1...1...1.11..1.1.1..1..1111
c=11....1 :   .....111111.1.1.11..11.111.11.1..1..111...1.1111..1.1...11....1
```

Figure 41.5-A: All m-sequences for $n = 2, 3, 4, 5$, and 6. Dots denote zeros.

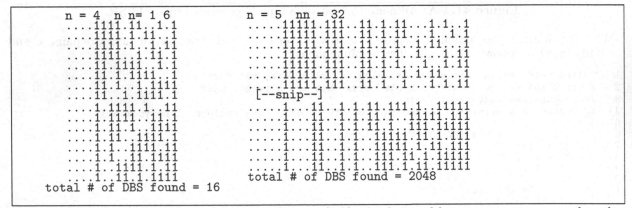

```
    n = 4  n n= 1 6          n = 5  nn = 32
    ....1111.11..1.1          ....11111.111..11.1.11...1.1..1
    ....1111.1.11..1          ....11111.111..11.1.11...1..1.1
    ....1111.1..1.11          ....11111.111..11.1.1...1.11...1
    ....1111..1.11.1          ....11111.111..11.1.1..1...1.11
    ....11.1111...1.1          ....11111.111..11.1.1...1.11..1
    ....11.1..1.1111          ....11111.111..11.1.1..1.1.11...1
    ....11..1.1111.1          ....11111.111..11.1.1...1.1.11
    ....11...1.1111.1          [--snip--]
    ....1.1111.1..11          .....1...11..1.1.11.111.1..11111
    ....1.1111..11.1          .....1...11..1.1.11.1...11111.111
    ....1.11.1...1111          .....1...11..1.1...11111.11.111
    ....1.11..1111.1          .....1...11..1.1...11111.111.111
    ....1.1..1111.11          .....1...11..1.1..11111.1.11.111
    ....1.1..11.1111          .....1...11..1.1...111.11.1.11111
    ....1..11.1.1111          .....1...11..1.1..111.11.1.11111
    .....1..11.1.1111         .....1...11..1.1...111.1.11.11111
 total # of DBS found = 16     total # of DBS found = 2048
```

Figure 41.5-B: All De Bruijn sequences for $n = 4$ (left), the first and last sequence correspond to the two m-sequences for $n = 4$. The first and last few De Bruijn sequences for $n = 5$ (right).

If a zero is inserted to the (unique) run of $n-1$ zeros in an m-sequence, then a *De Bruijn sequence* (DBS) is obtained. A DBS contains all binary words including the all-zero word.

For all $n \geq 4$ given there exist more DBSs than m-sequences. For example, for $n = 6$ there are 6 m-sequences and 67,108,864 DBSs. An exhaustive search for all DBSs of given length $L = 2^n$ is possible only for tiny n. The program [FXT: bits/all-dbs-demo.cc] finds all DBSs for $n = 3, 4, 5$. Its output with $n = 4$ and $n = 5$ (partly) is shown in figure 41.5-B.

The total number of DBSs equals

$$S_n = 2^x \quad \text{where} \quad x = 2^{n-1} - n \tag{41.5-1}$$

The two DBSs for $n = 3$ are [...111.1] and [...1.111]=[1.111...], reversed sequences are considered different by the formula. The first few values of S_n are shown in figure 41.5-C. The sequence is entry A016031 in [312]. We have $S_{n+1} = S_n^2 L_{n-1}$, equivalently $x_{n+1} = 2 x_n + n - 1$.

The general formula for the number of length-n base-m DBSs is $S_n = m!^{m^{n-1}}/m^n$, as given in [215, sect.7.2.1.1]. A graph theoretical proof of the formula for $m = 2$ can be found in [234, p.56], see also [358, entry "De Bruijn graph"]. For a more efficient approach to generate all DBSs of given length see section 20.2.2 on page 395.

$n:$	$L_n = 2^n$	$x = 2^{n-1} - n$	$S_n = 2^x$
1:	2	0	1
2:	4	0	1
3:	8	1	2
4:	16	4	16
5:	32	11	2,048
6:	64	26	67,108,864
7:	128	57	144,115,188,075,855,872
8:	256	120	1,329,227,995,784,915,872,903,807,060,280,344,576

Figure 41.5-C: The number S_n of DBSs of length L_n.

We note that there are several ways to generalize the idea of the De Bruijn cycles to *universal cycles* for combinatorial objects as described in [103]. An explicit construction for universal cycles for permutations is given in [293]. The problem of finding a rectangular pattern such that all different patterns of given size appear is discussed in [188]. De Bruijn sequences for words with forbidden substrings are discussed in [254].

41.6 Auto-correlation of m-sequences

```
 1:  [ .1..11.1.1111... ]  C= +15 -1 -1 -1 -1 -1 -1 -1 -1 -1 -1 -1 -1 -1 -1  <--=
 2:  [ .1..1111.1.11... ]  C= +15 -1 -1 -1 -1 +3 -5 -1 -1 -5 +3 -1 -1 -1 -1
 3:  [ .1.1..11.1111... ]  C= +15 -1 -1 -1 -1 +3 -5 -5 +3 -1 -1 -1 -1 -1 -1
 4:  [ .1.1..1111.11... ]  C= +15 -1 -1 -1 -1 +3 -1 -5 -5 -1 +3 -1 -1 -1 -1
 5:  [ .1.11..1111.1... ]  C= +15 -1 -1 -1 -1 -5 +3 -1 -1 +3 -5 -1 -1 -1 -1
 6:  [ .1.11.1..1111... ]  C= +15 -1 -1 -1 -9 -1 +3 +3 +3 +3 -1 -9 -1 -1 -1
 7:  [ .1.1111..11.1... ]  C= +15 -1 -1 -1 -1 -5 +3 -1 -1 +3 -5 -1 -1 -1 -1
 8:  [ .1.1111.1..11... ]  C= +15 -1 -1 -1 -1 -1 -5 +3 +3 -5 -1 -1 -1 -1 -1
 9:  [ .11..1111.11... ]   C= +15 -1 -1 -1 -1 -1 -5 +3 +3 -5 -1 -1 -1 -1 -1
10:  [ .11.1..1.1111... ]  C= +15 -1 -1 -1 -9 +3 -1 +3 +3 -1 +3 -9 -1 -1 -1
11:  [ .11.1.1111..1... ]  C= +15 -1 -1 -1 -1 +3 -5 -1 -1 -5 +3 -1 -1 -1 -1
12:  [ .11.1111..1.1... ]  C= +15 -1 -1 -1 -1 +3 -1 -5 -5 -1 +3 -1 -1 -1 -1
13:  [ .1111..1.11.1... ]  C= +15 -1 -1 -1 -9 -1 +3 +3 +3 +3 -1 -9 -1 -1 -1
14:  [ .1111.1..1.11... ]  C= +15 -1 -1 -1 -9 +3 -1 +3 +3 -1 +3 -9 -1 -1 -1
15:  [ .1111.1.11..1... ]  C= +15 -1 -1 -1 -1 -1 -1 -1 -1 -1 -1 -1 -1 -1 -1  <--=
16:  [ .1111.11..1.1... ]  C= +15 -1 -1 -1 -1 -1 +3 -5 -5 +3 -1 -1 -1 -1 -1
```

Figure 41.6-A: Cyclic auto-correlations for all truncated De Bruijn sequences for $n = 4$. Only first and the second last are m-sequences.

We have seen that a De Bruijn sequence (DBS) can be obtained from an m-sequence by inserting a single zero at the longest run of zeros. In the other direction, if we take a DBS and delete a zero from the longest run of zeros, then we get a sequence of length $N = 2^n - 1$ that contains every n-bit nonzero word. But these sequences are *not* m-sequences in general: most of them can not be generated with an n-bit LFSR and miss an important property of m-sequences.

For a sequence M of $N - 1$ zeros and ones define the sequence S via

$$S_k \quad := \quad \begin{cases} +1 & \text{if } M_k = 1 \\ -1 & \text{otherwise} \end{cases} \tag{41.6-1}$$

Then, if M is a length-L m-sequence, we have for the cyclic auto-correlation (or *auto-correlation function*, ACF) of S

$$C_\tau \quad := \quad \sum_{k=0}^{L-1} S_k\, S_{k+\tau \bmod L} = \begin{cases} L & \text{if } \tau = 0 \\ -1 & \text{otherwise} \end{cases} \tag{41.6-2}$$

where $L = N - 1$ and $N = 2^n$. That is, C_0 equals the length of the sequence, all other entries are of minimal absolute value: they cannot be zero because L is odd.

This property does not hold for most of the 'truncated' DBS (where one zero in the single run of n consecutive zeros is removed). Figure 41.6-A shows all (signed) truncated DBS for $n = 4$ and their auto-correlations. Only 2 out of the 16 truncated DBS have an auto-correlation satisfying relation 41.6-2 on the previous page, these are exactly the m-sequences for $n = 4$.

For every odd prime q there are sequences of length $L = q$ whose ACF satisfies

$$\sum_{k=0}^{L-1} S_k \, S_{k+\tau \bmod L} \;=\; \left\{ \begin{array}{ll} L-1 & \text{if } \tau = 0 \\ -1 & \text{otherwise} \end{array} \right. \tag{41.6-3}$$

The sequences start with a single zero: set $S_0 = 0$, and for $1 \le k < q$ set $S_k = 1$ if k is a square modulo q, else $S_k = -1$. A method to determine whether a number is a square modulo a prime is given in section 39.8 on page 781. The first three such sequences for primes of the form $4\,k+1$ and their ACFs are:

```
  5:   S: [0, +1, -1, -1, +1]
       C: [4, -1, -1, -1, -1]

 13:   S: [ 0, +1, -1, +1, +1, -1, -1, -1, -1, +1, +1, -1, +1]
       C: [12, -1, -1, -1, -1, -1, -1, -1, -1, -1, -1, -1, -1]

 17:   S: [ 0, +1, +1, -1, +1, -1, -1, -1, +1, +1, -1, -1, -1, +1, -1, +1, +1]
       C: [16, -1, -1, -1, -1, -1, -1, -1, -1, -1, -1, -1, -1, -1, -1, -1, -1]
```

With primes of the form $q = 4\,k+3$ we can construct a sequence of length $L = q$ satisfying relation 41.6-2 on the preceding page by simply setting $S_0 = 1$ ($S_0 = -1$ also works) in the sequence just constructed. The sequences for the first three primes $q = 4\,k+3$ and their ACFs are:

```
  3:   S: [+1, +1, -1]
       C: [ 3, -1, -1]

  7:   S: [+1, +1, +1, -1, +1, -1, -1]
       C: [ 7, -1, -1, -1, -1, -1, -1]

 11:   S: [+1, +1, -1, +1, +1, +1, -1, -1, -1, +1, -1]
       C: [11, -1, -1, -1, -1, -1, -1, -1, -1, -1, -1]
```

These sequences can be used for the construction of Hadamard matrices, see chapter 19 on page 384.

41.7 Feedback carry shift registers (FCSR)

There is an analogue of the LFSR in the modulo world, the *feedback carry shift register* (FCSR). With the LFSR we needed an irreducible ('prime') polynomial C where x has maximal order. The powers of x modulo C did run through all different (nonzero) words. Now take a prime c where 2 has maximal order (that is, 2 is primitive root modulo c, see section 39.5 on page 774). Then the powers of 2 modulo c run through all nonzero values less than c.

An implementation of an FCSR is [FXT: class fcsr in bpol/fcsr.h]:

```
1    class fcsr
2    {
3    public:
4        ulong a_;      // internal state (a_0*2**k modulo c),  1 <= a < c
5        ulong w_;      // word of the SRS,  1 <= w <= mask
6        ulong c_;      // a prime with primitive root 2, e.g. 37 = 1..1.1
7        ulong mask_;   // mask  e.g. (with above)    mask == 63 == 111111
8
9    public:
10       fcsr(ulong c)
11       {
12           c_ = c;
13           const ulong h = highest_one(c_);
14           mask_ = ( h | (h-1) );
15           set_a(1);
16       }
17
18       ~fcsr()  { ; }
19
20       ulong next()
21       {
22           a_ <<= 1;                    // a *= 2
```

```
        c = 1..1.1  = 37

            0 :    a= .....1 =      1      w= .1..11 =     19
            1 :    a= ....1. =      2      w= 1..11. =     38
            2 :    a= ...1.. =      4      w= ..11.. =     12
            3 :    a= ..1... =      8      w= .11... =     24
            4 :    a= .1.... =     16      w= 11.... =     48
            5 :    a= 1..... =     32      w= 1..... =     32
            6 :    a= .11.11 =     27      w= .....1 =      1
            7 :    a= .1...1 =     17      w= ....11 =      3
            8 :    a= 1...1. =     34      w= ...11. =      6
            9 :    a= .11111 =     31      w= ..11.1 =     13
           10 :    a= .11..1 =     25      w= .11.11 =     27
           11 :    a= ..11.1 =     13      w= 11.111 =     55
           12 :    a= .11.1. =     26      w= 1.111. =     46
           13 :    a= ..1111 =     15      w= .111.1 =     29
           14 :    a= .1111. =     30      w= 111.1. =     58
           15 :    a= .1.111 =     23      w= 11.1.1 =     53
           16 :    a= ..1.1 =      9      w= 1.1.11 =     43
           17 :    a= .1..1. =     18      w= .1.11. =     22
           18 :    a= 1..1.. =     36      w= 1..11. =     44
           19 :    a= 1...11 =     35      w= ..11..1 =     25
           20 :    a= 1....1 =     33      w= 11..11 =     51
           21 :    a= .111.1 =     29      w= 1..111 =     39
           22 :    a= .1.1.1 =     21      w= ..1111 =     15
           23 :    a= ...1.1 =      5      w= .11111 =     31
           24 :    a= ..1.1. =     10      w= 11111. =     62
           25 :    a= .1.1.. =     20      w= 1111.. =     60
           26 :    a= ....11 =      3      w= 111..1 =     57
           27 :    a= ...11. =      6      w= 11..1. =     50
           28 :    a= ..11.. =     12      w= 1..1.. =     36
           29 :    a= .11... =     24      w= ..1... =      8
           30 :    a= ..1.11 =     11      w= .1...1 =     17
           31 :    a= .1.11. =     22      w= 1...1. =     34
           32 :    a= ..1111 =      7      w= ..1.1 =      5
           33 :    a= ..1111 =     14      w= ..1.1. =     10
           34 :    a= .111.. =     28      w= .1.1.. =     20
           35 :    a= .1..11 =     19      w= 1.1..1 =     41

           36 :    a= .....1 =      1      w= .1..11 =     19  <-- period restarts
           37 :    a= ....1. =      2      w= 1..11. =     38
           38 :    a= ...1.. =      4      w= ..11.. =     12
```

Figure 41.7-A: Successive states of an FCSR with modulus $c = 37$.

```
23          if ( a_ > c_ )  a_ -= c_;   // reduce mod c
24
25          // update w:
26          w_ <<= 1;
27          w_ |= (a_ & 1);
28          w_ &= mask_;
29
30          return w_;
31      }
32
33      [--snip--]
34
35      void set_a(ulong a)
36      {
37          w_ = 0;
38          ulong t = c_;
39          while ( (t>>=1) )
40          {
41              if ( 0==(a & 1) )  a >>= 1;
42              else
43              {
44                  a = (a & c_) + ((a ^ c_) >> 1);
45              }
46          }
47          a_ = a;
48          next_w();
49      }
50
51      ulong get_a()  const  { return a_; }
52      ulong get_w()  const  { return w_; }
53  };
```

The routine corresponds to the Galois setup described (for the LFSR) in section 41.2 on page 867, see also [162]. Figure 41.7-A shows the successive states of an FCSR with modulus $c = 37$. It was created with the program [FXT: gf2n/fcsr-demo.cc]. Note that w does not run through all values $< c$ but through a subset of $c - 1$ distinct values $< 2^6$.

```
    x:   p prime with 2 a primitive root, 2**x < p < 2**(x+1)
    1:   3
    2:   5
    3:   11 13
    4:   19 29
    5:   37 53 59 61
    6:   67 83 101 107
    7:   131 139 149 163 173 179 181 197 211 227
    8:   269 293 317 347 349 373 379 389 419 421 443 461 467 491 509
    9:   523 541 547 557 563 587 613 619 653 659 661 677 701 709 757
         773 787 797 821 827 829 853 859 877 883 907 941 947 1019
   10:   1061 1091 1109 1117 1123 1171 1187 1213 1229 1237 1259 1277
         1283 1291 1301 1307 1373 1381 1427 1451 1453 1483 1493 1499
         1523 1531 1549 1571 1619 1621 1637 1667 1669 1693 1733 1741
         1747 1787 1861 1867 1877 1901 1907 1931 1949 1973 1979 1987
         1997 2027 2029
```

Figure 41.7-B: List of primes $p < 2048$ where 2 is s primitive root.

A list of all primes less than 2048 for which 2 is a primitive root is shown in figure 41.7-B. The shown sequence is entry A001122 in [312]. For further information on the correspondence between LFSR and FCSR see [208].

41.8   Linear hybrid cellular automata (LHCA)

Linear hybrid cellular automata (LHCA) are 1-dimensional cellular automata (with 0 and 1 the only possible states for each cell) where two different rules are applied dependent on the position, therefore the 'hybrid' in the name. The computation of the next state with an LHCA can be implemented as follows [FXT: bpol/lhca.h]:

```
1    inline ulong lhca_next(ulong x, ulong r, ulong m)
2    // LHCA := (1-dim) Linear Hybrid Cellular Automaton.
3    // Return next state (after x) of the LHCA with
4    // rule (defined by) r:
5    //    Rule 150 is applied for cells where r is one, rule 90 else.
6    //    Rule 150 := next(x) = x + leftbit(x) + rightbit(x)
7    //    Rule 90  := next(x) = leftbit(x) + rightbit(x)
8    // Length defined by m:
9    //    m has to be a burst of the n lowest bits (n: length of automaton)
10   {
11       r &= x;
12       ulong t = (x>>1) ^ (x<<1);
13       t ^= r;
14       t &= m;
15       return t;
16   }
```

Note that the routine is branch free and implementation in hardware is trivial.

The naming convention for the rules is as follows: draw a table of the eight possible states of a cell together with its neighbors, then draw the new states below:

```
XXX  XXO  XOX  XOO  OXX  OXO  OOX  OOO
 O    X    O    X    X    O    X    O
```

Now read the lower row as a binary number, the result equals $01011010_2 = 90$, so this is rule 90. Rule 150 corresponds to $10010110_2 = 150$:

```
XXX  XXO  XOX  XOO  OXX  OXO  OOX  OOO
 X    O    O    X    O    X    X    O
```

A run of successive values for the length-16 weight-2 rule vector $r = 4001_{16}$ starting with 1 is shown on the left side of figure 41.8-A. For certain rule vectors r all $m = 2^n - 1$ nonzero values occur, the period is maximal. This is demonstrated in [FXT: gf2n/lhca-demo.cc], which for $n = 5$ and rule $r = 1$ gives the output shown in the middle of figure 41.8-A. Rule vectors with minimal weight that lead to maximal period are given in [94]. The list in [FXT: bpol/lhcarule-minweight.cc] is taken from that source:

```
1    #define R1(n,s1)     (1UL<<s1)
2    #define R2(n,s1,s2)  (1UL<<s1) | (1UL<<s2)
```

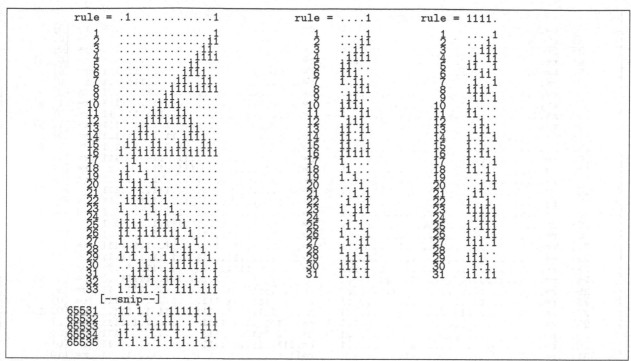

Figure 41.8-A: Partial run of a 16-bit LHCA (left) and complete runs of two 5-bit LHCAs (middle and right). The LHCAs shown have maximal periods.

```
3    extern const ulong minweight_lhca_rule[]=
4    // LHCA rules of minimum weight that lead to maximal period.
5    {
6           0,  // (empty)
7    R1(  1,  0),
8    R1(  2,  0),
9    R1(  3,  0),
10   R2(  4,  0, 2),
11   R1(  5,  0),
12   R1(  6,  0),
13   R1(  7,  2),
14   R2(  8,  1, 2),
15   R1(  9,  0),
16   R2( 10,  1, 6),
17   R1( 11,  0),
18   R2( 12,  2, 6),
19   R1( 13,  4),
20   [--snip--]
21   };
```

Up to $n = 500$ there is always a rule with weight at most 2 that leads to the maximal period. The full list of these rules is given in [FXT: data/minweight-lhca-rules.txt].

41.8.1 Conversion of LHCAs to binary polynomials

To convert a length-n LHCA to a binary polynomial proceed as follows: initialize $p_{-1} := 0$, $p_0 := 1$, and iterate for $k = 1, 2, \ldots, n$:

$$p_k \quad := \quad (x + r_{k-1})\, p_{k-1} + p_{k-2} \tag{41.8-1}$$

where r_i denotes bit i of rule r. The degree of the returned polynomial p_n is n. An implementation of the algorithm is [FXT: bpol/lhca.h]:

```
1    inline ulong lhca2poly(ulong r, ulong n)
2    // Return binary polynomial p that corresponds to the length-n LHCA rule r.
3    {
```

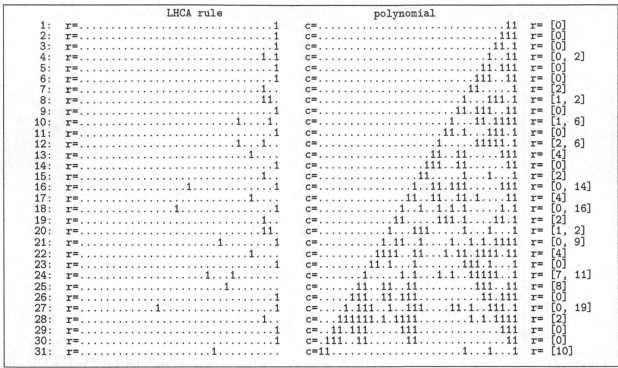

Figure 41.8-B: Minimum-weight LHCA rules and the corresponding binary polynomials.

```
4          ulong p2 = 0,  p1 = 1;
5          while ( n-- )
6          {
7              ulong m = r & 1;
8              r >>= 1;
9              ulong p = (p1<<1) ^ p2;
10             if ( m )  p ^= p1;
11             p2 = p1;  p1 = p;
12
13         }
14         return  p1;
15     }
```

The lexicographically first minimum-weight LHCA rules and their binary polynomials are shown in figure 41.8-B. The table was created by the program [FXT: gf2n/lhca2poly-demo.cc]. For rules of maximal period the polynomials are primitive.

An LHCA rule and its reverse give the identical polynomial. The polynomials corresponding to an LHCA rule and its complement are either both reducible or irreducible: if $p(x)$ corresponds to the LHCA rule r, then $p(x+1)$ corresponds to the rule that is the complement of r.

Figure 41.8-C shows a list of LHCA rules with maximal period where the highest bit lies in the lowest possible position. The list can be produced with [FXT: gf2n/lowbit-lhca-demo.cc]. For software implementation of LHCAs that need more than one machine word low-bit rules are advantageous. A table of low-bit LHCA rules corresponding to primitive polynomials up to $n = 400$ is given in [FXT: data/lowbit-lhca-rules.txt]. The maximal value of a rule that occurs is $r = 1293$ for $n = 380$ so the table can be stored compactly, for example, in an array of 16-bit integers.

Figure 41.8-D shows a list of LHCA rules that have minimal weight and the highest bit in the lowest possible position. The list can be produced with [FXT: gf2n/minweight-lowbit-lhca-demo.cc].

```
            LHCA rule                          polynomial
  1:  r=.............................1   c=.............................11  r= [0]
  2:  r=.............................1   c=............................111  r= [0]
  3:  r=.............................1   c=...........................11.1  r= [0]
  4:  r=...........................1.1   c=..........................1..11  r= [0, 2]
  5:  r=.............................1   c=.........................11.111  r= [0]
  6:  r=.............................1   c=........................111...11 r= [0]
  7:  r=............................1..  c=.......................11.....1  r= [2]
  8:  r=...........................11.   c=...................1...111.1     r= [1, 2]
  9:  r=.............................1   c=....................11.111..11   r= [0]
 10:  r=.........................1111   c=.................1.111111.11      r= [0, 1, 2, 3]
 11:  r=.............................1   c=.................11.1...111.1    r= [0]
 12:  r=.........................1.11   c=..................11.1.1....11    r= [1, 2, 4]
 13:  r=...........................1..1 c=................1.11..1.1111.1    r= [0, 3]
 14:  r=.............................1   c=..................111..11.....11 r= [0]
 15:  r=...........................1..   c=..............11.....1...1...1   r= [2]
 16:  r=.........................1.1.1   c=...........11.1..1111...1.111    r= [0, 2, 4]
 17:  r=............................11   c=..............1.1111..11......11 r= [0, 1]
 18:  r=.........................1.11.   c=...........11...11.1.1..1..1.1   r= [1, 2, 4]
 19:  r=...........................1..   c=...........11.....111.1....11.1  r= [2]
 20:  r=...........................11.   c=............1..111....1...1...1  r= [1, 2]
 21:  r=........................11..1.   c=........1111.11.1111.1...1.11.1  r= [1, 4, 5]
 22:  r=.........................1.11   c=.........11.1.111..11.11.11.1.11  r= [0, 1, 3]
 23:  r=.............................1   c=........11.1...1....111.1...1    r= [0]
 24:  r=........................1.111.   c=......1.1..1.1...11....1..1..1   r= [1, 2, 3, 5]
 25:  r=.........................1.11   c=.:....111....1.1..1.11.1....1.1   r= [0, 1, 3]
 26:  r=.............................1   c=....111..11.111........11.111    r= [0]
 27:  r=.......................111..   c=...1111.1.1111...1......1.1111     r= [2, 3, 4]
 28:  r=...........................1.   c=...111111.1.1111........1.1.1111  r= [2]
 29:  r=.............................1   c=..11.111.....111..........111    r= [0]
 30:  r=.............................1   c=.111..11......11..........11     r= [0]
 31:  r=.......................11.1.   c=11111.1....1.11.......1....1.11    r= [1, 3, 4]
```

Figure 41.8-C: Low-bit LHCA rules and the corresponding binary polynomials.

```
            LHCA rule                          polynomial
  1:  r=.............................1   c=.............................11  r= [0]
  2:  r=.............................1   c=............................111  r= [0]
  3:  r=.............................1   c=...........................11.1  r= [0]
  4:  r=...........................1.1   c=..........................1..11  r= [0, 2]
  5:  r=.............................1   c=.........................11.111  r= [0]
  6:  r=.............................1   c=........................111..11  r= [0]
  7:  r=...........................1..  c=....................11.....1      r= [2]
  8:  r=...........................11.   c=......................1...111.1  r= [1, 2]
  9:  r=.............................1   c=...................11.111..11    r= [0]
 10:  r=.......................1....1.   c=................1...11.1111       r= [1, 6]
 11:  r=.............................1   c=...................11.1...111.1  r= [0]
 12:  r=......................1...1..   c=.................1.....11111.1     r= [2, 6]
 13:  r=.....................1.          c=................11..11.....111   r= [4]
 14:  r=.............................1   c=..................111..11.....11 r= [0]
 15:  r=...........................1..  c=................11.....1...1...1  r= [2]
 16:  r=......................1.1....   c=.................1........111111  r= [4, 6]
 17:  r=......................1.....   c=..............11..11..11.1.....11  r= [4]
 18:  r=......................1...1.   c=..........1...11.11.1111111.1      r= [1, 5]
 19:  r=...........................1..  c=.............11.....111.1....11.1 r= [2]
 20:  r=...........................11.   c=.............1...111.....1...1...1 r= [1, 2]
 21:  r=.....................11.....   c=..........1.1...1.......1.1.1....1 r= [5, 6]
 22:  r=......................1.....   c=........1111...11...1.11.1111.11   r= [4]
 23:  r=.............................1   c=........11.1...1.......111.1...1 r= [0]
 24:  r=...................1...1.....   c=......1.....1.1...1.1..11111..1   r= [7, 11]
 25:  r=..................1.           c=......11..11..11.........111..11  r= [8]
 26:  r=.............................1   c=....111..11.111.........11.111   r= [0]
 27:  r=......................1..1..   c=......1.1....1..1..11111......1.1  r= [3, 6]
 28:  r=...........................1.   c=...111111.1.1111........1.1.1111  r= [2]
 29:  r=.............................1   c=..11.111.....111..........111    r= [0]
 30:  r=.............................1   c=.111..11......11..........11     r= [0]
 31:  r=..................1.......... c=11.....................1...1....1   r= [10]
```

Figure 41.8-D: Minimum-weight low-bit LHCA rules and the corresponding binary polynomials.

41.8.2   Conversion of irreducible binary polynomials to LHCAs

Computing the LHCA corresponding to an irreducible binary polynomial $p(x)$ proceeds in two steps. Firstly, the following quadratic equation over $GF(2^n)$ must be solved for Z:

$$Z^2 + (x^2 + x)\, p'(x)\, Z + 1 \;=\; 0 \quad \mathrm{mod}\, p(x) \tag{41.8-2}$$

The algorithm is given in section 42.4 on page 896. The second step is a GCD computation. Set $Z_{n-1} := p$, $Z_{n-2} := Z$, and compute successively $Z_{n-3}, Z_{n-4}, \ldots, Z_0$ such that

$$Z_{n-1} \;=\; (x + r_0)\, Z_{n-2} + Z_{n-3} \tag{41.8-3a}$$

$$Z_{n-2} \;=\; (x + r_1)\, Z_{n-3} + Z_{n-4} \tag{41.8-3b}$$

$$\vdots$$

$$Z_2 \;=\; (x + r_{n-3})\, Z_1 + 1 \tag{41.8-3c}$$

$$Z_1 \;=\; (x + r_{n-2})\, Z_0 + 1 \tag{41.8-3d}$$

$$Z_0 \;=\; (x + r_{n-1})\, 1 + 0 \tag{41.8-3e}$$

Each step consists of a computation of polynomial quotient and remainder (see section 40.1 on page 822). The vector $[r_{n-1}, r_{n-2}, \ldots, r_0]$ is the LHCA rule. An implementation of the method can be given as follows [FXT: bpol/bitpol2lhca.cc]:

```
1   ulong
2   poly2lhca(ulong p)
3   // Return LHCA rule corresponding to the binary polynomial P.
4   // Must have: P irreducible.
5   {
6       ulong dp = bitpol_deriv(p);
7       const ulong h = bitpol_h(p);
8
9       ulong b = dp;
10      b ^= bitpolmod_times_x(b, p, h); // p' * (x+1)
11      b = bitpolmod_times_x(b, p, h);  // p' * (x^2+x)
12
13      ulong r0, r1;  // solutions of  1 + (p'*(x*x+x))*z + z*z == 0 modulo p
14      bool q = bitpolmod_solve_quadratic(1, b, 1, r0, r1, p);
15      if ( 0==q )  return 0;
16
17      // GCD steps:
18      ulong r = 0;  // rule vector
19      ulong x = p,  y = r0;  // same result with r1
20      while ( y )
21      {
22          ulong tq, tr;
23          bitpol_divrem(x, y, tq, tr);
24          r <<= 1;
25          r |= (tq & 1);
26          x = y;
27          y = tr;
28      }
29
30  //     r = revbin(r, bitpol_deg(p));
31      return r;
32  }
```

The described algorithm is given in the very readable paper [93] which is recommended for further studies. Note that the paper uses the reversed rule. To use the reversed rule, uncomment the line just before the final return statement. The program [FXT: gf2n/poly2lhca-demo.cc] converts a given polynomial into the corresponding LHCA rule.

41.9   Additive linear hybrid cellular automata

The algorithm for the conversion of LHCA rules to binary polynomials is a special case of a general method for additive cellular automata. An automaton is called additive if, for all words a and b,

$$N(a) + N(b) \;=\; N(a + b) \tag{41.9-1}$$

where $N(x)$ is the next state after the state x and addition is bit-wise (XOR).

41.9.1 Conversion into binary polynomials

For additive automata the action of N on a binary word can be described by a matrix over GF(2): Let e_k be the word where only bit k is set. We seek the matrix whose k-th row is $N(e_k)$. We use a *cyclic LHCA* (CLHCA) as an example. A CLHCA is a LHCA with cyclic boundary condition. Its action N can be implemented as [FXT: bpol/clhca.h]

```
1    ulong clhca_next(ulong x, ulong r, ulong n)
2    {
3        r &= x;
4        ulong t = x ^ bit_rotate_right(x, 1, n);
5        t ^= r;
6        return t;
7    }
```

The action of a CLHCA with rule $r := [r_0, r_1, \ldots, r_{n-1}]$, as the matrix, is

$$
M_r := \begin{bmatrix}
\overline{r}_0 & & & & & & & 1 \\
1 & \overline{r}_1 & & & & & & \\
 & 1 & \overline{r}_2 & & & & & \\
 & & 1 & \overline{r}_3 & & & & \\
 & & & \ddots & \ddots & & & \\
 & & & & 1 & \overline{r}_{n-3} & & \\
 & & & & & 1 & \overline{r}_{n-2} & \\
 & & & & & & 1 & \overline{r}_{n-1}
\end{bmatrix}
\tag{41.9-2}
$$

where $\overline{r}_k$ is the complement of r_k and blank entries denote zero. The binary polynomial corresponding to the automaton is the characteristic polynomial of the matrix M_r:

```
1    inline ulong clhca2poly(ulong r, ulong n)
2    // Compute the binary polynomial corresponding to the length-n CLHCA with rule r.
3    {
4        ALLOCA(ulong, M, n);
5        for (ulong k=0; k<n; ++k)  M[k] = clhca_next( 1UL<<k, r, n );
6        ulong c = bitmat_charpoly(M, n);
7        return c;
8    }
```

To compute the polynomial for any additive automaton, replace `clhca_next()` by the update for the automaton. The routine `bitmat_charpoly()` is given in [FXT: bmat/bitmat-charpoly.cc], it uses an algorithm from [110, p.55].

41.9.2 Properties of the CLHCA

```
         r = .111     r = 1.11     r = 11.1     r = 111.

    1:     ...1         ...1         ...1         ...1
    2:     1...         1...         1...         1..1
    3:     11..         .1..         .1..         11.1
    4:     111.         .11.         ..1.         1111
    5:     1111         .111         ..11         111.
    6:     .111         1111         1.11         .111
    7:     1.11         1.11         1111         1.1.
    8:     .1.1         11.1         11.1         .1.1
    9:     1.1.         1.1.         111.         1.11
   10:     11.1         .1.1         .1.1         11..
   11:     .11.         111.         1.1.         .11.
   12:     ..11         ..11         .111         ..11
   13:     1..1         1..1         1..1         1...
   14:     .1..         11..         11..         .1..
   15:     ..1.         ..1.         .11.         ..1.
```

Figure 41.9-A: Rules of identical weight lead to essentially identical CLHCA: all tracks in the successive states of all weight-3 (length-4) automata are cyclic shifts of each other.

```
       k       r =   CLHCA rule              c = binary polynomial
       0:      r =   .................       c = 11.............1.
       1:      r =   ................1       c = 1.........1111111111111111.1
       2:      r =   ...............11       c = 11111111111111111.1
       3:      r =   ..............111       c = 1.1.1.1.1.1.1.1...1   P
       4:      r =   .............1111       c = 11..11..11..11...1
       5:      r =   ............11111       c = 1...1...1...1...1...1   P
       6:      r =   ...........111111       c = 1111....1111....1   P
       7:      r =   ..........1111111       c = 1.1.....1.1.....1
       8:      r =   .........11111111       c = 11.......11.......1
       9:      r =   ........111111111       c = 1.........1.......1
      10:      r =   .......1111111111       c = 11111111..........1
      11:      r =   ......11111111111       c = 1.1.1.1...........1   P
      12:      r =   .....111111111111       c = 11..11............1   P
      13:      r =   ....1111111111111       c = 1...1.............1
      14:      r =   ...11111111111111       c = 1111..............1   P
      15:      r =   ..111111111111111       c = 1.1...............1
      16:      r =   .1111111111111111       c = 11................1
      17:      r =   11111111111111111       c = 1.................1
```

Figure 41.9-B: Binary polynomials (right) corresponding to rule vectors for the length-17 cyclic linear hybrid cellular automata (left) with k bits set. Automata with maximal period are marked with 'P'.

```
       w=2:  r=...11           w=3:  r=..111           w=1:  r=....1
       1:      ...1            1:      ...1            1:      ...1
       2:     1....            2:     1....            2:     1....
       3:     11...            3:     11...            3:     11...
       4:     1.1..            4:     1.1..            4:     1.1..
       5:     1111.            5:     11.1.            5:     1111.
       6:     1..11            6:     1.1.1            6:     1...1
       7:     .1..1            7:     .1.1.            7:     .1...
       8:     111.             8:     .11.1            8:     .11..
       9:     1..1.            9:     1111.            9:     .1.1.
      10:     11..1           10:     1.111           10:     .1111
      11:     ..1..           11:     .1.11           11:     11...1
      12:     ..11.           12:     111.1           12:     ..1..
      13:     .111.           13:     ...11           13:     ..11.
      14:     1.111           14:     ...11           14:     .1.1
      15:     .1111           15:     1...1           15:     1.11.
      16:     11.11           16:     .1...           16:     111.1
      17:     ...1.           17:     .11..           17:     ...1.
      18:     1.11.           18:     .111.           18:     ;..11
      19:     11111           19:     .1111           19:     1..11
      20:     ;...11          20:     11111           20:     .1.11
      21:     1...1           21:     ...111          21:     11111
      22:     .1...           22:     1..11
      23:     .11..           23:     .1..1
      24:     .1.1.           24:     111..
      25:     .11.1           25:     1.11.
      26:     11.1.           26:     11.11
      27:     1.1.1           27:     ..1.1
      28:     .111.           28:     1..1.
      29:     .1.11           29:     11..1
      30:     111.1           30:     ...1..
      31:     ...1.           31:     ...1.
```

Figure 41.9-C: Successive states of the length-5 CLHCA with weights 2, 3, and 1 (left to right).

The polynomials for the given automata depend only on the number of bits set in the rule r. Figure 41.9-A shows the successive states for all length-4 CLHCA with rules of weight 3. As there are essentially only $n+1$ different automata of length n, we only need to investigate the rules with the lowest k bits set for $k = 0, 1, \ldots, n$. The polynomials for the length-17 automata are shown in figure 41.9-B. If we write $C_{n,k}(x)$ for the polynomial for the length-n rule with k set bits, then $C_{n,n-k}(x) = C_{n,k}(x+1)$. Indeed, they can be given in the closed form

$$C_{n,k}(x) \;=\; 1 + x^k \, (1+x)^{n-k} \tag{41.9-3}$$

Thus the polynomials can be computed with the simple routine [FXT: bpol/clhca.h]

```
1    inline ulong clhca2poly(ulong r, ulong n)
2    {
3        ulong c = 1UL << n;
4        for (ulong k=0; k<n; ++k)  if ( 0==(r & (1UL<<k)) )  c ^= (c>>1);
```

```
        n   w:        c = polynomial
        2   1:        c = 111
        3   1:        c = 1.11
        4   3:        c = 11..1
        5   2:        c = 1111.1
        6   1:        c = 11..111
        7   1:        c = 1.1.1.11
       [8]
        9   4:        c = 11..11...1
       10   3:        c = 1111111..1
       11   2:        c = 11......11.1
     [12,13,14]
       15   4:        c = 1111....1111...1
       [16]
       17   3:        c = 1.1.1.1.1.1.1.1..1
       18   7:        c = 1111....1111......1
       [19]
       20   3:        c = 11............11..1
       21   2:        c = 1111..........1111.1
       22  21:        c = 11..............1...1
       23   5:        c = 1.1............1.1....1
       [24]
       25   3:        c = 1.1.1.1........1.1.1.1..1
     [26,27]
       28   9:        c = 1111....1111....1111.....1
       29   2:        c = 1111....1111....1111....1111.1
       [30]
```

Figure 41.9-D: The polynomials (c, right) corresponding to rules of lowest weight (w) such that the length-n ($n \leq 30$) CLHCA has maximal period.

```
5        c ^= 1;
6        return c;
7    }
```

With $n = 5$ there are just two rules that lead to maximal periods, $r = [0, 0, 0, 1, 1]$ (weight 2) and $r = [0, 0, 1, 1, 1]$ (weight 3). The successive states for both rules are shown in figure 41.9-C. The polynomials corresponding to the rules of minimal weight for all length-n automata where $n \leq 30$ are given in figure 41.9-D. The sequence of values n where a primitive length-n CLHCA exists starts as:

2, 3, 4, 5, 6, 7, 9, 10, 11, 15, 17, 18, 20, 21, 22, 23, 25, 28, 29, 31, 33, 35, 36, 39, 41, 47, 49, 52, 55, 57, 58, 60, 63, ...

It coincides with entry A073726 in [312], values n such that there is a primitive trinomial of degree n. The sequence was computed with the program [FXT: gf2n/clhca-demo.cc]. A list of CLHCA rules with maximal period is given in [FXT: data/clhca-rules.txt].

Chapter 42

Binary finite fields: $\mathrm{GF}(2^n)$

We introduce the binary finite fields $\mathrm{GF}(2^n)$. The polynomial representation is used for stating some basic properties. The underlying arithmetical algorithms are given in chapter 40. An introduction of the representation by normal bases follows. Certain normal bases are advantageous for hardware implementations of the arithmetical algorithms. Finally, several ways of computing the number of irreducible binary normal polynomials are given.

Binary finite fields are important for applications like error correcting codes and cryptography.

42.1 Arithmetic and basic properties

In section 39.6 on page 776 we discussed the finite fields $\mathbb{Z}/p\mathbb{Z} = \mathrm{GF}(p)$ for p a prime. The 'GF' stands for *Galois Field*, another symbol often used is $\mathbb{F}_p$. The arithmetic in $\mathrm{GF}(p)$ is the arithmetic modulo p.

There are more finite fields: for every prime p there are fields with $Q = p^n$ elements for all $n \geq 1$. All elements in a finite field $\mathrm{GF}(p^n)$ can be represented as polynomials modulo a degree-n irreducible polynomial C with coefficients over the field $\mathrm{GF}(p)$. The arithmetic to be used is polynomial arithmetic modulo C. As in general there is more than one irreducible polynomial of degree n it might seem that there is more than one field $\mathrm{GF}(Q)$ for given $Q = p^n$. There isn't. Using different polynomials as modulus leads to isomorphic representations of the same field. The field $\mathrm{GF}(p^n)$ is called an *extension field* of $\mathrm{GF}(p)$. The field $\mathrm{GF}(p)$ is called the *ground field* (or *base field*) of $\mathrm{GF}(p^n)$.

When speaking about an element of $\mathrm{GF}(Q)$, think of a polynomial modulo some fixed irreducible polynomial C (modulus). For example, the product of two elements can be computed as the polynomial product modulo C. For the equivalent construction using the polynomial $x^2 + 1$ with real coefficients that leads to the complex numbers see section 39.12 on page 804.

The polynomial C used as modulus is called the *field polynomial*.

The elements zero, the neutral element of addition, and one, the neutral element of multiplication, are the constant polynomials with constant zero and one, respectively. This does not depend on the choice of the modulus.

Multiplication with an element of the ground field is called *scalar multiplication*. In this section an element of the ground field is denoted by u. Scalar multiplication corresponds to the multiplication of every coefficient of (the polynomial representing) the field element a by u.

We restrict our attention mostly to $Q = 2^n$, that is, the *binary finite field* $\mathrm{GF}(2^n)$ as we have seen the algorithms for the underlying arithmetic in chapter 40 on page 822.

42.1.1 Characteristic and linear functions

The *characteristic* of the field $\mathrm{GF}(p^n)$ is p: we identify two elements if their difference is a multiple of p (when adding any element of the field p times to 0 the result will be 0). For infinite fields such as $\mathbb{C}$ the characteristic is 0: two elements are identified if their difference is a multiple of 0 (that is, the underlying

J. Arndt, *Matters Computational: Ideas, Algorithms, Source Code,*
DOI 10.1007/978-3-642-14764-7_42, © Springer-Verlag Berlin Heidelberg 2011

equivalence relation is equality, see section 3.5.2.1 on page 149). Note that the notion "multiplication is repeated addition" is meaningless in an extension field $\mathrm{GF}(p^n)$.

For $\mathrm{GF}(p^n)$ we have

$$(u+v)^p = u^p + v^p \tag{42.1-1}$$

because the binomial coefficients $\binom{p}{k}$ are divisible by p for $k = 1, 2, \ldots, p-1$. For $\mathrm{GF}(2^n)$:

$$(u+v)^2 = u^2 + v^2 \tag{42.1-2}$$

We call a function f *linear* if the relation

$$f(u_1 \cdot a + u_2 \cdot b) = u_1 \cdot f(a) + u_2 \cdot f(b) \tag{42.1-3}$$

holds for u_1 and u_2 from the ground field. The linear functions in $\mathrm{GF}(p^n)$ are of the form

$$f(x) = \sum_{k=0}^{n-1} u_k \cdot x^{p^k} \tag{42.1-4}$$

where the u_k are again in the ground field. Linear functions can be computed using lookup tables. In $\mathrm{GF}(2^n)$ these are all functions of the form

$$f(x) = \sum_{k=0}^{n-1} u_k \cdot x^{2^k} \tag{42.1-5}$$

42.1.2 Squaring

Squaring (and raising to any power 2^k) is a linear operation in $\mathrm{GF}(2^n)$. The linearity can be used to accelerate the computation of squares. Write

$$\left(u_0 + u_1\,x + u_2\,x^2 + \ldots + u_{n-1}\,x^{n-1}\right)^2 = u_0 + u_1\,x^2 + u_2\,x^4 + \ldots + u_{n-1}\,x^{2\,(n-1)} \tag{42.1-6a}$$

$$=: u_0\,s_0 + u_1\,s_1 + u_2\,s_2 + \ldots u_{n-1}\,s_{n-1} \tag{42.1-6b}$$

One has to precompute the values $s_i = x^{2\,i} \bmod C$ for $i = 0, 1, 2, \ldots, n-1$. For successive square computations it is only necessary to add (that is, XOR) those s_i corresponding to nonzero u_i. For example, with $n = 13$ and the polynomial modulus $C = x^{13} + x^4 + x^3 + x^1 + 1$ one obtains the table

```
S0  = ...........:.1
S1  = .........:.1.:..
S2  = .......:.1.:....
S3  = .....:.1.:......
S4  = ...:.1.:........
S5  = .:.1.:..........
S6  = .1.:............
S7  = .........11.11.:
S8  = .......11.11....
S9  = .....11.11......
S10 = .:.11.11.:..:.11
S11 = .:.11.11.:.11.11
S12 = .11....:.1.11.1.
```

The squares $s_0, s_1 \ldots s_{\lfloor (n-1)/2 \rfloor}$ are simply $s_i = x^{2\,i}$ which can be used to further accelerate the computation.

42.1.3 Computation of the trace

The *trace* of an element u in $\mathrm{GF}(2^n)$ is defined as

$$\mathrm{Tr}(a) := a + a^2 + a^4 + a^8 + \ldots + a^{2^{n-1}} = \sum_{j=0}^{n-1} a^{2^j} \tag{42.1-7}$$

The trace of any element is either 0 or 1. The trace of 0 is always 0. The trace of 1 in $\mathrm{GF}(2^n)$ equals 1 for odd n, else 0, that is, $\mathrm{Tr}(1) = n \bmod 2$. Exactly half of the elements have trace 1.

The trace of the sum of two elements is the sum of the traces of the elements:

$$\mathrm{Tr}(a+b) \;=\; \mathrm{Tr}(a) + \mathrm{Tr}(b) \tag{42.1-8}$$

With u zero or one (an element of the ground field $\mathrm{GF}(2)$) we have

$$\mathrm{Tr}(u \cdot a) \;=\; u \cdot \mathrm{Tr}(a) \tag{42.1-9}$$

The trace function is linear: for u_1 and u_2 from the ground field we have

$$\mathrm{Tr}(u_1 \cdot a + u_2 \cdot b) \;=\; u_1 \cdot a + u_2 \cdot b \tag{42.1-10}$$

A fast algorithm to compute the trace uses the *trace vector*, a precomputed table $t_i = \mathrm{Tr}(x^i)$ for $i = 0, 1, 2, \ldots, n-1$, and the linearity of the trace

$$\mathrm{Tr}(u) \;=\; \sum_{i=0}^{n-1} u_i \, t_i \tag{42.1-11}$$

where the u_i are zero or one. Precompute the trace vector **tv** whose bits are the traces of the powers of x and later compute the trace of an element via [FXT: bpol/gf2n-trace.h]:

```
1    inline ulong gf2n_fast_trace(ulong a, ulong tv)
2    // Fast computation of the trace of a
3    //  using the pre-calculated table tv.
4    { return  parity( a & tv ); }  // scalar product over GF(2)
```

Given the trace vector it is also easy to find elements of trace zero or one by simply taking the lowest unset or set bit of the vector, respectively. There are polynomials such that the trace vector contains just one nonzero bit, see section 42.3.3 on page 896.

42.1.4 Inverse and square root

The number of elements in $\mathrm{GF}(Q)$ equals Q. For any element $a \in \mathrm{GF}(Q)$ one has

$$a^Q \;=\; a \tag{42.1-12}$$

and so $a^{Q-1} = 1$. So we can compute the *inverse* a^{-1} of a nonzero element a as

$$a^{-1} \;=\; a^{Q-2} \tag{42.1-13}$$

We have seen this technique of inversion by exponentiation in section 39.7.4 on page 781 for the special case $\mathrm{GF}(p)$.

All elements except zero are invertible in a field. That is, the number of invertible elements (units) in $\mathrm{GF}(Q)$ equals $|\mathrm{GF}(Q)^*| = Q - 1 = p^n - 1$.

Every element a of $\mathrm{GF}(2^n)$ has a unique *square root* s which can be computed as

$$s \;=\; a^{Q/2} \;=\; a^{2^{n-1}} \tag{42.1-14}$$

It can be computed by squaring the element $n-1$ times. But the square root is a linear function, so we can again apply table lookup methods. A method that uses the precomputed value $\sqrt{x}$ is described in [145]: for an element $a = \sum_k a_k \, x^k$ we have

$$\sqrt{a} \;=\; \sum_{k \text{ even}} a_k \, x^{k/2} + \sqrt{x} \sum_{k \text{ odd}} a_k \, x^{(k-1)/2} \tag{42.1-15}$$

The only nontrivial operation is the multiplication with $\sqrt{x}$. If the field polynomial is of the form $C = B^2 x + 1$, then $\sqrt{x} = B x$. If the polynomial B has low weight, then the multiplication by $\sqrt{x}$ is cheap. Moreover, no reduction by C is required when computing the product with $\sqrt{x}$ on the right side of relation 42.1-15, see [26]. Polynomials of this form also have a trace vector with only a single one, see section 42.3.3 on page 896.

Also every binary polynomial C can be expressed as $C = A^2 + x\,B^2$, so $\sqrt{x}$ can be computed via modular division as

$$\sqrt{x} \;=\; \frac{A}{B} \bmod C \tag{42.1-16}$$

The method given as relation 42.1-15 can be generalized for higher roots: for example, for the third root we have

$$\sqrt[3]{a} \;=\; S(0) + \sqrt[3]{x}\,S(1) + \left(\sqrt[3]{x}\right)^2 S(2) \tag{42.1-17a}$$
$$=\; S(0) + \sqrt[3]{x}\left[S(1) + \sqrt[3]{x}\,S(2)\right] \tag{42.1-17b}$$

where $S(m)$ is defined as

$$S(m) \;:=\; \sum_{k\equiv m \bmod 3} a_k\, x^{(k-m)/3} \tag{42.1-18}$$

42.1.5 Order and primitive roots

The *order* of an element a is the least positive exponent r such that $a^r = 1$. The maximal order of an element in $\mathrm{GF}(2^n)$ equals $2^n - 1 = Q - 1$. An element of maximal order is called a *generator* (or *primitive root*) as its powers 'generate' all nonzero elements in the field. The order of a given element a in $\mathrm{GF}(2^n)$ can be computed as follows (compare to section 39.7.1.2 on page 779):

```
1    function order(a, n)
2    {
3        if a==0 then   return 0  // a not a unit
4
5        h := 2**n - 1  // number of units
6        e := h
7        {np, p[], k[]} := factorization(h)  // h==product(i=0..np-1, p[i]**k[i])
8
9        for i:=0 to np-1
10       {
11           f := p[i]**k[i]
12           e := e / f
13           g1 := a**e  // modulo polynomial
14           while g1!=1
15           {
16               g1 := g1**p[i]  // modulo polynomial
17               e := e * p[i]
18               p[i] := p[i] - 1
19           }
20       }
21
22       return e
23   }
```

The C++ implementation is given in [FXT: bpol/gf2n-order.cc]:

```
1    ulong gf2n_order(ulong g, ulong c, ulong h, const factorization &mfact)
2    // Return order of g \in GF(2**n) with field polynomial c.
3    // c must be irreducible
4    // h must be equal 1<<(deg(c)-1)
5    // mfact must contain the factorization of 2**deg(c)-1
6    // The routine may loop if either:
7    //   - the polynomial c is reducible
8    //   - deg(g) >= deg(c)
9    //   - h is not set correctly
10   //   - mfact is not set correctly
11   {
12       if ( 0==g )  return 0;  // not in multiplicative group
13
14       ulong m = mfact.product();
```

```
15        ulong e = m;
16        for (int i=0; i<mfact.nprimes(); ++i)
17        {
18            long p = mfact.prime(i);
19            long f = mfact.primepow(i);
20
21            e /= f;
22
23            ulong g1 = bitpolmod_power(g, e, c, h);
24            while ( g1!=1 )
25            {
26                g1 = bitpolmod_power(g1, p, c, h);
27                e *= p;
28            }
29        }
30
31        return e;
32    }
```

Let a be an element of order r, then the order of a^k is

$$\text{ord}(a^k) \;=\; \frac{r}{\gcd(k,r)} \tag{42.1-19}$$

The order remains unchanged if $\gcd(k,r) = 1$. Let $N = 2^n - 1$ and g a generator of $GF(2^n)$. Then all $\varphi(N)$ generators are of the form g^k where $\gcd(k,N) = 1$. For N a (Mersenne) prime the order of all invertible elements except 1 is N.

42.1.6   Implementation

A C++ class for computations in the fields $GF(2^n)$ with n not greater than BITS_PER_LONG is [FXT: class GF2n in bpol/gf2n.h]:

```
1    class GF2n
2    // Implementation of binary finite fields GF(2**n)
3    // with the arithmetic operations.
4    {
5    public:
6        ulong v_;
```

The static (that is, class global) elements support the computations:

```
1    public:
2        static ulong n_;    // the 'n' in GF(2**n)
3        static ulong c_;    // polynomial modulus
4        static ulong h_;    // auxiliary bit-mask for computations
5        static ulong mm_;   // 2**n - 1 == max order (a Mersenne number)
6        static ulong g_;    // a generator (element of maximal order)
7        static ulong tv_;   // trace vector
8        static ulong sqr_tab[BITS_PER_LONG]; // table for fast squaring
9        static factorization mfact_; // factorization of max order
10       static char* pc_;   // chars to print zero and one: e.g.  "01" or ".1"
11       [--snip--]
12       static GF2n zero; // zero (neutral element wrt. addition) in GF(2**n)
13       static GF2n one;  // one (neutral element wrt. multiplication) in GF(2**n)
14       static GF2n tr1e; // an element with trace == 1
```

Note all data is public, making many methods 'get_something()' unnecessary. You can modify the data, but unless you know *exactly* what you are doing the results of subsequent computations are undefined. The constructors from other types are 'explicit' to avoid surprises:

```
1    public:
2        explicit GF2n()  { ; }
3        explicit GF2n(const ulong i) : v_(i & mm_)  { ; }
4        GF2n(const GF2n &g) : v_(g.v_)  { ; }
5        ~GF2n()  { ; }
```

One has to call the initializer before doing any computations [FXT: bpol/gf2n.cc]:

```
1    // if INIT_ASSERT is defined, asserts are C asserts,
2    // else init() returns false if one of the tests fail:
3    #define INIT_ASSERT
```

```
4
5    bool // static
6    GF2n::init(ulong n, ulong c/*=0*/, bool normalq/*=0*/, bool trustme/*=0*/)
7    // Initialize class GF(2**n) for 0<n<=BITS_PER_LONG.
8    // If an irreducible polynomial c is supplied it is used as modulus,
9    // else a primitive polynomial of degree n is used.
10   // Irreducibility of c is asserted.
11   // If normalq is set, then a primitive normal polynomial is used,
12   // if in addition c is supplied, then normality of c is asserted.
13   // If trustme is set, then the asserts are omitted.
14   {
15      [--snip--]
16          if ( n_ < BITS_PER_LONG )  // test only works for polynomials that fit into words
17          {
18              if ( ! trustme )
19              {
20   #ifdef INIT_ASSERT
21              jjassert( bitpol_irreducible_q(c_, h_) );
22   #else
23              if ( ! bitpol_irreducible_q(c_, h_) )  return false;
24   #endif
25          }
26      }
27      [--snip--]
28   }
```

```
     n = 4  GF(2^n)
     c = 1..11 == x^4 + x + 1  (polynomial modulus)
     mm= .1111   == 15  =  3 * 5  (maximal order)
     h = .1...  (aux. bit-mask)
     g = ...1.  (element of maximal order)
     tv= .1...  (traces of x^i)
   tr1e= .1...  (element with trace=1)

     k   :    f:=g**k  Tr(f)   ord(f)    f*f     sqrt(f)
     ...  :      ...1    0        1      ...1     ...1
     ...1 :      ..1.    0       15      .1..     :1.1
     ..1. :      .1..    0       15      ..11     ..1.
     ..11 :      1...    1        5      11..     1.1.
     .1.. :      ..11    0       15      .1.1     .1..
     .1.1 :      .11.    0        3      .111     .111
     .11. :      11..    1        5      1111     1...
     .111 :      1.11    1       15      1..1     111.
     1... :      .1.1    0       15      ..1.     ..11
     1..1 :      1.1.    1        5      1...     1111
     1.1. :      .111    0        3      .11.     ..11.
     1.11 :      111.    1       15      1.11     11.1
     11.. :      1111    1        5      1.1.     11..
     11.1 :      11.1    1       15      111.     1..1
     111. :      1..1    1       15      11.1     1.11
```

Figure 42.1-A: Powers of the generator $g = x$ in $GF(2^4)$ with a primitive polynomial modulus.

The class defines all the standard operators like the binary operators '+' and '-' (which are the same operation in $GF(2^n)$), '*' and '/', the comparison operators '==' and '!=', also the computation of inverse, powering, order, and trace. The algorithms used for the arithmetic operations are described in section 40.3 on page 832. We give the method for the inverse and the arithmetic shortcut operators as examples:

```
1    GF2n inv()  const
2    {
3        GF2n z;
4        z.v_ = bitpolmod_inverse(v_, GF2n::c_);
5        return z;
6    }
7    [--snip--]
8
9    friend inline GF2n & operator += (GF2n &z, const GF2n &f)
10   { z.v_ ^= f.v_;  return z; }
11
12   friend inline GF2n & operator -= (GF2n &z, const GF2n &f)
13   { z.v_ ^= f.v_;  return z; }
14
15   friend inline GF2n & operator *= (GF2n &z, const GF2n &f)
16   { z.v_ = bitpolmod_mult(z.v_, f.v_, GF2n::c_, GF2n::h_);  return z; }
17
```

```
      n = 4  GF(2^n)
      c = 11111 [normal] [NON-primitive]
        = =x ^ 4 x ^ 3 x 2 + x + 1  (polynomial modulus)
     mm= .1111   == 15 =  3 * 5  (maximal order)
      h = .1... (aux. bit-mask)
      g = ...11 (element of maximal order)
     tv= .111. (traces of x^i)
   tr1e= ...1. (element with trace=1)

      k  :      f:=g**k  Tr(f)    ord(f)       f*f      sqrt(f)
      ...1 :      ...1      0        1        ...1      ...1
      ...1 :      ..11      1       15        .1.1      1..1
      ..1. :      .1.1      1       15        111.      ..11
      ..11 :      1111      1        5        1...      .1..
      .1.. :      111.      1       15        1..1      .1.1
      .1.1 :      11.1      0        3        11..      11..
      .11. :      1...      1        5        ..1.      1111
      .111 :      .111      0       15        1.1.      1.11
      1... :      1..1      1       15        ..11      111.
      1..1 :      .1..      1        5        1111      ...1.
      1.1. :      11..      0        3        11.1      11.1
      1.11 :      1.11      0       15        .111      .11.
      11.. :      ..1.      1        5        1.11      11..
      11.1 :      .11.      0       15        1.11      1.1.
      111. :      1.1.      0       15        .11.      .111
```

Figure 42.1-B: Powers of the generator $x + 1$ in GF(2^4) with a non-primitive polynomial modulus.

```
18      friend inline GF2n & operator /= (GF2n &z, const GF2n &f)
19      { z *= f.inv();  return z; }
```

A simple demonstration of the class usage is the program [FXT: gf2n/gf2n-demo.cc]. It prints the successive powers of a primitive root, their squares and square roots. By default computations in GF(2^4) are shown, both for a primitive polynomial modulus (figure 42.1-A) and for a non-primitive polynomial modulus (figure 42.1-B).

42.2 Minimal polynomials

The *minimal polynomial* of an element a in GF(2^n) is defined as the polynomial of least degree which has a as a root. The minimal polynomial can be computed as the product

$$p_a(x) := \prod_{k=0}^{r-1} \left(x - a^{2^k} \right) \tag{42.2-1}$$

where r is the smallest positive integer such that $a^{2^r} = a$. The minimal polynomial of any element is irreducible and its degree is a divisor of n.

The zeros of the polynomial are $a, a^2, a^4, a^8, \ldots, a^{2^{r-1}}$. Note that $(a^{2^{r-1}})^2 = a$, that is, $p_a = p_{a^2} = p_{a^4} = \ldots = p_{a^{2^{r-1}}}$. The elements $a^2, a^4, \ldots$ are called the *conjugates* of a. For the field GF(p^n) the minimal polynomial has the form $\prod_{k=0}^{r-1} (x - a^{p^k})$.

It can be seen from the definition that the coefficients of the minimal polynomial lie in GF(2^n). However, all of them are either zero or one, they lie in GF(2). The computation has to be carried out using the arithmetic in GF(2^n) but the final result is a binary polynomial [FXT: bpol/gf2n-minpoly.cc]:

```
1   ulong gf2n_minpoly2(GF2n a, ulong &bp)
2   // Compute the minimal polynomial p(x) of a \in GF(2**n).
3   // Return the degree of p().
4   // The polynomial p() is written to bp
5   {
6       GF2n p[BITS_PER_LONG+1];
7       ulong n = GF2n::n_;
8       for (ulong k=0; k<=n; ++k)  p[k] = 0;
9       p[0] = 1;
10      ulong d;
```

```
n = 6  GF(2^n)
c = 1....11 == x^6 + x + 1  (polynomial modulus)
mm= .111111    == 63  =  3^2 * 7   (maximal order)

 k         :   f:=g**k  ord(f) Tr(f)  p:=minpoly(f)  deg(p)
 0 = ...... : .....1        1     0    ......11         1
 1 = .....1 : ....1.       63     0    .1....11         6
 2 = ....1. : ...1..       63     0    .1....11         6
 3 = ....11 : ..1...       21     0    .1.1.111         6   N
 4 = ...1.. : .1....       63     0    .1....11         6
 5 = ...1.1 : 1.....       63     1    .11..111         6
 6 = ...11. : ....11       21     0    .1.1.111         6   N
 7 = ...111 : ...11.        9     0    .1..1..1         6   N
 8 = ..1... : ..11..       63     0    .1....11         6
 9 = ..1..1 : .11...        7     0    ....11.1         3
10 = ..1.1. : 11....       63     1    .11..111         6
11 = ..1.11 : 1...11       63     1    .11.11.1         6
12 = ..11.. : ...1.1       21     0    .1.1.111         6   N
13 = ..11.1 : ..1.1.       63     0    .1.11.11         6
14 = ..111. : .1.1..        9     0    .1..1..1         6   N
15 = ..1111 : 1.1...       21     1    .111.1.1         6   N
16 = .1.... : .1..11       63     0    .1....11         6
17 = .1...1 : 1..11.       63     1    .11..111         6
18 = .1..1. : ..1111        7     0    ....11.1         3
19 = .1..11 : .1111.       63     0    .1.11.11         6
20 = .1.1.. : 1111..       63     1    .11..111         6
21 = .1.1.1 : 111.11        3     1    .....111         2
22 = .1.11. : 11.1.1       63     1    .11.11.1         6
23 = .1.111 : 1.1..1       63     1    .111..11         6
24 = .11... : .1...1       21     0    .1.1.111         6   N
25 = .11..1 : 1...1.       63     1    .11.11.1         6
26 = .11.1. : ...111       63     0    .1.11.11         6
27 = .11.11 : ..111.        7     0    ....1.11         3
28 = .111.. : .111..        9     0    .1..1..1         6   N
29 = .111.1 : 111...       63     1    .111..11         6
30 = .1111. : 11..11       21     1    .111.1.1         6   N
31 = .11111 : 1..1.1       63     1    .11....1         6
32 = 1..... : ..1..1       63     0    .1....11         6
33 = 1....1 : .1..1.       21     0    .1.1.111         6   N
34 = 1...1. : 1..1..       63     1    .11..111         6
35 = 1...11 : ..1.11        9     0    .1..1..1         6   N
36 = 1..1.. : .1.11.        7     0    ....11.1         3
37 = 1..1.1 : 1.11..       63     1    .11.11.1         6
38 = 1..11. : .11.11       63     0    .1.11.11         6
39 = 1..111 : 11.11.       21     1    .111.1.1         6   N
40 = 1.1... : 1.1111       63     1    .11..111         6
41 = 1.1..1 : .111.1       63     0    .1.11.11         6
42 = 1.1.1. : 111.1.        3     1    .....111         2
43 = 1.1.11 : 11.111       63     1    .111..11         6
44 = 1.11.. : 1.11.1       63     1    .11.11.1         6
45 = 1.11.1 : .11..1        7     0    ....1.11         3
46 = 1.111. : 11..1.       63     1    .111..11         6
47 = 1.1111 : 1..111       63     1    .11....1         6
48 = 11.... : ..11.1       21     0    .1.1.111         6   N
49 = 11...1 : .11.1.        9     0    .1..1..1         6   N
50 = 11..1. : 11.1..       63     1    .11.11.1         6
51 = 11..11 : 1.1.11       21     1    .111.1.1         6   N
52 = 11.1.. : .1.1.1       63     0    .1.11.11         6
53 = 11.1.1 : 1.1.1.       63     1    .111..11         6
54 = 11.11. : .1.111        7     0    ....1.11         3
55 = 11.111 : 1.111.       63     1    .11....1         6
56 = 111... : .11111        9     0    .1..1..1         6   N
57 = 111..1 : 11111.       21     1    .111.1.1         6   N
58 = 111.1. : 111111       63     1    .111..11         6
59 = 111.11 : 1111.1       63     1    .11....1         6
60 = 1111.. : 111..1       21     1    .111.1.1         6   N
61 = 1111.1 : 11...1       63     1    .11....1         6
62 = 11111. : 1....1       63     1    .11....1         6
```

Figure 42.2-A: Minimal polynomials of the powers of a generator in GF(2^6). Polynomials of degree $n = 6$ that are non-primitive are marked with an 'N'. The trace of an element equals the coefficient of x^{n-1} of its minimal polynomial.

```
11          GF2n s = a;
12          for (d=1; d<=n; ++d)
13          {
14              for (ulong k=d; 0!=k; --k)  p[k] = p[k-1];
15              p[0] = 0;
16              for (ulong k=0; k<d; ++k)  p[k] += p[k+1] * s;
17              s = s.sqr();
18              if ( s == a )  break;
19          }
20
21          // Here all coefficients are either zero or one,
22          //  so we can fill them into a binary word:
23          ulong p2 = 0;
24          for (ulong j=0; j<=d; ++j)  p2 |= (p[j].v_ << j);
25          bp = p2;
26
27          return  d;
28      }
```

The algorithm needs $O(n^2)$ space. An algorithm requiring only space $O(n)$ is given in [161]. Compute the element $m_a \in GF(2^n)$ as

$$m_a \quad := \quad \prod_{k=0}^{r-1} \left(x - a^{2^k} \right) \tag{42.2-2}$$

where x is a root of the field polynomial and r is the smallest positive integer such that $a^{2^r} = a$. If $r = \deg(c)$ then return $m_a + c$, otherwise return m_a. The returned value has to interpreted as a polynomial. An implementation is

```
1   ulong
2   gf2n_minpoly(GF2n a, ulong &bp)
3   {
4       if ( a.v_ < 2 )  { bp = 2 ^ a.v_;  return 1; }
5
6       const GF2n x(2UL);  // a root of the polynomial GF2n::c_
7       GF2n s = a;
8       GF2n m(1UL);  // minpoly
9       ulong d = 0;  // degree
10      do
11      {
12          m *= (x - s);  // x - a^(2^d)
13          ++d;
14          s = s.sqr();
15      }
16      while ( s != a );
17
18      if ( d==GF2n::n_ )  m.v_ ^= GF2n::c_;
19      bp = m.v_;
20
21      return  d;
22  }
```

Versions of the routines that do not depend on the class GF2n are given in [FXT: bpol/bitpolmod-minpoly.cc]. The program [FXT: gf2n/gf2n-minpoly-demo.cc] prints the minimal polynomials for the powers of a primitive element g, see figure 42.2-A. The polynomials (of maximal degree) that are non-primitive are marked by an 'N'. The minimal polynomials for g^k are non-primitive or of degree $< n$ whenever $\gcd(k, 2^n - 1) \neq 1$.

Let C be an irreducible polynomial of degree n and a an element such that $r = \mathrm{ord}_C(a)$ is the order of a modulo C. Then the order of x modulo the minimal polynomial of a is also r. Thus a primitive polynomial can be determined from an irreducible polynomial C and a generator g modulo C by computing the minimal polynomial of g.

With a primitive polynomial (and the generator $g = x$) the minimal polynomial of the element x^k is primitive if k is a Lyndon word and $\gcd(k, n) = 1$. With a fast algorithm for the generation of Lyndon words we can therefore generate all primitive polynomials as shown in section 40.10 on page 856.

42.3 Fast computation of the trace vector

We give two methods for the computation of the trace vector and some properties of the trace vector for certain field polynomials.

42.3.1 Computation via Newton's formula

Let $C(x)$ be a polynomial with n roots $a_0, a_1, \ldots, a_{n-1}$

$$C(x) = \prod_{k=0}^{n-1} (x - a_k) = \sum_{k=0}^{n} c_k \, x^k \qquad (42.3\text{-}1)$$

Following [335, sec.32] we define

$$s_k := a_0^k + a_1^k + \ldots + a_{n-1}^k \qquad (42.3\text{-}2)$$

Then, for $m = 1, \ldots, n$, we have *Newton's formula*:

$$m \, c_{n-m} = -\sum_{j=0}^{m-1} s_{m-j} \, c_{n-j} \qquad (42.3\text{-}3)$$

Now let $C = c_0 + c_1 \, x + c_2 \, x^2 + \ldots + c_n \, x^n$ be an irreducible polynomial with coefficients in $\mathrm{GF}(p)$. Its roots are a, (and the conjugates) $a^p, a^{p^2}, a^{p^3}, \ldots, a^{p^{n-1}}$. Let $t_0 = n$ and $t_i = \mathrm{Tr}(a^i)$ (computationally x is a root of C, so $t_i = \mathrm{Tr}(x^i)$). Note that $t_0, \ldots, t_{n-1}$ are the elements of the trace vector, see relation 42.1-11 on page 888. Using $c_n = 1$ (monic polynomial C) and $t_j = s_j$ we rewrite Newton's formula as

$$t_1 = -1 \, c_{n-1} \qquad (42.3\text{-}4\text{a})$$
$$t_2 = -c_{n-1} t_1 - 2 \, c_{n-2} \qquad (42.3\text{-}4\text{b})$$
$$t_3 = -c_{n-1} t_2 - c_{n-2} t_1 - 3 \, c_{n-3} \qquad (42.3\text{-}4\text{c})$$
$$t_4 = -c_{n-1} t_3 - c_{n-2} t_2 - c_{n-3} t_1 - 4 \, c_{n-4} \qquad (42.3\text{-}4\text{d})$$
$$t_5 = -c_{n-1} t_4 - c_{n-2} t_3 - c_{n-3} t_2 - c_{n-4} t_1 - 5 \, c_{n-5} \qquad (42.3\text{-}4\text{e})$$
$$\vdots$$
$$t_k = -c_{n-1} t_{k-1} - c_{n-2} t_{k-2} - \ldots - c_{n-k-1} t_1 - k \, c_{n-k} \qquad (42.3\text{-}4\text{f})$$

To compute the trace vector for the field $\mathrm{GF}(p^n)$, make the assignments in the given order, and finally compute $t_0 = n \bmod p$. The computation does not involve any polynomial modular reduction so the method can be worthwhile even for the determination of the trace of just one element.

With binary finite fields, the components with even subscripts can be computed as $t_{2k} = t_k$. During the computation we set $t_0 = 0$ and correct the value at the end of the routine. An implementation of the implied algorithm is [FXT: bpol/gf2n-trace.cc]:

```
1    ulong gf2n_trace_vector_x(ulong c, ulong n)
2    // Return vector of traces of powers of x, where
3    //   x is a root of the irreducible polynomial C.
4    // Must have:  n == degree(C)
5    {
6        c &= ~( 2UL<<(n-1) );  // remove coefficient c[n]
7
8        ulong t = 1;  // set t[0]=1, will be corrected at the end
9        for (ulong k=1; k<n; ++k)
10       {
11           if ( k & 1 )  // k odd: use recursion
12           {
13               ulong cv = c >> (n-k);  // polynomials coefficients [n-1]..[n-k]
14               cv &= t;                // vector (j=1, k,   c[n-j]*t[k-j])
15               cv = parity(cv);        //     sum (j=1, k,   c[n-j]*t[k-j])
```

```
16                t |=  (cv<<k);
17           }
18           else  // k even:  copy t[k/2] to t[k]
19           {
20                t |= ( (t>>(k/2)) & 1 ) << k;
21           }
22      }
23
24      // correct t[0]:
25      t ^= ((n+1)&1);   // change low bit if n is even
26
27      return t;
28  }
```

The routine involves n computations of the parity. The equivalent routine for large n is $O(n^2)$ (n computations of sums with $O(n)$ summands).

42.3.2   Computation via division of power series

The following variant of the algorithm, suggested by Richard Brent [priv. comm.], shows that the computation is equivalent to a division of power series. Let R be the reciprocal polynomial of C, then (see [76, p.135])

$$\log\left(R(x)\right) \;=\; -\sum_{j=1}^{\infty} t_j\, x^j / j \tag{42.3-5}$$

Differentiating both sides gives

$$\frac{R'(x)}{R(x)} \;=\; -\sum_{j=1}^{\infty} t_j\, x^{j-1} \tag{42.3-6}$$

When using Newton's method for the inversion we have a computational cost of $\gamma M(n)$ where $M(n)$ is the cost for the multiplication of two power series up to order x^n and γ is a constant (the method is also given in [153, p.24]). The constant γ equals 3 if the division is done by one inversion, which is two multiplications with the second order Newton iteration, and one final multiplication with $R'(x)$, see section 29.1.1 on page 567. For large n the multiplications should be done by either one of the splitting schemes suggested in [59] or by FFT methods such as given in [303].

42.3.3   Some properties of the trace vector

For a binary polynomial C of odd degree n and all nonzero coefficients c_i at odd indices i we obtain $t_0 = 1$ and $t_i = 0$ for all $i \neq 0$, so the trace of any element is just the value of its lowest bit. In [57] it is shown that for $n \equiv \pm 3 \bmod 8$ the first nonzero coefficient c_k (with $k < n$) must appear at a position $k \geq n/3$.

With even degree and all nonzero odd coefficients c_i, c_j, c_k, ... at positions $i, j, k, \cdots < n/2$ the only nonzero components of the trace vector are t_{n-i}, t_{n-j}, t_{n-k}, ... Thus polynomials of even degree with just one nonzero coefficient c_k where $k < n/2$ lead to only t_{n-k} being nonzero. A special case are trinomials $C = x^n + x^k + 1$ of even degree n and $k < n/2$ (k must be odd else C is reducible). In the trace vector for all-ones polynomials ($C = \sum_{k=0}^{n} x^k$, see section 40.9.9 on page 852) the only zero component is t_0. A detailed discussion of the properties of the trace vector is given in [5].

42.4   Solving quadratic equations

We want to solve, in GF(2^n), the equation

$$a\, x^2 + b\, x + c \;=\; 0 \tag{42.4-1}$$

Extracting a square root of an arbitrary element in GF(2^n) is easy, but this does not enable us to solve the given equation. The formula $r_{0,1} = \left(-b \pm \sqrt{b^2 - 4ac}\right)/(2a)$ that works fine for real and complex numbers is of no help here: how should we divide by 2?

```
       n = 5   GF(2^n)
       c = 1..1.1 == x^5 + x^2 + 1   (polynomial modulus)
       mm= .11111   == 31 (prime)    (maximal order)
       h = .1.... (aux. bit-mask)
       g = ....1. (element of maximal order)
       tv= ..1..1 (traces of x^i)
     tr1e= .....1 (element with trace=1)

       k:   f:=g**k  Tr(f)    RootOf(z^2+z=f)
       0:   ....1    1
       1:   ...1.    0        .1..1
       2:   ..1..    0        .1.11
       3:   .1...    1
       4:   1....    0        .1111
       5:   ..1.1    1
       6:   .1.1.    1
       7:   1.1..    0        ....1
       8:   .11.1    0        11111
       9:   11.1.    1
      10:   1..1.    1
      11:   ..111    1
      12:   .111.    1
      13:   111..    1
      14:   111.1    0        1....
      15:   11111    0        11..1
      16:   11.11    0        1..1.
      17:   1..11    1
      18:   ...11    1
      19:   ..11.    0        ...1.
      20:   .11..    1
      21:   11...    1
      22:   1.1.1    1
      23:   .1111    1        1.11.
      24:   1111.    1
      25:   11..1    0        11.11
      26:   1.111    1
      27:   .1.11    0        111.1
      28:   1.11.    0        .11.1
      29:   .1..1    0        1.1..
      30:   1..1.    0        ..11.
```

Figure 42.4-A: Solutions of the equation $z^2 + z = f$ for all elements $f \in \mathrm{GF}(2^5)$ with trace zero.

Instead we transform the equation into a special form: divide by a: $x^2 + (b/a)\,x + (c/a) = 0$, substitute $x = z\,(b/a)$ to get $z^2\,(b/a)^2 + (b/a)^2\,z + (c/a) = 0$, and divide by $(b/a)^2$ to obtain

$$z^2 + z + C = 0 \quad \text{where} \quad C = \frac{a\,c}{b^2} \tag{42.4-2}$$

If r_0 is one solution of this equation, then $r_1 = r_0 + 1$ is the other one: $z\,(z+1) = C$. The equation does not necessarily have a solution at all: the trace of C must be zero because we have $\mathrm{Tr}(C) = \mathrm{Tr}(z^2 + z) = \mathrm{Tr}(z^2) + \mathrm{Tr}(z) = \mathrm{Tr}(z) + \mathrm{Tr}(z) = 0$ for all $z \in \mathrm{GF}(2^n)$.

The following function checks whether the reduced equation has a solution and if so, returns true and writes one solution to the variable r [FXT: bpol/gf2n-solvequadratic.cc]:

```
1   bool gf2n_solve_reduced_quadratic(GF2n c, GF2n& r)
2   // Solve  z^2 + z == c
3   {
4       if ( 1==c.trace() )  return  false;
5
6       GF2n t( GF2n::tr1e );
7       GF2n z( GF2n::zero );
8       GF2n u( t );
9       for (ulong j=1; j<GF2n::n_; ++j)
10      {
11          GF2n u2 = u.sqr();
12          z = z.sqr();   z += u2*c;   // z = z*z + c*u*u
13          u = u2 + t;                 // u = u*u + t
14      }
15      r = z;
16
17      return  true;
18  }
```

```
------ k=1: ------
    u=t^2 + t
    z=c*t^2
  z^2=c^2*t^4
z^2+z=c^2*t^4 + c*t^2

------ k=2: ------
    u=t^4 + t^2 + t
    z=(c^2 + c)*t^4 + c*t^2
  z^2=(c^4 + c^2)*t^8 + c^2*t^4
z^2+z=(c^4 + c^2)*t^8 + c*t^4 + c*t^2

------ k=3: ------
    u=t^8 + t^4 + t^2 + t
    z=(c^4 + c^2 + c)*t^8 + (c^2 + c)*t^4 + c*t^2
  z^2=(c^8 + c^4 + c^2)*t^16 + (c^4 + c^2)*t^8 + c^2*t^4
z^2+z=(c^8 + c^4 + c^2)*t^16 + c*t^8 + c*t^4 + c*t^2
     =(c^8 + c^4 + c^2)*t    + c*(t^8 + t^4 + t^2)    [using t^16=t]
     =( c + trace(c)  )*t    + c*( t + trace(t) )     [using x^8+x^4+x^2=x+trace(x)]
     = (c + 0  ) * t   + c * ( t + 1 )                [using trace(c)=0, trace(t)=1]
     =                          c                     [ z^2+z==c ]
```

Figure 42.4-B: Solving the reduced quadratic equation $z^2 + z = c$ in GF(2^4).

Figure 42.4-A shows the solutions to the reduced equations $x^2 + x = f$ for all elements f with trace zero [FXT: gf2n/gf2n-solvequadratic-demo.cc].

The implementation of the algorithm takes advantage of a precomputed element with trace one. At the end of step $k \geq 1$ we have

$$u_k = \sum_{j=0}^{k} t^{2^k} \tag{42.4-3a}$$

$$z_k = \sum_{j=0}^{k-1} \left[t^{2^k} \sum_{i=0}^{k-1} c^{2^i} \right] \tag{42.4-3b}$$

Figure 42.4-B shows (for GF(2^4)) that this expression is the solution sought.

For GF(2^n) with n odd the solution of the reduced quadratic equation $z^2 + z = A$ can be computed via the *half-trace* of A which is defined as

$$H(A) = A + A^4 + A^{16} + \ldots + A^{4^{(n-1)/2}} \tag{42.4-4}$$

We have $H(A)^2 + H(A) = \mathrm{Tr}(A) + A$, so $H(A)$ is a solution of the reduced quadratic if $\mathrm{Tr}(A) = 0$. The half-trace of an element A in the field with field polynomial C can be computed as follows [FXT: bpol/gf2n-trace.cc]:

```
1   ulong
2   gf2n_half_trace(ulong a, ulong c, ulong h)
3   {
4       ulong t = a;
5       ulong d = h;
6       while ( d>>=2 )
7       {
8           t = bitpolmod_square(t, c, h);
9           t = bitpolmod_square(t, c, h);
10          t ^= a;
11      }
12      return  t;
13  }
```

The following routine computes both solutions. It transforms the equation into the reduced form, solves it, and finally transforms back [FXT: bpol/gf2n-solvequadratic.cc]:

```
1   bool gf2n_solve_quadratic(GF2n a, GF2n b, GF2n c, GF2n& r0, GF2n& r1)
2   // Solve  a*x^2 + b*x + c == 0
3   // Return  whether solutions exist.
```

```
4    // If so, the solutions are written to r0 and r1.
5    {
6        GF2n cc = a*c;
7        cc /= (b.sqr());   // cc = (a*c)/(b*b)
8        GF2n r;
9        bool q = gf2n_solve_reduced_quadratic(cc, r);
10       if ( !q ) return  false;
11
12       GF2n s = b / a;
13       r0 = r * s;
14       r1 = (r+GF2n::one) * s;
15
16       return  true;
17   }
```

Routines for the solution of quadratic equations that do not depend on the class `GF2n` are given in [FXT: bpol/bitpolmod-solvequadratic.cc].

42.5 Representation by matrices ‡

```
    n = 4  GF(2^n)
    c = 1..11 == x^4 + x + 1   (polynomial modulus)

    k:   f:=g**k
    0:   ...1
    1:   ..1.
    2:   .1..        1...1..11.1.111
    3:   1...        .1..11.1.1111
    4:   ..11        ..1..11.1.1111.
    5:   .11.        ...1..11.1.1111
    6:   11..
    7:   1.11
    8:   .1.1        M_0 =   M_1 =   M_2 =   M_3 =   M_4 =   M_5 =
    9:   1.1.        1...    ...1    ..11    .1..    11.1    .11
    10:  .111        .1..    1..1    ..11    .11.    11.1    1.1.1
    11:  111.        ..1.    .1..    1..1    ..11    .11.    11.1
    12:  1111        ...1    ..1.    .1..    1..1    ..11    .11.
    13:  11.1
    14:  1..1
```

Figure 42.5-A: Powers of the primitive element in $GF(2^4)$ with field polynomial $x^4 + x + 1$ (left), the list of powers rotated counter clockwise by 90 degree (top right), and the matrices obtained by taking 4 consecutive columns of the list (bottom right).

With a primitive polynomial modulus $C(x)$ a representation of the elements of $GF(2^n)$ as matrices can be obtained from the powers of the generator ('x') as follows: take row k through $k+n-1$ as the columns of matrices M_k, as shown in figure 42.5-A. Now we have $M_k = M_1^k$, so we can use the matrices to represent the elements of $GF(2^n)$.

The matrix $M := M_1$ is the *companion matrix* of the polynomial modulus g. The companion matrix of a polynomial $p(x) = x^n - \sum_{i=0}^{n-1} c_i x^i$ of degree n is defined as the $n \times n$ matrix

$$M = \begin{bmatrix} 0 & 0 & 0 & \cdots & 0 & c_0 \\ 1 & 0 & 0 & \cdots & 0 & c_1 \\ 0 & 1 & 0 & \cdots & 0 & c_2 \\ \vdots & \vdots & \vdots & & \vdots & \vdots \\ 0 & 0 & 0 & \cdots & 0 & c_{n-2} \\ 0 & 0 & 0 & \cdots & 1 & c_{n-1} \end{bmatrix} \qquad (42.5\text{-}1)$$

For polynomials $p(x) = \sum_{i=0}^{n} a_i x^i$ set $c_i := -a_i/a_n$.

The *characteristic polynomial* $c(x)$ of an $n \times n$ matrix M is defined as

$$c(x) := \det(x\, E_n - M) \qquad (42.5\text{-}2)$$

where E_n is the $n \times n$ unit matrix. The roots of the characteristic polynomial are the eigenvalues of the matrix. The characteristic polynomial of the companion matrix of a polynomial $p(x)$ equals $p(x)$. If $p(x)$ is the characteristic polynomial of a matrix M, then $p(M) = 0$ (non-proof: set $x = M$ in relation 42.5-2, for a proof see [101]).

```
     k:    [ p_k(x) ]^d              k:    [ p_k(x) ]^d
   -------------------------       -------------------------
     0:   [     11 ]^4              7:   [  1..11 ]^1
     1:   [  11..1 ]^1              8:   [  11..1 ]^1
     2:   [  11..1 ]^1              9:   [  11111 ]^1
     3:   [  11111 ]^1             10:   [    111 ]^2
     4:   [  11..1 ]^1             11:   [  1..11 ]^1
     5:   [    111 ]^2             12:   [  11111 ]^1
     6:   [  11111 ]^1             13:   [  1..11 ]^1
                                   14:   [  1..11 ]^1
```

Figure 42.5-B: Characteristic polynomials of the powers of the generator x with the field GF(2^4) and the polynomial $x^4 + x + 1$.

Let $c_k(x)$ be the characteristic polynomial of the matrix $M_k = M^k$ and $p_k(x)$ the minimal polynomial of the element $g^k \in$ GF(2^n). Then

$$c_k(x) \;=\; [p_k(x)]^d \quad \text{where} \quad d = n/r \tag{42.5-3}$$

where r is the smallest positive integer such that $M_k^{2^r} = M_k$. For example, for the primitive modulus $C(x) = x^4 + x + 1$ the sequence of characteristic polynomials of the powers of the generator 'x' are shown in figure 42.5-B.

The trace of the matrix M^k is the d-th power of the *polynomial trace* of the minimal polynomial of g^k. The polynomial trace of $p(x) = x^n - (c_{n-1} x^{n-1} + \cdots + c_1 x + c_0)$ equals c_{n-1} as can be seen from relation 42.5-1.

By construction, picking the first column of M_k gives the vector of the coefficients of the polynomial x^k modulo $C(x)$:

$$M^k [1, 0, 0, \ldots, 0]^T \;\equiv\; x^k \bmod C(x) \tag{42.5-4}$$

Finally, the characteristic polynomial of an element $a \in$ GF(2^n) in polynomial representation can be written as

$$p_a(x) \;:=\; \prod_{k=0}^{n-1} \left(x - a^{2^k} \right) \tag{42.5-5}$$

Compare to relation 42.2-1 on page 892 for minimal polynomials.

42.6   Representation by normal bases

So far we used the n basis vectors $x^0, x^1, x^2, x^3, \ldots, x^{n-1}$ to represent an element $a \in$ GF(2^n) (as a vector space over GF(2)):

$$a \;=\; \sum_{k=0}^{n-1} a_k x^k \tag{42.6-1}$$

The arithmetic operations were the polynomial operations modulo an irreducible polynomial modulus C.

For certain irreducible polynomials (which are called *normal polynomials* or *N-polynomials*) it is possible to use the *normal basis* $x^1, x^2, x^4, x^8, \ldots, x^{2^{n-1}}$ to represent elements of GF(2^n):

$$a \;=\; \sum_{k=0}^{n-1} a_k x^{2^k} \tag{42.6-2}$$

To check whether a polynomial C is normal, compute $r_k = x^{2^k} \bmod C$ for $1 \leq k \leq n$, compute the nullspace of the matrix M whose k-th row is r_k. If the nullspace is empty (that is, $M \cdot v = 0$ implies $v = 0$), then the polynomial is normal.

The normality of a polynomial is equivalent to its roots being linearly independent. See section 40.5.1 on page 841 for the equivalence of computations modulo a polynomial and computations with linear combinations of its roots.

An element $f \in \mathrm{GF}(2^n)$ where $f^1, f^2, f^4, f^8, \ldots, f^{2^{n-1}}$ are linearly independent is called a *normal element* (or *free element*). The minimal polynomial of a normal element f is normal.

Addition and subtraction with a normal basis is again a simple XOR. Squaring is a cyclic shift by one position. Taking the square root is a cyclic shift in the other direction.

In normal basis representation the element one is the all-ones word. So adding one is equivalent to complementing the binary word.

The trace can be computed easily with normal bases, it equals the parity of the binary word.

42.6.1 Multiplication and test for normality

For the multiplication of two elements we use the *multiplication matrix* M. Given two elements $a, b \in \mathrm{GF}(2^n)$ in normal basis representation

$$a = \sum_{k=0}^{n-1} a_k\, x^{2^k}, \qquad b = \sum_{k=0}^{n-1} b_k\, x^{2^k} \tag{42.6-3}$$

their product $p = a \cdot b$ can be computed as follows: for the first component p_0 of the product we have

$$p_0 = a^T \cdot M \cdot b \tag{42.6-4}$$

and in general

$$p_k = \left(a^{-2^{k-1}}\right)^T \cdot M \cdot b^{-2^{k-1}} \tag{42.6-5}$$

That is, all components of the product are computed like the first, but with a and b cyclically shifted.

```
Normal poly:   c=11111 =^= 4,3,2,1,0       Normal poly:   c=111.11 -^= 5,4,2,1,0

   A=          A^-1=                        A=          A^-1=
   .1..        1111                            .1...       11111
   ..1.        1...                            ..1..       1....
   1111        .1..                            ....1       .1..1.
   ...1        ...1                            .1.1.       1..1.
                                               1.111       ..1..
   C^T=        D=A*C^T*A^{-1}=
   .1..        .1..                         C^T=        D=A*C^T*A^{-1}=
   ..1.        ...1                            .1...       .1..1.
   ....1       1111                            ..1..       1..1.
   1111        ..1.                            ...1.       ...11
                                               ....1       .11..
   Multiplication matrix:  M=                  111.1       ..1.1
   ..1.
   ..11                                     Multiplication matrix:  M=
   11..                                        .1...
   .1.1                                        1..1.
                                               ...11
                                               .11..
                                               ..1.1
```

Figure 42.6-A: Matrices that occur with the computation of the multiplication matrix for the field polynomials $c = 1 + x + x^2 + x^3 + x^4$ (left) and $c = 1 + x + x^2 + x^4 + x^5$ (right).

An algorithm to check whether a given polynomial c is normal and, if so, compute the multiplication matrix M can be given as follows:

1. If the polynomial c is reducible, return false.

2. Compute the matrix A whose k-th row equals x^{2^k} mod c. If A is not invertible, then (the nullspace is not empty and) c is not normal, so return false.

3. Set $D := A \cdot C^T \cdot A^{-1}$ where C is the companion matrix of c.

4. Compute the multiplication matrix M where $M_{i,j} := D_{j',i'}$, $i' := -i$ mod n and $j' := j - i$ mod n. Return (true and) the matrix M.

An implementation is given in [FXT: bpol/bitpol-normal.cc]. Examples of the intermediate results for two different field polynomials are given in figure 42.6-A.

A C++ function implementing the multiplication algorithm is [FXT: bpol/normal-mult.cc]:

```
1   ulong
2   normal_mult(ulong a, ulong b, const ulong *M, ulong n)
3   // Multiply two elements (a and b in GF(2^n)) in normal basis representation.
4   // The multiplication matrix has to be supplied in M.
5   {
6       ulong p = 0;
7       for (ulong k=0; k<n; ++k)
8       {
9           ulong v = bitmat_mult_Mv(M, n, b);  // M*b
10          v = parity( v & a );  // a*M*b (dot product)
11          p ^= ( v << k );
12          a = bit_rotate_right(a, 1, n);
13          b = bit_rotate_right(b, 1, n);
14      }
15      return  p;
16  }
```

The routine for the multiplication $M \cdot v^T$ of a binary vector by a matrix is given in [FXT: bmat/bitmat-inline.h]:

```
1   inline ulong bitmat_mult_Mv(const ulong *M, ulong n, ulong v)
2   {
3       ulong p = 0;
4       for (ulong j=0; j<n; ++j)
5       {
6           ulong t = parity( M[j] & v );
7           p |= (t<<j);
8       }
9       return p;
10  }
```

A multiplication $v \cdot M$ is more efficient:

```
1   inline ulong bitmat_mult_vM(const ulong *M, ulong n, ulong v)
2   {
3       ulong p = 0;
4       for (ulong j=0; j<n; ++j)
5       {
6           if ( v&1 )  p ^= M[j];
7           v >>= 1;
8       }
9       return p;
10  }
```

So we modify two lines in the loop:

```
1           ulong v = bitmat_mult_vM(M, n, a);  // a*M
2           v = parity( v & b );  // a*M*b (dot product)
```

The algorithm for multiplication with normal bases is much more attractive for hardware implementations than for software, see [120]. An alternative test for normality is given in section 42.6.4 on page 908.

```
Normal poly:   c=1111.1 == x^5 + x^4 + x^3 + x^2 + 1
     k =        :    f=g**k  Tr(f)   x^2+x==f
     0 = ....   :    11111   1
     1 = ....1  :    ....1   1
     2 = ...1.  :    ...1.   1
     3 = ...11  :    .111.   1
     4 = ..1..  :    ..1..   1
     5 = ..1.1  :    1.111           x=.11.1
     6 = ..11.  :    111..   1
     7 = ..111  :    .11.1   1
     8 = .1...  :    .1...   1
     9 = .1..1  :    111.1   .        x=.1.11
    10 = .1.1.  :    .1111   .        x=..1.1
    11 = .1.11  :    ...11   .        x=...1.
    12 = .11..  :    11..1   1
    13 = .11.1  :    11...   .        x=.1...
    14 = .111.  :    11.1.   1
    15 = .1111  :    1.1..   .        x=.11..
    16 = 1....  :    1....   1
    17 = 1...1  :    ..111   1
    18 = 1..1.  :    11.11   .        x=.1..1
    19 = 1..11  :    1.11.   1
    20 = 1.1..  :    1111.   .        x=.1.1.
    21 = 1.1.1  :    ...11   .        x=...1.1
    22 = 1.11.  :    .11..   .        x=..1..
    23 = 1.111  :    ..1.1   .        x=..11.
    24 = 11...  :    1..11   1
    25 = 11..1  :    .1.11   1
    26 = 11.1.  :    1...1   .        x=.1111
    27 = 11.11  :    ..1.1   .        x=...11
    28 = 111..  :    1.1.1   1
    29 = 111.1  :    1..1.   .        x=.111.
    30 = 1111.  :    .1..1   .        x=..111
```

Figure 42.6-B: Solving the reduced quadratic equation $x^2 + x = f$ for powers $f = g^k$ of the generator $g = x$. The equation is solvable if the trace is zero, that is, the number of ones in the normal representation is even. The (primitive) field polynomial is $1 + x^2 + x^3 + x^4 + x^5$.

42.6.2   Solving the reduced quadratic equation

The reduced quadratic equation $x^2 + x = f$ has two solutions if $\text{Tr}(f) = 0$. One solution $x = [x_0, x_1, \ldots, x_{n-1}]$ can be computed as $x_k = \sum_{j=0}^{k} f_k$ where $f = [f_0, f_1, \ldots, f_{n-1}]$. This follows from

$$x^2 + x = [x_0 + x_{n-1},\ x_0 + x_1,\ x_1 + x_2,\ \ldots,\ x_{n-2} + x_{n-1},\ x_{n-1} + x_0] \qquad (42.6\text{-}6)$$

Now equate $x^2 + x = f$ and set $x_{n-1} = 0$ (setting $x_{n-1} = 1$ gives the complement which is also a solution). In C++ this translates to (see section 1.13.5 on page 32) [FXT: bpol/normal-solvequadratic.h]

```
1    inline ulong normal_solve_reduced_quadratic(ulong c)
2    // Solve x^2 + x = c
3    // Must have:  trace(c)==0,  i.e. parity(c)==0
4    // Return one solution x, the other solution equals 1+x,
5    // that is, the complement of x.
6    {
7        return  inverse_rev_gray_code(c);
8    }
```

The highest bit of the result is zero if and only if the equation is solvable: $\text{Tr}(c) = 0$, the vector c has an even number of ones. The reversed Gray code is given in section 1.16.6 on page 45.

A function to compute the trace and solve the reduced quadratic (if possible) is

```
1    inline ulong normal_solve_reduced_quadratic_q(ulong c, ulong &x)
2    // Return t, the trace of c.
3    // If t==0 then x^2 + x = c is solvable
4    // and a solution is written to x.
5    {
6        x = inverse_gray_code(c);
7        ulong t = ( x & 1 );
8        x >>= 1;  // immaterial if t==1, but avoid branch
9        return t;
10   }
```

The program [FXT: gf2n/normalbasis-demo.cc] prints the powers g^k of a generator g in normal basis representation and solves $x^2 + x = g^k$ when possible, see figure 42.6-B. By default a primitive normal polynomial from [FXT: bpol/normal-primpoly.cc] is used.

42.6.3 The number of binary normal bases ‡

$n:$	A_n	$n:$	A_n	$n:$	A_n	$n:$	A_n
1:	1	11:	93	21:	27783	31:	28629151
2:	1	12:	128	22:	95232	32:	67108864
3:	1	13:	315	23:	182183	33:	97327197
4:	2	14:	448	24:	262144	34:	250675200
5:	3	15:	675	25:	629145	35:	352149525
6:	4	16:	2048	26:	1290240	36:	704643072
7:	7	17:	3825	27:	1835001	37:	1857283155
8:	16	18:	5376	28:	3670016	38:	3616800768
9:	21	19:	13797	29:	9256395	39:	5282242875
10:	48	20:	24576	30:	11059200	40:	12884901888

Figure 42.6-C: The number A_n of degree-n binary normal polynomials up to $n = 40$.

$n:$	B_n	$n:$	B_n	$n:$	B_n	$n:$	B_n
1:	1	11:	87	21:	23579	31:	28629151
2:	1	12:	52	22:	59986	32:	33552327
3:	1	13:	315	23:	178259	33:	78899078
4:	1	14:	291	24:	103680		
5:	3	15:	562	25:	607522		
6:	3	16:	1017	26:	859849		
7:	7	17:	3825	27:	1551227		
8:	7	18:	2870	28:	1815045		
9:	19	19:	13797	29:	9203747		
10:	29	20:	11255	30:	5505966		

Figure 42.6-D: The number B_n of degree-n binary primitive normal polynomials up to $n = 33$.

The number A_n of degree-n binary normal polynomials up to $n = 40$ is given in figure 42.6-C. A table of the values A_n for $1 \leq n \leq 130$ and their factorizations is given in [FXT: data/num-normalpoly.txt]. The sequence A_n is entry A027362 in [312]. The number B_n of degree-n binary primitive normal polynomials up to $n = 33$ is given in figure 42.6-D. This is sequence A107222 in [312].

42.6.3.1 Computation via exhaustive search

For small degrees all normal polynomials can be generated by selecting from the irreducible polynomials those that are normal. Using the mechanism that generates all irreducible polynomials via Lyndon words, which is described in section 40.10 on page 856, the computation is a matter of minutes for $n < 25$. The program [FXT: gf2n/all-normalpoly-demo.cc] prints all normal polynomials of a given degree n, its output for $n = 9$ is shown in figure 42.6-E We can compute the number of normal (A_n) and primitive normal (B_n) binary polynomials for small degrees n using that program. The table of the values B_n in figure 42.6-D was produced with the mentioned program, the computation up to $n = 30$ takes about 90 minutes. As noted in [165], no formula for the number of primitive normal polynomials is presently known. The proof that primitive normal bases exist for all finite fields is given in [231].

42.6.3.2 Cycles in the De Bruijn graph

Quite surprisingly, it turns out that A_n equals the number of cycles in the De Bruijn graph (see section 41.5 on page 873 and section 20.2.2 on page 395). Therefore for n a power of 2 the number A_n equals the

```
 1: c =  11..11...1    P ==   x^9 + x^8 + x^5 + x^4 + 1
 2: c =  11...1..11    P ==   x^9 + x^8 + x^4 + x + 1
 3: c =  11111...11    P ==   x^9 + x^8 + x^7 + x^6 + x^5 + x + 1
 4: c =  11.11.1.11    P ==   x^9 + x^8 + x^6 + x^5 + x^3 + x + 1
 5: c =  111....1.1    P ==   x^9 + x^8 + x^7 + x^2 + 1
 6: c =  111...1111    P ==   x^9 + x^8 + x^7 + x^3 + x^2 + x + 1
 7: c =  11.......1      ==   x^9 + x^8 + 1
 8: c =  11.111..11    P ==   x^9 + x^8 + x^6 + x^5 + x^4 + x + 1
 9: c =  1111.1.1.1    P ==   x^9 + x^8 + x^7 + x^6 + x^4 + x^2 + 1
10: c =  1111..1.11    P ==   x^9 + x^8 + x^7 + x^6 + x^3 + x + 1
11: c =  11.1.11.11    P ==   x^9 + x^8 + x^6 + x^4 + x^3 + x + 1
12: c =  11.1..1..1      ==   x^9 + x^8 + x^6 + x^3 + 1
13: c =  1111111.11    P ==   x^9 + x^8 + x^7 + x^6 + x^5 + x^4 + x^3 + x + 1
14: c =  1111...111    P ==   x^9 + x^8 + x^7 + x^6 + x^2 + x + 1
15: c =  11..1.11.1      ==   x^9 + x^8 + x^4 + x^2 + 1
16: c =  11.1..1111    P ==   x^9 + x^8 + x^6 + x^3 + x^2 + x + 1
17: c =  11...11111    P ==   x^9 + x^8 + x^4 + x^3 + x^2 + x + 1
18: c =  111.111..1    P ==   x^9 + x^8 + x^7 + x^5 + x^4 + x^3 + 1
19: c =  1111.11..1    P ==   x^9 + x^8 + x^7 + x^6 + x^4 + x^3 + 1
20: c =  11..111.11    P ==   x^9 + x^8 + x^5 + x^4 + x^3 + x + 1
21: c =  11.11.11.1    P ==   x^9 + x^8 + x^6 + x^5 + x^3 + x^2 + 1
```

Figure 42.6-E: All normal binary polynomials of degree 9. Primitive polynomials are marked with 'P'.

number of binary De Bruijn sequences of length $2n$. No isomorphism between both objects (paths and binary normal polynomials) is presently known.

42.6.3.3 Invertible circulant matrices

```
L=1......        L=1.11...  [S]      L=11111..
 M =              M =                 M =
 1......          1.11...             11111..
 .1.....          .1.11..             .11111.
 ..1....          ..1.11.             ..11111
 ...1...          ...1.11             1..1111
 ....1..          1...1.1             11..111
 .....1.          11...1.             111..11
 ......1          .11...1             1111..1

L=111....        L=11..1..            L=1111.1.
 M =              M =                 M =
 111....          11..1..             1111.1.
 .111...          .11..1.             .1111.1
 ..111..          ..11..1             1.1111.
 ...111.          1..11..             .1.1111
 ....111          .1..11.             1.1.111
 1....11          ..1..11             11.1.11
 11....1          1..1..1             111.1.1

L=11.1...  [S]   L=1.1.1..            L=111.11.
 M =              M =                 M =
 11.1...          1.1.1..             111.11.
 .11.1..          .1.1.1.             .111.11
 ..11.1.          ..1.1.1             1.111.1
 ...11.1          1..1.1.             11.111.
 1...11.          .1..1.1             .11.111
 .1...11          1.1..1.             1.11.11
 1.1...1          .1.1..1             11.11.1
```

```
n=7    #invertible=7   #singular=2
```

Figure 42.6-F: The length-7 Lyndon words of odd weight and the corresponding circulant matrices. Singular matrices are marked with '[S]'. Dots denote zeros.

The number A_n of binary normal bases also equals the number of invertible circulant $n \times n$ matrices over GF(2). This is demonstrated with [FXT: gf2n/bitmat-circulant-demo.cc], the output for $n = 7$ is shown in figure 42.6-F. The search uses only Lyndon words, as periodic words would trivially lead to singular matrices. Further, Lyndon words with an even number of ones can be skipped as the vector $[1, 1, 1, \ldots, 1]$ is in the nullspace of the corresponding matrices.

If the set $\{\alpha, \alpha^2, \alpha^4, \alpha^8, \ldots, \alpha^{2^{n-1}}\}$ is a normal basis of GF(2^n), we say that α generates the normal basis. Consider the first row of a circulant matrix as some element β in a normal basis representation. Then the following rows are $\beta^2, \beta^4, \beta^8, \ldots, \beta^{2^{n-1}}$ and the matrix is invertible if β generates a normal basis. If

α generates a normal basis, then an element $\beta = \sum_{i=0}^{n-1} a_i \alpha^{2^i}$ generates a normal basis if and only if the polynomial $\sum_{i=0}^{n-1} a_i x^i$ is relatively prime to $x^n - 1$. Thus, with a fast algorithm to generate Lyndon words, determine all elements that generate normal bases if one such element is known as follows: select the Lyndon words with an odd number of ones and test whether $\gcd(L(x), x^n - 1) = 1$ where $L(x)$ is the binary polynomial corresponding to the Lyndon word. If n is a power of 2, then $x^n - 1 = (x - 1)^n$ and all Lyndon words with an odd number of ones are coprime to $x^n - 1$.

```
  L(x) = 111.11.   W(x) = 1....11        L(x) = 1.1.1..   W(x) = 1..1111

      M =           M^-1 =                  M =            M^-1 =
    111.11.        1....11                 1.1.1..        1..1111
    .111.11        11....1                 .1.1.1.        11..111
    1.111.1        111....                 ..1.1.1        111..11
    11.111.        .111...                 1..1.1.1        111..1
    .11.111        ..111..                 .1..1.1        11111..
    1.11.11        ...111.                 1.1..1.        .11111.
    11.11.1        ....111                 .1.1..1        ..11111
```

Figure 42.6-G: The inverse of an $n \times n$ circulant matrix can be found by computing the inverse $W(x)$ of its first row as a polynomial $L(x)$ modulo $x^n - 1$.

If the Lyndon word under consideration is taken as a polynomial $L(x)$ over GF(2), then the corresponding matrix is invertible if and only if $\gcd(L(x), x^n - 1) = 1$. The first row of the inverse of a circulant matrix over GF(2) can be found by computing $W(x) = L(x)^{-1} \bmod x^n - 1$ where $L(x)$ is the binary polynomial with coefficients one where the Lyndon word has a one. As the inverse of a circulant matrix is also circulant, the remaining rows are cyclic shifts of $W(x)$. Two examples with $n = 7$ are shown in figure 42.6-G.

The equality of the number of invertible circulants and normal bases can also be seen as follows: choose a normal basis and test for each element f whether the elements $f^1, f^2, f^4, f^8, \ldots, f^{2^{n-1}}$ are linearly independent. As squaring is a cyclic shift, the matrices to be tested are the circulants we considered.

42.6.3.4   Factorization of $x^n - 1$

The factorization of the polynomial $x^n - 1$ over GF(2) can be used for the computation of A_n. The file [FXT: data/polfactdeg.txt] supplies the necessary information:

```
# Structure of the factorization of x^n-1 over GF(2):
 1:   [1]   [1*1]
 2:   [2]   [1*1]
 3:   [1]   [1*1 + 1*2]
 4:   [4]   [1*1]
 5:   [1]   [1*1 + 1*4]
 6:   [2]   [1*1 + 1*2]
 7:   [1]   [1*1 + 2*3]
 8:   [8]   [1*1]
 9:   [1]   [1*1 + 1*2 + 1*6]
10:   [2]   [1*1 + 1*4]
11:   [1]   [1*1 + 1*10]
12:   [4]   [1*1 + 1*2]
13:   [1]   [1*1 + 1*12]
14:   [2]   [1*1 + 2*3]
15:   [1]   [1*1 + 1*2 + 3*4]
16:  [16]   [1*1]
17:   [1]   [1*1 + 2*8]
```

An entry: n: [e] [m1*d1 + m2*d2 + ...] says that $(x^n - 1) = P(x)^e$ and $P(x)$ factors into m1 different irreducible polynomials of degree d1, m2 different irreducible polynomials of degree d2 and so on. As an example, for $n = 6$ we have

$$x^6 - 1 \;\; = \;\; \left[x^3 - 1\right]^2 \;\; = \;\; \left[(x+1)\left(x^2 + x + 1\right)\right]^2 \tag{42.6-7}$$

x^6 is the square ($e = 2$) of a product of one irreducible polynomial of degree 1 and one of degree 2. Therefore we have the entry: 6:   [2] [1*1 + 1*2]. Another example, $n = 15$,

$$x^{15} - 1 \;\; = \;\; \left[(x+1)\left(x^2 + x + 1\right)\left(x^4 + x + 1\right)\left(x^4 + x^3 + 1\right)\left(x^4 + x^3 + x^2 + x + 1\right)\right]^1 \tag{42.6-8}$$

corresponding to the entry   `15:   [1] [1*1 + 1*2 + 3*4]`.

For the number of normal polynomials we have

$$A_n = \frac{2^n}{n} \prod_i \left(1 - \frac{1}{2^{d_i}}\right)^{m_i} \tag{42.6-9}$$

Note that the quantity e does not appear in the formula. For example, with $n = 6$ and $n = 15$ we find

$$A_6 = \frac{2^6}{6} \cdot \left(1 - \frac{1}{2^1}\right)^1 \cdot \left(1 - \frac{1}{2^2}\right)^1 = \frac{64}{6} \cdot \frac{1}{2} \cdot \frac{3}{4} = 4 \tag{42.6-10a}$$

$$A_{15} = \frac{2^{15}}{15} \cdot \left(1 - \frac{1}{2^1}\right)^1 \cdot \left(1 - \frac{1}{2^2}\right)^1 \cdot \left(1 - \frac{1}{2^4}\right)^3 = 675 \tag{42.6-10b}$$

42.6.3.5   Efficient computation

It is possible to compute the number of degree-n normal binary polynomials without explicitly factorizing the polynomial $x^n - 1$. We have

$$x^n - 1 = \prod_{d \backslash n} Y_d(x) \tag{42.6-11}$$

where $Y_d(x)$ is the d-th cyclotomic polynomial (see section 40.11 on page 857). We further know that $Y_d(x)$ factors into $\varphi(d)/r$ polynomials of degree r where $r - \operatorname{ord}_d(2)$ is the order of 2 modulo d. Let $a_n := A_n / \left(\frac{2^n}{n}\right)$, then a_n can for odd n be computed as

$$a_n = \prod_{d \backslash n} \left(1 - \frac{1}{2^r}\right)^{\varphi(d)/r} \tag{42.6-12}$$

The following GP code works all odd n:

```
1    p=2 /* global */
2    num_normal_p(n)=
3    {
4        local( r, i, pp );
5        pp = 1;
6        fordiv (n, d,
7            r = znorder(Mod(p,d));
8            i = eulerphi(d)/r;
9            pp *= (1 - 1/p^r)^i;
10       );
11       return( pp );
12   }
```

The number A_n can be computed (for arbitrary n) as $A_n = a_q \left(\frac{2^n}{n}\right)$ where q odd and $n = q\,2^t$:

```
1    num_normal(n)=
2    {
3        local( t, q, pp );
4        t = 1;   q = n;
5        while ( 0==(q%p), q/=p; t+=1; );
6        /* here: n==q*p^t */
7        pp = num_normal_p(q);
8        pp *= p^n/n;
9        return( pp );
10   }
```

The quantity t is not used in the computation. The implementation is quite efficient: the computation of A_n for all $n \leq 10{,}000$ takes less than three seconds. The computation of A_n for $n = 1234567 = 127 \cdot 9721$ (A_n is a number with $371{,}636$ decimal digits) takes about 200 milliseconds.

42.6.4   Dual and self-dual bases

Let $A = \{a_0,\, a_1,\, a_2,\, \cdots,\, a_{n-1}\}$ be a basis of GF(2^n). A basis $B = \{b_0,\, b_1,\, b_2,\, \cdots,\, b_{n-1}\}$ such that

$$\text{Tr}\,(a_k\, b_j) \;=\; \delta_{k,j} \qquad \text{for} \quad 0 \le k, j < n \tag{42.6-13}$$

is called the *dual basis* (or *complementary basis*, or *trace-orthonormal basis*) of A. A basis that is its own dual is called *self-dual*. We consider only normal basis here. If α is a root of a normal polynomial C, then $A = \{\alpha,\, \alpha^2,\, \alpha^4,\, \cdots,\, \alpha^{2^{n-1}}\}$ is a normal basis.

```
                 C              T              C*         D = T^-1 (mod x^n-1)

      1:   11..11...1    .11....111   P      1111.1.1.1   .1.1111.11
      2:   11...1..11    .1..11..11   P      111....1.1   ..111111.1
      3:   11111...11    .1.1111.11   P      11..111.11   .11....111
      4:   11.11.1.11    ..1..111.1   P      1111111.11   .111..1111
      5:   111....1.1    ..111111.1   P      11...1..11   .1..11..11
      6:   111...1111    ..111111.1   P      11...1.1.1   .1..11..11
      7:   11......1     .11....111          1111.11..1   .1.1111.11
      8:   11.111..11    .......1     P  S   11.111..11   .......1
      9:   1111.1.1.1    .1.1111.11   P      11..11...1   .11...111
     10:   1111.1.11     111...1111   P      11.1.11..11  ..1.11.11
     11:   11.1.11.11    ..1.11.1.1   P      1111...1.11  .111..1111
     12:   11.1..1..1    .......1        S   11.1..1..1   .......1
     13:   1111111.11    ..11..1111   P      11.11.1..1   ..1..11..1
     14:   1111....11    .111..1111   P      11.11.11.1   .1.11.1.1
     15:   111...1.1.1   .1..11..11   P      111....1111  .111111.1
     16:   11.1..1111    .1...1..1    P  S   11.1..1111   ..111111.1
     17:   11...11111    .1.....11    P      111.111..1   ..111111.1
     18:   111.111..1    ...111111.1  P      11...11111   .1..11..11
     19:   1111.11..1    .1.1111.11   P      11......1    .11....111
     20:   11..111.11    .11.....111  P      11111...111  .1.1111.11
     21:   11.11.11.1    ..1.11.1.1   P      1111...111   .111..1111
```

Figure 42.6-H: All normal polynomials C of degree 9 and their polynomials T (left), their duals C^* and $D = T^{-1}$ (right). Primitive polynomials are marked with 'P', self-dual $C = C^*$ are marked with 'S'.

Let C be an irreducible polynomial, α a root of C, and define $t_k = \text{Tr}(\alpha \cdot \alpha^{2^k})$ for $0 \le k < n$. We can compute the binary vector $[t_0, t_1, \ldots, t_{n-1}]$ as follows [FXT: bpol/normalpoly-dual.cc]

```
1    ulong
2    gf2n_xx2k_trace(ulong c, ulong deg)
3    // Return vector T of traces T[k]=trace(ek),
4    // where ek = x*x^(2^k), k=0..deg-1, and
5    //    x is a root of the irreducible polynomial C.
6    // Must have:  deg == degree(C)
7    {
8        if ( c==3 )  return 1UL;  // x+1 is self-dual
9
10       const ulong tv = gf2n_trace_vector_x(c, deg); // traces of x^k
11       ulong rt = 2UL;  // root of C
12       const ulong h = 1UL << (deg-1);  // aux
13
14       ulong v = 0;
15       for (ulong k=0; k<deg; ++k)
16       {
17           ulong ek = bitpolmod_times_x(rt, c, h);   // == x*x^(2^k)
18           ulong tk = gf2n_fast_trace(ek, tv);       // == sum(ek[i]*tk[i])
19           v |= (tk<<k);
20           rt = bitpolmod_square(rt, c, h);
21       }
22
23       return  v;
24   }
```

Now define the polynomial T as

$$T \;=\; t_0 + t_1\, x + t_2\, x^2 + \ldots + t_{n-1}\, x^{n-1} \tag{42.6-14}$$

The polynomial C is normal if and only if T has an inverse $D \equiv T^{-1} \bmod (x^n - 1)$. Therfore normality of C can be tested as follows [FXT: bpol/bitpol-normal.cc]:

```
1    bool
2    bitpol_normal2_q(ulong c, ulong n)
3    // Return whether polynomial c (of degree n) is normal.
4    // Must have: c irreducible.
5    {
6        const ulong t = gf2n_xx2k_trace(c, n);
7        const ulong xn1 = (1UL<<n) | 1UL;   // x^n-1
8        return ( 1 == bitpol_gcd(t, xn1) );
9    }
```

If $D = T$ then basis under consideration is self-dual. But as $D = T^{-1}$ we must have $T = 1$. Therefore the following statements can be used to test whether the roots of C are a self-dual (normal) basis:

```
1        // C == an irreducible polynomial of degree n
2        ulong T = gf2n_xx2k_trace(C, n);
3        if ( T==1 )  /* C is normal, its roots are a self-dual (normal) basis */
```

To compute the dual basis, write

$$D \;=\; d_0 + d_1\, x + d_2\, x^2 + \ldots + d_{n-1}\, x^{n-1} \tag{42.6-15a}$$

Then β defined by

$$\beta \;=\; d_0\, \alpha + d_1\, \alpha^2 + d_2\, \alpha^4 + \ldots + d_{n-1}\, \alpha^{2^{n-1}} \tag{42.6-15b}$$

is a root of a normal polynomial C^*, and $B = \{\beta, \beta^2, \beta^4, \cdots, \beta^{2^{n-1}}\}$ is the dual (normal) basis of A. The following routine computes T, D, and C^*:

```
1    ulong
2    gf2n_dual_normal(ulong c, ulong deg, ulong ntc/*=0*/, ulong *ntd/*=0*/)
3    // Return the minimal polynomial CS for the dual (normal) basis
4    //   with the irreducible normal polynomial C.
5    // Return zero if C is not normal.
6    // Must have:  deg == degree(C).
7    // If ntc is supplied it must be equal to gf2n_xx2k_trace(c, deg).
8    // If ntd is nonzero, ntc^-1 (mod x^deg-1) is written to it.
9    {
10       if ( 0==ntc )  ntc = gf2n_xx2k_trace(c, deg);
11       const ulong d = bitpolmod_inverse(ntc, 1 | (1UL<<deg) );  // ntc=d^-1 (mod x^deg-1)
12       if ( 0==d )  return 0;  // C not normal
13       if ( 0!=ntd )  *ntd = d;
14
15       const ulong h = 1UL << (deg-1);  // aux
16       ulong alpha = 2UL;  // 'x', a root of C
17       ulong beta = 0;     // root of the dual polynomial
18       for (ulong m=d; m!=0; m>>=1)
19       {
20           if ( m & 1 )  beta ^= alpha;
21           alpha = bitpolmod_square(alpha, c, h);
22       }
23
24       ulong cs;  // minimal polynomial of beta
25       bitpolmod_minpoly(beta, c, deg, cs);
26
27       return cs;
28   }
```

Figure 42.6-H shows the normal polynomials C of degree 9 and the polynomials C^*. It was created with the program [FXT: gf2n/normalpoly-dual-demo.cc]. A list of all polynomials with self-dual bases is given in section 40.9.13 on page 855.

42.6.5 The number of self-dual normal basis

Figure 42.6-I gives the number S_n of self-dual normal basis (top) and the number Z_n of such basis where the field polynomial is primitive (bottom). The field polynomial is the minimal polynomial of any of the basis elements. The sequence of values S_n is entry A135488 in [312], the values Z_n are entry A135498. No formula for the numbers Z_n is known, the values were computed with the program [FXT: gf2n/normalpoly-dual-demo.cc]. An expression for S_n is given in [195, theorem 5]. The following routine for computing the values S_n (for $p = 2$) is given by Max Alekseyev [priv. comm.]:

$n:$	S_n	$n:$	S_n	$n:$	S_n	$n:$	S_n	$n:$	S_n
1:	1	9:	3	17:	17	25:	205	33:	3267
2:	1	10:	4	18:	48	26:	320	34:	4352
3:	1	11:	3	19:	27	27:	513	35:	4095
4:	0	12:	0	20:	0	28:	0	36:	0
5:	1	13:	5	21:	63	29:	565	37:	7085
6:	2	14:	8	22:	96	30:	1920	38:	13824
7:	1	15:	15	23:	89	31:	961	39:	20475
8:	0	16:	0	24:	0	32:	0	40:	0

$n:$	Z_n	$n:$	Z_n	$n:$	Z_n	$n:$	Z_n	$n:$	Z_n
1:	0	9:	2	17:	17	25:	200	33:	2660
2:	1	10:	3	18:	25	26:	215	34:	2917
3:	1	11:	3	19:	27	27:	428	35:	
4:	0	12:	0	20:	0	28:	0	36:	
5:	1	13:	5	21:	57	29:	562	37:	
6:	1	14:	4	22:	60	30:	997	38:	
7:	1	15:	11	23:	87	31:	961	39:	
8:	0	16:	0	24:	0	32:	0	40:	

Figure 42.6-I: Number of self-dual normal basis (S_n, top) and self-dual normal basis where the field polynomial is primitive (Z_n, bottom). No self-dual normal basis exists for n a multiple of 4.

```
1   sdn(m,p) =
2   \\ Number of distinct self-dual normal bases of GF(p^m) over GF(p) where p is prime
3   {
4       local(F, f, g, s, c, d);
5       if ( p==2 && m%4==0, return(0) );
6
7       if ( !(m%p), /* p divides m */
8           s = m\p;
9           return( p^((p-1)*(s+(s*(p+1))%2)/2-1) * sdn(s,p) );
10      , /* else */
11          F = factormod( (x^m - 1)/(x - 1), p );
12          c = d = [];
13          for (i=1, matsize(F)[1],
14              f = lift(F[i,1]);
15              g = polrecip(f);
16              if ( f==g,  c = concat( c, vector(F[i,2],j,poldegree(f)/2) ); );
17              if ( lex(Vec(f), Vec(g))==1 ,
18                  d = concat( d, vector(F[i,2],j,poldegree(f)) );
19              );
20          );
21          return( 2^(p%2) * prod(i=1,#c, p^c[i] + 1) * prod(j=1,#d, p^d[j] - 1) / m );
22      );
23  }
```

We note that duality is defined for any basis, but no self-dual polynomial basis exists. See [156] and [232] for more information. Algorithms for the construction of self-dual normal bases are given in [229].

42.7 Conversion between normal and polynomial representation

If the field polynomial C is normal, then conversion between the representations in polynomial and normal basis can be done as follows: Let Z be the $n \times n$ matrix whose k-th column equals $x^{2^k} \bmod C$ where n is the degree of C. If a is the polynomial representation, then the normal representation is $b = Z^{-1} \cdot a$.

The implementation [FXT: class GF2n in bpol/gf2n.h] allows the conversion to the normal representation if the field polynomial is normal. In the initializer the matrices Z (n2p_tab[]) and Z^{-1} (p2n_tab[]) are computed with the lines

```
  k = bin(k):    f= g**k   ==  (normal)  trace(f)
  0 = .....  :    ....1    ==  11111       1
  1 = ....1  :    ...1.    ==  ....1       1
  2 = ...1.  :    ..1..    ==  ...1.       1
  3 = ...11  :    .1...    ==  .111.       1
  4 = ..1..  :    1....    ==  .1.1.       1
  5 = ..1.1  :    111.1    ==  1.111       .
  6 = ..11.  :    ..111    ==  111..       .
  7 = ..111  :    .111.    ==  .11.1       1            P2N=
  8 = .1...  :    111..    ==  .1...       1            11...
  9 = .1..1  :    ..1.1    ==  111.1       .            1.11.
 10 = .1.1.  :    .1.1.    ==  .1111       .            1..11
 11 = .1.11  :    1.1..    ==  ...11       .            1..1.
 12 = .11..  :    1.1.1    ==  11..1       1            1....
 13 = .11.1  :    1.111    ==  11...       .
 14 = .111.  :    1..11    ==  11.1.       1
 15 = .1111  :    11.11    ==  1.1..       .            N2P=
 16 = 1....  :    .1.11    ==  1....       1            ....1
 17 = 1...1  :    1.11.    ==  ..111       1            1...1
 18 = 1..1.  :    1...1    ==  11.11       .            .1.1.
 19 = 1..11  :    11111    ==  1.11.       1            ...11
 20 = 1.1..  :    ...11    ==  1111.       .            ..11.
 21 = 1.1.1  :    ..11.    ==  ...11       .
 22 = 1.11.  :    .11..    ==  .11..       .
 23 = 1.111  :    11...    ==  .1.1.       .
 24 = 11...  :    .11.1    ==  1..11       1
 25 = 11..1  :    11.1.    ==  .1.11       1
 26 = 11.1.  :    .1..1    ==  1...1       .
 27 = 11.11  :    1..1.    ==  1..1.       .
 28 = 111..  :    11..1    ==  1.1.1       1
 29 = 111.1  :    .1111    ==  1..1.       .
 30 = 1111.  :    1111.    ==  .1..1       .
```

Figure 42.7-A: Conversion between normal and polynomial representation with the (primitive) polynomial $c = 1 + x^2 + x^3 + x^4 + x^5$. The conversion matrices are given as P2N= Z^{-1} and N2P= Z.

```
1        // conversion to and from normal representation:
2        for (ulong k=0,s=2;  k<n_;  ++k)
3        {
4            n2p_tab[k] = s;
5            s = bitpolmod_square(s, c_, h_);
6        }
7        bitmat_transpose(n2p_tab, n_, n2p_tab);
8        is_normal_ = bitmat_inverse(n2p_tab, n_, p2n_tab);
```

The last line records whether the field polynomial is normal (Z is invertible).

The functions [FXT: bpol/gf2n.cc]

```
1    ulong // static
2    GF2n::p2n(ulong f)
3    { return  bitmat_mult_Mv(p2n_tab, n_, f); }
4
5    ulong // static
6    GF2n::n2p(ulong f)
7    { return  bitmat_mult_Mv(n2p_tab, n_, f); }
```

allow conversions between the normal and polynomial representations. To get the normal representation of a given element, use the method

```
    ulong get_normal()  const  { return p2n(v_); }
```

This is demonstrated in [FXT: gf2n/gf2n-normal-demo.cc] where both the polynomial and the normal representation are given, see figure 42.7-A.

If the last argument of the initialization routine of the C++ class **GF2n**, **init(n, c, normalq)**, is set, then a (primitive) normal polynomial will be used as field polynomial. A list of primitive normal polynomials is given in [FXT: bpol/normal-primpoly.cc].

42.8 Optimal normal bases (ONB)

The number of nonzero terms in the multiplication matrix determines the complexity (operation count) for the multiplication with normal bases. It turns out that for certain values of n there are normal bases of GF(2^n) whose multiplication matrices have at most two nonzero entries in each row (and column). Such bases are called *optimal normal bases* (ONB).

Optimal normal bases are especially interesting for hardware implementations because of both the highly regular structure of the multiplication algorithm and the minimal complexity with ONBs.

42.8.1 Type-1 optimal normal bases

A *type-1 optimal normal basis* exists for n when $p := n + 1$ is prime and 2 is a primitive root modulo p (and for $n = 0$ and $n = 1$). The sequence of such n is (entry A071642 in [312])

$$0, 1, 2, 4, 10, 12, 18, 28, 36, 52, 58, 60, 66, 82, 100, 106, 130, 138, 148,$$
$$162, 172, 178, 180, 196, 210, 226, 268, 292, 316, 346, 348, 372, 378, 388,$$
$$418, 420, 442, 460, 466, 490, 508, \ldots$$

One has always $n \equiv 2$ or $n \equiv 4$ modulo 8. A list of the corresponding primes is given in figure 41.7-B on page 878. The field polynomial corresponding to a type-1 ONB is the all-ones polynomial

$$c = \frac{x^p - 1}{x - 1} = 1 + x + x^2 + x^3 + \ldots + x^n \tag{42.8-1}$$

The order of these polynomials is $n + 1$ (for $n > 1$) so they are non-primitive for all $n \geq 3$.

```
      Normal poly:   c=11111111111

      A:              A^-1:          C^T:          D=A*C^T*A^{-1}:  Mult. matrix M:
.1........          1111111111     .1........     .1........       ......1...
..1.......          1.........     ..1.......     ........1.       ......11..
...1......          .1........     ...1......     ....1.....       ...1....1.
....1...1.          ..1.......     ....1.....     ......1...       ..1......1.
..1                 ..1.......                    ........1        ......1.1
1111111111          ...1......     .....1....     1111111111       11........
........1           ....1.....     ......1...     ....1.....       .1......1.
...1....1..         .....1....     .......1..     ..1.......       ..1.1.....
....1.....          ......1...     ........1.     .1........       ....1.1...
.......1...         .......1...    111111111      .......1..       ....1....1
```

Figure 42.8-A: Matrices that occur with the computation of the multiplication matrix for the field polynomial $c = 1 + x + \ldots + x^{10}$.

The multiplication matrices are sparse: there is one entry in the first row and column, and two entries in the other rows and columns. That is, the multiplication matrices for GF(n) with optimal normal basis have $2n - 1$ nonzero entries. For example, with $n = 10$ we obtain the matrix shown at the right of figure 42.8-A. The equivalent data for $n = 4$ is shown in figure 42.6-A on page 901.

42.8.2 Type-2 optimal normal bases

A *type-2 optimal normal basis* exists for n if $p := 2n + 1$ is prime and either

- $n \equiv 1$ or $n \equiv 2$ modulo 4 and the order of 2 modulo p equals $2n$.

- $n \equiv 3 \mod 4$ and the order of 2 modulo p equals n.

A type-2 basis exists for the following $n \leq 200$ (entry A054639 in [312]):

$$1, 2, 3, 5, 6, 9, 11, 14, 18, 23, 26, 29, 30, 33, 35, 39, 41, 50,$$
$$51, 53, 65, 69, 74, 81, 83, 86, 89, 90, 95, 98, 99, 105, 113, 119$$
$$131, 134, 135, 146, 155, 158, 173, 174, 179, 183, 186, 189, 191, 194$$

The corresponding polynomials p_n (see figure 42.8-B) can be computed via the recurrence

$$p_0 := 1, \qquad p_1 := x + 1 \tag{42.8-2a}$$
$$p_k := x\,p_{k-1} + p_{k-2} \tag{42.8-2b}$$

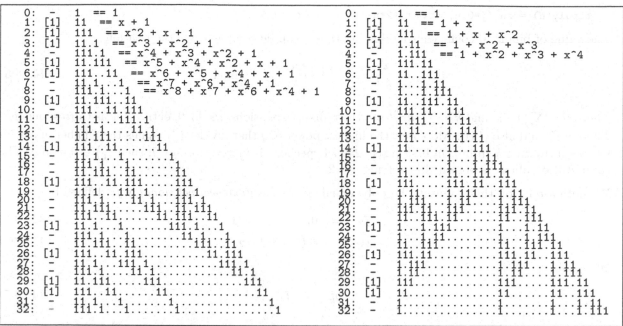

Figure 42.8-B: The polynomials p_k as binary strings, high coefficients aligned left and right. The entry in the second column is '[1]' if the polynomial is irreducible (a field polynomial for a type-2 ONB).

Compare to the recursion that transforms a linear hybrid cellular automaton into a binary polynomial relation 41.8-1 on page 879: the type-2 ONBs correspond to the simplest LHCA defined by the rule having a single one as the lowest bit of the rule word.

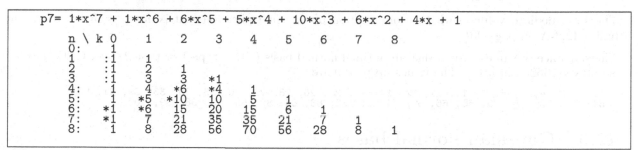

Figure 42.8-C: Locations (starred entries) of the coefficients of the polynomial p_7 in Pascal's triangle.

Expressions for the polynomials p_n are

$$p_n = \sum_{j=0}^{n} \binom{n - \lfloor (j+1)/2 \rfloor}{\lfloor j/2 \rfloor} x^{n-j} = \sum_{j=0}^{n} \binom{\lfloor n/2 + j/2 \rfloor}{j} x^j \tag{42.8-3}$$

The locations of the coefficients of the polynomials p_n in Pascal's triangle (figure 6.1-A on page 176) lie on a rising diagonal. For p_7 they are shown in figure 42.8-C. The following relations hold over GF(2) (but not over $\mathbb{Z}$):

$$p_n = \sum_{j=0}^{n} \binom{2n - j}{j} x^{n-j} = \sum_{j=0}^{n} \binom{n+j}{n-j} x^j \tag{42.8-4}$$

The binomial coefficient $\binom{n}{k}$ modulo 2 equals 1 if the binary expansion of k is a subset of the expansion of n. With the trick from section 1.9.1 on page 23 we obtain a fast method for the computation of the polynomials p_n (using the first equality in 42.8-4):

```
1    t2poly(n) = sum(j=0,n, (bitand(2*n-j, j)==j)*x^(n-j));
```

The value of binomial coefficients modulo a prime q can be computed via the relation

$$\binom{n}{k} \equiv \prod_{j=0}^{\infty} \left[\binom{n_j}{k_j} \right] \qquad \mathrm{mod}\ q \tag{42.8-5}$$

where $n = \sum_j n_j\,q^j$ and $k = \sum_j k_j\,q^j$ are the radix-q expansions, see [349, entry "Lucas Correspondence Theorem"] and also [141]. Moreover, the highest power of q that divides $\binom{n}{k}$ equals the number of carries when subtracting k from n in base q, see [249]. Especially, if $k_j > n_j$ for any j, then $\binom{n}{k} \equiv 0 \bmod q$. The computation above is obtained by setting $q = 2$.

We note a relation that connects the polynomials p_k to the *Fibonacci polynomials* f_k defined by

$$f_0 := 0, \qquad f_1 := 1 \tag{42.8-6a}$$
$$f_k := x\,f_{k-1} + f_{k-2} \tag{42.8-6b}$$

We have

$$p_k^2 = f_{2k+1} \tag{42.8-7}$$

As with type-1 ONBs, the multiplication matrices are sparse. The polynomials and multiplication matrices for $n = 6$ and $n = 9$ are

```
6,5,4,1,0    9,8,6,5,4,1,0
.1...1.      .1....1....
i....ii.     1....1..i..
.ii...i      ....1..i.ii
...i.i       .ii...i11..
             ...i.i.i11.
             ...i.i1....
             ...1....1
```

The intermediate values with the computation of the multiplication matrix for $n = 5$ are shown in figure 42.6-A on page 901.

The sequence of values n such that an optimal normal basis (either type-1 or type-2) over $\mathrm{GF}(2^n)$ exists is entry A136250 in [312]. The values up to 100 are

```
1, 2, 3, 4, 5, 6, 9, 10, 11, 12, 14, 18, 23, 26, 28, 29, 30, 33, 35, 36, 39, 41, 50,
51, 52, 53, 58, 60, 65, 66, 69, 74, 81, 82, 83, 86, 89, 90, 95, 98, 99, 100
```

42.9 Gaussian normal bases

The *type-t Gaussian normal basis* (GNB) generalize the optimal normal basis. The type-1 and type-2 GNBs are the corresponding ONBs. The multiplication matrices for type-t GNBs for $t > 2$ have more nonzero entries than the ONBs.

A type-t GNB exists for n if $p := t\,n + 1$ is prime and $\gcd(n, t\,n/r_2) = 1$ where r_2 is the order of 2 modulo p. For n divisible by 8 no GNB exist. Figure 42.9-A shows, for $t \le 10$, the first values n such that a type-t GNB exists. The sequences for $1 \le t \le 7$ are the following entries in [312]: A071642 (type-1), A054639 (type-2), A136415 (type-3), A137310 (type-4), A137311 (type-5), A137313 (type-6), A137314 (type-7), and A101284 (type-8). We implement the test using GP:

```
1    gauss_test(n, t)=
2    { /* test whether a type-t Gaussian normal basis exists for GF(2^n) */
3        local( p, r2, g, d );
4        p = t*n + 1;
5        if ( !isprime(p), return( 0 ) );
6        if ( p<=2, return( 0 ) );
7        r2 = znorder( Mod(2, p) );
8        d = (t*n)/r2;
9        g = gcd(d, n);
10       return ( if ( 1==g, 1, 0) );
11   }
```

```
 1:   2,  4, 10, 12, 18, 28, 36, 52, 58, 60, 66, 82, 100, 106, 130
 2:   1,  2,  3,  5,  6,  9, 11, 14, 18, 23, 26, 29, 30, 33, 35
 3:   4,  6, 12, 14, 20, 22, 46, 52, 54, 60, 70, 76, 92, 94, 116
 4:   1,  3,  7,  9, 13, 15, 25, 37, 43, 45, 49, 67, 73, 79, 87
 5:   2, 12, 20, 26, 36, 42, 84, 92, 98, 108, 114, 132, 140, 164, 188
 6:   1,  2,  3,  5,  6,  7, 10, 11, 13, 17, 23, 26, 27, 30, 33
 7:   4, 28, 30, 54, 60, 70, 78, 94, 100, 108, 118, 126, 166, 196, 214
 8:   5,  9, 11, 17, 29, 35, 39, 51, 65, 71, 77, 95, 101, 107, 117
 9:   2,  4, 18, 20, 34, 42, 44, 58, 60, 68, 82, 84, 92, 98, 124
10:   1,  6,  7, 10, 13, 18, 19, 21, 27, 31, 42, 43, 46, 49, 54
```

Figure 42.9-A: For $t \in \{1, 2, \ldots, 10\}$: lowest values n such that a type-t GNB exists for $\mathrm{GF}(2^n)$.

42.9.1 Computation of the multiplication matrix

An algorithm to compute the multiplication matrix for a type-t GNB proceeds as follows (we use a vector $F[1, 2, \ldots, p-1]$):

1. Set $p = tn + 1$ (this is a prime) and compute an element r of order t modulo p.

2. For $k = 0, 1, \ldots, t-1$ do the following: set $j = r^k$ and for $i = 0, 1, \ldots, n-1$ set $F[j\,2^i] = i$.

3. Set the multiplication matrix M to zero.

4. For $i = 1, 2, \ldots, p-2$ add one to $M_{F[p-i], F[i+1]}$.

5. If t is odd, set $h = n/2$ and do the following: for $i = 0, 1, \ldots, h-1$ increment $M_{i, h+i}$ and $M_{h+i, i}$.

Implementation in GP:

```
1    gauss_nb(n, t)=
2    { /* return multiplier matrix for type-t Gaussian normal basis */
3      /* returned matrix is over Z and has to be multiplied by Mod(1,2) */
4        local(p, r, F, w, x, nh, m, ir, ic);
5
6        p = t*n + 1;
7        r = znprimroot(p);   r = r^(n);   /* r has order t */
8        F = vector(p-1);
9        w = Mod(1, p);
10       for (k=0, t-1,
11           j = lift(w);
12           for (i=0, n-1,
13               F[j] = i;
14               j+=j;  if (j>=p, j-=p);   /* 2*j mod p */
15           );
16           w *= r;
17       );
18
19       m = matrix(n, n);
20       for (i=1, p-2,
21           ir = F[p-i];  ic = F[i+1];
22           m[ ir+1, ic+1 ] += 1;
23       );
24
25       if ( 1==(t%2),
26           nh = n/2; /* odd t ==> even n */
27           for (i=0, nh-1,
28               ir = i;   ic = nh + i;
29               ir += 1;  ic += 1;
30               m[ir, ic] += 1;
31               m[ic, ir] += 1;
32           );
33       );
34
35       return ( m );
36   }
```

```
        n=7, t=4                              n=12, t=3

      M=          M mod 2=                M=              M mod 2=
   .1..2..      .1.....              ...1.1.,..1.       ...1.1.,..1.
   1.1..11      1.1..11              ...1.111...       ...1.111...
   .1.111.      .1.111.              ...1..12..,      ...1..1...,
   ..12.1.      ..1..1.              .11..1...1..      .11..1...1..
   2.1...1      ..1....1             1....1.11.,      1....1.11.,
   .111..1      .111..1              .1.1...,..1.1      .1.1...,..1.1
   .1..111      .1..111              11....2.....      11..........
                                     .,11.1....,1.      .,11.1....,1.
                                     ..2.....1.1      ...,.....1.1
                                     1....1.1...,1      1....1.1...,1
                                     ....1..1.11      .....1..1.11
```

Figure 42.9-B: Multiplication matrices over $\mathbb{Z}$ and GF(2) for Gaussian normal bases with $n = 7$, $t = 4$ (left) and $n = 12$, $t = 3$ (right). Dots denote zeros.

The implementation computes M with entries in $\mathbb{Z}$, so M has to be reduced modulo 2 before usage. Figure 42.9-B gives two examples.

The file [FXT: data/gauss-normal-types.txt] lists for each $2 \leq n \leq 1032$ the smallest ten values of t such that there is a type-t GNB of GF(2^n). Note that different values of t do not necessary lead to different multiplication matrices, especially for small values of n. For example, the modulo 2 reduced multiplication matrices for $n = 6$ and the 10 smallest values of t are:

```
  t=2:     t=3:     t=6:     t=10:    t=11:    t=23:    t=27:    t=30:    t=35:    t=55:
 .1...,    ..11.1   .1....   .1....   ..11.1   1.11.    1.11.    .1....   1.11.    .1.11.
 1...1.    .,11,    1.11.1   1.11.1   .,11,    1.111.   1.111.   1...1.   1.111.   1.111.
 ...11,    11..11   .1...1   .1...1   11..11   .1...1   .1...1   ...11,   .1...1   .1...1
 .,1..1    ...,..1  .,1..1   .1...1   11.....  11.....  11.....  .,1..1   11.....  11...,
 .11...    .,1..1   .,1..1   .,1..1   .,1..1   111..1   111..1   .11...   111..1   111..1
 ...1.1    1.1.11   .11.11   .11.11   1.1.11   ....11   ....11   ....11   ....11   ....11
                    ==t=6    ==t=3             ==t=23   ==t=2             ==t=23   ==t=23
```

42.9.2 Determination of the field polynomial

We give algorithms to compute the field polynomial corresponding to a given pair (n, t) such that a type-t GNB exists over GF(2^n). A list of the polynomials for $n \leq 63$ and $1 \leq t \leq 11$ is given in [FXT: data/gauss-normal-polys.txt].

42.9.2.1 Algorithm with complex numbers

```
     n=4 t=1:  p=5
       a(1)=2  w(1)=(-0.809016994374947 + 0.587785252292473 I)
       a(2)=4  w(2)=(+0.309016994374947 - 0.951056516295154 I)
       a(3)=3  w(3)=(-0.809016994374947 - 0.587785252292473 I)
       a(4)=1  w(4)=(+0.309016994374947 + 0.951056516295154 I)
     z(x)=x^4 + x^3 + x^2 + x + 1
     p(x)=x^4 + x^3 + x^2 + x + 1

     n=4 t=3:  p=13
       a(1)=2  w(1)=(-1.15138781886600  + 1.72542218842201 I)
       a(2)=4  w(2)=(+0.651387818865997 - 0.522415803456408 I)
       a(3)=8  w(3)=(-1.15138781886600  - 1.72542218842201 I)
       a(4)=3  w(4)=(+0.651387818865997 + 0.522415803456408 I)
     z(x)=x^4 + x^3 + 2*x^2 - 4*x + 3
     p(x)=x^4 + x^3 + 1

     n=4 t=7:  p=29
       a(1)=2  w(1)=(-1.59629120178363  - 0.509187583844044 I)
       a(2)=4  w(2)=(+1.09629120178363  + 2.64399848798351 I)
       a(3)=8  w(3)=(-1.59629120178363  + 0.509187583844044 I)
       a(4)=16 w(4)=(+1.09629120178363  - 2.64399848798351 I)
     z(x)=x^4 + x^3 + 4*x^2 + 20*x + 23
     p(x)=x^4 + x^3 + 1
```

Figure 42.9-C: Numerical values with the computation of the field polynomial for $n = 4$ and types $t \in \{1, 3, 7\}$. Note that the final result is identical for the types $t = 3$ and $t = 7$.

The normal polynomial corresponding to a type-t Gaussian basis can be computed as follows:

```
        n=11 t=2:   p=23
          a(1)=2     w(1)=(+1.7088388090929771051 - 1.175494350822287508 E-38 I)
          a(2)=4     w(2)=(+0.9201300754623042520 + 5.877471754111437540 E-39 I)
          a(3)=8     w(3)=(-1.1533606442297342825 - 5.877471754111437540 E-39 I)
          a(4)=16    w(4)=(-0.6697592243419723039 - 2.938735877055718770 E-39 I)
          a(5)=9     w(5)=(-1.5514225814088396141 + 1.763241526233431262 E-38 I)
          a(6)=18    w(6)=(+0.4069120261052675797 + 1.193861450053885750 E-39 I)
          a(7)=13    w(7)=(-1.8344226030109060357 + 1.028557556969501569 E-38 I)
          a(8)=3     w(8)=(+1.3651062864373081657 + 1.175494350822287508 E-38 I)
          a(9)=6     w(9)=(-0.1364848267293419518 - 1.205340887073634651 E-39 I)
          a(10)=12   w(10)=(-1.9813718920726615047 + 2.277520304718182046 E-38 I)
          a(11)=1    w(11)=(+1.9258345746955985900 - 2.938735877055718770 E-38 I)

        z(x)=x^11 + x^10 - 10*x^9 - 9*x^8 + 36*x^7 + 28*x^6 - 56*x^5 \
                - 35*x^4 + 35*x^3 + 15*x^2 - 6*x - 1
        p(x)=x^11 + x^10 + x^8 + x^4 + x^3 + x^2 + 1

        n=11 t=6:   p=67
          [--snip--]
        z(x)=x^11 + x^10 - 30*x^9 - 63*x^8 + 220*x^7 + 698*x^6 - 101*x^5 \
                - 1960*x^4 - 1758*x^3 - 35*x^2 + 243*x - 29
        p(x)=x^11 + x^10 + x^8 + x^5 + x^2 + x + 1

        n=11 t=8:   p=89
          [--snip--]
        z(x)=x^11 + x^10 - 40*x^9 - 19*x^8 + 482*x^7 + 84*x^6 - 2185*x^5 \
                + 102*x^4 + 3152*x^3 - 781*x^2 + 57*x - 1
        p(x)=x^11 + x^10 + x^8 + x^5 + x^2 + x + 1

        n=11 t=18:   p=199
          [--snip--]
        z(x)=x^11 + x^10 - 90*x^9 - 115*x^8 + 2349*x^7 + 943*x^6 - 26327*x^5 \
                + 21284*x^4 + 102168*x^3 - 217794*x^2 + 148930*x - 30647
        p(x)=x^11 + x^10 + x^8 + x^7 + x^6 + x^5 + 1
```

Figure 42.9-D: Numerical values with the computation of the field polynomial for $n = 11$ and types $t \in \{2, 6, 8, 18\}$. The final results for $t = 6$ and $t = 8$ are identical.

1. Set $p = t\,n + 1$ and determine r such that the order of r modulo p equals t.

2. For $1 \leq k \leq n$ compute $w_k = \sum_{j=0}^{t-1} \exp(a_k\, 2\,\pi\, i/p)$ where $a_k = 2^k\, r^j \bmod p$.

3. Let $z(x) = \prod_{k=1}^{n} (x - w_k)$, this is a polynomial with real integer coefficients.

4. Return the polynomial with coefficients reduced modulo 2.

The computation of the polynomial $z(x)$ uses complex (inexact) arithmetic. The coefficients should be close to real integers, which can be used as a check. The following GP routine computes the complex polynomial:

```
1    gauss_zpoly(n, t)=
2    { /* return field polynomial for type-t Gaussian normal basis
3          as polynomial over the complex numbers */
4
5        local(p, r, wk, tk1, tk, a, zp);
6        p = n*t + 1;
7        r = znprimroot(p)^n;   \\ r has order t (mod p)
8
9        zp = 1;
10       tk1 = Mod(2,p);   tk = Mod(1,p);
11       for (k=1, n,
12           tk *= tk1;   \\ == Mod(2,p)^k;
13           wk = 0;
14           a = tk;
15           for (j=0, t-1,
16               wk += exp(2.0*I*Pi*lift(a)/p);
17               a *= r;
18           );
19           zp *= (x-wk);
20       );
21
22       return ( zp );
23   }
```

The final step uses GP's function round() which rounds all coefficients of its polynomial argument:

```
1    gauss_poly(n, t)=
2    { /* return field polynomial for type-t Gaussian normal basis */
3        local(pp, zp);
4        zp = gauss_zpoly(n, t);
5        pp = round(real(zp));  /* rounds all coefficients */
6        pp *= Mod(1,2);  /* coefficients modulo 2 */
7        return( pp );
8    }
```

The results for type-1 bases can be verified using relation 42.8-1 on page 912, results with type-2 bases with relations 42.8-2a and 42.8-2b. The values occurring with the computation for $n = 4$ and the types $t \in \{1, 3, 7\}$ are shown in figure 42.9-C, the values for $n = 11$ and $t \in \{2, 6, 8, 18\}$ in figure 42.9-D.

The computation can be optimized by using a trigonometric recursion as described in section 21.3.2 on page 417. We further exploit symmetry and use real values if the type t is even:

```
1    vexp(p, t)=
2    {
3        local( ve, ph, c, s, al, be,  cp, sp, tt );
4        tt = 2.0*Pi/p;  \\ angle increment
5        c = 1.0;  s = 0.0;  ga = ph;  al = 2.0*(sin(0.5*tt))^2; be = sin(tt);
6        ve = vector(p);  ve[1] = 1.0;
7        if ( t&1,  /* odd t, need complex values */
8            for (j=1, (p-1)>>1,
9                tt = c;
10               c -= (al*tt+be*s);
11               s -= (al*s -be*tt);
12               ve[j+1]   = c + I*s;
13               ve[p-j+1] = c - I*s;
14           );
15       , /* even t: can use real values */
16           for (j=1, (p-1)>>1,
17               tt = c;
18               c -= (al*tt+be*s);
19               s -= (al*s -be*tt);
20               ve[j+1]   = c + s;
21               ve[p-j+1] = c - s;
22           );
23       );
24       return( ve );
25   }
```

The computation of the field polynomial needs two changes for even t:

```
1    gauss_vpoly(n, t)=
2    {
3        [--snip--]
4        ve = vexp(p, t);  \\ precompute trigonometric values
5        [--snip--]
6                wk += ve[lift(a)+1];  \\ was:  wk += exp(2.0*I*Pi*lift(a)/p);
7        [--snip--]
8    }
```

For odd t we only need $n/2$ of the loop iterations:

```
1        for (k=1, n\2,  \\ note: n/2 times
2            tk *= tk1;  \\ == Mod(2,p)^k;
3            wk = 0;
4            a = tk;
5            for (j=0, t-1,
6                wk += ve[lift(a)+1];
7                a *= r;
8            );
9            \\ use (x-(a+I*b))*(x-(a-I*b)) == x^2 - 2*a*x + (a^2 + b^2):
10           zp *= (x^2-2*real(wk)*x+norm(wk));
11       );
```

Note that the polynomial is always real throughout the computation.

42.9.2.2 Algorithm working in GF(2)

The following algorithm is a variation of what is given in [340].

```
  n=4  t=3:  p=13  \\ integer computation
      r= Mod(3, 13)  ord(r)=3 ==  t
    M= x^12 + x^11 + x^10 + x^9 + x^8 + x^7 + x^6 + x^5 + x^4 + x^3 + x^2 + x + 1

    ------- k=1
    Z= x^9 + x^3 + x
    F= x^9 + x^3 + 2*x
    ------- k=2
    Z= x^6 + x^5 + x^2
    F= x^11 + x^10 + x^9 + x^8 + 2*x^7 + 2*x^6 + x^5 + x^4 + 2*x^3 + 3*x^2 + x
    ------- k=3
    Z= -x^11 - x^9 - x^8 - x^7 - x^6 - x^5 - x^3 - x^2 - x - 1
    F= -x^11 - x^10 - 2*x^9 + x^7 + 2*x^6 + x^3 - 1
    ------- k=4
    Z= x^11 + x^8 + x^7
    F= x^4 - x^3 + 2*x^2 + 4*x + 3

  ==> x^4 - x^3 + 2*x^2 + 4*x + 3   ==   x^4 + x^3 + 1 (mod 2)
```
```
  n=4  t=3:  p=13  \\ computation over GF(2)
      r= Mod(3, 13)  ord(r)=3 ==  t
    M= x^12 + x^11 + x^10 + x^9 + x^8 + x^7 + x^6 + x^5 + x^4 + x^3 + x^2 + x + 1

    ------- k=1
    Z= x^9 + x^3 + x
    F= x^9 + x^3 + 2*x
    ------- k=2
    Z= x^6 + x^5 + x^2
    F= x^11 + x^10 + x^9 + x^8 + x^5 + x^4 + x^2 + x
    ------- k=3
    Z =x ^ 1+1x^9 + x ^ 8 x^7 + x^6 + x^5 + x^3 + x^2 + x + 1
    F= x^11 + x^10 + x^7 + x^3 + 1
    ------- k=4
    Z= x^11 + x^8 + x^7
    F= x^4 + x^3 + 1

  ==>  x^4 + x^3 + 1
```

Figure 42.9-E: Computation of the field polynomial for $n = 4$ and $t = 3$ with polynomials over the integers (top) and polynomials over GF(2) (bottom).

1. Set $p = tn + 1$ and determine r such that the order of r modulo p equals t.

2. Set $M = \sum_{k=0}^{p-1} x^k$. All computations are done modulo M.

3. If t equals 1, then return M.

4. Set $F_0 = 1$ (modulo M).

5. For $1 \leq k \leq n$:

   (a) Set $Z_k = \sum_{j=0}^{t-1} x^{a(k,j)}$ (modulo M) where $a(k, j) = 2^k r^j \bmod p$.

   (b) Set $F_k = (x + Z_k) F_{i-1}$ (modulo M).

6. Return F_n.

The intermediate quantities in the computation for $n = 4$ and $t = 3$ are shown at the top of figure 42.9-E. The result is a polynomial over the integers identical to the one computed with the algorithm that uses complex numbers. When all polynomials are taken over GF(2) the computation proceeds as shown at the bottom of figure 42.9-E. Implementation in GP:

```
1   gauss_poly2(n, t)=
2   { /* return field polynomial for type-t Gaussian normal basis */
3       local(p, M, r, F, t21, t2, Z);
4
5       p = t*n + 1;
6       r = znprimroot(p)^n;  \\ element of order t mod p
7       M = sum(k=0, p-1, 'x^k);  \\ The polynomial modulus
8       M *= Mod(1,2);  \\ ... over GF(2)
9       if ( 1==t,  return( M ) );  \\ for type 1
10
11      F = Mod(1, M);
```

```
12        t21 = Mod(2,p);   t2 = Mod(1,p);
13        for (k=1, n,
14            Z = sum(j=0, t-1, Mod('x^lift(t2*r^j), M) );
15            F = ('x+Z)*F;
16            t2 *= t21;
17        );
18        return ( lift(F) );
19    }
```

While the algorithm avoids inexact arithmetic, the polynomial modulus M is of degree $p-1 = nt$ which is large for large t. The computation with complex numbers is much faster in practice. It finishes in less than a second for $n = 620$ and $t = 3$ (and a working precision of 150 decimal digits), the exact method needs about two minutes.

Using the redundant modulus $x^p - 1 = (x - 1) \cdot M$ gives a significant speedup:

```
1    gauss_poly2(n, t)=
2    {
3        local(p, M, r, F, t21, t2, Z);
4        p = t*n + 1;
5        r = znprimroot(p)^n;  \\ element of order t mod p
6        M = 'x^p - 1;  \\ Use redundant modulus (instead of sum(k=0, p-1, 'x^k))
7        M *= Mod(1,2);  \\ ... over GF(2)
8
9        if ( 1==t,  return( sum(k=0, p-1, 'x^k) ) );  \\ for type 1
10
11       [--snip--]   \\ main loop as before
12
13       \\ final reduction for redundant modulus:
14       M = sum(k=0, p-1, 'x^k);  \\ The polynomial modulus
15       F = lift( Mod( lift(F), M) );
16       return ( F );
17   }
```

Now computation of the polynomial for $n = 620$ and $t = 3$ takes less than nine seconds. The final reduction can be simplified by observing that no reduction is needed if the constant coefficient is one, else all coefficients just have to be negated. So the end of the routine can be changed to

```
1        \\ final reduction for redundant modulus (simplified):
2        F = lift(F);
3        if ( 0==polcoeff(F,0), F=sum(k=0, n, (1-polcoeff(F,k))*'x^k) );
4        return ( F );
5    }
```

"Ever tried. Ever failed. No matter.
Try Again. Fail again. Fail better."

— Samuel Beckett

Appendix A

The electronic version of the book

The electronic version of this book is available free of charge at `http://www.jjj.de/fxt/#fxtbook`, it is identical to the printed version.

Copyright and license

Copyright © Jörg Arndt.

The electronic version is distributed under the terms and conditions of the Creative Commons license "Attribution-Noncommercial-No Derivative Works 3.0". You are free to copy, distribute and transmit this book under the following conditions:

- **Attribution.** You must attribute the work in the manner specified by the author or licensor (but not in any way that suggests that they endorse you or your use of the work).

- **Noncommercial.** You may not use this work for commercial purposes.

- **No Derivative Works.** You may not alter, transform, or build upon this work.

For any reuse or distribution, you must make clear to others the license terms of this work. The best way to do this is with a link to the web page below. Any of the above conditions can be waived if you get permission from the copyright holder. Nothing in this license impairs or restricts the author's moral rights.

For more information about the license, visit `http://creativecommons.org/licenses/by-nc-nd/3.0/`.

How to make the hyperlinks work on your computer

The hyperlink showing as [FXT: bits/revbin.h] points to `file:.fxtdir/src/bits/revbin.h`. To make this work on your machine you may want to create (in the directory where the viewer is started) a soft-link to the directory of the FXT sources. For example, assuming that the package is located at `~/work/fxt`, execute the following statement:

```
ln -sv ~/work/fxt ~/.fxtdir
```

Similarly, for hfloat, do

```
ln -sv ~/work/hfloat ~/.hfloatdir
```

Test with the hyperlink [hfloat: src/hf/funcsrt.cc] which points to `file:.hfloatdir/src/hf/funcsrt.cc`.

For xdvi you may want to add the following lines to your `file:~/.mailcap`:

```
text/plain;/usr/bin/emacs -no-site-file %s &
text/x-csrc;/usr/bin/emacs -no-site-file %s &
text/x-chdr;/usr/bin/emacs -no-site-file %s &
text/x-c++src;/usr/bin/emacs -no-site-file %s &
text/x-c++hdr;/usr/bin/emacs -no-site-file %s &
```

Here the editor emacs is used for viewing plain text, C and C++ sources and headers.

Mozilla based browsers do not handle local links correctly, so you may want to use an alternative browser for this book, expecially with the pdf files.

Appendix B

Machine used for benchmarking

The machine used for performance measurements is an AMD64 (Athlon64) clocked at 2.2 GHz with dual channel double data rate (DDR) clocked at 200 MHz ('800 MHz'). It has 512 kB (16-way associative) second level cache and separate first level caches for data and instructions, each 64 kB (and 2-way associative). Cache lines are 64 bytes (8 words, 512 bits). The memory controller is integrated in the CPU.

The CPU has 16 general purpose (64 bit) registers that are addressable as byte, 16 bit word, 32 bit word, or 64 bit (full) word. These are used for integer operations and for passing integer function arguments. There are 16 (128 bit, SSE) registers that are used for floating-point operations and for passing floating-point function arguments. The SSE registers are SIMD registers. Additionally, there are 8 (legacy, x87) FPU registers.

The parts of the information reported by the CPUID instruction that are relevant for performance are:

```
Vendor: AuthenticAMD
Name: AMD Athlon(tm) 64 Processor 3500+
  Family: 15,  Model: 47,  Stepping: 2
Level 1 cache (data):  64 kB,  2-way associative.
  64 bytes per line,  lines per tag: 1.
Level 1 cache (instr):  64 kB,  2-way associative.
  64 bytes per line,  lines per tag: 1.
Level 2 cache:  512 kB,  16-way associative
  64 bytes per line,  lines per tag: 1.

Max virtual addr width: 48
Max physical addr width: 40
Features:
  lm: Long Mode (64-bit mode)
  nx: No-Execute Page Protection
  mtrr: Memory Type Range Registers
  tsc: Time Stamp Counter
  fpu: x87 FPU
  3dnow: AMD 3DNow! instructions
  3dnowext: AMD Extensions to 3DNow!
  mmx: Multimedia Extensions
  mmxext: AMD Extensions to MMX
  sse: Streaming SIMD Extensions
  sse2: Streaming SIMD Extensions-2
  sse3: Streaming SIMD Extensions-3
  cmov: CMOV instruction (plus FPU FCMOVCC and FCOMI)
  cx8: CMPXCHG8 instruction
  fxsr: FXSAVE and FXRSTOR instructions
  ffxsr: fast FXSAVE and FXRSTOR instructions
  lmlahf: load/store flags to ah (LAHF/SAHF) in 64-bit mode
```

Special instructions as SIMD, prefetch and non-temporal moves are not used unless explicitly noted.

See [169] for a comparison of instruction latencies and throughput for various x86 CPU cores. You do want to study the cited document *before* buying an x86-based system.

The compiler used was the GNU (C and C++) compiler [146].

Appendix C

The GP language

We give a short introduction to GP, the language of the pari calculator [266]. From the manual page (slightly edited):

```
NAME        gp - PARI calculator

SYNOPSIS    gp [-emacs] [-f] [-test] [-q] [-s stacksize] [-p primelimit]

DESCRIPTION
        Invokes the PARI-GP calculator. This is an advanced programmable calcu-
        lator, which computes symbolically as  long  as  possible,  numerically
        where  needed,  and  contains  a  wealth  of number-theoretic functions
        (elliptic curves, class field theory...).  Its basic data types are

        integers, real numbers, exact rational numbers,  algebraic  numbers,
        p-adic numbers, complex numbers,
        modular integers,
        polynomials and rational functions,
        power series,
        binary quadratic forms,
        matrices, vectors, lists,
        character strings,
        and recursive combinations of these.
```

Interactive usage

To use GP interactively, just type gp at your command line prompt. A startup message like the following will appear:

```
            GP/PARI CALCULATOR Version 2.3.4 (released)
        amd64 running linux (x86-64 kernel) 64-bit version
            compiled: Oct 14 2008, gcc-4.2.1 (SUSE Linux)
            (readline v5.2 enabled, extended help available)

                Copyright (C) 2000-2006 The PARI Group

PARI/GP is free software, covered by the GNU General Public License, and
comes WITHOUT ANY WARRANTY WHATSOEVER.

Type ? for help, \q to quit.
Type ?12 for how to get moral (and possibly technical) support.

parisize = 8000000, primelimit = 500000
?
```

The question mark in the last line is a prompt, the program is waiting for your input.

```
? 1+1
%1 = 2
```

Here we successfully computed one plus one. Next we compute a factorial:

```
? 44!
%2 = 2658271574788448768043625811014615890319638528000000000000
```

Integers are of unlimited precision, the practical limit is the amount of physical RAM. For floating-point numbers, the precision (number of decimal digits) can be set as follows

```
? default(realprecision,55)
%3 = 55
? sin(1.5)
%4 = 0.9974949866040544309417233711414873227066514259221158219
```

The history numbers %N (where N is a number) can be used to recall the result of a prior computation:

```
? %4
%5 = 0.99749498660405443094172337114148732270665142592211158219
```

The output of the result of a calculation can be suppressed using a semicolon at the end of the command. This is useful for timing purposes:

```
? default(realprecision,10000)
%5 = 10000
? sin(2.5);
? ##
  ***   last result computed in 100 ms.
```

The command `##` gives the time used for the last computation.

The printing format can be set independently of the precision used:

```
? default(realprecision,10000);
? default(format,"g.15");
? sin(2.5)
%6 = 0.598472144103956
```

Command line completion is available, typing `si`, then the tab-key, gives a list of built-in functions whose names start with `si`:

```
? si
  sigma      sign        simplify   sin      sinh       sizebyte  sizedigit
```

You can get the help text by using the question mark, followed by the help topic:

```
? ?sinh
  sinh(x): hyperbolic sine of x.
```

A help overview is invoked by a single question mark

```
? ?
Help topics: for a list of relevant subtopics, type ?n for n in
   0: user-defined identifiers (variable, alias, function)
   1: Standard monadic or dyadic OPERATORS
   2: CONVERSIONS and similar elementary functions
   3: TRANSCENDENTAL functions
   4: NUMBER THEORETICAL functions
   5: Functions related to ELLIPTIC CURVES
   6: Functions related to general NUMBER FIELDS
   7: POLYNOMIALS and power series
   8: Vectors, matrices, LINEAR ALGEBRA and sets
   9: SUMS, products, integrals and similar functions
  10: GRAPHIC functions
  11: PROGRAMMING under GP
  12: The PARI community
```

Select a section by its number:

```
? ?7
 0                     deriv             eval              factorpadic
 intformal             padicappr         polcoeff          polcyclo
 poldegree             poldisc           poldiscreduced    polhensellift
 polinterpolate        polisirreducible  pollead           pollegendre
 polrecip              polresultant      polroots          polrootsmod
 polrootspadic         polsturm          polsubcyclo       polsylvestermatrix
 polsym                poltchebi         polzagier         serconvol
 serlaplace            serreverse        subst             substpol
 substvec              taylor            thue              thueinit
```

You should try both of the following

```
? ??tutorial
  displaying 'tutorial.dvi'.
? ??
  displaying 'users.dvi'.
```

A short overview (which you may want to print) of most functions can be obtained via

```
? ??refcard
  displaying 'refcard.dvi'.
```

A session can be ended by either entering `quit` or just hitting control-d.

Built-in operators and basic functions

There are the 'usual' operators +, -, *, /, ^ (powering), and % (modulo). The operator \ gives the integer quotient without remainder. The assignment operator is =. C-style shortcuts are available, for example t+=3 is the same as t=t+3.

The increment by 1 can be abbreviated as t++, the decrement as t--. [Technical note: these behave as the C-language pre-increment (and pre-decrement), that is, the expression evaluates to t+1, not t. There is no post-increment or post-decrement in GP.]

Comparison operators are ==, != (alternatively <>), >, >=, <, and <=. Logical operators are && (and), (or), and ! (not)

Bit-wise operations for integers are

```
bitand  bitneg  bitnegimply  bitor  bittest  bitxor
```

and

```
shift(x,n): shift x left n bits if n>=0, right -n bits if n<0.
shiftmul(x,n): multiply x by 2^n (n>=0 or n<0)
```

One can also use the operators >> and <<, as in the C-language, and the shortcuts >>= and <<=.

An overview of basic functions is obtained as

```
? ?2
Col          List        Mat          Mod         Pol           Polrev       Qfb
Ser          Set         Str          Strchr      Strexpand     Strtex       Vec
Vecsmall     binary      bitand       bitneg      bitnegimply   bitor        bittest
bitxor       ceil        centerlift   changevar   component     conj         conjvec
denominator  floor       frac         imag        length        lift         norm
norml2       numerator   numtoperm    padicprec   permtonum     precision    random
real         round       simplify     sizebyte    sizedigit     truncate     valuation
variable
```

Here are a few:

```
sign(x): sign of x, of type integer, real or fraction.
max(x,y): maximum of x and y.
min(x,y): minimum of x and y.
abs(x): absolute value (or modulus) of x.

floor(x): floor of x = largest integer<=x.
ceil(x): ceiling of x=smallest integer>=x.
frac(x): fractional part of x = x-floor(x)
```

An overview of sums, products, and some numerical functions:

```
? ?9
intcirc          intfouriercos     intfourierexp      intfouriersin
intfuncinit      intlaplaceinv     intmellininv       intmellininvshort
intnum           intnuminit        intnuminitgen      intnumromb
intnumstep       prod              prodeuler          prodinf
solve            sum               sumalt             sumdiv
suminf           sumnum            sumnumalt          sumnuminit
sumpos
```

For example:

```
sum(X=a,b,expr,{x=0}): x plus the sum (X goes from a to b) of expression expr.
prod(X=a,b,expr,{x=1}): x times the product (X runs from a to b) of expression.
```

Basic data types

Strings:

```
? a="good day!"
  "good day!"
```

Integers, floating-point numbers (real or complex), and complex integers:

```
? factor(239+5*I)
  [-I 1]
  [1 + I 1]
  [117 + 122*I 1]
```

Exact rationals:

```
? 2/3+4/5
  22/15
```

Modular integers:

```
? Mod(3,239)^77
  Mod(128, 239)
```

Vectors and matrices:

```
? v=vector(5,j,j^2)
  [1, 4, 9, 16, 25]
? m=matrix(5,5,r,c,r+c)
  [2 3 4 5 6]
  [3 4 5 6 7]
  [4 5 6 7 8]
  [5 6 7 8 9]
  [6 7 8 9 10]
```

The vector is a row vector, trying to right-multiply it with the matrix fails:

```
? t=m*v
  ***   impossible multiplication t_MAT * t_VEC.
```

The operator ~ transposes vectors (and matrices), we multiply with the column vector:

```
? t=m*v~
%14 = [280, 335, 390, 445, 500]~
```

The result is a column vector, note the tilde at the end of the line.

Vector indices start with one:

```
? t[1]
%15 = 280
```

Symbolic computations

Univariate polynomials:

```
? (1+x)^7
  x^7 + 7*x^6 + 21*x^5 + 35*x^4 + 35*x^3 + 21*x^2 + 7*x + 1
? factor((1+x)^6+1)
  [x^2 + 2*x + 2 1]
  [x^4 + 4*x^3 + 5*x^2 + 2*x + 1 1]
```

Power series:

```
? (1+x+O(x^4))^7
  1 + 7*x + 21*x^2 + 35*x^3 + O(x^4)
? log((1+x+O(x^4))^7)
  7*x - 7/2*x^2 + 7/3*x^3 + O(x^4)
```

Types can be nested, here we compute modulo the polynomial $1 + x + x^7$ with coefficients over GF(2):

```
? t=Mod(1+x, Mod(1,2)*(1+x+x^7))^77
  Mod(Mod(1, 2)*x^3 + Mod(1, 2)*x + Mod(1, 2), Mod(1, 2)*x^7 + Mod(1, 2)*x + Mod(1, 2))
? lift(t)   \\ discard modulo polynomial
  Mod(1, 2)*x^3 + Mod(1, 2)*x + Mod(1, 2)
? lift(lift(t))   \\ discard modulo polynomial, then modulus 2 with coefficient
  x^3 + x + 1
```

Symbolic computations are limited when compared to a computer algebra system: for example, multivariate polynomials cannot (yet) be factored and there is no symbolic solver for polynomials.

An uninitialized variable evaluates to itself, as a symbol:

```
? hello
  hello
```

To create a symbol, prepend a tick:

```
? w=3
  3
? hello='w   /* the symbol w, not the value of w */
  w
```

Here is a method to create symbols:

```
? sym(k)=eval(Str("A", k))
? t=vector(5, j, sym(j-1))
  [A0, A1, A2, A3, A4]
```

The ingredients are eval() and Str():

```
eval(x): evaluation of x, replacing variables by their value.
Str({str}*): concatenates its (string) argument into a single string.
```

Some more trickery to think about:

```
sym(k)=eval(Str("A", k))
t=vector(5, j, sym(j-1));  print("1: t=", t);
{ for (k=1, 5,
    sy = sym(k-1);
    v = 1/k^2;
    /* assign to the symbol that sy evaluates to, the value of v: */
    eval( Str( Str( sy ), "=", Str( v ) ) );
); }
print("2: t=", t); /* no lazy evaluation with GP */
t=eval(t);   print("3: t=", t);
```

The output of this script is

```
1: t=[A0, A1, A2, A3, A4]
2: t=[A0, A1, A2, A3, A4]
3: t=[1, 1/4, 1/9, 1/16, 1/25]
```

More built-in functions

The following constants and transcendental functions are available:

```
? ?3
Euler         I             Pi            abs           acos          acosh         agm           arg
asin          asinh         atan          atanh         bernfrac      bernreal      bernvec       besselh1
besselh2      besseli       besselj       besseljh      besselk       besseln       cos           cosh
cotan         dilog         eint1         erfc          eta           exp           gamma         gammah
hyperu        incgam        incgamc       lngamma       log           polylog       psi           sin
sinh          sqr           sqrt          sqrtn         tan           tanh          teichmuller   theta
thetanullk    weber         zeta
```

To obtain information about a particular function, use a question mark:

```
? ?sinh
  sinh(x): hyperbolic sine of x.
```

Transcendental functions will also work with complex arguments and symbolically, returning a power series:

```
? sinh(x)
%9 = x + 1/6*x^3 + 1/120*x^5 + 1/5040*x^7 + 1/362880*x^9 \
    + 1/39916800*x^11 + 1/6227020800*x^13 + 1/1307674368000*x^15 + O(x^17)
```

The line break (and the backslash indicating it) was manually entered for layout reasons. The 'precision' (that is default order) of power series can be set by the user:

```
? default(seriesprecision,9);
? sinh(x)
%11 = x + 1/6*x^3 + 1/120*x^5 + 1/5040*x^7 + 1/362880*x^9 + O(x^10)
```

One can also manually give the $O(x^N)$ term:

```
? sinh(x+O(x^23))
%12 = x + 1/6*x^3 + 1/120*x^5 + 1/5040*x^7 + \
  [--snip--] \
  + 1/121645100408832000*x^19 + 1/51090942171709440000*x^21 + O(x^23)
```

Functions operating on matrices are (type `mat`, then hit the tab-key)

```
matadjoint       matalgtobasis    matbasistoalg    matcompanion
matdet           matdetint        matdiagonal      mateigen
matfrobenius     mathess          mathilbert       mathnf
mathnfmod        mathnfmodid      matid            matimage
matimagecompl    matindexrank     matintersect     matinverseimage
matisdiagonal    matker           matkerint        matmuldiagonal
matmultodiagonal matpascal        matrank          matrix
matrixqz         matsize          matsnf           matsolve
matsolvemod      matsupplement    mattranspose
```

Built-in number theoretical functions are

```
? ?4
addprimes       bestappr        bezout          bezoutres       bigomega        binomial
chinese         content         contfrac        contfracpnqn    core            coredisc
dirdiv          direuler        dirmul          divisors        eulerphi        factor
factorback      factorcantor    factorff        factorial       factorint       factormod
ffinit          fibonacci       gcd             hilbert         isfundamental   ispower
isprime         ispseudoprime   issquare        issquarefree    kronecker       lcm
moebius         nextprime       numbpart        numdiv          omega           precprime
prime           primepi         primes          qfbclassno      qfbcompraw      qfbhclassno
qfbnucomp       qfbnupow        qfbpowraw       qfbprimeform    qfbred          qfbsolve
quadclassunit   quaddisc        quadgen         quadhilbert     quadpoly        quadray
quadregulator   quadunit        removeprimes    sigma           sqrtint         zncoppersmith
znlog           znorder         znprimroot      znstar
```

Functions related to polynomials and power series are

```
? ?7
0                       deriv           eval                    factorpadic
intformal               padicappr       polcoeff                polcyclo
poldegree               poldisc         poldiscreduced          polhensellift
polinterpolate          polisirreducible pollead                pollegendre
polrecip                polresultant    polroots                polrootsmod
polrootspadic           polsturm        polsubcyclo             polsylvestermatrix
polsym                  poltchebi       polzagier               serconvol
serlaplace              serreverse      subst                   substpol
substvec                taylor          thue                    thueinit
```

Plenty to explore!

Control structures for programming

Some loop constructs available are

`while(a,seq)`: while a is nonzero evaluate the expression sequence seq. Otherwise 0.

`until(a,seq)`: evaluate the expression sequence seq until a is nonzero.

`for(X=a,b,seq)`: the sequence is evaluated, X going from a up to b.

`forstep(X=a,b,s,seq)`: the sequence is evaluated, X going from a to b in steps of s (can be a vector of steps)

`forprime(X=a,b,seq)`: the sequence is evaluated, X running over the primes between a and b.

`fordiv(n,X,seq)`: the sequence is evaluated, X running over the divisors of n.

The expression seq is a list of statements:

```
for ( k=1, 10,   stat1; stat2; stat3; )  /* last semicolon optional */
for ( k=1, 10,   stat1; )
for ( k=1, 10,   ; )  /* zero statements (do nothing, ten times) */
```

(The comments enclosed in /* */ were added manually.)

The loop-variable is local to the loop:

```
? for(k=1,10, ; )  /* do nothing, ten times */
? k
k /* not initialized in global scope ==> returned as symbol */
```

A global variable of the same name is not changed:

```
? k=7
7
? for(k=1,3, print("  k=",k))
  k=1
  k=2
  k=3
? k
7 /* global variable k not modified */
```

For the sake of clarity, avoid using global and loop-local variables of the same name.

A loop can be aborted with the statement `break()`. The n enclosing loops are aborted by `break(n)`. With `next()`, the next iteration of a loop is started (and the statements until the end of the loop are skipped). With `break(n)` the same is done for the n-th enclosing loop.

And yes, there is an `if` statement:

`if(a,seq1,seq2)`: if a is nonzero, seq1 is evaluated, otherwise seq2. seq1 and seq2 are optional, and if seq2 is omitted, the preceding comma can be omitted also.

To have more than one statement in the branches use semicolons between the statements:

```
if ( a==3, /* then */
    b=b+1;
    c=7;
    , /* else */
    b=b-1;
    c=0;
  );
```

Non-interactive usage (scripts)

Usually one will create scripts that are fed into gp (at the command line):

```
gp -q < myscript.gp
```

The option `-q` suppresses the startup message and the history numbers `%N`.

If the script contains just the line

```
exp(2.0)
```

the output would be

```
7.3890560989306502272304274605750078131
```

To also see the commands in the output, add a `default(echo,1);` to the top of the file. Then the output is

```
? exp(2.0)
7.3890560989306502272304274605750078131
```

You should use comments in your scripts, there are two types of them:

```
\\ a line comment, started with backslashes
/* a block comment
   can stretch over several lines, as in the C-language */
```

Comments are not visible in the output. With the script

```
default(echo, 1);
\\ sum of square numbers:
s=0;  for (k=1, 10, s=s+k*k);  s
```

the output would be

```
? default(echo,1);
? s=0;for(k=1,10,s=s+k*k);s
  385
```

Note that all blanks are removed (on input) and are therefore missing in the output.

A command can be broken into several lines if it is enclosed within a pair of braces:

```
{ for (k=1, 10,
      s=s+k*k;
      print(k,":   s=", s);
  ); }
```

This is equivalent to the one-liner

```
 for (k=1, 10,  s=s+k*k;  print(k,":   s=", s);  );
```

User-defined Functions

Now we define a function:

```
powsum(n, p)=
{ /* return the sum 1^p+2^p+3^p+...+n^p */
    local(t);
    t = 0;
    for (k=1, n,
        t = t+k^p);  \\ '^' is the powering operator
```

```
    return( t );
}
```

The statement `local(t);` makes sure that no global variable named `t` (if it exists) would be changed by the function. It must be the first statement in the function. The variable `k` in the `for()`-loop is automatically local and should not be listed with the locals. Note that each statement is terminated with a semicolon. The output would be

```
? powsum(n,p)=local(t);t=0;for(k=1,n,t=t+k^p);return(t);
? powsum(10,2)
  385
```

Note how the function definition is changed to a one-liner in the output.

If you have to use global variables, list them at the beginning of your script as follows:

```
global(var1, var2, var3);
```

Any attempt to use the listed names as names of function arguments or local variables in functions will trigger an error. Note the use of `global()` is deprecated in later versions of GP.

Arguments are passed by value. There is no mechanism for passing by reference, global variables can be a workaround for this.

Arguments can have defaults, as in

```
powsum(n, p=2)= /* etc */
```

Calling the function as either `powsum(9)` or `powsum(9,)` would compute the number of the first 9 squares. Defaults can appear anywhere in the argument list, as in

```
abcsum(a, b=3, c)= return( a+b+c );
```

So `abcsum(1,,1)` would return 5.

All arguments are implicitly given the default zero, so the sequence of statements

```
foo(a, b, c)= print(a,":",b,":",c);
foo(,,)
foo()
foo
```

will print three times `0:0:0`. This feature is rarely useful and does lead to obscure errors. It will hopefully be removed in future versions of GP.

Bibliography

A
---

[1] Milton Abramowitz, Irene A. Stegun, (eds.): **Handbook of Mathematical Functions**, National Bureau of Standards, 1964, third printing, (1965). 277, 604, 686, 687, 689, 691, 696, 697

[2] Ramesh C. Agarwal, James W. Cooley: **New algorithms for digital convolution**, IEEE Transactions on Acoustics, Speech, and Signal Processing, vol.ASSP-25, pp.392-410, (October-1977). 551

[3] Simon Joseph Agou, Marc Deléglise, Jean-Louis Nicolas: **Short Polynomial Representations for Square Roots Modulo** p, Designs, Codes and Cryptography, vol.28, pp.33-44, (2003). 784

[4] Manindra Agrawal, Neeraj Kayal, Nitin Saxena: **PRIMES is in P**, Annals of Mathematics, vol.160, no.2, pp.781-793, (September-2004). URL: http://annals.math.princeton.edu/annals/2004/160-2/p12.xhtml. 804

[5] Omran Ahmadi, Alfred Menezes: **On the number of trace-one elements in polynomial bases for** $\mathbb{F}_{2^n}$, Designs, Codes and Cryptography, vol.37, no.3, pp.493-507, (December-2005). URL: http://citeseerx.ist.psu.edu/viewdoc/summary?doi=10.1.1.5.2051. 896

[6] Omran Ahmadi, Alfred Menezes: **Irreducible polynomials of maximum weight**, Utilitas Mathematica, vol.72, pp.111-123, (2007). URL: http://www.math.uwaterloo.ca/~ajmeneze/research.html. 853

[7] W. R. Alford, Andrew Granville, Carl Pomerance: **There are infinitely many Carmichael numbers**, Annals of Mathematics, vol.139, pp.703-722, (1994). 786

[8] Jean-Paul Allouche, Jeffrey Shallit: **The ubiquitous Prouhet-Thue-Morse sequence**, In: C. Ding, T. Helleseth, H. Niederreiter, (eds.), Sequences and Their Applications: Proceedings of SETA'98, pp.1-16, Springer-Verlag, (1999). URL: http://www.cs.uwaterloo.ca/~shallit/papers.html. 44, 729

[9] Jean-Paul Allouche, Michael Cosnard: **The Komornik-Loreti constant is transcendental**, Amer. Math. Monthly, vol.107, pp.448-449, (2000). URL: http://www.lri.fr/~allouche/. 729

[10] Advanced Micro Devices (AMD) Inc.: **AMD Athlon Processor, x86 code optimization guide**, Publication no.22007, Revision K, (February-2002). URL: http://www.amd.com/. 19

[11] Advanced Micro Devices (AMD) Inc.: **Software Optimization Guide for AMD64 Processors**, Publication no.25112, Revision 3.06, (September-2005). URL: http://www.amd.com/. 6

[12] Advanced Micro Devices (AMD) Inc.: **Software Optimization Guide for AMD Family 10h Processors**, Publication no.40546, Revision 3.1, (May-2009). URL: http://www.amd.com/. 6

[13] Advanced Micro Devices (AMD) Inc.: **AMD64 Architecture Programmer's Manual. Volume 3: General-Purpose and System Instructions**, Publication no.24594, Revision 3.15, (November-2009). URL: http://www.amd.com/. 26

[14] Ray Andraka: **A survey of CORDIC algorithms for FPGA based computers**, In: Proceedings of the Sixth ACM/SIGDA International Symposium on Field-Programmable Gate Arrays (FPGA '98), ACM, pp.191-200, (1998). URL: http://www.andraka.com/papers.htm. 650

[15] George E. Andrews: **The theory of partitions**, Addison-Wesley, (1976). 344

[16] George E. Andrews: **Euler's Pentagonal Number Theorem**, Mathematics Magazine, vol.56, no.5, pp.279-284, (November-1983). 346

[17] George E. Andrews, Richard Askey, Ranjan Roy: **Special functions**, Cambridge University Press, (1999). 346, 348, 589, 686, 692, 702

[18] François Arnault: **Rabin-Miller Primality Test: Composite Numbers Which Pass It**, Mathematics of Computation, vol.64, no.209, pp.355-361, (January-1995). 791

[19] Jörg Arndt, Christoph Haenel: **Pi − Unleashed**, Springer-Verlag, (2000). Translation of: **Pi. Algorithmen, Computer, Arithmetik**, (1998). 615

[20] Jörg Arndt: **Arctan relations for Pi**, (May-2006). URL: http://www.jjj.de/arctan/arctanpage.html. 639

[21] Jörg Arndt: **FXT, a library of algorithms**, (1996-2009). URL: http://www.jjj.de/fxt/. xi

[22] Jörg Arndt: **hfloat, a library for high precision computations**, (1995-2009). URL: http://www.jjj.de/hfloat/. xi, 530

[23] Jörg Arndt: **Testing polynomial irreducibility without GCDs**, INRIA research report RR-6542, Nancy, France, (May-2008). URL: http://hal.inria.fr/inria-00281614/en/. 839, 840

[24] Jörg Arndt: **Generating Random Permutations**, PhD thesis, Australian National University, Camberra, Australia, (10-March-2010). URL: http://www.jjj.de/pub/. 117

[25] Mikhail J. Atallah, Samuel S. Wagstaff, Jr.: **Watermarking With Quadratic Residues**, In: Proc. of IS-T/SPIE Conf. on Security and Watermarking of Multimedia Contents, SPIE vol.3657, pp.283-288, (1999). URL: http://homes.cerias.purdue.edu/~ssw/water.html. 784

[26] Roberto Maria Avanzi: **Another Look at Square Roots (and Other Less Common Operations) in Fields of Even Characteristic**, Lecture Notes in Computer Science, vol.4876, pp.138-154, (2007). 889

B

[27] John C. Baez: **The Octonions**, Bulletin of the American Mathematical Society, vol.39, no.2, pp.145-205, (2002). URL: http://www.ams.org/journals/bull/2002-39-02/home.html. 816

[28] David H. Bailey: **FFTs in External or Hierarchical Memory**, Journal of Supercomputing, vol.4, no.1, pp.23-35, (March-1990). URL: http://crd.lbl.gov/~dhbailey/dhbpapers/. 438

[29] David H. Bailey, P. N. Swarztrauber: **The Fractional Fourier Transform and Applications**, SIAM Review, vol.33, no.3, pp.389-404, (September-1991). URL: http://crd.lbl.gov/~dhbailey/dhbpapers/. 456

[30] David H. Bailey, Jonathan M. Borwein, Peter B. Borwein, Simon Plouffe: **The Quest for Pi**, The Mathematical Intelligencer, vol.19, no.1, pp.50-57, (January-1997). URL: http://crd.lbl.gov/~dhbailey/dhbpapers/. 617, 618

[31] David H. Bailey, Richard E. Crandall: **On the Random Character of Fundamental Constant Expansions**, Experimental Mathematics, vol.10, no.2, pp.175-190, (June-2001). URL: http://www.expmath.org/. 626

[32] David H. Bailey: **Some Background on Kanada's Recent Pi Calculation**, manuscript, (16-May-2003). URL: http://crd.lbl.gov/~dhbailey/dhbpapers/dhb-kanada.pdf. 640

[33] Wilfrid Norman Bailey: **Products of generalized hypergeometric series**, Proceedings of the London Mathematical Society, Series 2, vol.s2-28, no.1, pp.242-254, (1928). 693

[34] Wilfrid Norman Bailey: **Generalized hypergeometric series**, Cambridge University Press, (1935). 692

[35] Robert Baillie, S. Wagstaff, Jr.: **Lucas Pseudoprimes**. Mathematics of Computation, vol.35, no.152, pp.1391-1417, (October-1980). 801

[36] Jean-Claude Bajard, Sylvanus Kla, Jean-Michel Muller: **BKM: A New Hardware Algorithm for Complex Elementary Functions**, IEEE Transactions on Computers, vol.43, no.8, (August-1994). URL: http://perso.ens-lyon.fr/jean-michel.muller/BKM94.pdf. 650

[37] Dominique Roelants van Baronaigien: **A Loopless Gray-Code Algorithm for Listing k-ary Trees**, Journal of Algorithms, vol.35, pp.100-107, (2000). 333

[38] Friedrich L. Bauer: **An Infinite Product for Square-Rooting with Cubic Convergence**, The Mathematical Intelligencer, vol.20, pp.12-13, (1998). 684

[39] M. Beeler, R. W. Gosper, R. Schroeppel: **HAKMEM**, MIT AI Memo 239, (29-February-1972). Retyped and converted to html by Henry Baker, (April-1995). URL: http://home.pipeline.com/~hbaker1/hakmem/hakmem.html. 59, 63, 85, 86, 672, 727

[40] Hacène Belbachir, Farid Bencherif: **Linear Recurrent Sequences and Powers of a Square Matrix**, INTEGERS: The Electronic Journal of Combinatorial Number Theory, vol.6, (2006). URL: http://www.integers-ejcnt.org/vol6.html. 667

[41] Jordan Bell: **Euler and the pentagonal number theorem**, arXiv:math/0510054v2 [math.HO], (17-August-2006). URL: http://arxiv.org/abs/math.HO/0510054. 346

[42] Fabrice Bellard: **Computation of 2700 billion decimal digits of Pi using a Desktop Computer**, technical notes, (11-February-2010). URL: http://bellard.org/pi/pi2700e9/. 454

[43] A. A. Bennett: **The four term Diophantine arccotangent relation**, Annals of Mathematics, Second Series, vol.27, no.1, pp.21-24, (September-1925). 638

[44] F. Bergeron, J. Berstel, S. Brlek: **Efficient computation of addition chains**, Journal de Théorie des Nombres de Bordeaux, vol.6, no.1, pp.21-38, (1994). URL: http://www.numdam.org/numdam-bin/item?id=JTNB_1994__6_1_21_0. 565

[45] Lennart Berggren, Jonathan Borwein, Peter Borwein, (eds.): **Pi: A Source Book**, Springer-Verlag, (1997). 615

[46] E. R. Berlekamp: **Factoring polynomials over finite fields**, Bell System Technical Journal, vol.46, pp.1853-1859, (1967). 858

[47] Bruce C. Berndt, S. Bahrgava, Frank G. Garvan: **Ramanujan's Theories of Elliptic Functions to Alternative Bases**, Transactions of the American Mathematical Society, vol.347, no.11, pp.4163-4244, (1995). URL: http://www.math.ufl.edu/~frank/publist.html. 613

[48] Bruce C. Berndt: **Flowers which we cannot yet see growing in Ramanujan's garden of hypergeometric series, elliptic functions and q's**, In: J. Bustoz, M. E. H. Ismail, S. K. Suslov, (eds.): Special Functions 2000: Current Perspective and Future Directions Kluwer, Dordrecht, pp.61-85, (2001). URL: http://www.math.uiuc.edu/~berndt/publications.html 612

[49] Pedro Berrizbeitia, T. G. Berry: **Generalized Strong Pseudoprime tests and applications**, Journal of Symbolic Computation, no.11, (1999). 792

[50] Eli Biham, Rafi Chen: **Near-Collisions of SHA-0**, Advances in Cryptology - CRYPTO'04, Lecture Notes in Computer Science, vol.3152, pp.290-305, (2004). URL: http://eprint.iacr.org/2004/146.ps. 870

[51] Eli Biham, Rafi Chen, Antoine Joux, Patrick Carribault, Christophe Lemuet, William Jalby: **Collisions of SHA-0 and Reduced SHA-1**, Lecture Notes in Computer Science, vol.3494, pp.36-57, (2005). 870

[52] James R. Bitner, Gideon Ehrlich, Edward M. Reingold: **Efficient generation of the binary reflected Gray code and its applications**, Communications of the ACM, vol.19, no.9, pp.517-521, (September-1976). 207

[53] Andreas Björklund, Thore Husfeldt, Petteri Kaski, Mikko Koivisto: **Fourier meets Möbius: fast subset convolution**, Proceedings of the thirty-ninth annual ACM Symposium on Theory of Computing, San Diego, California, USA, pp.67-74, (2007). URL: http://arxiv.org/abs/cs.DS/0611101. 496

[54] Ian F. Blake, Shuhong Gao, Ronald C. Mullin: **Explicit Factorization of $x^{2^k} + 1$ over $\mathbb{F}_p$ with Prime $p \equiv 3 \bmod 4$**, Applicable Algebra in Engineering, Communication and Computation 4, pp.89-94, (1993). URL: http://www.math.clemson.edu/~sgao/pub.html. 807

[55] Ian F. Blake, Shuhong Gao, Robert J. Lambert: **Construction and Distribution Problems for Irreducible Trinomials over Finite Fields**, In: D. Gollmann, (ed.): Applications of finite fields, pp.19-32, (1996). URL: http://www.math.clemson.edu/~sgao/pub.html. 851

[56] Leo I. Bluestein: **A linear filtering approach to the computation of the discrete Fourier transform**, IEEE Transactions on Audio and Electroacoustics, vol.18, pp.451-455, (December-1970). 455

[57] Antonia W. Bluher: **A Swan-like theorem**, Finite Fields and Their Applications, vol.12, pp.128-138, (28-June-2006). URL: http://arxiv.org/abs/math/0406538v2. 896

[58] Arnaud Bodin: **Number of irreducible polynomials in several variables over finite fields**, arXiv:0706.0157v2 [math.AC], (11-June-2007). URL: http://arxiv.org/abs/0706.0157v2. 843

[59] Marco Bodrato: **Towards Optimal Toom-Cook Multiplication for Univariate and Multivariate Polynomials in Characteristic 2 and 0**, Lecture Notes in Computer Science, vol.4547, pp.116-133, (2007). URL: http://bodrato.it/papers/.831, 896

[60] Marco Bodrato, Alberto Zanoni: **What About Toom-Cook Matrices Optimality?**, Technical Report 605, Centro Vito Volterra, Università di Roma Tor Vergata, (October-2006). URL: http://bodrato.it/papers/. 552, 555

[61] Marco Bodrato, Alberto Zanoni: **Integer and Polynomial Multiplication: Towards Optimal Toom-Cook Matrices**, Proceedings of the 2007 International Symposium on Symbolic and Algebraic Computation, pp.17-24, (2007). URL: http://portal.acm.org/citation.cfm?id=1277548.1277552. 553, 555

[62] Miklós Bóna: **Combinatorics of Permutations**, Chapman & Hall/CRC, (2004). 278

[63] J. M. Borwein, P. B. Borwein: **Cubic and higher order algorithms for** π, Canadian Mathematical Bulletin, vol.27, no.4, pp.436-443, (1984). URL: http://www.cecm.sfu.ca/~pborwein/PAPERS/papers.html. 619

[64] J. M. Borwein, P. B. Borwein: **More quadratically converging Algorithms for** π, Mathematics of Computation, vol.46, no.173, pp.247-253, (January-1986). URL: http://www.cecm.sfu.ca/~pborwein/PAPERS/papers.html. 615

[65] J. M. Borwein, P. B. Borwein: **An explicit cubic iteration for** π, BIT Numerical Mathematics, vol.26, no.1, (March-1986). URL: http://www.cecm.sfu.ca/~pborwein/PAPERS/papers.html. 620

[66] J. M. Borwein, P. B. Borwein: **Pi and the AGM**, Wiley, (1987). 601, 606, 616, 617, 621, 622, 692, 702

[67] J. M. Borwein, P. B. Borwein: **On the Mean Iteration** $(a, b) \leftarrow \left(\frac{a+3b}{4}, \frac{\sqrt{ab}+b}{2} \right)$, Mathematics of Computation, vol.53, no.187, pp.311-326, (July-1989). URL: http://www.cecm.sfu.ca/~pborwein/PAPERS/papers.html. 611, 621

[68] J. M. Borwein, P. B. Borwein: **A cubic counterpart of Jacobi's Identity and the AGM**, Transactions of the American Mathematical Society, vol.323, no.2, pp.691-701, (February-1991). URL: http://www.cecm.sfu.ca/~pborwein/PAPERS/papers.html. 611, 619

[69] J. M. Borwein, P. B. Borwein, F. Garvan: **Hypergeometric Analogues of the Arithmetic-Geometric Mean Iteration**, Constructive Approximation, vol.9, no.4, pp.509-523, (1993). URL: http://www.cecm.sfu.ca/~pborwein/PAPERS/papers.html. 611, 614

[70] J. M. Borwein, P. B. Borwein, F. G. Garvan: **Some cubic modular identities of Ramanujan**, Transactions of the American Mathematical Society, vol.343, no.1, pp.35-47, (May-1994). URL: http://www.math.ufl.edu/~frank/publist.html. 617

[71] J. M. Borwein, F. G. Garvan: **Approximations to** π **via the Dedekind eta function**, CMS Conference Proceedings, vol.20, pp.89-115, (1997). URL: http://www.math.ufl.edu/~frank/publist.html. 619, 620

[72] R. N. Bracewell, O. Buneman, H. Hao, J. Villasenor: **Fast Two-Dimensional Hartley Transform**, Proceedings of the IEEE, vol.74, no.9, pp.1282-1283, (September-1986). 530

[73] Florian Braun, Marcel Waldvogel: **Fast Incremental CRC Updates for IP over ATM Networks**, In: Proceedings of the 2001 IEEE Workshop on High Performance Switching and Routing, (2001). URL: http://marcel.wanda.ch/Publications/braun01fast. 871

[74] Richard P. Brent: **Algorithms for minimization without derivatives**, Prentice-Hall, (1973) (out of print). 588

[75] Richard P. Brent: **Fast multiple-precision evaluation of elementary functions**, Journal of the ACM (JACM), vol.23, no.2, pp.242-251, (April-1976). URL: http://www.rpbrent.com/. 615

[76] Richard P. Brent: **On computing factors of cyclotomic polynomials**, Mathematics of Computation, vol.61, no.203, pp.131-149, (July-1993). URL: http://www.rpbrent.com/. 802, 896

[77] Richard P. Brent: **On the periods of generalized Fibonacci recurrences**, Mathematics of Computation, vol.63, no.207, pp.389-401, (July-1994). URL: http://wwwmaths.anu.edu.au/~brent/pub/pubsall.html. 669

[78] Richard P. Brent: **Computing Aurifeuillian factors**, in: Computational Algebra and Number Theory, Mathematics and its Applications, vol.325, Kluwer Academic Publishers, Boston, pp.201-212, (1995). URL: http://www.rpbrent.com/. 802

[79] Richard P. Brent, Alfred J. van der Poorten, Herman J. J. te Riele: **A comparative Study of Algorithms for Computing Continued Fractions of Algebraic Numbers**, Lecture Notes in Computer Science, vol.1122, pp.35-47, (1996). URL: http://wwwmaths.anu.edu.au/~brent/pub/pubsall.html. 719

[80] Richard P. Brent, Samuli Larvala, Paul Zimmermann: **A Fast Algorithm for Testing Irreducibility of Trinomials mod 2 and some new primitive trinomials of degree 3021377**, Mathematics of Computation, vol.72, pp.1443-1452, (2003). URL: http://www.rpbrent.com/. 842

[81] Richard P. Brent: **Primality Testing**, Slides of talk to the Oxford University Invariant Society, (25-November-2003). URL: http://wwwmaths.anu.edu.au/~brent/talks.html. 804

[82] Richard P. Brent, Paul Zimmermann: **Algorithms for finding almost irreducible and almost primitive trinomials**, in: Primes and Misdemeanours: Lectures in Honour of the Sixtieth Birthday of Hugh Cowie Williams, Fields Institute Communication FIC/41, The Fields Institute, Toronto, pp.91-102, (2004). URL: http://www.rpbrent.com/. 850

[83] Richard P. Brent: **Fast Algorithms for High-Precision Computation of Elementary Functions**, slides of talk at RNC7, Nancy, (12-July-2006). URL: http://wwwmaths.anu.edu.au/~brent/talks.html. 658

[84] Richard P. Brent, Paul Zimmermann: **A Multi-level Blocking Distinct Degree Factorization Algorithm**, Finite Fields and Applications: Contemporary Mathematics, vol.461, pp.47-58, (2008). URL: http://www.rpbrent.com/. 842

[85] Richard P. Brent, Pierrick Gaudry, Emmanuel Thomé, Paul Zimmermann: **Faster Multiplication in $GF(2)[x]$**, INRIA Technical Report RR-6359, (November-2007). URL: http://hal.inria.fr/inria-00188261/ or http://www.rpbrent.com/. 832

[86] Dany Breslauer, Devdatt P. Dubhashi: **Combinatorics for Computer Scientists**, BRICS Lecture Series, LS-95-4, (August-1995). URL: http://www.brics.dk/LS/95/4/BRICS-LS-95-4/BRICS-LS-95-4.html. 707

[87] David M. Bressoud: **A generalization of the Rogers-Ramanujan identities for all moduli**, Journal of Combinatorial Theory, Series A, vol.27, no.1, pp.64-68, (July-1979). 347

[88] John Brillhart, Derrick H. Lehmer, John L. Selfridge: **New primality criteria and factorizations of $2^m \pm 1$**, Mathematics of Computation, vol.29, no.130, pp.620-647, (April-1975). 795

[89] J. Brillhart, D. H. Lehmer, J. L. Selfridge, B. Tuckerman, S. S. Wagstaff, Jr.: **Factorizations of $b^n \pm 1$** $b = 2, 3, 5, 6, 10, 11$ **up to high powers**, Contemporary Mathematics, vol.22, second edition, American Mathematical Society, (1988). URL: http://www.ams.org/. 797, 804, 842

[90] Bette Bultena, Frank Ruskey: **An Eades-McKay Algorithm for Well-Formed Parentheses Strings**, Information Processing Letters, vol.68, no.5, pp.255-259, (1998). URL: http://www.cs.uvic.ca/~ruskey/Publications/. 329

[91] Ronald Joseph Burthe, Jr.: **Further Investigations with the Strong Probable Prime Test**, Mathematics of Computation, vol.65, no.213, pp.373-381, (January-1996). 790

$$\boxed{\text{C}}$$

[92] David G. Cantor: **On arithmetical algorithms over finite fields**, Journal of Combinatorial Theory, Series A, vol.50, no.2, pp.285-300, (March-1989). 832

[93] K. Cattel, S. Zhang, X. Sun, M. Serra, J. C. Muzio, D. M. Miller: **One-Dimensional Linear Hybrid Cellular Automata: Their Synthesis, Properties, and Applications in VLSI Testing**, tutorial paper, (2009). URL: http://webhome.cs.uvic.ca/~mserra/CA.html. 882

[94] Kevin Cattel, Shujian Zhang: **Minimal Cost One-Dimensional Linear Hybrid Cellular Automata of Degree Through 500**, Journal of Electronic Testing: Theory and Applications, vol.6, pp.255-258, (1995). URL: http://www.cs.uvic.ca/~mserra/CA.html. 878

[95] Kevin Cattell, Frank Ruskey, Joe Sawada, Micaela Serra, C. Robert Miers: **Fast Algorithms to Generate Necklaces, Unlabeled Necklaces, and Irreducible Polynomials over** GF(2), Journal of Algorithms, vol.37, pp.267-282, (2000). URL: http://www.cis.uoguelph.ca/~sawada/pub.html. 374, 856

[96] Heng Huat Chan: **On Ramanujan's cubic transformation formula for** $_2F_1(\frac{1}{3}, \frac{2}{3}; 1; z)$, Mathematical Proceedings of the Cambridge Philosophical Society, vol.124, pp.193-204, (September-1998). 611

[97] Heng Huat Chan, Kok Seng Chua, Patrick Solé: **Quadratic iterations to** π **associated with elliptic functions to the cubic and septic base**, Transactions of the American Mathematical Society, vol.355, pp.1505-1520, (2003). URL: http://www.ams.org/tran/2003-355-04/S0002-9947-02-03192-6/. 611, 620, 621

[98] W. Chaundy: **On Clausen's hypergeometric identity**, The Quarterly Journal of Mathematics, Oxford, vol.9, no.1, pp.265-274, (1958). 692

[99] William Y. C. Chen, Amy M. Fu: **Cauchy augmentation for basic hypergeometric series**, Bulletin of the London Mathematical Society, vol.36, pp.169-175, (2004). 344

[100] Howard Cheng, Guillaume Hanrot, Emmanuel Thomé, Eugene Zima, Paul Zimmermann: **Time- and Space-Efficient Evaluation of Some Hypergeometric Constants**, International Symposium on Symbolic and Algebraic Computation, ISSAC'07, pp.85-91, (2007). URL: http://hal.inria.fr/inria-00177850/. 656

[101] Busiso P. Chisala: **A Quick Cayley-Hamilton**, The American Mathematical Monthly, vol.105, no.9, pp.842-844, (November-1998). 900

[102] D. V. Chudnovsky, G. V. Chudnovsky: **The computation of classical constants**, Proceedings of the National Academy of Sciences of the United States of America, vol.86, no.21, pp.8178-8182, (1-November-1989). 651

[103] Fan Chung, Persi Diaconis, Ronald Graham: **Universal cycles for combinatorial structures**, Discrete Mathematics, vol.11, pp.43-59, (1992). URL: http://www-stat.stanford.edu/~cgates/PERSI/papers/92_06_universal_cycles.pdf. 875

[104] Jaewook Chung, M. Anwar Hasan: **Asymmetric Squaring Formulae**, Centre for Applied Cryptographic Research, University of Waterloo, Ontario, Canada, (3-August-2006). URL: http://www.cacr.math.uwaterloo.ca/tech_reports.html. 551, 553, 557

[105] Frédérick Chyzak, Peter Paule, Otmar Scherzer, Armin Schoisswohl, Burkhard Zimmermann: **The construction of orthonormal wavelets using symbolic methods and a matrix analytical approach for wavelets on the interval**, Experimental Mathematics, vol.10, no.1, pp.67-86, (2001). 547

[106] Mathieu Ciet, Jean-Jacques Quisquater, Francesco Sica: **A Short Note on Irreducible Trinomials in Binary Fields**, (2002). URL: http://www.dice.ucl.ac.be/crypto/publications/2002/poly.ps. 850

[107] Douglas W. Clark, Lih-Jyh Weng: **Maximal and Near-Maximal Shift Register Sequences: Efficient Event Counters and Easy Discrete Logarithms**, IEEE Transactions on Computers, vol.43, no.5, pp.560-568, (May-1994). 850

[108] Thomas Clausen: **Ueber die Fälle, wenn die Reihe von der Form** $y = 1 + \frac{\alpha}{1} \cdot \frac{\beta}{\gamma} x +$ $\frac{\alpha.\alpha+1}{1.2} \cdot \frac{\beta.\beta+1}{\gamma.\gamma+1} x^2 +$ **etc. ein Quadrat von der Form** $z = 1 + \frac{\alpha'}{1} \cdot \frac{\beta'}{\gamma'} \cdot \frac{\delta'}{\epsilon'} x + \frac{\alpha'.\alpha'+1}{1.2} \cdot \frac{\beta'.\beta'+1}{\gamma'.\gamma'+1} \cdot \frac{\delta'.\delta'+1}{\epsilon'.\epsilon'+1} x^2 +$ **etc. hat**, Journal für die reine und angewandte Mathematik, vol.3, pp.89-91, (1828). URL: http://www.digizeitschriften.de/main/dms/toc/?PPN=PPN243919689_0003. 691

[109] Thomas Clausen: **Beitrag zur Theorie der Reihen**, Journal für die reine und angewandte Mathematik, vol.3, pp.92-95, (1828). URL: http://www.digizeitschriften.de/main/dms/toc/?PPN=PPN243919689_0003. 708

[110] Henri Cohen: **A Course in Computational Algebraic Number Theory**, Springer-Verlag, (1993). Online errata list at http://www.ufr-mi.u-bordeaux.fr/~cohen/. 13, 636, 782, 784, 795, 804, 860, 863, 883

[111] Henri Cohen, Fernando Rodriguez Villegas, Don Zagier: **Convergence acceleration of alternating series**, Experimental Mathematics, vol.9, no.1, pp.3-12, (2000). URL: http://www.expmath.org/. 662

[112] Henri Cohen: **Analysis of the sliding window powering method**, Journal of Cryptology, vol.18, no.1, pp.63-76, (January-2005). Preprint titled "Analysis of the flexible window powering method" URL: http://www.math.u-bordeaux.fr/~cohen/. 565

[113] Stephen D. Cohen: **The Explicit Construction of Irreducible Polynomials Over Finite Fields**, Designs, Codes and Cryptography, vol.2, no.2, pp.169-174, (June-1992). 855

[114] Stephen A. Cook: **On the minimum computation time of functions**, PhD thesis, Department of Mathematics, Harvard University, (1966). URL: http://www.cs.toronto.edu/~sacook/. 551

[115] Thomas H. Cormen, Charles E. Leiserson, Ronald L. Rivest, Clifford Stein: **Introduction to Algorithms**, MIT Press, second edition, (2001). 134, 579

[116] Richard Crandall, Barry Fagin: **Discrete Weighted Transforms and Large-Integer Arithmetic**, Mathematics of Computation, vol.62, no.205, pp.305-324, (January-1994). 449

[117] Richard E. Crandall, Ernst W. Mayer, Jason S. Papadopoulos: **The twenty-fourth Fermat number is composite**, Mathematics of Computation, vol.72, no.243, pp.1555-1572, (6-December-2002). 795

[118] Richard Crandall, Carl Pomerance: **Prime Numbers: A Computational Perspective**, second edition, Springer-Verlag, (2005). 792, 804

[119] Reiner Creutzburg, Manfred Tasche: **Parameter Determination for Complex Number-Theoretic Transforms Using Cyclotomic Polynomials**, Mathematics of Computation, vol.52, no.185, pp.189-200, (January-1989). 808

D

[120] Ricardo Dahab, Darrel Hankerson, Fei Hu, Men Long, Julio Lopez, Alfred Menezes: **Software Multiplication using Normal Bases**, IEEE Transactions on Computers, vol.55, pp.974-984, (2006). Online as technical report CACR 2004-12 at http://www.cacr.math.uwaterloo.ca/. 902

[121] Ivan B. Damgård, Peter Landrock, Carl Pomerance: **Average case error estimates for the strong probable prime test**, Mathematics of Computation, vol.61, no.203, pp.177-194, (July-1993). 790

[122] Ivan B. Damgård, Gudmund Skovbjerg Frandsen: **An extended quadratic Frobenius primality test with average and worst case error estimates**, IEEE Transactions on Computers, vol.19, pp.783-793, (February-2003). URL: http://www.brics.dk/RS/03/9/index.html. 792

[123] Leonard Eugene Dickson: **History of the Theory of Numbers, vol.I, Divisibility and Primality**, Carnegie Institute of Washington, 1919, unaltered reprint of the AMS, vol.1-3, (2002). 342, 707

[124] Alfred Cardew Dixon: **The elementary properties of the elliptic functions, with examples**, Macmillan, (1894). URL: http://www.archive.org/details/117736039. 604

[125] Geoffrey Dixon: **Division Algebras, Galois Fields, Quadratic Residues**, Acta Applicandae Mathematicae, vol.50, no.1-2, pp.111-120, (January-1998). URL: http://arxiv.org/abs/hep-th/9302113. 818

[126] Christophe Doche: **Redundant Trinomials for Finite Fields of Characteristic 2**, Lecture Notes in Computer Science, vol.3574, pp.122-133, (2005). URL: http://www.ics.mq.edu.au/~doche/redundant.pdf. 850

[127] R. W. Doran: **The Gray Code**, Journal of Universal Computer Science, vol.13, no.11, pp.1573-1597, (2007). URL: http://www.jucs.org/jucs_13_11/the_gray_code/. 44

[128] Gabriele Drauschke, Manfred Tasche: **Prime factorizations of values of cyclotomic polynomials in** $\mathbb{Z}[i]$, Archiv der Mathematik, vol.49, no.4, pp.292-300, (October-1987). 802

[129] P. Duhamel, H. Hollmann: **Split radix FFT algorithm**, Electronics Letters, vol.20, no.1, pp.14-16, (5-January-1984). 427

[130] Pierre Duhamel: **Implementation of "split-radix" FFT algorithms for complex, real and real-symmetric data**, IEEE Transactions on Acoustics, Speech and Signal Processing, vol.34 pp.285-295, (1986). 434

[131] G. Duhamel, M. Vetterli: **Fast Fourier transforms: a tutorial review and a state of the art**, Signal Processing, vol.19, no.4, pp.259-299, (1990). 458

[132] Richard Durstenfeld: **Algorithm 235: random permutation**, Communications of the ACM, vol.7, no.7, p.420, (July-1964). 111

[133] Jacques Dutka: **On Square Roots and Their Representations**, Archive for History of Exact Sciences, vol.36, no.1, pp.21-39, (March-1986). 684

E

[134] Peter Eades, Brendan McKay: **An algorithm for generating subsets of fixed size with a strong minimal change property**, Information Processing Letters, vol.19, p.131-133, (19-October-1984). 183

[135] H.-D. Ebbinghaus, H. Hermes, F. Hirzebruch, M. Koecher, K. Mainzer, J. Neukirch, A. Prestel, R. Remmert: **Zahlen**, second edition. English translation: **Numbers**, Springer-Verlag, (1988). 58, 816, 818

[136] Karen Egiazarian, Jaako Astola: **Discrete Orthogonal Transforms Based on Fibonacci-type recursions**, IEEE Digital Signal Processing Workshop Proceedings, pp.405-408, (September-1996). URL: http://citeseerx.ist.psu.edu/viewdoc/summary?doi=10.1.1.40.3844. 513

[137] Gideon Ehrlich: **Loopless Algorithms for Generating Permutations, Combinations, and Other Combinatorial Configurations**, Journal of the ACM, vol.20, no.3, pp.500-513, (July-1973). 254

[138] Doron Zeilberger ('Shalosh B.EKHAD'): **Forty "Strange" Computer-Discovered Hypergeometric Series Evaluations**, (12-October-2004). URL: http://www.math.rutgers.edu/~zeilberg/pj.html. 687

[139] Arthur Erdélyi, Wilhelm Magnus, Fritz Oberhettinger, Francesco G. Tricomi: **Higher Transcendental Functions**, McGraw–Hill, New York, vol.1-3, (1953). 686, 691, 693, 702, 705, 706

F

[140] Steven R. Finch: **Mathematical Constants**, Cambridge University Press, (2003). List of errata online at http://algo.inria.fr/bsolve/. 692, 744

[141] N. J. Fine: **Binomial Coefficients Modulo a Prime**, The American Mathematical Monthly, vol.54, no.10, pp.589-592, (December-1947). 914

[142] N. J. Fine: **Infinite Products for k-th Roots**, The American Mathematical Monthly, vol.84, no.8. pp.629-630, (October-1977). 684

[143] Philippe Flajolet, Robert Sedgewick: **Analytic Combinatorics**, Cambridge University Press, (2009). URL: http://algo.inria.fr/flajolet/Publications/AnaCombi/anacombi.html. 173

[144] Agner Fog: **Software optimization resources**, (2010). URL: http://www.agner.org/optimize/. 6

[145] K. Fong, D. Hankerson, J. López, A. Menezes: **Field inversion and point halving revisited**, Technical Report, CORR 2003-18, Department of Combinatorics and Optimization, University of Waterloo, Canada, (2003). URL: http://www.cacr.math.uwaterloo.ca/techreports/2003/tech_reports2003.html. 888

[146] The Free Software Foundation (FSF): **GCC, the GNU Compiler Collection**, version 4.2.1. URL: http://gcc.gnu.org/. 21, 922

[147] The Free Software Foundation (FSF): **Other built-in functions provided by GCC**, section 5.47 of the documentation for GCC version 4.2.1. URL: http://gcc.gnu.org/onlinedocs/gcc-4.2.1/gcc/Other-Builtins.html. 21

G

[148] Yves Gallot: **Cyclotomic polynomials and prime numbers**, Note, revised version, (5-January-2001). URL: http://perso.wanadoo.fr/yves.gallot/papers/cyclotomic.html 802

[149] Shuhong Gao: **Normal Bases over Finite Fields**, PhD thesis, University of Waterloo, Ontario, Canada, (1993). URL: http://www.math.clemson.edu/~sgao/pub.html. 807, 855

[150] Shuhong Gao, Daniel Panario: **Tests and Constructions of Irreducible polynomials over Finite Fields**, In: F. Cucker, M. Shub, (eds.): Foundations of Computational Mathematics, Springer-Verlag, pp.346-361, (1997). URL: http://www.math.clemson.edu/~sgao/pub.html. 839

[151] Frank Garvan: **Cubic modular identities of Ramanujan, hypergeometric functions and analogues of the arithmetic-geometric mean iteration**, Contemporary Mathematics, vol.166, pp.245-264, (1993). URL: http://www.math.ufl.edu/~frank/publist.html. 611

[152] Frank Garvan: **Ramanujan's theories of elliptic functions to alternative bases – a symbolic excursion**, J. Symbolic Computation, vol.20, no.5-6, pp.517-536, (1995). Revised 16-December-2005 edition URL: http://www.math.ufl.edu/~frank/publist.html. 614

[153] Joachim von zur Gathen, Victor Shoup: **Computing Frobenius maps and factoring polynomials**, Computational Complexity, vol.2, pp.187-224, (1992). URL: http://www.shoup.net/papers/. 896

[154] Joachim von zur Gathen, Jürgen Gerhard: **Modern Computer Algebra**, Cambridge University Press, second edition, (2003). List of errata URL: http://www-math.upb.de/mca/. 704, 804, 863

[155] Pierrick Gaudry, Alexander Kruppa, Paul Zimmermann: **A GMP-based implementation of Schönhage-Strassen's large integer multiplication algorithm**, Proceedings of the 2007 International Symposium on Symbolic and Algebraic Computation (ISSAC'07), Waterloo, Ontario, Canada, pp.167-174, (2007). URL: http://portal.acm.org/citation.cfm?id=1277548.1277572 and http://www.loria.fr/~gaudry/publis/issac07.pdf. 561

[156] Willi Geiselmann, Dieter Gollmann: **Self-dual bases in** $\mathbb{F}_{q^n}$, Designs, Codes and Cryptography, vol.3, pp.333-345, (1993). 910

[157] S. Georgiou, C. Koukouvinos, J. Seberry: **Hadamard matrices, orthogonal designs and construction algorithms**, in: Designs 2002: Further Combinatorial and Constructive Design Theory, Kluwer Academic Publishers, Norwell, Massachusetts, pp.133-205, (2002). URL: http://works.bepress.com/jseberry/75/. 390

[158] (GMP developers): **GNU MP: The GNU Multiple Precision Arithmetic Library**, ver.4.3.0, (14-April-2009). URL: http://gmplib.org/. 681

[159] Solomon W. Golomb: **Cyclotomic Polynomials and Factorization Theorems**, The American Mathematical Monthly, vol.85, no.9, pp.734-737, (November-1978). 802

[160] Daniel M. Gordon: **A survey of fast exponentiation methods**, Journal of Algorithms, vol.27, no.1, pp.129-146, (1998). URL: http://www.ccrwest.org/gordon/jalg.pdf. 565

[161] J. A. Gordon: **Very simple method to find the minimum [sic] polynomial of an arbitrary nonzero element of a finite field**, Electronics Letters, vol.12, no.25, pp.663-664, (9-December-1976). 894

[162] Mark Goresky, Andrew Klapper: **Fibonacci and Galois Representations of Feedback with Carry Shift Registers**, IEEE Transactions on Information Theory, vol.48, no.11, pp.2826-2836, (November-2002). URL: http://www.math.ias.edu/~goresky/. 877

[163] Édouard Goursat: **Sur l'équation différentielle linéaire, qui admet pour intégrale la série hypergéométrique**, Annales scientifiques de l'École Normale Supérieure, Sér.2, vol.10, pp.3-142 (supplement), (1881). URL: http://www.numdam.org/item?id=ASENS_1881_2_10__S3_0. 691

[164] Édouard Goursat: **Mémoire sur les fonctions hypergéométriques d'ordre supérieur (seconde partie)**, Annales scientifiques de l'École Normale Supérieure, Sér.2, vol.12, pp.395-430, (1883). URL: http://www.numdam.org/item?id=ASENS_1883_2_12__395_0. 692

[165] Johannes Grabmeier, Alfred Scheerhorn: **Finite Fields in AXIOM**, AXIOM Technical Report no.ATR/5, (1992). URL: http://citeseerx.ist.psu.edu/viewdoc/summary?doi=10.1.1.46.7813. 904

[166] R. L. Graham, D. E. Knuth, O. Patashnik: **Concrete Mathematics**, second printing, Addison-Wesley, New York, (1988). 173, 277, 278, 331, 686, 689, 725, 754

[167] R. L. Graham, M. Grötschel, L. Lovász (eds.): **Handbook of combinatorics**, Elsevier, (1995). 173

[168] Torbjörn Granlund, Peter L. Montgomery: **Division by Invariant Integers using Multiplication**, SIGPLAN Notices, vol.29, pp.61-72, (June-1994). URL: http://gmplib.org/~tege/. 3

[169] Torbjörn Granlund: **Instruction latencies and throughput for AMD and Intel x86 processors**, (18-November-2009). URL: http://gmplib.org/~tege/x86-timing.pdf. 922

[170] Andrew Granville: **It is easy to determine whether a given integer is prime**, Bulletin of the American Mathematical Society, vol.42, no.1, pp.3-38, (2005). URL: http://www.ams.org/journals/bull/2005-42-01/. 804

[171] David Gries, Jinyun Xue: **Generating a random cyclic permutation**, BIT Numerical Mathematics, vol.28, no.3, pp.569-572, (September-1988). 112

[172] S. Gudvangen: **Practical Applications of Number Theoretic Transforms**, NORSIG-99, Norwegian Signal Processing Symposium, (1999). URL: http://www.ux.uis.no/norsig/norsig99/Articles/gudvangen.pdf. 542

[173] Jesús Guillera: **Easy Proofs of Some Borwein Algorithms for** π, arXiv:0803.0991v1 [math.NT], (7-March-2008). URL: http://arxiv.org/abs/0803.0991v1. 616

H

[174] Bruno Haible: **CLN, a class library for numbers**, (1996). URL: http://www.ginac.de/CLN/. 656

[175] Bruno Haible, Thomas Papanikolaou: **Fast multiprecision evaluation of series of rational numbers**, Technical Report, no. TI-7/97, (18-March-1997). URL: http://www.informatik.th-darmstadt.de/TI/Veroeffentlichung/TR/Welcome.html. 655

[176] G. H. Hardy, E. M. Wright: **An Introduction to the Theory of Numbers**, Oxford University Press, fifth edition, (1979). 346, 347, 707

[177] R. V. L. Hartley: **A More Symmetrical Fourier Analysis Applied to Transmission Problems**, Proceedings of the IRE, vol.30, pp.144-150, (March-1942). 515

[178] B. R. Heap: **Permutations by Interchanges**, The Computer Journal, vol.6, pp.293-294, (1963). URL: http://comjnl.oxfordjournals.org/cgi/content/abstract/6/3/293. 249

[179] Gerben J. Hekstra, Ed F. A. Deprettere: **Floating Point Cordic (extended version)**, Technical Report ET/NT 93.15, Delft University of Technology, (8-March-1993). URL: http://citeseerx.ist.psu.edu/viewdoc/summary?doi=10.1.1.56.7269. 650

[180] Nicholas J. Higham: **The Matrix Sign Decomposition and its Relation to the Polar Decomposition**, Linear Algebra and its Applications, 212-213, pp.3-20, (1994). URL: http://www.maths.manchester.ac.uk/~higham/papers/matrix-functions.php. 579

[181] Nicholas J. Higham: **Stable Iterations for the Matrix Square Root**, Numerical Algorithms, vol.15, no.2, pp.227-242, (1997). URL: http://www.maths.manchester.ac.uk/~higham/papers/matrix-functions.php. 579

[182] David Hilbert: **Ueber die stetige Abbildung einer Linie auf ein Flächenstück**, Mathematische Annalen, vol.38, pp.459-460, (1891). 83

[183] Charles A. R. Hoare: **Quicksort**, The Computer Journal, vol.5, no.1, pp.10-16, (1962). URL: http://comjnl.oxfordjournals.org/cgi/content/abstract/5/1/10. 135

[184] Christian W. Hoffmann: π **und das arithmetisch-geometrische Mittel**, Swiss Federal Research Institute WSL, (9-April-2002). URL: http://www.wsl.ch/staff/christian.hoffmann/pi.pdf. 620

[185] Alston S. Householder: **Polynomial Iterations to Roots of Algebraic Equations**, Proceedings of the American Mathematical Society, vol.2, no.5, pp.718-719, (October-1951). 586

[186] Alston S. Householder: **The Numerical Treatment of a Single Nonlinear Equation**, McGraw-Hill, (1970). 587, 588, 589, 592, 593, 598

[187] Thomas D. Howell, Jean-Claude Lafon: **The Complexity of the Quaternion Product**, Technical Report TR-75-245, Department of Computer Science, Cornell University, Ithaca, NY, (June-1975). URL: http://home.pipeline.com/~hbaker1/. 818

[188] Glenn Hurlbert, Garth Isaak: **On the de Bruijn Torus problem**, Journal of Combinatorial Theory, Series A, vol.64, no.1, pp.50-62, (September-1993). URL: http://math.la.asu.edu/~hurlbert/papers/DBTP.pdf. 875

I J

[189] F. M. Ives: **Permutation enumeration: four new permutation algorithms**, Communications of the ACM, vol.19, no.2, pp.68-72, (February-1976). 270

[190] Michael J. Jacobson, Hugh C. Williams: **Solving the Pell equation**, Springer-Verlag, (2009). 815

[191] Gerhard Jaeschke: **On strong pseudoprimes to several bases**, Mathematics of Computation, vol.61, no.204, pp.915-926, (October-1993). 789

[192] T. A. Jenkyns: **Loopless Gray Code Algorithms**, Technical Report CS-95-03, Brock University, Canada, (July-1995). URL: http://www.cosc.brocku.ca/Department/Research/TR/cs9503.ps. 206, 214

[193] Selmer M. Johnson: **Generation of permutations by adjacent transposition**, Mathematics of Computation, vol.17, no.83, pp.282-285, (July-1963). 254

[194] W. P. Johnson: **How Cauchy Missed Ramanujan's** $_1\psi_1$ **Summation**, American Mathematical Monthly, vol.111, no.9, pp.791-800, (November-2004). 344

[195] Dieter Jungnickel, Alfred J. Menezes, Scott A. Vanstone: **On the Number of Self-Dual Bases of** $GF(q^m)$ **Over** $GF(q)$, Proceedings of the American Mathematical Society, vol.109, no.1, pp.23-29, (May-1990). URL: http://www.math.uwaterloo.ca/~ajmenezes/publications/sdb.pdf. 909

K

[196] Bahman Kalantari, Jürgen Gerlach: **Newton's Method and Generation of a Determinantal Family of Iteration Functions**, Technical Report DCS-TR 371, Dept. of Computer Science, Rutgers University, New Brunswick, NJ, (1998). URL: http://citeseerx.ist.psu.edu/viewdoc/summary?doi=10.1.1.55.2629. 592

[197] Bahman Kalantari, Y. Yin: **On Extraneous Fixed-Points of the Basic Family of Iteration Functions**, BIT Numerical Mathematics, vol.43, no.2, pp.453-458, (June-2003). 593

[198] Dan Kalman: **A Singularly Valuable Decomposition: The SVD of a Matrix**, preprint, College Math Journal, vol.27, no.1, (January-1996). URL: http://www.american.edu/academic.depts/cas/mathstat/People/kalman/pdffiles/index.html. 581

[199] K. Karamanos: **From symbolic dynamics to a digital approach**, International Journal of Bifurcation and Chaos, vol.11, no.6, pp.1683-1694, (2001). 735

[200] Anatoly A. Karatsuba, Y. Ofman: **Multiplication of multidigit numbers on automata**, Soviet Physics Doklady, vol.7, no.7, pp.595-596, (January-1963). Translated from Doklady Akademii Nauk SSSR, vol.145, no.2, pp.293-294, (July-1962). 550

[201] Richard Kaye: **A Gray Code For Set Partitions**, Information Processing Letters, vol.5, no.6, pp.171-173, (December-1976). URL: `http://www.kaye.to/rick/`. 357

[202] Wilfried Keller: **Fermat factoring status**, (prime factors $k \cdot 2n + 1$ of Fermat numbers F_m and complete factoring status). URL: `http://www.prothsearch.net/fermat.html`. 796

[203] Adalbert Kerber: **A matrix of combinatorial numbers related to the symmetric groups**, Discrete Mathematics, vol.21, no.3, pp.319-321, (1978). 368

[204] Yong Sup Kim, Arjun K. Rathie: **A generalization of Preece's identity**, Communications of the Korean Mathematical Society, vol.14, no.1, pp.217-222, (1999). URL: `http://www.mathnet.or.kr/mathnet/kms_tex/64609.pdf`. 693

[205] Andrew King: **Generating Indecomposable Permutations**, Discrete Mathematics, vol.306, no.5, pp.508-518, (2006). 281

[206] Louis V. King: **On the Direct Numerical Calculation of Elliptic Functions and Integrals**, Cambridge University Press, (1924). URL: `http://www.archive.org/details/ondirectnumerica00kinguoft`. 606, 615, 627

[207] V. Kislenkov, V. Mitrofanov, E. Zima: **How fast can we compute products?**, in ISSAC: Proceedings of the ACM SIGSAM International Symposium on Symbolic and Algebraic Computation, (1999). URL: `http://citeseerx.ist.psu.edu/viewdoc/summary?doi=10.1.1.27.9121`. 565

[208] Andrew Klapper, Mark Goresky: **Feedback Shift Registers, 2-Adic Span and Combiners With Memory**, Journal of Cryptology, vol.10, pp.111-147, (1997). URL: `http://www.math.ias.edu/~goresky/EngPubl.html`. 58, 878

[209] Konrad Knopp: **Theorie und Anwendung der unendlichen Reihen**, fifth edition, Springer-Verlag, (1964). URL: `http://gdz.sub.uni-goettingen.de/no_cache/dms/load/img/?IDDOC=264078`. English translation: **Theory And Application Of Infinite Series**, (1954). URL: `http://www.archive.org/details/theoryandapplica031692mbp`. 709, 712

[210] Donald E. Knuth: **Structured programming with go to statements**, ACM Computing Surveys, vol.6, no.4, (December-1974). 147

[211] Donald E. Knuth: **Efficient representation of perm groups**, Combinatorica, vol.11, no.1, pp.33-44, (1991). URL: `http://www-cs-staff.stanford.edu/~knuth/`. 323

[212] Donald E. Knuth: **The Art of Computer Programming**, third edition, Volume 1: Fundamental Algorithms, Addison-Wesley, (1997). Online errata list at `http://www-cs-staff.stanford.edu/~knuth/`. 644

[213] Donald E. Knuth: **The Art of Computer Programming**, third edition, Volume 2: Seminumerical Algorithms, Addison-Wesley, (1997). Online errata list at `http://www-cs-staff.stanford.edu/~knuth/`. 58, 60, 111, 560, 565, 589, 595, 768, 860

[214] Donald E. Knuth: **The Art of Computer Programming**, second edition, Volume 3: Sorting and Searching, Addison-Wesley, (1997). Online errata list at `http://www-cs-staff.stanford.edu/~knuth/`. 134, 708, 709

[215] Donald E. Knuth: **The Art of Computer Programming**, pre-fascicles for Volume 4. URL: `http://www-cs-staff.stanford.edu/~knuth/`. 16, 18, 55, 80, 183, 191, 222, 224, 257, 266, 278, 343, 874

[216] Wolfram Koepf: **Orthogonal Polynomials and Computer Algebra**, In: R. P. Gilbert et al., (eds.): Recent Developments in Complex Analysis and Computer Algebra, Kluwer, pp.205-234, (1999). URL: `http://www.mathematik.uni-kassel.de/~koepf/Publikationen/index.html`. 612

[217] Kenji Koike, Hironori Shiga: **A three terms Arithmetic-Geometric mean**, Journal of Number Theory, vol.124, pp.123-141, (2007). 611

[218] D. Kolba, T. Parks: **A prime factor FFT algorithm using high-speed convolution**, IEEE Transactions on Acoustics, Speech and Signal Processing, vol.25, no.4, pp.281-294, (August-1977). 458

[219] Richard B. Kreckel: **decimal**(γ) $\approx$ 0.57721566[0 − 9]{1001262760}39288477, online note, (19-January-2008). URL: `http://www.ginac.de/~kreckel/news.html#EulerConstantOneBillionDigits`. 656

[220] Donald L. Kreher, Douglas R. Stinson.: **Combinatorial algorithms: generation, enumeration, and search**, CRC Press, (1998). 391

[221] Ramanujachary Kumanduri, Cristina Romero: **Number theory with computer applications**, Prentice-Hall, (1998). 718, 784, 787, 812

[222] Ernst Eduard Kummer: **Über die hypergeometrische Reihe** $y = 1 + \frac{\alpha \cdot \beta}{1 \cdot \gamma} x + \frac{\alpha(\alpha+1)\beta(\beta+1)}{1 \cdot 2 \cdot \gamma(\gamma+1)} x^2 + \frac{\alpha(\alpha+1)(\alpha+2)\beta(\beta+1)(\beta+2)}{1 \cdot 2 \cdot 3 \cdot \gamma(\gamma+1)(\gamma+2)} x^3 + \ldots$, Journal für die reine und angewandte Mathematik, vol.15, pp.39-83 and pp.127-172, (1863). URL: `http://www.digizeitschriften.de/resolveppn/GDZPPN00214056X` and `http://www.digizeitschriften.de/resolveppn/GDZPPN002140616`. 602, 691, 700, 701

L

[223] Clement W. H. Lam, Leonard H. Soicher: **Three new combination algorithms with the minimal change property**, Communications of the ACM, vol.25, no.8, pp.555-559, (August-1982). 183

[224] Susan Landau, Neil Immermann: **The Similarities (and Differences) between Polynomials and Integers**, International Conference on Number Theoretic and Algebraic Methods in Computer Science (1993), pp.57-59, version of (8-August-1996). URL: `http://citeseerx.ist.psu.edu/viewdoc/summary?doi=10.1.1.42.7692`. 560

[225] Glen G. Langdon, Jr.: **An algorithm for generating permutations**, Communications of the ACM, vol.10, no.5, pp.298-299, (May-1967). 266

[226] D. H. Lehmer: **On arccotangent relations for** π, American Mathematical Monthly, vol.45, pp.657-664, (1938). 638

[227] D. H. Lehmer: **Interesting series involving the central binomial coefficient**, American Mathematical Monthly, vol.92, no.7, pp.449-457, (1985). 338

[228] Charles E. Leiserson, Harald Prokop, Keith H. Randall: **Using de Bruijn Sequences to Index a 1 in a Computer Word**, MIT Lab for Computer Science, Cambridge, MA, (June-1998). URL: `http://supertech.csail.mit.edu/papers.html`. 14

[229] Abraham Lempel, Marcelo J. Weinberger: **Self-complementary normal bases in finite fields**, SIAM Journal on Discrete Mathematics, vol.1, no.2, pp.193-198, (May-1988). 910

[230] Arjen K. Lenstra: **Integer Factoring**, Designs, Codes and Cryptogaphy, vol.19, pp.101-128, (2000). URL: `http://citeseerx.ist.psu.edu/viewdoc/summary?doi=10.1.1.93.5587`. 804

[231] H. W. Lenstra, Jr., R. J. Schoof: **Primitive Normal Bases for Finite Fields**, Mathematics of Computation, vol.48, no.177, pp.217-231, (January-1987). 904

[232] Qun Ying Liao, Qi Sun: **Normal bases and their dual-bases over finite fields**, Acta Mathematica Sinica, English Series, vol.22, no.3, pp.845-848, (May-2006). 910

[233] Rudolf Lidl, Harald Niederreiter: **Introduction to finite fields and their applications**, Cambridge University Press, revised edition, (1994). 842

[234] J. H. van Lint, R. M. Wilson: **A Course in Combinatorics**, Cambridge University Press, (1992). 390, 874

[235] W. Lipski, Jr.: **More on permutation generation methods**, Computing, vol.23, no.4, pp.357-365, (December-1979). 250

[236] Charles Van Loan: **Computational Frameworks for the Fast Fourier Transform**, SIAM, (1992). 465

[237] Daniel Loebenberger: **A Simple Derivation for the Frobenius Pseudoprime Test**, Cryptology ePrint Archive, entry 2008/124, (17-March-2008). URL: `http://eprint.iacr.org/2008/124.pdf`. 792

[238] Lisa Lorentzen, Haakon Waadeland: **Continued Fractions and Applications**, North-Holland, (1992). 624, 725

[239] Ya Yan Lu: **Computing the Logarithm of a Symmetric Positive Definite Matrix**, Applied Numerical Mathematics: Transactions of IMACS, vol.26, no.4, pp.483-496, (1998). URL: `http://citeseerx.ist.psu.edu/viewdoc/summary?doi=10.1.1.37.759`. 624

M

[240] Robert S. Maier: **A generalization of Euler's hypergeometric transform**, arXiv:math/0302084v4 [math.CA], (14-March-2006). URL: `http://arxiv.org/abs/math.CA/0302084`. 689, 691

[241] Robert S. Maier: **Algebraic hypergeometric transformations of modular origin**, arXiv:math/0501425v3 [math.NT], (24-March-2006). URL: `http://arxiv.org/abs/math.NT/0501425`. 611, 614

[242] Robert S. Maier: **On rationally parametrized modular equations**, arXiv:math.NT/0611041v4, (7-July-2008). 614

[243] Robert S. Maier: **P-symbols, Heun identities, and $_3F_2$ identities**, arXiv:0712.4299v2 [math.CA], (30-December-2007). URL: `http://arxiv.org/abs/0712.4299`. 689

[244] Kei Makita, Yasuyuki Nogami, Tatsuo Sugimura: **Generating prime degree irreducible polynomials by using irreducible all-one polynomial over $\mathbb{F}_2$**, Electronics and Communications in Japan (Part III: Fundamental Electronic Science), vol.88, no.7, pp.23-32, (2005). 847

[245] Conrado Martínez, Alois Panholzer, Helmut Prodinger: **Generating random derangements**, Proceedings of the 10th ACM-SIAM Workshop on Algorithm Engineering and Experiments (ALENEX) and the 5th ACM-SIAM Workshop on Analytic Algorithmics and Combinatorics (ANALCO), pp.234-240, (2008). URL: `http://www.siam.org/proceedings/analco/2008/analco08.php`. 117

[246] Keith Matthews: **Solving $Ax^2 - By^2 = N$ in integers, where $A > 0$, $B > 0$ and $D = AB$ is not a perfect square and $\gcd(A, B) = \gcd(A, N) = 1$**, online note, (13-September-2007). URL: `http://www.numbertheory.org/notes.html`. 813

[247] M. D. McIlroy: **A Killer Adversary for Quicksort**, Software Practice and Experience, vol.29, p.1-4, (1999). 136

[248] James Mc Laughlin, Andrew V. Sills, Peter Zimmer: **Rogers-Ramanujan-Slater Type Identities**, The Electronic Journal of Combinatorics, dynamic survey no.15, (2008). URL: `http://www.combinatorics.org/Surveys/index.html`. 344

[249] K. R. McLean: **Divisibility Properties of Binomial Coefficients**, The Mathematical Gazette, vol.58, no.403, pp.17-24, (March-1974). 914

[250] A. Menezes, P. van Oorschot, S. Vanstone: **Handbook of Applied Cryptography**, CRC Press, (1996). URL: `http://www.cacr.math.uwaterloo.ca/hac/`. 766

[251] Helmut Meyn, Werner Götz: **Self-reciprocal Polynomials Over Finite Fields**, Séminaire Lotharingien de Combinatoire, B21d, (1989). URL: `http://www.emis.de/journals/SLC/`. 847

[252] Peter L. Montgomery: **Modular Multiplication Without Trial Division**, Mathematics of Computation, vol.44, no.170, pp.519-521, (April-1985). 766

[253] Peter L. Montgomery: **A Survey of Modern Integer Factorization Algorithms**, CWI Quarterly, vol.7, no.4, pp.337-365, (1994). URL: `http://citeseerx.ist.psu.edu/viewdoc/summary?doi=10.1.1.32.2831`. 804

[254] Eduardo Moreno: **De Bruijn graphs and sequences in languages with restrictions**, PhD thesis, Universidad de Chile, (May-2005). URL: `http://emoreno.uai.cl/Publications.html`. 875

[255] James A. Muir, Douglas R. Stinson: **Minimality and Other Properties of the Width-w Nonadjacent Form**, Technical report CORR 2004-08, Centre for Applied Cryptographic Research

(CACR) at the University of Waterloo, Canada, (2004). URL:
http://www.cacr.math.uwaterloo.ca/techreports/2004/tech_reports2004.html. 62

[256] Jean-Michel Muller: **Elementary Functions: algorithms and implementation**, Birkhäuser, (1997). 642, 650

[257] David R. Musser: **Introspective Sorting and Selection Algorithms**, Software Practice and Experience, vol.8, pp.983-993, (1997). 136

[258] Wendy Myrvold, Frank Ruskey: **Ranking and unranking permutations in linear time**, Information Processing Letters, vol.79, pp.281-284, (2001). URL:
http://www.cs.uvic.ca/~ruskey/Publications/. 239

N O

[259] Eugen Netto: **Lehrbuch der Combinatorik**, Teubner Verlag, (1901). URL:
http://www.archive.org/details/lehrbuchdercomb00nettgoog. 267

[260] Harald Niederreiter: **An enumeration formula for certain irreducible polynomials with an application to the construction of irreducible polynomials over the binary field**, Applicable Algebra in Engineering, Communication and Computing, vol.1, no.2, pp.119-124 (September-1990). 855

[261] Albert Nijenhuis, Herbert S. Wilf: **Combinatorial Algorithms for Computers and Calculators**, Academic Press, second edition, (1978). URL:
http://www.math.upenn.edu/~wilf/website/CombAlgDownld.html. 354

[262] Henri J. Nussbaumer: **Fast Fourier Transform and Convolution Algorithms**, second edition, Springer-Verlag, (1982) (out of print). 451

[263] Carl Douglas Olds: **Continued Fractions**, Random House (1963), republished as vol.9 of the New Mathematics Library, the Mathematical Association of America, (1977) (out of print). 725, 812

[264] Michael Orchard: **Fast bit-reversal algorithms based on index representations in** $GF(2^n)$, IEEE International Symposium on Circuits and Systems, (1989), vol.3, pp.1903-1906, (1989). 873

P

[265] Igor Pak: **Partition Bijections, a Survey**, Ramanujan Journal, vol.12, pp.5-75, (2006). URL:
http://www.math.umn.edu/~pak/research.htm. 349

[266] The PARI Group (PARI): **PARI/GP**, version 2.3.5, (5-February-2010). URL:
http://pari.math.u-bordeaux.fr/. 923

[267] Michael S. Paterson, Larry J. Stockmeyer: **On the number of nonscalar multiplications necessary to evaluate polynomials**, SIAM Journal on Computing, vol.2, no.1, pp.60-66, (March-1973). 658

[268] Peter Paule: **On identities of the Rogers-Ramanujan type**, Journal of Mathematical Analysis and Applications, vol.107, no.1, pp.255-284, (April-1985). 347

[269] W. H. Payne, F. M. Ives: **Combination Generators**, ACM Transactions on Mathematical Software (TOMS), vol.5, no.2, pp.163-172, (June-1979). 183

[270] Richard G. E. Pinch: **Some primality testing algorithms**, AMS Notices, vol.40, no.9, pp.1203-1210, (November-1993). Corrected version URL:
http://www.chalcedon.demon.co.uk/rgep/publish.html#42. 804

[271] J. M. Pollard: **The Fast Fourier Transform in a Finite Field**, Mathematics of Computation, vol.25, no.114, pp.365-374, (April-1971). 542

[272] Carl Pomerance, J. L. Selfridge, S. Wagstaff, Jr.: **The Pseudoprimes to** $25 \cdot 10^9$. Mathematics of Computation, vol.35, no.151, pp.1003-1026, (July-1980). 789, 801

[273] Peter John Potts: **Computable Real Arithmetic Using Linear Fractional Transformations**, Report, Department of Computing, Imperial College of Science, Technology and Medicine, London, (June-1996). URL:
http://citeseerx.ist.psu.edu/viewdoc/summary?doi=10.1.1.24.7373. 687, 691

[274] A. D. Poularikas: **The Transforms and applications handbook**, second edition, CRC Press, (2000). 456

[275] Helmut Prodinger: **On Binary Representations of Integers with Digits -1, 0, +1**, INTEGERS: The Electronic Journal of Combinatorial Number Theory, vol.0, (14-June-2000). URL: http://www.integers-ejcnt.org/vol0.html. 62

Q R

[276] Michael O. Rabin: **Probabilistic algorithms in finite fields**, Technical Report MIT-LCS-TR-213, Massachusetts Institute of Technology, (January-1979). URL: http://publications.csail.mit.edu/. 838

[277] Charles M. Rader: **Discrete Fourier Transforms When the Number of Data Samples is Prime**, Proceedings of the IEEE, vol.56, iss.6, pp.1107-1108, (June-1968). 458

[278] Janusz Rajski, Jerzy Tyszer: **Primitive Polynomials Over GF(2) of Degree up to 660 with Uniformly Distributed Coefficients**, Journal of Electronic Testing: Theory and Applications, vol.19, pp.645-657, (2003). 853

[279] David Rasmussen, Carla D. Savage, Douglas B. West: **Gray code enumeration of families of integer partitions**, Journal of Combinatorial Theory, Series A, vol.70, no.2, pp.201-229, (1995). URL: http://www.csc.ncsu.edu/faculty/savage/papers.html. 343

[280] I. S. Reed, T. K. Truong: **The use of finite fields to compute convolutions**, IEEE Transactions on Information Theory, vol.21, no.2, pp.208-213, (March-1975). 808

[281] I. S. Reed, T. K. Truong, R. L. Miller: **A new algorithm for computing primitive elements in the field of Gaussian complex integers modulo a Mersenne prime**, IEEE Transactions on Acoustics, Speech, and Signal Processing, vol.27, no.5, pp.561-563, (October-1979). 808

[282] Phillip A. Regalia, Sanjit K. Mitra: **Kronecker Products, Unitary Matrices and Signal Processing Applications**, SIAM Review, vol.31, no.4, pp.586-613, (December-1989). 465

[283] Paulo Ribenboim: **The Little Book of Bigger Primes**, second Edition, Springer-Verlag, (2004). 804

[284] Hans Riesel: **Prime Numbers and Computer Methods for Factorization**, Birkhäuser, (1985). 799, 804

[285] Kenneth H. Rosen, John G. Michaels, Jonathan L. Gross, Jerrold W. Grossman, Douglas R. Shier (eds.): **Handbook of Discrete and Combinatorial Mathematics**, CRC Press, (2000). 707

[286] Gian-Carlo Rota: **On the foundations of combinatorial theory I. Theory of Möbius Functions**, Probability Theory and Related Fields, vol.2, no.4, pp.340-368, (January-1964). 707

[287] Frank Ruskey, Carla Savage, Terry MinYih Wang: **Generating Necklaces**, Journal of Algorithms, vol.13, pp.414-430, (1992). 377

[288] Frank Ruskey: **Simple combinatorial Gray codes constructed by reversing sublists**, Lecture Notes in Computer Science, vol.762, pp.201-208, (1993). URL: http://www.cs.uvic.ca/~ruskey/Publications/. 363

[289] Frank Ruskey, Joe Sawada: **An Efficient Algorithm for Generating Necklaces with Fixed Density**, SIAM Journal on Computing, vol.29, no.2, pp.671-684, (1999). URL: http://www.cs.uvic.ca/~ruskey/Publications/. 383

[290] Frank Ruskey, Joe Sawada: **Generating Necklaces and Strings with Forbidden Substrings**, Lecture Notes in Computer Science, vol.1858, pp.330-339, (July-2000). URL: http://www.cs.uvic.ca/~ruskey/Publications/. 383

[291] Frank Ruskey, Aaron Williams: **Generating combinations by prefix shifts**, Lecture Notes in Computer Science, vol.3595, pp.570-576, (2005). URL: http://www.cs.uvic.ca/~ruskey/Publications/. 180

[292] Frank Ruskey, Aaron Williams: **Generating Balanced Parentheses and Binary Trees by Prefix Shifts**, CATS 2008, Computing: The Australasian Theory Symposium, Wollongong, Australia, (2008). URL: http://www.cs.uvic.ca/~ruskey/Publications/. 330

[293] Frank Ruskey, Aaron Williams: **An explicit universal cycle for the $(n-1)$-permutations of an n-set**, ACM Transactions on Algorithms, (2008). URL: http://www.cs.uvic.ca/~ruskey/Publications/. 875

S

[294] Eugene Salamin: **Computation of π Using Arithmetic-Geometric Mean**, Mathematics of Computation, vol.30, no.135, pp.565-570, (July-1976). 615

[295] Eugene Salamin: **Application of Quaternions to Computation with Rotations**, Working Paper, Stanford AI Lab, (1979). Edited and TeX-formatted by Henry G. Baker, (1995). URL: http://home.pipeline.com/~hbaker1/. 576

[296] Sandra Sattolo: **An algorithm to generate a random cyclic permutation**, Information Processing Letters, vol.22, no.6, pp.315-317, (1986). 112

[297] Carla Savage: **Generating Permutations with k-Differences**, SIAM Journal on Discrete Mathematics, vol.4, no.4, pp.561-573, (November-1990). 266

[298] Carla Savage: **A Survey of Combinatorial Gray Codes**, SIAM Review, vol.39, no.4, pp.605-629, (December-1997). URL: http://www.csc.ncsu.edu/faculty/savage/papers.html. 172, 264

[299] Joe Sawada: **Generating Bracelets in Constant Amortized Time**, SIAM Journal on Computing, vol.31, no.1, pp.259-268, (2001). URL: http://citeseerx.ist.psu.edu/viewdoc/summary?doi=10.1.1.22.6949. 371

[300] Joe Sawada: **A fast algorithm to generate necklaces with fixed content**, Theoretical Computer Science, vol.301, no.1-3, pp.477-489, (May-2003). 383

[301] Fred Schneider, Keith Strickland: **Planet Claire**, in: The B52's, (1979). 20

[302] Arnold Schönhage, Volker Strassen: **Schnelle Multiplikation grosser Zahlen**, Computing, vol.7, no.3-4, pp.281-292, (September-1971). 560

[303] Arnold Schönhage: **Schnelle Multiplikation von Polynomen über Körpern der Charakteristik 2**, Acta Informatica, vol.7, no.4, pp.395-398, (December-1977). 832, 896

[304] Ernst Schröder: **Ueber unendlich viele Algorithmen zur Auflösung der Gleichungen**, Mathematische Annalen, vol.2, no.2, (June-1870). English translation: **On Infinitely Many Algorithms for Solving Equations**, URL: http://citeseerx.ist.psu.edu/viewdoc/summary?doi=10.1.1.22.1497. 588, 589

[305] Robert Sedgewick: **Permutation Generation Methods**, ACM Computing Surveys (CSUR), vol.9, no.2, pp.137-164, (June-1977). URL: http://www.princeton.edu/~rblee/ELE572Papers/. 250

[306] Robert Sedgewick: **Algorithms in C++. Parts 1-4: Fundamentals, Data Structures, Sorting, Searching**, third edition, Addison-Wesley, (1998). 134, 138

[307] Robert Sedgewick: **Algorithms in C++. Part 5: Graph Algorithms**, third edition, Addison-Wesley, (2001). 391

[308] Victor Shoup: **A New Polynomial Factorization Algorithm and its Implementation**, Journal of Symbolic Computation, vol.20, pp.363-397, (1995). URL: http://www.shoup.net/papers/. 863

[309] Victor Shoup: **A Computational Introduction to Number Theory and Algebra**, Cambridge University Press, (2005). Updated version URL: http://www.shoup.net/papers/. 784

[310] Andrew V. Sills: **Finite Rogers-Ramanujan Type Identities**, The Electronic Journal of Combinatorics, vol.10, (2003). URL: http://www.combinatorics.org/Volume_10/v10i1toc.html. 349

[311] Lucy Joan Slater: **Further Identities of the Rogers-Ramanujan Type**, Proceedings of the London Mathematical Society, Series 2, vol.s2-54, no.2, pp.147-167, (1952). 347

[312] N. J. A. Sloane: **The On-Line Encyclopedia of Integer Sequences**, (2009). URL: http://oeis.org/classic/?blank=1. xii, 9, 10, 44, 45, 53, 59, 60, 62, 71, 72, 73, 74, 78, 88, 90, 95, 99, 100, 119, 129, 151, 248, 257, 277, 279, 280, 281, 282, 309, 312, 314, 315, 318, 320, 321, 322, 331, 337, 345, 346, 347, 348, 349, 350, 351, 352, 353, 358, 360, 366, 368, 369, 373, 380, 383, 389, 390, 408, 493, 610, 627, 649, 703, 706, 708, 710, 726, 727, 728, 729, 730, 731, 732, 733, 735, 739,

740, 742, 744, 745, 750, 753, 754, 755, 756, 758, 759, 776, 780, 784, 786, 788, 789, 797, 802, 813, 817, 820, 840, 843, 848, 849, 850, 851, 853, 855, 874, 878, 885, 904, 909, 912, 914

[313] N. J. A. Sloane: **A Library of Hadamard Matrices**, online document, (2008). URL: http://www.research.att.com/~njas/hadamard/index.html. 390

[314] David M. Smith: **Efficient multiple precision evaluation of elementary functions**, Mathematics of Computation, vol.52, pp.131-134, (1989). 658

[315] Jerome A. Solinas: **Generalized Mersenne Numbers**, Technical report CORR 99-39, University of Waterloo, Canada, (1999). URL: http://www.cacr.math.uwaterloo.ca/. 768

[316] Hong-Yeop Song: **Examples and Constructions of Hadamard Matrices**, Dept. of Electrical and Electronics Engineering, Yonsei University, Korea, (June-2002). URL: http://calliope.uwaterloo.ca/~ggong/710T4/Song-lecture.ps. 390

[317] H. Sorensen, D. Jones, C. Burrus, M. Heideman: **On computing the discrete Hartley transform**, IEEE Trans. on Acoustics, Speech and Signal Processing, vol.33, no.5, pp.1231-1238, (October-1985). 524

[318] Henrik V. Sorensen, Douglas L. Jones, Michael T. Heideman, C. Sidney Burrus: **Real-Valued Fast Fourier Transform Algorithms**, IEEE Transactions on Acoustics, Speech and Signal Processing, vol.35, no.6, pp.849-863, (June-1987). 434

[319] Richard P. Stanley: **Enumerative combinatorics**, Cambridge University Press, vol.1, (1997), vol.2, (1999). List of errata at http://math.mit.edu/~rstan/ec/. 173, 323

[320] Richard P. Stanley: **Exercises on Catalan and Related Numbers**, online note, (23-June-1998). URL: http://www-math.mit.edu/~rstan/ec/. 323

[321] Richard P. Stanley: **Catalan Addendum**, online note, (5-May-2010). URL: http://www-math.mit.edu/~rstan/ec/. 323

[322] Damien Stehlé, Paul Zimmermann: **A Binary Recursive Gcd Algorithm**, INRIA research report RR-5050, (December-2003). 768

[323] William Stein: **Elementary Number Theory**, Springer-Verlag, (November-2008). URL: http://wstein.org/ent/. 784

[324] Ralf Stephan: **Divide-and-conquer generating functions. Part I. Elementary sequences**, arXiv:math/0307027v1 [math.CO], (2003). URL: http://arxiv.org/abs/math.CO/0307027. 740

[325] Paul K. Stockmeyer: **The Tower of Hanoi: A Bibliography**, online note, (2005). URL: http://www.cs.wm.edu/~pkstoc/h_papers.html. 737

[326] Carl Størmer: **Sur l'application de la théorie des nombres entiers complexes a la solution en nombres rationnels** x_1 x_2 ... x_n c_1 c_2 ... c_n k **de l'équation:** c_1 **arc tg** x_1 + c_2 **arc tg** x_2 + ... + c_n **arc tg** $x_n = k\frac{\pi}{4}$, Archiv for Mathematik og Naturvidenskab, B.XIX, Nr.3, (vol.19, no.3), pp.1-96, (1896). 634

[327] Richard G. Swan: **Factorization of polynomials over finite fields**, Pacific Journal of Mathematics, vol.12, no.3, pp.1099-1106, (1962). 850

[328] Paul N. Swarztrauber: **Bluestein's FFT for Arbitrary N on the Hypercube**, Parallel Computing, vol.17, pp.607-617, (1991). URL: http://www.cisl.ucar.edu/css/staff/pauls/papers/bluestein/bluestein.html. 455

$$\boxed{\text{T}}$$

[329] Tadao Takaoka, Stephen Violich: **Combinatorial Generation by Fusing Loopless Algorithms**, In: Computing: The Australasian Theory Symposium (CATS2006), Hobart, Australia. Conferences in Research and Practice in Information Technology (CRPIT), vol.51. Barry Jay, Joachim Gudmundsson, (eds.), (2006). 329

[330] M. A. Thornton, D. M. Miller, R. Drechsler: **Transformations Amongst the Walsh, Haar, Arithmetic and Reed-Muller Spectral Domains**, International Workshop on Applications of the Reed-Muller Expansion in Circuit Design (RMW), pp.215-225, (2001). URL: http://engr.smu.edu/~mitch/publications.html. 486

[331] John Todd: **A problem on arc tangent relations**, Amer. Math. Monthly, vol.56, no.8, pp.517-528, (October-1949). 638

[332] Mikko Tommila: **apfloat, A High Performance Arbitrary Precision Arithmetic Package**, (1996). URL: http://www.apfloat.org/. 809

[333] J. F. Traub: **Iterative Methods for the Solution of Equations**, Chelsea, (1964). 588, 589, 597

[334] H. F. Trotter: **Algorithm 115: Perm**, Communications of the ACM, vol.5, no.8, pp.434-435, (August-1962). 254

[335] H. W. Turnbull: **Theory of Equations**, fifth edition, Oliver and Boyd, Edinburgh, (1952). 895

U V

[336] Abraham Ungar: **Generalized Hyperbolic Functions**, The American Mathematical Monthly, vol.89, no.9, pp.688-691, (November-1982). 688

[337] Vincent Vajnovszki: **Generating a Gray Code for P-Sequences**, Journal of Mathematical Modelling and Algorithms, vol.1, pp.31-41, (2002). 329

[338] Vincent Vajnovszki, Timothy R. Walsh: **A loop-free two-close Gray-code algorithm for listing k-ary Dyck words**, Journal of Discrete Algorithms, vol.4, no.4, pp.633-648, (December-2006). 333

[339] Raimundas Vidūnas: **Expressions for values of the gamma function**, arXiv:math.CA/0403510, (30-March-2004). URL: http://arxiv.org/abs/math/0403510. 610

[340] San C. Vo: **A Survey of Elliptic Cryptosystems, Part I: Introductory**, NASA Advanced Supercomputing (NAS) Division, (August-2003). URL: http://www.nas.nasa.gov/News/Techreports/2003/2003.html. 918

[341] Edward R. Vrscay, William J. Gilbert: **Extraneous fixed points, basin boundaries and chaotic dynamics for Schröder and König rational iteration functions**, Numerische Mathematik, vol.52, no.1, pp.1-16, (January-1987). 592, 593

W

[342] Timothy R. Walsh: **The generalized Towers of Hanoi for space-deficient computers and forgetful humans**, The Mathematical Intelligencer, vol.20, no.1, pp.32-38, (March-1998). 737

[343] Timothy Walsh: **Generating Gray codes in $O(1)$ worst-case time per word**, In: DMTCS 2003, C. S. Calude et al. (eds.), Lecture Notes in Computer Science, vol.2731, pp.73-88, (2003). 172

[344] Xiaoyun Wang, Dengguo Feng, Xuejia Lai, Hongbo Yu: **Collisions for Hash Functions MD4, MD5, HAVAL-128 and RIPEMD**, Cryptology ePrint Archive, Report 2004/199, revised version, (17-August-2004). URL: http://eprint.iacr.org/2004/199/. 870

[345] Zhong-De Wang: **New algorithm for the slant transform**, IEEE Transactions on Pattern Analysis and Machine Intelligence, vol.4, no.5, pp.551-555, (September-1982). 483

[346] Henry S. Warren, Jr.: **Hacker's delight**, Addison-Wesley, (2003). Additional material and revisions at URL: http://www.hackersdelight.org/. 3

[347] André Weimerskirch, Christoph Paar: **Generalizations of the Karatsuba Algorithm for Polynomial Multiplication**, (March-2002). URL: http://citeseerx.ist.psu.edu/viewdoc/summary?doi=10.1.1.13.4028. 827, 831

[348] André Weimerskirch, Christoph Paar: **Generalizations of the Karatsuba Algorithm for Efficient Implementations**, Technical Report, Ruhr-Universität-Bochum, Germany, corrected version, (2003). URL: http://www.crypto.ruhr-uni-bochum.de/en_publications.html. 827

[349] Eric Weisstein: **MathWorld**. URL: http://mathworld.wolfram.com/. 338, 359, 610, 687, 914

[350] Mark B. Wells: **Generation of Permutations by Transposition**, Mathematics of Computation, vol.15, no.74, pp.192-195, (April-1961). 252

[351] Ernst Joachim Weniger: **Nonlinear sequence transformations for the acceleration of convergence and the summation of divergent series**, arXiv:math/0306302v1 [math.NA], (19-June-2003). URL: http://arxiv.org/abs/math/0306302v1. 665

[352] Mark Weston, Vincent Vajnovszki: **Gray codes for necklaces and Lyndon words of arbitrary base**, Pure Mathematics and Applications (PU.M.A.), vol.17, no.1-2, pp.175-182, (2006). URL: http://homelinux.capitano.unisi.it/~puma/. 375

[353] Michael Roby Wetherfield, Hwang Chien-lih: **Lists of Machin-type (inverse integral cotangent) identities for Pi/4**, URL: http://www.machination.eclipse.co.uk/. 638

[354] Michael Roby Wetherfield: **The enhancement of Machin's formula by Todd's process**, The Mathematical Gazette, vol.80, no.488, pp.333-344, (July-1996). 638

[355] Francis John Welsh Whipple: **A fundamental relation between generalized hypergeometric series**, Journal of the London Mathematical Society, Series 1, vol.s1-1, no.3, pp.138-145, (1926). 693

[356] E. T. Whittaker, G. N. Watson: **A Course of Modern Analysis**, Cambridge University Press, fourth edition, (1927), reprinted (1990). 608, 686, 687, 689, 692

[357] Mladen Victor Wickerhauser: **Adapted Wavelet Analysis from Theory to Software**, AK Peters, Wellesley, Massachusetts, (1994). 546

[358] (Wikipedia contributors): **Wikipedia, The Free Encyclopedia**, (2008). URL: http://en.wikipedia.org/. 2, 534, 560, 607, 874

[359] Herbert S. Wilf: **generatingfunctionology**, second edition, Academic Press, (1992). URL: http://www.math.upenn.edu/~wilf/DownldGF.html. 279

[360] Aaron Williams: **Loopless Generation of Multiset Permutations using a Constant Number of Variables by Prefix Shifts**, ACM-SIAM Symposium on Discrete Algorithms (SODA09), (2009). URL: http://www.siam.org/proceedings/soda/2009/soda09.php. 299

[361] Hugh C. Williams: **Éduard Lucas and primality testing**, Wiley, (1989). 804

[362] Mark C. Wilson: **Random and exhaustive generation of permutations and cycles**, arXiv:math/0702753v1 [math.CO], (25-February-2007). URL: http://arxiv.org/abs/math/0702753. 112

X Y Z

[363] Limin Xiang, Kazuo Ushijima: **On $O(1)$ Time Algorithms for Combinatorial Generation**, The Computer Journal, vol.44, pp.292-302, (2001). 329

[364] Shmuel Zaks: **A new algorithm for generation of permutations**, BIT Numerical Mathematics, vol.24, no.2, pp.196-204, (June-1984). 245

[365] Zhenxiang Zhang: **Finding strong pseudoprimes to several bases**, Mathematics of Computation, vol.70, no.234, pp.863-872, (April-2001). 791

[366] Zhenxiang Zhang, Min Tang: **Finding strong pseudoprimes to several bases. II**, Mathematics of Computation, vol.72, no.244, pp.2058-2097, (30-May-2003). 791

[367] Paweł Zieliński, Krystyna Ziętak: **The Polar Decomposition – Properties, Applications and Algorithms**, Annals of the Polish Mathematical Society, vol.38, (1995). URL: http://citeseerx.ist.psu.edu/viewdoc/summary?doi=10.1.1.50.3541. 577

[368] Neal Zierler: **On a Theorem by Gleason and Marsh**, Proceedings of the American Mathematical Society, vol.9, no.2, pp.236-237, (April-1958). 842

Index

Printed in the United States
By Bookmasters